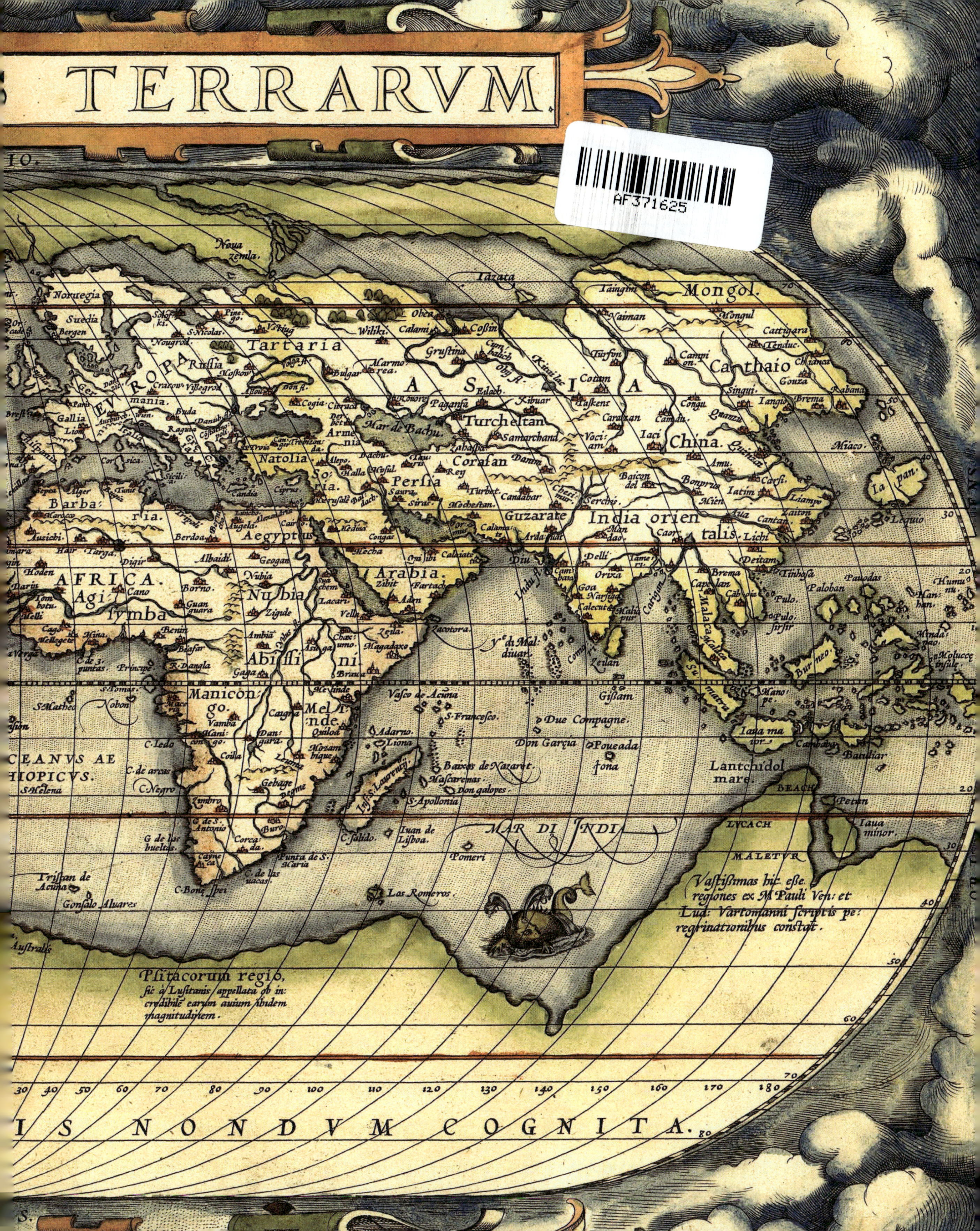
TERRARVM.
10.
IS NONDVM COGNITA.
Nova zemla.
Tazata
Taingin
Mongol.
Norvegia
Suedia
Bergen
Naiman
Mongul
Cattigara
Tenduc.
Tartaria
Obea
Wiliki
Calami
Cossin
Grustina
Kinsia
Turfon
Campi on
Canthaio
Chiarea
Gouza
Russia
Craeow
Vyssegrod
Moskow
Bulgar
Marmo rea
Cotum
Congu
Singui
Iangiu
Brema
Rabana
mania.
Buda
Cogia
Chirack
Paganfu
Sedach
Kibuar
Taskent
Caraxan
Camdin
Gallia
Lion
Ragula
Danubio
Per beta
Mar de Bachu
Turcheltan
Samarchand
Voci am
Iaci
China.
Macao.
Natolia
So ria.
Alepo
Balla
Armenni
Bachu
Corasan
Danim
Turbut
Baicon del
Bonpron
Amu.
Iatim
Cacsi.
La pan.
Ciprus.
Persia
Saura
Candabar
Mochestan.
Serchis
Mien
Cantan
Lequio
Barba ria.
Aegyptus
Mecha
Ielsolē
Calama
Ardant
Mandao
Caor
India orientalis
Lichi
Deitam
Hoden
Albaidi
Geogan
Ormus
Delli
Tame
Brema
Cape lan
Tinhofa
Palobos
Humi nu.
AFRICA.
Agi fymba
Nubia
Borno
Cano
Guan guara
Zigde
Arabia.
Zibit
Aden
Vella
Zula
Fartach
Goa
Narfinga
Calecut
Kalipur
Malacca
Pulo
Pulo fifort
Manhan.
Anda gao.
Moluccæ infulæ
Abissini
Branca
Magadaxo
y de Mal diuar
Zeilan
Burneo
Manicon go.
Yamba
Cangra
Mel Inde
Giffam
Mano pe.
Iana ma ior.
S. Matheo
Nobon
Quiloa
Adarno
Liona
S. Francesco
Due Compagne
Don Garçia
Poueada fona
Lantchidol mare
Camboya
Batuliar
CEANVS AE
HIOPICVS.
S. Helena
C. de arcos
C. Negro
Mombaza
Gebage
Lago Laurentij
Baixes de Nazaret
Mascarenas
Don qalopes
S. Apollonia
BEACH
Peten
Iaua minor.
Trifian de Acuna
Gonfalo Aluares
C. Bone fpei
Corca da.
C. falido.
Iuan de Lisboa.
Pomeri
MAR DI INDI
LVCACH
MALETVR
Auftralis
Las Romeros
Vaftifimas hic effe regiones ex M. Pauli Ven: et Lud: Vartomanni fcriptis pe: regrinationibus conftat.
Pfitacorum regio, fic à Lufitanis appellata ob in: credibile earum auium ibidem magnitudinem.
30 40 50 60 70 80 90 100 110 120 130 140 150 160 170 180

THE COMMONALITY OF HUMANS THROUGH ART

Created and edited by Stuart Handler

Cover and concept design by Stuart Handler

ISBN 978-1-913645-65-6

Library of Congress Control Number: 2024901148

Produced by Paul Holberton Publishing, London
www.paulholberton.com

For enquiries about large quantity orders, or anything else, contact: enquiries@tcohta.com

Copyeditor: Lisa Bessette
Photo editor: Christian Ruiz

Printed by E-Graphic, a division of 4Flying Srl, Verona, Italy

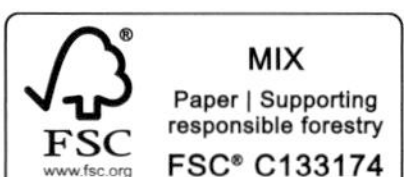

Front cover:
Kneeling Mother and Child
Djenne-Jeno culture, Inner Niger Delta, Mali
1170–1330
Terracotta, 13 in., 33 cm
Blanpain Collection

Back cover:
Female Figure
Egypt
Predynastic, Naqada Ila Period, 3500–3400 BCE
Terracotta
11 ½ × 5 ½ × 2 ¼ in., 29.2 × 14 × 5.7 cm
Brooklyn Museum, New York

Page 574:
Detail of *White Clouds and Red Trees* (Chapter 5, fig. 32)
Li Jian (China, active second half of 1700s), 1788
Hanging scroll, ink and color on silk
49 ¹¹⁄₁₆ × 20 ¾ in., 126.2 × 52.7 cm
Cleveland Museum of Art, Purchase from
the J. H. Wade Fund, 1972.42

THE COMMONALITY OF HUMANS THROUGH ART

HOW ART CONNECTS MANKIND THROUGH THE AGES

CREATED AND EDITED BY **STUART HANDLER**

CONTENTS

ABOUT THE AUTHORS

Alex W. Barker

Alex W. Barker is director of the Arkansas Archeological Survey, University of Arkansas System. He was formerly the director of the Museum of Art and Archaeology and the Museum of Anthropology at the University of Missouri. He was president of the American Anthropological Association in 2017–19 and is the recipient of many grants, honors, and awards.

Herbert M. Cole

Herbert M. Cole is professor emeritus of art history at the University of California, Santa Barbara, and has authored, co-authored, and edited eleven books on African arts and over sixty essays and articles. His most recent book is *Maternity: Mothers and Children in the Arts of Africa*.

David H. Dye

David H. Dye is professor of archaeology and faculty advisor at the University of Memphis. His latest book, *War Paths, Peace Paths*, explores the relationship of conflict and cooperation throughout prehistory in the Eastern Woodlands and reveals new insights into the political and religious nature of warfare.

Stuart Handler

Stuart Handler is a prominent collector of pre-Columbian art and an industrialist. He is the editor and an author of the book *Traveling with Cortés and Pizarro: Discovering Fine Pre-Columbian Art*.

Lark E. Mason

Lark E. Mason is an expert on Chinese art and antiquities. He was formerly a senior vice president at Sotheby's in charge of Chinese Works of Art and director of Online Auctions. He has regularly appeared on the PBS television series *Antiques Roadshow*. He was president of the Appraiser's Association of America in 2019–21 and is currently president of Lark Mason Art Advisory.

Todd J. Pesek, MD

Todd J. Pesek, MD, is a physician practicing preventive, integrative holistic healthcare. He is the founding director of the Center for Healing Across Cultures and an associate professor in the School of Health Sciences at Cleveland State University. He has written several books and many articles on multicultural healing practices.

Robert B. Pickering

Robert B. Pickering is professor emeritus of anthropology at the University of Tulsa and founding director of the Museum Science and Management program at the university. He has been the recipient of many research grants, honors, and awards and is the author of scores of essays, articles, books, and papers.

John F. Scott

John F. Scott is professor emeritus of art history at the University of Florida and has taught courses on far-ranging areas of art practice in cultures throughout human history. Recipient of numerous fellowships and grants, he has been a prominent presenter of papers, a lecturer at many art symposiums, has written scores of articles for academic journals, and is author of *Latin American Art: Ancient to Modern*, nominated for the Arvey Book Award.

Barbara C. Sproul

Barbara C. Sproul is the former chair of the department of Religion at Hunter College, City University of New York (CUNY), and professor emerita of religion. She is the author of many articles and essays, and of the book *Primal Myths: Creation Myths Around the World*.

Wilfried van Damme

Wilfried van Damme has taught at various Belgian and Dutch universities, most recently at Leiden University (2004–21). He studied art history, archaeology, and cultural anthropology, and received his doctoral degree in art history from Ghent University, Belgium. His main interests are in aesthetics, which he approaches from an intercultural and interdisciplinary perspective.

Dahlia W. Zaidel

Dahlia W. Zaidel is adjunct professor of Behavioral Neuroscience, department of Psychology, and member of the Brain Research Institute, University of California, Los Angeles. A Fulbright scholar, she has studied and written extensively on the brain and art and has ninety-eight publication and research credits to her name.

ACKNOWLEDGMENTS

I would not have been able to start this book without the help of John Buxton, the owner of ArtTrak and a long-time appraiser on the PBS television series *Antiques Roadshow*. From the very beginning, when I first called him and told him about my idea for this book, he got its meaning and significance to art literature. He was enthusiastic and supportive of my undertaking this huge project and proceeded to graciously open his rolodex and call potential authors about writing the chapters.

I also would not have been able to produce this book without the skill and patience of my copy editor, Lisa Bessette. She became my partner in ensuring that essays about complex subjects written by scholars were understandable to a lay audience without losing their deeper meanings and nuances.

I want to commend the book's designer, Paul Sloman, for interpreting my vision of the project in a creative, thoughtful way without losing sight of his own vision of it. My congratulations to Paul Holberton for creating a company that allows limited market, limited profitability fine art books to be published so the world can be nourished by the unique gift that humankind has been given.

Above all, my eternal gratitude to the scholar authors of the book for their enthusiasm for the project and the passion they showed in their writing.

I also want to express my deep appreciation to the artists, known and unknown, who made the wonderful artworks reproduced in the book and to the artists of our day who continue to help us better understand the human experience.

Last, but not least, my thanks and love for my partner and wife of over fifty years, Susan, who heard about the book every night and commiserated with me over the problems and struggles of tackling such a complex subject in a form that had never been attempted before.

A book is a journey that its creator takes along with the reader. My goal was to make the end of this journey the beginning of another journey for each reader: to get through art a better understanding of their own life from the lives of humans that lived before. I hope I have achieved that.

Note to readers

You will see in the book that no dimensions are given
for some of the artworks reproduced. As hard as we
tried, we were unable to locate this information for every
object. We apologize for these omissions, but felt it was
important to include every piece of extraordinary art, even
if dimensions were not available.

Many of the photos shown in this book were taken
from the website Wikipedia Commons or provided by
museums who have made their collections open access.
I am very grateful for their mission in making available
free visual information to the world.

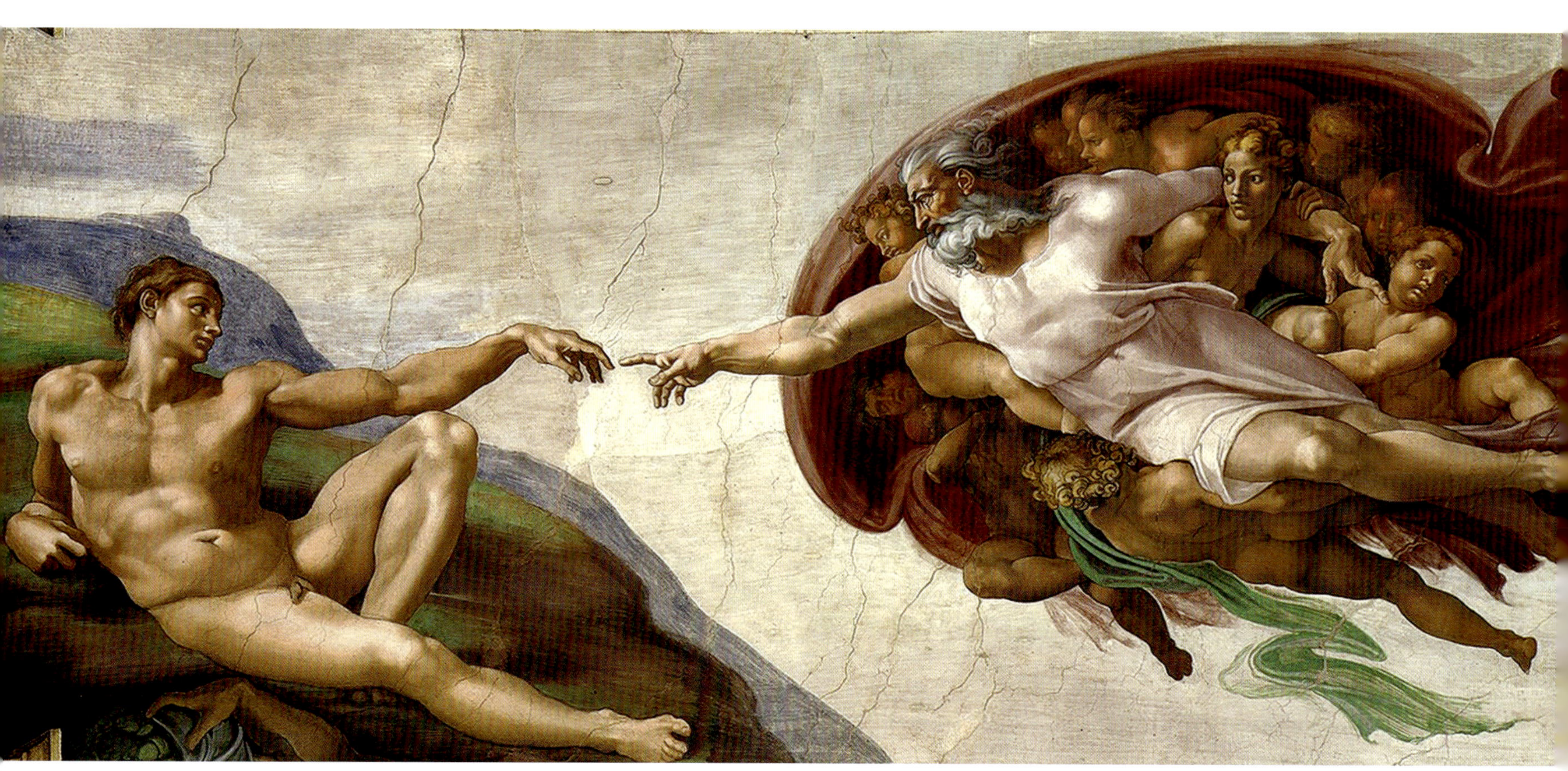

Creation of Adam

Detail of ceiling of Sistine Chapel
Michelangelo Buonarroti (Italy, 1475 – 1564)
1508 – 1512
Fresco
Vatican Palace, Vatican City

Art is the stored honey
of the human soul.

Theodore Dreiser

THE BOOKENDS OF COMMONALITY OVER THIRTY THOUSAND YEARS

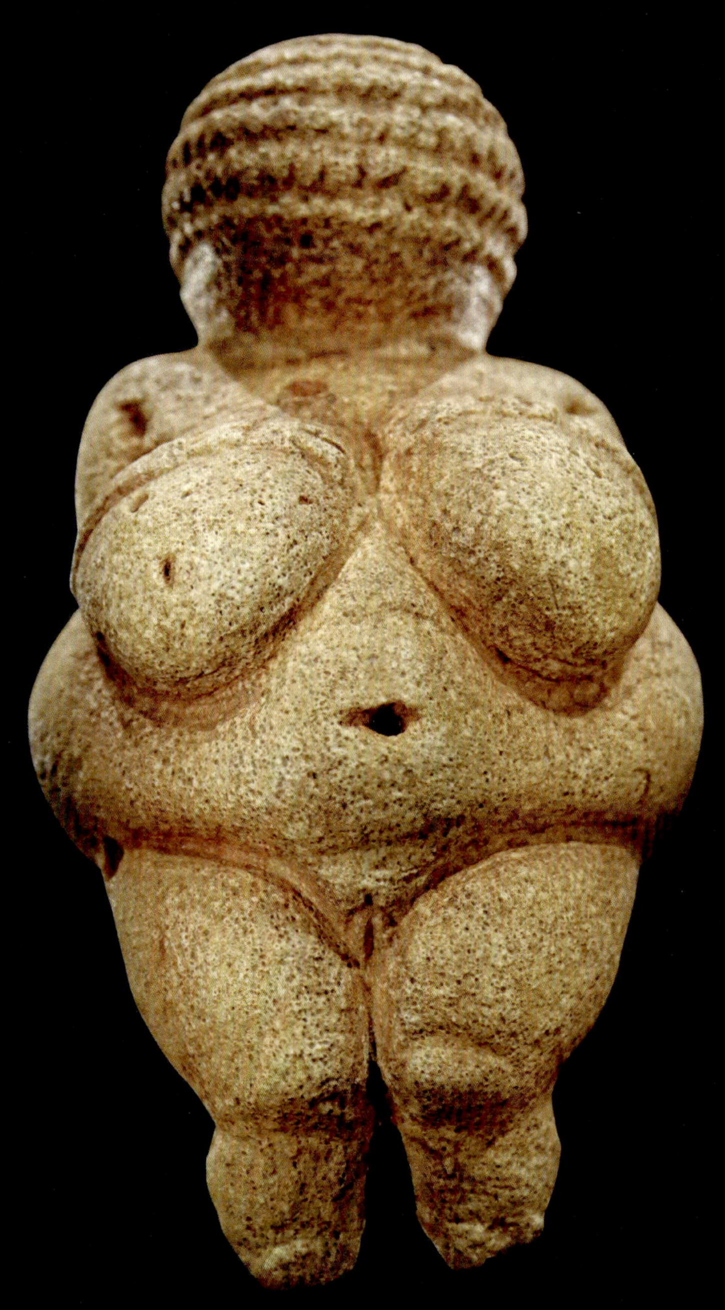

Venus of Willendorf

Paleolithic site near Willendorf, Austria
30,000 – 25,000 BCE
Oolitic limestone, 4 ⅜ in., 11.1 cm,
Natural History Museum, Vienna, Austria

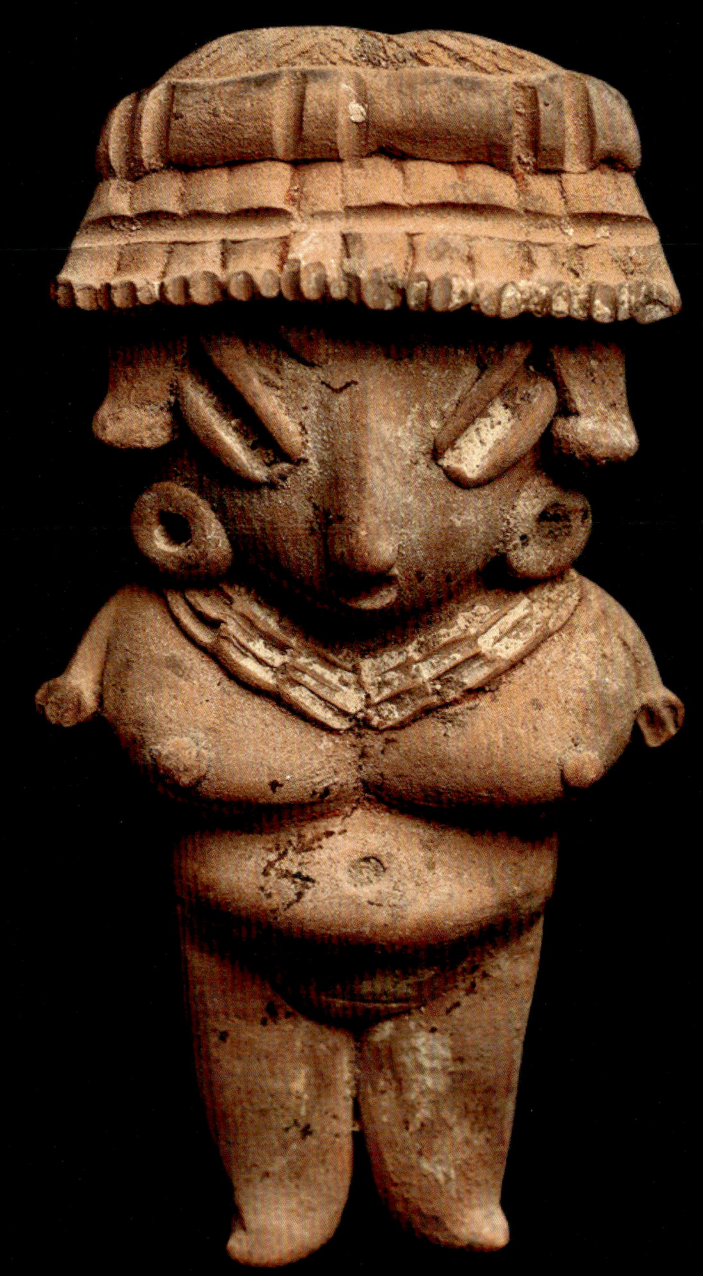

Pretty Lady

Chupicuaro culture, Mexico
400 – 100 BCE
Terracotta, 4 ⅜ in., 11.11 cm,
Arte Primitivo Gallery, New York
Photo by Gregory J. Adams

INTRODUCTION

Stuart Handler

This book was very challenging to assemble because the subject is so vast and complex. Initially, I hoped to see a museum mount an exhibition on the subject, but when I approached a major museum to do it with significant funding from me, I was told it would be too difficult. So rather than shop my idea around to other museums, I decided to put together my own vision of such an exhibition in book form. As it turned out, I came to realize that a book does far greater justice to the subject than a museum exhibition could. It would not have been possible, for example, for a museum to gather together in one place so many art objects from the world's great museums and private collections, as this book has, and to explain their full context with as much scholarship. On top of this, a book is forever and a museum exhibition is not. I understood the enormity of the task ahead of me and the responsibility to get it right.

It is too easy to think that people who lived at another time and in another place across the world from us are inexplicably different. But when we look at their lives through their art, we see similarities with our own lives and similarities in the art they made. To some, this commonality may seem obvious. After all, we are all human beings with similar brains, so why should we not think alike in certain ways? But considering the different ideologies, morals, and lifestyles that many cultures have tried to impose on each other throughout history, it is easy to lose sight of the commonality among us: that humans have had the same basic needs and emotions since time immemorial. As individuals we are unique, but we are also familiar to each other, as you will see in the art that follows on these pages. You will also see different styles infused with unique cultural context and individual personality, all the art showing the incredibly inventive, creative nature of the human mind.

We often forget that cultures communicate to each other by expressing their lives through art. We can learn about the experiences of the peoples of past cultures by looking at and studying this art—it is true that pictures often speak louder than words. This bridge enables us to deal with our own lives in ways that we otherwise might not. Few ancient and tribal cultures had a written language that allowed them to pass down stories about their lives, but they did have art, which they used as a language to teach their descendants and future cultures about living and dying. To this day we continue to use art to help us understand and deal with our complex, difficult lives, which, in turn, will help subsequent cultures better cope with their own.

The phenomenon of human connection in art is extraordinary and should be given greater attention. The genesis of my interest in the subject began while I was collecting pre-Columbian art. While looking for new pieces over the past thirty years, I saw many examples of tribal and ancient art that resembled the art in my collection in certain ways. Often this art had similar forms and meanings despite being different in style and materials. This led me to search for books explaining this phenomenon. I found only one: *Patterns That Connect*, written by Carl Schuster and Edmund Carpenter and published in 1996. I thought the book was an excellent start but did not go far enough geographically or chronologically, and it was not documented by photographs of the beautiful art I had seen.

A particularly clarifying moment of my personal discovery of this pattern of connection was seeing the famous Venus of Willendorf figure, made some 30,000 years ago, which strikingly resembled some of the West Mexican Chupicuaro figures created during the pre-Columbian period. For me, these were the bookends of a continuum of commonality in the art made by different cultures over time. Seeing this small, carved figure of a woman with large breasts and distended stomach made by a human being in a cave, possibly as a fertility icon, and similar figures made thirty millennia later spanning from the European continent to the North American continent was enlightening and inspired me to explore this pattern further.

The most challenging part of putting this book together was finding the proper people to write about the subjects I considered important to the story. In this age of specialization, generalists who can write broadly and in depth on any subject are rare. I sought people who, while specialists in a particular culture, were willing to work outside of their comfort zone and to think about other cultures alongside their own specialties. I started my search by reaching out to everybody I have come to know over the many years I have been collecting pre-Columbian art. I hoped to build a network of people who knew somebody who could write with authority on the subjects from a multicultural perspective over the history of mankind and to select examples of art that amplified their writing. Over the course of my search,

all the scholars I talked to were enthusiastic about the subject and thought a more comprehensive book about it was long overdue. In the end, I believe I have put together a group of scholars who tell an important story illustrated in a visually stunning way.

In thinking about this subject for so long and about how I would plan an exhibition of this kind, I always came back to the same organizing principle: the stages or events in a human being's life. Before I took the reader into these life experiences, however, I thought it was important to start with the brain and how humans are uniquely wired to make art for art's sake. In the first chapter, Dahlia W. Zaidel explains how the human brain has evolved over time to create more complex forms of art to express an ever more complex life. To complement this idea, I thought the narrative needed to be expanded into aesthetics and culture: how human beings choose forms, designs, and materials to show how they feel about themselves, their lives, and the world around them. Wilfried van Damme leads a discussion of why so many cultures have the same concept of beauty and take pleasure from art objects. These chapters naturally lead to creation myths, which are explored by Barbara C. Sproul. These are stories that in most cultures create the lens through which people view the world around them. I have always been struck by the similarities between the creation myths of different cultures and have come to believe that they set the stage for how people view life and how they express it through art. Professor Sproul provides many examples of these similarities in cultures throughout the world and throughout history.

Human life begins with birth and moves forward from there. Nearly all human cultures celebrate this process. Herbert M. Cole discusses motherhood and the family, considering art portraying women in labor, giving birth, nursing and caring for children, and family groupings. He explains how different cultures look at procreation and the care of their children and the similarities and differences in how they express these life experiences through art. This chapter is an important part of the book because the will to survive and to reproduce is such an innate part of the human species. The subject has also been expressed in some of the greatest art in human history.

Humans have realized since their evolution that they are not alone on this earth and have shown us through their art how they view the world around them. Lark E. Mason explores the commonalities in how cultures over time have viewed the plants, animals, and heavens of their world and how these views have been shaped by exchange with other cultures. Their art shows the reverence they had for the plants and animals that fed and healed them, and for the world they shared. Conflict and warfare have always been a part of human life and David H. Dye helps us to understand the dynamics of this behavior: the irony of why war both repels and attracts people, and how cultures have expressed it in their art. John F. Scott explores the evolution of representations of the human figure—the very essence of artmaking since the earliest images drawn on the walls of caves during Paleolithic times—and how they relate to a society's political organization.

The will to survive is organic to the human species and as people got sick, they found creative ways to heal themselves. Dr. Todd J. Pesek writes about how various cultures have treated sickness and facilitated healing by making medicines from the plants and animals around them and by communicating with the energetic or spiritual realm. All human life experience comes together in religion and rituals and all cultures have belief systems expressed through art that enable them to work through the problems of living. Alex W. Barker explains how beliefs and rituals arose from creation myths and were expanded through a culture's life experience to make the unknown meaningful, connect with the transcendent, foster community and group identity, and achieve a sense of power over the unknown. The art expressing this part of life shows striking similarities between cultures. Death is the final stage in human life, and in our final chapter, Robert B. Pickering shows how cultures throughout time have expressed concepts of death and the afterlife in beautiful and powerful art.

Like the chapters in our own lives, the chapters in the book intertwine, relating to and affecting each other. Creation myths affect the development of religious systems and rituals. Beliefs affect the cultural meanings of motherhood and the family. The art expressing the world around us is also affected by religious beliefs and other life experiences, as are political systems leading to conflict and warfare. Traditions and beliefs affect how we view ourselves and others, and the rituals and meaning of death. You will see that as humans evolved, the life events expressed through their art evolved alongside them, giving the art ever deeper and more nuanced meanings. References in the chapters to modern art show how humans continue to deal with the problems that the ancients faced in everyday living.

In essence, the art collected in this book reflects the human behaviors that led to its making and shows the needs and emotions of humans since they first evolved on earth. As you take your own journey through this book, you will realize, as I did in putting it together, how small we really are as individuals in the scheme of things. How insignificant we are in our place and time in the history of the universe. How we are just another animal on this planet focused on meeting our basic needs. It puts our self-importance in perspective in a humbling way. We still face the conundrum of having to deal with the important problems of everyday living, of how to survive and thrive, as did the people of past cultures whose art is portrayed on these pages.

To me, the commonality expressed through art means hope. It signals our mutual connection to humanity and to each other. Though it often seems like we have lived throughout history against a background of conflict and war, humankind will continue to endure because of this connection. Art shows us that we are indelibly bound to each other. It shows us that we have never been alone, nor will we ever be, in our common struggle to live and survive.

The chapters in this book represent hundreds of years of combined scholarship by their authors, men and women who are esteemed in their fields and approached their subjects with passion and dedication. Their research, ideas, and insights produced some remarkable writing. We looked at thousands of artworks to arrive at the examples that tell the story of each chapter, and the final selection represents some of the finest art ever created. But humans have made many millions of artworks over their history and the ones collected here are merely a fraction of what we know and an even smaller fraction of what still lays under the ground, yet to be discovered.

So, this book is not meant to be the final word on the subject. It surveys a swath of cultures throughout human history to show that we share the same brain structure and are compelled to make art, often with similar form and intent, to express ourselves. It is true that this subject is vast and complex, but a journey begins with a single step and I hope this book exhibition is the beginning of many books and museum exhibitions that will explore this fascinating subject. For when we realize that we as human beings are all essentially the same, maybe we can learn to better understand each other and, consequently, live in a more peaceful world.

I

THE BRAIN AND ART

DAHLIA W. ZAIDEL

Art is created in every human society, small and large, on all continents throughout the world. Enormous energy is invested in producing it—artists sometimes devote weeks, months, and even years to their works. The Italian Renaissance artist Leonardo da Vinci (1452–1519) is said to have spent four years painting the *Mona Lisa* (and some have suggested fourteen). Since art does not have the same immediate survival value as food, drink, and shelter, why all the effort? This has always been puzzling to scholars and philosophers. They have debated the reasons for this investment of time and the very nature of art for more than two thousand years without reaching consensus.

Recently, however, advances in multiple scientific fields have contributed to the insight that art, like language, is a communicative system for sharing ideas with others, supported by the remarkable human brain, which subserves extraordinary cognition.[1] Neuroscientists in particular have unraveled a great deal about the brain and art. For early humans, *Homo sapiens* (we are all *Homo sapiens* on earth today), who from the very dawn of their emergence in Africa around 315,000 years ago lived in social groups, harmonious interactions were critical. Evolutionary structural brain changes supporting communication between people, in addition to language, helped in achieving that goal.

Social communication enables comprehension of words, metaphors, symbols, and artistic representations. It is subserved by humans' unique capacity for symbolic cognition.[2] Only humans are endowed with such highly developed cognition, which enables us to have art and explains why animals do not. When we see a drawing or a sculpture of a horse, we understand instantaneously that we are not looking at a real, living horse, even when the representation is life-size. When we see Picasso's drawing *Dancer* (1954), we understand the work refers to a woman dancer, even though we are looking at a line drawing, not at a realistic depiction (1). This capacity to understand the difference between what is real and what is a representation is already present in babies and young children. Distinguishing between them is enabled with symbolic cognition.[3] When it comes to language communication, the operations of symbolic cognition are tied to semantic cognition, through which we grasp the meaning of words. We comprehend the meaning of the spoken word "cup," for example, without having to physically see a cup. Arbitrary sounds can be grouped to form a language whose meaning is understood by members of the society in which it originated. This is also true of representations in art, which likewise communicate ideas, notions, and concepts.

In broad terms, art is comprised of the visual arts (paintings, drawings, sculptures, film, and so on), music, dance, and literature. The formats familiar to us today only gradually, step-wise, became cultural behaviors. Early humans relied on intra-group cooperation and cohesion for survival.[4] Exploring the circumstances of art's origins in early human culture suggests that the practice held an evolutionary survival value and grew into an adaptive

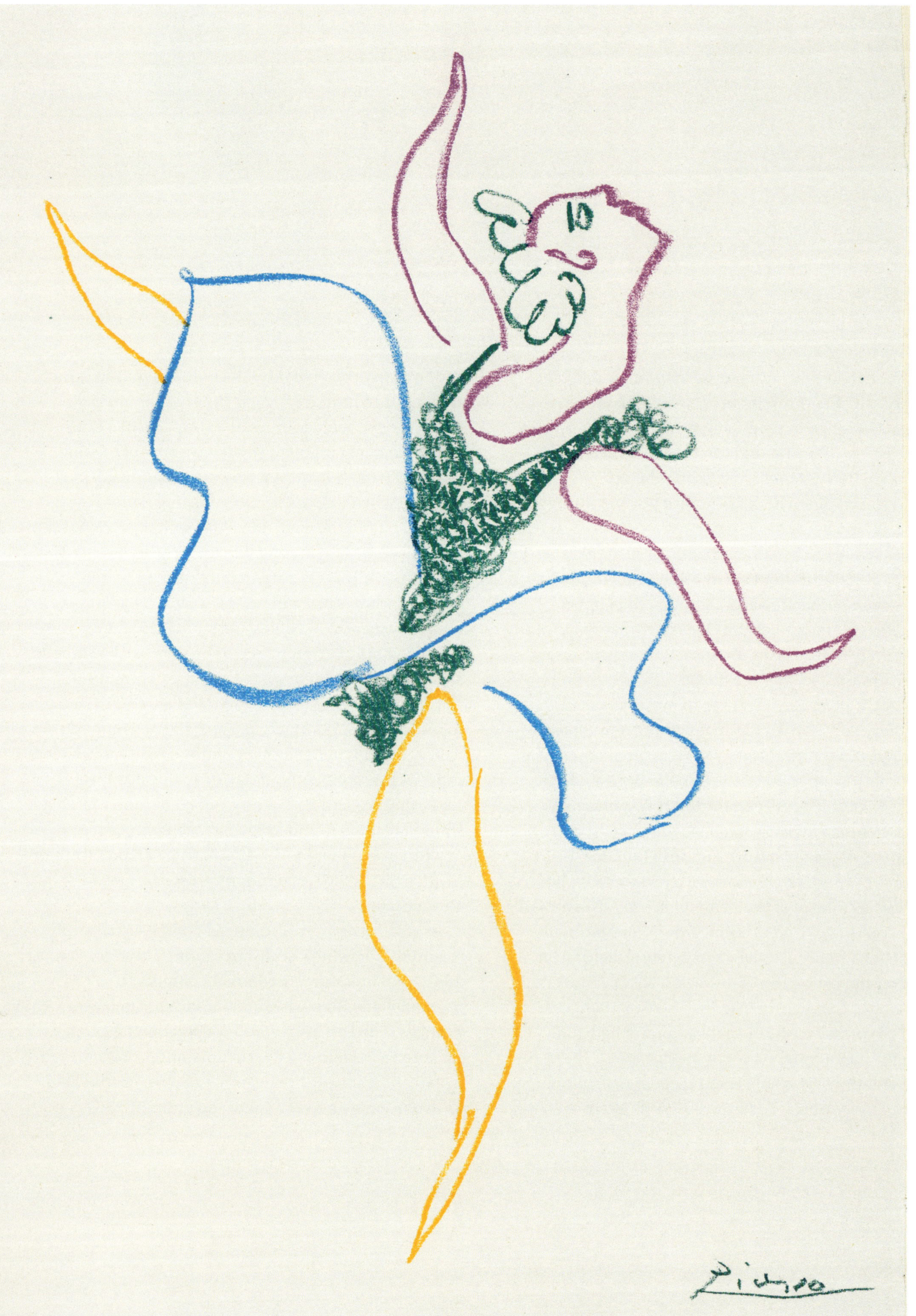

1 Ballet Dancer

Pablo Picasso (Spain, 1881 – 1973)
1954
Lithograph
12 ³⁄₁₆ × 8 ¹¹⁄₁₆ in., 31 × 22 cm
Museum of Modern Art, New York
Gift of Mrs. Bertha M. Slattery

practice. Humans would not be creating such a great variety of art today and investing so much effort in doing so if the practice did not hold this value. Early art expressions powerfully denoted group unity—indeed the earliest material art that has been found is strung sea shell beads that are thought to have provided a visible sign of belonging to a social group. The social message was the critical part and they included the practice of art in their cultural repertoire for that purpose. From an evolutionary perspective, art expression maximized biological survival, which led to its permanent adoption as a system of communication.[5]

Art and the Injured Brain

Research from the past 180 or so years has increased our understanding of how the brain controls multiple human abilities, such as speaking, reading, memory, emotions, attention, cognition, and so on. Much of what is now known about the brain and art has come from studying acquired brain injuries in visual artists who have spent a lifetime painting, drawing, and sculpting.[6] Acquired brain injury results in fractionation of behavior into fragments (components) that reveal what the whole behavior consists of. Neurologists, neuropsychologists, and neuroscientists study the behavioral aftermath of the injury. Typically, the scientific questions concern the relationship between the location of the injury and the impairments, if any, that follow. Studies of artists with a healthy brain that sustained injury in adult life as a

result of a stroke, tumor, or dementia have shown that regardless of which hemisphere of the brain (left or right) was damaged or the location of the injury within the hemisphere, they continued to create their art. This indicates that neither hemisphere has exclusive control over art making, and no single specific region controls the artistic endeavor. From the inception of the idea to the completion of an artwork, the steps require recruiting several widely spread regions of the brain.

We have also learned that when an established artist suffers a sudden brain injury localized in the parietal lobe in the right hemisphere (**2**), a particular perceptual impairment unrelated to their artistic cognition and abilities can emerge, albeit for a relatively short time. These artists have difficulties completing the work in the left half of the canvas due to an attentional issue (known as hemi-inattention) common in non-artists with a similar injury. Excessive attention is paid to the right half of the canvas, and the left half is not filled or only partially filled. The condition expresses itself in daily life, too, for example in neglecting to comb the hair on the left side of the head or not eating food on the left side of the plate. When the artists recover from the perceptual disorder, they are able to attend to the entire canvas. We have also found that when established adult artists experience sudden brain injury, there does not appear to be a dramatic shift to a new artistic style (genre) or subject matter, nor is there a loss of skill, talent, or creativity. A loss would suggest that specific brain regions control these components of art making.

In general, certain aspects of artistic skill can be learned and perfected through experience. Talent appears to be inborn, but creativity draws upon accumulated knowledge, experience, problem solving, dedication to the work, and imagination. Both talent and creativity are elusive in the sense that it is hard to quantify them.[7] Currently, there is no known single region (or two or three) in the brain exclusively dedicated to supporting talent or skill. Most likely, multiple, widely spread regions subserve their expression and providing they were spared by neural injury, no alteration in these aspects of art would be expected.

In cases of artists with brain injury resulting in paralysis of the right hand (the dominant hand for most activities in the majority of people), they shifted to using their left hand. In cases of dementia, which typically results in injurious alterations in multiple interconnected brain regions, artists continued to create art for many years into the disease.[8] Eventual cessation of artistic productivity in such cases is associated with loss of ability to control movements, extensive problems with perceptual distortions, and growing damage to brain regions normally subserving accumulated knowledge, memory, and mental concepts.

Even more unexpected is the finding that in most writers with injury to the left hemisphere, the main site for language specialization (speaking, writing, reading, comprehension), there was no loss of the capacity for creative writing. Instead, it would appear that well-practiced skills (exercised for many years) can be retained through the intact parts of the brain. In general, an artist's ability to continue making art despite brain injury that impairs their speech, some of their perceptual abilities, or movements of their dominant hand is maintained by brain regions that have been spared, though the exact mechanism and neural circuitry are not understood. Taken together, the study of brain injury in artists has revealed that there is no single brain region that subserves the whole process involved in producing art.

The Brain and Its Neural Networks in Art Making

What enabled artists like Michelangelo, Vincent Van Gogh, Claude Monet, and Pablo Picasso to create their now famous works was controlled by multiple brain regions in both the left and right cerebral hemispheres. Decades ago, a popular theory posited that the right hemisphere specializes in the creation and perception of art. The theory was not grounded in solid empirical findings and was incomplete in its assumptions; eventually, it was abandoned for lack of robust scientific evidence.[9] The attribution of creativity to right hemisphere specialization alone has also been doubted.[10] Studies that include neuroimaging of the brain (which allows scientists to see a person's brain activity on a computer screen) revealed that multiple cognitive functions in the left and right hemispheres have a functional role in the final artistic product.

2 A side view of the major subdivisions of the brain's cerebral cortex showing the frontal, temporal, parietal, and occipital lobes. Illustration by Dahlia W. Zaidel

Thinking, problem solving, imagining, concept and idea formation, memory, comprehension, art making, art perceiving, and so on, are all subserved by the cortex. There are two sets of these subdivisions, one in the left side, one in the right side, known as the left and right hemispheres.

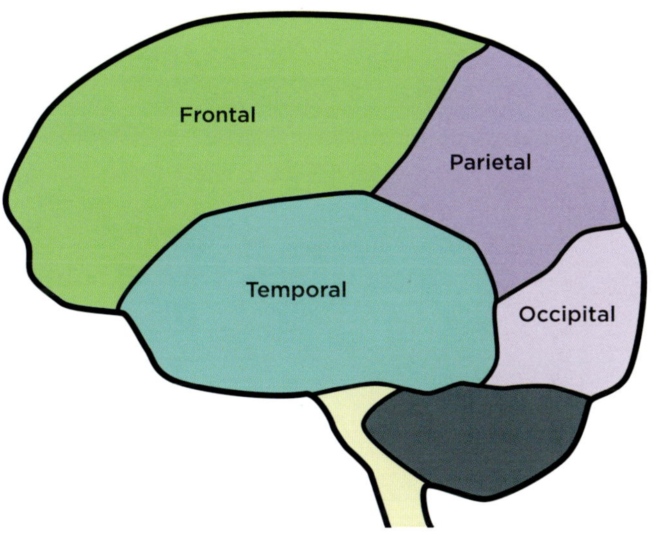

Once an idea is formed in the mind, regardless of whether or not it involves art, it is brought to fruition through neural activity. There is no clear understanding of which brain region or regions lead to the formation of ideas. Both the left and right hemispheres are involved. Imagination, an integral component of ideas, represents several domains of thinking—knowledge of existing facts, memory, networks of concepts, logical reasoning, problem solving—as well as the ability to mentally visualize ideas and their modes of execution in the mind's eye. Parts of the brain in the occipital, parietal, and temporal lobes are active in mental visualization (**2**). Interestingly, they are the parts that are also active when we use our eyes to see. The components of the imagination are subserved by interconnected neural regions.

Located in the frontal lobes of the brain, the pre-frontal region enables planning actions for reaching an idea's goal, directing the steps needed to realize the work, monitoring the steps, knowing when to start and stop, evaluating and error correcting, and maintaining sustained attention. The part of the brain controlling the movement of hands and legs, known as the motor cortex (in the back of the left and right frontal lobes), enables fine dexterous finger-hand movements for painting, drawing, sculpting, playing musical instruments, and the leg, arm, and whole-body movements involved in dancing. Eye-hand coordination is a critical component in the final work, recruiting adequate control through connections between the occipital lobes (the main vision processing areas) and the motor cortex (controlling execution of movements) in the frontal lobes. Added to that are the actions of the cerebellum (the dark grey area in figure 2, below the occipital lobes), which critically controls the timing and coordination of muscle movements used in speaking and to maintain posture balance in walking, dancing, and sitting. These brain regions and their connectivity to each other contribute to the quality of the artwork, whether painting, dancing, musical composition, or performance.

The parietal lobe in the right hemisphere enables the mental rotation of images or objects in the "mind's

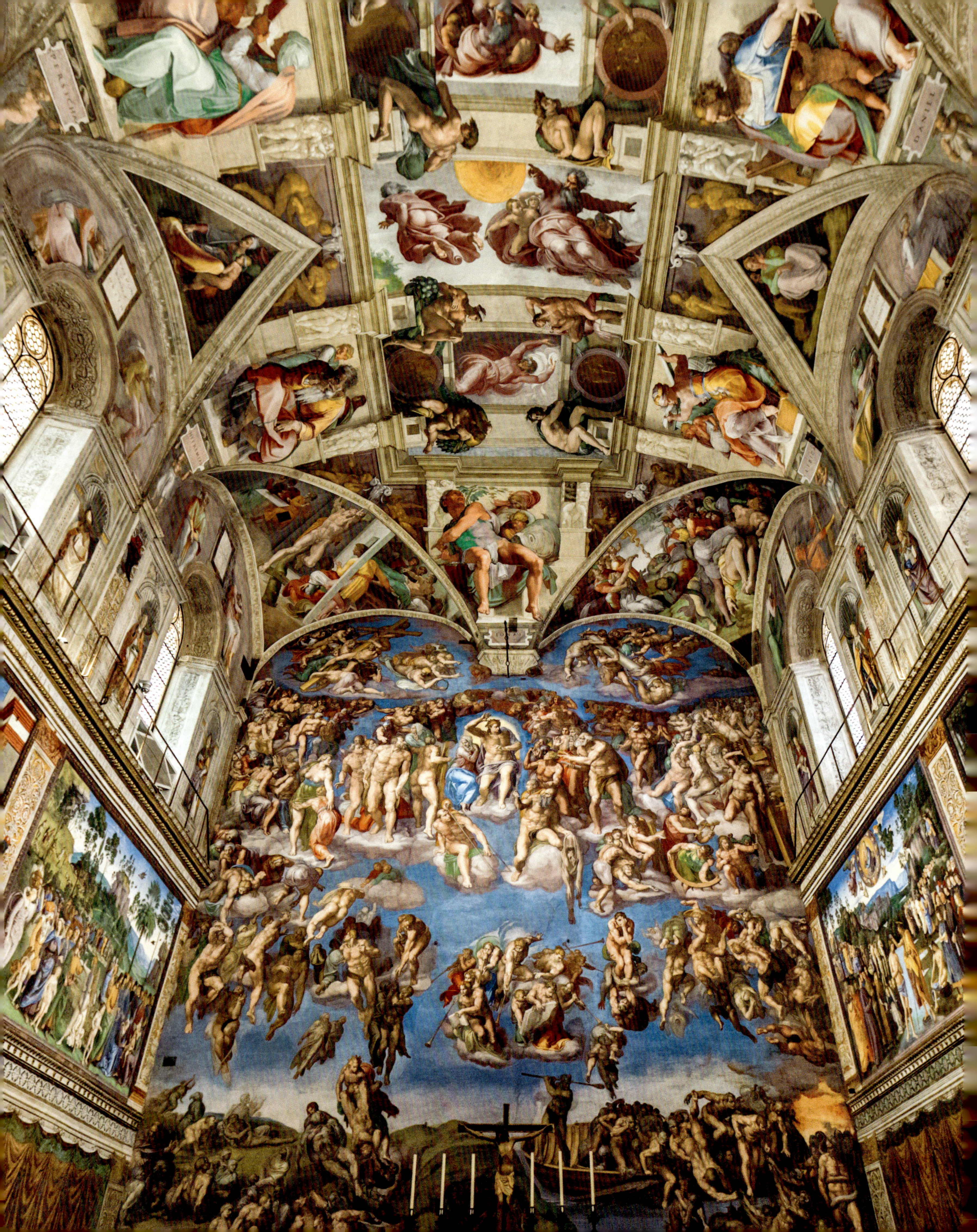

eye" for spatially accurate depictions or for executing the totality of the design envisioned by the artist, whether the representation is figurative or abstract. In our visual environment and in paintings, we often come across objects that are blocked from view, and we need to infer what is hidden. The ability to fill in gaps in patterns, whether obscured by shadows or occluded, is also a function of the right parietal lobe. This ability allowed Italian Renaissance artist Michelangelo to mentally visualize how the paintings on the ceiling of the Sistine Chapel would appear to viewers looking up from the floor below (**3**). He had to consider the subject matter for each of the panels and their implied meaning, taking into account the perspective of each figure from the viewer's vantage point. And while painting, he would have had to come down periodically to consider whether or not his work-in-progress matched his original calculations. Monitoring progress and recognizing that adjustments are in order draws upon error correction capability subserved by the frontal lobes. In the end, Michelangelo's artistic endeavor reflected the high quality of his artistic cognition, remarkable skills, talent, and creativity.

Have you noticed artists stepping back from their paintings periodically, taking in the work in its totality from a short distance away? When they do so, they are evaluating the global appearance, assessing the whole configuration with the help of the right parietal lobe. When Leonardo da Vinci painted the *Mona Lisa*, he had to keep in mind that people would view her likeness two-dimensionally on canvas, not three-dimensionally as he saw her in real life. Like all portrait painters, he had to add subtle shadows in just the right spaces on the canvas to translate a three-dimensional view into a two-dimensional representation. In doing so, he masterfully conveyed both his artistic skills and his face recognition specialization (supported by regions in the right occipital and temporal lobes).

Similarly, in creating his pointillist paintings, nineteenth-century French artist Georges Seurat had to place his tiny brush strokes on canvas in such a way that figures seem to emerge from the sum total of differently colored dots (**4**). To do so required mental visualization of the final work, drawing on, among other regions, the functions subserved by the right parietal lobe. Similarly, the splattered paint artworks by Jackson Pollock, the geometrical abstractions of Piet Mondrian, and Cubist works by Pablo Picasso and Georges Braque all involved mental visualization of the entire composition, how a collection of small and large shapes would merge into a coherent, two-dimensional artistic whole. But simultaneously with mental visualization, the parietal lobe in the left hemisphere also plays a functional role in these works, contributing cognition that allows the logical, detailed steps to its realization. The left parietal lobe enables retrieval of lifelong accumulated semantic knowledge (knowing the meaning of things) derived from lived experiences, including some linguistic and non-linguistic knowledge; logical step-wise reasoning; and attention to details. When artists work on the details, this part of the brain is active. Problem solving,

4   **A Sunday on La Grande Jatte**

Georges Seurat (France, 1859 – 1891)
1884 – 1886
Oil on canvas
81.7 × 121.25 in., 207.6 × 308 cm
Art Institute of Chicago
Helen Birch Bartlett Memorial Collection

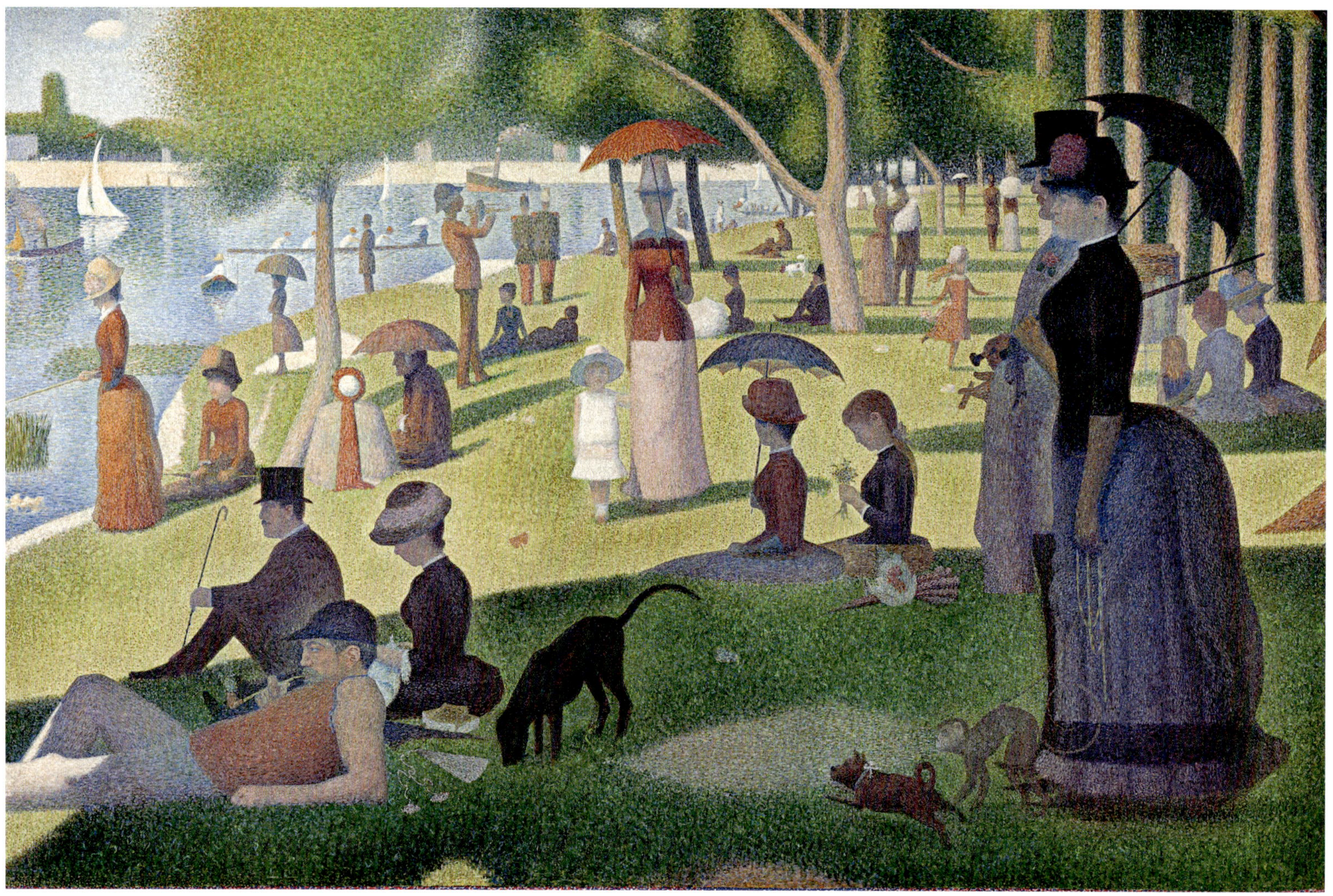

In the Pointillism tradition, tiny brush strokes are placed on the canvas in such a way that figures emerge from the sum total of differently colored dots. This required Seurat to mentally visualize the final work, being guided by functions subserved by the right parietal lobe.

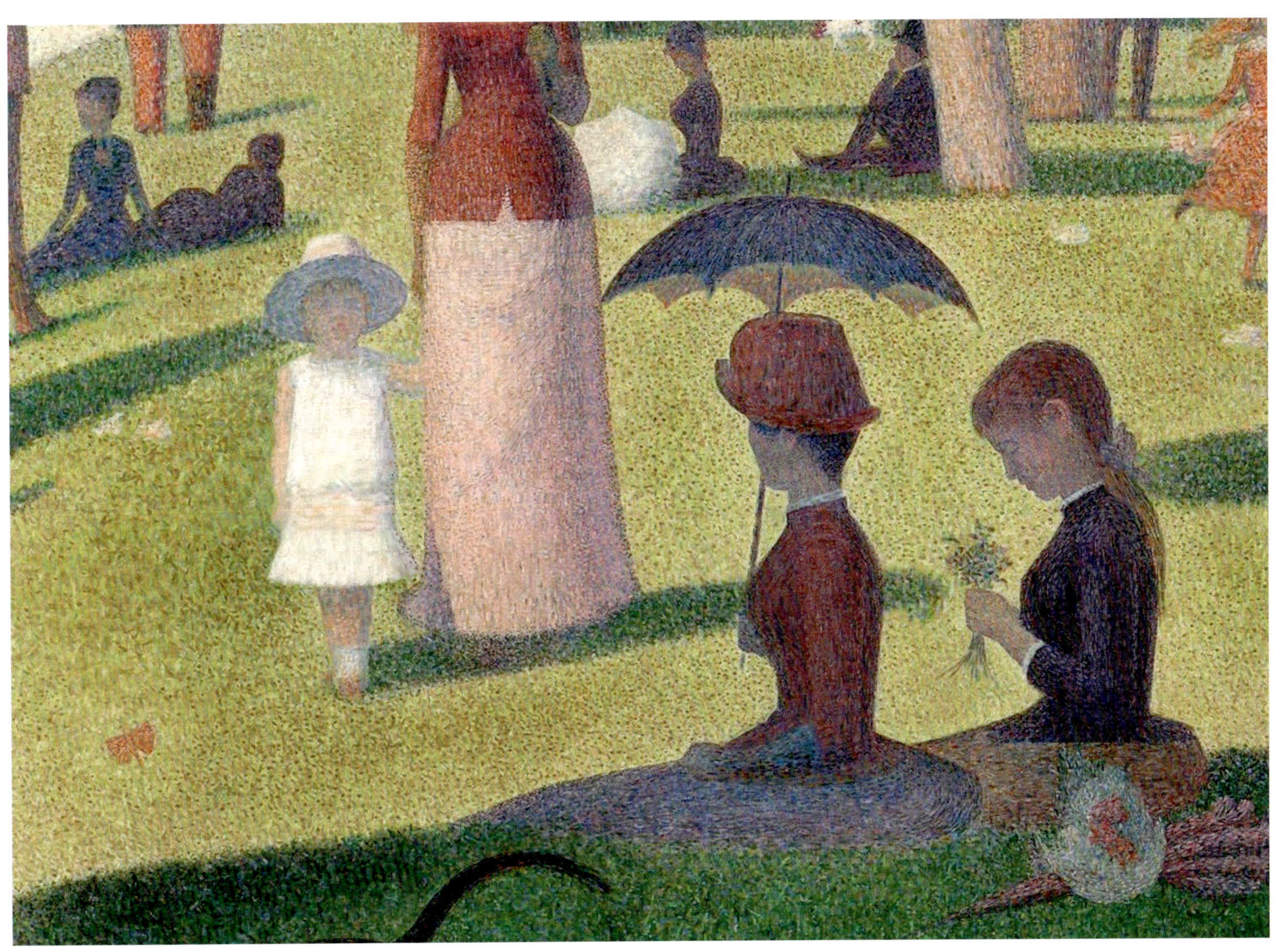

arithmetical calculations, comprehending word-labels for left-right orientation, and knowledge of body parts are similarly subserved by the left parietal lobe and end up contributing to the final artistic product. Ultimately, visual artists rely on abilities subserved by both parietal lobes. The two sides of the brain (cortex) communicate with each other through a large interconnecting structure known as the corpus callosum and in this way both sides contribute to the final artistic product.

Sounds, memory processes, and visual computation recruit the activity of different areas within the temporal lobes. Understanding the meaning of language sounds, music, or environmental sounds (fire engines, church bells), as well as memory for various facts and events are processed in the temporal lobes. Visual images, acuity, and colors are initially processed in the occipital lobes, located in the back of the brain, before engaging the parietal and temporal lobes for further processing, giving rise in particular to perceptual and meaningful understanding of what we are seeing.

The Evolution of Homo Sapiens, the Brain, and Art

By itself, all of the foregoing does not explain how and why art making originated in human culture. Our biological ancestors, the hominins, diverged from chimpanzees approximately 7 million years ago in Africa, but there is no archaeological evidence that they created visual art for a few million years afterward. The brain first underwent structural changes (over millions of years) in our immediate biological ancestors, the non-human primates. As hominins evolved, their brains grew in size, their survival skills began to include handmade stone tools, and they continued to live in small social groups, but still in that early period they did not produce art that left physical traces.

By around 315,000 years ago, based on unearthed skull fossils, the first *Homo sapiens* evolved, also in Africa. While brain tissue does not survive the passage of hundreds of thousands of years, by measuring the volume and shape of the skulls, scientists have been able to infer the size and some features of the brains of our *Homo sapiens* ancestors. The measurements indicate that they developed brains similar to ours today and surviving archaeological artifacts suggest that they could already have possessed aspects of semantic knowledge and symbolic cognition that supported imagination, language communication, and possibly some non-material art forms (such as dance, music, storytelling, and body painting). While the artifacts they left behind suggest they used clever survival strategies, material art was not a feature of their culture. By around 230,000 years ago, *Homo sapiens* were anatomically similar to modern humans with still no substantial evidence for visual art making.[11]

The brain regions and their functions discussed above evolved to promote non-art survival purposes such as navigating the environment (leaving and returning to the home base after hunting and food gathering), visualizing the topography in the mind's eye, remembering the exact locations of water sources, interpreting environmental sounds, distinguishing animal vocalizations, remembering faces and language utterances, speaking, reasoning, problem solving, comprehending new events, and recognizing colors of ripe fruits and vegetables. With this type of cognition, early humans were able to not only orient themselves, find their way in their surroundings, and remember specific geographical layouts, they were also able to hammer stones into fine tools for use in hunting, digging for edible roots, trapping and skinning animals, and multiple other life-saving purposes. Given early *Homo sapiens'* fine hand-finger dexterity and clever know-how with stone tool technology, one wonders why they did not extend their abilities to art sculpting, carving, and engraving. The likely explanation is that cultural and belief systems at the time imposed rules and norms for behaviors that prevented potential artistic abilities from being expressed.

Collective effort ensured stability and safety for the small groups of early *Homo sapiens* evolving in Africa. They survived major, long-lasting environmental upheavals and climatic changes, such as prolonged droughts that affected water and food resources, including animals they depended on for meat, skin, and bones. Despite such adversity, they continued to refine their stone tools and improve their hunting abilities, and they had the mental and physical abilities to deal with the consequences of weather instability. In the face of threats to their very existence, personal competitiveness would have only hindered survival. The symbolic art expressions that initially emerged and were practiced are not likely to have emphasized artistic virtuosity (meaning, who is the best artist or who can make the most beautiful art) but rather communal displays of art representations denoting unity, such as communal dancing and group choral singing.

The intersection of social-cultural conditions and environmental survival needs has shaped evolutionary pressures on brain structure. Today, *Homo sapiens* share the same genome containing the genetic instructions for our body and brain, the underpinning of cognition, sensory organs (eyes, ears, nose, and so on), emotions, social needs, and attitudes to social rules and norms. The changes were substantial in humans, enabling comprehension of artistic symbolic expressions of beliefs and experiences. Cultural habits in and of themselves are thought to contribute to the evolutionary process of brain development.

The major and most significant human migration away from Africa was around 60,000 years ago. This resulted in the successful establishment of human societies throughout the world. Those who left the continent were equipped with adaptive (useful) cultural practices, early art expressions (described below), and solid social values and norms. All of this, as well as knowledge of stone tool technology, material for extracting pigments from geological rocks, and navigation skills, aided in staking out new habitats where food and water were bountiful. Universal themes and motifs that we observe in art today despite cultural diversity and geographical remoteness—the emphasis on objects used in daily life, facial and body appearance, the sight and sounds of surrounding wildlife, cultural practices, and beliefs—highlight this shared beginning of brain evolution and cultural development.

The Early Non-Material Arts

The archaeological record indicates that material visual art (paintings, carvings, sculptures) was initiated into cultural practice remarkably slowly. The creation of non-material forms of art, the kinds that do not leave physical traces behind and are difficult to verify now with the passage of time, could have been underway more than 300,000–400,000 years ago. Given their successful social existence, early humans were clearly capable of symbolic thinking, the necessary cognitive ingredient to this kind of art making. Collective forms of display deeply anchored in biological traits involving rhythmical movements, touching, and synchrony, such as communal moving and swaying dance formations and choral melodious vocalization, would have been an important symbol of cohesion. Cooperation and social harmony were, and remain, crucial for survival in socially oriented human life. These art forms "could have all been practiced for their socially unifying value, and at the same time represented coded systems that referred to symbolic meaning understood by members of the group."[12] This type of artistic expression signified coordinated social life and was practiced to ensure social harmony.

Communal dancing formations in particular reinforced the concept of group togetherness and effort: "Slipping into collective formations while swaying, holding, shuffling, and clapping in unison is a natural act that seems rooted in biological needs of primates for social comfort, closeness, and touch. Synchronizing rhythmically to a beat. . . . is achieved by current modern humans, and recently has been found to be displayed to some extent in fireflies, in certain pet birds, sea lions, elephants, horses and other animals. Dancing is clearly a natural human expression; very young children spontaneously break into rhythmical body dance motion in response to music without prior instructions. There is no reason to assume that rhythmic motoric synchrony was not present at the dawn of early anatomically modern humans and grew to obtain meaningful symbolic purpose."[13] Creating melodious music by singing in chorus or through communal rhythmical percussion of stones (or clapping hands or hand-held wooden sticks) could have been practiced for symbolic displays as well. Repeated shaping of tools from stones would have resulted in man-made sound percussion as tapping, chipping away, and knapping one stone against another created a melodious chorus of sounds with low and high pitches, tempos, and timbre. Additional sounds came from birds, mammals, nocturnal organisms, and weather conditions. It has been reasonably suggested that music making was one of the earliest forms of artistic expression.

There was a physiological lure to participating in collective singing, humming, clapping, and dancing; touching others and maintaining body closeness created pleasurable sensations, which entrenched the practices. And participation would have been within the capability of all—young, old, men, and women. Because traits of dance and music, such as rhythm and beat, have deep evolutionary origins (inherited from our biological ancestry), their initial expression may have been spontaneous and eventually re-formulated into an art form for their symbolic value. Importantly, through characteristic stylistic formats that distinguish social groups from one another, communal dance and music signify group identity. The adaptive nature of the practice was preserved after the dispersion away from Africa, developing and growing into today's folk dances, ballet, hip-hop, rave music dancing, and symphonies, concertos, operas, and so on. The key here is that the original social purpose in human society was preserved due to its adaptive value while still providing a flexible basis for further expansion.[14]

Another possible early art form is storytelling, which probably occurred around the fire where the group congregated.[15] The earliest hearths date to around 400,000 years ago in Africa. Small, socially oriented groups shared their food in a centrally located space within the boundaries of the campsite, typically around the fire hearth, where food was cooked, and warmth, light, and some protection from predators were afforded. Congregating in that way provided opportunities for rehashing events, sharing new information, friendly and adversarial encounters, learning and teaching, and planning. At the same time, the hearth could have set the stage for oral storytelling and theater-related acting, both of which expressed the imagination, enshrined past experiences and observations, and, importantly, linked the community together. We cannot be certain that such art forms were practiced in this way in the distant evolutionary past of *Homo sapiens* because there are no physical traces in the archeological record, but it is reasonable to contemplate such a scenario. Today, storytelling is a universally practiced art. In tribal societies throughout the world, gathering around the fire to make announcements, tell stories about the distant past, engage in singing, and consume food signifies shared intentions and declares social identification. In modern societies, the art of storytelling has expanded to literature, poetry, and film making.

Marking the body with painted motifs or skin tattoo designs is another art form that has not left a trace in the archeological record. This practice, too, symbolizes whole group affiliation or status within a group. Visually recognizing such marks from a distance in peace and war would also hold obvious advantages. In the early prehistoric past, color pigments were derived from ocher clay with varying concentrations of minerals that yielded yellow, red, purple, orange, pink, brown, and in-between shades. Evidence for its mining and use can be traced to around 300,000 years ago in Africa, where it was used in tanning animal skin hides, the preparation of adhesives, and to protect the skin from insects and sun. There is also evidence that pigment was used on stone and bone tools, and that early humans walked great distances to mine different shades. This, and the fact that clumps of clay were transformed in various ways—pounded into powder, fashioned into crayon-like shapes, heated, and scraped—suggests that it was manipulated and altered to be used on different surfaces for symbolic purposes. With body painting, which is still practiced as an art form among tribal people, the purpose would have been to express group or group-level identity.

In the archaeologically rich Blombos Cave in South Africa, evidence dated to 70,000 years ago suggests that differently pigmented ocher was heated in separate abalone shells.[16] Heating alters the clay into the preferred consistency for painting some surfaces, possibly the body. Although the specific use cannot be ascertained given the passage of time and lack of preserved body tissue, scholars argue the heating could have been meant for symbolic applications. Significantly, while early humans sheltered in caves and a range of pigments were available, they did not leave behind evidence of wall paintings or carvings. They would have been artistically capable of doing so considering their finely chiseled stone tools at that time, made with carefully chosen materials and requiring dexterity and mental visualization. Future discoveries might help shed light on the reasons.

The Early Material Arts

Well over 250,000 years elapsed from the time *Homo sapiens* evolved around 315,000 years ago in Africa to the "explosion" of visual artmaking around 45,000–35,000 years ago. A glimpse of the early beginnings of material art can be had by tracking the timeline of dated artifacts. The reasons for the percolation of art expression in the distant evolutionary dawn of *Homo sapiens* hold keys to the current worldwide practice of art making, the social-cultural constraints placed upon it, and its universal commonalities.

The earliest visual art-related object we have is a necklace made of seashell beads dated to approximately 77,000 years ago found in a cave in South Africa. After this there is a time gap of tens of thousands of years with only a trickle of material art. In another cave in South Africa, over 400 shards of painted ostrich egg shells dating to around 60,000 years ago were found. Ostrich eggs are very large and the shells have walls thick enough to serve as water containers. Rectangular or squarish grids had been scratched onto the shells, which were also painted with a reddish, ocher-based material and regularly spaced black dots. Some shards had engraved or painted grids with no dots. The markings and colors are thought to have provided information on the water content inside and group identity. Both the seashell beads and the egg shell markings are considered visual symbolic expressions signifying collective identity and affiliation.

Around 45,000–35,000 years ago, in a period known as the Upper Paleolithic, mostly in western Europe, we see the beginning of material art creations in the form of sculptures from ivory and engraving on animal bones, stones, and antlers. Currently there is no evidence to indicate that the period coincided with specific brain changes. Rather, it is thought that the explosion in art making likely reflects the fortuitous intersection of several factors that include new social-cultural dynamics, the growth of social group size, an abundance of food sources, and changes in environmental and living circumstances. The Ice Age might have played a major role in this development,[17] as major swaths of land being covered in ice and snow and exceptionally low temperatures forced people to stay indoors, which at that time meant retreating inside natural rock caves with plenty of free time.[18] Whatever the triggers might have been, social-cultural norms supported the practice of making material art.

By this time, other parts of the world were also inhabited by *Homo sapiens*. The oldest figurative art painting made by them was found in Leang Tedongnge Cave in Indonesia and dates to 45,500 years ago. The painting was created with pigment extracted from red clay (ocher), and it depicts a single, nearly life-size side view of a native small pig of a type that can still be found on the island today. The oldest cave paintings in Europe, found in Chauvet Cave in France and dating to 36,000–32,000 years ago, depict multiple animals. Painted on and etched into the walls in six chambers of a single cave, they demonstrate considerable artistic skill and talent. The animals are presented in head-on and profile views, and they are shown stationary, resting, and galloping. Painted with charcoal and red ocher, they include herds of horses, single horses, groups of rhinoceroses, the ancestors of current domestic cattle, eurochs (now extinct), bison, mammoths, and lions. The engraved animals include owls, rhinoceroses, and horses, and in their attempts to render the images as realistically as possible, the artists made use of bumps and recesses in the walls.

In a chamber located deep within Altamira Cave in northern Spain, over 100 images of animals in various positions, including bison, horses, wild boars, and goats, were painted and engraved with pigments also made of charcoal and reddish ocher clay, diluted to achieve different shades (5). Here, too, natural perturbations in the walls were used to add dimension and realism. The images were not created in a single cave-occupation time period but in successive occupations stretching over a period of 35,000–15,000 years. They were either drawn from memory or possibly from sketches made on stone tablets when observing the animals in their habitat (though no such tablets have yet been found).

In Pech Merle Cave in southeastern France, wall paintings of horses with black spots (blown on using the mouth or imprinted with fingers) have been dated to 25,000 years ago. Current genetic research shows that such horses existed at the time, suggesting that artists were depicting realistic images of wildlife. However, in other chambers there are line drawings of mammoths with red spots, which are not true to life.

Countless other caves with realistic animal paintings and rock engravings from that period in the Upper Paleolithic, mostly depicting animals, have now been

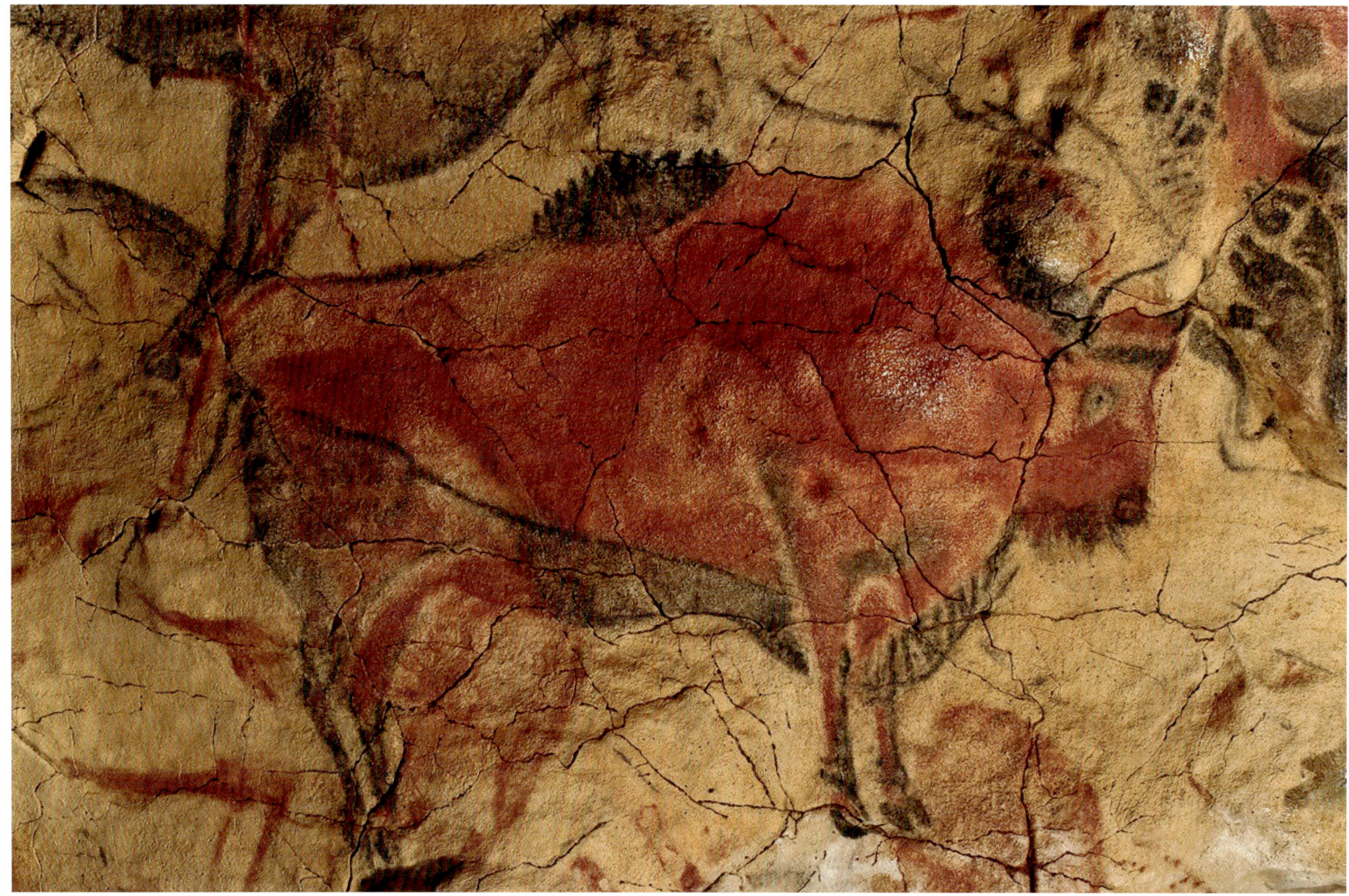

Realistic drawings of wildlife by the people who lived in this cave in Spain approximately 35,000 – 15,000 years ago, known as the Upper Paleolithic period in Europe.

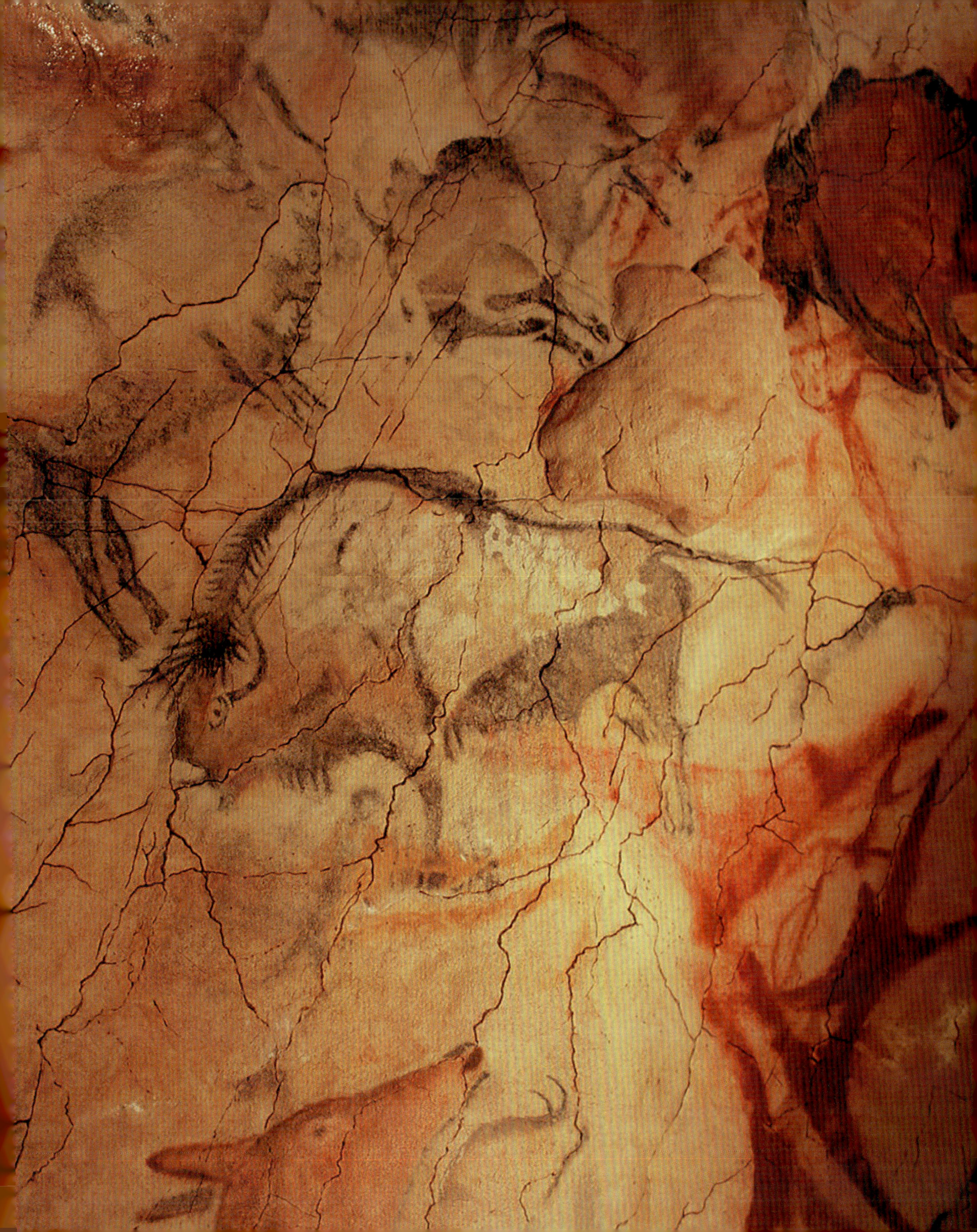

discovered in France, Spain, Portugal, and Italy. In some of these places and in Germany, small statues and carvings made from ivory tusks, bone, wood, and antlers were unearthed as well. At that point of *Homo sapiens* evolution, highly skilled individuals, with talent not unlike what we see today, were able to exhibit their artistic virtuosity. In addition to the paintings, stenciled hand marks of both adults and children have been found on cave walls throughout the world. These are believed to signify symbolic group affiliation, as if to say "we are one, we live here." They were created either by dipping the hand in liquified red pigment derived from ocher clay and then pressing it against the wall, or by positioning the hand on the wall and then spit-blowing pigmented liquid on it.

There has been much speculation regarding the purpose of all of these depictions. They may have served spiritual functions or acted as emotional reminders of nature's bounty outside the cave. It is likely that while isolated in caves during the Ice Age, artists imagined the outside world, wanting to be surrounded by animals and to return to more hospitable times. We cannot know, of course, but the evidence points to a remarkable expansion in artistic expression and cultural approval of such a time-consuming occupation. Acceptance of the work of individual artists is determined by society; it reflects time allotted to the endeavor by the most talented, levels in the allocation of responsibilities and duties, and hierarchical structure and organization. Acknowledging that some group members are

capable of expressing concepts not directly associated with the procurement of food, drink, warmth, and defense indicates the presence of established security and comfort.

The Brain, Biology, and Beauty

Although beauty plays a role in our attraction and attention to artistic representations, and on the surface may seem the sole reason for why we have art in the first place, the practice of making art evolved into an integral and powerful communicative system in human societies for depicting universal concerns ranging from daily experiences, emotions, thoughts, concepts, and symbols to technological advances. Artistic talent and skills articulate the essence of the communication.

Beauty is said to be subjective, something that exists in "the eye of the beholder." In fact, aesthetic reactions to art have underpinnings in the brain, but they are not art-specific. Those brain regions normally process non-art material as well. They are involved in attention, memory, vision, emotions, memory, thinking, and experiencing pleasure. Through neuroimaging scientists have been able to study what goes on in the brain when people judge a painting for its beauty, and it turns out that no single part of the brain is dedicated exclusively to assessing beauty in art. The same brain areas active in aesthetic reactions, which include vision processing in the occipital lobes and the posterior temporal lobes, memory-related parts in the hippocampus and connected areas, and emotion processing sections of the posterior cingulate gyrus and the insula are involved. Thinking and attention processes in the precuneus in the parietal lobe associated with self-reflection (self-consciousness), autobiographical memory, imagery, and spatial perception are all highly active in the evaluation of art. In addition, some studies have found activity in a neural network associated with the feeling of pleasure upon positive reactions to visual artworks, which, again, is not an art-dedicated network, since it normally becomes active in the context of experiences such as addiction to drugs, food, sex, and rewards.[19]

Because of their immediate reactions to artworks, most people think that the purpose of art is to beautify and give pleasure. But when the practice of artmaking began at the dawn of the evolution of *Homo sapiens*, sources of natural beauty abounded, from colorful sunrises to sunsets, wide vistas, fields of flowers, animals, faces, waterfalls, and so on. Adding human-made beauty would not have contributed to social group survival.[20] Beauty is not likely to have been the reason the balance was tipped in favor of introducing art into cultural practice.

Scientists link aesthetic experiences to inherited biological factors. Beauty is what attracts our attention to the artwork and helps us attend to its message.[21] The biological parallel is the displays animals put on to attract potential mates for procreation, which are meant to exhibit their genetic health and fitness qualities. The males of many species invest a great deal of time in elaborate displays to females, who attentively inspect them, rejecting males with poor health signals. In this way females maximize the chances for health-related traits to be passed on genetically to their offspring, which predicts offspring survival, a critical consideration in the continuation of the species. When artists exhibit their work, they are not trying to attract a mate or display their physical health. What is being displayed is their artistic cognition, talent, skill, and creativity, all of which are subserved by the brain. The brain of the viewer similarly assesses the artistic traits through attention-attraction to works with excellent artistic genetic qualities.[22] Neuroimaging the brains of viewers tasked with evaluating the aesthetics of visual artworks indicates that several considerations enter into their assessment. The artistic qualities attract our attention to the work, but once attracted, our aesthetic judgement relies on memory, emotions, attention, thinking, imagery, and other aspects of our mental processes subserved by interconnected brain parts.

The Social Basis of Art Styles

Today, and in the preceding thousands of years, myriad art styles, movements, schools, and techniques have emerged throughout the globe. As already discussed, incorporating art expressions into cultural practice early on had an evolutionary use value; art became an adaptive strategy for enhancing biological survival. This usefulness to society is what eventually led to the adoption of characteristic styles. The definition of "useful" has undergone changes in parallel with the growth of different social groups, unshared geographical spaces, advances in general knowledge, social control hierarchies, as well as political and dominant cultural belief systems. Neither viewers' aesthetic preferences nor artistic talent, creativity, or skill alone determines the trends. Because of the social communicative role of art, constraints on expressions are sometimes imposed by central societal norms, and the final appearance of the work reflects a combination of entrenched artistic habits and cultural expectations.[23] In the end, regardless of where they are practiced, distinctive signature styles grow from social-cultural approval.

Enduring styles convey stability through their very continuity, serving as threads connecting us to the past and symbolizing a coherent society with far reaching roots, and thus with permanence, providing security in shared history and self-identification. Renaissance art, which emerged in the 1400s in Europe, reflected a major new change to an entrenched art style that had persisted for hundreds of years previously. Ancient Egyptian paintings were created in a style that remained practically the same for nearly 3000 years. Styles in ancient Greek art, expressed in sculptures, vase paintings, and carvings, lasted for hundreds of years before changing in response to social, intellectual, and political shifts. Indeed, throughout history styles have transitioned in response to a society's cultural values. Even now, social attitudes drive distinctive trends in art.

The sense of shared history and identification is a powerful uniting concept in human life that is reinforced by art. Even the earliest strung sea shell beads provided visible signs of group belongingness and affiliation. In the brain, the desire for social identity is subserved by several regions,[24] including the amygdala, which processes general emotional responses such as fear, anger, and threat, and directs attention to salient social features that involve interactions with others. Another region in this network, the fusiform gyrus, especially in the right hemisphere, is sensitive to face recognition, social categories, and social context. Regions in the frontal lobes subserve anticipation of others' intentions, opinions, and perspectives. An additional region is involved in subjective evaluation of group members and is implicated in feelings of group belongingness.

The Sensory Organs and Universal Commonalities in Art

While art distinctively expresses belonging to specific cultural groups, there are also universal commonalities in art that cut across geographical distance, spoken language, and cultural origin.[25] These reflect the fact that we are all *Homo sapiens* on earth today, and we have the same human brain, which ultimately controls the whole process of artmaking. We also share similar basic social interests, emotions, and perceptual and sensory limitations. Commonalities in art can be partly explained by the characteristics and limitations of human sensory organs

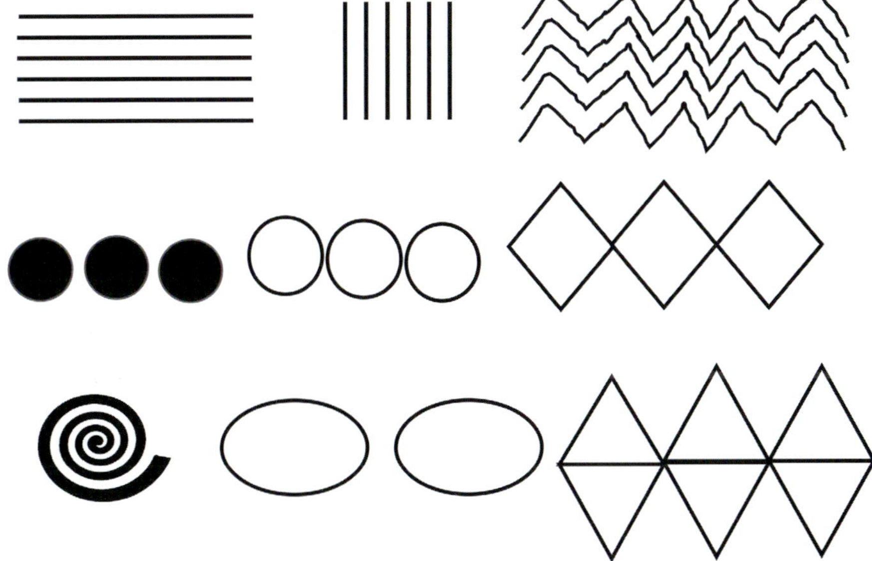

(such as eyes). The prevalent use of red, for example, is related to the color vision capabilities of the human eye (in both the artist and the viewer). Special receptors in the retina known as cones, located in the back of each eye, enable us to see/perceive colors (actually, the cones react to lightwaves and then the brain "tells" us what color we are seeing).[26] The central part of the retina (known as the fovea), where visual acuity is the sharpest, is particularly sensitive to reds. Yellows, greens, and blues are processed slightly off that central spot. One reason red stands out and attracts our attention is that we see it with the greatest clarity.

The occipital lobes (**2**), located in the back of the brain, contain neurons that specialize in reacting to specific features of the visual environment. Some respond only to shape contours, others to line orientations, luminance (degree of brightness), colors, and contrast, either alone or in combination. Both artists and viewers have these neurons. Their activity gives rise to the world we see with our eyes and allows us to understand art that represents that world.[27]

In left-right symmetry, another common, universal tendency in art, the two sides of a work appear as mirror-images of each other. This technique is frequently found in traditional face masks in parts of Africa and in wooden totem poles by First Nations people in the Pacific Northwest of Canada. Although these artifacts serve as visual symbols, cultural beliefs alone cannot explain the tendency toward left-right symmetry. There are two competing possible explanations. One is the ease with which the total design can be assembled—symmetrical patterns are easier to copy and reproduce than asymmetrical designs. The other explanation is that left-right symmetry is harder to reproduce because perfect mirror-image duplication demands extraordinary skill, which, in turn, is highly valued and justifies serving as an important symbol representing the society.

Some visual patterns that appear in art are common across geographically distant cultures (**6**). The universal application of drawn, painted, and etched parallel lines—straight, wavy, or zig zagged—in artistic compositions has been documented.[28] Dots, filled or not, are another universally repeated motif that appears on various surfaces going back many thousands of years.[29] Although dots can be created in multiple ways, the ease with which they can be made by both artists and non-artists allows them to convey powerful messages in symbolic communication. A non-artist would find it difficult to freely draw naturalistic faces, scenery, human figures, or animals, while simple patterns made of dots and lines can be copied with relative ease by all members of the community, facilitating the passing on of ancestral traditions to future generations.

Summary and Conclusions

Brain researchers have found that there is no single brain region that controls and specializes in the production of art or in the aesthetic reaction to it. A network of regions in both the left and right hemispheres of the brain that is recruited in making and perceiving art is also involved in a broad range of non-art cognition, such as thinking, emotions, attention, problem solving, and motoric movements.

Aesthetic reactions to art only seem to be subjective because not everyone shares the same opinion. These reactions have underpinnings in the brain, but they are not art-specific. Brain regions active in aesthetic reactions also provide neural support for functions such as memory, emotions, attention, thinking, spatial perception, vision, and pleasure. Although beauty plays a role in our attraction and attention to artistic representations, and on the surface may seem the sole reason for why we have art in the first place, the practice of making art evolved into an integral and powerful communicative system in human societies for depicting universal concerns ranging from daily experiences, emotions, thoughts, concepts, and symbols to technological advances.

Only humans create art, investing enormous energy and resources in doing so. Art is now created in all societies across the world. We, *Homo sapiens*, evolved in Africa, and from there dispersed to all continents. The shared evolutionary origins of all humans on earth today explains how, despite the wide diversity in cultural habits and languages around the globe, there are universal commonalities in art. These can be seen in themes, subject matter, motifs, portrayals of lived experiences, pigments, and attitudes signifying group affiliation. The commonalities reflect shared brain structure and the cognition supported by it, constraints imposed by sensory modalities, the evolutionary trajectory of survival through socially oriented life, and the cultural origins in the distant past. There is greater permanence to art than to the sounds of language. In this sense, art represents a powerful lasting proof of the lived life of a society.

1. D. W. Zaidel, "Art in Early Human Evolution: Socially Driven Art Forms Versus Material Art," *Evolutionary Studies in Imaginative Culture* 1, no. 1 (2017): 149–58.

2. T. W. Deacon, *The Symbolic Species: The Co-evolution of Language and the Brain* (New York: W. W. Norton, 1998).

3. D. W. Zaidel, "Co-evolution of Language and Symbolic Meaning: Co-opting Meaning Underlying the Initial Arts in Early Human Culture," *Cognitive Science* 11, no. 2 (2020): e1520.

4. J. Tooby and L. Cosmides, "Human Cooperation Shows the Distinctive Signatures of Adaptations to Small-scale Social Life," *Behavioral and Brain Sciences* 39 (2016): e54.

5. Zaidel, "Art in Early Human Evolution," 15.

6. D. W. Zaidel, *Neuropsychology of Art: Neurological, Biological and Evolutionary Perspectives*, 2nd ed. (Hove, UK: Psychology Press, 2015).

7. Zaidel, *Neuropsychology of Art*, 206.

8. Zaidel, *Neuropsychology of Art*, 149.

9. D. W. Zaidel, "Split-brain, the Right Hemisphere, and Art: Fact and Fiction," *Progress in Brain Research* 204 (2013): 3–17.

10. J. E. Bogen and G.M. Bogen, "Creativity and the Corpus Callosum," *Psychiatric Clinics of North America* 11 (1988): 293–301.

11. C. M. Schlebusch et al., "Southern African Ancient Genomes Estimate Modern Human Divergence to 350,000 to 260,000 Years Ago," 358, no. 6363 (2017): 652–55, and C. M. Vidal et al., "Age of the Oldest Known Homo Sapiens from Eastern Africa, *Nature* 601, no. 7894 (2022): 579–83.

12. Zaidel, "Art in Early Human Evolution," 151.

13. Zaidel, "Art in Early Human Evolution," 152–53.

14. S. A. Mehr et al., "Universality and Diversity in Human Song" *Science* 366, no. 6468 (2019): 970. These experiences are practiced and shared by humans across cultures.

15. K. Coe, N. E. Aiken, and C. T. Palmer, "Once upon a Time: Ancestors and the Evolutionary Significance of Stories," *Anthropological Forum* 16, no. 1 (2006): 21–40.

16. C. S. Henshilwood, F. d' Errico, and I. Watts, "Engraved Ochres from the Middle Stone Age Levels at Blombos Cave, South Africa," *Journal of Human Evolution*, 57, no. 1 (2009): 27–47.

17. D. Lewis-Williams, *The Mind in the Cave: Consciousness and the Origins of Art* (London: Thames and Hudson, 2002), 320.

18. P. J. Richerson and R. Boyd, *Not by Genes Alone: How Culture Transformed Human Evolution* (Chicago: University of Chicago Press, 2005).

19. M. Skov and M. Nadal, "Art Is Not Special: An Assault on the Last Lines of Defense Against the Naturalization of the Human Mind," *Reviews in the Neurosciences* 29, no. 6 (2018): 699–702, and O. Vartanian and M. Skov, "Neural Correlates of Viewing Paintings: Evidence from a Quantitative Meta-analysis of Functional Magnetic Resonance Imaging Data," *Brain and Cognition* 87 (2014): 52–56.

20. D. W. Zaidel, "The Evolution of Aesthetics and Beauty," in *The Oxford Handbook of Empirical Aesthetics*, ed. M. Nadal and O. Vartanian (Oxford: Oxford University Press, 2019), 183–95.

21. D. W. Zaidel, "Neuroesthetics Is Not Just About Art," *Frontiers in Behavioral Neuroscience* 9 (2015): 80.

22. Zaidel, "Neuroesthetics Is Not Just About Art."

23. Zaidel, "Art in Early Human Evolution," 154.

24. J. F. Guassi Moreira, J. J. Van Bavel, and E. H. Telzer, "The Neural Development of 'Us and Them'," *Social Cognitive and Affective Neuroscience* 12, no. 2 (2016): 184–96.

25. C. Schuster and E. Carpenter, *Patterns That Connect: Social Symbolism in Ancient and Tribal Art* (New York: Harry N. Abrams, 1996).

26. Zaidel, *Neuropsychology of Art*, 52.

27. M. Livingstone, *Vision and Art: The Biology of Seeing* (New York: Abrams, 2014), 54.

28. Zaidel, "Art in Early Human Evolution," 154.

29. B. O. Alpert, "The Meaning of the Dots on the Horses of Pech Merle," *Arts* 2, no. 4 (2013): 476–90.

II

AESTHETICS AND HUMAN CULTURES

WILFRIED VAN DAMME

Addressing the aesthetic from the perspective of humanity and its cultures may be a daunting affair, but it has at least one major advantage: the "view from afar" or "satellite perspective" alerts one to fundamental questions about the aesthetic as a dimension of being human. What are the evolutionary origins of the human aesthetic? Are there aesthetic universals, and what do we mean by that? How do we account for cultural diversity in aesthetic preference? What is the place and role of the aesthetic in humans' varied modes of sociocultural existence?

Remarkably, scholarship has mostly ignored these fundamental questions about humans as aesthetic beings. This chapter will attempt to tackle some of them, drawing on data and insights from various disciplines. Our emphasis throughout will be on finding commonalities in aesthetic preferences worldwide. This search for "aesthetic universals" will address two types of commonalities. In its most familiar guise, the idea of universals in aesthetics—here, visual aesthetics—refers to properties of form that are experienced as perceptually pleasing by all human beings, regardless of cultural background. For the sake of analytical clarity, we may call these properties "substantive aesthetic universals": actual or concrete stimulus features that routinely prompt a pleasurable response in members of our species. The possible existence of visual characteristics with panhuman appeal, especially as they apply to the visual arts, will occupy us in the first half of the chapter.

Our quest for common denominators, however, will also lead us to consider aesthetic universals of a less straightforward type, consisting of commonalities situated on a deeper level of analysis. Could it be that underlying the apparent diversity in aesthetic preference there are structuring principles that are essentially the same across cultures? Are there perhaps interculturally recurring mechanisms or pancultural processes that produce variety on a surface level when operative in varying sociocultural contexts? As the noted anthropologist Claude Lévi-Strauss has suggested, the ultimate task for students of human culture is not to map observable similarities and differences but to establish "what is *common to the differences* among societies."[1] In the second part of this chapter we will take up the challenge of finding "unity in diversity" in visual preferences around the globe. Any governing principles or processes involved may then be called "structural aesthetic universals": underlying anthropological constants in the formation of aesthetic preference that generate variants on the level of culture.

By way of introduction to our search, we will provide a few observations on the ubiquity and antiquity of the aesthetic in human existence, with the latter topic leading us right into the issue of universals. The aesthetic experience is a crucial feature of being human, making the quest for common denominators in visual preference a worthwhile endeavor, however exploratory at present. In pursuing our search, we will draw especially on empirical data furnished by ethnography; our explanatory framework will be basically evolutionary.

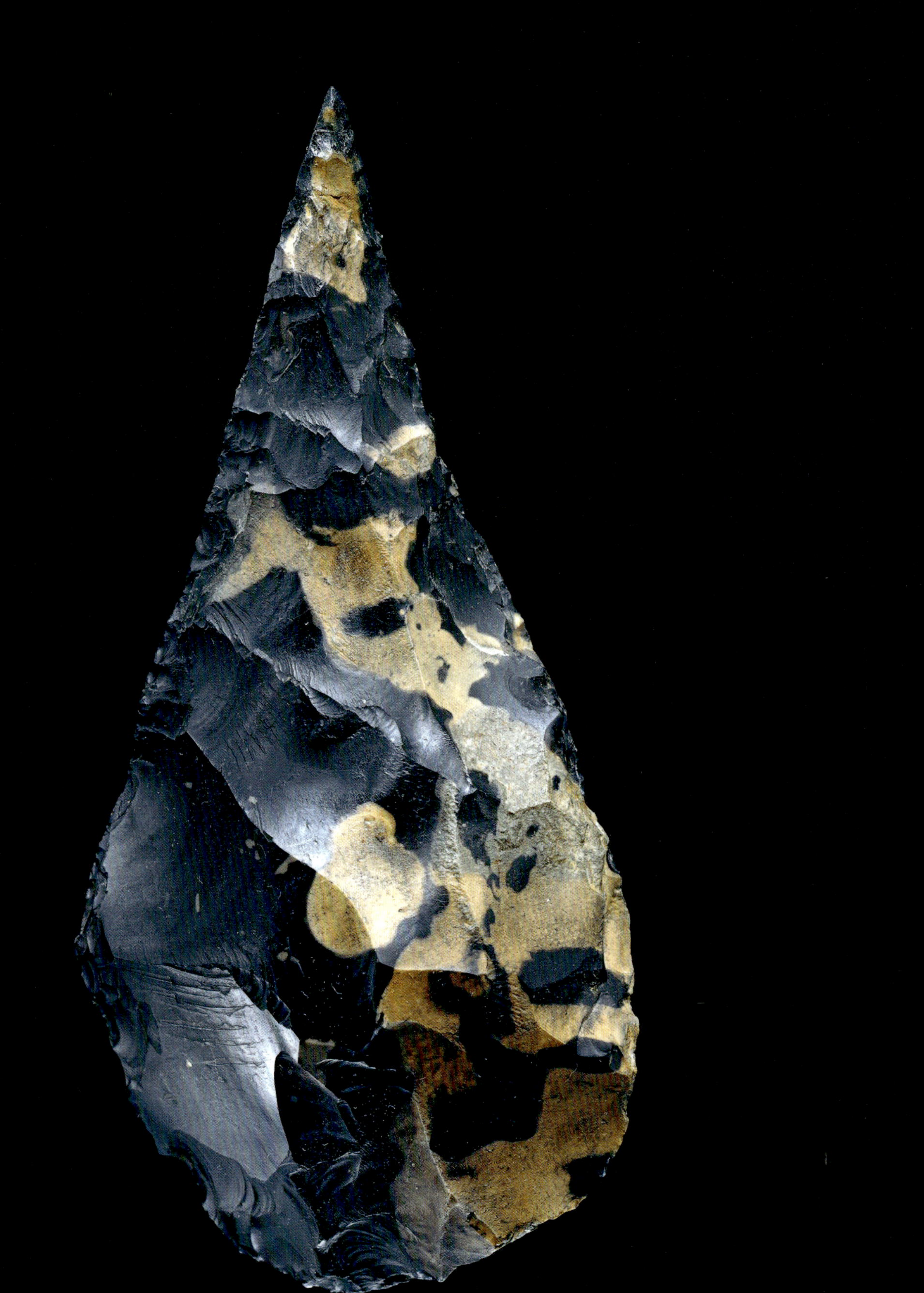

1 **Pointed Handaxe**

Hoxne, Suffolk
Lower Paleolithic, around 400,000 years ago
Stone
Society of Antiquaries, London, England

The Significance of the Aesthetic in Human Existence

Many educated people still associate the aesthetic first and foremost with the rarefied world of the fine arts and especially the lofty or high-minded experiences these arts may engender in perceivers. However, if we relax this stringent and limited conception of our topic and descend to a more mundane level, we find that the aesthetic is all around us. Humans evaluate people's visual appearance as attractive or unattractive, assess natural environments as pleasing or displeasing, experience the dwellings and public buildings they pass by as appealing or unappealing, and so on.

Humans do not only passively experience the aesthetic, we also act on our perceptual likes and dislikes. This happens, for example, when we create or strive to acquire objects that appeal to our visual sense. Indeed, if we have a choice, we tend to surround ourselves with objects that please the eye—from kitchen utensils and furniture to the pictures we hang on walls—and we tend to avoid items we experience as unpleasant. Humans also use aesthetic objects in a variety of individual and communal contexts, often with a particular purpose in mind. We may dress ourselves up and beautify our living spaces in order to make a good impression on visitors, or embellish shrines in hopes of propitiating some supernatural entity. In these examples we deploy the aesthetic to have an impact on others, but others may also try and influence us. One may think here of various forms of visual propaganda that intend to exploit our aesthetic sensibilities in order to get some message across: political, religious, or commercial. Attested across time and space, these forms of visual persuasion, frequently including what we would call today works of art, characteristically prompt intensified types of visual pleasure that we experience in more diluted forms in everyday life. Already these few examples and observations—from the ordinary to the extraordinary, from the secular to the religious—demonstrate that the aesthetic is intensely interwoven in the fabric of human existence.

Paleoaesthetics

The aesthetic is not only ubiquitous and meaningfully integrated into individual and collective human life, it is also ancient, having deep evolutionary roots. In humans, and indeed their precursors as well as many other animal species, evolution has built in affect-laden responses, notably attraction and repulsion, to a range of sensorial stimuli recurrent in a species' environment. The qualitative perceptual responses triggered by these environmental cues serve to economically guide individuals in seeking out things conducive to survival and reproduction (such as nutritious foods, suitable habitats, and fit mates) and in steering clear of those things that are evolutionarily disadvantageous.

Aesthetic sensibility being ancient and firmly rooted in our evolved neurobiology, it may be asked when our ancestors first started *making* objects that appeal to that sensibility. At which point in human evolution does the archaeological record suggest the emergence of artifacts that have an aesthetic dimension? It has been intimated that the earliest material evidence we have of humans creating objects that command attention through their visual qualities is a category of carefully produced pear-shaped handaxes. Stone handaxes were made beginning around 1.5 million years ago, but between roughly 500,000 and 200,000 years ago (that is, in the period immediately preceding the emergence of modern humans in Africa), a significant percentage of these artifacts display a striking symmetry (1). Some of these exquisitely crafted objects have other intriguing features: they show no traces of use-wear, even under a microscope, and some are too big, or too small, to perform the practical tasks for which they appear to be designed. In addition, the materials from which these handaxes are made (often glistening stone, exceptionally with a fossil in the middle of the finished product) seem to have been carefully selected, partly for visual effect.

Neurobiologist Marek Kohn and archaeologist Steven Mithen have suggested an intriguing interpretation of these objects by drawing on evolutionary theory and specifically the concept of sexual selection, which concerns mate choice and its implications.[2] Kohn and Mithen propose that the carved stones served to signal to members of the opposite sex that their maker, probably male, has "good genes": he is able to secure resources,

capable of planning ahead, skillful, has endurance, and enough leisure to engage in the production of nonutilitarian objects. To be clear, this signalling need not involve a deliberate intention on the part of the maker or some conscious consideration on the part of the beholder—let alone knowledge of genetics. Evolutionary thinking proposes that members of the opposite sex who happened to be drawn to "sexy handaxe" producers as mates made advantageous choices when it came to the survival of their genes in their physical and sociocultural environments. The competitive offspring of the admirers and creators of the objects—creators who might have simply been enjoying what they did well— would then inherit the same interest in the production and perception of symmetrical handaxes. The objects could thus be considered "indexes" of certain motor and mental capacities, as determined by an analyst, similar to conceptualizing a peacock's large and colorful tail as an index of the animal's genetic qualities and an attractor to peahens (although in human evolution, associations and deliberations are likely to play an increasingly important role).

As for the conspicuous imposed symmetry of the stone tools, Kohn and Mithen argue that while it makes the artifact sit comfortably in the hand, it goes beyond utilitarian requirements (experiments show that handaxes taking less time and skill to produce do as well). Its presence in the context of females' sexually selecting males (or perhaps vice versa) is elucidated with reference to a "perceptual bias" for symmetry. In other words, early humans had already evolved a sensitivity to symmetry as a property of stimuli other than made objects, notably the human body (where symmetry counts as a reliable indicator of stable development and good health, and hence as an index of physical fitness). The creators of these handaxes are suggested to have exploited this perceptual bias, producing artifacts that caught the attention and elicited the appreciation of members of the opposite sex.

Aesthetic Universals: Visual Properties with Panhuman Appeal

Symmetry is to this day commonly mentioned as an aesthetic universal, meaning here a visual feature that is held to appeal to all human beings. Indeed, in discussions that broach the subject, symmetry is frequently cited as the only ready example of an aesthetic universal, although "visual regularity" or "visual pattern" are sometimes mentioned as well. The prominence of symmetry is probably based in large part on the observation that artistic objects from around the world, over space and in time, often display bilateral symmetry (2–5).

Are there perhaps other such aesthetic universals? In pondering this question, readers may well be reminded of the so-called golden section or ratio. This mathematically intriguing proportion, involving the irrational number phi (φ), or 1.618 … (which corresponds in the visual realm to a roughly eight-to-five ratio), is said to be favored by artists and designers and to have a special visual appeal to humans. In fact, the small body of empirical research devoted to the issue does not support claims for the aesthetic specialness of the golden ratio, either from a global perspective or even in Western contexts, where the claims arose.

The topic of panhuman commonalities in aesthetic preference generally has so far received only very slight attention from researchers, whether they be philosophers, psychologists, or anthropologists. The subject is even considered anathema by some scholars, especially in the more radically relativist branches of cultural anthropology (which strongly influenced postmodern philosophy). Yet it is precisely ethnography that provides us with the most elaborate and convincing data to suggest the existence of shared aesthetic likes and dislikes among human beings. Scholars carrying out so-called fieldwork in the world's various cultures— not only anthropologists but increasingly also art historians—have at times made quite extensive inquiries into local people's visual predilections. Using "aesthetic ranking tests" and other methodological procedures, they have asked people not only to indicate their visual preferences but to expound on their evaluations by articulating the standards they use in aesthetic assessment. This has resulted in the establishment of a number of culturally consensual aesthetic criteria in a wide variety of living cultures across the globe. A comparative analysis of the results produces the following aesthetic standards that appear widespread, if not universal, in human cultures.[3]

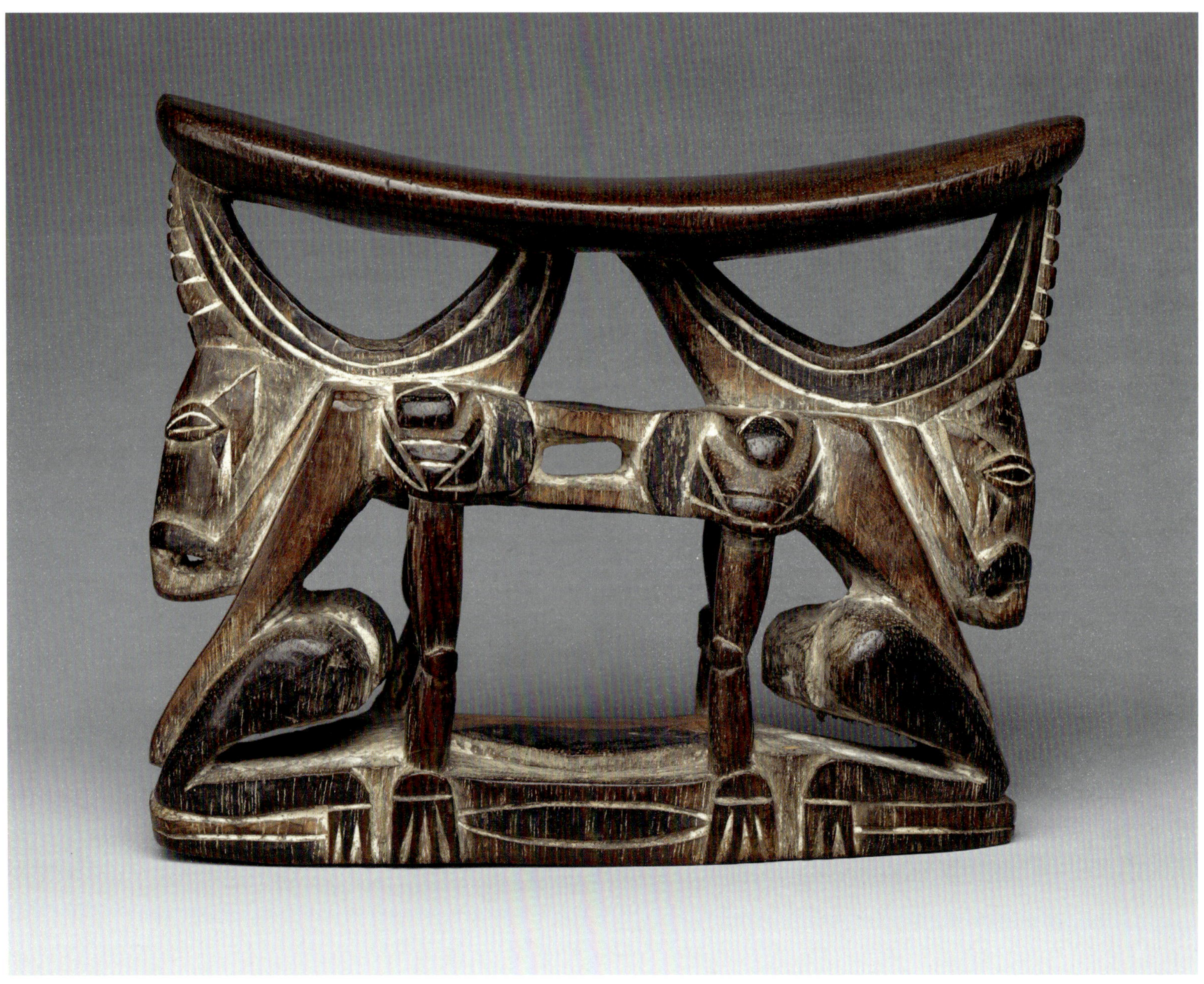

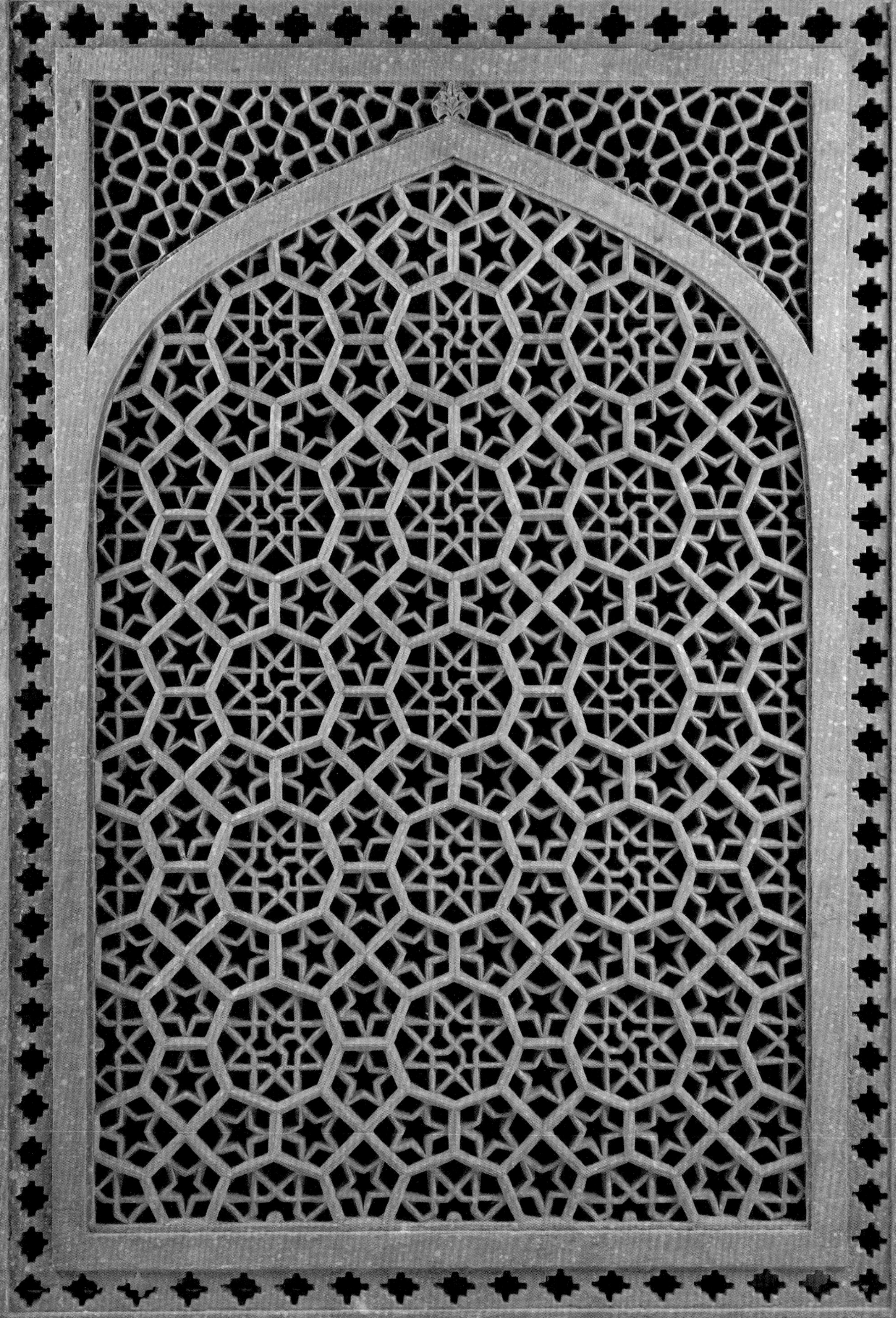

4   **Wearing Blanket**

Navajo culture, Arizona or
New Mexico
1860 – 1870
Wool
69 × 48 in., 175.3 × 121.9 cm
Metropolitan Museum of Art, New York
The Michael C. Rockefeller Memorial Collection,
Bequest of Nelson A. Rockefeller, 1979

5   **Seated Male Figure**

Ameca/Etzatlan style,
Jalisco, Mexico
100 BCE – 250 CE
Terracotta
20 ⅝ in., 52.39 cm
The Stuart Handler Collection

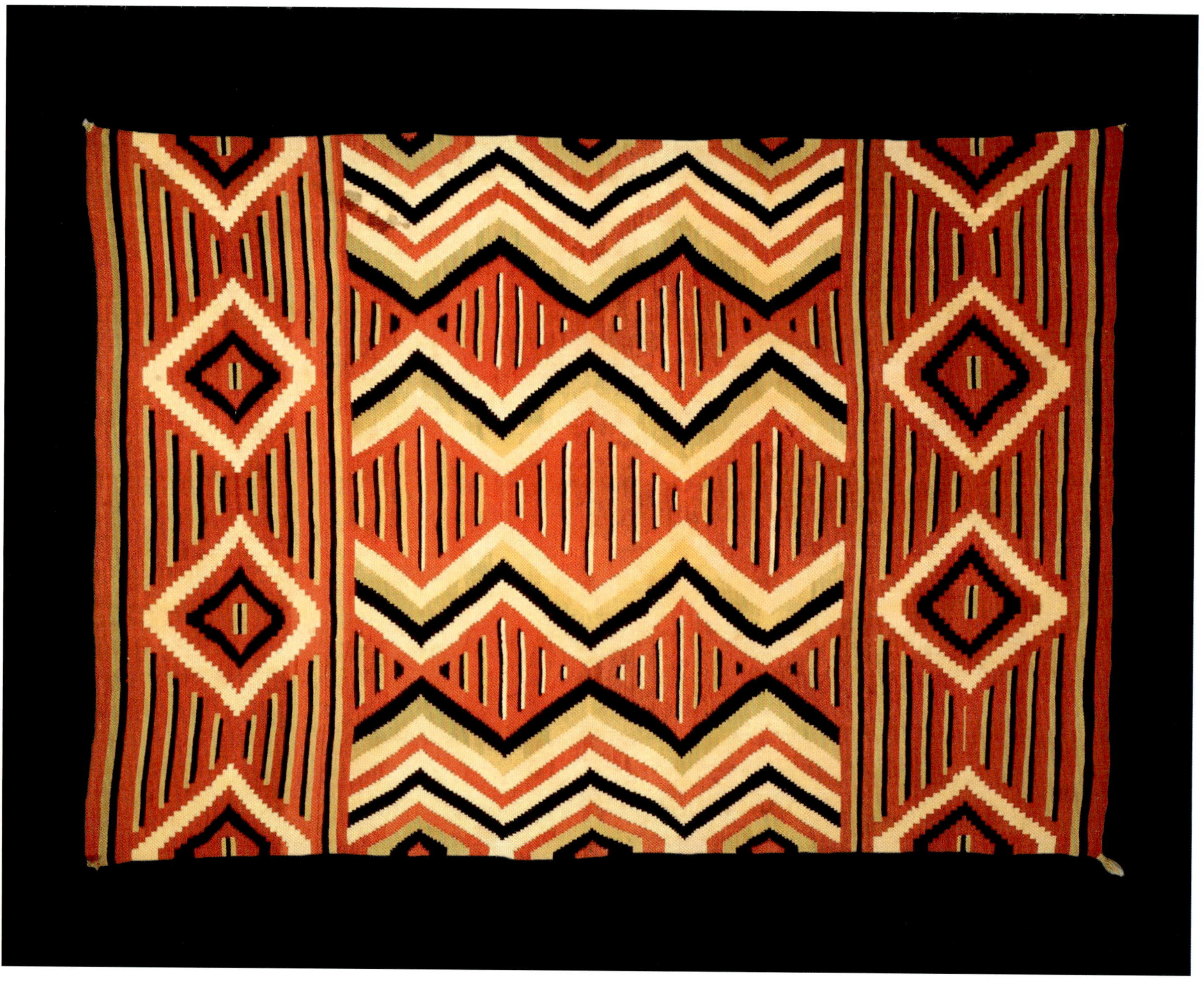

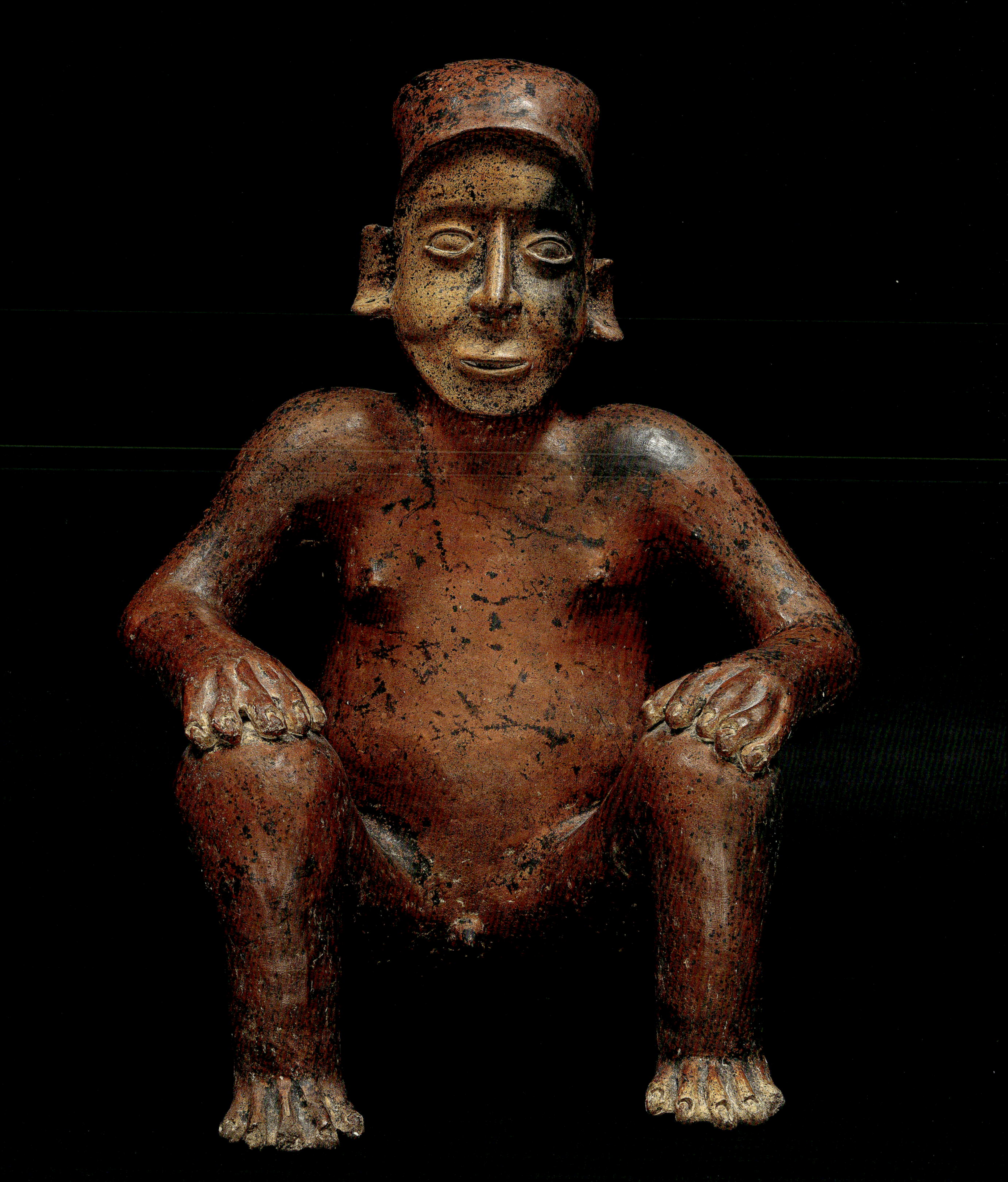

  Court Dancer

China
Han dynasty, 206 BCE – 220 CE
Terracotta
18.1 × 14.1 in., 46 × 36 cm
Collection Galerie Golconda, France

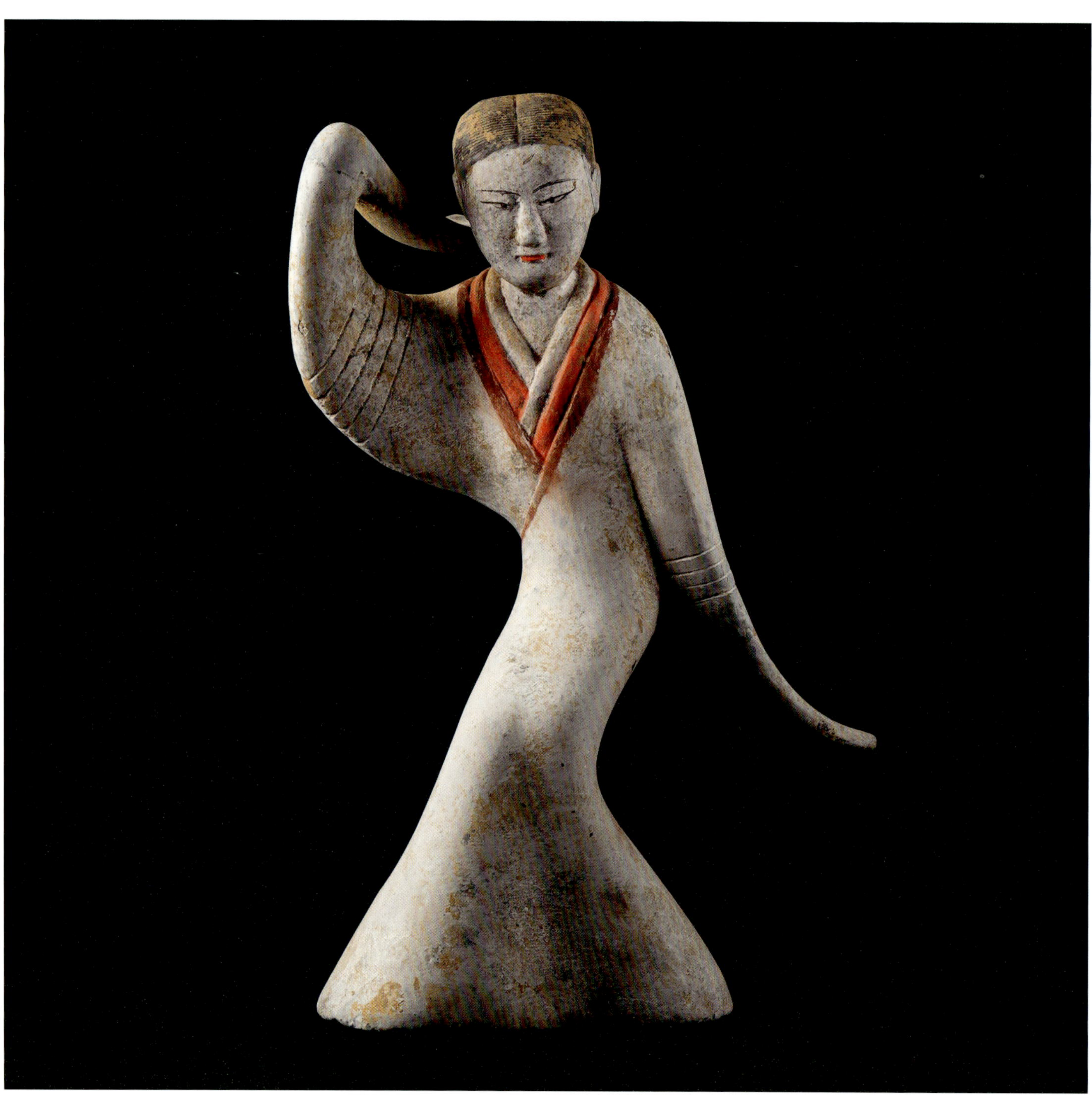

7 **Laocoön and His Sons**

Copy after a Hellenistic original found in the
baths of Trajan, Rome, Italy, in 1506
40 – 30 BCE
Marble
8 feet, 2.4 meters
Museo Pio-Clementino, Octagon, Laocoön Hall
Vatican Museums, Vatican City

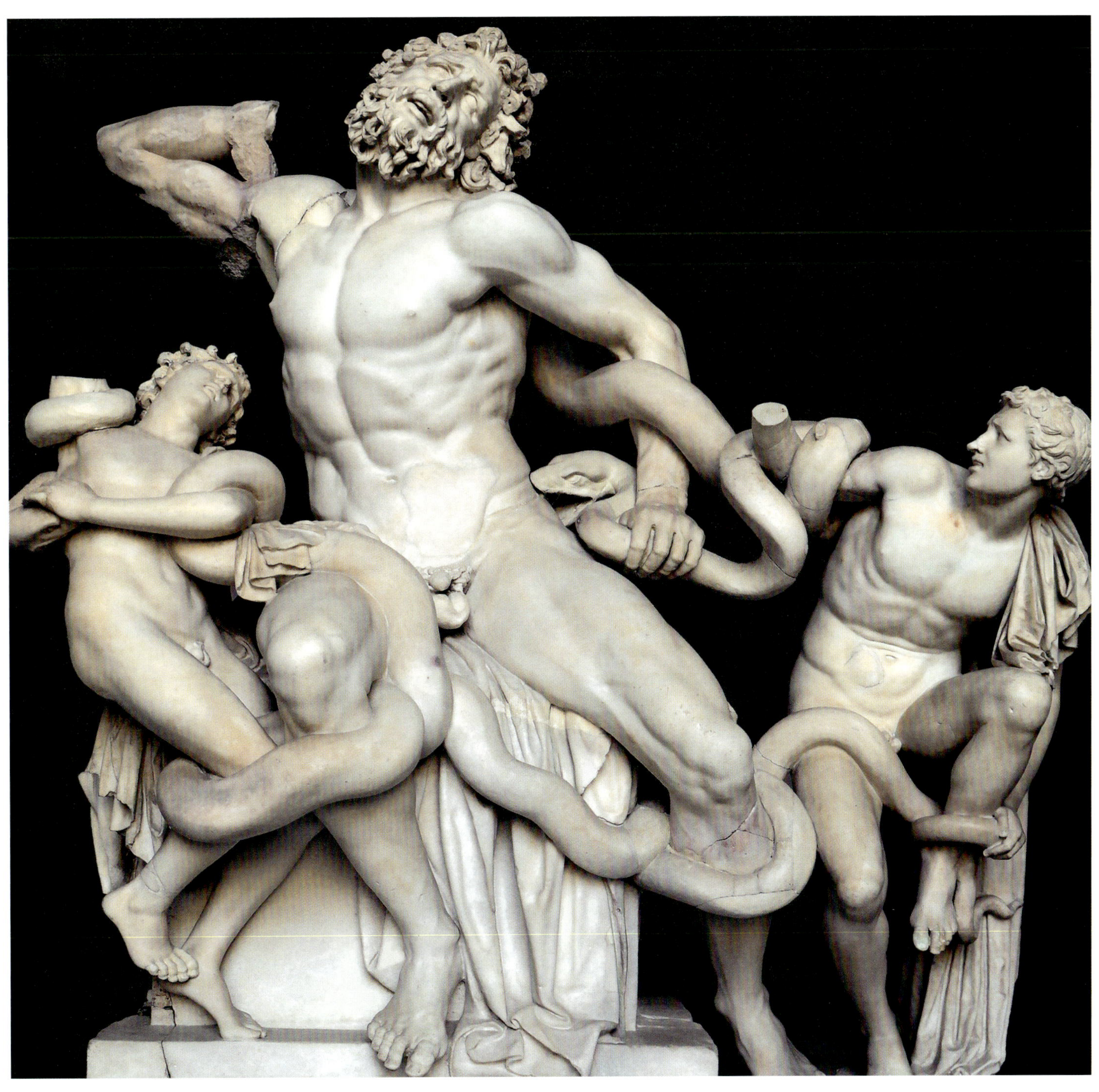

Symmetry and Balance

Among the standards that people worldwide are found to apply in their aesthetic evaluations we find first of all what in Western terms would be called symmetry and balance. These two terms are frequently bracketed together, or even used interchangeably, yet they have their own nuances. Symmetry may in a general sense be said to refer to the more or less exact match along a—usually vertical—axis between two sides that are the same in both size and shape. The term balance, on the other hand, commonly signifies a less tangible type of equilibrium, articulating what is felt to be an equilibrated relationship between two or more non-identical forms or between unequal sets of visual characteristics (**6–8**).

When ethnographic reports on research into aesthetic assessment provide indigenous terms that are used to indicate symmetry or balance, these sometimes correspond to the idea of symmetry rather than balance. The Canadian Inuit, for example, employ the word *idluriik* ("two equals as a pair") in reference to the bilateral symmetry they admire in visual stimuli. Yet local concepts frequently encompass types of visual equilibrium that go beyond strict symmetry. In these instances, the latter appears to be regarded as one possible, and indeed common, manifestation of the former. Thus, among the Yoruba of Nigeria the qualifier *didogba* may point to symmetry, but the term is also used to signify balance. Its range of application includes, for example, the visual equilibrium between light and dark zones in sculpture or between areas that are smooth and those that are incised with designs. In the case of the concept of *gula* in the Trobriand Islands in Melanesia, emphasis would clearly seem to be on balance rather than bilateral symmetry. Sculptors there use the term to indicate the equilibrium that should obtain between the two objectively asymmetrical sides of a canoe prowboard (**9**).

Clarity

A second widespread standard is that of clarity or visibility. The criterion of clarity may be summarized as denoting a preference for easily recognizable visual configurations made up of readily perceptible parts. Thus, in sculpture, people favor clearly defined volumes produced by sharp renderings of line and mass (**10–12**). A distinct use of color, including color contrast, contributes to visual clarity as well, either in sculpture or in other art forms (**13–14**). Research in African cultures, for instance, has shown the importance of the standard of visibility among the Bamana in Mali (where the term *jɛya* expresses clarity and discernibility), the Mende of Sierra Leone (who use the expression *ma ja-sahein*), the Nigerian Yoruba (employing the term *ifarahan*), and a dozen or so other West and Central African peoples. The idea of clarity has also been reported to play a major role in aesthetic assessments among several Melanesian, Aboriginal Australian, and Native American cultures. Among the Alaskan Inuit, for instance, clarity is considered so important that in visual

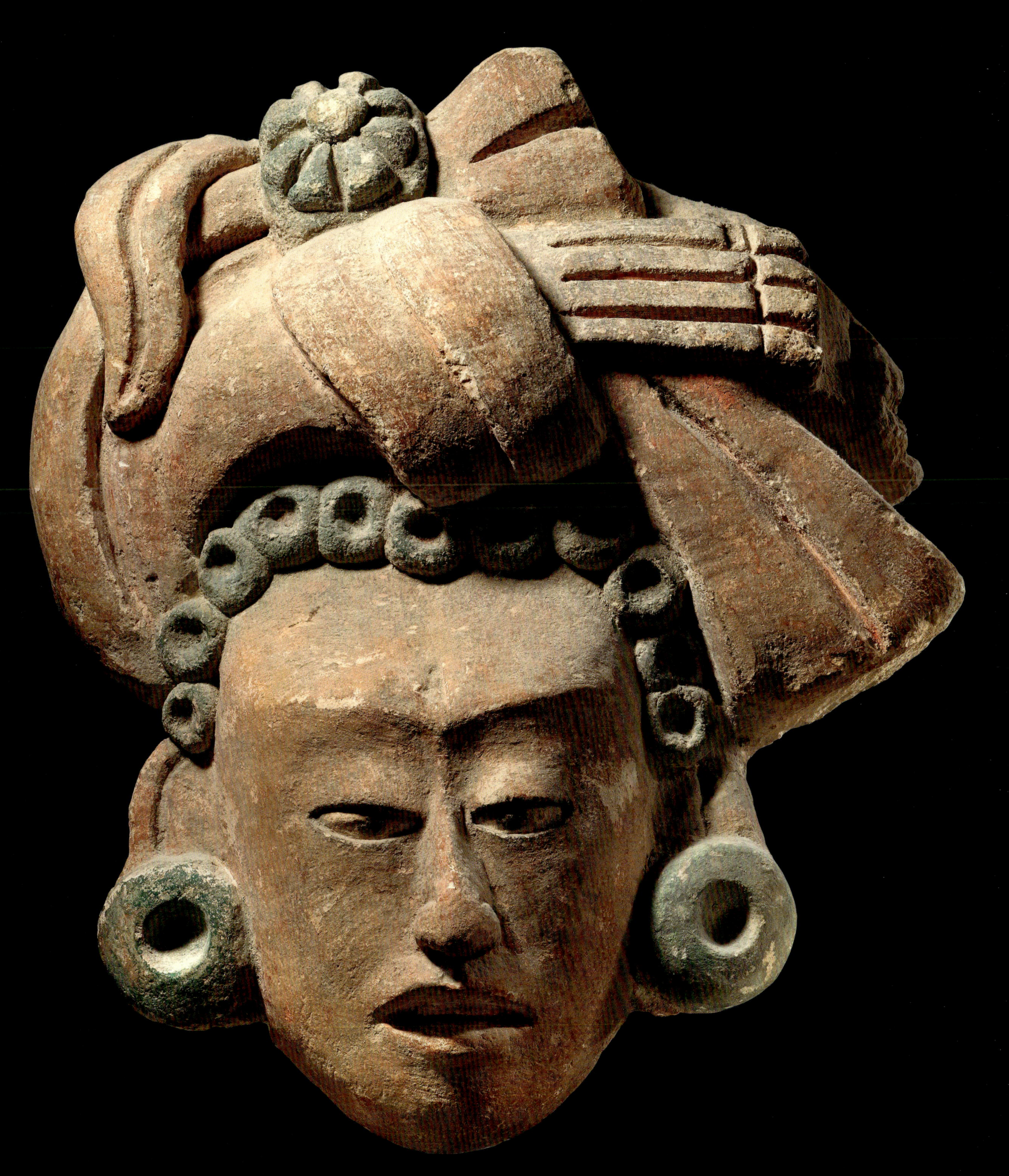

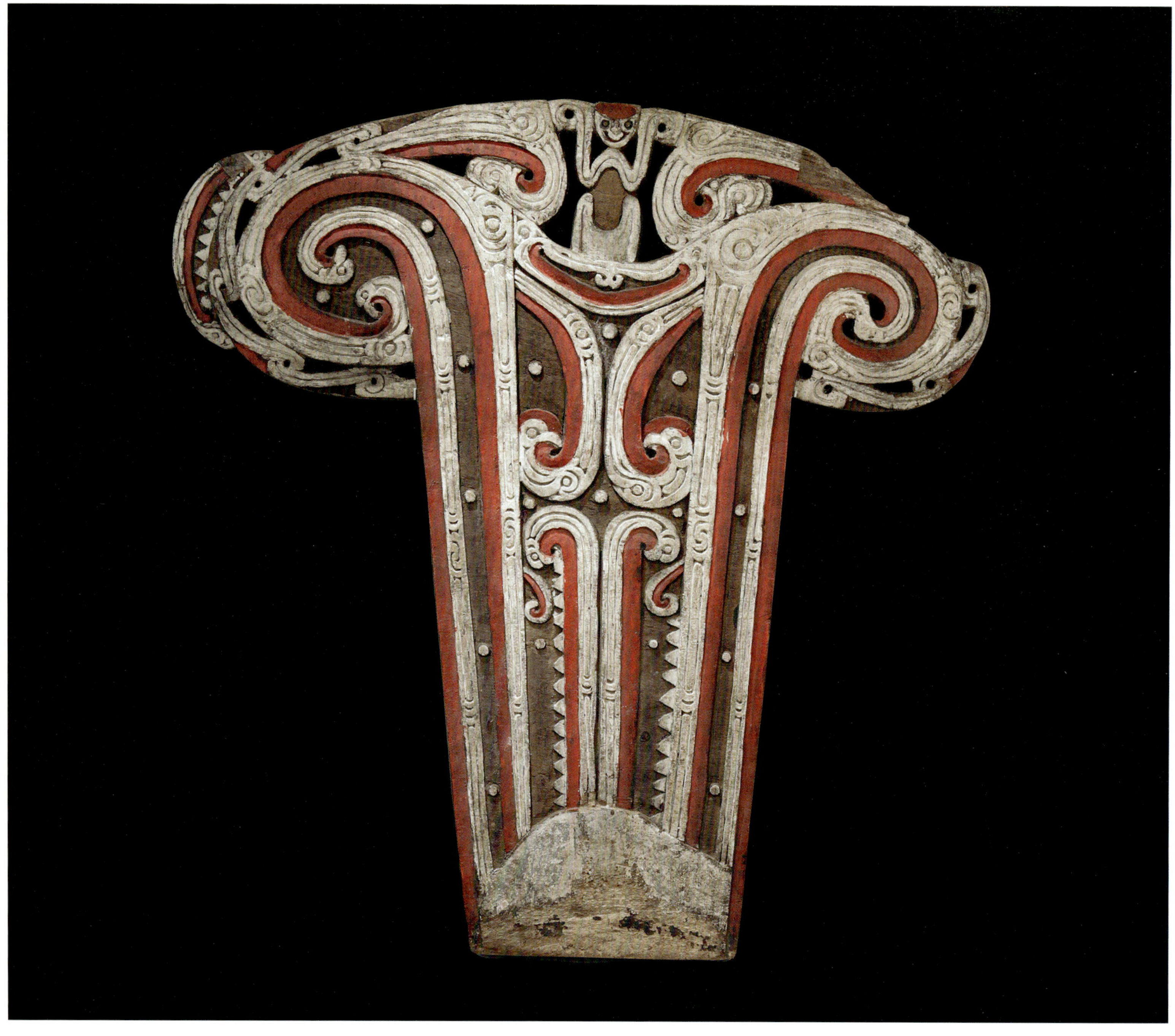

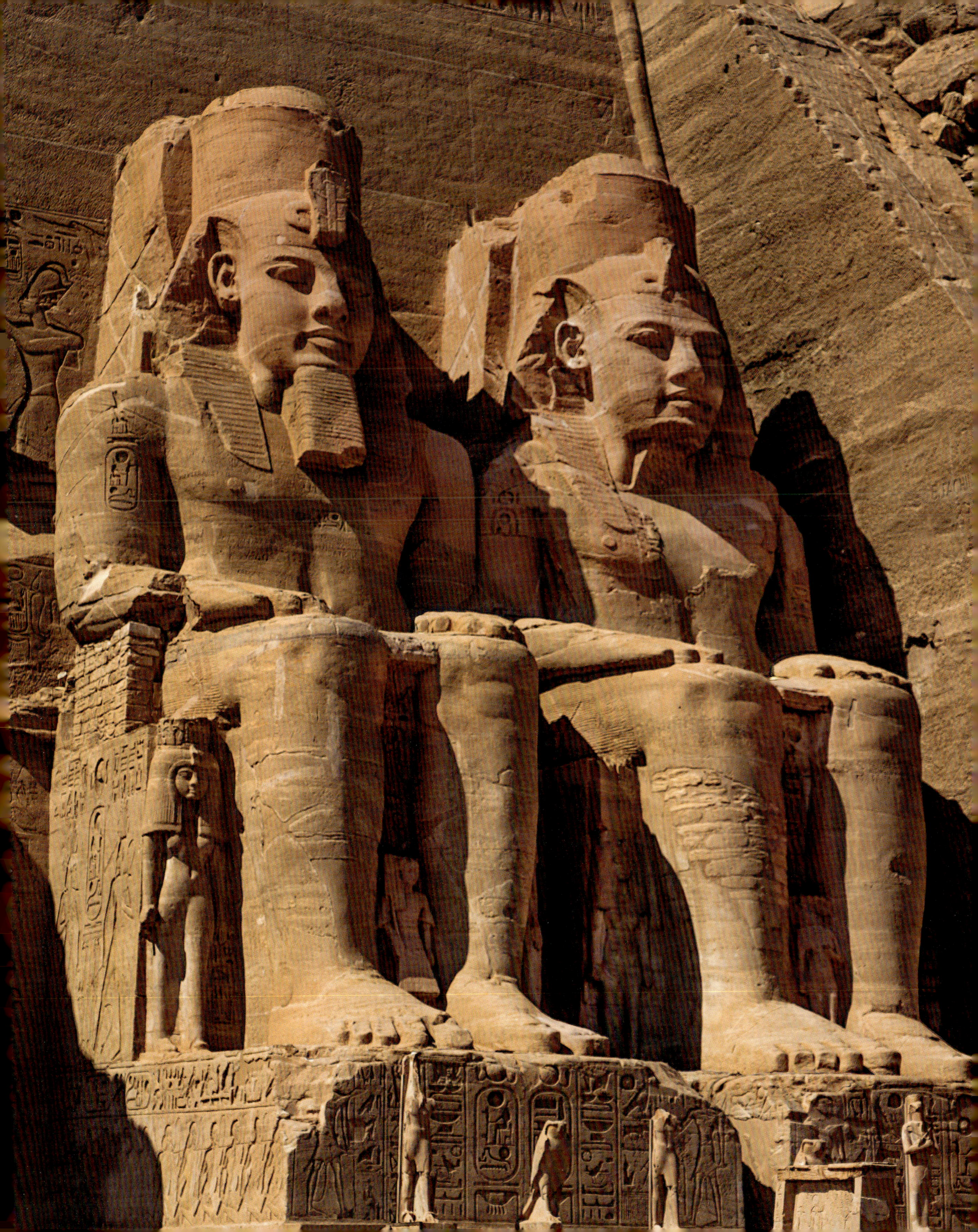

compositions objects are sometimes depicted in a place where normally they should not be, if by doing so the clarity or visibility of the composition is enhanced.

Smoothness and Brightness

One of the most frequently noted criteria employed in assessing visual appeal is smoothness, which may include a preference for shininess or brightness. The standard of smoothness appears to be applied especially when judging the attractiveness of human skin. Among the Melpa of the New Guinea Highlands, for example, a body is admired when its surface is *mbongena*, meaning "without blemish or scars," thus suggesting youth and health. In comparison with old, wrinkled, and loose skin, moreover, tight, smooth, and youthful skin better reflects the light and thus attains the admired shiny quality that the Melpa call *kuki ndaep*, meaning "the gleam or bloom of the skin." To enhance this quality, people rub their body with pig grease or tree oil. Smoothness has been reported to be admired in numerous other cultures, not only as a property of the human body but also as a characteristic of its rendering in sculpture. The standard is applied as well to several types of human-made objects other than anthropomorphic sculpture, although a relationship with the human body can in some instances still be perceived. For example, the Batammaliba of Togo and Benin identify houses with human beings, and just as the Batammaliba consider smooth skin attractive in people, so they finish and beautify their dwellings by adding a smooth silt plaster.

The quality of brightness, frequently implied in local notions of smoothness, is sometimes found to function as an aesthetic standard per se. This is the case among the Australian Yolngu, where *bir'yun*, meaning "brilliance" or "brightness," is considered the most important criterion in judging paintings. In order for a Yolngu bark painting to be deemed successful, it should possess a shimmering brilliance that is produced by completing the work through cross-hatching. For the Yolngu, however, *bir'yun* is much more than just a pleasurable visual quality, as shimmering brightness is considered to emanate from the world of the ancestors and thus endows paintings with spiritual power. The Yolngu case demonstrates— and the same can be said of most of the other examples discussed here—that although a particular visual quality may well appeal to all human beings, we should always take into account the culturally determined reasons that contribute to its appreciation in a given sociocultural context.

Youthfulness

In anthropomorphic sculpture, the depiction of smooth and shiny skin is one typical feature of the application of the standard of youthfulness that in many cultures is employed in aesthetically evaluating representations of the human form. The criterion refers to a preference for the portrayal of people who are physically in the prime of life (**15–19**). In addition to smooth and unblemished skin, this standard characteristically encompasses preferences for other signs of youthfulness and its associated qualities of health, strength, and fertility, such as an upright posture,

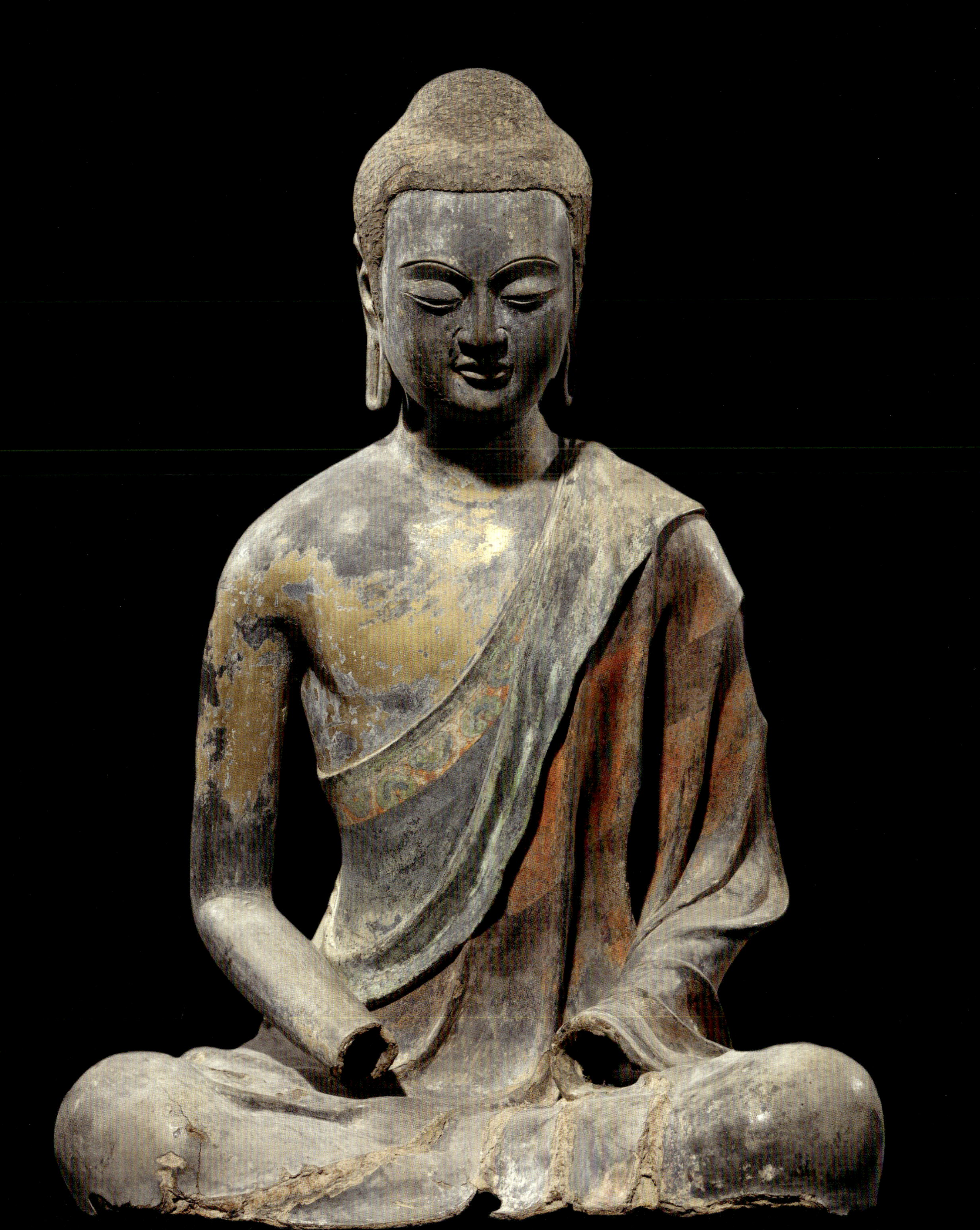

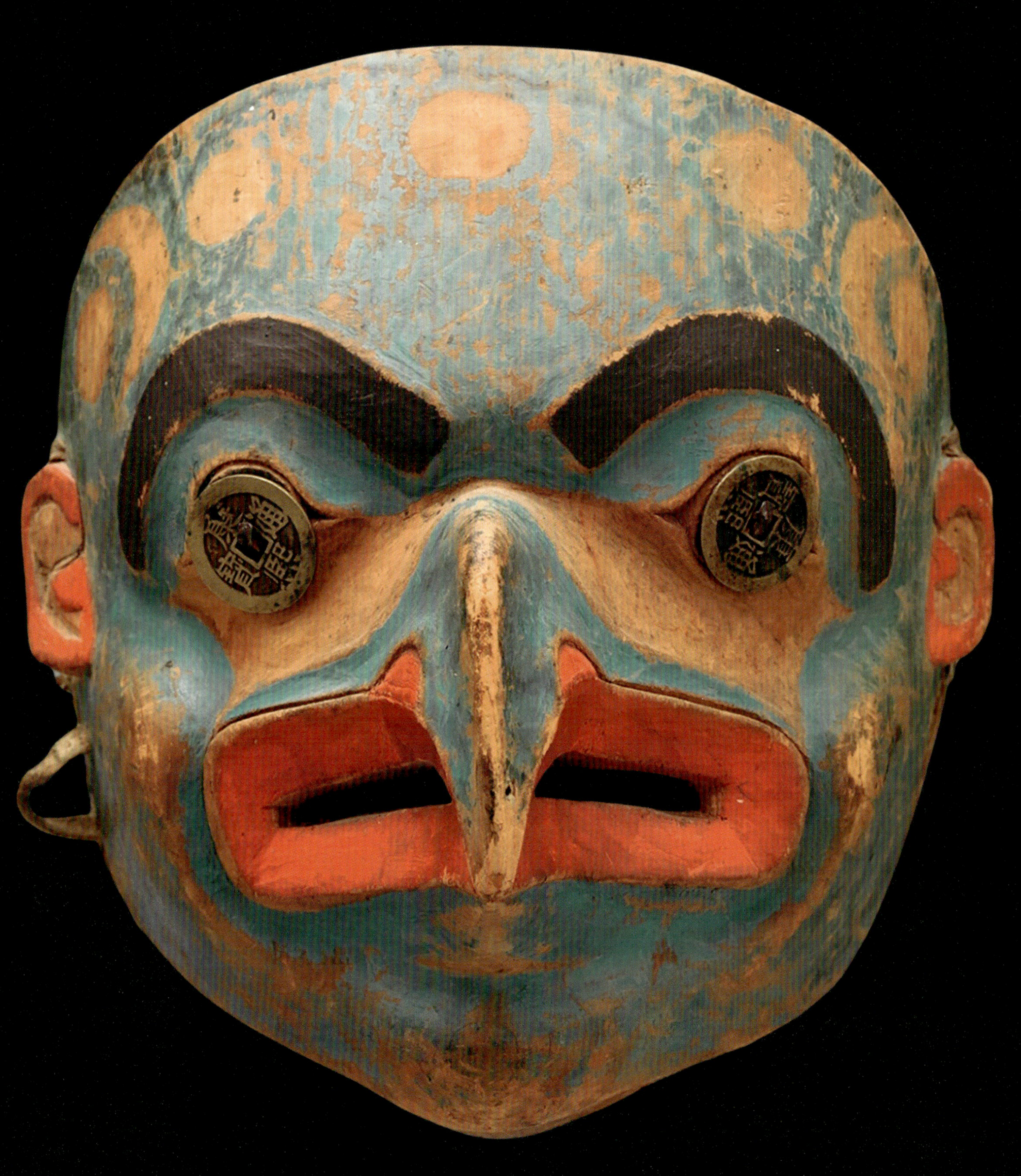

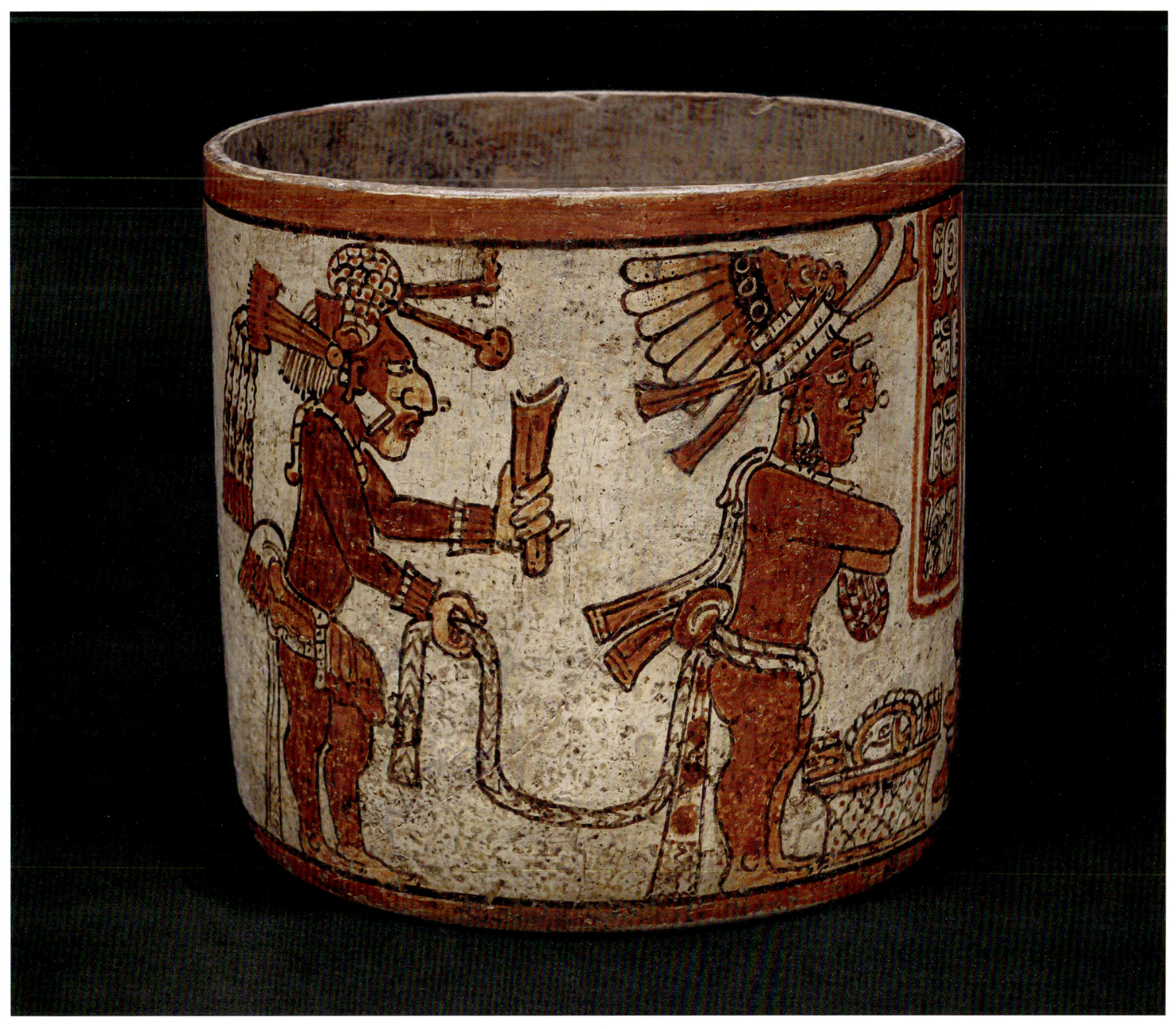

14 Feather Cloak

Maui, Hawaiian Islands
Collected 1842
Plant fiber, bird feathers, net textile
Pitt Rivers Museum,
University of Oxford, England

15 Kroisos Kouros

Funerary statue found on the grave of Kroisos
Attic culture, Greece
530 BCE
Marble
National Archaeological Museum
of Athens, Greece

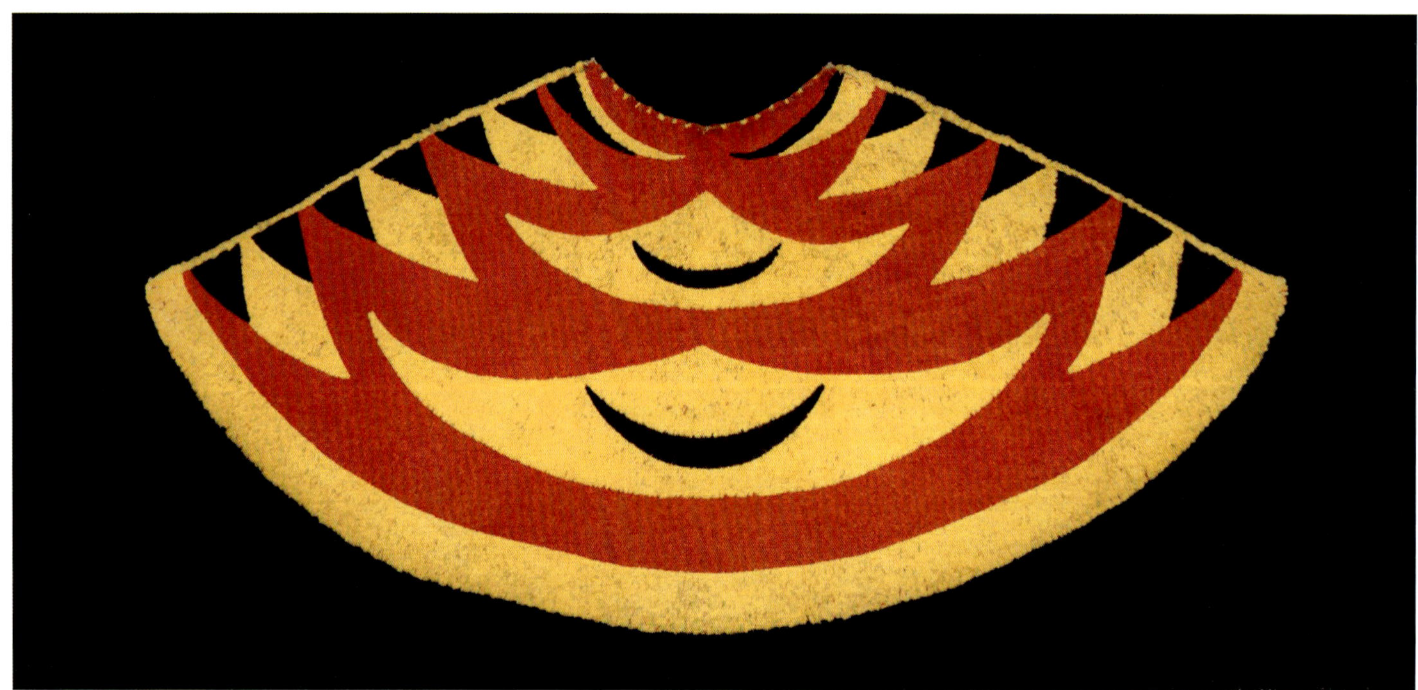

a robust body in men, and in women, a slender waist and firm breasts—features that are often exaggerated in order to create what ethologists and neuropsychologists call a supernormal stimulus, its amplified properties heightening an already pleasurable response (**20**). The standard of youthfulness can be held to more generally express a predilection for vitality and energy.

Novelty

A last widespread standard to mention here is novelty, commonly referring to a moderate degree of innovation in the arts. To be experienced as pleasurable, these innovations typically are not only moderate in nature but are perceived as somehow fitting, in a non-disturbing way, into pre-existing visual frames. Among the Pokot of Kenya, for example, the idea of novelty—*pachigha*—plays a major role in visual appeal, whether it be a wooden milk pot with innovative design features, a basket that has an uncommon weaving pattern, or a house that introduces new elements of style. Novel objects or features that are considered extraordinarily attractive are more specifically called *wechigha*.

The admiration for moderate innovation in the visual arts, notably including the appreciation of novelty in dress and hairstyle, has been observed in many cultures

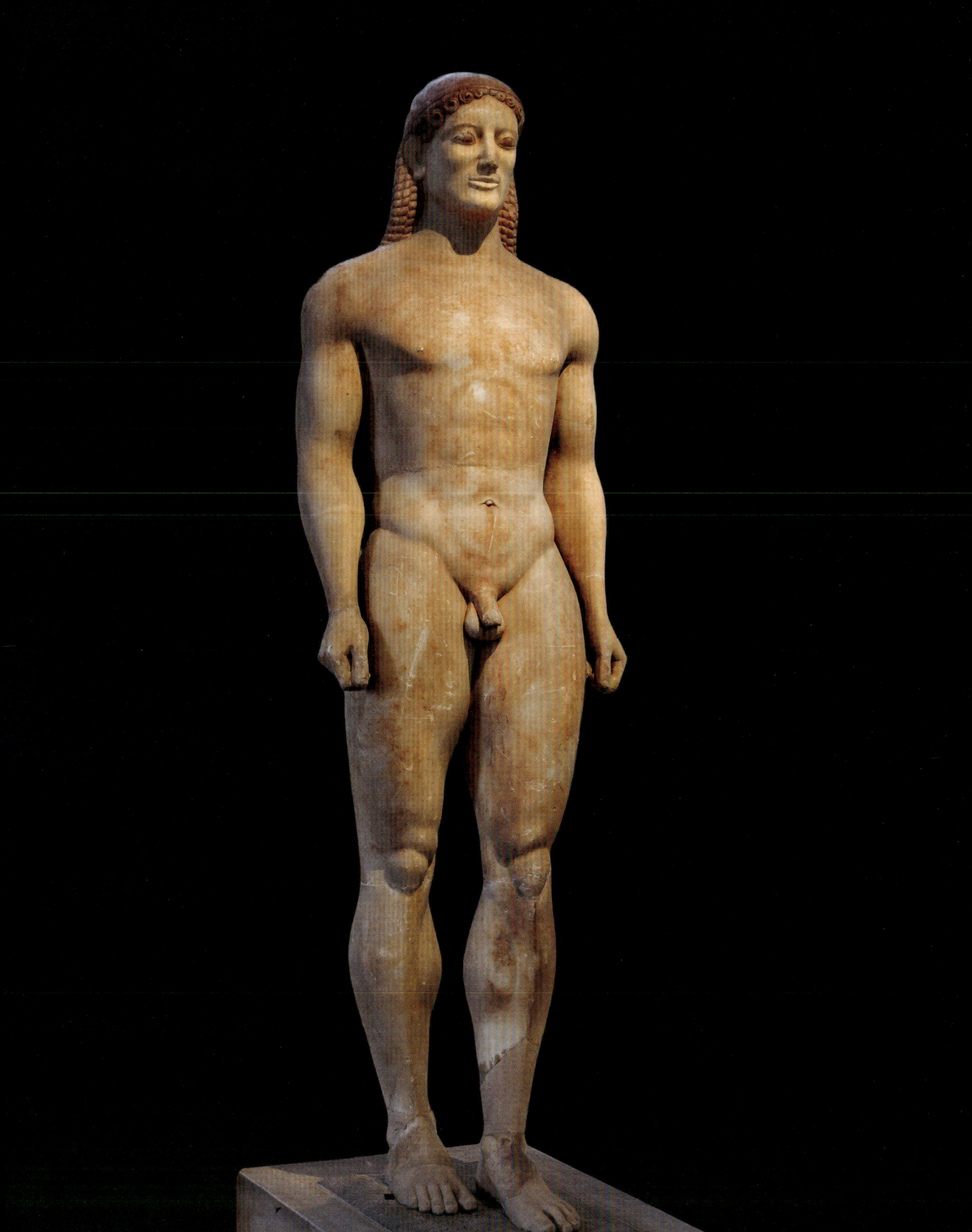

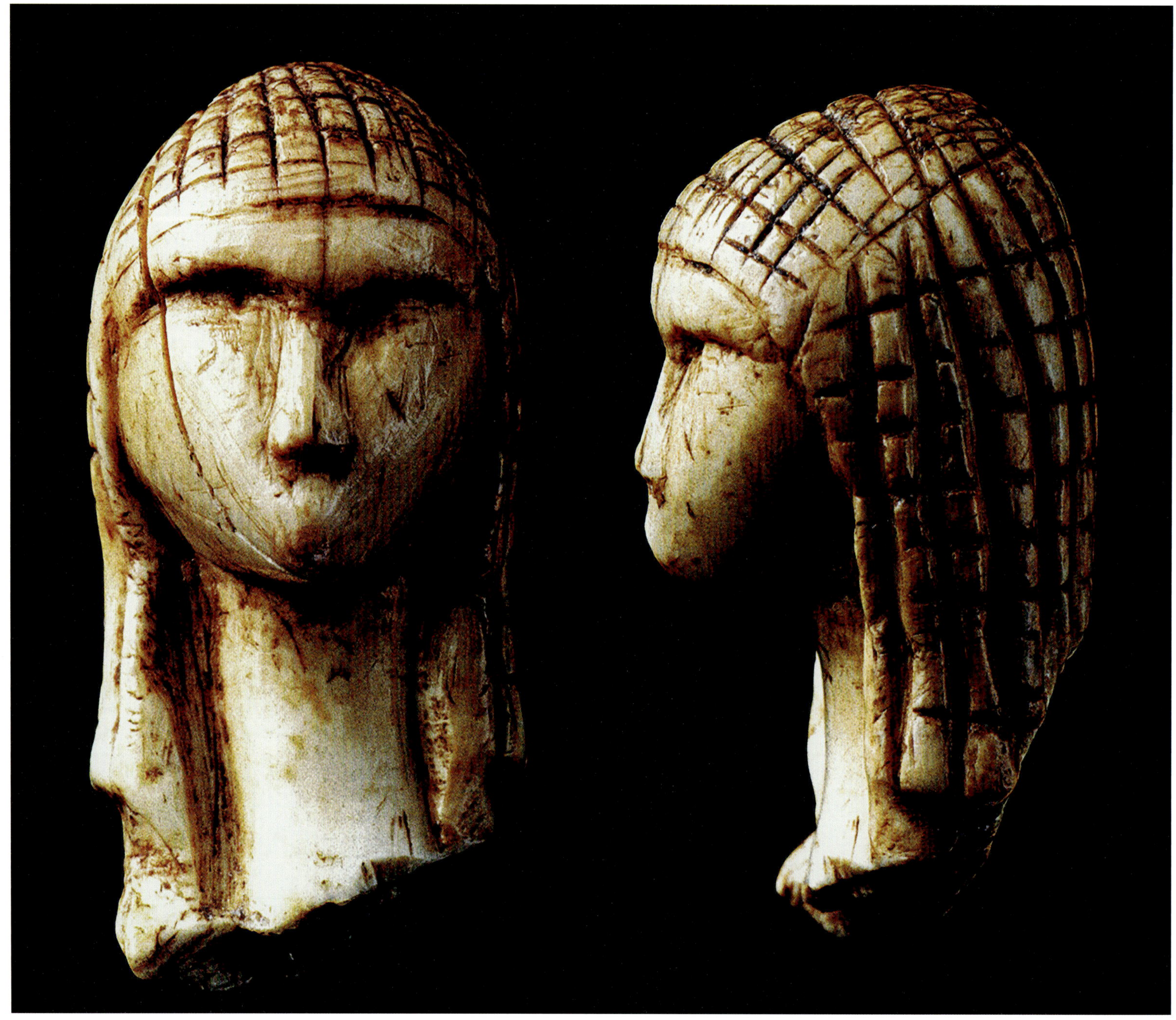

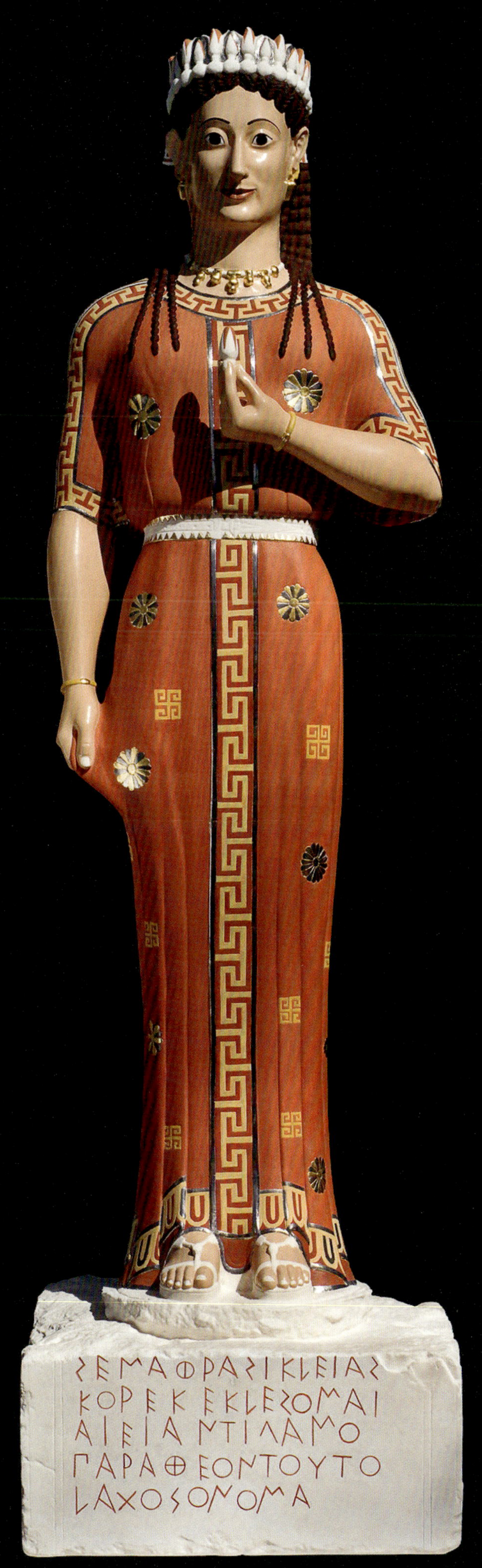

ΣΕΜΑΦΡΑΣΙΚΛΕΙΑΣ
ΚΟΡΕΚΕΚΛΕΣΟΜΑΙ
ΑΙΕΙΑΝΤΙΓΑΜΟ
ΠΑΡΑΘΕΟΝΤΟΥΤΟ
ΛΑΧΟΣΟΝΟΜΑ

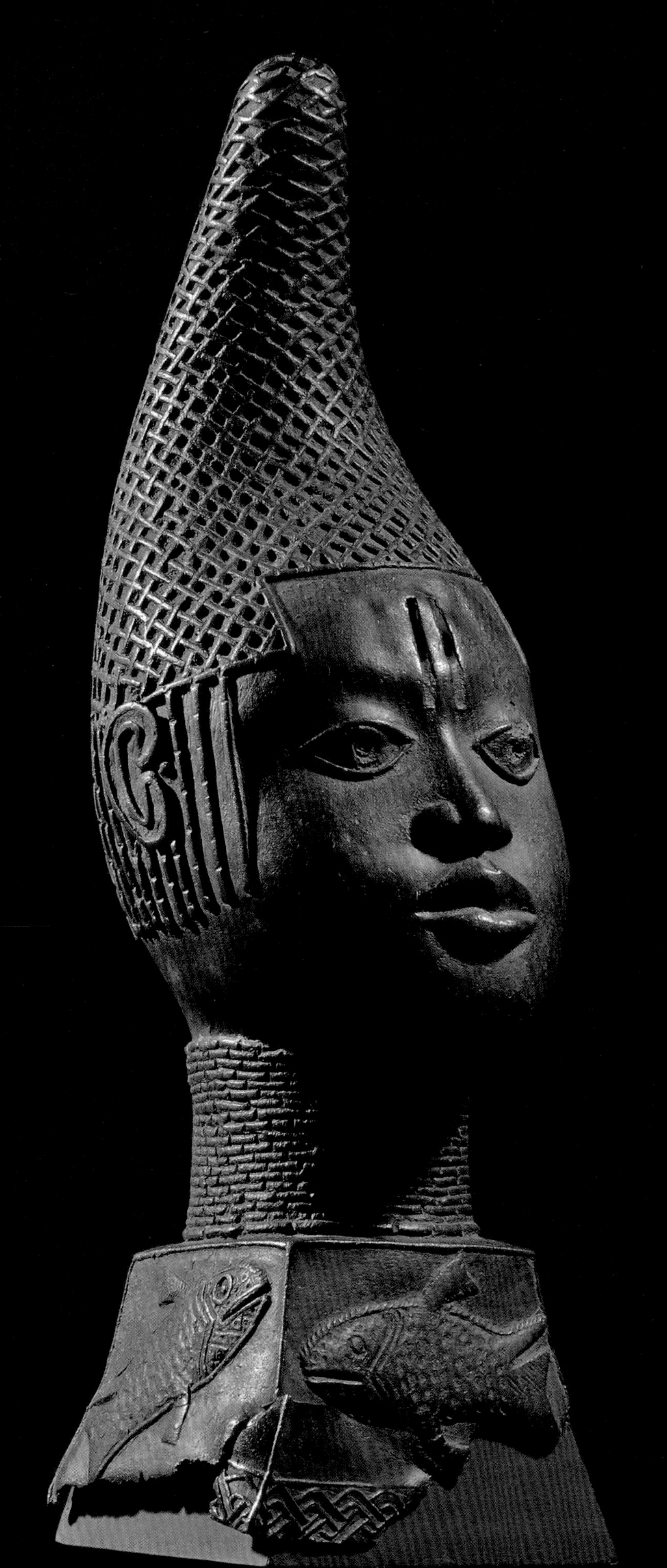

18 Head of Queen Mother (*Iyoba*)

Kingdom of Benin, Nigeria
Early 1500s
Gun bronze
20.08 × 6.30 × 7.09 in.,
51 × 16 × 18 cm
Humboldt Forum, Berlin, Germany

19 Cooling Off at Shijō

Tsukioka Yoshitoshi (Japan, 1839 – 1892)
1885
Woodblock print
14.5 × 9.5 in., 36.83 × 24.13 cm
Ronin Gallery, New York

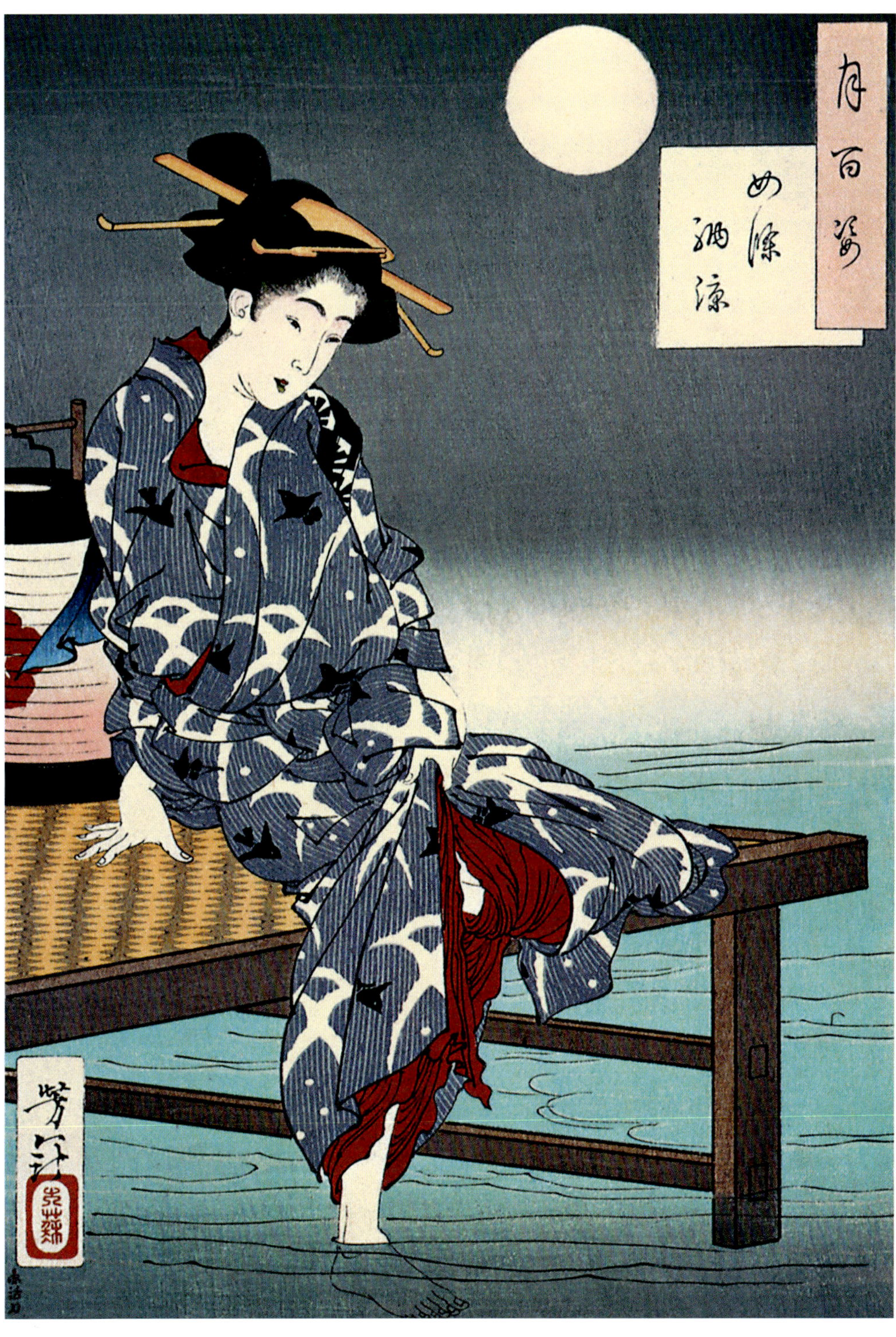

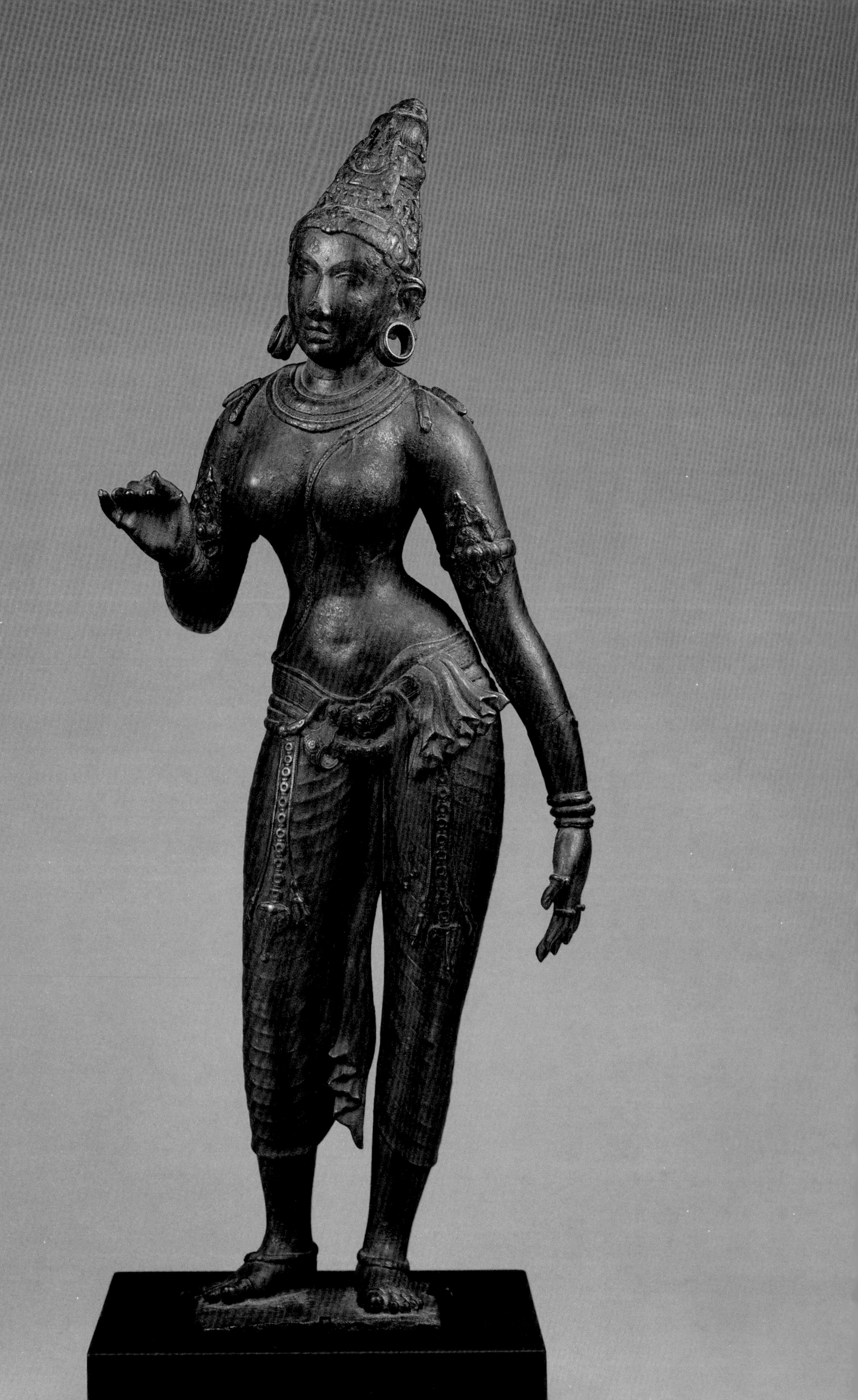

around the world. However, precisely which visual characteristics are experienced as novel will depend to a significant extent on the perceiving subject's previous experiences, not only as an individual but also, importantly, as a member of a culture. The property of novelty therefore is largely an attribute that in a culturally determined manner is ascribed to particular visual stimuli. In this regard, the standard of novelty does not quite fit the category of substantive aesthetic universals, meaning those that denote actual visual features considered attractive by all people. In fact, it introduces the idea of pancultural principles underlying surface diversity in aesthetic preference. We will return to these structural aesthetic universals below.

Accounting for Universal Aesthetic Properties

The list of aesthetic standards that appear widespread in human cultures would seem to be confirmed by a closer inspection of the world's visual arts, as well as in descriptive and normative art writing from around the globe. The list, basic as it is, may also resonate with readers' own experiences and their observations of the aesthetic preferences expressed by their fellow human beings. The next logical step would then be to try and explain the worldwide adherence to the aesthetic standards just enumerated. In an attempt to do so, we will continue to approach aesthetic preference through the lens of bio-evolution.[4]

The panhuman appreciation of symmetry may well reside, as was hinted at above, in an innate preference resulting from the evolutionary processes of random genetic variation and non-random selection. A normally developing and healthy human body has a symmetrical build, which makes visual symmetry an index of physical fitness. Ancestral people who, through arbitrary genetic changes, became sensitive to bodily symmetry then tended to choose more healthy mates than did others, which led on average to a better chance of seeing their genes survive into the next generation. Due to its evolutionary advantages, the innate preference for bodily symmetry then spread through the population and finally became a feature of the species as a whole. The inborn human preference for symmetry could then be exploited by individuals who created artifacts intended to be visually attractive.

Bodily symmetry is a prominent characteristic of the youthful presentation of the human figure that is universally admired. The preferences for other properties of youthfulness, such as a smooth skin and an overall impression of physical bloom, can be similarly accounted for by evolutionary incentives, as these visual features have been treated in medical literature as objective indexes of health and fertility. Innate predilections for these features are thus instrumental in selecting mates with reproductive potential.

The case of balance is more complex to explain in evolutionary terms and probably involves not only perceptual dimensions, of which more below, but also the basic pleasure involved in the sensorimotor experience of bodily equilibrium, and especially its restoration. This encompasses our constant striving to balance the body and its activities, a feat we learn with some difficulty when young and cherish ever after, thus optimizing the efficacy of our actions.

The aesthetic standard of clarity expresses the pleasure people feel when encountering visual stimuli that are readily perceptible, with both parts and whole being easily identified. Clarity seems to function as a kind of "container standard," as symmetry, balance, smoothness, brightness, and color contrast may all contribute to the pleasurable experience of visual comprehensibility. So may such varying features as right angles, parallel lines, and any other form of visual pattern or regularity that facilitates the perceptual process. Ancestral people who, due to chance genetic changes, became more attracted to one or more of these perceptibility-enhancing properties were able to make better sense of visual stimuli in their surroundings, resulting in a more efficient identification of landscape features, predators, food sources, and more. Since a heightened ability to extract information from the visual environment is easily seen to be valuable to survival and reproduction, the increase in this ability may be considered selectively advantageous. Future generations will then inherit the genetic codes involved

in developing neural circuits that entail an above-average attraction, followed by sustained attention, to visual properties that aid visual discrimination and detection. In human-made objects created to provide visual pleasure, the amplification of these properties (by presenting them in purified and concentrated forms) then tends to produce a relatively strong, agreeable perceptual effect in human beings.

In the case of novelty, an evolutionary account may propose that individuals who, on a genetic basis, became more attracted to novelty tended to display more exploratory behavior than others—motivated by the anticipated rewards of encountering something new, they would have more frequently ventured beyond the familiar. Exploratory behavior may well be seen as instrumental in finding such essentials as water, food, and mates; in spotting dangers; in discovering escape routes; and so on—all behaviors with adaptive value. If an increased display of exploratory behavior (up to a certain point) indeed provides an evolutionary edge, then people endowed with this tendency are more likely to pass on their genes. The heritable neural programming that involves a heightened attraction to novelty then spreads among the human species, together with the type of behavior it inspires.

Aesthetic Universals:
Structural Principles of Pleasing Form

In addition to taking account of visual properties that have a panhuman appeal, or what we have called substantive aesthetic universals, when examining common denominators in qualitative visual discernment we also need to consider interculturally recurring principles in the formation of aesthetic preference that may not entail such universally admired properties. That is, we need to consider structuring principles of pleasing form operative in many or all cultures regardless of whether the application of these principles in a given culture results in visual features that elicit panhuman appreciation. The widespread standard of novelty illustrates the existence of such principles, or what we have labelled structural aesthetic universals: what will be experienced as novel in one culture need not be experienced thus in another, where the principle itself may nonetheless equally apply. Incidentally, the example of novelty also demonstrates that a bio-evolutionary approach may account on a panhuman basis for particular cultural or regional *differences* in visual preference.

In what follows, we will examine a somewhat more complex example of a structural principle that I suggest underlies human aesthetic appreciation. The commonality we will consider may go some way to explaining the cultural relativism in aesthetic preference we encounter around the world, overlaying the basic panhuman visual property preferences discussed above.

Over the last century or so, both culture historians and especially cultural anthropologists have consistently argued that aesthetic preference is culture-bound. Yet attempts to systematically account for this cultural relativism in aesthetics have been virtually absent. A comparative analysis of a few well-documented cases of the aesthetic in its societal and cultural settings suggests, however, that light may be shed on the issue by considering an interculturally recurring relationship that methodically relates aesthetic preference to a particular dimension of its cultural context. The regularity I will argue for entails that a given community's visual predilections are informed by its sociocultural values or ideals. If so, then cultural relativism in aesthetics may be explained by arguing that differing sociocultural values lead to differing aesthetic preferences—again, above and beyond visual properties with panhuman appeal.

In order to substantiate this thesis, we will consider aesthetic preferences in three African cultures and demonstrate how they relate to the sociocultural value systems of these cultures. By sociocultural values or ideals, I mean communally endorsed notions of what is to be preferably achieved in individual and collective sociocultural strivings. Any convincing case study then needs to provide us with valid data on people's actual aesthetic preferences; a decent knowledge of consensual local views regarding what is worth attaining in a sociocultural sense; and a good understanding of the ways meanings are locally communicated through form—or how visual stimuli translate or signify these meanings in the culture. Case studies providing solid data on all three fronts are rare. This explains the emphasis on Africa in what follows, as empirical and contextual approaches to aesthetics have so far been mainly applied in sub-Saharan settings.[5]

The Baule:
Beauty and the Behavioral Mean

The first case study concerns people who identify as Baule. The analysis draws mainly on the work of art historian Susan Vogel, who studied Baule art, aesthetics, and culture between the late 1960s and the mid-1990s.[6]

Numbering about three million, the Baule people inhabit large parts of central Côte d'Ivoire in West Africa. Consisting mainly of agriculturalists, their society has been described as democratic and egalitarian. Baule life has also been described as highly collectivistic. This blend of egalitarianism and collectivism entails that the stress on people's equality is accompanied by an emphasis on the average, meaning that individuals are expected always to conform to the mean as defined by the community. In fact, being regarded as different from the average community member has been called one of the greatest fears of a Baule person, who thereby risks becoming isolated from the group. This brings us to a first sociocultural value or ideal among this people, namely always observing the mean in one's conduct and avoiding any excesses or extremes.

The Baule are first and foremost farmers, with both men and women being involved in field labor; the ability and the willingness to work hard are highly praised. This work ethic is another major value, which in itself relates to several other sociocultural qualities. Thus, there is the value placed on excellent physical condition, which is necessary to work hard. Good health is also a prerequisite for fertility, yet another sociocultural value. Like so many other African peoples, the Baule feel that having children is one of the greatest goods in life, and it is in fact necessary if a person is to earn respect and esteem in the community.

Good health, in turn, depends in part on taking care of the body, as well as on other types of cleanliness. Indeed, a Baule person highly values personal hygiene, taking at least one hot bath per day. More generally, the Baule attach much importance to a well-cared for appearance, with special attention being given to hairstyle and scarification. These two forms of body decoration are considered signs of civilization, or, as the Baule would have it, they characterize the individual as a *klo sran*, a "person of the village." This expression refers to an honorable man or woman who ideally embodies the whole cluster of Baule sociocultural values, including restraint and conformation to the mean, health, cleanliness, fertility, and the ability to work hard.

The Baule produce finely sculpted anthropomorphic statues—or they did so until at least the turn of the century. These figures are made in connection with two kinds of spirits that may be diagnosed as the source of a variety of misfortunes. To put an end to these, a diviner may advise having a statue carved for the trouble-causing spirit. The statue should be as beautiful as possible and hence attractive to the spirit. The attractiveness of the statue is thereby judged according to the same standards that are used to evaluate the beauty of the human body. So which visual qualities or criteria do the Baule use to evaluate the beauty of human beings and statues? To answer this question Vogel carried out empirical research into Baule aesthetic preferences.

It turned out that the Baule regard as attractive exactly those visual properties of a statue that aptly signify the sociocultural values esteemed in their community. This is shown, for example, in the appreciation of a well-finished and polished surface, which denotes smooth and glossy skin. The Baule associate such skin with a series of interrelated sociocultural values. Smooth and shiny skin is said to indicate cleanliness, demonstrating that the individual takes care of his or her personal hygiene. And since it is unblemished by traces of tropical skin diseases, smooth skin also signifies health. Health and the related notion of fertility are qualities that are associated predominantly with youthful people. So it is no surprise that according to Baule critics, an anthropomorphic sculpture should always depict a person in the prime of life. Healthy young people also possess the ability to perform hard physical labor. In this respect, Baule evaluators almost invariably commented upon a figure's calves, consistently preferring ones that are full and round—an indication that the person is strong and able

to perform exacting tasks in the fields. The value of hard work also informs the assessment of the neck. In both people and statues, the Baule prefer a straight, relatively long, and strong neck, which suggests that the person is able to transport the heavy loads traditionally carried on the head.

Now, the visual preference for smooth and shiny skin, full calves, and long, strong necks can be related rather easily to sociocultural values, since the local meanings these features signify are quite evident in a contextual analysis. It appears, however, that the same linkage between preferred form and sociocultural qualities can also be established with respect to a more abstract, allegedly purely formal criterion of beauty. Vogel concludes that the most important aesthetic standard by far among the Baule is *sɛsɛ*, a term that references the "golden mean." For example, although a beautiful figure should have scarifications, their number should be moderate: not too few, not too many. Similarly, hairstyles should be carefully crafted but never over-elaborate. Baule also stress the mean in the execution of the different parts of a figure's body: the buttocks should be neither too flat nor too developed, just as a neck should be neither too short nor too long.

We have seen that the mean or the average is of central importance in the sociocultural value system of the Baule as well. It could therefore be argued that, like full calves or smooth and shiny skin, the presence of *sɛsɛ* in a figure elicits culturally valued meaning in a Baule beholder. Indeed, it could even be proposed that a stimulus displaying this most abstract and dominant criterion of beautiful form signifies what in the egalitarian and collectivistic society of the Baule can be considered the most general and important sociocultural value, namely the behavioral mean.

This brief contextual examination of Baule aesthetic preferences has introduced us to the thesis that the visual features considered aesthetically pleasing in a given community reference the community's sociocultural values or ideals. If this contention is valid, then we should be able to demonstrate that a different sociocultural value system gives rise to different aesthetic preferences, or in other words, that a different view of beauty can be linked to a different sociocultural ideal. In order to do so, we shall take a closer look at aesthetic preference among the Igbo, which has been the subject of several publications by art historian Chike Aniakor, who is himself Igbo.[7]

The Igbo:
Beauty and Achievement

The Igbo live in southeast Nigeria and today number about thirty million. Their economy is based on agriculture, but trade has always been of great importance as well. The Igbo are subdivided into several hundred so-called village groups that are governed by different types of associations and especially by these associations' title holders. There are several hierarchical title systems in Igboland that place political and moral authority in groups of mature, relatively wealthy men. Indeed, among the Igbo, authority combines with wealth in that a man can move from lower,

inexpensive grades with little power, to more costly and exclusive grades that allow him to exercise considerable influence. Among the Igbo, titles are not inherited but acquired by individuals who gain enough wealth through personal efforts to purchase them, gaining political power and social status.

From this it is clear that personal success, whether in farming, trade, or other activities, is much valued by the Igbo. Indeed, several scholars, both Igbo and non-Igbo, consider the notion of individual achievement to be the sociocultural ideal of this people. Attaining this ideal presupposes physical and mental strength as well as determination. Strength and perseverance may lead to an increase of resources and finally wealth, which via the title system is translated into high sociopolitical status, influence, and privilege. This pursuit of personal wealth and status also implies a considerable amount of socioeconomic competition and rivalry among individuals. Thus, whereas the Baule stress restraint and conformity to the mean, the Igbo encourage individuals to excel and distinguish themselves from the average.

As for Igbo aesthetic preferences, Aniakor's work suggests that the quality that above all others makes a stimulus visually attractive for the Igbo is *igwogo ngwogo*, which may be translated as "curvilinear elaboration," the term *igwo* meaning "curve" or "coil." Coiled forms and ornaments are indeed characteristic of many Igbo art forms, from body paintings and house decorations to pottery and wood sculpture (**21**). *Igwogo ngwogo* also expresses a preference for visual elaboration or even complexity, features that are typical of the superstructures

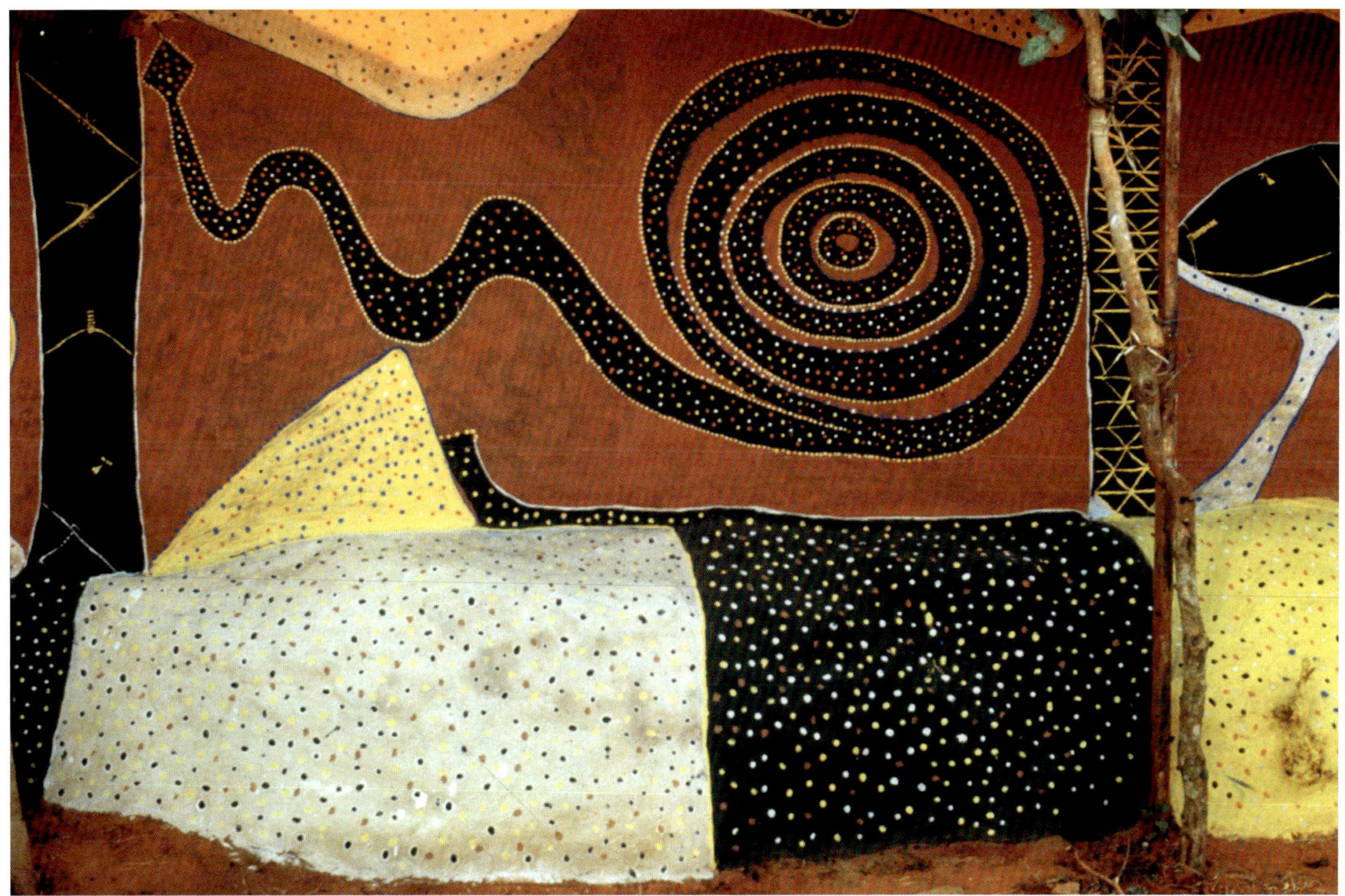

of certain face masks and several other visual art forms. Structural and ornamental elaboration often combines with curvilinearity, which is a visual feature conducive to the creation of intricate designs and complex forms. Three-dimensional examples of this can be seen in stools that serve as the emblems of title holders (**22**).

So why is curvilinear elaboration admired by the Igbo? To understand this from the perspective proposed here, we should try to connect the visual preference for curvilinear elaboration to the Igbo ideal of individual achievement and the qualities it encompasses. We may first consider the idea of curvilinearity. Curvilinear forms are typical, for example, of *Ikenga* sculptures (**23**). These wooden carvings show an anthropomorphic figure, frequently seated on a stool, carrying an object such as a curved horn in its hands. The figure is crowned by at least two upthrusting and coiling motifs but may have a much more elaborate superstructure dominated by curvilinear

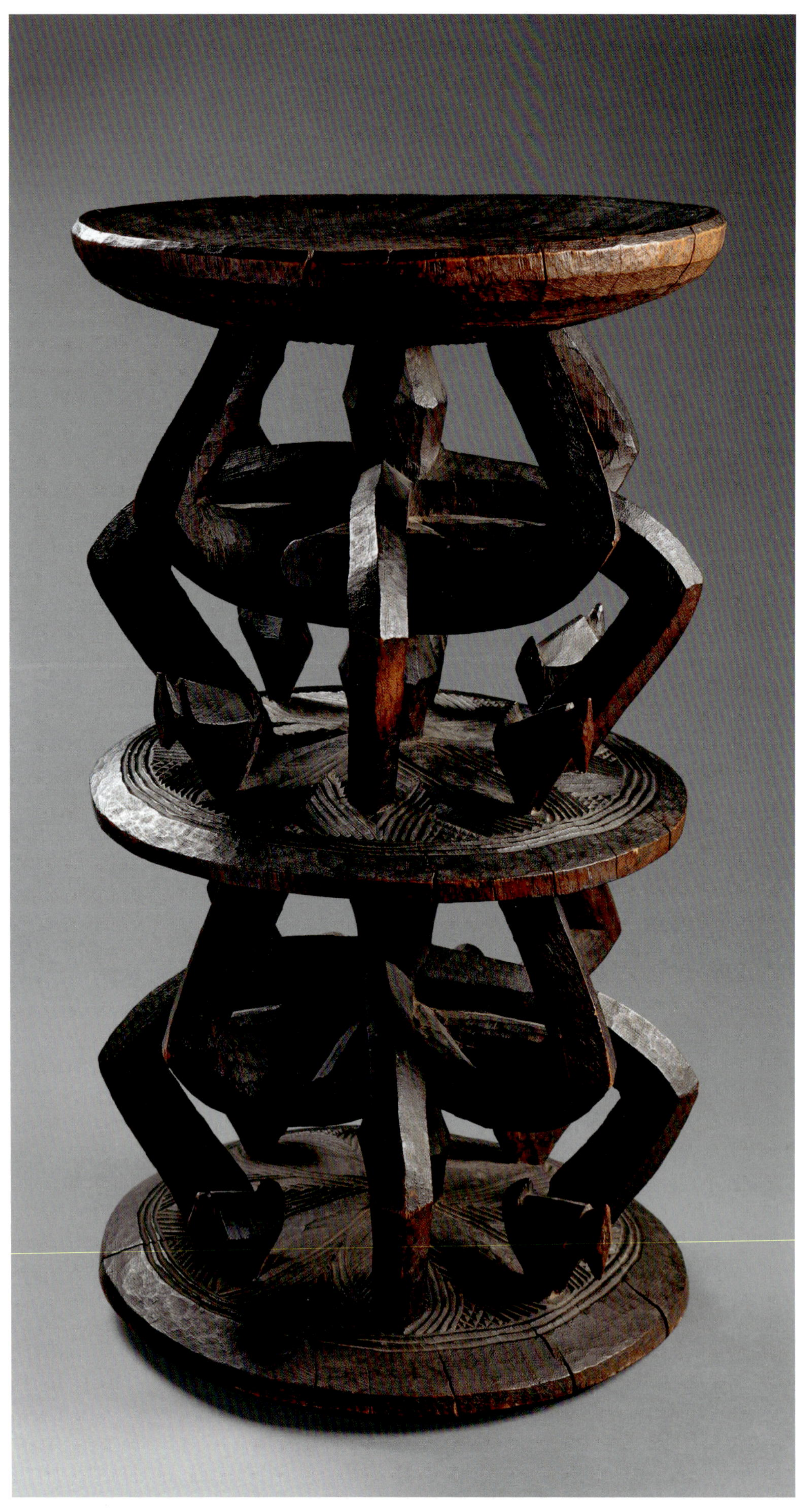

22 Prestige Stool (*Oche Ozo*)

Igbo culture,
Southeastern Nigeria
Iroko wood
23 ¼ in., 59 cm
Private Collection

23 Figure (*Ikenga*)

Igbo culture,
Southeastern Nigeria
1900 – 1950
Wood and paint
45 ¹¹⁄₁₆ × 11 ¹³⁄₁₆ × 11 ¹³⁄₁₆ in.,
116 × 30 × 30 cm
Princeton University Art Museum,
New Jersey
Museum Purchase, Fowler
McCormick, Class of 1921, Fund

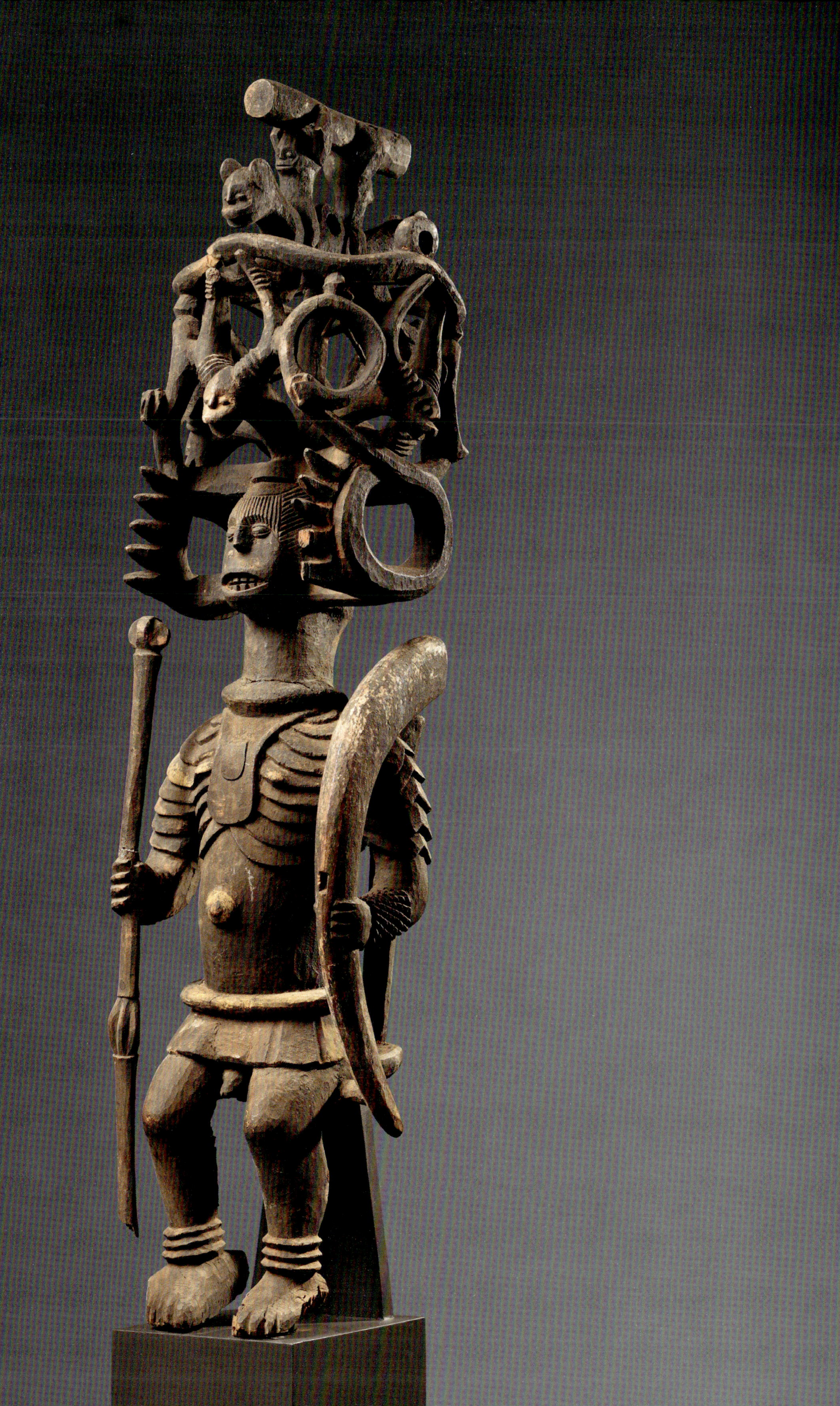

forms. The sculptures are used in individual cults that celebrate a man's—and sometimes a woman's—personal achievements. In *Ikenga* figures, curvilinear motifs actually depict or seem to be inspired by horns. Among the Igbo, as in so many African cultures, horns signify vital force and strength. In addition, the curves or coils of a horn are thought to convey growth and increase. Horns could thus be said to signify vital, expansive strength. The horns of an *Ikenga* sculpture, moreover, are usually identified by the Igbo as those of a ram, an animal known for its stubborn determination—a characteristic it shares with a man of high achievement. Curvilinear forms inspired by horns could thus be said to signify important prerequisites to and features of the Igbo ideal of achievement, namely strength, perseverance, and expansion. The same qualities are evoked by the curvilinear designs that women use to decorate Igbo houses and bodies. Called *uli* designs, they are inspired by such organic forms as young, growing leaves and plant tendrils and likewise signify vitality, tenacity, and growth.

To understand the Igbo praise of that other characteristic of pleasing form, elaboration, we must consider what Aniakor believes to be a crucial factor in their aesthetics: The less time a work takes, the less money it costs and the less elaborate the sculptural elaboration. Conversely, the more time it takes, the higher the cost and the more complex the sculptural elaboration. Because they consume time and money, sculptural elaboration and complexity are thus signs of riches and prestige. Indeed, only men of achievement can afford elaborately worked, visually complex *Ikengas* and intricately carved stools.

We may then conclude that the Igbo seem to aesthetically prefer exactly those visual stimuli that evoke their sociocultural ideal of achievement. Curvilinearity thereby signifies the vitality and tenacity needed to be successful in farming, trade, or any other human endeavour, and at the same time it refers to the ideas of growth or expansion that accompany the notion of achievement. Elaboration references the wealth, status, and prestige that result from the successful application of energy and determination to one's enterprises.

The Asante:
Beauty and Sociocultural Change

If a given community regards as visually pleasing stimuli that aptly signify its sociocultural ideal, it is implied that when this ideal changes, aesthetic predilection will also change. A consideration of Asante visual preferences recorded in a period of value change suggests that this is indeed the case. The following analysis is primarily based on the research of anthropologist Harry Silver.[8]

The Asante (or Ashanti), who number about three million, inhabit large parts of what is today central and southern Ghana. Trade centering around gold, and later slaves, has traditionally been of considerable importance to Asante economy. When European merchants became involved in their business networks at the end of the sixteenth century, trade not only began to supply the Asante with iron tools, which increased agricultural productivity, but also firearms. Both contributed to the Asante conquest of surrounding territories. Around 1700, the Asante headed a confederacy of small states and towns that gradually expanded and was to dominate central and southern Ghana for the next two centuries.

Being interested in slaves and the large gold reserves of the Asante territory, European nations, and Great Britain in particular, tried to establish peaceful relationships with the powerful Asante Empire. In the first decades of the nineteenth century, British efforts led to an Anglo-Asante treaty. British interference in internal affairs increased, however, and around 1900, the Asante territory and surrounding areas became a British crown colony named Gold Coast. In 1957, the Asante and other peoples, who had been forcibly united by the British into what was now called Ghana, became independent under President Nkrumah.

Following half a century of colonization, modernization forcefully arrived in post-independence Ghana. Opinions on how to respond to changing circumstances and needs, however, diverged considerably. According to national government policy, modernization should be seen in terms of "intertribal homogenization," meaning the elimination of all ethnic distinctions within the borders of present-day Ghana. But the Asante, who have been typified as fiercely proud of their past and confident of their superiority, were strongly opposed to this. The prospect of being lumped together with peoples who once were their subordinates or with peoples living farther to the north (who, unlike the largely Christianized Asante, are generally Muslim) was experienced by the Asante as a threat to their strongly felt ethnic identity, or "Asanteness."

Rather than following the official policy of intertribal homogenization, the Asante confronted the challenge of modernization in terms of their own history, in which they generally consider the West to have played a positive role. Indeed, in spite of the negative sides of colonization, in the first half of the twentieth century the Asante continued to be sympathetic toward the West, adopting its technologies and cultural traits. When confronted with the need to modernize, then, the Asante opted to harmoniously assimilate into their culture Western influences and values. The new Asante sociocultural ideal that arose in the wake of independence may thus be described in terms of a smooth blend of traditional Asante values and modern Western ones.

In order to learn about Asante aesthetic preferences, Silver conducted an experiment in the mid-1970s that involved twenty-five contemporary Asante sculptures that were rated and commented upon by more than one hundred respondents. The test items may be grouped into four categories. The first consists of traditional Asante carvings such as *akuamma*, so-called fertility figures. Women carry *akuamma* (singular *akuaba*) on the back to help induce conception and to ensure the birth of handsome children. The figures emphasize salient characteristics of ideal human beauty as conceived by the Asante, namely an oval-shaped face with a broad forehead and full eyebrows, and a straight, long neck with a series of rings or folds around it. These neck rings represent small rolls of fat and are considered a sign of prosperity and beauty. Traditional *akuamma* display these features in a highly stylized manner. The emphasis is clearly on the flatly rendered oval head that usually occupies more than a third of the figure, whereas the rest of the body is abstracted into a slender, tubular form with two short horizontal extensions representing the arms.

Already in the 1930s, innovative Asante sculptors started to create more naturalistically executed fertility figures. The head continued to be proportionally large, but facial features and later also the body were rendered in more anatomically correct detail. For the Asante, naturalism in style is definitively a Western borrowing introduced by means of photographs, advertisements, and Christian religious iconography. The modern *akuamma* fall into the second category of test items, which encompasses innovative treatments of traditional themes. The third group was made up of sculptures inspired by several West African mask styles and mainly sold to tourists. The fourth category consisted of so-called genre carvings, such as the depiction of a woman pounding *fufu*, a favorite Asante food. These are not traditional art forms, but unlike the sculptures based on other African art styles, they draw upon indigenous Asante experience.

Reporting on his aesthetic ranking test, Silver observed that the most popular pieces were those that translated traditional themes into new, naturalistic forms. The highest ratings were indeed given to genre figures and naturalistic *akuamma*. One of the two favorites of the Asante critics was a genre carving depicting a naturalistically portrayed seated man in traditional robes holding an open book. Asante critics praised the literacy of this Westernized figure and said that he was clearly a man to respect, the type who would play a central role in Ghana's future. Yet this modern leader was also a traditional man: he sits rigidly in his African robe, displaying the dignity and composure typical of an Asante chief. The figure thus signifies enduring qualities of traditional Asante culture while at the same time referring to the West and its values. In other words, the Asante appeared to give the highest praise to a sculpture that offered a harmonious synthesis of traditional and Western elements, pithily signifying their contemporary sociocultural ideal in visual form.

The other favorite of Asante respondents consisted of a rather naturalistically rendered *akuaba* figure. On the one hand, critics appreciated such traditionally valued features as an oval head, broad forehead, prominent eyebrows, and a layered neck. On the other hand, they praised the figure's modern appearance, especially the naturalistic details of both face and body. As with the figure of the modern chief, the sculpture aptly evokes the sociocultural ideal of merging traditional Asante values and modern Western ones. In this case, too, this fusion is to a large extent achieved by smoothly blending stylization, which is a hallmark of traditional Asante culture, and naturalism, which is seen as distinctive of Western culture.

Accounting for the Connection between Aesthetic Preference and Sociocultural Values

The analysis of these three case studies proposes that visual metaphors of local sociocultural values—works that succinctly and suggestively evoke these values through visual form—elicit a pleasurable perceptual experience in local viewers. Importantly, in our examples this evocation is to a significant degree achieved by way of seemingly abstract or purely formal features such as visual restraint or elaboration, or the mixture of stylization and naturalism. In other instances, non-iconic characteristics such as color or even medium may be involved. Indeed, readers might ponder the relationship between sociocultural ideals and notions of beauty in other cultural contexts, including other subcultural contexts (for example generational subcultures, social subcultures, as well as mixtures of these and various other subcultures). The full range of empirical data ideally needed for the type of analysis presented above, however, may well be lacking.

If visual stimuli that concisely and evocatively elicit communal values routinely prompt a positive aesthetic response, we need to next ask why this would be the case. The answer may seem simple: the meanings signified by these visual stimuli are not neutral for local perceivers but denote what is consensually seen as preferred modes of individual and collective behavior in the community or culture. This turns these meanings into what are commonly known as values, a concept to which we tend to ascribe an emotional valence. But this begs the ultimate question, highly relevant in the context of aesthetics: Why would people respond *affectively* to what they identify as communally endorsed behavioral guidelines, rather than merely register them? Why would a qualitative dimension be involved in discerning collective strivings, including here their signification on the level of visual form?

We may offer the following evolutionary explanation of the positive affective response that people appear to experience when confronted with concise and evocative visual articulations of consensual guidelines for ideal behavior. We may approach the topic as follows: Having evolved to live in groups, humans recurrently face the problem of social inclusion. Social inclusion would seem to require that at given times, individuals display at least an elemental type of conformity to the behavioral principles or values of the community into which they have been enculturated. Indeed, people who do not display some minimal observance to these behavioral guidelines face the risk of ostracization. Especially in the foraging and hunter-gatherer contexts in which the mental predispositions of humans evolved over hundreds of thousands of years, such casting-out is likely to have severely reduced an individual's prospects of survival and reproduction. Conversely, some measure of endorsement of communal behavioral norms may benefit a human organism and those sharing its genes. This compliance would seem to be instrumental, for example, in the organization and effectuation of various forms of cooperation, such as gathering and distributing food or warding off danger. These forms of cooperation may then be held on average to confer advantages to the survival and reproductive success of the individual members of the group, as well as their kin.

Social conformity in humans, and the social inclusion and effective cooperation it entails, may thus be regarded as a recurring problem that is subject to selection pressure. One may then speculate that selective processes, acting on the adaptive problem of sociality, favor people who are predisposed, in given conditions, to respond in a positive affective manner to what enculturation teaches them to be communal norms and to subsequently act on them. In this case, as in so many others, emotional responses would serve as economic motivators of behavior that on average proves beneficial to gene survival. If so, visual metaphors that pithily signify local sociocultural values may be able to trigger a relatively intense affective response with an innate basis.

Conclusion

The quest for human commonalities has not been very popular in scholarship over the last century or so. Intercultural studies have rather focused on dissimilarities, from anthropology's insistence on cultural relativism, to postmodern philosophy's emphasis on the fragmented and the unstable, to today's ubiquitous concerns with difference. Add to this the humanities' loss of interest in the aesthetic category of "the beautiful" over the same time period—"beauty" went from being considered antithetical to the artistic aims of the modernist avant-garde to being construed as elitist and oppressive in more recent years—and one begins to understand why the search for commonalities in aesthetic preference has languished in scholarship, however interesting and legitimate the topic is. This chapter has nonetheless tried to shed some light on the issue of common denominators in human visual predilections, especially by taking into account the results of empirical research that ethnographers have carried out in a variety of cultures. A comparative analysis of these results produces a basic list of substantive aesthetic universals—visual properties that people anywhere experience as pleasing to the eye, including symmetry, balance, clarity, and visual signs of youthfulness. It also suggests the existence of structural aesthetic universals: recurring principles underlying some of the observable differences in aesthetic preferences around the globe. This chapter has highlighted one such principle, involving the influence that local sociocultural ideals exert on people's qualitative visual experiences. Evolutionary accounts would seem to clarify the existence of both types of commonalities, proposing that they are firmly rooted in humans' evolved neurobiology of affect. Aesthetic universals, including those that may systematically account for cultural diversity in taste, deserve to be taken seriously, and they need to be explored further if we are to better understand what is arguably a fundamental feature of human nature, namely our tendency to relate to the world by means of aesthetic response. In human-made objects meant to please the eye (including what are labelled works of art), innately pleasurable visual properties are enlisted (as in the case of symmetry), enhanced (as in the case of clarity), or even exaggerated (as in the case of youthfulness). The presence of such substantive aesthetic universals in works from cultures unfamiliar to the perceiver may allow enjoyment of these works' aesthetic qualities. The existence of structural aesthetic universals, such as the proposed relationship between notions of beauty and sociocultural ideals, may then invite us to more closely examine these works in their cultural context and, by doing so, perhaps lead us to a point where we start seeing aesthetic excellence in terms of the culture concerned.

1   As quoted in a translation from the French by Ino Rossi, *People in Culture: A Survey of Cultural Anthropology* (New York: Praeger, 1980), 4 (emphasis in the original).

2   Marek Kohn and Steven Mithen, "Handaxes: Products of Sexual Selection?," *Antiquity* 73, no. 281 (1999): 518–26. See also Mark White and Frederick Foulds, "Symmetry is its Own Reward: On the Character and Significance of Acheulean Handaxe Symmetry in the Middle Pleistocene," *Antiquity* 92, no. 362 (2018): 304–19.

3   The discussion of this list of standards is based on a more extensive analysis provided in Wilfried van Damme, *Beauty in Context: Towards an Anthropological Approach to Aesthetics* (Leiden: E. J. Brill, 1996); chapter three: "Universalism in Aesthetics," includes references to the original studies on which the survey draws.

4   For a more detailed introduction to "evolutionary aesthetics," see Wilfried van Damme, "World Aesthetics: Biology, Culture, and Reflection," in *Compression vs Expression: Containing and Explaining the World's Art*, ed. John Onians (New Haven: Yale University Press, 2006), 165 ff. In the study of the human aesthetic, evolutionary aesthetics, focusing on humans as evolved neurobiological beings, needs to be complemented by both "contextual aesthetics," zooming in on humans as sociocultural beings, and "philosophical aesthetics," concentrating on humans as reflective beings. For an introduction to this three-layered approach in the study of Homo aestheticus, see Wilfried van Damme. "Beauty and Ugliness in African Art and Thought," in *The Language of Beauty in African Art*, ed. Constantine Petridis (New Haven: Yale University Press, 2022), 120 ff.

5   For more detailed and more fully referenced expositions of the case studies to follow, see van Damme, *Beauty in Context: Towards an Anthropological Approach to Aesthetics*.

6   See Susan Mullin Vogel, *Beauty in the Eyes of the Baule: Aesthetics and Cultural Values, Working Papers in the Traditional Arts* 6 (Philadelphia: Institute for the Study of Human Issues, 1980) and *Baule: African Art, Western Eyes* (New Haven: Yale University Press, 1997).

7   See Chike C. Aniakor, "Structuralism in Ikenga: An Ethno-Aesthetic Approach to Traditional Igbo Art," *The Conch* 6, no. 1–2 (1974): 1–14; Chike C. Aniakor, "Igbo Aesthetics (An Introduction)," *Nigeria Magazine* 141 (1982): 3–15; and Herbert M. Cole and Chike C. Aniakor, *Igbo Arts: Community and Cosmos* (Los Angeles: University of California Press, 1984).

8   See Harry L. Silver, "Beauty and the 'I' of the Beholder: Identity, Aesthetics, and Social Change among the Ashanti," *Journal of Anthropological Research* 35, no. 2 (1979): 192–207 and "Selective Affinities: Connoisseurship, Culture, and Aesthetic Choice in a Contemporary African Community" *Ethos* 11, no. 1/2 (1983): 87–126.

III

CREATION MYTHS

BARBARA C. SPROUL

At first there was nothing.
Time passed and nothing became something.
Time passed and something split in two:
the two were male and female.
These two produced two more, and these two
produced P'an Ku, the first being,
the Great Man, the Creator.

The Myth of P'an Ku

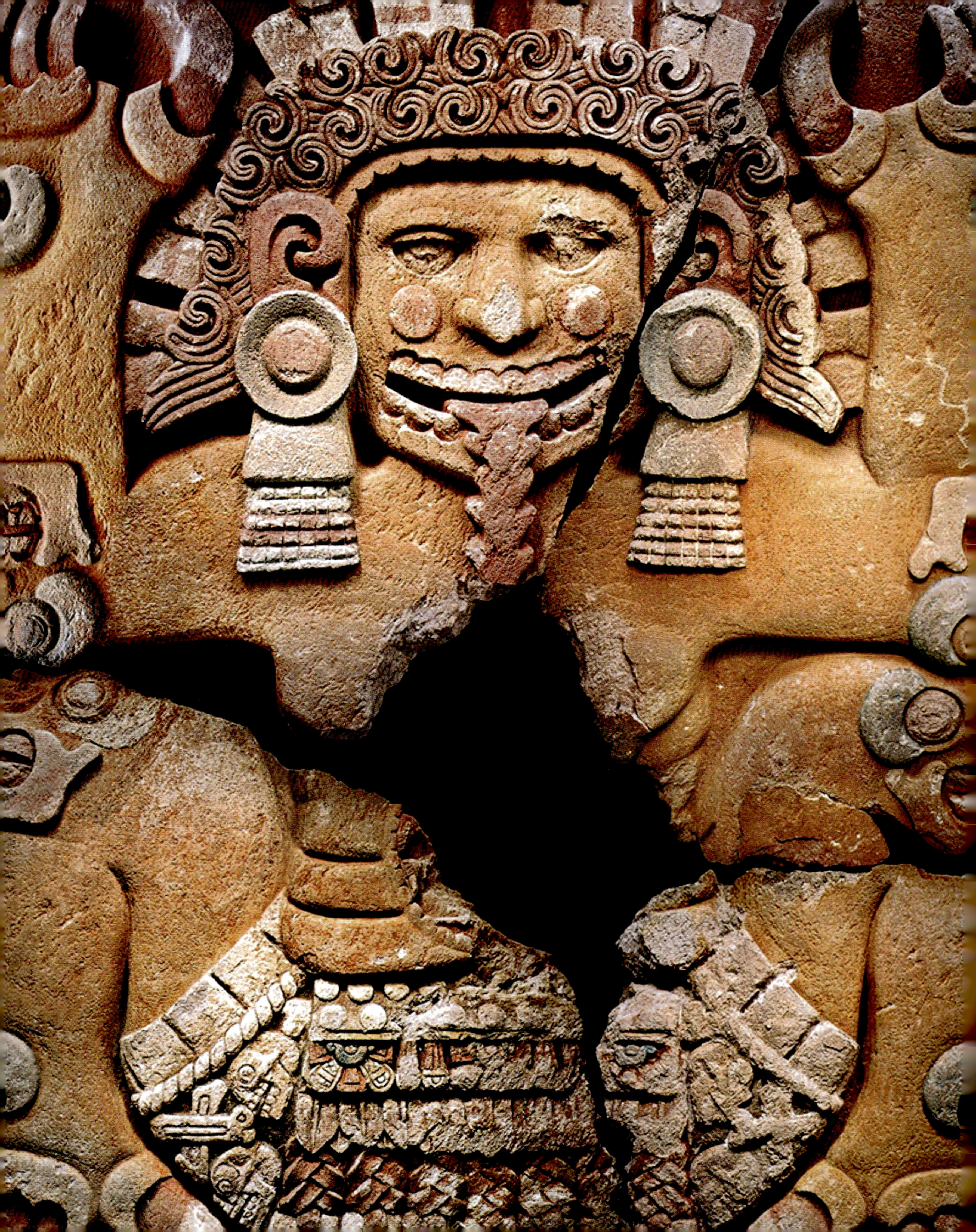

Religion, like art, is a universal response by people to the world in which they find themselves. *What was before anything was? How it is that we exist at all—that existence exists? What sustains us? How should we live successfully, purposefully, meaningfully?* These are some of the most basic questions facing all people throughout time, and the cultures they have created show evidence of their answers in the forms both of religious mythologies and of art.

Science now dates the Big Bang to 13.8 billion years ago, but it can say nothing about *before* that time—before Time/Being/Space-Itself—and people have wondered about that as long as we have evidence of human thought. These are not merely idle questions. They are the most fundamental questions about the mysteries of our daily being and they are the special realm of creation mythology. What was before the before?

Three answers present themselves: *Something, Nothing,* and *I don't know,* and religions try them all. One of the most profound myths in world culture is from the Rig Veda, a canonical text of early Hinduism (ca. 1200 BCE) that speaks of Reality-Itself, the One, before it has split into two or the "many":

> *When neither Being nor Not-Being was*
> *Nor atmosphere, nor firmament, nor what is beyond*
> *What did it encompass? Where? In whose protection?*
> *What was water, the deep, unfathomable?*
> *Neither death nor immortality was there then,*
> *No sign of night or day.*
> *That One breathed windless, by its own energy:*

> *Nought else existed then.*
> *In the beginning was darkness swathed in darkness;*
> *All this was but unmanifested water.*
> *Whatever was, the One, coming into being,*
> *Hidden by the Void,*
> *Was generated by the power of heat.*
> *In the beginning this [One] evolved,*
> *Became Desire, first seed of mind.*
> *Wise seers, searching within their hearts,*
> *Found the bond of Being in Not-Being.*
> *Their cord was extended athwart.*
> *Was there a below? Was there an above?*
> *Casters of seed there were, and powers:*
> *Beneath was energy, above was impulse.*
> *Who knows truly? Who can here declare it?*
> *When it was born, whence is this emanation.*
> *By emanation of this, the gods only later [came to be].*
> *Who then knows whence it has arisen?*
> *When this emanation hath arisen,*
> *Whether [God] disposed it, or whether he did not,—*
> *Only he who is its overseer in highest heaven knows.*
> *[He only knows], or perhaps he does not know![1]*

Here all potentiality is still swirling, undefined reality, like the images our telescopes reveal of nebulae where liquids, solids, and gasses have not yet separated into recognizable worlds of stars and planets, but all the forces and elements are potentially present. Such nebulae, first recorded by the Persian astronomer Abd al-Rahman al-Sufi in the tenth century, and within the next hundred years by both Chinese and Arabian astronomers, are visible examples of this process that help us understand what ancient peoples were talking about when they tried to envision the beginning of all being, not just one galaxy. Throughout the world, religions agree that what they consider the Holy is akin to this One that the Hindus imagined. All affirm it is *absolute* (always the case), *eternal* (transcending temporality), and *infinite* (transcending spatiality). While all relative realities are dependent on others, what is truly Holy must by definition be *omnipotent*—all powerful—and thus *independent*.

On Fifth Avenue in New York City, there is a statue of the Greek god Atlas holding up the world. But what makes him a god is not his bulging arm and shoulder muscles: those only make him more powerful than anyone else. He is stronger than we are, maybe even the strongest, but those are still only relative, comparative achievements. What makes Atlas divine within his tradition is that he is not standing on Fifth Avenue, but on his own two feet. Representing Power-in-itself, Atlas is holding himself up. He is the source of his own power, his own being. Such an understanding of the Holy echoes throughout the world. "Kiho had no parents," a creation myth of the Tuamotuan people of the South Pacific, describes divine self-origination in human, anthropomorphic terms: "He had no friend; he had no mate; there was none but him; he was not the root; he was the stability."[2] And religious texts around the world concur. As the Qur'an declares, Allah is One, independent and self-generated.[3]

The major insight of such thinking is that the nature of the *Something* or *Nothing* imagined as descriptions of the Holy One transcends duality. Such potent No-thing-ness is not the opposite of Being-Itself but, paradoxically, another way of describing it. *Some-thing-like-no-other* is *No-thing-like-any-other*: this Reality is not finite, not limited by time and space or positive or negative descriptions. On the contrary, it is their very context and condition.

Infinite and eternal, transcendent in every regard, it is simultaneously the essence of immanence—the very power we employ in considering it, the ground and core of our thinking as well as of our being. As Hinduism's Kena Upanishad (ca. 600–300 BCE) notes, it is "what cannot be thought with the mind, but that whereby the mind can think."[4] We cannot stand apart and contemplate it. On the contrary, as the Qur'an states, Allah is "nearer to you than your jugular vein."[5] This echoes the understanding of the Biblical author of Exodus, who depicts God speaking out of the burning bush, describing himself as "I am what I am"[6]—first person, singular, infinitely and eternally present: unlike anything in its transcendence, hence "Other" and yet simultaneously the core, root, and ground of everything. Here the mind-blowing nature of divinity is fully apparent: we cannot stand outside or separate from this Reality; we cannot make it a finite thing and objectify it. We cannot *know* it. Our perspective shifts with the religious realization that we are in it and of it, as it is within and of all.

While all religions agree that the Holy is the absolutely Real—independent, eternal, infinite—they struggle to

describe the Indescribable. One creation chant of the
Maori of New Zealand imagines creation occurring
spontaneously out of thought, through dark nothingness
into light and being. There is no deity doing the thinking
here; no attribution of power to one identifiable force.
Reality-Itself is inherently creative; matter and mind
are one:

First Period: Thought
From the conception the increase.
From the increase the thought.
From the thought the remembrance,
From the remembrance the consciousness,
From the consciousness the desire.
Second Period: Night
The world became fruitful;
It dwelt with the feeble glimmering;
It brought forth night:
The great night, the long night,
The lowest night, the loftiest night,
The thick night, to be felt,
The night to be touched,
The night not to be seen,
The night of death.
Third Period: Light
From the nothing the begetting.
From the nothing the increase,
From the nothing the abundance,
The power of increasing
The living breath.

It dwelt with the empty space
And produced the atmosphere which is above us,
The atmosphere which floats above the earth;
The great firmament above us dwelt with the early dawn,
And the moon sprung forth;
The atmosphere above us dwelt with the heat,
And thence proceeded the sun;
They were thrown up above,
As the chief eyes of heaven:
Then the heavens became light,
The early dawn, the early day,
The mid-day,
The blaze of day from the sky.[7]

The Maori understanding of the infinite fertility of
No-thing-ness requires a shift in common Western
materialistic thinking, where Nothingness is usually
considered the dead opposite of life and being. But here,
as in many other religious traditions, Nothingness is the
very source of all that is. The wonderful and abstract Hindu
Tantric painting of the life force (the "Vee" of feminine
fertility) within the core of Nothingness is expressed
in a painting stemming from seventeenth-century
meditative symbols (1).

While the most sophisticated creation myths all posit
the absolute, eternal, infinite, and independent One as the
ground and essence of the manifold beings of creation,
many do so in anthropomorphic terms, envisioning
the Holy as an omnipotent God, female or male. As
female, she is the Great Mother, inherently fertile and

productive—a character familiar to many in the so-called Venuses found in Neolithic European caves. But images of her are to be found throughout the world, as is evidenced by these figurines from the Halaf culture of Mesopotamia (6000–5100 BCE, **2**) and from Mehrgarh in the Indus Valley, ca. 3000 BCE (**3**).

Pachamama is a primal Mother Earth goddess of the indigenous people of the Andes. The source not only of the earth and all its creatures, she is also cited as the origin of the four Quechua elements of water, earth, sun and moon, but mostly in her later incarnations, she is associated with the fertile powers of the earth, at home in (and even personified by) mountains and expressed in her musings by earthquakes. Sometimes she is depicted as a dragon of wild chaos from which people are born and to which they return.

As is common when religions expand, missionaries tried to incorporate the power of such local deities into their theological frameworks when they sought to convert people to Christianity. To this end, throughout Latin America, while denying her any independent reality, they related Pachamama to the Virgin Mary, another Mother of God, and the new world of spiritual insight to which she gives birth. In images reflecting this conflation, she is often portrayed as a woman/mountain, her robes forming its sides, and all creatures living within them (**4**).

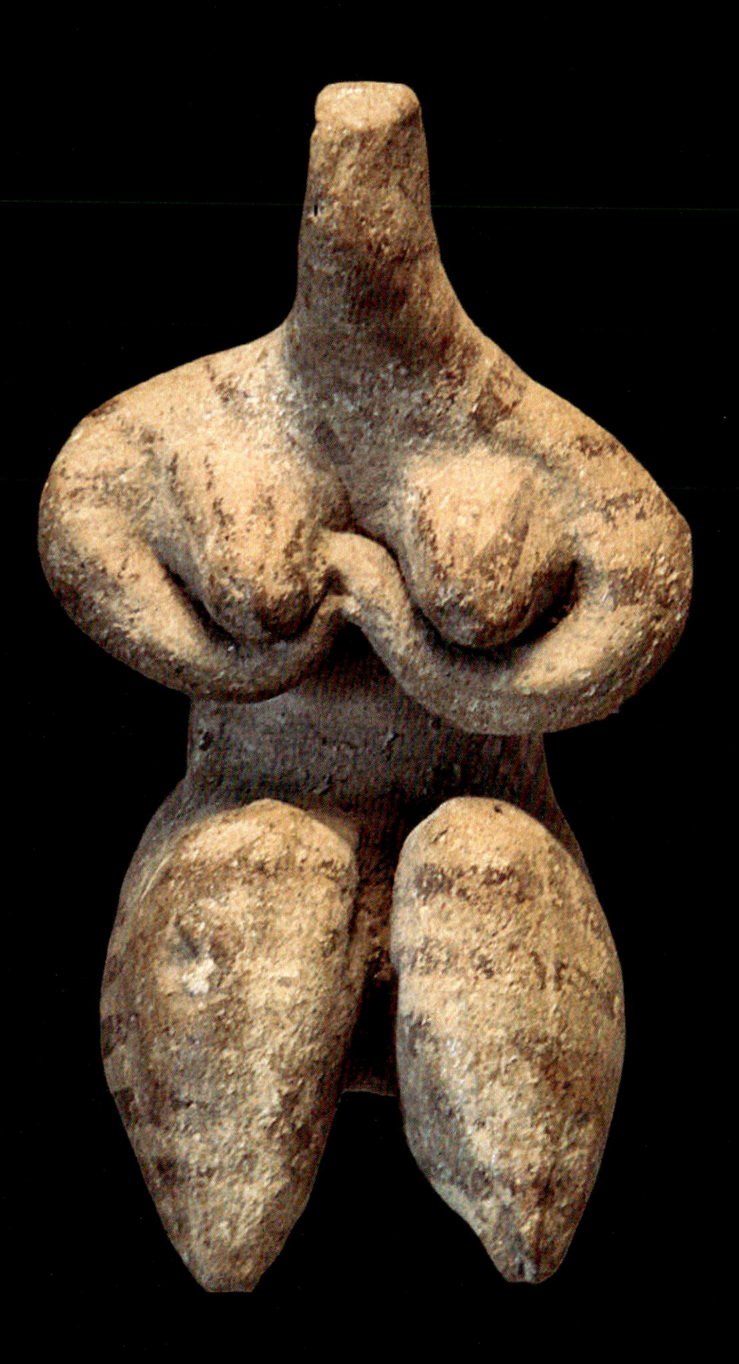

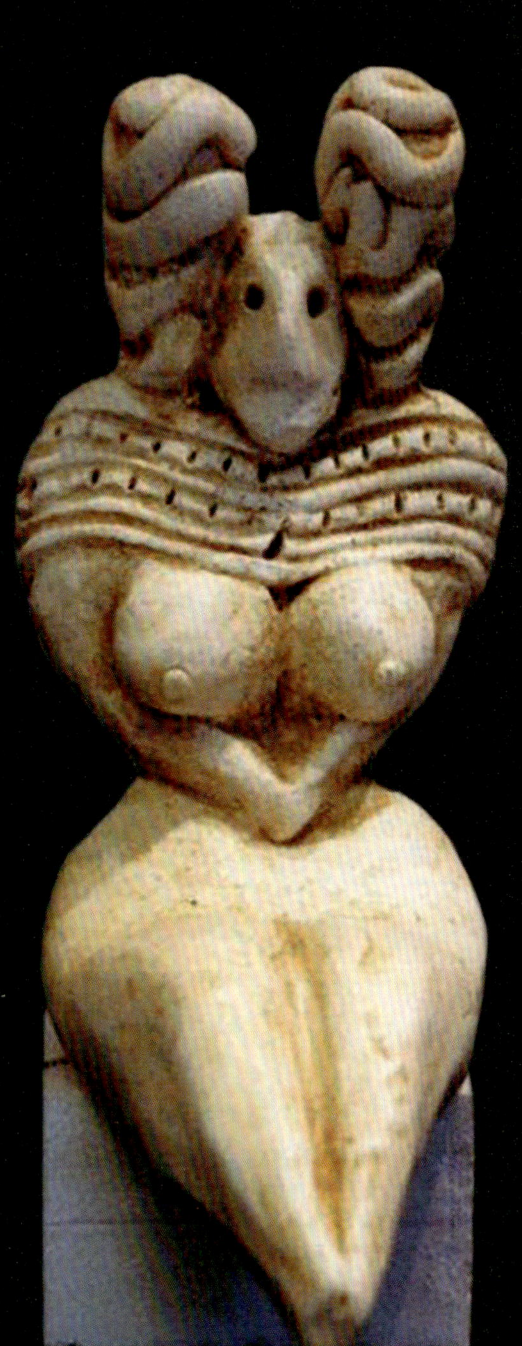

More frequently, the Goddess retains her connection to the phallic snake and to the moon and water, two of the other natural forces with which she is commonly associated. The lovely Snake Goddess of Crete (ca. 1650–1550 BCE) was found in the main sanctuary of the Palace of Knossos (**5**).

This concept takes a different turn in theological considerations of the Aztec deity Coatlicue, who—much like so many other personifications of Chaos—is ultimately sacrificed by her children, becoming the stuff of creation. The mother of Huitzilopochtli (the power of the sun and of war) and hundreds of others, she is a still-wild primal Force with ponderous human breasts, claws for hands, and garlands of snakes framing her fearsome face (**6**).

In many instances the pure sexual power of the Mother is emphasized, as it is in the alluring beauty of the statue of the dancing Dakini (seventeenth century) of Nepalese Buddhism, representing the potentiality of all possible manifestations (**7**).

In others, she is a great Mother. The Baga people of southern Guinea in West Africa traditionally recognized Nimba as a personification of the pervasive power of the feminine. Carved as an enormous mask to be worn over a dancer's shoulders and in practice bedecked with a raffia skirt covering the participant's body, the Nimba often stands eight feet tall. Her full breasts indicate her success as a mother who has reared many children; her braided hair mimics the rows of crops planted in local fields; and the scarification on her face and upper torso demonstrates her ability to alter her condition as she does the weather and features of the natural environment: she is the fertile power of the earth, of the harvest, of birth into life as well of into death, where she initiates the dead into their new state (**8**).

While many traditions depict the infinite creative power of the One as female, others imagine it in masculine form. At the early cult center of Heliopsis in Egypt (ca. 2500 BCE), Atum ("the complete one") was envisioned as emerging from the watery chaos and creating the world. By the time of the Pyramid Texts (ca. 2400–2300 BCE), he was associated with the sun god Ra, his rising being equated with the dawn's vanquishing of the chaos of darkness.

Like all myths that personify the Source of all as a solo god, the ancient Egyptian myths have to account for how the one became two and then the many. A sequence of ancient Egyptian myths shows how this is accomplished in various and related ways. In the first, "The Books of the Knowing of the Evolutions of Re" from the cult center at Heliopis (ca. 2500 BCE), Neb-er-tcher (Lord of the Limit and one of the incarnations of the Sun God) rises up out of the chaotic waters of Nu and takes the form of Khepera ("He who comes into existence"). Nothing else existed—not the heaven or earth: Khepera was alone. Awakening to consciousness, he made a plan and in a semi-androgenous manner, "he had union with his clenched hand and joined himself in an embrace with his shadow"[8] (his passive feminine element) and poured his seed into his mouth

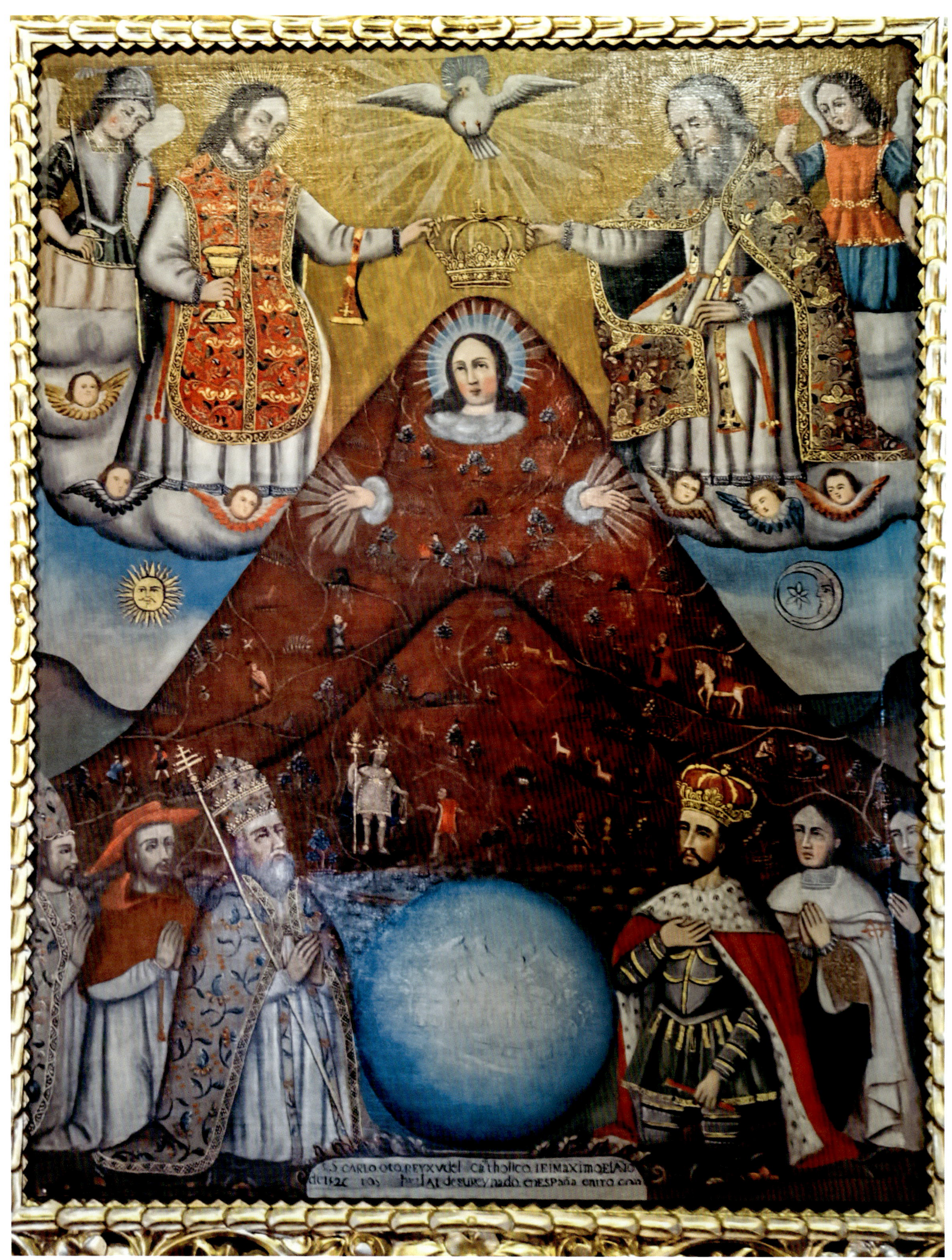
S. CARLO Q.TO REY X V DEL CATHOLICO Y EL MAXIMO ELA[N]O
DE 1520 AÑOS HA[BI]LA[S] DE SU REYNADO EN ESPAÑA ENTRO CON

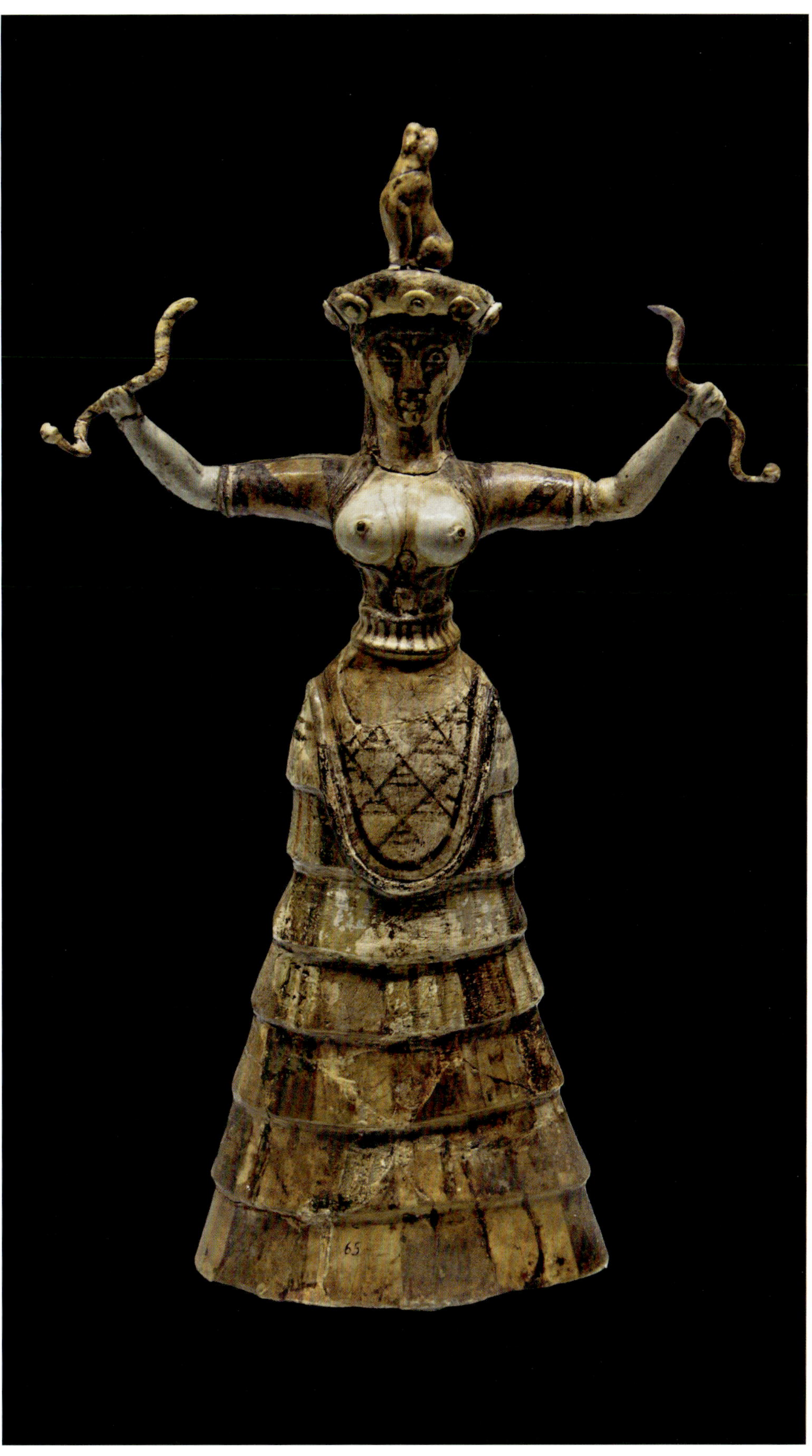

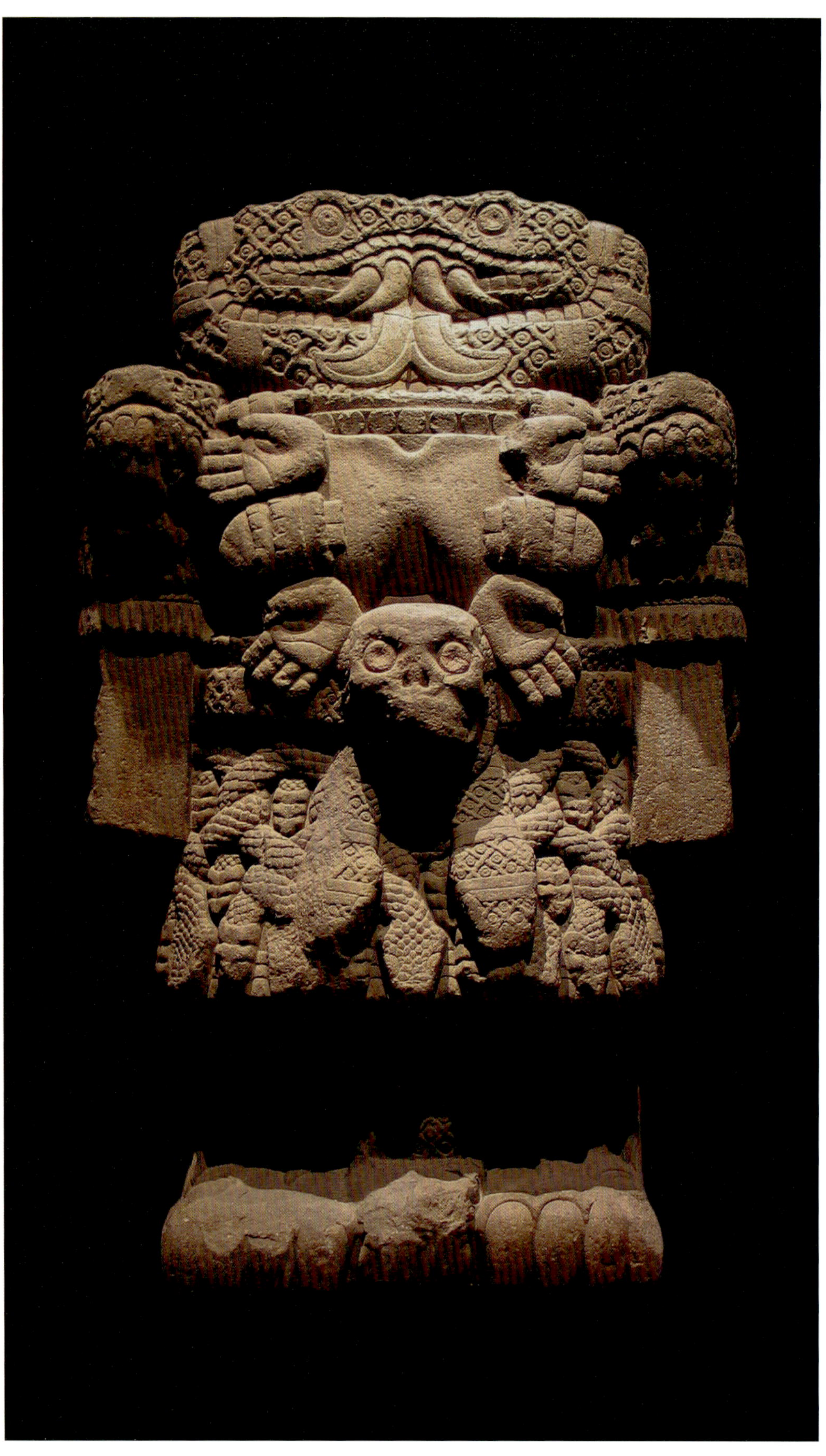

6 Coatlicue

Aztec culture, Mexico
1439 – 1491
Terracotta
8.3 feet, 2.52 meters
National Museum of
Anthropology, Mexico City

7 Dakini Dancing

Nepal
1600 – 1800
Gilded bronze
7 ¼ × 5 in., 18.42 × 12.7 cm
Asian Art Museum, San Francisco
The Avery Brundage Collection

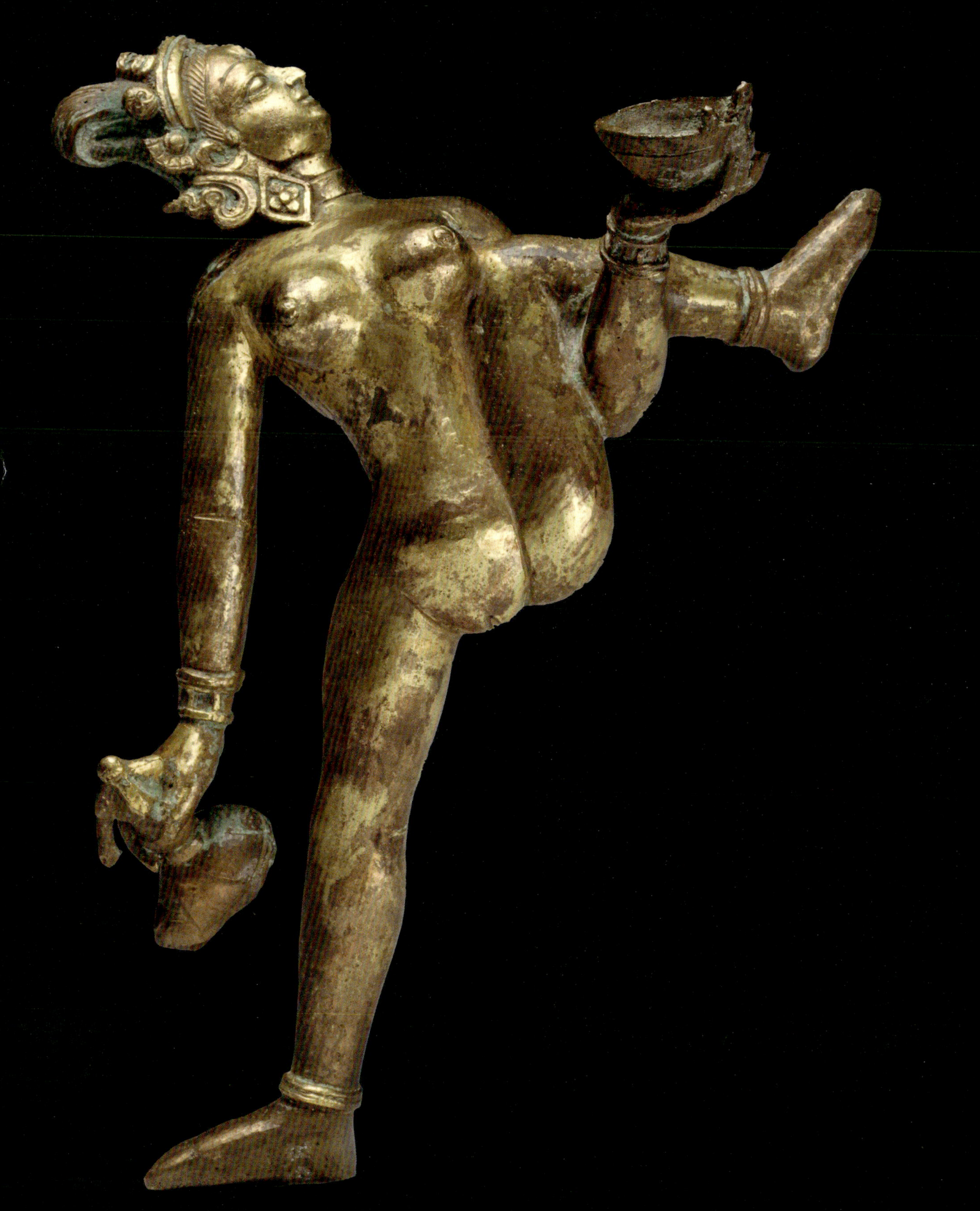

Shoulder Mask (*D'mba*)

Baga culture, Guinea Coast
Late 1800s
Wood, copper alloy
51 15/16 × 13 3/8 × 24 3/16 in.,
132 × 34 × 61.5 cm
Saint Louis Art Museum
Gift of Morton D. May

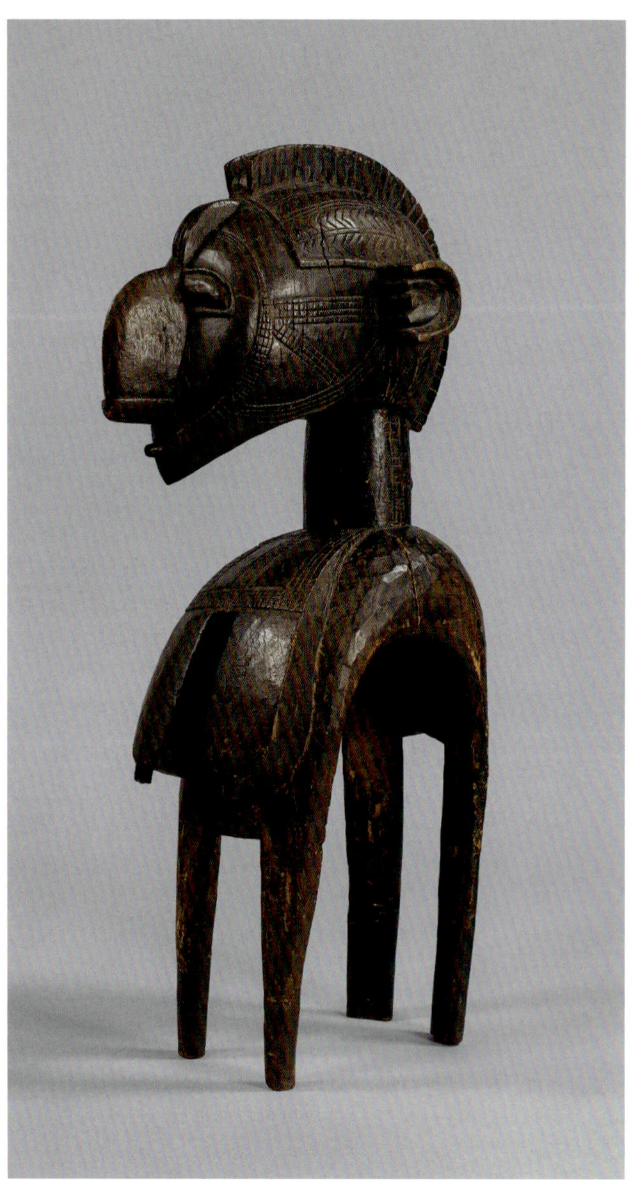

(the equivalent here of a womb) and, now fertilized, spit forth Shu (God of air and principle of life) and his daughter Tefnut (goddess of moisture and principle of world order). People were created from Neb-er-cher's tears and plants and animals later came forth from him as well (**9**).

In later renderings of this myth, the act of masturbation is transformed. In one version, the heart serves as the forming agent and saliva the raw material of creation: the god spits creation. In a still later version, his divine mind is the forming agent and his words serve as the basic matter: in this version, the god speaks creation. In all these myths, the great Egyptian deities are identified externally as male but clearly have some feminine aspects as well, allowing them to create by these kinds of internalized means. Atum indeed contains all opposites within himself, being not only the Lord of Creation but also of Destruction who will devolve everything at the end of the world and return to the form of a primeval serpent.

The father god Karora of the Aranda people of Australia also creates the world out of himself. Resting within the perpetual darkness—almost as if he were its symbolic personification—Karora slept and dreamed. Out of his head arose a great *tratantja*—a ceremonial center pole used by the nomadic Aranda use to locate "here" when they are traveling and religiously symbolizing spiritual connection between the realms of earth and sky. In this instance the *tratantja* was covered with skin, symbolically representing a sacred phallus and emphasizing the fertile power of Karora's thoughts. And as he dreamed, "wishes and desires flashed through his mind and bandicoots began to come out of his naval and armpits."[9] As dawn

Atum Having Intercourse with His Shadow: Creating the World with his Semen

Egypt
Stone

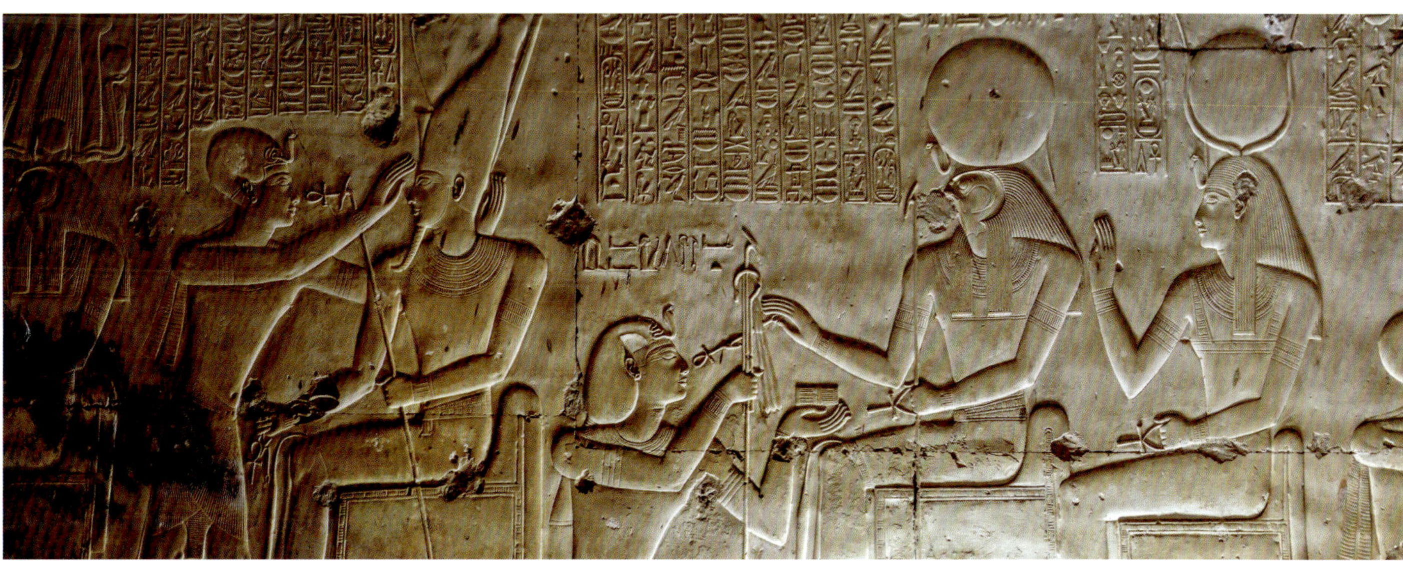

broke, he birthed and then united with his own son, creating all others. Eventually, he sank back into eternal sleep in the core of darkness. A son here, a shadow in the Egyptian myth: the Other with whom the male god mates is ultimately another (feminine) aspect of himself.

Perhaps the images of creation by a father God most familiar to Westerners are those offered in the Hebrew Bible. The Book of Genesis relates two different versions of creation. The earliest story of Adam and Eve, dating from the ninth century BCE, envisions God using the Void as the raw material out of which he molds all the creatures of the earth. The later account—but first in Genesis—is generally agreed to have been written after the Babylonian Exile, in the fourth century BCE. Here again, some suggestion is

made of a duality of God and the Void/Darkness. Unlike the Australian myth, however, in the Hebrew Bible God is not considered an expression of that Void but is depicted as independently acting upon it, speaking creation and organizing the chaotic nature of pre-Being (**10**):

In the beginning God created the heavens and the earth. The earth was without form and void, and darkness was upon the face of the deep; and the Spirit of God was moving over the face of the waters.

And God said, "Let there be light": and there was light And God saw that light was good; and God separated the light from the darkness. God called the light Day and the darkness he called Night.[10]

And so God continued for the next five days separating the waters from the heavens, creating earth and vegetation, forming the stars, sun, and moon, commanding the being of all the creatures of the sea and land, and finally human beings. While the Babylonians from whom the Hebrews had recently been freed described seven major sacred powers accomplishing creation, the Hebrews demonstrated in this account that their One God could accomplish all by himself the same divine task that had required so many Babylonian deities—and he could even take one day off at the end (**11**)!

The Abrahamic tradition's depiction of the Father God's creation out of his wisdom and via his word is most powerfully expressed later in Christianity's Gospel of John in the Bible's New Testament. Assumed by most scholars to have been written by a Jewish Greek evangelist around 90 CE, the Gospel proclaims: "In the beginning was the Word, and the Word was with God, and the Word was God. He was in the beginning with God; all things were made through him, and without him was not anything made that was made." And it continues to declare that this Word of God, this expression of his deepest being, "became flesh and dwelt among us, full of grace and truth: we have beheld his glory, glory as the only Son from the Father . . . No one has ever seen God; the only Son, who is in the bosom of the Father, he has made him known."[11]

In Islam, God is also envisioned commending creation into being with his word. In the Qur'an's Surah al-hijr 40, The Believer, it is written "It is He who giveth life and death; and when he decreeth a thing, He only saith 'Be'

and it is."[12] In all of these understandings, the Primordial One creates the world out of Himself: his Word, the outward expression of his innermost self, is revealed as the essential creative agent of all that is. As Surah al-ikhlas CXII, The Oneness, decrees: "Say, 'He's the one God (one and only), He is eternal (endures), he has no son and wasn't born, and there's no one who is like him'."[13]

The dualities implicit within many religions' understandings of the primal One are often made explicit in their artistic representations of the personifications of this Reality. Such power incarnated, when expressed anthropomorphically, is frequently understood as androgynous. Fertility—the power to be, grow, and reproduce—is both female and male. One of the earliest of such images is realized in this figurine from Valdivian culture of coastal Ecuador (3500–1500 BCE), formed with both female and male characteristics (**12**).

A similar series of dualities is understood to be contained in the Incan creator God Viracocha, who is conceived of as the infinite ground and fertile essence of all—above and below, male and female, life and death, body and word:

> *O Uira-cocha! Lord of the universe;*
> *Whether thou art male,*
> *Whether thou art female,*
> *Lord of reproduction,*
> *Whatsoever thou mayest be,*
> *O Lord of divination,*
> *Where art thou?*[14]

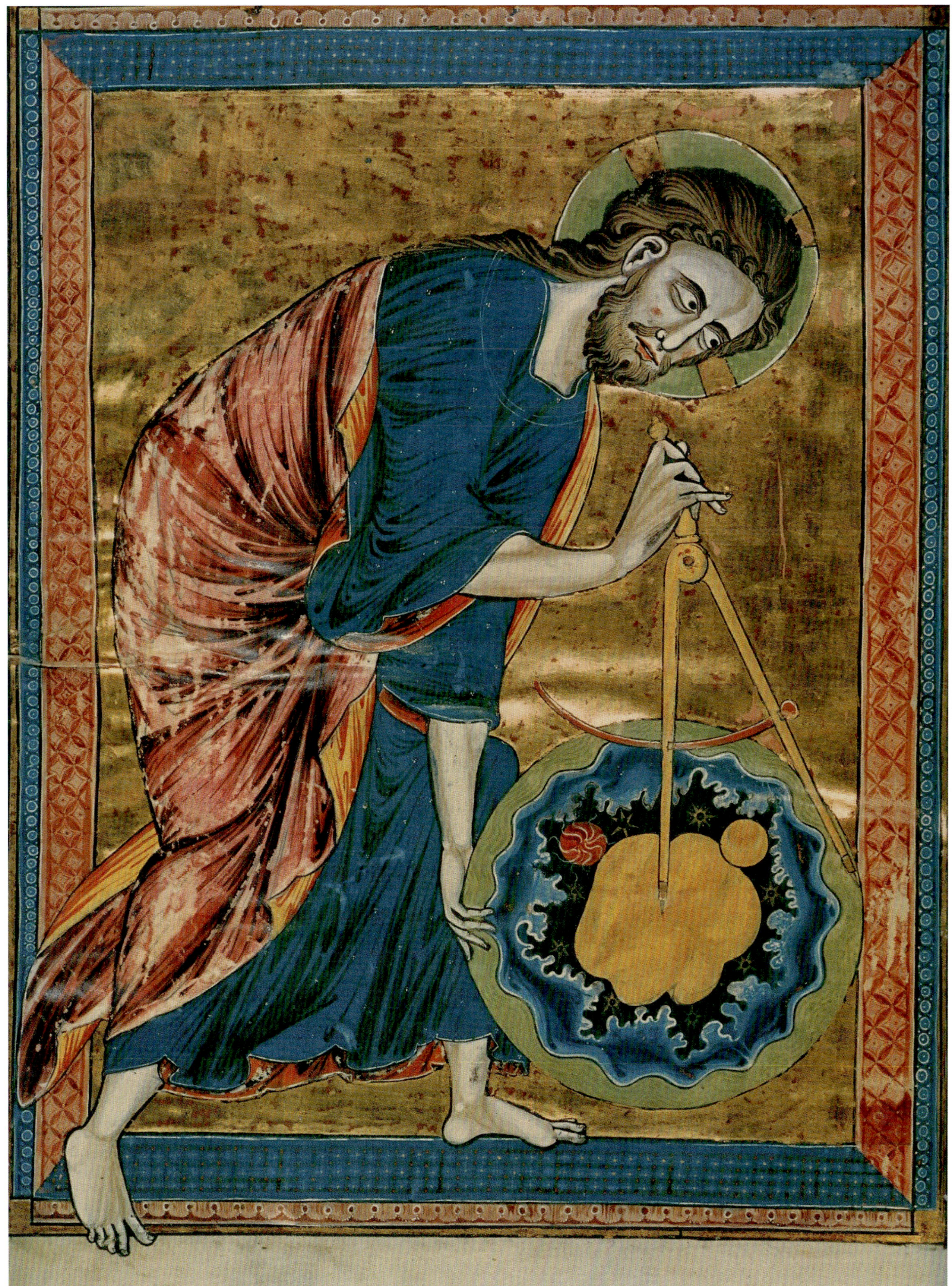

  Tapestry of the Creation

Girona, Spain
1000 – 1100
11 × 9.7 × 14 feet, 9.2 in., 3.6 × 4.5 meters
Museum of the Cathedral of Girona, Spain

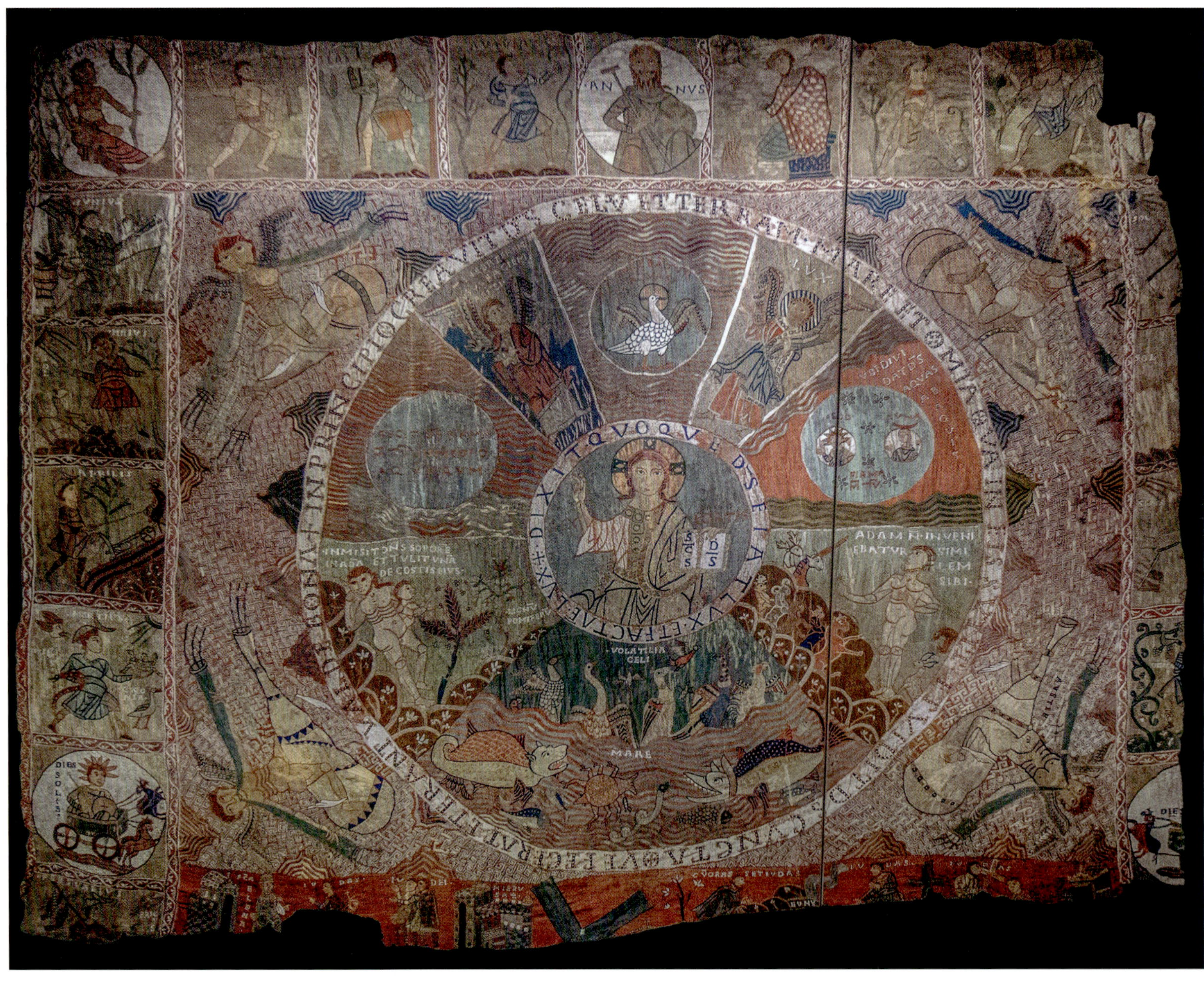

12 **Androgenous Deity**

Valdivia culture, Ecuador
2200 – 2000 BCE
Terracotta
4 × 1¼ × 1 in., 10.2 × 3.2 × 2.5 cm
Metropolitan Museum of Art, New York
Gift of Timothy, Peter, and
Jonathon Zorach, 1980

Viracocha creates both by the word as well as by self-sacrifice, saying, "'Let this be a man!'"" and "'Let this be a woman!' Thou madest them and gavest them being!"[15]

Hinduism as well features several androgyne deities, not only those depicting Siva and Parvati—the male and female aspects of Brahman, later worshipped as separate deities in their own rights—but portrayed as Ardhanarishvara in a tenth-century Nepalese sculpture. Ardhanarishvara demonstrates how the masculine and feminine powers of the One are unified in their deepest essence. They are inseparable, and their union is the root and womb of all that is and is not (**13**).

How to describe the breaking of the Original Unity is a challenge to all religious traditions, which ask the question about the creation of being and non-being most profoundly, trying to describe the indescribable Origin of origins.

The duality inherent in the One becomes clearer in various myths that portray the creation as the result of the union of divine world parents. The Wuraka people of Arnhem Land in the north of Australia portray divinities as personifications of the enormous powers of fertility striding through the ocean's waters. Maintaining the theme of the life force coalescing the fertile energies of dark No-thing-ness and rising out of the ground of death, the Djanggawul gods (a male "brother" and his female elder and younger "sisters") were thought to have come from the land of the dead and before that "some unknown place" to found the world of Australia. The Djanggawul were so fertile and their genitalia so enormous that the

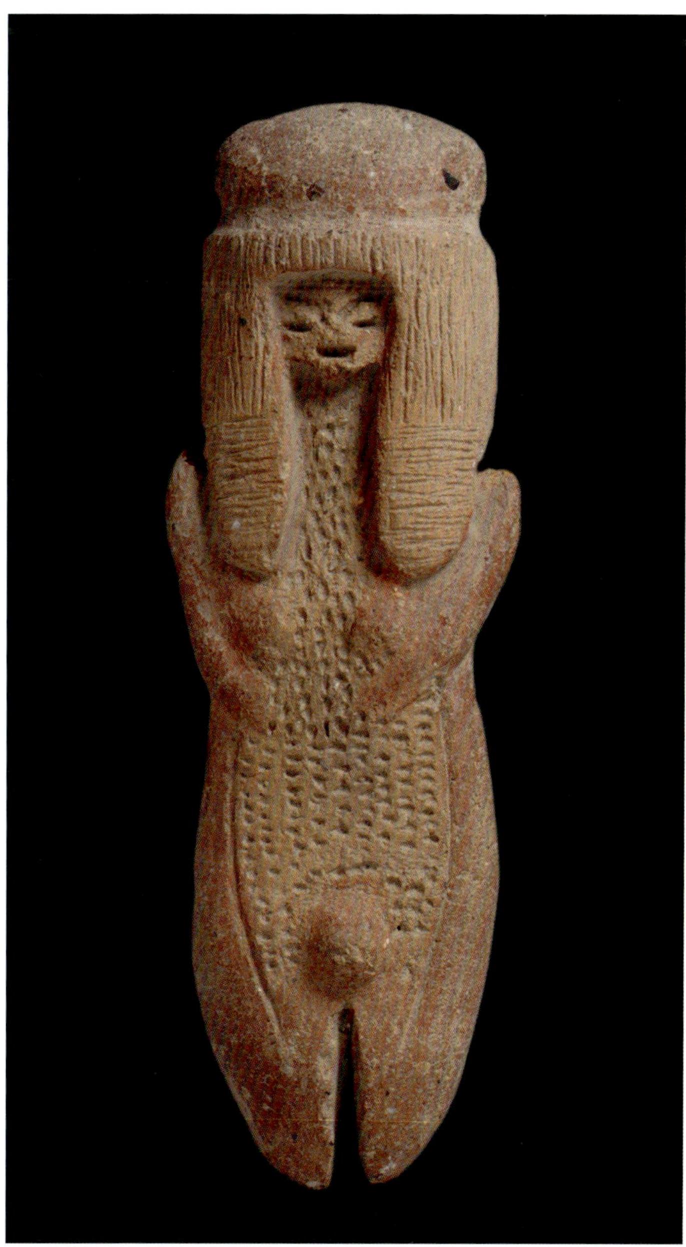

  God Shiva as Lord Who Is Half-Male,
Half-Female (Ardhanarishvara)

Tamil Nadu, India
1301 – 1400
Granite
45 ⅝ × 23 ⅜ × 10 ¾ in.,
123.5 × 59.4 × 27.3 cm
Art Institute of Chicago
Gift of the Alsdorf Foundation

grooves formed as they dragged their penis and clitorises along the ground can still be seen. Acting together, they journeyed throughout the land creating sacred places and beings.

Separating the original parental unity is a task myths usually assign to the younger gods—the "children" of Mother Earth and Father Sky, like the natural powers of ocean and land, forest and mountains. In another Maori myth from New Zealand, Rangi (personifying the powers of the sky) and Papa (portraying those of the earth) lay close to each other, forming such a unity that their offspring were crushed between them, hidden in darkness: "At last the beings who had been begotten by Heaven and Earth, worn out by the continued darkness, consulted amongst themselves, saying 'Let us now determine what we should do with Rangi and Papa, whether it would be better to slay them or to rend them apart.'"[16] Finally, it was agreed: "'It is better to rend them apart and to let the heaven stand far above us and the earth lie beneath our feet. Let the sky become a stranger to us, but let the earth remain close to us as a nursing mother.'"[17] Only the power of the wind demurred and decided to stay with his sky father; the other powers took turns trying to force their parents apart. Many of the lesser deities made the attempt, but failed (**14**):

Then at last, slowly uprises Tane-mahuta, the god and father of forests, of birds and of insects, and he struggles with his parents; in vain he strives to rend them apart with his hands

and arms. Lo, he pauses; his head is now firmly planted on his mother, the earth, his feet he raises up and rests against his father the skies, he strains his back and lifts with mighty effort. Now are rent apart Rangi and Papa, and with cries and groans of woe they shriek aloud. "Wherefore slay you thus your parents? Why commit you so dreadful a crime as to slay us, as to rend your parents apart": But Tane-mahuta pauses not, he regards not their shrieks and cries; far, far beneath him, he presses down the earth; far, far above him he thrusts up the sky . . . . No sooner was heaven rent from earth than the multitude of human beings were discovered whom they had begotten, and who had hitherto lain concealed between the bodies of Rangi and Papa.[18]

Another common way for religions worldwide to evoke the potential for duality inherent in the primal Unity is through the symbol of a cosmic Egg, representing the totality from which all creation emerges. Some cultures envisage it as the form of the original unity in itself, like the enigmatic Zero containing the possibilities of all numbers. Others depict it as a kind of coalescence of the original chaotic void, the result of an internal ordering, arising spontaneously out of the formless chaos. Still others imagine a wondrous (pre-creation) bird of some sort, usually associated with a prominent deity, laying the egg on top of the waters. However it appears, the Egg serves as a familiar solution to the theoretical problem of describing how the One becomes two—the basis of all fundamental oppositions—and then develops into

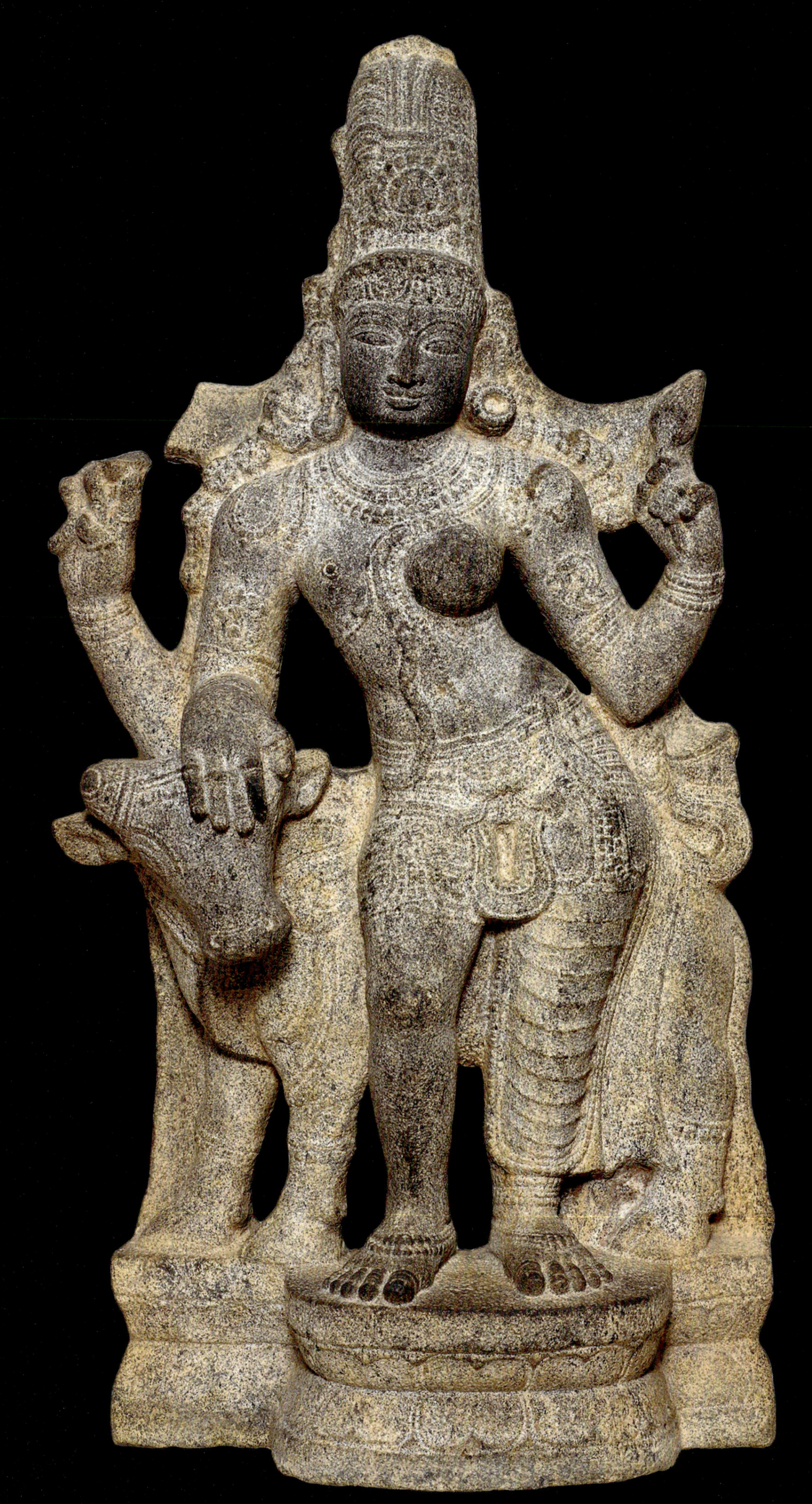

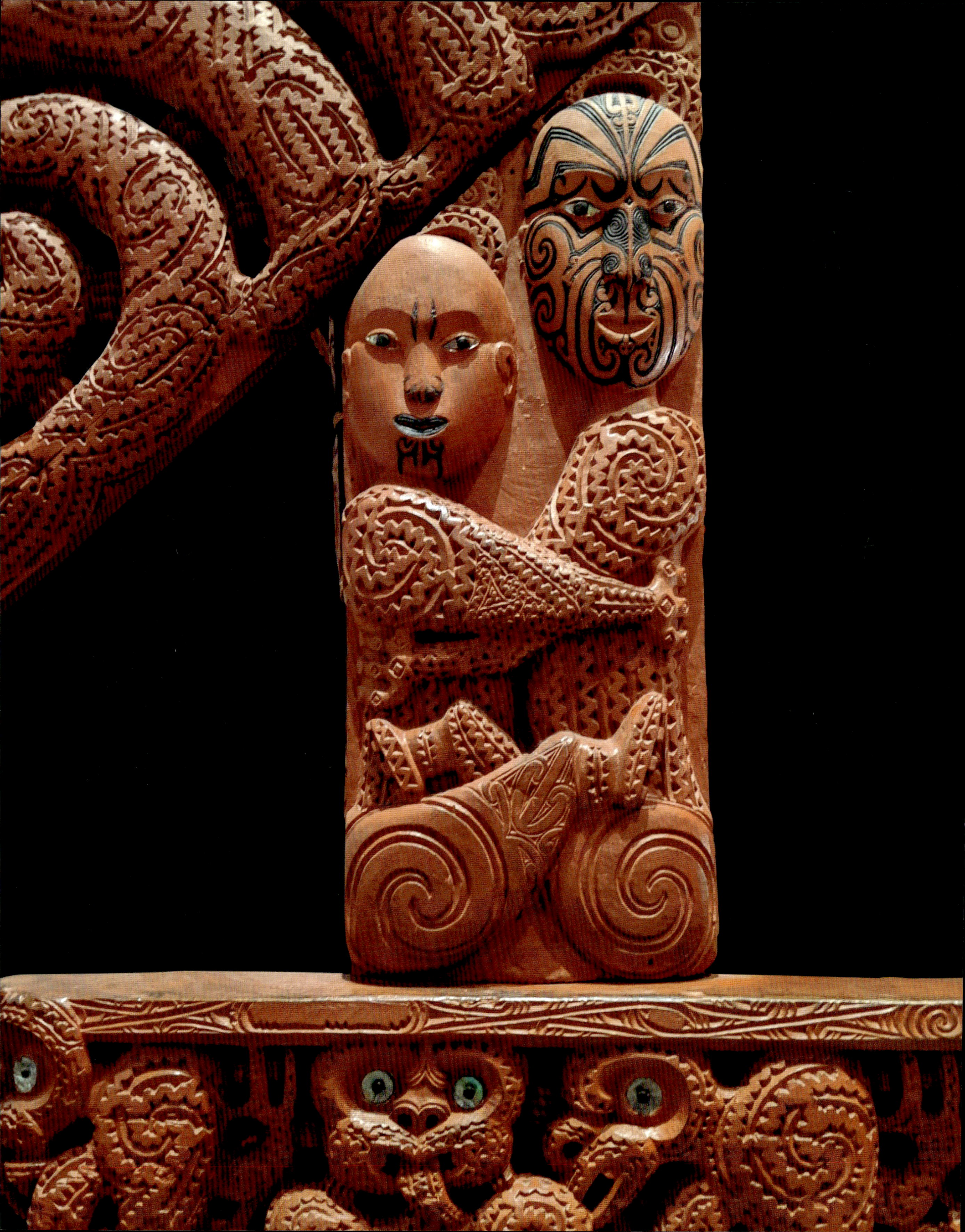

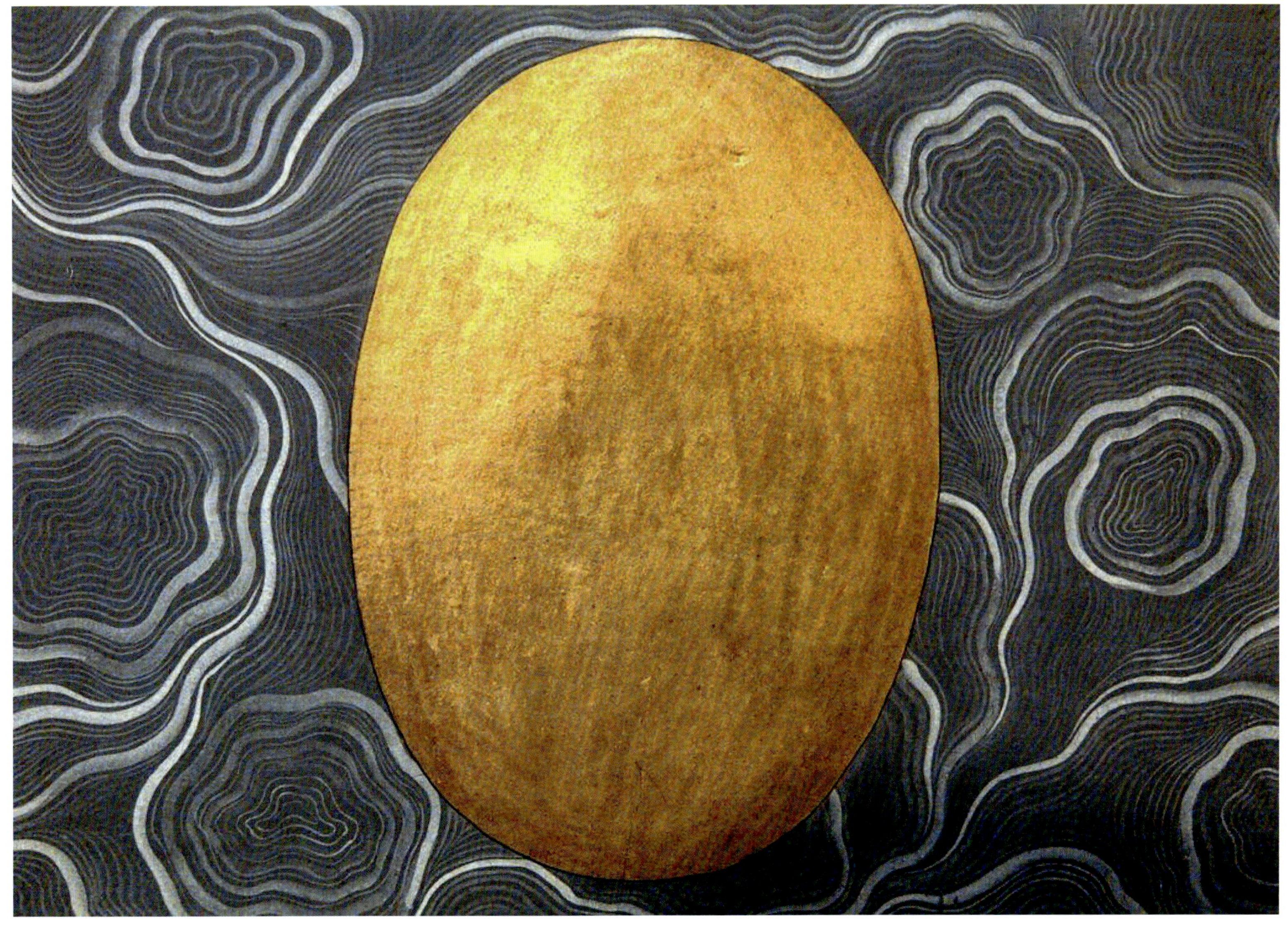

the many of the "manifold creatures," as the ancient texts described the ever-changing multiplicities of the created world.

An Egyptian New Kingdom period (1569–1085 BCE) manuscript contains the earliest reference to a cosmic Egg emerging from the primal waters. Some speak of it as their soul—an essence of the Void. Alternative variations amplify the role of whatever divine figure achieved particular prominence in the varying theologies of the day: sometimes the Egg was most closely associated with Thoth (representing the power of the moon), or Re (the solar force), or Seb (the earth god), or even Khuum (a creator god), who was said to have fashioned the Egg on his potter's wheel. But whatever image is employed, they are consistent in finding that within that Egg are all the elements of universal creation and all the opposites whose interactions create all beings and things.

Several Hindu creation myths, even those stemming from different periods, adopt similar imagery. The Vedas speak of Prajapati, lord of creation, initially in the form of a Golden Embryo, evolving out of the waters as a self-created Egg of fire (**15**):

> When the mighty waters moved, conceived the All
> as an Embryo, giving birth to fire,
> Then did he evolve,
> The One life force (asu) of the gods . . .[19]

Still other Hindu texts, like the Brahmanas (1000 BCE and later), note that the intermingling of the two is key to the formation of the Egg. The amorphous potentials of the unformed forces coalesce in this turmoil eventually—after a divine year—to form Prajapati. The god's connection here to manifest time is clear, as it is in several similar myths, since space, time, and being are innately bound to one another, and once they are made manifest, change begins. The transcendent aspect of eternity rests in the No-thing-ness, while in its immanence, it is ever-present within the moment. Eternity is always now:

> Verily, in the beginning this (universe) was water, nothing but
> a sea of water. The waters desired, "How can we be reproduced?"
> They toiled and performed fervid devotions, when they were
> becoming heated, a golden egg was produced. The year indeed
> was not then in existence: this golden egg floated for as long as
> the space of a year . . .[20]

After hatching out and beginning to speak—creating the Earth (*bluh*), air (*bluvah*) and sky (*svah*)—in this manner, Prajapati "laid the power of reproduction upon his own self. By the breath of his mouth he created the gods"[21]—all the various powers and forces of the world.

In one of the early Chinese myths of creation involving P'an Ku (or P'an Gu), the Egg is said to have contained the primal chaos within itself:

> First there was the great cosmic egg. Inside the egg was
> chaos and floating in chaos was P'an Ku, the Undeveloped,
> the divine Embryo. And P'an Ku broke out of the egg, four
> times larger than any man today, with an adze in his hand

*(or a hammer and chisel) with which he fashioned the
world. Two great horns grew out of his head . . . and two
long tusks grew from his upper jaw, and he was covered
with hair . . . P'an Ku went to work, mightily, to put the
world in order. He chiseled the land and sky apart. He piled
up the mountains on earth and dug the valleys deep and
made courses for the rivers.*[22]

Most creation myths using the symbol of the egg
approach the issue of the breaking of the primal One and
the separation of opposing forces nascent within it—the
first step in the evolution of creation—into several stages.
Just for the original unformed Chaos or No-thing-ness to
coalesce into some form of Being like the Egg requires
an initial internal separation; after that, breaking the egg
into further oppositions is secondary.

In the Kalevala, the Finnish national epic compiled in
1835 but containing material that is far older, a beautiful
teal is imagined flying over the primeval waters. Finally,
the Mother of the Waters lifts a wave of her knee for the
teal to land upon and build her nest:

*And her nest she there established,
And she laid her eggs all golden
Six gold eggs she laid within it,
And a seventh she laid of iron.*[23]

Heat (or passion or desire) again plays an important role
here as the teal uses it to hatch the eggs, which fall into
the sea and in breaking up, form the parts of the world
that become the sky, sun, moon, stars, and clouds.

Across the globe, the Tahitians also envision their
creator initially contained within an Egg as a kind of core
or essence of the chaotic void. The relation of inner power
to its outer manifestations is clearly drawn here, evolving
into a dichotomy of mind and matter; the god is hidden
within a series of shells:

*For a long period, Ta'aroa dwelt in his shell (crust). It was round
like an egg and revolved in space in continuous darkness. There
was no sun, no moon, no land, no mountains; all was in a
confluent state . . . But at last Ta'aroa was filliping his shell, as
he sat in close confinement, and it cracked and broke open . . . So
he overturned his shell and raised it up to form a dome for the
sky . . . and he slipped out of another shell that covered him, that
he took for rock and sand.*[24]

Eventually he uses his own body—the shell of his
intention—to create the rest of the beings of the world (**16**).

The image of a primal Egg is endemic in West Africa and
is often symbolized ritually in the form of the calabash.
In a sacrificial altarpiece from the Fon people of Benin, a
calabash encrusted with the patina of sacrificed blood
and palm oil contains figures of people and animals and
bits of shell and cloth and metal—all the elements of
creation (**17**).

The innate dualities within that One can be expressed
in terms of many different oppositions as we have seen:
being and not-being, activity and passivity, day and night,
life and death. And while any given myth may emphasize

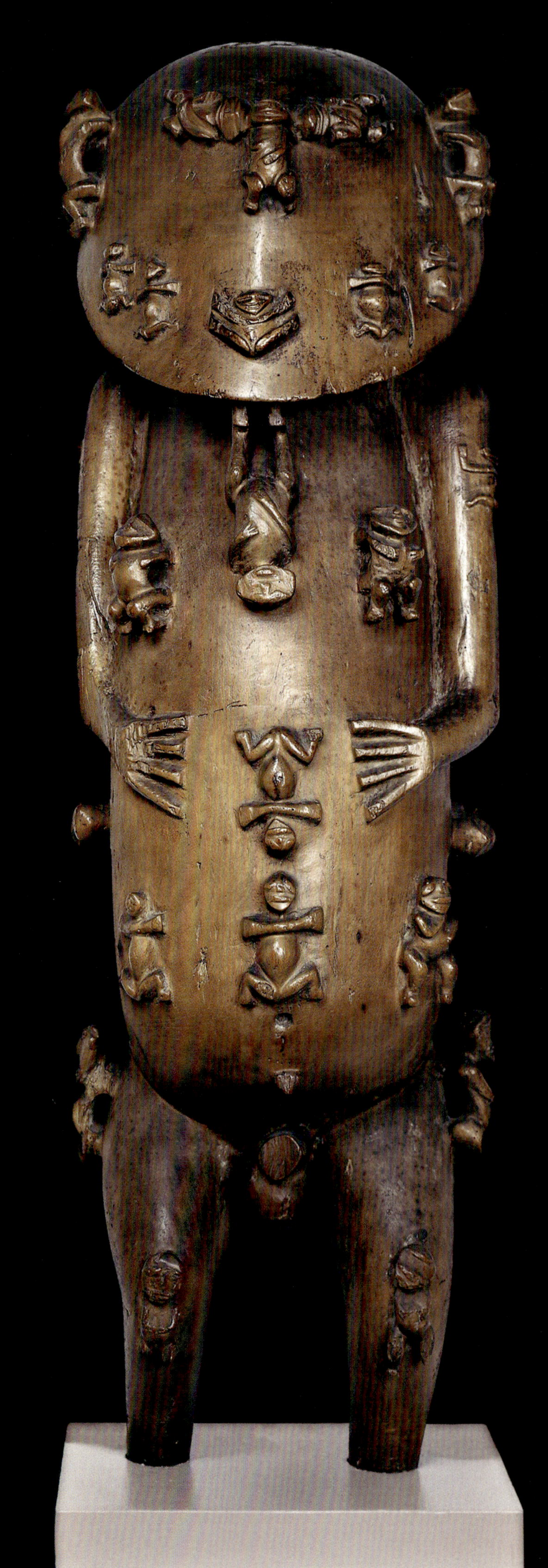

one of these oppositions, the others are usually present as well. The lesson in all of these myths is about the interrelation of the opposites: they are interdependent and mutually creative as the great insightful yin/yang symbol of Taoism shows. The core of each one is its opposite. A most powerful truth sounded in many of these myths is the relation of life and death, and nowhere is this clearer than in myths describing creation as the result of a sacrifice of the primary unity. As the Veda said, "Wise seers, searching within their hearts, Found the bond of Being in Not-Being."[25]

Only when the One splits into the two does creation really get underway. The lesson of these creation myths is that the multiplicity of life is created out of the breaking of original Unity.

Myths of the sacrifice of this One are universal and have the effect not only of reminding us of the profound interrelatedness of opposites, but also of showing all aspects of relative reality stem from the Divine. A different myth of P'an Ku, popular in southern China from the third to sixth century, related that this personification of Chaos formed the basis of all:

> The world was never finished until P'an Ku died. Only his death could perfect the universe: from his skull was shaped the dome of the sky, and from his flesh was formed the soil of the fields; from his bones came the rocks, from his blood the rivers and the seas; from his hair came all vegetation. His breath was the wind; his voice made thunder; his right eye became the moon, his left eye, the sun. From his saliva or sweat came rain. And from the vermin which covered his body came forth mankind.[26]

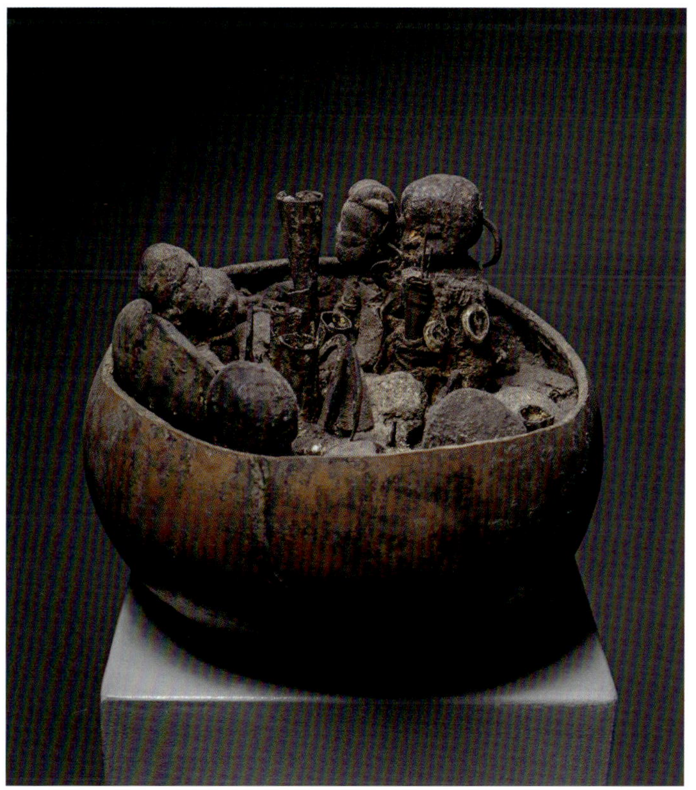

No ecology text could be clearer than this about the interdependence of all parts of nature: the myth underscores the unity of all the apparent differences and distinctions we make in our understandings of the relative world. This theme is extended even into human culture in the Rig Veda's Hymn to Purusha, portrayed here as "Primal Man." This holy figure is said to retain three quarters of Himself as unmanifest and absolute, while the material and temporal world and all its creatures—and even its social structures—are fashioned from the manifest quarter of his infinite Reality. Some parts of his body become the sun, moon, and stars; others are transformed into the features of the earth, the plants, animals, people, and more:

> *When they divided [primal] Man,*
> *Into how many parts did they divide Him?*
> *What was his mouth? What his arms?*
> *What are his thighs called? What are his feet?*
> *The Brahman was his mouth*
> *His arms were made the princes*
> *His thighs the common people,*
> *And from his feet the serf was born . . .*[27]

Even these very religious texts containing these lines are included here: the sacred books of the Vedas themselves are understood to be manifestations of the sacrificed divine Reality. This first sacrifice (from the Latin *sacer*, meaning "sacred," and *facere*, meaning "to make"), this divine self-giving shows that the destruction of a body in one form becomes a religious act of sacred creation. The assertion of the life-giving properties of death, initial No-thing-ness, is reiterated again and again throughout the world's religions.

Thought to have been derived from pre-Zoroastrian cultures in Iran, the Mithraic mysteries were a most popular form of religion (and major competitor to early Christianity) in the first- through the fourth-century Roman Empire. Described as having been born from a rock (an earth egg?), Mithra emerged as the great power whose primal act was to slaughter the wild bull of Chaos (**18**). Instantly, creation was born: the moon sprung forth and was placed in Mithra's cloak, which became the sky with all the planets and stars in place. The bull's tail and blood became the grains and grapes, and every creature on earth was born from his seed. Day and night were made and began to alternate as temporality evolved along with space and being. And as one inscription on the wall of a Mithraic temple rejoiced in the grounding of the finite in the Infinite: "Thou hast redeemed us too by shedding the eternal blood."[28]

A very early expression of this common theme was sounded in the great Babylonian creation myth, the Enuma Elish from ca.1750 BCE. There it is related that the hero god Marduk (formerly a symbol of storm power, but now as civilized as the people of his great home city) fought the monsters and demons Chaos had assembled to war with him: untamed nature is not controlled without a mighty struggle. Lord of the young gods, Marduk made war on Chaos itself in the form of Tiamat (from *tamtu*,

All of these myths demonstrate the life-giving power of the sacrifice of the original unity, but the specific connection between death and life is perhaps made most clearly in the myths of pre-Columbian Mesoamerica (present-day Mexico and central America), specifically those about Tlaltecuhtli, the monstrous power of the earth—usually depicted as female but referred to as the Lord of the Earth and Underworld in primarily Aztec myths (ca. 1500). At the beginning of time in the fifth world, they say the great gods Quetzalcoatl and Tezcatlipoca began to create our realm but were thwarted by Tlaltecuhtli's destructiveness. Turning themselves into giant serpents, they wrapped themselves around the goddess until they tore her body into two pieces: one half became the dome of the sky, while the other half was transformed into the earth and its mountains and rivers, her eyes becoming caves and wells, her hair the trees and plants. Here the principle of death giving life became connected to the idea that the sacrifice had to be mutual: Tlaltecuhtli was thought to demand sacrifices in return, to keep the exchange of the Life Force flowing. A giant monolith of Tlaltecuhtli discovered in Mexico City in 2006 shows her to be a most fearsome creature, with blood dripping out of her open mouth, terrifying claws on her hands and feet, and the skulls of the dead making up her joints (**21**).

As Chaos is increasingly conquered and even often considered to be the basis of ordered life, the development of the idea of duality from the physical oppositions of light and dark, sky and earth, energy and matter into the moral realm of good and evil begins to occur more frequently in various religious traditions. Issues of morality do not usually become relevant in creation myths until humankind is fashioned, but in the deeply dualistic Zoroastrian tradition and later in the Abrahamic faiths it influenced, it is one of the dualisms present in myths focusing on establishment of the land, and sometimes it is even seen as endemic to the establishment of the universe itself.

Creation myths employing the symbol of earth divers usually envision the Void as primordial formless waters over which the god is pondering how to create land. In some, the celestial powers are depicted as coming from the void of the sky realm and creating land out of the formless waters. The "Chronicles of Japan" (the Nihongi, composed in 720), for instance, tell of the divine forces of Izanagi and Izanami ("Male-who-invites" and "Female-who-invites"), newly separated from one another, who stood

> *on the floating bridge of Heaven, and held counsel together, saying, 'Is there not a country beneath?' Thereupon they thrust down the jewel-spear of Heaven, and groping about therewith found the ocean. The brine which dripped from the point of the spear coagulated and became an island which received the name of Ono-goro-jima ("Spontaneously-congealed-island").*[30]

Descending to the land they had just created, they circled the center pole formed out of their potent spear—a connection between earth and heaven replicated later in human rituals of marriage—and from their subsequent union arose the islands of Japan and all their mountains,

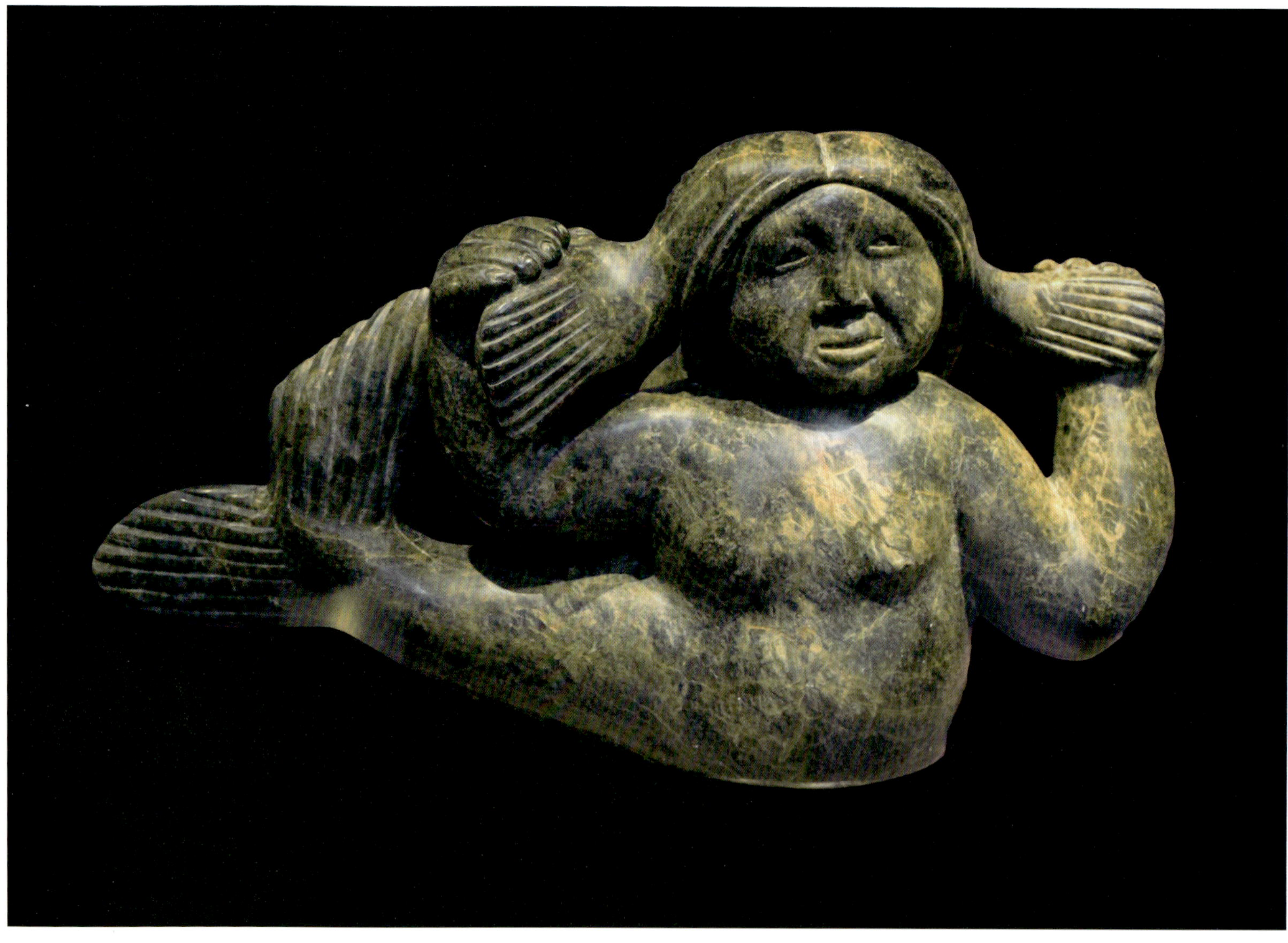

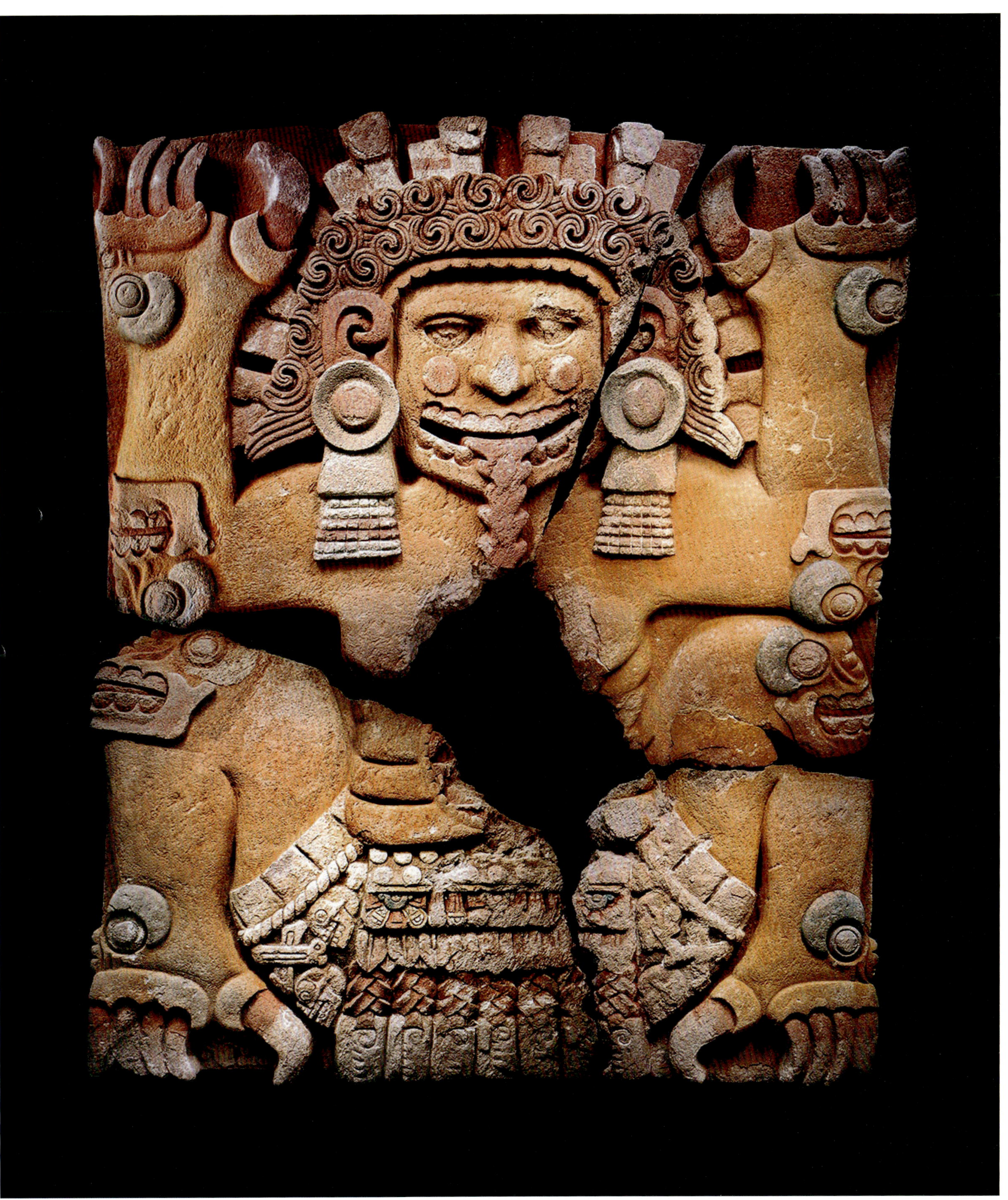

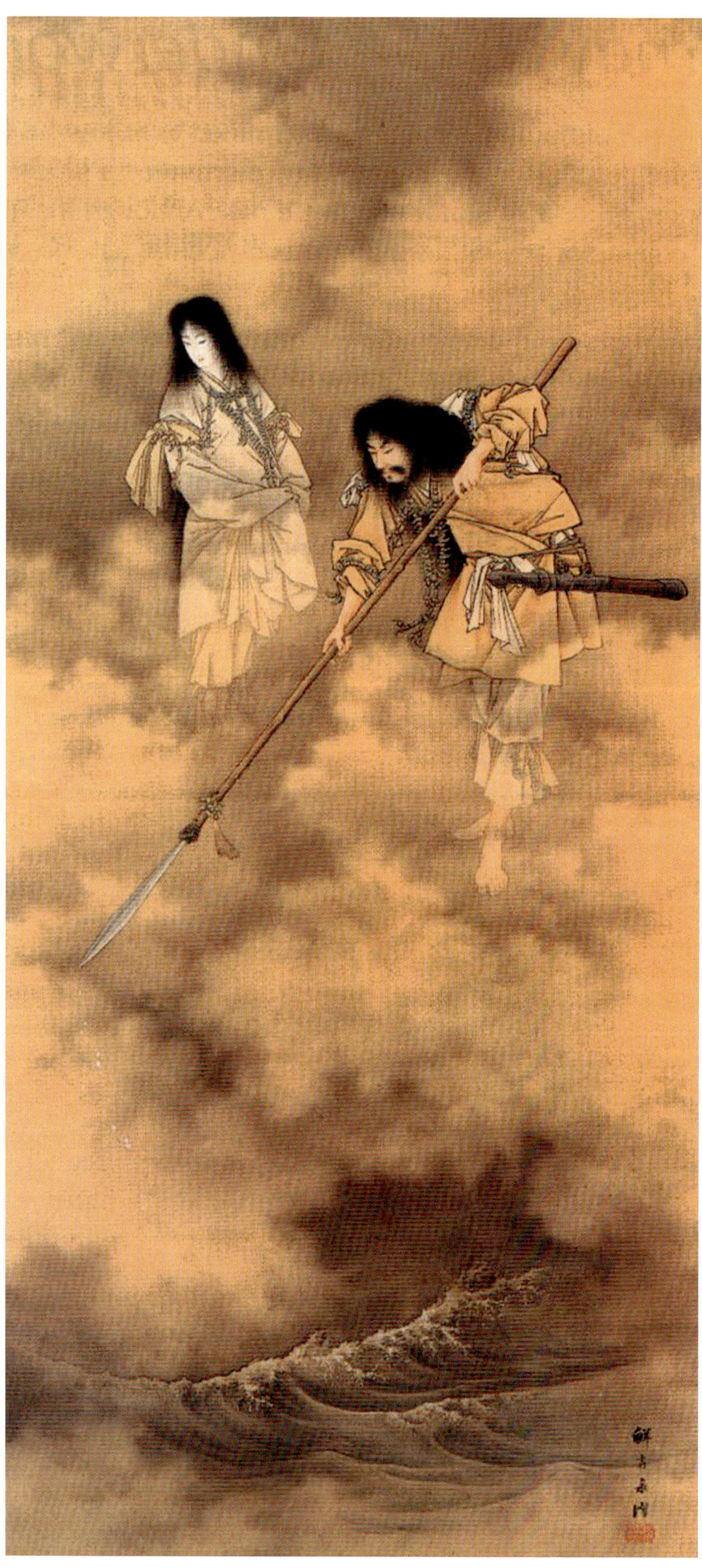

Kobayashi Eitaku (Japan, 1843 – 1890)
1885
Hanging scroll; ink and color on silk
49 ⅝ × 21 ½ in., 126 × 54.6 cm
Museum of Fine Arts, Boston
William Sturgis Bigelow Collection

seas, rivers, and trees, and eventually even the sun and moon (**22**).

What seems clear about such earth diver myths is that they start from a later point in the sequence that most religious traditions envision as the process of creation. Being and Not-Being have already split out of the One—either born from Chaos Itself or from a Great Mother or Father or Egg or already imagined as two World Parents. Often the One has not only split into two, but into many: the "lesser gods"—concentrations of great powers seen populating so many of the pantheons common in many religious traditions. In indigenous African religions, like so many others, Father Sky and Mother Earth are described as the Great Gods and their "children," Ocean and Land, have in turn produced the lesser powers of rivers and mountains and forests and fields. The One source of all is hidden within all these.

This point is made most dramatically in the great Hindu epic, the Bhagavad Gita (ca. 500 BCE and after), when Krishna, an avatar of Vishnu here serving as charioteer to the prince Arjuna, explains to him the nature of reality and his role within it. At one point in the general revelation that the book explores, Krishna reveals to Arjuna his true form (**23**):

And Arjuna saw in that form countless visions of wonder: eyes from innumerable faces, numerous celestial ornaments, numberless heavenly weapons . . . The Infinite Divinity was facing all sides, all marvels in him containing . . . If the light of a thousand suns suddenly arose in the sky, that splendor might be compared to the radiance of the Supreme Spirit. And Arjuna saw in that radiance the whole universe in its variety, standing in a vast unity in the body of the God of gods. Trembling with awe and wonder, Arjuna bowed his head, and joining his hands in adoration he this spoke to his God: "I see in thee all the gods, O my God; and the infinity of the beings of thy creation . . . All around I behold thy Infinity: the power of thy innumerable arms, the visions from innumerable eyes, the words from thy innumerable mouths, and the fire of life of thy innumerable bodies. Nowhere I see a beginning or middle or end of thee, O God of all, Form Infinite!"[31]

What becomes clear in many of these myths is that the One is not the opposite of the Many, but their source and essence. There are not only many different ways for people to approach the Holy, there are infinite expressions of it within the world, and potentially infinite lesser gods. Like their images—and even their verbal descriptions—none of these confines the Holy, which can be expressed in all (**23**).

For those disinclined to mystical visions of the holy One uniting all, there remain various theological understandings of God designating parts of himself via sacrifice or more conscious appointment. Sons—or in matrilineal cultures where the line of succession runs through the women, nephews—agents, avatars, appointees of one kind of another: creation myths outline any number of ways in which the divine One manifests His power within the temporal, relatively understood, knowable world. As we saw in the myth of Purusha, where it was understood that three-quarters of the infinite God remained unmanifest, there is an understanding in many religious traditions that there are layers or intensities of holiness. The heart, the core, may be conceptualized as having degrees of interiority. The Maori of New Zealand, for instance, describe varying levels and qualities of No-thing-ness evolving way before the beginning of the beginning of light and being ever occurred:

> *Te-Po-te-kitea, the unseen Po.*
> *Te-Po-te-whaia, the unpossessed Po.*
> *Te-Po-te-wheau, the unpassing Po.*
> *Te-Po-tangotango, the Po of utter darkness.*
> *Te-Po-te-whawha, the untouched and untouchable Po.*[32]

Others describe the interiority of the Holy in more psychological terms. Na Arean, God of the Maiana Island, southeast of the Marshall Islands, is envisioned as sitting alone in space, *"as a cloud that floats in nothingness"*:[33]

> *So he remained for a great while until a thought came into his mind. He said to himself "I will make a thing." . . . As he said this, a great swelling grew in his forehead, until on the third day it burst, and a little man sprang forth. "Thou art my thought," said Na Arean. "Thou art the picture of my thought. Thy name is Na Arean the younger."*[34]

And Na Arean sent his thought to make the world, separating the cleaving-together of the elements and making room for light to come into being. Na Arean's

thought—a product of a self-reflecting mind—is one step away from his core. Going forth to make the world is a second step. The Christian New Testament similarly describes God speaking his Word as the embodied Jesus Christ, through whom all creation was accomplished. Other religions also define creative agents as outgoing or exterior expressions—visible evidence—of Absolute Power still mostly reserved to itself.

Such distinctions are similar to how we often speak of ourselves, clarifying differences between "me," "myself," and "I": "me" referring to aspects of self that can be objectified or stand in relation to others; "myself" being objectified only within; and "I" evoking the innermost subject. Other religions that perceive the split between the Holy and its creation more radically (like various forms of Zoroastrianism), and envision the Creator as more profoundly separate from the creation, still identify sacred connectors between the infinite and finite. Their religious rituals, texts, and places, as well as a host of special spiritual beings—lesser gods, angels, saints, icons, etc.—not to mention in the world itself, all provide evidence of the infinite omnipresence of the Divine. As the Biblical psalmist observes: "The heavens declare the glory of God; the firmament showeth his handiwork."[35]

Finally, though, the message of all these myths remains that all power truly belongs to the One, that the existence of everything and everyone else is dependent, given. In Hinduism's Kena Upanishad (sixth century BCE), there is a pivotal passage in which Brahman, there identified with the Spirit Supreme, encounters several of the lesser gods.

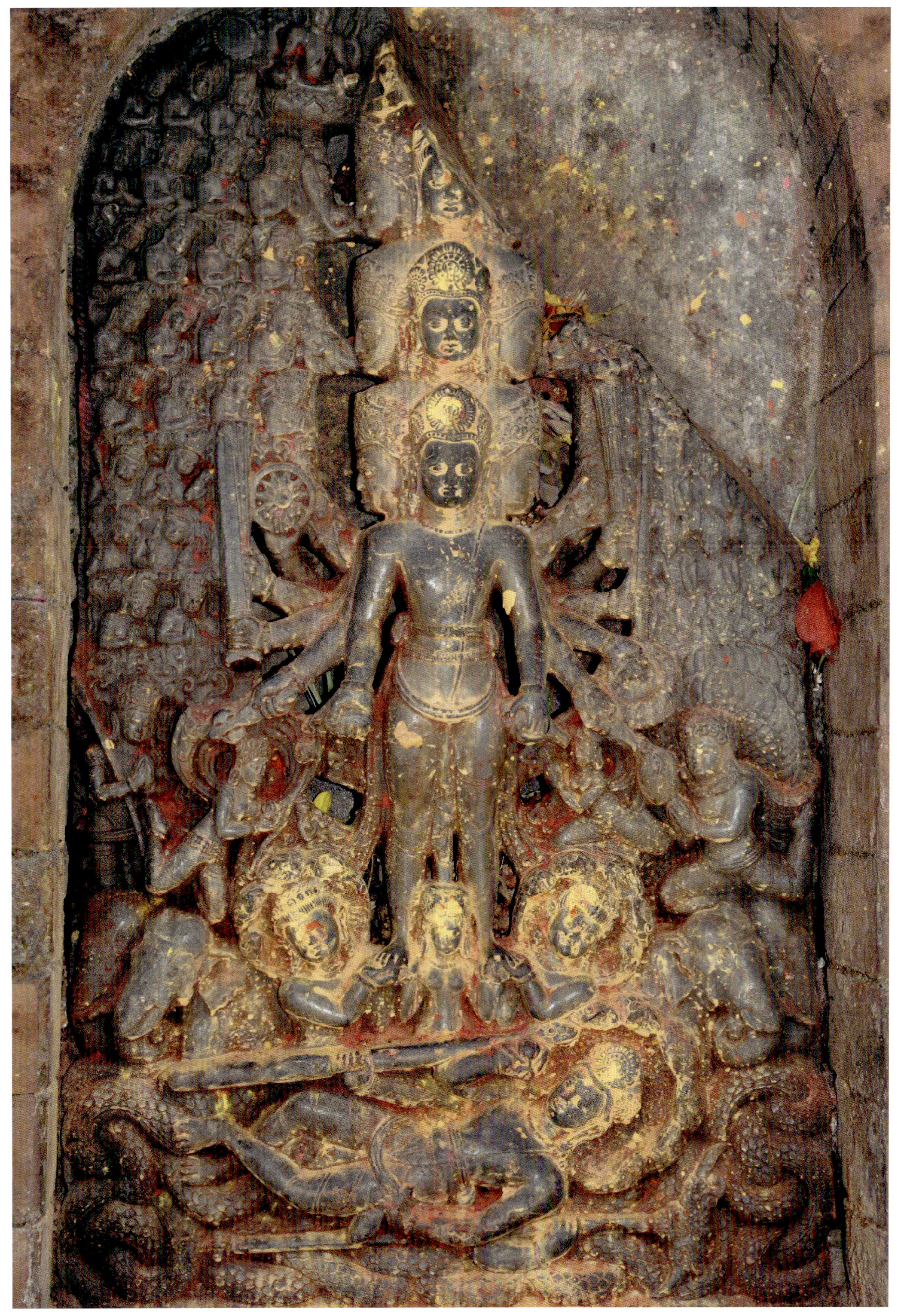

Agni, symbolizing the power of fire, is the first to present himself, and Brahman enquires about his identity:

I am the god of fire", [Agni] said, "the god who knows all things."
"What power is in you?" asked Brahman. "I can burn all things
on earth." And Brahman placed a straw before him saying:
"Burn this." The god of fire strove with all his power, but was
unable to burn it.[36]

Only after several of the lesser deities have gone through the same process does the story relate that they consulted Uma, personification of divine wisdom, who revealed to them the truth that the Being who filled them with such wonder in these meetings was indeed Brahman, source and essence of every power. Only at that point do they—and we—understand the true nature of their existence—of all existence. The illusion of independent being—of power, life, existence itself belonging to any creature—is the source of what Asian religions generally call ignorance and what Abrahamic religions term sin.

Once cultures begin thinking about that stage of creation involving humankind, the ambiguities of temporal life often become the emphasis. The big picture may depict one Reality evolving into two and then many, but from the point of view of individual identity relatively understood—of each person in the world considered in terms of others—the differences between opposites seem overwhelming. Light and darkness, male and female, good and evil, rich and poor, free and slave, and especially life and death: how can these very separate realities be navigated? How can all the trials and tribulations people experience be appreciated? What is our role? Where can we find any meaning that transcends such oppositions, especially the existential threats of condemnation, death, and non-being?

Some traditions posit few reasons for human exceptionalism. After the Babylonian god Marduk has finished ordering Chaos into the world's various natural powers, he turns to a final creation and addresses Ea, a personification of the power of water:

When Marduk hears the words of the gods,
His heart prompts (him) to fashion artful works.
Opening his mouth he addresses Ea
To impart the plan he addresses Ea
To impart the plan he had conceived in his heart:
"Blood I will mass and cause bone to be.
I will establish a savage, "man" shall be his name.
Verily, savage man I will create.
He shall be charged with the service of the gods
That they might be at ease! The ways of the gods I will
artfully alter.[37]

Some myths, like that of P'an Ku, declare right from the beginning that people are totally dependent on the earth—they are parasitic vermin, no less, with no other purpose or possibility of hope even mentioned. But other cultures—particularly those stemming from peoples who have settled down, created cities, and live in fixed locations, having tamed at least the surface powers of nature—are far more anthropocentric, proclaiming humankind as superior to all and valuing people as essentially different from other creatures, sometimes even as the culmination of universal creation. These more anthropocentric cultures see the various powers of destruction in a negative light, characterizing them as accidents of some sort, mistakes of sacred evolution, or the product of some lesser evil deity creating all the unpleasant realities that present challenges within human experience.

Whether because of evil, stupidity, or simple inattention on the part of the creative powers, many religions agree that the creation of humans is a difficult and risky process, full of potential and real errors, often requiring many tries.

The omniscience and omnipotence of the gods seem to falter here. The Popol Vuh (Book of the Community) is the sacred text of the Quiche Maya, recounting their history from the creation through the Mayan kings in 1550. Its myth begins with many of the same themes sounded by other images of creation:

> *This is the account of how all was in suspense, all calm, in silence; all motionless, still, and the expanse of the sky was empty . . . There was neither man nor animal, birds, fish, crabs, trees, stones, caves, ravines, grasses, nor forests; there was only the sky . . . There was nothing brought together, nothing which could make a noise, nor anything which might move, or tremble . . . There was nothing standing; only the calm water, the placid sea, alone and tranquil. Nothing existed.*

> *There was only immobility and silence in the darkness, in the night. Only the Creator, the Maker, Tepeu, Gucumatz the Forefathers, were in the water surrounded with light. They were hidden under green and blue feathers, and were therefore called Gucumatz. By nature they were great sages and great thinkers. In this manner the sky existed and also the Heart of Heaven, which is the name of God and thus he is called.*[38]

All these forces—the world parents of Tepeu and Gucumatz (feminine and masculine deities, already combining opposites in their symbolic representations of fire and water)—the light and darkness, sea and sky, and then the Heart of Heaven—the Huracan representing the energies of powerful storms we experience as lightning, thunder, wind and rain—all of these participate in the moment of creation:

> *Then came the word. Tepeu and Gucumatz came together in the darkness, in the night, and Tepeu and Gucumatz talked together. They talked then, discussing and deliberating; they agreed and they united their words and their thoughts . . . Then the earth was created by them . . . "Earth!" They said, and instantly it was made.*[39]

It was after the creation of animals that problems became apparent. The myth relates that the gods wanted the animals to praise them, but finding that the only noises they could make were hisses, screams, and cackles, they relegated those first creatures to the ravines and the woods, condemning them to be hunted and killed.

A second attempt to fashion humankind was made using mud, but this, too, proved unsuccessful, as the creatures were soft and melted. Again, they were destroyed and again the gods tried to create people. Consulting other powers now evolved, they next formed people out of the wood of trees. These people could walk, talk, even procreate, but still "they did not have souls, nor minds, they did not remember their Creator, their Maker; they walked on all fours, aimlessly." A great flood destroyed most of them and the survivors became monkeys: "And therefore the monkey looks like man, and is an example of a generation of men which were created and made but were only wooden figures."[40]

So, the gods tried yet again and this time, with the help of many of the animals, they gathered plants—mainly corn and beans, the primary foods of the region—and made four people out of them. While their names are difficult to translate with certainty, the first men seem to represent the cardinal directions, so their existence can be understood to have helped establish geographical order as well as human existence. What is clear is that they were very great creatures with extraordinary powers, gifted with such wisdom and understanding that they actually frightened the gods, who limited their abilities before proceeding with the creation of four women (whose names all indicate connection with water) to be their mates. Finally, the dawn broke, the sun transformed all the dangerous creatures into stone, and the people rejoiced. The world was established, and with it, people's roles: they were to understand themselves in terms of the creation, to praise the gods and sustain the world order—

to define themselves in terms of the Absolute Reality of their creation, not relatively in terms of other created beings and things.

While many religions recount difficulties in the creation of human beings, necessitating a series of attempts on the part of the gods to get it right, several blame the problem on the people themselves. In the Hopi creation story, after the heavens, earth, and water had all been properly arranged by Tiaowa's nephew Sotuknang, and the magnetic poles fixed and the vibratory centers of earth's energies established so all sound could express the voice of the Creator, the powerful Spider Woman was directed to make people. This she did, using the four colors of earth—yellow, red, white, and black, representing the four directions—mixed with her own saliva. She formed eight beings and covered them with her white substance-cape, which was the creative wisdom itself, so they would understand their role in the world. Once uncovered, the people stirred to life and completed their birth as the night eased into dawn and daylight. Sotuknang was summoned to make the final touches, to give people their own abilities to create: the powers to speak and reproduce, to make something out of nothing—God-like powers:

All at once, with the sound as of a mighty wind, Sotuknang appeared in front of them: "I am here. Why do you need me so urgently?"

Spider Woman explained. "As you commanded me, I have created these First People. They are fully and firmly formed; they are properly colored; they have life; they have movement. But they cannot talk. This is the proper thing they lack. So I want you to give them speech. Also the wisdom and power to reproduce, so that they may enjoy their life and give thanks to the Creator."

So Sotuknang gave then speech, a different language to each color, with respect for each other's differences. He gave them the wisdom and the power to reproduce and multiply.

Then he said to them, "With all these I have given you this world to live on and to be happy. There is only one thing I ask of you. To respect the Creator at all times. May wisdom, harmony and respect for the love of the Creator who made you. May it grow and never be forgotten among you as long as you live."[41]

But the people forgot. They began to use their powers solely for earthly purposes, no longer remembering to carry out the plan of the Creator. Gradually they started thinking relatively, egocentrically, paying attention to their differences—"the differences between people and animals, the differences between the people themselves by reason of the color of their skins, their speech and belief in the plan of the creator."[42] By the time people started to war with each other, Sotuknang and Taiowa decided to destroy this evil. They told those good people who remained to migrate to a special place where they could join the Ant People below the earth. There they would be safe while Sotuknang unleashed the volcanoes and drew fire from the sky, destroying the first world. There they could also learn the ants' wisdom, understanding how to be industrious and live in peace with one another.

The second world was also destroyed, this time because of human greed. Though they had everything they needed, people began to want more and eventually acquisitiveness and commercialism led to wars and such global imbalance that Sotuknang removed the forces guarding the earth's magnetic poles and the planet teetered and spun around crazily, eventually freezing into solid ice. Again, the good people had been forewarned to migrate to the place of the Ant People and be saved. When the ground thawed sufficiently, they emerged once again out of the earth to establish the third world.

But once again, people forgot their purpose. While they had advanced in many ways, building cities and civilizations, they were still self-centered and corrupt. Greed once again led to war, and the gods once again decided to destroy the world. This time Spider Woman helped the few good people to survive by hiding them in hollow reeds that floated on the waters Sotuknang had loosed to flood the world. When they finally emerged, the good people traveled east over the formless waters for ages seeking dry land, sometimes on raft boats they made from the reeds. Passing small islands along the way—the tips of the mountains rising up from the flooded third world—they finally came to their proper place of emergence: the fourth and present world. Each group was instructed by Sotuknang to follow their stars and migrate to the land reserved for them, and this is where they are today.

Images of people emerging out of the (mother) earth, or even its trees (or reeds), are as common as those in earlier myths that depicted gods or eventually the land itself rising up out of the waters. The idea of birth from dark interiority is universal. And successive creations—now necessitated by the destruction of initial and corrupted realms—are also frequently encountered in religious cosmologies dealing with the creation of man.

The Mesopotamian Epic of Gilgamesh (ca. 2100 BCE) relates how Enlil, god of the air, storm, and waters, tried to eradicate humankind because people had overpopulated the land and were making too much noise. He wanted to destroy all living things by flood, but when other gods overheard Enlil's plan, they warned the good man Utnapishtim to tear down his house, build a boat, and save himself, his household, and the seeds of all other creatures. This he did, surviving the flood and repopulating the earth.

The Hebrew Bible recounts a similar story. Formed from dirt and animated by the very breath of God, at first man is portrayed as being close to the Creator in every regard. His world of Eden is imagined as a paradise, a land of innocence and bounty. There "the Lord God commanded the man saying 'You may eat freely of every tree of the garden; but of the tree of the knowledge of good and evil, you shall not eat, for in the day you eat of it you shall die.'"[43] Originally as unselfconscious as every child, once Adam and Eve had obtained that forbidden knowledge, they became aware of their own creatureliness and mortality; they became self-conscious. The myth describes this as their inability then to partake of the fruit of eternal life and their subsequent exile from the bliss of their original innocence. Thinking selfishly, they are cut off from their connection to the eternal essence and cast out of paradise. Separated from being able to understand their closeness to God, they now live in the realm of the sins

that stem from such relative thinking. Like people in the Hopi myth, they forgot their purpose. And after several generations of increasing human corruption and chaos, God is described as having decided to destroy this once perfect world. As in the Epic of Gilgamesh, a good man— here Noah—is advised to take his wife and children and a pair of all the creatures on earth onto an ark to survive the coming storm (**24**).

In the rains that follow, creation is undone. Whereas initially, God had separated the waters above the earth from those below, forming dry land, now he opened the "windows of heaven" and the "fountains of the deep" so that the formless waters once again covered everything. Animals and finally people are all drowned, "returned to clay" as the Epic of Gilgamesh had described it. Only the ark and its inhabitants are saved to begin a new world, and God promises with the sign of a rainbow not to destroy the world again.[44]

Other religious traditions also imagined a series of successive creations, but they did not necessarily connect these to matters of moral failure. Hinduism speaks of immeasurable *kalpas*, periods of enormous duration: the texts dazzle with numbers. The Vishnu Purana (a pre-ninth-century Hindu work) figures that a *kalpa* consists of 4.32 billion years—just one day in the life of the god Brahma—after which there is a night of the same length. At the end of each *kalpa*, the world is destroyed by fire and then recreated. And within these vast periods of existence, the creator Time never stops, rolling along like one of the twenty-four wheels surrounding the Temple at Konark, India (**25**).

Edward Hicks (United States, 1780 – 1849)
1846
Oil on canvas
26 ⁵⁄₁₆ × 30 ⅜ in., 66.8 × 77.2 cm
Philadelphia Museum of Art, Pennsylvania,
Bequest of Lisa Norris Elkins, 1950

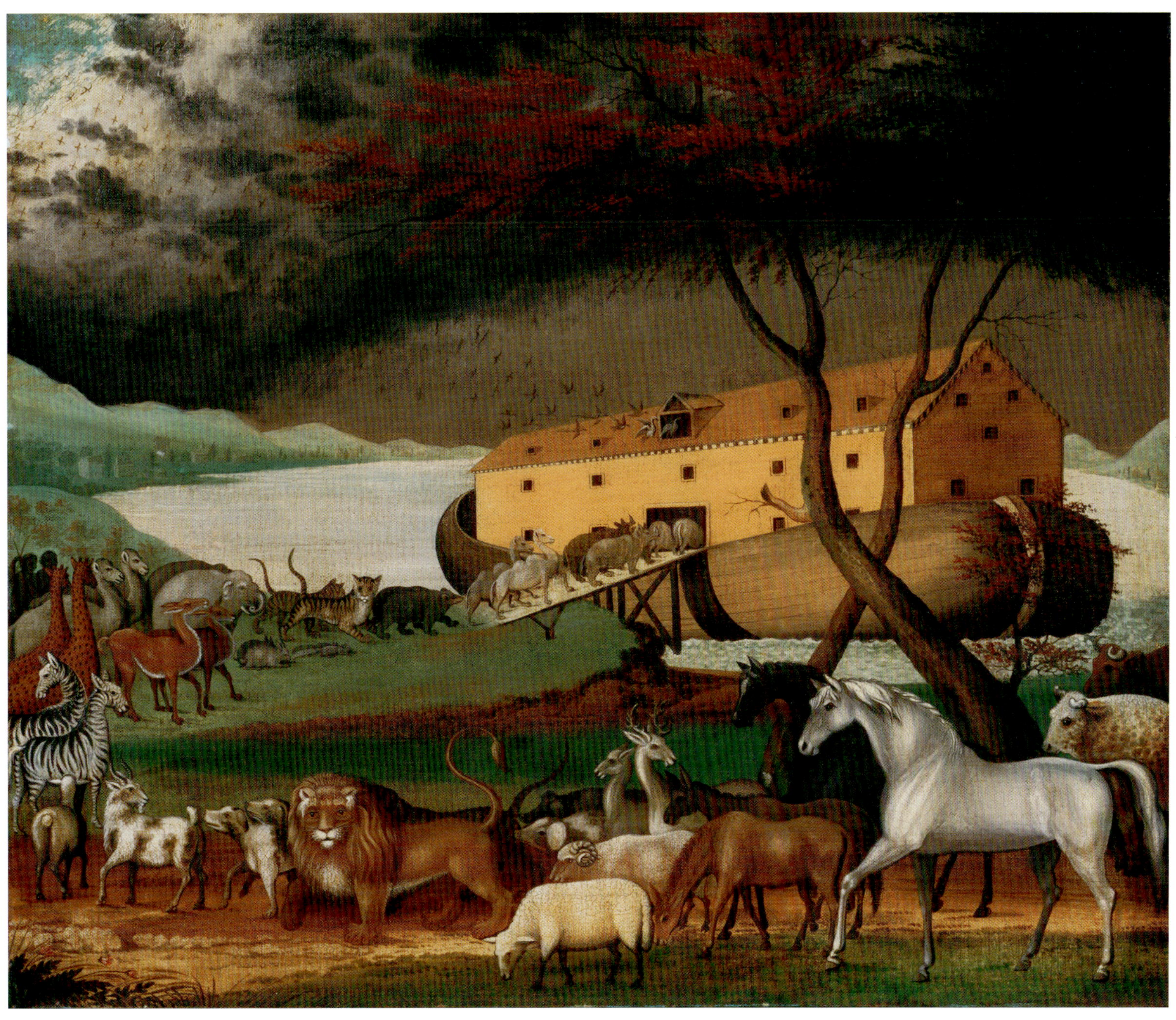

Konark, Odisha, India
1200 – 1300
Stone
117 in., 297.18 cm in diameter

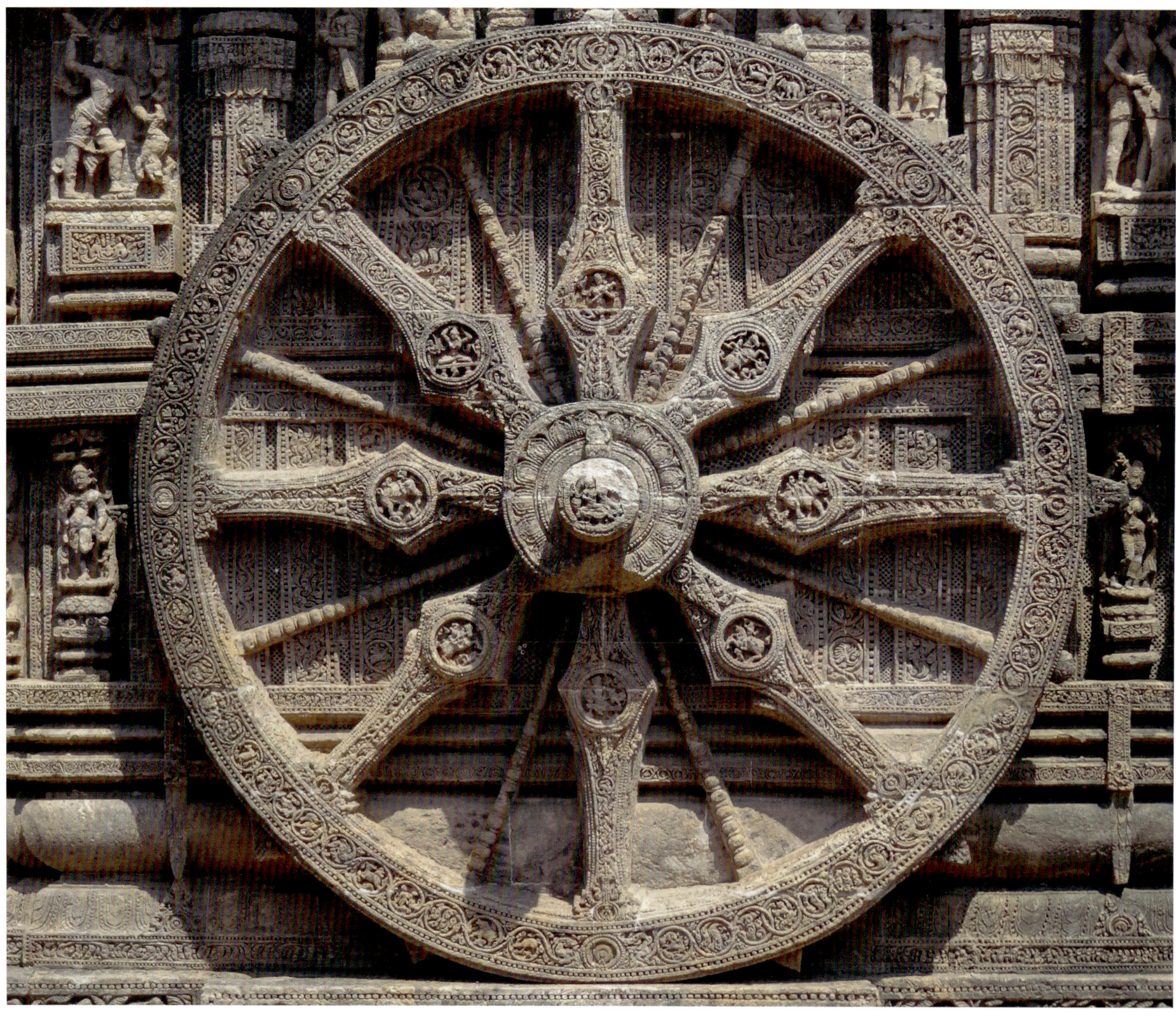

26 Sun Calendar

Aztec culture, Mexico
1502 – 1520
Stone
11.8 feet, 3.6 meters in diameter
National Museum of Anthropology,
Mexico City

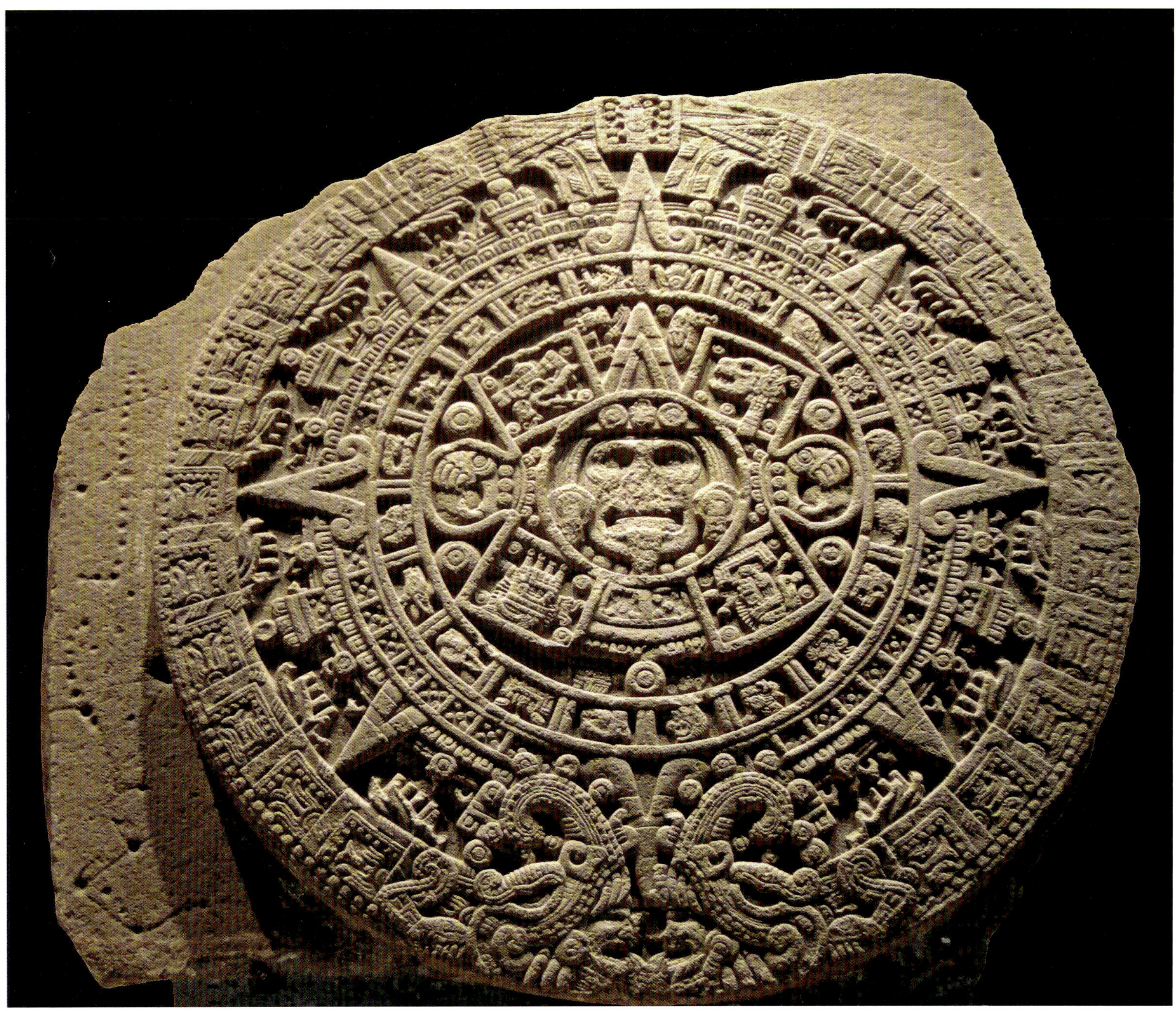

The Aztecs, like many who conceived of the creator in temporal terms, envisioned Eternity's wheel rotating through the ages, grinding out (and grinding up) all creatures. Not only did they often proclaim multiple different ages or even successive creations, but they also carefully recorded our place in relative time now—giving us temporal orientation. The Aztecs focused on Time as just such a great creator/destroyer, understanding its passage as endlessly creating change and newness. Their complex calendar system followed the movement of the planets and stars, providing a proper accounting of sacred dates. Each day not only had a unique name and number but was represented by its own deity: the power of a day. The 260-day cycle was subdivided into periods of twenty days each, which ran alongside a second group of thirteen numbered days. After all possible combinations of names and numbers had been passed through, one 260-day year had concluded.

Yet another cog in the complex wheel of Aztec time was based on the solar calendar of 365 days, divided into eighteen groups of twenty days each. They, too, each had religious significance and marked the holy-days, times when people were called upon to understand themselves in terms of Existence-Itself. When all the possible variations of the different temporal periods coincided every fifty-two years, it was a most sacred time of endings and renewal—the Aztec "century"—a completion and new beginning.

At the center of the monumental Aztec Sun or Calendar Stone (probably created in the reign of Moctezuma II (1502–1520; **26**), is a figure that most scholars identify as Tonatiuh, the Sun god, with a tongue like the blade of a sacrificial knife and his clawed hands (to the side of his face) holding human hearts. Himself the product of sacrifice, the creation of life out of death, he demands to be fed by more sacrifice in order keep being. Surrounding his face in the great carving, four squares depict symbols for a jaguar, the wind, fire, and water—the four ways the prior worlds were destroyed. This fifth world, it is predicted, will be brought down by earthquakes. The circle beyond the innermost one represents the twenty days of the cycles and beyond that the solar rays point in the cardinal directions, connecting space to both time and being. The encircling snakes may represent the fertile essence and eternality of Time-Itself.

Buddhism addresses the issue of successive creations from a radically different theoretical premise, denying the possibility of any original creation: "Not to be discovered is any first beginning of beings."[45] The Buddha's primary doctrine of radical interdependence and change is the understanding that no thing or being has any independent existence; all are constantly evolving interdependently with all other things and beings. As there are no fully separate beings at all, Buddhism argues, there could be no separate Creator. Ordinary understandings of space and time—which measure the momentary dimensions of beings *as if* they were permanent—are finally illusory as well. Within this context of understanding, Buddhism envisages an eternal succession of creations, each lasting for unimaginable

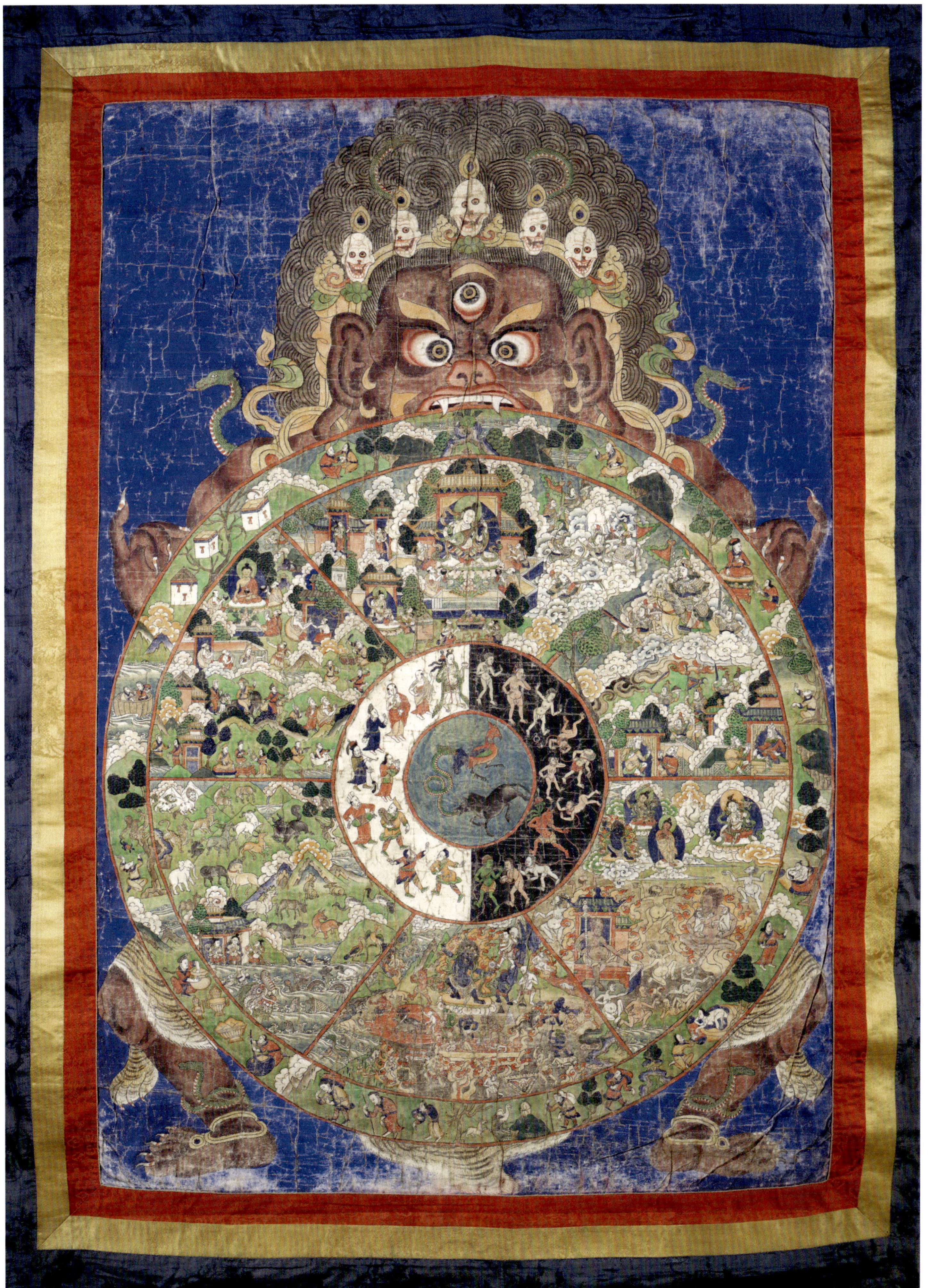

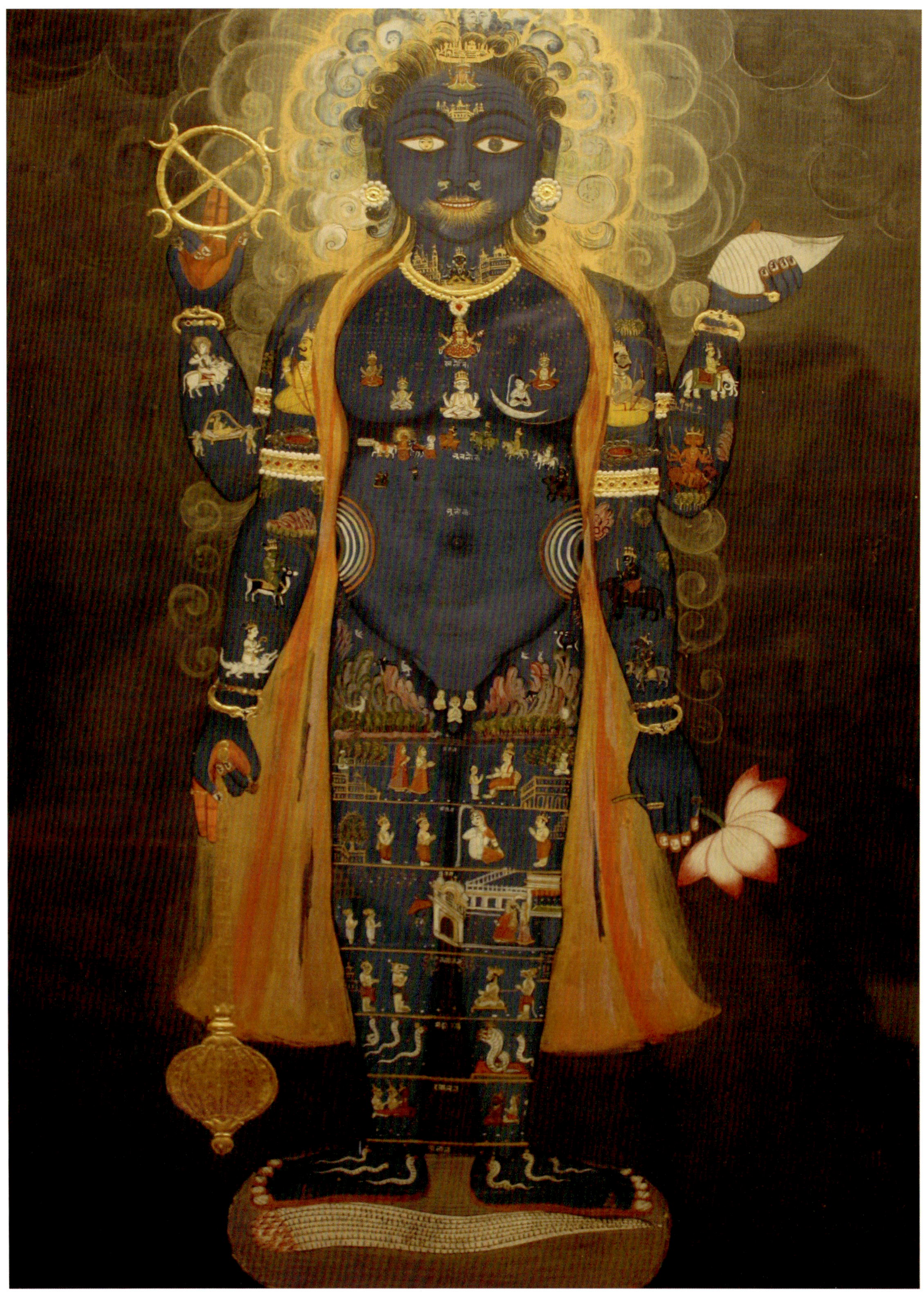

periods of time, evolving out of one another. These periods of time are so long that they are not really even worth thinking about:

> *Were a man to take a piece of cloth of this most delicate texture [of fine cotton], and therewith to touch in the slightest possible manner, once in a hundred years, a solid rock, free from earth, a yojana [~14 miles] high, and as much broad, the time would come when it would be worn down, by this imperceptible trituration, to the size of a mung or undu seed. This period would be immense in its duration; but it has been declared by Buddha that it would not be equal to a Maha Kalpa.*[46]

Tantric Buddhist images of universal reality show Yama, the power of death, perpetually about to swallow all present beings and things: endless change is symbolized by the wheel of dependent origination. We suffer because we become attached to temporal realities (especially the idea of self). In a Buddhist painting of the Wheel of Life, at the core of our world of illusion and misery—this realm of *samsara*—are the rooster of attachment, the green snake of hatred, and the black pig of ignorance (**27**). Surrounding them are the good and evil possibilities of action, reminding us of the karmic consequences of our deeds, and outside of that are the six realms of possible future births—hell, hungry ghosts (those incapable of satisfaction), animals, human beings, demigods, and gods. And finally on the outer rim are the twelve steps of dependent origination showing how one stage leads to the next and the next. While ignorance is the weakest link in the circle, it is the basic condition of birth: had we been enlightened, we would have been freed from the cycle of rebirth into the unity of No-Thing-ness. So, the great number of Buddhist images seek to help us understand Reality and dissolve our ignorance.

Another great religious tradition from the sixth-century BCE Ganges Basin in India, Jainism was founded by Mahavira ("The Great Hero") whose principal understanding was that the universe existed eternally. As the monk Jinasena declared in the Mahapurana, the major Jain text of the ninth century, "Know that the world is uncreated, as Time itself is, without beginning and end, and is based on the principles, life and the rest."[47] According to Jainism, there is no creator: the universe itself—and its nine basic elements—is eternal and absolute. Yet within it, there are multiple periods of temporality and several distinct realms. In this tradition the cosmic wheel of time rotates continuously and repeatedly through six different periods within two eons—a first in which life and being evolve, and a second in which they devolve. We are currently in the fifth period of the second eon, a period of increasing immorality and misery.

The Jains also imagine Space to be absolute, with three upper realms of beings of various degrees of enlightenment: those fully liberated from the curse of rebirth are imagined at the very top in the crescent cap of the universal man; one middle realm at the waist where humans and animals were thought to dwell; and seven realms of underworlds where different kinds of hellish beings presumably resided until they could expiate enough negative karma to be able to be reborn into another opportunity for enlightenment. This

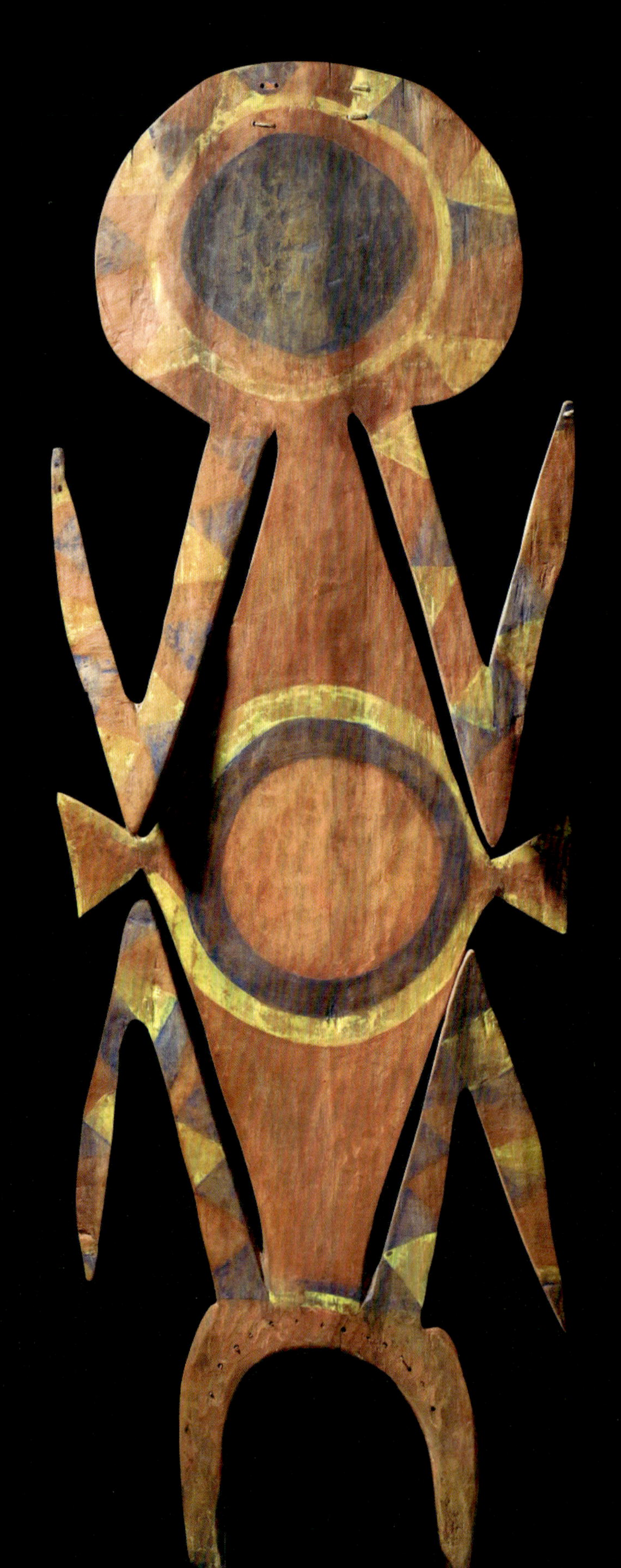

29 **Siane Board Depicting the Universe**

Siane culture, Eastern Highlands Province, Papua New Guinea
Around 1955
Wood
Los Angeles County Museum of Art (LACMA)
Purchased with funds provided by the Eli and Edythe Broad
Foundation, with additional funding by Jane and Terry Semel,
The David Bohnett Foundation, Camilla Chandler Frost, Gayle
and Edward P. Roski, and the Ahmanson Foundation

anthropomorphic image of the universe also conveys the understanding of the interrelatedness of all, as well as the relation of the microcosm to the macrocosm. The myth and its resultant images of the universe as a kind of primal man convey the lesson that the universe is of a piece— though souls are on separate paths of enlightenment, everything is interconnected through the effect we have on each other and the karma created by our deeds; accordingly, we need to act kindly and without violence.

Time, Space, and Being are three ways of describing one universal Reality. Religions that chose Being as the primary focus of their creation myths usually describe the creator anthropomorphically, like a person, using the most familiar example we have. Here the Holy is depicted personally and is often understood as expressing its own very being in the world's existence. Such a practice is global. Not only did the Jains create such images, but so did the Hindus, the Dogon of Mali, and people of Oceania. We noted the myth of Purusha being sacrificed to become all the elements of the world, but within the fluid theologies that comprise Hinduism, other gods may be similarly imagined. In a nineteenth-century painting from Rajasthan, Vishnu is depicted as the universe, each of his four hands clutching the symbols of his powers—the conch shell, a lotus flower, a mace and his circular wand—and his flesh embodying all the people and creatures of the world (**28**). God is omnipresent, and understood in this context, people are temporal expressions of holy Being. The resultant ethic is clear: each is of absolute value.

Other cultures make a similar point: a sculpted wooden board made by the Siane people of the Eastern Highlands in New Guinea also appears to be in the abstracted shape of a human but actually is a *wenena gerua*, a figure evoking the universal order (**29**). Here the head represents the sun and the body the moon. The limbs outline the various ways the two great powers communicate with each other. The sculpted figure is worn atop the head of the family at tri-annual rituals, where is it danced so that the young initiates are tutored in the eternal realities of existence.

Another way in which cultures whose thinking is grounded in spatial imagery express their understanding is to begin with images of emptiness and the void, often eventually situating numerous different realms within it. As common as the idea of various epochs of universal existence is that of various spatial realms of being, often seen to be arranged hierarchically in layers and frequently connected by a great world tree, serving as an *axis mundi*, the center pole of the world rising up through them all, permitting travel between levels of being.

The Prose Edda, a Norse epic compiled in the thirteenth century by Snorri Sturluson from earlier sources, described a universe of three major tiers. The giant Ymir was first formed when the ice of Niflheim (the cold, dark, dead aspect of Reality) met the burning heat of Muslepheim (the polar opposite aspect of fire and light). The product of the merger of these two primal forces, Ymir became the father of all the lesser gods. From his sweat and various body arose sons and daughters—progenitors of the gods who, in turn, like their counterparts in other

Oluf Olufsen Bagge (Denmark, 1780 – 1836)
1859
Print
Boston Public Library
Norman B. Leventhal Map Center Collection

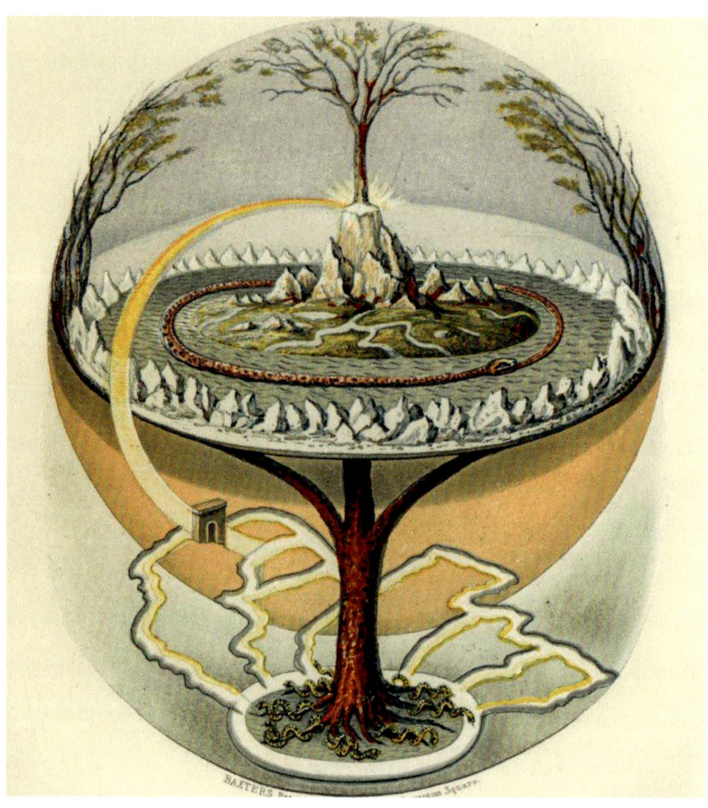

mythic traditions, sacrificed Ymir to make the world as we know it. They formed the sky from Ymir's skull, clouds from his brains, the earth from his flesh, and mountains from his bones. His eyelashes became the fence surrounding Middle Earth, the realm of mankind. The great tree of Yggdrasil serves as the *axis mundi*—the central core of the world—uniting all the realms and forms and marking not only a crucial point of absolute orientation but also a figurative connection between the realms (**30**).

Mesoamerican traditions also emphasize spatial orientations in their cosmologies. The world tree imagined in the Codex Ferjérváry-Mayer (a late fifteenth- or early sixteenth-century Aztec manuscript; **31**), usually described as a grand Cieba tree, not only rises up through the nine levels of the underworld, the one level of the middle world, and the thirteen levels of the upper world, but it is fundamentally related to the ideas of the five directions—the four cardinal points and the center. In the complex design shown in the Codex Ferjérváry-Mayer, the central figure is Xiuhtecutli, the Fire-Deity who is both mother and father of the gods and dwells in the navel of the earth. Placed in the middle realm with a spear and spear-thrower, Xiuhtecutli sends the formative power of divine life blood out into the four directions. Each directional realm has its own tree of life, its own pair of deities, its own references to days and times, creating an image of all aspects of reality: existential, temporal, and spatial. One encircling realm enclosed by red represents the east, where the sun rises; a second surrounded by yellow is the north, where death and the jaguar reign; a

 Aztec Five Realms

First page of the Codex Ferjérváry-Mayer
Veracruz, Mexico
Before 1521
Deerskin parchment
World Museum Liverpool, England

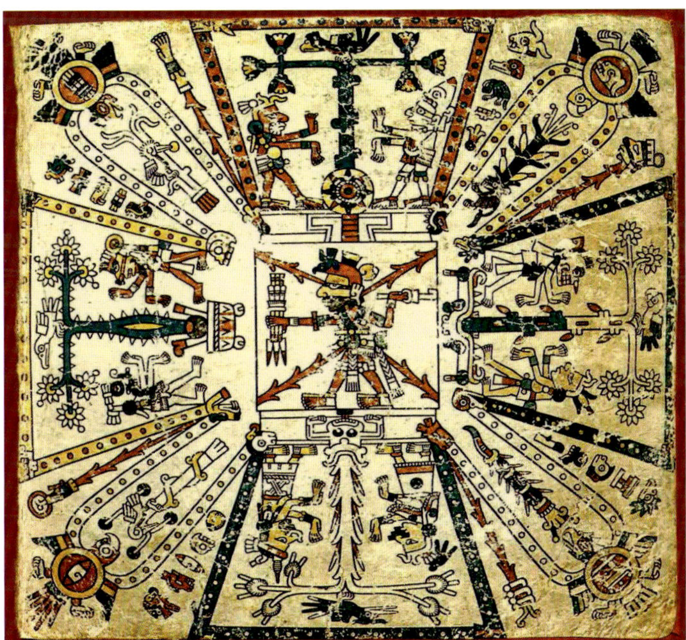

third with its edge of blue depicts the west, where the sun dies; and the fourth, defined by green is the south, a realm of air. Birds and other symbols indicate distinct periods of time, both long and short, so that the painting orients the viewer in space, time, and being: the one world of sacred reality.

While Islam eschews any attempt to describe the Infinite through finite forms and thus discourages portraiture, in the designs of its architecture, it powerfully depicts the glorious relation of the One and the many. For instance, in the ceiling from the dome of the Sheikh Lotfollah Mosque in Isfahan, Iran (completed in 1619), the splendor of the countless emanations from their central point and the profound harmony of their interrelations call the faithful to understand themselves more profoundly (**32**).

All of these images serve to proclaim the unity of the manifold world, the mysterious oneness of apparent dualities, the interrelatedness of all created beings and things. They direct their followers to understand themselves not just relatively, in terms of other people and temporal things, but absolutely, in the context of Reality itself, asserting that Eternity is now; Infinity is here; Being is animating all.

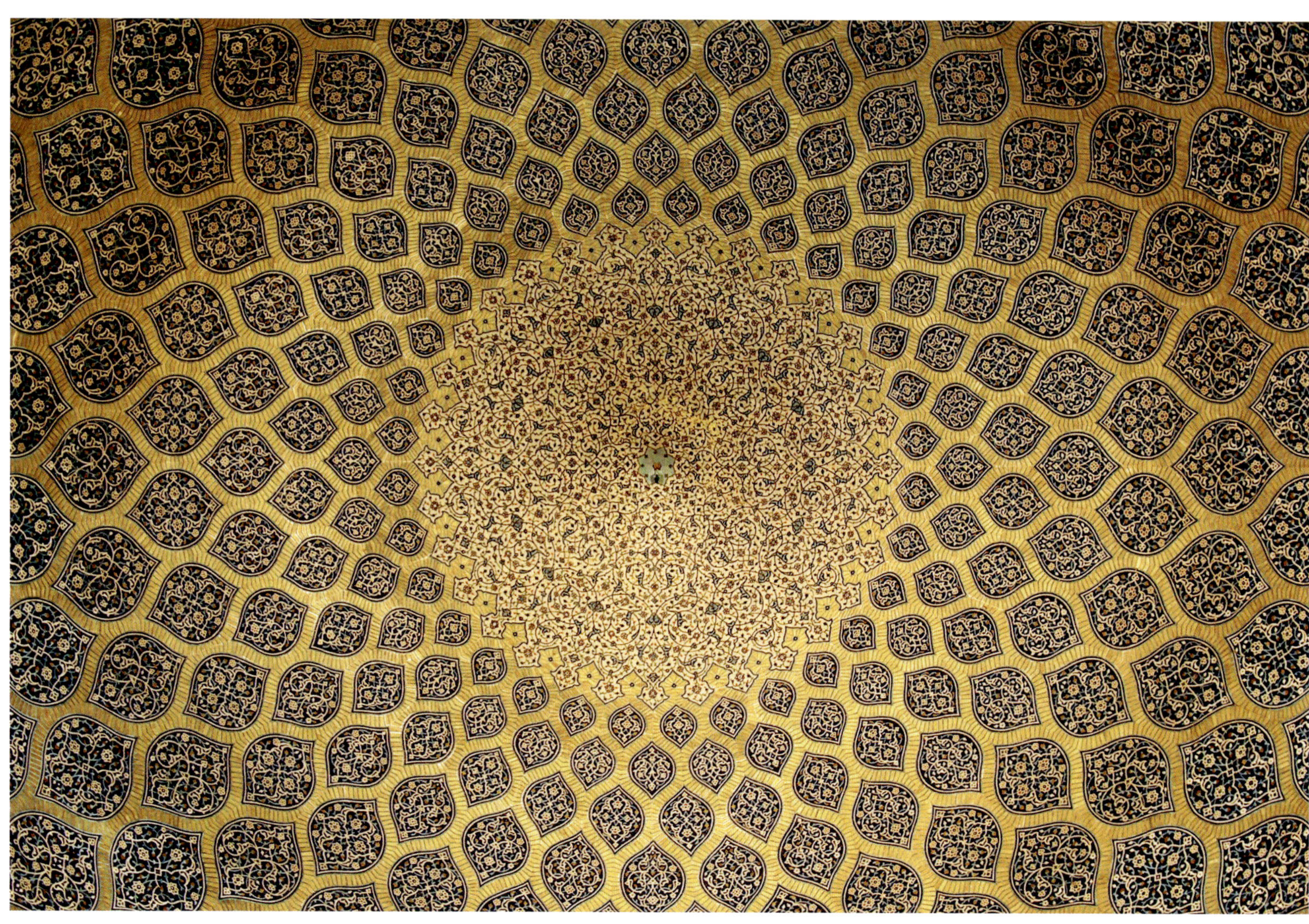

1   R. C. Zaehner, *Hindu Scriptures* (London: J. M. Dent, 1966), 11–12.

2   Frank J. Stimson, *Tuamotuan Religion*, Bernice P. Bishop Museum Bulletin 103 (Honolulu: Bishop Museum Press, 1933), 12.

3   Qur'an 112:1–4.

4   Juan Mascaro (trans.), *The Upanishads* (London: Penguin Books, 1965), 51.

5   Qur'an 50:16.

6   Bible, Exodus 3:14 (New English Version).

7   Richard Taylor, *Te Ika a Maui* (London: Wertheim and Macintosh, 1855). Quoted in A. W. Reed, *Treasury of Maori Folklore* (Wellington, New Zealand: A. H. and A. W. Reed, 1963), 19.

8   E. A. Wallis Budge, *The Gods of the Egyptians*, vol. 1 (New York: Dover, 1969), 309.

9   T. G. H. Strehlow, *Aranda Traditions* (Melbourne: University of Melbourne Press, 1947), 7.

10 Bible, Genesis 1:1–5 (Revised Standard Version).

11 Bible, Gospel of John 1:1–18.

12 Qur'an 40:70.

13 Qur'an 112:1–4.

14 Sir Clements Robert Markham, *The Inca of Peru* (London: Smith, Elder & Co., 1912), 100.

15 Markham, *The Inca of* Peru, 33.

16 Sir George Grey, "The Children of Heaven and Earth," in *Polynesian Mythology and Ancient Traditional History* (Aukland: H. Brett, 1885), 1.

17 Ibid., 1.

18 Ibid., 3.

19 Zaehner, *Hindu Scriptures*, 10.

20 Julius Eggeling (trans.), "Sátapatha-Brāhmaṇa XI, I, 6," in *The Sacred Books of the East Series*, vol. 44 (Oxford: Clarendon Press, 1900), 15.

21 Ibid., 12.

22 Maria Leach, *The Beginning* (New York, Funk and Wagnalls: 1956), 224.

23 W. F. Kirby, *Kalevala: The Land of the Heroes*, vol.1. (London: J.M. Dent, 1907), 5–7.

24 Teuira Henry, *Ancient Tahiti*, Bernice P. Bishop Museum Bulletin 48 (Honolulu: Bishop Museum Press, 1928), 339.

25 Zaehner, *Hindu Scriptures*, 12.

26 Leach, *The Beginning*, 225.

27 Zaehner, *Hindu Scriptures*, 9–10.

28 Reinhold Merkelbach, "Mithraism: Mythology and Theology" in *Encyclopaedia Britannica*, 8th ed. (Chicago: Encyclopaedia Britannica, 2009), https://www.britannica.com/topic/Mithraism/Mythology-and-theology.

29 E. A. Speiser (trans.), "The Enuma Elish" in *Ancient Near Eastern Texts Relating to the Old Testament*, ed. James B. Pritchard (Princeton: Princeton University Press, 1950), 65.

30 W. G. Aston (trans), *The Nihongi* (London: George Allen and Unwin, 1956), 2–3.

31 Gita 11, 9–16. Juan Mascaro (trans.), *The Bhagavad Gita* (London: Penguin Books, 1962), 53.

32 A. W. Reed, *Treasury of Maori Folklore* (Wellington, New Zealand: A. H. and A. W. Reed, 1963), 18.

33 A. Grimble, "Myths from the Gilbert Islands," in *Folklore* 33, no. 1 (1922): 106.

34 Ibid., 106–7.

35 Bible, Psalm 19:1 (Revised Standard Version).

36 Mascaro, *The Upanishads*, 52–53.

37 Speiser (trans.), "The Enuma Elish," 67.

38 Adrian Recinos (trans), Delia Goetz, and Sylvanus G. Morley (English trans.), *The Popul Vuh* (Norman: University of Oklahoma Press, 1950), 81.

39 Ibid.

40 Ibid., 91–92.

41 Frank Waters, *The Book of the Hopi* (New York: Viking Press, 1963), 8.

42 Ibid., 15.

43 Bible, Genesis 2:16–17 (Revised Standard Version).

44 Bible, Genesis 9:13–17.

45 *Samyutta-Nikaya* XV, 13, quoted in Barbara C. Sproul, *Primal Myths: Creating the World* (New York: Harper and Row, 1979), 194.

46 Daniel John Gogerly, David de Silva, and John Scott, "Buddhism: A Lecture Delivered before the Colombo Young Men's Christian Association," *Journal of the Ceylon Branch of the Royal Asiatic Society* 14, pt. 1 (1867–70): 96–97.

47 William Theodore de Bary (ed.), *Sources of Indian Tradition*, vol. 1 (New York: Columbia University Press, 1966), 78.

IV

MOTHERHOOD AND THE FAMILY

HERBERT M. COLE

Who makes seed grow in women,
Who makes people from sperm;
Who feeds the son in his mother's womb
Who soothes him to still his tears,
Nurse in the womb,
Giver of breath,
To nourish all that he made.

The Great Hymn to the Aten,
14th century BCE

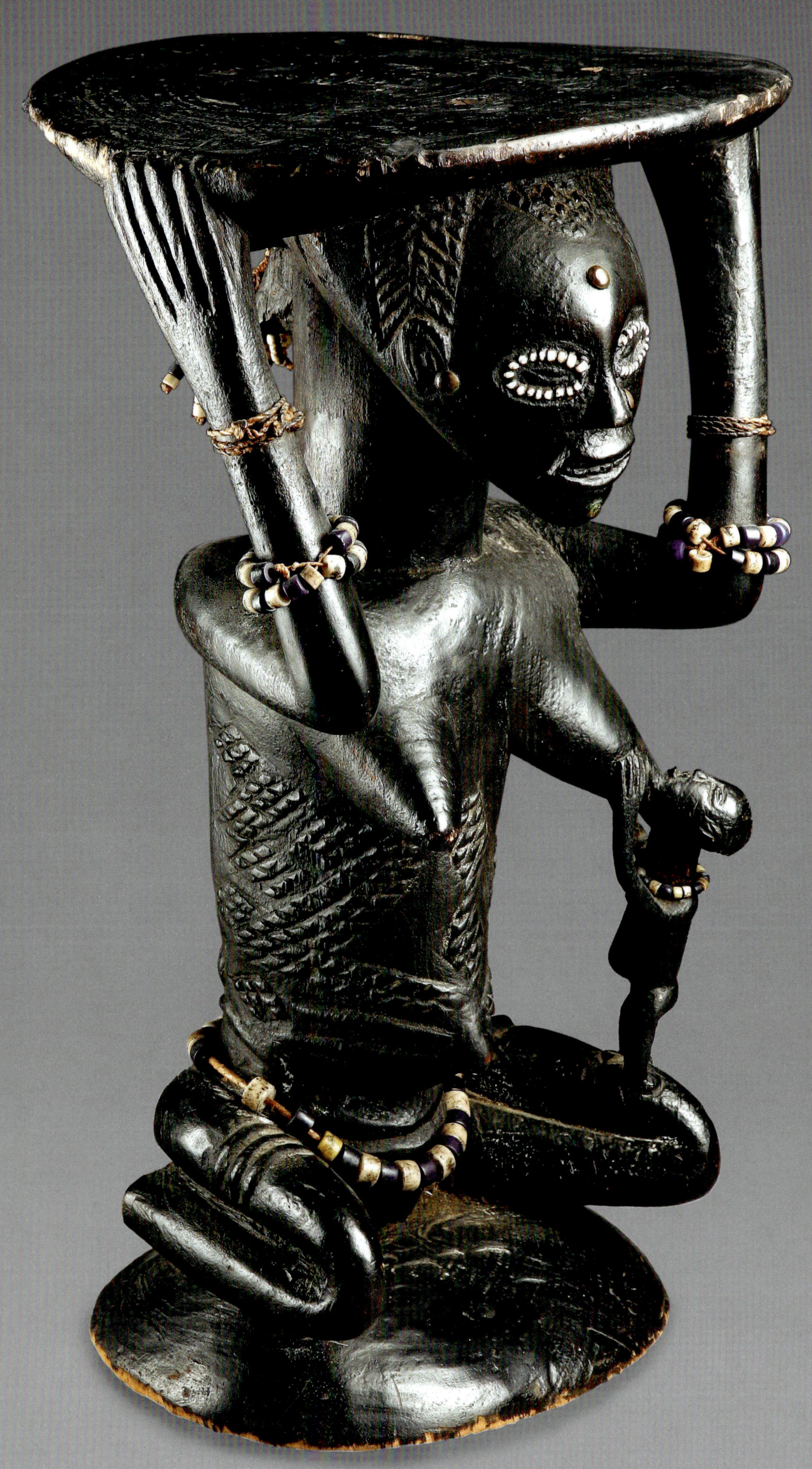

Royal Stool

Mother Earth, the Madonna, Isis, Great Mother, Cybele, Fertility Goddesses, Artemis, Guanyin, Coatlique, Universal Mother, Shasthi, Virgin Goddess, Demeter, Inanna, Black Virgin, Magna Mater— these and other personifications of motherhood and regeneration are embodied in hundreds of thousands of images across the world. The vast, almost unimaginable power of many such depictions depends on the merging of image and prototype—of an object, a thing, with its human or spiritual model—as David Freedberg has amply proven.[1] And at the same time, that fusion arises from the depth and strength of belief. God, often a female goddess, or a human female, is in and of the image, especially when properly prepared, decorated, consecrated, and physically established in a sacred place; the image is the locus of the spirit or deity or woman. The image often *is* the deity or the person. The unseen god or ancestor exists, is seen by supplicants as alive, is felt, and sometimes even has the ability to act. Image and prototype are mystically fused.

Stories and arts about cosmic and human origins are populated with female and male figures, the former often nursing or holding a child. Here we explore these images and the ideas surrounding them. Art forms, myths, and beliefs are linked together across vast reaches of time and space in countless nuanced styles and variations. If our main focus is maternity—the mother-and-child unit—its genesis in life, of course, is the sexual union of male and female, sometimes explicit in art, but usually not. We impute meaning to objects that we designate as works

of art displaying our themes.[2] The representations, these tangible things, often have no explicit ideas linked to them, so our starting point, invariably, is human biology: male fertilizes female who, after about nine months of pregnancy, gives birth to a child, whom the new mother may nurse at her breast. These biological facts are the same everywhere in the world. These three humans—father, mother, baby—constitute a type of nuclear family. Yet depictions of these facts in art are always products of culture that rarely exist simply to record biology. Rather, they fulfill needs of many sorts. They are culturally determined things, with a constellation of reasons for being, uses, functions, and meanings that may or may not be supported by local information. In the case of archaeological objects from the distant past, we rarely have much more to go on than the things, the images themselves, yet we nevertheless seek to place them within a network of ideas, beliefs, values, and activities. That is to say, we do not regard them as simple records of biology; we place them within human culture. When we come to objects informed by careful research and firm knowledge about local practices, we will see that biological explanations fall very short of understanding those local contexts and meanings, and that these three phenomena—works depicting the male-female couple, the mother-with-child, and the family—have a variety of cultural meanings that are not necessarily legible or perceptible in the artworks we are examining. So, reading back in time from thoroughly understood local settings, we must also conclude that earlier representations of sexual union, motherhood, and family almost certainly have a great variety of culturally generated meanings and uses almost entirely unknown to us and therefore very hard to discern. We must then be cautious when imputing meaning to them. Our journey with these objects will be roughly chronological, beginning in pre-historic eras and proceeding through the centuries up to the beginning of modern times.

Paleolithic female figures constitute a remarkable corpus of roughly 150 sculptures made between 40,000 and 9000 BCE, an enormously long period populated by bands of hunters and gatherers across a vast geographic Old World area that stretched from modern Spain to central Siberia. Rarely, if ever, were these people unified within what we call civilizations that embraced thousands of people in one socio-political organization. We illustrate some of the best known of these ample-fleshed females—often called "Venus" as an honorific but without a shred of local factual evidence of a named or even known deity—from Höhle Fels (Germany), Willendorf (Austria), Dolni Vestonice (Czech Republic), and Menton (Italy) (1–3). These venerable sculptures share several physical traits: overall corpulence, wide hips, large pendulous breasts, and small size. Some appear to be pregnant. Rarely are any facial features shown, while arms and legs are frequently minimized. The figures are fashioned from varied kinds of rock, as well as ivory and fired clay (terracotta). Virtually all scholars consider the figures sacred, often designating them earth mothers and/or goddesses associated with fertility, nurture, and regeneration: the perpetuation of the race. Yet all such suggestions of content and ritual use are conjectural—of course no one really knows what beliefs and ritual practices existed twenty or thirty thousand years ago. Meanings and uses are based entirely on the figures' appearances, along with the large quantity of quite similar small, portable images. Such numbers would *seem* to suggest some kind of broad cross-cultural and temporal meaning, and possibly cults that once featured these archetypal important women, or as Erich Neumann called them in his classic 1955 study, "Great Mothers."[3] Many writers, including some scholars, have long posited a cross-cultural "mother goddess" complex for these many prehistoric female figures, but recently this "goddess movement" has been challenged due to a striking lack of archaeological evidence.[4] And no myths survive from such a distant period of time. It seems very unlikely that small hunting and gathering bands of human beings would share beliefs about these female figures over the vast geographic range from which they come.

The female figure carved from ivory and found in a cave site called Hohle Fels in 2008, dated to ca. 40,000–35,000 BCE, is the earliest undisputed depiction of a human being in history (1). While the figure is headless, there is a small perforated protrusion where her neck would

1 **Venus of Höhle Fels**	**2** **Venus of Dolni Vestonice**	**3** **Venus of Menton**
Unearthed in 2008 in Höhle Fels, a cave Near Schelklingen, Germany 40,000 – 35,000 BCE Mammoth ivory 2.4 in., 6 cm Prehistoric Museum of Blaubeuren, Germany	Paleolithic settlement of Dolni Vestonice, Moravia, Czech Republic 27,000 – 23,000 BCE Terracotta 4.4 × 1.7in., 11.18 × 4.32 cm Moravian Museum, Brno, Czech Republic	Barma Grande Cave, Grimaldi, Wintimiglia, Italy Upper Paleolithic, 24,000 – 19,000 BCE Yellow steatite (soapstone) 1.89 in., 4.8 cm National Archeological Museum, Saint-Germain-en-Laye, France

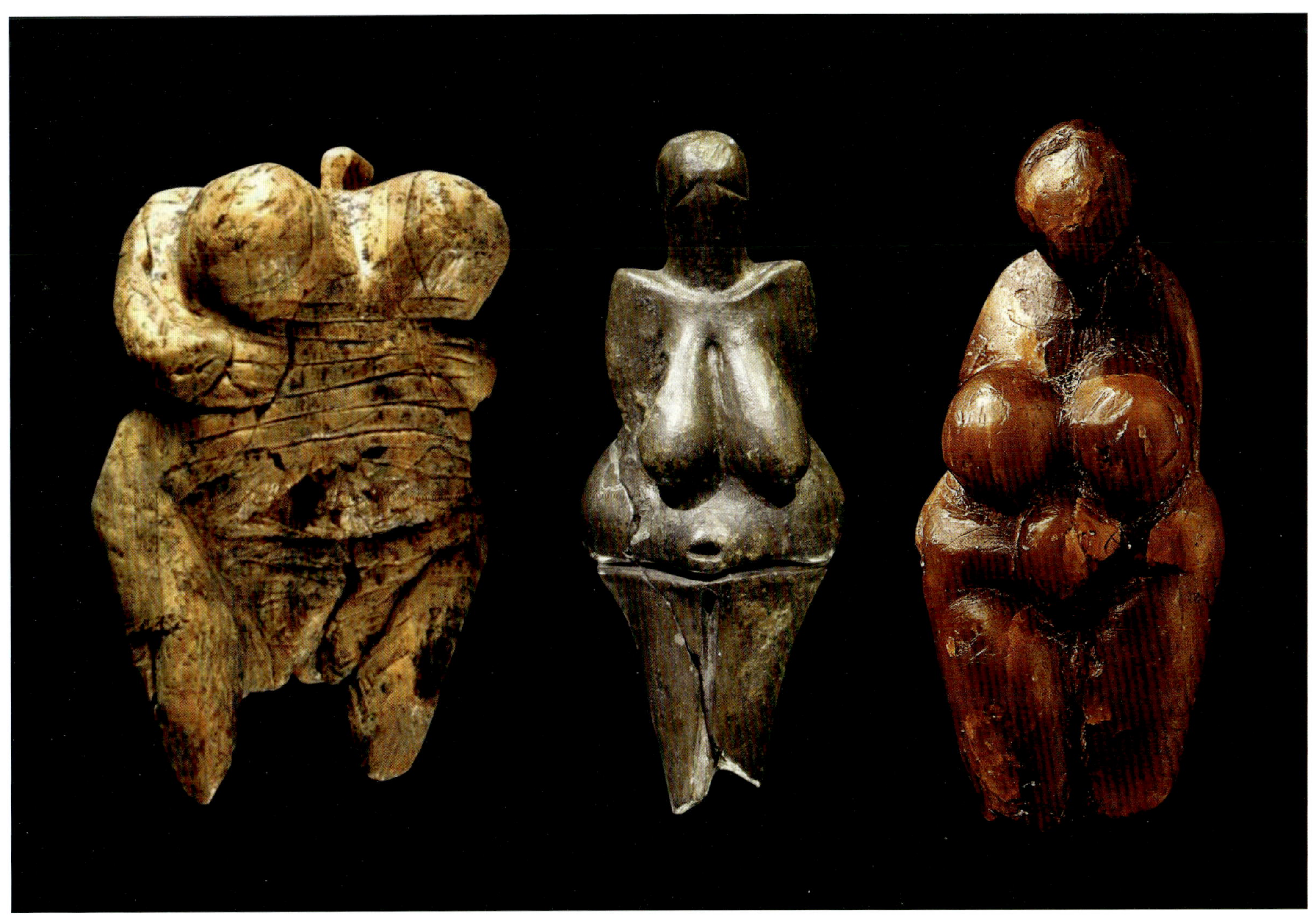

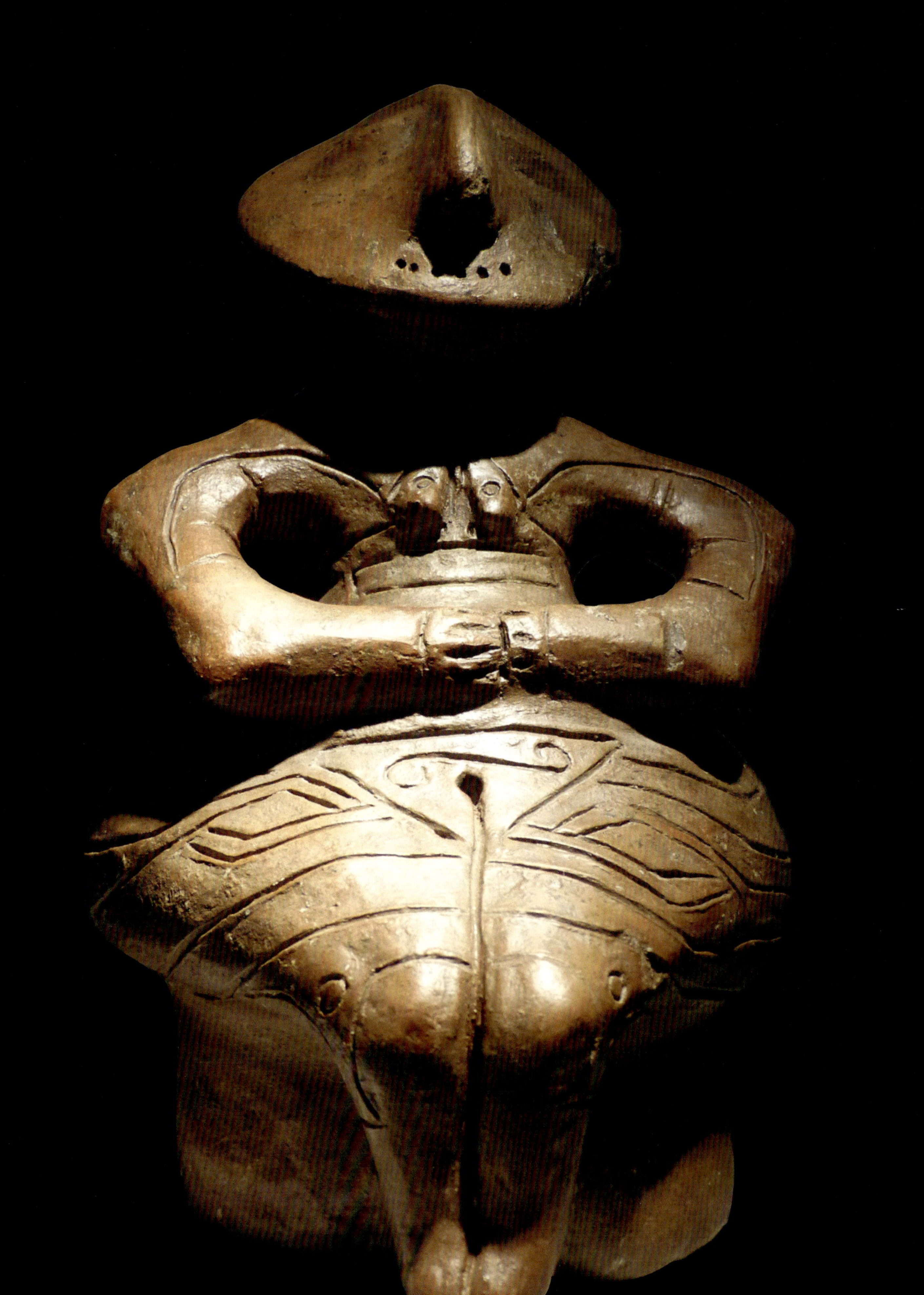

4 **Lady of Pazardzhik**

Pazardzhik, Bulgaria
Neolithic period, Karanovo VI culture,
4500 BCE
Terracotta
Natural History Museum,
Vienna, Austria

be, suggesting that the sculpture may have been worn as an amulet. Her large abdomen also suggests pregnancy, a condition paralleled in other female figures in this large corpus. The best known of these corpulent ladies is the so-called Venus of Willendorf, sculpted of limestone, dating to ca. 30,000–25,000 BCE, and named after her find spot (Handler, Introduction, p. 12). Radically obese with large breasts and wide hips, yet with negligible arms and no feet, she has a braided cap or hairstyle over what might have been a face. Like all her sister-sculptures, the use and meaning of this sculpture are unknown yet perhaps had to do with fertility and a possible matriarchal cult. The fact that fewer male images come from the same areas enhances the probability of a widespread reverence for females, possibly mothers, as the only gender that can conceive and bear children, surely a mystical process then, as it is today despite the understandings of science. The four different female figures illustrated here are a small sample from more than 150 analogous Paleolithic examples, many found in Europe and a few farther east, and one as far as Siberia. None of them can definitively be called a goddess, although most have uncritically been so labeled. Perhaps we are safe in assuming the images were sacred, but much more than that is only speculation.

The distribution of other, later female figures, often mothers with children, is also very wide in time and space, with a greater variety of forms and, most probably, disparate original purposes and meanings. Cyprus, Crete, and other European sites, the ancient Near East, predynastic Egypt, and the Indus Valley of south Asia are among the origin sites of these mostly female statuettes. Though the dates of many remain uncertain, the simplest sculptures may be the oldest, dating from the sixth millennium BCE to a few centuries before the start of the Common Era, the period known as Neolithic. From ca. 4500 BCE comes an apparently pregnant female terracotta seated figure from central Bulgaria with very broad hips and buttocks and small breasts, called a vegetation or fertility goddess (**4**).[5] She has incised patterns suggesting tattoos and a prominent pubic triangle also set off by incising, but the circumstances of her discovery and hence her meaning and purpose are not really known. The earth and women as mothers are logical constructs as agriculture developed and began to flourish in this period. Many cultures see human and agricultural fertility as similar or nearly the same, and the same rituals in some cultures encourage both. Analogous wide-hipped, standing terracotta females, some holding children and others holding their breasts, come from Cyprus and date to about 2500–1450 BCE (**5**). Many have especially prominent incised pubic triangles, as if to stress their female sexuality and thus perhaps fertility. Again, they were probably sacred, but we cannot call them goddesses with any assurance. They might have aided fertility, but

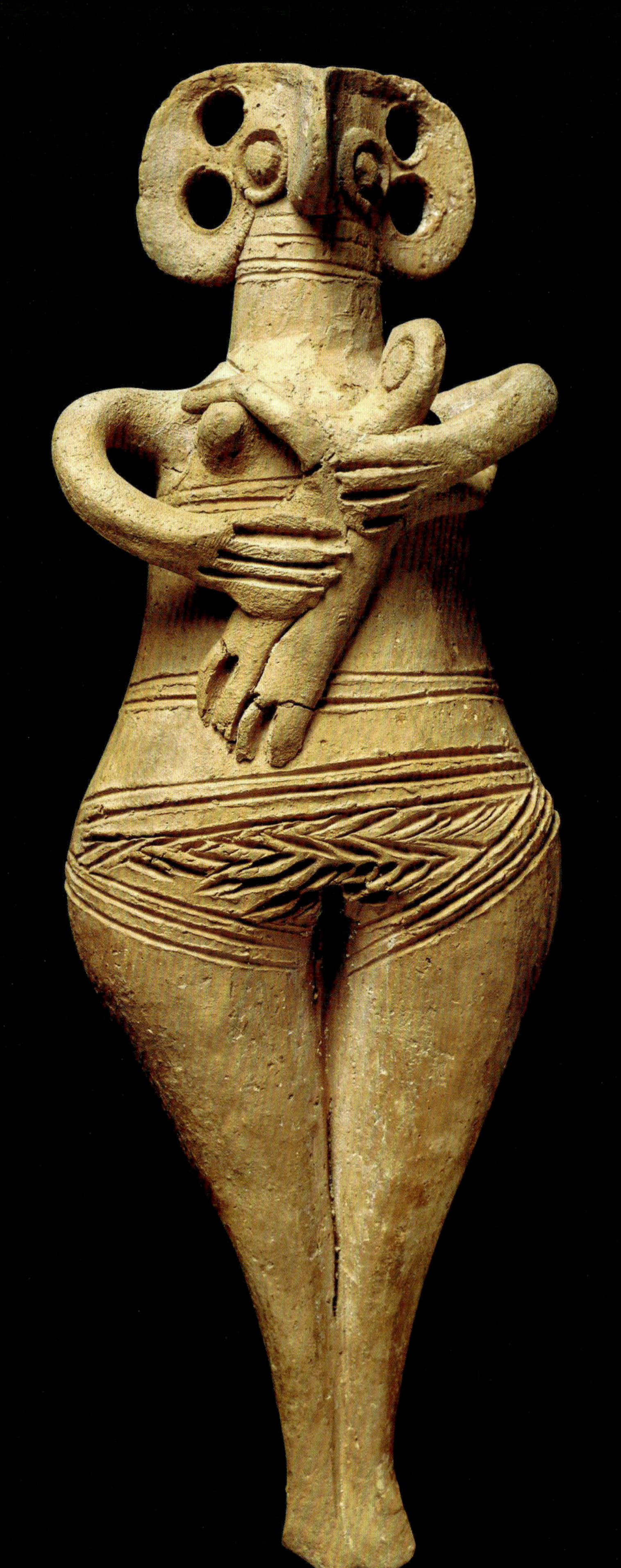

5 Female Figure Holding Infant

Cyprus
Late Cypriot II, 1450 – 1200 BCE
Terracotta
7.6 × 1.7 × 2.4 in., 19.20 × 4.20 × 6.20 cm
British Museum, London, England

**6 Disk Pin Showing a Woman
Giving Birth Between
Two Antelopes**

Luristan, Iran
Iranian iron age, 1500 – 650 BCE
Bronze
Louvre Museum, Paris, France

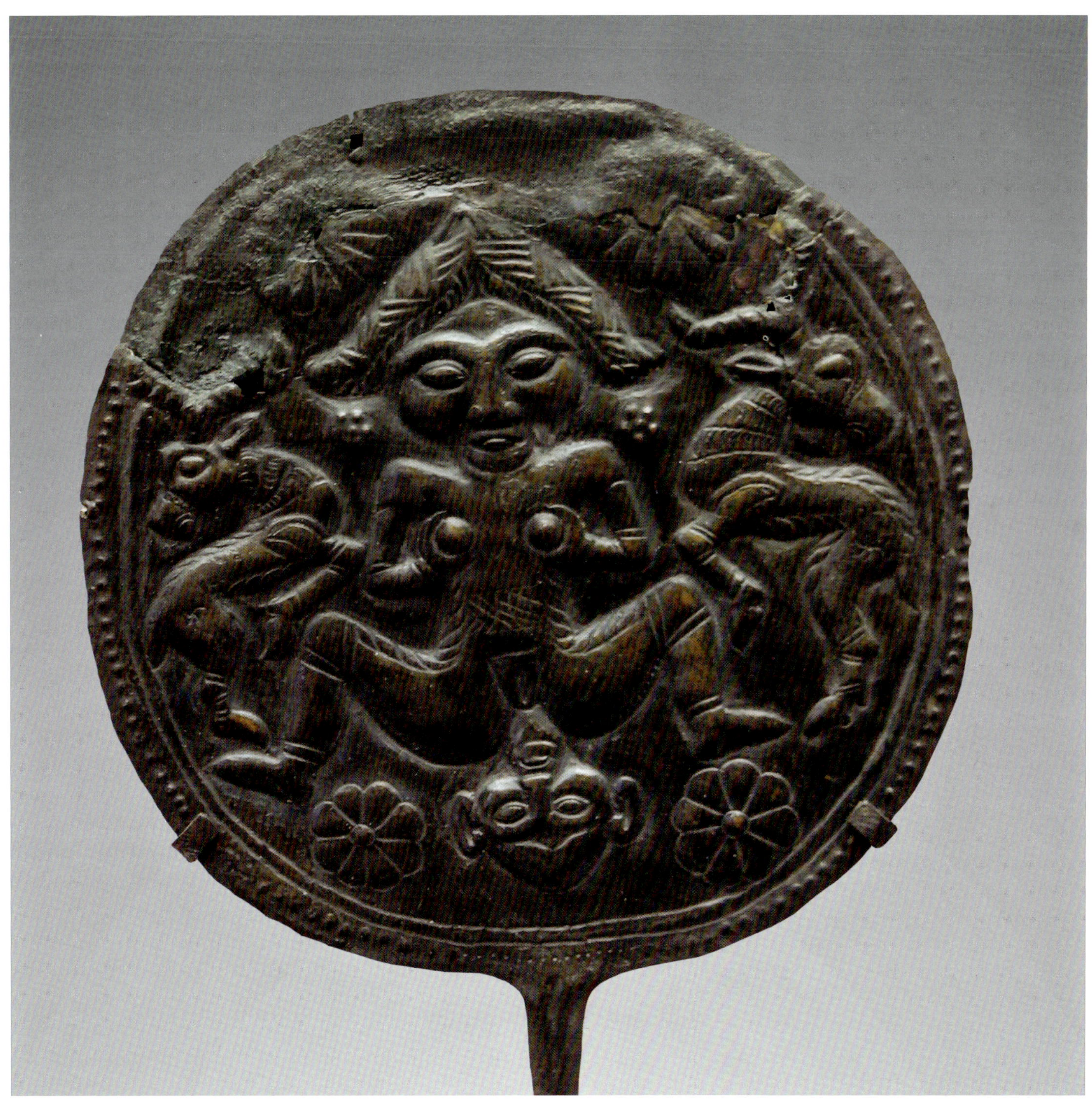

they might also have been girls' playthings, dolls, or servants to accompany the dead.

Two quite different bronzes from Luristan (Iran-Persia, ca. 1500–650 BCE) again suggest female abundance. A standing sculpture of a slender woman holds her breasts; bird heads sprout from her shoulders. Several other bronzes show broad-hipped female figures controlling animals. Images interpreted as Inanna or Ishtar, the Mesopotamian (a region in present-day Iraq) goddess of fertility, love, and war—known from Sumerian (a Bronze Age civilization) myths—show her holding her breasts. The same breast-offering gesture is seen on a Luristan circular relief plaque, where the woman's legs are spread as she is in the act of giving birth to a human head (**6**). Holding or offering breasts is often interpreted as nurturing, implying an abundance of milk, but that gesture could have other meanings. The graphic depiction of birth must surely have had an important local meaning not yet deciphered for this era with any certainty. From the Sumerian urban complex Ur, also in Mesopotamia, comes a series of slender females, some of whom nurse a child (**7**). Many scholars have interpreted these as mother goddesses, a conclusion drawn in part from the relative absence of male figures. A final, later example from the Hittite Empire (a fourteenth-century BCE civilization in present-day Iraq), dated to the fourteenth to thirteenth century BCE, is a more detailed gold casting of a seated mother with a child seated on her lap between her

arms (**8**). This frontal image is interpreted as possibly the sun goddess Arinna, known from later New Kingdom Hittite (ca. 1190 BCE) mythology, and also referred to as a mother, earth goddess, and "queen of the land." She protected the king and kingdom as the chief deity in an extensive state pantheon and had children with her husband, a weather god. The halo-like crescent on her head is possibly a solar disc.

A quite different yet equally evocative terracotta female dated to ca. 6500 BCE and interpreted as giving birth comes from the site of çatalhöyük in what is now Turkey (**9**). In her corpulence, she reminds us of the Paleolithic females, yet her seated position between two felines (the head of one was missing and is restored in the photograph, as is the woman's head) is more elaborate and suggests royal or at least elevated status. This headless figure was recovered from a grain bin, once more suggesting a parallel between agricultural and human fertility and abundance. And farther east, from the extensive urban site of Mohenjo Daro in the Indus Valley (in what is now Pakistan), come several more terracotta female figures with ample breasts and wide hips, also interpreted by many, but with scant evidence, as goddesses. They date to ca. 4500 BCE. All the Neolithic and Bronze Age female images shown here—and this is only a small sampling from a much larger corpus— are associated with earth, maternity, and fertility cults by many scholars, so my skepticism in the absence of firm empirical data and clear written records may be misplaced.

  Lizard-Headed Nude Woman Nursing a Child

Ur, Mesopotamia
4000 BCE
Terracotta
Iraq Museum, Baghdad

  Seated Goddess with a Child

Hittite Empire, Central Anatolia
1300 – 1200 BCE
Gold
1 11/16 × 11/16 × 3/4 in., 4.3 × 1.7 × 1.9 cm
Metropolitan Museum of Modern Art, New York
Gift of Norbert Schimmel Trust, 1989

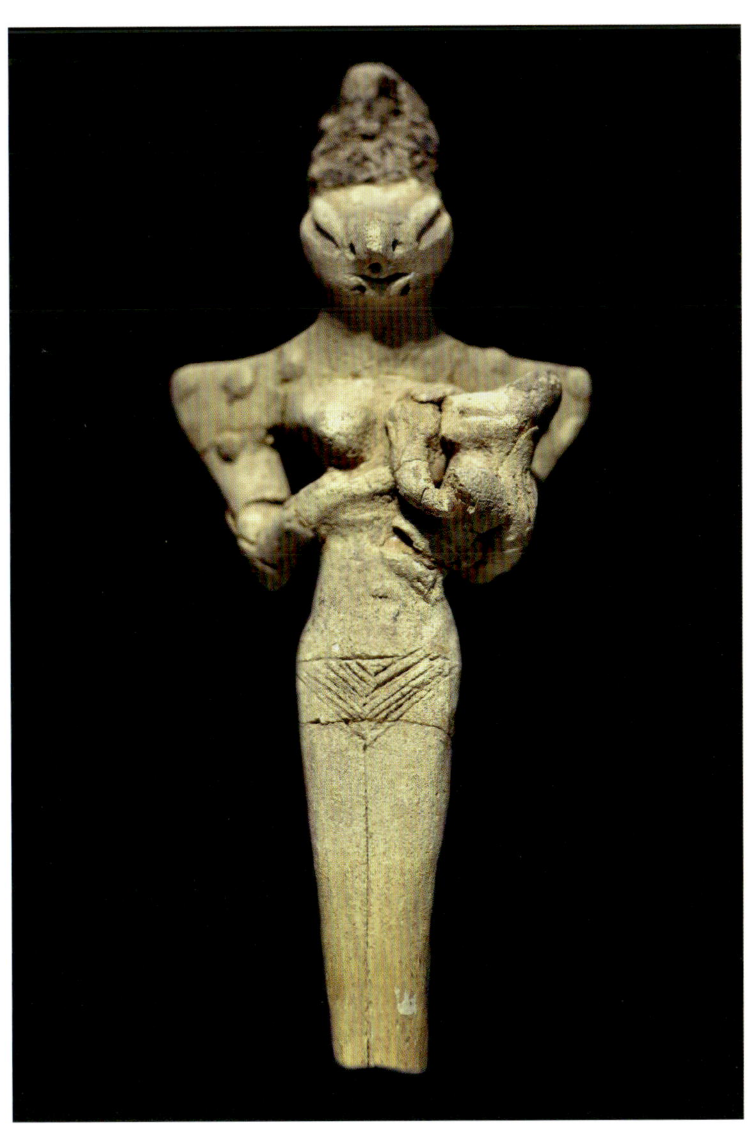

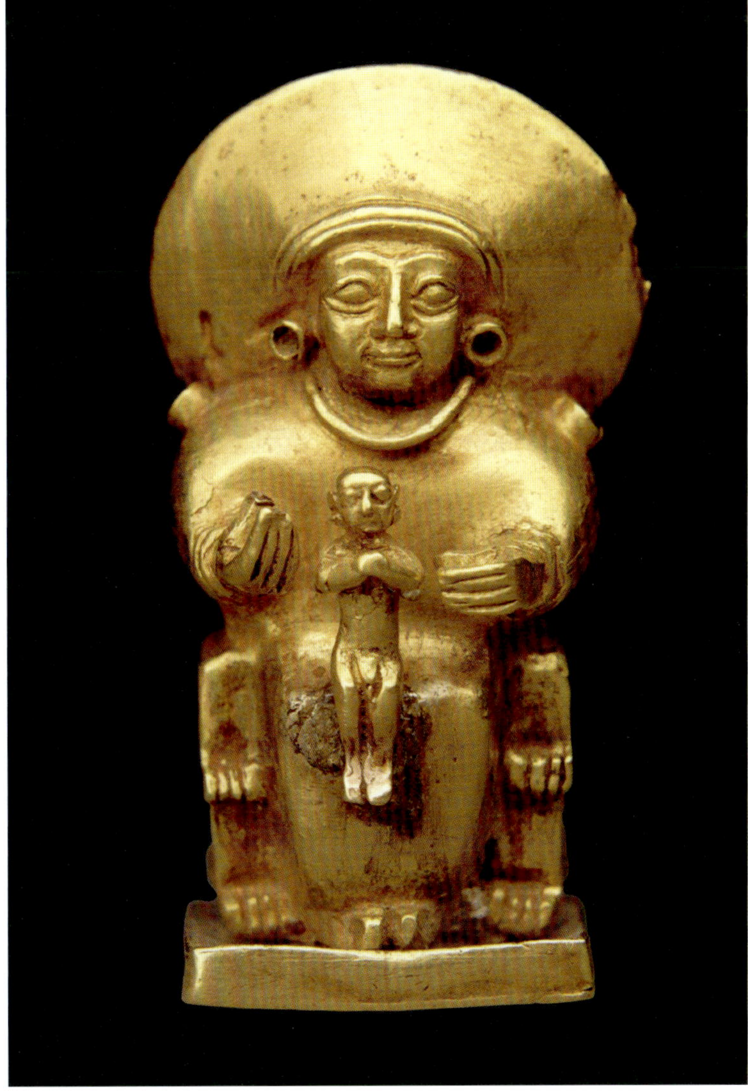

9   Seated Woman of Çatalhöyük

The head and the proper left handrest are restored
Çatalhöyük, Turkey
Neolithic period, 6500 BCE
Terracotta
Museum of Anatolian Civilizations,
Ankara, Turkey

10   Two-Figure Female

Cycladic culture, Cyclades
3200 – 2200 BCE
Marble
18.35 in., 46.6 cm
Private Collection

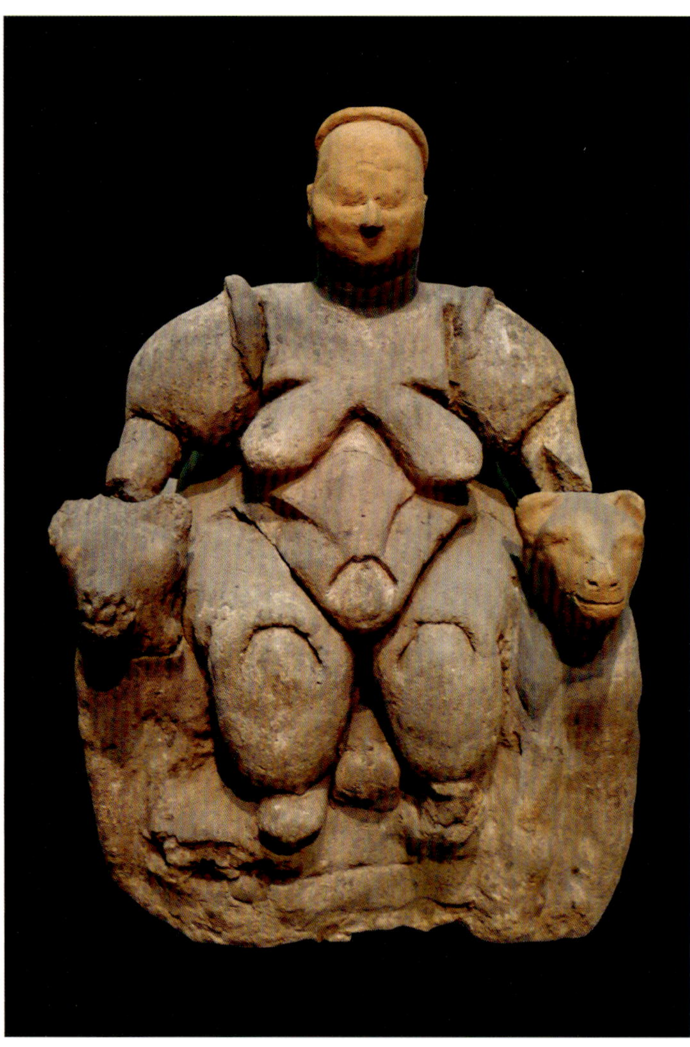

Still, I am reluctant to call any female figure a goddess when sufficient evidence is lacking.

Another, somewhat anomalous version of a possible maternity figure is the marble sculpture of a pregnant woman with a small, identical yet not pregnant figure standing atop her head (**10**). This is the only known image among many hundreds of white marble female Cycladic sculptures that can be interpreted as a maternity figure, although several other female images in this tradition appear to be pregnant, suggesting that fertility and birth were among the reasons why at least some of these fine sculptures were made in Greece and its many islands between 4500 and 2200 BCE. The fact that female images far outnumber male images suggests but does not prove that the figures may have aided fertility in some way. Our sculpture dates from the middle of this period and was almost certainly recovered from a grave of a person of some status, where most smaller Cycladic sculptures were found in the relatively few controlled Cycladic excavations conducted by trained archaeologists.[6]

Indeed, the fact that this and many of the other prehistoric artworks shown here were interred in graves tells us something about the people who made them. Whether meant to accompany or guide deceased persons to the hereafter, to be gifts to or representations of spirits or gods, to serve as symbols of renewal in their life after death, or to protect or help them in some way, the images

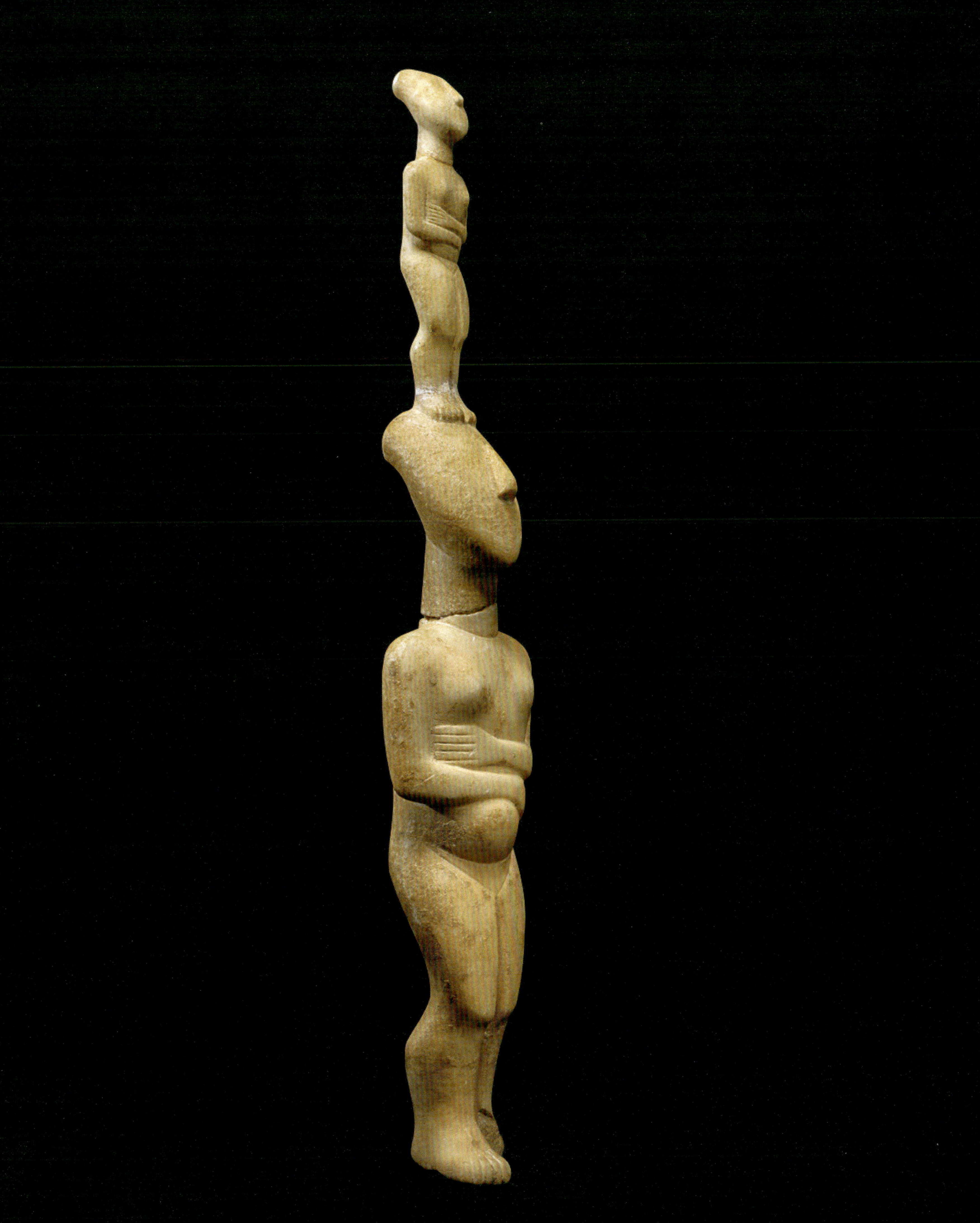

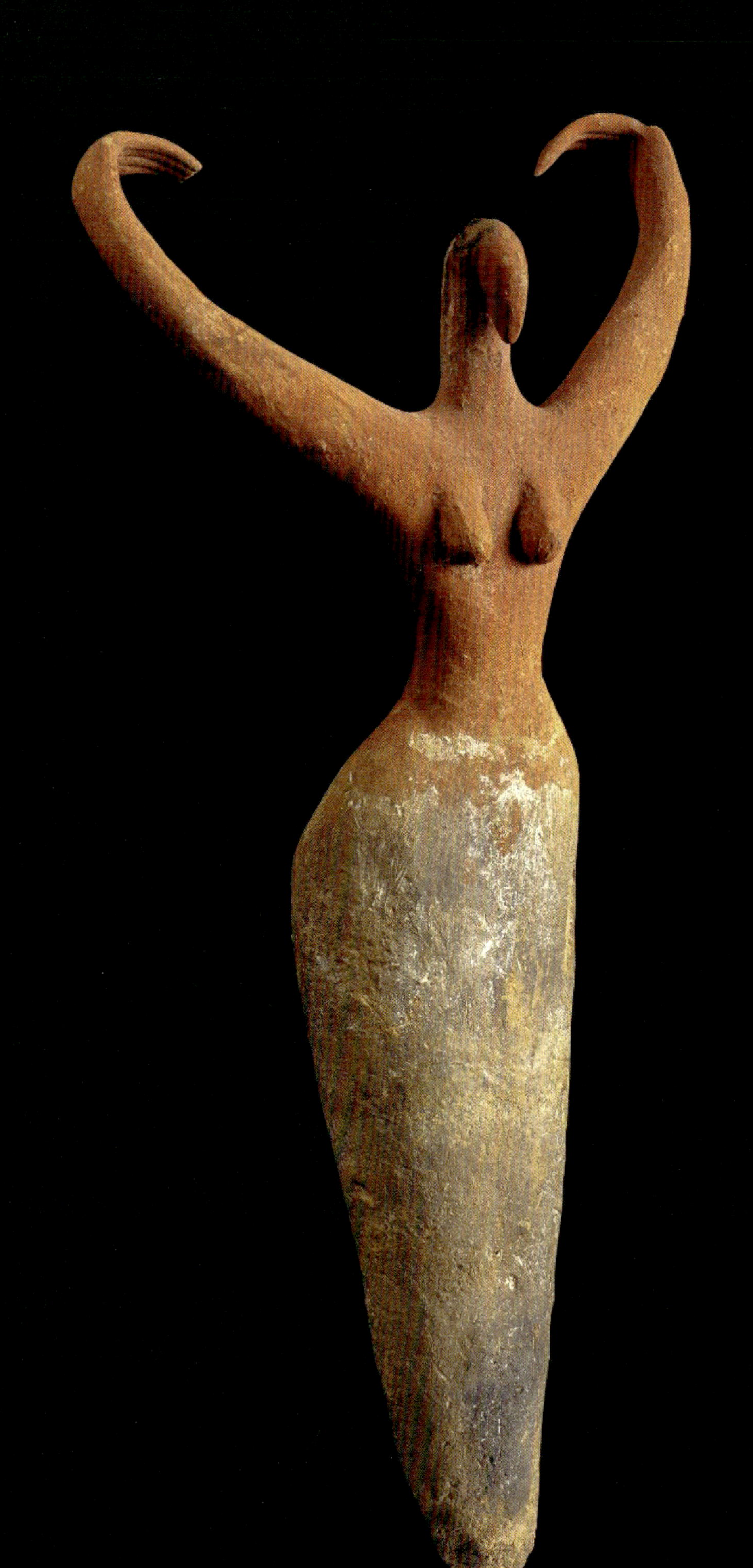

11   Female Figure

Egypt
Predynastic, Naqada IIa period,
3500 – 3400 BCE
Terracotta
11 ½ × 5 ½ × 2 ¼ in.,
29.2 × 14 × 5.7 cm
Brooklyn Museum, New York

fulfilled an affirmative purpose for their people. When objects are carefully, artistically crafted in labor-intensive, intractable materials such as stone, ivory, or cast metal, we can be sure that they were considered both precious and necessary, even essential, to their makers and owners, just as they remain valuable to us many centuries later, often because we are impressed and moved by their artistic quality. When the art forms are maternity figures, it is only logical to suppose they had something to do with the importance of motherhood, childbirth, and children, as many such images from historic and recent times are documented to do. On the other hand, Christian maternity images—the Virgin Mary with her son, Jesus— were almost never made to accompany the dead even though many surely have done so. Below we will explore some of their reasons for being and some of their settings.

A final pair of predynastic Egyptian figures are quite different from each other: one a slender yet broad-hipped terracotta female with a bird-like head and arms raised in a delicate curve (**11**), the other a spare, simplified, nearly abstract rendering of a female in silver and gold (**12**). The black, oxidized silver of the latter is highlighted with contrasting gold accents: breasts, booties, and four circular decorations on the abstracted head that are probably eyes and ear ornaments. This female figure, described by curators at the Boston Museum of Fine Arts as the great Anatolian mother goddess, more than likely served wealthy people, as evidenced by its

precious materials alone. The terracotta, one of many similar examples, was likely made for people of lesser status. These early figures lead us into Egyptian dynastic eras when rich and extensive recorded mythology and hieroglyphic texts intersect with varied artistic renderings, resulting in a more satisfying body of credible, explicit information on mother deities and associated burial and ritual practices.

The ancient Egyptian deity Isis is a commanding mother goddess, perhaps the first to be fully understood in her well-documented complexity. The interpretive lore surrounding Isis is extensive, as is that of her husband/ brother, Osiris, and their son, Horus (**13**). Egyptian mythology has the sister/brother, Isis/Osiris pair as the progeny of the sky-goddess Nut and the earth god Geb, establishing an equivalence of cosmic, spiritual, and human birth; Isis then maintains the mystical connections between the spiritual and human realms, and indeed she is credited with giving birth to all the other gods as well as to human beings. The qualities ascribed to Isis became critical for the success of Egyptian social, economic, political, and spiritual life for nearly four millennia, as captured in the rhapsodic words of Isis scholar R.E. Witt: "There, in the beginning was Isis. Oldest of the old, she was the goddess from whom all Becoming arose. She was the Great Lady—Mistress of the Two Lands of Egypt, Mistress of shelter, Mistress of Heaven, Mistress of the House of Life, Mistress of the Word of god. She was

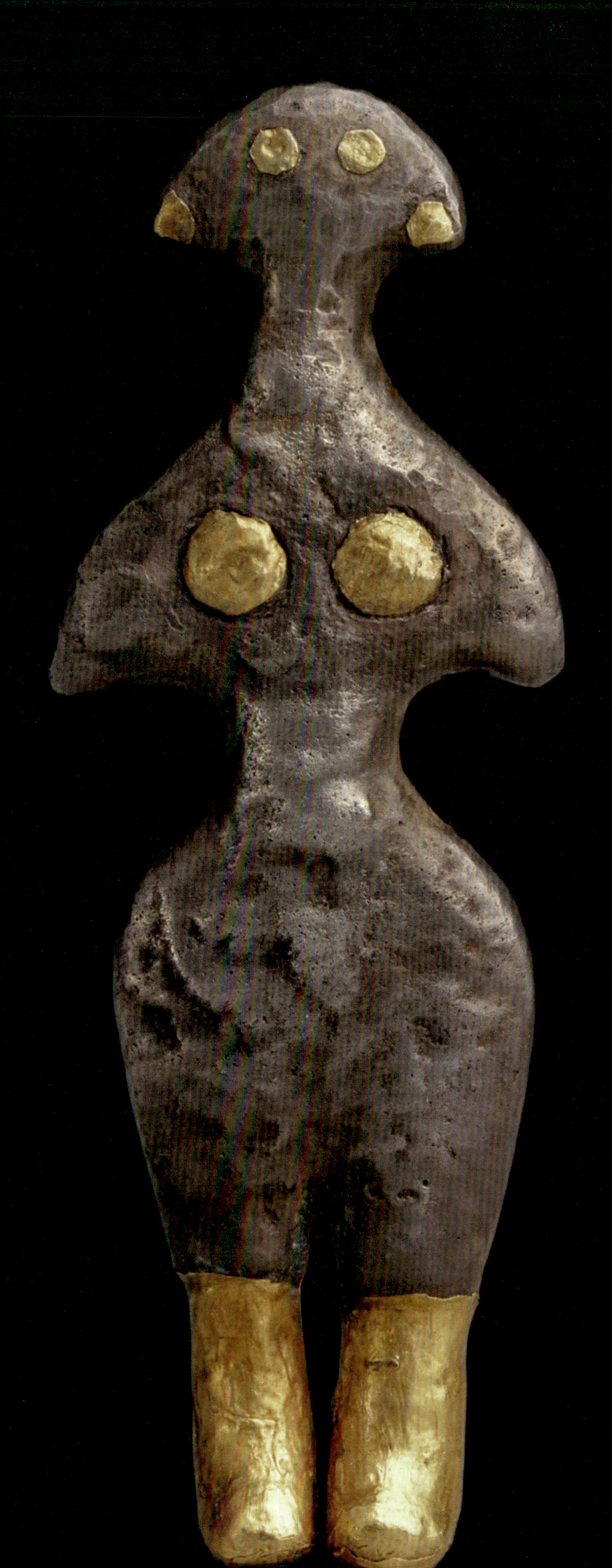

  Figurine of a Goddess

Near Eastern, Anatolian
Early Bronze Age, 2500 – 2300 BCE
Silver and gold
5 in., 12.7 cm
Museum of Fine Arts, Boston
Anonymous gift in memory of
James Bishop Peabody

the Unique. In all her great and wonderful works she was a wiser magician and more excellent than any other god."[7]

On a cosmic scale, Isis separated earth from sky and revealed the stars' paths; she also invented and presided over seafaring, over the winds, and over thunder.[8] A magician and culture-bringer, she is referred to as the first lady of the sky and queen of the underworld.[9] Her tears magically caused the annual flooding of the River Nile, enabling agriculture to flourish. As fertility goddess and mother of the first pharaoh, Horus, yet known also as a virgin, Isis was the mother of all subsequent pharaohs, who were seen as incarnations of Horus. Her hieroglyph was a throne, so all the pharaohs sat upon her lap; she was their mother and figuratively, their throne. She introduced spinning flax and weaving to produce garments and canvas sails for boats. She fostered the growth of barley and thus the brewing of beer and the baking of bread. She was a savior, protector of all children, and a skilled healer who discovered the mysteries of birth, life, and death; she raised Osiris from the dead. Her miracles are legion. She was considered the ideal wife and mother, and the preeminent goddess of all Egyptian families. Isis was also the avatar of many animals, including the asp (cobra), falcon, ibis, gazelle, dog, crocodile, and vulture. Thousands of mother-and-child icons, both large and small, of Isis and her son Horus exist; she is often shown nursing, as in our fine gilt bronze example from the Cairo Museum (**14**). Such images were placed on household

and community altars, and hundreds have been found in burials. They are in varied materials: gilded bronze, gold, faience (glazed ceramic ware), different stones, and they were undoubtedly made of wood as well. Very small ones were personal amulets or charms. The number of these images and the varied contexts in which they have been found are testimony to the manifold powers of the Isis cult (and/or the cults of related deities) over broad regions and a long period of time. Isis maternity images assuredly influenced later icons of the Virgin Mary and Christ in many ways, in both two- and three-dimensional artworks and as objects of worship on domestic and community altars and shrines.

While Isis, Osiris, and Horus are a storied nuclear family, ancient Egyptian art features many other families, especially those of its leaders. Pharaoh Amenophis (also known as Akhenaten, 1372–1336 BCE) and Queen Nefertiti appear with their three children in an elegant, Amarna-style sandstone relief, to cite one charming example among many (**15**). All five figures are quite informally and actively posed; they display motion along with familial affection. This shallow relief presents a graphic picture of domestic, even anecdotal family life. In contrast to the intimacy and casual informality of this relief is the stiff, hieratic, three-dimensionality of King Menkaura, the Goddess Hathor (Isis by another name), and the deified Hare nome (an anthropomorphized depiction of an administrative division of ancient Egypt, **16**). This rigidly

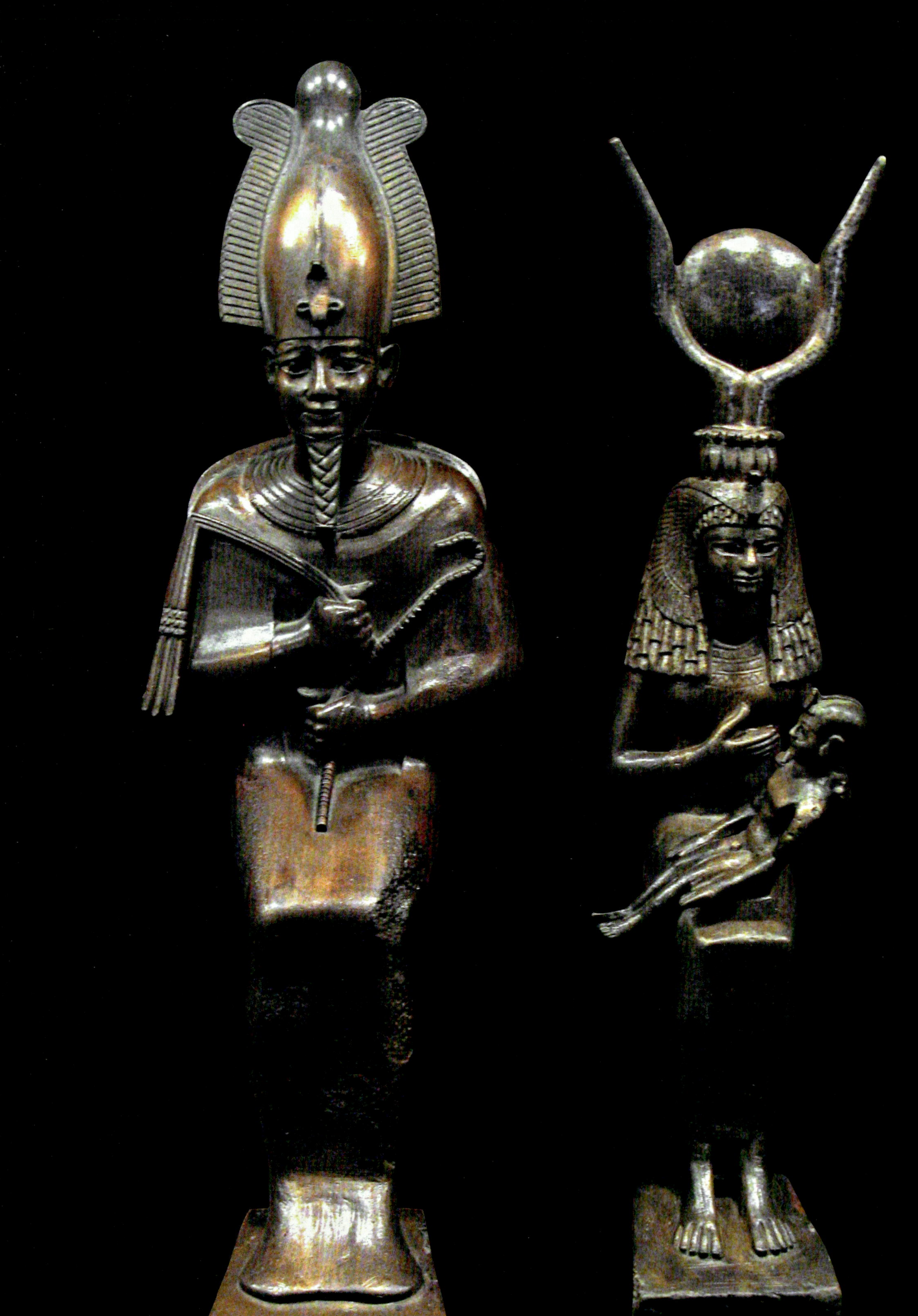

13 Osiris and Isis with the Infant Horus

Egypt
Dynasty 26, 664 – 525 BCE
Bronze
15 in., 38.1 cm
Hermitage Museum,
St. Petersburg, Russia

14 Statuette of Isis Breastfeeding Infant Horus

From the treasure of Tutankhamun
Egypt
New Kingdom, Dynasty 18,
1550 – 1292 BCE
Gold and silver
23.62 × 34.65 in., 60 × 88 cm
Egyptian Museum, Cairo

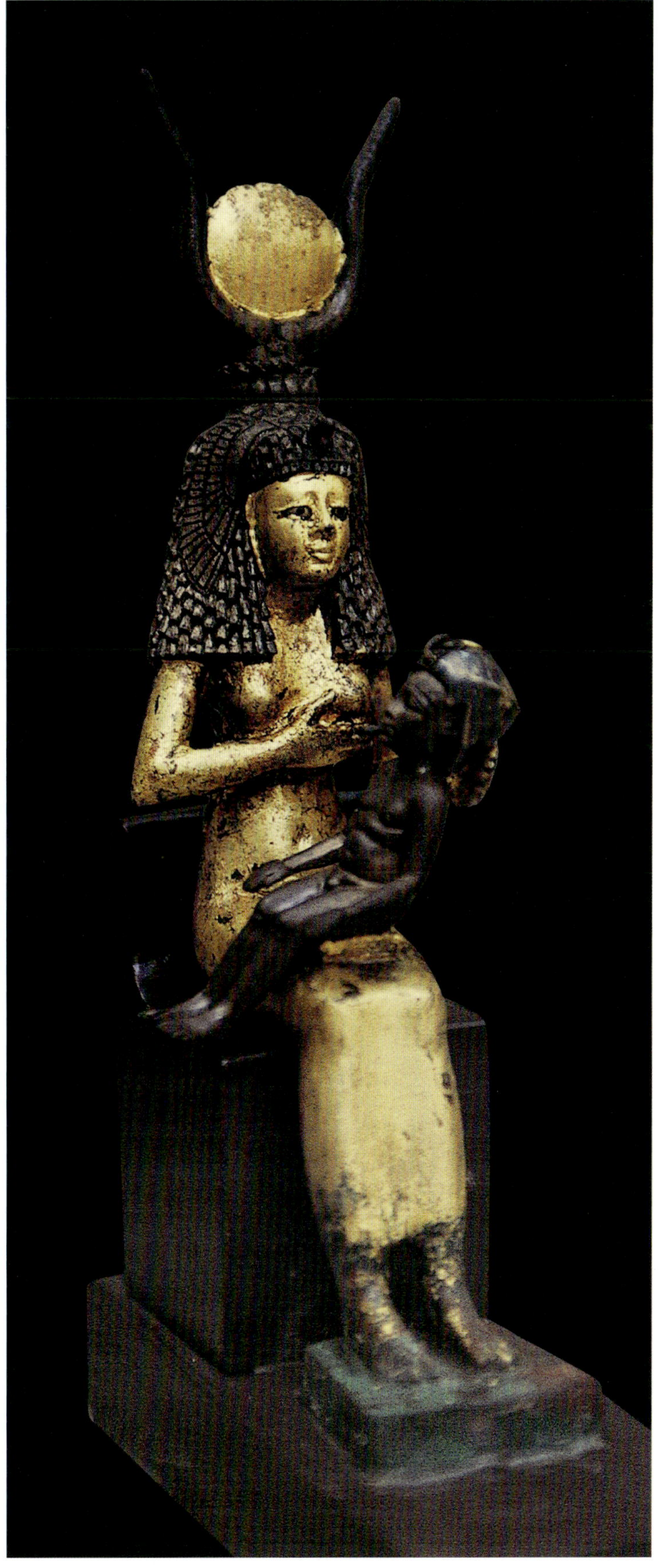

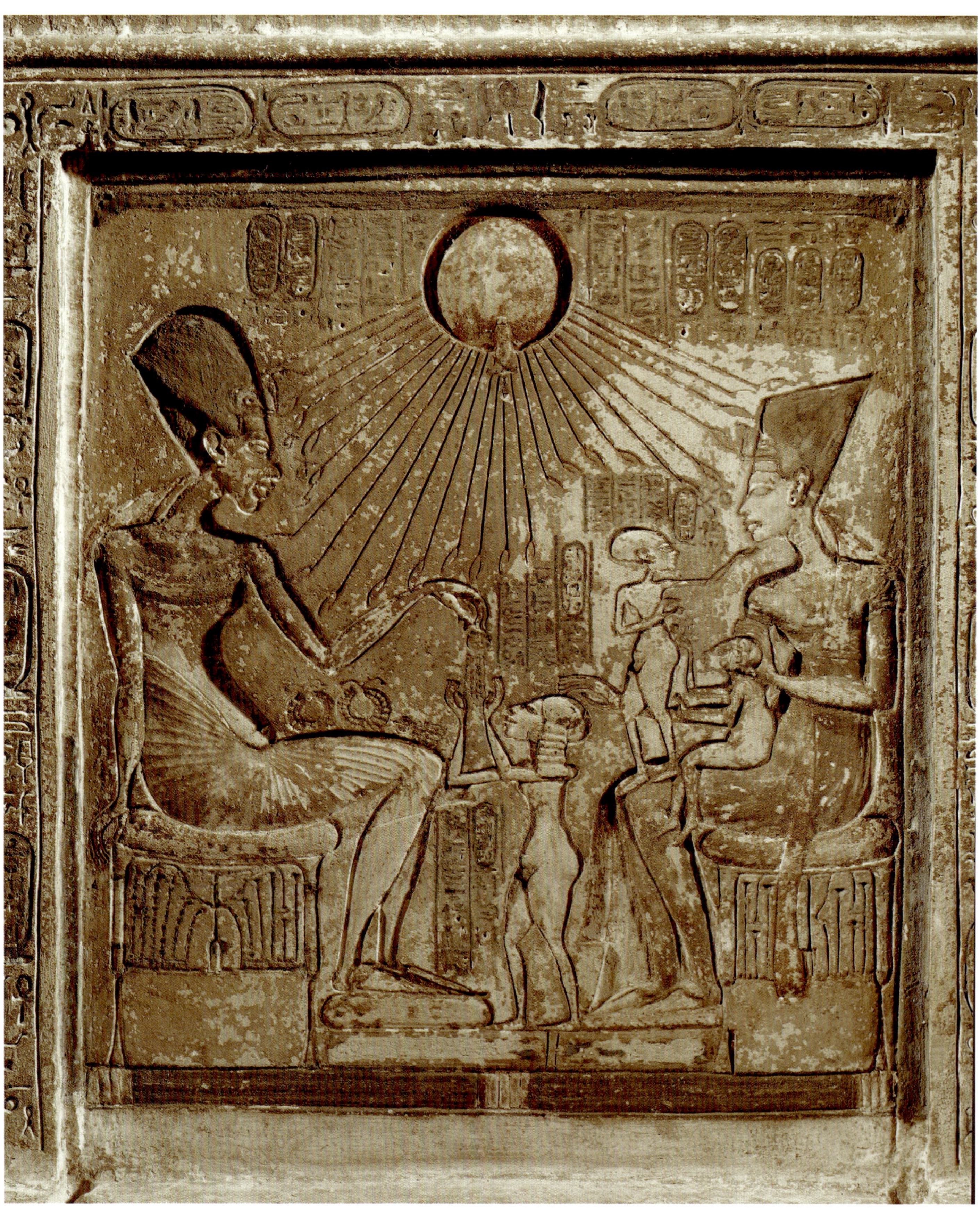

frontal sculpture, in hard greywacke sandstone, shows the mother deity Hathor central and larger than the other figures, with her left arm embracing the king to her left (the viewer's right), and a third figure, suggesting a family of leaders.

Isis was merged with the Virgin Mary in Rome and early Christianity. Under many different names, the pagan cult of Isis spread widely in space, across North Africa, to Greece and Rome, and beyond. In Greece, Isis became identified with the virgin Demeter/Diana. The mother goddess Cybele, first worshipped as a black stone, reached Rome from Anatolia in Asia Minor (now part of Turkey), where these goddesses fused with the Virgin Mary in early and Coptic (indigenous Egyptian) Christianity. That Ephesus (in present-day Turkey) was said to be where the Virgin Mary spent her later years helps link this Greek and Roman goddess with still later images of Mary. At Ephesus in 431, Mary was proclaimed the Mother of God.[10] The several statues of the multi-breasted Diana of Ephesus signal the plurality of types, names, and ascribed powers of many images with claims as mother goddesses. A second-century marble sculpture of Diana has a black head, neck, hands, and feet (of bronze), signaling Diana as precursor of Black Virgin sculptures found in many European shrines and churches (**17**). The Roman deity Diana is indistinguishable from the Greek Artemis, a woodland or nature deity, mistress of forest animals, and maiden of the hunt. Both were seen as fertility deities

and were invoked to help with conception and childbirth. Both protected and educated children. Artemis was worshipped as a moon goddess; as the fertile, productive powers of the earth; and as the virgin mother of all life. At Diana's shrine at Roman Aricia (Italy), worshipers left terracotta votive images of babies and wombs. In the second century, Cybele was the supreme deity in Lyon (now France), where a Black Virgin cult flourishes to this day,[11] and the same Roman Cybele was replaced by the Black Virgin at Rocamadour (also France), and the Greek virgin goddess Anath was succeeded by the Black Virgin, the Daurade of Toulouse (France) (**18**). Many Black Virgins are ascribed miraculous powers, among them the ability to confer fertility on women and raise the dead, echoes of the miracles of Isis.

The Virgin Mary assumed many attributes of Isis, Artemis/Diana, Demeter, Cybele, and other deities in the beliefs, rituals, and iconography of the late Roman Empire between about 200 and 450. Eventually, pagan Isis cults (and others) waned or were stamped out, but her influence prevailed in some places until the fourteenth century of our era, and images of Isis (and other female deities) morphed into the Christian Virgin Mary, the Christ child, and not infrequently into Black Virgins.[12]

The miracles of Isis continue with early Christian, Coptic, and medieval images of the Virgin Mary. A wealthy Egyptian family sought immortality from the nursing Mary depicted in the Egyptian Red Monastery (**19**) with

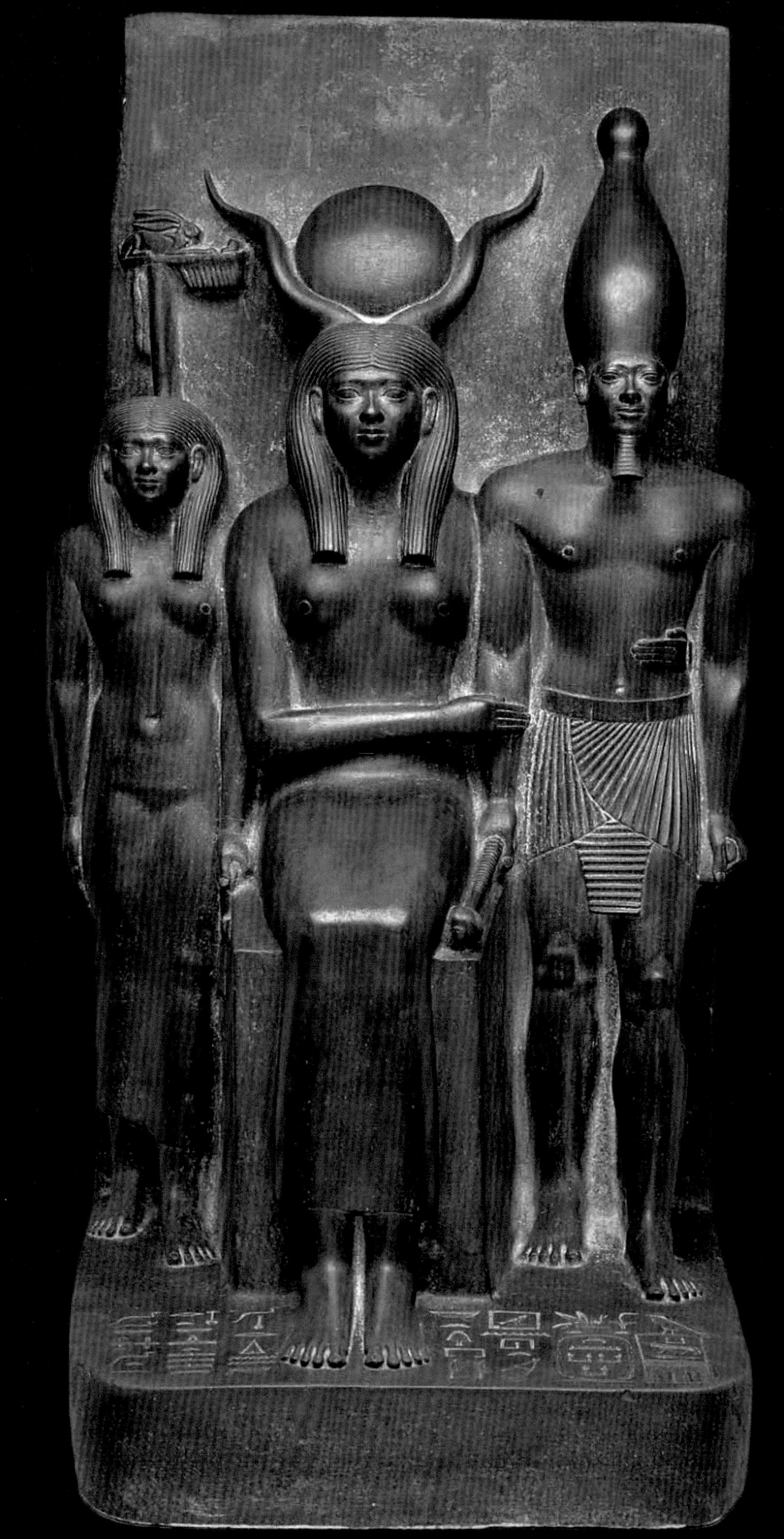

16 **King Menkaura, the Goddess Hathor, and the Deified Hare Nome**

Menkaura Valley temple, Giza, Egypt
Old Kingdom, Dynasty 4,
2490 – 2472 BCE
Greywacke sandstone
17 ⅛ × 33 ¼ × 19 ⁵⁄₁₆ in.,
43.5 × 84.5 × 49 cm
Museum of Fine Arts, Boston
Harvard University, Boston Museum
of Fine Arts Expedition, 1908

17 **Diana of Ephesus**

Greece
150 – 200 CE
Bronze and alabaster
51.18 in., 130 cm
National Archaeological Museum,
Naples, Italy

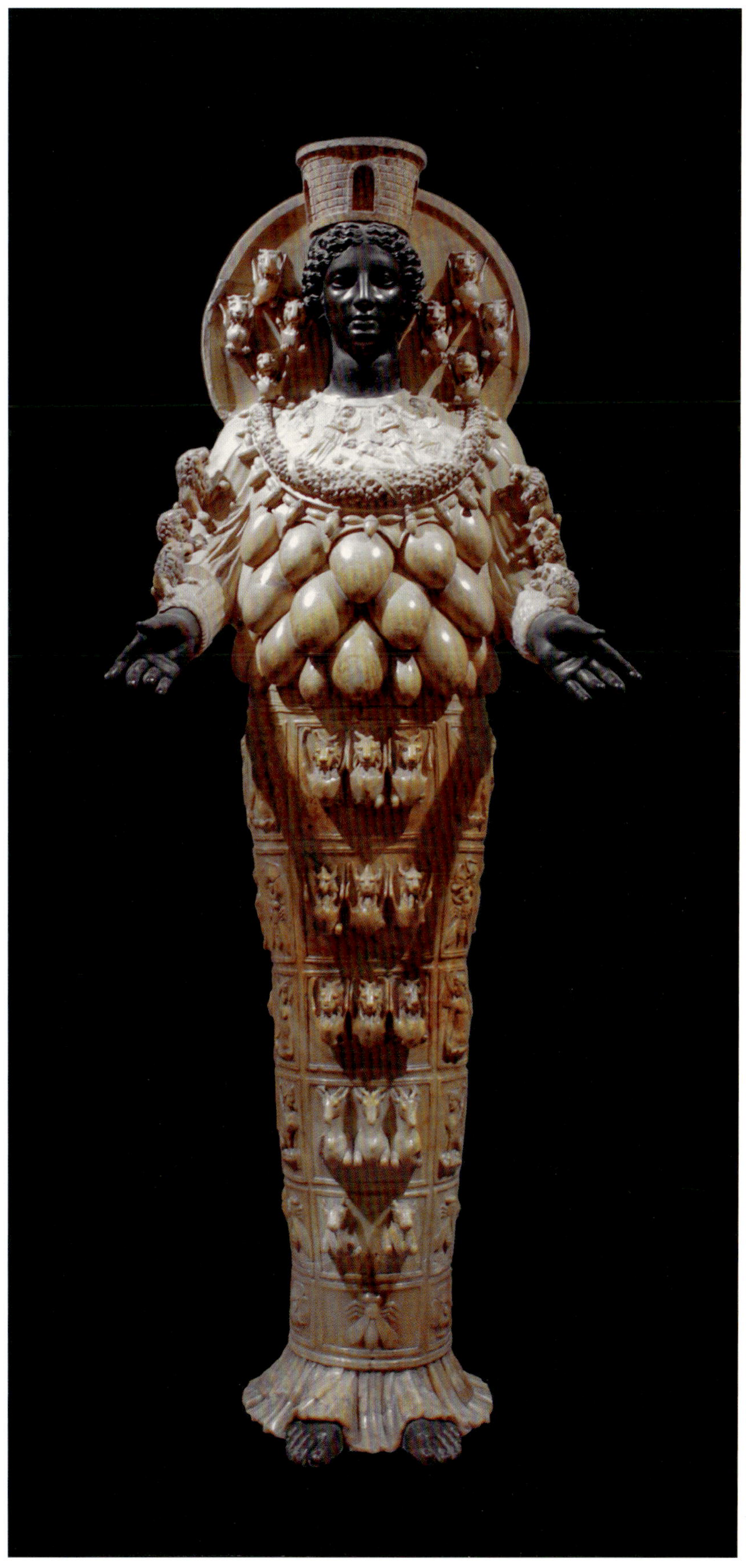

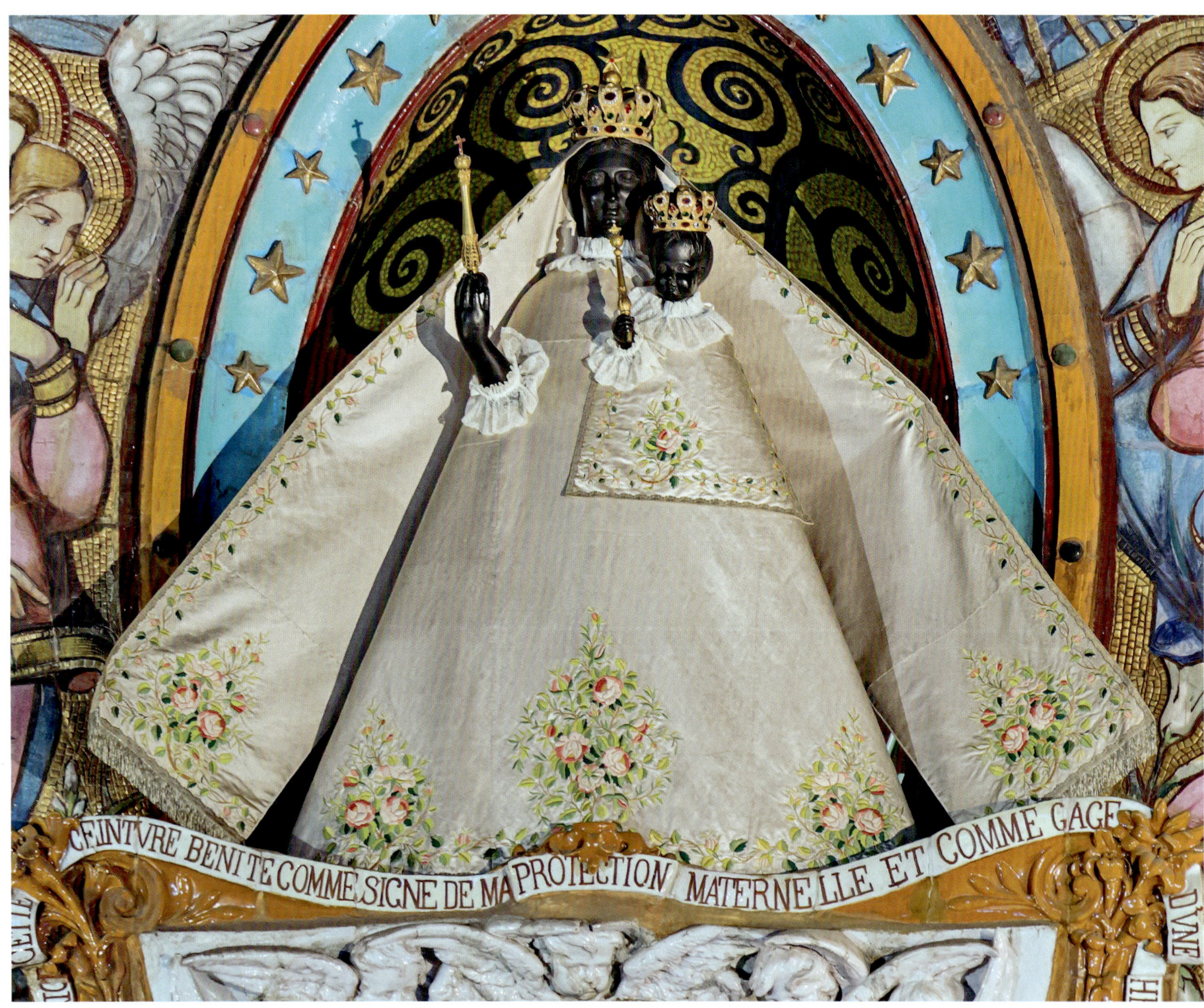
CEINTVRE BENI TE COMME SIGNE DE MA PROTECTION MATERNELLE ET COMME GAGE

20 Virgin and Christ
Coptic Egypt
100 – 200 CE
Terracotta
8.74 in., 22.2 cm
Royal Ontario Museum, Toronto, Canada
Gift of Walter Massey

21 Our Lady of Rocamadour
Notre Dame de Rocamadour, France
Wood and blackened silver
16 in., 40.64 cm

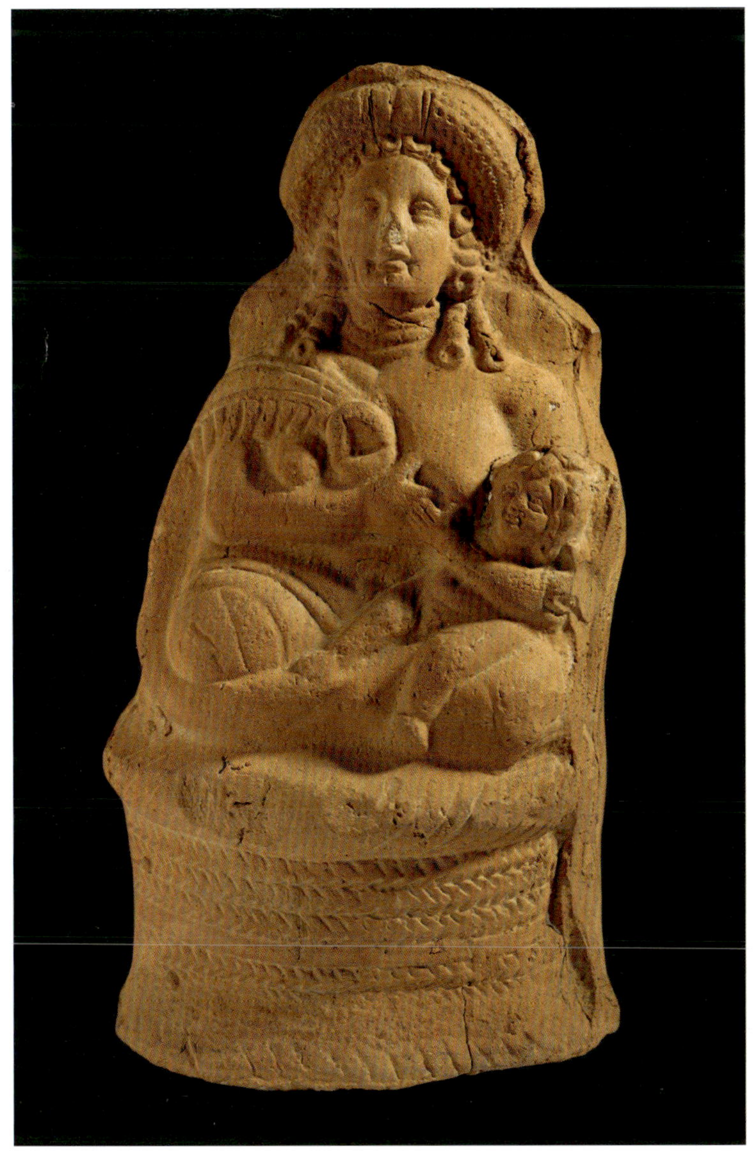

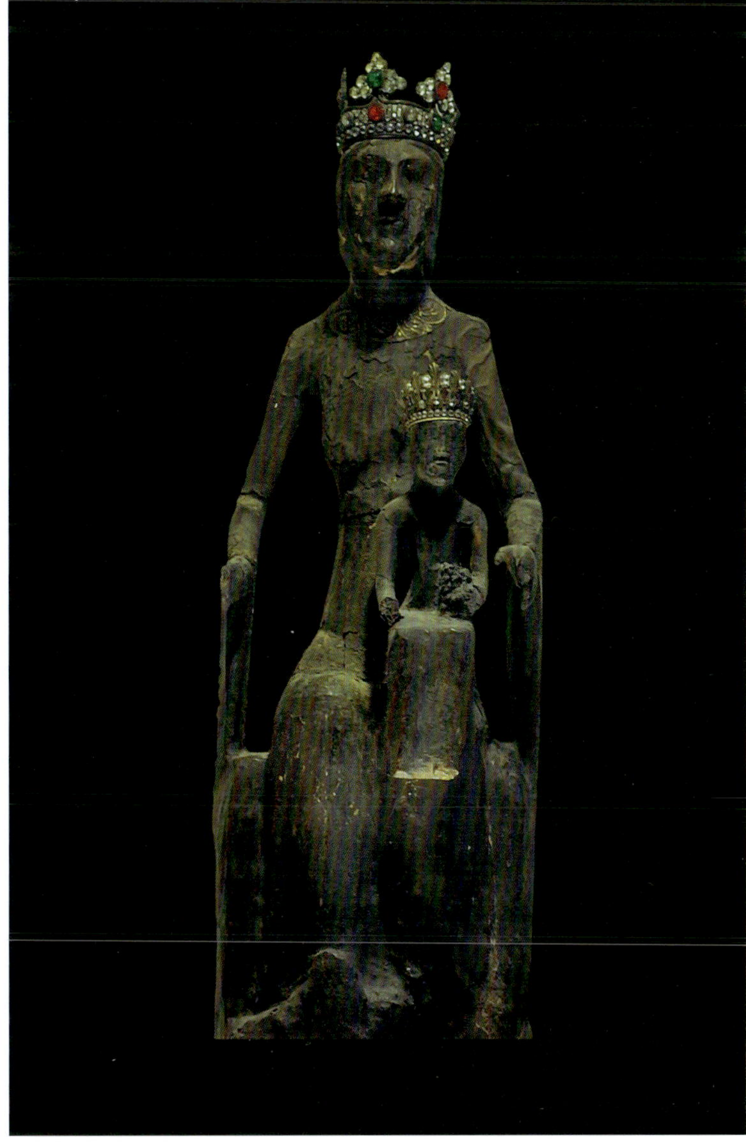

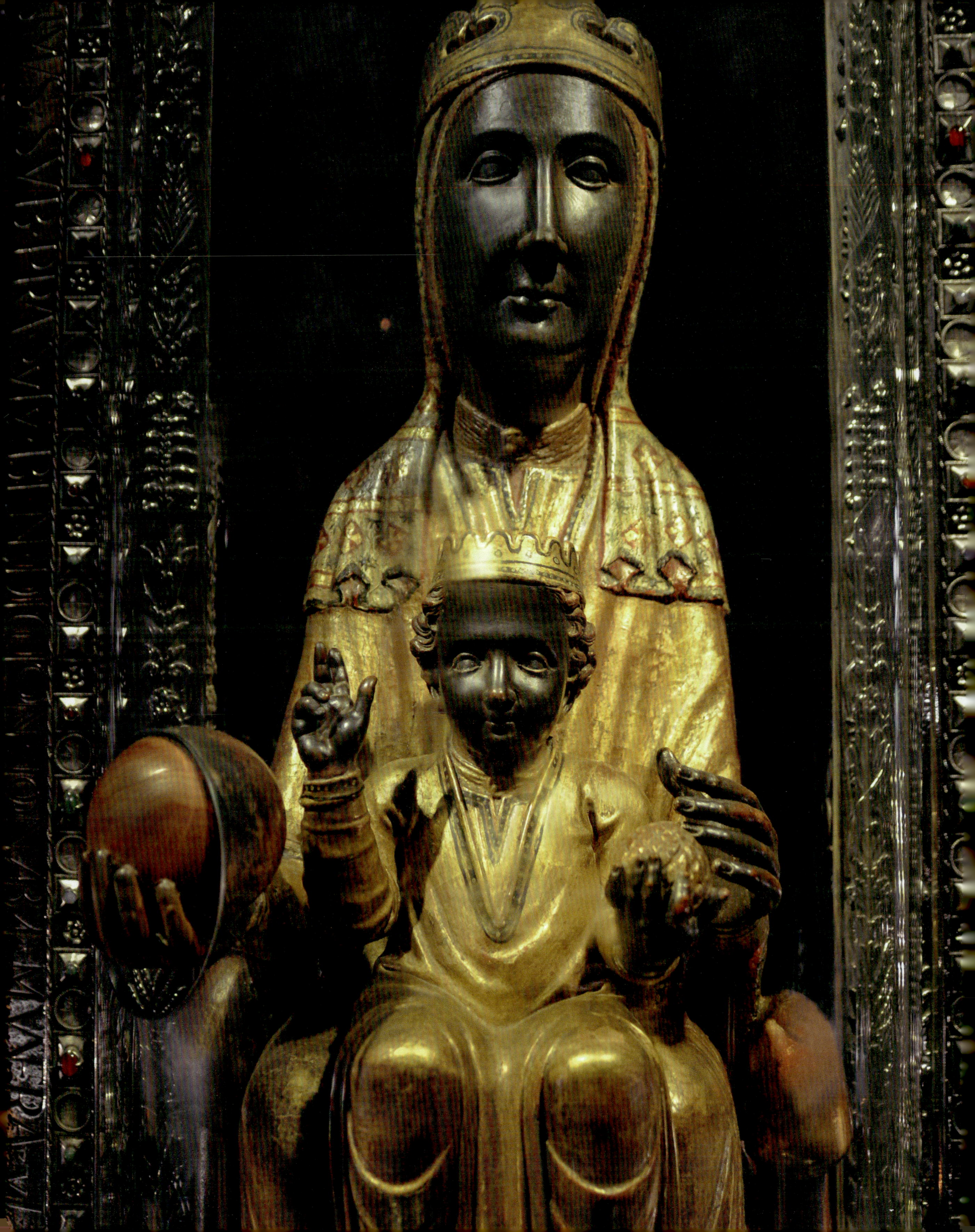

Christianity entered Ethiopia in the fourth century, but maternity imagery only became common in the fifteenth century, and its forms were more influenced by late medieval (14th to 15th century) Italian paintings of the Virgin and Child than by Coptic versions. King Dawit (reigned 1382–1413) commissioned a translation of the Miracles of Mary from Arabic into Ge'ez (the liturgical language of the Ethiopian Orthodox church), with illuminations including the Virgin and Child. His son Zara Yacob (1399–1468) fiercely promoted the cult of Mary, with great artistic, religious, and political effects. During his reign, he unified Ethiopia and extended the spiritual hegemony of Christianity through his zealous institutionalization of the Marian cult. He insisted on the creation of thousands of images of Mary and mandated that an altar to her must be found in every church in the land. He decreed that thirty-two Marian festivals should be held throughout the year and that the twenty-ninth day of each month should be observed as a Festival of the Nativity. Zara Yacob used the cult of Mary and its imagery to help consolidate his empire politically. He required church attendance every week and on all Marian festival days. Believing he owed his life to Mary and considering himself her slave, Yacob called her the Mother of the Church, and his subjects were her children. He insisted that passages such as these from the twelfth-century *One Hundred Miracles of Mary* be read at every church service:

"Salutation unto thee, O my Lady Mary, thou Mother of our Lord Jesus Christ . . . O my Lady, mother of Salvation, Mother of Light, Mother of Incense, Mother of Offering, Mother of Fire, thou only Mother, Mother of the King, Mother of Christ the messiah. Oh Mother divine and awe-inspiring."[18] Yacob encouraged the Ethiopian people to wear a pendant or carry an amulet with an image of Mary or Christ and decreed that they prostrate themselves whenever three names were mentioned: Jesus Christ, Mary, and Zara Yacob. By elevating himself in this manner to the level of Christ and Mary, Yacob promoted his own divinity as his empire's leader and at the same time controlled and unified his people in Mary's name. Again, we have a clear example of the politics of maternity, plus further evidence of the power of maternity imagery.

Some Ethiopian images of Mary and her Beloved Son were accorded mystical powers to punish sinners and others to cure diseases and intercede in petitions to God, and some were actually believed to have the power to see, talk, and even take action.[19] Oaths were sworn on Marian icons, which were clearly seen to embody or possess divine powers. In short, starting at least as early as the fifteenth century, Ethiopians have accorded images of Mary and Christ enormous agency. That countless paintings and other images of Mary and her Beloved Son exist to this day owes much to the policies of Zara Yacob. Many styles of Virgin and Child paintings

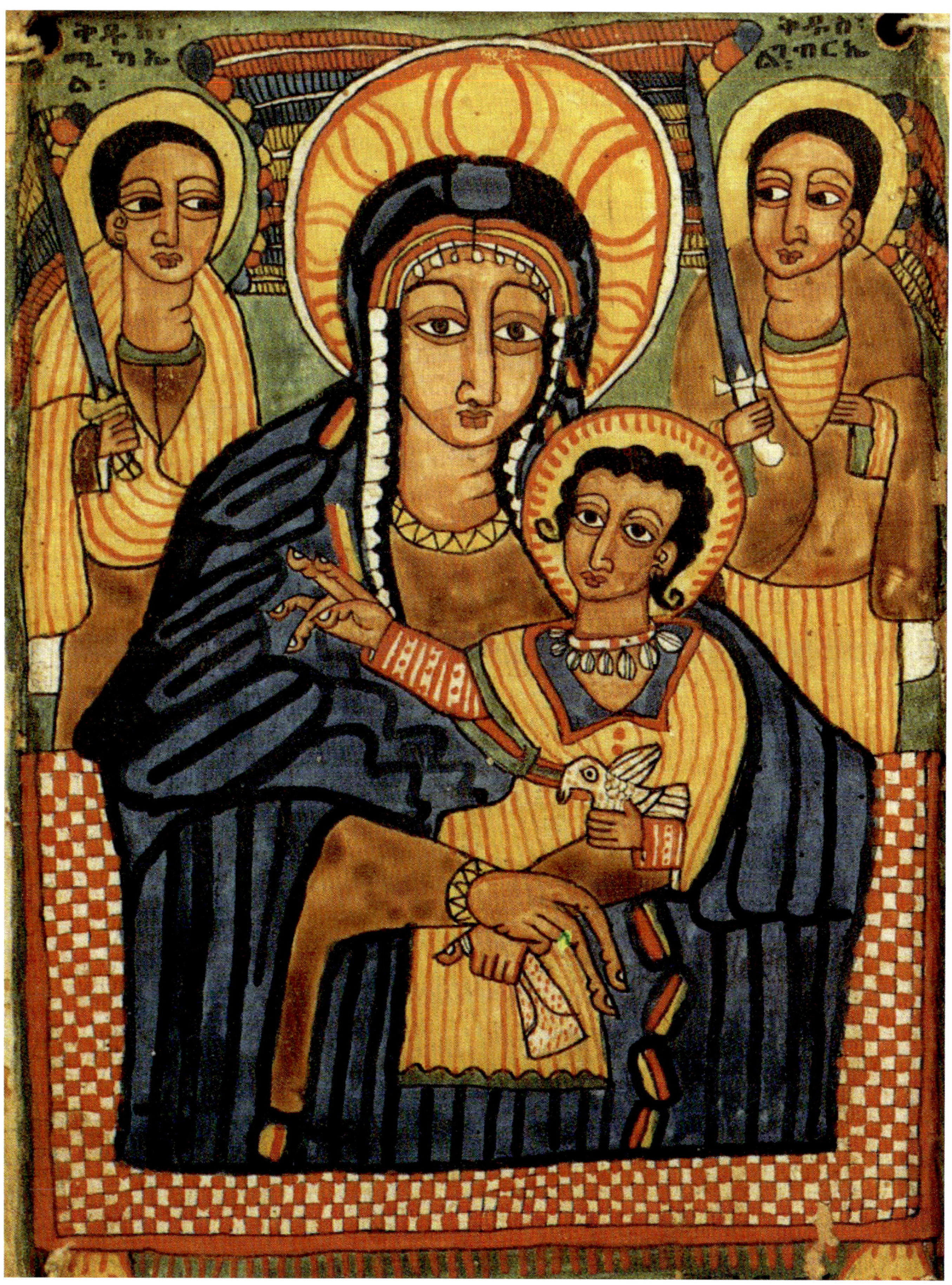

can be identified by period and region (**23**). Most are vividly colored, with a directness of rendering and a relative simplicity of line and form, typically in frontal postures, with stylized facial features, large eyes, halos around the heads of holy figures, and schematically rendered drapery. Hundreds of thousands of Ethiopian maternity images exist. Most devout people have one or more in their homes and/or on their persons. The more than one thousand churches in Ethiopia sometimes have a dozen or more such images, and hundreds of shops sell images of different sorts and sizes to local believers and to tourists. Western museums also contain hundreds of Ethiopian Virgin and Child icons.

The Inland Delta region of the great Niger River in Mali is the site of hundreds of archaeological terracotta sculptures, among them more than two dozen maternity images dated to between ca. 1000 and 1600 and associated with the trading center and civilization of Djenne, just south of the Sahara Desert. This was a period coeval with the emergence of Black Virgin worship in Europe, but no one posits a formal or spiritual relationship between the two cultures. Djenne people were animists (worshippers of local nature deities) until the arrival of Islam in the thirteenth century, but the terracottas are not associated with Islam. One terracotta mother-and-child sculpture is illustrated on this book's cover. It is possibly a kind of "visual reporting" of a common, natural biological

process in life, but a deeper if unknown cultural meaning is far more likely. To this point is a more exceptional, unusual example: a seated mother embracing four small people, surely understood to be children, although modeled with adult features and proportions (**24**). Two small figures caress the woman's chest as she holds them affectionately with her right arm and hand; the other two embrace one another at her back as she holds them to her with her left arm. The notion of a mother with four children, all of the same size and age, is neither lifelike nor plausible. Another maternity image has two small figures, one of whom is bearded, and thus clearly adult. The mother of four, as she is surely intended to be understood, is a woman of some status, as revealed by her elaborate necklace. There is also a puzzling small snake that stretches from her nose, over the top of her head, then downward. Many other terracotta human figures from this tradition have snakes, often several of varied size, all over their bodies, as well as boils and other skin eruptions that signal diseases such as small pox. Snakes appear in myths, epic legends, and rituals among peoples living today in the areas where these images were found; some snakes are associated with the beginnings of agriculture and many in the region are considered messengers of the gods. Nearly all the hundreds of terracotta sculptures from this region and time were recovered from archaeological digs, most sadly illegal, that destroyed

24 Female Figure with Four Children

Jenne-Jeno culture, Sahel, Inner Niger Delta, Mali
1100 – 1400
Terracotta with traces of red slip
13 ¾ × 8 ⁷⁄₁₆ × 7 ⁵⁄₁₆ in.,
35 × 21.5 × 18.5 cm
Yale University Art Gallery, New Haven
Charles B. Benenson,
B.A. 1933 Collection

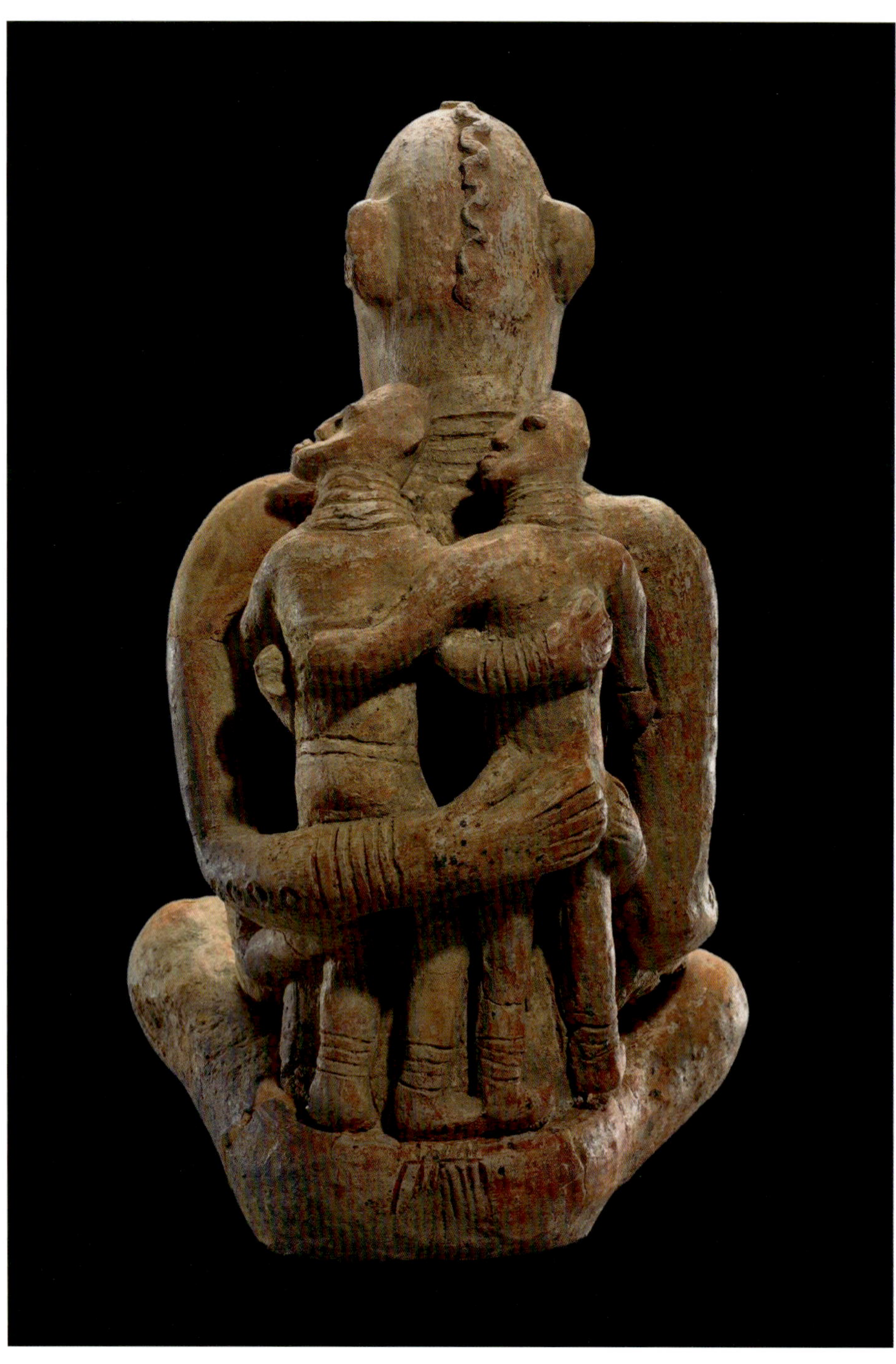

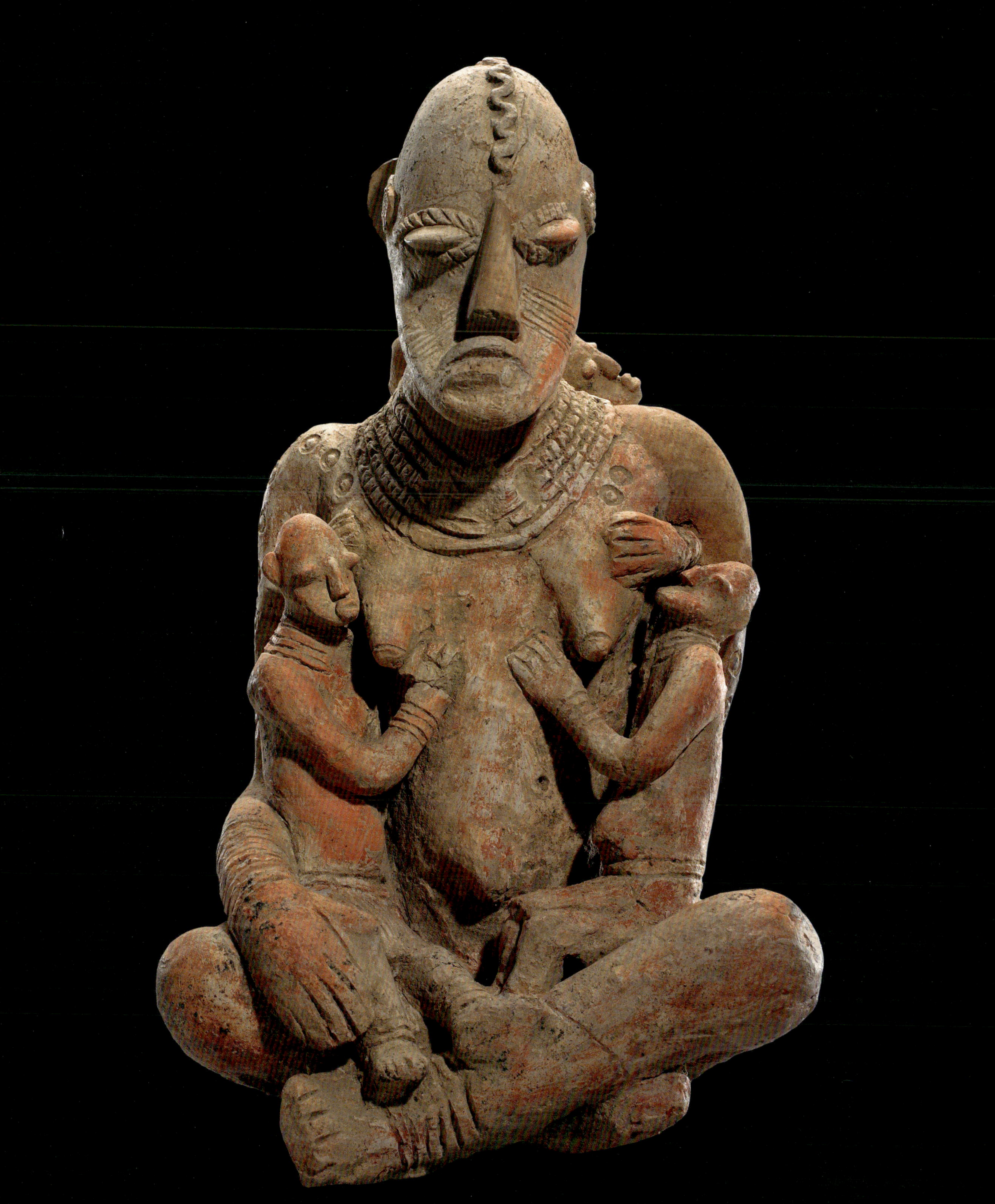

evidence of their contexts, so we know almost nothing about their original functions and meanings. Yet from the iconography we can surmise that many were intended as symbolic expressions, metaphors, or references to now-lost legends. Many represent elite people, their status signaled by their personal decoration, and some may well depict gods. The diseased maternity figures perhaps addressed health problems, and the mothers with two, three, or four children may suggest potentiality, as well as fertility and prosperity. Several, too, are mothers of twins, which are now revered among the cultures of this region. But because of the stress twins and other multiple births impose upon mothers and families, they are an ambivalent "blessing," like the snakes living in trees, on land, deep underground, and in water. So, the full meanings of these maternity figures remain enigmatic.

Other more recent African cultures south of the Sahara Desert yield more detailed data on the nature of maternity and its images, the latter also mainly sculptures. Most records are from the first seventy years of the twentieth century, when anthropological and art historical research became intense. My own interest in this subject began in 1966, when I first saw a large maternity sculpture in a *mbari* house among Igbo peoples in southeastern Nigeria (**25**), followed by more than a year of research on the *mbari* institution.[20] By a roadside, I was surprised to see, front and center in a shrine-like structure populated with many figures, a larger-than-life sun-dried earthen figure of Ala, the earth goddess, flanked by two children, and before

her the sacred python messenger. This powerful deity is the mother of all other gods, plants, animals, and the human family and community (**26**). For over a hundred years *mbari* houses were built in a ritualized process that, with the building itself, was offered as a major community sacrifice to this most powerful deity. An *mbari* was occasionally built to avert disaster brought on by human or natural causes, or in thanks for blessings such as peace after warfare. Specially selected men and women were initiated as spirits into the ritualized process for a year or longer for large *mbari* (containing fifty to 200 images) constructed in the 1930s, during the halcyon years of *mbari* (the 1920s to 1930s). Professional artists modeled *mbari* inhabitants, along with people and scenes of everyday life, and spirit workers did most of the painting. Ala is featured larger than life-size, an older woman (past child-bearing age), seen as a "man among women," yet a mother with one or two children on her lap or by her side, while most other figures are about half life-size.

Could it be that the god responsible for morality and ethics, and the source and keeper of tradition, achieved these characteristics because she was seen as the mother of all? This is well asserted by the children with her and by the other modeled family members, deities, and villagers in her house. The meaning of the knife she holds is ambivalent; with it "she peels yam for her people" as gifts, but local Igbo people also told me that she may use it to kill those who offend by polluting her (e.g., by spilling blood). Like many deities, Ala has both positive

25 *Mbari* House dedicated to
Ala, Earth Goddess

Igbo culture, Umuogote Orishaeze,
Imo State, Nigeria
Photo: Herbert M. Cole, 1966

26 Ala (Earth) and Children in the
Mbari to ObiAla (detail)

By the artist Nnanti Obube Vlakwo
Photo: Herbert M. Cole, 1966

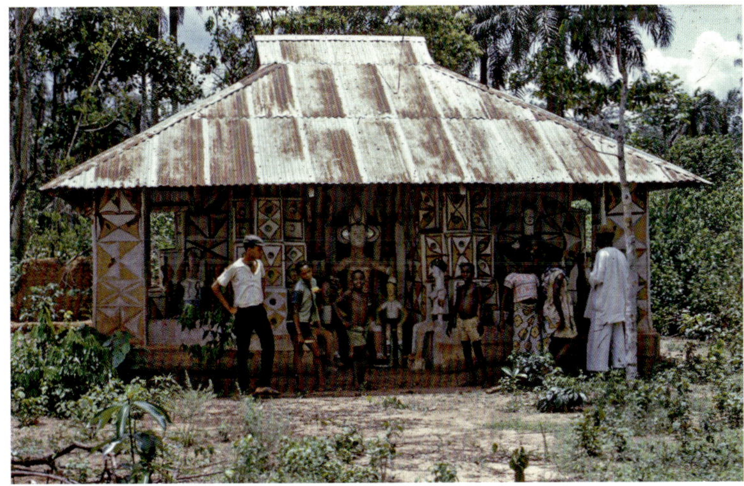

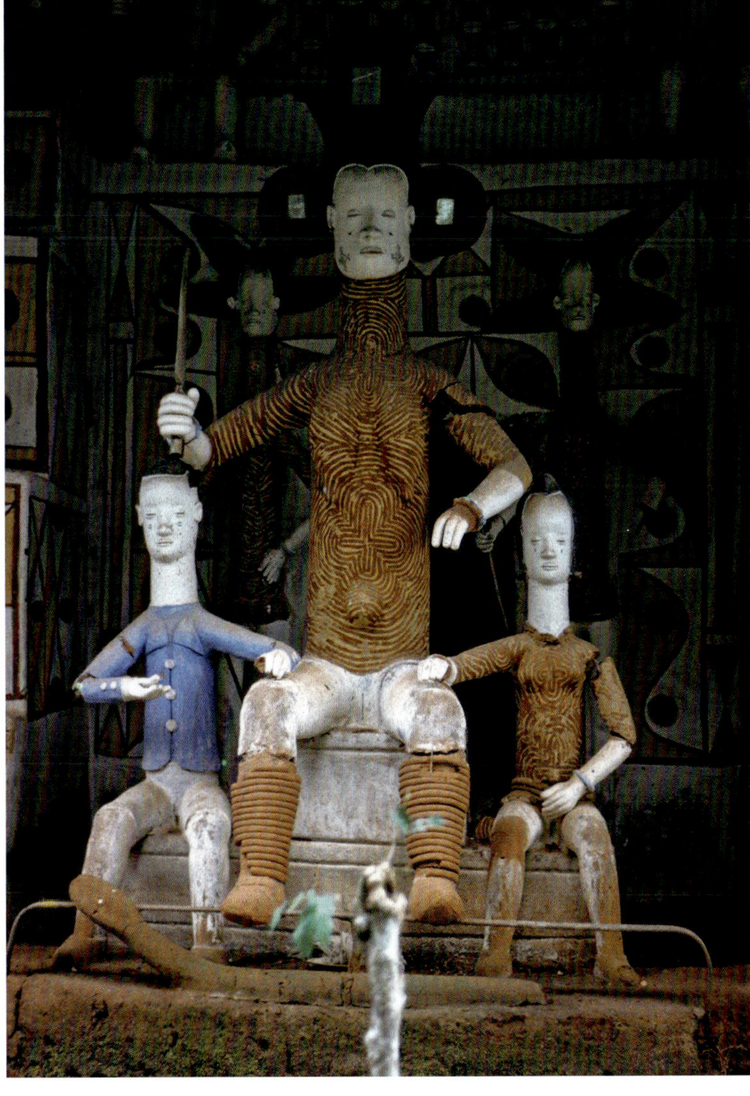

and negative attributes; how she exercises her power depends on the behavior of her people. If the close bonds in life between a mother and her children help account for their character, their moral and ethical values as well as their adherence to the cultural traditions she inculcates, then the same might be true of the most powerful of local gods and Igbo families and the community.

The deified Earth is sometimes thought of in conjunction with her fertilizing partner, Amadioha, god of thunder, lightning, and rain. He was often given his own *mbari*, usually much smaller than those for Ala. All *mbari* images are modeled in clay taken by initiates from deep within sacred termite mounds and pulverized with water in mortars to become the consistency of pounded yam, the staple Igbo prestige food.[21] Twice processed, by termites and then by women as if preparing food, this unusual sculptural medium is in fact called *fufu*—the local name for balls of pounded yam readied for eating— just as *mbari* spirit workers say they are going to the "yam farm" when leaving at night to dig up spirit-infused termite hill clay. The fact that a queen termite hatches as many as 13 million eggs per year is not insignificant. This numinous clay becomes a visible symbol of the productive, sacred, nurturing earth that supports us, and it is also understood as a powerful if unseen deity. Ala, as the mother of all, is the genetrix, the true ground of being for the Owerri Igbo: she is the font of fertility

and morality, the source of family and community tradition and, therefore, culture. She is nature and culture simultaneously, inseparably joined. Once consecrated and opened to the public, the *mbari* sacrifice was accepted by Ala and the building and its figures were never repaired. After some years, the structure and figures of an *mbari*, including Ala, melt back to fertilize the earth, repeating the cycle of regeneration.

Ancient Mother, usually depicted nursing a child, is a form of creator deity and cultural beacon for many Senufo groups in Ivory Coast (27). She is considered head of the male initiation institution that prepares boys to become men through rigorous instruction, tests, and ordeals over many years. Ancient Mother is said to nurture male initiates with "the milk of knowledge," a telling metaphorical statement about mothers' teaching that demonstrates the deeply cultural nature of many maternity images not only in Africa but around the world. As the culture-historian Ellen Dissanayake has written: "The mother-infant duet is the archetypal origin of affiliative, sympathetic, and moral capacities that make (and have made) human culture—and human existence—possible."[22] Whenever we know a lot about the values, rituals, and beliefs surrounding images of maternity, their powerful cultural importance is so clear that we can rightly speak of "cultures of maternity" that are different from one part of the world to another, just as we see them vary significantly on the African continent.

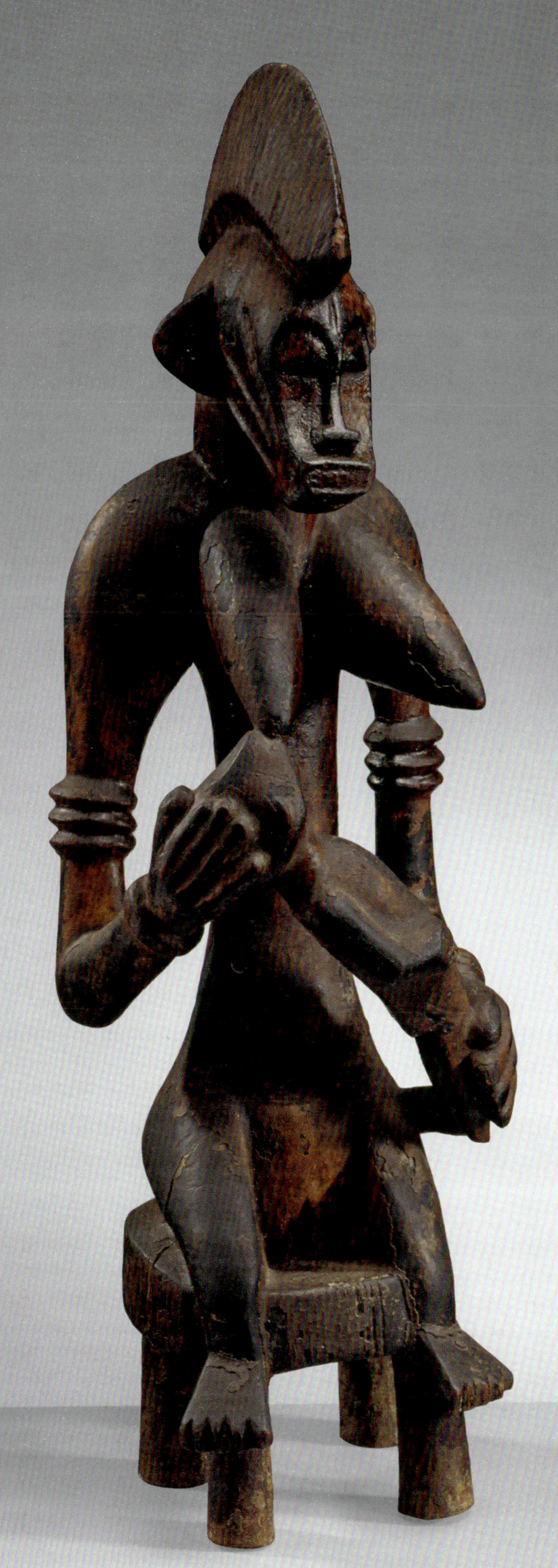

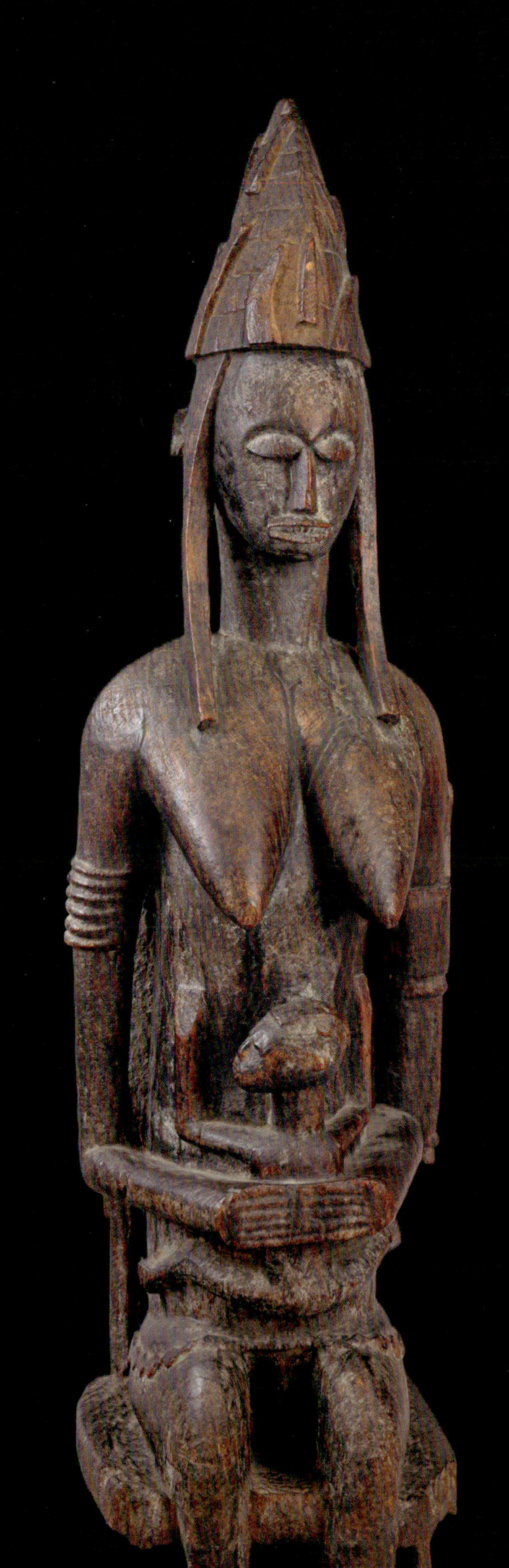

The carved wood Bamana (a people in Mali) maternity figure (**28**), called Gwandusu, has a male counterpart; together, and often with other family members in their shrine-like building, they are leaders of ritual associations called Jo and Gwan, which are devoted to promoting the fertility of the fields and the human population. This female-male couple indicates that female principles typically have balancing, complementary male qualities, expressed among the Bamana in the concepts of *badenya* (mother-childness) and *fadenya* (father-childness). Mother-childness is linked with centripetal social forces such as stability, unity, and cooperation, which pull a person back into the group, toward the hearth and mother, one could say. Father-childness is centrifugal, allied with individuality, competition, self-promotion, and heroics—traits that spin a person outside his domestic and social field.[23] Both genders have components of each quality and are essential for prosperity. But Bamana women, who normally desire above all to be mothers, are anchored in *badenya,* as embodied in the reality of maternity and its carved wood image. A woman can make her mark or help others become innovators or heroes—showing her *fadenya* qualities—but it is traditionally males that do so. For Bamana women, "children are a source of pride, self-fulfillment, and status in the community; their absence brings anxiety, shame, and often a diminished role in the family and village … Children are a woman's most valued possession and most respected accomplishment."[24] Jo and Gwan maternity sculptures epitomize the forces that hold society together and advance it, yet show her with a weapon lashed to her arm and potent charms on her hat. She is powerful enough to pass greatness on to her children, as stated in the proverb "everyone is in his mother's hands" and in a song verse, "a man's power comes from his mother"—again, her *fadenya* traits. Gwan is a female initiatory association with the express purpose of promoting childbirth, and it is also an association of blacksmiths who carve Gwan figures. Explicitly, Gwan celebrates both childbirth and the metaphoric "birthing" of iron from the female furnace. The word *gwan* also means "smelting furnace."[25] Some Gwan and other power-endowed figures were carved from trees that grew out of termite mounds, with both trees and mounds embodying fertile spiritual energy (*nyama*) that is also inherent in *badenya* and *fadenya*.

Note, too, that human language is called the "mother-tongue." A father-tongue does not exist.

A fifth African example, from Congo, is the finial sculpture that surmounts an important chief's house among the Eastern Pende peoples (**29**). The statue shows a woman—the chief's wife—holding a child in one arm and a knife in the other. The house she protects and presides over contains the secrets and artifacts of chiefly power; the "stomach" of the house, its innermost sanctum, is beneath the central pole that also support the roof figure.

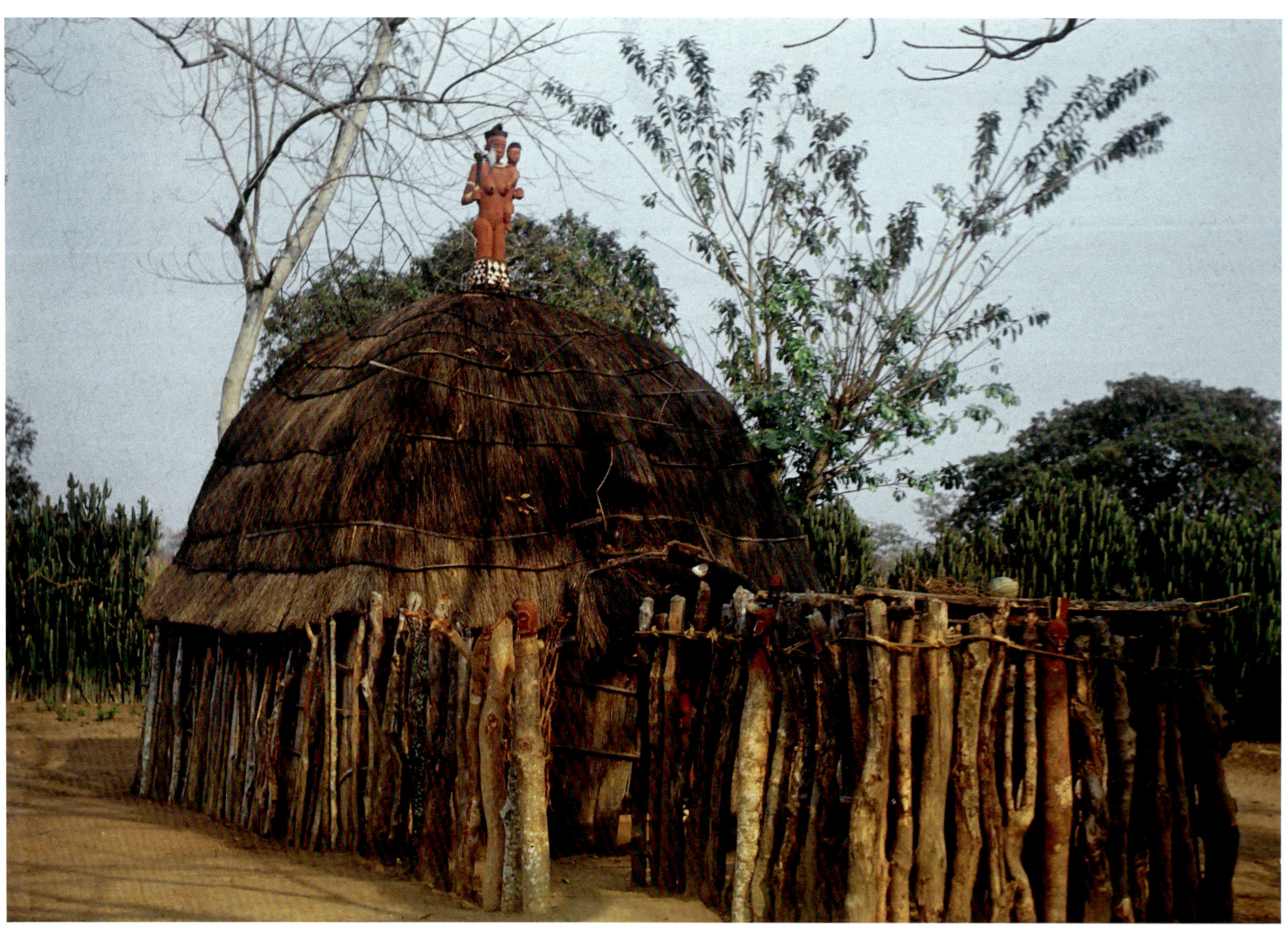

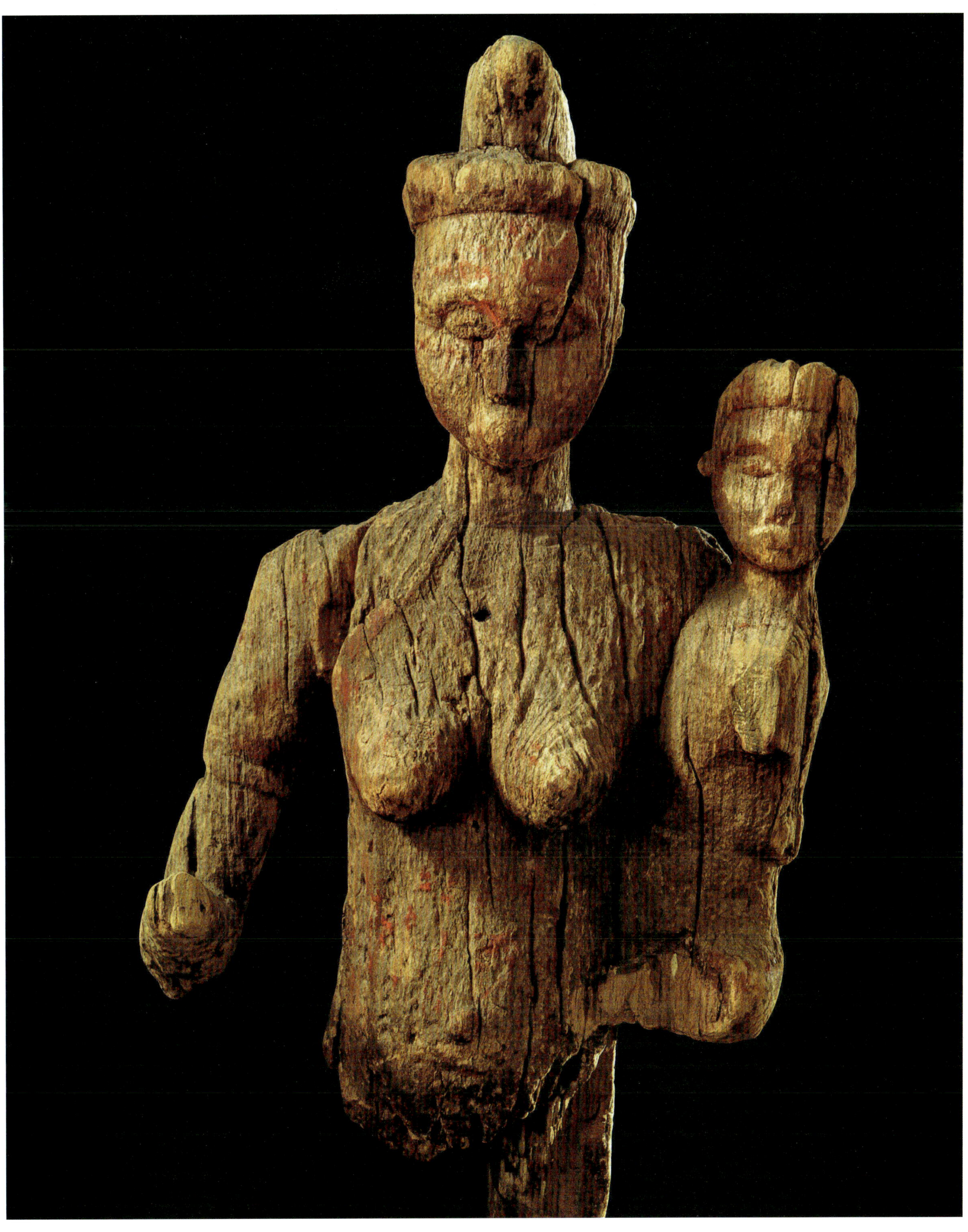

Within this stomach are placed a few of all the seeds and grains grown locally, plus protective medicines. A prayer intoned in darkness the morning these items are placed and the house is ritually opened indicates that this sanctum and its contents are a microcosm of the Pende world. That morning, the chief's invocation to his ancestors and his constituents is:

You are the center pole of the house, you are the village with its people, fields, and forest. We have given you all the seeds for cultivation so that you may grip the earth as the seeds [roots] grip the earth over there. All seeds grow, may you grow [as] the seeds grow, so that the women may give birth, so that there may be lots of palm wine, so that the hunters may kill [their prey] with their guns.[26]

The axe-wielding maternity sculpture atop the house is the public declaration of these ideas, visible at a distance because of its size and elevated placement. This figure lacks her right hand and her knife, and its weathered condition suggests a possible nineteenth-century origin (**30**). Under ancestral sanctions, this woman is the symbolic protector of the chief and his realm. Her knife is surely a warning to anyone with evil intent (as is Ala's knife among the Igbo). As the chief's first wife, she has several ritual duties regarding agriculture and is a socio-political force. At her husband's investiture, she dances with a knife, then hands it to him: he beheads a sacrificial

dog with one strike, symbolic of his power. The maternity figure's child represents the continuity of her matrilineal line: the future of her people.

The Yoruba of Nigeria are the continent's most prolific makers and users of maternity images; many thousands are known, mostly made of wood, but also made from ivory and cast copper alloys. The Yoruba people tell us that nearly all such images depict worshippers of the gods rather than the gods themselves, and most maternity figures are offerings given to shrines in thanks for gifts from the gods or petitions to them, often for children, the greatest blessing for a Yoruba family. Carved figures of women giving birth appear but are not very common on the continent, yet a few Yoruba carvers have made them for shrines of gods promoting fertility and childbirth (**31**).

The cultures of the Pacific Islands have laid little stress on either maternity or family imagery in their visual arts in comparison with Africa, but this does not mean that people of the South Seas are any less concerned about having and raising children and healthy families. A few interesting exceptions exist, especially among the Polynesian Maori of New Zealand, whose creation mythology is symbolized by images of sexual union. Some carved nineteenth-century wood boxes (*waka huia*) that contained tribal and family treasures, such as valuable feathers and heirloom jade pendants, had lids showing a male and female copulating in the high relief characteristic of Maori style. Finely carved and difficult

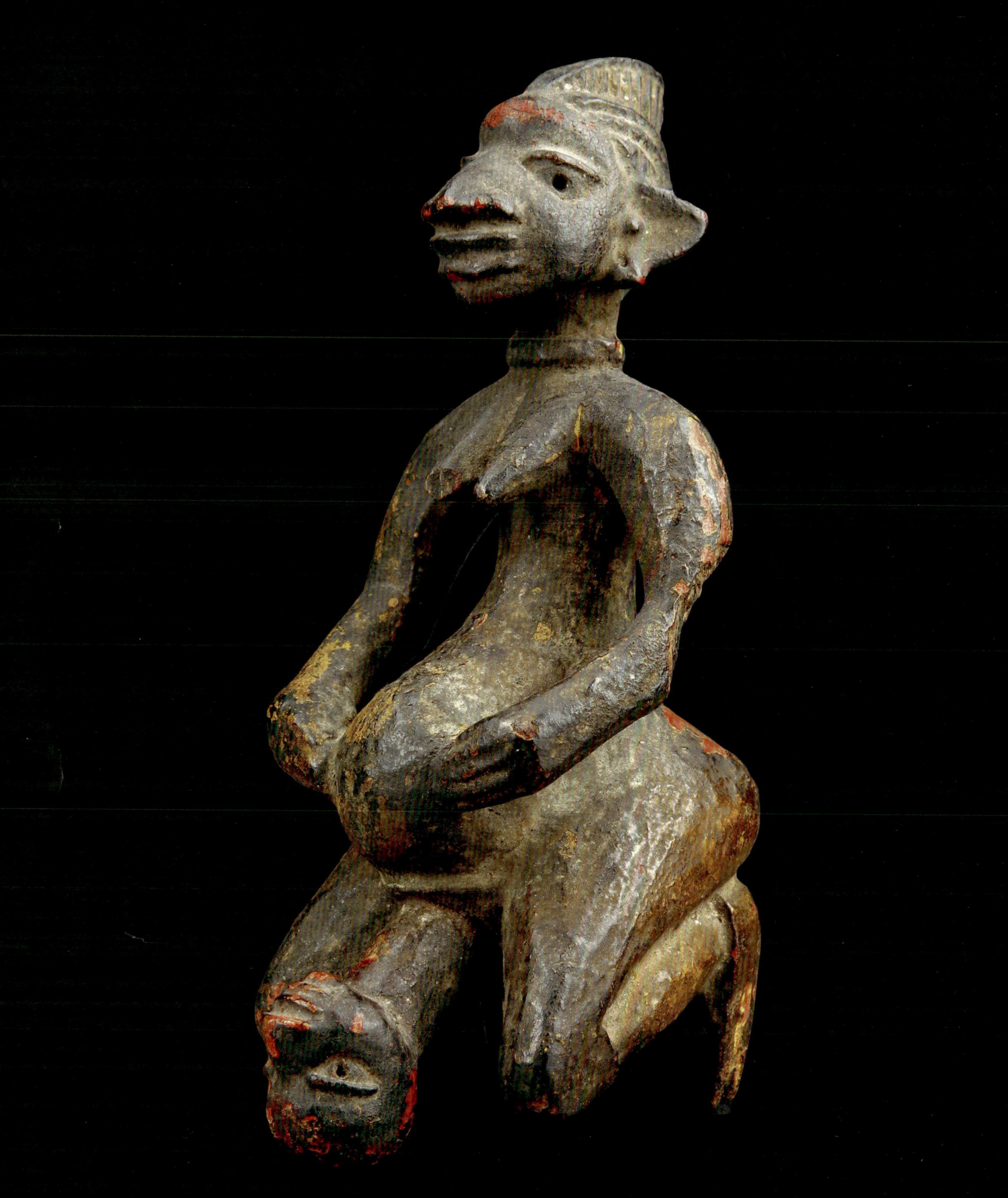

to read for people unfamiliar with intricate Maori surface detailing, the two figures are interpreted as Rangini (aka Rangi, meaning "great heavens" or "sky father") and Papatuanuku (aka Papa, meaning "earth mother"). From their union and in darkness, Papa gave birth to all life and to all other nature gods (sea, forests, storms, volcanos, etc.) and, eventually, to human beings. These gods tried to separate Rangi and Papa, to banish darkness and bring light, but failed repeatedly until Tane, god of forests, pushed them apart with his great trees, bringing light to the world. The figures on these treasure boxes are also interpreted as the founders of different Maori tribes, subtribes, and families. A more chaste rendering of the Rangi and Papa coupling is depicted on an exterior panel of a council house, the meeting place of tribal leaders, in a twentieth century, more naturalistic style. Once again female/male relationships relate to cosmic beginnings and forces and the legendary deities responsible for both the universe and human life itself.

Under the influence of Christian missionaries in the nineteenth century, Maori artists also produced at least two finely carved maternity figures in a traditional style representing the Virgin holding the Christ child. The carver of this figure gave the Virgin Mary full facial tattoo (*moko*), likening her to a Ariki Tapairu, the first-born female in a high-status family; such women were invested with special sacredness. Yet mother-and-child carvings were not part of the traditional Maori canon, and this Virgin sculpture was at first rejected when offered to churches around 1890. A non-Maori priest refused to accept the tattooed carving for his church, as he found it offensive. Catholic and other missionaries sometimes failed to understand traditional Maori responses to Christianity and, presumably, the patently non-naturalistic style of Maori carving, which was so different from the relatively naturalistic European renderings of the Virgin Mary and Christ.

Missionary influence probably also accounts for another South Seas woman-and-child group from the Solomon Islands in Melanesia. The color difference in these figures—dark mother and light child—suggests that the child may not be biologically related to the woman, unless he is her albino child. Alternatively, he may be a European child in the care of a nanny.[27] The lifelike naturalism of these figures is a striking departure from the usual conventions of Solomon Islands style. Suspension hooks (used to hang valuables in large community houses) are common artifacts from many Sepik River cultures of New Guinea; human figures are repeated subjects, but I believe only three or four maternity carvings are among them, all by the same hand, and most likely dating from the early twentieth century (**32**).

Australian native peoples celebrate their legendary ancestors with rituals that portray creation myths. Such

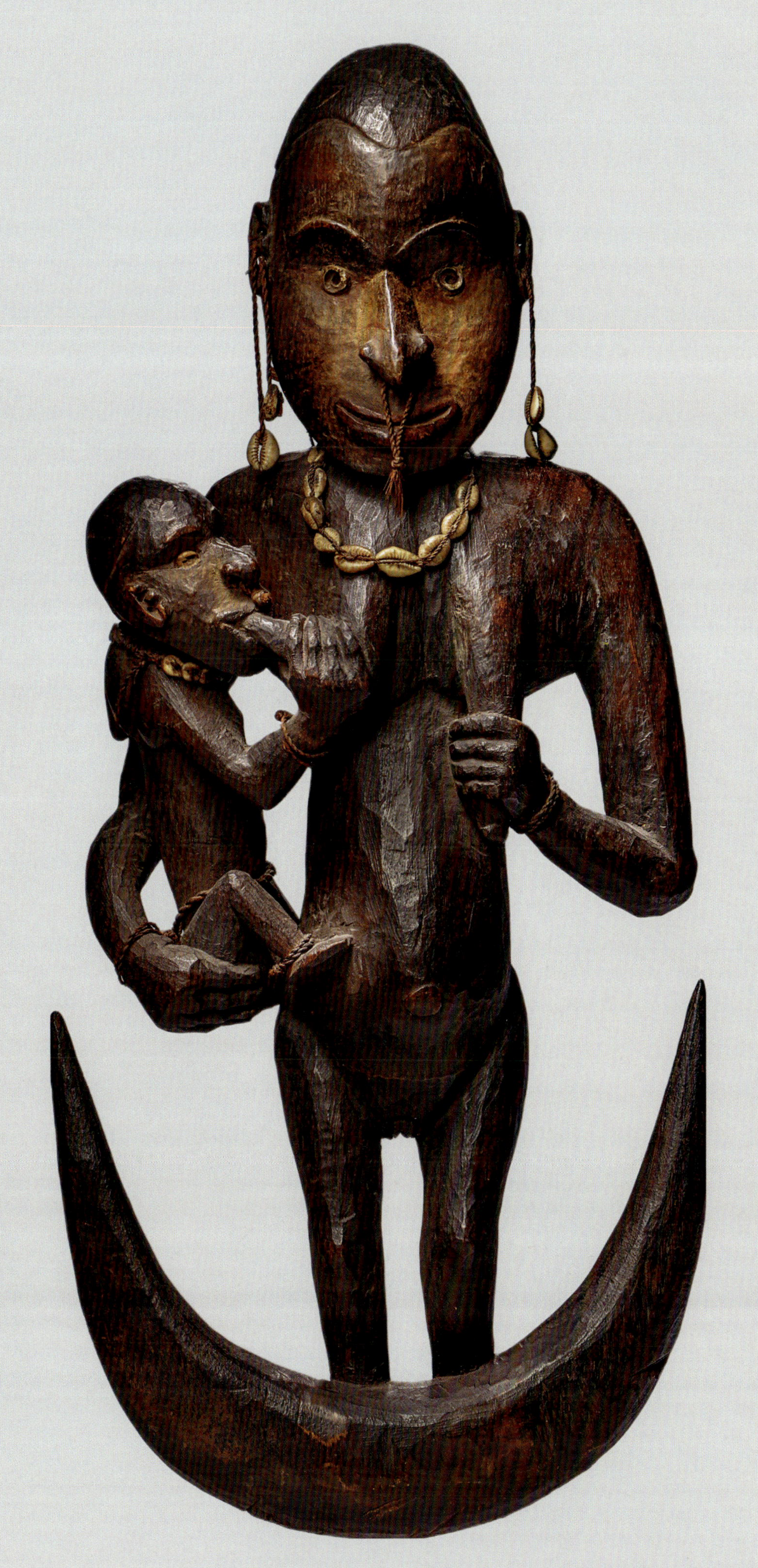

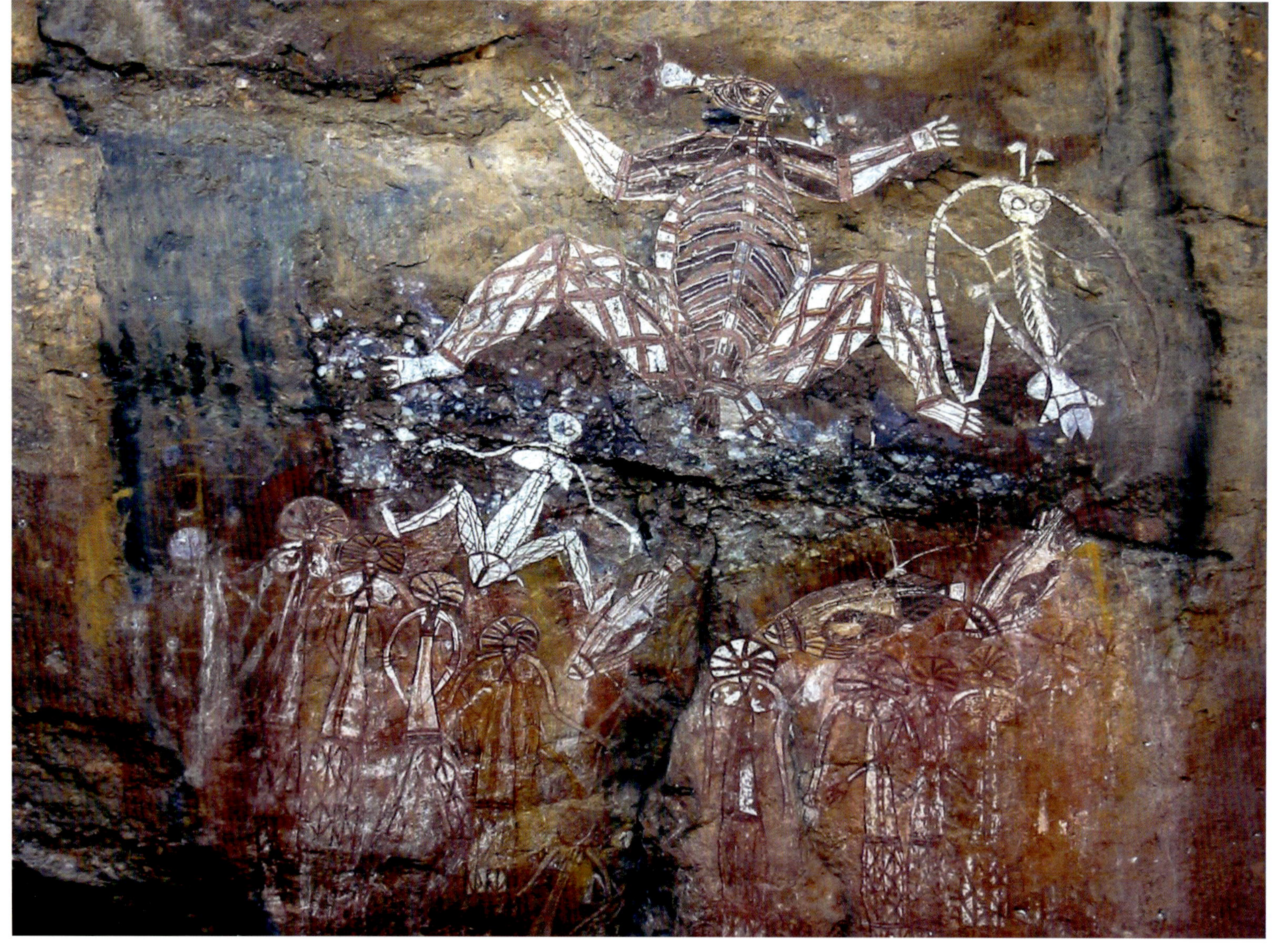

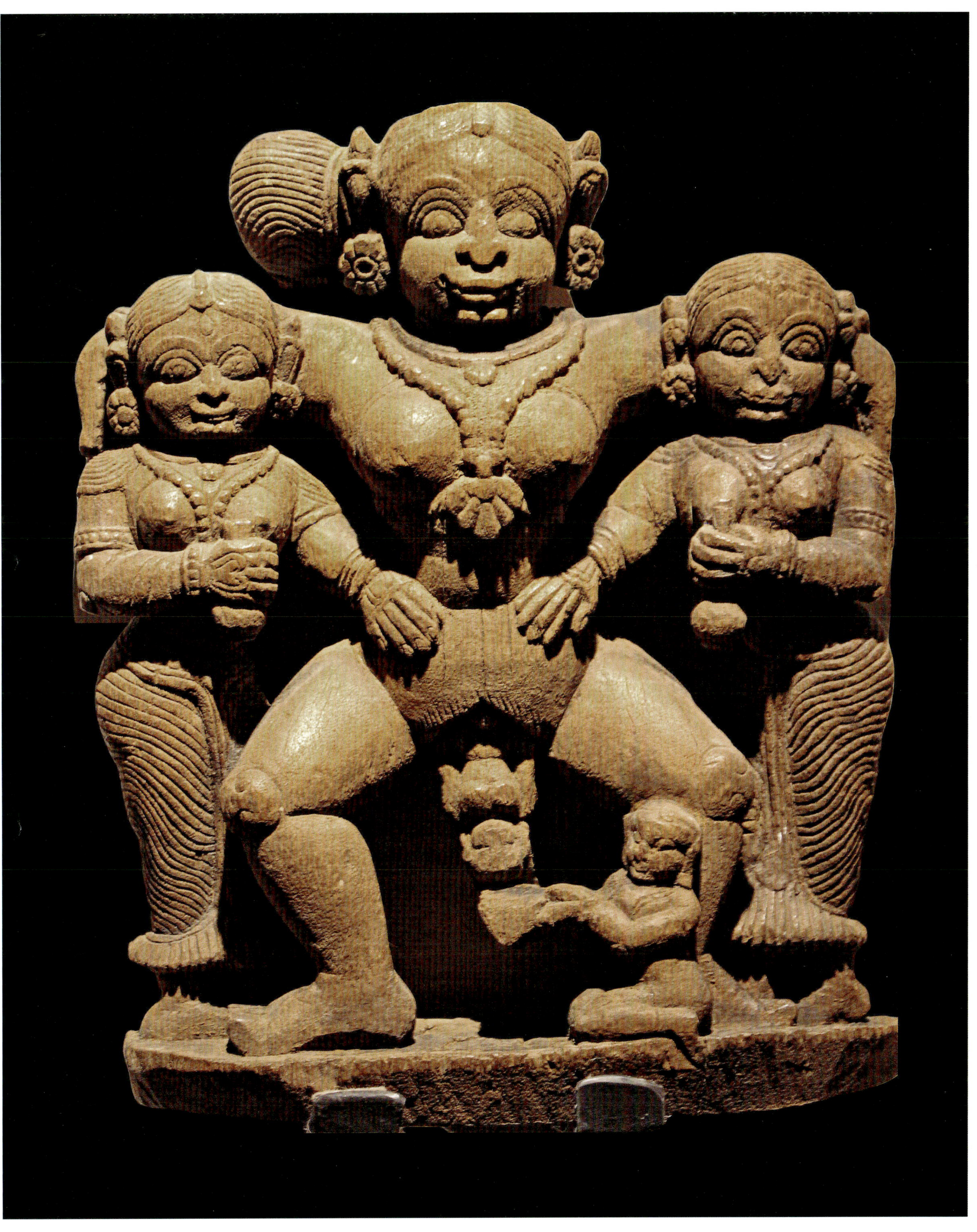

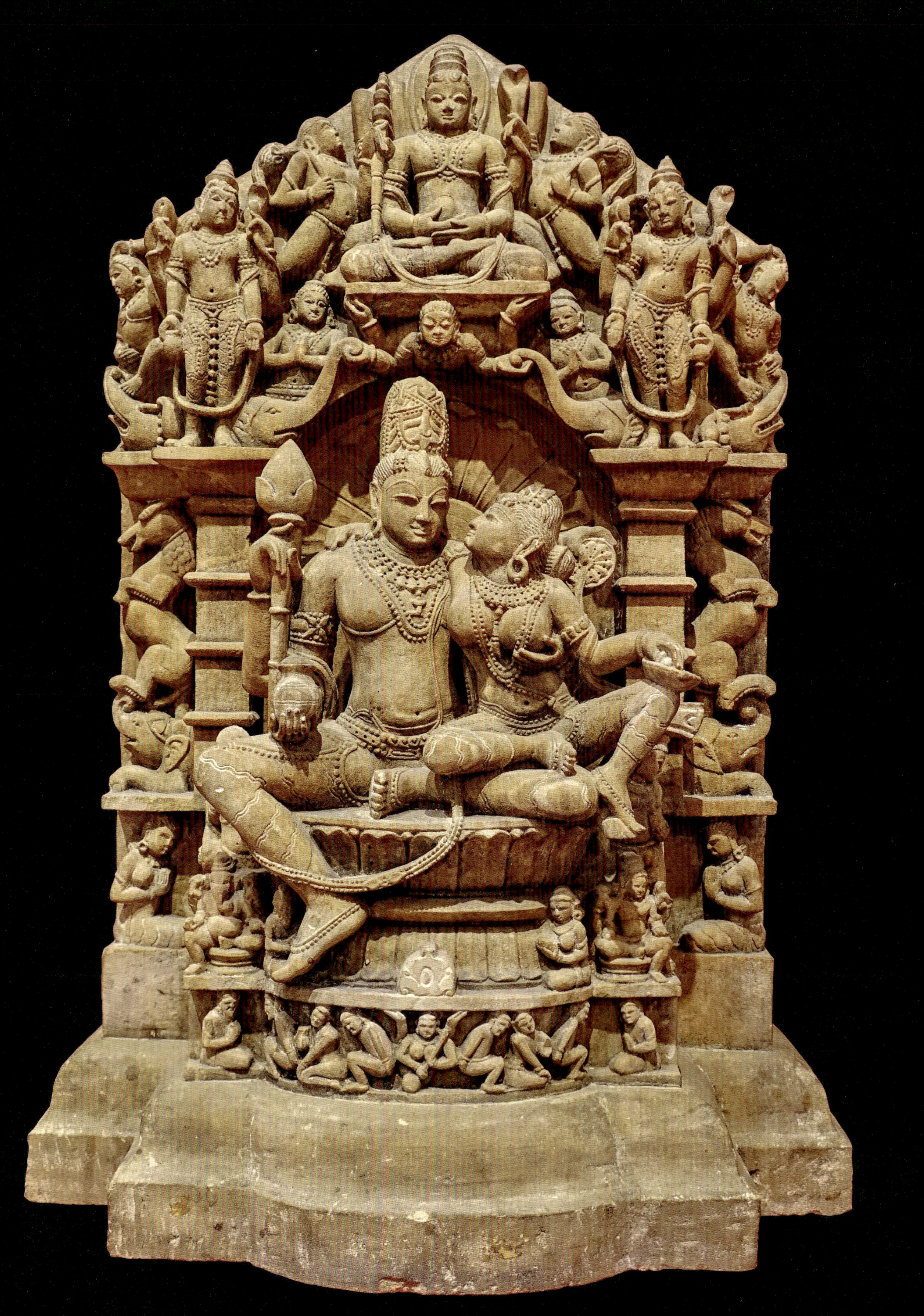

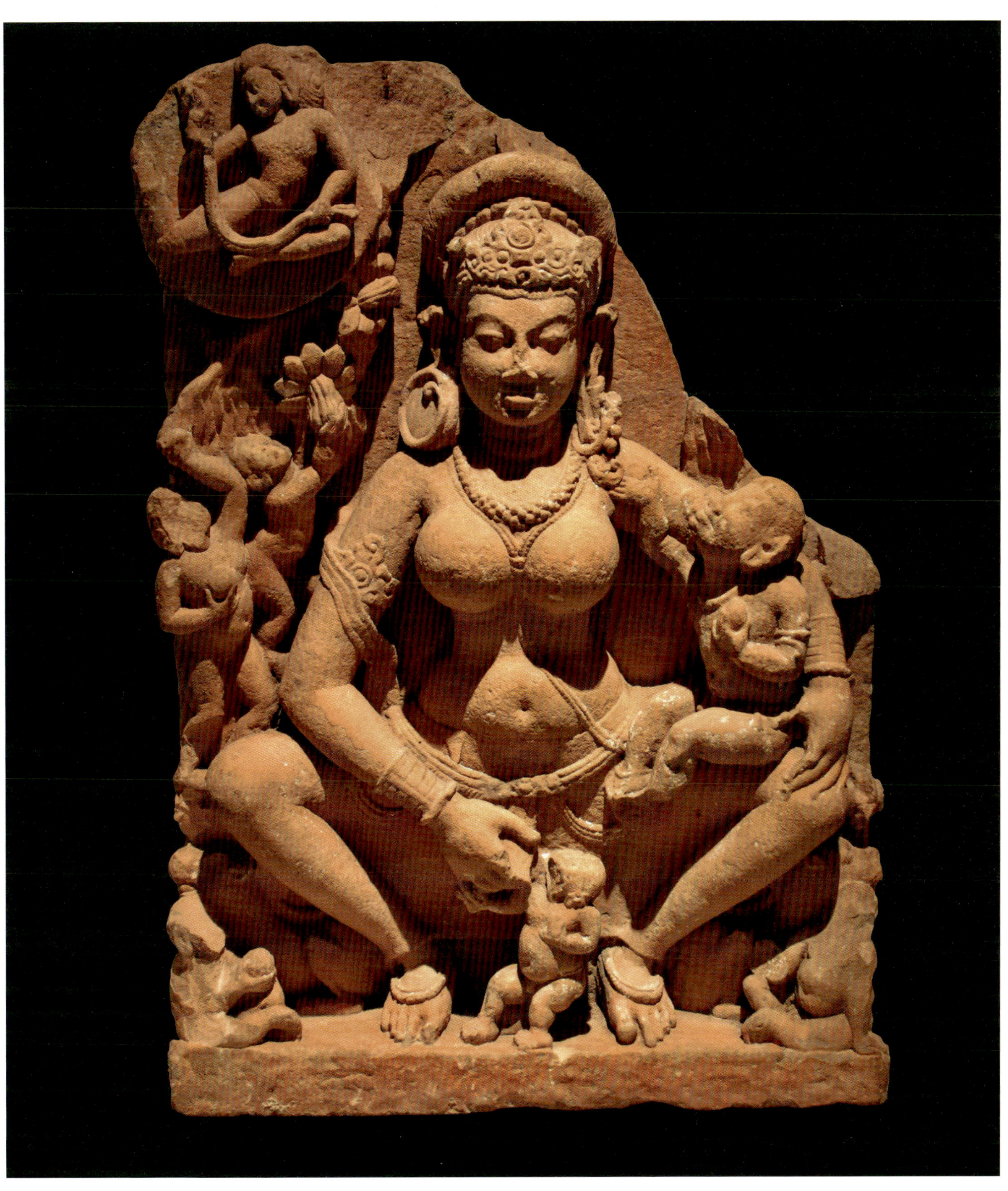

Bagbazar, Kolkata,
West Bengal, India

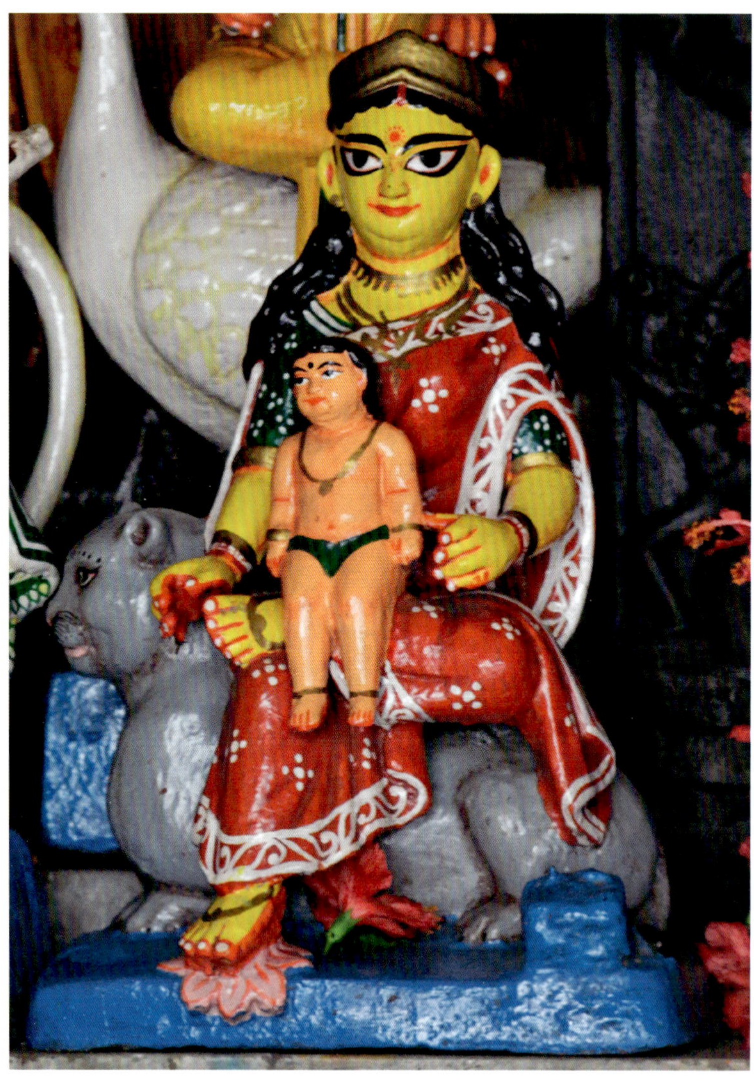

38 **Goddess Kali**

Ravi Varma (India, 1848 – 1906)
1910
Oil on canvas
19.69 × 13.78 in., 50 × 35 cm
The Hemamalini and Ganesh Shivaswamy
Collection, Bengaluru, India

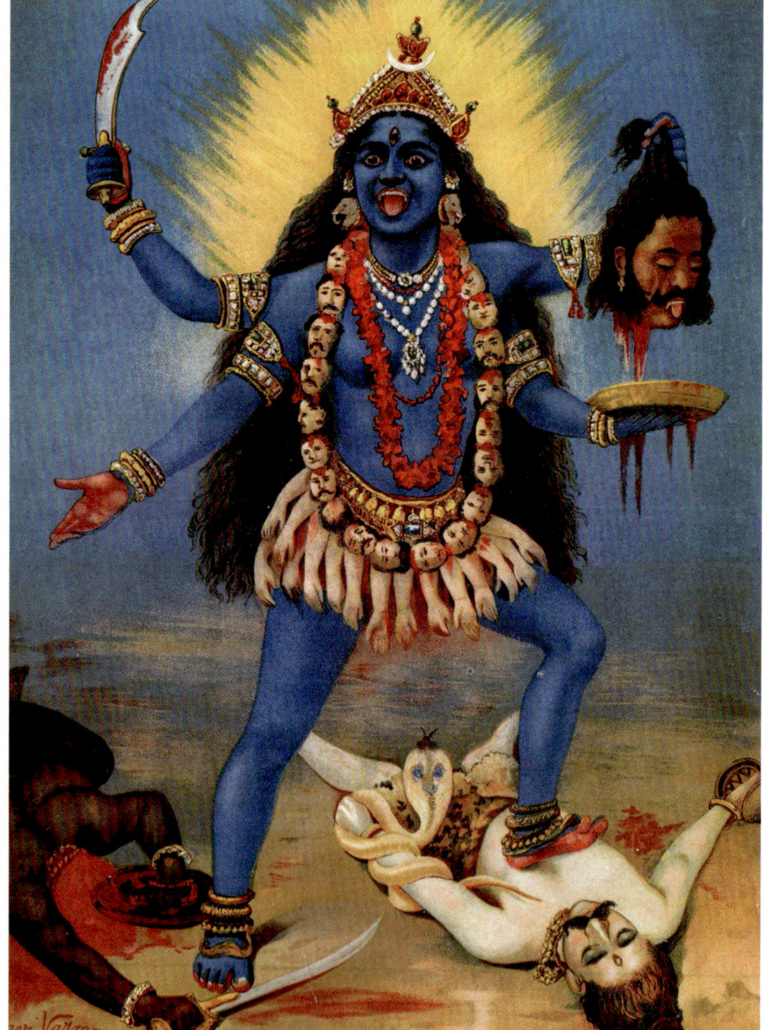

rites were often accompanied by the repainting of sacred ancestral images either in representational styles, as in our rock painting (**33**), or in what are to outsiders abstract patterns that nevertheless for the painters reenact the emergence of the people from revered sites and their travels across the sacred landscape from which they emerged in primordial times. Our image shows these creators in "X-ray style," with their bones and inner organs rendered schematically. The male in this painting is larger than the female, whose genitals are exaggerated, suggesting she has just given birth.

South Asia yields an extraordinary bounty of images of both females and mother goddesses, as well as more secular representations of mothers with children from Hindu and Buddhist cultures of India, Pakistan, Bangladesh, Tibet, Nepal, and Korea, spanning thousands of years. Our selection here is a mere sampling. Many are descendants of earlier goddess images, as well as *yoni* (vulva) and *linga* (phallus) symbols from the Indus Valley, yet in later times there are many textual accounts of numerous, multi-named and multivalent gods and goddesses in human form who are members of both celestial realms and the human world of couples and families. Shakti, Parvati, Durga, Sita, Lakshmi, Kali, and other female deities, usually with male counterparts, populate a bewildering landscape of mythology and history in such texts as the Vedas, Puranas, Upanishads, and the Ramayana. Numerous stone-cut temples contain an abundance of imagery, and there are as well thousands of portable sculptures of varying sizes, along with many paintings depicting a vast polytheistic pantheon not always easy to understand and align with specific texts. South Asian arts are also wonderfully, openly sensual and erotic, as expressed especially in Tantric practice and imagery, which many believers and practitioners see as paths to spiritual enlightenment. Indeed, the gods and goddesses are models for human behavior, and the vulva and phallus, as well as other aspects of female-male dualism, are widely depicted in symbolic and literal forms, far from complete here, in much art from this region. Further, what is symbolic of human beings and deities is often at the same time cosmological.

A wood sculpture of a birthing scene (**34**), for example, could refer to Aditi (Infinity) giving birth to the gods, including the male god Daksha (Dexterity)—as in a Vedic poem that says "After this the quarters of the sky, and the earth, were born from her who crouched with legs spread"[28]—at the beginning of time, when cosmic existence was created from nonexistence. Infinity and Dexterity created one another, a paradox of Hindu belief, when the creator creates himself, or the creatrix creates herself, as in circular time repeating itself. There are several versions of this birthing sculpture in wood and stone, showing a central mother deity with varied attendants supporting and helping her, that date to the first to fourth centuries.[29]

The gods, too, are both multi-named and ambiguous: representing humans, aspects of the larger world, human body parts, and abstract principles. Shakti is a great goddess, wife of Shiva, both a great god and, while male, possessing *shakti*, seen as the female principle and mother-womb power that permeates all creation, which is especially prominent in major male deities. Shiva and another wife, Parvati, together known as Uma-Maheshvara, appear in a loving, intimate embrace, dominant and central in a high relief stone sculpture from a central Indian temple (**35**). Parvati's right arm rests on Shiva's shoulder, while Shiva's left hand cups her breast. Near them are smaller images of family members: Ganesha, the elephant-headed god of the common people is below the couple to the left, and below them to the right is probably Skanda, general of the gods. But these children were not born of Parvati, who is barren (although Ganesha comes from the kneaded dirt shed by Parvati while bathing), but rather of Shiva, whose *shakti* is Parvati. These four deities do not constitute a family in the human sense, as each has separate qualities and roles in Hinduism, and the children are not born in the usual biological way.[30] Yet Parvati has many manifestations and names. She is a nurturing mother goddess who gives birth to all life forms (plants, animals, minerals), which she nourishes with her body, yet she later re-absorbs these life forms back into herself, devouring them, feeding upon them as the power of

death to produce new life. Thus, she is both creative and destructive. Another mother goddess with numerous small figures we can interpret as children comes from Madhya Pradesh or Rajasthan (**36**). The mother in this high-relief limestone temple fragment embraces and points to her children affectionately as other probable children cavort nearby.

The complex ambiguity of Indian art and religion is shown in the relationship between Shakti (deity) and *shakti* (principle), and from Wendy Doniger's account of Shiva as midwife and both female and a mother:

> *A devotee's daughter was about to give birth to her first child. Her mother could not cross the flooding Kaveri River in time to help her waiting daughter. So Shiva took the form of the old mother—"back bent like the crescent moon, hair white as moonlight, a bamboo staff in hand"—and came to her house. Uma (Parvati, Shiva's wife, and Ganga (the river [Ganges], often said to be a wife of Shiva) had been sent ahead with bundles. When labor began, Shiva played midwife; a boy was born and Mother Shiva cradled and cared for him as if he were Murukan (a deity also known as Skanda, also a son of Shiva). Soon the floods abated, and the real mother appeared on the doorstep. Shiva began to slip away. Seeing the two women, the young couple were amazed. "Which is my mother?" cried the girl. Before her eyes, Shiva disappeared into the sky like lightning.*[31]

39 Mother and Child

Rajasthan, Tanesar-Mahadeva, India
500 – 550 CE
Foliated dark green schist
30 × 10 × 6 in., 76.2 × 25.4 × 15.24 cm
Los Angeles County Museum of Art (LACMA),
Nasli and Alice Heeramaneck Collection,
Museum Associates Purchase

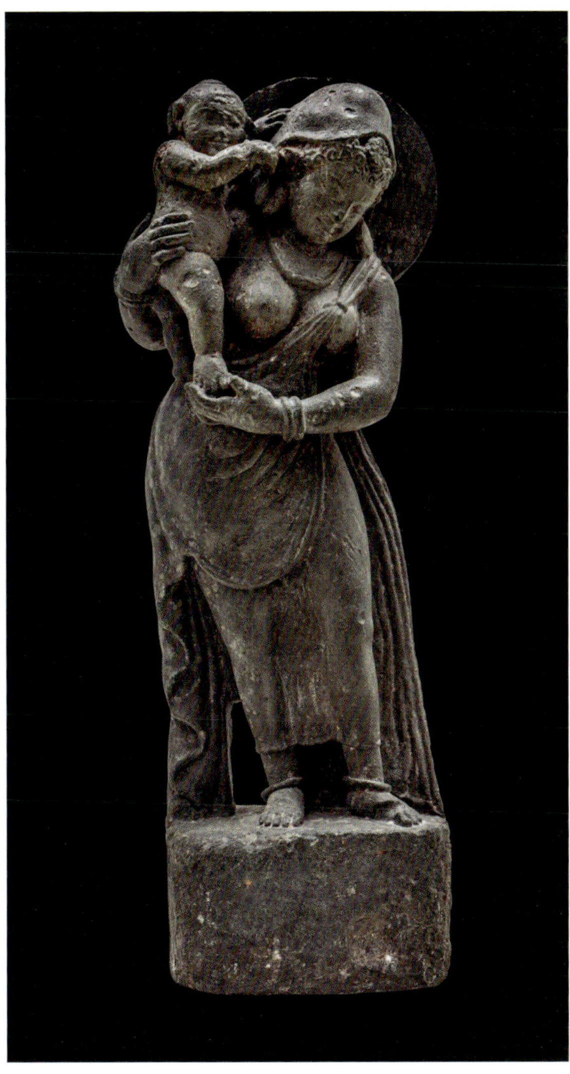

To further confuse the reader (as it has the writer!), Shasthi is the Bengali Hindu goddess of childbirth, whose devotees make images of her in their own likeness, often pregnant, with a newborn child at her breast, on her hip, or on her lap (**37**), a practice analogous to women in Ghana (West Africa) taking "child figures" to shrines so the resident deity will empower them to assist with conception and to ensure a safe pregnancy and healthy, handsome children. Our image of Shasthi is modern, from a temple near Bagbazar not far from Kolkata, proving the persistence of gods and beliefs a thousand or more years old.

Durga, another wife of Shiva, is a Hindu mother goddess associated with protection, war, and destruction. Her dark side is manifest especially in Kali, the *shakti* or female creative force that emerged from Shiva, who is also both benevolent and fearsome, thus exemplifying the dualistic nature of Hindu belief. Kali, too, embodies both positive and negative powers. She is considered the mother of all things, including language and human beings, worshipped by many sects as a divine mother, protector, and mother of the universe; she is the active cosmic power of eternal time. Yet she also destroys evil to protect goodness. In annihilation, through death and destruction, new creation and the seed of life emerge. At her annual festivals, the Durga Puja, many human sacrifices were offered before this practice was prohibited in 1835, and even today many water buffalo, sheep, pigs,

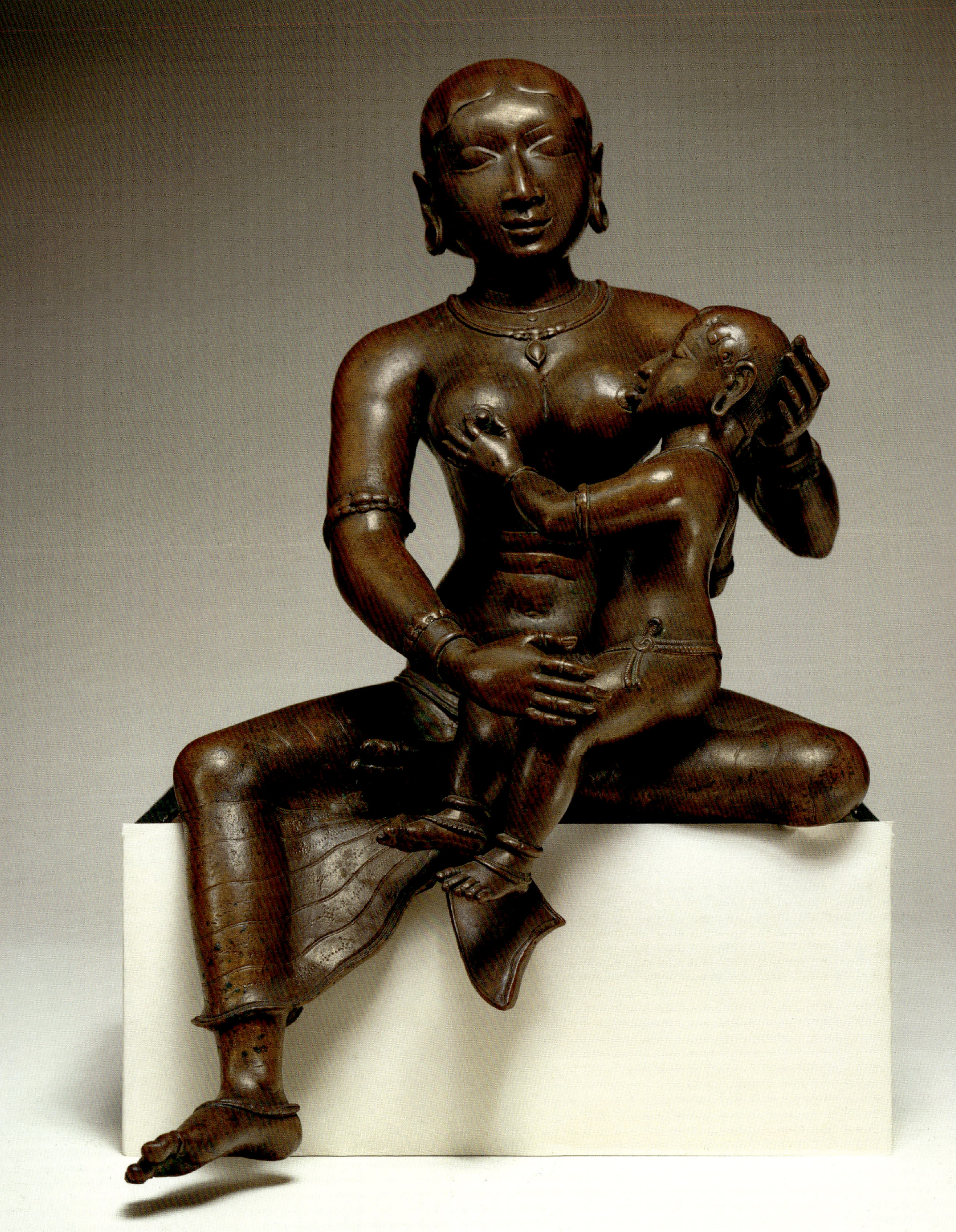

Tamil Nadu, Pudukkottai, and Tanjavur Districts, India
Early 1100s
Copper alloy
17 ½ × 11 ¹³⁄₁₆ × 10 ⅞ in., 44.5 × 30 × 27.6 cm
Metropolitan Museum of Art, New York
Purchase, Lita Annenberg Hazen Charitable Trust
Gift, in honor of Cynthia Hazen
and Leon B. Polsky, 1982

and fowl are immolated in her rituals. Kali's image is a complex of competing symbols: with black or blue skin, white teeth, red sunken eyes, disheveled hair, a garland of human skulls (symbolizing wisdom and power), a severed head in one of her left hands and a sword dripping blood in the other, gifts and blessings in her right hands, and a belt of human hands signifying *karma* (**38**). Her right foot rests on the prostate body of Shiva, her "father." There are many other forms of Kali as well, signaling her diverse, numerous, and multivalent attributes.

Among the thousands of South Asian figural sculptures, many are strongly naturalistic, and many radiate a powerful eroticism. Some of these may be as-yet-unidentified deities, while others are likely idealized depictions of real people (**39** and **40**). The informally posed stone statue of a standing woman holding a child on her shoulder, the child reaching for her hair, is a tender rendering of maternal affection, in a stop-motion, life-like pose. Details of draped clothing, jewelry, and posture contribute to its realism. The facial expression of the seated mother with her suckling child, somewhat stylized in smoothly finished brass, is impassive—but both mother and child are nevertheless portrayed as tangible, fleshy people, the mother's full breasts reflecting that she is in the prime of new motherhood. She affectionately holds her young child, who is no longer an infant.

The arts of China and Japan do not often feature images of mothers with children or show parental affection toward young children. In many periods and places in both cultures, pregnancy and childbirth were considered unsavory subjects, unfit for polite or public discourse, and women were often isolated during pregnancy and childbirth. Mothers with infants were therefore rarely depicted in painting and sculpture, which were mainly made for the elite. Exceptions are the Chinese Buddhist bodhisattva Guanyin and her Japanese counterpart, Kannon. Both are derived from the male Indian bodhisattva (a spiritually enlightened person who stays on earth as an example for faithful Buddhists to venerate and follow) Avalokiteśvara. Both are earthly divinities who embody qualities of compassion, mercy, and love, and both were and still are worshipped by women desiring children. While these Asian deities developed independently from the Virgin Mary in the West and Byzantium, their ascribed qualities are similar, just as the statues are analogous in their postures (shown embracing a son), in their varied materials and different sizes, and in their placement in shrines, temples, churches, and domestic altars. An elegant sixteenth-century Chinese Ming dynasty ivory carving of Guanyin, known as "bestower of sons," is depicted holding her son, shown as a diminutive adult—just as Christ is seen in many renderings of him in his mother's arms (**41**). The graceful curve of Guanyin's body, followed as well in the meticulous details of her draped garment, comes from the gentle curve of the elephant tusk from which the exquisite

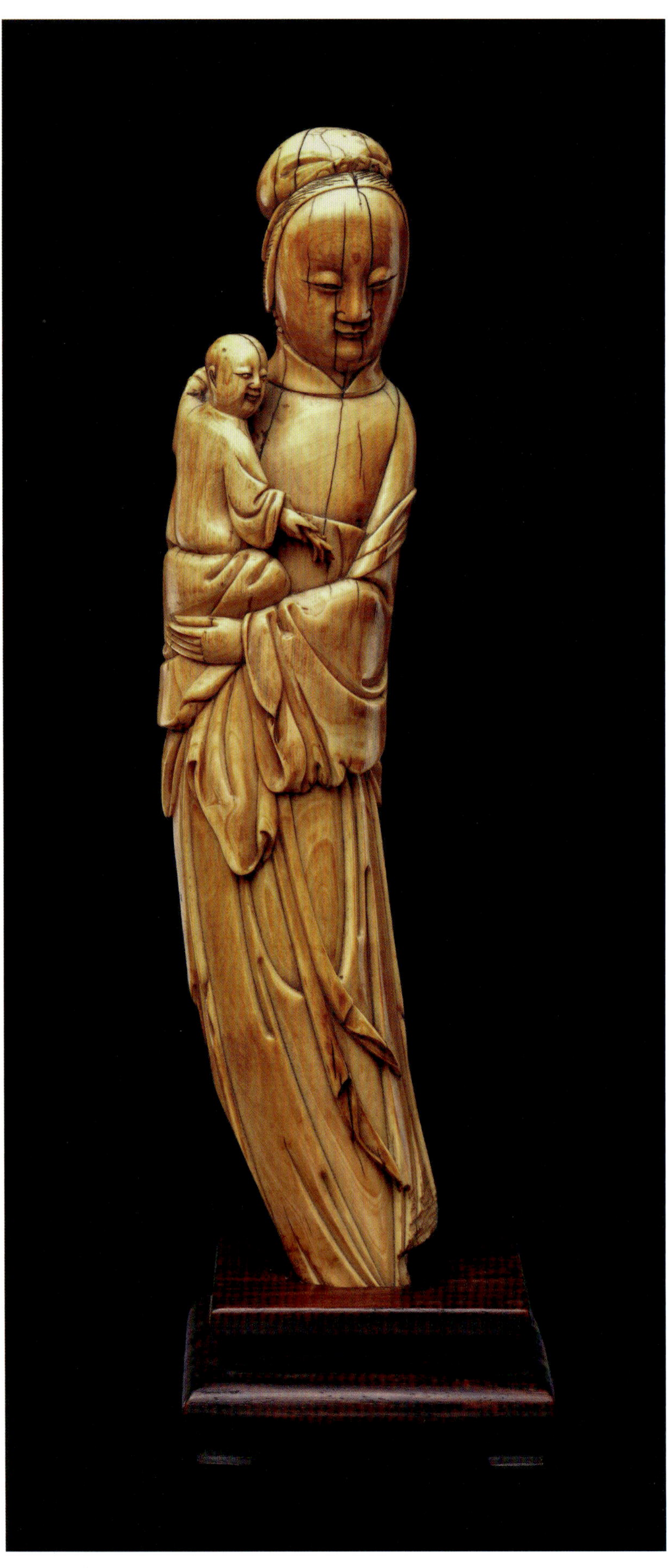

41 Bodhisattva Guanyin

China
Ming dynasty, 1500 – 1600
Ivory
9 ¾ in., 24.8 cm
Metropolitan Museum of Art, New York,
Rogers Fund, 1913

**42 Guanyin, Goddess of Mercy with
Child and Four Companions**

China
Ming dynasty, 1368 – 1644
Ceramic
14 in., 35.5 cm
Hallwyl Museum, Stockholm, Sweden

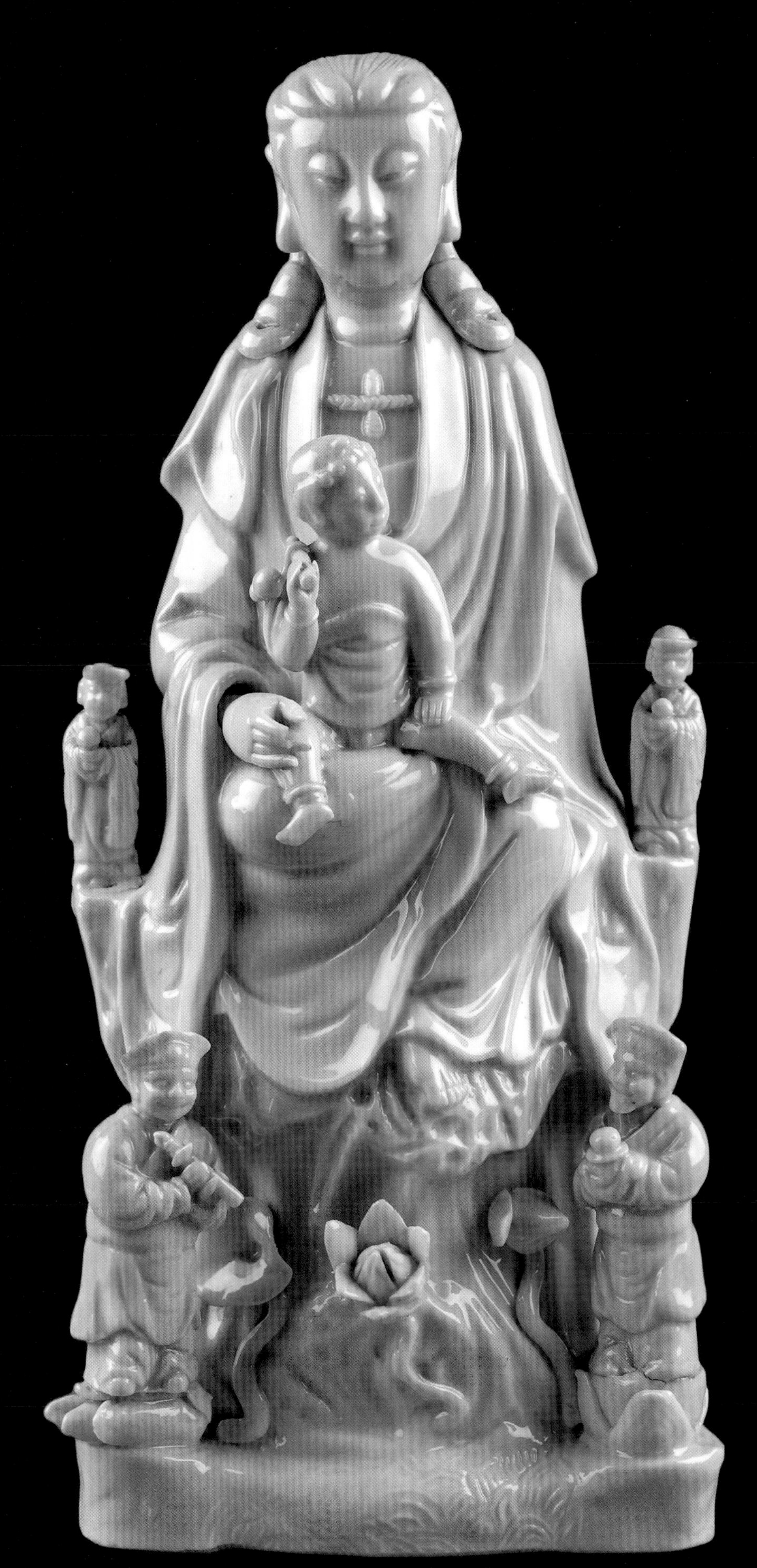

sculpture was carved. Ivory was a rare and sought-after material, symbolic of purity and goodness. A second image of Guanyin, this time with her son seated on her lap, is rendered in white porcelain, another symbol of purity (**42**). She also has two small guardian figures flanking a lotus flower in front of her throne and sits between two small figures, probably also guardians, on the arms of her throne. Such images were placed on small domestic altars in homes, while public temples featured more monumental images. A third Guanyin adorns a scroll painting from the late sixteenth-century Ming dynasty (1368–1644). She sits on a royal lion and holds a male child wearing emblems of high rank, with two attendants nearby (**43**). The style is refined and detailed; undoubtedly the scroll was owned by a person of high status and wealth.

Kannon, the Japanese rendering of Guanyin, is a very popular deity to this day. Kannon entered Japan from China in the late sixth century. Daikannon, a 328-foot-tall statue of Kannon located in Sendai, near Hokkaido, is among the largest statues in the world (**44**), and there are several other smaller but still enormous outdoor, public images of Kannon, who is also featured in temples and domestic shrines. While earlier depictions render Kannon as male, in more recent depictions, Kannon is represented as a female; she is the divine mother, the child-giver, the protector, the savior. She prevents sickness and disaster, fosters fertility and safe childbirth, and assists in educating and raising children—all sought at her shrines and temples. The Jibo Kannon—*jibo* means

"compassionate mother"—who in recent centuries is depicted holding a child in her arms, reached Japan from China in the seventeenth century, stimulated by Christian images of the Virgin and Child; she is sometimes called the Maria Kannon. Sculptures and paintings of Kannon are numerous and very diverse over the centuries, as are her attributes. She is also, for example, the bodhisattva of mariners and fish, protector of pets and other animals. At the time of writing this chapter, six images of Guanyin and Kannon are among the twenty tallest sculptures in the entire world, testimony to the enormous appeal of these deities.

Among the arts of the pre-Columbian Americas are many maternity and related sculptures from different eras and geographic regions, including some tableaus that can be interpreted as depicting families. Virtually all have been unearthed from burials and other ancient sites, too few of which have been excavated by archaeologists. The result is a corpus of material, the specific uses and meanings of which are too often unknown or unclear. Rarely do we have much insight into the early American cultures (e.g., classic or pre-classic periods) of maternity that are parallel, for example, to the African examples discussed earlier, until later, precolonial and post-conquest eras. Maternity imagery, too, is very unevenly distributed in the New World. It is sparse in North America north of the Rio Grande, plentiful in Mesoamerica (Mexico and Central American countries), and relatively sparse in South America. It is difficult to argue from absence; why some

43 **Guanyin the Bringer of Sons**

China
Ming dynasty, late 1500s
Hanging scroll; ink, color, and gold on silk
47 ½ × 23 ¾ in., 120.7 × 60.3 cm
Metropolitan Museum of Art, New York
Purchase, Friends of Asian Art Gifts, 1989

44 **Sendai Kannon**

Daikanmitsuji Temple,
Sendai, Japan
1991
328 feet

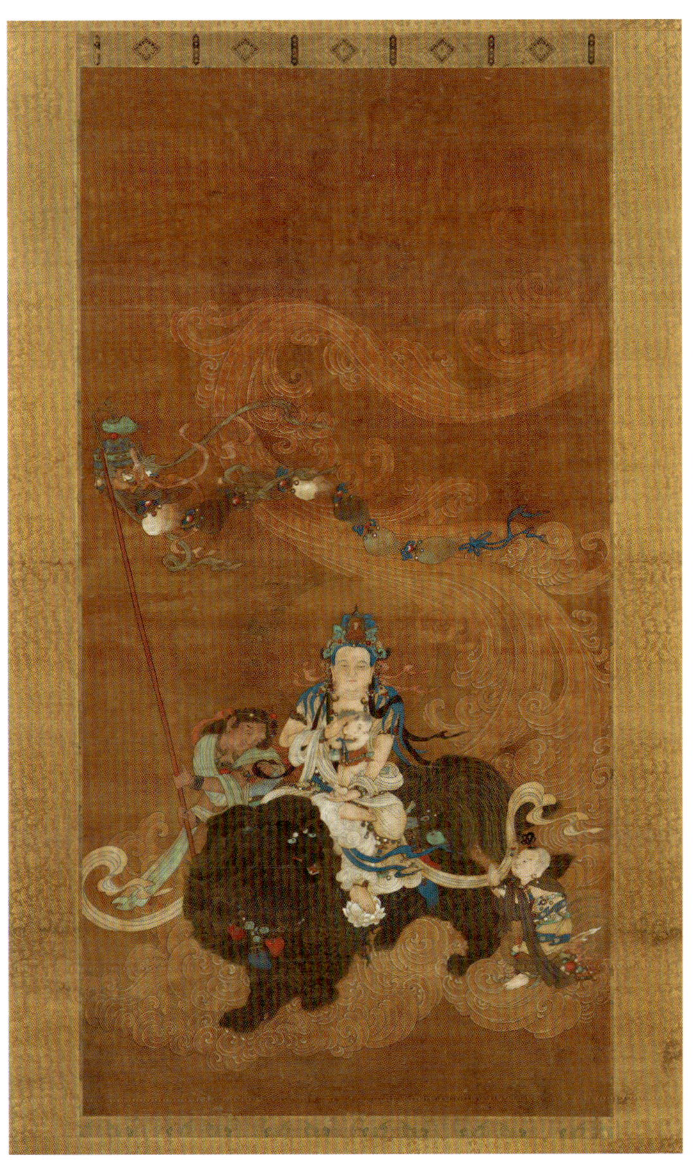

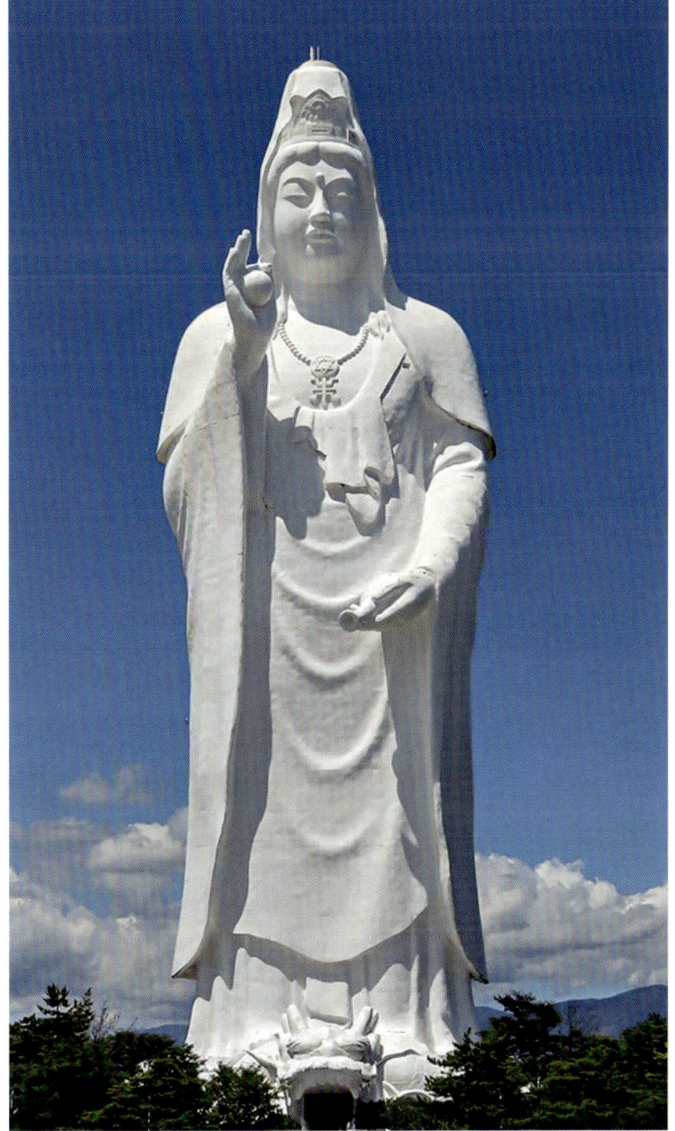

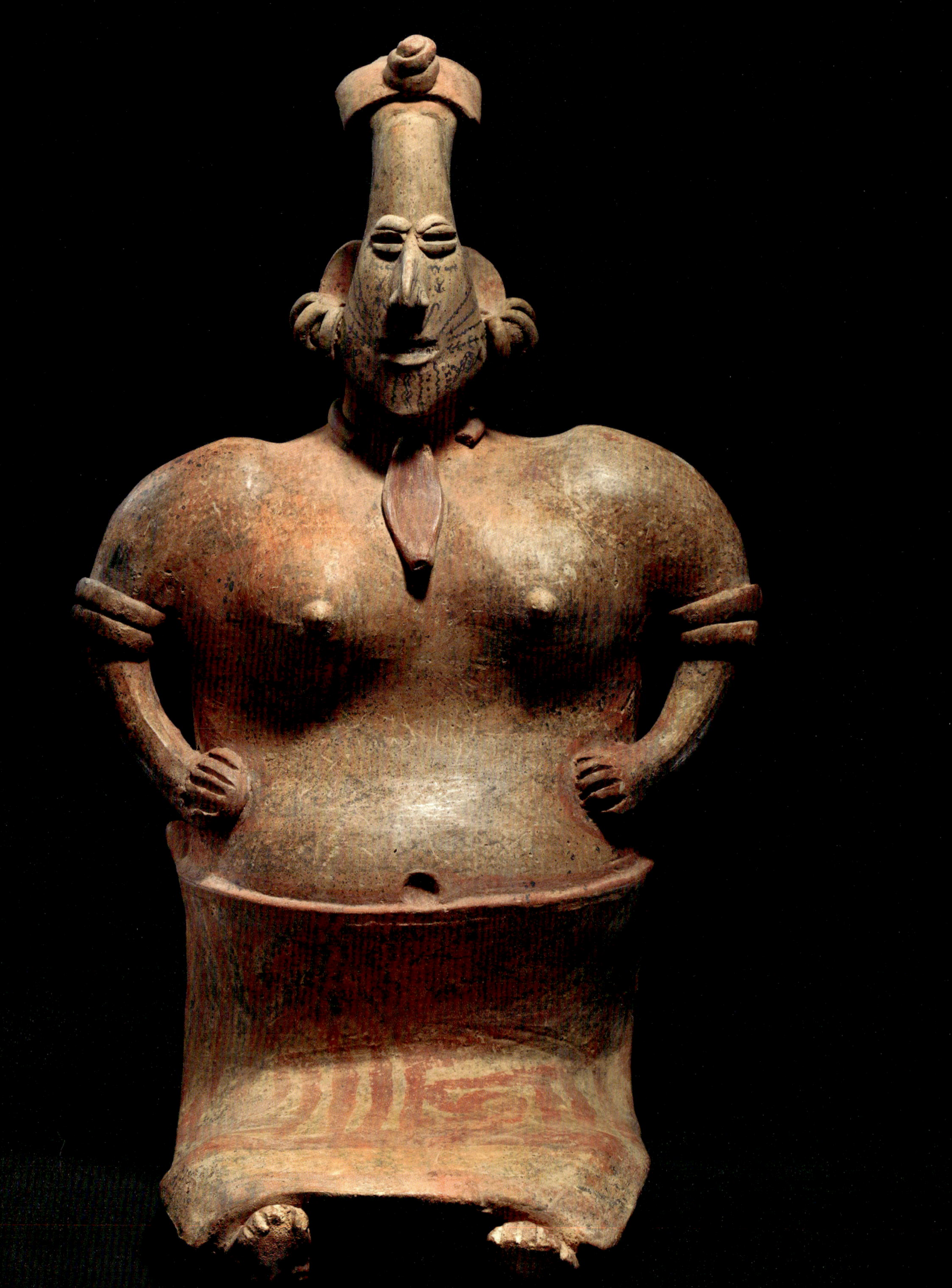

45 Jalisco Seated Female Figure

Arneca-Etzatlan style, West Mexico
100 BCE – 250 CE
Terracotta
24 in. high, 61 cm
The Stuart Handler Collection

46 Nayarit Figure of a Woman in Labor

San Sebastian style, West Mexico
100 BCE – 250 CE
Terracotta
27 in. high, 69.58 cm
The Stuart Handler Collection

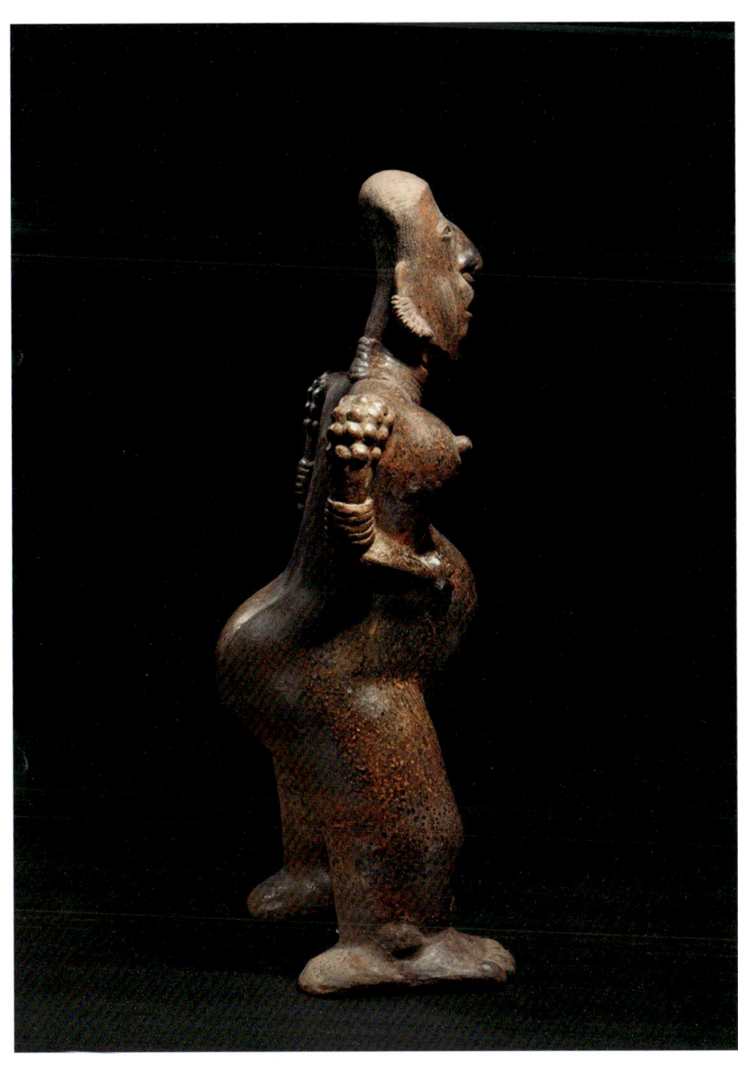

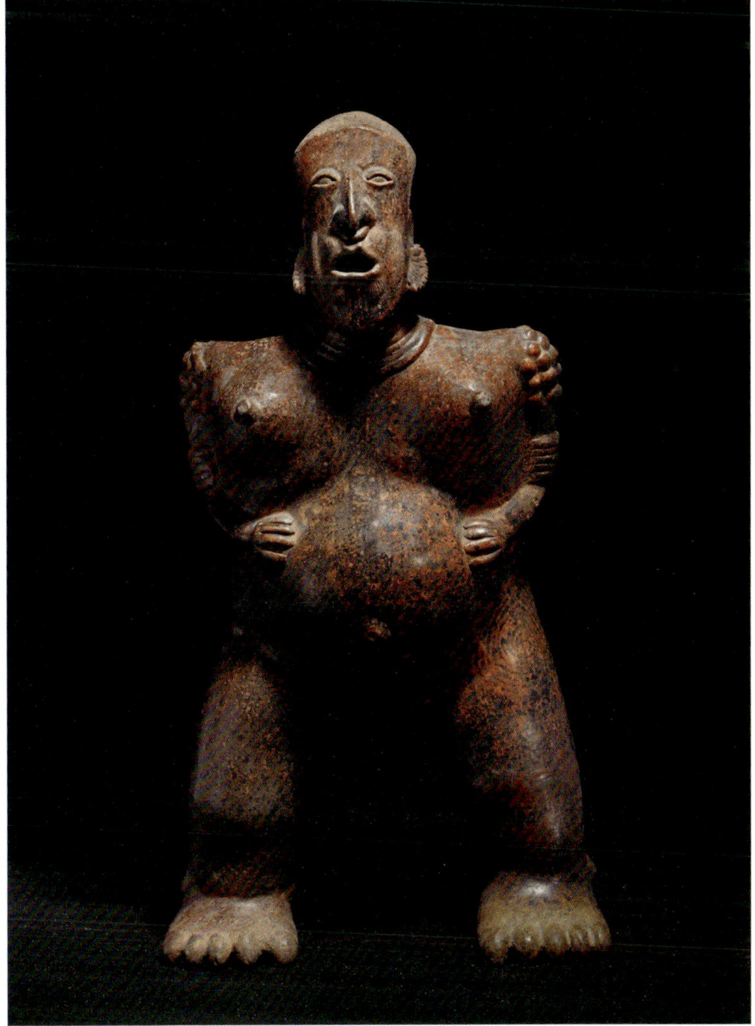

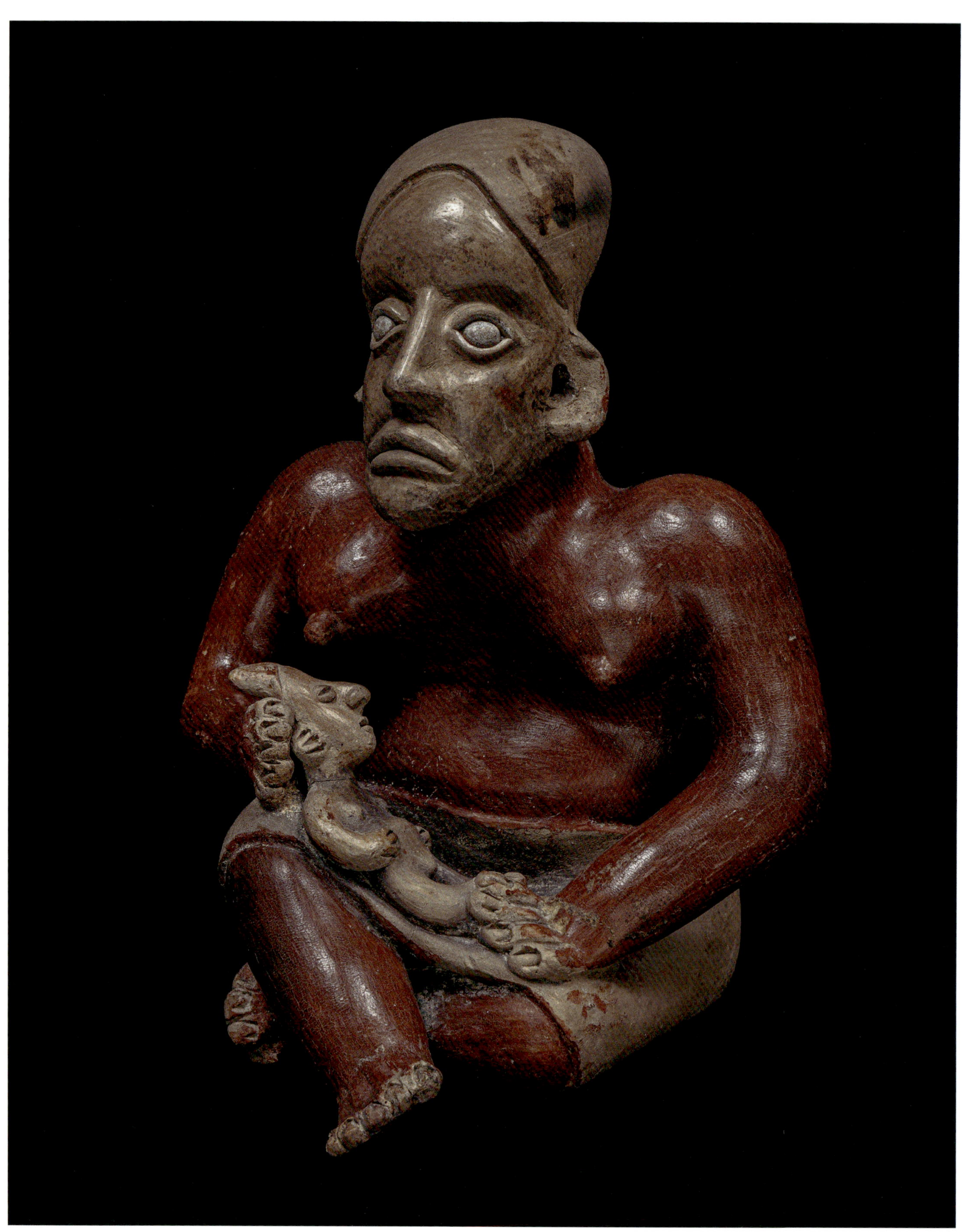

47 Jalisco Maternity Figure

State of Jalisco, Mexico
200 BCE – 200 CE
13 ½ in., 34.29 cm
Private Collection

48 Small House with Six People, a Dog, and Food

Ixtlan del Rio, Nayarit, Mexico
100 BCE – 250 CE
Terracotta
Anthropos Gallery,
Laguna Beach, California

cultures embrace maternity figures in their arts and others do not is very difficult to determine unless there is a stated rationale, as in China and Japan.

What we do have, especially in Mesoamerica, is a huge variety of poses, postures, and gestures in maternity and related imagery from virtually all regions and eras. The West Mexican cultures of Colima, Nayarit, and Jalisco produced dozens, and probably hundreds, of versions. Most are from pre-classic periods (ca. 500 BCE–400 CE). Nearly all have come from poorly excavated graves, so their particular roles in association with either living or dead people are not known, even if we can speculate that maternal affection toward infants and young children was keenly observed by the artists who modeled and fired these clay images. Many are quite small, only five or six inches high, while others, such as two pregnant females—a seated one from Nayarit, perhaps already in labor as her open mouth implies, and a standing woman from Jalisco—are more than two feet tall, suggesting that these depictions of pregnancy had considerable importance to the local people when the figures were made (**45** and **46**). While the rendering of the head and body of the standing woman is quite conventionalized—she has short arms and a very narrow cranium—the sculptor has nevertheless carefully depicted robust shoulders and torso along with a headdress, earrings, neck pendant,

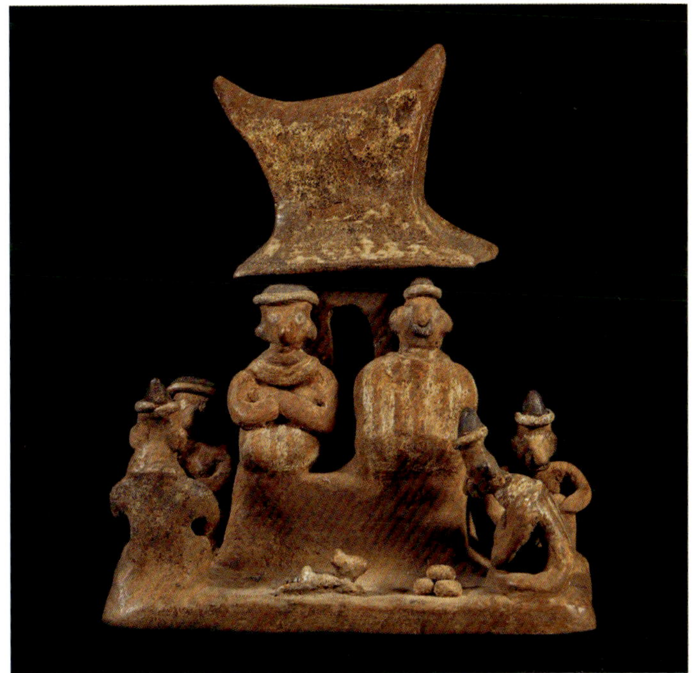

armlets, and precise facial markings, perhaps tattoos. All were almost certainly observed from life, indicating the person represented was of some status. A third pre-classic period West Mexican image is a mother-and-child from Jalisco (**47**). The broad-shouldered mother holds her child in her lap, yet she looks out past the child, showing no visible emotion, which can be observed in other maternity images from these sites. Nayarit and other West Mexican sites also have yielded several quite complex scenes, miniature terracotta versions of rituals, village life, ballgames, and families. Our example shows what is surely a family scene of people gathered near a small building (**48**). Two larger central figures, raised on a dais, are flanked by four smaller people, including a mother-and-child, plus hearthstones or fruit, and a dog.

The Olmec are often considered the mother culture of later Mesoamerican civilizations; their primary sites were in Veracruz near the Gulf of Mexico. While Olmec cosmology is not fully understood, the so-called were-jaguar infant, with a cleft head, in the lap of a person neither clearly female nor male, is said to personify maize sprouts, the center and organizing principle of the four-cornered Olmec (and later Maya) world, thus linking childhood to cosmology (**49**). Recent scholars say the subject is a priest preparing to sacrifice a child. Here, as elsewhere in the world, the cultural construction of childbirth relates it to cosmic events. As a Metropolitan Museum of Art text has it: "The baby, this maize sprout made manifest, then stands in for the center of the world. The preoccupation of Olmec peoples with child-rearing and the mythological connections between the life cycles of infants and agriculture transcend time and space."[32] The recurring presence of apparent children in Olmec monuments and of Olmec-influenced babies or children in later Mesoamerican cultures distant from the Olmec heartland would seem to speak to the importance of children themselves, and perhaps mothers with children. This refined, carefully observed child from the Las Bocas site in Puebla state is made of hollow, fired clay (**50**). It is an unsexed, fleshy baby with a jowly face and down-turned mouth, seated with splayed legs, infantile proportions and posture, its right hand raised to its mouth, the left hand resting on its left thigh. What this sculpture represents is not clear, although Olmec infant sacrifice was known and such figures may have been substitutes for actual babies. They could also represent mythological beings, or be portraits or some sort of ritual agent or memorial. Though their function and identity remain enigmatic, their considerable numbers would seem to reveal the importance of children in Olmec cosmology and ritual, and thus in peoples' lives.

A graphic representation of childbirth is the subject of a two-spouted terracotta vessel from Calima in Colombia, dated ca. 200 BCE–600 CE (**51**). The mother lies back in a supine position, hands placed symmetrically behind her head, legs apart. Her facial features, while simple, seem

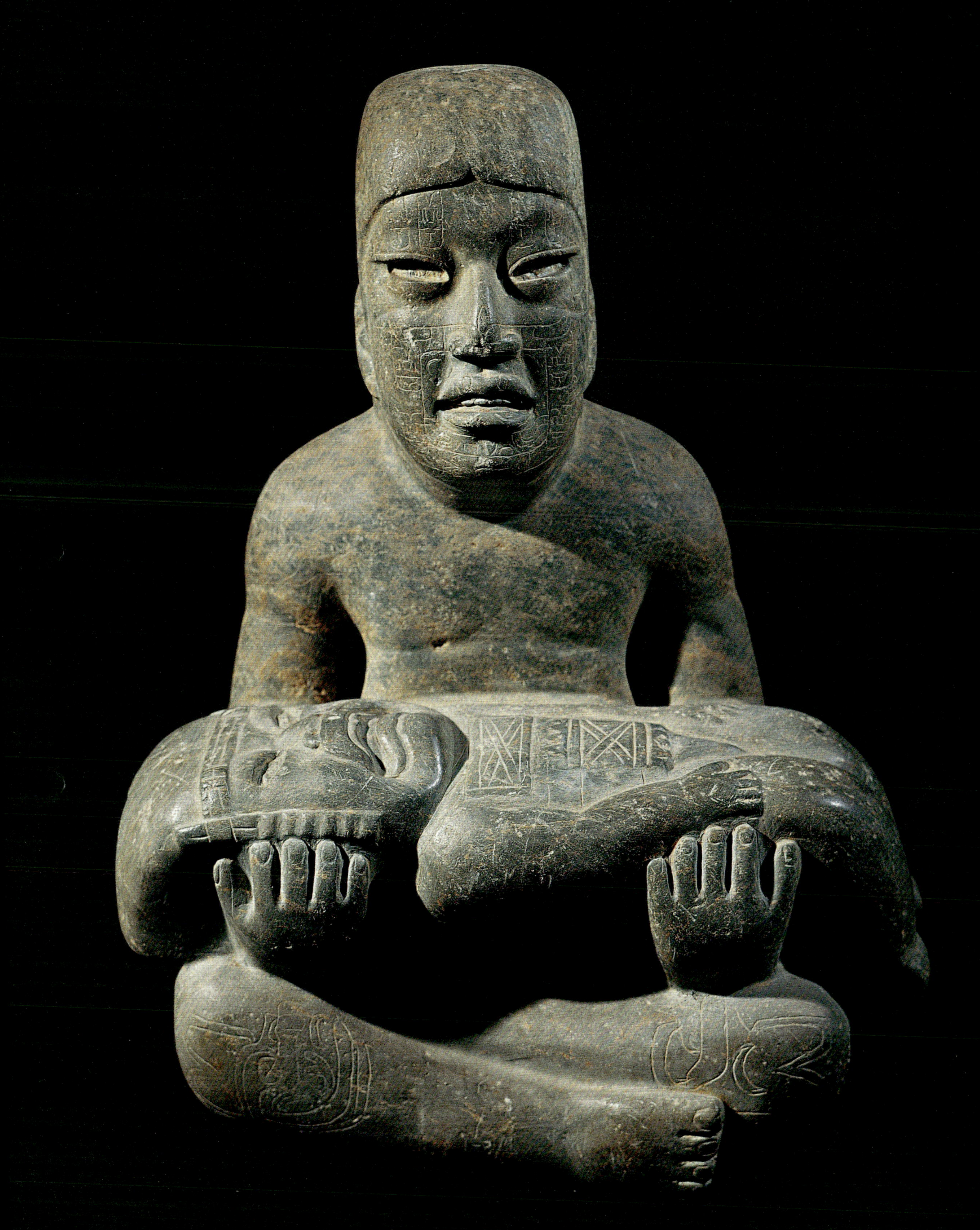

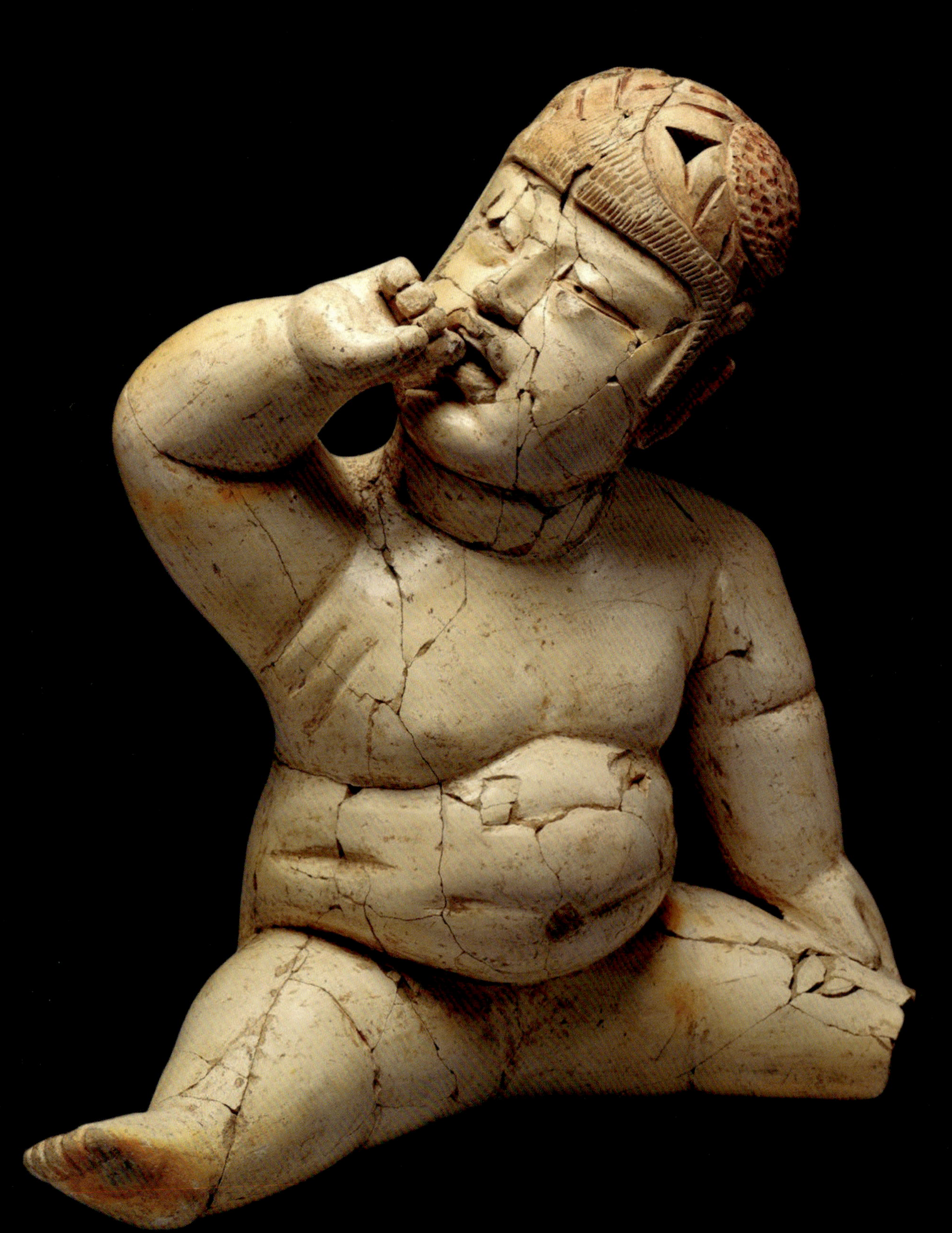

to express pain, which is understandable as the head of her child descends visibly from her birth canal. The faces of both mother and child are white, while her body is red with incised lines showing a necklace emphasizing her projecting breasts, and possibly wristlets and anklets. While common in life, childbirth is quite rarely represented in art, although several such scenes are found in the pre-Columbian corpus, from West Mexico through Central America to Colombia and the Moche culture of Peru. We have seen above images of pregnancy and mothers with infants; these birth vessels continue the cycle, completed at death.

Another South American sculpture, a charming seated mother with a child in her lap—whether alive or dead is unclear—comes from a Jama-Coaque site in Ecuador (dated 350 BCE–400 CE, **52**). Elaborately dressed, with jewelry, the mother appears to be of elite status. Perched beside her are two birds whose meaning is not clear.

The lid of a classic Maya incense burner from Tiquisate, Guatemala—copal (a tree resin) incense was burned ritually to communicate with gods and ancestors—shows another elaborately dressed and bejeweled woman of high status holding her child, whose front teeth have been modified, a common Maya practice (**53**). Such implements were common and have been found in temple ruins, caves, shrines, and in burials, proving the importance of incense in Maya rites. It is not known why a maternity

is featured here, but it is possibly because women seeking children worshipped at the shrine served by this incense burner, a shrine that perhaps served the cult of one among many Maya fertility deities. The Maya moon goddess reflects that culture's linkage between the female body and moon cycles. She is associated with sexuality, fertility, healing, procreation, motherhood, the growth of both human beings and vegetation, water in various forms, weaving and other women's crafts, and disease. Her image is painted on a Maya drinking vessel, a symbol of the crescent moon shown behind the seated goddess. In other artworks, the moon goddess appears with the complementary male maize god, suggesting a kind of fused, even androgynous identity.

Other later Mesoamerican and South American peoples produced an abundance of artworks relating to our themes, akin to texts that prove the vital importance of maternity. There are many classic Maya sculptures of male and female couples showing affection to one another, and mothers with children, as in a terracotta from Jaina dated ca. 600–900 (**54**). These figurines were excavated from tombs on Jaina Island and inland valley sites near the Usumacinta River, and many were found on the chests of interred individuals, suggesting they were probably made specifically for burials; some may have been portraits of those interred, while others may have been deities, although the subjects of the sculptures do not necessarily

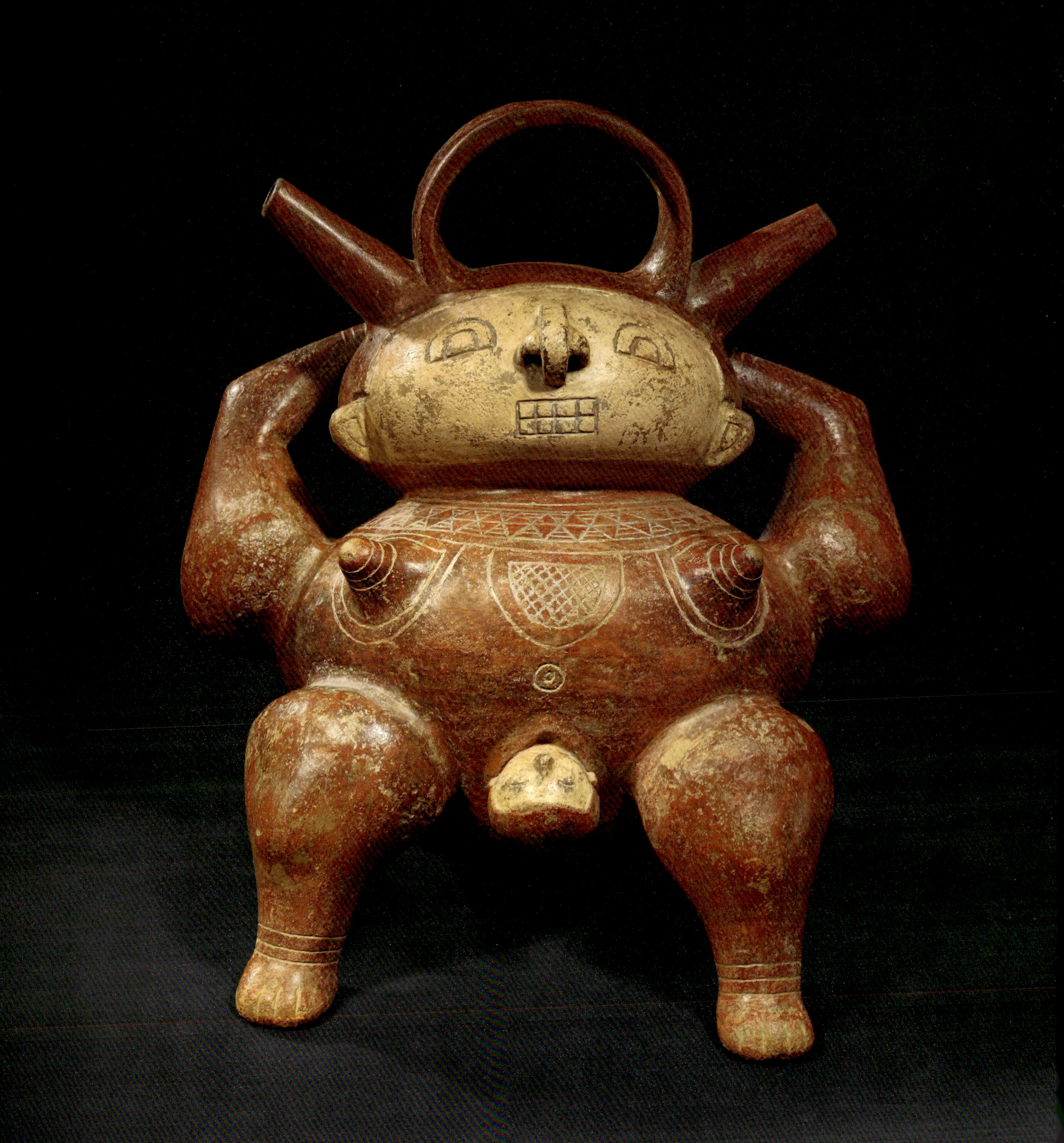

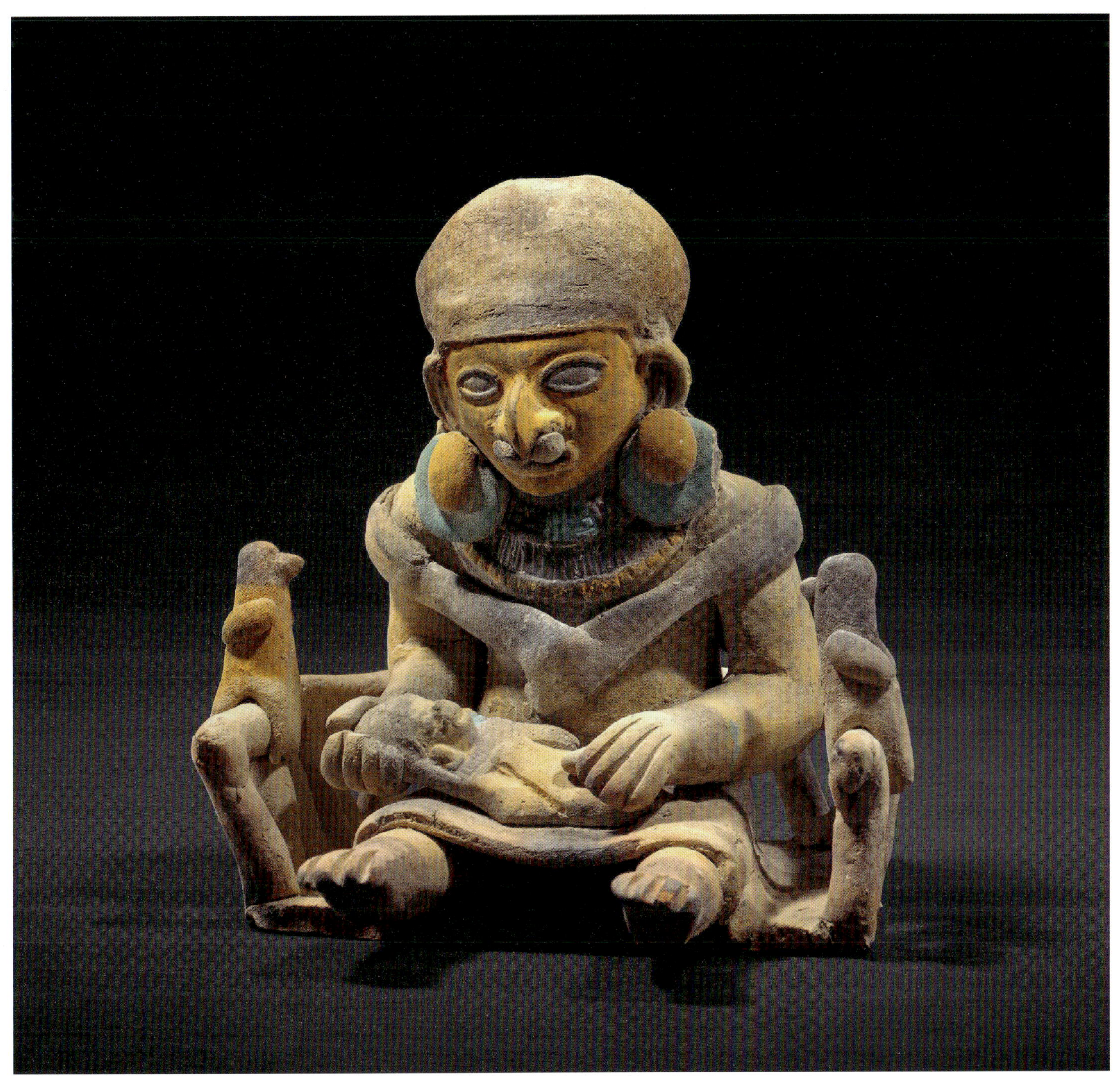

53   Figural *Incensario* Lid

Maya culture, Tiquisate,
Escuintla, Guatemala
400 – 700 CE
Terracotta
19 ½ in., 49.53 cm
Private Collection

54   Noblewoman with a Small Child

Jaina, Campeche, Mexico
600 – 900 CE
Terracotta

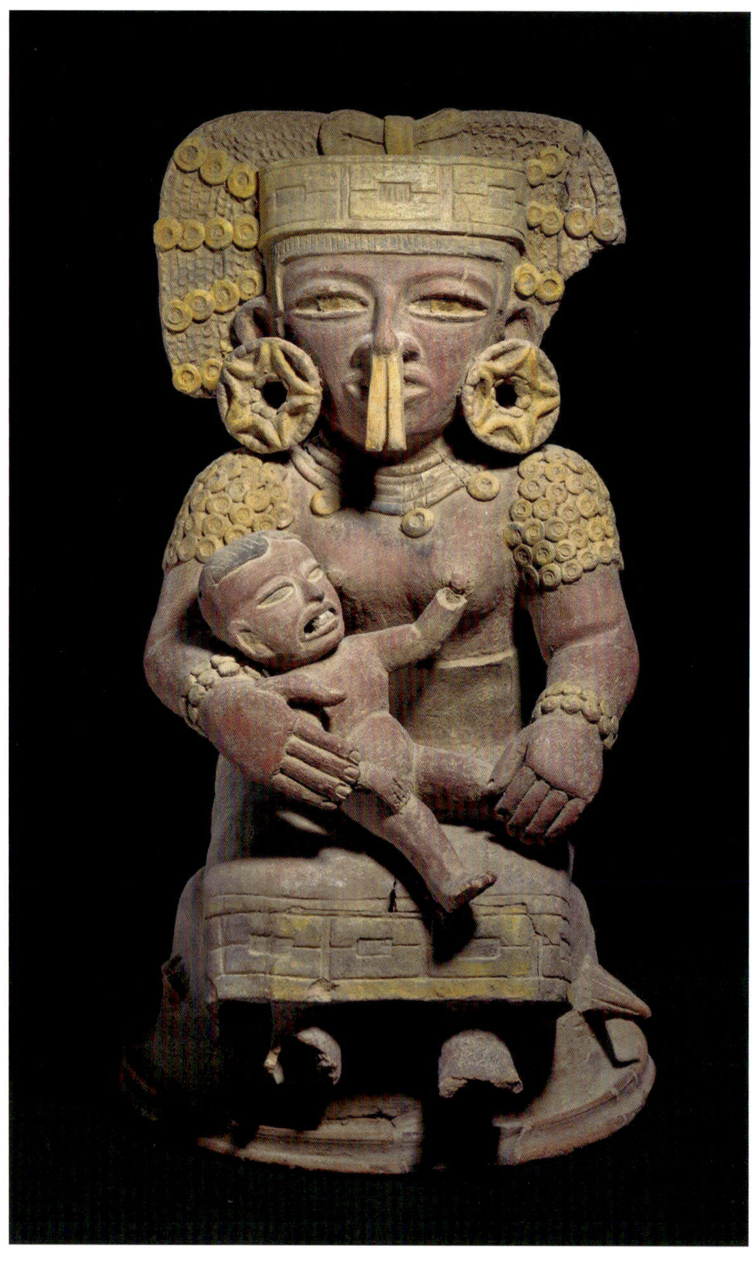

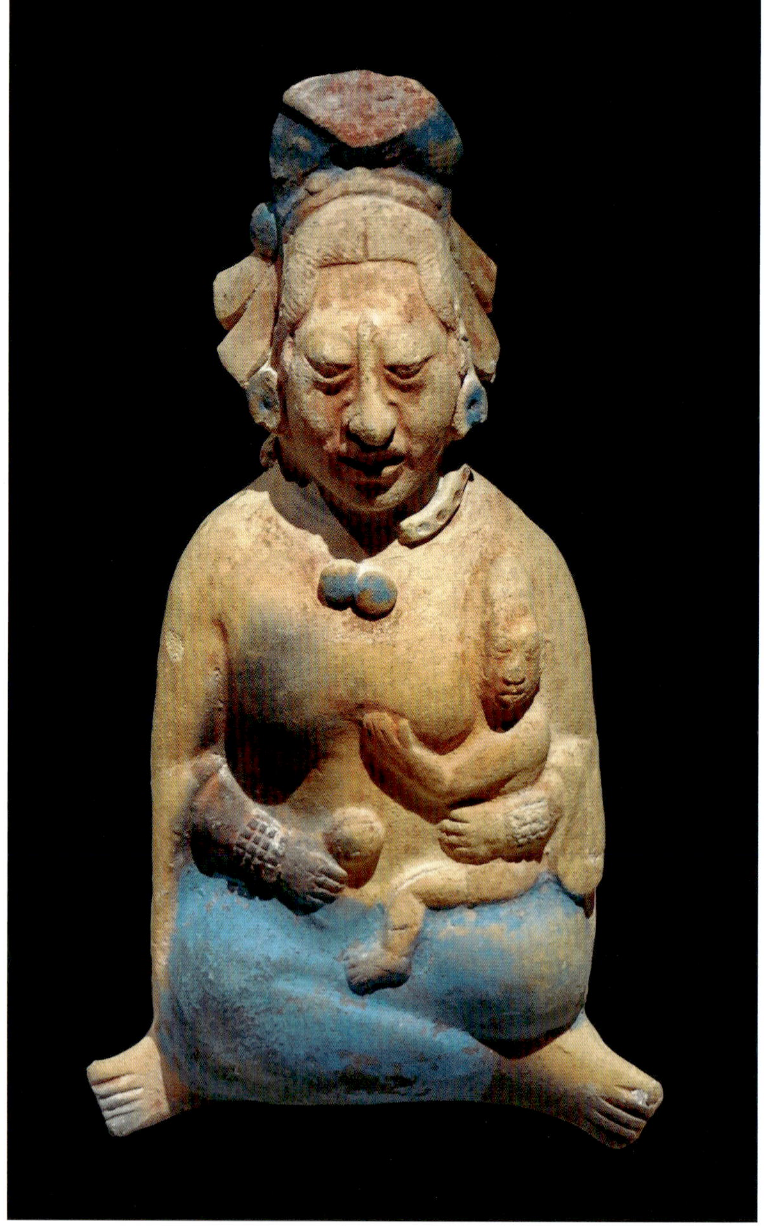

 Great Goddess of Teotihuacan

Reproduction of one of the murals from the Tepantitla
apartment complex located at Teotihuacan
National Museum of Anthropology, Mexico City

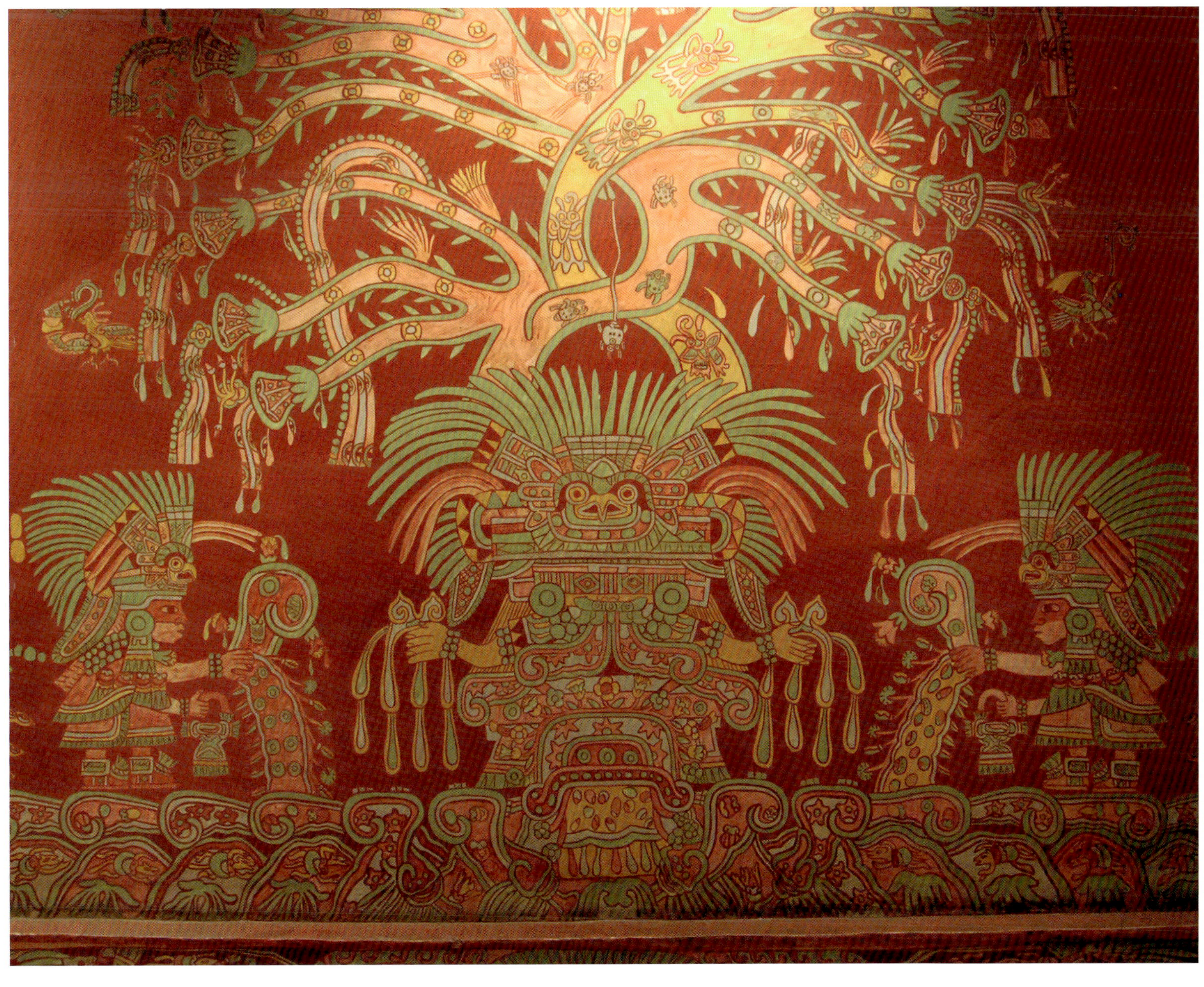

accord with the dead person. A maternity figure could be found with the corpse of a male, for example, and a warrior figure might be found in a woman's grave.

In the great central Mesoamerican civilization at Teotihuacan (ca. 100 BCE–700 CE), several complex fresco wall paintings at Tepantitla, a house believed to have been a residence of high-status people, have been identified as aspects of the great goddess of Teotihuacan. She was an underworld deity associated with darkness, water, war, and possibly creation as a mother goddess, as well as being linked with vegetation and fertility. The painting shows an aspect or version of her with elaborate flowering plants growing from behind her head, with spiders, considered creatures of darkness, nearby; her hands also give out gifts of water, seeds, and jade (**55**). This deity is also sometimes interpreted as male or of mixed gender, and for this reason relates to the Mayan maize god, also a male creator, even as maize itself was seen as female. Like other Mesoamerican deities, this one has ambivalent positive and negative attributes.

One of pre-Columbian America's larger and most famous monumental sculptures is the post-classic Aztec goddess Coatlicue, meaning "Snakes-her-skirt" in Nahuatl. This colossal image was found in 1790 in the Templo Mayor (Great Temple) of Tenochtitlan, the early sixteenth century Aztec capital in what is now Mexico City (**56**). It is an amalgam of what are for us somewhat grisly symbols: a skirt of writhing rattlesnakes; a necklace of human hearts and hands centered on a human skull; and a head comprised of converging, fanged serpent heads. Her arms and legs are also formed of serpents. We see in this important sculpture a strong contrast with the benign, fairly naturalistic renderings of mothers and children from several earlier pre-Columbian cultures, and, thankfully, we know quite a lot about this and other gods in the large Aztec pantheon. As recorded in legends and written codices, Coatlicue was the primordial Aztec earth and mother goddess who gave birth to the supreme male deity, Huizilopochtli. She, along with other female creators, including Xochiquetzal (see below), bore other gods and four hundred sons and five daughters who gave up their lives to give birth to a new era—the "fifth sun," the moon and stars—thus to "help create a habitable world."[33] Coatlicue's snake skirt is also interpreted as a magical garment, comprised of several woven cloth panels, of the sort venerated for its power to help women conceive and give birth, and to cure sick children. As Cecelia Klein puts it: "Coatlicue sacrificed herself voluntarily to provide the Mexica with the warmth, light, and changing seasons that brought them crops, food, and good health."[34] And the deity returned to life—aided by the serpent skirt that is her name—and became a major force, even a political force, in Aztec society. Like Kali in Hindu religion, Coatlicue is creative yet also has a dark side.

Aztec culture relied on periodic human sacrifice to maintain the cycles of life: day and night—the return of

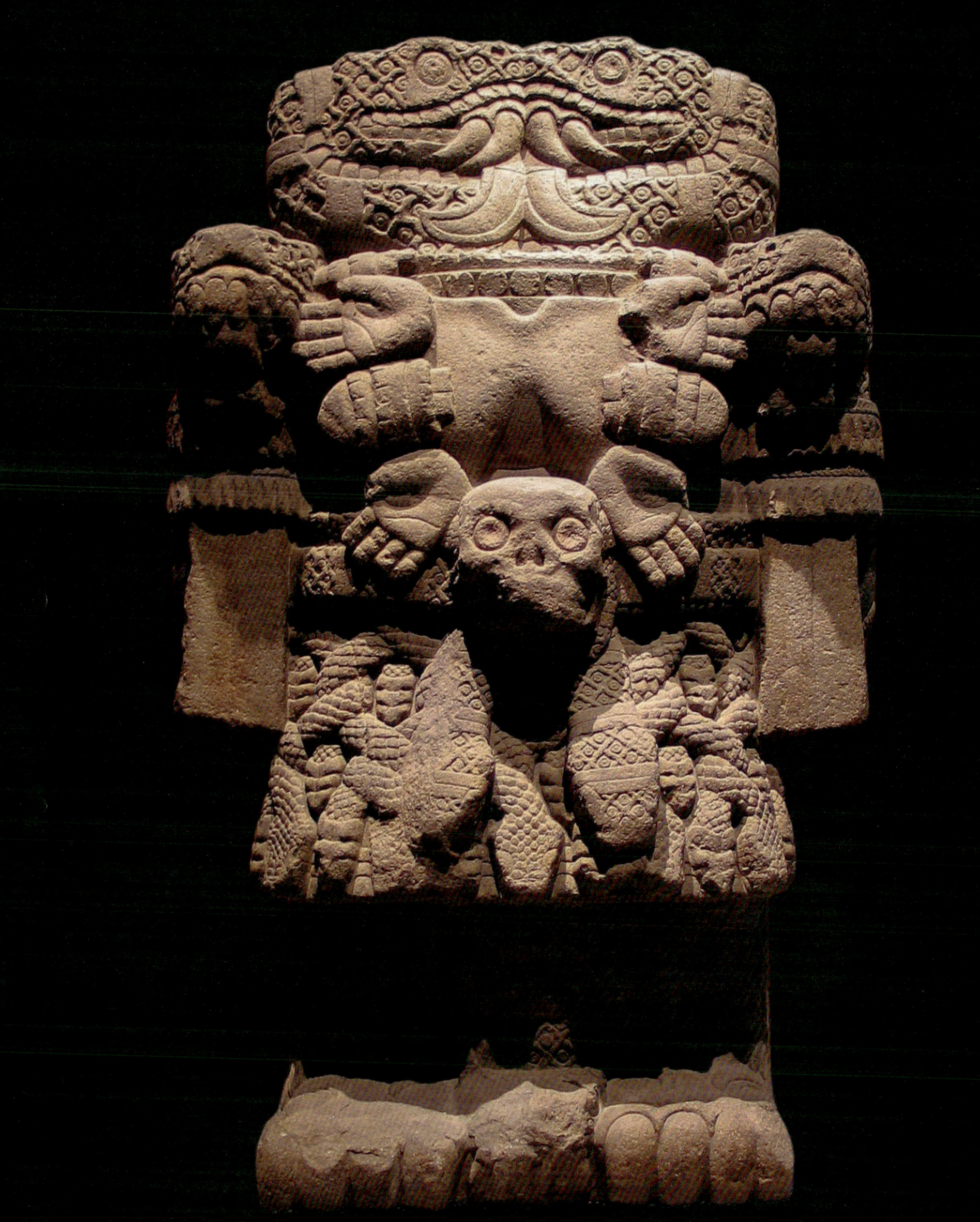

the sun—and, indeed, life on earth. The Aztec also had several gods who dealt with fertility and childbirth, which they saw as tied into and indeed the result of human sacrifice. For Aztecs, as for many, both birth and death were fraught processes and subjects. Both infant and maternal mortality were common in pre-colonial and earlier times, so midwifery was valued and important, and some deities were patrons of midwives, who were powerful older women. Childbirth was sometimes compared to warfare, and women who died in childbirth were honored as fallen warriors, as if they were heroes who sacrificed themselves or were sacrificed on altars so the life cycle could be maintained. Regeneration is among the prime tenets of Aztec thought and ritual activity. After death, a human is in the "deathly underworld," as is the sun at night. Dawn brings rebirth; the souls of young warriors slain in battle help the sun to rise again.[35]

Cihuacoatl—meaning "Woman Snake" in Nahuatl—was another Aztec fertility and motherhood deity remembered in early colonial times as a primordial creator, a founding ancestor, and protector of midwives and childbearing women, as well as being the patron of women who died in childbirth. And like Coatlicue, Cihuacoatl had a dark, destructive side; she was thought to haunt crossroads and steal children. Certain medicinal plants used to help with childbirth problems are also associated with her, yet the same plants could also have negative effects. Klein has argued that Cihuacoatl evolved into a more malevolent deity in late post-classic times, which would account for the statue (from Calixtlahuaca) identified as representing her in the National Museum of Anthropology in Mexico City, which includes the dark symbols of skulls and severed hands.[36] In burials outside the Aztec capitol, numerous miniature figures also holding children have been found, some seeming to be images of this "mother." These small sculptures, some examples of which have been recovered from domestic settings, may have been associated with childbirth deities and their cults (**57**).[37]

Xochiquetzal—meaning "Precious Flower" in Nahuatl— is the young and beautiful Aztec goddess of youth, sexual love, beauty, and household crafts practiced by women, such as weaving, embroidery, and other arts.[38] In a codex illustration, she is shown as a richly attired, youthful maiden holding a child to her breast, sprouting feathers from her headdress, and facing a flowering plant (**58**). She was believed to preside over pregnancy and childbirth, as well as being a guardian of young mothers.

The myths and legends about Aztec gods, as well as Maya and earlier deities, symbolism, and the rituals addressing them are too complex to probe and analyze further here, and their images too numerous. Yet they clearly link daily life, including human birth, death,

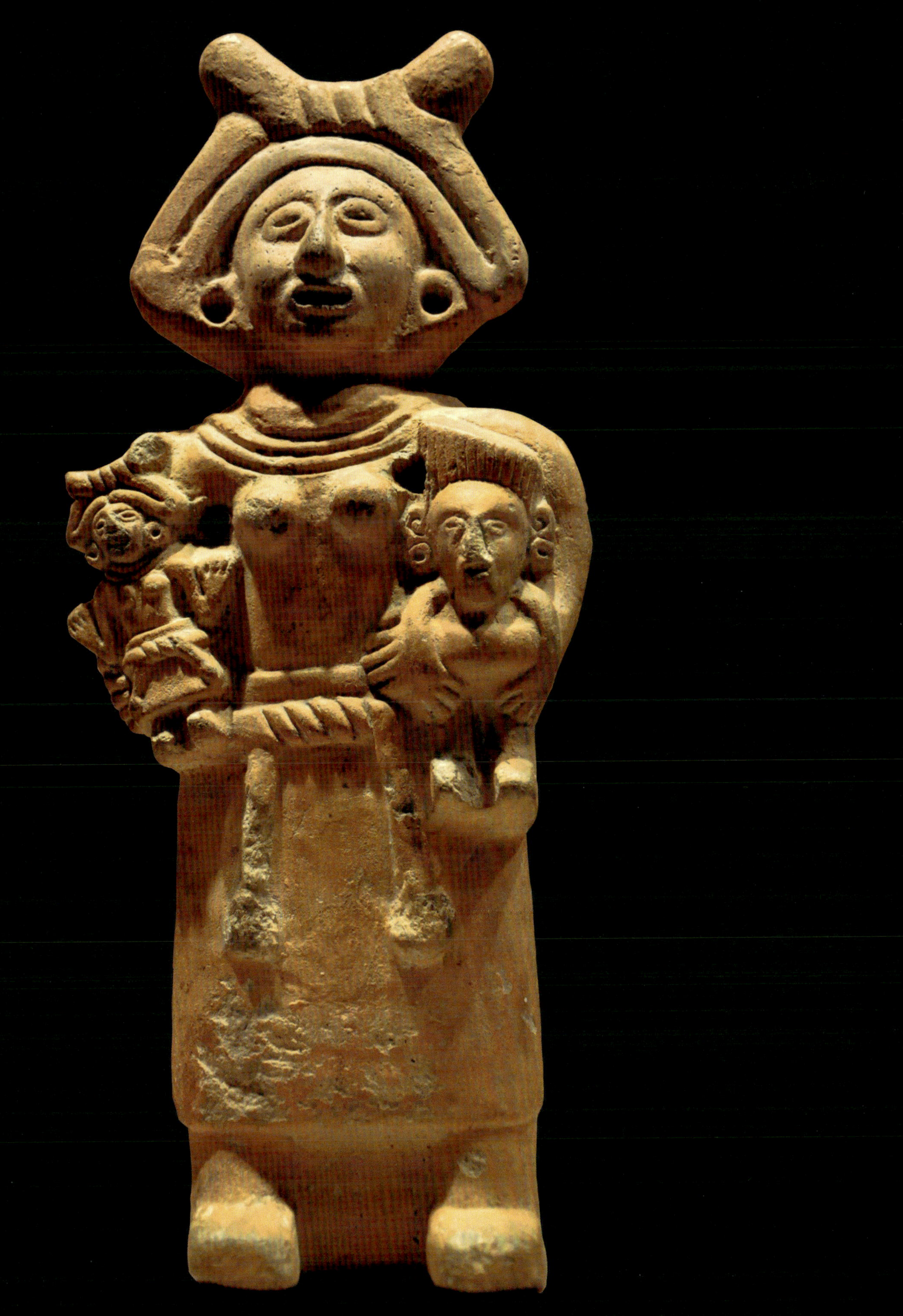

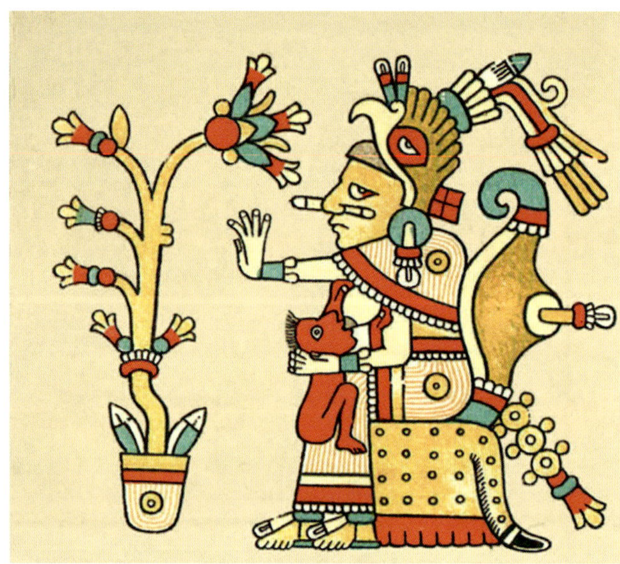

and sacrifice, to the rhythm of the seasons and thus to cosmology and the regeneration of the greater world and all its creatures.

•

To summarize, the biology of conception and birth is only a starting point for maternity imagery, which is endlessly repeated throughout the world and simultaneously

magical. In most cultures surveyed here, the mother figure is a center of existence: a ground, hearth, or furnace from which plants, other beings, and crucial substances such as iron emerge or radiate. That the mother deity is often a virgin proves her mystical powers. Semantic, philosophical, and cosmological elaborations are found in the beliefs about and actions of maternity deities almost everywhere. As a dominant image and idea, motherhood is a transformative, generative, yet ambivalent local reality, a centripetal nexus extending outward from its biological prototype to amplify many other dimensions of life. The mother-child group, often a female-male dyad, embodies a complex set of complementary ideas, values, and ritual actions simultaneously, even as these vary greatly among different geographical regions. Beliefs in a sky father and earth mother, and/or sun father and moon mother, are echoed in a female mother holding her male son, just as females have male qualities and vice versa. The world contains both good and evil, benevolent and malevolent ideas, deities, creatures, and actions. Snakes, as ambivalent, liminal, mysterious creatures, also figure in several religious traditions that were never in historical contact.

As an artistic, material object, the sculptured or painted maternity dyad might seem to be a fixed image, but it is more than that, for it represents and evokes temporal processes akin to a mother's essential activity in raising and teaching her children, which is to say, carrying out her role in replenishing human society. The dyad, as a deity, also embodies the duality of creation and destruction inherent in the world, or if not those stark opposites, then light and dark. Mothers have a fundamental role in creating the world, its plants, animals, and people. Yet as aspects of their ambivalent beings—every creature has positive and negative possibilities, of both good and evil—these gods often promote human or animal sacrifice; death is necessary for rebirth not only of human beings, but for society and the cosmos itself. Every body, every plant, every thing must die. Earth as mother is re-fertilized, replenished when people and plants die, so that new life again may emerge, so that the sun will rise again. As a mother gives birth, so is the world renewed.

Female creatures are refashioned into mothers when they create new life. Their children are often depicted as adults rather than infants, suggesting that the mother/child unit in art is more symbol than a naturalistic or realistic rendering. It is not static either, as fire and motherhood are not; maternity images are products of human imagination: compressed symbols of human development and social change that depend upon and result from nurturing, language, learning, and many other activities required for success and prosperity. The maternity archetype, then, goes far beyond a mother nursing her child to evoke education and the conversion of children into responsible adults, to evoke the succession of leaders and the regeneration of entire populations—the future of human civilization. The mother by herself, and vitally, with her child, is a tightly packed metaphor for active regeneration/destruction, growth/decline; yet the image itself is essentially positive, as it looks to the fruitfulness of family, field, and forge, as well as to protection, beauty, integrity, leadership, prosperity, and all other good things sought in human society, along with implied, inevitable darkness and negativity. The recurring maternity image across the world represents the desire and indeed the imperative of children as crucial to the cultural enterprise. It is as if the regenerating promise of nature—despite the negatives—so fully embodied in a mother with her child is fulfilled in the complexity and grandeur of culture in an enlightened community of people, activities, and ideas.

As a final note, I would suggest that despite the commonalities identified here, every mother and child relationship—of which there have been and continue to be billions—is in fact unique. They are all dependent on both the unique genetics of the two people plus their equally unique historical and cultural environments. No two mother and child interactions have ever been duplicated. Such uniqueness is, for me, yet another magical dimension of human existence.[39]

1   See David Freedberg, *The Power of Images: Studies in the History and Theory of Response* (Chicago: University of Chicago Press, 1989).

2   Esther Pasztory, *Thinking with Things: Toward a New Vision of Art* (Austin: University of Texas Press, 2007.

3   Erich Neumann, *The Great Mother: An Analysis of the Archetype* (New York: Pantheon, 1955).

4   Lucy Goodison and Christine Morris, eds., *Ancient Goddesses: The Myths and the Evidence* (Madison: University of Wisconsin Press, 1998); Peter J. Ucko *Anthropomorphic Figurines of Predynastic Egypt and Neolithic Crete*, Royal Anthropological Institute Occasional Paper 24 (London: Andrew Szmidla, 1968); and Andrew Fleming, "The Myth of the Mother Goddess," *World Archaeology* 1, no. 2: 247–61.

5   Elinor W. Gadon, *The Once and Future Goddess: A Symbol of Our Time* (New York: Harper and Row, 1989), 49.

6   See Pat Getz-Preziosi, *Early Cycladic Sculpture; An Introduction* (Malibu: J. Paul Getty Museum, 1994).

7   R. E. Witt, *Isis in the Ancient World* (Baltimore: Johns Hopkins University Press, 1971), 14, adapted from Maria Muenster, *Untersuchungen zur Goettin Isis: vom Alten Reich bis zum Ende des Neuen Reiches: mit hieroglyphischem Textanhang* (Berlin: Hessling, 1968).

8   Witt, *Isis in the Ancient World*, 106–7.

9   Witt, *Isis in the Ancient World*, 121.

10 Ian Begg, *The Cult of the Black Virgin* (London: Routledge and Kegan Paul, 2018), 53.

11 Begg, *Cult of the Black Virgin*, 57.

12 Witt, *Isis in the Ancient World*, 274.

13 Herbert M. Cole, *Maternity: Mother and Children in the Arts of Africa* (Brussels and New Haven: Mercatorfonds and Yale University Press, 2017), 11.

14 Begg, *Cult of the Black Virgin*, 3, 14.

15 Begg, *Cult of the Black Virgin*, 135.

16 Freedberg, *Power of Images*, 28.

17 Freedberg, *Power of Images*, 108.

18 Cole, *Maternity*, 45.

19 Stanilaw Chojnacki, *Ethiopian Icons: Catalogue of the Collection of the Institute of Ethiopian Studies, Addis Ababa University* (Addis Ababa: Addis Ababa University, 2000), 21.

20 See Herbert M. Cole, *Mbari: Art and Life among the Owerri Igbo* (Bloomington: Indiana University Press, 1982).

21 This west African yam is a white-fleshed tuber that is often twelve to eighteen inches long, weighing four to ten pounds, and very dissimilar to our "sweet potato."

22 Ellen Dissanayake, *Art and Intimacy: How the Arts Began* (Seattle: University of Washington Press, 2000), 70.

23 Cole, *Maternity*, 142–43.

24 Kate Ezra, *A Human Ideal in African Art: Bamana Figurative Sculptures* (Washington, DC: National Museum of African Art, Smithsonian Institution, 1986), 143.

25 Ezra, *A Human Ideal*, 142–43.

26 Ezra, *A Human Ideal*, 161.

27 C. Howarth, personal communication, 2022

28 Rig Veda Hymn 10.72 in Wendy Doniger, *The Rig Veda* (New York, Penguin Books, 2005).

29 Wendy Doniger, *The Hindus: An Alternative History* (New York: Penguin Books, 2009), 127.

30 Doniger, *Hindus*, 398.

31 Doniger, *Hindus*, 337.

32 From James Doyle, "Seated Bench Figure," on the Olmec serpentine bench figure of a person with a "child" on his lap (Metropolitan Museum of Art, The Michael C. Rockefeller Collection, Bequest of Nelson A. Rockefeller, 1979.206.940). Available at http://www.metmuseum.org/about-the-museum/now-at-the-met/2015/olmec-babies.

33 See Cecelia Klein, "A New Interpretation of the Aztec Statue Called Coatlicue, "Snakes-Her-Skirt," *Ethnohistory* 55, no. 2 (2008): 229–50, at 235. Much of this Aztec data comes from this article and from Mary Ellen Miller and Karl Taube, *The Gods and Symbols of Ancient Mexico and the Maya: An Illustrated Dictionary of Mesoamerican Religion* (New York: Thames and Hudson, 1993).

34 Klein, "A New Interpretation," 244–45.

35 Miller and Taube, *Gods and Symbols*, entries on Birth, Dawn, Death, and Creation.

36 Cecelia Klein, "From Clay to Stone: The Demonization of the Aztec Goddess Cihuacoatl," in *Sorcery in Mesoamerica*, ed. Jeremy D. Coltman and John M. D. Pohl (Louisville: University Press of Colorado, 2020), 330–80, 359 ff.

37 Klein, "From Clay to Stone." I have simplified much of the detailed data in this and Klein, "A New Interpretation."

38 And also a Toltec deity at Tula, a civilization that succeeded Teotihuacan, lasting from ca. 900–1150 in the post-classic period.

39 I would like to thank the following for their help in locating images or providing useful references: Matiu Baker, Chloe Beauvais, Bernard DeGrunne, Michael Hamson, Crispin Howarth, Cecelia Klein, Susan Kloman, Alisa LaGamma, Alexis Maggiar, Lark Mason, Ian Mursell. I also appreciate the careful editing by Lisa Bessette.

Further reading

Ardren, Traci, ed. *Ancient Maya Women*. Walnut Creek, London: Altamira Press, 2002.

Bean, Wendell Charles. *Myth, Cult and Symbols in Sakta Hinduism: A Study of the Indian Mother Goddess*. Leiden: E.J.Brill, 1967.

Berlo, Janet C. and Ruth B. Phillips. *Native North American Art*. New York and Oxford: Oxford University Press, 1998.

Berrin, Kathleen, and Virginia M. Fields, eds. *Olmec: Colossal Masterworks of Ancient Mexico*. San Francisco: The Fine Arts Museums of San Francisco, 2010.

Burkert, Walter. *Ancient Mystery Cults*. Cambridge, MA: Harvard University Press, 1987.

Campbell, Joseph. *Primitive Mythology: The Masks of God*. New York: Penguin Books, 1959.

Campbell, Joseph. *The Mythic Image*. Princeton, N.J.: Bollingen Series C, Princeton University Press, 1974.

Diehl, Richard A. *The Olmecs: America's First Civilization*. London: Thames and Hudson, 2004.

Downing, Christine. *The Goddess: Mythological Images of the Feminine*. New York: Crossroad Publishing, 1984.

Gimbutas, Marija. "Vulvas, Breasts and Buttocks of the Goddess Creatrix," in G Buccellari and C. Speroni, *The Shape of the Past: Studies in Honor of Franklin D. Murphy*. Los Angeles: University of California Press, 1981.

Gimbutas, Marija. *The Goddesses and Gods of Old Europe: Myth and Cult Images*. Los Angeles: University of California Press, 1982.

Hutchinson, R.W. *Prehistoric Crete*. Baltimore: Penguin, 1962.

James, E.O. *The Cult of the Mother Goddess*. New York: Praeger, 1959.

Mookerjee, Ajit and Madhu Khanna. *The Tantric Way: Art, Science, Ritual*. Boston: New York Graphic Society, 1977.

Ochshorn, Judith. *The Female Experience and the Nature of the Divine*. Bloomington: Indiana University Press, 1981.

Oda, Mayumi. *Goddesses*. Berkeley: Lancaster-Miller Publishers, 1981.

Olsen, Carl. *Book of the Goddess Past and Present: An Introduction to her Religion*. New York: Crossroad Publishing, 1983.

Stone, Merlin. *When God Was a Woman*. New York: Dial Press, 1976.

V

THE WORLD AROUND US

LARK E. MASON

Those who contemplate the beauty of the earth find
reserves of strength that will endure as long as life
exists. There is something infinitely healing in the
repeated refrains of nature—the assurance
that dawn comes after night, and spring after winter.

Rachel Carson,
Silent Spring,
1962

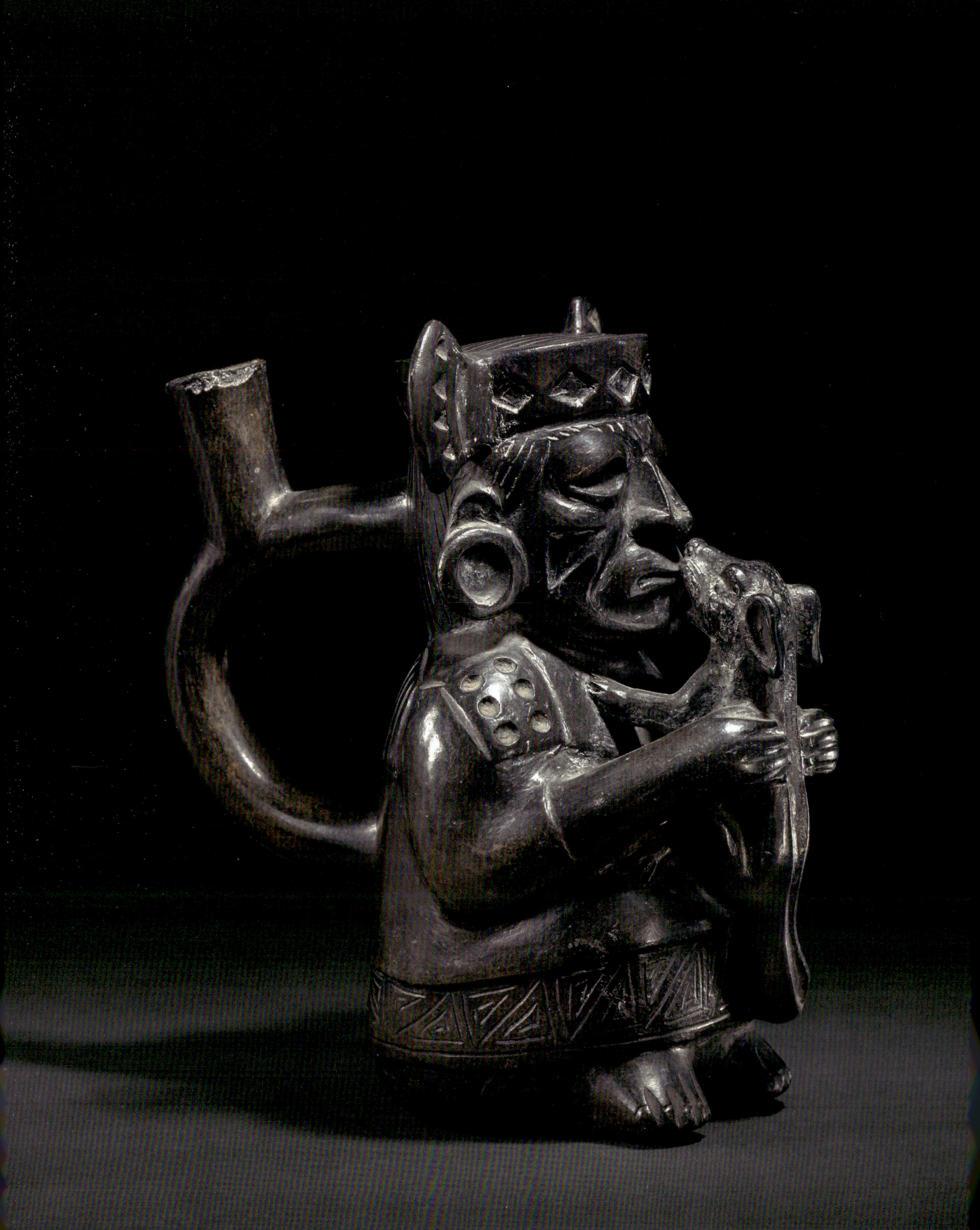

1 Stirrup Spout Vessel of Man with Animal

Moche culture, North Coast Peru
200 – 500 CE
Terracotta
6 ¾ in., 17.15 cm
Private Collection

The Universal Language of Nature

All humans past and present are linked by a shared experience of living in a natural and human-influenced world. We relate to our environments based on our senses, local circumstances, and the collective cultural experiences that those who came before us communicated in writing, stories, models, and images. Our relationship to flora and fauna, indeed the entire natural world, is also shaped by exchange with other cultures. Through trade, the spread of religions, the sharing of scientific discoveries, and conquest, regional and larger communications networks expose cultural groups to outside ideas that influence how they see the world. In the course of trade, familiar and unfamiliar images have been exchanged as woven patterns on clothing; incised designs on utilitarian vessels; tools with human, plant, and animal attributes; religious images, and other forms. These exchanges expanded the knowledge of a group's immediate environment, which was then shared with other groups, resulting in the adoption of new forms into their vocabulary of design.

In an effort to understand their surroundings, humans have long made images of familiar species and objects. We usually do not know how an object was perceived when it was created, but we do know that the image was important enough that someone took the time to make it. The choice to adorn an object or structure with a frieze of repeating vines, fruit, animals, the sun or moon, or other elements from the natural world was made by an artisan as a result of cultural influences. And yet many

representations of the surrounding world by cultures with no known connection can be very similar. Objects from different cultures and times that are visually similar may be made of like materials, use nature as a source, and have similar functions. For all their cultural diversity, humans are physically similar with the same basic needs, and thus there is a commonality in our depictions of the natural world that transcends time and place. Cave drawings of fluid, simple lines in the Grotto of Lascaux and other locations in the Dordogne area of southwestern France represent the world seen by the inhabitants of 10,000 BCE. There is much conjecture about prehistoric art, but the visual similarity of works from hunter-gatherer peoples is notable in spite of differences in location and time. It implies that there was a direct transmission via trade or observation, and supporting evidence sometimes proves or disproves this connection. In instances where no direct connection can be established, we are left to accept that artisans selected familiar natural materials and imagery as inspiration and represented these in a manner similar to those from a culture with which there was no contact. The human creative source is the connection. Humans of the past and of today create images that are realistic, meant to show an actual plant or animal, and fanciful images that represent the essence of something beyond comprehension.

The Moche stirrup spout vessel that introduces this chapter (1), made in Peru around 200–500, highlights the problem faced by modern observers when analyzing objects from the past. We wonder what this object is; when, where, and why it was made; how was it made; and who made it. We do not have answers to most of these questions because we have only the mute object and we are separated from the circumstances in which it was created. Most often, the answers come grudgingly. For example, what we know about the Moche stirrup spout vessel is that it models an interaction between a male human, possibly of some stature based on our conjecture that the headdress is a mark of importance, and a canine or similar animal. We know the form is a vessel, and we know the material is clay. We know that it took skill and practice to create it for an audience, inferring it had value at the time it was made. We do not know the reasons it was made nor the meaning of the interaction between the man and the animal.

When we look at this vessel, we do so through the lens of our own cultural experiences. When we "respond" to the vessel, we are by extension "responding" to the ideas and motivations of its creator-craftsman, whose inspiration came from the culture in which he lived. Though it was made by someone for a purpose that is obscure to us, it was not obscure to the person who created it, and the object is a means of communication. This is a definitive aspect of the commonality that exists between humans, outside of time and culture. Though we are not members of the culture in which this object was created, we have a shared understanding with the creator that time, skill, and materials were devoted to it, giving it an emotional and practical value beyond the hourly pay of the maker, the cost of the clay, and the amount of wood used to fire the kiln.

Attempting to understand the layers of importance of the vessel; the value of the time, training, manufacturing, and materials used to make it; the emotions it communicated; and its function, we look at it through the lens of our experiences. Our relationship with nature, our knowledge of humans and animals, suggest interpretations that may be about companionship, survival, spirituality, tradition, or something else. But we do not know whether or how much these motivated the vessel's creator. What we do know is that someone with skill made it to communicate something, perhaps as part of a special ceremony or event, for a third-party, and we, like that unknown third-party, are recipients of that communication.

The relationships between humans and nature expressed through art involve the creator, the audience, and the subject. The creator was human but the audience could be either human or spirit. Though we are disconnected from the culture of the creator, the object retains power because humans react to images, whether ancient Troglodyte cave drawings of the Loire River valley, or cartoon sketches in the Sunday paper. Natural images of flora and fauna elicit intellectual and emotional responses, even if the plant or animal or natural feature are not specifically known to us.

With the Moche vessel, the man is not just standing beside an animal, showing the viewer that dogs or some other animal were part of their culture; he is holding the animal up to his face. The animal is not struggling but rather stretches toward the lips of the man, whose eyes are shut in transcendence, as if bridging the divide between species. Works of art created over many millennia were meant to convey grandiosity, cultural dominance, and foundational ideals of empires to a large audience; well-known examples include the sculptural friezes adorning the Parthenon (447 BCE) atop the Athenian Acropolis, the architecture, sculpture, and stone carvings of Angor Wat (1110–1150) in Cambodia, or the vast temple complexes of the Aztecs and Maya of Central and South America. But, like this vessel depicting a man and an animal, other works are much more intimate, their meaning directed to a small group of people in the context of a communal or ritual event.

Three-dimensional objects made to contain materials essential for survival, such as food or liquid, were often decorated with images of flora and fauna associated with the plant or animal represented and the purpose of the vessel. The primary purpose of two-dimensional representations of the natural world is to convey an idea or record an event. The value of these works is usually not in the materials, such as clay and pigments, but in the workmanship, ideas, and associations represented by the images. The gold ground on a late medieval Italian religious painting, for example, may augment the meaning of the image, but the message is conveyed primarily through the images. Objects made of gold or incorporating precious stones use these materials to emphasize the importance of the images, and because

gold and precious stones are valued by us today, we experience these works closer to the original intent of the artisan or intended audience. The materials, imagery, and skilled representation convey meaning to those of the past and to us today.

The transmission of ideas using images of the world around us could be isolated and intended for a local audience or meant to be shared across cultures, in effect as a universal visual language. Sometimes the message conveyed was perfectly transmitted, such that the recipient had a full understanding of the meaning of the object, but other times the meaning would be only partially understood. During the late eighteenth century, for example, Lord McCartney (1737–1806) was charged with representing British interests to the Chinese emperor at a formal meeting that took place in 1793 in the Qianlong Emperor's (1711–99) private hunting palace north of Beijing. The British diplomats sought to impress the emperor with mechanical clocks encased in jeweled and gilded-bronze cases as well as other examples of British industry. The Qianlong emperor was dismissive of the gifts, which he considered an unserious, condescending gesture that failed to recognize him as the equal or better of the British monarch. The mismatch between the messages intended by the British and those received by the Chinese emperor is similar to our attempts to understand the purpose and meaning of objects from past cultures. When objects are accompanied by written communications that explain their social, diplomatic, and religious influences, we can better understand the contexts surrounding them, but otherwise we are like the diplomats in the McCartney Mission with a partial perspective.

Objects carry clues to their meaning from the originating culture. Representational imagery from the natural and imaginary worlds transmits messages of power, dominance, or mystery, as in the *taotie* (monster) masks on ancient bronze ritual vessels from China created during the Shang dynasty (1766–1122 BCE) or fearsome images conjured by visions of hell by Netherlandish painter Hieronymous Bosch (ca. 1450–1516). All aspects of nature represented on works of art depicting animals, plants, or the heavens were intended to intellectually and emotionally affect the viewer. The response is dependent upon the culture, time, and purpose behind the image. For instance, the symbol of the Roman legion was the Aquila (eagle); for peoples under Roman rule, this image represented either oppression and fear or pride and respect. For cultures remote from Rome, the eagle had different meanings. A thistle was symbolic of resiliency and nobility to a Sottish person, but it does not have that meaning to most people. Humans use nature and the heavens as a visual language, but not all humans have the same understanding of that language. When objects are shared across cultures as gifts and through trade, or are seen by non-native viewers, only part of the object's message will be understood. An animal held to the lips of a pre-Columbian priest conveys something entirely different from a dog held to the lips of someone from a culture that prizes dog meat or to a modern pet lover.

Often images taken from nature are distilled into designs that incorporate reality and myth. Some natural objects become reduced or changed into highly stylized and abstract forms. Others are realistic representations of humans or animals or plants shown in a combination that would never appear in nature, as in this sculpture of the mythological Serpent King Muchalinda, in which cobras form a protective niched platform and arched canopy over Buddha (**2**). The entwined serpents are less cobra and more pattern, their sinuous, intertwined, rope-woven design heightening the image of the placid, seated meditative figure in a black, polished, contrasting stone. The large stone sculpture was likely a central image in a temple, where it would have been viewed by a single person at a time or by audiences of people participating in a solemn ceremony within a grand, awe-inspiring setting that included secondary objects meant to collectively enhance the experience of the participants.

The space likely included censers, with coils of smoke rising to the ceiling; some might be in a fanciful animal shape called a *luduan*, a beast incorporating elements from living and mythical creatures (**3**). When we see a *luduan* censer in isolation from the temple setting, we are only partially aware of the purpose and meaning that would be understood by someone from the culture and space where it was displayed. This *luduan* dates to the seventeenth century and is made of porcelain, but similar vessels were made in bronze. The blue is from cobalt, brought from central Asia to the porcelain workshops of Jingdezhen in central China.[1] Though Chinese, the *luduan* incorporates

2 **Buddha Sheltered by the Serpent King Muchalinda**

Kathmandu Valley, Nepal
1001 – 1200
Schist
17 ⅜ × 13 ³⁄₁₆ × 5 ¹¹⁄₁₆ in.,
44.2 × 33.5 × 14.5 cm
Art Institute of Chicago
Gift of Marilynn B. Alsdorf

3 **Censer in the Form of a Mythical Beast**

China
Ming dynasty, early 1600s
Porcelain painted in underglaze blue
13 in., 33 cm
Metropolitan Museum of Art, New York
Purchase, Bequests of William Rhinelander Stewart
And Matilda E. Frelinghuysen, Gift ofR. Thornton Wilson,
In memory of Florence Ellsworth Wilson, Purchase by
Subscription, and Gift of Edgar Worch, by exchange, 2018

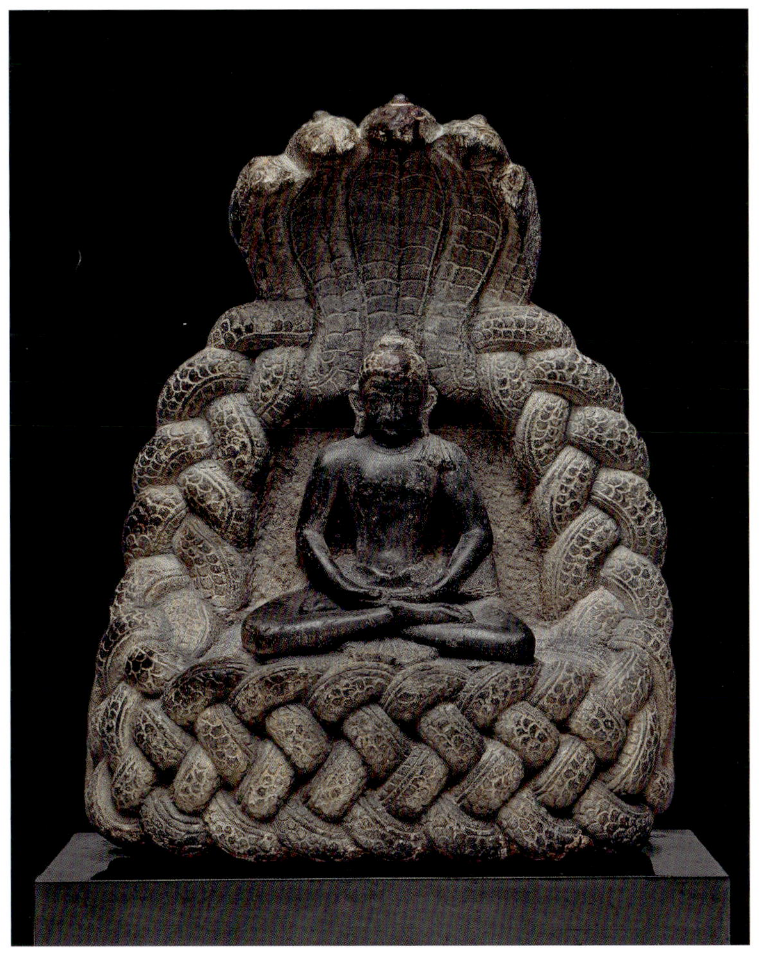

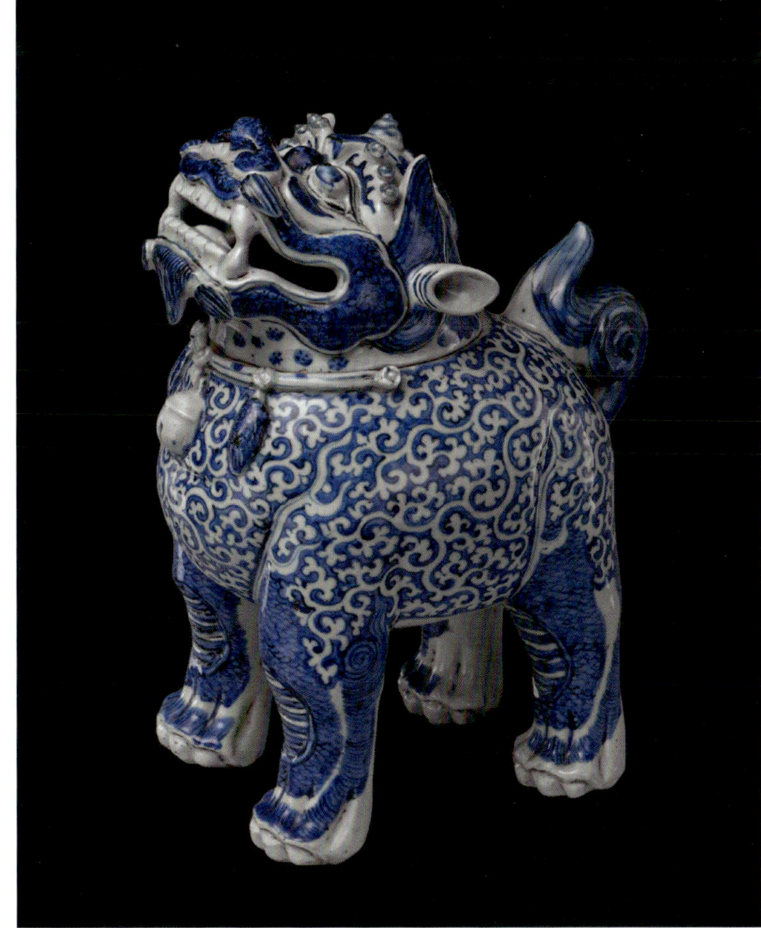

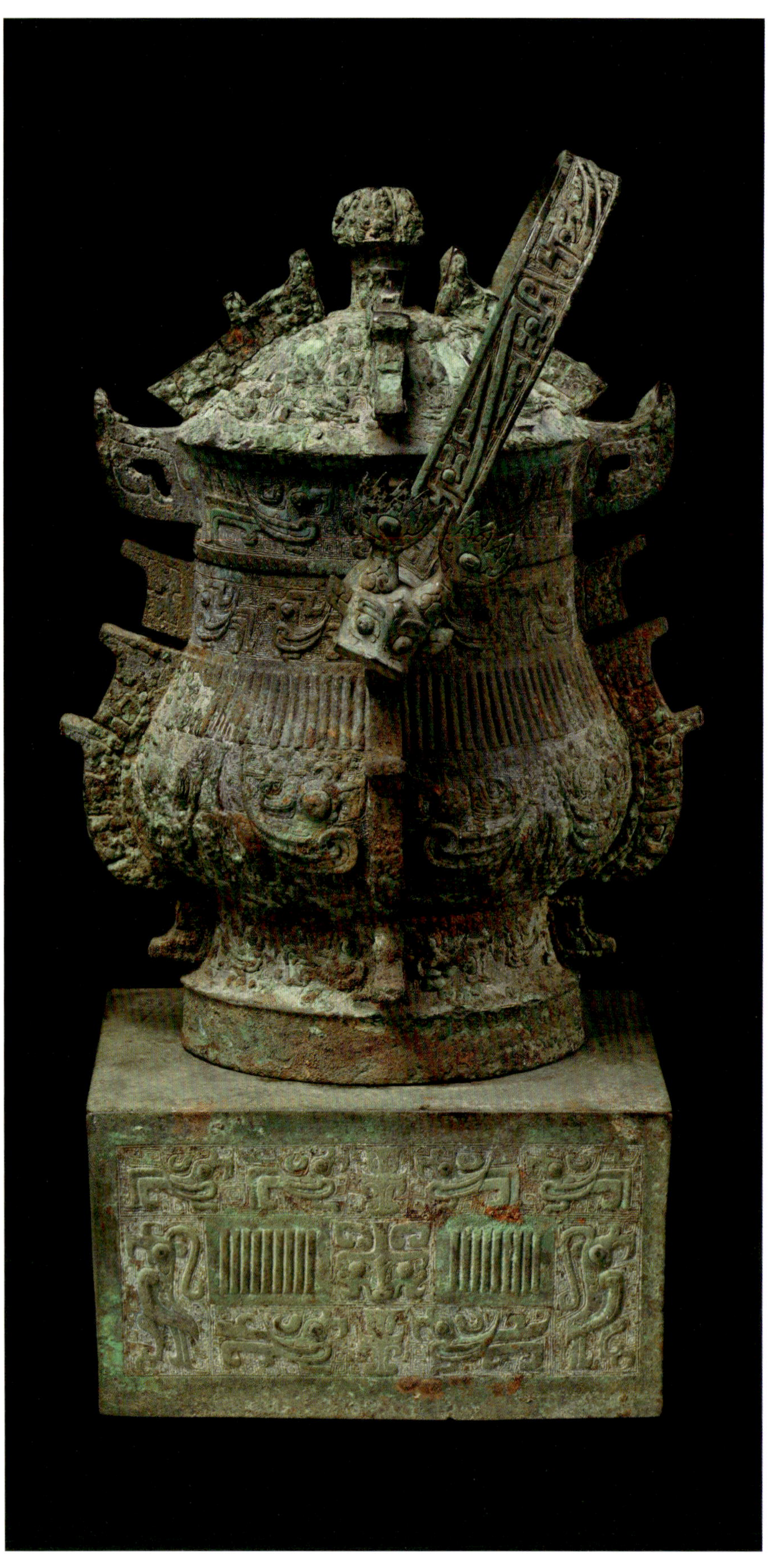

4 **Ritual Wine Container (*Yu*)
with Lid and Pedestal**

China
Western Zhou dynasty, late 1000s BCE
Bronze
13 ½ × 9 ½ × 9 in., 34.3 × 24.1 × 22.9 cm
Metropolitan Museum of Art, New York
Munsey Fund, 1931

5 **Jaguar Effigy Tripod Vase**

Guanacaste culture, region of Nicoya,
Costa Rica, Nicaragua
Period VI, 1200 – 1400
Buffware with polychrome paints
15 in., 38.1 cm
The Stuart Handler Collection

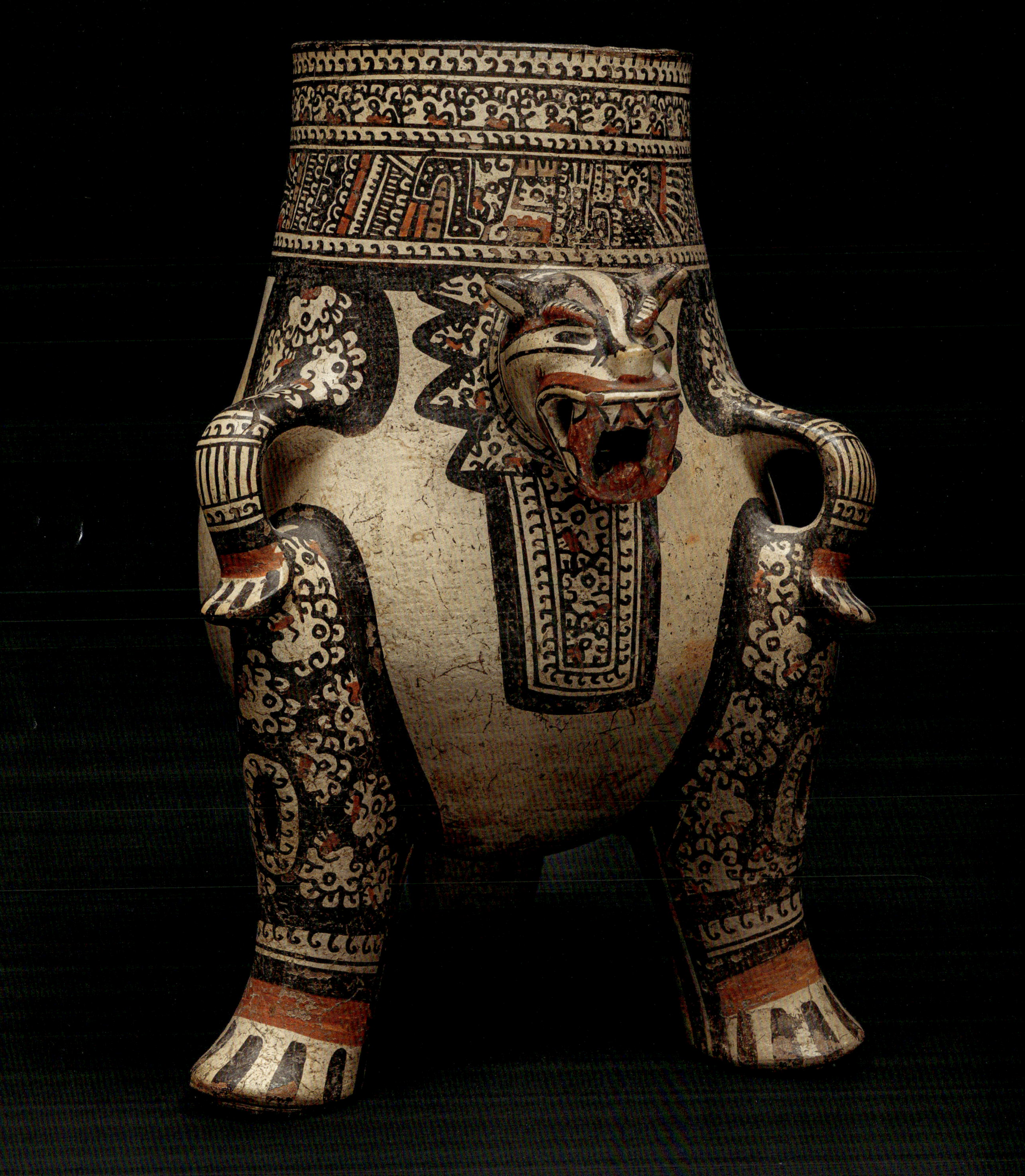

influences from the Mongolian steppes with stylized scrollwork patterns, as well as rounded-animal-body vessels from Persia.

Vessels from the Bronze Age in China were created for ritual use as food and wine containers, incorporating a combination of natural forms that are recognizable, such as bovine heads and fanciful *taotie* masks (**4**). Early Chinese bronze vessels were important symbols of power with ritual significance and were included in burial chambers for the deceased. Many have inscriptions dedicating them to a particular location or person. These ancient bronze forms assumed a less ritualistic purpose over time and began to incorporate gold, silver, and other precious materials, emphasizing their sumptuous aspect. By the Han dynasty (206 BCE–220 CE), the ritual significance had disappeared and the vessels were either ostentatious displays of wealth or utilitarian and almost devoid of decoration.

Examples of pre-Columbian pottery have a superficial similarity to some early Chinese bronze vessels and later Chinese and Japanese bronze and ceramic forms that incorporate similar imagery. This pre-Columbian pottery vessel has a spout on the side and handles that are stylized arms, with panels of design around the upper body and on the legs and arms (**5**). The Kingdom of Nicoya, which produced the vessel, was centered around the Pacific coast of Costa Rica, and by the time Europeans arrived and settled, between 1502 and 1524, the capital was the most important population center of the area. Though similar in appearance, the Chinese vessel served an entirely different purpose than the pre-Columbian vessel and the objects would have been perceived differently by the cultures in which they were created, as each incorporates religious and cultural imagery with a purpose that is distinct to that culture.

Depicting the Natural World

Why create objects representing the natural world? While this question is clouded by our own cultural perspectives, humans have always had a need for protection from harsh surroundings, whether from excesses in temperature or from animate and inanimate threats to survival—the natural world was providential and terrifying, constant and variable. The importance of the flora and fauna around us is heightened when these elements are recognized as essential or inimical to survival. Paintings or models of flora and fauna represent their significance to the person or society where they were created. Animals and plants used for food or security were often the earliest representations. Supernatural traits were shown by exaggerated or zoomorphic mixes of features that express the otherworldliness of the incomprehensible.

The Sun

Most flora and fauna vary by geographic location due to climate, soil, and other conditions. Desert cultures have in common the types of creatures and plants acclimated to the absence of water and the presence of extreme heat; cultures in colder climes have a similarly specialized variety of flora and fauna. One of the constants across all cultures is the heavens: The sun, moon, and stars feature in representations from many cultures.

The concept of the sun as creator and sustainer of life has ancient origins. This is not surprising since without the sun, we would not have life. The ancient Egyptian belief in an afterlife and in rebirth is referenced in many works of art. Though not a direct image of the sun, this necklace made around 2040–1783 BCE references its power with its turquoise-glazed faience beads and falcon-head finials and small tubular beads festooned with faceted drops and gilded beads (**6**). The green color is evocative of new growth and life, and the golden sheen of the life-giving sun. In Egypt, the sun was famously celebrated in the enormous complex of Heliopolis, associated with the cult of the sun god Atum, then Ra, and then Horus. The pharaoh Akhenaten (ca. 1350 BCE) elevated the worship of Aten and the city continued as a cult center for worship of the sun through the Roman period.

Masks personifying the sun were made by many cultures to explain existence and the origin of life. Myths developed to represent the sun and other heavenly bodies, and to explain and humanize these astronomical features.

In tribal northwest American cultures, painted wood sun masks were used by prominent families in elaborate ceremonies (**7**). These masks have radiating beams, and this example has a white ground with black, green, and red pigments, likely signifying the growth of new life and the radiance of the sun and the darkness of night. A sun image from Rajasthan (India) dating from the nineteenth century has male stylized features and is similar to other images in developed and primitive cultures (**8**).

Far remote from ancient Egypt and Asia, the Italian artist Giovanni Lanfranco (1582–1647) created an engraving after a work by Raphael (1483–1520), with rays radiating from the sun in a manner similar to images from other cultures (**9**). The sliver of light from the moon is visible and the triangle rising above the earth and between the sun and moon has the Hebrew characters for the name of God, YHWH, a reference to the account of creation in the bible: "In the beginning God created the heavens and the earth. Now the earth was formless and empty, darkness was over the surface of the deep, and the Spirit of God was hovering over the waters. And God said, 'Let there be light,' and there was light. God saw that the light was good, and he separated light from the darkness" (Genesis 1:1–4).[2] A modern viewer understands the importance of the sun, but prior to the advent of electrical lighting, gilded surfaces were necessary to reflect light, as were faceted glass or polished stone surfaces. The Hall of Mirrors at the palace of Versailles in France, completed

6 **Broad Collar**

Egypt
2040 – 1783 BCE
Faience (glazed silica)
6 ⅛ × 25 in., 15.6 × 63.5 cm
Minneapolis Museum of Art
Gift of Edward S. Harkness

7 **Sun Mask**

Kwakwaka'wakw culture, Canada
1860
Wood, metal, pigment, cord, cloth
17 ¼ × 15 ¾ × 4 ⅞ in., 43.82 × 40.01 × 12.38 cm
Minneapolis Institute of Art
The Putnam Dana McMillan Fund and
Purchase through Art Quest 2003

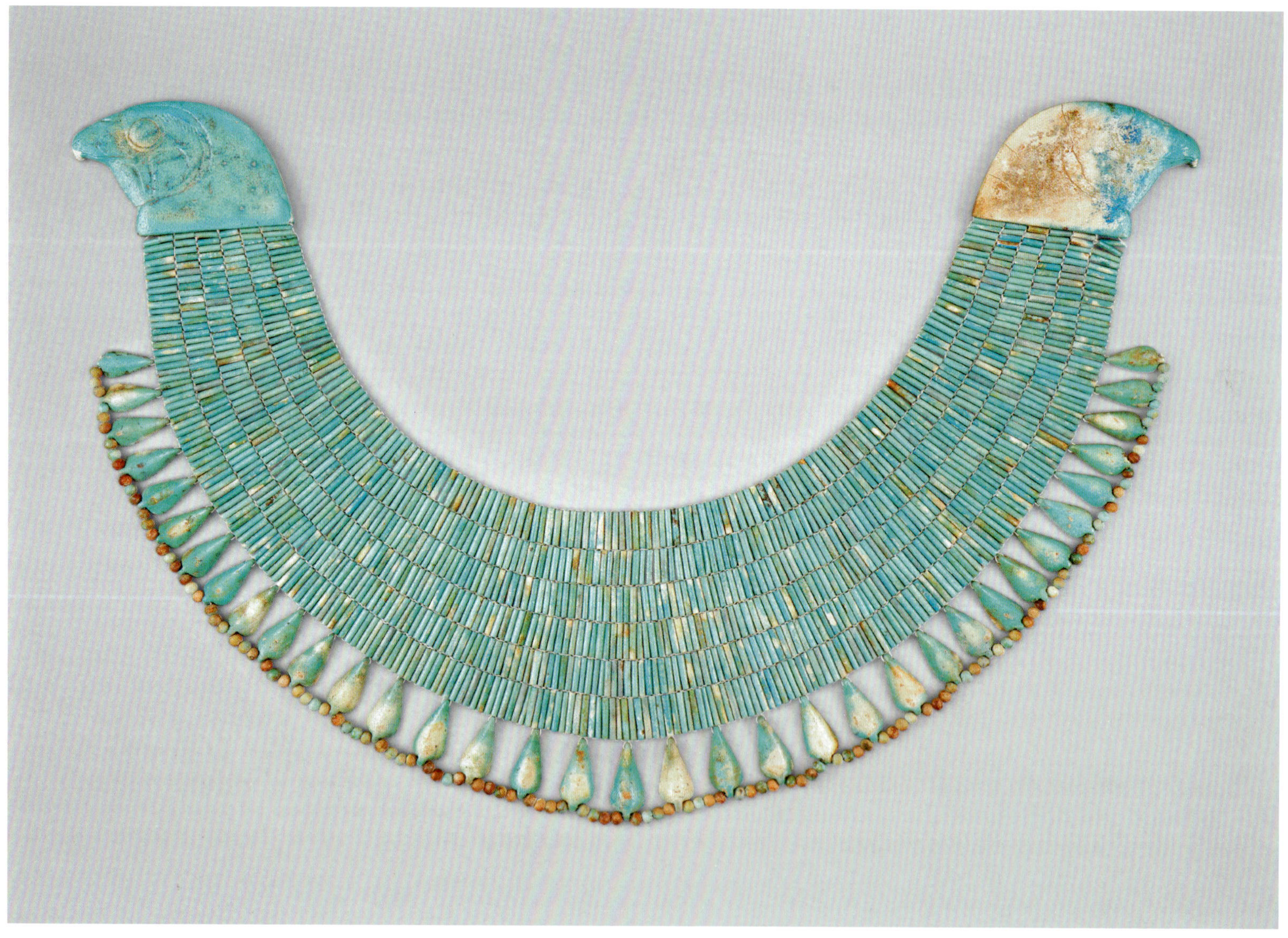

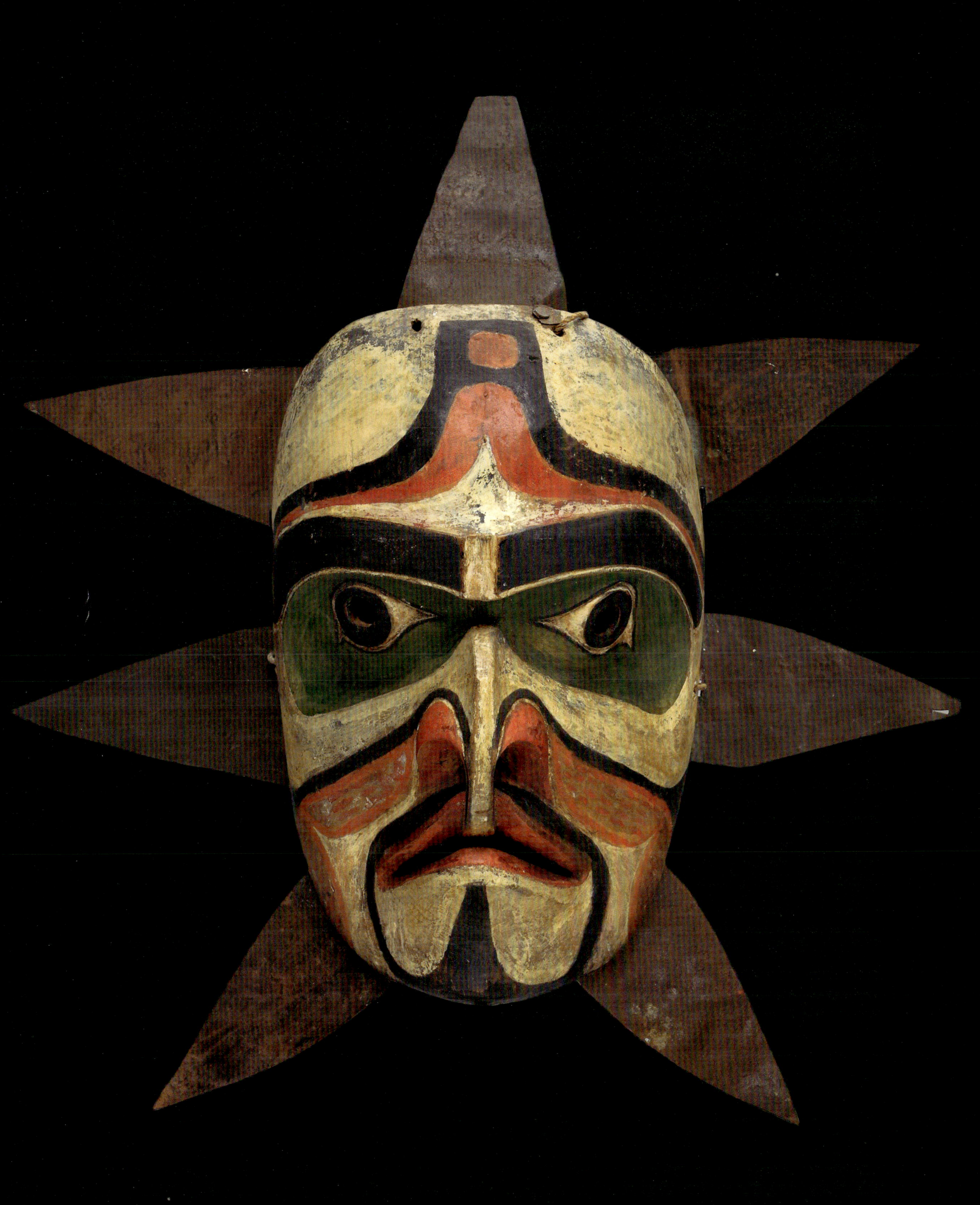

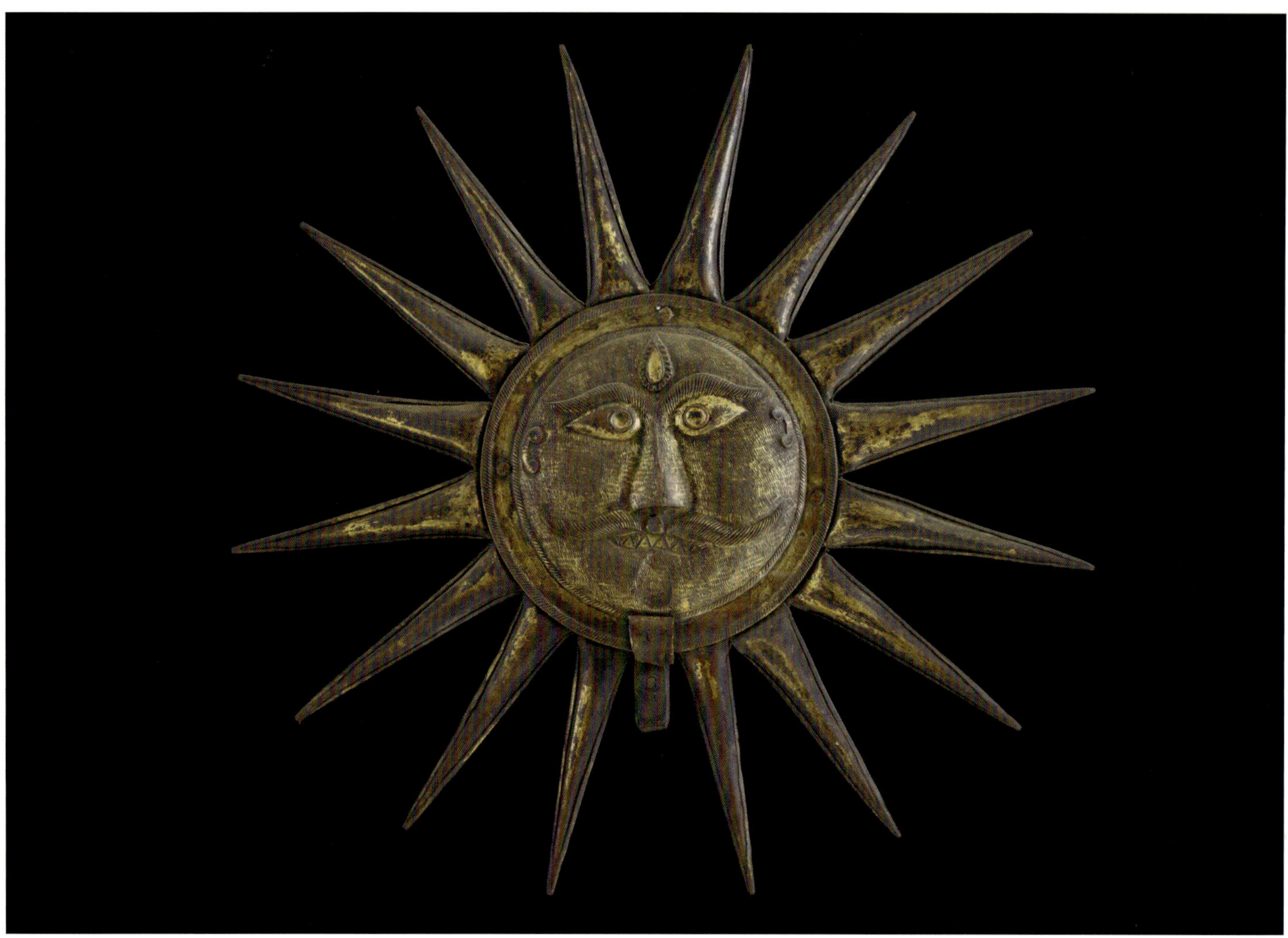

in 1644, was a sensation at the time because it reflected enough light to maintain activities into the night, pushing out darkness and extending the day, leading to Louis XIV (1638–1715) being called the Sun King.

Scientific advances in the understanding of time entered into people's lives through horological advances. A French clock made in Paris in 1789 features a popular image of the rising sun atop a lyre-shaped support associated with Apollo, the ancient Greek god of the sun, and Johannes Kepler (1571–1630), the famed German mathematician, astronomer, and musician who postulated that the paths of the planets produced sounds with different tones, converting into a continuous Music

8 **Personified Sun Emblem**

Rajasthan, India
1900
Copper alloy repoussé with gilding
14 ³⁄₁₆ × 1 ½ in., 36.04 × 3.81 cm
Los Angeles County Museum of Art (LACMA)
Bequest of Oppi Untracht

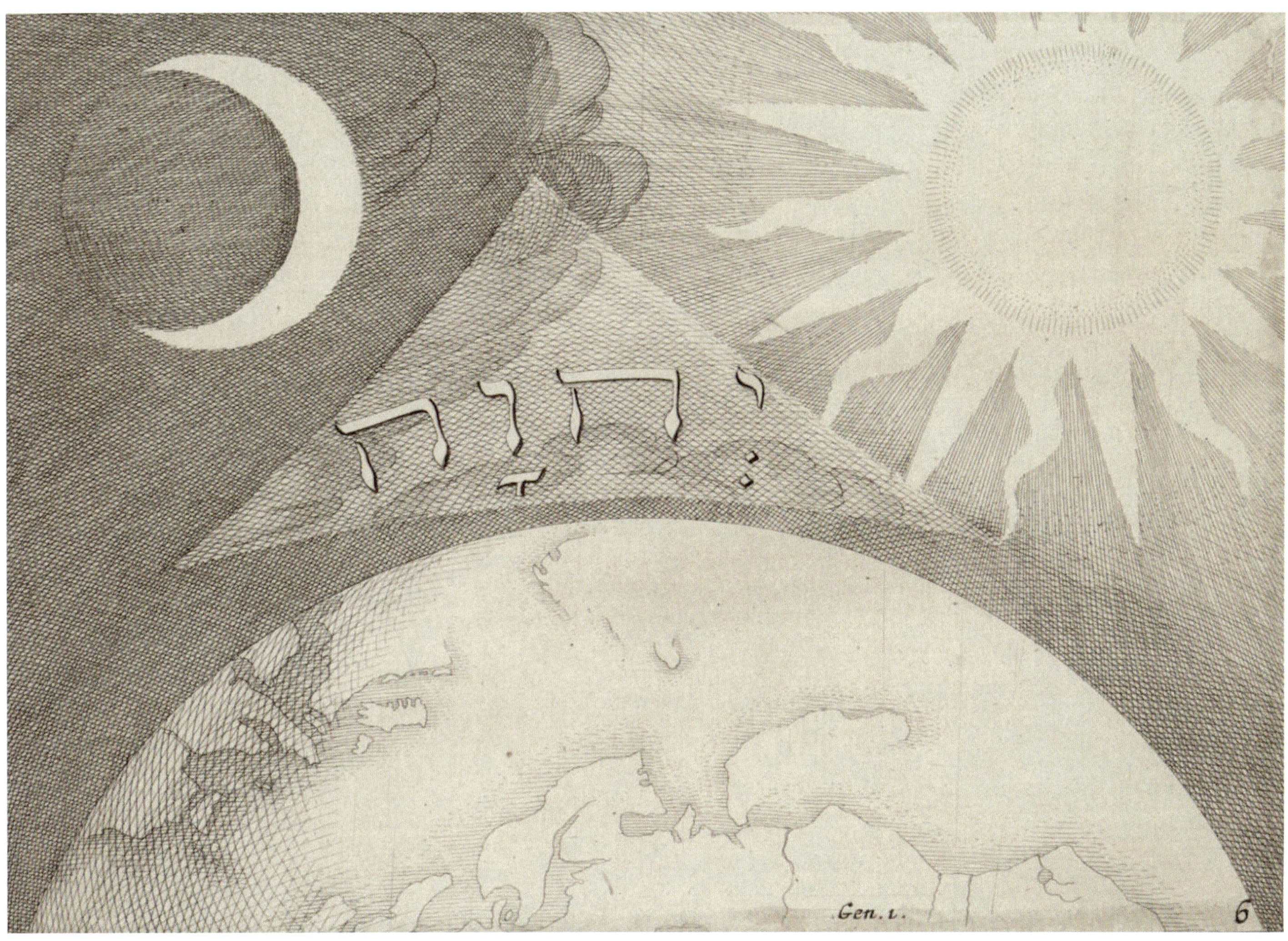

of the Spheres that, though inaudible, was orderly and harmonious (**10**). The gilded bronze mounts and the white marble base and supports are entwined with laurel leaves. During the Enlightenment in Europe (1685–1815), scientific inquiry aligned with classical sources of design and individual liberty. Freedom was represented by classically inspired motifs and materials associated with ancient Greek and Roman art, such as white marble and gilded bronze, which also referenced scientific progress. The ingenious time-keeping mechanism behind the central clock dial, twelve subsidiary world-capital clock dials, and dials for the rising and setting of the sun are mechanically advanced connections to past cultures.

9　**God Separating the Sun and Moon**

Giovanni Lanfranco (Italy, 1582 – 1647)
1607 – 1638
Etching
5 ¼ × 7 ³⁄₁₆ in., 13.3 × 18.2 cm
Philadelphia Museum of Art
The Muriel and Phillip Berman Gift, Acquired from the John S. Phillips bequest of 1876 to the Pennsylvania Academy of the Fine Arts, with funds contributed by Muriel and Phillip Berman, gifts (by exchange) of Lisa Norris Elkins, Bryant W. Langston, Samuel S. White 3rd and Vera White, with additional funds contributed by John Howard McFadden, Jr., Thomas Skelton Harrison, and the Phillip H. and A.S.W Rosenbach Foundation, 1985

Jean-Antoine Lépine (France, 1720 – 1814)
Painter: Joseph Coteau (France, 1740 – 1801)
1789
Marble, gilt bronze
29 ½ × 27 × 7 ¾ in.,
74.93 × 68.58 × 19.69 cm
Minneapolis Museum of Art
Gift of Funds from Mrs. Carolyn Groves

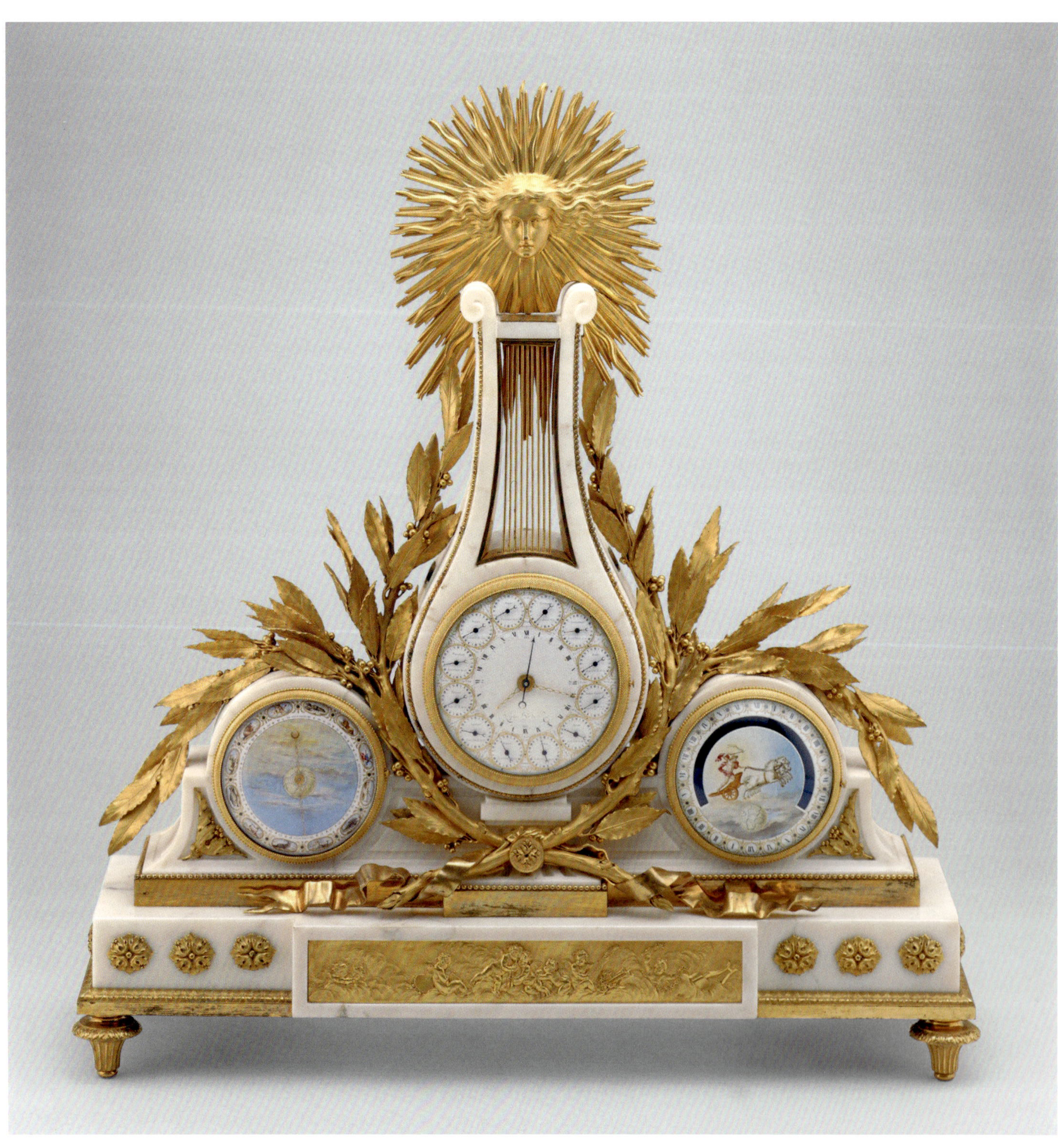

Nonetheless, the sentiments expressed in this clock are similar to those of much less advanced cultures: the primacy of the sun to survival, the notion of time and our limited lives, and the importance of light for growth and sustenance.

Animals

Ceramicists, painters, stonemasons, wood carvers, metalworkers, and other skilled craftspeople responded to the cultural impulses of their society by creating works of art from familiar forms, including domestic animals, which were sources of food, protection, and companionship, and a means of transport. Domesticated animals are among the earliest images made by humans and feature strongly in the artistic representations of most cultures. Animals were initially bred for food and for a variety of by-products, such as leather, which offered protection against harsh surroundings in the form of garments and housing. Human domestication of animals began between 15,000 and 20,000 years ago with the dog, followed by other animals including, around 6,000 years ago, the horse.

Throughout history representations of canines and other animals appear in a variety of materials but most commonly in pottery or stone. Dogs from the Americas, Europe, and Asia display features that highlight companionship and domesticity. Though radically different culturally, similar relationships existed between the owner and the animal, which was considered a beloved pet, companion, or reliable guardian. This Roman terracotta model in the shape of a reclining dog had a utilitarian function as an oil container (**11**). A ceramic pre-Columbian dog from the Colima culture was a funerary model, made to accompany and protect the deceased in the afterlife (**12**). Both are realistic images, but they have different functions. Realistic depictions of animals exist across cultures, particularly those in which interactions between human and domesticated animals were common; they are meant to convey the practical and emotional connections between humans and animals. The stone Cypriot dog made in the Mediterranean region around the fourth to third century BCE is a realistic portrayal likely created to guard the entrance to a tomb (**13**), as was the small green-glazed pottery example made in China during the Han dynasty (**14**). Though different culturally, the Colima, Cypriot, and Chinese models were all created for inclusion in a tomb to accompany the deceased to the afterlife.

The earliest horse breeds were from Central Asia and horses were replicated in pottery models created for burial in Chinese tombs, with many of the most striking examples made during the Han dynasty. Without this tomb association, the purposes of these models would be difficult to determine—they could have served as artistic representations, as reminders of favorite animals, as symbols of a trade, or they may have had a religious or a cultural function. In China, ceramic tomb models were meant to be physical representations of the essence of the living animal that would accompany the deceased to the afterlife. Pottery horses created for burial in Chinese

Roman culture, Italy
100 – 200 CE
Terracotta
5.91 × 4.72 in., 15 × 12 cm
Metropolitan Museum of Art, New York
Bequest of Nanette B. Kelekian, 2020

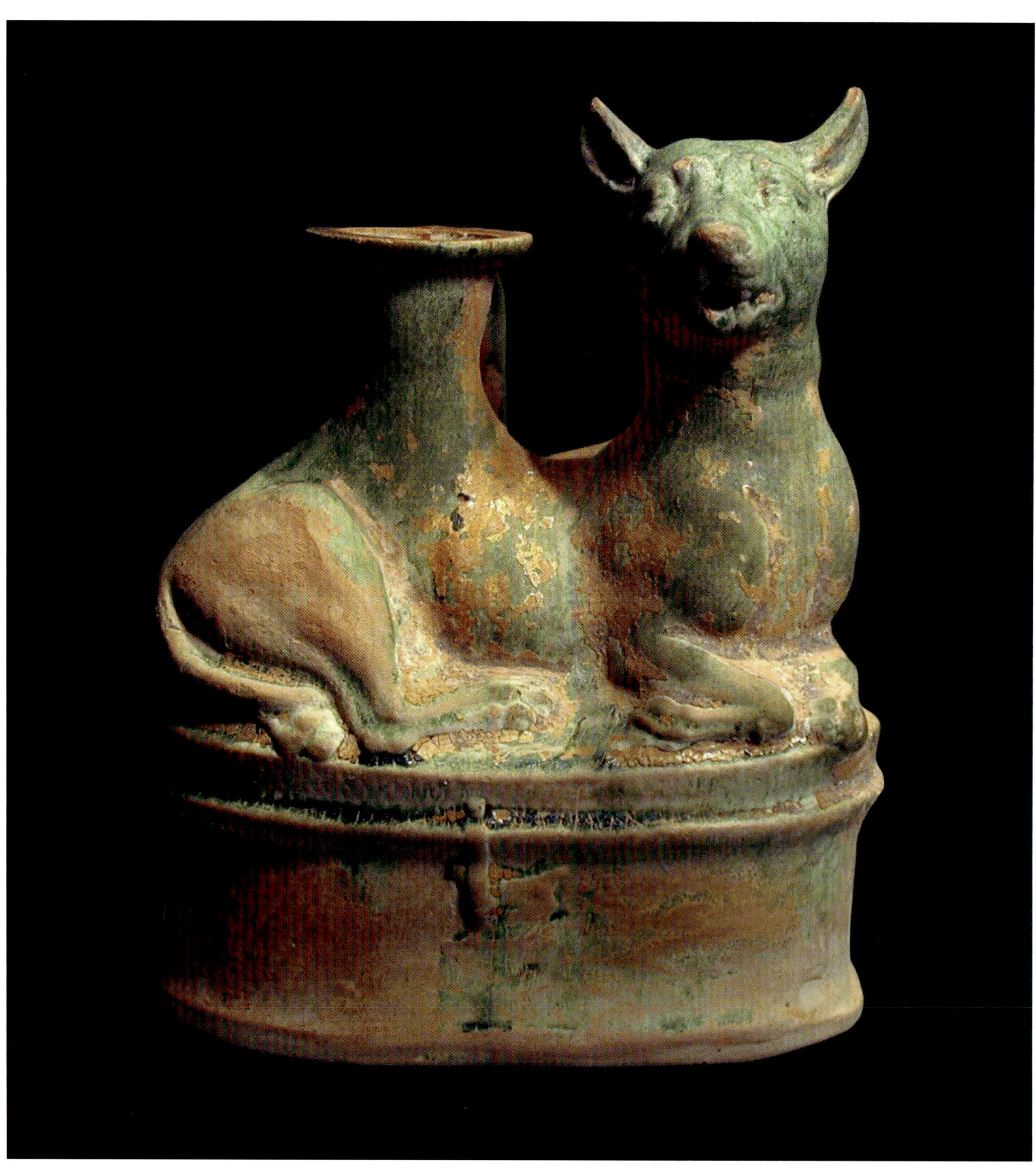

12 Figure of a Dog

Colima culture, Mexico
1 – 200 CE
Terracotta
12 × 18 in., 30.5 × 45.7 cm
Art Institute of Chicago
Ruth Falkenau Fund

13 Figure of a Dog

Late Classical or early Hellenistic, Cyprus
300 – 200 BCE
Limestone
17 ¾ × 6 ⅜ × 11 in.,
45.1 × 16.2 × 27.9 cm
Metropolitan Museum of Art, New York
The Cesnola Collection, Purchased by
Subscription, 1874 – 76

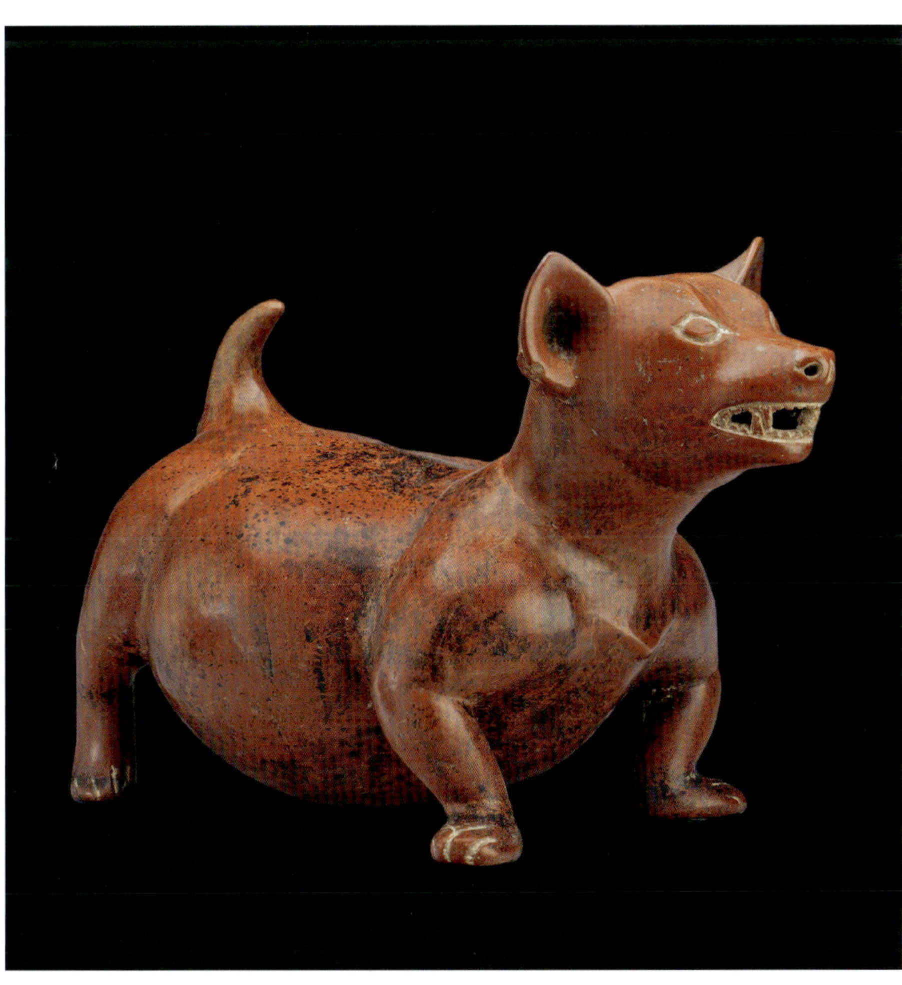

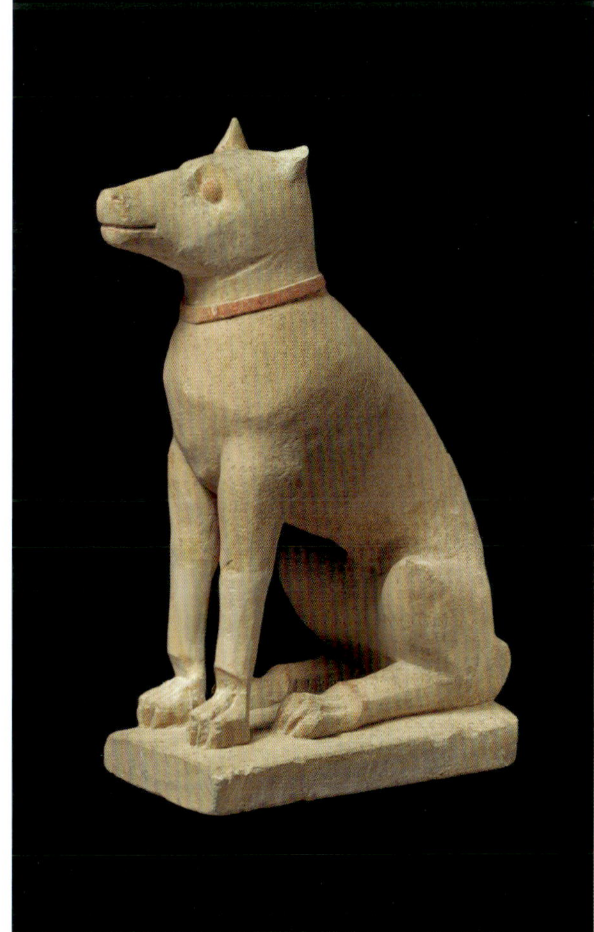

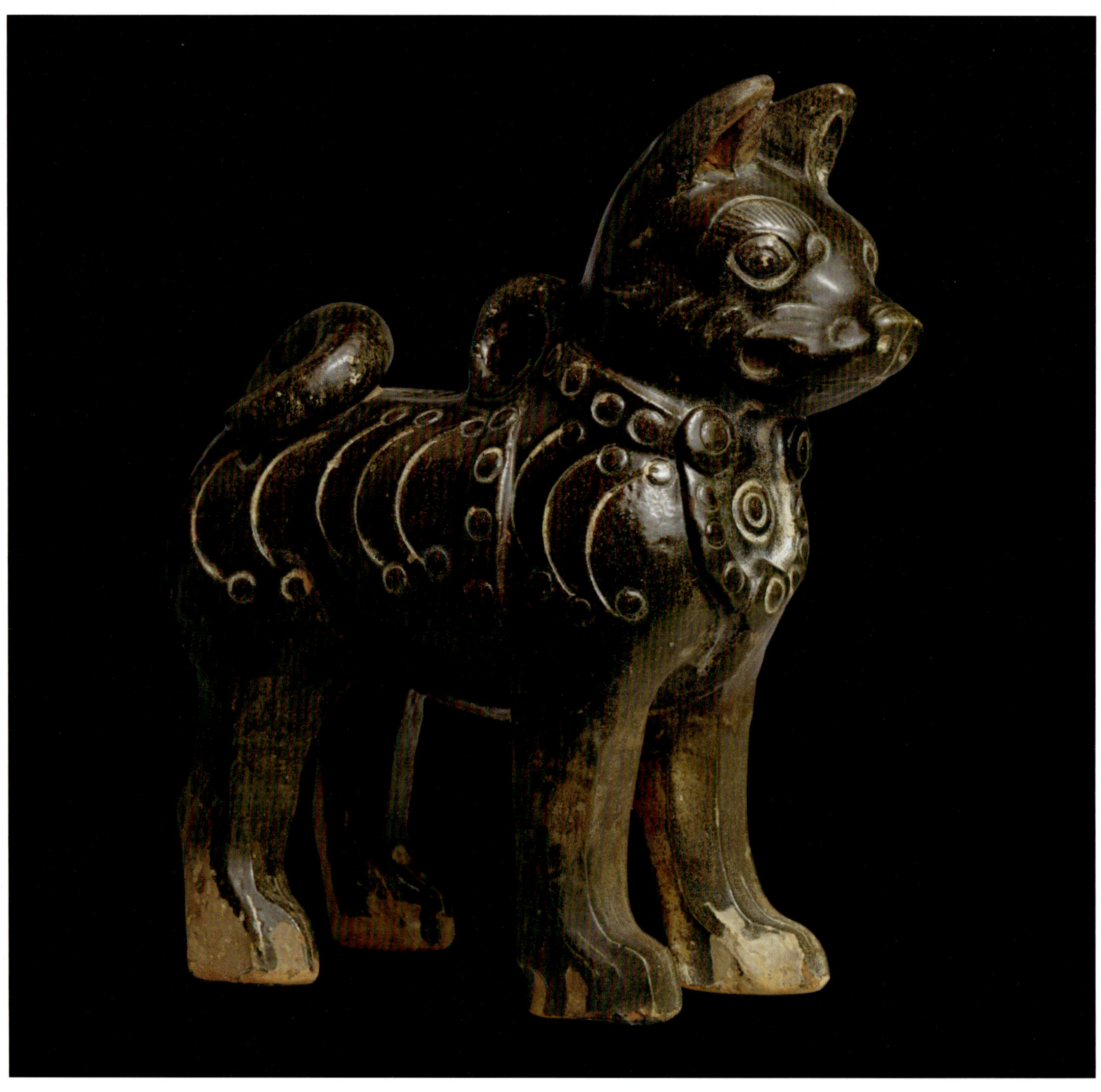

<table>
<tr><td valign="top">

14 **Figure of a Dog**

China
Eastern Han dynasty, 25 – 220 CE
Earthenware with dark green glaze
10 ½ × 4 ½ × 9 ½ in.,
26.7 × 11.4 × 24.1 cm
Metropolitan Museum of Art, New York
Gift of Stanley Herzman,
in memory of Adele Herzman, 1991

</td><td valign="top">

15 **Prancing Horse**

China
1 – 200 CE
Earthenware with traces of pigment
42 × 36 ½ × 11 ½ in.,
106.68 × 92.71 × 29.21 cm
Minneapolis Museum of Art
Gift of Ruth and Bruce Dayton

</td></tr>
</table>

tombs are usually idealized representations, strong and muscular, with arched necks, trimmed manes, and docked tails, portrayed as if they are moving forward with a trained, regular gait. An earthenware horse would have been one of many models included in the deceased's tomb (**15**).[3] These models represented the needs of the deceased in the afterlife and the inclusion of numerous models represented wealth and status to the inhabitants of the next world.

Greek bronze models of horses were made in roughly the same period (late 2nd–1st century BCE) as Chinese pottery models of the Han dynasty, but for a different purpose (**16**). This Greek bronze model is smaller and less muscular than the Chinese example, but it has a similar forward prancing stance. It has a proudly arched neck and raised head, and a trimmed mane indicating care by a groom. The Greek horse was likely created as a trophy or memorial for a favorite animal, but horse models from Greece and other cultures show the animals as important for transport, commerce, recreation, and warfare. Horses were essential to society and the finest were celebrated in images that accentuated ideal characteristics, determined by the purpose for which the horse was to be used. For racing, this would have been an animal that was lean, strong, and swift with a long gait, like the Greek example. The model made for the Chinese tomb shows a horse that was bred for battle with a large, muscular frame.

By the Renaissance period in Europe (ca. 1400–1600), images of Chinese and Greek horses had been long inculcated into the cultures that created them and into surrounding cultures that saw these or similar images. People viewed horses in the context of their own culture and in the context of works filtered from the past. Horses that originated in central Asia were brought to China and adopted by adjoining cultures because of the military or economic benefits they provided. Alexander the Great's (356–323 BCE) horse cavalry, called the Companions, were shock troops that swept across central Asia, leaving an indelible imprint on the region by establishing cities that became major trading centers joining Asia and the Western world. These populations long remembered and celebrated Alexander's accomplishments, and travelers who passed through shared Alexander's exploits with those farther east and west, influencing the depiction of horses as regal and muscular, like that of the Chinese pottery warhorse from the Han dynasty tomb.

An engraving from 1586 by Dutch artist Hendrick Goltzius is based on his drawing of the Roman dictator and general Titus Manlius Torquatus, who lived in the Roman Republic of the fourth century BCE (**17**). The type of war horse in the print is very similar to the Chinese pottery model, with a cropped mane and the taut features of a highly trained animal under the control of an equally powerful rider. Alexander's horse "imprint" resonates in both the Chinese Han dynasty horse and in Goltzius's horse. We react to these horse images based on our experiences. Most of us do not associate horses with combat or transport, seeing them primarily as animals for recreation and sport, but culturally the horse was viewed by most of humanity in roughly the same way from the

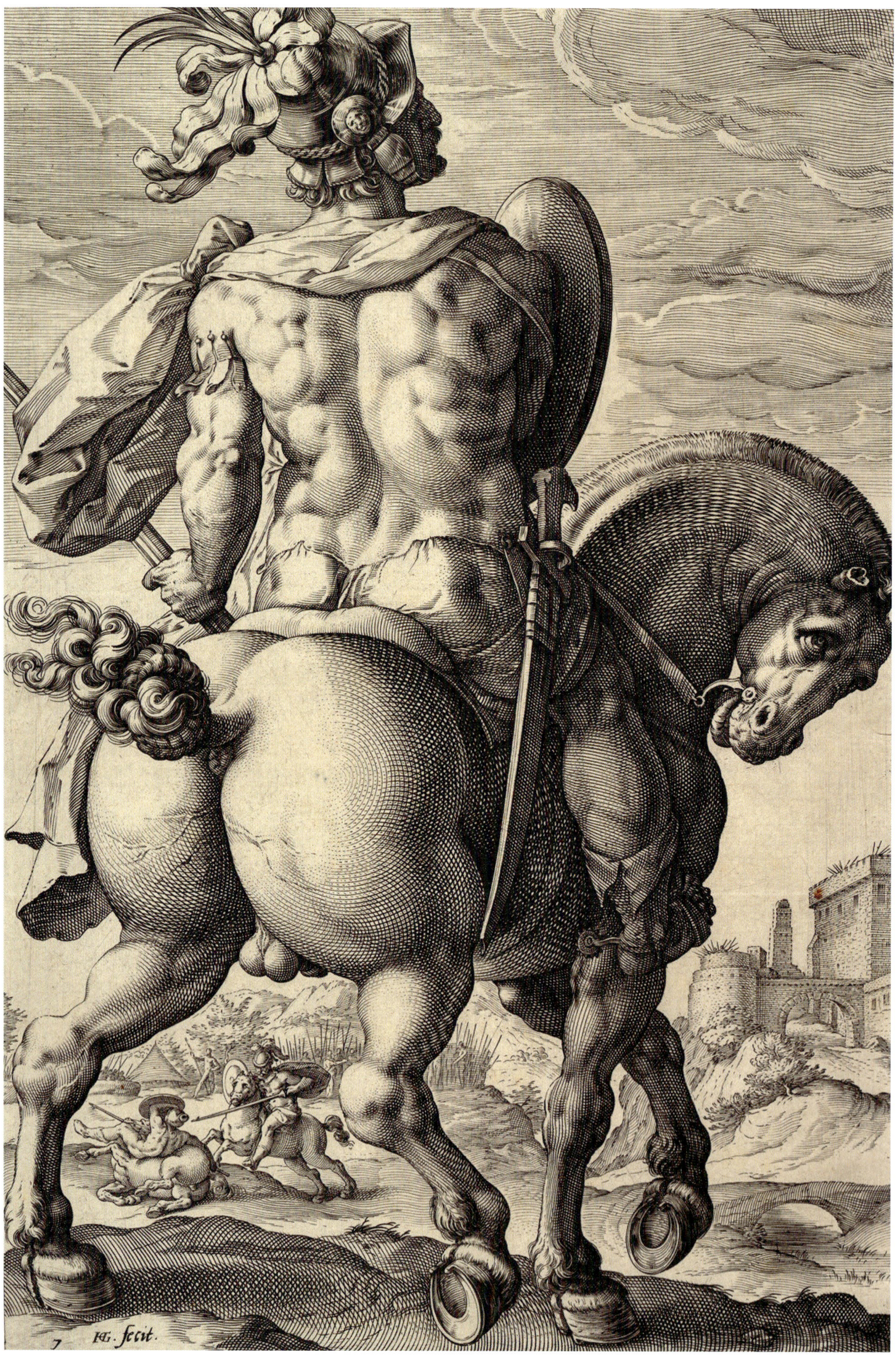

17 *Titus Manlius Torquatus*,
  from the Series *The Roman Heroes*

Hendrick Goltzius (Netherlands, 1558 – 1617)
1586
Engraving; second state
14 ½ × 9 ³⁄₁₆ in., 36.9 × 23.4 cm
Metropolitan Museum of Art, New York
The Elisha Whittelsey Collection,
The Elisha Whittelsey Fund, 1951

time of Alexander up through the end of the nineteenth century. Our "horse lens" changes the way we relate to and represent horses, just as Alexander changed the perceptions about horses during his short lifetime.

Animals are frequently depicted on ritual objects, often vessels, from ancient Egypt to the pre-Columbian cultures of Central and South America (**18** and **19**). Zoomorphic objects mix the practical aspects of a utilitarian vessel meant to hold liquid or dry materials with animal features. The Mayan jar with a pelican head is painted with stylized feathers on both the cover and the body. The rounded vessel represents the body of the animal, with short feet and a tabular tail that serve as supports. There is a balance between sculpture and function in this object. Vessels made to solely represent the animal or plant would likely have a more symbolic or ritual purpose than vessels made for functionality. Early cultures were intimately bound to nature for survival and as part of their belief systems, so animal-form vessels were not just for storage—they were connected by the image to the living creatures represented on or in the form.

Ritual objects were often decorated with flora and fauna relevant to their ceremonial purposes. The Tairona culture of Colombia, dating back to 200 BCE, was particularly noted for objects in gold used for personal adornment and shamanic rituals in which the wearer would assume powers from the represented animal. This gold bird pendant, made ca. 1000–1500, has a superficial similarity to bronze mounts on ritual vessels in China during the Western Zhou period (1045–771 BCE), but aside

from the visual similarity, there is no known connection between early Chinese and pre-Columbian peoples (**20**). The similarity of the forms is likely the result of a mutual, shamanistic-type belief and expression of these distilled bird-like elements into a stylized form, which is found in abstracted zoomorphic imagery among many cultures.

This bone fragment from the Chavin culture in Peru's central highlands ca. 600–200 BCE is fully carved with deeply and finely incised lines that wrap around the body (**21**). The bone has been shaped to be a sharp instrument and is heightened with color in a design of disembodied animal and human elements with a form that is less dagger than fang or claw. The design suggests forest predators like the jaguar, caiman, or anaconda, but the elements are so fragmented that no full image is present. The design is unsettling, evoking ritual, danger, and mysticism. The work is probably a *tupus*, a long pin used to secure a cloak in place, but it might have been used for bloodletting or sacrifice. Such abstraction can leave the modern viewer uncertain about what is depicted and opens the possibility of a number of options taken from natural sources, but the original viewer would not have had this cultural barrier and the imagery would have been clear.[4] What we perceive as abstract images were not seen that way by the cultures that created them. We do not know exactly how this vocabulary of design was received by the creating culture, but we know that it meant more to them than it does to us because we are viewers who stand outside of their cultural traditions and observe from our own cultural position.

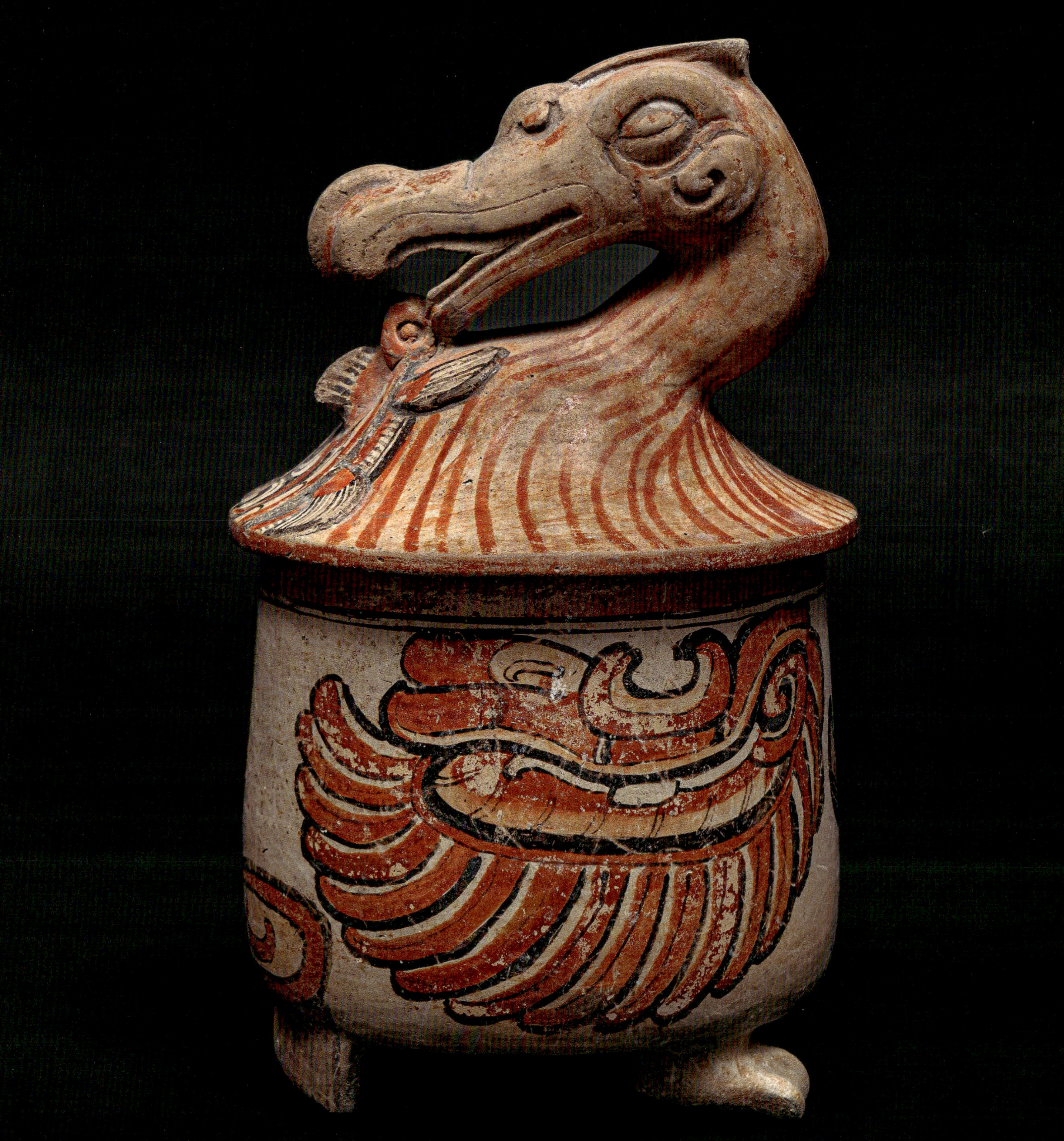

18   Lidded Polychrome Effigy Vessel

Maya culture, Mexico
Early Classic period, 250 – 450 CE
Terracotta
9 in., 22.86 cm
Private Collection

19   Falcon Stirrup Vessel

Paracas culture, south coast of Peru
600 – 100 BCE
Terracotta
7 × 8 in., 17.78 × 20.32 cm
Private Collection

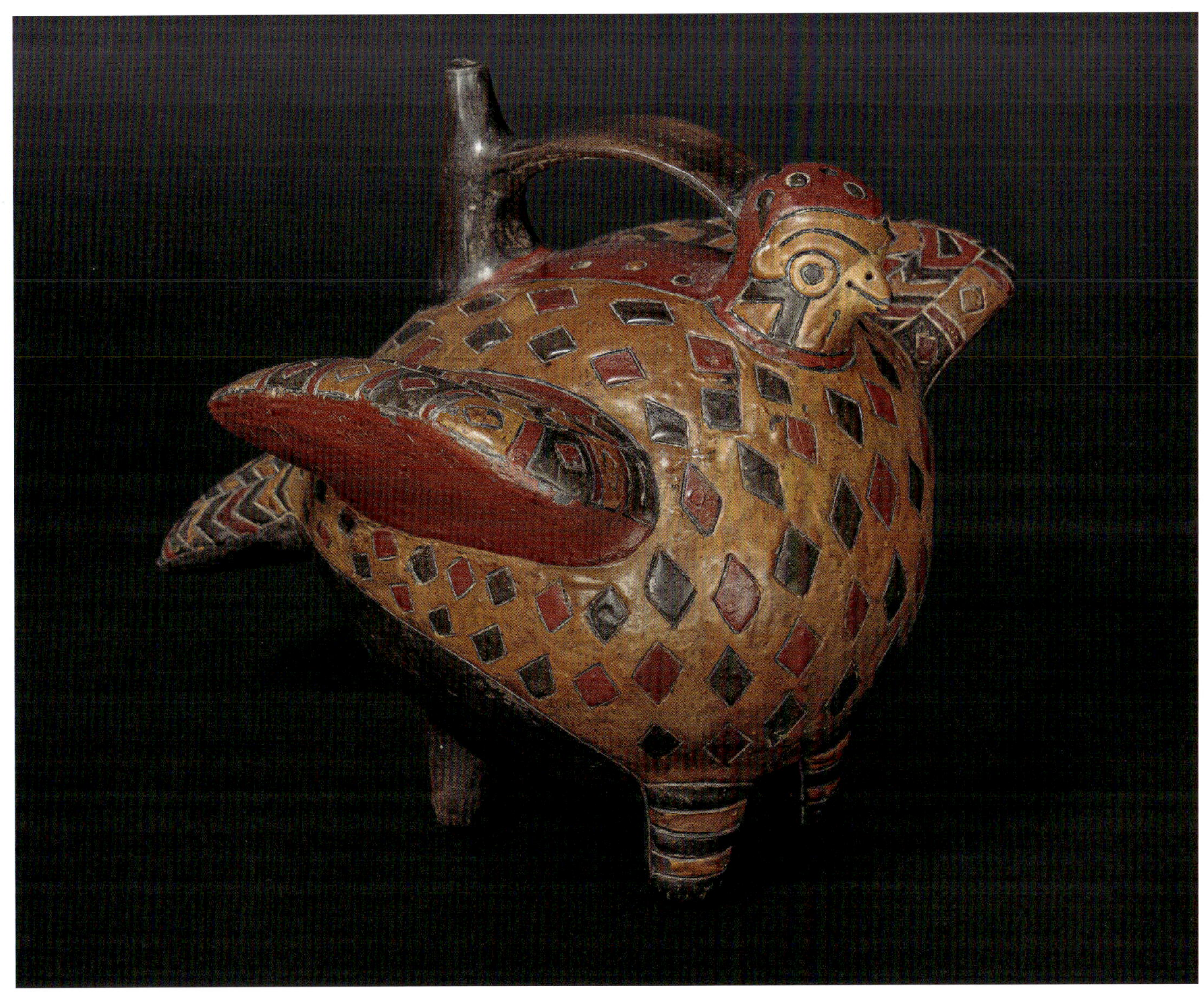

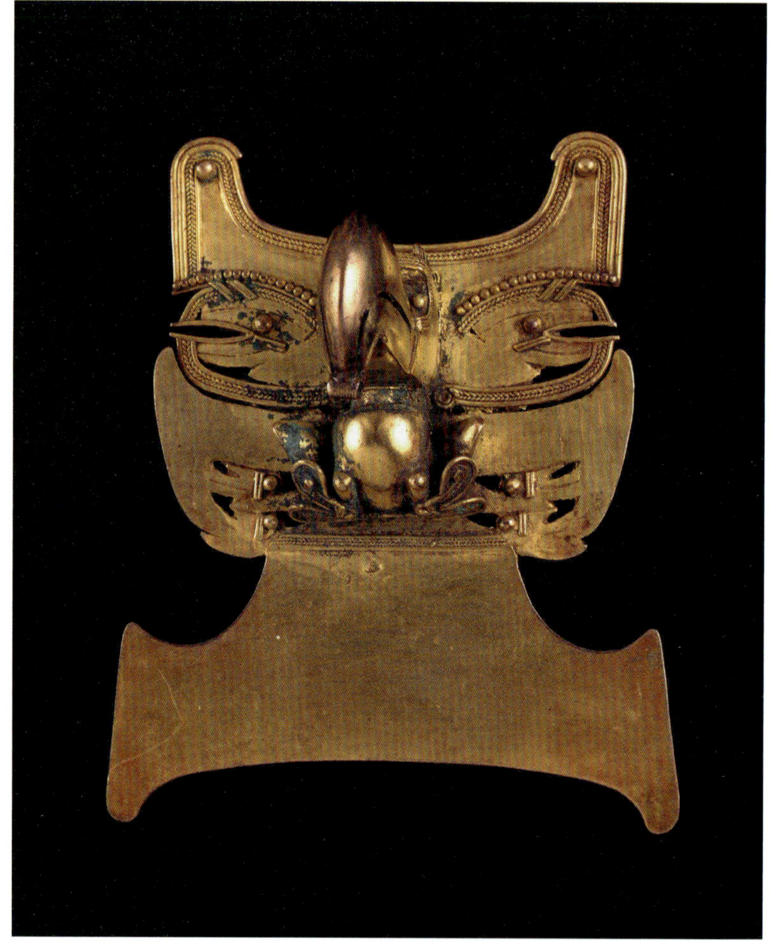

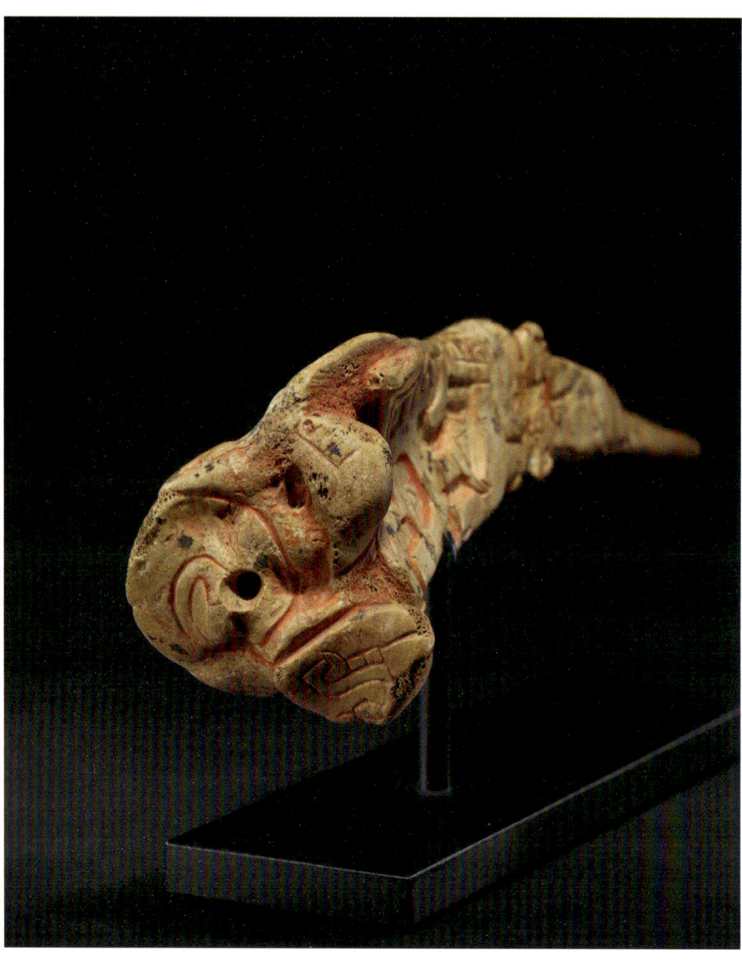

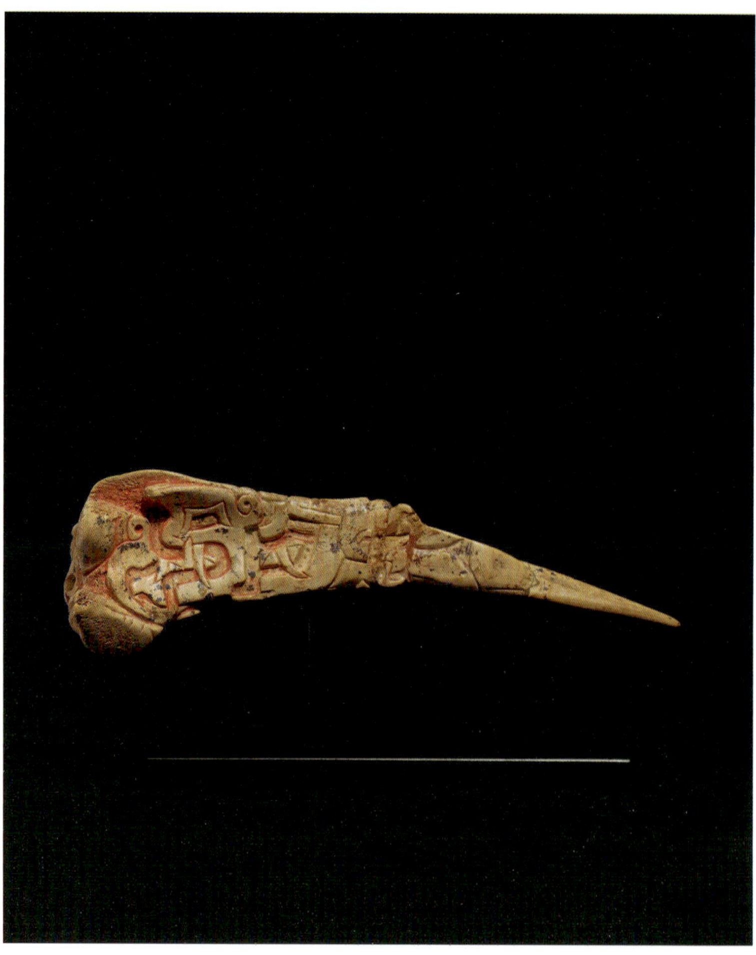

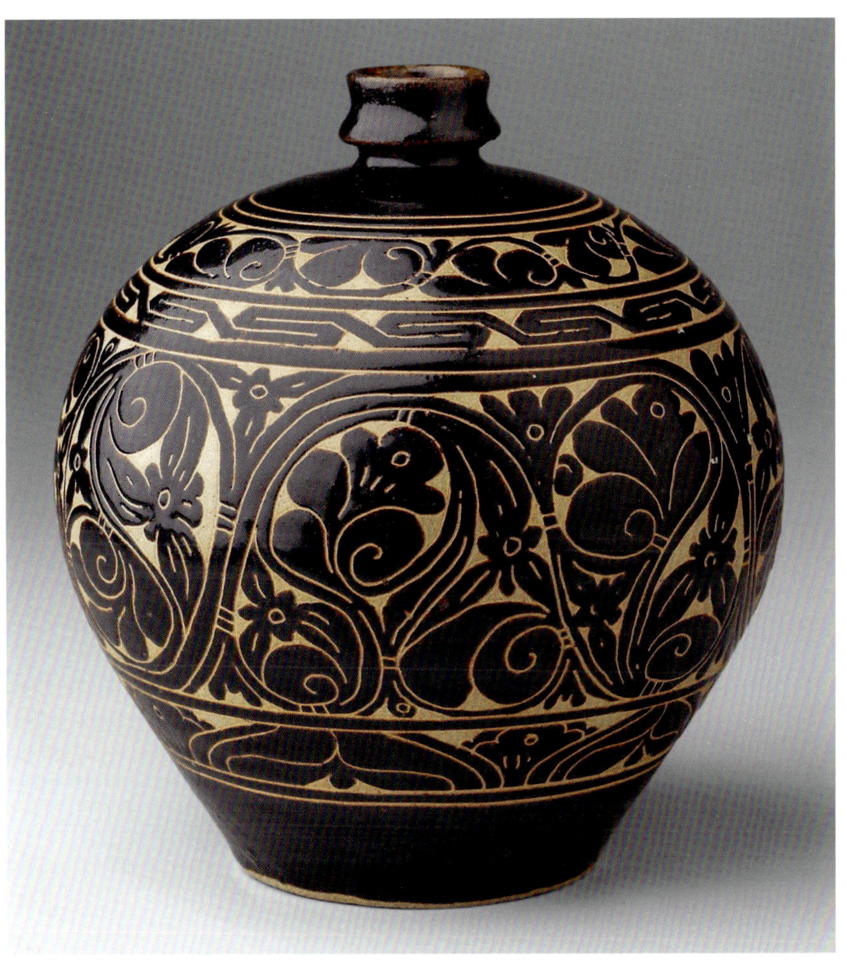

22 Ovoid Bottle

China
Late 1100s
Huai-Jen ware stoneware with dark brown
glaze and "cut-glaze" decoration
8 9/16 × 7 11/16 in., 21.75 × 19.53 cm
Minneapolis Museum of Art
Gift of Ruth and Bruce Dayton

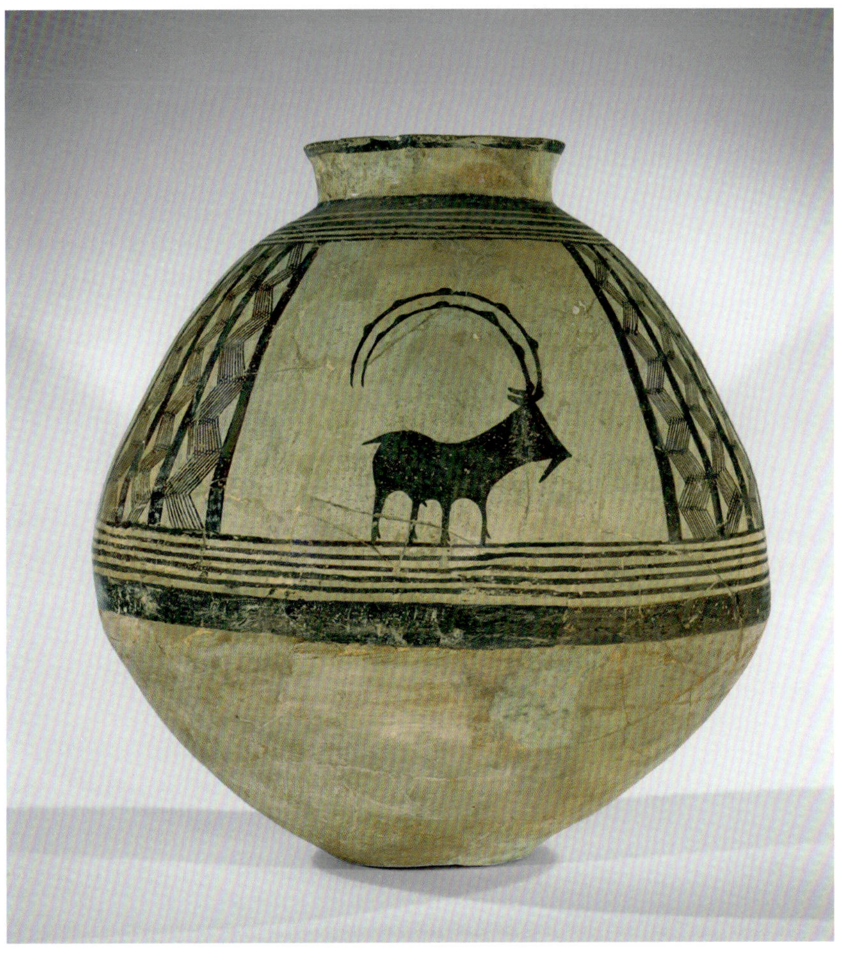

23 Storage Jar Decorated with Mountain Goats

Central Iran
Chalcolithic period, 4000 – 3600 BCE
Terracotta
21 in., 53.3 cm
Metropolitan Museum of Art,
New York, Purchase,
Joseph Pulitzer Bequest, 1959

This starkly abstract vessel made during the late twelfth century in China could easily be mistaken as a work from a European workshop of the early twentieth century (**22**).[5] The rounded body shape is for holding liquid and the narrow spout reduces spillage and evaporation. The design is repetitive and incorporates natural forms that would have been familiar to the viewer, but to us they are highly stylized, with rounded outlines and contrasts between light and dark in the glaze and buff colored body. The recipient of the vase would have been familiar with the images and associated them with local plants. Similarly, Iranian artists, working in one of the most sophisticated of ancient cultures with a long tradition of trade within the region, created utilitarian vessels decorated with scenes that would have been understood by viewers, such as this storage vessel from ca. 4000–3600 BCE depicting mountain goats (**23**).

Nature and Fantasy

Images of dragons, griffins, and other fantastic animals are found within most cultures.[6] Fanciful beasts explained the mysteries and terrors of the unknown and usually incorporated observations taken from living sources or second-hand observations shared by individuals who had no context to explain the unusual. Whether depicted naturalistically or stylized, the animal often was believed to be a living but rare creature, though some cultures recognized that it was fanciful. Early depictions of dragons were believed to represent living creatures. Belt hooks in ancient China were made of jade, metal, and other materials, and the elaborate examples made during the Eastern Zhou and Warring States periods were of bronze inlaid with gold and silver. The body frequently was modeled as a dragon with other stylized natural forms incorporated into the design. Usually, the dragon head is recognizable and the body is abstract, often with inlays or patterns cast into the bronze.

While dragons are often associated with Asia and especially China, they are found in mythology and art from outside of Asia. Cultural exchanges from the Roman and earlier periods through the Middle Ages and into the Renaissance and modern world included works of art and written and verbal accounts of myth and science. Facts about the known world mixed with mythology rooted in both Western and Eastern sources. Both myth and reality inform this twelfth-century gilt-copper disk with green, stylized leafy patterns encircling a swordsman and his antagonist, the dragon; the circular form is suggestive of the known world (**24**). This scene may represent the Arthurian hero Tristan, a figure who represented knightly love that emerged from Celtic legends of the twelfth century, or it may be a generalized reference to similar tales. The stylized patterns recall works in red carved lacquer created in China in the twelfth century,[7] and early Roman/Byzantine enamel wares.[8]

24 **Warrior Fighting a Dragon**

Anglo-Norman, England or France
1170 – 1180
Gilded copper, enamel
2 ⁹⁄₁₆ × ⅛ in., 6.5 × 0.3 cm
Cleveland Museum of Art
Purchase from the J. H. Wade Fund

This aquamanile was created in Nuremberg between 1425 and 1450 (**25**). Aquamanile were water vessels used for washing hands during a meal or as part of the Christian Eucharist ceremony, in which adherents memorialized the life and teachings of Jesus. They were made in a variety of materials but most surviving examples are in bronze or copper alloys. This one is in the form of a griffin, with a neck of stylized, leaf-like feathers and a flame-form mane with eagle talon legs. Unicorns, griffins, and fanciful creatures were either believed to be living but rare and naturally occurring, or mythological. The undiscovered world was immense and new species were constantly being discovered, making it easy to believe in the existence of creatures that were imaginary.

An exquisite dragon pendant, made in Spain between 1575 and 1600 of gold with colored enamels and pearl, is a contrast of terror and beauty, the fantastic and the natural (**26**). The riches of the newly discovered Americas are represented by gold and pearls. The pendant is accentuated by contrasting colors and gilded, reflective surfaces. The high-quality workmanship is evident from a few steps away, and the subject matter of a beautiful and dangerous animal subdued by the owner would have been understood by observers as a metaphor for the fragility of life.

The dragon and the phoenix, mythical animals represented in many cultures, are often depicted together, as in this drawing by an artist working in the mid-sixteenth century in the Ottoman Empire, which spanned east Asia to Egypt (**27**). The painter was probably familiar

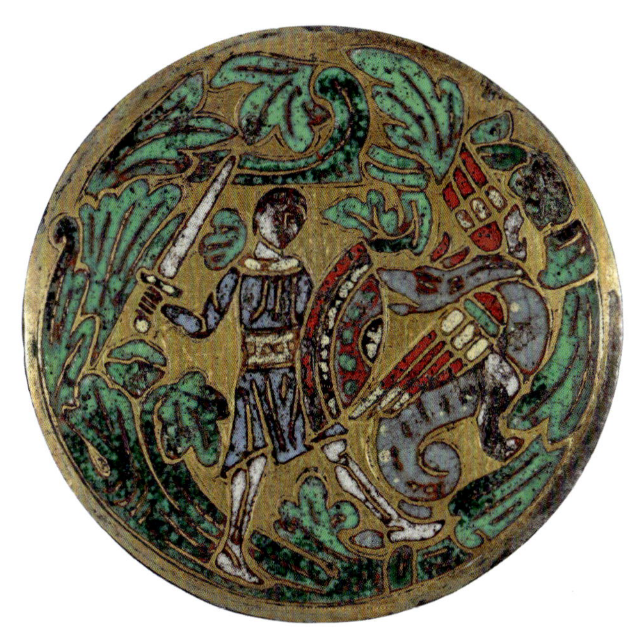

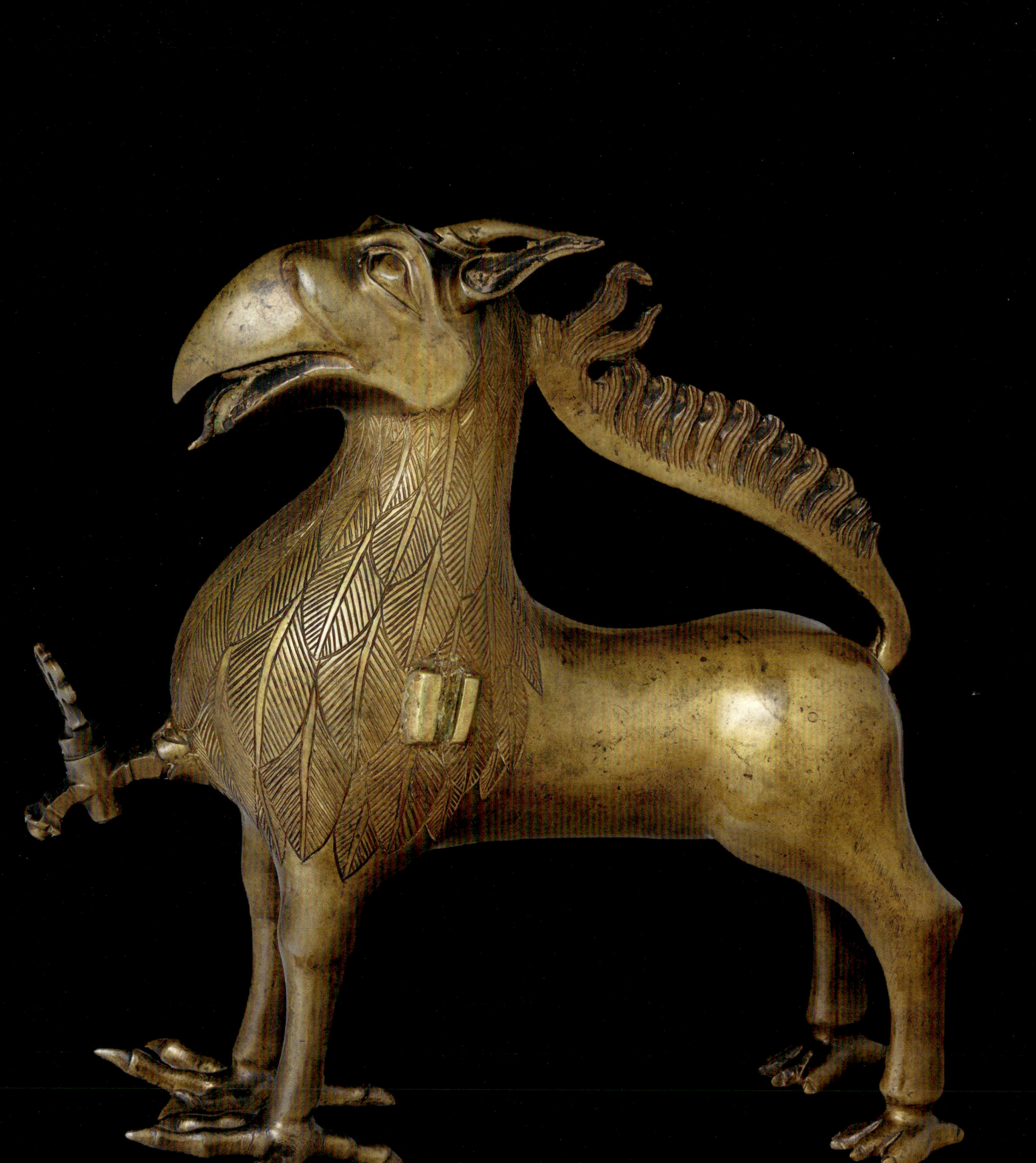

25 Aquamanile in the Form of a Griffin

Nuremberg, Germany
1425 – 1450
Bronze
12.60 in., 31.9 cm
Metropolitan Museum
of Art, New York
Robert Lehman Collection, 1975

26 Pendant Shaped as a Dragon

Spain
1575 – 1600
Gold, enamel, and baroque pearls
3 1/16 × 1 7/8 in., 7.8 × 4.7 cm
Art Institute of Chicago
Gift of Marilynn B. Alsdorf

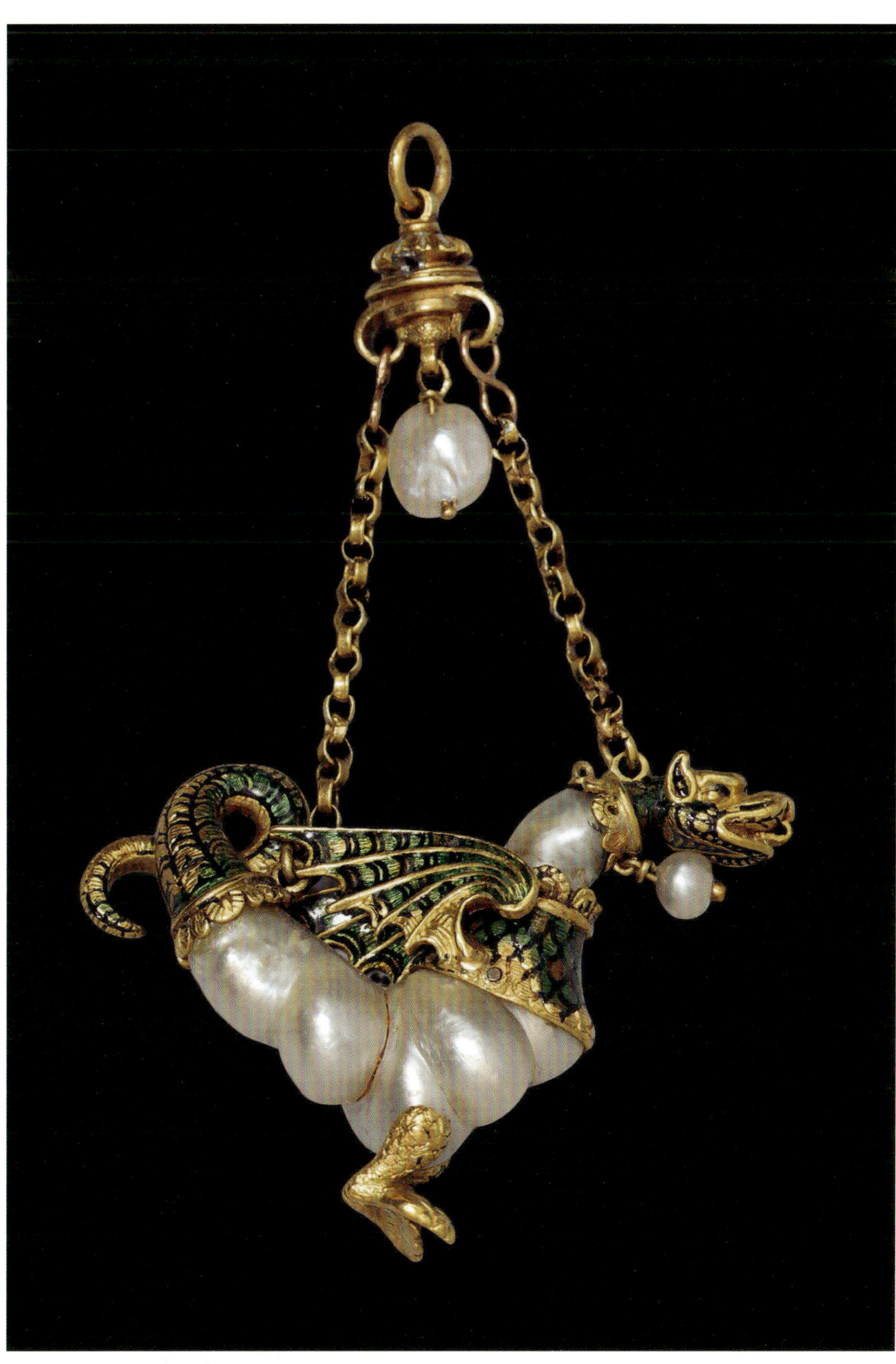

27 **Dragon in Foliage with Lion and Phoenix Heads**

Attributed to Sahkulu (Turkey, active 1526 – 1556)
1550
Ink, gold, opaque watercolors on paper
6 ¹³⁄₁₆ × 15 ¹³⁄₁₆ in., 17.3 × 40.2 cm
Cleveland Museum of Art
Purchase from the J. H. Wade Fund

28 **Griffin Protome**

Greece
Ionian period, 625 – 575 BCE
Bronze
5 ½ in., 13.9 cm
Cleveland Museum of Art
The Charles W. Harkness
Endowment Fund

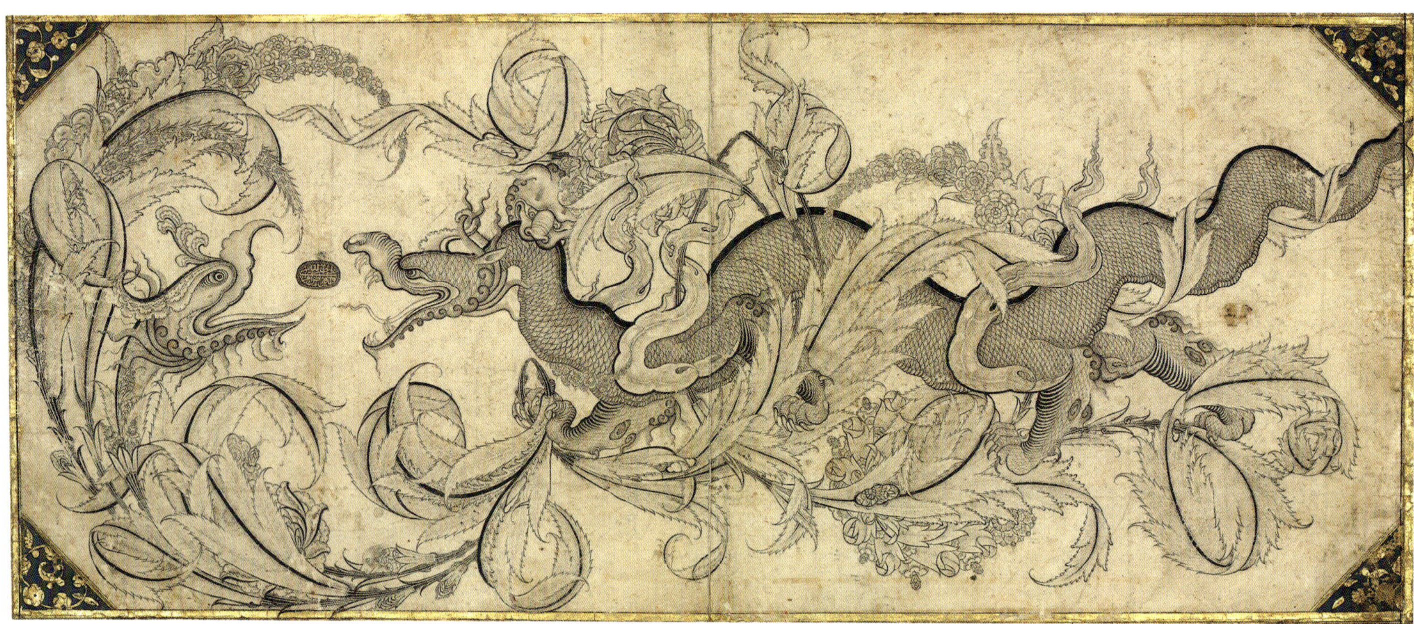

with the Iranian artist Sahkulu, who introduced this style of work, with leafy vines emanating from the phoenix, in Istanbul in 1526. In a defensive action, the phoenix is transforming itself into foliate forms. The contrast of the two combatants with the flowering vines encircling them recalls the struggle between the armed swordsman and the dragon on the champlevé enamel gilded copper medallion in a setting of familiar, though stylized, foliage (**24**).

The griffin is a mythical animal incorporating bird and lion elements that has origins in ancient Greece and other cultures and was represented in stone, bronze, and other materials. The bird perched atop this Greek bronze finial

dating to the sixth century closely resembles a griffin (**28**); it was likely attached to the shoulder of a large bronze cauldron.[9] The beak, upright ears, and single horn may have been sourced from rhinoceros or even fossilized bones. Cultural exchanges over the Silk Road trade route introduced this and other forms from the West to Asia and from Asia to the West.[10] Though this depiction is representational and includes parts of actual animals, it is of an animal that does not exist in nature. The stylized carved stone head of a pelican made in Guatemala ca. 550–950 is a *hacha*, a Spanish term for axe (**29**). *Hacha* were used as markers within the arena in which the ballgame was played, an important practice within the Mayan culture,

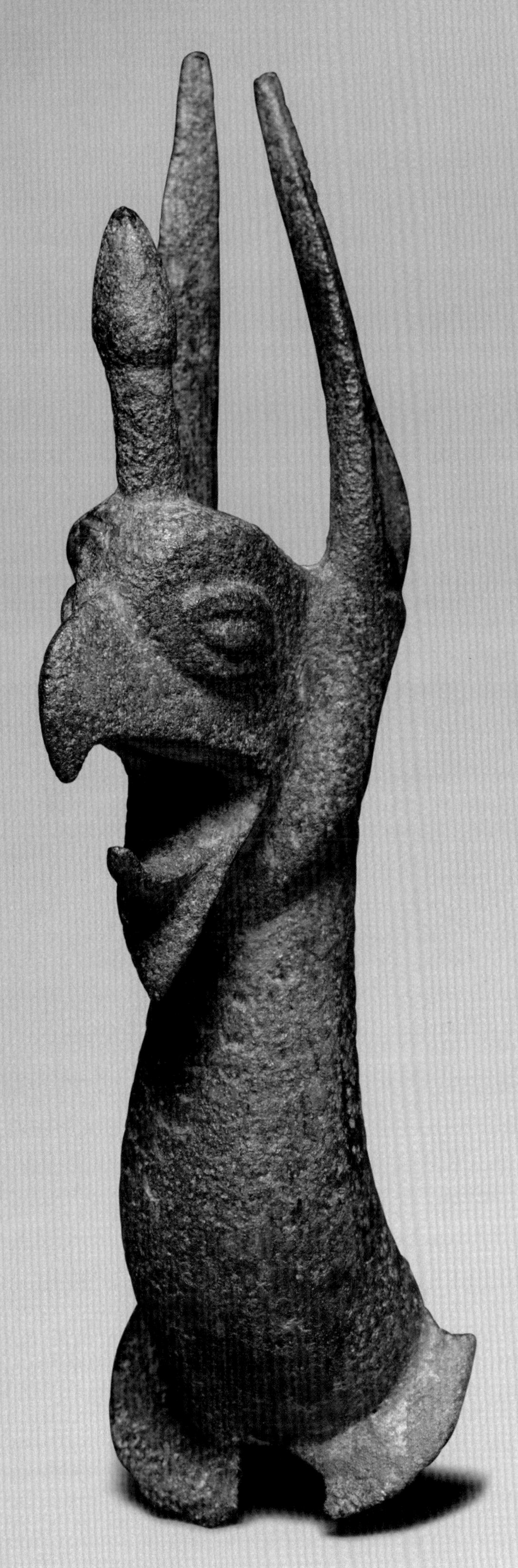

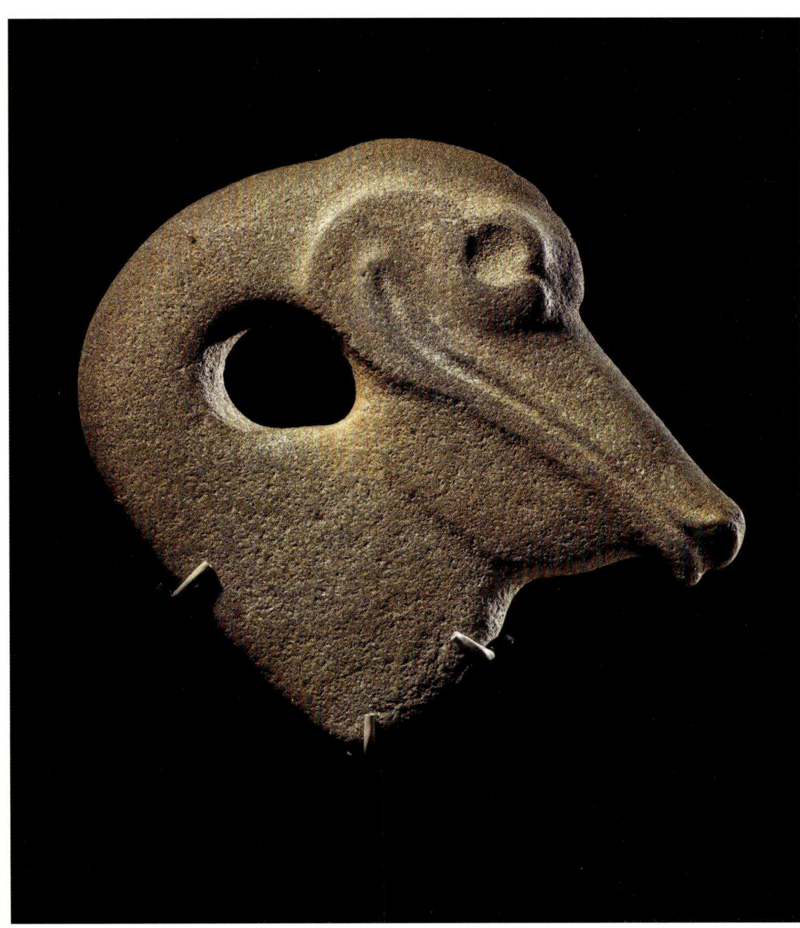

centered in what is now Guatemala, that originated over three thousand years ago. The pelican, with its curved neck merging into the lowered head, is representational and based on a living creature; it is not a stylized representation of a mythical creature.

The co-existence of natural and imaginary creatures is not unique to ancient cultures. In our modern culture we regularly encounter humans depicted with mythological powers, or animals and plants that speak and have human characteristics. We know these to be myth not nature. Our forebears likely had a similar perspective of the unknown spirit world that exists beyond life.

Creating Paradise: The Human Manipulation of Nature

In our Anthropocene age, in which humans are a dominant part of the ecosystem, we are both part of nature and the shapers of nature. We cultivate crops, we breed animals, we eradicate creatures that are detrimental to our health and well-being and to the species under our care and call them pests. We are the inheritors of paradise and the scourge of it. The legendary Hanging Gardens of Babylon, the grand vistas of English landscape architect Capability Brown (1716–1783), and the magnificent parks of American Fredrick Law Olmstead (1822–1903) were

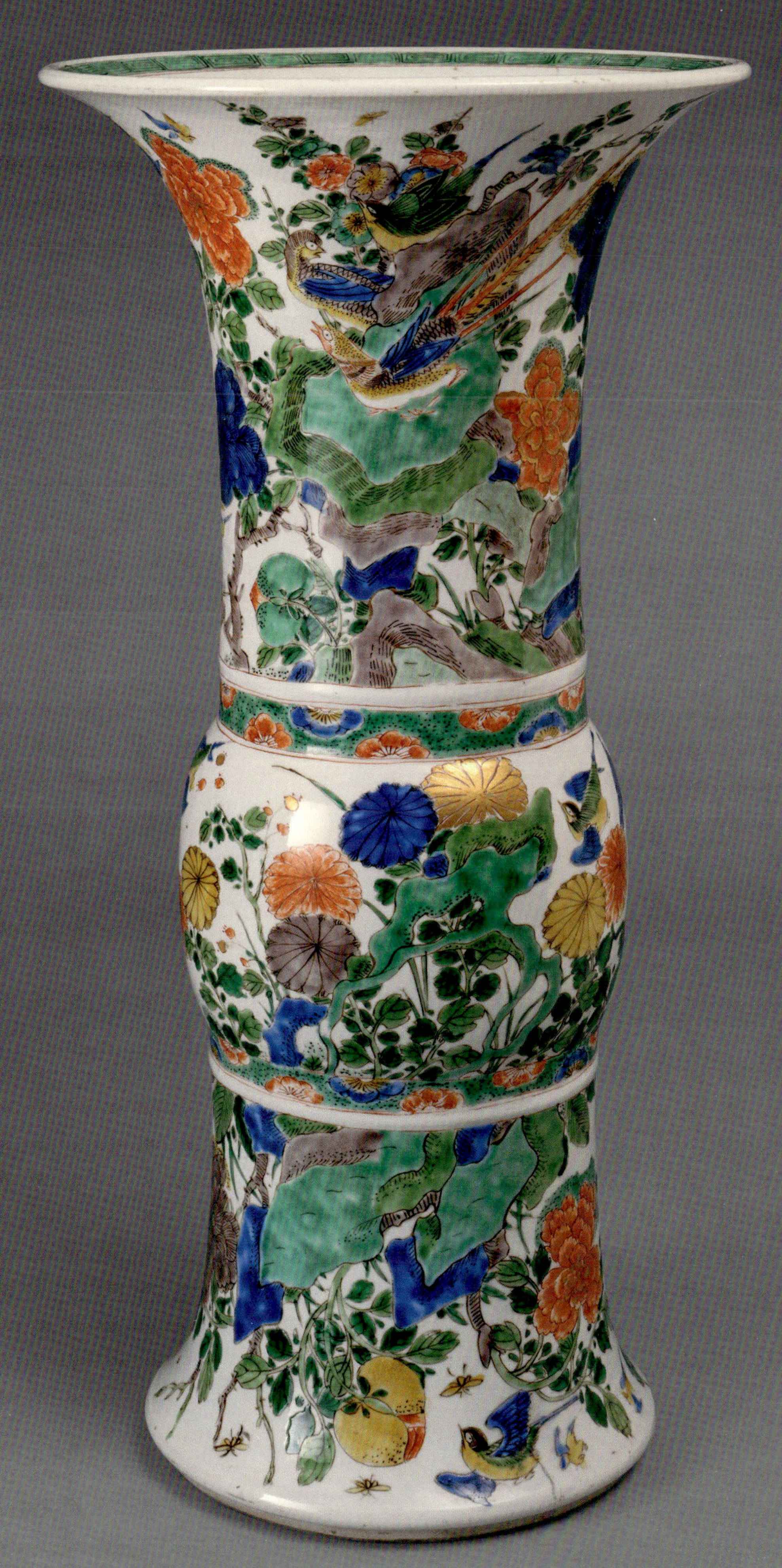

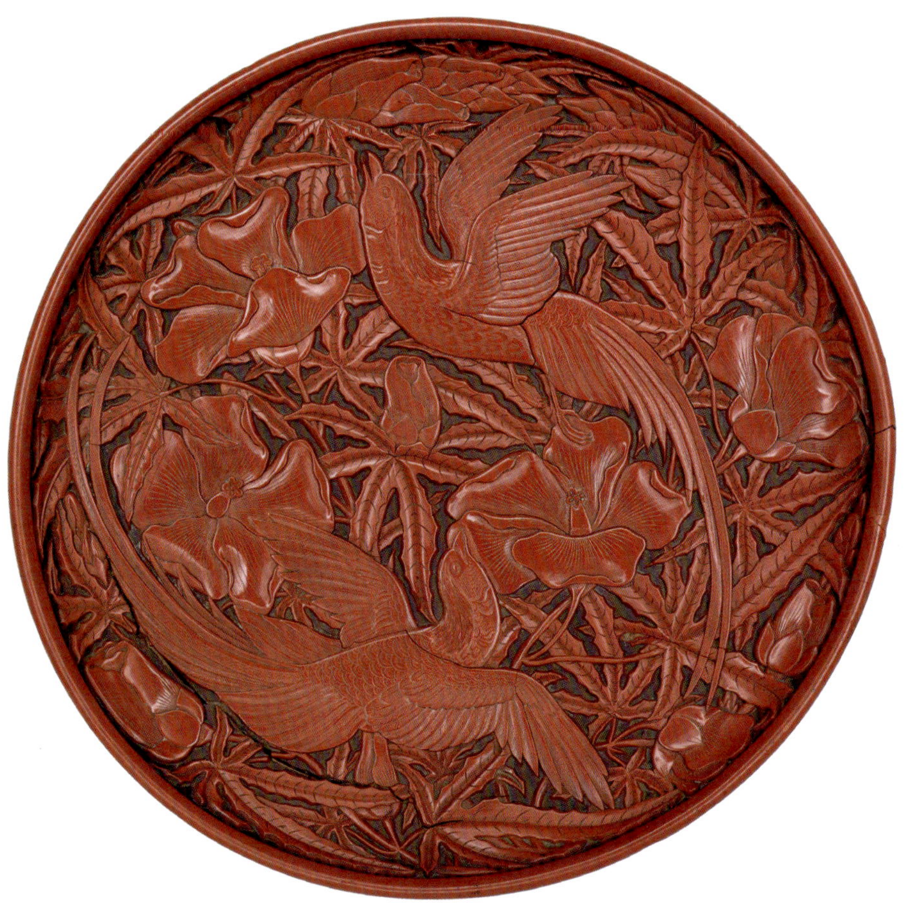

all manipulations of nature meant to suit human preferences. Nature accommodated the change, but none of these changes would have occurred without human intervention.

Parks, earthworks, and public gardens reflect the culture of those who created them, just as small-scale representations of flowers and animals clustered together on a pottery jar are reflections of the culture in which the artisan who created them lived. The scale is different but the motivations are similar. In this Chinese vase from the late seventeenth to early eighteenth century (**30**), nature is shown in an artistic apogee of clustered, colorful enamels on a clay and glaze vessel modeled after an original design (called a *gu*) first made in bronze over a thousand years earlier. Though it depicts "nature," the image is a compacted, compartmentalized version that exists only by human representation. The profusion of flowers might approximate a garden but the plants, rock work, insects, blooming flowers, and birds would never be found like this in a natural setting. It is an idealized view, idyllic only to humans and not to the creatures and plants that are represented. It is the creation of a human designer who thought it a perfect representation of nature, seen by human eyes. It is a heightened, filtered, and curated image that was meant to emotionally affect the human audience, who would have recognized the connection between the shape of the vase and its archaic bronze ancestor. The stark white body accentuates the

 White Clouds and Red Trees

Li Jian (China, active second half of 1700s)
1788
Hanging scroll; ink and color on silk
49 ¹¹⁄₁₆ × 20 ¾ in., 126.2 × 52.7 cm
Cleveland Museum of Art
Purchase from the J. H. Wade Fund

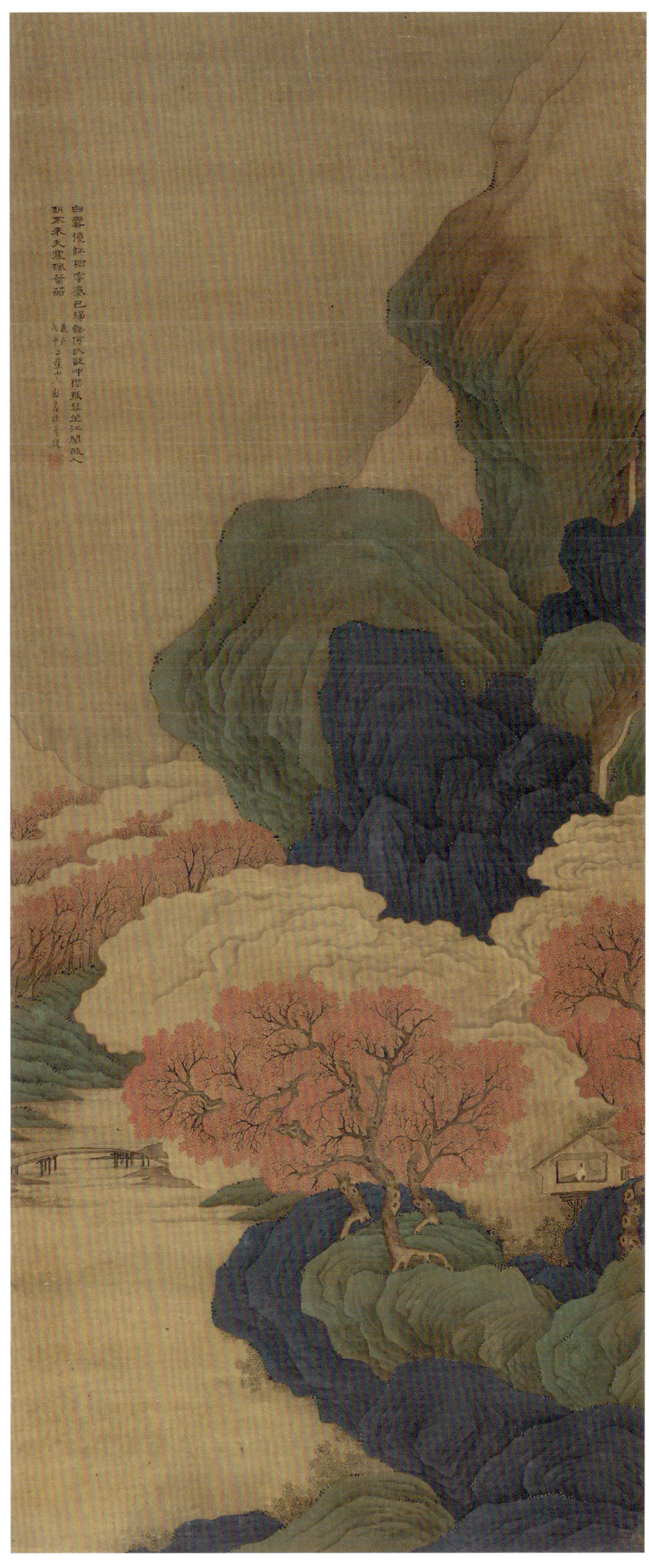

33 Storage Chest

Tlingit culture, Alaska
1880
Wood, paint
20 ¼ × 30 ⅝ × 20 ½ in., 51.5 × 77.8 × 52.1 cm
Metropolitan Museum of Art, New York
The Michael C. Rockefeller Memorial Collection,
Bequest of Nelson A. Rockefeller, 1979

34 Cinerary Urn

Roman culture, Italy
Early Imperial period, Julio-Claudian dynasty,
100 – 150 CE
Marble
14 ¼ × 21 ¼ × 16 ⅛ in., 36.2 × 54 × 41 cm
Metropolitan Museum of Art, New York
Purchase, Philodoroi Gifts, 2002

perfection and otherworldliness of the plants, rock work, birds, and insects. It reminds us of a better world, a perfect harmony, a place of peace.[11]

This carved red lacquer dish has some of the same features as the Kangxi porcelain vase but it depicts two birds among hibiscus (**31**). Though the birds and flowers are recognizable, the design is idealized and reality is accentuated. The carved design is meant to elicit an emotional response. The sense of balance and the placement of the flowers and birds is pleasing to a human viewer. It is not a natural scene, for nothing like this appears in nature. It has been manipulated to appeal to human sensibilities. It is a smaller version of a landscaped garden with plants that would not naturally appear together but arranged as we would like to see them. This dish is like other works of art that incorporate natural imagery, composed in a way that pleases the audience and showcases the skills of the artist and artisan. While landscapes are meant to capture a location's topography, flora, and fauna, they are often idealized views, with heightened emphasis on color and light. Two hundred and fifty years ago the Chinese painter Li Jian created an ordered landscape with blocks of color that defy natural experience (**32**). Instead, Jian's hanging scroll painting of white clouds and red trees conveys a sentiment of order, harmony, and perfection.

Figural representation of the natural world can be stylized, naturalistic, or fanciful, regardless of culture. A late nineteenth-century cedar storage box from the Tlingit culture of the northwest coast of the American

continent, for example, has a stylized mask design that is balanced and abstract (**33**). The Tlingit occupied an area rich in natural resources and had a strong matrilineal clan social structure; the box was for storage and decorated with symbols of power and prestige. Like the Tlingit storage box, this Roman marble container from the first century is profusely carved with images, but it serves an entirely different purpose as a repository for the ashes of the deceased (**34**). It is adorned with trophies of war, indicating that the owner was an important military figure. Both the Tlingit and Roman boxes use natural imagery to address the living and the spirit worlds. To the living, the images were symbolic of current and past time, while to the spiritual audiences, they were symbolic of the future. The Tlingit approached the natural images with abstraction and the Romans approached them with realism, but both are in settings that are removed from nature.

As with nature, we manage our environment and the depictions of our environment. In a living tableau, such as a garden or a park, we create a natural setting that heightens what we want nature to be, not what nature is. In some settings, such as an old-growth forest or national park, we experience nature in an untouched and unmanipulated state. We value these experiences but cannot live within these environments without affecting them. We bring them to us in the objects we create, which are distillations of nature, provided to us by a skilled individual who is valued by us as the interpreter of nature and the natural world. When we view the

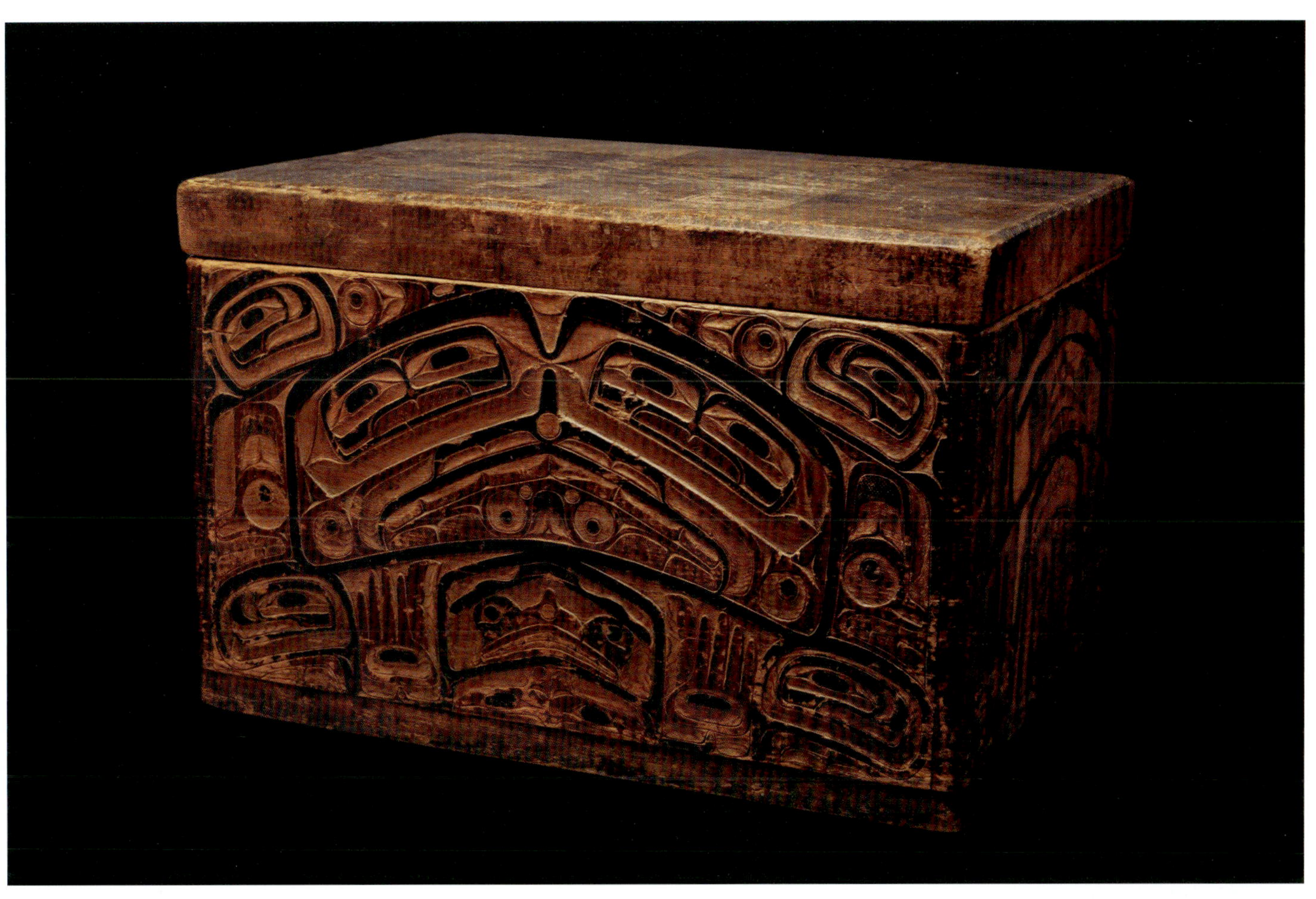

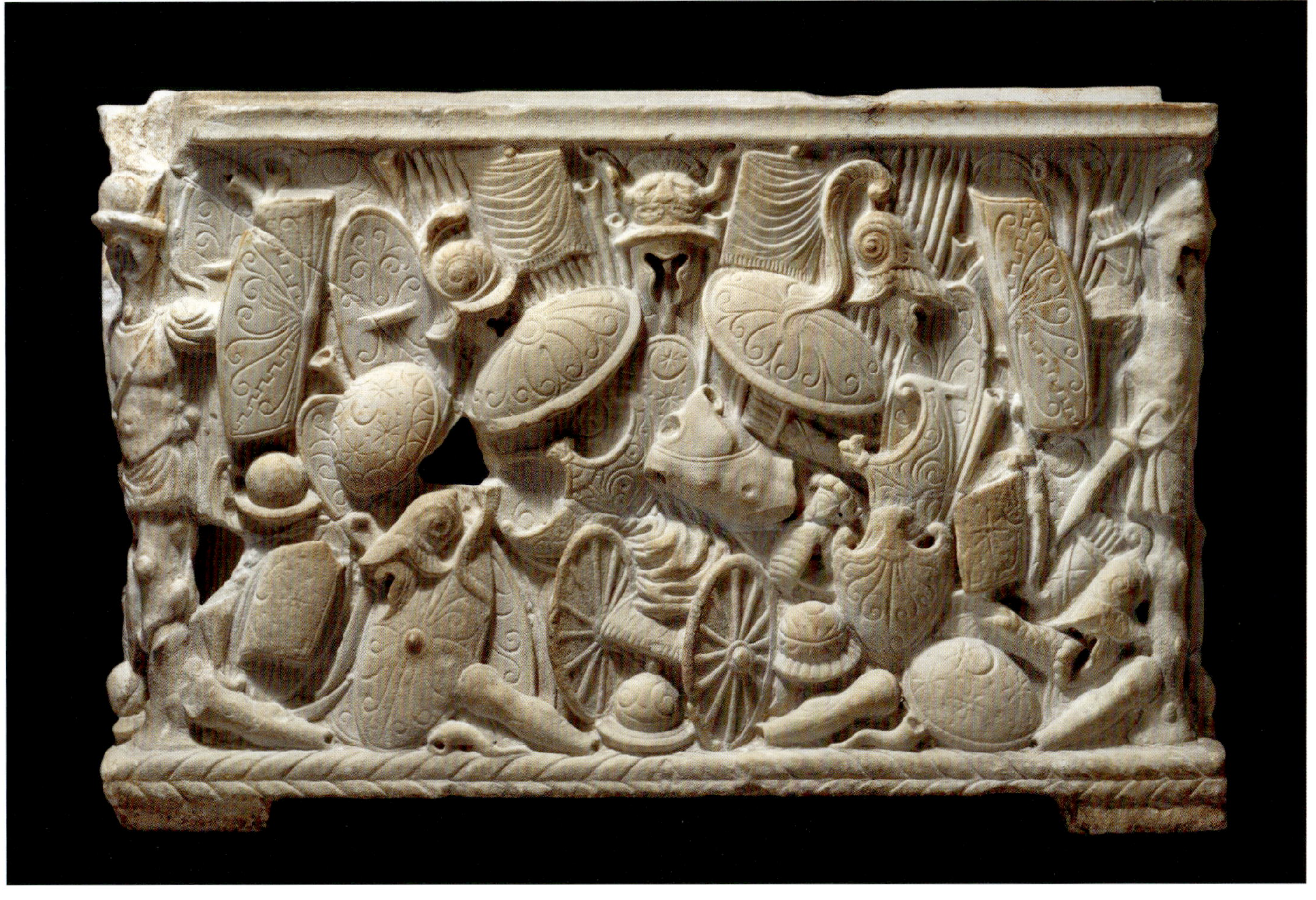

lacquer dish, we are seeing a representation of hibiscus and long tailed birds through the creative eyes of the artisan who sketched the design and those who carried out the work (**31**). The artist imbued his creation with his experiences, his culture, the immediate environment, and other internal and external influences. The dish, like other works of art, is a window into fourteenth-century China, as well as the creator of the dish, the owner of the dish, and those who appreciated the dish through the centuries up to the present day. Regardless of culture, humans have an inquisitive spirit that seeks to better understand our place in creation while also managing the created world that surrounds us.

Travel, Religion, Commerce, and Creativity

Humans are communal, and as we interact, we adapt to our environment and to each other, and we take ideas from our interactions to create works of art. There is commonality in our experiences and interactions and these lead to a similarity in how we represent nature and the world around us. An interaction with a plant that causes a rash leads us to avoid it in the future, while finding that a plant is edible leads to its cultivation. Experiences lead to exchanges of information with nearby groups. Sharing a harvest from cultivated plants with a group that does not have those plants creates a mutually beneficial relationship. Taking a storehouse of lumber

from a group without compensation is not mutually beneficial. In both instances, individuals gain experience from interacting that informs future actions.

Travel

We think of the ancient world and the Middle Ages as a time of seclusion and limited travel, but there was extensive travel during these periods, facilitating the sharing of manufacturing techniques, materials, and designs, and trade routes extended over ocean and land. The cultural exchanges brought by trade seeded new ideas and perspectives about design and works of art. Objects of personal adornment, such as jewelry, belts, or cloak clasps, that accompanied the wearer on his or her travels were observed by individuals outside the wearer's culture. As traders and pilgrims made their way across the myriad trade routes that ran through all continents, those who came into contact with them would have seen their clothing and personal articles in addition to the goods brought for trading purposes. This seal, used as a stamp to ensure authenticity of authorship, was created at a time when early Middle Eastern civilizations were extending their reach by overland and sea-based trade; such objects would have been shared extensively throughout trading networks (**35**). Dating to around 2000 BCE, it features a profile portrait with a mythical animal near an altar or censer or similar object, though the relationship between the animal and the object is speculative. Images of single-

 Seal with Unicorn and Inscription

Indus Valley civilization, Pakistan
2000 BCE
Soapstone
1⅜ × 1⁷⁄₁₆ in., 3.5 × 3.6 cm
Cleveland Museum of Art
Purchase from the J. H. Wade Fund

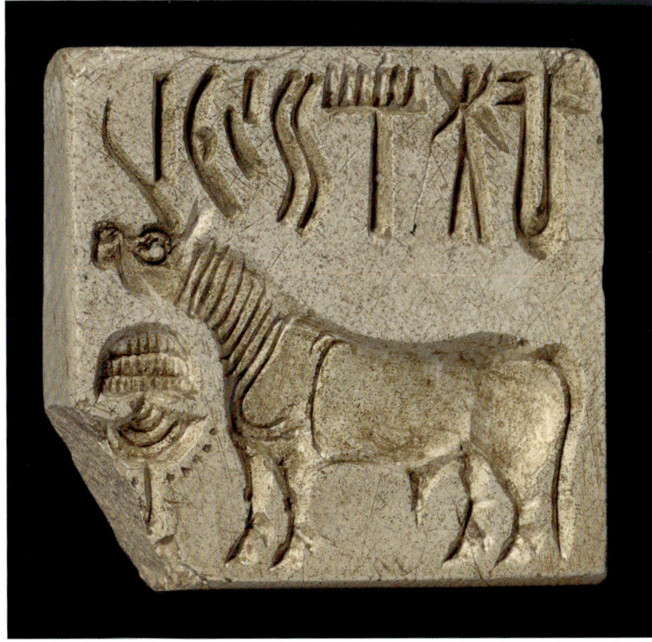

horned bovines, identified as unicorns, were found at a very early date in the Indus Valley, most often as seals. Representations of single-horned animals also appear in Chinese pottery and other materials as well as in ancient Greek art, where the griffin has bird-like features but also a single vertical horn or spike.

Religion

Buddhism, originating in India, spread across central Asia and left influences within diverse, already existing cultural traditions. Christianity and Islam likewise emerged from western Asia and rapidly expanded over Roman trade routes. Cultural exchange brought Asian and Western influences to the Byzantine court in Constantinople (present-day Istanbul) and these were in turn spread to diverse locations. The expansion of Islam, Christianity, and Buddhism also increased cultural exchange. Islamic tileworks, metalwork, and fabrics incorporated natural designs that were adopted and modified by cultures in Spain and other European locations, with trading networks that extended into Buddhist and Islamic commercial centers, resulting in a sharing and modification of ideas and designs.[12]

Christianity arose in the Mediterranean crossroads of Judea within the Roman Empire and was initially suppressed, but by the reign of the emperor Constantine (280–337), it was supported by the power of the Roman state. Christianity spread rapidly over the centuries, supplanting ancient belief systems throughout Asia, Europe, and Africa. With the powerful network of trading routes protected by the Roman state, the far-flung regions of Roman control were connected in spite of long distances and diverse cultures. With the expansion of the Eastern empire, Byzantine trade and Christianity continued to expand, even after the Western empire fell in the fifth century. This pattern of trade, Christian

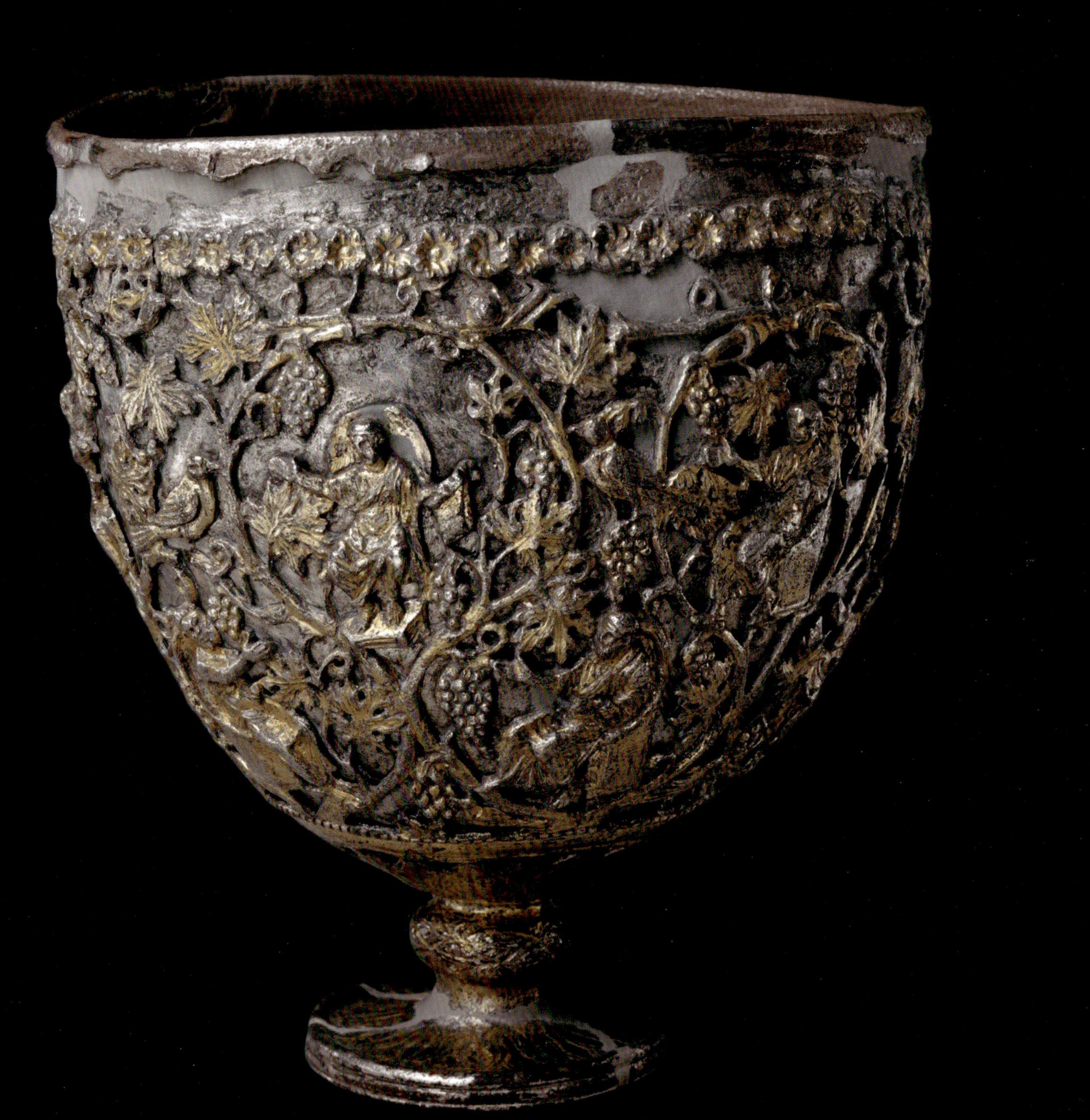

36 Antioch Chalice

Byzantine culture,
Antioch or Kaper Koraon, Syria
500 – 550 CE
Silver, silver gilt
7 ¹¹⁄₁₆ × 7 ¹⁄₁₆ × 6 in., 19.6 × 18 × 15.2 cm
Metropolitan Museum of Art, New York
The Cloisters Collection, 1950

evangelism, and a shared interest in scientific discoveries was not the only means of cultural exchange across vast land areas. Islam, Buddhism, and other religions traveled the same trade routes, as did the conquering armies of Genghis Khan (1162–1227) and other empires.

The Antioch chalice was discovered near Antioch, Syria, in the early twentieth century (**36**). At that time the chalice, which includes a plain silver cup encased with a filigree silver shell was thought to be the "grail," the cup said by Christians to be used by Jesus at the Last Supper. More recent scholarship suggests the chalice was probably created during the sixth century.[13] Antioch was one of the most important cities of the ancient world for commerce, administrative rule, and culture before, during, and after the Roman period, and it was an important Christian center with a population that exceeded 500,000 people by the first century, when it was the third largest city in the Roman Empire. Trade and travelers passed through Antioch from the East and West. The silver indicates that the chalice's purpose merited a material of value and substance, and the high-quality workmanship indicates it had a greater purpose than just a drinking vessel. The exterior reticulated shell of the chalice is decorated with twelve figures seated on high-backed chairs amid scrolling grape vines, grapes, and animals, including an eagle, rabbit, and lamb. The exact meaning of these images is not settled, though the cup is usually agreed to have been used in the Eucharist.

The chalice's design encapsulates images and ideas of surrounding cultures and Asia. The shape is egg-like, deep bodied, with a tracery design that shows influences from East and West. The small, circular foot has a band of outward facing leaves and the knob in the short stem is of braided leaves, echoing the designs found on architectural elements of Roman columns and friezes. Images of scrolling grapevines and grapes are found in ceramics and architecture of central Asia as well as China. The seated figures are in long robes, usually associated with Greek or Roman sources but also found in the region of Parthia, located in northwest Iran, which was conquered and settled by Alexander the Great.

Religious imagery was often the vehicle for the transmission of design elements from one culture to another, spread by trade and travel. A painted and leaded glass panel made in Germany or Switzerland around 1515 includes both a unicorn and the Virgin Mary, mixing a hunting scene with the Christian story of the Annunciation—the announcement to Mary that she would bear a child who would be the son of God (**37**). The principal image is a female figure in a highly stylized posture standing alongside a heraldic image of the Lichtenfel family, framed within a pair of tree-trunk columns and foliate devices that merge into armor. Swirls of leafy, gilt foliage with oversized heraldic emblems reminiscent of ancient Roman trophies dominate the image of the pair of trunks supporting a lintel of Mary

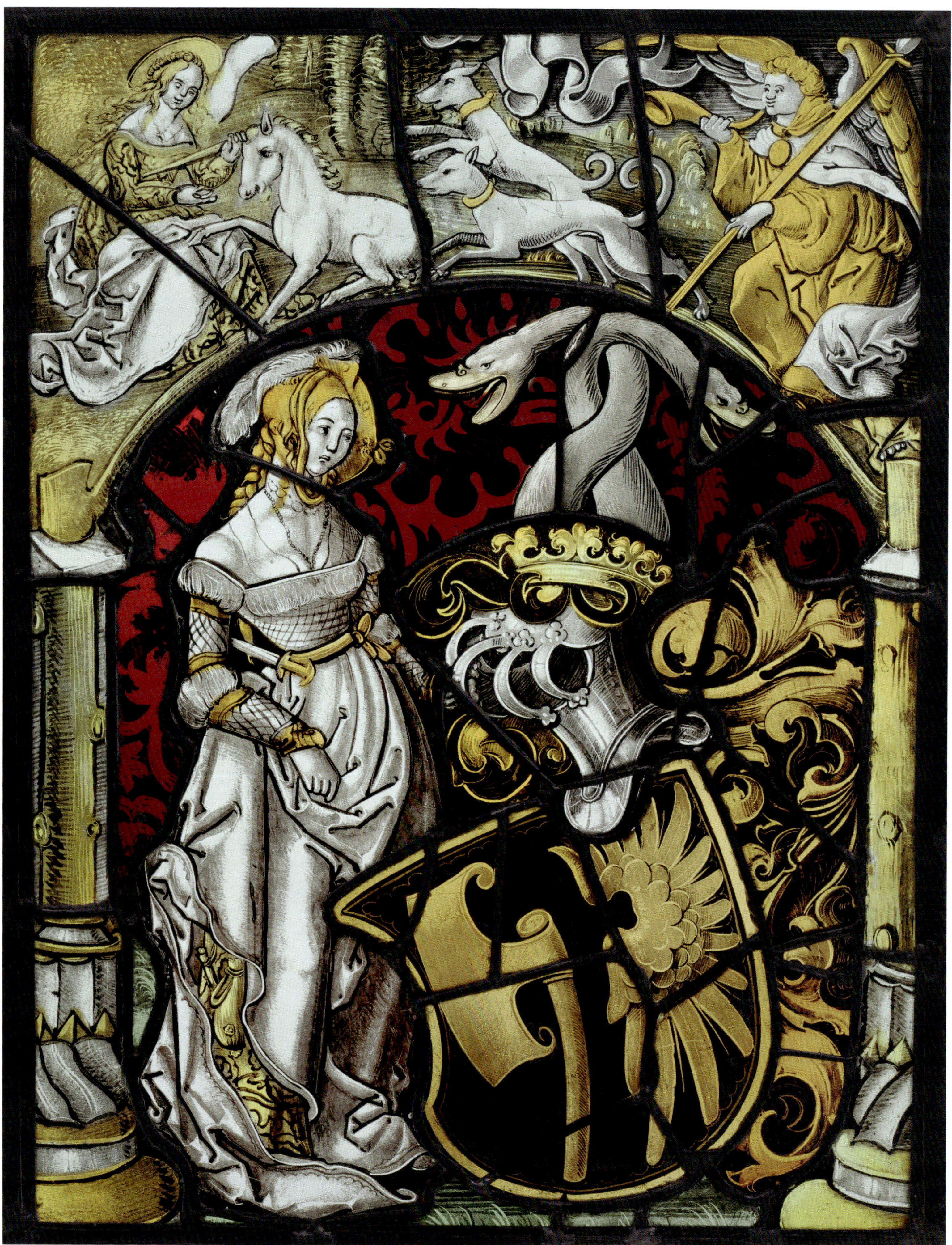

Germany or Switzerland
1515
White glass with silver stain and pot metal
15 ⅜ × 11 ⅜ in., 39.1 × 28.9 cm
Cleveland Museum of Art
Purchase from the J. H. Wade Fund

holding the unicorn's horn. The ground behind the slender female figure in the foreground is red with indistinct black, leafy, amoebic forms, similar to the twelfth-century gilded copper panel depicting a warrior fighting a dragon (**24**). The imagery suggests the fluidity between the temporal and the heavenly worlds, much as is shown by similar imaginative works from other cultures.

Commerce

Exchange may be based on barter, where goods are traded, or on a mutually agreed upon unit of value, usually involving a precious commodity, such as gold. The exchange of a good or service for other goods or services is called trade; it takes many forms and it occurs with and fosters communication and understanding between groups of people. Local trade might involve the bartering of animal skins for food, or of iron, silver, or gold for timber or woven fibers. Those involved in trade meet their counterparts and from that interaction become familiar with the other party, their dress, foods, customs, religions, and artwork. The exchange of foodstuffs, finished goods, and precious materials formed the backbone of most trade. In ancient Greece, wine and olive oils dominated most shipping. Spanish conquistadors sought cities of gold

in Central and South America, and the gold that was taken in trade and by force traveled across the oceans to Asia, to be exchanged for cargoes of spices and other exotica. The sharing of ideas through association with other peoples included designs in works of art, which are the physical manifestations of our perceptions of the world around us.

During the Tang dynasty (690–705 CE) in China, caravans ranged over the Silk Road, the most famous of the Eastern trade routes. The Silk Road was not a single strategic highway of the ancient world but a series of trading centers stretching from Constantinople into central Asia and ending at the Tang capital of Xian. Traders would not make the entire journey but would travel across segments of the route, exchanging their items for local goods that would then be traded for other items. The exchange of ideas, of shapes, of materials, and of workmanship flowed across these trading pathways. This example of eighth-century white porcelain Xing ware is likely influenced by central Asian metal forms that would have been transported over the Silk Road (**38**). The cover of the vessel is removable and fits over the curved, shallow spout as if to form the neck of the animal, and then the body swells downward to a large, rounded stylized bird-form resting on a short stem and circular foot. The upright handle at the upper part also echoes the bird's plumage, creating a form that is both highly stylized and representational.

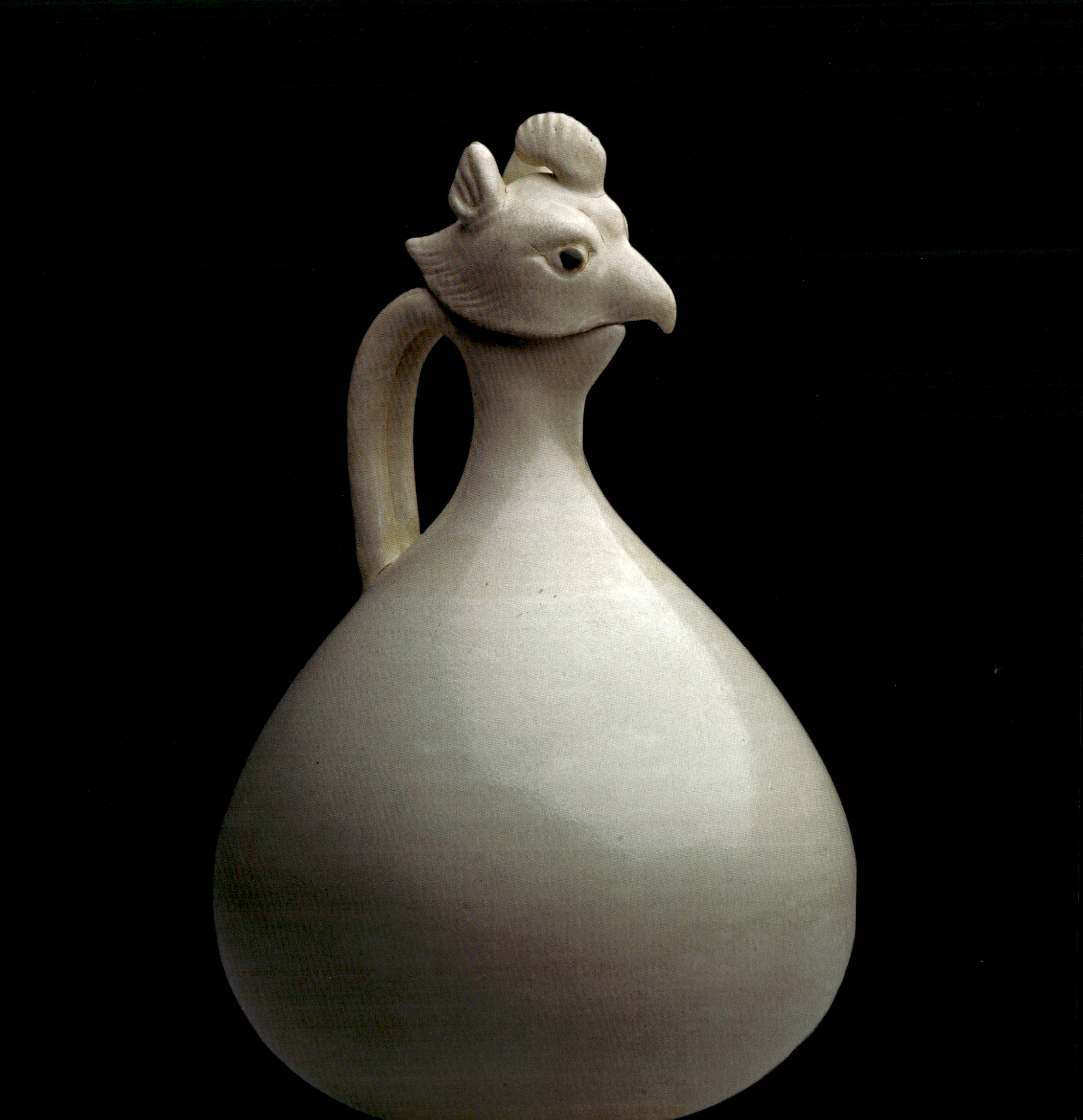

38   Ewer with Pheasant Head-Stopper

China
700 – 800 CE
Porcelain
12 in., 30.48 cm
Minneapolis Institute of Art
The Ethel Morrison Van Derlip Fund

The movement of peoples as a result of climatic change is not new: vast migrations of people took place in ancient and more modern times and these were augmented by disruptions caused by famine, war, religious persecution, economic failures, and pestilence. Trade alone was not responsible for all transmissions of design elements between cultures, but it was particularly important because it involved the movement of physical objects made for commercial purposes. Other transmissions of ideas through stories or written sources led to the widespread adoption of designs, myths, and shapes.

Cultural exchange among peoples with little in common except trade meant that Asian, European, and other cultures could draw from a variety of design sources. In these interactions, cultural exchanges influenced objects meant for religious and secular purposes, such as vessels for pouring water. A form that maximized storage and minimized weight would have been noticed by a culture with inferior storage vessels. In a similar manner, the exoticness of images on a utilitarian vessel might be more desirable than imagery commonly seen on a local vessel. Subtle changes in shapes based on practical improvements doubtless led to the adoption of forms like the ancient Greek amphora throughout the Mediterranean coastal area and the adoption of imagery that had different associations between the source culture and the adopting cultures.

Greek design and culture were widely admired in the ancient world. Designs created in Greece were copied by the Etruscans (8th–2nd century BCE) and Romans, who adopted some elements and modified others. This terracotta krater, used for mixing wine and water, is a Greek form with Greek-style figural designs, but modified to reflect Etruscan taste (**39**). The adoption of shapes, images, and materials from one culture to another occurred as a consequence of trade and communication networks. The wide, swelled body and upright loop handles are derived from the amphora form, used not just for wine vessels but also for smaller containers in metal and glass that likely were transported directly over the Silk Road. Discoveries of vases of this shape and others during excavations in Italy and Greece during the seventeenth and eighteenth centuries popularized revival versions of classical designs in Europe during the late eighteenth and nineteenth century. The eighteenth-century designers of these forms were part of the Enlightenment movement in Europe, which sought to discover the classical sources for art, design, philosophy, and governance, and directly tied ancient designs to the American and French revolutions and other reform movements.

Other landlocked cultures adopted the amphora as a result of recognizing the original purpose and efficiency of the shape. The high-shouldered amphora has a tapered foot so it can be securely wedged against other amphora in a cart or in the hold of a ship. This shape was adopted by surrounding cultures connected by trade, such as China. Other cultures may have adopted aspects of the form because of the novelty and social cachet of something from a distant land. Chinese amphora from the Tang dynasty have roughly the same form as the Greek original: the Chinese vessel has a wide, swelled upper body tapering to a narrow foot with sharply incurved neck and a deep, open mouth with a pair of dragon handles (**40**). It is not ideal for transport. The amphora shape was brought to China from central Asia, likely through a Byzantine trading network, and Chinese potters and their buyers modified it from its functional form, adding the Chinese feature of the double-dragon handles.[14]

Like the ubiquitous amphora, many early Central and South American cultures engaged in trade and shared design elements, particularly in their depictions of the human figure and zoomorphic elements incorporating both mythical and natural forms. In pre-Columbian societies, ceramic vessels with loop handles are often associated with Peruvian cultures, but this feature appears on vessels from Mexico, Guatemala, and other locations. It was a practical innovation, enabling the safe handling of a vessel that otherwise might be awkward to hold. Cultural exchanges occurred over the major trading networks in Peru, Mexico, and the Mississippian culture of the eastern and southeastern United States, along with numerous regional networks of trade between the Aztec and Maya, Olmec and Mokaya, and other surrounding cultures.

Trade routes and the exchange of goods from one culture to another have existed for thousands of years in all locations where there is human habitation. The tribal cultures of Africa, Asia, Europe, and the American continents traded with those in close proximity, and with the advent of improved transportation, trade expanded across continents and oceans. Trade often was a mutually beneficial exchange of one product or material for another, but it could also be forced: empires are built on trade. Spain and the explorers who established Spanish control over much of the Americas exploited the natural resources of these lands and also the wealth of the conquered cultures, primarily in the form of works in gold, silver, and precious stones. Brought back to Europe by ship, the wealth of the Americas enabled Spain to establish a trading network extending to Asia. Together with Portugal, Spain created a competitive trading empire built on spices, gold, and silver that led to domination of the Asian trading routes and the sharing of Spanish and Portuguese design elements in works of art, architecture, and paintings. This pattern continued as other European states joined in the rush for trading dominance. Whether establishing trading centers in conquered lands or with local trading partners, the objects exchanged also transmitted designs that were incorporated into the local cultures or brought back to Europe as cultural imports. Spanish and Portuguese trading colonies in Asia and the Americas were among the earliest trade routes established by European powers.[15]

Trade entails risk. There was risk for those who captained and manned the ships, for the investors who financed the voyages, and for those whose products were transported. Managing risk was an impetus for the collaboration between investors, whose interests

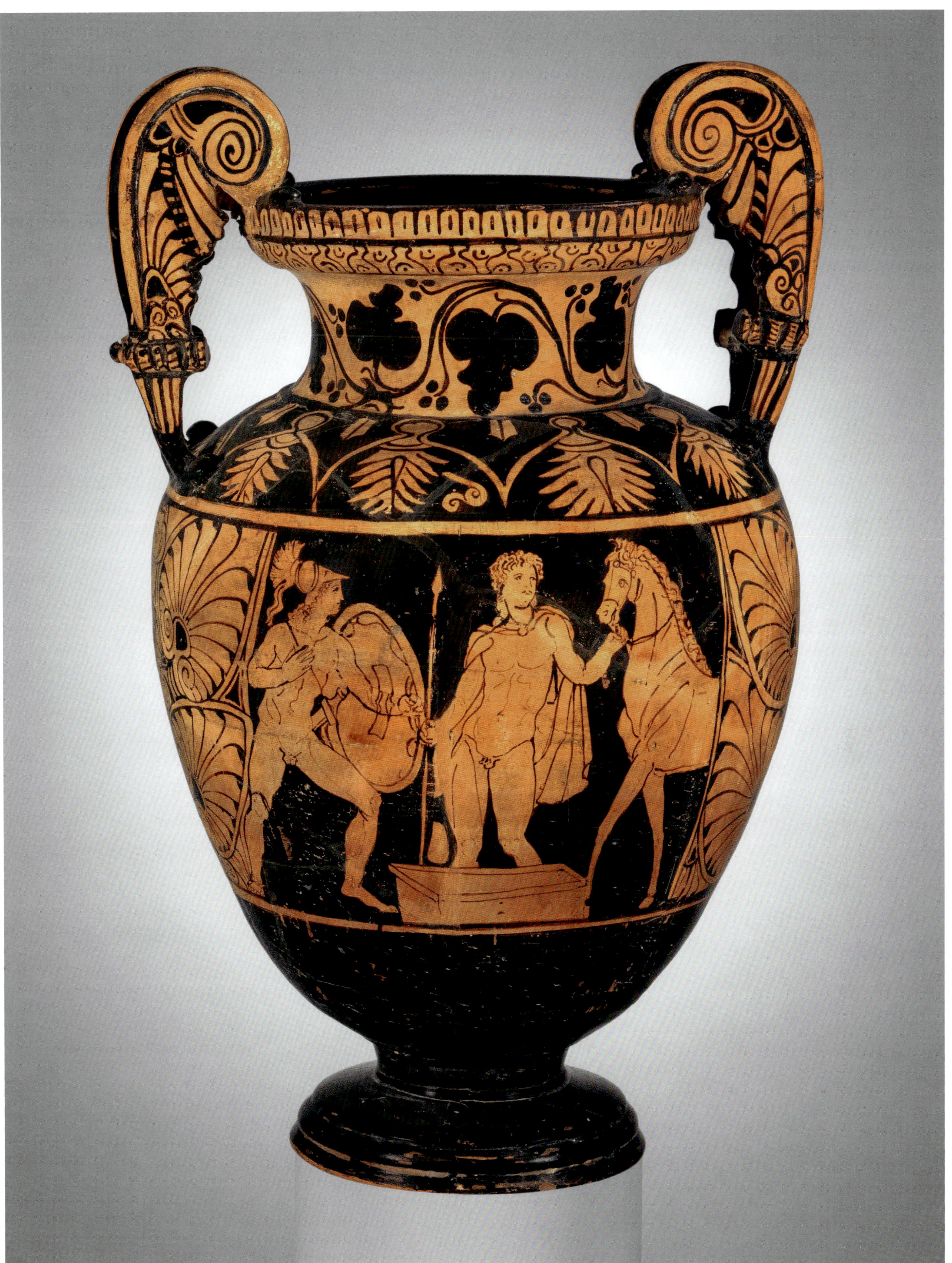

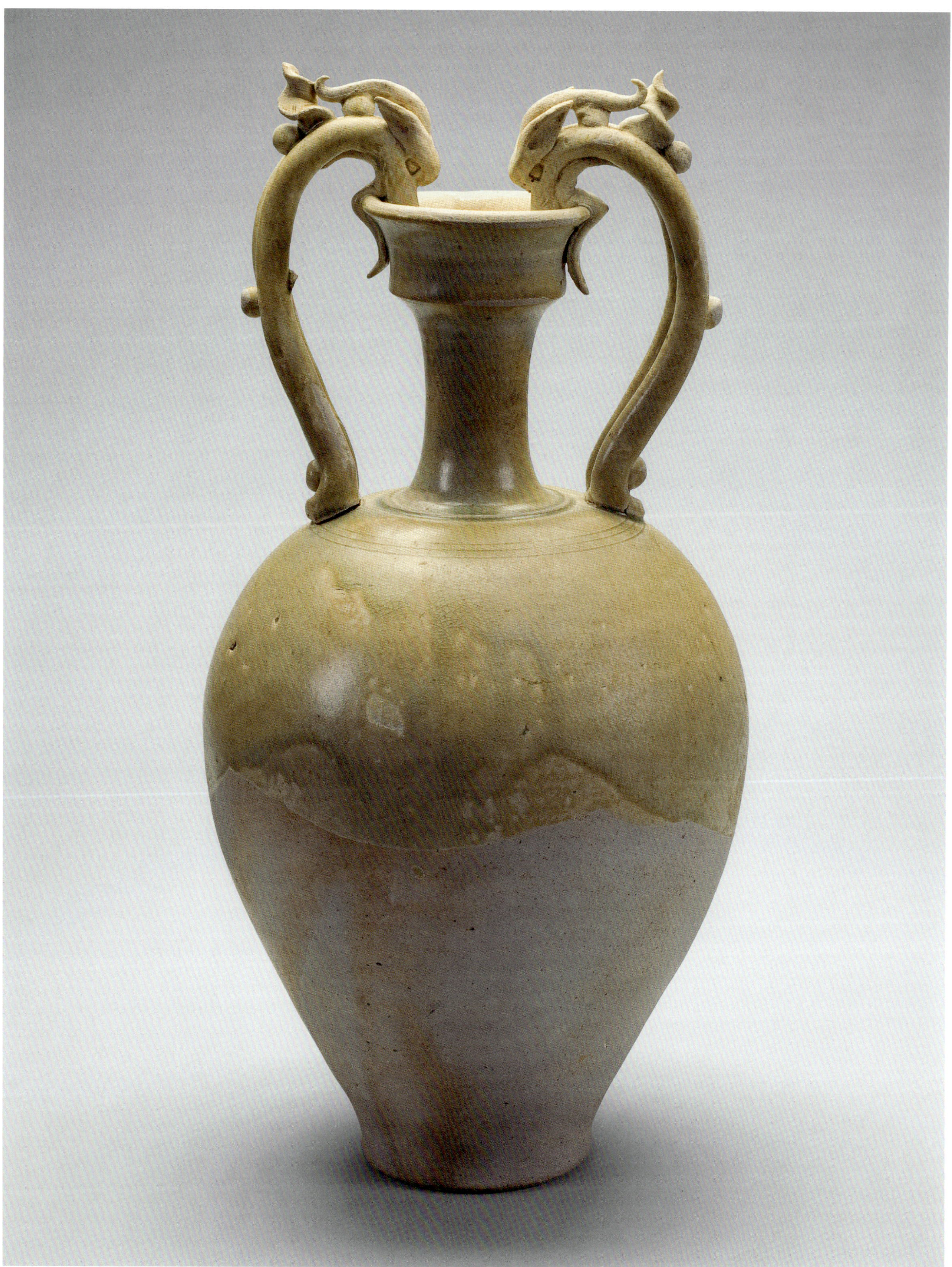

China
Tang dynasty, 600 – 700 CE
Stoneware with incised
and applied decoration under celadon glaze
17 ⅛ in., 43.5 cm
Saint Louis Art Museum
Spink Asian Art Collection
Bequest of Edith J. and C. C. Johnson Spink

were protected contractually by the creation of the modern corporation, which allowed risk to be shared and profits to be reinvested and shared. The Dutch East India Company was the first multinational corporation, eventually employing over a million people, and through trade it created enormous profits for thousands of individual stock owners. The company, whose initials VOC (Verenigde Oostindische Compagnie) were emblazoned on many of the products brought in trade, had headquarters in Amsterdam and Jakarta, Indonesia, and the thousands of ships in its transport system brought spices and other goods from Asia to Europe and European goods to other locations throughout the world. The Dutch formed commercial alliances with local trading partners, fought against European and regional competitors, and created international and localized trading networks. Silver was exchanged for Chinese silk and other materials, including spices and porcelain, the latter highly prized because the recipe for its manufacture was unknown in Europe. Porcelain was durable, bright, and often colorfully decorated in patterns of underglaze blue heightened with gold and enamel colors. It was also exotic, coming from the Far East, and these factors made it extremely desirable to European audiences and therefore a highly profitable trade commodity.

European wine glasses and other glass objects began to be made in wealthy trading centers where designs from the East and West flowed along with trade.[16] Dragon-stemmed glasses or serpent glasses were made in Venetian workshops and other locations during the sixteenth and seventeenth centuries. The stem of this glass, made in the south Lowlands of Germany in the seventeenth century, is supported by a wide, circular foot and features a number of Eastern design elements, including the interlaced pair of dragons that form a spade or heart-device with shoulders of brilliant blue in a zoomorphic, plumage, or serpent form (**41**). The flat foot has a flared, single stem that spreads at the base and top, as if rising from the earth and supporting the heavens. The complicated, interlaced patterns set between the clear, deep cup and the clear, circular base heighten the effect of the contrasting colors and designs.

Dutch traders came to Japan in 1609 as competitors to long-established Portuguese traders who enjoyed a monopoly with the Japanese silver trade. With the opening of Japan to Western trade and diplomatic relations by Commodore Perry (1794–1858) between 1852 and 1854, Japanese design was brought to the West, and by the 1870s it was popularized through works made by artists such as Louis Comfort Tiffany (1848–1933) and others. This hammered surface pitcher by Tiffany incorporates copper, silver, and gilded surfaces in a pattern taken from Japanese woodblock prints, paintings, fabrics, metalwork, and other items (**42**). During the late nineteenth century, Japanese taste became popular in the West, and the style was called "Japonisme." Tiffany and Company produced creations in silver that incorporated mixed metals in a style reminiscent of Japanese design.[17] The naturalistic scene on the pitcher compares with underglaze blue water, plant, and animal panels on

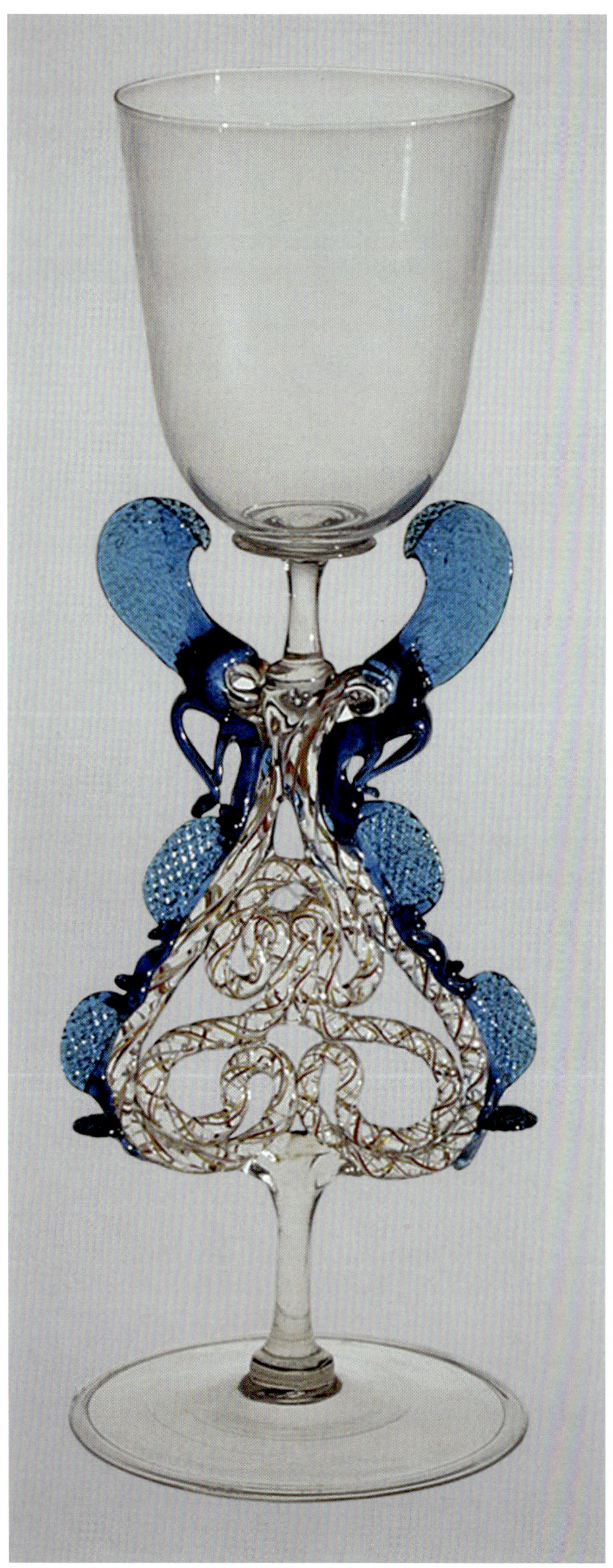

41 Goblet

Facon de Venise, probably South
Lowlands of Germany
1600 – 1700
Glass
11 1/16 in., 28.1 cm
Metropolitan Museum of Art, New York
Robert Lehman Collection, 1975

42 Pitcher

Tiffany and Company, New York
1878 – 1880
Silver and copper with gilding
8 13/16 × 7 1/2 × 5 3/8 in., 22.4 × 19.1 × 13.7 cm
Saint Louis Art Museum
Marjorie Wyman Endowment Fund,
the Richard Brumbaugh Trust in memory of
Richard Irving Brumbaugh and Grace Lischer
Brumbaugh, the Gary Wolff Family; and Museum
Shop Fund, gift of Dr. and Mrs. Graham T. Lusk,
Mr. and Mrs. Harvard Hecker, Mrs, Thomas T.
Hoopes, Olivia Vogel, and Mr. and Mrs. Stanley
Goodman, bequest of Richard Brumbaugh, and
Museum Purchase, by exchange

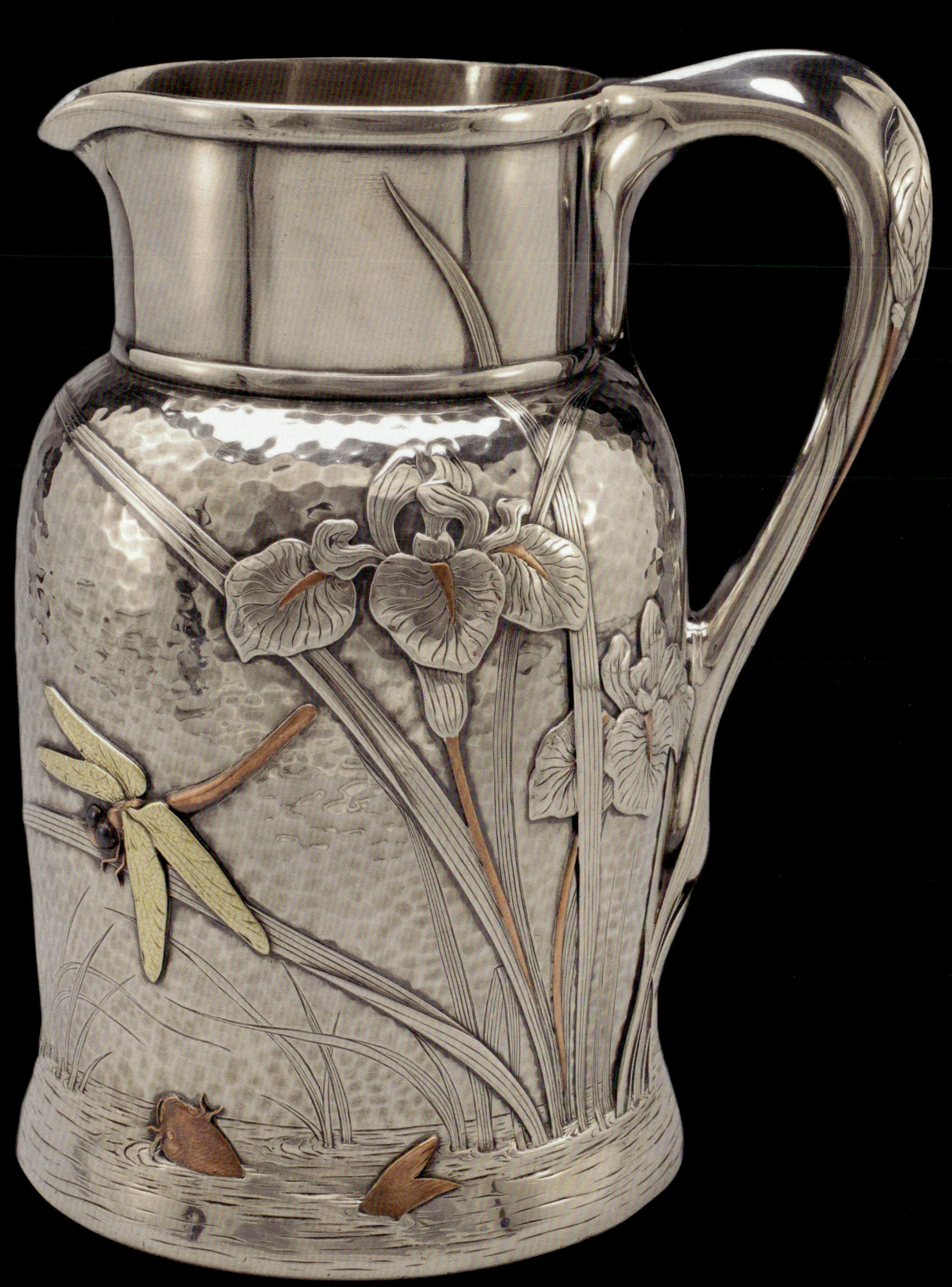

Karnataka, Bidar, India
1675 – 1700 CE
Bidri ware inlaid with silver and brass
(tarkashi and tehnishan techniques)
¾ × 13 in., 1.91 × 33.02 cm
Los Angeles County Museum of Art (LACMA)
Gift of Anna Bing Arnold and the
Indian Art Special Purpose Fund

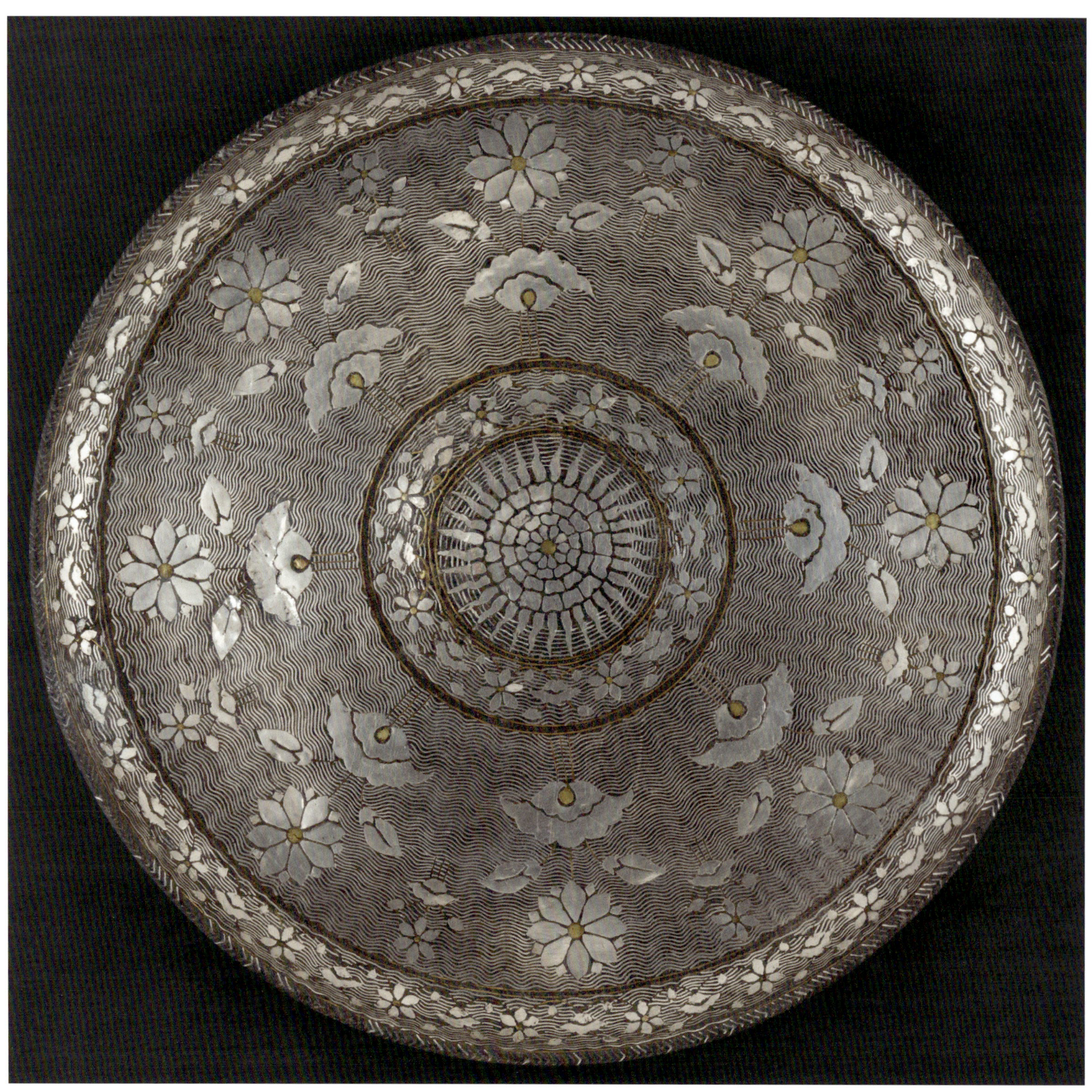

Chinese porcelain from the Yuan (1271–1368) and early Ming (1368–1644) dynasties and later works of the Kangxi dynasty (1644–1722). The Tiffany pitcher was the precursor to the European Art Nouveau designs of the late nineteenth and early twentieth century and the British Arts and Crafts Movement (1875–1920), which began in response to rapid industrialization at the expense of skilled craftsmen. The hammered surface, mixed metals, and form purposely highlighted the handwork still present in the arts of Japan and of less industrial cultures.

Though the Tiffany silver pitcher was made in the United States in the late nineteenth century, the design was based on Japanese works of art and aesthetics as interpreted by Western designers. Works from other countries also emphasized naturalistic forms within utilitarian objects. This large tray made in India around 1675–1700 is an example of Bidriware, a white brass with a high zinc content with copper, inlaid with silver blackened to contrast with the surrounding material (**43**). The tray mixes designs incorporating flowerheads and leaves within a circular format that has a rounded edge with a continual pattern of flowers and leaves, with the center of the tray presented as a stamen with radiating petals. The wavy line surface gives an impression of water. The overall effect is that of a stylized pond, hundreds of years in advance of the similar visions by French artist Claude Monet (1840–1926) in his *Water Lillies* (ca. 1919) paintings. The circular panel is also sun-like, with radiating rays shining onto a pond of flowers and water plants. It could be viewed as a metaphor for the earth, with the sun at the center and the earth with a watery surface and scattered flowers and plants. The integration of the earth and the heavens within the scope of a single, circular tray speaks to the interaction of humans within creation.

Conclusion

In the process of trade, ideas are passed between cultures; some are adopted and some are modified. When the Spanish arrived in Central America from the Iberian Peninsula, they brought with them a rich, European cultural heritage that was a mix of Celtic and native populations, of Roman habitation, Islamic conquest, and influences from trade routes that extended to North Africa and Carthage, Egypt, and the eastern Mediterranean. They also brought with them their personal observations of flora and fauna from their homelands. As Spanish trade expanded to Asia, Asian cultural traditions and designs became part of the mix, connecting the New World of the Americas to the Old World of the European continent (**44**).

Local plants, animals, and the heavens were creatively represented in drawn images and objects based on an artisan's and viewer's cultural experiences. When these regional and geographically based designs were transported to distant cultures that did not have these plants, animals, and views of the heavens, objects that include these designs are often a radical mix of influences (**45**). Features of living creatures that were alien to

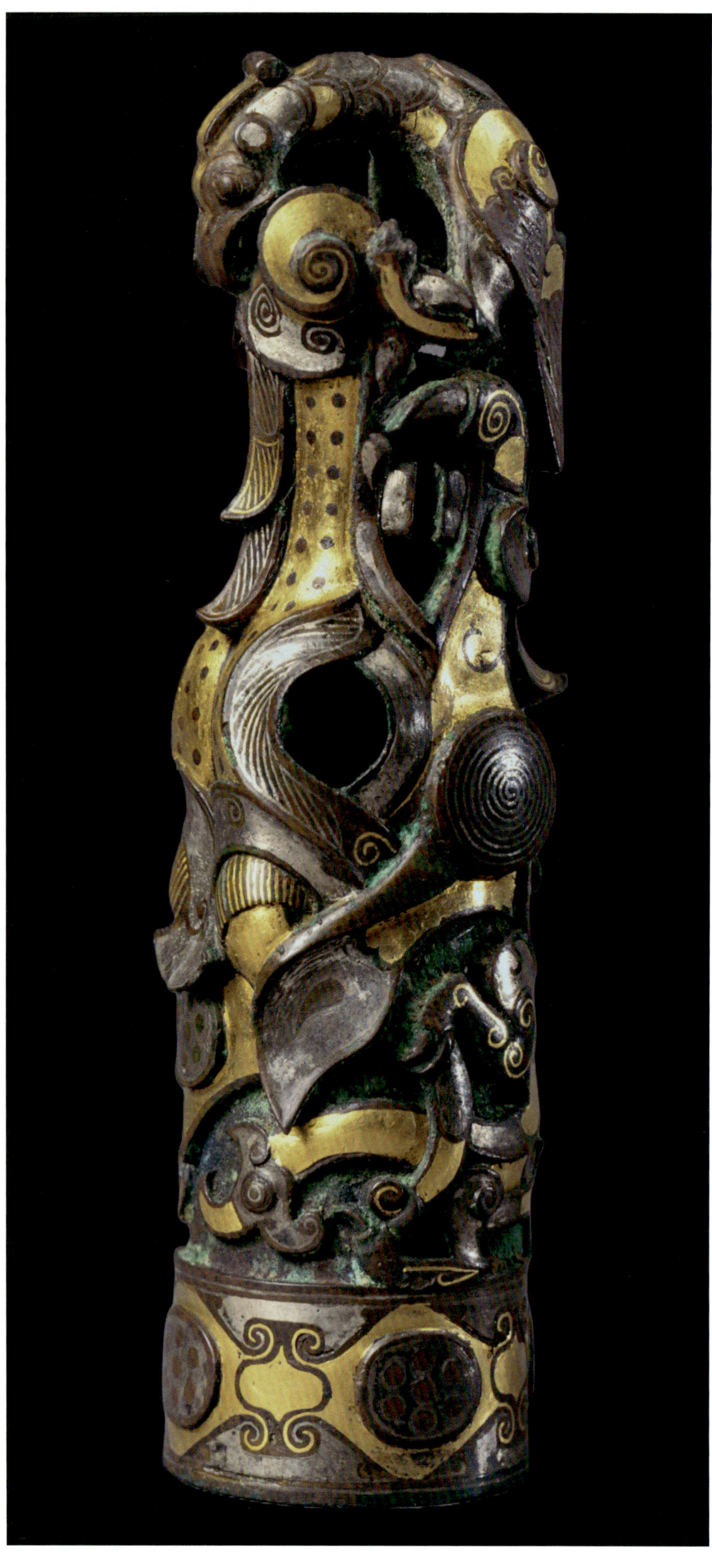

44 Finial

China
Jincun, Henan Province, China
Warring States period, 475 – 221 BCE
Bronze inlaid with gold and silver
5 ³⁄₁₆ in., 13.1 cm
Cleveland Museum of Art,
Purchase from the J. H. Wade Fund

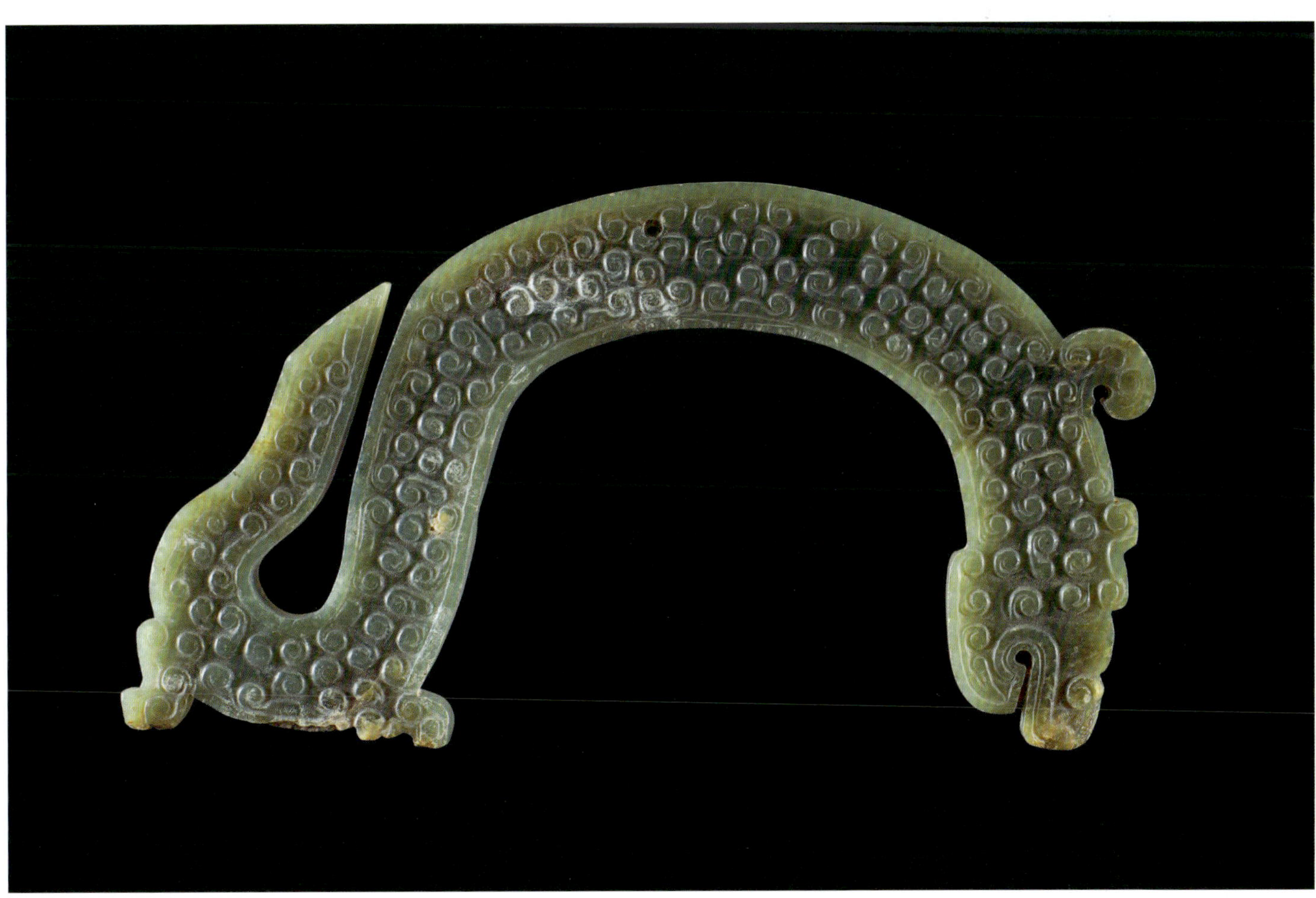

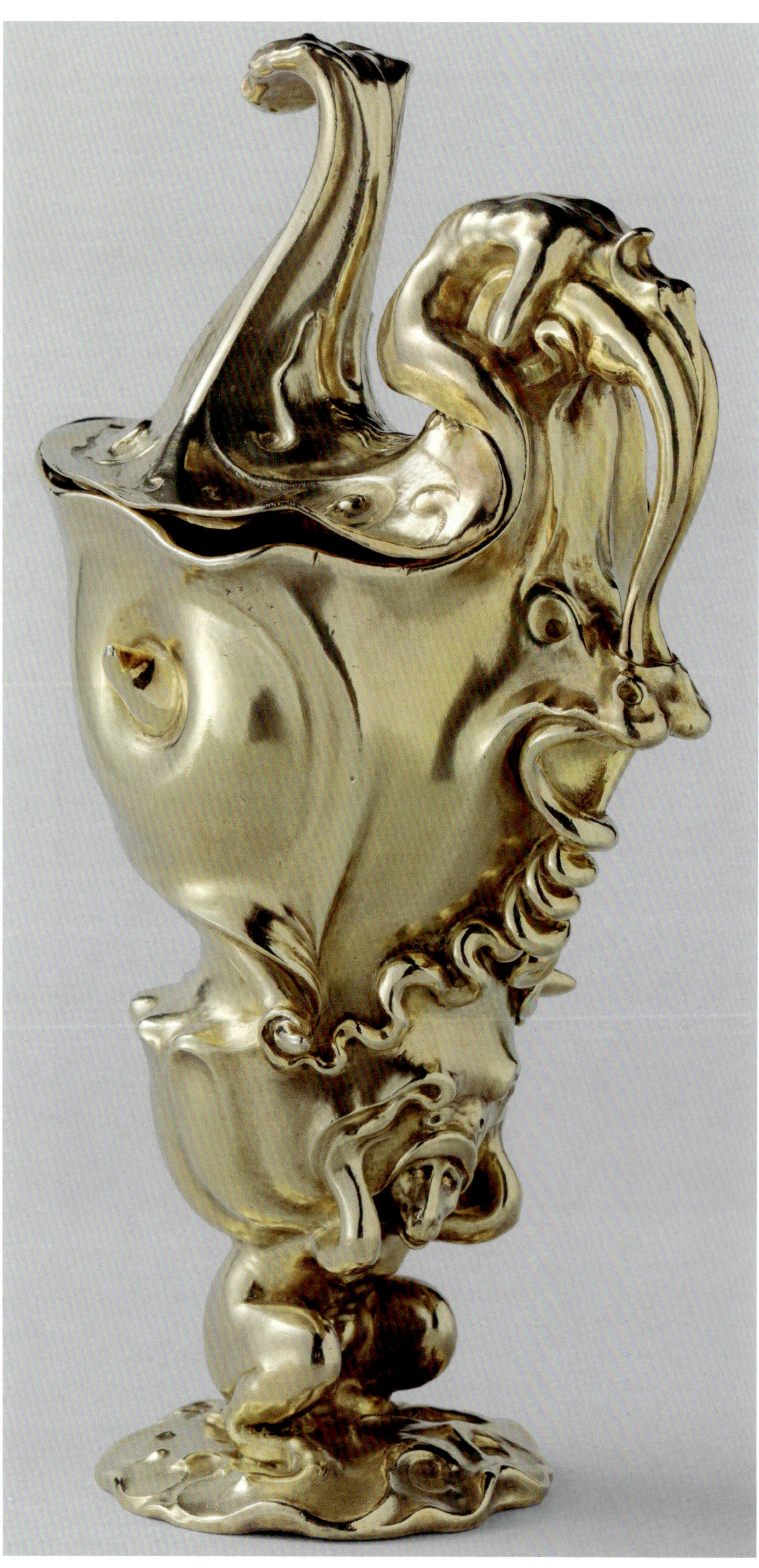

46 **Memorial Gilded Ewer for Amsterdam Guild in Memory of the Artist's Brother**

Adam van Vianen
(Netherlands, 1568 – 1627)
1614
Silver
9.84 × 5.51 × 3.54 in., 25 × 14 × 9 cm
Rijksmuseum, Amsterdam, Netherlands

 Platter

France
1575 – 1600
Lead-glazed earthenware
20 ½ × 15 ⅝ × 2 ¹³⁄₁₆ in., 52.1 × 39.7 × 7.1 cm
Metropolitan Museum of Art, New York
Gift of Julia A. Berwind, 1953

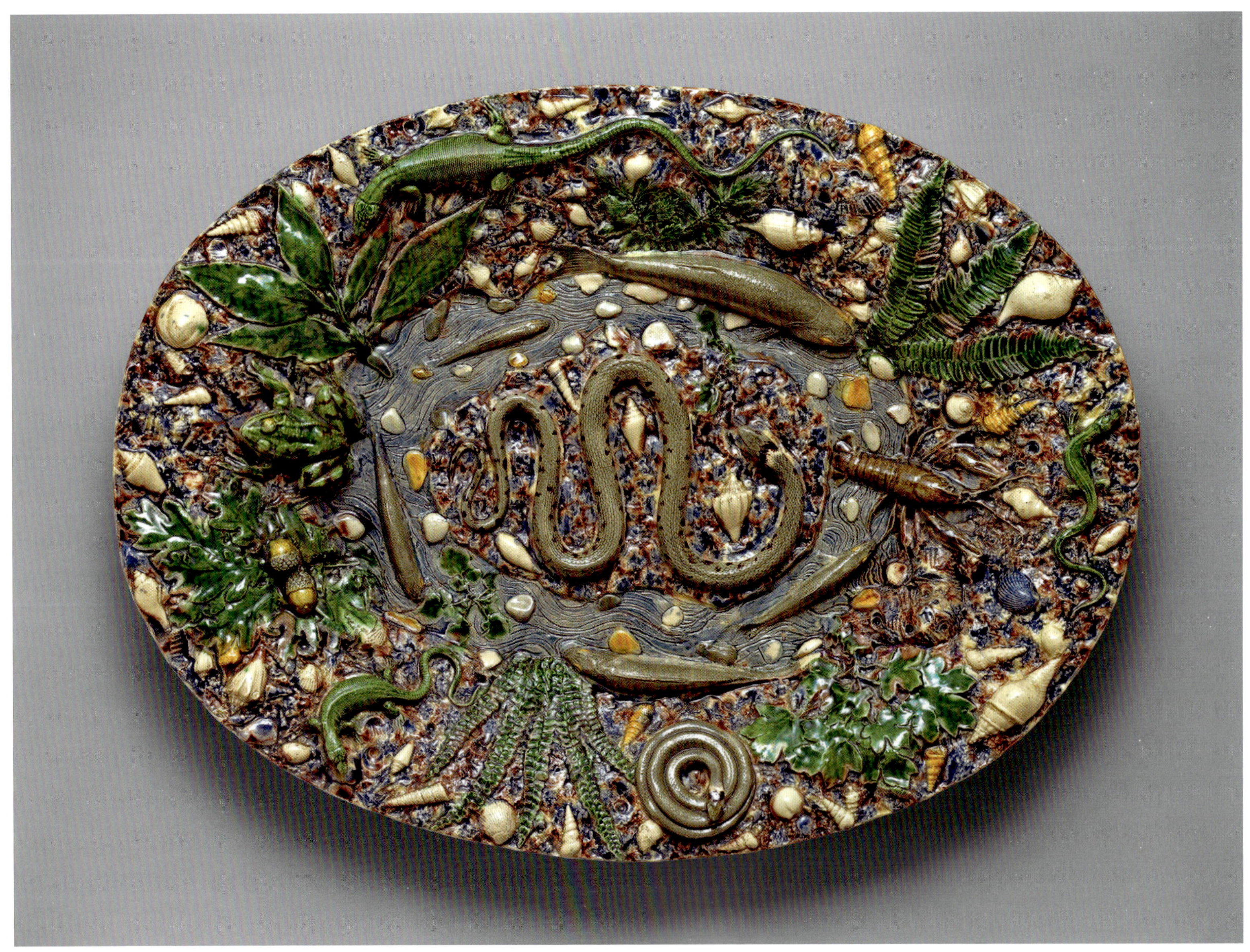

one culture become exaggerated and mythologized. Characteristics of commonly encountered geographic vistas become heightened and otherworldly (**46**). Color combinations can become muted or explosively brilliant. Elements that represented danger to one culture lose this association when adopted as a design by another culture, assuming a novel or exotic appearance.

Pulling apart the threads of design origins is not easy. The northern European nomadic tribes that swept across Roman outposts and created the outlines of modern Europe brought with them complex social and trade interactions similar to those that existed in Central America, South Asia, and the tribal cultures of North America. Trade facilitated the sharing and adoption of design elements, but human creativity and observations of nature were often the genesis of the original designs (**47**). Trading networks originating in the ancient world expanded over time and with this expansion, connections between cultures grew either directly or indirectly.[18] The undiscovered lands shown in European maps of the world were actually not isolated but rather separate networks apart from those that encompassed the European powers. The story of civilization is the story of shared experiences and the exchanges of ideas, products, peoples, and the animate and inanimate parts of creation, which are displayed in the works of art crafted by myriad peoples sharing the world around us and beneath the heavens.

1   For more on Chinese blue and white porcelain, see Anne Gerritsen, *The City of Blue and White: Chinese Porcelain and the Early Modern World* (Cambridge: Cambridge University Press, 2020); Laurie Barnes et al., *Chinese Ceramics: From the Paleolithic Period through the Qing Dynasty* (New Haven: Yale University Press, 2010).

2   New International Version.

3   For more on Chinese tomb pottery models, including horses, see Robert Jacobsen, *Celestial Horses and Long Sleeve Dancers: The David W. Dewey Collection of Ancient Chinese Tomb Sculpture* (Minneapolis: Minneapolis Institute of Arts, 2013).

4   For an example of a Chinese gilt bronze belt hook with a similarity to the Chavin bone *tupus*, see Belt Hook with Dragons, Western Han Dynasty (206 BCE–9 CE), Metropolitan Museum of Art, New York, 2002.201.170.

5   See, for example, Emile Jacques Ruhlmann, Ceramic Vase Mounted on a Bronze Base, ca. 1925, Sevres Porcelain Factory, Minneapolis Institute of Art, 98.276.89; Emile Lenoble, Glazed Stoneware, ca. 1925, Metropolitan Museum of Art, New York, 25.210.

6   For images of dragons in Western and Asian art, see the following examples from periods when dragons were both believed to be living creatures with mythical powers and from later periods, when they were recognized as mythological: Master AG, St. George and the Dragon, ca. 1480–90, Minneapolis Institute of Art, P.10,950; Ewer, ca. 1760, Vauxhall China Works, Minneapolis Institute of Art, 2005.159.3; P. Hertz, Fish Serving Set, 1905, Minneapolis Institute of Art, 98.5.3.1; Dragon, Spanish, after 1200, The Cloisters Collection, Metropolitan Museum of Art, New York, 31.38.2 a, b; Dragon, Urbino, ca. 1550, Metropolitan Museum of Art, New York, 32.100.386; Vivienne Tam,

Dragon Robe, Spring/Summer 1998, Metropolitan Museum of Art, New York, 2005.72.1.

7   For more on Chinese and other lacquer, see Julia M. White et al., *Masterpieces of Chinese Lacquer from the Mike Healy Collection* (Honolulu: Honolulu Academy of Arts, 2005); James C. Y. Watt and Barbara Brennan Ford, *East Asian Lacquer: The Florence and Herbert Irving Collection* (New York: Metropolitan Museum of Art, 1991); Oliver Impey, *Japanese Export Lacquer* (Amsterdam: Hotei Publishing, 2006); Oliver Impey, *Chinoiserie: The Impact of Oriental Styles on Western Art and Decoration* (London: Oxford University Press, 1977); Christiane Hertel, *Siting China in Germany: Eighteenth-Century Chinoiserie and its Modern Legacy* (University Park: Pennsylvania State University Press, 2019).

8   For more on Asian and Western enamels, see Elisabeth Taburet-Delahaye and Barbara Drake Boehm, *Enamels of Limoges 1100–1350* (New York: Metropolitan Museum of Art, 1996); Marilyn Stokstad, *Medieval Art*, 2nd ed. (New York, Routledge Publishing, 2018); Klaus Wessel, *Byzantine Enamels: From the 5th to the 13th Century* (Greenwich: New York Graphic Society, 1967); Marco Aimone, *The Wyvern Collection: Byzantine and Sassanian Silver, Enamels, and Works of Art* (London: Thames & Hudson, 2020).

9   See Parts of a Cauldron with Griffin Protomes, Probably from Samos or Ionia, ca. 625–600 BCE, Museum of Fine Arts Boston, 50.144a–d.

10   For more on the Silk Trade Routes and later Asian trade, see Susan Whitfield, *Life Along the Silk Road*, 2nd ed. (Berkeley: University of California Press, 2001); Teresa Canepa, *Silk, Porcelain and Lacquer: China and Japan and their Trade with Western Europe and the New World, 1500–1644* (London: Paul Holberton Publishing, 2016); Edward S. Cooke Jr., *Global Objects: Toward a Connected Art History* (Princeton: Princeton University Press, 2022).

11   For more on Chinese perspectives with objects within our natural world, see Zhenheng Wen, Tony Blishen, Craig Clunas, *Elegant Life of the Chinese Literati: From the Chinese Classic, "Treatise on Superfluous Things," Finding Harmony and Joy in Everyday Objects* (Shanghai: Shanghai Press, 2019).

12   For more on Islamic influences in Spain and Europe, see Jerrilynn D. Dodds, ed., *Al-Andalus: The Art of Islamic Spain*, (New York: Metropolitan Museum of Art, 1992); Mariam Rosser-Owen, *Islamic Arts from Spain* (London: V & A Publishing, 2010); Rose Walker, *Art in Spain and Portugal from the Romans to the Early Middle Ages: Routes and Myths* (Kalamazoo: Medieval Institute Publications, 2016); Diana Darke, *Stealing from the Saracens: How Islamic Architecture Shaped Europe* (London: Hurst Publishing, 2020).

13   For more on the Antioch Chalice, see Gustavus A. Eisen, *The Great Chalice of Antioch* (Whitefish: Kessinger Publishing, 2010); James M. Arnold, *The Evidence About the Antioch Chalice* (n.p.: Reel Art, 1970).

14   For more on the relationship between the Greek/Roman amphora and the Chinese version, see Rosemary Trentinella, "Roman Luxury Glass," in *Heilbrunn Timeline of Art History* (New York: Metropolitan Museum of Art, 2000–). http://www.metmuseum.org/toah/hd/rgls/hd_rgls.htm (October 2003).

15   See Hugh Thomas, *Rivers of Gold: The Rise of the Spanish Empire, From Columbus to Magellan* (New York: Random House, 2003); Kenneth Pomeranz, *The World That Trade Created: Society, Culture, and the World Economy, 1400 to the Present*, 4th ed. (New York, Routledge Publishing, 2018); Philip D. Curtin, *Cross Cultural Trade in World History* (Cambridge: Cambridge University Press, 1984); William J. Bernstein, *A Splendid Exchange: How Trade Shaped the World* (New York: Atlantic Monthly Press, 2008); Buddy Levy, *Conquistador: Hernan Cortes, King Montezuma, and the Last Stand of the Aztecs* (New York: Bantam Books, 2008).

16   For a guide to the history of glass, see Chloe Zerwick, *A Short History of Glass*, 2nd ed. (New York: Harry N. Abrams, 1990).

17   See John Loring, *Magnificent Tiffany Silver* (New York: Harry N. Abrams, 2001); Albert Soeffing, "The Battle of the Birds: Japanese Patterns of the 1870s," *Silver* (May/June 1995): 18–23; Lionel Lambourne, *The Aesthetic Movement* (London: Phaidon Press, 1996).

18   For more on the interconnected world and trade, see Niall Ferguson, *The Square and the Tower: Networks and Power, from the Freemasons to Facebook* (New York: Penguin Press, 2018); Michael Rank, *Off the Edge of the Map: Marco Polo, Captain Cook, and 9 Other Travelers and Explorers That Pushed the Boundaries of the Known World*, Five Minute Book (CreateSpace Independent Publishing Platform, 2014); Steven E. Sidebotham, *Berenike and the Ancient Maritime Spice Route* (Berkeley: University of California Press, 2019); Raoul McLaughlin, *The Roman Empire and the Silk Routes: The Ancient World Economy and the Empires of Parthia, Central Asia and Han China* (Barnsley: Pen & Sword History, 2016); Felipe Fernandez-Armesto, *Pathfinders: A Global History of Exploration* (Oxford: Oxford University Press, 2006); Raoul McLaughlin, *The Roman Empire and the Indian Ocean: The Ancient World Economy and the Kingdoms of Africa, Arabia, and India* (Barnsley: Pen & Sword Military, 2014); Felipe Fernandesz-Armesto, *1492: The Year the World Began* (New York: Harper Collins, 2009).

VI

CONFLICT AND WARFARE

DAVID H. DYE

They went with songs to the battle, they were young,
Straight of limb, true of eye, steady and aglow,
They were staunch to the end against odds uncounted;
They fell with their faces to the foe.

They shall grow not old, as we that are left grow old:
Age shall not weary them, nor the years condemn.
At the going down of the sun and in the morning
We shall remember them.

Lawrence Binyon,
"For The Fallen,"
1914

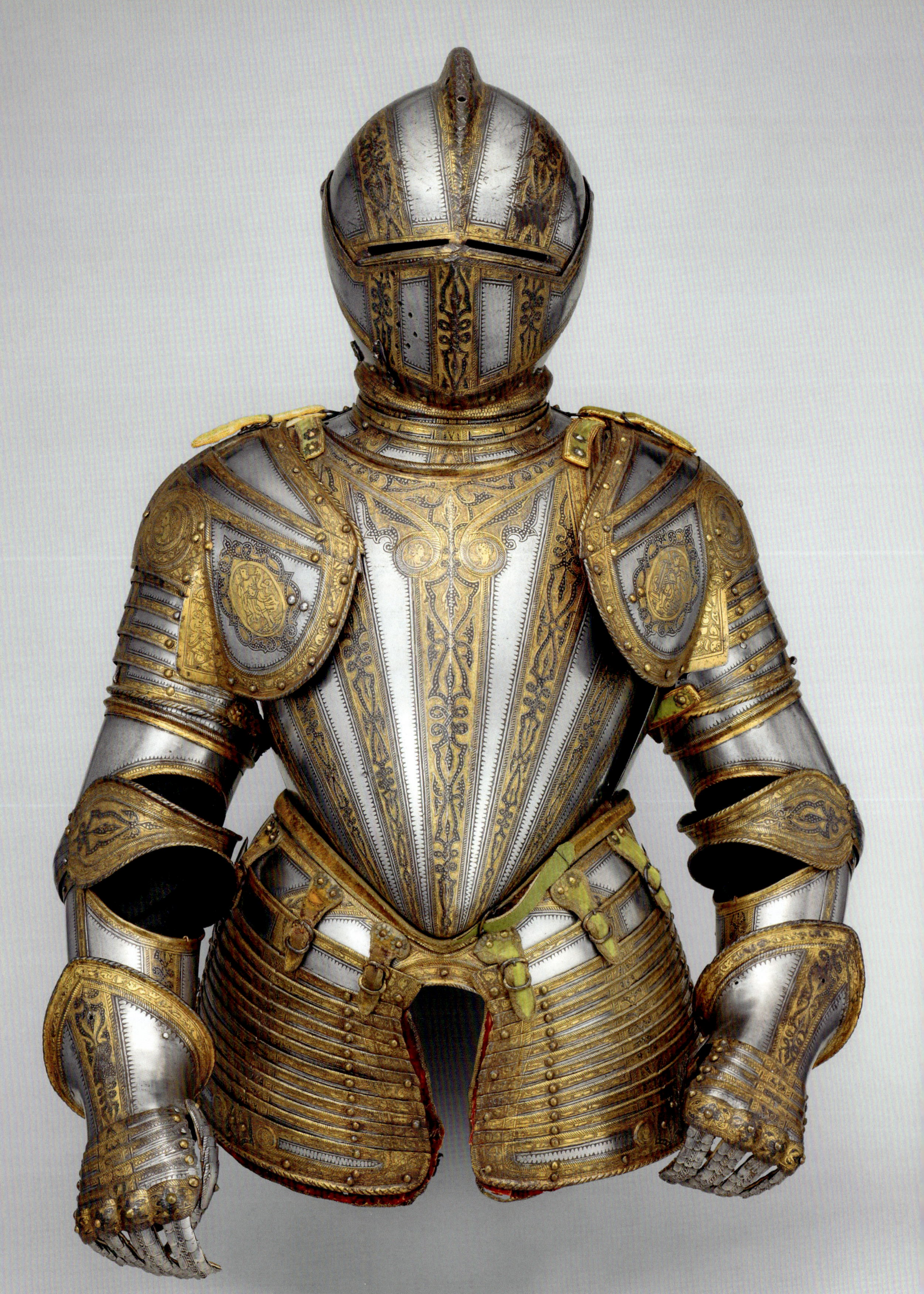

Garniture for Field and Foot Tourney at the Barriers

On the Nile's west bank at Luxor, Egyptian painters considered how best to depict the Macedonian pharaoh Ptolemy IV (Pilopator) (reigned 222–204 BCE) on the new temple's limestone walls. Although the temple had been dedicated to the goddess Hathor, the mural would depict Ptolemy making an offering to the war god Montu (1). The result of their deliberations may be witnessed today in the small but prominent building that stands within a mud-brick wall enclosure in a secluded valley of the Theban hills at the Place of Truth, Deir el-Medina.[1] The Hathor temple, built and decorated by Ptolemy IV, sits on the remains of earlier structures demolished for the construction of the new building. One of the best-preserved settlements of ancient Egypt, the village and its temples had been home to the artisans and workers who built the monuments and tombs at Thebes during Egypt's New Kingdom period (ca. 1550–1069 BCE).

The artisans portrayed Montu as a falcon avatar and the pharaoh with militaristic strength and vitality. As a sign of Montu's favor, Ptolemy IV decisively defeated Antiochus III the Great (reigned 222–187 BCE), the self-deified king of the Seleucid Empire (312–63 BCE), during the Fourth Syrian War (219–217 BCE). The battle of Gaza (or Raphia), which took place on June 22, 217 BCE, was one of the largest battles of the Hellenistic period (323–31 BCE). Interestingly, the battle pitted Asian elephants used by Antiochus III against African elephants employed by Ptolemy IV. The successful battle marked an important event in Ptolemaic history, but its glory was short-lived as the dynasty began to decline under Ptolemy IV.

In the early eighth century, Maya master artisans at Yaxchilán, a Maya city overlooking the Usumacinta River in Chiapas, Mexico, deliberated on the design for a carved limestone door lintel that would span the high-ranking priestess Lady K'abal Xook's personal house (2). Although once described as a war memorial, the structure is now considered the seat of Lady Xook's Tlaloc cult practices. Located in the West Acropolis, the building was dedicated to the Maya war god Tlaloc in 726, but the stone carvers would have been chosen and commissioned several years prior to the dedication so that the door lintels would be ready for the building's construction. The commissioned scene would depict Lady Xook celebrating her husband's accession to kingship in 681 through ritual blood sacrifice. Lady Xook conjures one of her venerated ancestors, an honored Tlaloc priestess, who emerges from the mouth of a double-headed caterpillar-serpent, a Tlaloc avatar.[2] Lady Xook's husband, the warrior king Itzamnaaj Bahlam the Great (Shield Jaguar III; reigned 681–742), ruled over Yaxchilán's territories along the Usumacinta River, during which time the ceremonial center would undergo a cultural renaissance and an explosive architectural building program. The door lintel is considered among the finest relief carvings to survive anywhere in the Maya region.

Lady Xook's blood offering to Tlaloc was meant not only to commemorate Itzamnaaj Bahlam's ascendancy to power but to garner success for him in the battles against the kingdom's enemies, especially his archrivals who ruled the Piedras Negras kingdom some forty kilometers downstream from Yaxchilán. The powerful deity Tlaloc had been appropriated from Central Mexico, where he was venerated as the storm god, but the Maya transformed him into a war god who could ensure a king's failure or success in battle and legitimacy to rule.

While separated by culture, history, space, time, and tradition, these two scenes were both royal commissions, and they highlight the ways in which depictions of warfare are entangled with kingship, political rhetoric, regalia, ritual practice, skilled artistry, and spectacular performance. Both were created by drawing upon ancient beliefs about ancestors, deities, and spirituality. As scholars have labored to decipher both Egyptian and Maya glyphs and sought to interpret their meanings, these ancient worlds have come into sharper focus, drawing our attention to works of art representing kings and gods as political statements. As symbolic images they express through ritual and theater how elites animated imagery and supplicated the gods for success in battle and military campaigns. The deities' blessings and favors underscored kingly success, which sent a strong message to both enemies and followers.

While there are broad and significant differences between the Egyptian and Maya worlds, both envisioned success in warfare as depending upon the performance of proper ritual protocols to gain divine favor. Artistic objects provided an abode for the spirits and established spiritual relationships between these objects and the kings who commissioned them. And by documenting critical ritual events and practices, images could serve as public pronouncements of political efficacy and power.

Similar depictions have been produced around the world by ceramicists, jewelers, masons, painters, sculptors, and smiths at the behest of their sovereigns, who used wealth and the talents of artisans appropriated through warfare to commemorate the blessings and favors of the gods.

Dramatic performance, image production, and ritual practice throughout the world, especially within the great artistic traditions of chiefly polities, archaic states, and expansive empires, reflect the many dimensions of past human behavior and culture and highlight the role violence and warfare plays in political machinations and social behavior. Works of art pertaining to conflict and warfare and their expressive and symbolic functions are discussed in this chapter as a means of gauging the interconnectedness of political life, religious beliefs, and ritual efficacy. Such depictions were inspired and created by the intellectual and spiritual experiences of the artisans who conceptualized and produced them, as well as by the rulers who commissioned them and deployed them for varied purposes. While the broad array of forms and styles speaks to the great diversity of peoples who created them, the artistic themes discussed here have also been depicted by numerous societies throughout the world well into the ancient past. While it is not always possible to readily apprehend and understand the original intents and meanings of these artistic expressions, interpretations obtained from archaeological excavations, ethnographic observations, and hieroglyphic records allow an appreciation of the ideas and inspirations that formed the basis for ancient and traditional artistic expressions and practice.

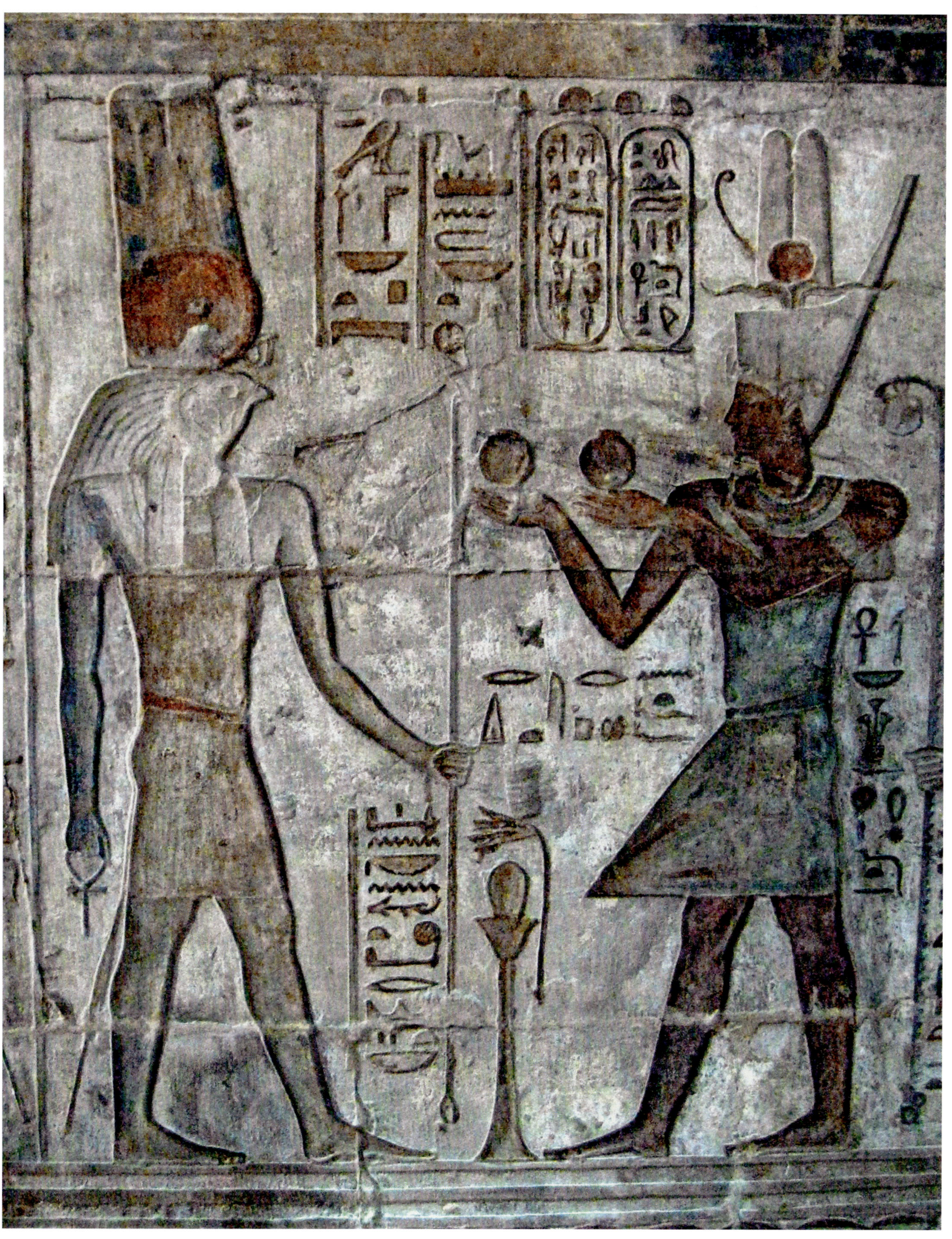

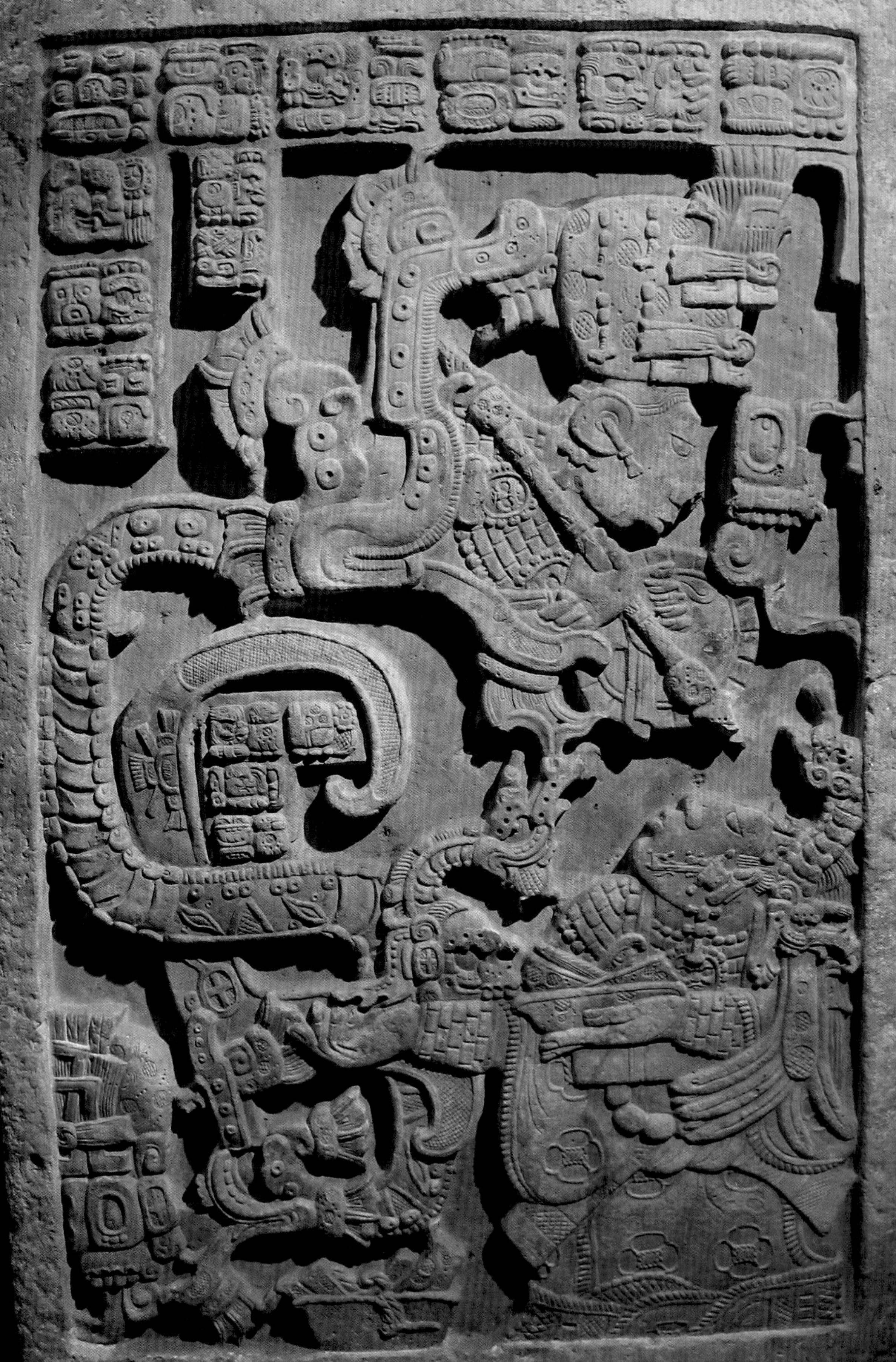

2 Yaxchilan Lintel 25

Maya culture, Chiapas, Mexico
Early 700s CE
Stone
British Museum, London, England

Rock Art and Mortal Combat

Representations of early human conflict, often depicting raids and skirmishes, become evident during the Neolithic period (ca. 5500–2500 BCE), when people developed increasingly complex forms of social organization. Retribution for homicides among egalitarian foragers often resulted from violence over women, but as people increasingly settled down in hamlets, towns, and villages and found new ways to organize larger fighting forces, they began to form community-based kin groups that engaged in collective aggression and violence. While humans have always had the potential for some level of violence, they have also possessed the means for resolving differences and pursuing cooperation and peace. But with greater degrees of social inequality, along with increased populations, larger settlements, and a stored surplus, their means for organizing social groups were transformed. In such cases, when attempts at peace failed, congregations of villagers often resorted to acts of socially based violence to resolve their grievances and to realign their political aspirations, social standing, and spiritual relations.

The earliest representations of organized aggression and violence are found not among egalitarian foragers but in nonegalitarian societies in which feuding stems from personal retaliatory justice undertaken by aggrieved parties, who typically seek blood revenge and social retribution through temporary but well-organized groups. While there is often no political objective in small-scale combat beyond the maintenance of group or personal honor, such feuds generally are settled by alliances among settlements or payments that compensate for death, injury, or insult. Complex and shifting forms of diplomacy and ritual practice bound communities and kin together as they engaged in violent reprisals.

Rock art in the Spanish Levant, the once fertile African Sahara, and the western coast of Sweden provides early artistic records of heroic combat and intercommunity raiding and violence. Some 5,500 years ago, artisans painted imagery depicting groups of archers pitted in deadly clashes in eastern Spain's mountainous coast bordering the Mediterranean Sea.[3] This Levantine art includes numerous small figures of game animals and humans. The style differs from that of the earlier Upper Paleolithic (ca. 40,000–10,000 BCE) paintings found in caves along the Pyrenees Mountains. For example, Upper Paleolithic art found in the dark zones of caves focuses attention not on humans but on Pleistocene megafauna that had become extinct because of climate change and increased hunting pressures following the last Ice Age. Levantine art on the other hand is frequently found on shallow cave and rock shelter walls, and it depicts humans either hunting or in combat in a "flying running" posture, with legs almost 180 degrees apart. Some rare battle scenes include dozens of people depicted in motion. These sites are not places of habitation but appear to be cosmoscapes—landscapes reflecting the beliefs and cosmology of the people who lived there.

3   Cave Painting of a Battle between Archers

Cueva del Roure, Morella la Vella,
Castellon, Valencia, Spain
Late Mesolithic period,
7000 – 5000 BCE

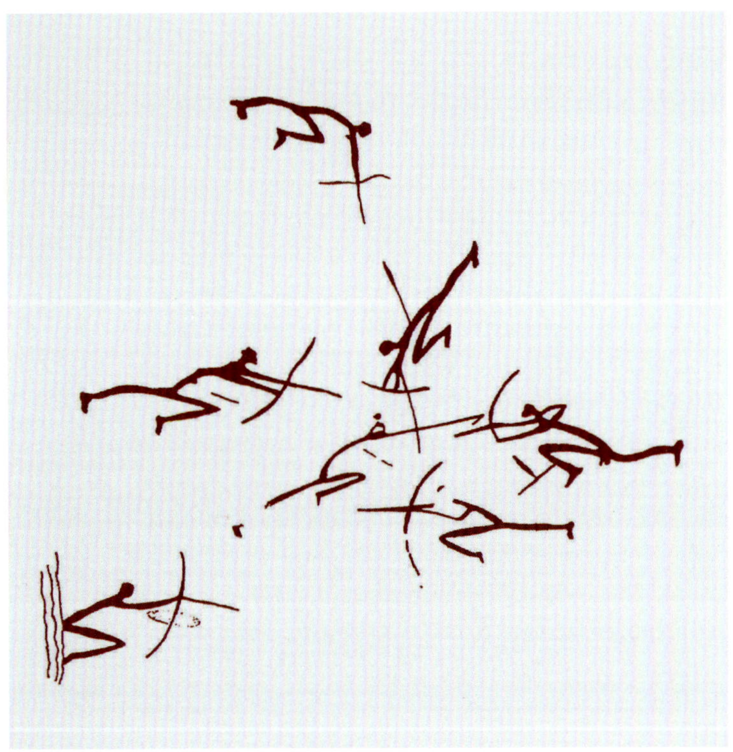

Art found on these rock-shelter walls illustrates the ways in which small enclaves of warriors engaged in violent clashes (3). These images represent one of the oldest artistic depictions of archery combat, with the longbow being the preferred weapon. This scene highlights two opposing sets of warriors in orchestrated violence, perhaps an act of retribution and revenge stemming from prior social conflict and violence. Such standardized images of stick figures running and shooting arrows suggest the depiction of actual combat rather than ritualized violence. Here we see two sets of opposed warriors with drawn bows engaged in group-based duels; one of the warriors outflanks an enemy and shoots them in the back. The lack of social distinctions suggests these are local kin groups in which markers of rank are minimized.

Similar organizational conflict is also depicted to the south in the once verdant north African Sahara Desert, where rock art images of combat may be contemporary with the Levantine art of Spain. Archaeologists have recorded battle scenes on sandstone rock faces at Sefar in the Tassili n'Ajjer National Park, a vast sandstone plateau in southeastern Algeria.[4] During the Neolithic period the Sahara was a massive savanna grassland teaming with antelopes, buffalo, elephants, giraffes, hippopotamus, rhinoceros, and warthogs. More than 15,000 petroglyphs (images created by removing part of a rock surface by carving or incising) and paintings have been identified on exposed rock faces, representing some 10,000 years of human occupation. The rock art transformed over time

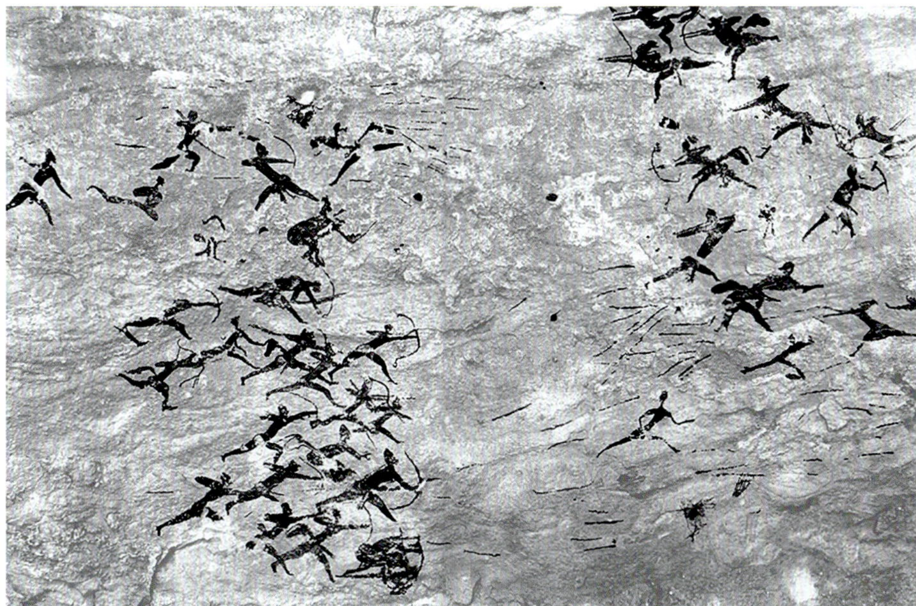

because of climate and cultural change. For example, as the African Humid period (ca. 10,000–6500 BCE) ended, the existing vegetation was destroyed by the introduction of livestock and the use of fire, resulting in desertification and human abandonment of the Sahara.

Conflict may have arisen among these Neolithic pastoralists who competed with one another as they moved their flocks seasonally between fixed summer and winter pastures. In this scene, twenty-four men to the left fight with thirteen people to the right (4). Each group is equipped with drawn bows and nocked arrows, and one person has an axe. Numerous arrows lie among the combatants, suggesting the attack has been ongoing for some time; bundles of arrows at the bottom edge of the scene may represent quivers. The two groups appear to surge toward one another in successive waves. For example, while the upper flank of the right party rushes at the enemy and shoots at them, their opponents on the left seem to be retreating.

Rock art offers one of the few visual depictions of organized violence in the Nordic Bronze Age (ca. 1750–500 BCE). In this example of chiefly combat, two solitary warriors engage in mortal violence (5). Such personal conflict may have erupted over access to exchange goods or trade routes. Highly desired items included bronze and gold, which were locally worked and exchanged for local exports such as amber, which has been found as far away as Egypt in the tomb of the New Kingdom pharaoh Tutankhamun (reigned 1333–1323 BCE). However, enslaved people may have been another important Scandinavian export. The ubiquity of bronze arrowheads, axes, daggers, spearheads, and swords in mortuary contexts testifies to the emphasis on heroic, personal combat by elite warriors.

The west coast of Sweden, especially northern Bohuslän, possesses the largest concentration of Bronze Age rock carvings in Europe. At the time the images were created, the granite bedrock hugged the Atlantic coastline; the rock art now stands some twenty-five meters above sea level as the landmass continues to rebound from the Scandinavian ice sheet that covered it during the last glaciation. This image consists of two men in a boat, brandishing axes as they face each other. While they may represent chiefly elites engaged in mortal combat, they may also depict Bronze Age beliefs in the Hero Twins, sons of the Sun God and the Sun Goddess. The Nordic twins came to the aid of ships in rough seas and rescued

  Two Men in a Boat, Holding Axes
and Facing Each Other

Fossum Panel, Tanum Rock Art Research Centre,
Northern Bohuslan Province, Sweden
Nordic Bronze Age,
1500 – 500 BCE
Stone
Photograph by David H. Dye

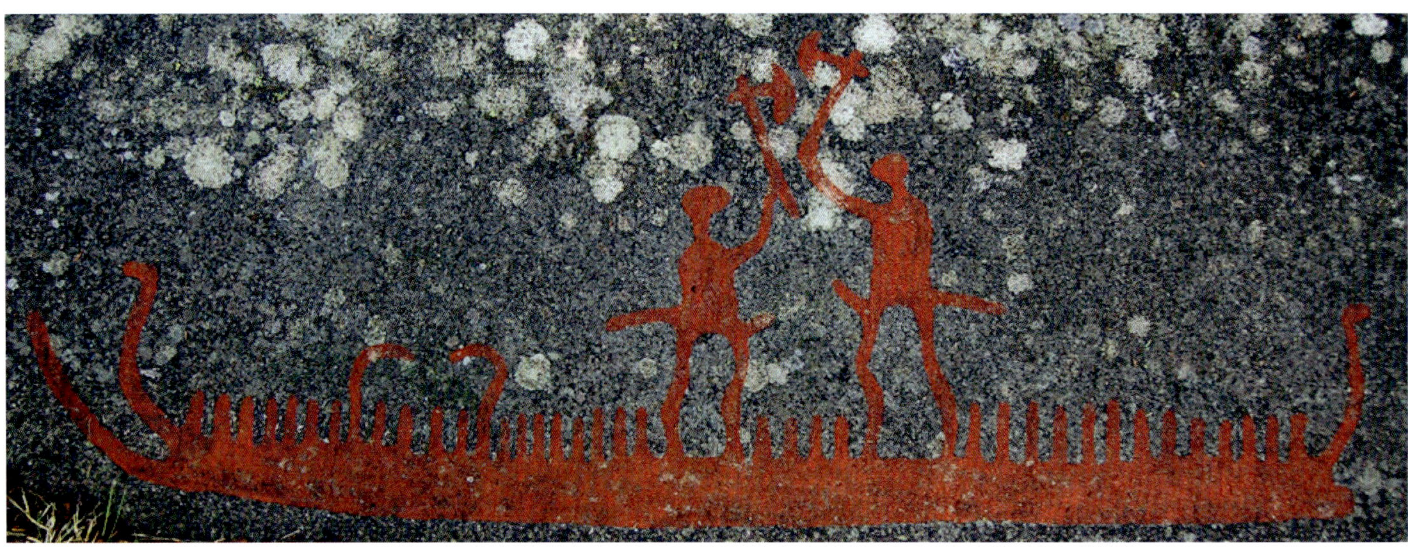

shipwrecked humans from drowning. While the rock carvings often depict everyday life, they also include scenes of heroic combatants, reflecting the Nordic warrior ethos with its emphasis on loyalty and prestige. Ornate daggers and swords, along with chain mail, helmets, and shields, were carried or worn by elite fighters not only for protection but also as ceremonial and status-defining regalia. Rock carvings in Bohuslan celebrate and chronicle a vibrant martial lifestyle, ideologically reinforcing warrior political dominance exercised through cultic rituals, moveable wealth, and social hierarchies.[5]

The rock art images from the Spanish Levant and the north African Sahara are particularly important as they are the earliest artistic depictions of social violence. While most rock art scenes portray hunting activities and ritual practices, combat is also a consistent theme. Such imagery typically focuses on clashes between small groups of mutually antagonistic archers. Violence between warring groups may have been a relatively rare occurrence but it was deadly when it took place. Given the rarity of such depictions, these events may have been experienced and recorded within only a few generations by a limited number of artists.

Blood feuds may have resulted in opportunistic battles precipitated by an insult, murder, or theft that had taken place within the group in the recent past. Revenge often stems from a prior murder or a death from natural causes that is perceived as an act of sorcery or witchcraft. The exclusive use of long-range weapons suggests the intent was to kill or wound individual combatants rather than to annihilate or "crush" the enemy, resulting in limited casualties rather than political gain. The aim, in other words, was not to wage a battle but to gain dominance without unnecessarily risking lives by senseless daring.

While rock art scenes may not represent ritual violence, ritual practice would have been important for success in these violent undertakings, especially by "complex" or transegalitarian hunter-gatherer societies beginning to exhibit nonegalitarian forms of social organization during the Late Neolithic period (ca. 7000–4500 BCE). Transegalitarian societies are those in which political leadership surpasses the boundaries of kinship yet lacks institutionalized power or clear political centralization. These depictions of violence have an almost photographic aspect, capturing the moment when the two sides clash. Pictorial messages may have been drawn for those involved in the melees to be viewed as realistic images of actual events; although stylized, they would have documented and preserved memories of the event for the community rather than portraying mythological scenes or the battles of deities.

Depictions of combat in Scandinavian Bronze Age rock art, in contrast, consist of two stylized warriors facing each other with raised axes and girded swords. Here we do not see images of victims or of people being killed, nor depictions of kin group coalitions and the movement of warrior lines. Nordic rock art reflects and records mythic narratives of mortal combat showcasing close combat weapons wielded by warriors

to demonstrate their might and power. The aim of heroic combat was to annihilate or humiliate the enemy, often with political intent, and thus the artwork glorified and personified conflict and violence. For example, the earliest depictions of violence in Egypt and Mesopotamia—the ancient region of southwestern Asia between the Tigris and Euphrates rivers—created around 3500 BCE, portrays scenes of heroic combat that adhere to canonical representations of kings and pharaohs, who are shown slaying their enemies. These later images illustrate idealized, mythological narratives, embodying formulaic artistic motifs that would have resonated within the community, attesting to the king's power and vitality.

Kings at War

Heroic individuals, often depicted as political leaders and mythic personages, are portrayed in victorious battle scenes and their aftermath to personify a civilization's wealth or a ruling family's military might. When eminent chiefs, emperors, kings, and warriors sponsored artwork depicting the armies they commanded, they bolstered their political clout and social prestige by emphasizing their glorious successes over the enemy. Kings, as well as deities, are represented in battle regalia brandishing weapons, capturing and humiliating prisoners, defeating and smiting their opponents, and personally sacrificing or trampling their enemies. These acts constitute dramatic performances,

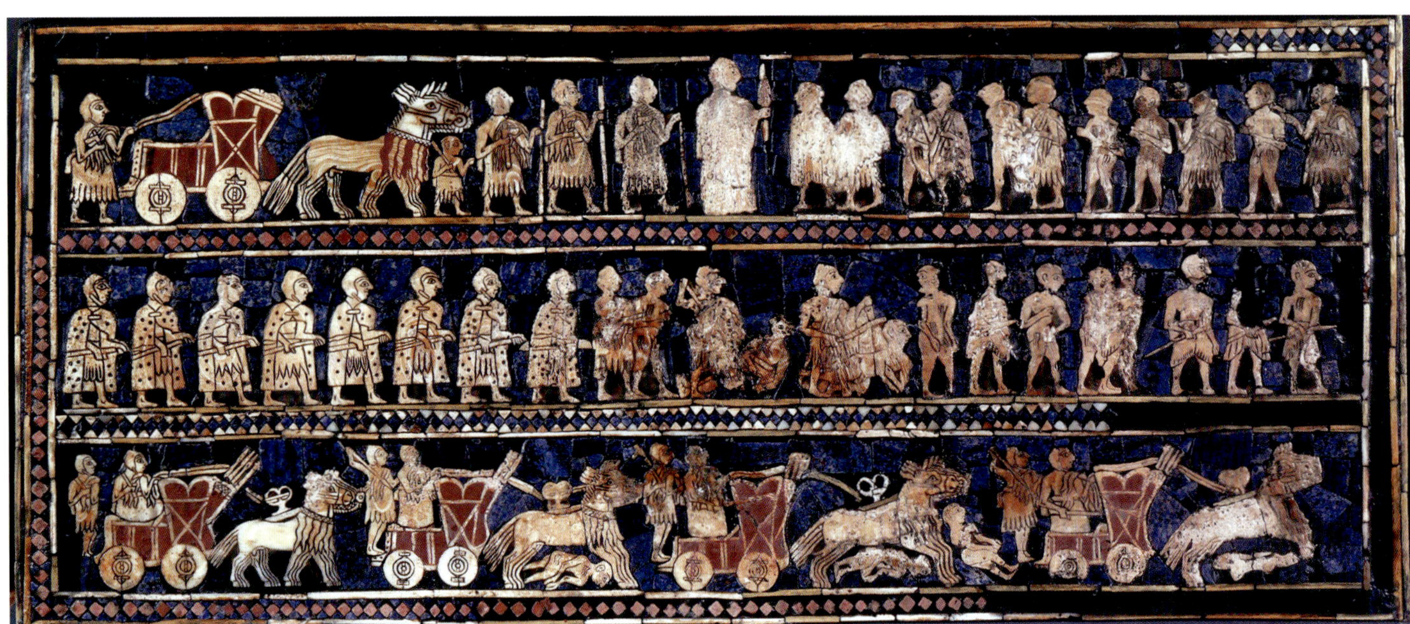

which were often reenacted on a large scale in public venues as propaganda and spectacle. The communal nature of performance and ritual, often in spacious arenas, plazas, and squares, aided in inculcating political agendas, social mandates, and worldviews. As military campaigns were funded by tribute revenues, compliance from those being taxed was rationalized by appeals to the blessings and the demands of heroes, deities, and gods. Coupled with supplication of the gods, carefully crafted images served to impress the general populace and to legitimize the actions and prerogatives of elite warriors and kings as battlefield commanders and leaders.

Perhaps one of the best examples of a depiction of a king at war is on the Sumerian Standard of Ur, an exquisitely crafted wooden box dating to the First Dynasty of Ur (ca. 26th to 25th century BCE), an important coastal city-state in ancient Mesopotamia (6). The Sumerian civilization flourished between around 4100 and 1750 BCE in southern Mesopotamia. Found in one of the largest Ur Royal Cemetery tombs, the box was associated with King Ur-Pabilsag, who died around 2550 BCE. The Royal Cemetery contained some sixteen tombs and provided evidence of mass mortuary rituals, including people sacrificed to accompany and to honor deceased royal

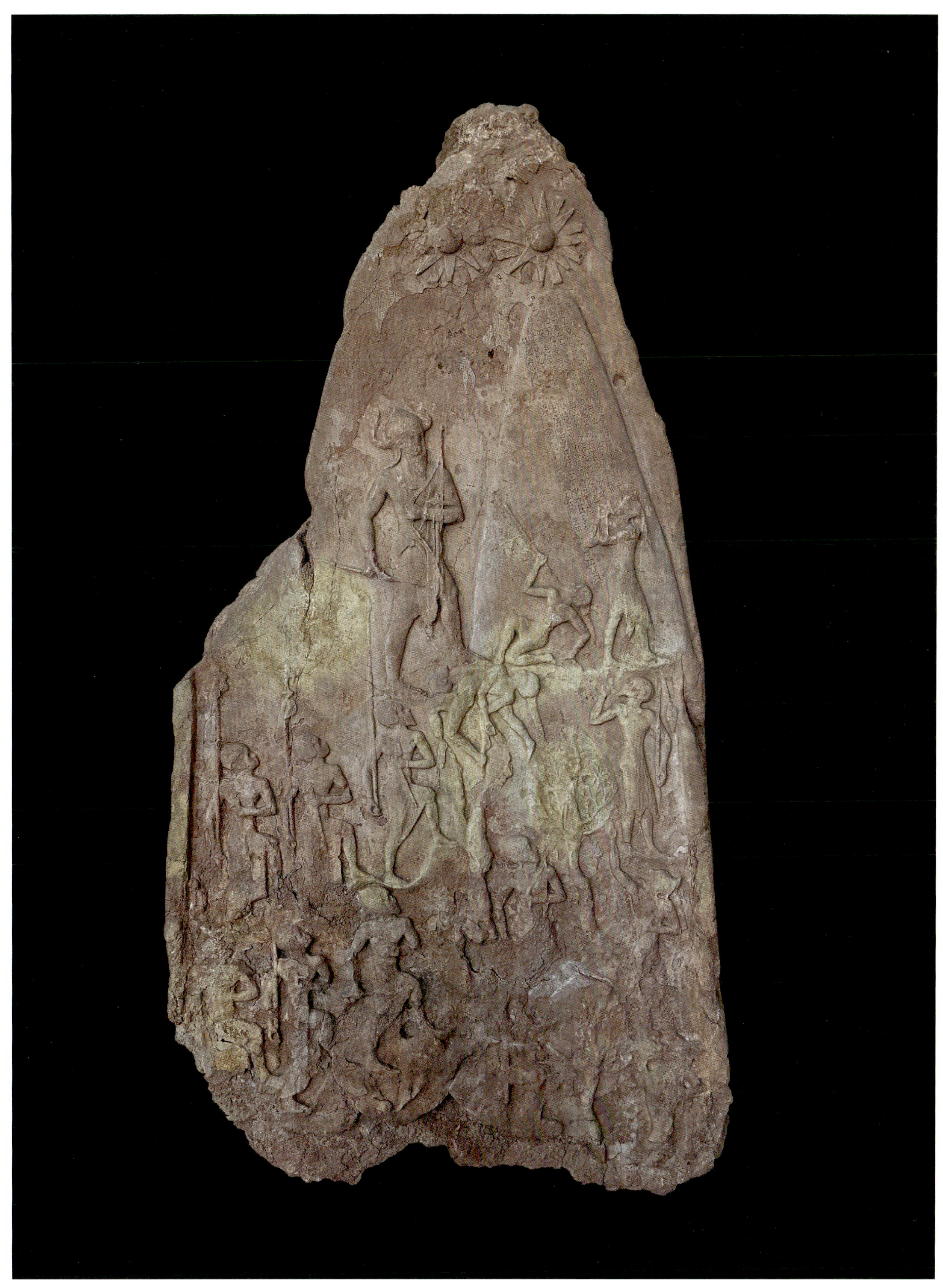

persons. Following a massive feast, abundant goods and provisions, along with animals, attendants, guards, and musicians, were interred with the principal person to meet their needs in the next world. The box, discovered in 1927–28 in fragmentary condition, had been placed next to a ritually sacrificed man who may have been its bearer or custodian. Originally thought to be a standard, its purpose remains unknown.

The ornate box has a "war" side and a "peace" side. While the peace side illustrates a military victory, the war side, shown here, is thought to represent a border skirmish. The scene portrays the king standing taller than the other figures, denoting his supreme status. He faces a row of nude and wounded prisoners with gashes on their chests and thighs—an artistic device that denotes debasement, defeat, and humiliation. The middle register depicts captured enemies being led away; the nudity of the captives and dead enemies does not depict how they appeared in real life but Mesopotamian beliefs linking nakedness with death.[6]

Mesopotamian political leaders accompanied their troops and appear in artistic renderings under the watchful protection of the gods. The victory stele of Naram-Sin, for example, illustrates the king as a self-deified leader, wearing a horned-helmet that proclaims his divinity and power (**7**). In fact, he is the first Mesopotamian king to claim divinity for himself, taking the title King of the Four Quarters, King of the Universe, and becoming a god of the city of Akkade. As a ruler known as the Beloved of the Moon God Sin, Naram-Sin ruled the Akkadian Empire (ca. 2254–2218 BCE). The stele depicts his defeat of King Satuni, who ruled Lullibi, a polity in the Zagros Mountains. Here Satuni implores Naram-Sin to spare his life as Naram-Sin tramples and spears his enemies. Naram-Sin strides before his standards and the ranks of his men, marching up the wooded slopes on a military campaign against the highlanders who lived to the east of his kingdom. He was famous for winning nine battles in a single year, and under his rulership the Akkadian Empire reached its maximum strength.[7] The Akkadian king is placed at the center of his monument, while the gods who witness his success are represented as astral symbols in the upper section. Naram-Sin is the most eminent and imposing figure in the stele not only because of his larger dimensions, but also because his human shape makes him recognizable by viewers as a deified king. The stele thus incarnates both his divine and human personas.

Kings are often depicted as commanders in battle, urging their forces forward and engaging in combat. Here the pharaoh Tutankhamun is portrayed in a battle scene painted on a plastered, wooden chest found in his tomb's antechamber (**8**).[8] The military scenes convey a sense of the young king's authority, power, and success over his enemies. Discovered in the Valley of the Kings by archaeologist Howard Carter in 1922, the tomb contained not only the chest, which held four pairs of sandals, a gilded headrest, necklaces, and embroidered ceremonial robes, but also body armor,

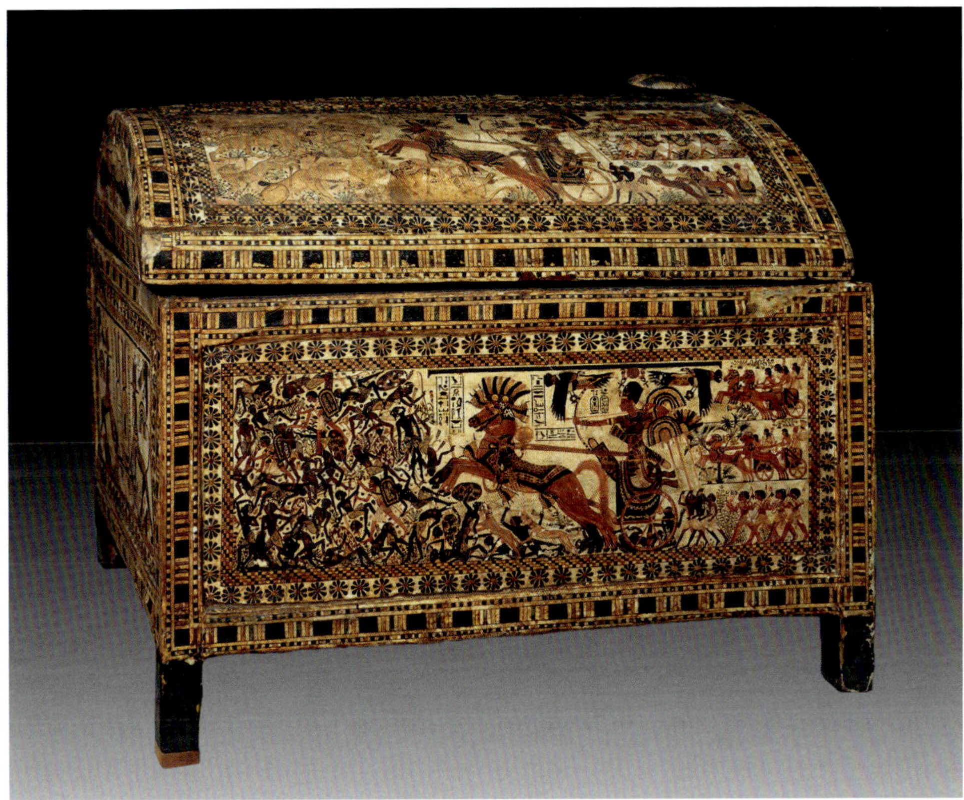

bows, and folding stools appropriate for military campaigns. Tutankhamun appears to have been trained in archery, and the Egyptian artisans placed him in his chariot in mid-battle, shooting arrows at opposing forces.

During Tutankhamun's reign the war chariot was a recent introduction to the Egyptians by the Hyksos, and it quickly became a powerful symbol of domination and royal regalia. Egyptologists speculate that Tutankhamun did not personally take part in such battles, as he had succumbed to severe bouts of malaria; additional disabilities required him to use a cane, several of which were found in the tomb among his belongings. However, his body armor indicates repeated use, suggesting he may have participated in battles or at least in the preparations for them. The inscription on the chest before Tutankhamun reads, "The good god, the Son of Amon, the Valiant one,

without his equal, A Possessor of strength who tramples hundreds of thousands, who makes them into a pile of corpses."[9]

Tutankhamun died at approximately eighteen years old, and afterwards he was venerated through mortuary cults and their associated temples, which included numerous painted scenes of his military career. The artists who painted these scenes for Tutankhamun's tomb depicted the enemy as a confused melee as opposed to the organized and orderly Egyptian military forces. A fierce confrontation takes place, with the pharaoh fighting against Nubians and Syrians. In the battle he shoots arrows into the fray, while three registers of subordinate personnel stand behind him. The two shorter sides portray Tutankhamun as a sphinx treading upon his enemies. The Egyptians frequently employed propaganda to promote the pharaohs and the interests of the state. For example, many temple

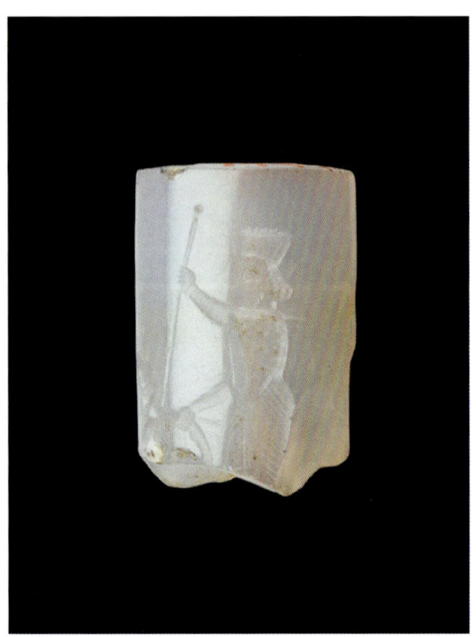

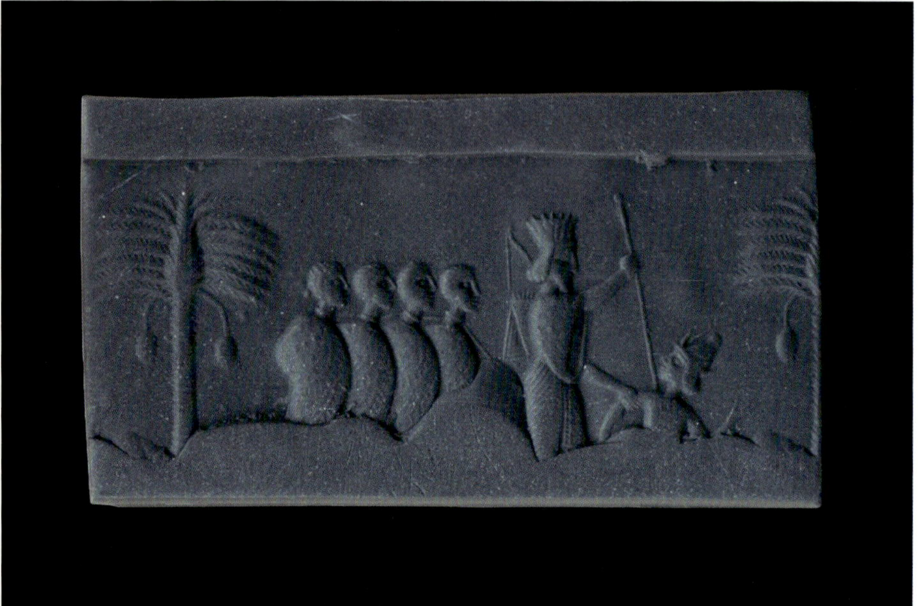

paintings depict overwhelming victories in wars that are known to have been lost to their enemies.

While images of leaders personally capturing their opponents in battles often portray idealized events, in many instances they reflect specific battles. For example, this cylinder seal features the image of the Persian king Darius the Great (reigned 522–486 BCE), who ruled the Achaemenid (Persian) Empire (ca. 550–330 BCE) at is greatest territorial extent (**9**). The empire spanned some 5.5 million square kilometers from the Balkans and ancient Egypt in the west to the Indus Valley in the east. Darius ascended the royal throne by overthrowing Bardiya, the

legitimate Achaemenid monarch, and then fabricating the story that Bardiya was an imposter. Here Darius wears a robe with wide flaring sleeves and a fluted crown, and he carries a bow and quiver of arrows over his shoulder while grasping an enemy by the arm and stabbing him from above. Behind the king is a row of prisoners tied to one another with ropes around their necks. The speared victim wears a version of the Egyptian royal crown, suggesting he is the defeated Egyptian rebel Pharaoh Petubastis IV (or III), who ruled around 522–520 BCE during the 27th Dynasty (First Egyptian Satrapy), a time when Egypt was effectively a province of the Achaemenid (Persian)

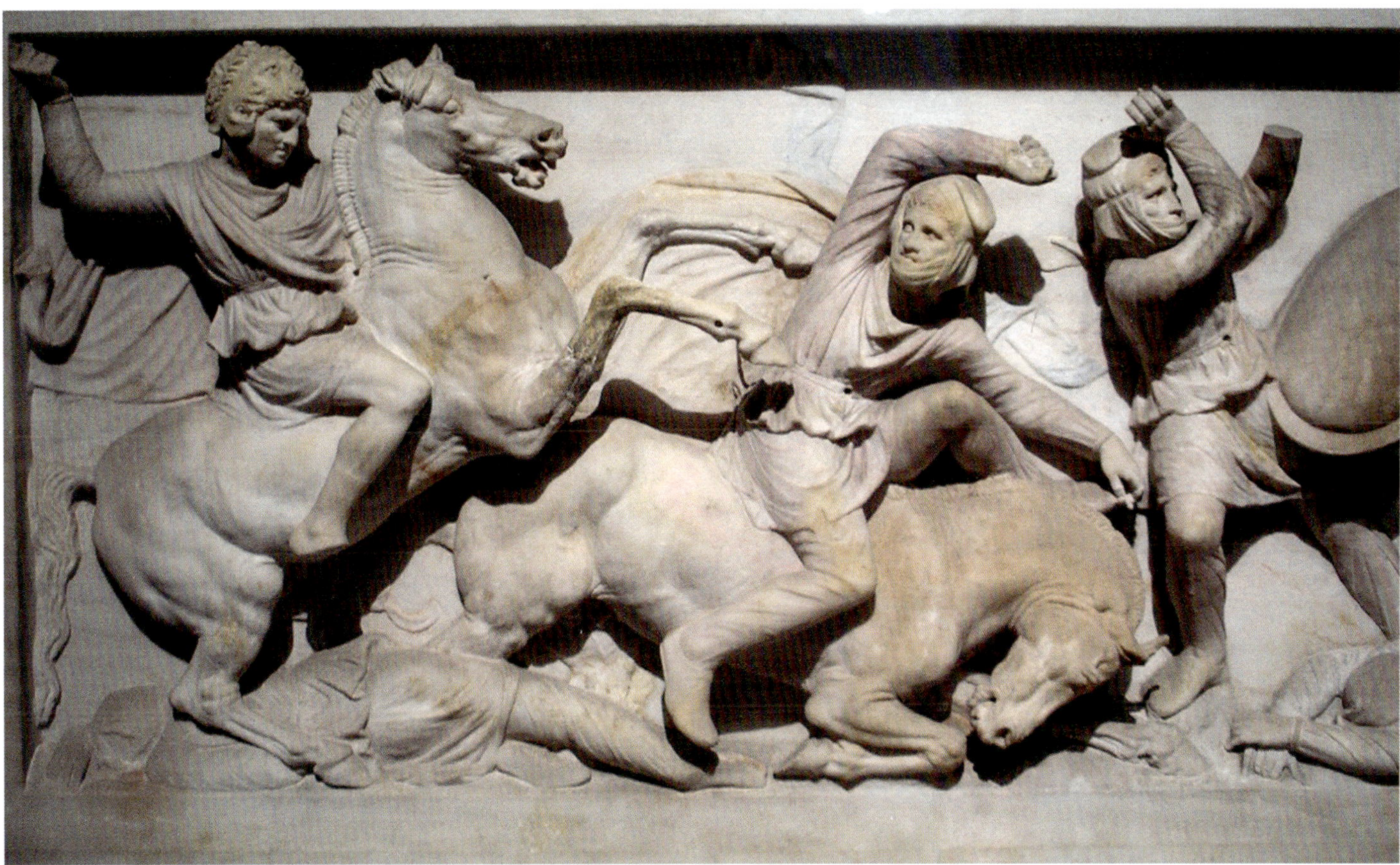

Empire.[10] Petubastis rebelled against Darius and ascended the Egyptian throne in early 521 BCE, only to be defeated by Darius and almost certainly executed, like other kings who rebelled against the Persian ruler. However, in a more general sense the image symbolizes the Persian subjugation of Egypt around 519 BCE.

The depiction of elites and rulers in battle is exquisitely represented by the Alexander Sarcophagus, commissioned around 332 BCE in Lebanon during the reign of Abdalonymus, a gardener of royal descent (**10**). The Hellenistic stone sarcophagus, discovered by archaeologists at the royal necropolis near Sidon, an ancient Phoenician port in what is today Lebanon, probably held the body of Abdalonymus, the king of Sidon, who was appointed to his position by Alexander the Great (356–323 BCE) in 333/332 BCE. Abdalonymus died around 311 BCE and the sarcophagus is thought to

have been commissioned by him and created by master artisans before his death. It is adorned with bas-relief carvings of mythological and historical scenes, including Alexander routing the Persians.[11] The relief carvings on one long side depict Alexander at the Battle of Issus (333 BCE), which resulted in the Macedonian defeat of the Persians; the Macedonian warriors fight in the nude, which is characteristic of Greek iconography. The sarcophagus, which at one time was intricately painted, consists of marble blocks adorned with alternating statuettes of women's heads, one of the which is possibly Atargatis, a Syrian fertility deity who protected those who offered sacrifices to her. She is thought to have been a later iteration of Bronze Age goddesses, including Anat, a war goddess.

Kings were not always successful in battle and their demise and later depiction by those who were victorious

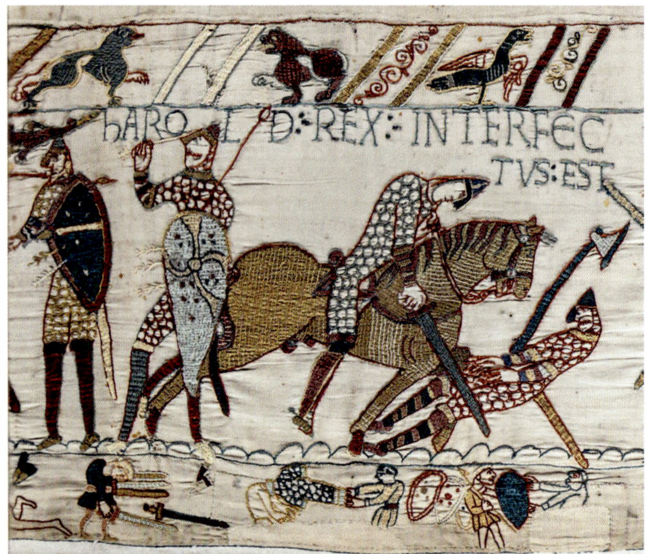

over them sent a powerful message of defeat. Within a few years after the Battle of Hastings, which was fought on October 14, 1066, in southeastern England, artisans produced the Bayeux Tapestry, an embroidered cloth some seventy meters long depicting the Norman Conquest (**11**). The tapestry was commissioned by William the Conqueror's maternal half-brother, Bishop Odo of Bayeux, who later became Earl of Kent. One of the supreme achievements of Norman secular Romanesque art, the tapestry consists of fifty-eight scenes detailing the events leading up to and including the battle, which was fought between the forces of William, duke of Normandy (1028–1087), who

challenged Harold II, king of England (ca. 1020–1066), for control of England.[12]

William, who became the first Norman king of England, led an army comprised of Norse descendants, the ancestors of whom had raided and settled Normandy since the late eighth century. The scenes on the tapestry, which portray the end of the Anglo-Saxon era and the beginning of the Norman period, are presented from the point of view of the conquering Normans; it was designed to assert the authority and sanctity of William's rule. Known as William the Bastard by his contemporaries, he was the son of the unmarried Robert I, duke of Normandy (1027–1035), and his mistress Herleva. While success in the battle legitimized William's claims to the throne and demonstrated God's blessing for his rulership, the tapestry was conceived and constructed by Anglo-Saxon artists and needleworkers in Kent.

While some images portray kings actively participating in battle, others provide a more static but powerful depiction of royal authority predicated on military success. The Kingdom of Benin or Edo Empire (ca. 1440–1897), home to the Edo-speaking peoples, is in the tropical rain forest region of western Africa and is famous for its court arts.[13] An old and venerated state within what is now southwestern Nigeria, it is not to be confused with the modern Republic of Benin, which was known as Dahomey from the seventeenth century to 1975. Brass was especially valued by the rulers (*obas*) of Benin, who obtained both brass and bronze through West African coastal trade routes from the Portuguese, who the Edo elite drew upon for their military and political clout.

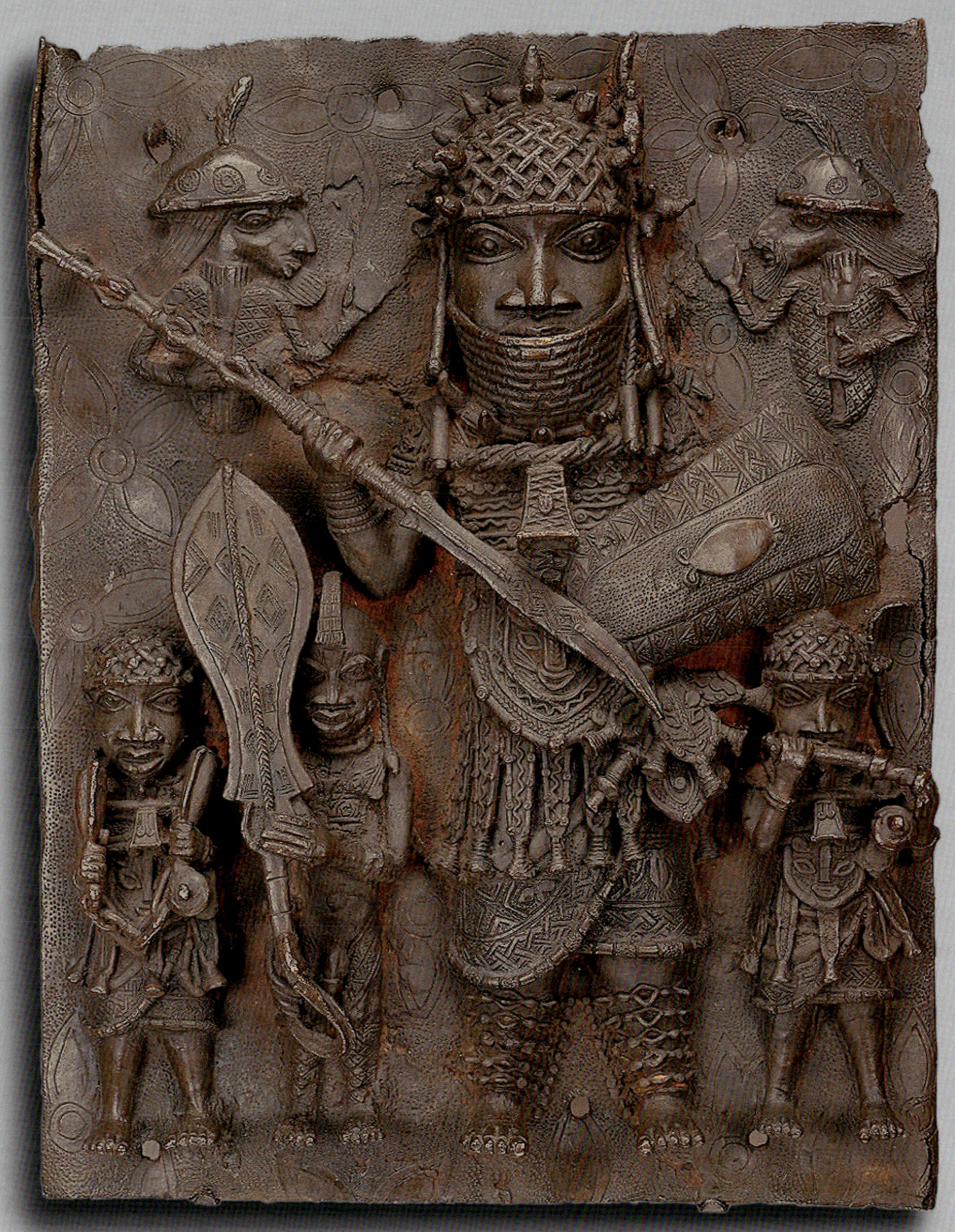

Members of the casting guild held the highest rank in the social hierarchy and their artistry adorned the royal court and courtiers. Their work with various copper alloys is referred to as either brass or bronze. This cast brass royal plaque once formed part of the decoration of the palace in Edo, described in 1668 by Dutch geographer Olfert Dapper (who never traveled outside of the Netherlands and relied on reports written by Jesuit missionaries and Dutch explorers) in his famous *Description of Africa*. The plaque depicts musicians and a court page flanking an *oba*, who holds a spear in his right hand and a shield on his left shoulder (**12**). His headdress is made of agate or coral and a quadrangular bell hangs from his neck. The coral choker of leopard's teeth proclaimed his rank. The small figure on the left sounds an elephant's tusk trumpet, while figures in profile hold books or tablets. The figural associations with elephants and leopards imbue the *oba* with great spiritual power. A nude attendant on the right holds a fanlike sword (*eben*), an example of symbolic weaponry that represents the *oba*'s royal authority and power.

Monuments and other artworks depicting combat manifest a ruler's achievements and thus serve as public records of their military accomplishments, which are often shown as individual combat scenes in which the ruler is depicted as symbolically fighting an individual who represents the enemy. In this sense, success in combat is typically predicated on relationships with the gods and a ruler's ritual supplication of the deities, which may take place in the context of feasting and mortuary events. These depictions focus our attention on the efforts of elite leaders who commissioned master painters and stone carvers to record their military exploits and present themselves as the gods' chosen instrument, extolling the near-mythic aspects of the nobility and thus legitimizing their claims to privilege and rulership.

Success on the battlefield and in combat demonstrates and underscores the favor and protection bestowed by the gods. In turn, failure in combat would signal the ancestors' and gods' disfavor, leading to civil unrest and competition with one's political rivals. The superiority of the state against its enemies is often portrayed by the king's participation in violent encounters and the subsequent celebration of victory. Such stylized combat scenes of king versus enemy are commemorated in various artistic genres and serve as both perpetual and public memorials to a king's ability to defeat the enemy and to forge links with the mythical past and the supernatural realm.

While much of the art of the Etruscan civilization, which flourished in ancient Italy from about 900 to 27 BCE, concerns the afterlife, battles were also an important artistic theme. Painted around 640 BCE, the Chigi Vase (or pitcher) was found in a tomb in Veii, an Etruscan city located a short distance northwest of Rome (**13**).[14] Veii was the richest city of the Etruscan League and for over 300 years it alternated between alliances and warfare with the Roman kingdom and later the Roman Empire. The pitcher is decorated with four friezes: hunts, horsemanship, the Judgement of Paris, and hoplite (citizen-soldiers of ancient Greece armed with spears, shields, and short

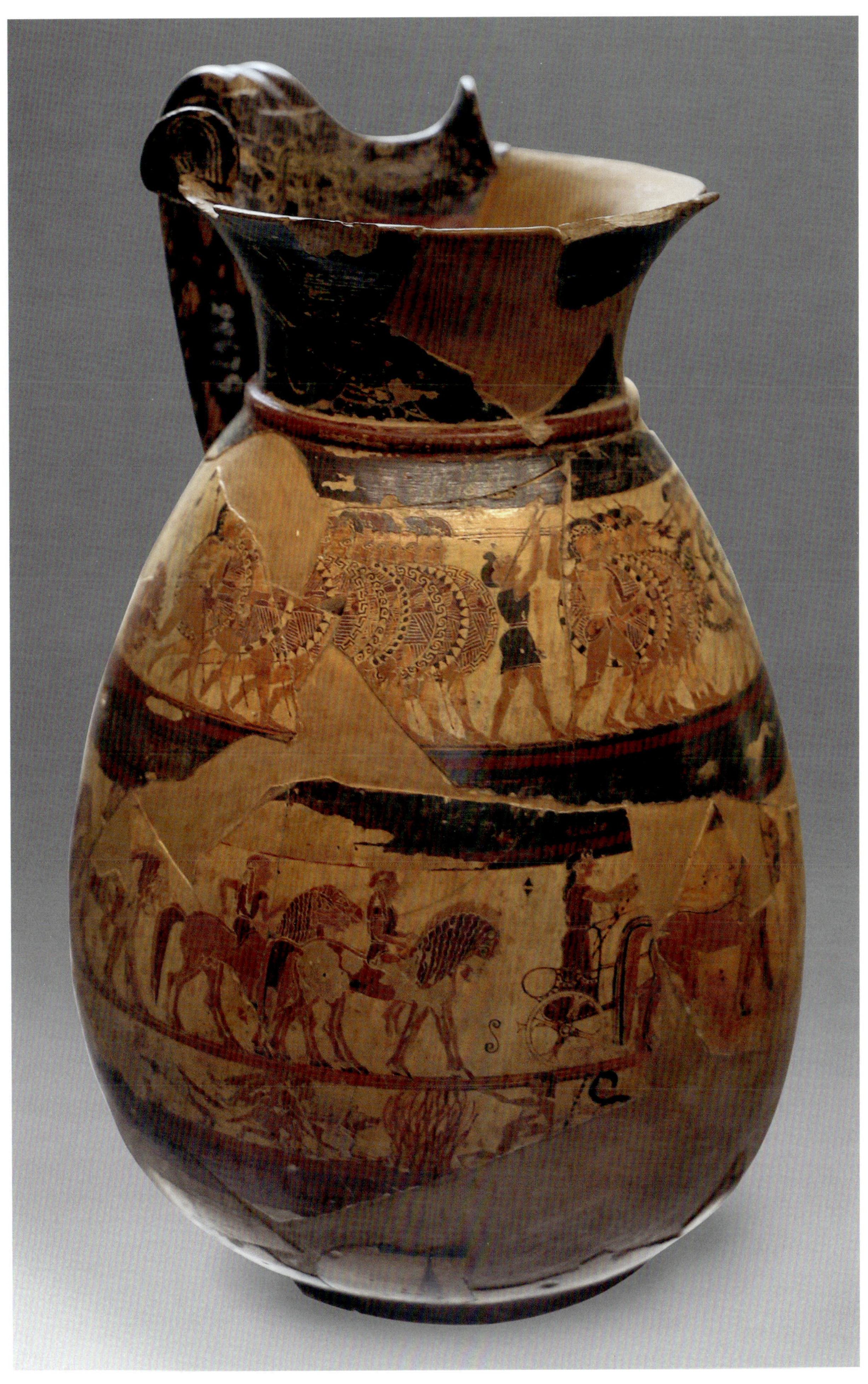

14 **Warrior with Weapon**

Edo culture, Kingdom of Benin, Nigeria
1500 – 1600
Brass
13 ⅜ × 11 ⅜ × 1 ⅞ in, 33.97 × 28.89 × 4.76 cm
Art Institute of Chicago
Samuel P. Avery Fund, 1933

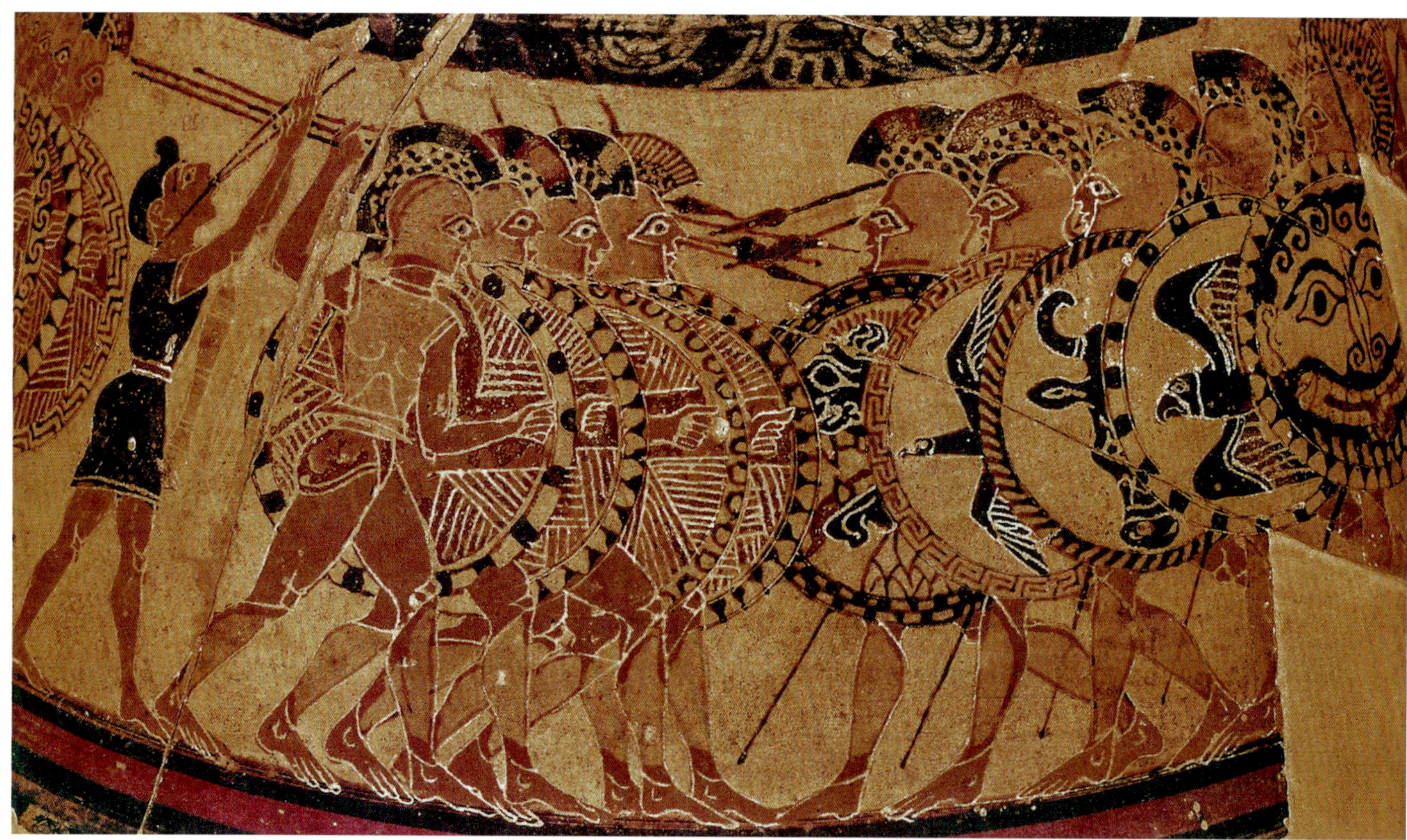

swords) phalanx formations. The battle scene, the earliest representation of the phalanx formation, shows hoplites carrying two spears—one for throwing (javelin) and one for thrusting; hoplite soldiers carried javelins on their backs and held thrusting spears in their hands. The success of the phalanx, which altered military tactics for hundreds of years, was based on ranks of warriors overlapping their shields, creating an impenetrable unit. This close order "shield wall" comprised of interlocking shields alternated with the "immediate order" phalanx in which the shield rims only touched; the former was used in combat, while the latter was employed during troop movements. A thrusting spear was crucial to wounding the shield bearers and breaking through the wall. Hoplite

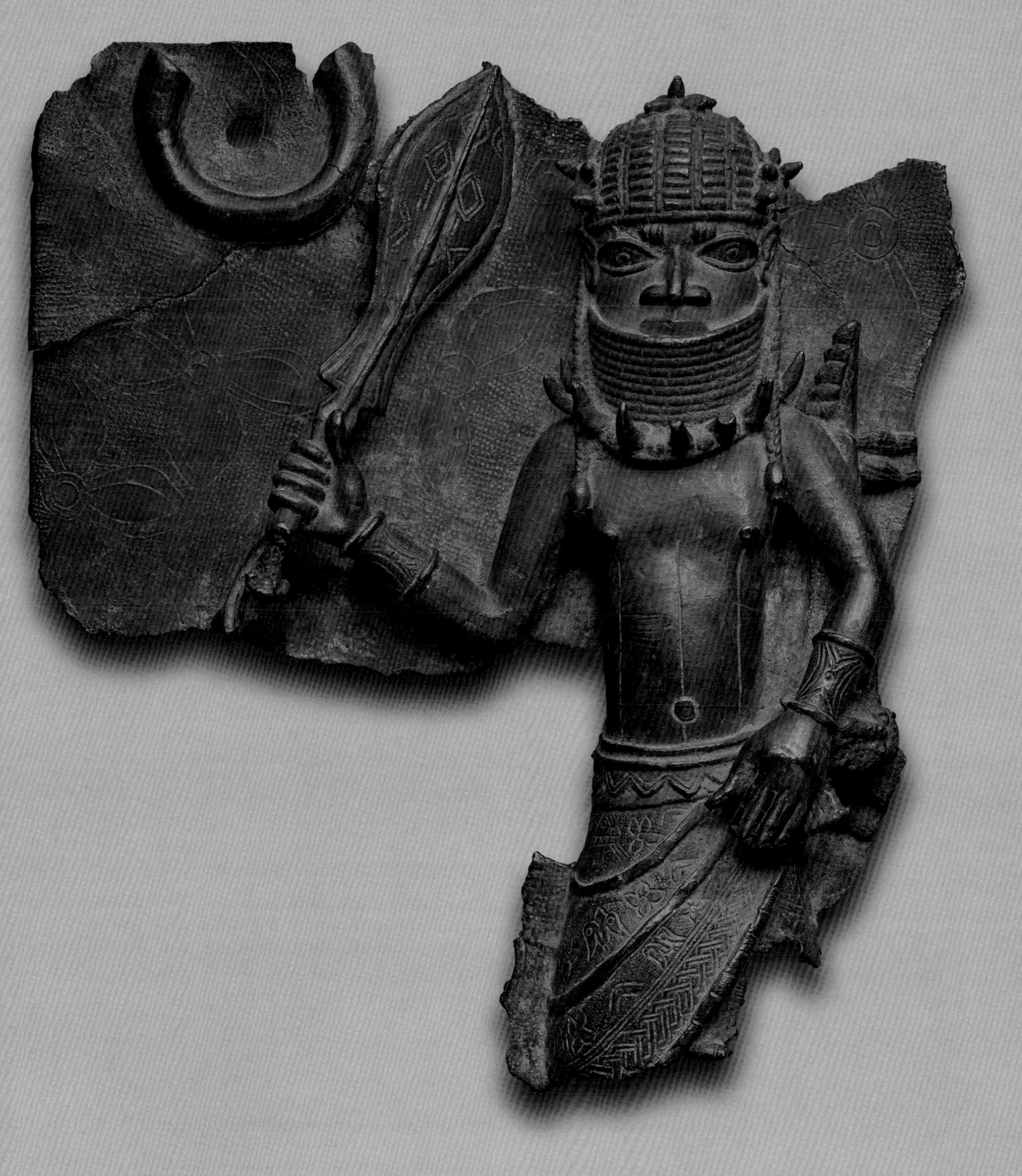

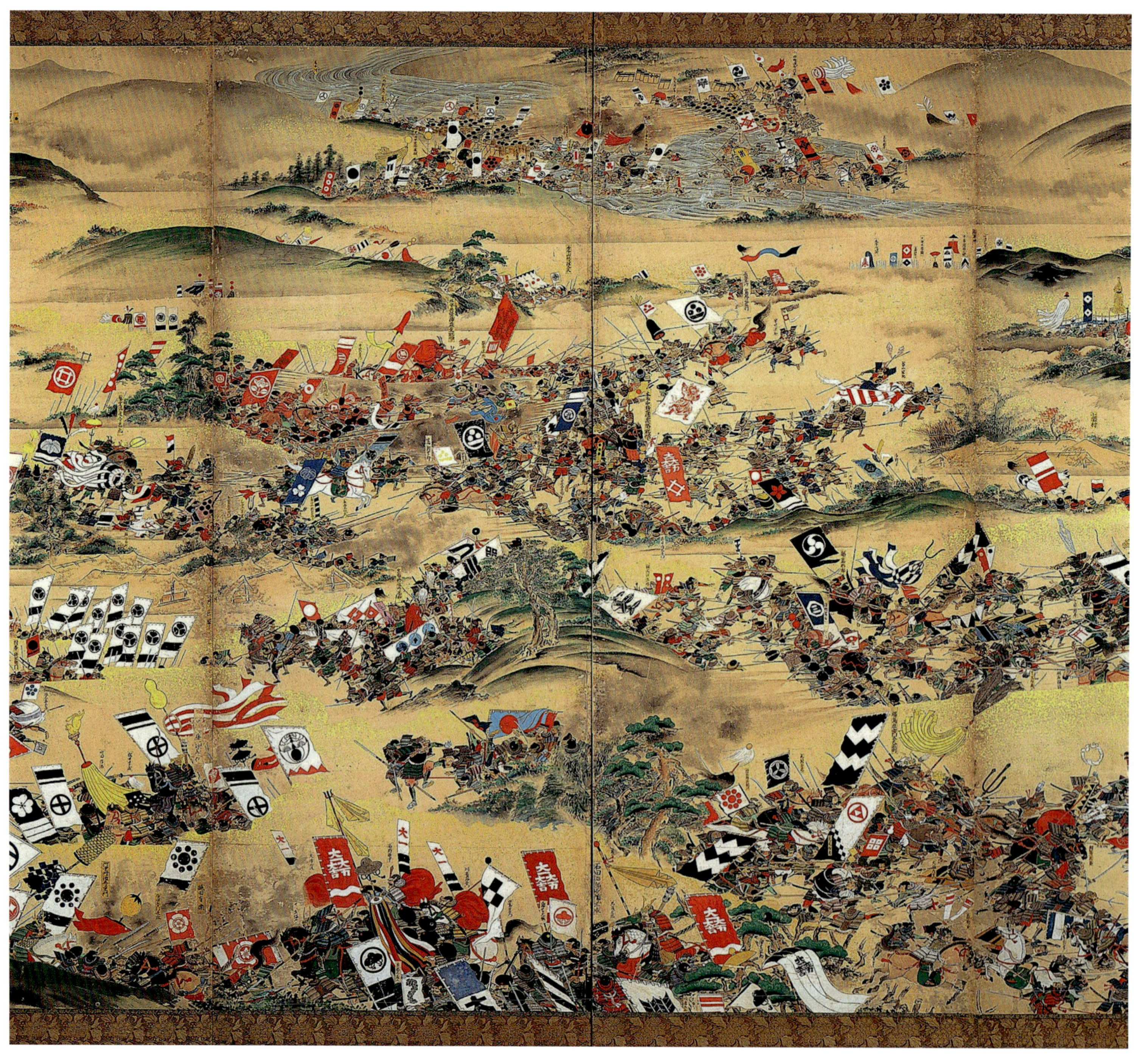

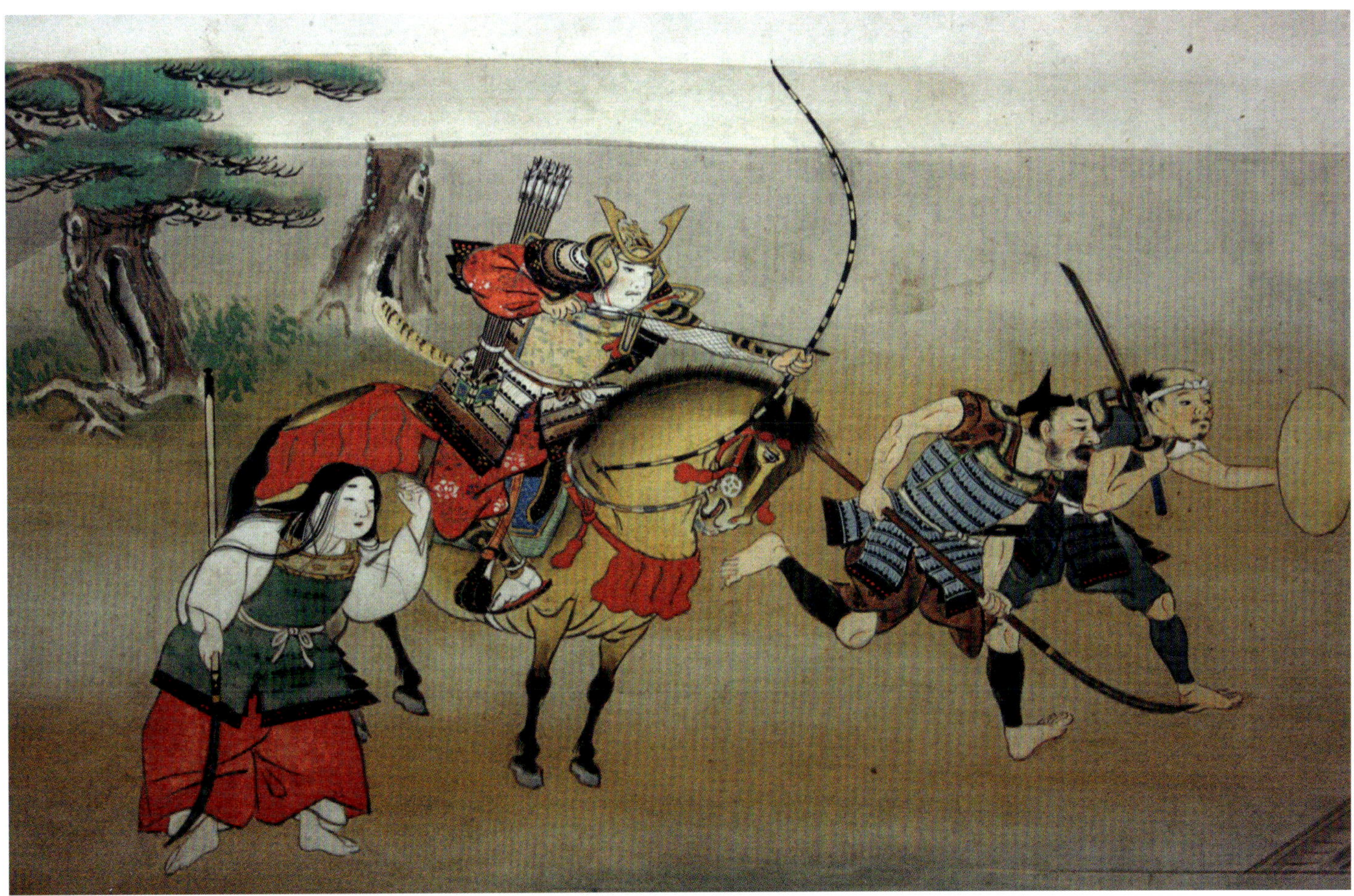

warfare relied on the unity of soldiers rather than expressions of individuals as heroic warriors, although individual fighting prowess and skill did play a role in battle. The painted pitcher expresses that phalanx success was due to organized teamwork.

Artworks commissioned by chiefs and kings served important political roles throughout the world. In West African kingdoms, skilled artisans produced art for the royal families, documenting their lifestyles and military prowess. Edo, the prosperous capital of the Kingdom of Benin, displayed cast brass and bronze for the *oba*, who commissioned ritual objects for the court (14). Oba Esigie (reigned 1504–50), a generous patron of the arts, commissioned master craftsmen to produce plaques that honored and glorified the warrior. These brass plaques

were commissioned for ancestral altars, as well as to validate a new *oba*. The Edo warrior depicted here dons a coral-studded cap and collar that symbolize his high rank; the club and regalia may represent royal authority and power.[15] The current *oba*, Erediauwa I, holds a royal court and continues to employ master craftworkers to produce works of bronze and ivory for the palace.

The long tradition of warrior art is influenced by political organization, with depictions of combat and victory serving the interests of chiefs, emperors, and kings. Perhaps one of the most decisive and significant battles in Japan was fought to establish which powerful family would rule the country. The Battle of Sekigahara took place on October 21, 1600, during the late Warring States (or Sengoku) period (1467–1615) in what is now

  Tomoe Gozen Wields a *Naginata* on Horseback

Toyohara Chikanobu (Japan, 1838 – 1912) with Uchida Ieyoshi
and Hatakeyama no Shiegetada
Late Heian period, 1899
Woodblock prints
20.5 × 10.1 in., 52 × 25.6 cm
Art Yoshikiri

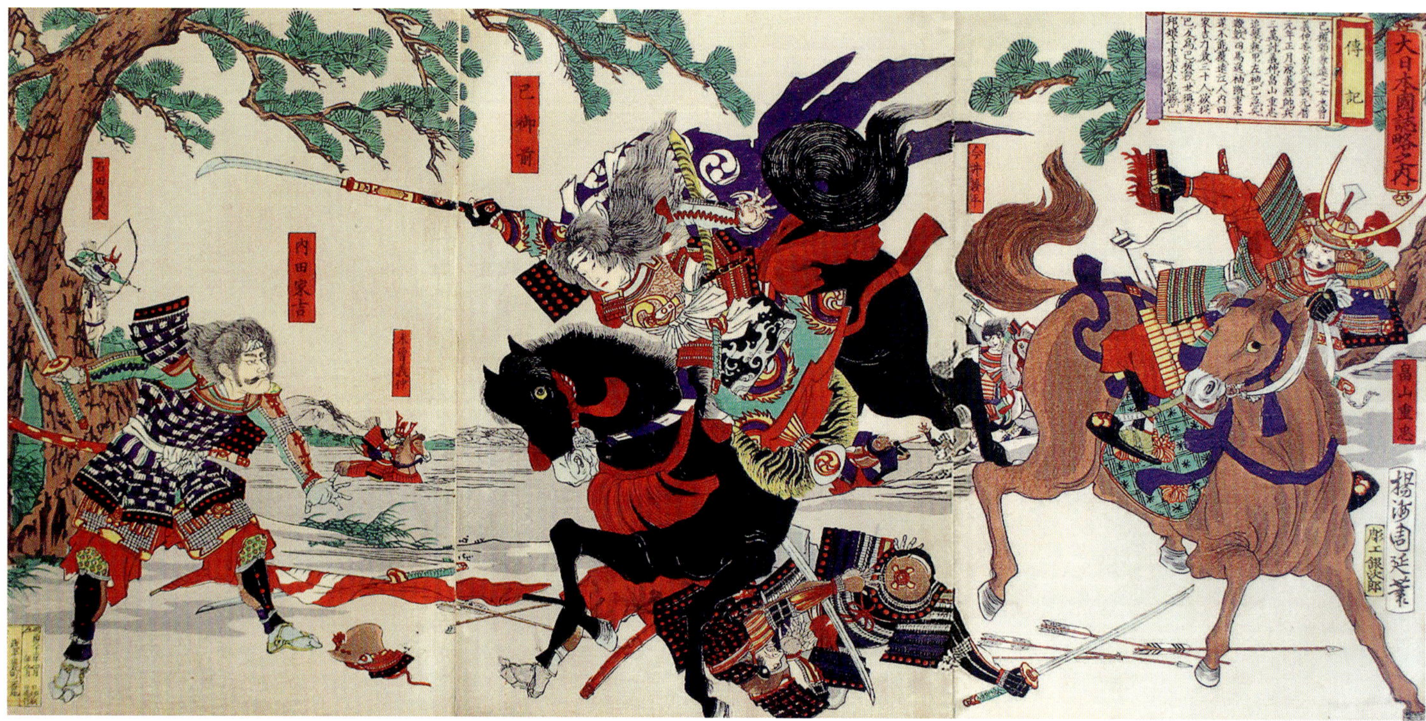

Gifu Prefecture.[16] A depiction of the battle was painted in 1854 during the Edo period (1603–1867) (**15**). The decisive seven-hour battle, which established the Tokugawa shogunate, was the largest and most important in Japanese feudal history, with some 160,000 soldiers facing each other; about 30,000 men died. The confrontation was fought between a coalition of Toyotomi loyalist clans commanded by *daimyō* Ishida Mitsunari based mostly in western Japan, against eastern *daimyō* forces fighting for Tokugawa Ieyasu. An intense rain fell the previous night and because of the fog and mist, the forces could not see more than thirty meters in front of themselves. Once the fog cleared, the attack began, with the forces using matchlock guns in addition to *naginata* and swords. The *naginata* is a pole weapon with a curved blade originally used by the samurai class, as well as by foot soldiers and warrior monks of feudal Japan; it is the iconic weapon of the female warrior of Japanese nobility (**16**). The Tokugawa shogunate went on to rule Japan for some two and a half centuries until 1868.

Women's roles in warfare are often overlooked and underappreciated, but Japanese images and historical narratives document female samurai in ancient Japan.

Cheyenne or Arapaho culture, United States
1884
Paper, pencil, watercolor, crayon, leather binding
Each page 11 ¾ in., 29.85 cm
Metropolitan Museum of Art, New York
The Michael C. Rockefeller Memorial Collection,
Purchase, Nelson A. Rockefeller Gift, 1968

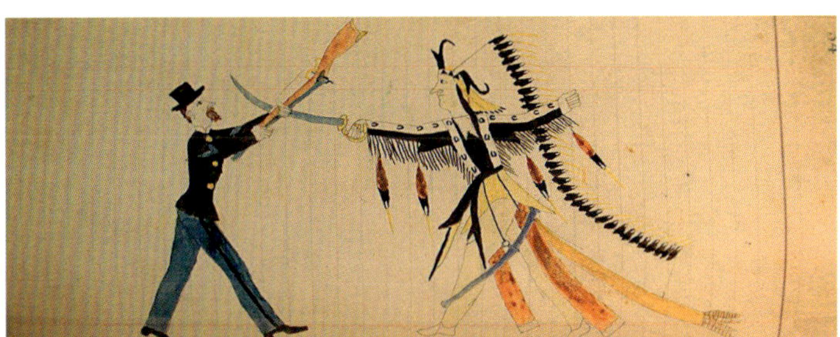

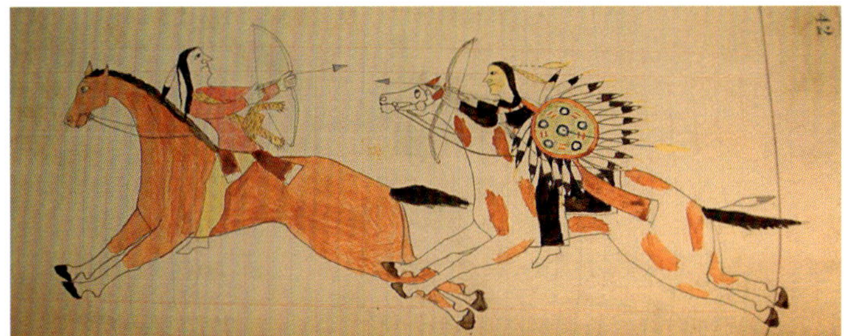

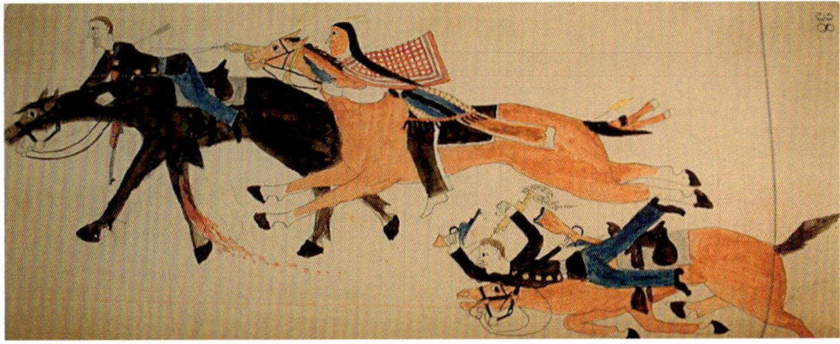

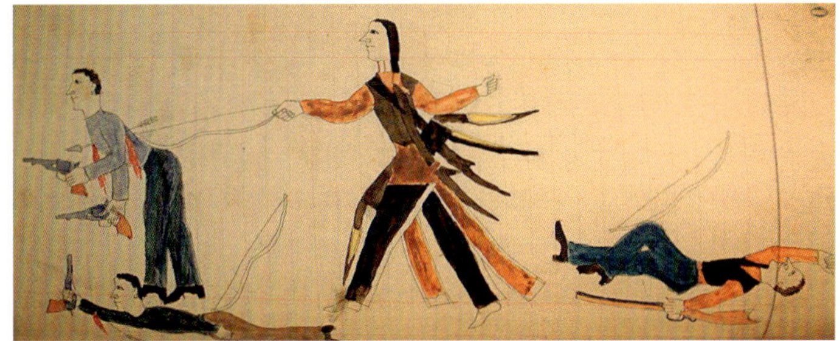

These woodblock prints depict Tomoe Gozen, an *onna-musha* (or female samurai) on horseback, wielding a *ko-naginata* (17). She served General Minamoto no Hoshinaka during the Genpei War (1180–85) and was part of the conflict that led to the first shogunate. This began the world of the shoguns, who held absolute power over their territory and turned the figure of the shogun into a hereditary and permanent position.

As a member of the *bushi* (warrior) class in feudal Japan, Tomoe Gozen was trained in the use of weapons such as the *naginata*. She had the reputation of being beautiful as well as undaunted and is known for killing Uchida Ieyoshi, a samurai warrior of the Kiso Minamoto clan, and beheading him. Her story is told in the *Tale of the Heike* (late twelfth or early thirteenth century), which recounts her participation in the Battle of Awasu in 1184 during the late Heian period (848–1185).[17] Her son, Asahina Saburo Yoshihide, is noted for his marvelous strength, and like his mother, is a legendary figure, though he, too, is likely based on a historical personage. She retired as a nun to the monastery of Tomomatsu in Echizen, a city known for its master metalsmiths, who for centuries forged high-caliber blades for weapons endowed with extraordinary value.

Of the many ways in which battles and individual acts of valor were recorded, perhaps one of the most intriguing is ledger art, which portrays warrior life on the American Great Plains. This genre begins in the early 1860s and continues into the 1920s. During this period, people painted their dreams, memories, and observations in accounting ledger books, an available source of paper in the late nineteenth century. Ledger art, which began to replace traditional drawings on animal hides, especially bison, continues the practice of depicting the warrior's desire for obtaining and demonstrating power bestowed by guardian spirit helpers. Upon being supplicated, a tutelary spirit—a guardian or protector—typically approaches the warrior through dreams or visions and provides the warrior with success and valor in combat. Proof of a warrior's spiritual connections and power is seen in ledger art depicting dominance and victory over enemies. These pictorial narratives document exploits of battle and combat—they are historical records that recall personal feats. For example, these four Cheyenne ledger drawings from the late nineteenth century depict warriors overcoming and killing their enemies (**18–21**). By recording individual success in battle, ledger art thus served as a type of public affirmation, which might be demonstrated and performed in public rituals, especially dances and songs that extolled and proclaimed personal combat success granted to the warrior by the deities and other spiritual forces. In this sense, the function of Plains ledger art is not to represent military success and connections to spiritual forces as much as to focus our attention on the ability of imagery to serve as an energized force that may be accessed through ritual supplication to personal guardian spirits.[18]

Art that manifests an elite or ruler's military achievements depicts more than the nature of the events being represented: it is a constant and public reminder that a leader is a deity's chosen instrument.

Indeed, images of ancient conflict and war remind us that socially constituted violence is based on elite legitimacy and political agendas and that success in combat is an expression of spiritual blessing and favor. Aggression is conveyed under varying circumstances, with both the intensity and prevalence of conflict and war being part of a complex, ongoing, dynamic social and political practice. While the artistic record depicts interpersonal and intercommunity feuding, raiding, and warfare stretching back to the ancient world, such expressions of conflict and war are rarely undertaken by neutral parties—they have decidedly political points of view and purposes.

Gods of War

Military victory is often tied to commissions of monumental art and their dedication to the gods who were believed to have empowered rulers and protected cities. Monuments portraying the king honoring and supplicating the gods through offerings, prayers, and sacrifices were considered crucial to military success and provided a powerful sign of divine blessings and sanctions. These depictions of the gods also served as models for elite behavior, military ethos, and martial codes of justice and morality. The public actions of kings, their ritual attire, and the sacrifices of captured prisoners were thought to bring sustenance to the earth and re-create the world for the benefit of the people. Fusing the identity of the gods with that of a king created a powerful and unassailable public statement: when a ruler dressed in the guise and regalia of a deity and re-created or reenacted the actions and events that lead to the creation of the cosmos in the distant past, supernatural beings and mythical time were actualized and made present through the king's body. Destroying the deities of one's enemies was equally important and provided a king with access to the ancestors and the deities of the conquered, which could then be appropriated as their own.

The gods of war were solicited for their blessings and aid in battle in many parts of the world. In the Kingdom of Kush (or Meroë) (ca. 300 BCE–250 CE) in northeast Africa, a region bounded by the Nile and Blue Nile, Apedamak was venerated as a major war deity, often depicted with a male body and a lion head (22). Naqa, an ancient city along the trade routes between Africa and the Mediterranean world, is the site of the Lion Temple, a ritual sanctuary within a major cultic center northeast of modern-day Khartoum, Sudan. The temple was constructed under the leadership of Natakamani (reigned 1 BCE–ca. 20 CE), shown holding an axe, with his Queen Amanitore, who wields a sword. In one scene they smite or subdue their enemies, perhaps captured prisoners. The lions at their feet are symbolic depictions of royal power. The image portrays Apedemak with three heads and four arms, but he is also represented on the temple emerging from a lotus flower as a tall, coiled serpent with a human upper body and his characteristic lion head. His consort is Amesemi, a Kushite protective goddess of conquest, military prowess, and warfare. Apedemak wears leather armor or a cuirass, carries a bow and arrow in his hand, and holds a chain of enemy warriors captured in battle. Although he has no Egyptian counterpart, he was closely associated with Amun and symbolized martial power for the Kushites.[19]

In the Roman Empire numerous gods controlled the lives of nobles and citizens, as well as the enslaved. Mars, the son of Jupiter and Juno, was a pre-eminent deity among the Roman army's military gods and was identified, although with some contempt, with the Greek god Ares. Because he sired Romulus and Remus, the founders of Rome, through his rape of Rhea Silvia, a vestal virgin, he is considered a father of the Roman people. He may have been initially a storm deity, associated with lightning and thunder. While usually portrayed nude or seminude, Mars typically wears a helmet and carries a spear to denote his status as a warrior when depicted in statuary or wall paintings (23). The stylized spear and shield of Mars symbolized both the male gender and the planet Mars. The spear possessed agency and animacy and was said to move or tremble when war was imminent or when the republic was endangered. The high priest of the Roman state cult of Mars led public ceremonies and rituals sacred to Mars. One of the priest's responsibilities included manipulating the sacred spears of Mars when the Roman army prepared for battle. While Mars was envisioned as a destructive force, his power was seen as the way to secure peace. As a vital force to be supplicated, he was crucial to Rome's defense and protection.[20]

The Indian subcontinent witnessed relentless conflict among competing chiefly polities and kingdoms and appeals for the gods' support was considered crucial for victory. Kartikeya, an ancient Hindu god of war, is an important deity whose narratives became widespread

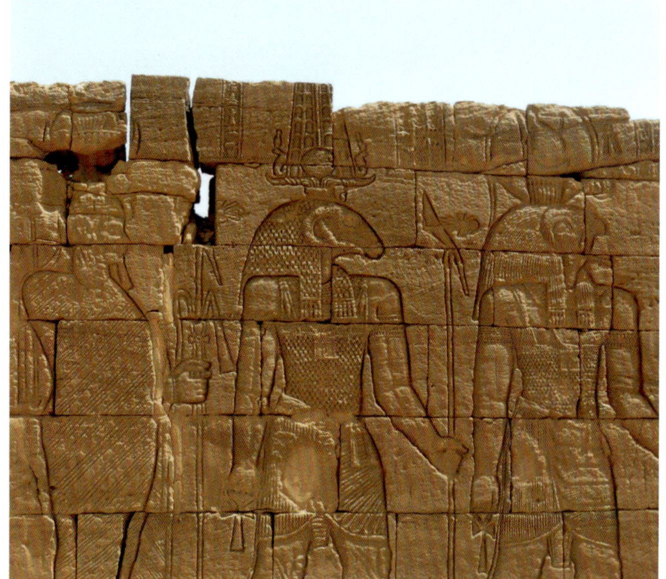

around 200 BCE in northern India. Also known as Murugan and Skanda—he has some 108 names in Sanskrit and Tamil religious accounts—he is the son of Parvati and Shiva, and he is portrayed in many different guises but most typically as an ever-youthful male riding an Indian peafowl: the tail feathers are visible behind his feet in this image (**24**). Kartikeya was charged by the gods to destroyed demons in widespread accounts, especially Hindu epics such as the Ramayana.[21]

Kartikeya was supplicated and venerated in early Hinduism during the Vedic period (ca. 1500–500 BCE) and is a primary deity in temples wherever Tamil people live. Like many war deities, Kartikeya is equipped with powerful weapons, such as a dagger and a *vel*, a divine javelin or spear; here his banner depicts a *vel* and the emblem of a rooster. While he is often shown with only one head, he sometimes has six, symbolizing the six stars of the Pleiades that were his mothers. He is also represented with twelve arms brandishing weapons: his multiple arms and heads denote the possession of supernatural powers and the rooster symbolizes his aggression and speed. He ages quickly, becoming a philosopher-warrior to teach his followers how to pursue an ethical way of life.

In many instances great war leaders become heroic figures over time and their accomplishments and deeds assume mythic proportions. An example includes Guan Yu, a Chinese general who served under Liu Bei, a powerful warlord during the era of the Three Kingdoms (220–280), who became lionized to the extent that he was deified (**25**).[22] His courtesy or style name is Yunchange, and he is considered to have been a talented warrior; he possessed a massive crescent-bladed weapon known as the Green Dragon. His deification took place during the Sui dynasty (581–618). As a great and mighty warrior who espoused a strict code of behavior and sense of honor, his military achievements have been the subject of generations of narratives, such as the historical novel *Romance of the Three Kingdoms*, written in the fourteenth century, as well as an authoritative historical text, the *Records of the Three Kingdoms*, which dates to the third century. Guan Yu is noted for his loyalty and

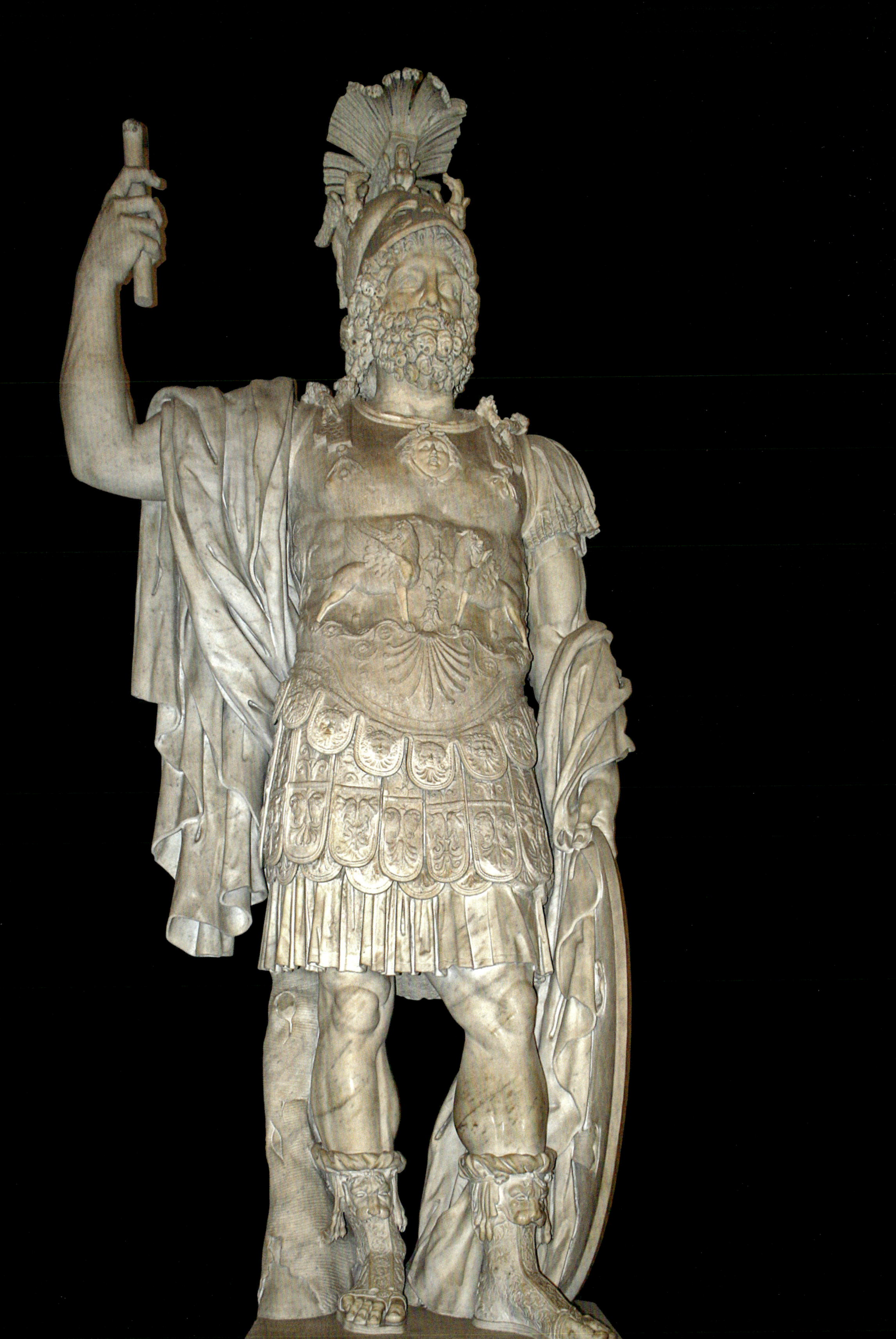

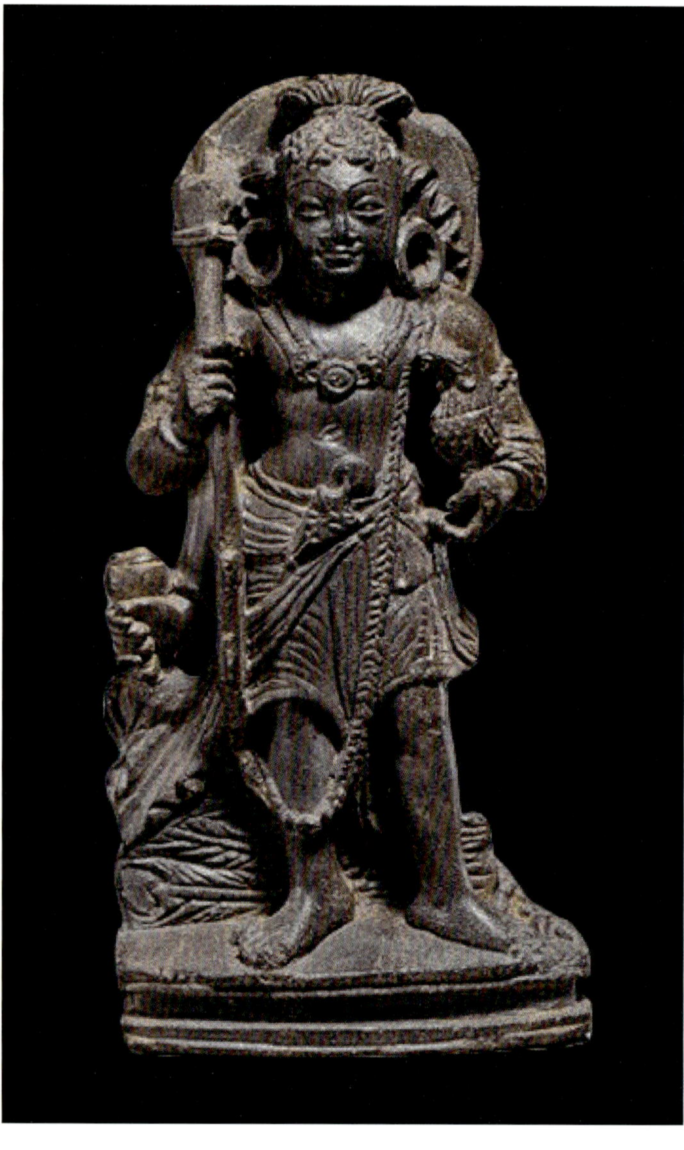

righteousness, symbolized by his red face in opera representations. He is worshipped as a deity in folk beliefs, as well as in Chinese Buddhism, Confucianism, and Taoism, and he is supplicated and venerated in numerous shrines throughout the modern world, including Chinese restaurants and shops. According to tradition, martial temples are dedicated to Guan Yu, and he is held in high esteem as a guardian deity who exerts control over evil spirits. The popularity of Guan Yu is seen in his large statue, which weighs some 1197 tons, in Jingzhou, China.

While images of gods of war are often created in stone, master Hawaiian artisans carved many of their figures in wood; the statues were then placed in temples dedicated to their veneration and worship. Kūkaʻilimoku, a Hawaiian war god known as Kū, the Snatcher of Land, epitomizes healing, strength, and warfare in Hawaiian beliefs.[23] As one of the four great Hawaiian gods, he is often depicted with bent knees and a wide, grimacing mouth, the latter a sign of disdain and disrespect toward his enemies and rivals. Incorporating stylized pig heads, perhaps symbolizing abundance and wealth, his coiffure suggests an identification with Lono, the god of agriculture, fertility, peace, and rain. Kūkaʻilimoku's spouse is Hina, a powerful creatrix, female force, and moon goddess with multiple identities and manifestations. This figure of Kūkaʻilimoku, the guardian of King Kamehameha 1 (reigned 1782–1819), represents one of his many manifestations; the image was commissioned

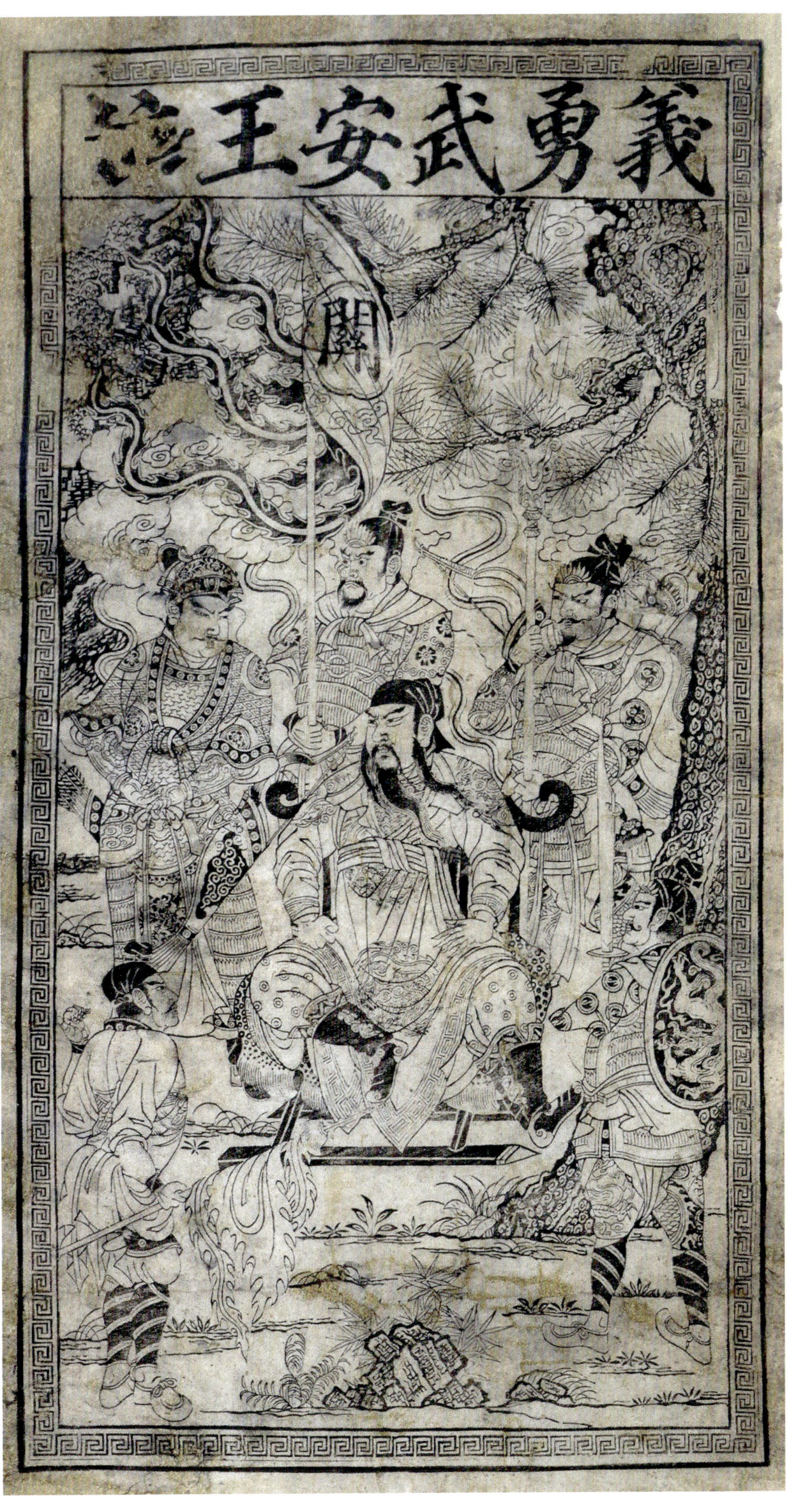

義勇武安王位
關

Kona style, Hawaii
1790 – 1810
Breadfruit tree wood
105.12 × 27.17 × 21.65 in., 267 × 69 × 55 cm
British Museum, London, England

by Kamehameha at the end of the eighteenth or the beginning of the nineteenth century (**26**).

Kamehameha built a number of temples as abodes to honor and supplicate Kūka'ilimoku for his support in unifying the Hawaiian islands. Human sacrifices were made to Kūka'ilimoku for success in warfare and as offerings for his support in defeating Kamehameha's enemies. Seeking victory over Hawaii's adjacent islands, Kamehameha ordered a great temple to be constructed for Kūka'ilimoku. Upon its completion and to earn the war god's support, Kamehameha summoned his brother to the temple and immediately sacrificed him. Kamehameha then launched a massive fleet of warships and took control of Maui. As is the case for many gods of war, Kūka'ilimoku's statuary is not considered a representation but rather a vehicle for the war god to enter and become manifest before supplicants.

Figures of war gods are not just representational—for many people the image is the abode of a spirit, and when approached and invoked, the spirit may ensure success, provide protection, and shape one's life. Many West African figures depict the theme of warfare, and warriors supplicate such imagery for aid and success in battle. The Ijo or Ijaw people of the Niger delta, comprising a population of some four million, are primarily Christians, but they also engage in traditional religious practices, including ancestor veneration and the supplication of water spirits. The latter are thought to be like humans, or at least people who lived among the water spirits before they were born. Egbesu, the

god of justice and warfare, is considered instrumental in combating evil; followers are organized as cultic institutions that venerate him for defense and to correct an injustice (**27**).[24] These images are perceived as invincible warriors as well as symbols of aggression, bravery, and power, which are reflected in their bared teeth. The figures are often dedicated to clan war gods for success in battle. Masks and statues are crafted to honor the spirits, who are persuaded by supplicants during celebrations and rituals to provide success in war. Ijo spirits respond to requests by supplicants through supernatural messages.

Throughout human existence, portrayals of other-than-human beings have served the needs of rulers in their acquisition and appropriation of power and wealth from their neighbors through military might and violent means. Religion and ritual, expressed in artwork and dramatic performances, serve the interests of those with power and demonstrate to the citizens of a polity an anointed ruler's divine right to rule when success in warfare is thought to reflect the benevolence of the war gods. Through the centuries, great chiefs and powerful kings have garnered political support that enhanced their own aggrandizement by producing artwork that pleased the gods. The gods of war are often portrayed in dramatic imagery, especially ceramic, stone, or wooden statues that may be animated through prayer as sentient deities able to provide success in warfare. Such objects are typically commissioned by powerful leaders who enjoy access to wealth obtained by plunder or tribute, which in turn underwrites craft guilds or workshops to produce ritual

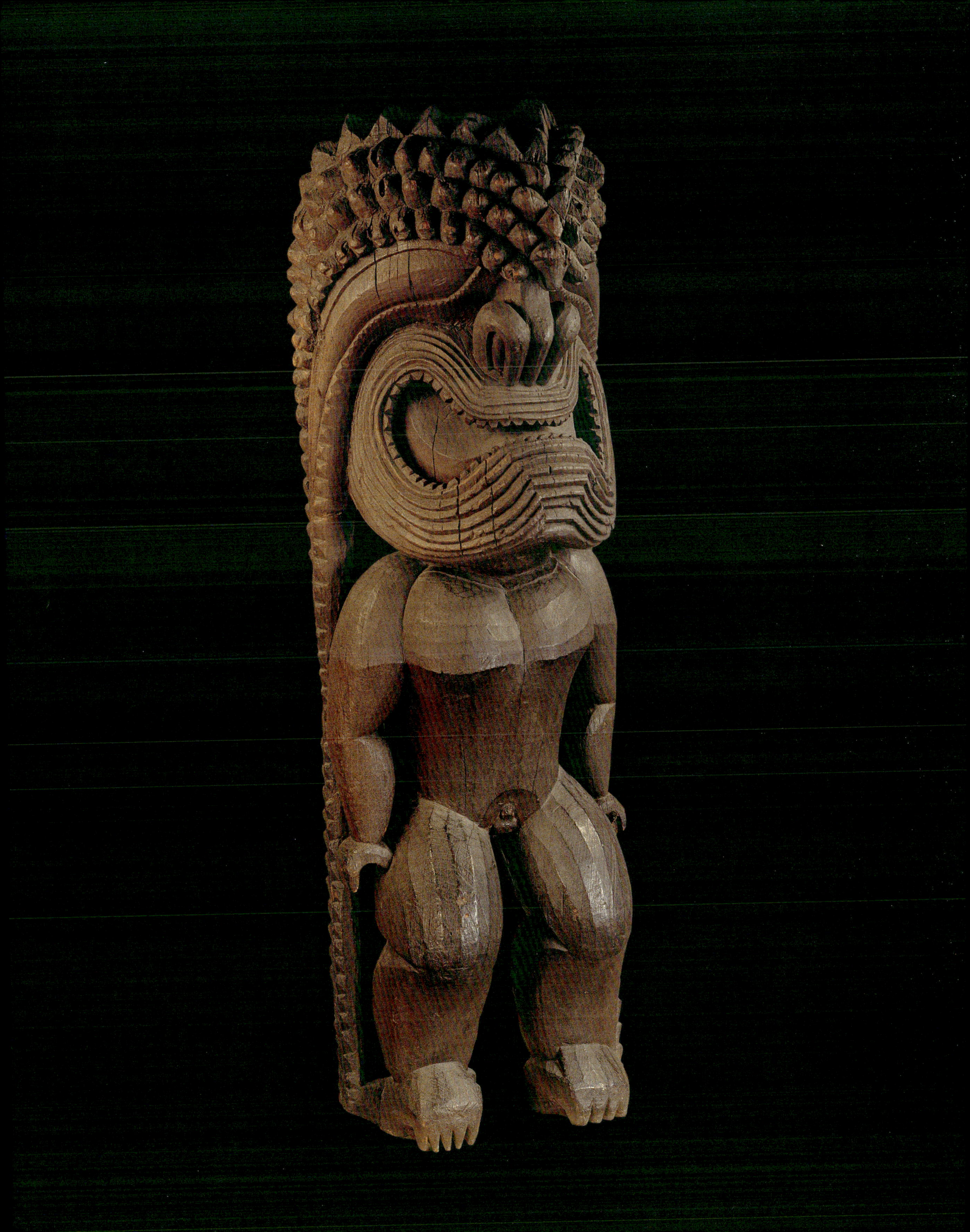

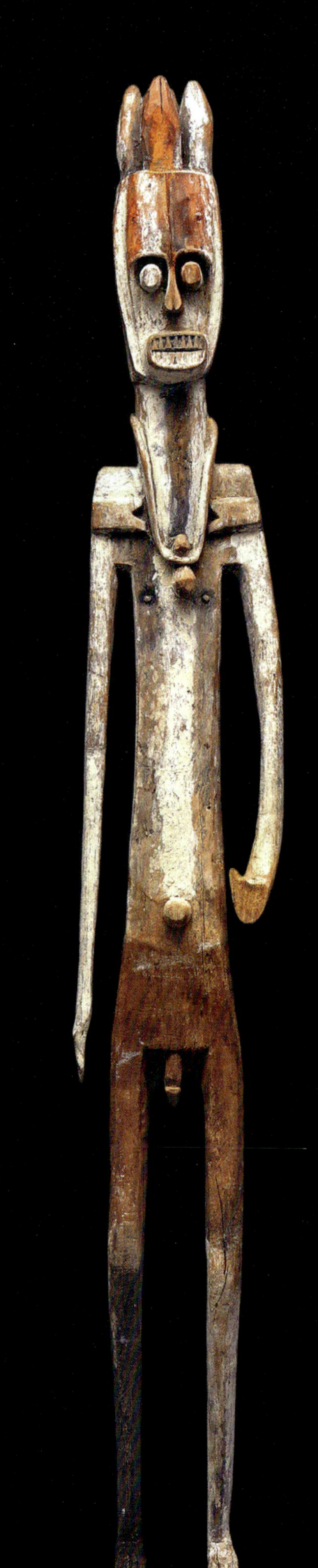

goods and regalia. For the cultures and societies that supplicated and venerated such artworks, they are the font of blessings and the answers to prayers for power and success.

Symbolic Weaponry

Military weapons, especially axes, clubs, and swords, have long been transformed by master artisans into exotic and often hypertrophic forms that were expensive to craft and, by their nature, rare. Such faux weapons, created from expensive materials, especially jewels and minerals like gold and silver, are decorated and embellished for an aristocratic and elite social class. What marks these goods as symbolic weaponry is that they exceed the artistic requirements for functional, mundane military weapons and were instead employed as political and ritual goods denoting privilege, rank, and status, communicating through metaphors and symbols the political potency of highly ranked and successful leaders.

In the ancient world, power was often based on wealth, and so symbolic weaponry identified the owner's social importance and prestige. The association of non-functional, exotic weapons with those in aristocratic positions was illustrated in artistic production as well as ritual performance. In many instances they were more than highly decorated objects—they were envisioned as weapons of the gods, imbued with agency and having a respected history, pedigree, and tradition. Thus, symbolic weapons possessed magical qualities that could be acquired, transferred, or transmitted to their owners through prayer, sacrifice, and supplication to the deities.

Symbolic weaponry often reveals mythic narratives that have long vanished, but the actors and motifs depicted on ancient art may be discerned or interpreted to some extent based on iconographic interpretations of the supernatural beings portrayed. This middle Bronze Age silver cast shaft-hole axe with gold foil depicts a complex cosmological scene replete with a bird-headed, other-than-human being that grapples with a horned, winged dragon and a wild boar (**28**).[25] The dragon-like being has a feline body; its bird talons, curled beard, single horn, and wings symbolize the Iranian Shimashki dynasty (ca. 2100–1900 BCE), which reigned in the ancient region of Elam, to the southeast of Babylonia. The exquisite axe comes from the western Central Asian Bactria-Margiana archaeological complex (Oxus civilization, ca. 2250–1700 BCE) in modern Afghanistan, Tajikistan, and Uzbekistan. The Oxus civilization rose from Neolithic populations that migrated into the northern reaches of the Middle East. Close ties with the Harappans, the Persians, and the Sumerians, as well as nomadic pastoralists of the Eurasian Steppe, suggest the Oxus civilization participated in widespread exchange and trade with the great civilizations of the ancient world located in the Indus Valley, the Iranian Plateau, and Mesopotamia. Such a mythic scene informs the contemporary and modern viewer of an ancient ruler defeating and subduing their neighboring enemies, one epitomized as a horned being and another as a wild boar.

While symbolic axes may have been functional to some extent, their primary purpose was to exhibit the

28 Shaft-Hole Axe Head with Bird-Headed Demon, Boar, and Dragon

Bactria-Margiana Archaeological Complex,
Turkmenistan
Bronze Age, 2300 – 1700 BCE
Silver and gold foil
4 ½ x 5 ⅞ in., 10.8 × 15 cm
Metropolitan Museum of Art, New York
Purchase, Harris Brisbane Dick Fund, and James N.
Spear and Schimmel Foundation Inc. Gifts, 1982

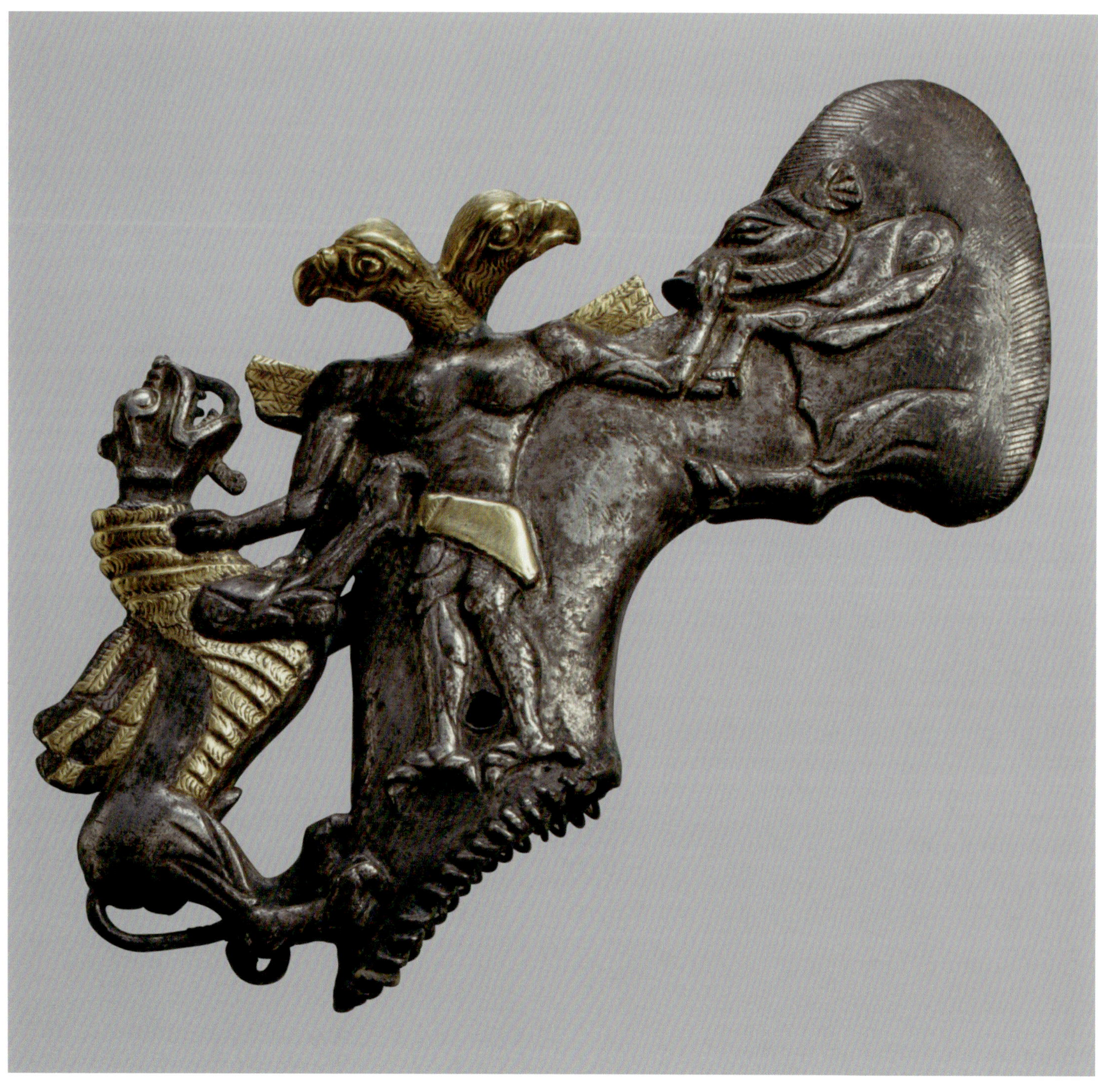

China
Tang dynasty, 618 – 907 CE
Gilt bronze
6 ¾ × 3 ⅞ in., 17.1 × 9.8 cm
Metropolitan Museum of Art, New York
Rogers Fund, 1916

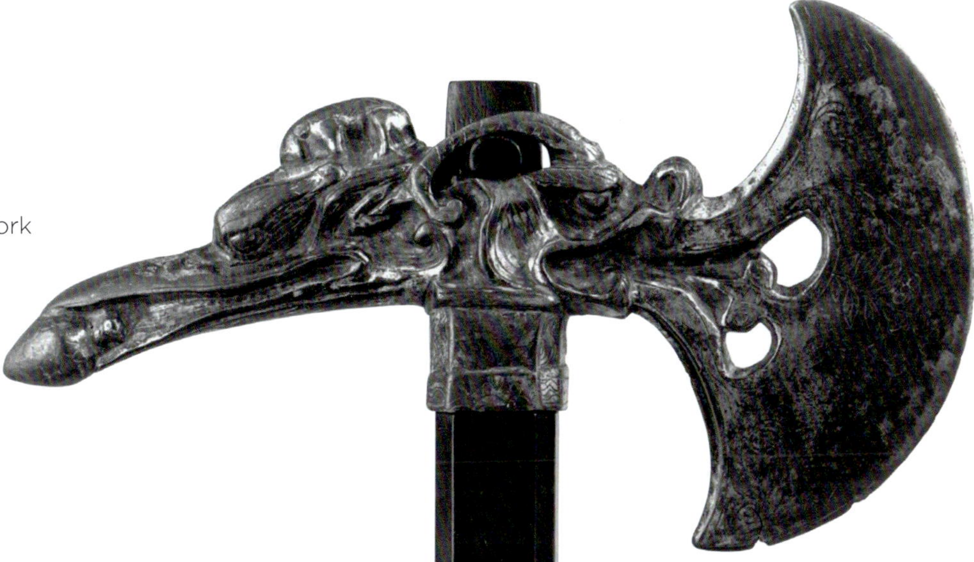

spiritual power of mythical beings in both their form and manufacture. The Chinese Tang dynasty (618–907) produced elite metalwork of superb quality, like this gilt bronze ceremonial axe depicting a composite mythological scene (**29**).[26] Such axes may have been the personal weaponry of guardsmen or warriors with sufficient status to possess weapons of fine workmanship appropriate for display and use in Tang imperial palaces. Symbolic weaponry, infused with spiritual power, denoted authority and nobility, providing the legitimacy of privileges and rank for the owner.

The Tang dynasty was founded by the Lǐ family, who seized power during the decline and collapse of the preceding Sui Empire (581–618), but was interrupted when Empress Wu Zetian (reigned 690–705), the only female emperor of imperial China, seized the throne. Scholars regard the Tang dynasty as a golden age of art and literature—the capital, Chang'an, was the world's most populous city at the time. Great achievements in art include a flowering of creativity in calligraphy, dance, literature, music, painting, poetry, and sculpture—over 48,900 poems were penned by some 2,200 poets. The Silk Road, an intercontinental trade route reopened by the Tang emperors in 639, provided contacts with India and the Middle East and promoted large-scale production of goods for overseas export. The Tang dynasty possessed a strong military based on a local militia system that could be quickly mobilized in time of war, which translated into an effective taxation and tribute system. In addition to axes, personal military offensive weapons included composite bows and crossbows, lances, and swords, prompting the creation of exotic and expensive symbolic weaponry.

Symbolic weaponry serves many functions, including display during ritual performances in which nobles and sovereigns proclaim their political clout. Another example is found in the Chimú civilization, also known as the Kingdom of Chimor, which flourished on the northern coast of Peru between the twelfth and fifteenth centuries. This was the second-largest empire in the Andean world, and their capital at Chan Chan covered some twenty square kilometers and had a population of up to 40,000 people, including some 26,000 craftspeople. Artisans were often forcibly removed from conquered polities to work in the various craft compounds at Chan Chan, creating elite prestige goods manufactured from precious minerals such as emeralds, gold, and silver. Popular designs and iconographic motifs include open-armed figures wearing headdresses and double-headed "rainbow" serpents.

30   Ceremonial Knife (*Tumi*)

Chimu culture, North Coast, Peru
1100 – 1470
Gold with turquoise inlays
13 ⅜ × 5 in., 34 × 12.7 cm
Art Institute of Chicago
Ada Turnbull Hertle Endowment

Symbolic weapons such as this Chimú gold *tumi* or ceremonial knife were made for rulers to hold as scepters, serving as signs of high office or being deployed as exotic sacrificial weapons during ritual theatrics (**30**). This *tumi* was created from gold with turquoise inlay between 1100 and 1470. As earlier Moche political dominance began to wane after about 750, new polities began to emerge; the first was Lambayeque between around 750 and 1375. The heroic founder, Naymlap, believed to have sprouted wings and flown into the sunset, is likely the figure depicted on the top of this symbolic knife. *Tumi* mimic mundane copper knives employed in sacrifices involving the decapitation of battle or war captives. Such weaponry was crafted in royal workshops by master artisans and awarded to high officials during ritual events as emblems of authority, privilege, and rank.[27] Dynastic Chimú rulers would have carried such weaponry during important ceremonies.

Ceremonial swords are important forms of symbolic weaponry for the West African Yoruba who live in modern Benin, Nigeria, and Togo, constituting one of the largest ethnic groups of Africa, with a population of more than 50 million people.[28] The Oyo Empire, a Yoruba state in present-day Nigeria, was one of the most important states in West Africa from the mid-seventeenth to the late eighteenth century. The empire was controlled by an *oba* with access to wealth through slavery, trade, and warfare. Oya, known for its ivory carving tradition, produced this Yoruba ceremonial dance sword (*udamalore*, meaning "sword of the well born") created from ivory with coconut shell inlay (**31**). This was the prestigious weaponry of a high-ranking *oba* worn by Owo rulers and their highest-ranking chiefs.[29] Sitting on the left hip above a distinctive skirt and hung over an elaborate belt, these ceremonial swords denote the chief's authority, power, status, and wealth; they were thrown into the air during public ceremonies and rituals. A coral, open-work cap sits on the figure's head, which has a coiffure of repeated chevrons; the eyes are augmented with dark, inlaid wood. The blade is decorated with two Solomon's knot patterns, which are quasi-heraldic symbols of Yoruba royalty. An Owo chief in ceremonial dress is depicted wearing an *udamalore* on the left hip. The *oba* holds an upraised, curved sword in his right hand; while this is a symbolic weapon, it mimics those used in combat. A bird perched on his left hand, pecking at his royal crown, symbolizes spiritual powers, especially of the ancestors, who protect the owner. The bird is also a metaphor for women's spiritual powers, which are crucial to a ruler's longevity.

Ceremonial dance swords were important ritual and status objects not only in the Owa kingdom but also in the royal courts of neighboring Benin. This mid- to late nineteenth-century iron wedge-shaped sword and its leather sheath would have been brandished during Benin court ceremonies by Edo nobles and kings (**32**).[30] The single-edge sword enlarges to the end and has an ivory handle that terminates in the head of a leopard, the eyes of which are inlaid with lead. Two serpents decorate the pommel's base. The scabbard has alternating human and tortoise figures on green plush and red cloth and the sword's belt terminates in tassels. The Solomon's knot symbolizes Benin royalty. The sword's spiritual potency

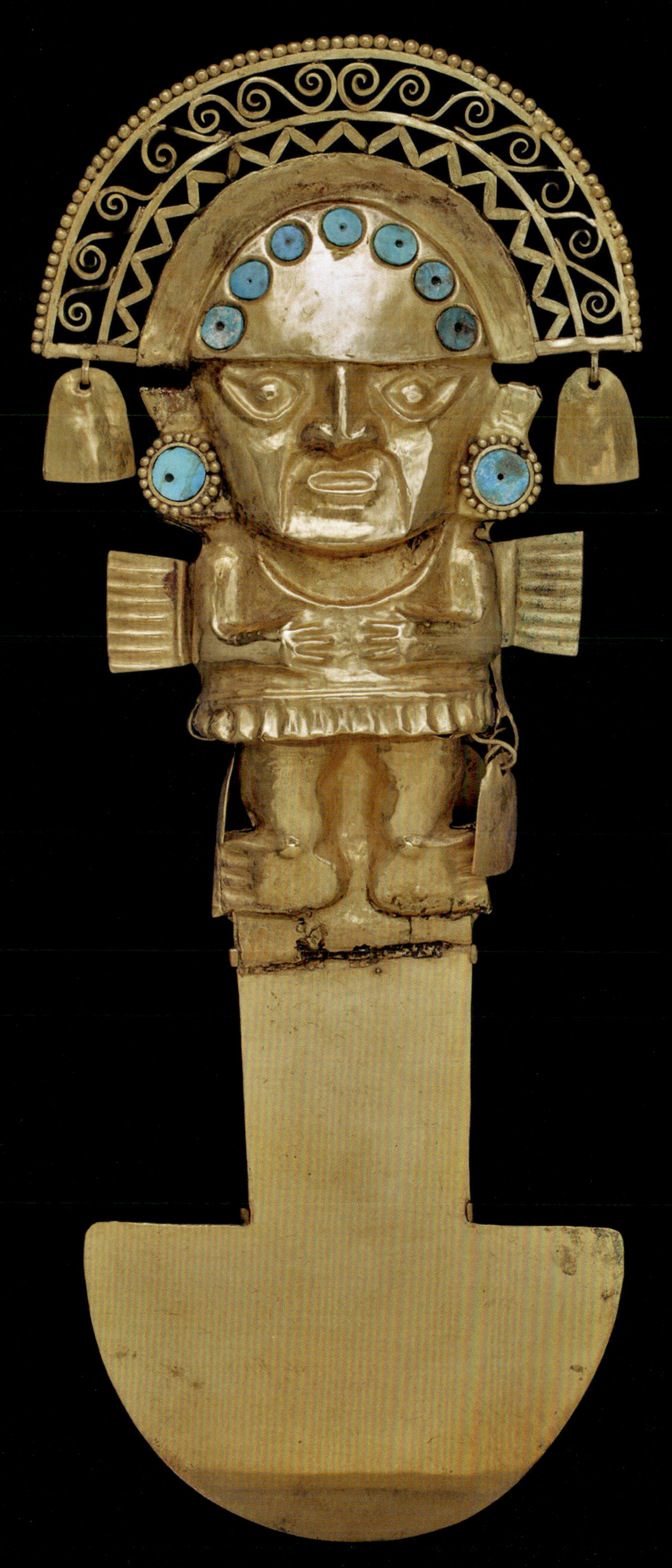

31 Ceremonial Sword (*Udamalore*)

Yoruba culture, Nigeria
1600 – 1800
Ivory, wood, or coconut shell inlay
5 × 2 × 19 ¼ in., 12.7 × 5.1 × 48.9 cm
Metropolitan Museum of Art, New York
Gift of Mr. and Mrs. Klaus G. Perls, 1991

32 Ceremonial Sword and Sheath

Edo culture, Court of Benin, Nigeria
1856 – 1897
Iron, ivory, silk, wool, cotton, yarn, leather,
metal tacks, staples
24 ⅛ × 7 ⅜ × 1 ½ in., 61.3 × 18.7 × 10.8 cm
Metropolitan Museum of Art, New York
Purchase, Rogers Fund and Frederick R. Mebel,
Fred and Rita Richman, and Noah-Sadie K. Wachtel
Foundation Inc. Gifts, 1994

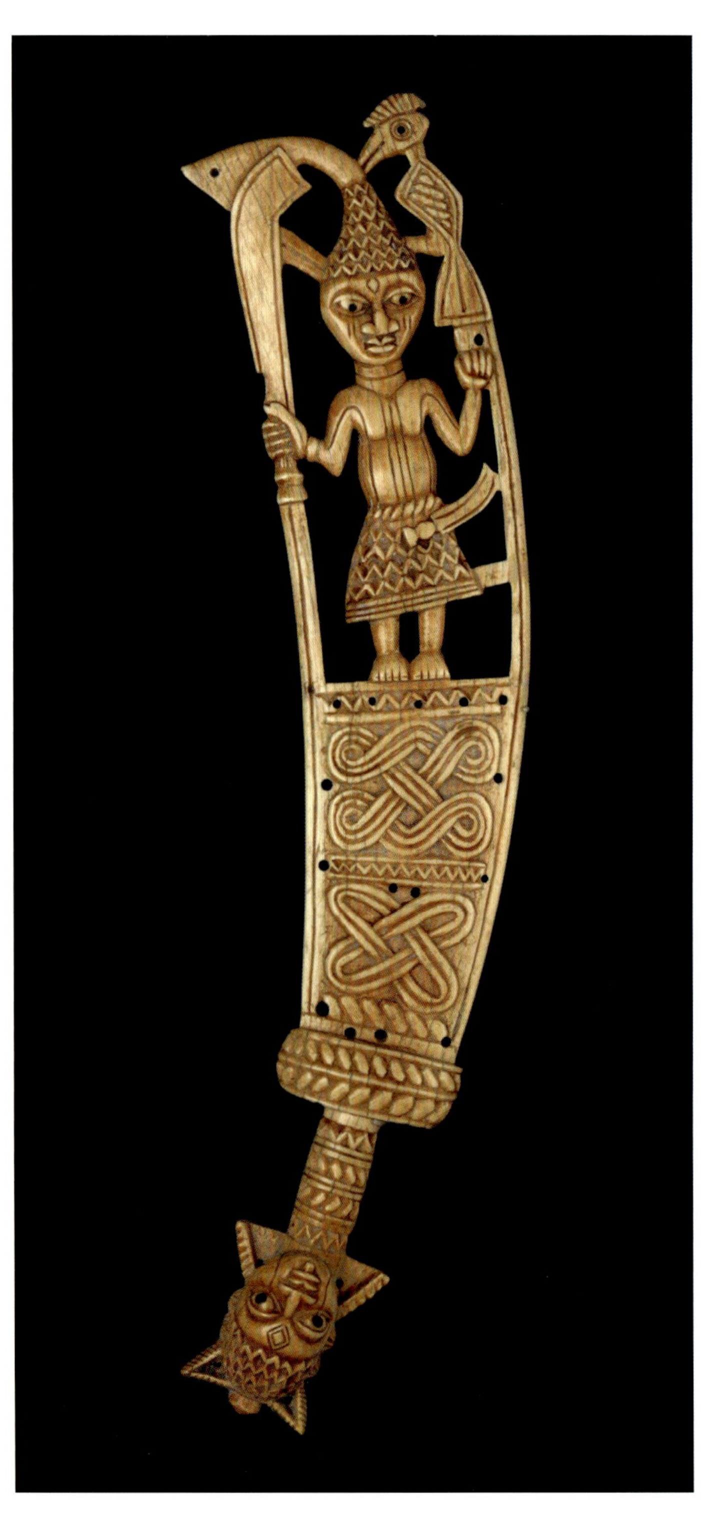

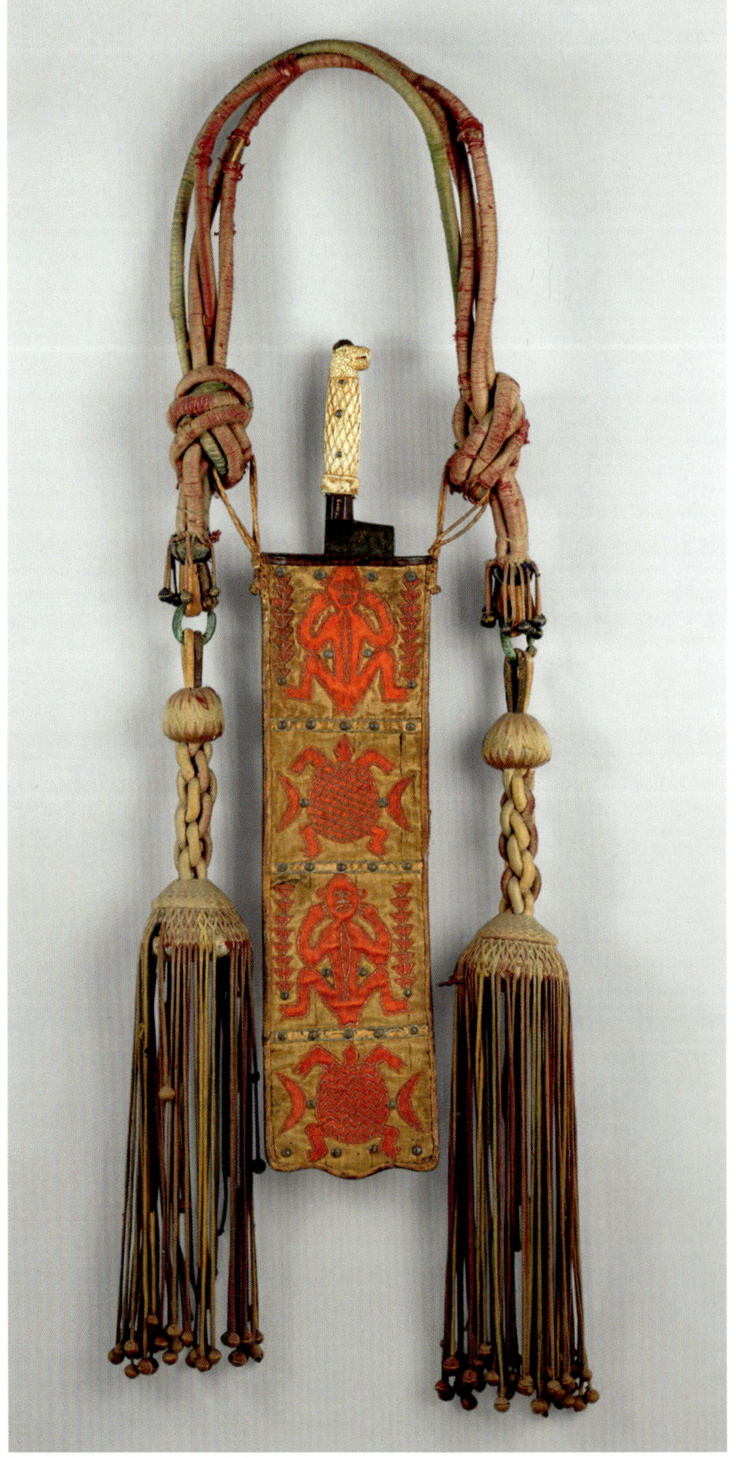

is proclaimed in its remarkable iconography, especially the cosmological associations with powerful West African animals such as elephants, leopards, and serpents.

High-ranking nobles in the Benin kingdom own dance swords that are important components of royal regalia today. During annual festivals and rituals, especially those honoring the king's ancestors, members of the court dance with their swords, tossing them in the air and swirling them about. As they approach the ancestral shrine, they touch the sword to the shrine to transfer power from one to the other. The king, as the chief priest, officiates in important rituals where the display of symbolic weaponry demonstrates prowess in warfare and efficacy in ceremonial events.

Symbolic weaponry was a crucial element of regalia in the ancient world for rulers and their noble congregations, serving the interests of elites as a display of wealth and in theatrical performances during court and palace ceremonies. Brandished, exhibited, swirled, thrown, wielded, and worn by chiefs, emperors, kings, rulers, and high-ranking elites, expensive and exotic weaponry has for millennia proclaimed the owner as a person of great influence, high status, and immense renown. The components and iconography of these symbolic weapons derives from, and is indicated by, their spiritual association with powerful other-than-human beings. For example, the inclusion of ivory in West African dance swords connects the sword with the elephant as a powerful being and a source of tremendous spirituality. The iconography of regalia weaponry often contains symbolic representations of spiritual connections to

a dangerous and powerful cosmoscape—a world of ancestors and culture heroes, deities, gods, and spirits, as well as animal masters and guardian tutelars. By demonstrating these connections to the powers residing in the other world, symbolic weapons become potent ritual implements that express the owner's authority and legitimacy.

Depictions of War Captives

Scenes of subjugation for political propaganda are widely depicted throughout history—indeed the portrayal of capture is the subject of numerous artistic expressions in which those who are victorious proclaim their dominance and power over the vanquished. These illustrate not only the capture of rivals, often noble members of adjacent polities, but also the appropriation and blessings of spiritual forces and connections to deities and gods. In this section we examine the ways in which captives are treated by rulers and represented in various artistic media to further political ends and kingly aspirations.

While the treatment of captive prisoners around the world and throughout time varies widely, the portrayal of people as living captives, mutilated prisoners, and war trophies was often meant to impress the viewer with the might and power of an elite class or powerful and prominent families. Such representations are especially vivid and widespread in the visual culture of empires, kingdoms, and states where rulers portray themselves as defenders and protectors of their borders, the faith, and

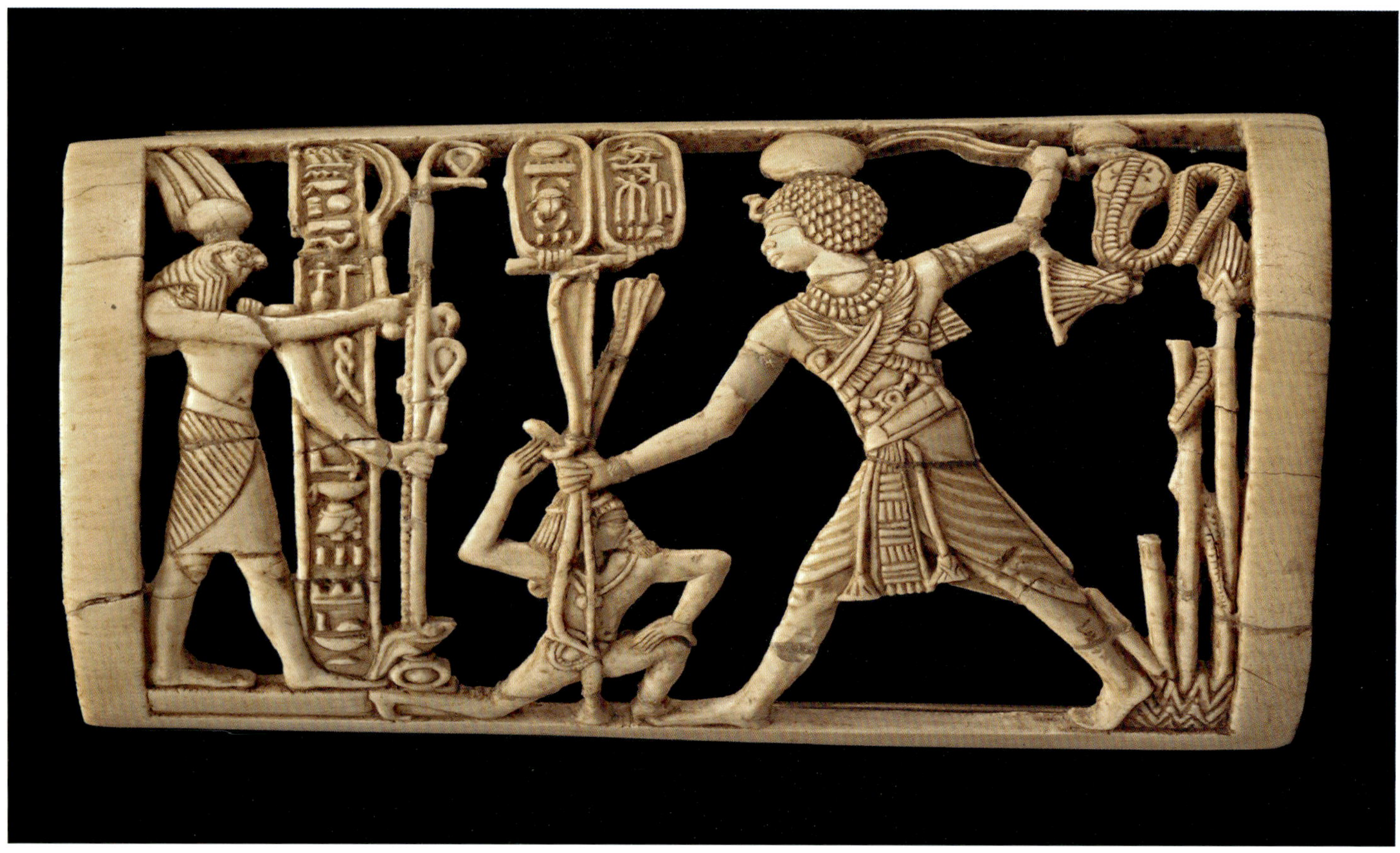

the realm. These often-violent tableaus reveal the darker side of ancient politics and showcase the aggrandizing prerogatives of leaders, especially their proclivities for aggression and violence, which were rationalized by their status as anointed and sanctioned by the gods.

Images of kings capturing, humiliating, or killing foreign elites, often their rivals on the world political stage, are commonplace in the ancient world. This intricately carved ivory arm bracer or wrist guard, for example, illustrates Thutmose IV (reigned 1400–1390 BCE) slaying an Asiatic prisoner before a god (33). Thutmose was an Egyptian pharaoh who ousted his older brother and then usurped the throne. While the depiction of Thutmose IV here may portray an actual historical event, it is more likely a symbolic representation of his punishment of rebellious Palestinian or Syrian vassals. Thutmose is crowned with a solar disc, indicating

he is being watched by or under the protection of the war-god Montu.[31]

The pharaoh was responsible for leading Egypt in times of war and Thutmose IV commanded the Egyptian army and led them into battle. If the pharaoh achieved success, he returned home as a hero. The pharaoh was responsible for defending and maintaining Egypt's borders, erecting fortifications along the Nile River, and stationing troops at strategic points along the border, thus ensuring Egypt's safety, security, and sovereignty. The pharaoh also had to deal with problems abroad by harshly crushing uprisings, as well as stamping out civil unrest. Thutmose IV exemplified his role as commander when he squashed a rebellion in Syria by leading his army into battle and defeating his enemies. This victory proved him to be an effective and powerful ruler who had the blessings of the gods, especially Montu.

Enemies and foes were treated violently throughout the world, and the ancient kingdoms of South America were no exception. The Nasca, famous for their depictions of trophy heads and weaponry, lived in the arid south coast of Peru from around 100 BCE to 800 CE. Sometime around 300 CE, ceramic depictions of trophy heads became increasingly popular in Nasca imagery. For example, this Nasca ceramic drum portrays violent themes, including depictions of elite men with trophy heads, supernatural beings brandishing decapitated heads, and warriors taking heads in armed combat (**34**). Deities and priests carry bleeding trophy heads, as a line of warriors, shown below, hold more heads and sacrificial knives while a victim is being offered for sacrifice. On the bottom level, ritually attired and masked figures brandish implements and instruments that will be used in the sacrifices. On the upper level, composite supernatural creatures combine felines, fish, and predatory bird forms, whose representations reflect the powers of the earth, sea, and sky. Another vessel illustrates a warrior figure holding a trophy head by the hair and grasping a two-handed war club (**35**).

These otherworldly beings are often depicted consuming human captives, emphasizing their role as potent symbols of elite status, magical fertility, and political efficacy.[32] Images of Nasca warriors holding weapons and trophy heads and wearing masks and headdresses of composite supernatural figures profoundly illustrate how their power derives from supernatural beings. Nasca elites and artisans chose to express political authority and social preeminence by employing violent symbols in their imagery: decapitation and trophy heads, sacrificial consumption, and victorious warriors. While these were statements of power, they also aided in invoking the magical efficacy of body parts, especially heads. Gifts to deities and violent rituals that involved human heads helped maintain cosmic balance and order for the Nasca.

Like the Nasca, the Moche of the South American Andes provide an important example of warrior ethos and the treatment of their enemies. The Moche state flourished on the north coast of Peru between 100 and 800 and master ceramicists created pottery that provides a wealth of information on Moche conflict, violence, and warfare. Warriors and their activities are commonly depicted, but much of their armed conflict appears to be ceremonial or ritual rather than militaristic. Artistic representations have been accepted by scholars as direct evidence of warfare, but art and ceremony did not always mirror the intentions or intensity of conflict and warfare.

In Moche depictions, combat is not typically expressed in terms of battles between armies, but rather as ritualized duels between high-status warriors, as indicated by their elaborate armament, dress, and ornaments. Warriors who participated in such contests might be compared with the knights of medieval Europe, who adorned themselves in their finest armor and regalia in jousting events. The focus of such ritualized combat included stunning one's rival and then capturing them, appropriating their attire as regalia trophy, leading them away nude and bleeding, and eventually displaying and ritually sacrificing them. This sequence of events is

 Container Depicting Warriors, Rulers, and Winged Beings with Trophy Heads

Nazca culture, Peru
180 BCE – 500 CE
Ceramic
50 × 45 × 45 in., 127 × 114.3 × 114.3 cm
Art Institute of Chicago
Gift of Edward and Betty Harris

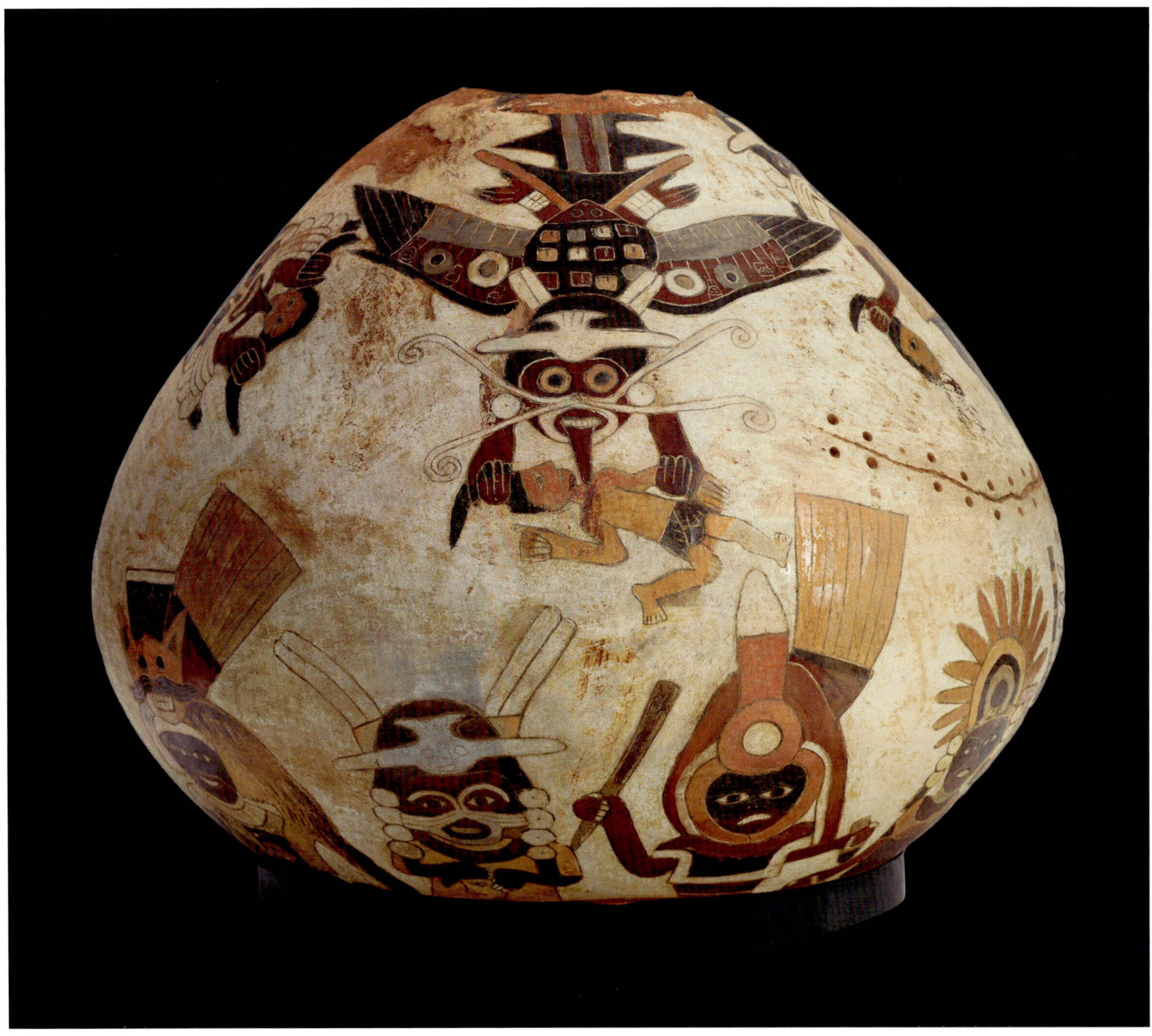

Nazca culture, Peru
100 BCE – 800 CE
Terracotta
Museum zu Allerheiligen
Schaffhausen, Switzerland

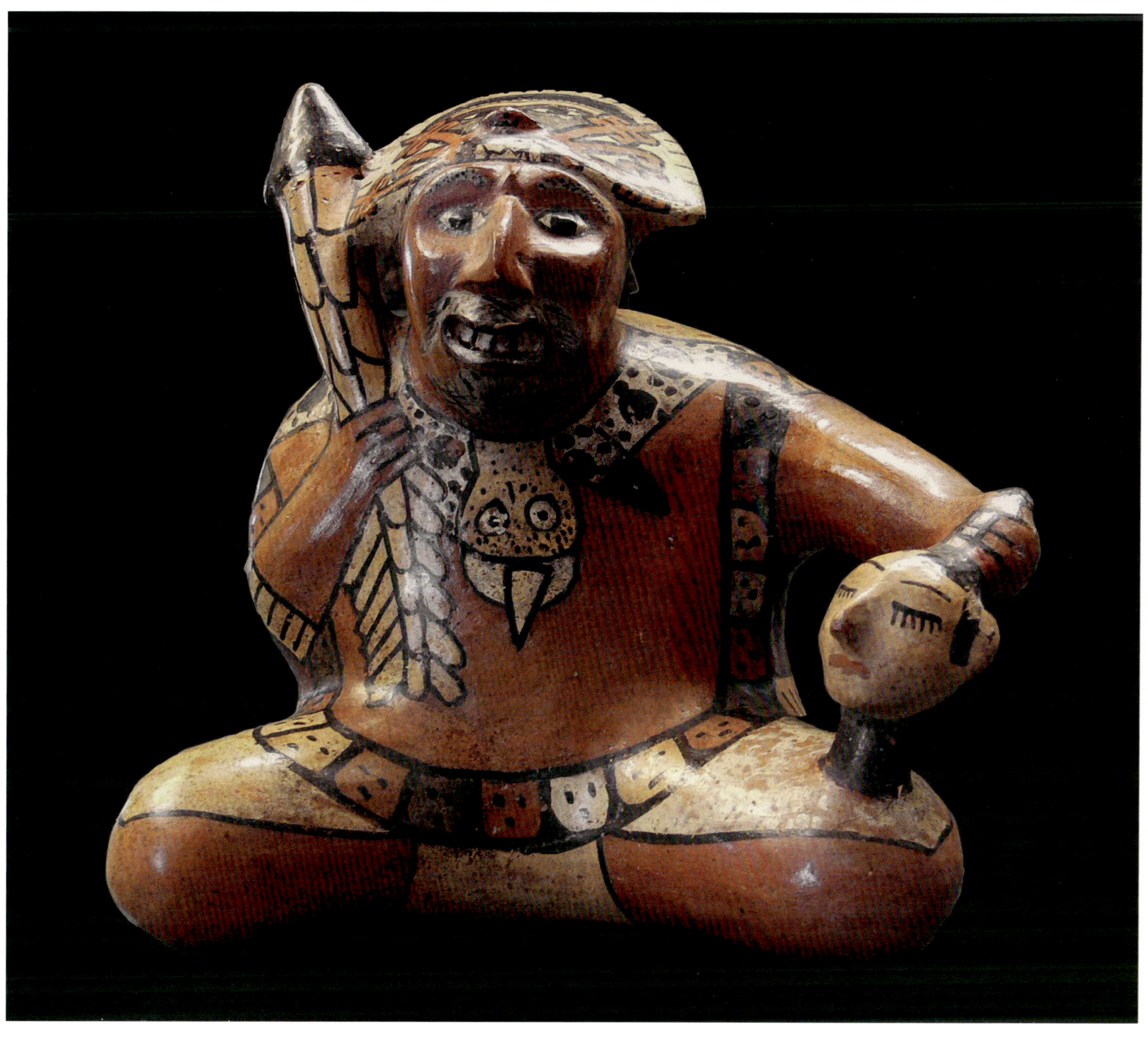

presided over by a supernatural being in whose honor the victims are taken.

The fate of such individuals is vividly illustrated in Moche ceramic art, such as this portrait vessel depicting a captive (**36**). Victors are shown stripping prisoners, draping their attire over a club, and placing a rope around the victim's neck as they are led away for eventual sacrifice. Portrait vessels also show bound prisoners awaiting judgement. Duels and subsequent sacrifices were generally staged between rival courts that competed for godly favor, prestige, and tribute. These theatrical mortal contests served as a substitute for all-out warfare, but they were nonetheless deadly and violent.[33] When pairs of warriors engaged in hand-to-hand combat, they typically fought with clubs, shields, and slings, as well as spears propelled from spear throwers (*atlatls*). The war club, employed in close combat, was a versatile hand-to-hand weapon that demonstrated a heroic form of warrior behavior in battle; in symbolic form it proclaimed office, power, and prestige.

The ancient Mesoamerican ballgame, perhaps originating earlier than 2000 BCE, was a sport with ritual overtones. Probably similar to racquetball, the object of the game was to keep the solid rubber ball in play by using only the forearms or hips. The ballgame had many layers of ritual meaning, some of which were associated with battle and decapitation. For example, enemies captured during battles might be forced to play the ballgame and then, after losing a fixed game in which they were starved and then forced to compete against veteran players,

they would be sacrificed in elaborate rituals in honor of the gods.

The Classic Veracruz culture, found in the Mexican state of Veracruz, flourished from roughly 100 to 1000. A defining characteristic of this culture is the carved stone *palma*, which served as elaborate regalia worn by ballplayers to protect their chest from the hard rubber ball's impact during the violent game. Here the ballplayer stands on a platform and wears a kilt and a padded yoke on which rests a *palma* (**37**).[34] A Veracruz innovation, the Mesoamerican *palmas* references the shape of a palm frond. This example from Nautla on the Gulf Coast juxtaposes a pointed, triangular axe in one hand with a trophy head in the other.

Axes, used to decapitate a captive, were envisioned as thunderbolts by the Maya. Such lightning or thunderbolt axes were imbued with spiritual essences and could serve as companion guardian spirits, protecting a person and providing them with the strength to overcome their captured opponents in the ballgame as well as their enemies in battle. Those with access to such life forces were able to command the power that resided in the axe and achieve success through the spiritual strength the axe imparted. Axes provided a powerful message of dominance, prowess, and subjugation, reminding the viewer of the grim fate of prisoners.[35] In Mesoamerica, ballplayers retained the heads of their captives, which had been taken through the force of the axe, as trophies. These trophy heads were thought to possess the captive's life force, which could be reallocated or transferred to the

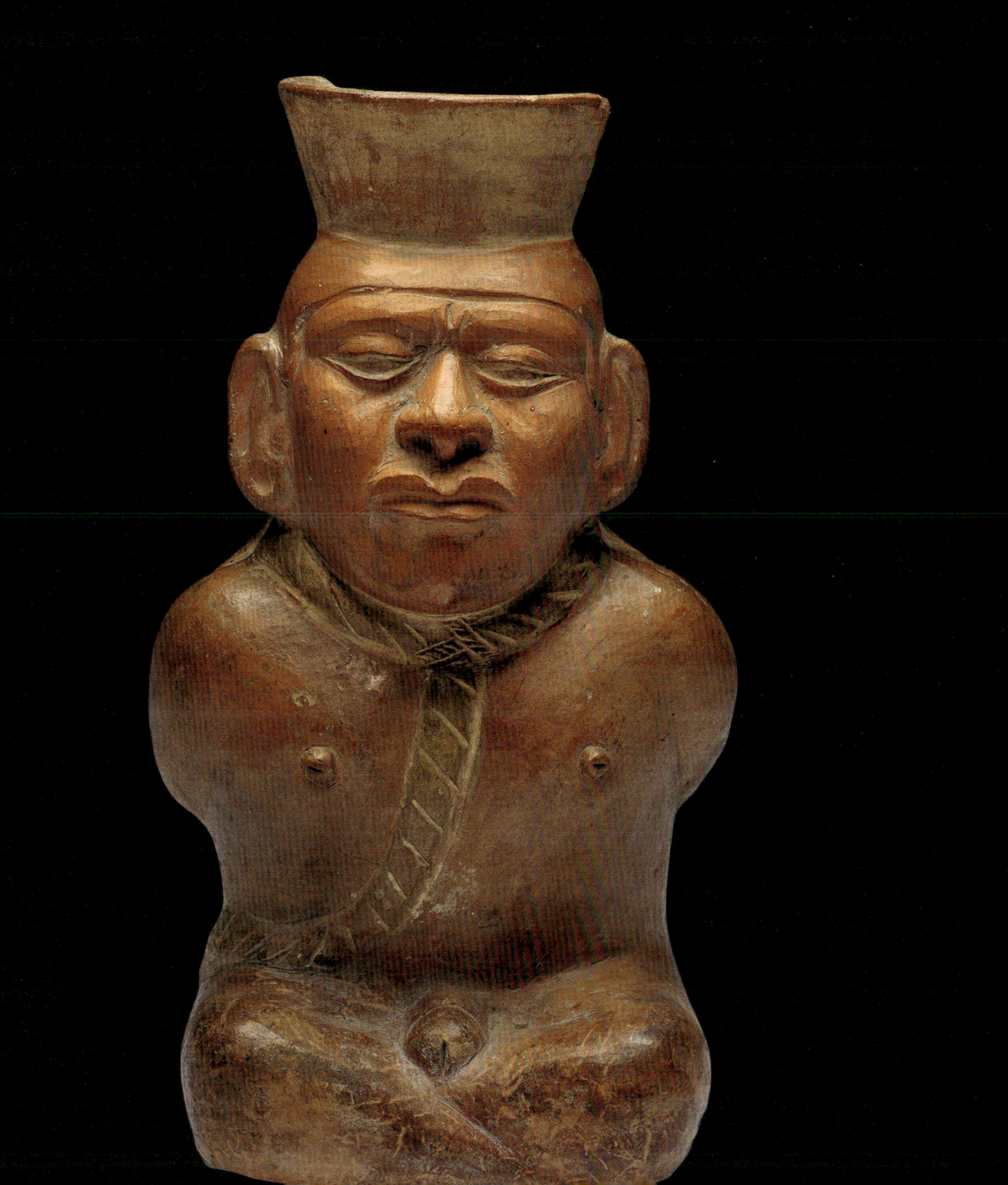

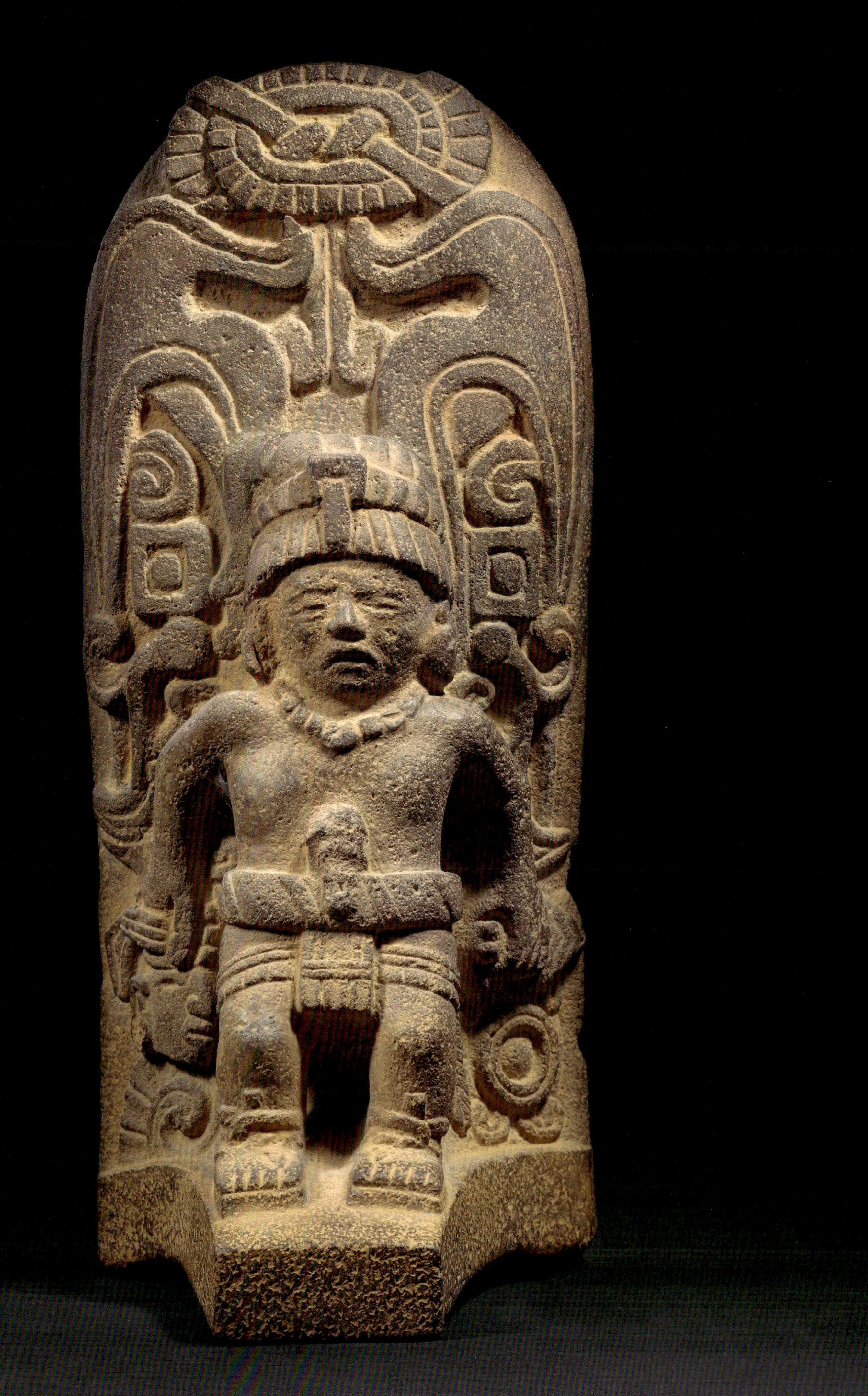

person who had obtained the head through capture and decapitation, thus prolonging their own life.

To the north of Mexico, the Mimbres people (1050–1150), a sub-group of the Mogollon culture, lived in southwestern New Mexico in compact adobe villages; they recorded their beliefs and cosmology on the interior of ceramic bowls.[36] This painted bowl depicts a decapitation scene, but rather than illustrating an historic event, the image portrays the Hero Twins engaging in one of many demonstrations of their performance of miraculous acts, including reviving the dead and shapeshifting (**38**). Here, one twin beheads his brother with a rabbit stick, a simple wooden throwing club used to hunt rabbits. Although seemingly dead, the decapitated twin is revived by his brother; a thin lifeline connects the severed head with the body.

Throughout North America the Hero Twins serve as powerful examples of how those with co-essences or spirit helpers could draw upon the powers of tutelars. The figural cape on the back of the twin holding the rabbit stick is a horned serpent, perhaps illustrating the source of the twins' supernatural efficacy. Such spiritual powers were demonstrated in dramatic legerdemain theatrics where animals and people were "killed" and then brought back to life. Such magical performances proved to spellbound audiences that some individuals, especially those who were members of medicine societies, possessed awesome powers, and that those powers could be deployed to heal the sick or to take life from one's enemies. Life essences obtained from one individual through decapitation of a captive, for example, could be used to add that person's remaining years

of life to those of the one who took the head or other body part. Illustrations of magical theatrics proclaimed one's access to spiritual powers bestowed by other-than-human beings.

Throughout the world, the political authority of kings was mediated through artistic portrayals, religious spectacles, and symbols of violence focusing on captives taken in battle. Political dynamics fomented by kings dominated court and state conflicts over captives, resources, and trade routes, resulting in highly competitive political landscapes consisting of interpolity conflicts, political intrigues, and sectional revolts. However, conflict and warfare often aided kings in acquiring sources of power and prestige based on their personal charisma and the wealth that enabled them to command and field armed forces. The capture of high-ranking enemies validated a king's connections with supernatural forces and provided justification and legitimation for further bloodshed and violence.

Conclusion

The record of violence that exists today in imagery represents some 5000 years of conflict and warfare based on the research of archaeologists, art historians, and epigraphers, which offers unique contributions to the study of human social conflict and violence through time. Depictions of political aggrandizement, self-deification, and social conflict alert us to the changing nature of violence and warfare, and the conditions under which

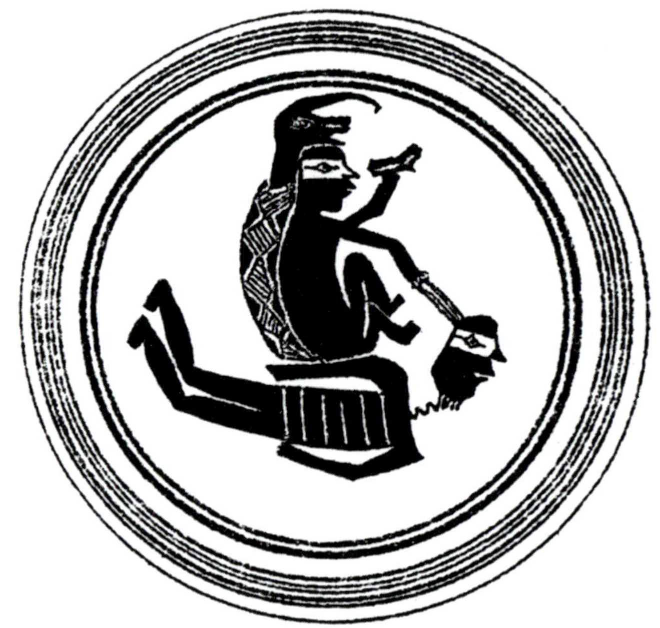

they existed. While levels of conflict varied, along with its intensity and scale, rulers invariably employed and escalated violence, often in tandem with overtures of alliance and cooperation, to achieve their goals. Common themes in the representation of violence may be identified, but several are central to societies throughout the world. Ancient cultures have engaged in the production of art depicting elites and violence, the portrayal of combat, the deities or gods of war, symbolic weaponry, and the treatment of captives. The importance of such artistic productions and the labor required to create them point to their significance as potent statements of the power and wealth of successful rulers and the devastation, misery, and suffering they inflicted on those who were defeated. Success in conflict and warfare revealed in artistic depictions routinely communicates that a ruler's connections to the supernatural realm and the gods to whom they prayed are the basis for their success.

Highly crafted images and performative acts expressed messages through records of conflict and violence. Often, two people are portrayed in combat, which serves as a metaphor for ruling elites and their battles against their rivals. Victory is the subject of many grand images that adorn defensive gates as well as palace walls, personal regalia, and ritual goods.

An additional genre of images includes warriors with weapons of battle. The gods of war include deities engaged in mortal combat and mythic scenes in which the gods serve as models for human behavior, demonstrating the ways ancient elites employed religion and ritual in their pursuit of political agendas. Symbolic weaponry directs our attention to the role played by martial regalia as a powerful form for legitimizing elite aggrandizement and authority through dramatic performance and sanctifying iconography. Finally, artistic depictions of ceremonies and rituals include the humiliation, enslavement, and sacrifice of captives and the crafting, display, and ritual use of body parts from vanquished enemies. These acts demonstrated in visual form the loss of power by rival polities and their leaders.

War in premodern societies changed over time and exhibits tremendous diversity. It may be infused with religious meanings, as well as being guided by cultural norms. But the practice of war and the creation of images of war were at their most basic level political acts and thus laden with political signals. Kings-as-warriors promoted imagery, propaganda, and spectacles that underscored the nature of political authority and this imagery permeated human social histories throughout the world.[37]

1   Günther Hölbl, *A History of the Ptolemaic Empire* (New York: Routledge, 2001).

2   Karen Bassie-Sweet, *Maya Gods of War* (Louisville: University Press of Colorado, 2021).

3   Antonio Beltran, *Rock Art of the Spanish Levant; The Imprint of Man* (New York: Cambridge University Press, 1982).

4   Roberto Risch and Harald Meller, "The Representation of Violence in the Rock Art of the Sahara and the Spanish Levant," in *European Archaeology: Identities and Migrations*, ed. Laurence Manolakakis, Nathan Schlanger, and Anick Coudart (Leiden: Sidestone Press, 2017), 371–85.

5   Åsa Fredell, Kristen Kristiansen, and Felipe C. Boado, eds., *Representations and Communications: Creating an Archaeological Matrix of Late Prehistoric Rock Art* (Oxford: Oxbow Books, 2010).

6   Richard L. Zettler, Lee Horne, Donald P. Hansen, and Holly Pittman, *Treasures from the Royal Tombs of Ur* (Philadelphia: University of Pennsylvania, Museum of Archaeology, 1998).

7   Davide Nadali, "When Ritual Meets Art. Rituals in the Visual Arts versus Visual Arts in Rituals: The Case Study of Ancient Mesopotamia," in *Approaching Rituals in Ancient Cultures*, ed. Claus Ambos and Lorenzo Verderame (Rome: Fabrizio Serra, 2013), 209–26.

8   Christine Desroches-Noblecourt, *Life and Death of a Pharaoh: Tutankhamen* (New York: New York Graphic Society, 1963).

9   http://inscriptionslibrary.bibalex.org/presentation/monument.aspx?lang=en&ins_id=13&mon_id=4125#ad-image-0.

10 Uzume Z. Wijnsma, "The Worst Revolt of the Bisitun Crisis: A Chronological Reconstruction of the Egyptian Revolt Under Petubastis V," *Journal of Near Eastern Studies* 77, no. 2 (2018): 157–73.

11 Olga Palagia, *Regional Schools in Hellenistic Sculpture* (Oxford: Oxbow Books, 1998).

12 David M. Wilson, *The Bayeux Tapestry* (New York: Thames and Hudson, 1985).

13 Barbara Plakensteiner, ed., *Benin: Kings and Rituals: Court Arts from Nigeria* (Chicago: Art Institute of Chicago, 2007).

14 Jeffrey M. Hurwit, "Reading the Chigi Vase," *Hesperia: The Journal of the American School of Classical Studies at Athens* 71, no. 1 (2002): 1–22.

15 Constantine Petridis, ed., *Speaking of Objects: African Art at the Art Institute of Chicago* (Chicago: Art Institute of Chicago, 2020).

16 Anthony J. Bryant, *Sekigahara 1600: The Final Struggle for Power*, Osprey Campaign Series 40 (Oxford: Osprey Publishing, 1995).

17 Helen C. McCullough, *The Tale of the Heike* (Palo Alto: Stanford University Press, 1988).

18 Janet C. Berlo, *Spirit Beings and Sun Dancers: Black Hawk's Vision of the Lakota World* (New York: Braziller, 2000).

19 Josefine Kuckertz and Angelika Lohwasser, *Introduction to the Religion of Kush* (Dettelbach: J. H. Röll Verlag, 2019).

20 Mary Beard, John North, and Simon Price, *Religions of Rome: A History* (New York: Cambridge University Press, 1998).

21 John Siudmak, "The Hindu-Buddhist Sculpture of Ancient Kashmir and Its Influences," in *Handbook of Oriental Studies: Section 2: South Asia* (Boston: Brill, 2013).

22 Barend J. ter Haar, *Guan Yu: The Religious Afterlife of a Failed Hero* (Oxford: Oxford University Press, 2017).

23 Peter Brunt and Thomas Nicholas, eds., *Oceania* (London: Royal Academy of Arts, 2018).

24 Elias Courson and Michael E. Odijie, "Egbesu: An African Just War Philosophy and Practice," *Journal of African Cultural Studies* 32, no. 4 (2020): 493–508.

25 Joan Aruz, ed., *Art of the First Cities: The Third Millennium B.C. from the Mediterranean to the Indus* (New York: Metropolitan Museum of Art, 2003).

26 Cao Yin, ed., *Tang: Treasures from the Silk Road Capital* (Sydney: Art Gallery of New South Wales, 2016).

27 Richard F. Townsend, *Indian Art of the Americas at the Art Institute of Chicago* (Chicago: Art Institute of Chicago, 2016).

28 Henry J. Drewal, *Yoruba: Nine Centuries of African Art and Thought* (New York: Center for African Art, 1989).

29 Kate Ezra, *Royal Art of Benin: The Perls Collection in the Metropolitan Museum of Art* (New York: Metropolitan Museum of Art, 1992).

30 Robin Poynor, "Edo Influence on the Arts of the Owo," *African Arts* 9, no. 4 (1976): 40–45, 90.

31 Richard H. Wilkinson, *The Complete Gods and Goddesses of Ancient Egypt* (New York: Thames and Hudson, 2003).

32 Elizabeth N. Arkush, *War, Spectacle, and Politics in the Ancient Andes* (New York: Cambridge University Press, 2022).

33 Townsend, *Indian Art of the Americas*.

34 Stuart Handler, Hugh Thomas, and Joanne Stuhr, *Traveling with Cortés and Pizarro: Discovering Fine Pre-Columbian Art* (Milan: 5Continents Publishing, 2018).

35 Carrie A. Berryman, "Captive Sacrifice and Trophy Taking Among the Ancient Maya: An Evaluation of the Bioarchaeological Evidence and Its Sociopolitical Implications," in *The Taking and Displaying of Human Body Parts as Trophies by Amerindians*, ed. Richard J. Chacon and David H. Dye (New York: Springer, 2007), 377–99.

36 Steven A. LeBlanc, *Painted by a Distant Hand: Mimbres Pottery from the American Southwest* (Cambridge, MA: Peabody Museum Press, 2005).

37 I am grateful to Stuart Handler for his invitation to participate in this wonderful volume and for his encouragement, insights, and support throughout the writing process. Lisa Bessette's editorial eye improved the text, sharpened the argument, and helped shape the contents. Christian Ruiz performed a remarkable job in helping to select and organize the chapter's images. Finally, I give my heartfelt thanks to my wife, Debbie, for whom all things are possible.

VII

PORTRAYING OURSELVES AND OTHERS

JOHN F. SCOTT

Said Life to Art—"I love thee best
Not when I find in thee
My very face and form, expressed
With dull fidelity,
But when in thee my craving eyes
Behold continually
The mystery of my memories
And all I long to be."

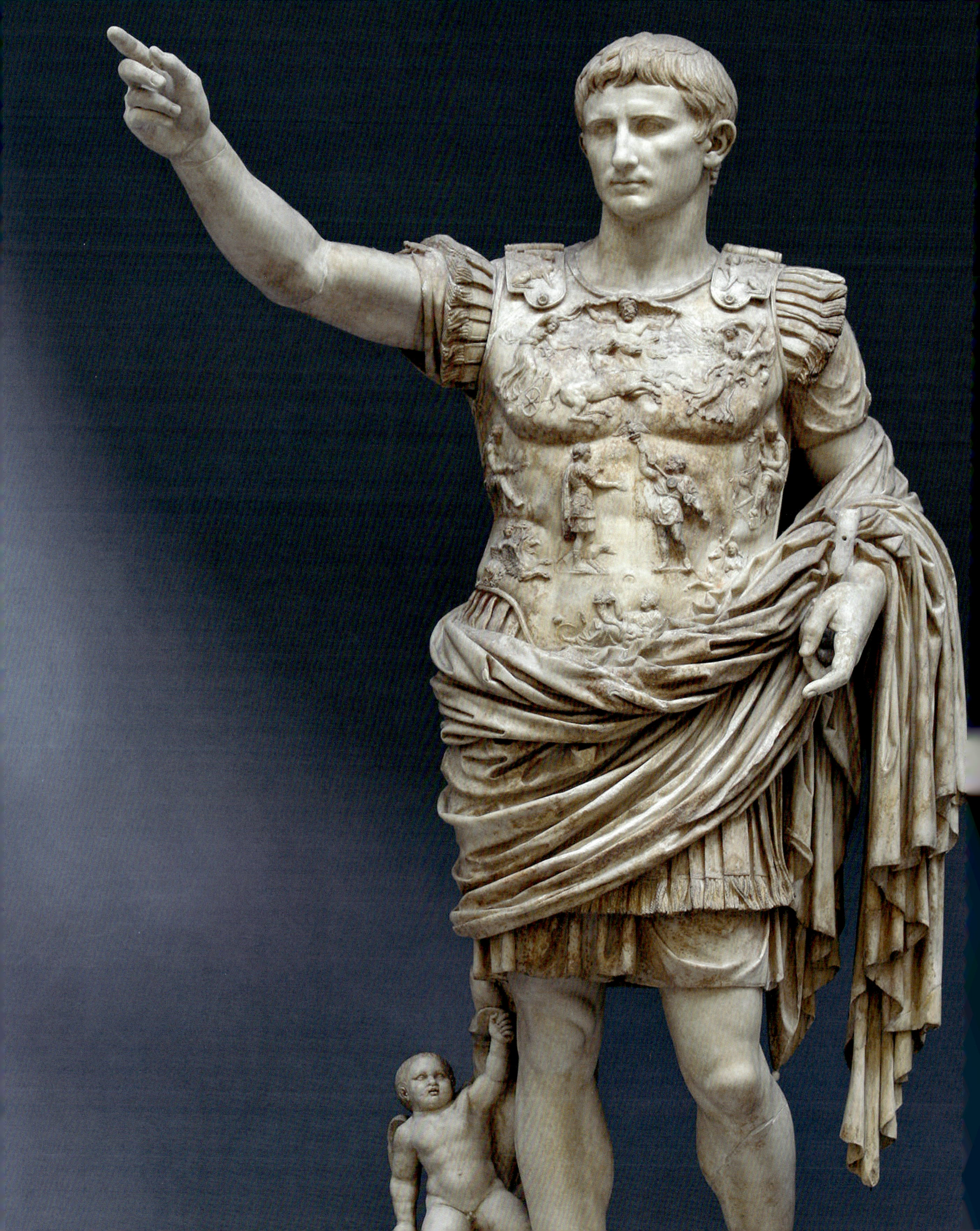

During the long history of humankind on earth, the way artists among different groups of people have chosen to represent them in their art has depended on the group's degree of social complexity and their relationship with nature. In this chapter, I divide human groups into five categories: small bands of hunter-gatherers surrounded by large mammals; nomadic larger bands in a world inhabited by smaller animal prey; horticultural settled villagers; larger agricultural towns ruled by hereditary chiefs; and city-states ruled typically by kings. This reflects the division of human societies proposed by the cultural anthropologist Elman Service: bands, tribes, chiefdoms, and states.[1] Each level imposed greater control over the vagaries of nature and provided its people with greater self-confidence. Artists from around the world in each of these groups reflected this self-confidence and created similar art, even sometimes using similar media. Indeed, people from different cultures and different time periods share a common expression in their art depending on how they relate to nature.

Art of Ice Age Bands

The earliest category of self-representation occurred in a world that no longer exists: the Ice Age, which ended around 10,000 BCE. We know of it mainly from Eurasia, during the period called the Upper Paleolithic, when large mammals provided the most challenging prey for hunters. Bands were comprised of modern humans, known in European archaeology as Cro-Magnons. Their art reflects that they saw humans as overpowered by those large mammals and that they did not have a high regard for themselves. They were dependent on the vagaries of nature; its great animals provided the vast majority of the subjects of cave painting, itself an attempt to capture the animals' spirits. The caves were places of transformation, where boys approaching puberty would be instructed in the lore of adult men, a practice that continued into the secret societies of horticultural settled villagers. They recorded the presence of these students by placing their hands on the cave walls and spraying pigment around them, creating a negative image. The individuality of these men is alluded to indirectly.

The only example of cave painting that represents an entire human is found in the deep well of the Lascaux cave in southwestern France (1). A giant bison, now almost extinct in Europe, has been wounded by spears thrown by humans and takes out his vengeance on what appears to be a stick figure of a man, whose gender is represented by an erect phallus but whose head is replaced by a bird-like profile. The bird might have symbolized the totem animal of the man's clan, another concept carried on into more complex groups of human society. Women are absent in the paintings found in these caves, which were not places of habitation but of mystery. They are represented instead by small, handheld sculptures that emphasize distinctive features of their gender: they have large breasts and vulvas, swollen abdomens, large hips, small legs and arms, and no facial features—these are not individual portraits (see Chapter 4: Motherhood and the Family, fig. 1). We refer to them as Venus figures but it is very doubtful that they represent goddesses, and certainly not the Roman goddess of love but rather the distinctive essence of womanhood. During the Paleolithic, humans had low regard for themselves as individuals, and their art reflects their opinion that nature was dominant and that people could only try to stay alive and reproduce themselves in order to have more help in their undertakings.

Art of Nomadic Bands

As the world warmed during the Holocene and the great Ice Age mammals went extinct, people became more numerous and achieved better control of their environments. They still were dependent on hunting and gathering, but the balance changed in favor of the latter. This era in Europe is called the Mesolithic and dates from about 10,000 to 6000 BCE. Technology became more varied as the stone tools humans created served a larger number of purposes and provided better accommodation to life's demands. People continued to paint on natural rock surfaces, but the location was more typically better lit overhanging shelters, not deep cave interiors. Humans make a regular appearance in these paintings, often in hunt scenes, where they are rendered as more equal foes to the smaller animals they pursue. The best European examples are found in the mountains of southeastern Spain, where the Valltorta Ravine painting shows a vertical line of hunters wielding bows and arrows confronting a herd of quadrupeds, likely deer (2). The surface acts as a map, plotted from above, while the men and animals are

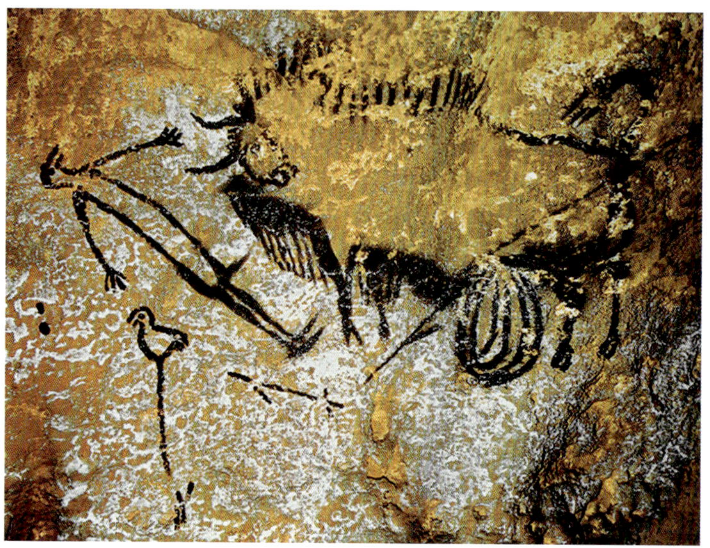

rendered in active profile positions. The proportions of the animals are quite naturalistic, but the humans are represented with exaggerated bent postures, as flexible as the bows they carry. The bodies of the men are rendered without interior details and there is no indication of facial features—the essence of individuality. While the men are subsumed as part of a group, in this case a hunting party, there is a marked confidence in the human ability to deal with nature together.

This culture of nomadic bands subsisting on gathering and hunting continued elsewhere as the great Ice Age mammals disappeared. South of the Mediterranean in the rocky outcrops of northern Africa, such cultures continued the tradition of rendering their activities on

Cave painting at Valltorta Gorge, Spain
8000 – 3000 BCE

Aboriginal culture, Ubirr,
Kadadu National Park,
Northern Territory, Australia
18,000 BCE

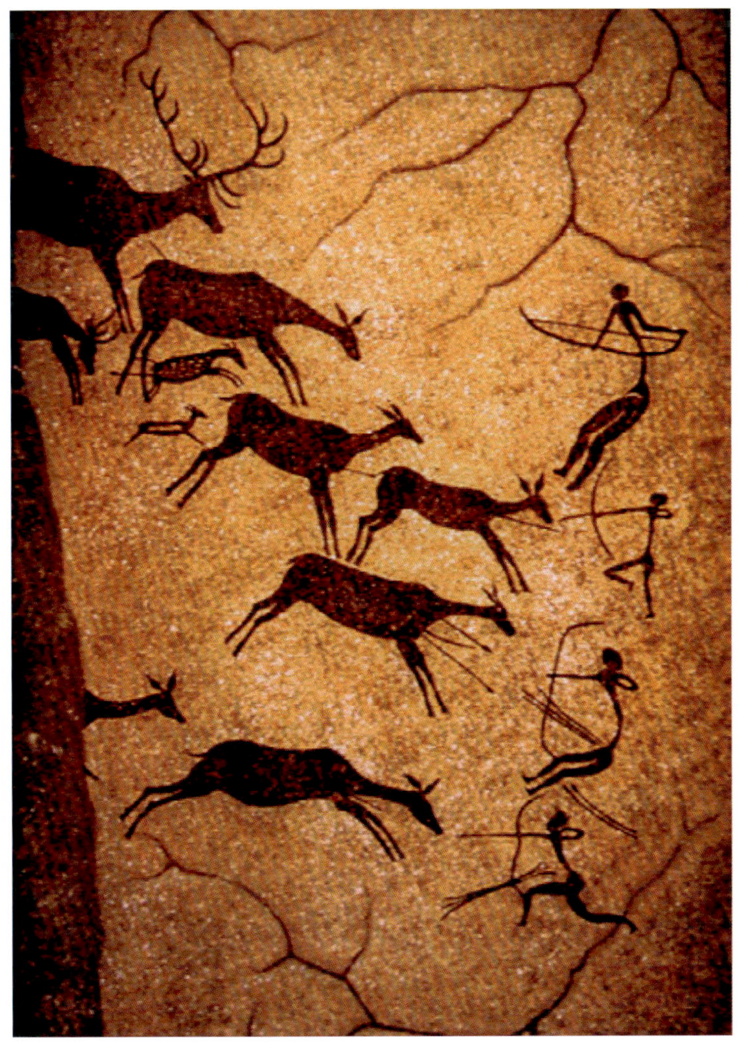

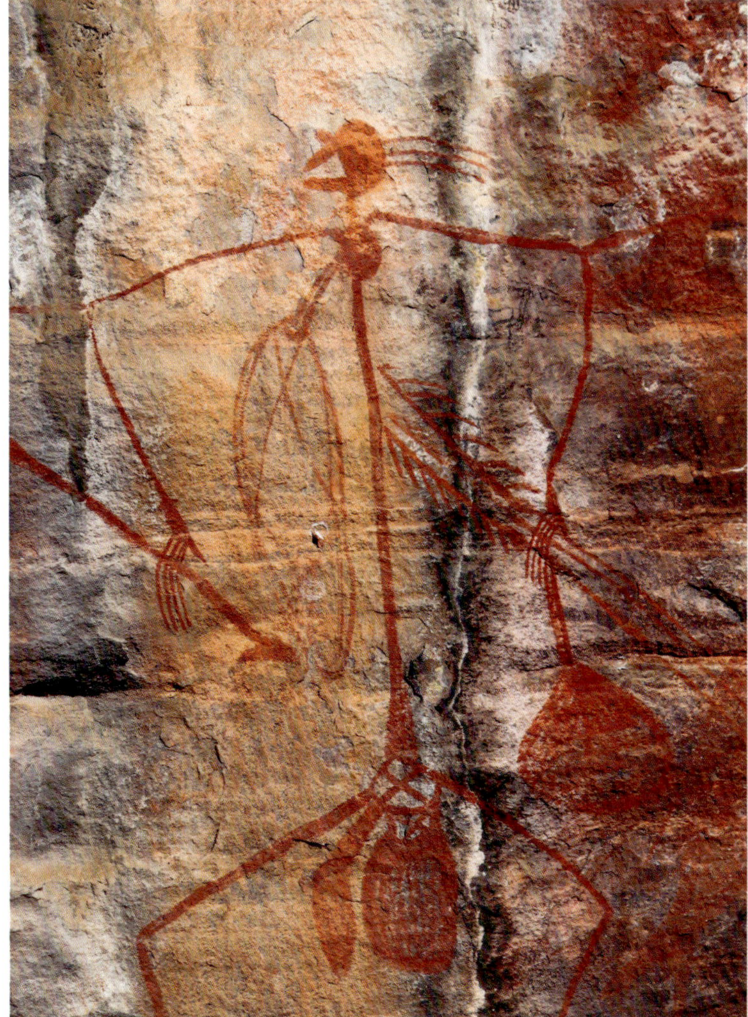

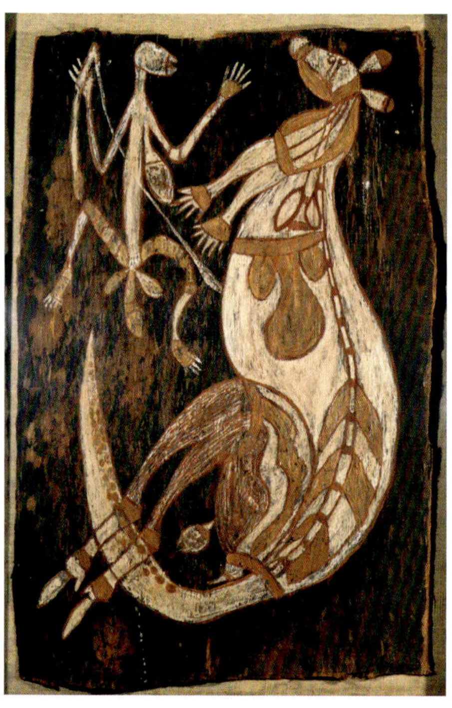

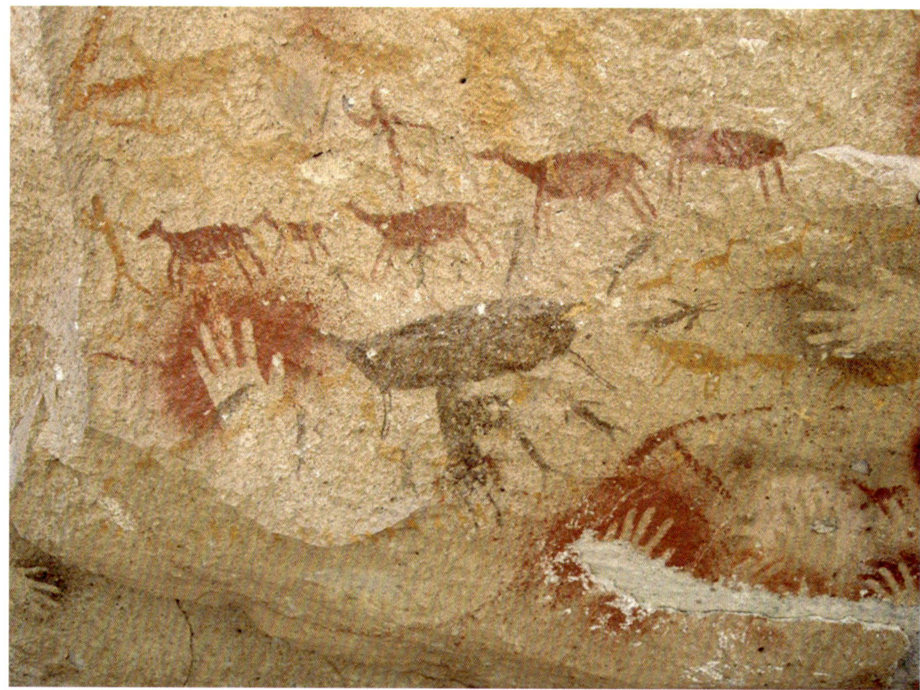

overhanging rock walls. What is now the Sahara Desert was then green and home to herds of antelopes and wild bovines, and mountainous areas rising from those plains in southern Algeria and Libya reveal painted images of hunts. Humans are rendered in somewhat more detail, with evidence of body painting—a characteristic of contemporary nomadic bands—and masking, including a woman wearing large cattle horns as part of her costume. Other nomadic groups used the plains of eastern Africa, well known today for enormous annual migrations, and documented their activities on rock paintings and in very low relief carvings. Cattle were domesticated there, and today herds are still an important source of tribal wealth. And in modern southern Africa, home to perhaps the earliest race of humans and their click languages, Khoisan—the Bushmen of modern Namibia, Botswana, and South Africa—have continued the tradition of painting their hunts and their large animal prey almost until the present day. One painting shows small, active, sword-bearing men battling much larger, shield-bearing men in what represents the conflict between the Bushmen and the Bantu-speakers who migrated south from central Africa around the seventeenth century. The Bushmen, or San, were pressed into less desirable desert areas by the Bantu, who by this time were herders of domesticated cattle. Leadership in Bushmen bands was achieved by proven prowess, not through any line of descent. The societies were basically egalitarian, the small numbers of band members requiring that different persons fulfill many roles, one of which was artist. This kind of group organization can be applied retroactively to the earlier nomadic gatherer-hunters whose artworks extend back to the beginning of the Holocene.

Australia was settled very early by Aboriginal groups, who also documented their presence by painting on rock outcroppings. Their subjects were ancestral spirits who lived during a Dream Time of mythical origin; these spirits introduced the Aborigines to their world and to the animals they should hunt. A rock painting shows a spirit figure, composed like a man but with very thin torso and limbs, his genitals emerging between his legs (**3**). He carries a dilly bag with items needed during travel, since Aborigines are migratory. The figure assumes a very active posture with arms and legs akimbo, dramatizing his attempt to control his environment. In a more recent Aboriginal bark painting, a similar ancestral spirit figure attacks a kangaroo, rendered in characteristic X-ray style with its internal organs visible (**4**). The more recent artist has appropriated his ancestors' rock art to create a portable object for modern use and sale.

Migratory bands of settlers filtered into the Americas via Alaska and in the course of following game, soon populated both the north and south continents. Paleoindian occupants of modern-day Chile provided one of the earliest well-documented dates for settlement in the Americas, 11,500 BCE, at the site of Monte Verde in northwestern Patagonia. On the Argentine side of the Andes in southern Patagonia are a number of rock shelter paintings that reflect the same focus on hunting that we see in Spain and Africa. The preferred prey was the herds of camelids such as wild guanaco and vicuña, the ancestors of the alpaca and llama later domesticated by Central Andean Indians. In a multicolored painting from Patagonia, we see profile humans rendered in red silhouette, running alongside what must be vicuña, given their small size (**5**). Other figures in yellow silhouette are in the lower right and above the vicuña, the latter confronted by a man. Larger camelids, possibly guanaco, are rendered below in grey silhouette; these likely were painted at a different time by bands who returned to the same outcropping at the start of the hunting season for ceremonies to ensure good hunts and to initiate pubescent boys. Negative handprints show a continuation of the Paleolithic tradition found in western Europe. Another painting from the area of Río Pinturas shows a technique of attacking the animals by surrounding them and driving them toward an opening, presumably where they would tumble off a cliff to their deaths, a successful technique used on horses in Paleoindian North America. The large size of the group— fifty-four figures can be counted—suggests that more

6   Mato-Tope with Wife and Son
George Catlin (United States, 1796 – 1872)
1854
Oil on canvas
Ethnological Museum, Berlin, Germany

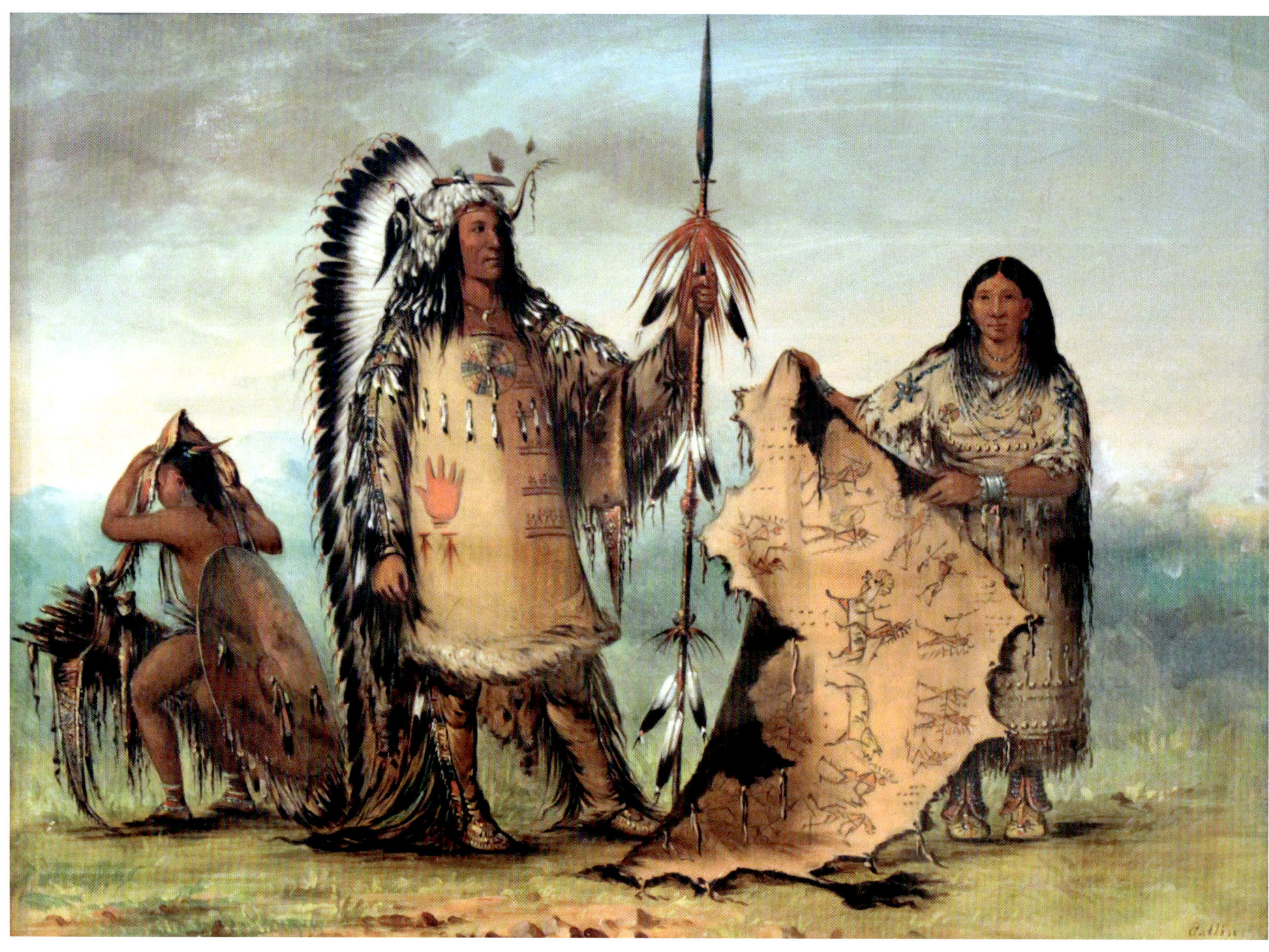

7 **Inlaid Pipe Bowl with Two Faces**
Sioux culture, Sisseton, South Dakota
Early 1800s
Catlinite (pipestone), lead
3 × 5 × 3 in., 7.6 × 12.7 × 7.6 cm
Brooklyn Museum, New York
Henry L. Batterman Fund
and the Frank Sherman Benson Fund

than one band got together for this drive, a technique also known in the North American Plains among Indigenous tribes. The numbers of participants, rather than individual prowess, seems important to these bands, so humans receive minimal detail.

Those Plains tribes in North America rendered their battles using a similar technique, as seen on teepee liners and exteriors. The exterior coverings, wrapped around poles in conical form and coming together at the top, were originally made of smoothed, dry, bison hide. They were painted to record the exploits of the leading man of the household in war and "counting coup," referring to acts of bravery where the man would touch an enemy or his horse and escape without being caught. The compositional technique was, like Mesolithic rock art, to distribute the figures in the scene from above but render each figure in profile. Like the Sahara Desert paintings, the figures displayed their body paint within the outline. In addition, each wore distinctive clothing and head gear. There was no indication of the landscape in which the scenes took place, nor was there any definition of where the composition ended—what its boundaries were. After the U.S. Army's conquest of the free-ranging Plains tribes in the late nineteenth century and their confinement to reservations, as well as the decimation of the bison herds, the paintings were done on muslin distributed by the government to the now-restricted tribes and also on ledger books given to warriors held in jails.

A painting by American artist George Catlin (1796–1872), made while he visited a Mandan village and its leader in modern North Dakota, shows various bison-hide objects

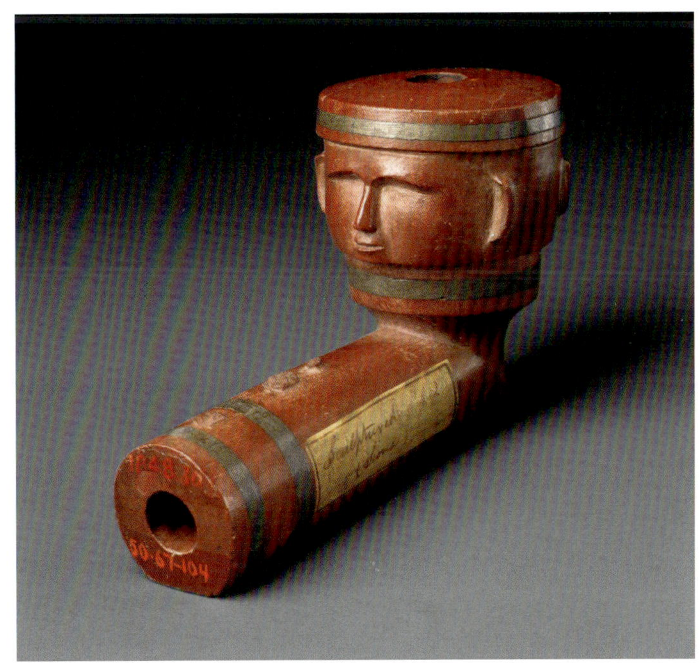

decorated with paintings of their owners' exploits (**6**). The chief himself, dressed in his long eagle-feather headdress, wears a shirt with a bloody hand on its front, testifying to his act of bravery in killing an enemy; his wife holds up a bison hide with details of other exploits, such as hand-to-hand combat and horse stealing; and his son, heading off to our left, carries a rawhide shield painted in four quadrants with horses and riders. The humans depicted on the hide are composed of simple triangular lines for the torso and circles for the head, with some elements of costume rendered. Simplified faces in front and looking back at the smoker adorn a peace pipe bowl made by a Dakota artist out of catlinite (**7**); this was a soft red rock quarried in southwest Minnesota by many tribes and named for George Catlin, who documented it in a painting. Lead acquired from white traders fill in grooves in the catlinite to make an attractive contrast between the light gray and the red. The Plains tribes brought this pipe-making tradition from their northeastern woodlands relatives who were not so nomadic. After Plains tribes acquired horses from seventeenth-century Spanish troops in the Southwest, they moved easily over long distances both for hunting and following seasonal harvests. The horses could drag the teepee poles and carry heavy bison-hide packages.

Among the latest Indigenous arrivals in the Americas were speakers of the Eskaleut family of languages, who settled along the coastal regions of easternmost Siberia, Alaska, Canada, and Greenland and subsisted on hunting and fishing. Their personal items, produced during the winter when they had leisure time, were decorated with incisions (on walrus ivory) or paint (on wood). For example, the Yupik owner of a small wooden box in the Smithsonian National Museum of Natural History, shaped like the body of a seal swimming through water, has painted on the underside of the lid scenes representing hunts of caribou and whales, rendered in black, while some of the men are rendered in red, shown nude in frontal view with their genitals visible between their legs. They are aided by giant mythical thunderbirds that grab the whales in their claws. Clearly this is a sign of favor for the hunt, some of the equipment for which was stored in the seal box. The Yupik traded on their skill in bone carving by catering to the requests for scrimshaw from visiting sailors and whalers, who themselves practiced this art during their long periods on calm oceans. Cribbage sets and pipes—foreign forms introduced by Euro-Americans—were skillfully carved with scenes of Indigenous environments and life. As with other nomadic bands, their art subordinated individuals to the group, and the power of both is minor in comparison to that of nature and the spirit world.

Art of Village Tribes

As the collecting of plant materials evolved into horticulture—the practice of growing plants in specific locations to have an assured supply—people began to settle down in one spot and build more permanent houses. Domestication of some of the animals that they had once hunted required corralling them, although

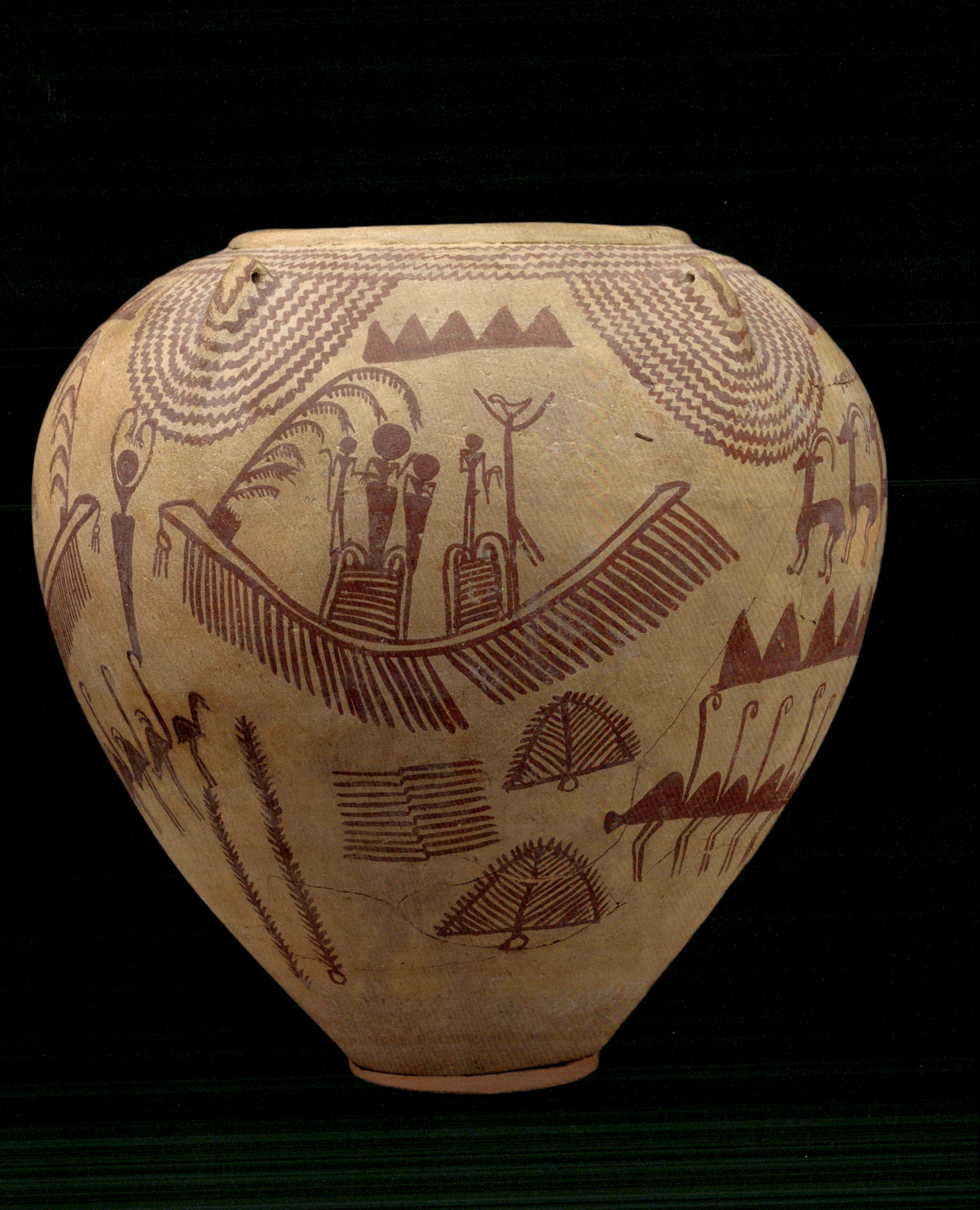

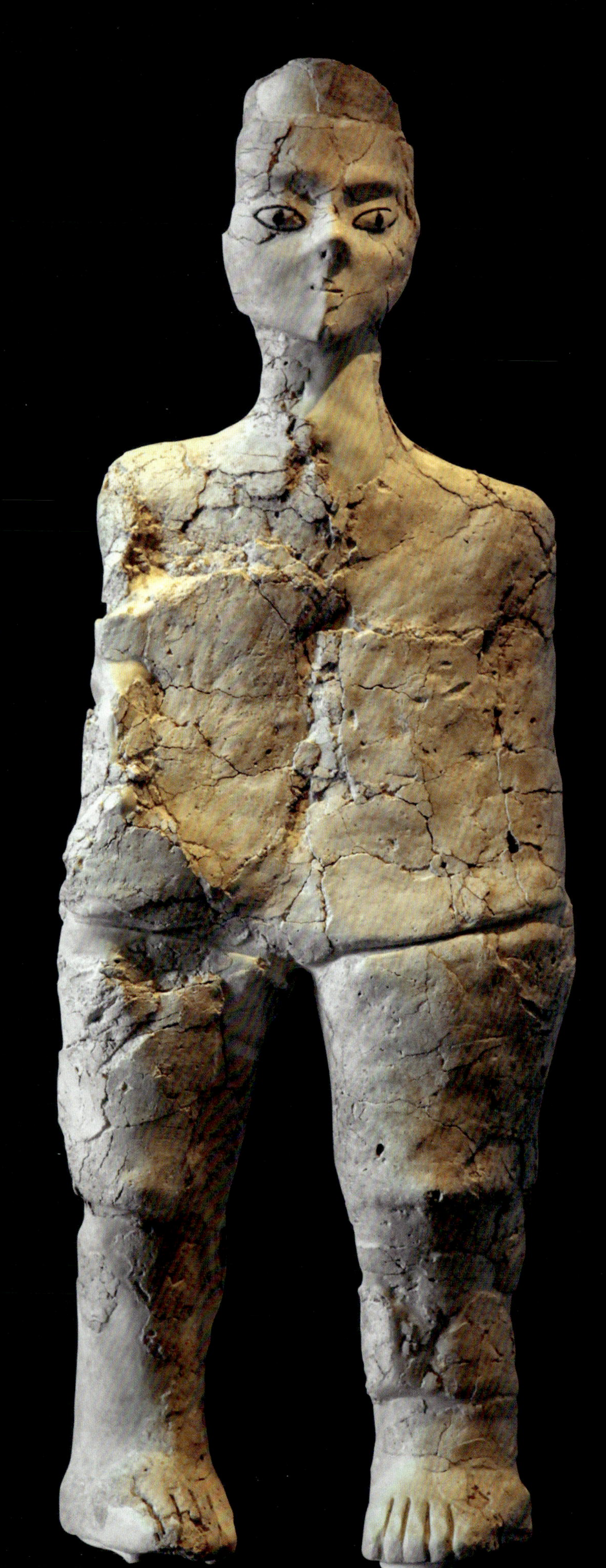

seasonal moves were often needed. In the ancient Middle East, this process began after 9000 BCE, and we call this period the Neolithic because of the smooth stone tools that were made. Documentation of this process is found in early villages such as Çatal Höyük in Turkey, Jarmo in Iraq, and Jericho in Palestine. The importance of ancestor worship in these cultures was reflected in the preservation of skulls within the household. In Jericho these skulls were overmodeled with clay to recreate their appearance in life and clam shells were inserted into the eye sockets to make them seem lifelike. In this period many other people whose political sway was limited to their village also showed a reverence to their ancestors' physical remains, including those surviving into the twentieth century. We call this level of political complexity tribal, with leaders determined by their proven abilities rather than by their family connections. These leaders may be called chiefs during the time they hold their positions, but a true chiefdom requires leadership to be passed on through descent.

After a while, pottery began to replace more flexible containers needed to survive migration. This provided a valuable source for art, both modeled and painted. In predynastic Egypt, around the fourth millennium BCE, vessels echoed the environment in which the artists lived and important cultural beliefs and practices. A large jar reflects funerary traditions along the Nile River, showing bundle-reed boats carrying the deceased to a necropolis away from the village where they lived (**8**). On the left, mourning women stand with their hands over

their heads, probably tearing out their hair. This posture is also found in a simplified female pottery figurine whose hands arch over her head (see back cover). Herds of antelopes are depicted on the shores of the landscape, although there is no vegetation. However, structures such as those on the central boat represent the human-made environment; inside one can see the mummified body being transported. A shrine inside Çatal Höyük is painted with a landscape of the village dominated by an erupting volcano. The compositions are limited in part by the natural barriers of the media: wall surfaces, pottery surfaces, and the warp and weft of weaving, another important innovation at this tribal level.

Figurines, made first of stone and then of ceramic after the introduction of pottery, are common in the pre-Columbian Americas during this tribal stage. They depict a generic rather than an individual presence. Large figures have been found in sites from the Neolithic Levant, both in Jericho, on the right bank of the Jordan River, and in Ain Ghazal, on its left bank (**9**). These are formed from plaster applied over a wooden armature; one of them is two-headed, a feature occasionally found in sculptures from Preclassic Mexico. In Jericho, where the figures were not so well preserved, their excavator believed that the group of three comprised a family. One of the figures from another group from Çatal Höyük would seem on first glance to be a Paleolithic Venus; however, this woman has a fully formed head and arms and her degree of obesity is consistent with what is possible in humans (see Chapter 4: Motherhood and the Family, fig. 9). She is also seated

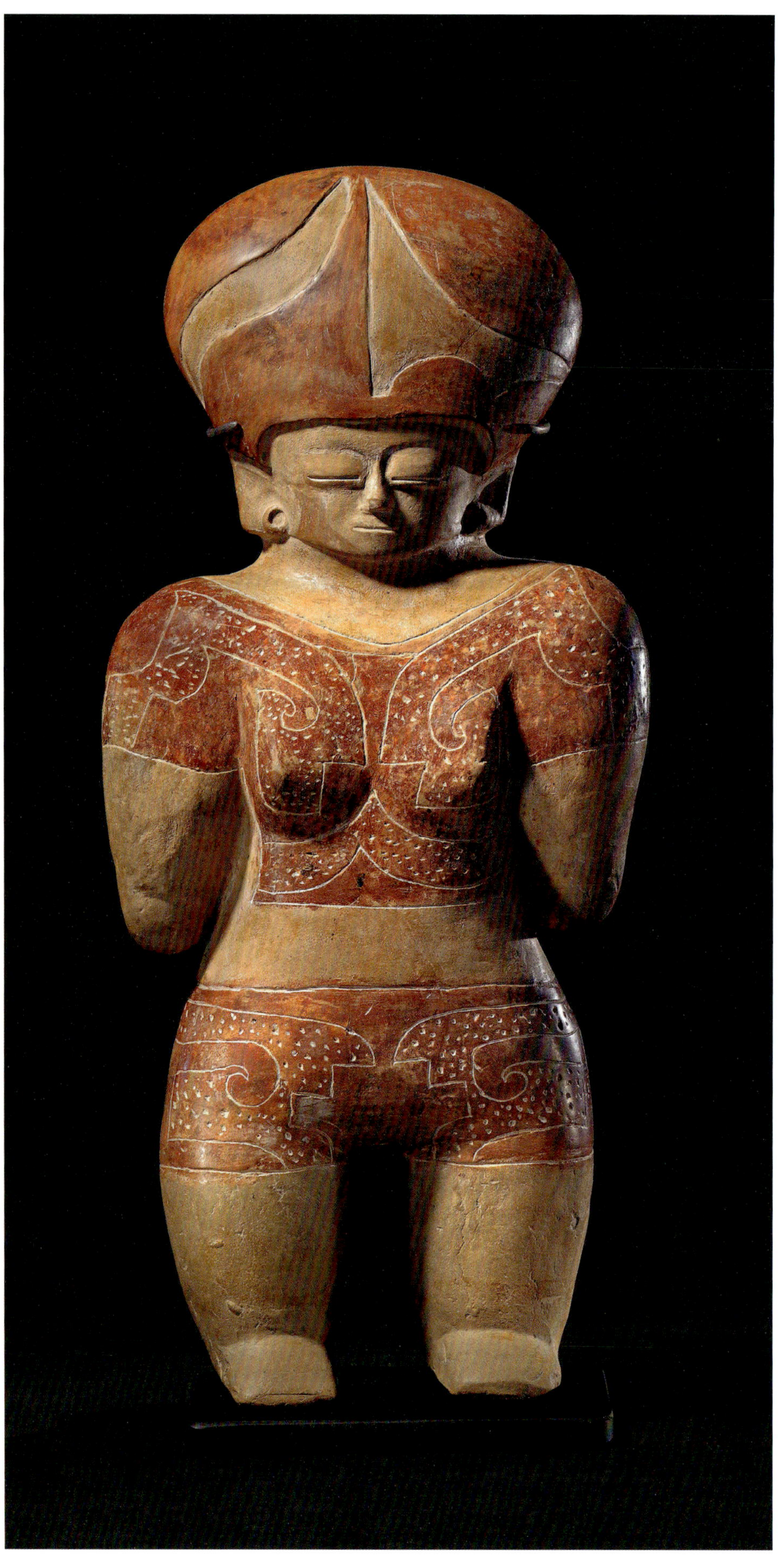

10 Standing Female Figure

Chorrera culture, Ecuador
900 – 300 BCE
Terracotta
15 × 6 ¾ in., 38.1 × 17.15 cm
Private Collection

11 Violin-Shaped Figure

Cycladic culture, Cyclades
3200 – 1050 BCE
Marble
Ashmolean Museum of Art and
Archaeology, University of Oxford,
England

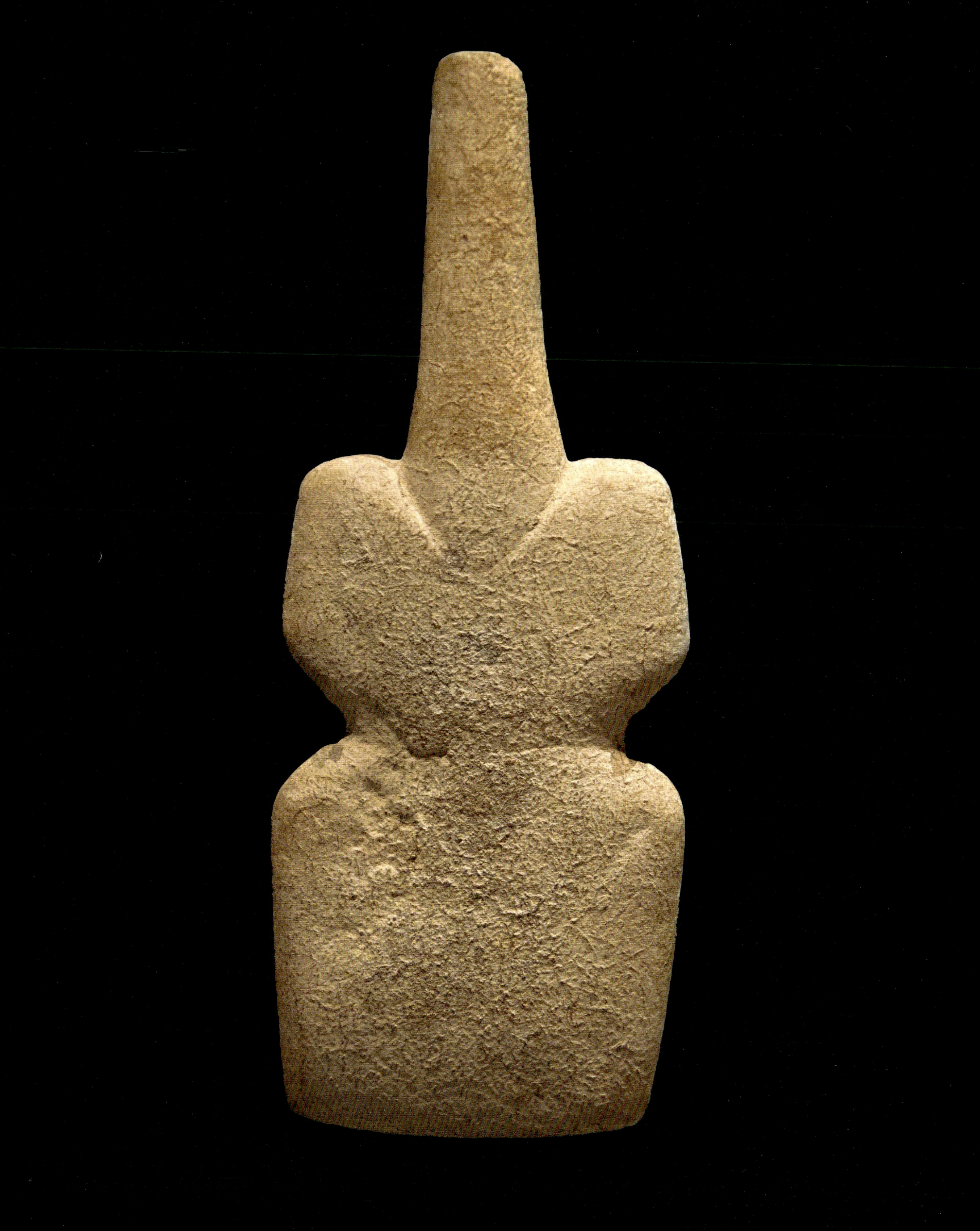

on a leopard throne, clearly indicating a commanding
if not divine personage. In coastal Ecuador, abstract
stone figurines were made from around 3000 to 2300 BCE,
at which point the sculptors changed over to ceramic
forms with more feminine curvature. The earliest known
ceramic figurine in Mexico, from 2300 BCE, shows a similar
feminine curvature in its lower half, but the treatment
of the head and arms is rudimentary. Later figurines
modeled in Mesoamerica after 1500 BCE had much regional
variation, sometimes reflecting the different purposes
they served in their village cultures.

With changes in pottery practices, larger figures began
to be modeled after 1200 BCE in both Mesoamerica and
in Ecuador. Making the figures hollow allowed heat to
escape through inconspicuously placed holes during the
firing process, reducing the risk of cracking. A beautiful
hollow figure in the Chorrera (or Engoroy) style created in
central coastal Ecuador is adorned with a headdress fully
rounded like a helmet (**10**). Its arms and legs are short,
creating childlike proportions, although the swelling
breasts and hips suggest a more mature female. Her tight-
fitting red clothing is decorated with incised lines that
also distinguish it from the ochre-slipped bare skin. Very
similar proportions are found in an early hollow figure
from Tehuacán, Mexico, of approximately the same date.

Although there is evidence of contact between Ecuador and
Mesoamerica because of trade in Spondylus shell, it did
not begin so early. A more reasonable conclusion would
be that the two cultures arrived at a similar bulbous style
of rendering humans independently, possibly because the
figures represented a generic stylization that merges child
and adult female images.

Cultures of the Woodland period in the eastern United
States (500 BCE–700 CE) produced numerous carved stone
images of animals in the bowls of pipes used for smoking
native tobacco in ceremonies at which significant decisions
were to be made. In burials on the sites of the houses
in which they had lived, the graves of the main men of
the Hopewell culture around Ohio include silhouettes of
astonishingly naturalistic forms of both animals and men
chipped out of mica sheets, such as a headless human
torso and a human hand. Their outlines are simplified into
beautiful convex and concave forms with no irregularities.
Some burials also included ceramic models of various
humans, from nursing mothers to a standing male, that
reflect the early figurine cults of Mesoamerica.

Stone female figurines appear in very abstract form on
the Cycladic Islands between Greece and Turkey as early
as 5300 BCE and spread up the Balkan Peninsula as far as
Hungary. A distinctive form is shaped like a violin (**11**).

12 Seated Figure

Djenné culture, Southern Mali
1200 – 1300
Terracotta
10 × 11 ¾ in., 25.4 × 29.9 cm
Metropolitan Museum of Art, New York
Purchase, Buckeye Trust and
Mr. and Mrs. Milton F. Rosenthal
Gifts, Joseph Pulitzer Bequest and
Harris Brisbane Dick and Rogers Funds, 1981

13 Figure of a Seated Musician

Dogon culture, Mopti Region, Mali
Late 1700s
Wood and iron
22 × 7 × 4 ¼ in., 55.8 × 17.7 × 10.8 cm
Brooklyn Museum, New York
Frank L. Babbott Fund

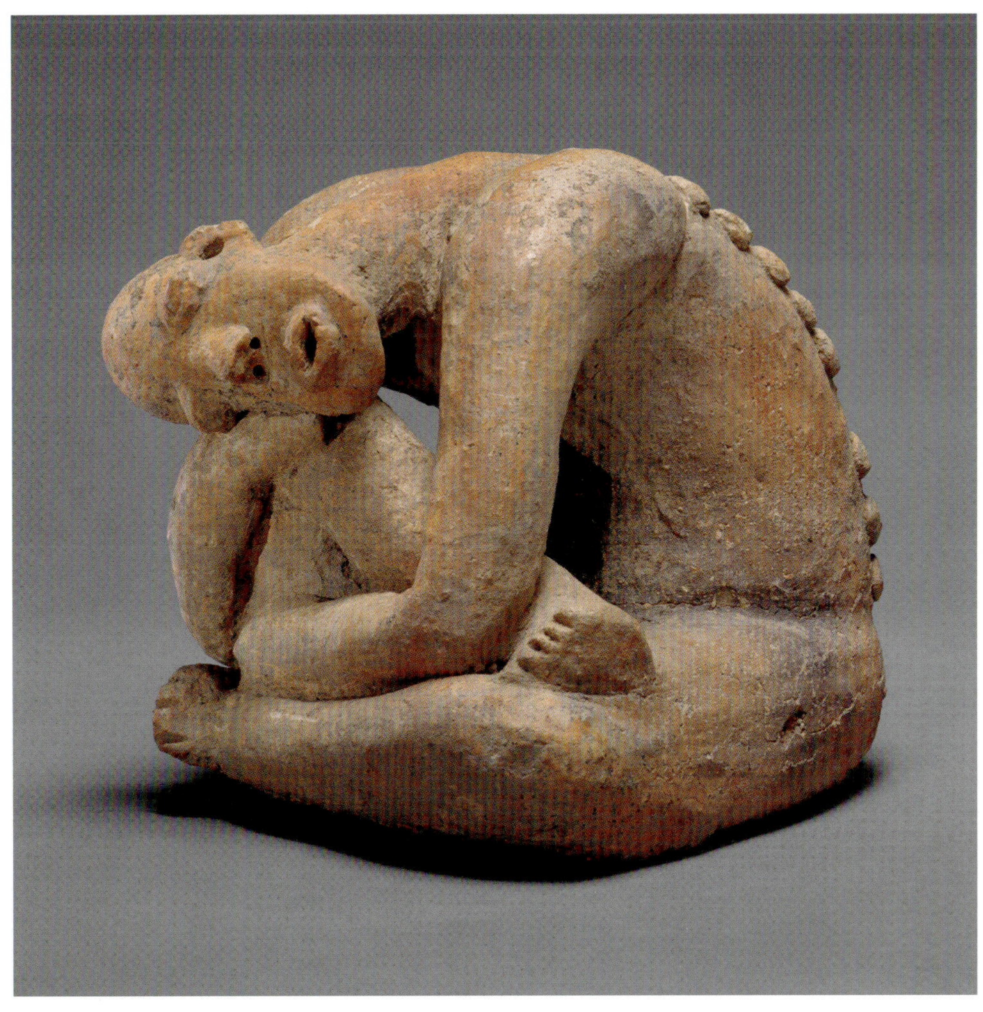

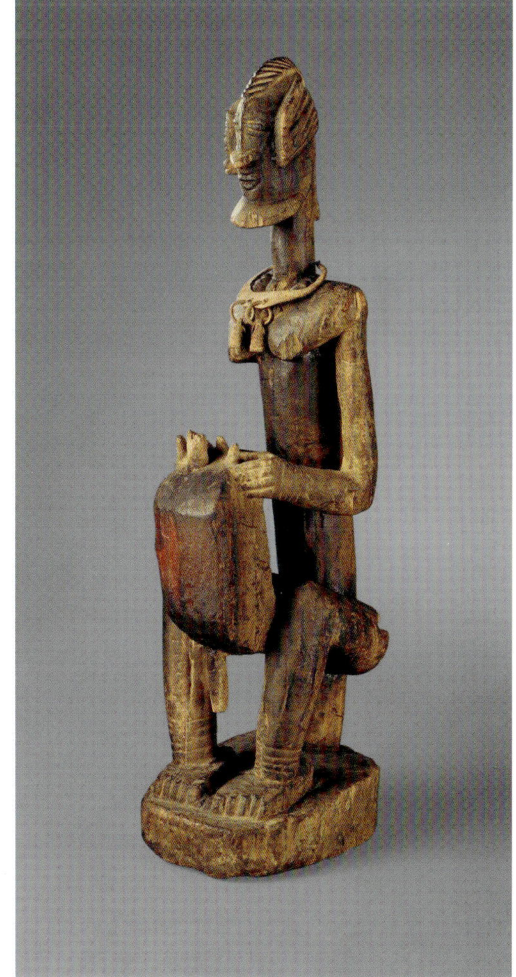

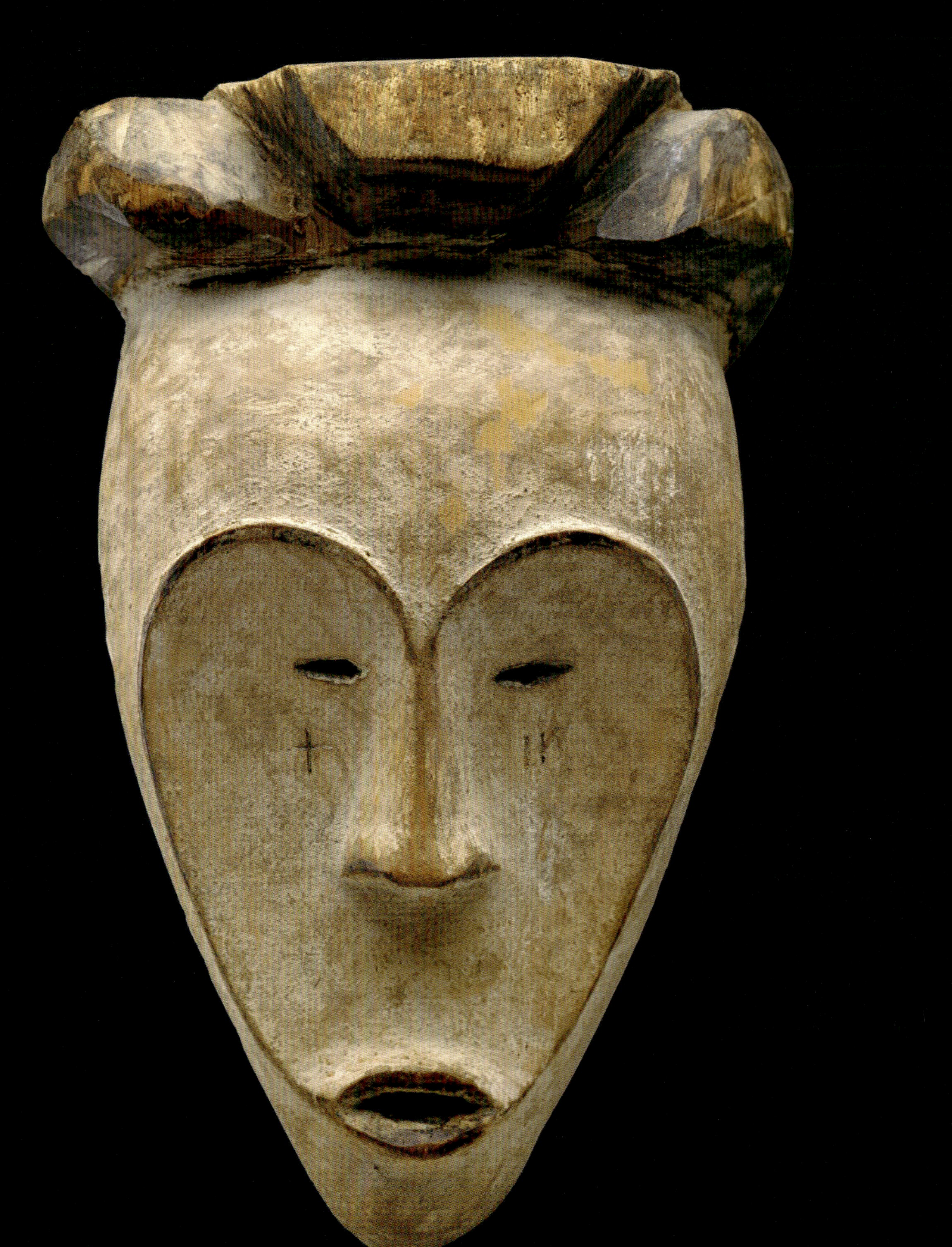

Carved of unblemished white marble found especially on the Cyclades, this example does not distinguish the arms and legs of the body, and its neck tapers upward like the handle of a violin, with no indication of a head. On other examples, limb division and minimal facial features are indicated by grooved lines. Such renderings of the human essence are typical of the Neolithic, when humans first struggled with the vagaries of nature to plant and sow crops and did not have a strong sense of their dominance; they were highly dependent on their domesticated animal herds, which had to be fed and protected around the clock against predators and disease.

In Sub-Saharan Africa, pottery led to the production of terracotta figures in the agricultural land well below the desert and along the Niger River. Though placed to commemorate the dead, these figures, too, had very generic features. An early type in Nigeria was produced by the Nok culture beginning around 900 BCE. Terracotta figures continued to be made in northwestern Nigeria and southern Niger until about 1200. A very angular sleeping figure with coarse facial features was made by a culture that arose in the inland Niger delta of Mali from 1100 to 1400, around the modern city of Djenné (**12**). His limbs and torso are cylindrical, and his facial features sit on the surface of his head. A continuation of this geometric tradition of rendering the human form is found among wood carvings of the Bamana and Dogon tribes of Mali, in the dry region known as the Sudan extending across the African continent. Earlier Dogon wood carvings known as *tellem* can be

dated before 1400. After being anointed with sacrificial material, they were placed in caves with the dead. French Colonial-era carvings continue to be geometric in approach, as in this seated male musician (**13**). He is playing an instrument known as a *kora*, his knees flexed to support it waist-high in front of him. His arms, legs, and torso are quite cylindrical, making little reference to his musculature. His facial features and beard sit on the surface of his head rather than being integrated into it. The cylindrical tree trunk from which the figure is carved remains visible and establishes the dominant limit of the sculpture. Agricultural dependence on nature in the Niger River and the dry Sudan zone made subsistence challenging; as in other village cultures, Sudanese art did not represent a confident reflection of humanity but rather an abstract geometric stylization of humans. Sculptures of wild animals also were more geometric, and they often combined features of several species to create a surreal being.

In central Africa during the colonial period, the faces of wood sculptures made in village societies often are carved in the shape of a concave heart. In Gabon, the Fang carved masks that were painted white to represent spirits (**14**). The neighboring Kota placed skull guardians in barrels with their ancestors' remains (see Chapter 10: Death, fig. 27). The guardians' bodies are reduced to a diamond shape that echoes arm placement, but the body is hollow and empty of detail. The head is flat, and the face is concave and covered with brass strips acquired from trade with the French to produce an unnatural glow.

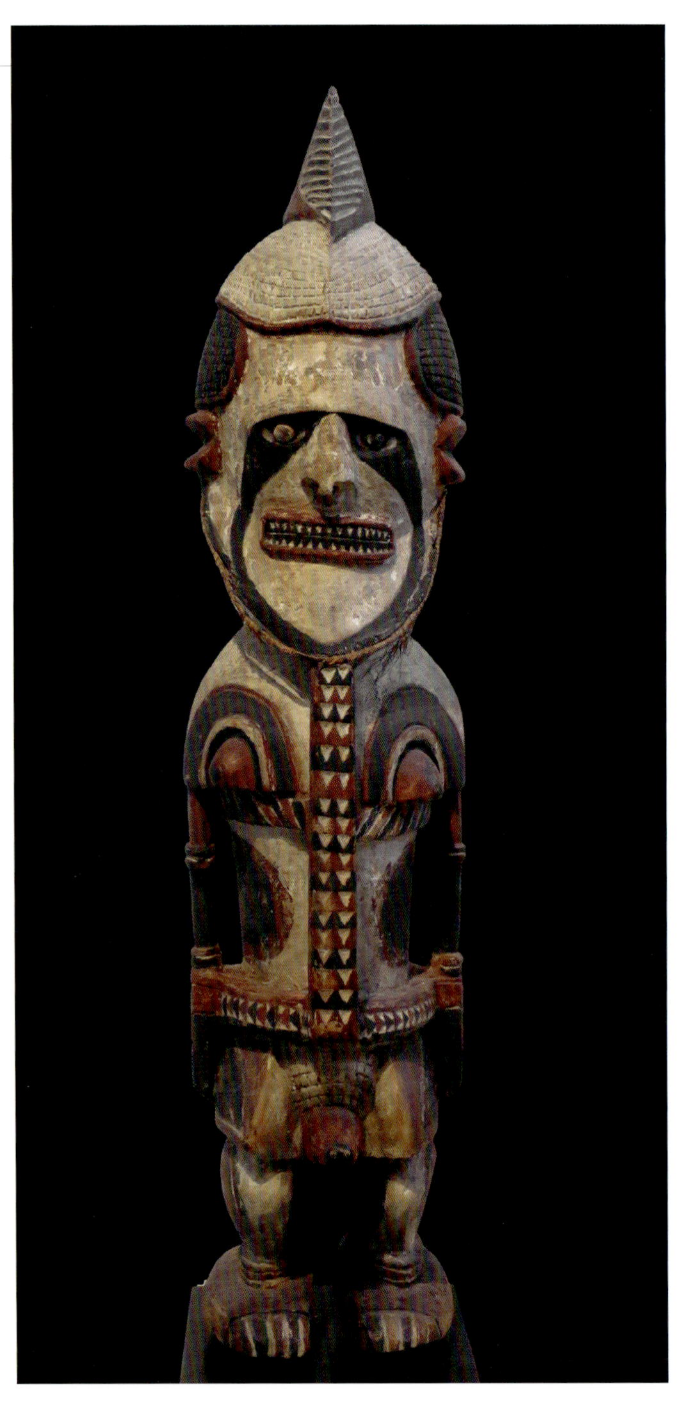

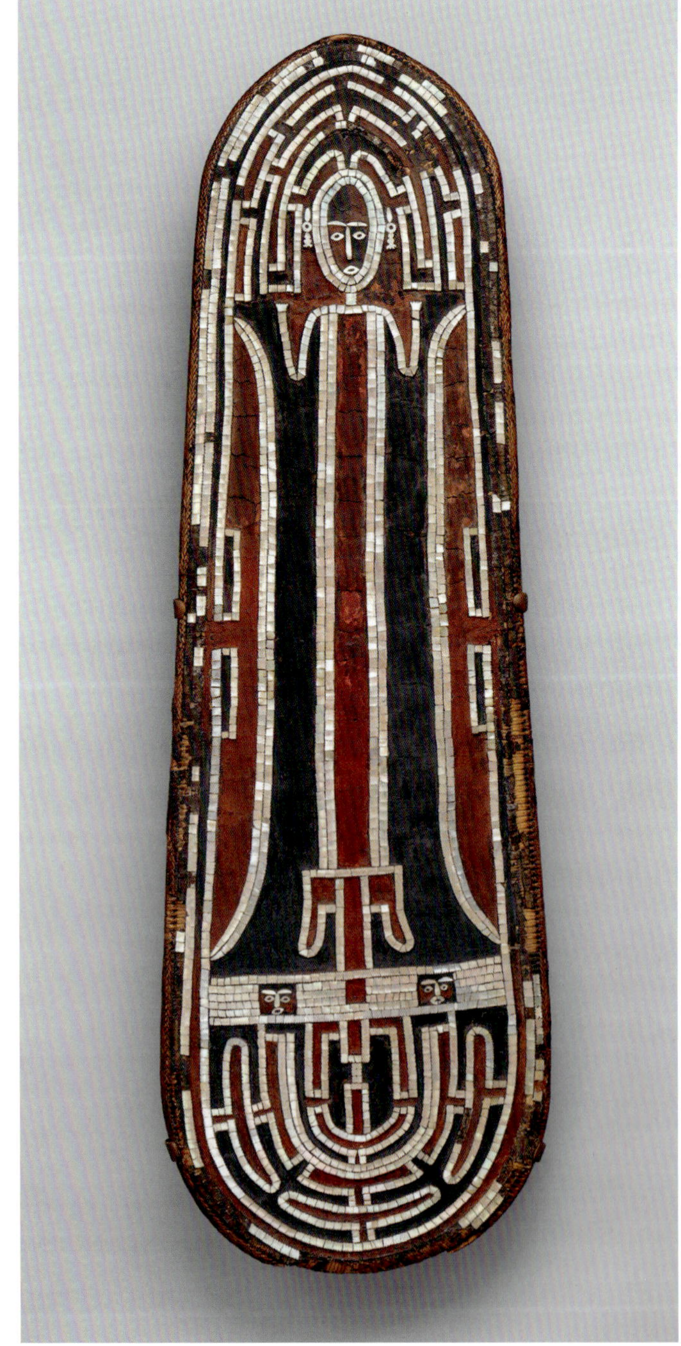

Much like the figures of Sudan societies in Africa, the powerful images carved by speakers of Malayo-Polynesian languages in the village societies in island Melanesia reflect the cylindrical limits of their raw material—wood trunks. The ancestor *uli* figure of New Ireland, on the eastern edge of the new republic of Papua-New Guinea, has bulky, massive proportions and a grimacing face expressing his fearsomeness (**15**). Other sculptures from New Ireland, used in the *malanggan* celebration commemorating ancestors who passed away during the intervening period, are spectacular displays of carving, with the standing human form surrounded by animal forms referring to their totem spirits, all painted in stripes of red, yellow, and black. This extravagant profusion of forms encasing a core human honors the recent ancestors. Farther southeast along the line of major Melanesian islands are the Solomon Islands, now an independent republic. Their inhabitants built large gable-roofed structures supported by main posts, some rendering highly simplified men with naturalistic proportions. The prows of their canoes are protected by half-bodied figureheads, their projecting jaws expressing determination that the canoe will reach its destination safely. Inlaid white Z-shaped shell contrasts dramatically with the painted black of the wooden figure. Battle shields are also inlaid with white shell that contrasts with a red and black background to form an attenuated human shape expressing a protective spirit facing the attacker (**16**). The geometric simplification found in much of village art is here used to ward off danger more effectively than the actual, probably ceremonial, shield.

Finally, the Indigenous pueblo towns of the southwestern United States convey the simplified geometry of much village art. Before the arrival of Europeans in the Americas, these towns subsisted on gardens planted with the Mesoamerican triad of corn, beans, and squash. In modern Arizona, the Hohokam culture centered on the Gila River watershed produced red on buff pottery, which also arrived from Mesoamerica around the beginning of the Common Era, as in this lobed bowl with painted line dancers circling its interior (**17**). Such dancers are commonly documented in more recent pueblo ceremonies in which villagers welcomed the spirit figures known as *kachinas*, who visited during specific seasons of the year. Prehistoric pottery from southwestern New Mexico known as Mimbres used the black-on-white palette typical of ancestral Pueblo to render natural forms but in a very unnatural, highly geometric way. A wooden doll representing a female *kachina* given to a child participating in her first visit of the *kachinas* was intended to remind her to be grateful for their assistance in controlling nature (**18**). The three-dimensional carving is comprised of highly simplified geometric forms, which are common in the art of village societies. Pueblo agriculture was extremely dependent on rainfall, which in several instances (documented by tree rings) caused the abandonment of cliff dwellings in parts of the ancestral Pueblo range. As we have seen, the geometric stylization of art is often found in village societies that prioritized the control of nature.

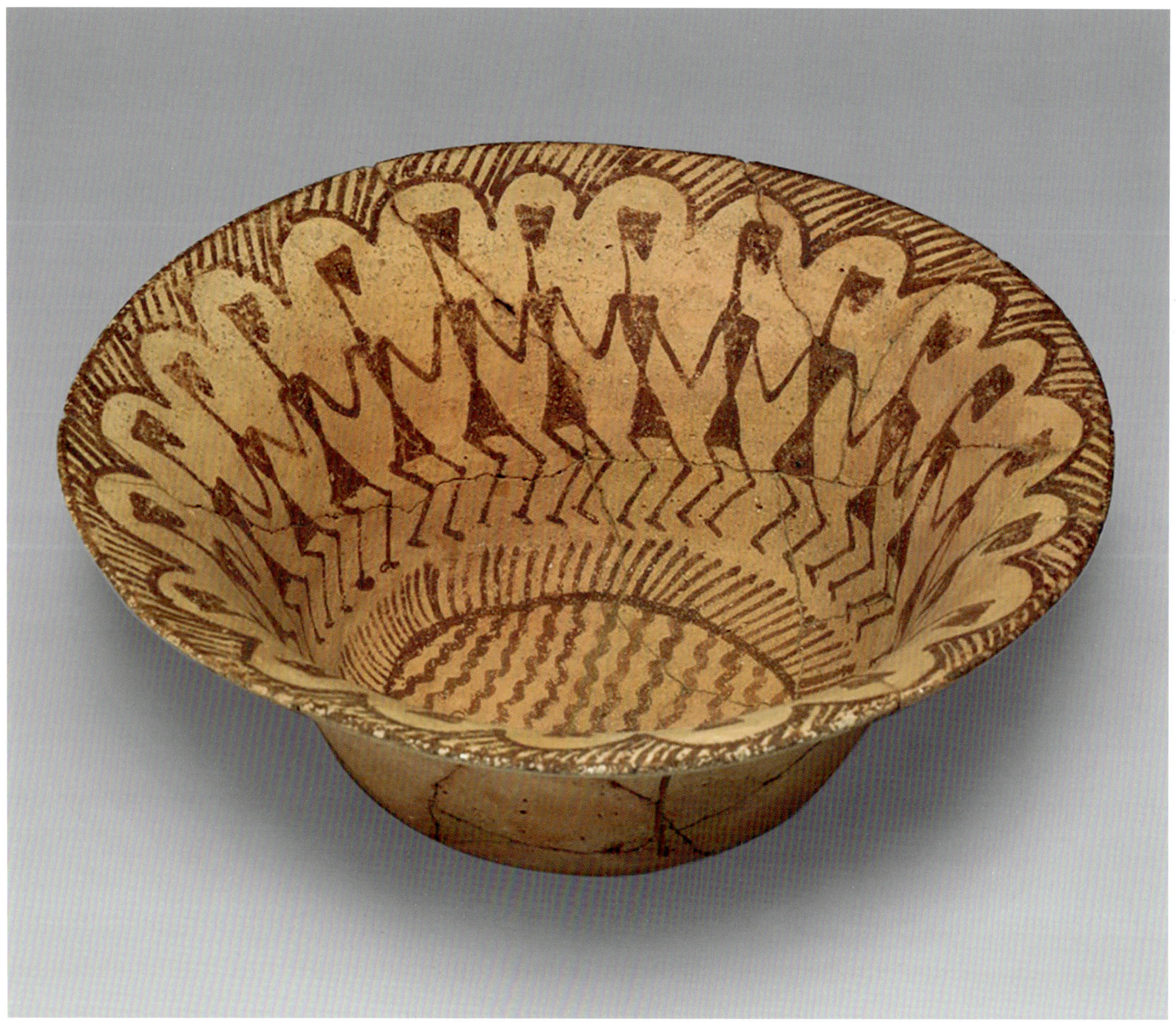

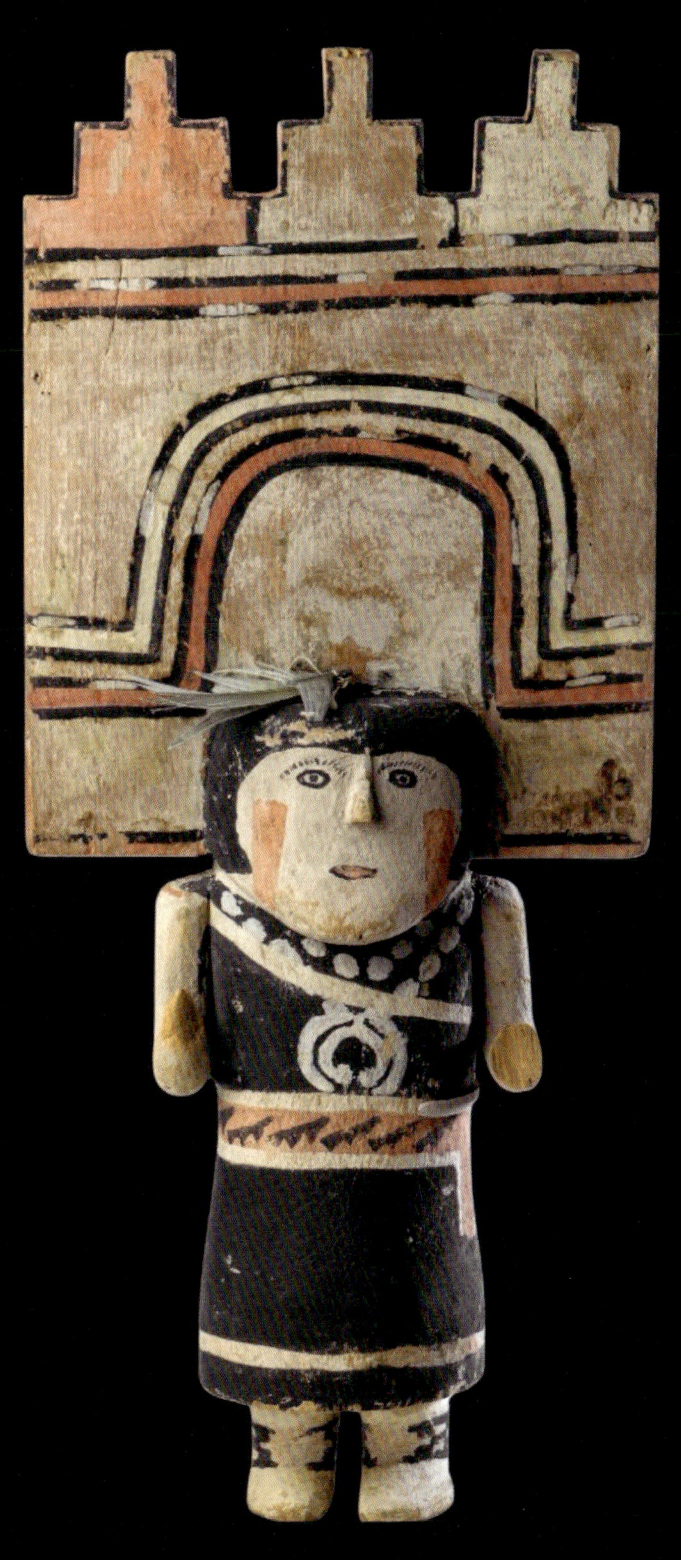

Art of Chiefdoms

Cultures that are ruled by hereditary chiefs control their environment through cooperative actions organized by chiefs or their subordinates. They comprise the third level of complexity as originally defined by Elman Service. Unlike bands and tribes, which are essentially egalitarian, chiefdoms have ranked hierarchies, or a noble class, who often used art to express their status and the prerogatives of rank. This created the need for trained artisans, quite different from the more self-taught and part-time artists of bands and tribes. The materials used could also be rare, acquired through trade networks. The rights of hereditary chiefs often were believed to derive from their close association with deities, and those deities often appeared in art. Tattooing was an art form that permanently branded an individual's status on their skin. The use of stools and chairs for sitting in assemblies called by the chief also identified their users as leaders. And chiefs were often buried under sizable earthen mounds. In two-dimensional art, the higher-ranked person was typically shown in larger scale than subordinates. Most of these traits continue into the art of states. While there is greater naturalism in the art of cultures ruled by hereditary chiefs, in contrast to the more imposed geometry of tribal art, the individuality of features is not represented. Bodies are generalized and proportions are not accurate, with heads being more important than limbs. But art in general exists in a richer context in chiefdoms and has a greater variety of expression.

In Europe before the dominance of the Roman Empire (27 BCE–476 CE), non-Latin-speaking ethnic groups were ruled by chiefs. Celtic-speaking groups, once dominant throughout mid-latitude Europe, buried their chiefs in large tumuli created by a sizable work force that transported the many baskets of earth required. A stone portrait of one such chief found in what is now the Czech Republic displays the distinctive features of the Celts as remarked on by their Mediterranean adversaries, the Greeks and Romans: mustachioed, with their hair worn in unwashed clumps (**19**). A famous Hellenistic Greek statue in the collection of the Capitoline Museum in Rome known as the Dying Gaul (another name for Celt) renders a Celtic man with a naturalism not seen in this head created by their own artists.

Jewelry worn on the clothing of Celts and other chiefly groups displayed the geometric forms popular in their art along with the zoomorphic so-called animal style brought in from the steppes of Eurasia. After the migrations of these "barbarian tribes" caused the collapse of the Roman Empire and the arrival of the Dark Ages in Western Europe in the fifth century, their styles replaced the realism of Roman art, reflecting the insecurity of the times. A merger of Celtic and Anglo-Saxon traditions in Britain, particularly in Christian monasteries along its coasts, is reflected in the manuscripts painted in their scriptoria. The symbolic rendering of the beginning of the Book of Matthew, part of the Echternach Gospels, produced in Lindisfarne Abbey in the seventh century, forms the

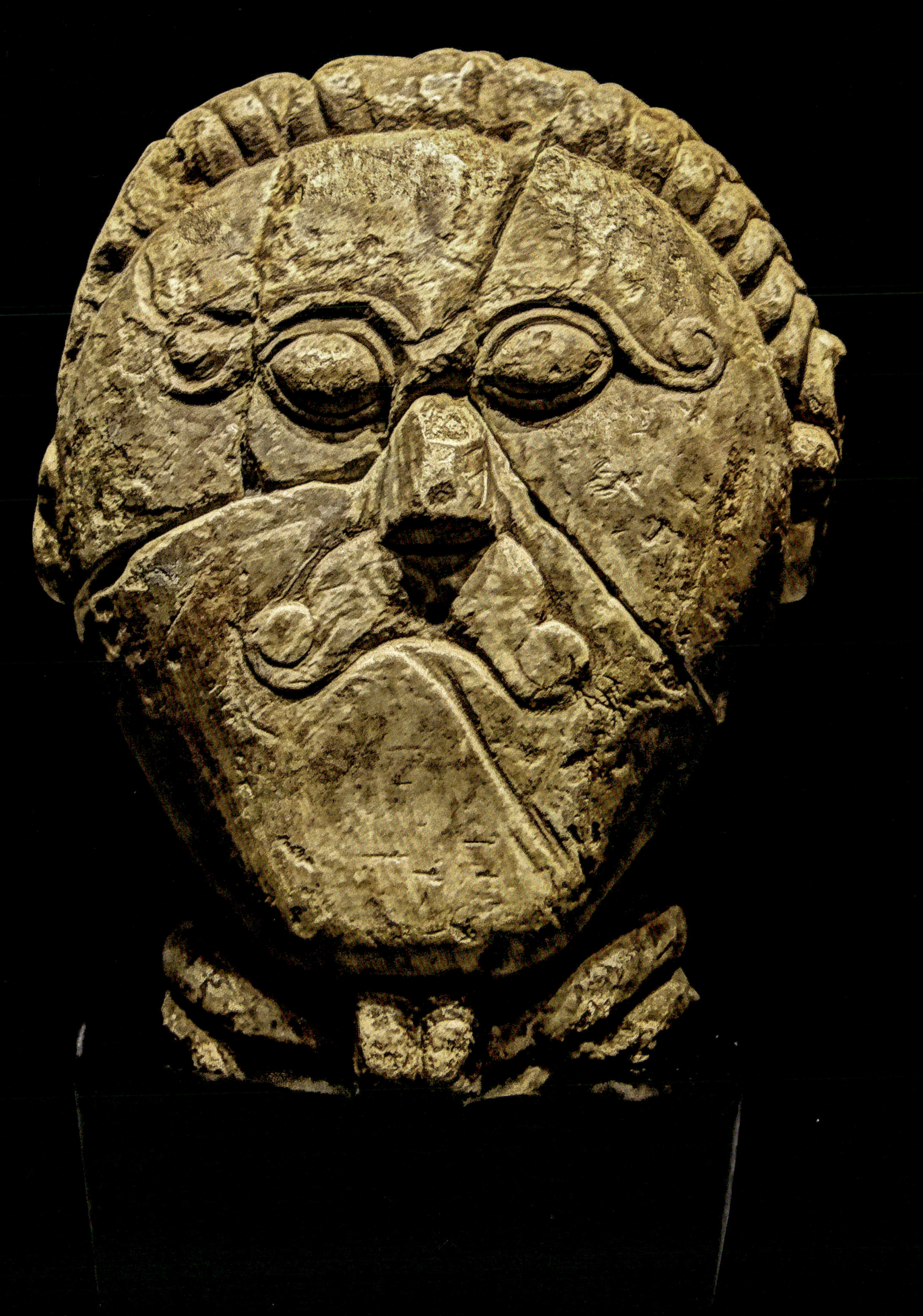

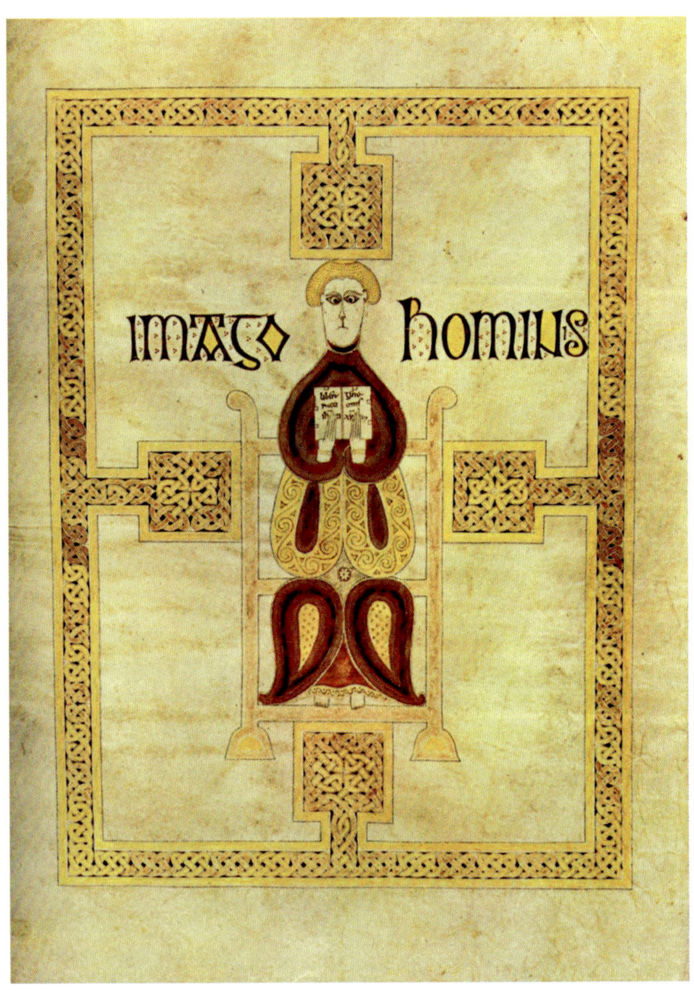

image of a man out of geometric jewels, tightly clamped into position by a cross coming from the center of the border (**20**). Border and image are on the same plane—a total rejection of Greco-Roman naturalism, but very much in the tradition of Germanic and Celtic tribes north of the Roman Empire.

In the far east of Eurasia at the same time, Japan began to establish a culture based on worship of their emperor, but in no way was this an urban civilization. Like the Celtic mounds built to house the bodies of their chiefs, the Japanese chiefs cooperated to construct giant keyhole-shaped tumuli defined by moats. Protecting these and other tombs for their chiefs were terracotta sculptures representing aspects of their society: houses, boats, horsemen, grooms, and warrior figures (**21**). These are simplified, idealized forms on hollow columnar bases set in the earth. Facial features consist of eyes and mouths slit into the interior of the column and a vertical pinched nose. The armor was much more detailed than the warrior himself, since it was important for the definition of the figure and his protection of the tomb. Raids on the islands by Koreans and Chinese created insecurity in Japanese society during this period, which is known as the Kofun (ca. 300–538), resulting in artists rendering humans with more generic and simplified forms.

In the pre-Columbian Americas, several art-producing tribes in peripheral regions also created art that was more generic and simplified. In the Mezcala region of the Balsas River, in the rugged mountains south of modern Mexico City, stone carvings based on those previously

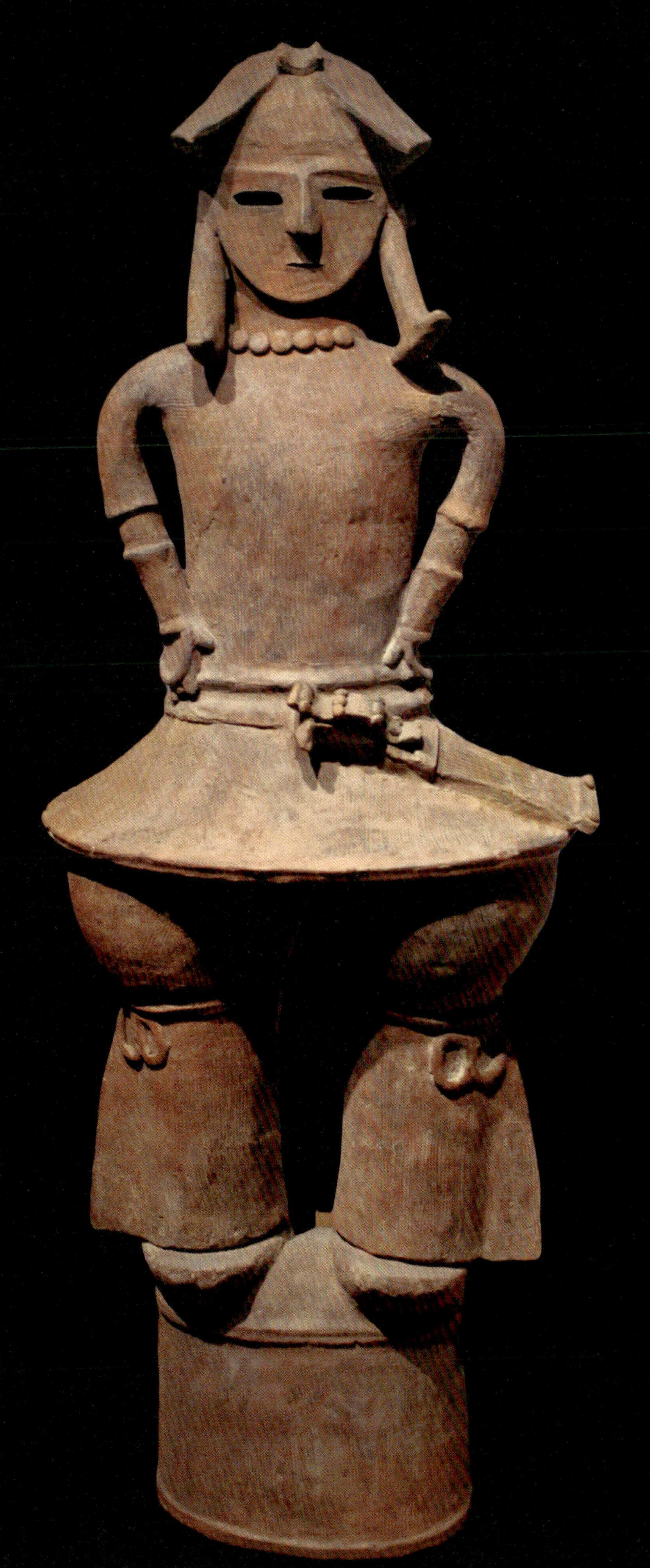

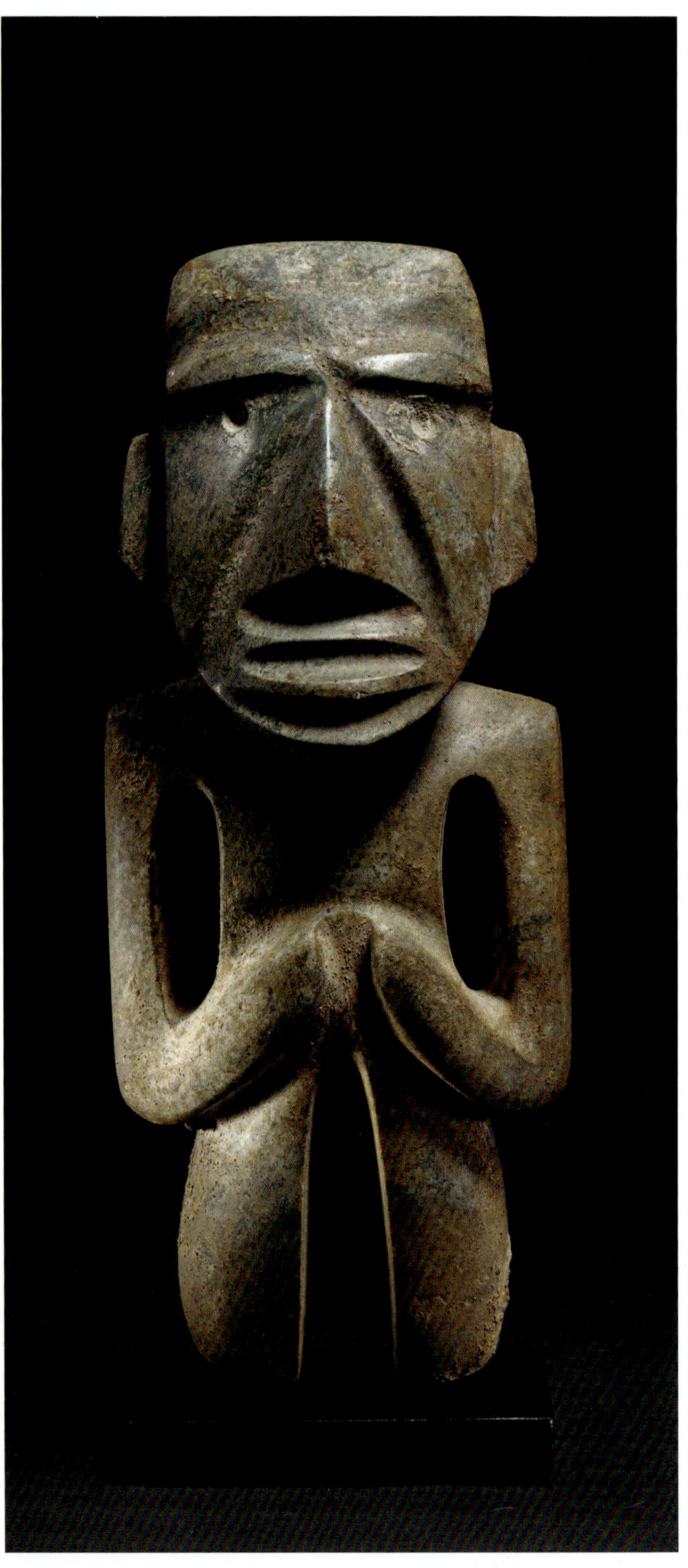

requested by Olmec traders (see Urban States below) simplified representations on ritual axes, rendering their deities only as grooved rough cuts. I have hypothesized that the Olmec preferred their greenstone imports to be just roughed out, with the detail provided by their own specialized lapidaries in their capital.[2] After the demise of the Olmec trade network, the local chiefdom around Mezcala elaborated the axe form into more fully articulated forms such as this human, but without details of body and clothing (22). They apparently did not use a circular drill for eyes or small jewelry, as the Olmec did. The mountainous terrain and periodical floods in Mezcala, in the western Mexican state of Guerrero, made for an environment with much insecurity, reflected in their art by greater simplification and lack of individualism.

Farther to the northwest in Mexico, chiefdoms based on growing agave for the ritual drink pulque commissioned sculptures of their leaders in ceramic effigies intended as gifts to their lieutenants; these usually ended up in shaft-and-chamber tombs beneath their homes. In this ceramic figure of a female chief (*cacica*) from a tomb near the modern Colima-Michoacán state line, her high status is conveyed by her sitting on a stool (23). Her political power is expressed by her extenuated torso and her generative power by her large vulva. Like most female figures in west Mexico, she proffers food, here holding out a bowl that probably contained actual food when it was first placed in the tomb. The more northern parts of West Mexico provide many examples of husband-wife pairs that were placed in tombs,

23 Seated Female Figure with Bowl (overleaf)
Colima culture, Coahuayana Style, Protoclassic
West Mexico
100 BCE – 250 CE
Terracotta
22 ½ in., 57.15 cm
The Stuart Handler Collection

suggesting that women in the area wielded considerable power. The ceramic figures of the Ameca tradition of Jalisco state have very naturalistic proportions, though they are without realistic facial features (see Chapter 4: Motherhood and the Family, fig. 47).

In the Intermediate Area, between the high cultures of Mesoamerica and the Central Andes, stools represented an important indicator of leadership among the pre-Columbian chiefdoms. The stunning gold figure of a chief of the Quimbaya culture of central Colombia conveys his power not only by the stool on which he sits but also by the rare material from which he is cast (**24**). The figure served as a container for powdered lime, which was chewed with coca leaves to put users in a trance, as this figure is, enabling them to commune with the spirit world. Along the mountainous border between Colombia and Ecuador, a stool-sitting figure chews coca in a projecting cud from his left cheek (see Chapter 8: Sickness and Healing, fig. 35). Stools from this area are sometimes rendered artistically, such as the wooden stools with spirit features of the Taino on the island of Hispaniola and the Savonarola-like stone stools supported by sculpted slaves used by the Manteño of coastal Ecuador. A handsome large-scale blackware figure of a Manteño chief expresses his power through his wide shoulders and chest, which swells like that of Superman (**25**). The large nose typical of the representation of Manteño faces gives an assertive power to all figures in this culture. Physical power is also conveyed by the Costa Rican warrior brandishing a knife and carrying a trophy head (**26**). Its aggressive masculinity

and muscular physique honored this warrior, probably a chief, in a sculpture that was placed on his grave mound. The construction of earthen grave mounds by cultures with chiefly organization—including the Japanese and the Celts—is a striking example of independent invention under similar cultural circumstances across the world.

In the eastern half of the United States, before European arrival disrupted the development of their cultures, chiefs ruled throughout the Mississippi River watershed. These chiefdoms, called Mississippian after their location, flourished between 700 and 1540. Their culture is also called the Temple Mound period because mounds, earlier used for burial, were increased in size and flattened to allow temples to be erected on their tops. The chiefs of these cultures commemorated themselves and their wives in stone carvings such as this example from eastern Tennessee (**27**). The carvings of chiefs produced in this region have the most realistic faces, although the torsos were depicted less naturalistically: they are smaller proportionally than the heads and not fully articulated, likely to avoid breaking the stone. Their faces have indications of some black tattooing, no doubt reflecting their heritage, which allowed them to serve as chiefs. These cultures also developed the sculptural complexity of pipe bowls, already part of eastern Woodland culture (like **7**), to include full-figure humans in flexible poses.

Among cultures observed and documented by experienced outsiders during periods of their flourishing, those of chiefly organization displayed similar expressions in their art, particularly renderings of their chiefs. Tribes

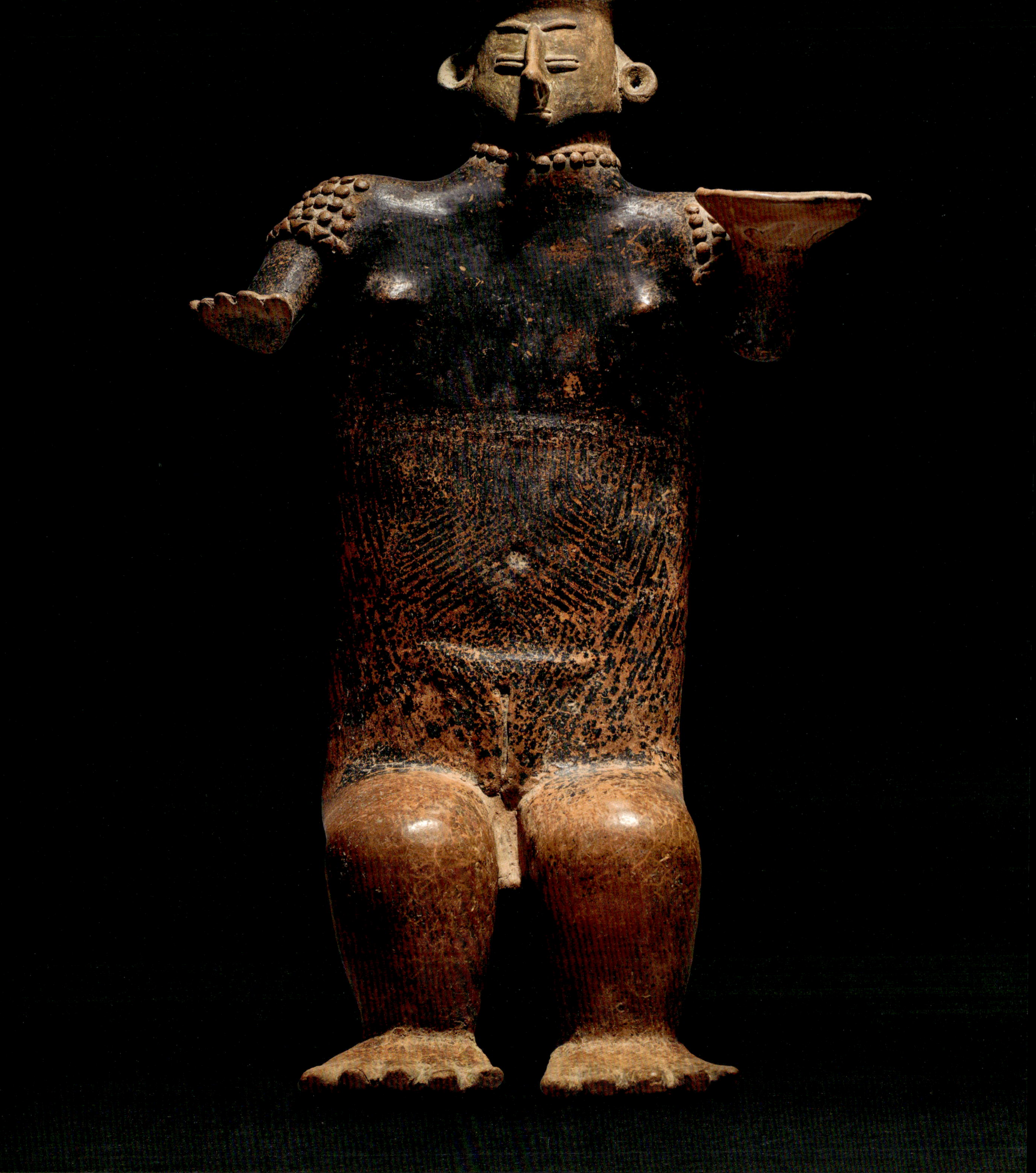

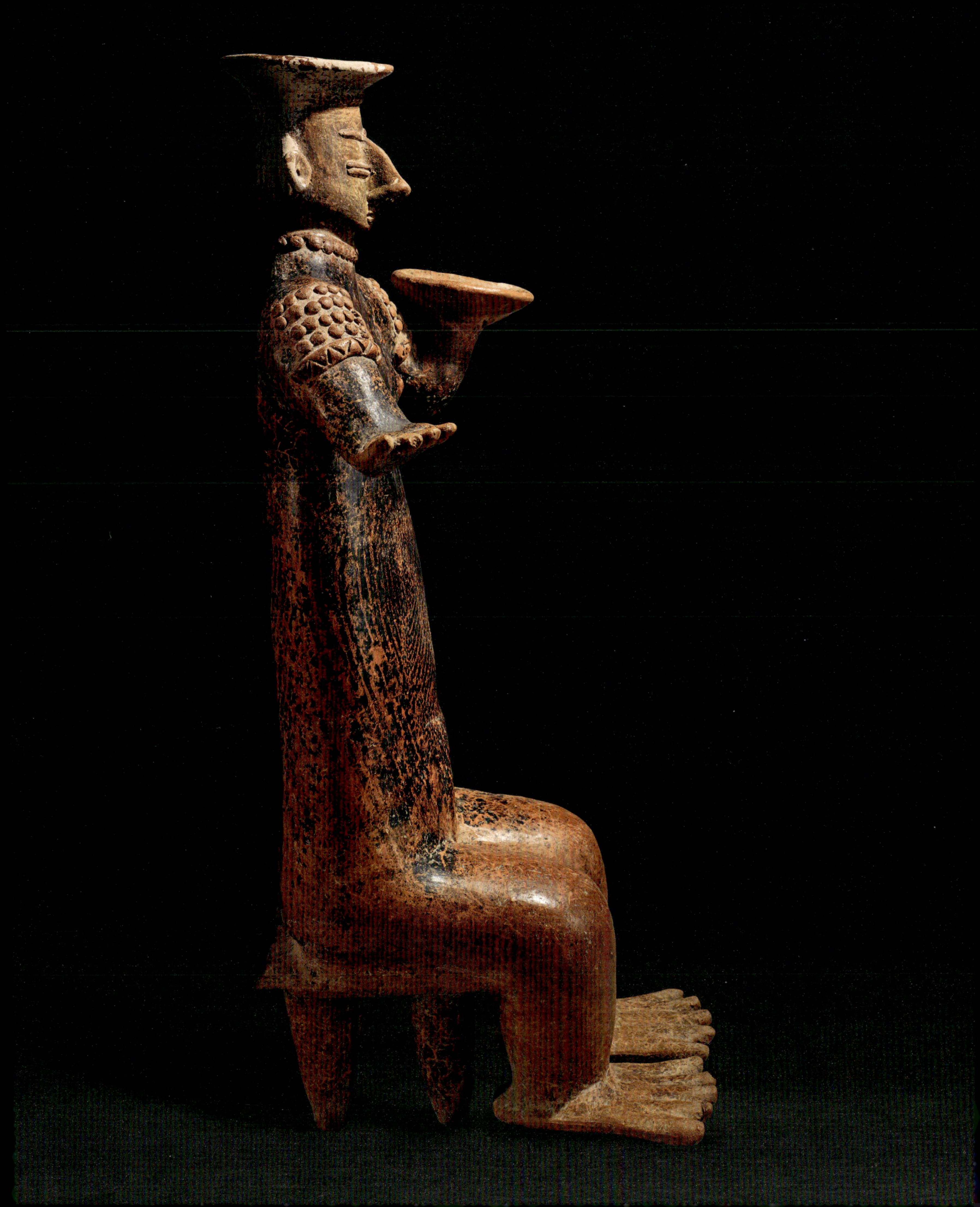

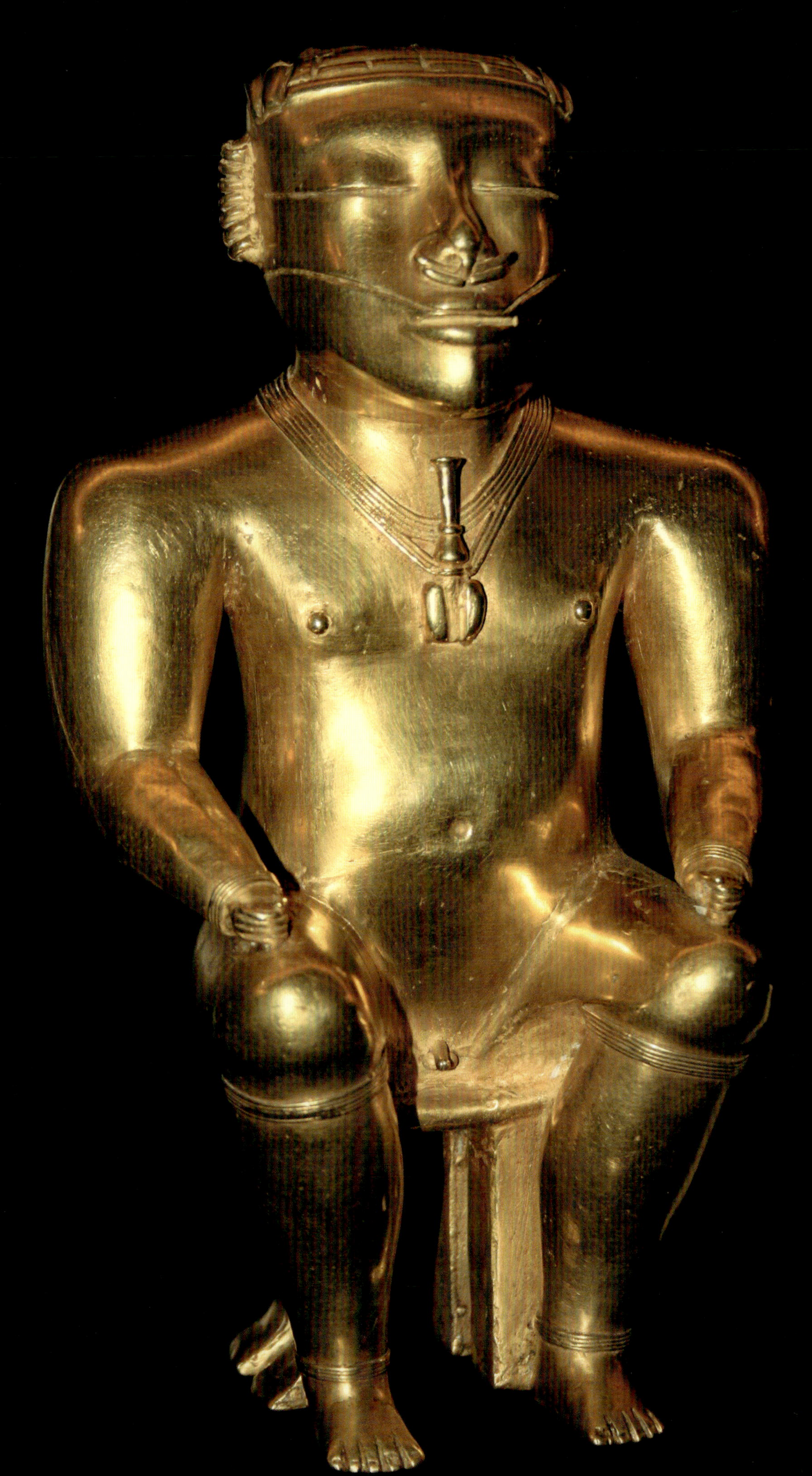

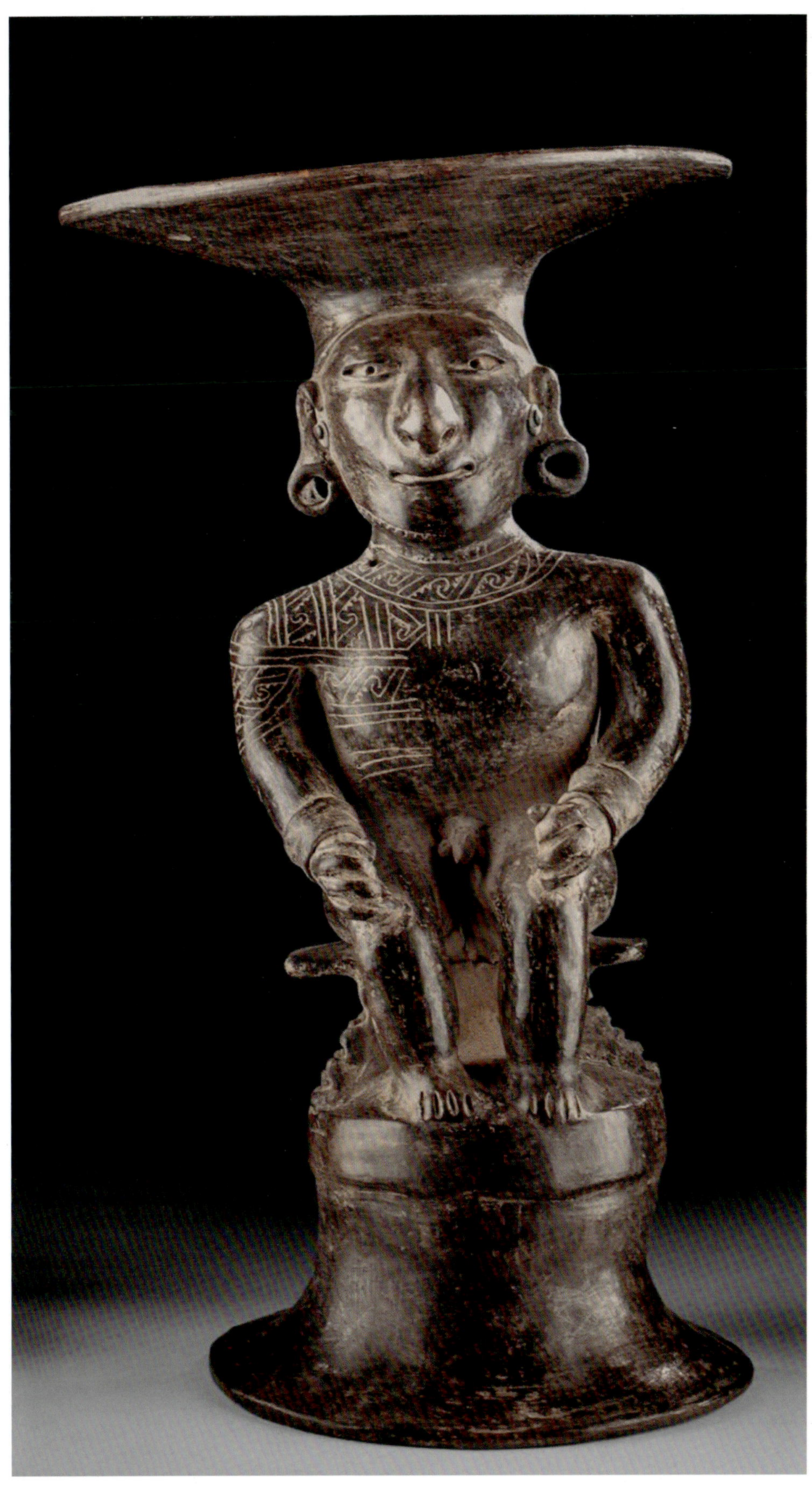

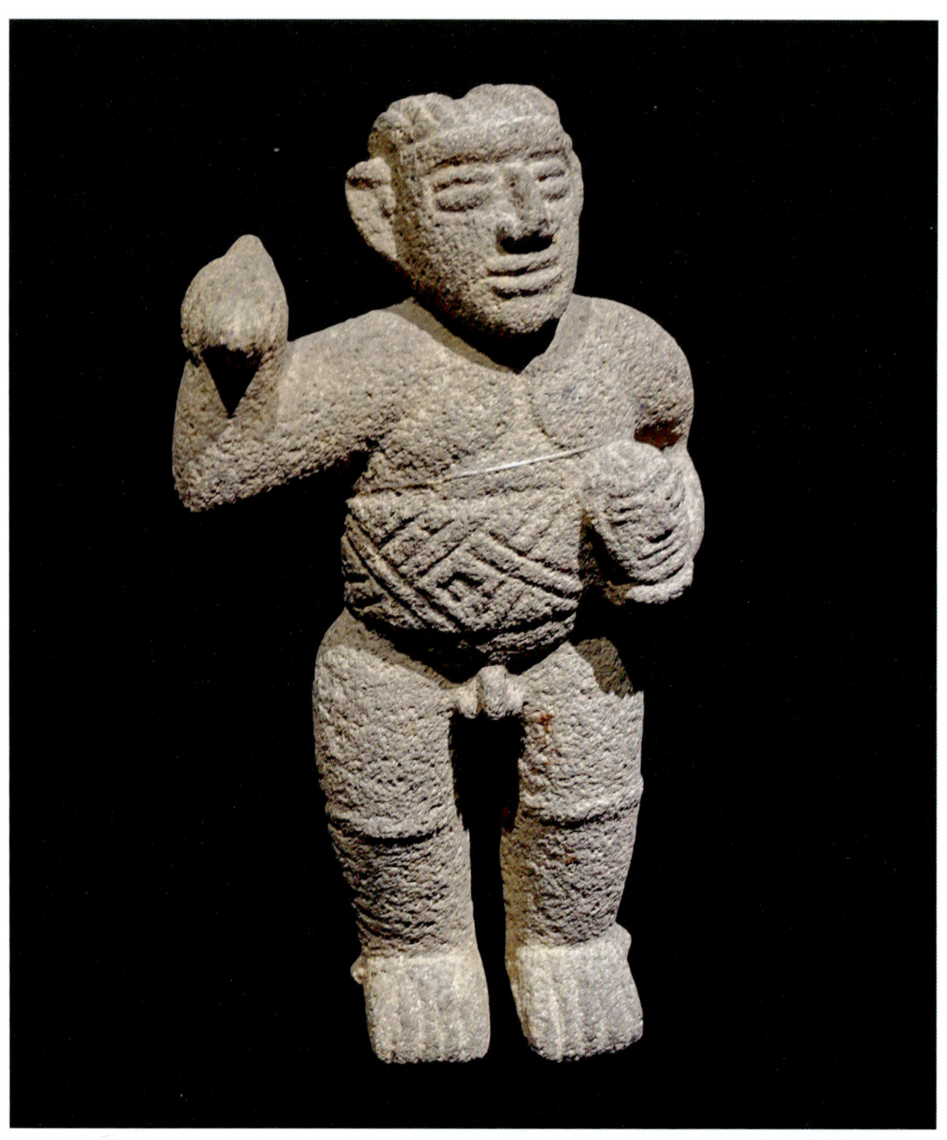

26 Warrior Figure with Trophy Head

Atlantic Watershed Zone,
Costa Rica
700 – 1100
Volcanic stone
Museum of Jade and the
Pre-Columbian Culture,
San Jose, Costa Rica

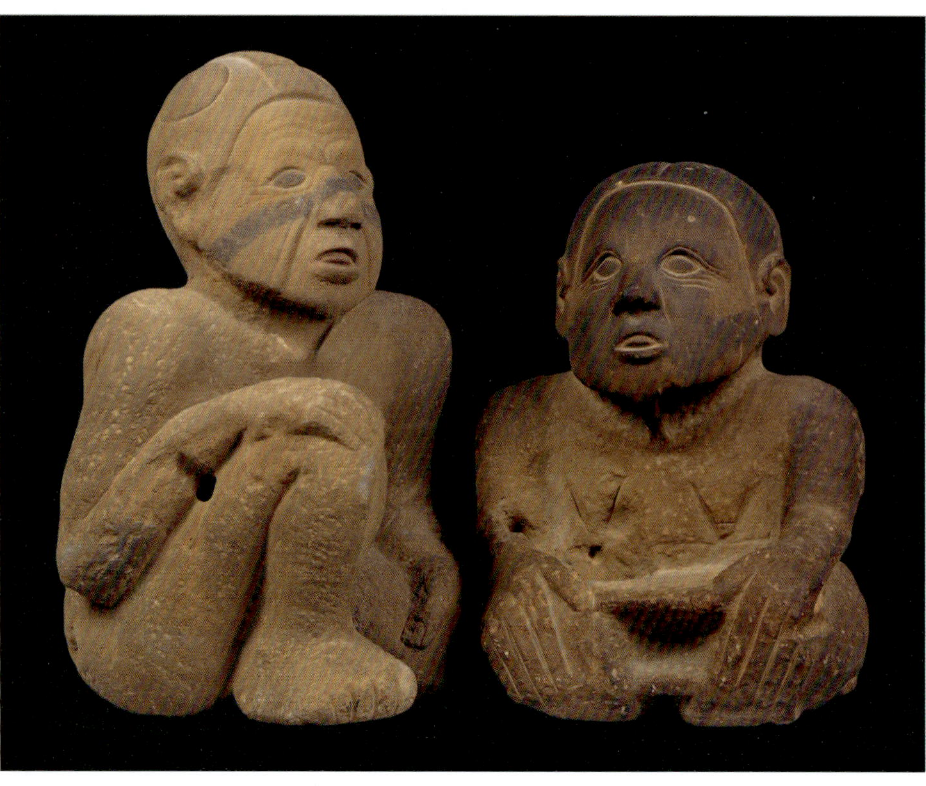

27 Male and Female Figures

Mississippian culture,
Cumberland Rivers region, Tennessee
1200 – 1400
Stone
18 ½ and 15 in., 46.99 and 38.10 cm

Male: McClung Museum of
Natural History & Culture,
Knoxville, Tennessee
Female: John C. Waggoner,
Jr. Collection
Photo: David H. Dye

28 **Figure of a Famous Kwakiutl Chief Holding a Ceremonial Copper Plate**

Kwakiutl culture,
British Columbia, Canada
1881
Wood
Ethnological Museum,
Berlin, Germany
Jacobsen Collection, 1881

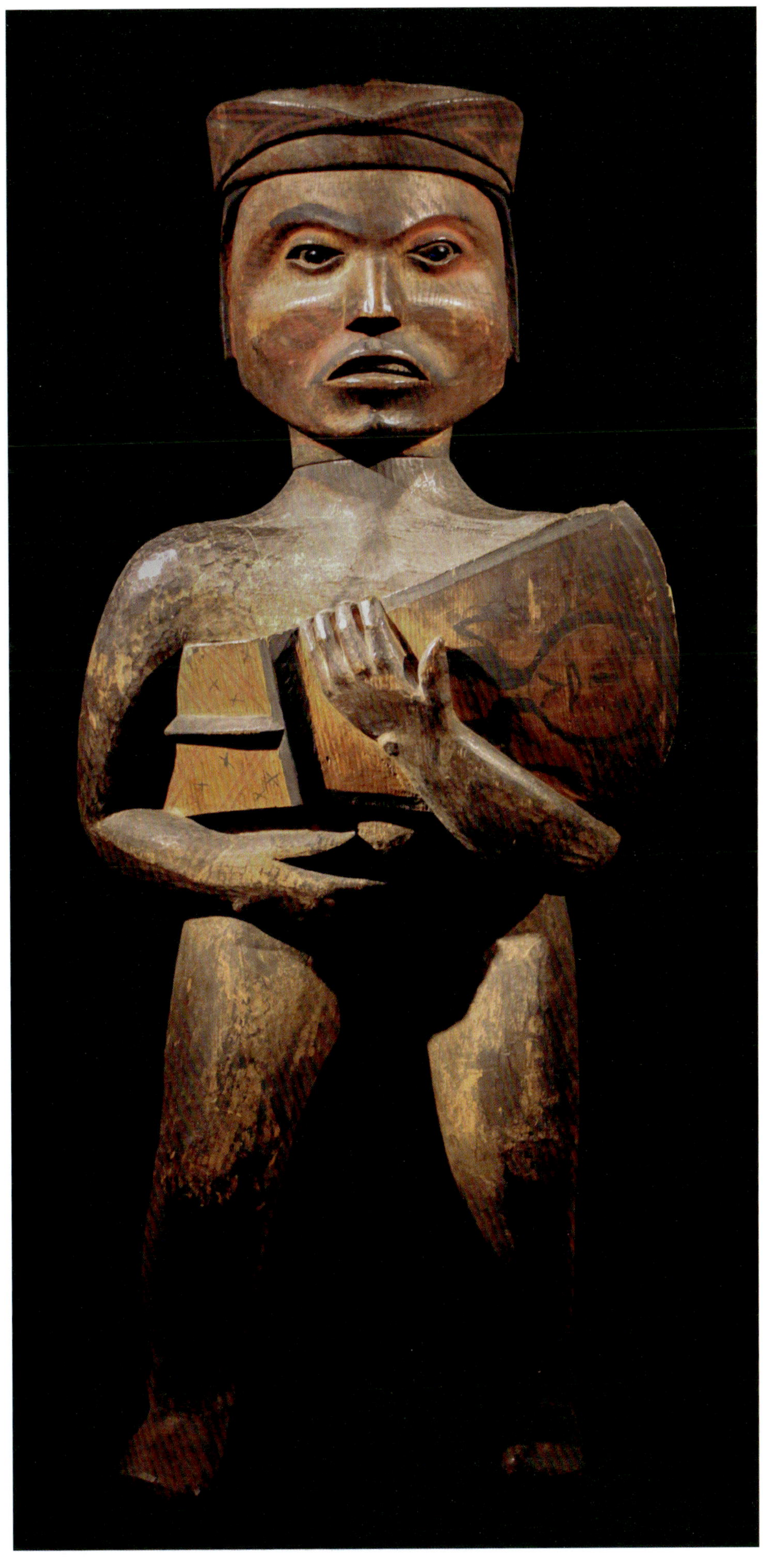

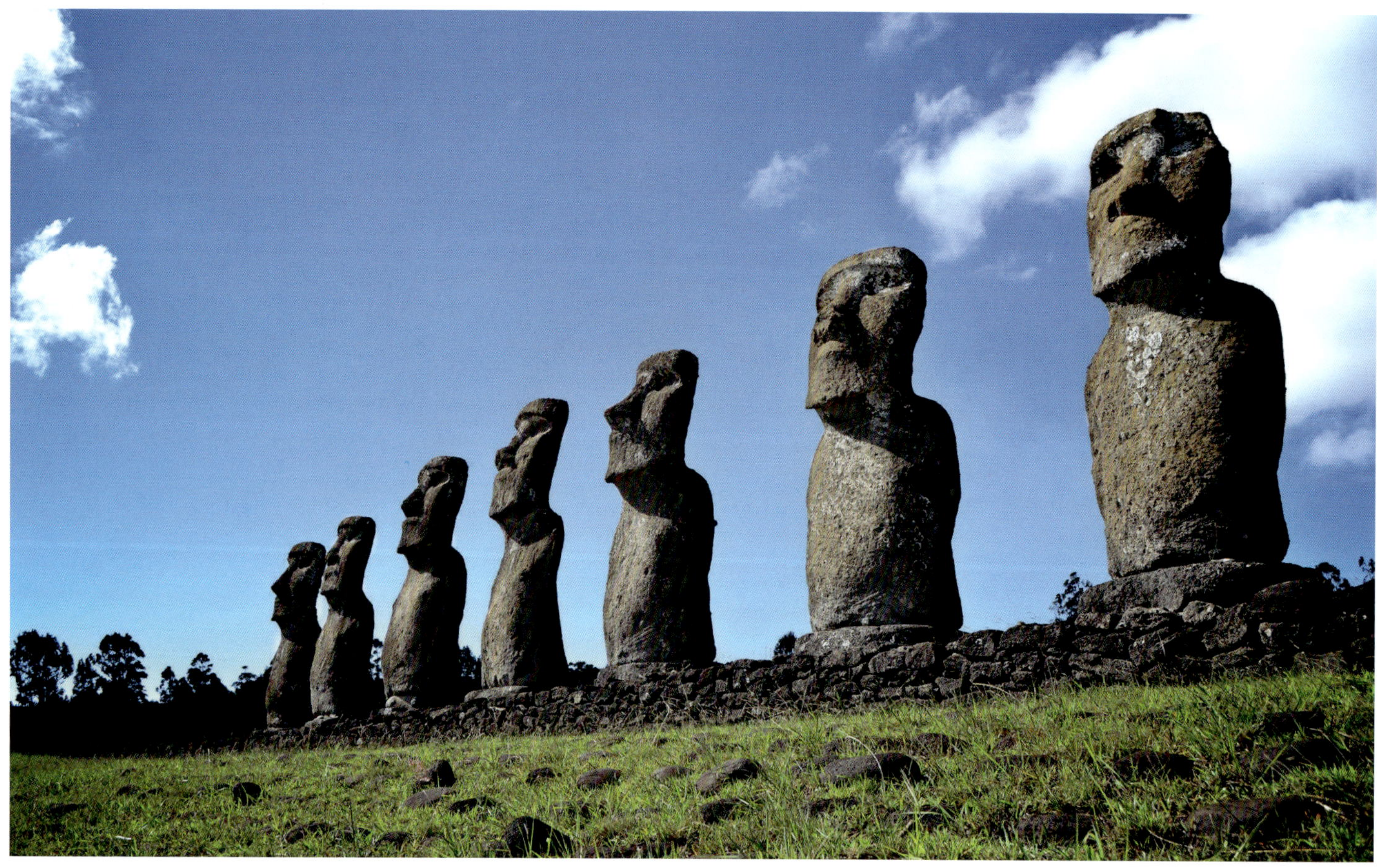

on the northwest coast of North America developed
a highly stratified society based on the abundance of
seafood and the heavy rainfall of the temperate forests
of mainly cedar that come down to the water's edge in
the archipelagos of Washington State, British Columbia,
and southeastern Alaska. Cedars were used to make large
gable-ended plank houses dominated by a male chief, the
structural poles of which were carved with the history of
his lineage and the stories associated with it (so-called
"totem-poles"). A Kwakiutl cedar carving represents a
chief holding a "copper," hammered in very distinctive
hexagonal outline trisected by ridges in its middle (**28**).

Such a copper is a mark of the chief's great wealth,
accumulated through hosting multiday potlatches—great
feasts at which he demonstrated his right to command
by dispersing much of his wealth in blankets and other
goods. The chief's face is generalized with idealized
features, although the sharp nose can be seen as a racial
marker. Unusual among chiefly societies, the Northwest
Coast natives had no need for agriculture because of the
wealth of their maritime environment.

Polynesian societies of the South Pacific during the age
of European exploration from the sixteenth through the
eighteenth centuries were dominated by chiefly societies;

Baule culture, Guinea Coast,
Ivory Coast
1800 – 1900
Wood, beads
Cleveland Museum of Art
Gift of Katherine C. White

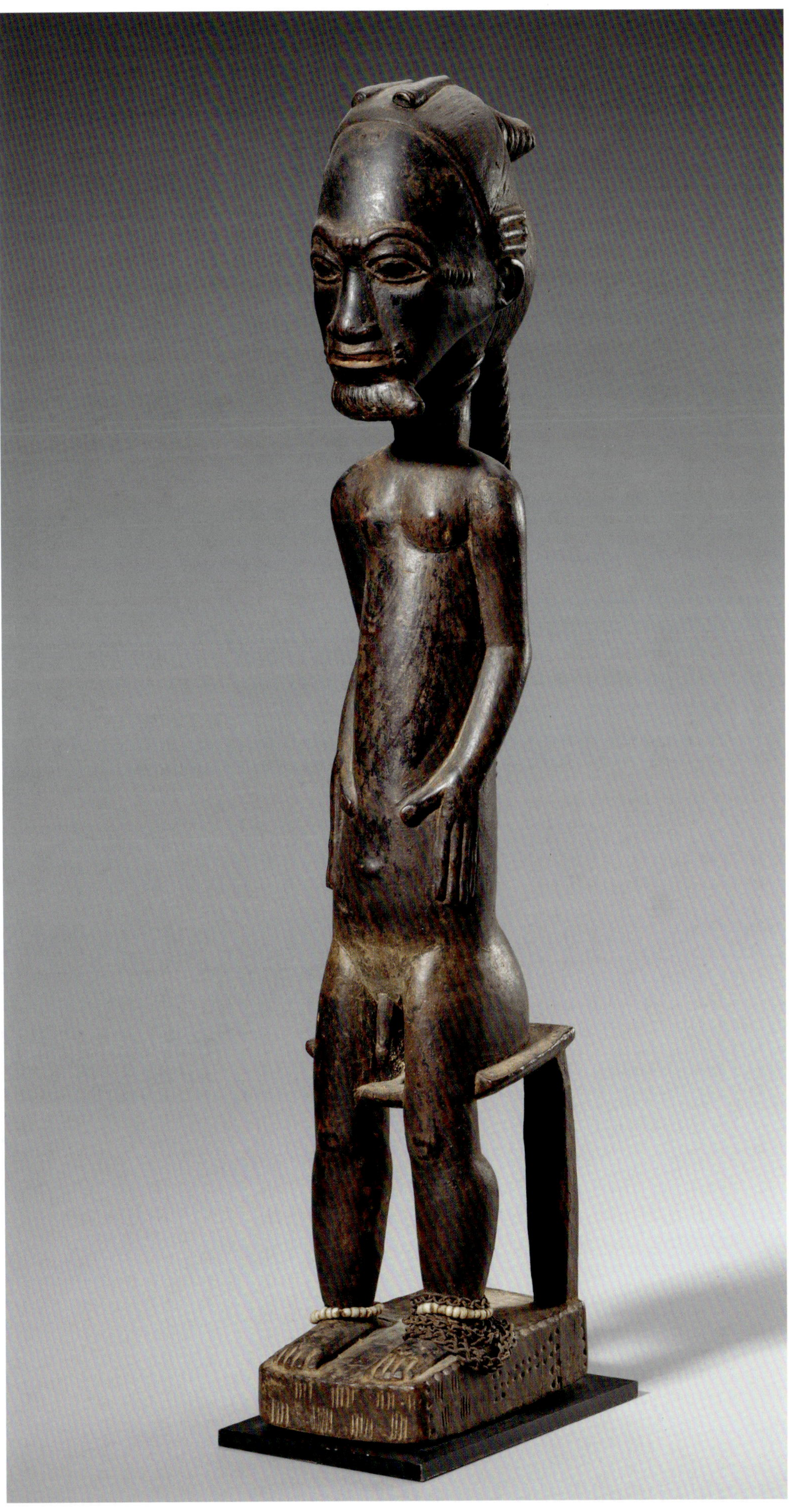

a few, such as Tahiti and the Hawaiian Islands, even became kingdoms, although without any large cities, so their art retains the characteristics of that of chiefdoms. Commemoration of their leaders after death was centered in large, open enclosures called *marae*. On Easter Island—Rapa Nui in the Polynesian language—*marae* were erected with gigantic stone statues of ancestors (**29**), quite an engineering feat for a pre-industrialized culture. Civil war had toppled these by the time Europeans arrived, but a few were re-erected sometime in the twentieth century. The gray volcanic stone of the figures themselves was obtained from the slopes of the sacred volcano, where many still lie, some still attached to its side. Upon their deaths, ancestors became endowed with supernatural *mana* (positive spiritual power), so their statues together brought great power to the *marae*. Some of the figures have torsos with attached arms that extend below their pelvises; these torsos have biomorphic curves that indicate their full bellies and chests. Their heads are elongated and have long earlobes and noses and projecting jaws, an aggressive feature typical of Polynesian sculpture. Distinctive tattooing, often very elaborate, was typical of Polynesian groups, again to document the divine attributes upholding the chiefs' right to rule.

Finally in Africa, the Akan-speakers of Ghana and the Ivory Coast all developed chiefdoms, some of which, like the Ashanti, approached kingdoms. The Baule of the Ivory Coast carved handsome naturalistic figures out of wood using metal adzes and knives. West Africa entered the Iron Age before the start of the Common Era, and metalworking was a highly respected craft. Baule

figures often depicted not ancestors but spirit lovers who had seduced their partners through black magic. Through appeasement and care for the statues carved to represent them, the earthly partners could lead a normal life. The skin of this male figure has been beautifully oiled by his owner as a way of showing this care (**30**). His facial features are integrated into his head, indicating naturalistic observation. The supple biomorphic curves of his elongated torso express dynamic life. He is rendered sitting on a chair, indicating his high rank in spiritual society. In the art of chiefdoms, we see a degree of naturalism, but not portrait-like realism, and an emphasis on the figure of the chief and his ability to transfer his spiritual power to his descendants.

Art of Urban States

An increased population made possible by more intensive agriculture and the concentration of people in urban centers required a more authoritarian type of government, usually a kingdom. The art produced by these societies continued to employ the greater naturalism established by chiefdoms but added more realism in the depictions of faces. Reliefs and paintings include the ground lines on which participants stand and an indication of landscape or architectural space in addition to people and animals found in previous art. Valuable materials are increasingly incorporated into these works. Some urban cultures developed writing systems and used them to identify the participants. This chapter will consider urban

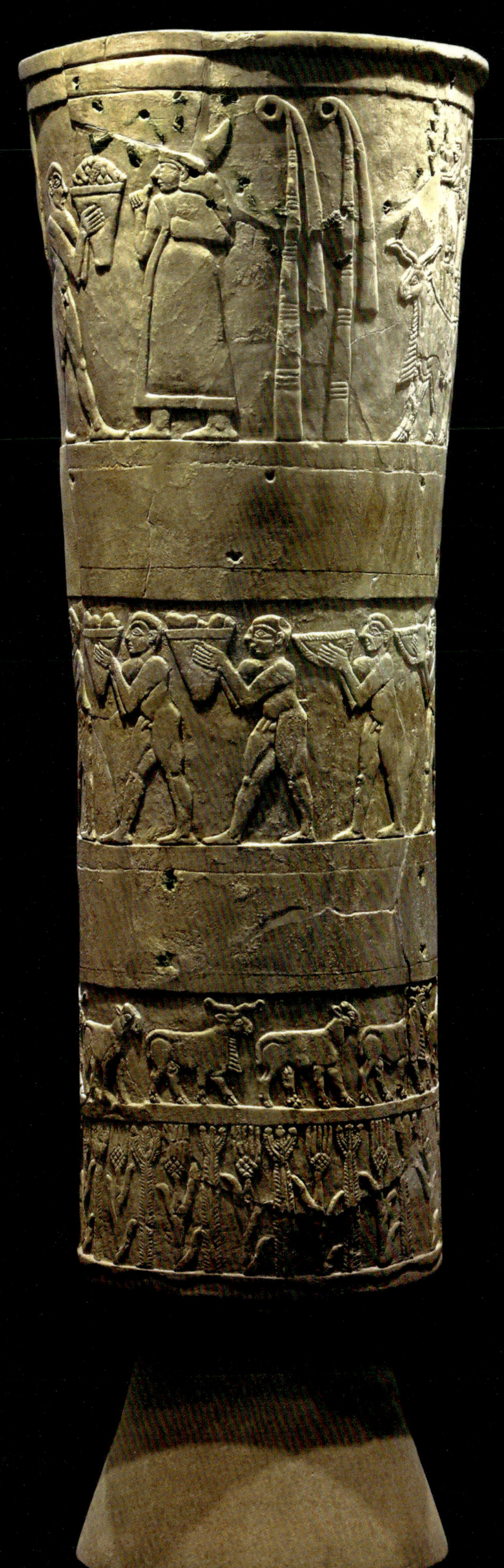

societies to the point where they develop the furthest in these directions but will not examine later variations on these themes.

The first civilization arose in Mesopotamia, the area between the Tigris and Euphrates rivers, in the thirty-fifth century BCE. This fertile land required considerable control to regulate its use, and the produce grown on the land caused an increase in population sufficient to inhabit a city. Early cities were independent entities we call city-states, the most important of which was the Sumerian city of Uruk, called Warka in the modern Arabic of Iraq. A large vase from Uruk summarizes key features of the society of its time: the bottom register shows the fruits of agriculture—wheat and date palms—while the next register up shows domesticated sheep (31). Above them are nude, shaven priests carrying baskets of produce given by the people for the maintenance of the temple and those priests. The top register shows the goddess Inanna receiving the produce, while behind the top priest stands a fragmentary relief of the ruler in a long skirt and train. Complete representations of this ruler on other works such as cylinder seals (used to roll an impression into wet clay) show him nude above the waist, full bearded, and wearing a hat with a rolled brim. This costume is also worn by a hero figure, predecessor of the Semitic legendary king Gilgamesh, who controls wild animals such as lions. This control of nature—through irrigation and organized division of the landscape—created a sense of confidence that was reflected in the naturalism of the art. A fragmentary bust of a figure with the attributes of

the ruler shows a muscular torso and the fists pressed together to flex the biceps (32). His back, not seen here, is also flexed—this is not the type of smooth surface seen in the art of less self-confident societies. The eyes, comprised of bitumen surrounding a colored stone inlay, stare intensely ahead, commanding our attention. Such ruler statues in later Sumerian culture are known to have been placed in temples to show perpetual reverence to the deity therein.

A Semitic culture known as the Akkadian conquered the Sumerian cities in the twenty-fourth century BCE and extended its reign well up into the Syrian and Iranian highlands, creating the first documented empire. A stone monument erected in the Iranian lowlands, at that time occupied by the Elamite people, shows in large scale the triumphant ruler, identified by cuneiform writing, at the top of a mountain, the sun shining directly on him (33). He wears a horned helmet, a symbol of his divinity; we will see that the ruler's claim of divinity characterizes many urban civilizations. Both the mountain and the undersized trees indicate the environment in which the actors participate, a feature almost unknown in the art of less advanced cultures. In a dramatic portrayal of the action, Akkadian warriors ascend the mountain to confront the four remaining enemies. It is more typical for two-dimensional renderings in early urban art to use a horizontal register line to represent the ground.

A Sumerian ruler figure appears on the relief carving on the handle of a knife from predynastic Egypt; it was probably copied from Mesopotamian cylinder seals

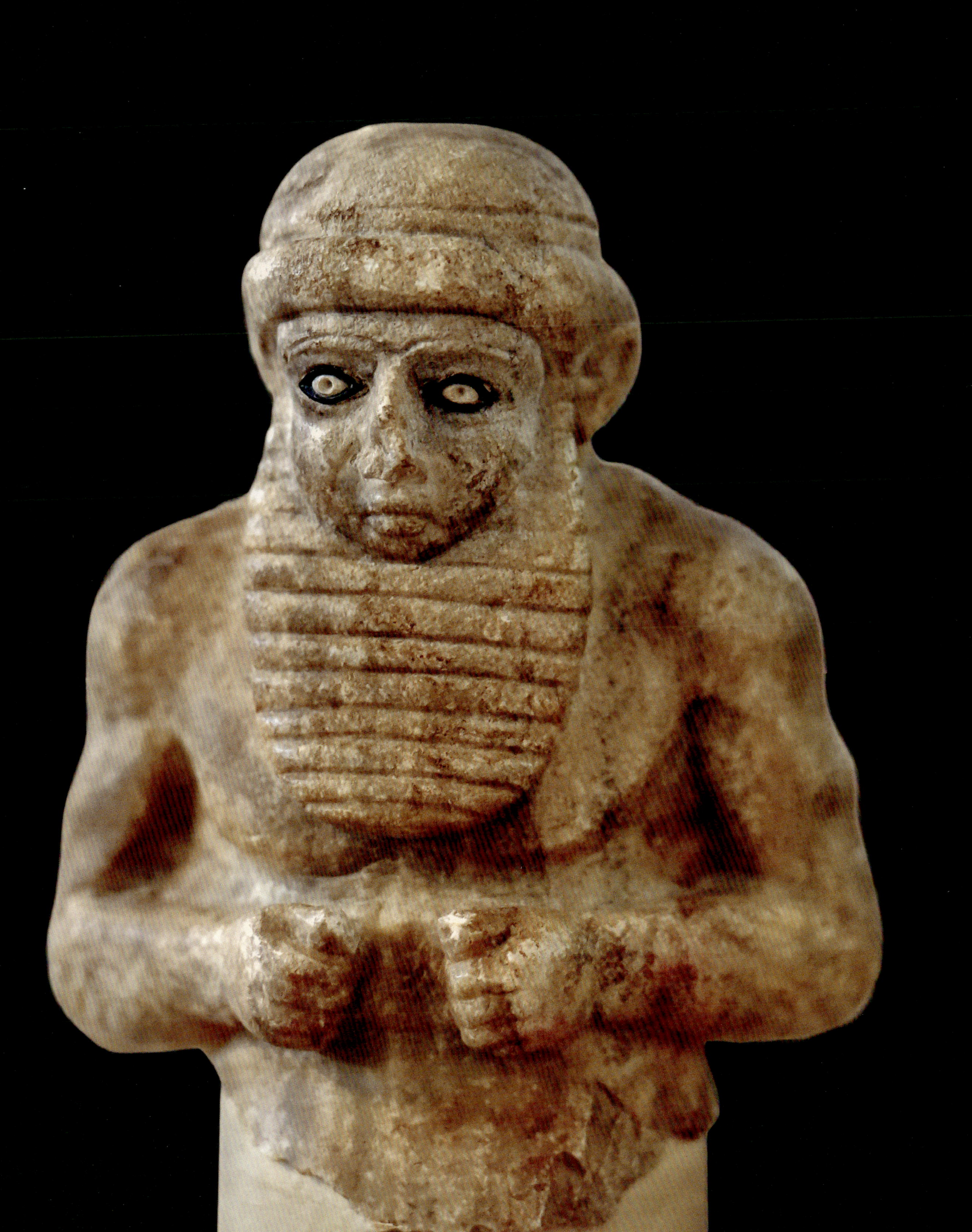

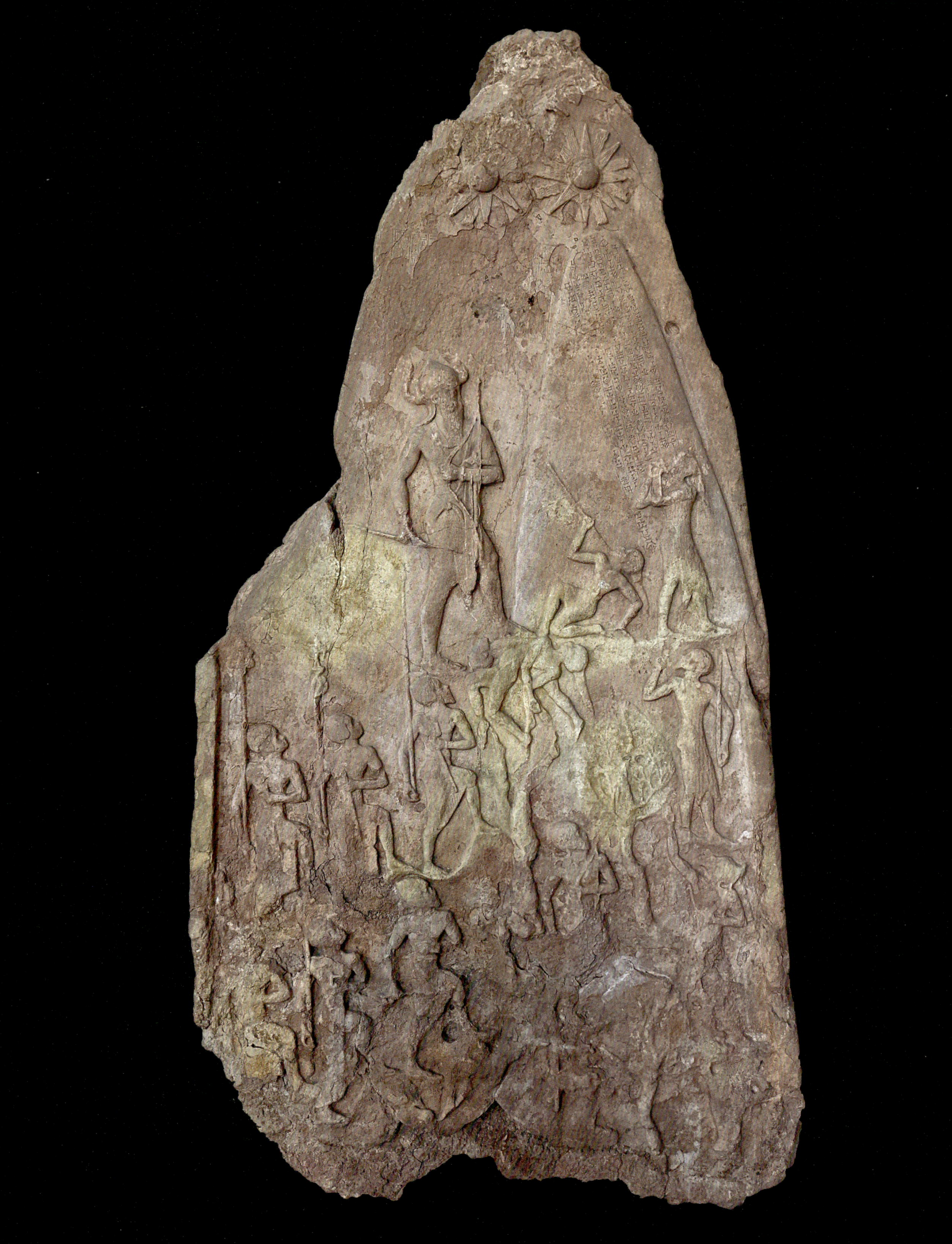

33 **Victory Stele of Naram-Sin**

Susa, Iran
Akkadian Empire, 2254 – 2218 BCE
Limestone
78.7 × 41.3 in., 200 × 105 cm
Louvre Museum, Paris, France

34 **Funerary Monuments from the Tomb of Hesi-Re**

Egypt
Old Kingdom, Dynasty 3, 2649 – 2575 BCE
Wood
Egyptian Museum, Cairo

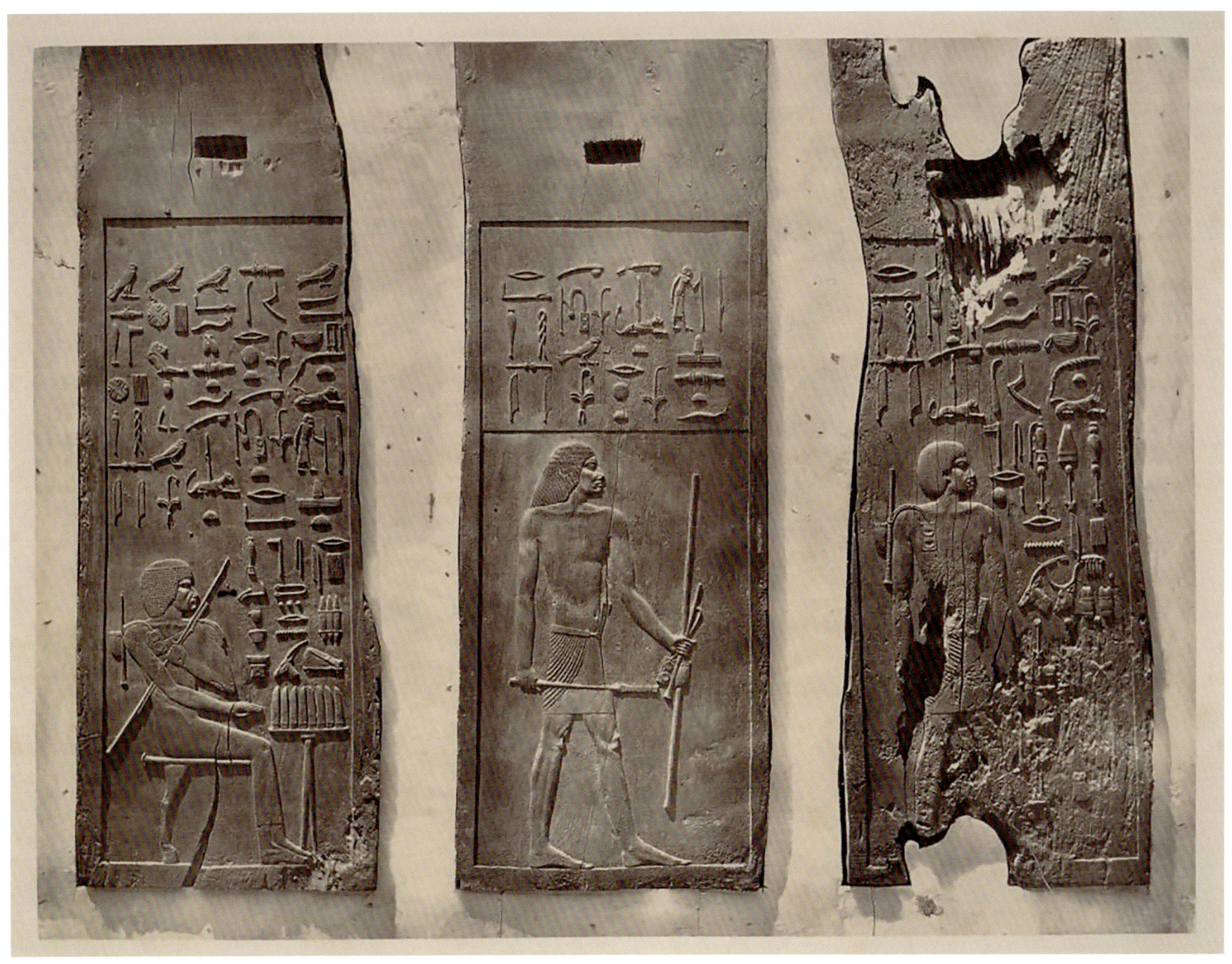

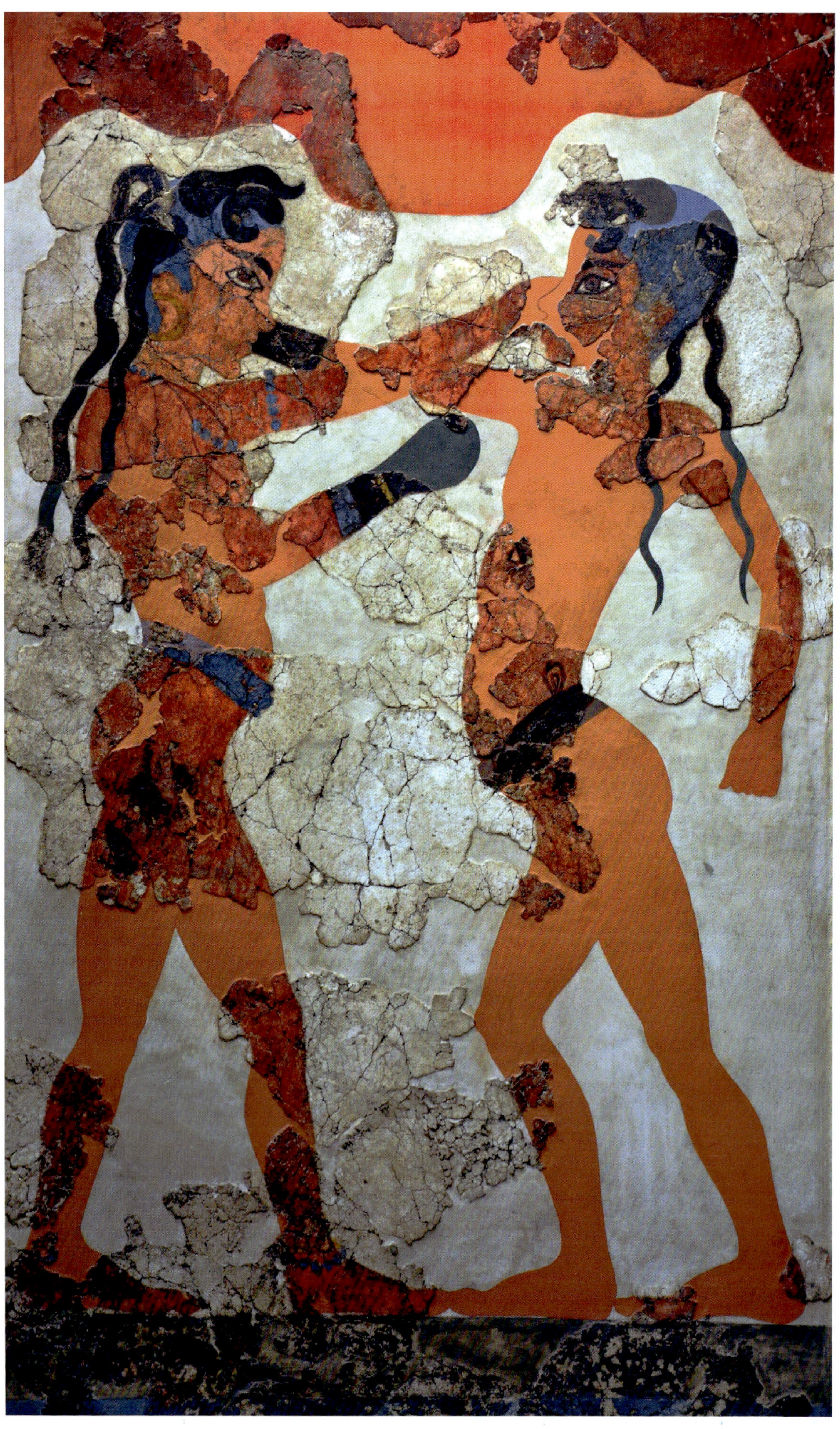

35 Boxers

Akrotiri, Thera (Santorini), Greece
1700 BCE
Fresco
National Archaeological Museum,
Athens, Greece

marking trade goods, indicating that Sumer developed urban civilization earlier than Egypt. By the time of the Old Kingdom (2665–2155 BCE), Egyptian kings had assumed divinity, which Mesopotamian rulers other than Sargon never did. Their control of agriculture in the Nile valley, with its predictable periodic floods, gave people a confidence in their dominance of nature that was reflected in their art. Menkaura, the pharaoh buried in the smallest of the three pyramids of Giza, had nearly life-size statues rendered of himself accompanied by two female deities, and their bodies have a swelling naturalism and accurate proportions (see Chapter 4: Motherhood and the Family, fig. 16). The gowns on the two goddesses cling to their bodies like wet T-shirts. Menkaura's face, smooth with the vigor of youth, is recognizable from other depictions. The figures seem somewhat stiff to our eyes because contrapposto (the depiction of weight shift) would not be utilized until fifth-century-BCE Greece. Their posture expresses a permanence appropriate to sculptures destined to provide a home to the souls of the deceased. A set of tomb reliefs identifiable through their hieroglyphic writing as belonging to Hesi-re, a noble, show him performing various roles useful to the rulers of the Old Kingdom (**34**). The naturalism comes through in the subtle relief of the torso, especially the chest and collar bones, but the overall body proportions are regulated by a grid system that required the elbow to fall at the same height on the figure whether or not the arm was extended—to our eyes the arm appears stretched. In addition, his torso is seen frontally, while his head and

lower limbs are shown in side view. All three figures of Hesi-re are placed firmly on a ground line, an important characteristic of the art of urban civilizations. Much of the background in these reliefs is taken up by hieroglyphs, which surround the figures. Their identification of the roles played by Hesi-re are as important as the depiction of him in these roles, the last of which takes place at his funerary banquet. Writing at this early stage of urban art had a magical quality and was restricted to very few people, one of whom was Hesi-re, "the chief of scribes."

Greater flexibility appears in the art of the Minoan civilization that was contemporary with the New Kingdom of Egypt and with which Egyptian and Levantine merchants traded. Recently discovered frescoes from the Aegean island of Thera (modern Santorini) show daily activities such as fishing and boxing, here with two boys (**35**). Their fluid postures seem very different from those of the Egyptians—one thrusts his torso forward and the backward arch of his back reflects his opponent's punch. Nevertheless, their feet are squarely planted on the base line. In another fresco showing acrobatic bull-leaping, the figures seem practically weightless, either standing on their toes or already springing over the back of the charging bull. The bull himself is in the flying gallop posture, with all four feet off the ground, a pose created by Minoan artists that continued to be used as a convention in the West until the nineteenth century, when Eadweard Muybridge's photography showed that at least one leg always stays in contact with the ground when a horse is running. The flowing curves in these paintings also characterizes the small sculpture of a snake priestess from the capital city of Knossos (see Chapter 3: Creation Myths, fig. 5). Before her bare breasts, a Minoan fashion at the time, she thrusts out her hands holding poisonous snakes, her back curving in response. This sculpture of faience, a glazed ceramic ware adopted from Egypt, seems much more delicate than Egyptian sculptures, which are often attached to a slab in the back. The maritime civilization of the Minoans made positive use of the sea and its bounty, so nature was its ally, not a threat.

Art of the New Kingdom in Egypt adopted some of the naturalistic flexibility of Minoan art, especially during the Amarna period, when the pharaoh Akhenaten (1352–1336 BCE) broke with religious convention to initiate exclusive worship of the solar disk. Representations of Akhenaten exaggerated his unusual features to such an extent that they border on caricatures, but they also broke with the strict grid proportionality of early Egyptian art (see Chapter 4: Motherhood and the Family, fig. 15). Akhenaten's son Tutankhamun (reigned 1332–1323 BCE) returned to the worship of the traditional pantheon, but his art retained some of the softness and fluidity of the Minoan style. This may be seen in the vast number of objects buried with him in the Valley of the Kings in 1327 BCE, such as a painted chest (see Chapter 6: Conflict and Warfare, fig. 8). The horses pulling his chariot are depicted in a more stable position than the flying gallop, with both of their rear legs on the ground line. In the hunting scene (top) and the battle scenes (front and back), he attacks his prey/enemies, who are plunging into a landscape; they are

in a chaotic environment, while he and his troops behind him stand securely on register lines. Egyptians found stability and confidence in an organized world, whereas their enemies or prey resided in wild nature. This sense of control allowed them to render humans with moderately accurate proportions, although high-status individuals were shown larger in scale than lower-status ones.

In the Assyrian Empire of the early first millennium BCE, which conquered all of the Near East and eventually Egypt, reliefs from palace walls depict courtiers as overly muscular, almost to the point of stripping off the skin on their legs and arms to show the forearm and calf muscles separate from the bones to which they are attached (**36**). Their body proportions otherwise are accurate, and the left foot, with each of its toes articulated, is distinguished from the right foot, on which only the big toe is rendered. This expresses the power of empire, even as these courtiers are rendering homage and bearing gifts of an ibex and flowers to the emperor.

Classic Greek art of the first millennium BCE demonstrates the process of studying nature to achieve fully naturalistic, and later realistic, depictions of the human form. As Greece emerged from the Dark Age (1200–900 BCE), when the "People of the Sea," as the Egyptians called them, caused chaos and insecurity by their migrations among the peoples of the eastern Mediterranean and surrounding lands, their art became almost abstract and geometric, a result of trying to impose order on their world, or at least its expression in their art. In the eighth century BCE, humans were still rendered with

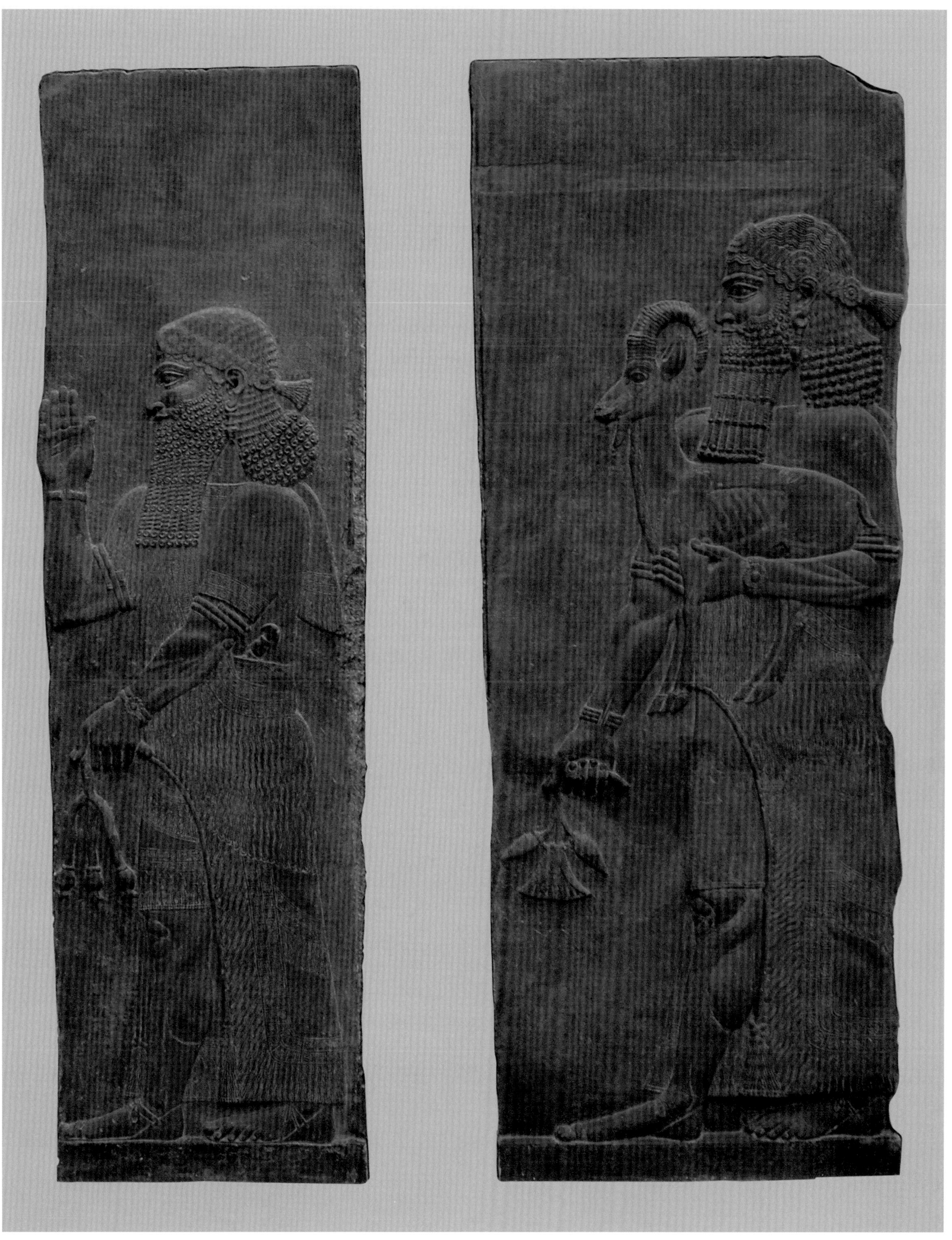

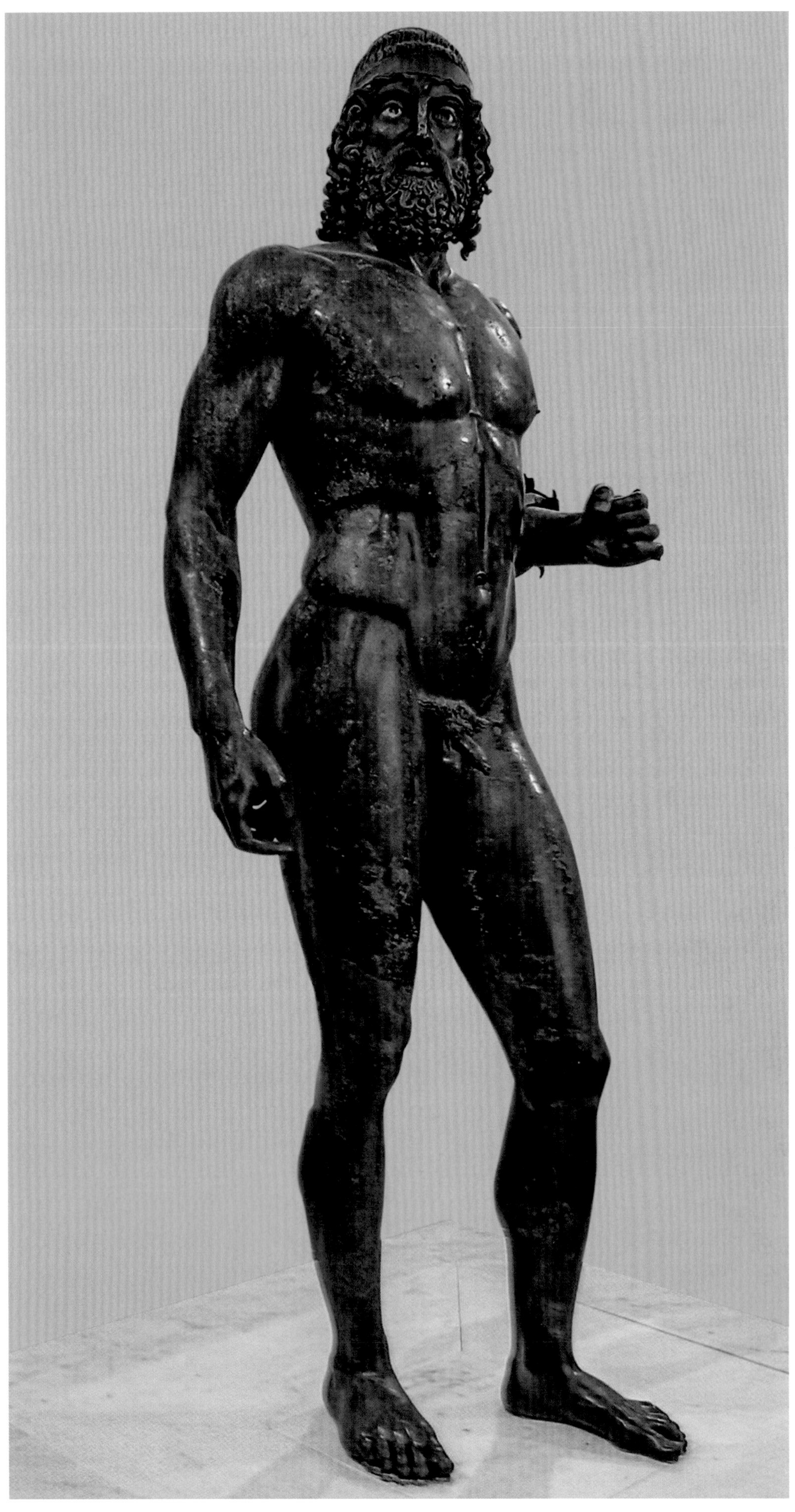

a geometric stylization, as we saw in village cultures. In the Archaic period of the sixth century, the depiction of humans emulated the stiff naturalism of dynastic Egypt, but more attention was paid to male anatomy and female drapery. In the fifth century, artists began to render figures in contrapposto, showing their weight shifted between an engaged leg supporting the body and a free leg trailing. Relative adjustments in the hips, spine, neck, and head followed, breaking from the rigidly frontal poses of the Egyptian sculptural canon. A sculpture by Polykleitos called the *Canon*, although usually known as the *Spear Bearer* (ca. 440 BCE), established the new Greek system that is believed to be based on geometric proportions of increasingly larger units of size. Recently discovered examples of bronze sculptures applying that canon were dredged out of the sea off Riace, southern Italy, where they had been shipwrecked (**37**). After patient cleaning, one warrior (missing his helmet, shield, and sword) demonstrated a fluid naturalism of the idealized male body. His eyes were inlaid with white colored stones, and he had teeth and eyelashes of silver and lips and nipples rendered with copper to provide a red color contrast against the bronze tan. In this period Greeks felt on top of their world, having settled throughout the Mediterranean in various colonies and defeated the Persian Empire in 480 BCE. Their art echoes this confidence, depicting the human body in its idealized perfection.

Female figures of the Early Classic period reflect the lower status of women in the Greek world. A grave stele of a woman named Hegeso, her name inscribed in capital Greek letters in the top frame, shows her seated, reflectively examining a piece of jewelry, originally depicted in colored paint, while her maid, shown in smaller scale, stands by with her jewelry box (**38**). Both figures are clothed in loosely hanging drapery, ensuring a modesty appropriate to women; it is not until the fourth century BCE that nude women were depicted and then only as goddesses. Vessels called *lekythoi* used to pour oil on gravesites were painted at this time with similar scenes of mourning loved ones standing by a tomb. The earlier red figures on a black ground were replaced on these *lekythoi* by a white ground with figures in natural colors. The tomb of Philip II of Macedon (382–336 BCE) in Vergina, Greece, shows how dramatically painting left behind the restrictions we best know from vase painting: only two colors, profile views, lack of shading. Instead, the scene of Pluto abducting Persephone is rendered in three-quarter view, with Pluto's chariot and horses coming toward us, their faces and bodies in white with heavier outlines where shade would be. The painting has a sketchy feel to it, and the bodies are not distinguished from the white color of the background. Even vase painting in southern Italy during the fourth century incorporates more natural colors, uses three-quarter views, and places figures in an environment of architecture and landscape.

In the subsequent Hellenistic period following the death of Alexander the Great in 332 BCE, Greek art and other arts that followed its lead, like those of Etruria and Republican Rome, introduced dramatic realism into the rendering of figures and depth of field in their placement

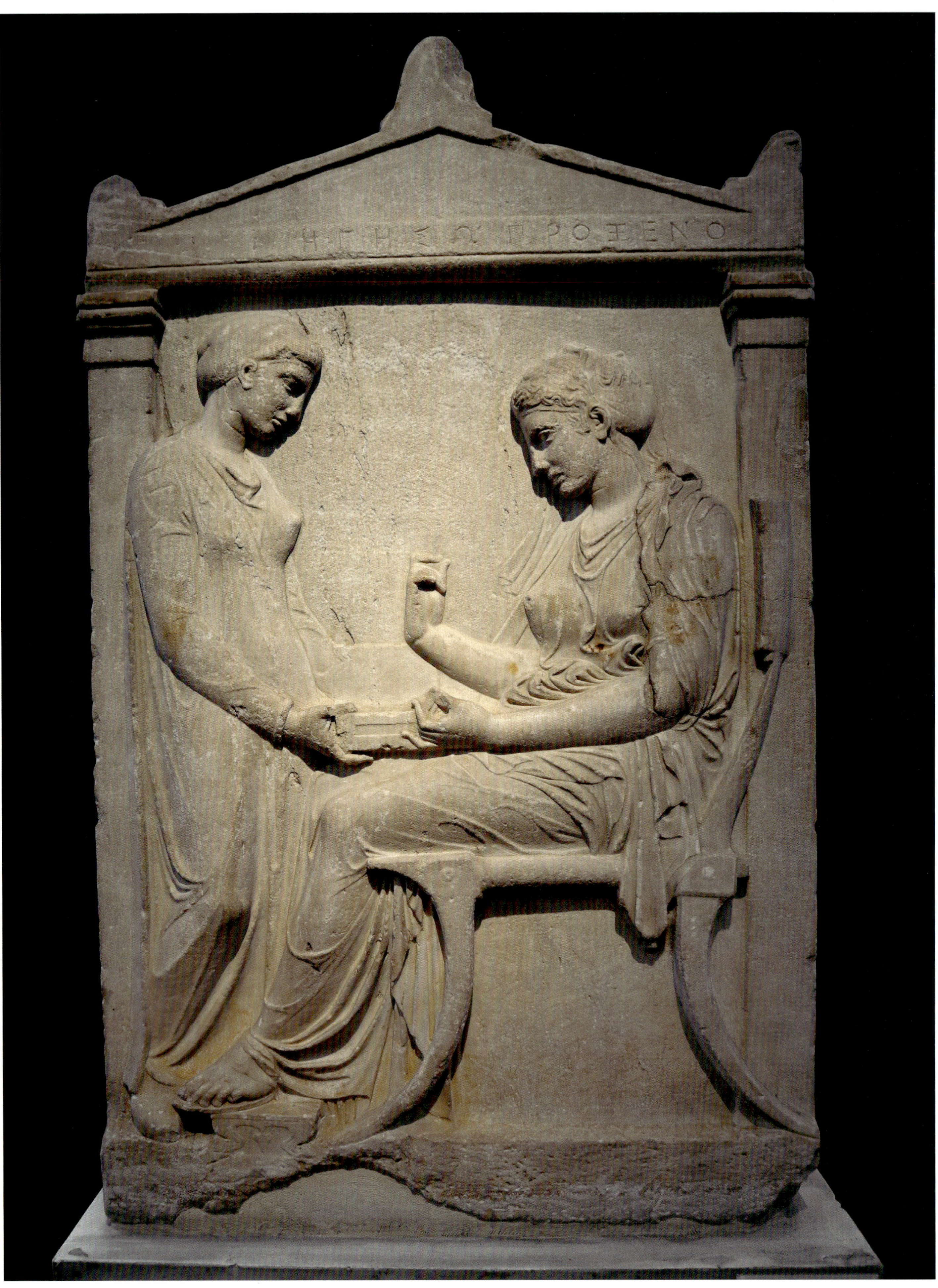

in their environment. By the time Augustus Caesar (63 BCE–14 CE) became a dictator and established his rule over the Roman Empire, he was considered partly divine. In the bronze original of the marble statue placed in his wife's villa at Primaporta, Cupid, a son of the goddess Venus, appears next to him at the base (p. 340). The artist documented a scene of surrender on an undulating ground line on Augustus's breastplate. Although the smooth features of his face and the clumps of his hair are somewhat idealized, Augustus is recognizable in this portrait—an aspect of realism introduced during the Hellenistic period. The earlier Classical period of Greek art is referenced in Augustus's posture, modeled after the *Canon* by Polykleitos. Much of Roman art copied famous works of that period, many of which were actually transported to Rome and its colonies, as was the Riace warrior when it was shipwrecked.

The Hellenistic period (332–30 BCE) spread Greek culture not only throughout the Mediterranean world but also as far east as modern Pakistan, where it came into contact with the Aryan peoples who had invaded India around 1500 BCE. In the northern part of India, Aryans displaced the native Dravidians, who around 2500 BCE had been the creators of the Indus Valley civilization, the first urban culture in the area. Stamp seals from that civilization reveal that it was literate, although they are still illegible to us, and had some deities related to later Hindu ones. A small stone bust survives, presumably of a ruler, rendered with naturalistic proportions. Two small stone sculptures represent male torsos with

notches for inserting erect phalluses and a very sensuous treatment of skin that foreshadows later treatment of the body in Hindu sculpture; one also has a tortional twist suggesting a dance posture, another important religious art form in later Hindu culture. But by the time of Hellenistic penetration into northern India, the dominant religion was not Hinduism but Buddhism, a reform movement derived from the sixth-century BCE teaching of Prince Siddartha Gautama, who became the Buddha (enlightened one). Art related to Buddhism in its early manifestation was symbolic and did not represent human forms, but the Hellenistic incursion triggered an impetus to represent humans. Excellent examples are found in the rock-cut temple of Karli, just south of Mumbai, India (**39**). They represent happy couples, swelling with life and sensuality, on either side of the central image of the Buddha. The sculptures grow out of the living rock itself, referring to the world mountain from which all creation emerged. Their smiles reflect the positivity that life can have if one follows Buddhist teachings. The asymmetry of their standing positions evokes Greek contrapposto, although not so systematically applied.

Renderings of the historic Buddha himself take on this happy expression but are more self-contained, and his naturalism transcends the more literal physicality of Greek sculpture (**40**). Many of the Buddha's features have symbolic meanings: the bony protuberance on top of his head is to contain his excess brain, the mole between his eyes symbolizes a third eye of wisdom, and a variety of hand positions called *mudras* have symbolic meaning. The

39 **Shrine in the Karla Caves**

A complex of ancient Indian Buddhist
rock-cut cave shrines located in Karli
near Lonavala, Maharashtra, India
100 BCE – 100 CE and 400 – 900 CE

40 **Seated Buddha Shakyamuni**

Gandhara culture, Central Asia, Pakistan, and Afghanistan
200 – 400 CE
Stucco
9 × 20.75 × 30 in., 22.9 × 52.7 × 69.8 cm
Private Collection
Artemis Gallery, Louisville, Colorado

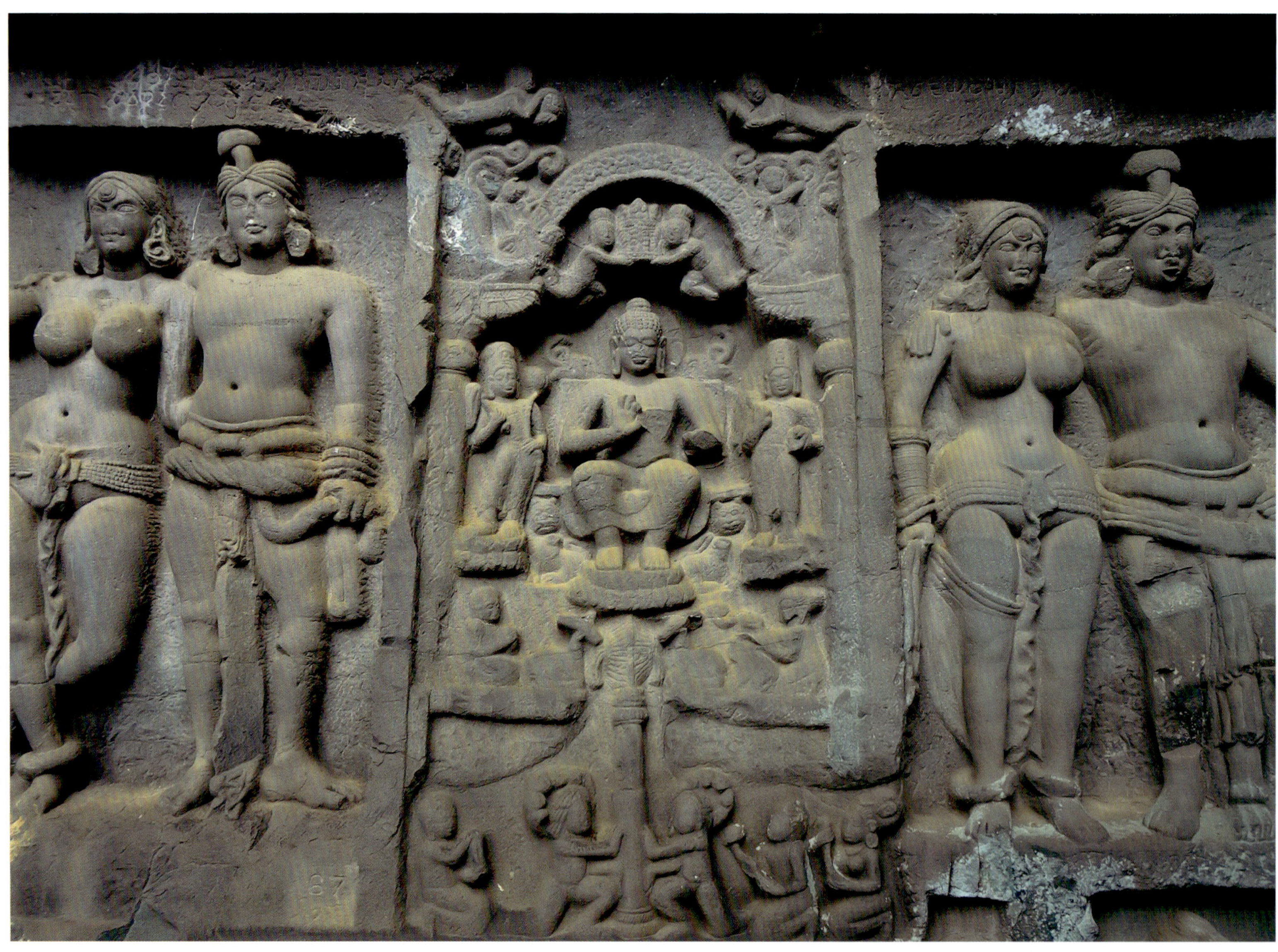

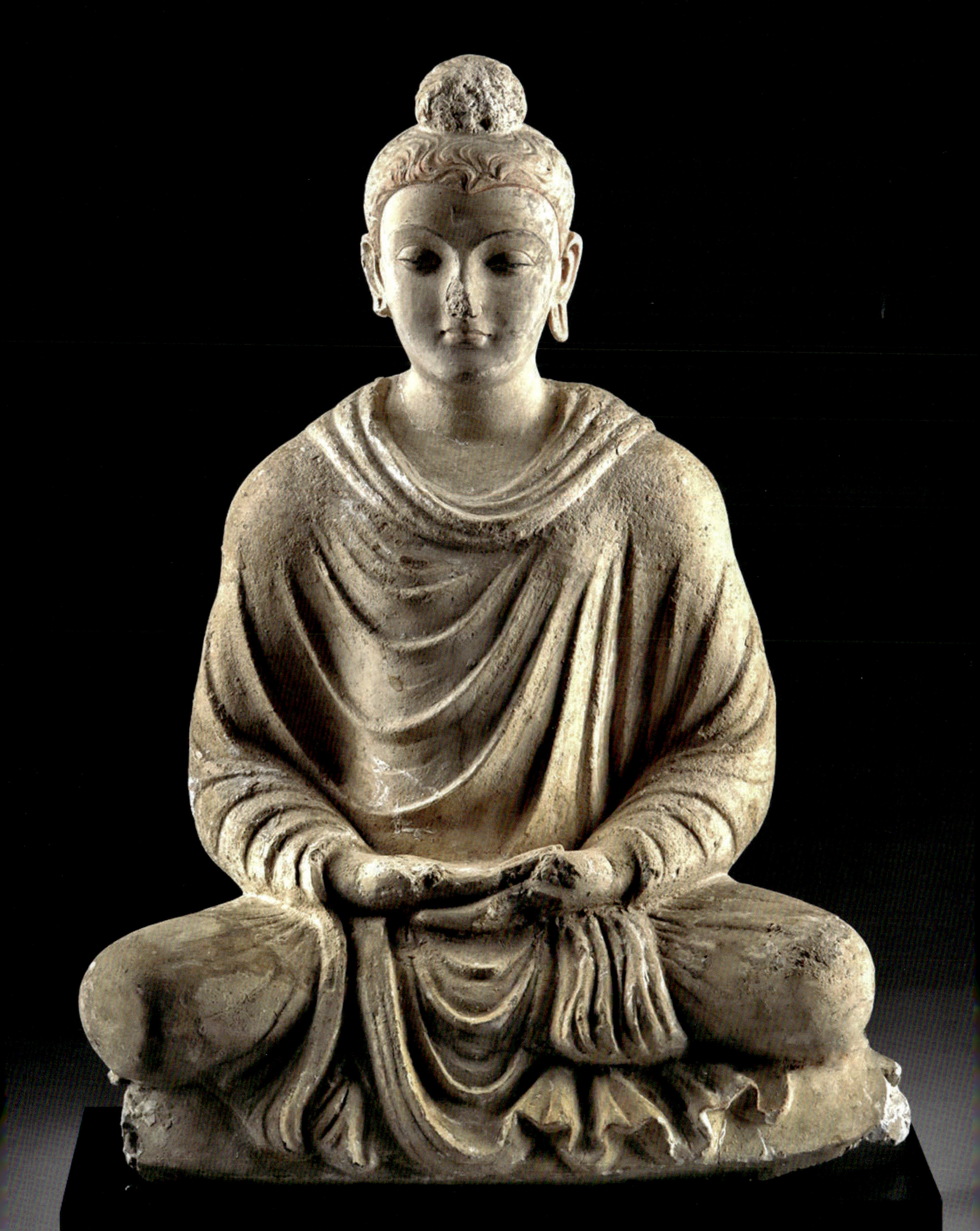

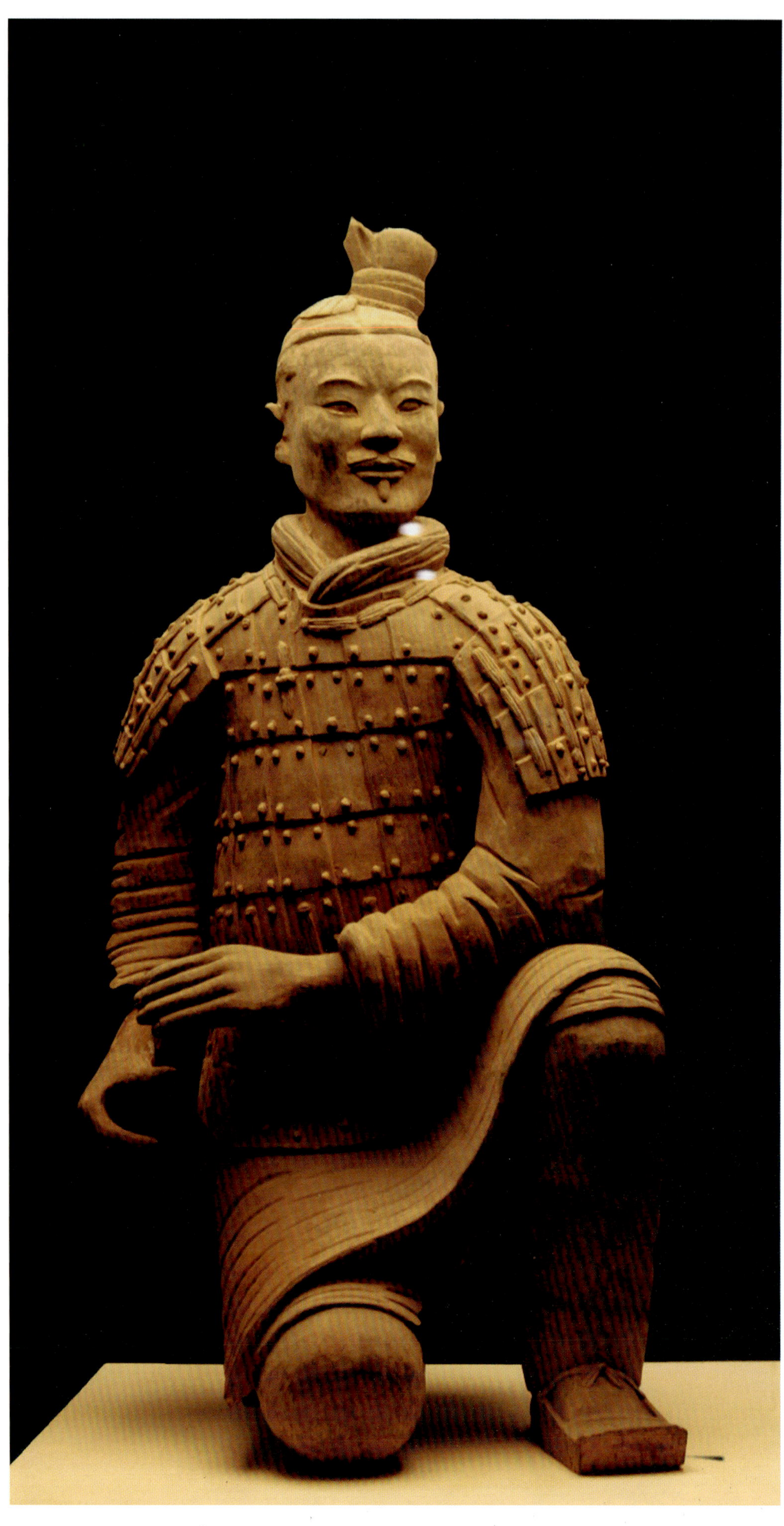

41 Kneeling Soldier
Xian, China
Qin dynasty, 221 – 206 BCE
Terracotta
Life-size
Xian, Shaanxi Province, China

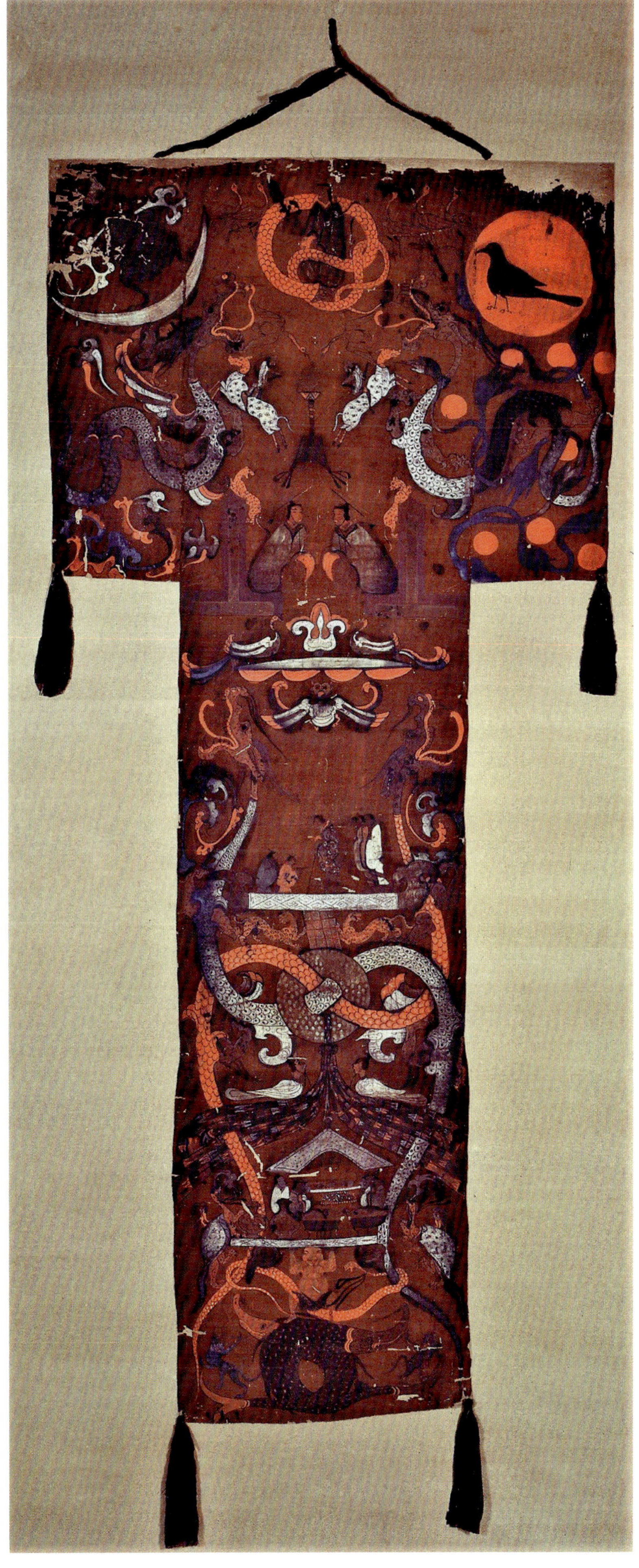

42 **Painting Depicting Heaven (Upper Part), the Human Realm (Middle), and the Netherworld (Bottom)**

China
Western Han dynasty,
206 BCE – 9 CE
Three layers of silk
80.71 in., 205 cm
Hunan Provincial Museum,
China

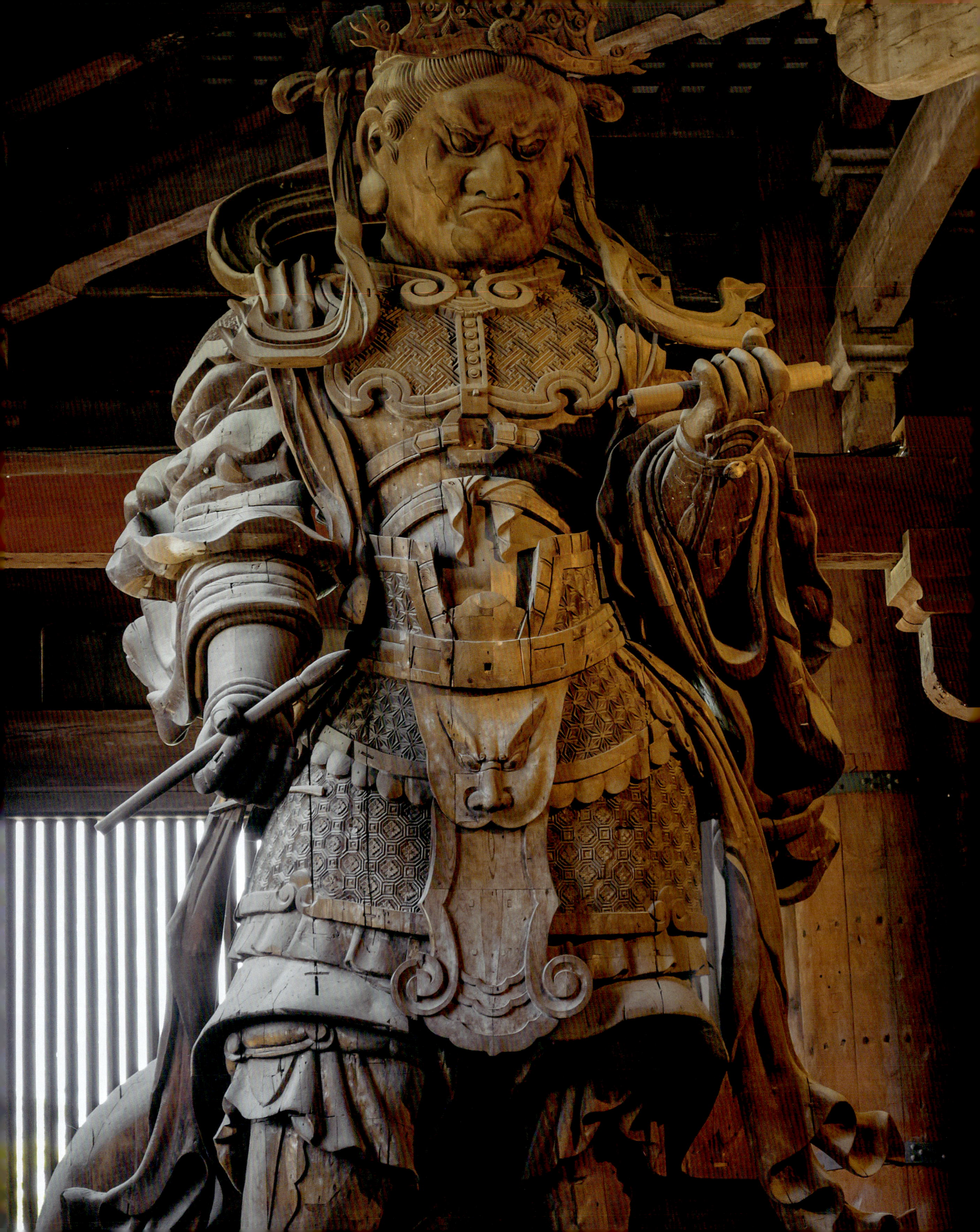

drapery is impossibly thin and hangs in rhythmic folds, unlike the irregular drapery of earlier Hellenistic art, and his body is visible beneath it but so smooth that it has lost its sensuousness. This Buddha comes from an area once known as Gandhara, presently northern Pakistan and adjoining Afghanistan. From here traders could access the Silk Road, a trade route that ran from China to the Middle East. Along this road Buddhist missionaries traveled to China to spread the faith from the first century, then on to Korea in the fourth century, and to Japan in the seventh century.

China before the arrival of Buddhism had two extremes of religion: Daoism, a spiritual worship of nature and man's submission to its principles; and Confucianism, dedicated to proper relationships and worshipful rites between people under the oversight of the emperor. The first emperor, Qin Xi Huang Di (221–210 BCE), who unified the country, was buried outside of Xian under an enormous earthen mound, much as we have seen built in chiefdoms. In the early dynasties, retainers and horses had been put to death to accompany a ruler. In Xian, however, the emperor ordered an entire army made of life-size ceramic replicas of men and horses of astonishing naturalism to accompany him to the afterlife (**41**). Their faces were idealized, so that one individual looks much like another. The details of their uniforms, however, are rendered with such great realism that they could be replicated today if need be. The standing men do not show contrapposto, although this relaxed posture would not be appropriate for soldiers at attention. Our

kneeling soldier was a crossbowman, who would need to stabilize himself on one knee, and his balance in that position is absolutely believable. Nature seems to have been domesticated by the time of the empire, and peace reigned throughout the realm, which must have been a relief following the well-named period of Warring States (475–221 BCE).

Portrayals of humans in the following Han dynasty (206 BCE–220 CE) continued the naturalism embraced by the first emperor. Noblemen throughout the empire had elaborate underground tombs built for themselves and their families. In the tomb of the Marchioness of Dai, a beautiful silk banner reveals the painting style that had evolved by that time (**42**). Much of the banner has mythical dragons twisting near the borders. Of more interest to our theme is the small scene on a white platform just below the center of the banner, which shows the funeral of the marchioness. The participants are graceful and rendered in three-quarter view, hardly typical of early art, and assume both standing and kneeling positions. It is likely that the Silk Road had brought China into contact with the naturalism of Hellenistic art, but we do not know how the process evolved in China itself. Art that has been preserved from the millennium before the first emperor consists mainly of bronze containers used in funerary banquets and decorated with spirits even more abstract than the dragons here. Inscriptions on these containers and on ritual bones contain precursors of the characters used in writing historical Chinese, which was codified by the Han dynasty.

China
Song dynasty, after 976
Hanging scroll; ink on silk
75.1 × 66.8 in., 191 × 169.7 cm
National Palace Museum, Taipei City, Taiwan

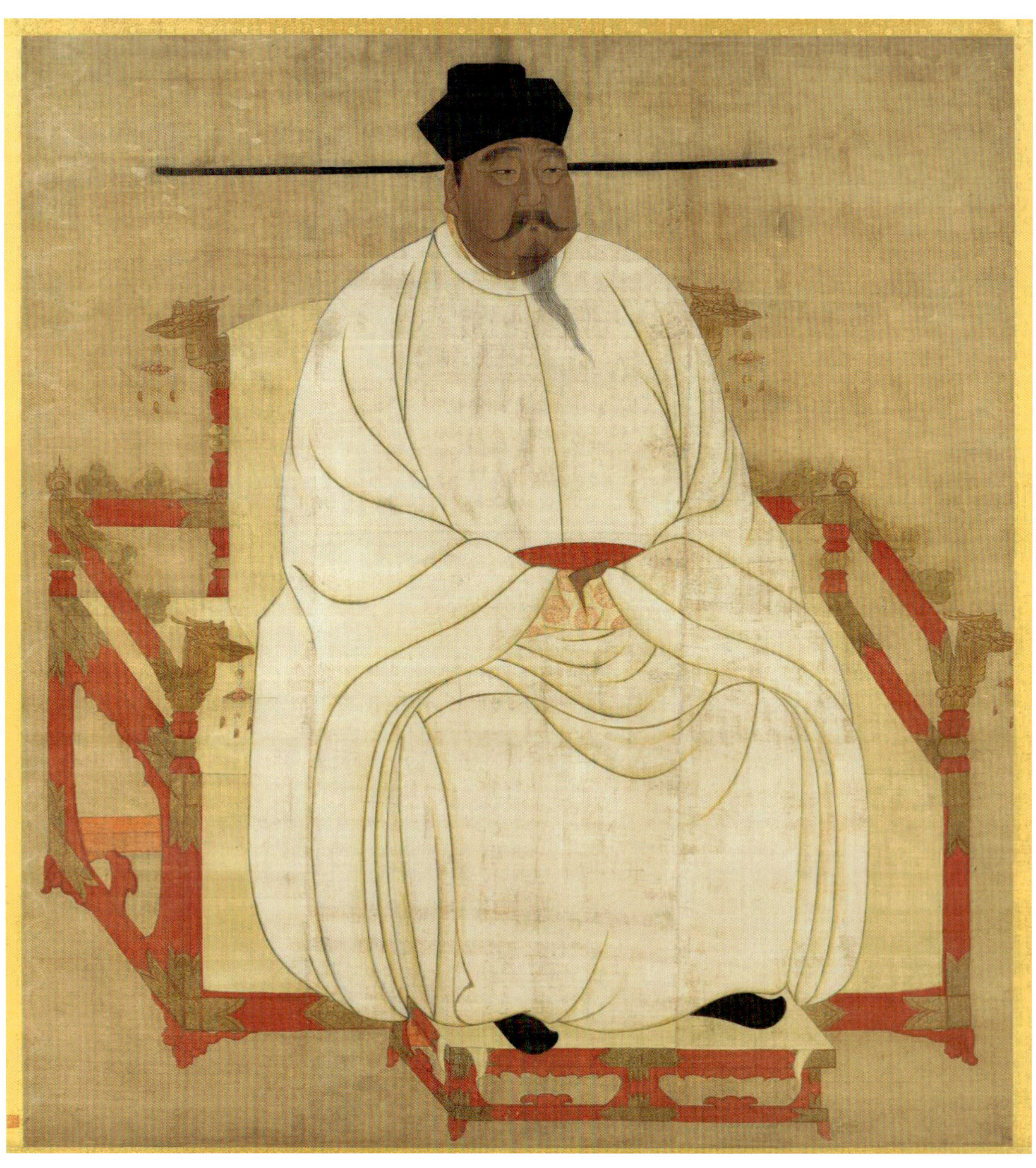

 Li Bai Strolling

Liang Kai (China, ca. 1140 – 1210)
Southern Song dynasty, early 1200s
Hanging scroll; ink on paper
31.93 × 12 in., 81.1 × 30.5 cm
Tokyo National Museum, Japan

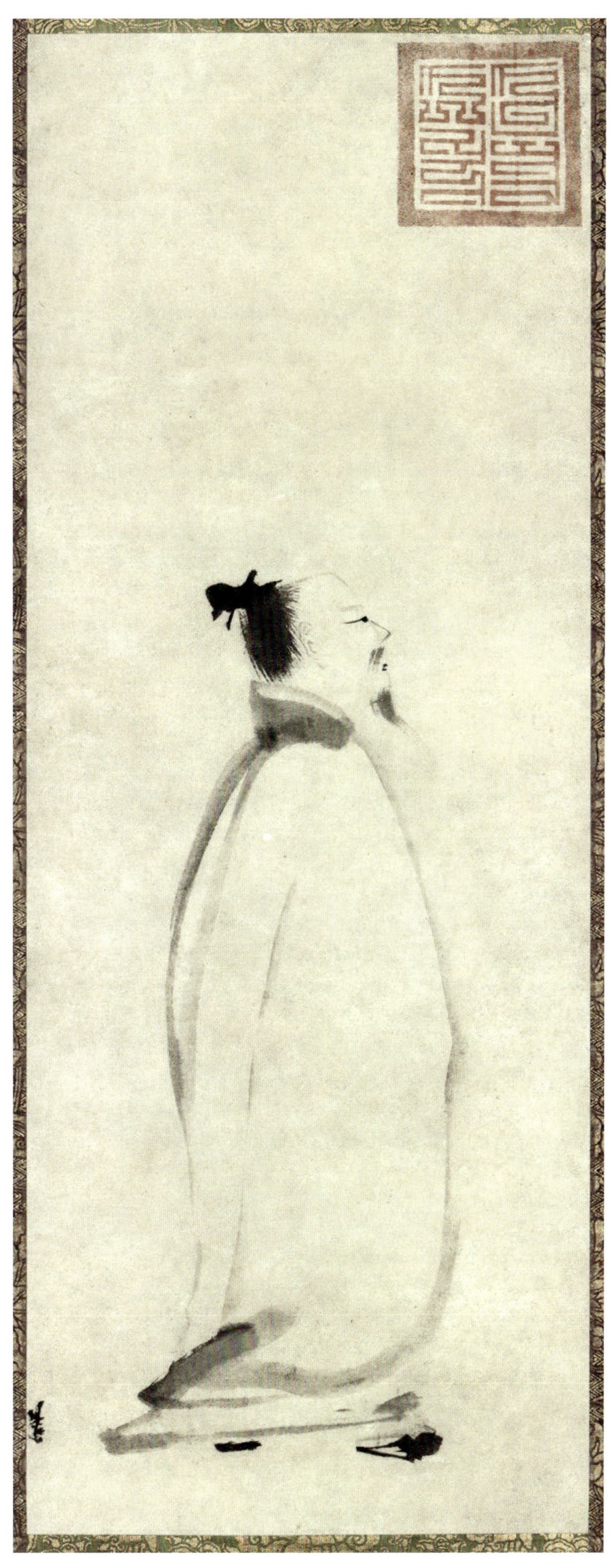

After the general acceptance of Buddhism in China, many caves along the Silk Road were carved with statuary of the Buddha, his manifestations in other reincarnations, Hindu deities who now protected the Buddhist figures, and bodhisattvas (followers of the Buddha who chose not to enter nirvana in order to serve humanity). Reliefs in the Binyang Cave were dedicated by a Northern Wei dynasty (386–535) emperor and his wife, who are shown accompanied by numerous female attendants that float like sylphs, hardly stepping on the ground beneath their long robes, their bodies elongated in three-quarter views. Statues of the Buddha from this dynasty are similarly elongated with elegant upswept lines and have a mandorla (body halo) behind them that is composed of flames. In spite of the shallowness of the relief, a sense of depth is achieved by the women behind the front row, whose heads in even shallower relief rise slightly above those of the empress and other figures in the front row.

More substantial human figures appear during the Tang dynasty (618–906) in China, when there was considerable exchange along the Silk Road with Central Asia and Iran. These include powerful horses and grooms from Ferghana, now outside of China in Tajikistan. All are ample in proportions, often with fleshy rolls under their chins. Contrapposto was more pronounced, adding to the weightiness of the figures. Japan was converted to Buddhism just prior to this period, and similarly proportioned, over life-size figures of the Buddha, his bodhisattvas, and fierce protectors filled the temples built at the time. The protectors of the four directions are derived from Hindu gods, now put into the service of Buddhism. A figure in the Todai temple in Nara, where it has always stood, is modeled in unfired clay, which allowed for great detail; his stocky body, heavily overmodeled with ornate straps and padding, extends asymmetrically into the space (**43**). His scowling face with inlaid black glass eyes is meant to terrify those who confront him and make them more respectful when approaching the Buddha statue.

Ink painting on silk scrolls has a long history in China and often references earlier works, sometimes even copying those of famous artists. A portrait of an early emperor of the Northern Song dynasty (960–1276), Song Taizu (960–976), replicates his specific facial features, including his beard, moustache, and even eyeglasses (**44**). His heavy white robe only vaguely reveals his body underneath. But the chair and footstool that he uses are rendered in the classic perspective technique of the Far East: isometric, with the front parts parallel to the bottom frame of the painting, while perpendicular parts are shown with their lines receding at the same angle. During the Italian Renaissance in Europe, beginning in the early fifteenth century, perspective is rendered with one or two vanishing points, to which all parallel lines converge. Roman perspective, while not rigorous, did use single vanishing points. But Far Eastern art consistently used isometric perspective until it adopted Western conventions in the later nineteenth century. A much more abbreviated approach is taken by the artist Liang Kai (active early 13th century) in his hanging silk scroll portrait of a Zen monk, Li Bai, strolling (**45**). Characteristic of Zen, a spontaneous, personalized version

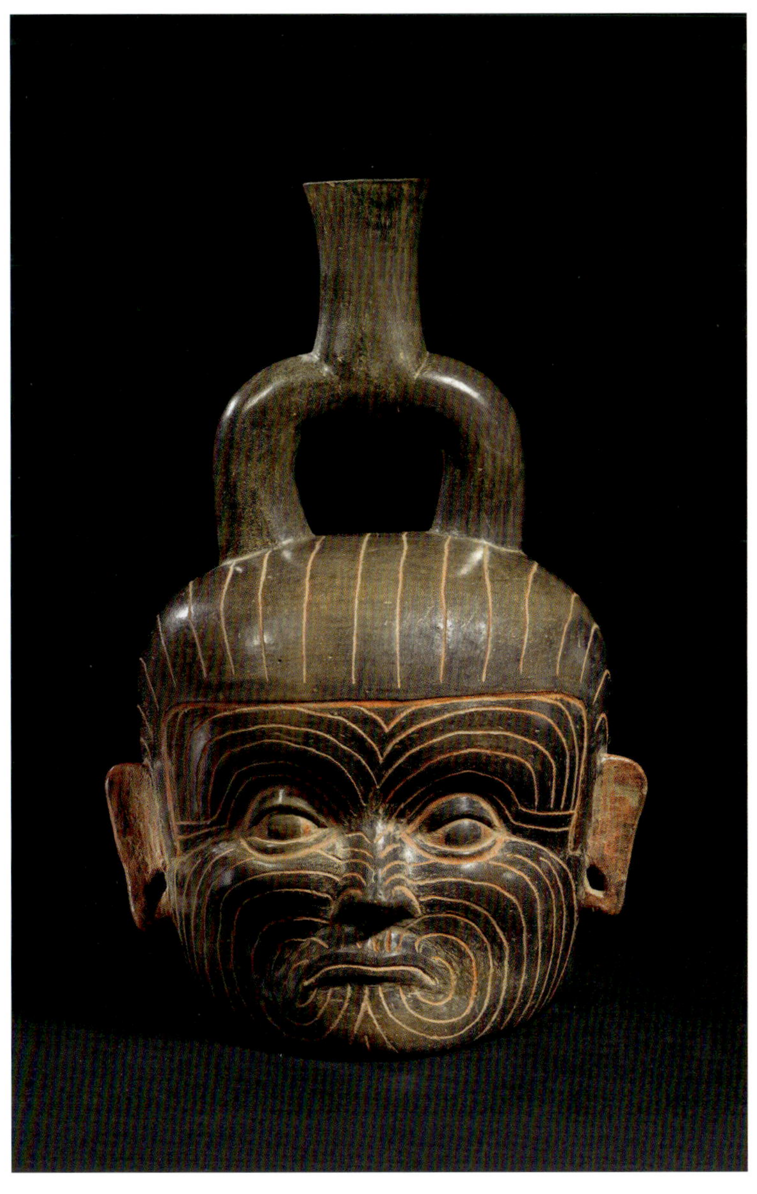

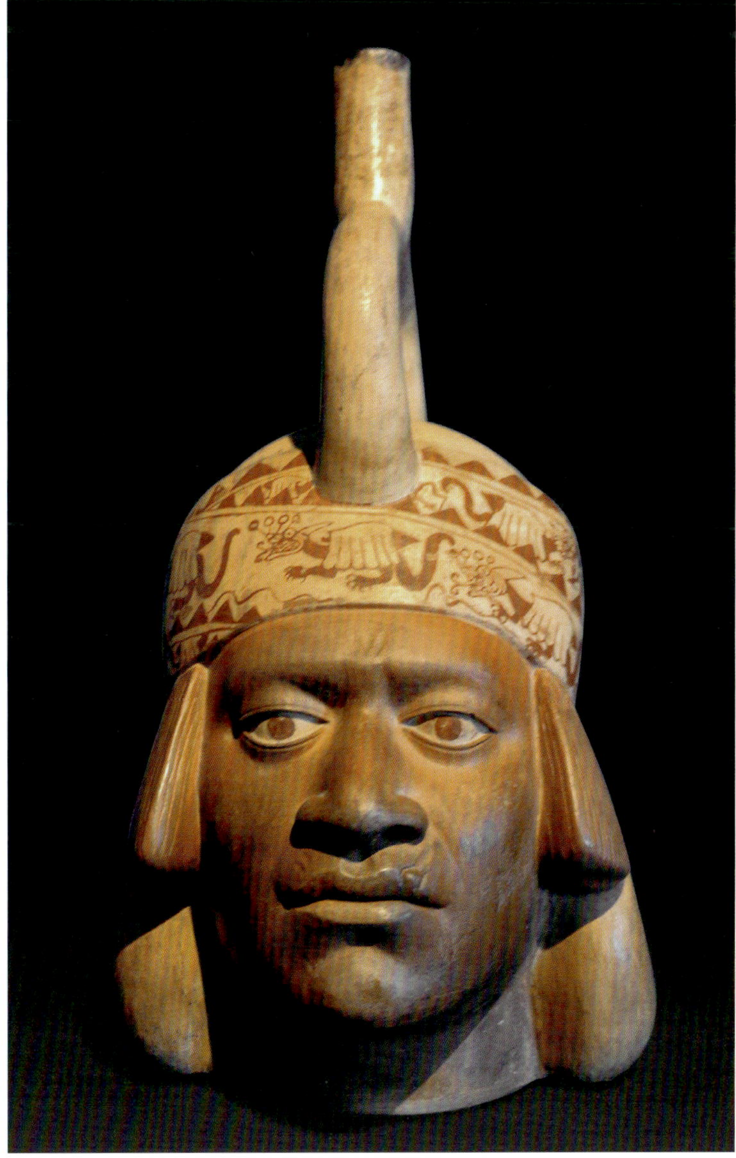

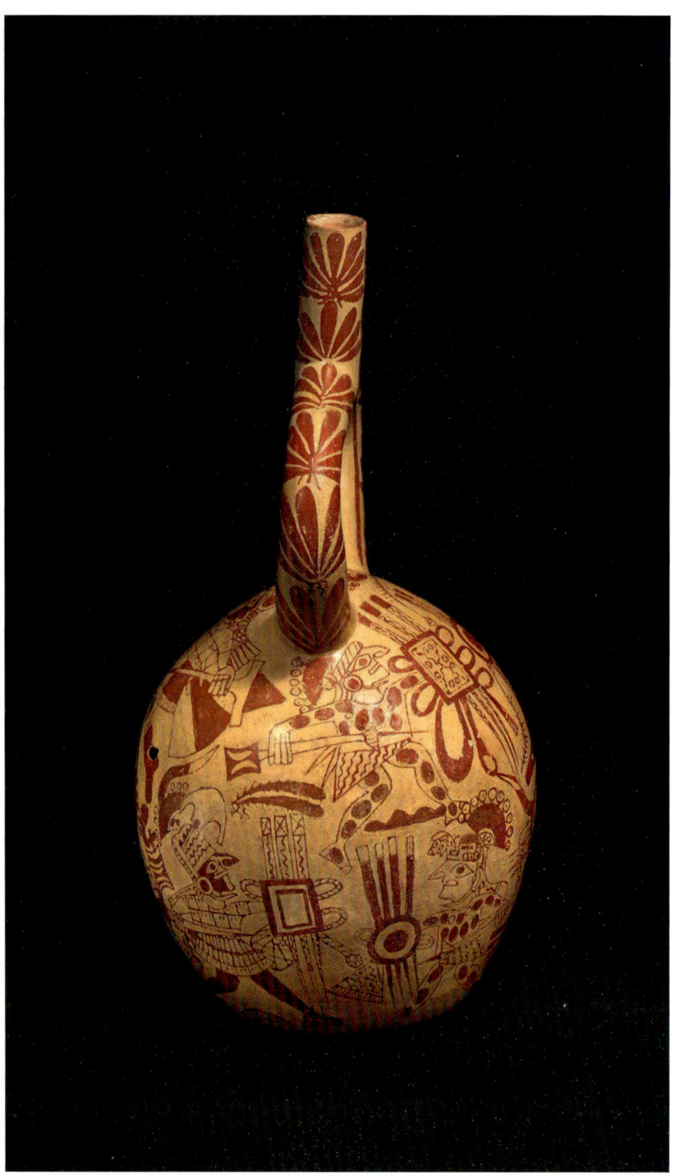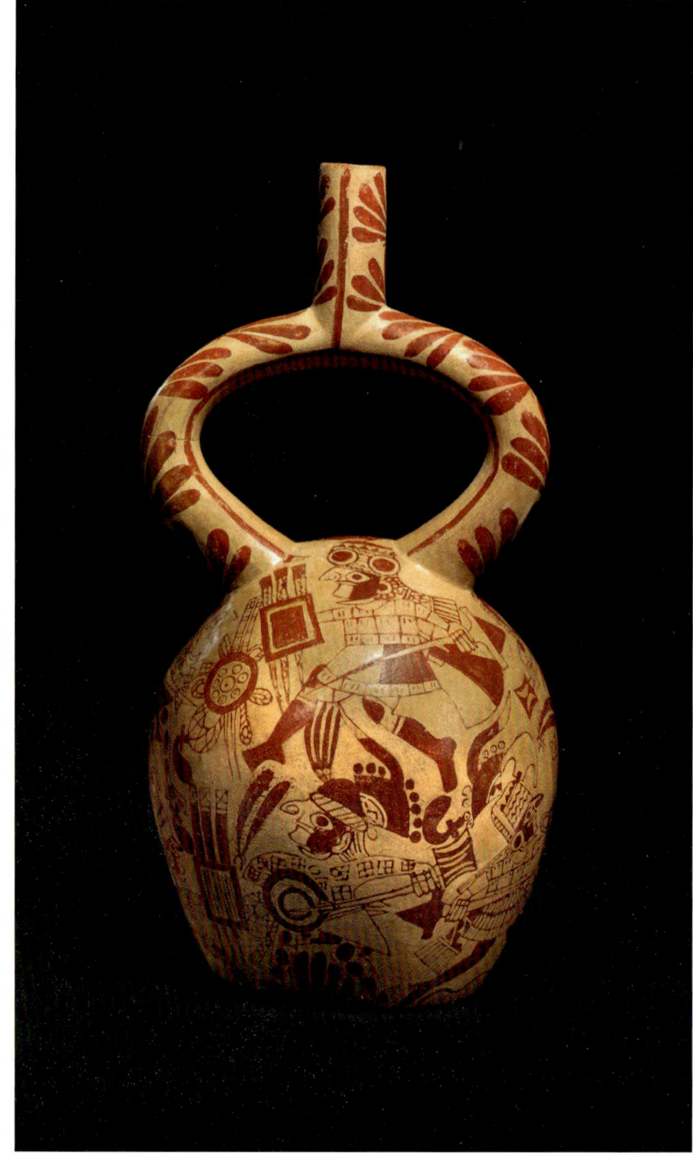

of Buddhism, this painting is rendered very quickly, with a minimum of strokes that nevertheless capture the essence of the person depicted. Much of the silk surface is left untouched, encouraging viewers to fill in the empty spaces with their imaginations. It is worth noting that this scroll is preserved in Japan, where Zen Buddhism achieved its greatest success.

The first urban civilizations in the Americas, which developed in Mesoamerica and the Central Andes, produced art that approximated the greater naturalism and realism of the Near Eastern and Mediterranean cultures. During the Initial Ceramic Period (1800–900 BCE), some very large settlements in the central coast of Peru can be considered urban, and their river irrigation systems instilled a confidence in their inhabitants' control of nature. A religious pilgrimage site called Chavín de Huántar in the north-central highlands of Peru brought together innovations from other areas during the Early Horizon (900–200 BCE). A stirrup-spouted head effigy bottle from the north coast at that time depicts an old man, somewhat idealized, with an even pattern of wrinkles incised into the clay surface rather than modeled (46). His hair is indicated by parallel stripes incised toward the back of the head. His face as a whole is naturalistically modeled with believable proportions, but this is not an individualized portrait. Stirrup-spouted bottles were used ritually in the north coast of Peru to reduce the rate of evaporation and ensure that when a libation was poured, it would emerge slowly.

The highest expression of naturalism in pre-Columbian Peru was achieved by the Moche culture of the north coast (1–700 CE). The rest of Peruvian art prioritized design over naturalism, with beautiful lines, handsome shapes, and harmonic colors. The Moche artists limited themselves to red on buff or overall black for their pottery colors, and copper and gold for metal objects. Their cities straddled major rivers descending from the high Andes, the waters of which were channeled into canals to feed their agriculture. Control of this canal system depended on the authority of their *curacas* (the Inca word for regional rulers). Their considerable effectiveness permitted large populations that were well fed and had confidence in their control of their environment. Only after dramatic changes in ocean currents brought by El Niño did the Moche culture fail due to disastrous flooding.

Moche leaders cemented their alliances with local leaders partly through gifts of stirrup-spout pots with their portraits, among the most realistic found in the ancient Americas (**47**). These pots eventually ended up in tombs, as evidence of the tomb owners' status. The same molds were used multiple times to make the pots, which were then given to local leaders to decorate as they wished. Many distinctive headdresses were painted on identical portrait jars, depending on the symbolism desired by the leader at the time. Here, the

intense eyes with large pupils give the impression that the figure is watching the viewer, although with a warm, friendly expression.

Mold-made jars also could portray the activities of leaders and their subjects. Scenes of oral and anal sex abound as evidence of the ruler's power. Llamas, the preferred sacrificial animal as well as a highly useful beast of burden, appear frequently. Religious scenes of composite animals with the distinctive fanged mouth of deities give us insight into their beliefs. Fine-line painting on functional bowls and jars provides complex scenes of both religious and warlike activities. One stirrup-spout bottle depicts a frenzied battle scene, with close combat between clear-faced, spotted-bodied troops and their foes, half of whose faces are painted red with their bodies unpainted (**48**). One of the former, on a side of the bottle directly under the spout attachment, stands straddling a small landscape of hills. Undulating sandy hills also appear on part of the base; in the middle of the body are spiny cactus plants and a vine. Such landscape features are characteristic of urban art. The Peruvian cultures lacked only one element characteristic of urban culture: writing. They had knotted-string *quipus*, however, which clearly provided counts of items in different colors, and some chroniclers claimed they could communicate much more.

To the north, in Mesoamerica, the Olmec culture developed a civilization based on powerful leaders who commemorated their rule through a series of colossal stone heads, each of which signaled the ruler's uniqueness through distinctive facial features,

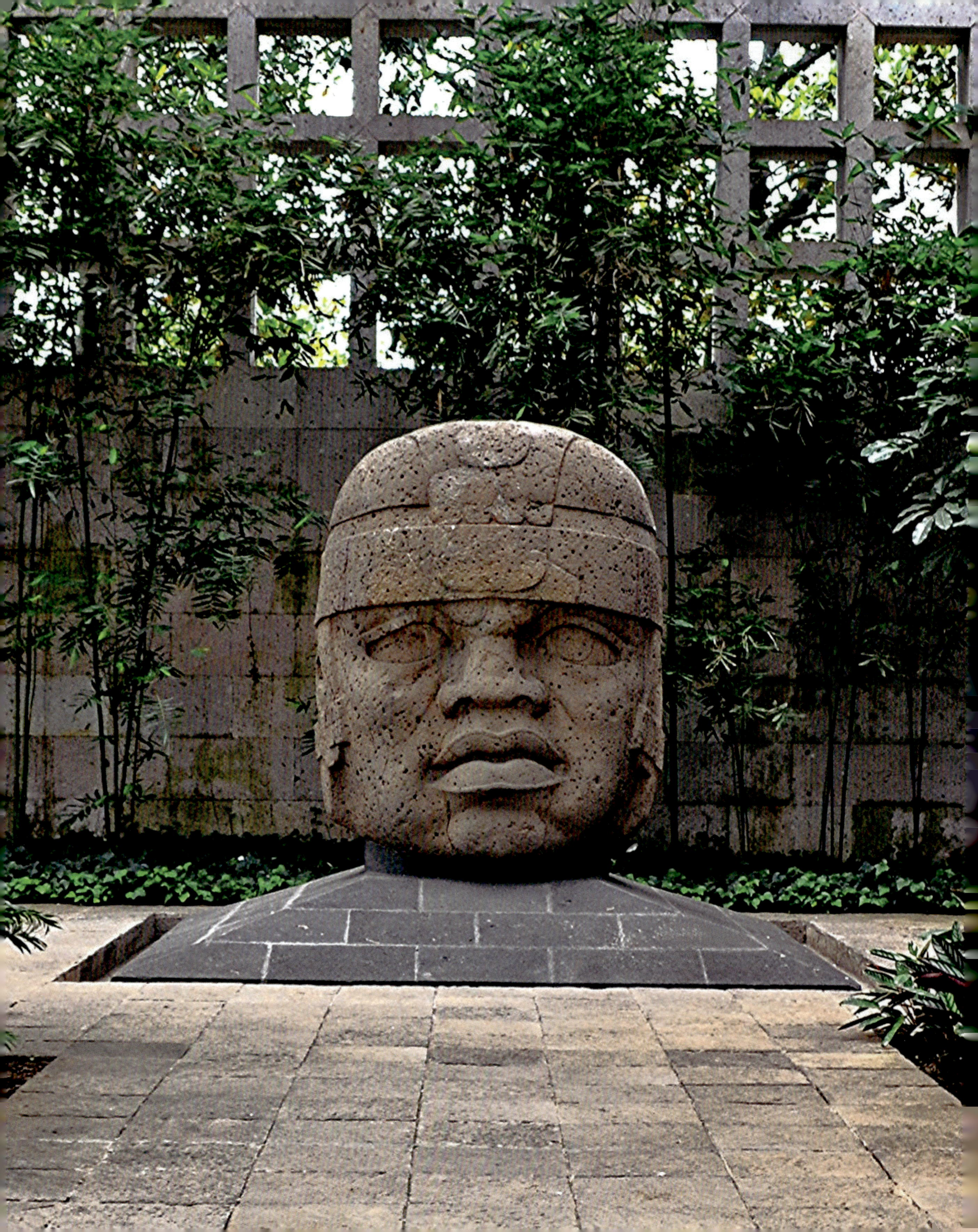

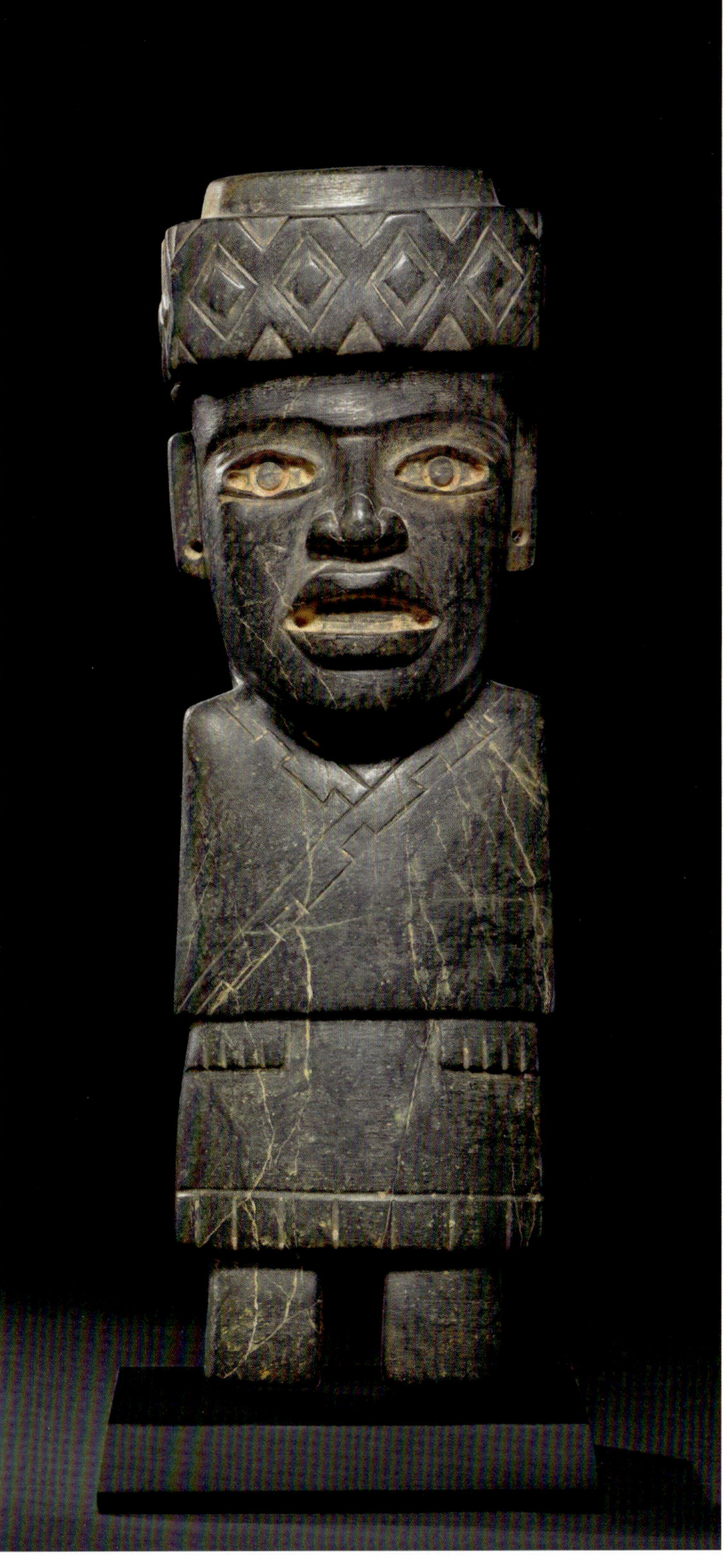

expressions, and headdresses (**49**). As evidenced by the site of San Lorenzo, located on a river not far inland from the Gulf of Mexico, the largest number of heads seems to have been made after 1200 BCE. The basalt used to make these heads came from a mountainous outcrop many miles to the north, whence the head could be floated on balsa raft down the Gulf and up the river. This required considerable labor, which clearly reflects the control the rulers had over their extensive population. They also maintained far-flung trading centers to obtain jade or other green stones, which symbolized water and agricultural life and were laboriously carved into celts (prehistoric axes of stone or metal, without perforations or grooves, for hafting) some with the face of a jaguar-human (see a similar figure from Las Limas being held like a baby on the lap of an adult man in Chapter 4: Motherhood and the Family, fig. 49). At the later Olmec capital of La Venta, a basalt sculpture named Altar 4 but now believed to be a throne has a powerfully muscled human figure emerging from a flame-filled cave; he must be the founder of the dynasty, upon whose shoulders the current ruler would sit. The Olmecs also began to create a writing system, which was fully developed by 100 BCE–100 CE in several states that followed the demise of the Olmec culture itself. Whereas San Lorenzo was only a ceremonial center, populated at times by people from

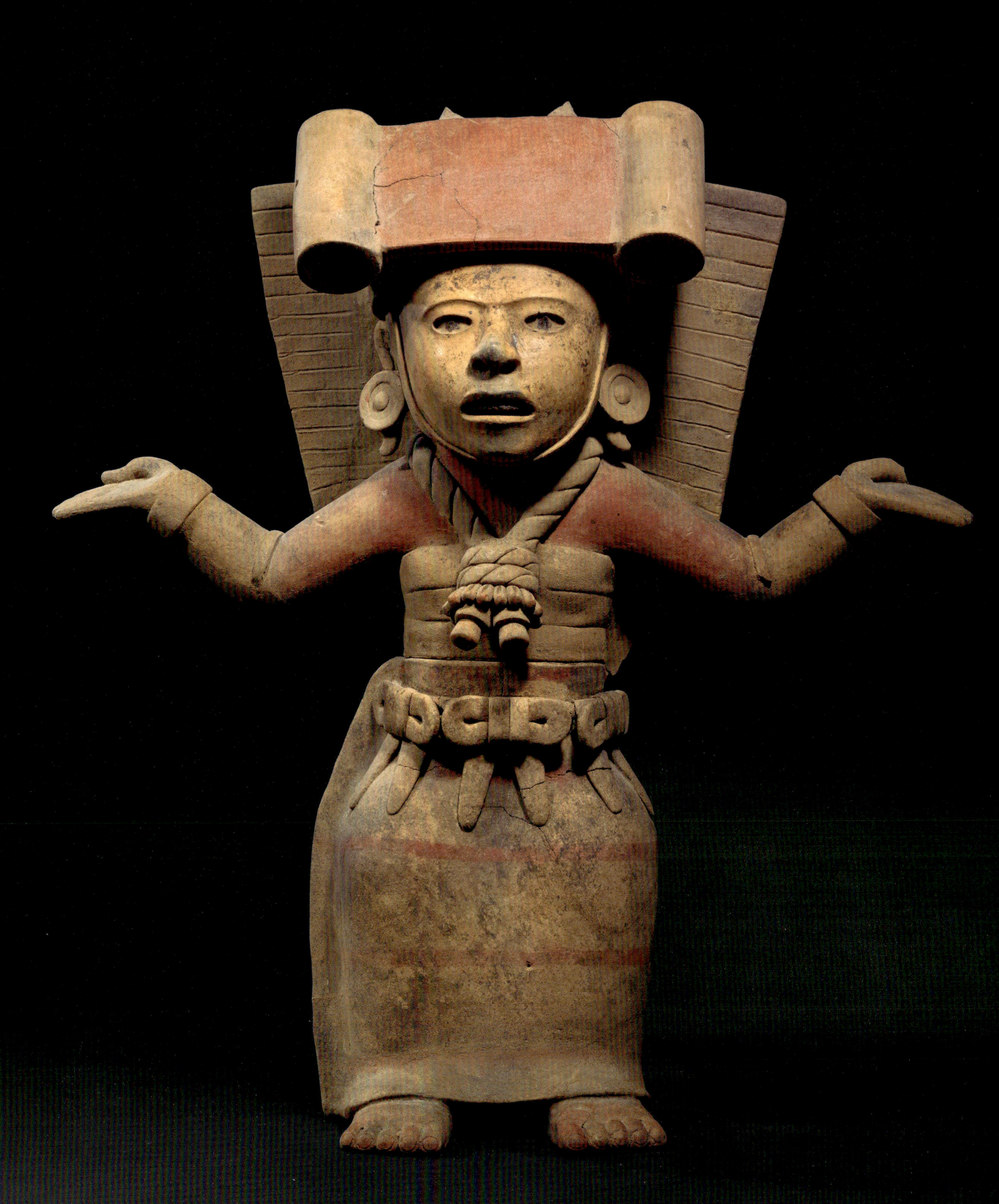

the surrounding towns, La Venta was a true city with several thousand inhabitants.

The greatest pre-Columbian urban complex was Teotihuacan, about 40 kilometers north of present-day Mexico City, considered to have been the most populous center in the world between 450 and 650 CE except for some Chinese cities. Its government seems not to have had a king, which one would expect as all the other Mesoamerican ethnic groups were ruled by people who were honored by portraits and identified by their names in hieroglyphs. Art historian Esther Pasztory believes Teotihuacan was ruled as a republic, without kings.[3] Some fresco paintings from the palace complex there show a procession of men identified by different names—this could refer to the current ruling group, all dressed as the same deity. Their individuality is not emphasized except by glyphs, and their proportions are too stumpy for naturalistic adults. An idealized standing woman sculpted in stone, also with flatly rendered, short bodily proportions, has a deeply carved face of considerable naturalism; she could represent a specific noble woman, perhaps of the ruling group, with normal female clothing that had no religious context (**50**). Only her diamond-patterned cap may convey her role or lineage.

During its apogee, Teotihuacan influenced the rest of Mesoamerica politically as well as artistically, particularly in the broad facial proportions of human representations. In Veracruz, a culture strongly influenced by Teotihuacan, a singing woman of considerable naturalism, including her body proportions, has that broad face (**51**). Groups of these large ceramic sculptures, so typical of Veracruz, would

have provided a chorus for the religious shrines. Artists in Oaxaca, a state to the southwest of Veracruz, created funerary urns contemporary with Teotihuacan that had the same wide facial proportions and firmly constructed bodies attached to cylindrical urns in back, suitable for offerings to the deceased. And on the Pacific Slope of Guatemala in the southern Maya area, a possible colony from Teotihuacan created complex frontal sculptures on the lids of ceramic incense burners (**52**); these reflected Teotihuacan incense burners, which had a rear chimney. In both locations a seated human figure is surrounded by plaques creating a proscenium stage-like construction.

The Maya of the central lowlands in Guatemala, Belize, adjacent Mexico, and western Honduras achieved the most naturalistic renderings of humans and the most highly developed writing system in the pre-Columbian Americas. In the past fifty years, their writing has been decoded beyond the numerical and calendrical glyphs known previously, revealing a great deal about their rulers, their rituals, and their beliefs. Ritual books made of deer-skin folded like an accordion contain astronomical rituals as well. Stone carved glyphs on standing steles, plaques, and architectural staircases document the histories and exploits of their cities' rulers. Pottery vases have inscriptions running around their rims that dedicate the vase to the consumption of foaming cacao, while vertical inscriptions identify the actors (**53**). In this case we have a seated lord on a jaguar-pelt throne, with a kneeling retainer behind him. Their bodily proportions are accurate, and the fluidity of their postures conveys an interest in human anatomy. Cylinder vases like this

Tiquisate, Escuintla, Guatemala
600 – 900 CE
Terracotta
21 in., 53.34 cm
The Stuart Handler Collection

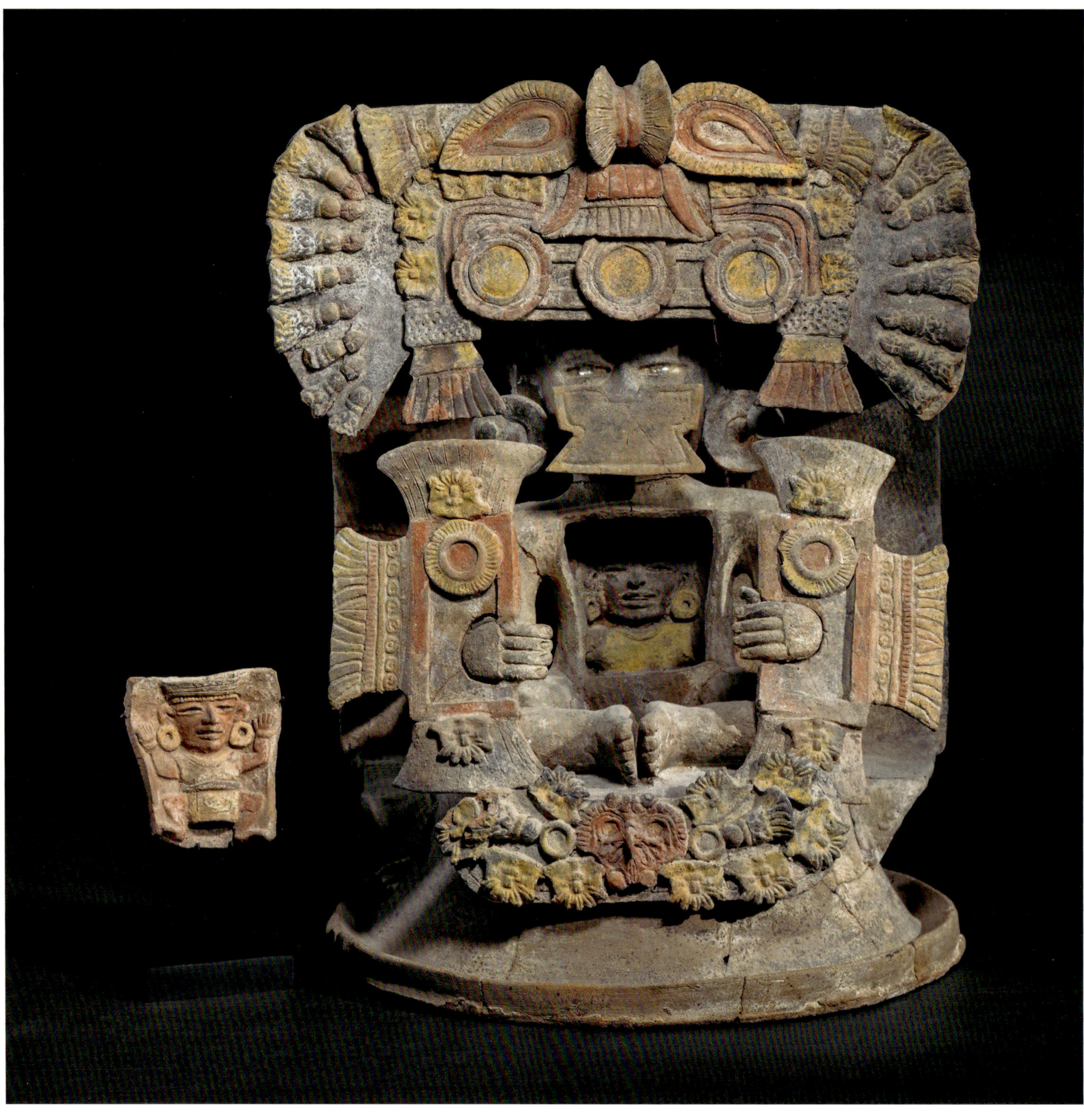

53 Cylinder Vase

Maya culture, Peten region, Guatemala
600 – 900 CE
Terracotta
Musée du Quai Branly, Paris, France

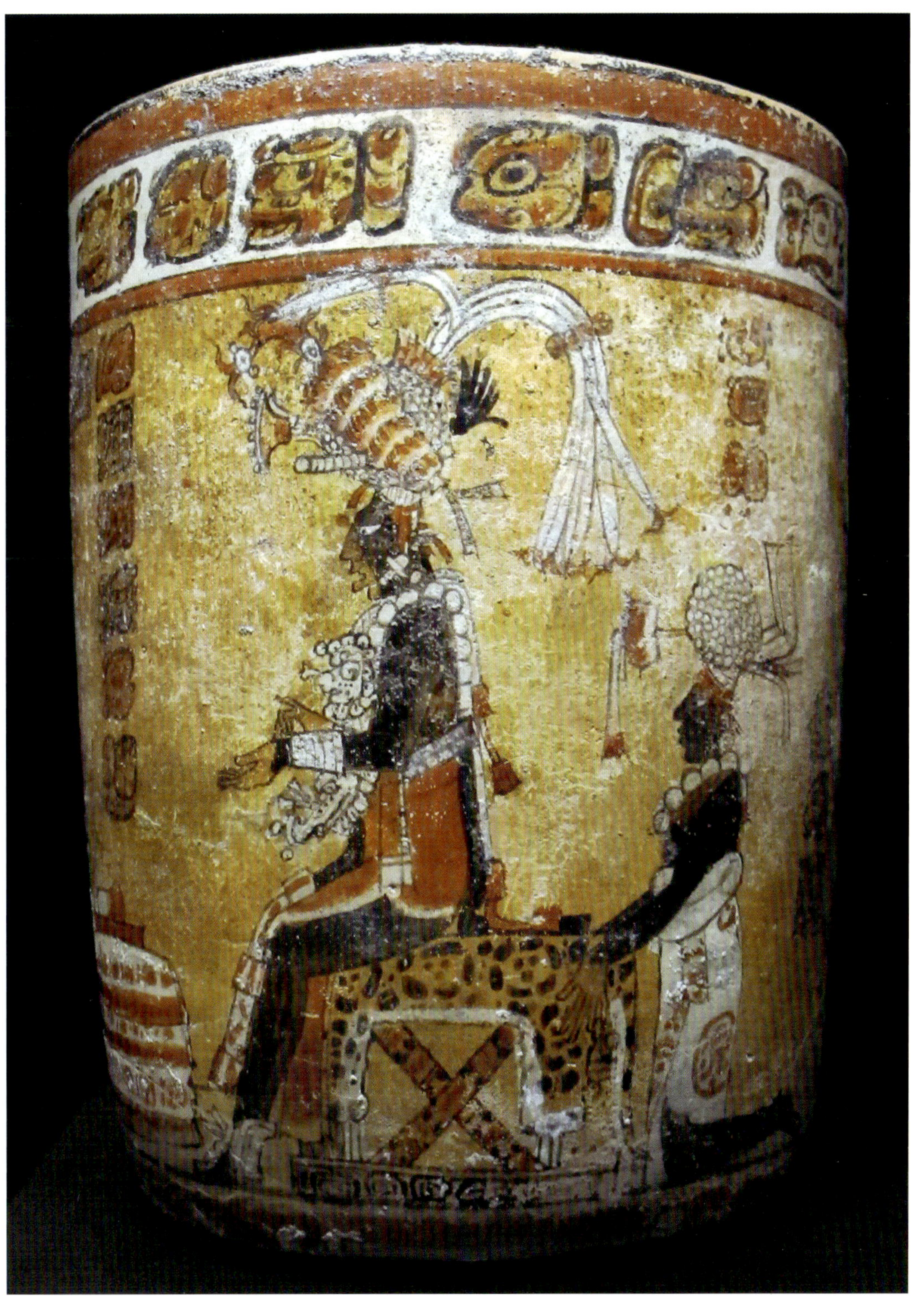

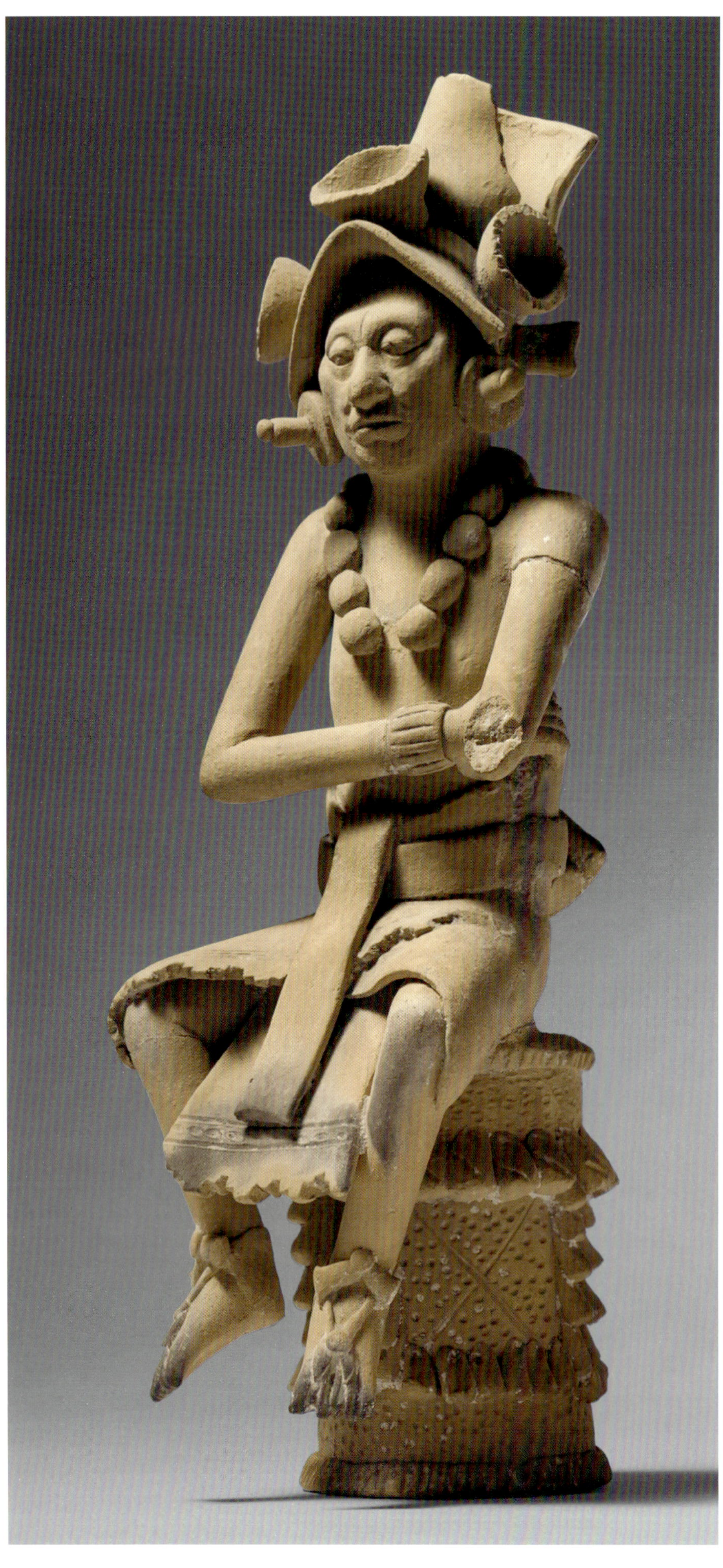

54 Figure of a Lord

Maya culture, Jaina Island
burial site, Mexico
500 – 950 CE
Terracotta
11 ⅜ in., 28.9 cm
Private Collection
Photo courtesy of Sotheby's,
New York

 Oni **Figure**

Ita Yemoo, Nigeria
1300 – 1400
Brass
18 ⁹⁄₁₆ in., 47.15 cm
Museum of Ife Antiquities,
Ife, Nigeria

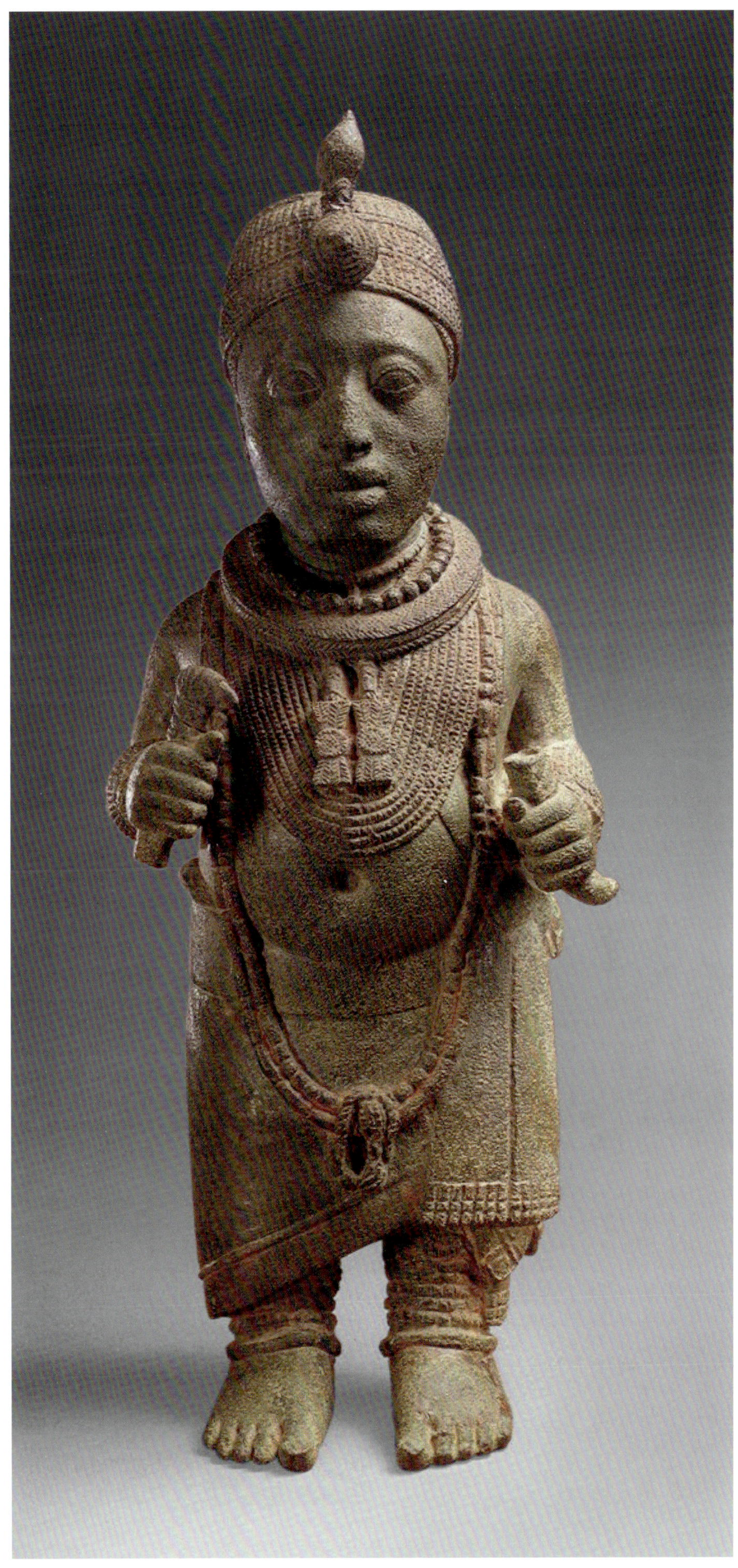

56 Queen Mother Pendant Mask (*Iyoba*)

Igun-Eronmwen guild, Court of Benin, Nigeria
1500 – 1600
Ivory, iron, copper (?)
9 ⅜ × 5 × 2 ½ in., 23.8 × 12.7 × 6.4 cm
Metropolitan Museum of Art, New York
The Michael C. Rockefeller Memorial Collection,
Gift of Nelson A. Rockefeller, 1972

would have been given at a banquet to a visiting lord, and he would treasure the gift throughout his life and have it buried with him after his death, as a reflection of the esteem in which he was held by his peers. Small ceramic figurines that accompanied the deceased show this fluid naturalism in three-dimensions, as in the example of this seated lord who wears jade earspools attached by perpendicular tubes penetrating his perforated ear lobes (**54**). Clearly visible is his elongated head, achieved by binding the heads of aristocrats from birth. Other heads have an extension of the nose up past the eyebrow ridge onto the forehead; we do not know of what material that was made or whether it was just an artistic convention (doubtful). Each Maya city was in theory an independent city-state with surrounding villages, but the many wars, as well as alliances achieved through battles and the marriage bed, led to larger but shifting groupings. In this way they recall the Greek city-states of the Classic era more than the ancient Roman Empire.

The final urban civilizations to be discussed are those of the Yoruba and Edo peoples in southwestern Nigeria. Today the Yoruba consider that they came originally from the city of Ife, now a major urban concentration, where a great artistic tradition flourished from the twelfth to the fifteenth centuries, predating the arrival of the first Europeans by ship in the late fifteenth century. Male heads rendered in brass have very realistic racial features. Holes perforated along the hair line and the beard into the hollow interior apparently allowed for the attachment of hair. The heads themselves have long necks intended for insertion into a body of other materials. Historic

Yoruba created life-size models of their ancestors at this scale, with the bodies made of a wooden armature and covered with real clothing. A full figure of the *oni* or king has stunted body proportions (**55**), perhaps like some later carved wooden figures among the Yoruba. The *oni*'s soft belly hangs out over his wrap-around skirt, and his legs are very short. His face is striated, perhaps to indicate tribal scarification but also possibly referencing dangling beads on modern Yoruba crowns that obscure the king's face. Other very naturalistic heads, some obviously female, are modeled in terracotta. Unlike most other early states, no indigenous writing system is known for Ife, although Arabic writing was known from nearby Muslim groups.

At the time of the Portuguese arrival along the coast of Africa in the late fifteenth century, the city of Benin had over fifty thousand Edo-speaking inhabitants and was dominated by the spire of the king's palace. Shrines inside the palace displayed bronze ancestor heads, some with carved elephant tusks curving out of holes in their tops. Early heads are the most naturalistic, since Edo craftsmen learned the art of casting directly from Ife metalsmiths. That naturalism is apparent in the carefully rendered whorls of the ears of a queen mother on a beautiful ivory belt mask from the sixteenth century, as well as her lips and nose (**56**). Her heavily lidded eyes seem characteristic of age. Abstracted Portuguese soldier heads encircle the top of her head and the collar underneath her chin; they alternate with mudfish, the symbol of Olokun, god of the sea. Portuguese soldiers symbolized power, having arrived in enormous ships with threatening cannons. Iron was inlaid in the iris of her eyes and on her forehead

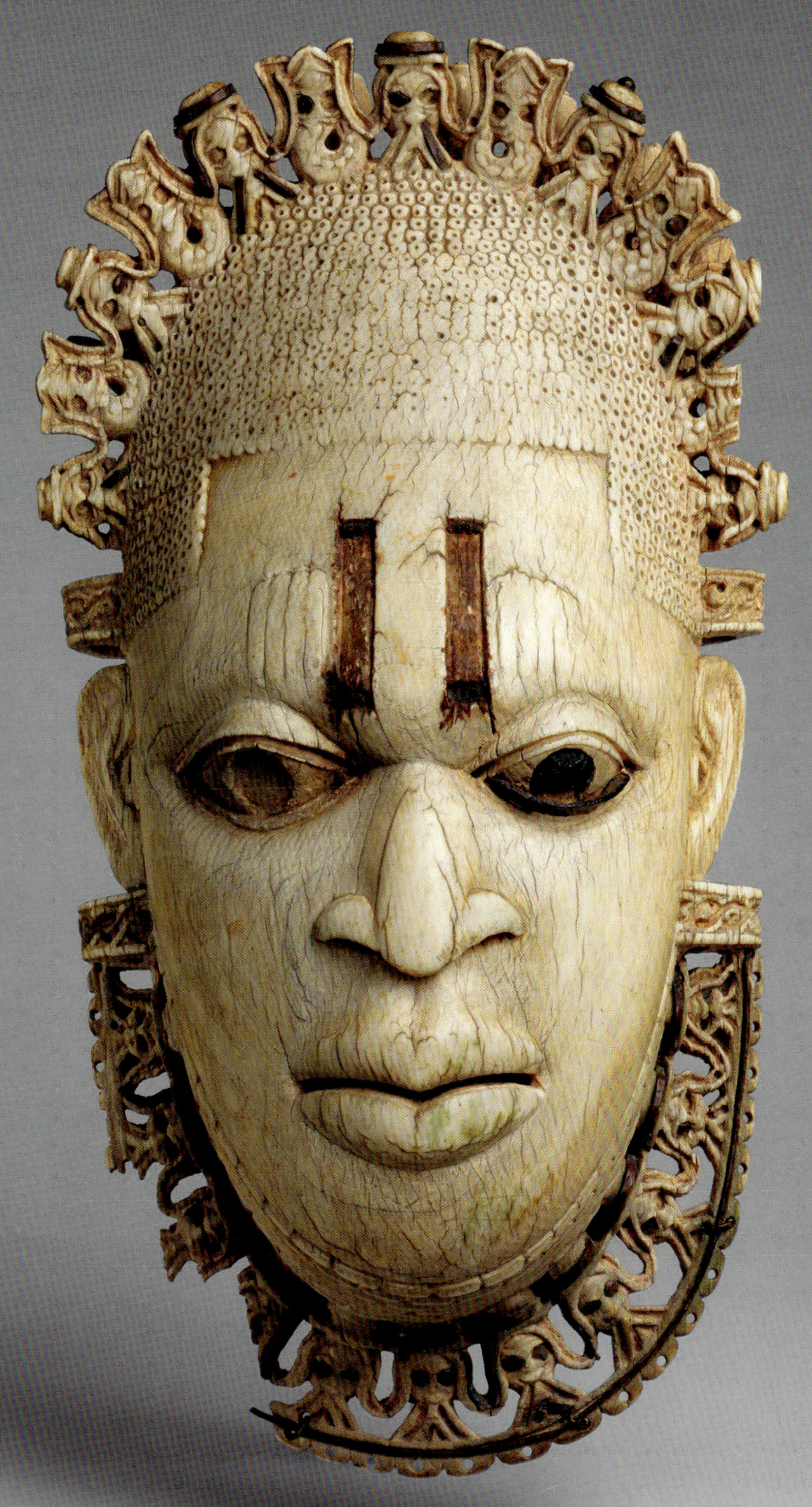

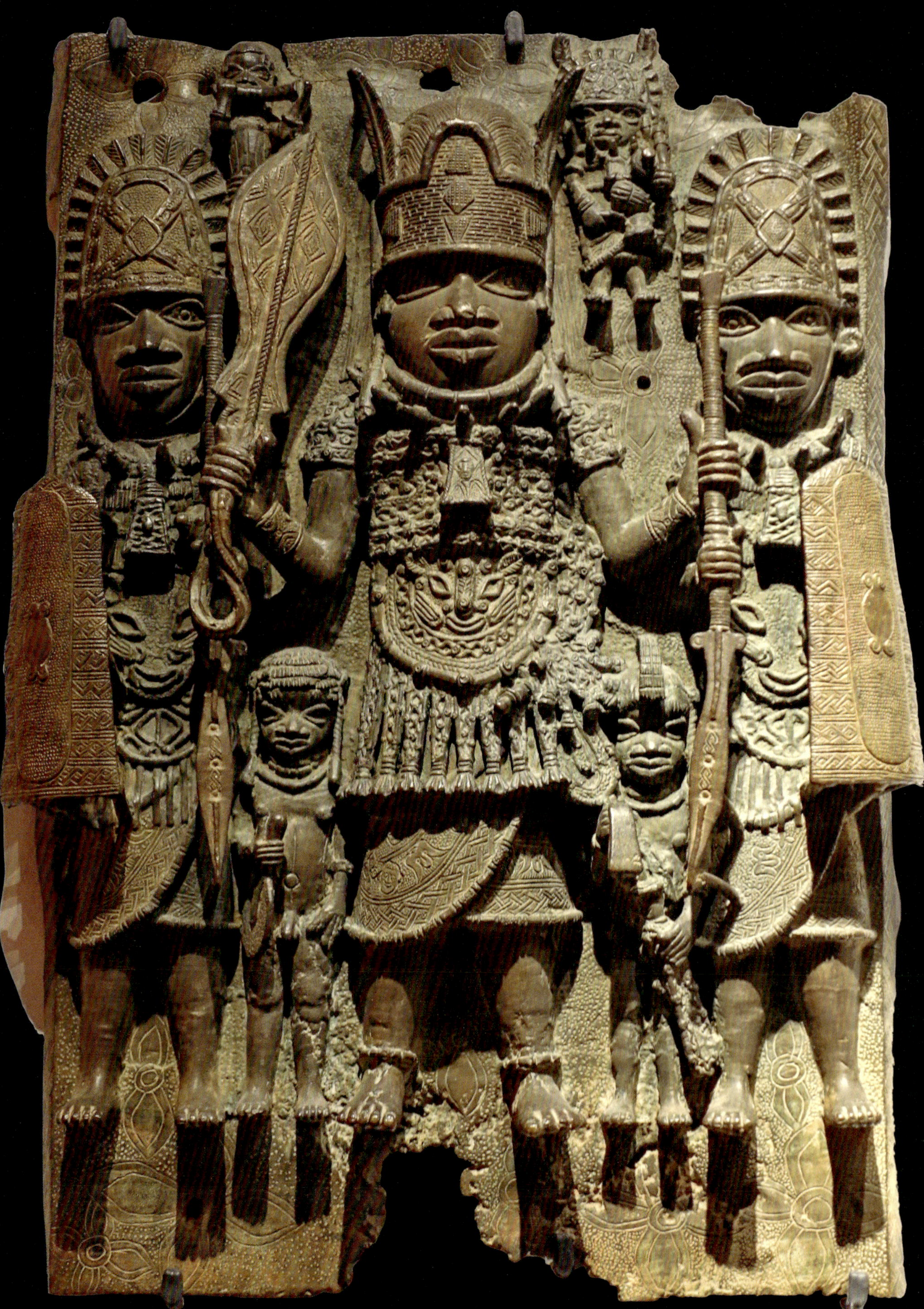

between the eyes. Later, after the British had acquired power over Nigeria at the Berlin conference of 1885, which divided up the African continent among the European colonizers, resistance by the Edo people to foreign rule caused the British to send a punitive expedition to sack the palace and strip it of the many bronze plaques documenting the history of the empire of Benin, which once extended as far west as the modern republic of Benin (formerly French Dahomey).[4] One plaque now in Berlin has frontal figures in very high relief ranked in importance by size, as in Egyptian reliefs, the largest central male taking up most of the height of the plaque with his slightly smaller lieutenants on either side (**57**). The abdomens of all three are covered by frontal leopard heads. Two very small children, almost nude, appear between the legs of the major three men, and all five stand on exactly the same level, implying a ground line. Two other very small figures, also soldiers, stand high in the background, suggesting they are a distance back from those in the front. A few plaques render architectural details, especially the palace with its tall tower.

In conclusion, the art of urban states renders humans with considerable naturalism and sometimes even realism, so that individuals can be identified. Their headdresses and other clothing are also used to identify their rank. Their environment is sometimes incorporated in the background. In most cultures, writing also is used to identify figures and their activities. Finally, valuable materials frequently are used as the media of these works.

Early urban civilizations had considerable confidence in their dominance of nature. As they matured and encountered difficulties, as we do today in our attempts to control nature, they often retreated from that confidence. I have chosen to stop my discussion of cultures after they begin to encounter these difficulties: the "People of the Sea" in the twelfth-century BCE Near East, the barbarian invasions beginning in the third century that finally toppled the Roman Empire, the disastrous El Niño flooding in northern Peru in the seventh century, the Maya collapse of the ninth century, the conquest of China by foreigners in the fourteenth century, and the cultural disruption by European slavers in Africa by the seventeenth century and colonization in the nineteenth century.

1   Elman Service, *Primitive Social Organization: An Evolutionary Perspective*, 2nd ed. (New York: Random House, 1971).

2   John F. Scott, "Post-Olmec Mesoamerica as Revealed in its Art," in *Actas del XLI Congreso Internacional de Americanistas, México, 2 al 7 de septiembre de 1974*, vol. 2 (Mexico City: Comisión de Publicación de las Actas y Memorias, 1976), 380–86.

3   Esther Pasztory, *Teotihuacan: An Experiment in Living* (Norman: University of Oklahoma Press, 1997).

4   Most ended up in museum collections in the Global North. European and American museums are now under political pressure to return the seized plaques to Nigeria, although it is doubtful they will ever be reinstalled on the royal palace walls.

VIII

SICKNESS AND HEALING

TODD J. PESEK, MD

Foolish the doctor who despises the knowledge acquired by the ancients.

Hippocrates

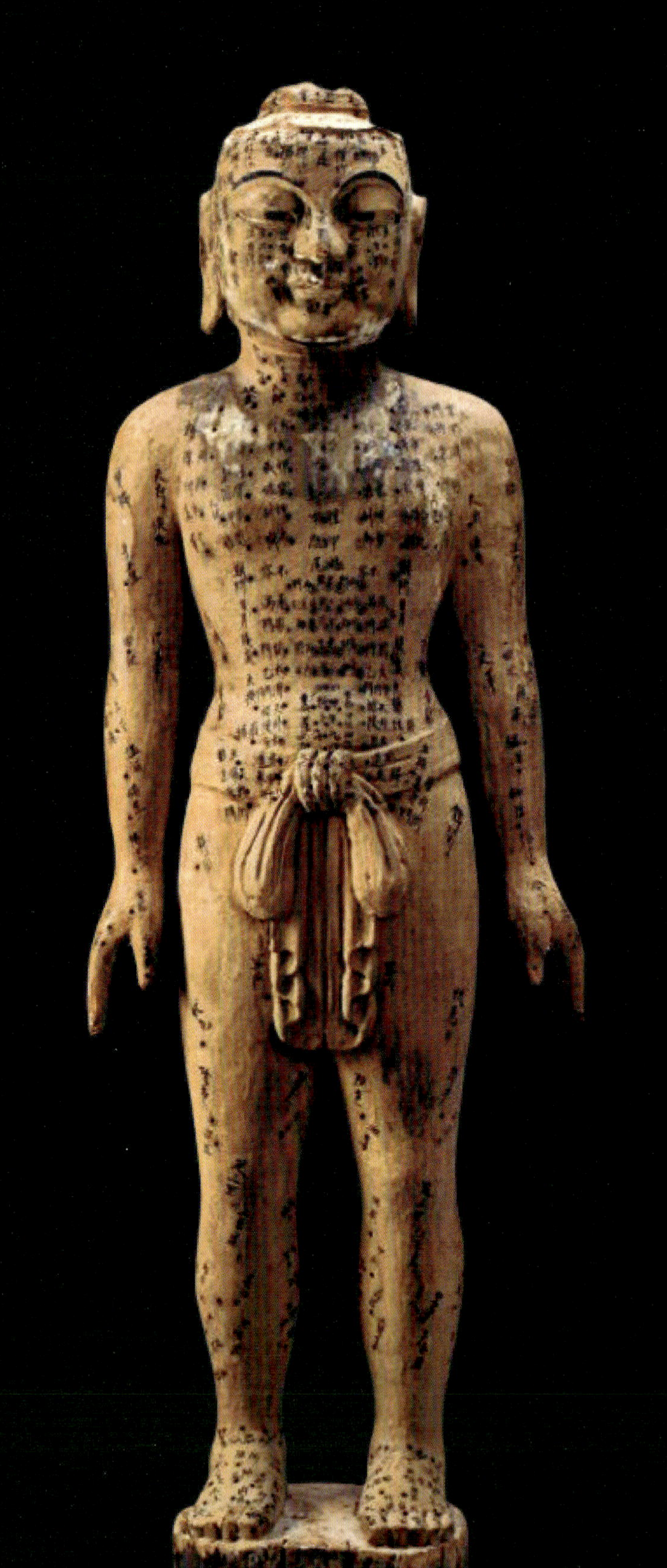

Since the dawn of humanity, there has been a need to promote health and longevity and mitigate and treat sickness, and our ancestors evolved complex strategies for imbuing overall health and wellness. They did this by using the only means available to them: the natural world and the energetic or spiritual realms that they perceived via their cultural systems of belief and their ways of being. Some healers specialized in the physical realm—for example the herbalist, the bonesetter, the midwife—and others specialized in the energetic and spiritual realm—the shamans (also known as *curanderos* in Latin America), the diviners, the light workers, the wizards, or on the flip side and in the shadow, the witch doctors or sorcerers (known as *brujos* in Latin America) and the vodou priests. Every culture, everywhere, from those of our earliest ancestors to the present day, has a version of these healers for the navigation of sickness and the promotion of healing.

Though the diversity of healing traditions matches that of humanity itself, there are unifying themes across cultures and through the ages that are not necessarily informed by the lateral transfer of knowledge. Rather, they were independently discovered and then developed by diverse peoples the world over for one reason—they were needed for survival and they worked. Successful healing traditions persisted and were initially passed via oral traditions to subsequent generations, evolving along the way. From various concepts of the physical nature of sickness and healing emerged complex pharmacopoeias from the plants, minerals, metals, and even animals of our ancestors' natural worlds. Similarly, concepts of energy and the supernatural realm engendered healing systems based on vital life force, whether this was called *prana*, *qi*, *oja*, or something else. Indeed, across prehistory, history, and cultures, we see a relatively uniform recognition of the fact that we are energetic beings with a connection to nature and the cosmos. Similar theories on energy flow, energetic channels, the elements, humors, and categorization of body types and their relative strengths and weaknesses based on characteristics emerged, along with corresponding methods of bringing balance to the system to avoid sickness and to bring about healing through diet, lifestyle, plant medicines, the use of hot and cold, bone-setting, surgery, balancing opposites, bloodletting, various forms of punctures and channel clearing, pressure releases and applications, body work, energetic balancing, protective and medicinal amulets, divination, shamanic journeying, and other healing rituals.

Indeed, one must consider the fact that for the vast majority of humanity, our ancestors embraced a worldview and existence of stewardship, realizing we are caretaker inhabitants of the land and inextricably intertwined with all that is around, above, and below us. Accordingly, our healing systems developed complex aspects of treating sickness and promoting healing and health maintenance that included elements of the mind-body, spirit, and environment—both the social and the natural worlds.[1]

**Container for Ritual Healing
(*Ngwarkandangra*)**

Nigeria
1925 – 1975
Terracotta
9 ½ × 5 ¾ in., 24.1 × 14.6 cm
Art Institute of Chicago
Gift of Keith Achepohl

Depictions of Sickness and Healing

Art depicting sickness and healing, from ancient
cave art and carvings to pottery and vessels and even
modern-day apothecaries used in ritual, healing,
and divination, is widely varied. A common theme,
however, is the effort made to give form to the pain
and discomfort experienced in sickness through
jagged scales and sharp points, bulges, or scabby
serrated patches, as in this twentieth-century vessel
from the lower Gongola River valley in Nigeria (1).
Such containers are also reminders of the worthy
but difficult journey of healing, as they are meant to
deliver elixirs and energetic brews that soothe the body
physically and also facilitate interactions with spirits
and cosmic realms. This *nkisi nkondi* is a spirit object
empowered with medicinal ingredients called *bilongo*,
here contained in the cap on the head and the packet
on the abdomen (2); the word *nkondi* references the
ability to counter or subdue wrongdoers or evil spirits
as the causative agents of sickness. Various types of
vessels and delivery objects, pipes, drums, whistles,
and rattles play prominent roles in healing rituals as
healing elixirs were often administered to participants
via sacred ceremonial vessels in conjunction with the
rhythmic oscillation of sound, a form of medicine that
induces entrainment and hypnotic trance states for
healing and divination.

The material record also shows that throughout
prehistory and history there has been a common
reliance by humans on protective and restorative

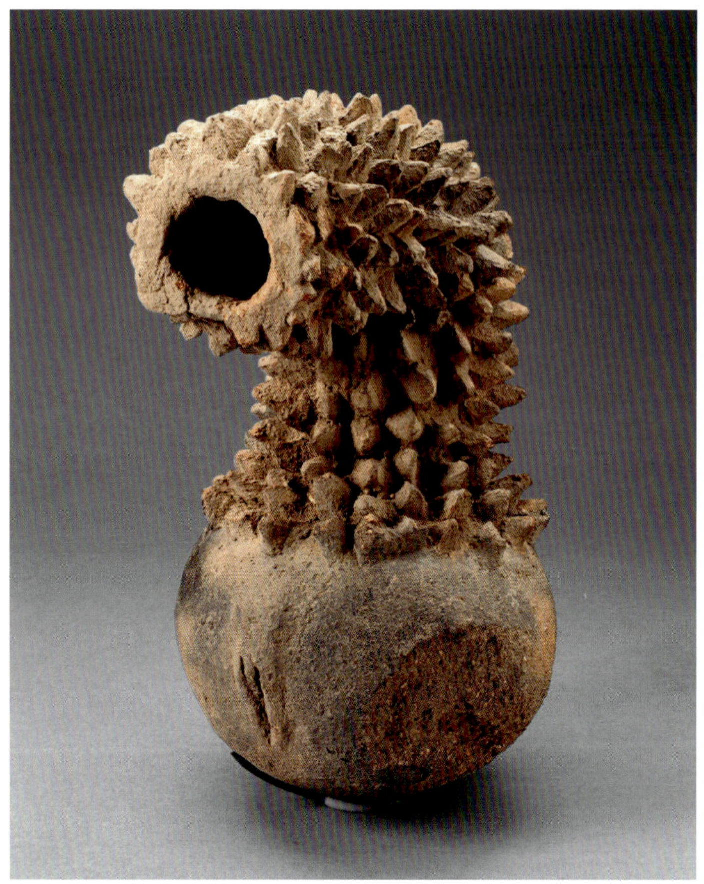

amulets. One of the most popular in ancient Egypt was the
wedjat (meaning "the one that is sound") eye, referring to
the eye of the god Horus (3). This eye represents healing,
rejuvenation, and protection, but also awakening and
enlightenment, including an ability to peer into and be in
higher realms of existence and consciousness. It is said to
depict the third eye or human pineal gland. In Hinduism,
this is called Ajna chakra, or third eye. Often depicted
in Kundalini yoga, the body's seven chakras represent
ascending energy and are frequently shown as snakes
intertwining about an axis or staff—this is known in Greek
mythology as the Caduceus and is also used as the symbol
of Western medicine today. These snakes intersect at the
seat of consciousness or Ajna chakra, which then leads to
divine consciousness or Sahasrara chakra.

There are also many depictions of the use of plants
and energetic realms in healing, as well as chests to carry

2 **Male Figure (*Nkisi Nkondi*)**

Republic of the Congo
1801 – 1875
Wood, metal, glass, fabric, fiber,
cowrie shells, bone, leather, gourd,
and feathers
28 ⅜ in., 72 cm
Art Institute of Chicago
Ada Turnbull Hertle Endowment

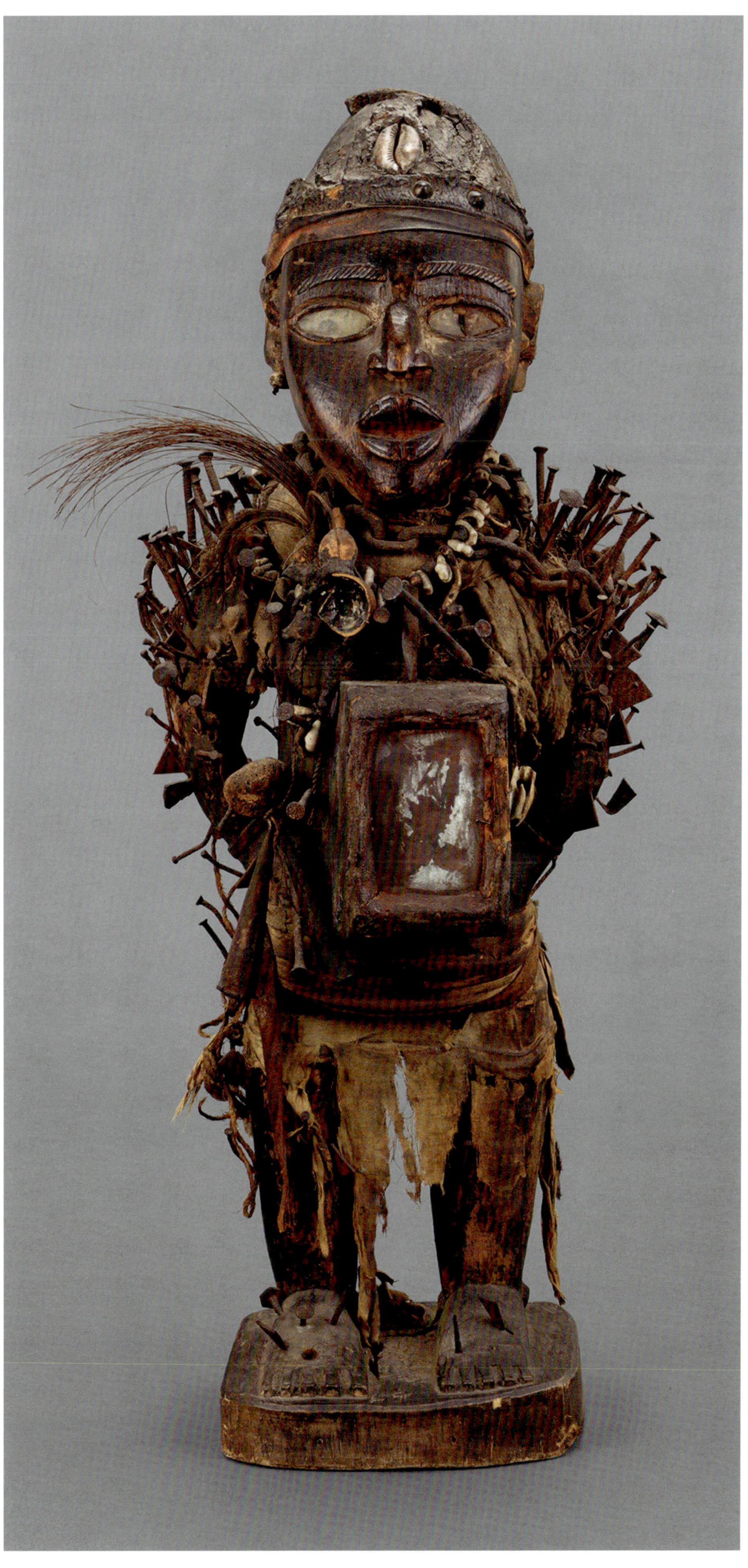

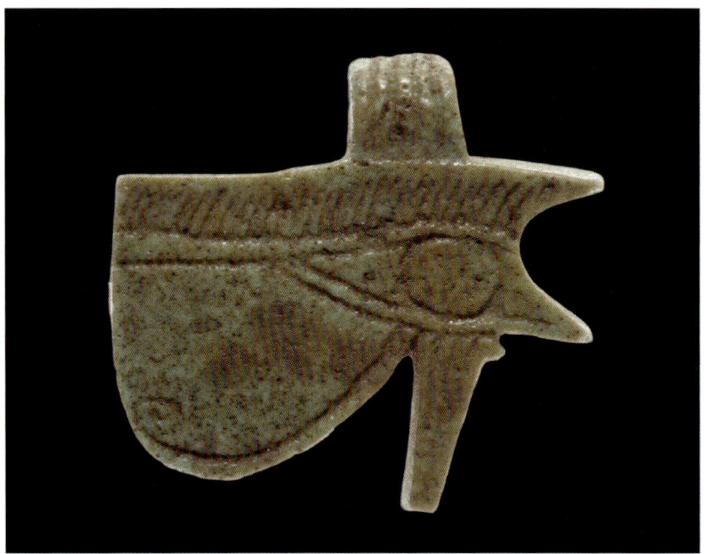

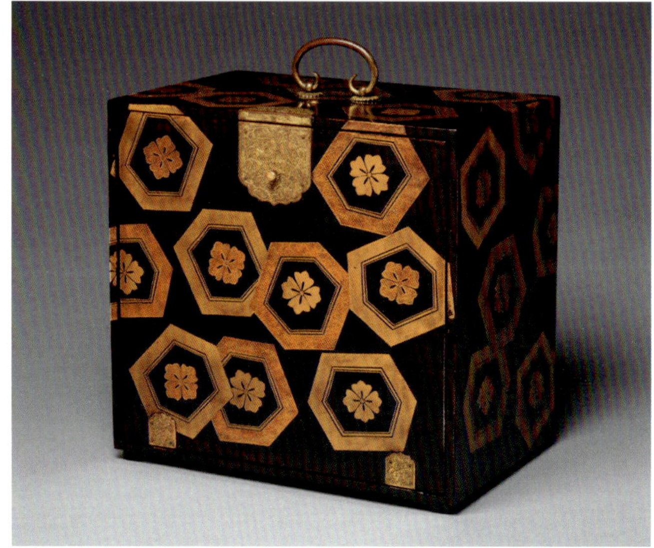

around plant medicines and the like. From Bronze Age animal hides to more elaborate medicine chests—this one decorated with tortoise patterns and cranes, which were associated in both China and Japan with healing and divine energy from a mythical mountain inhabited by immortals (**4**)— apothecary bottles (**5**) and traveling medicine cabinets or containers were common the world over and across many cultures as the healer often needed to transport their apothecary, including medicinal plants and healing accoutrements. A seventeenth-century traveling medicine case from Germany holds a silver garniture meant to contain the most precious of remedies, such as amulets or rare, exotic ingredients from faraway lands (like narwal horn, which was believed to come from

unicorns) and potent medicinal plants, crystals, bezoar stones, and the like all stored safely in their special places next to all the healer's local favorites (**6**).

A particularly common tool used in healing practices across cultures and history was the mortar and pestle, which were used to create medicines. To this day the mortar and pestle are a common symbol of medicinal apothecaries and pharmacological knowledge. They appear in the ancient Egyptian Ebers Papyrus scroll (along with 110 pages of medical knowledge) around 1500 BCE, at about the same time as they are mentioned in the ancient Indian Vedic texts, around 2000–1000 BCE. Examples of both everyday and ornate, ceremonial mortar and pestles have been discovered at archaeological sites across cultures.

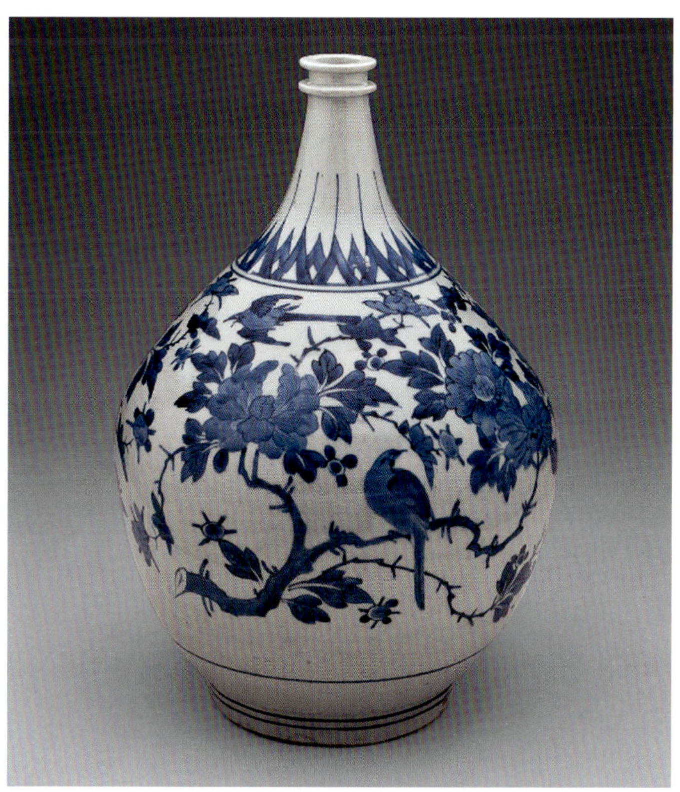

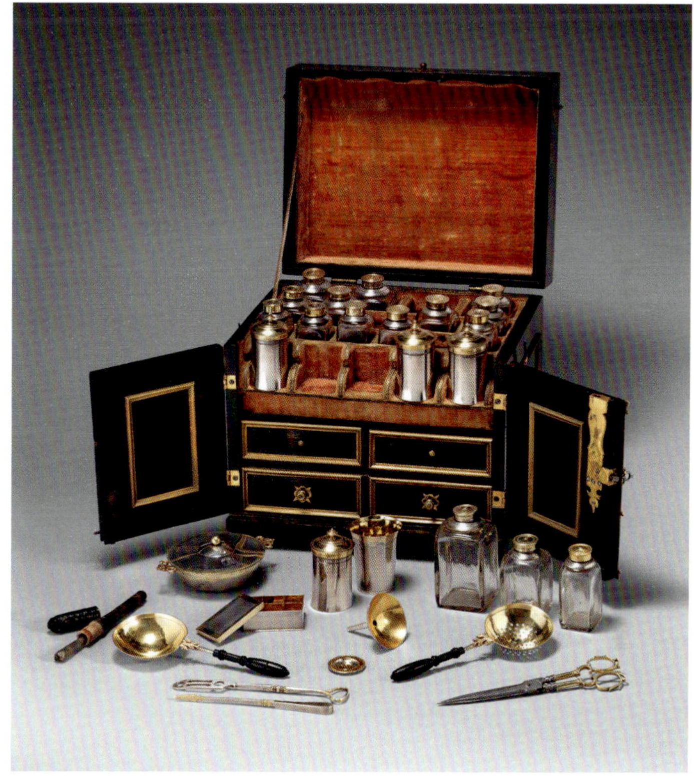

Later versions were made of expensive materials or took on elaborate and ritual forms (**7**). This Persian mortar and pestle from twelfth-century Iran is inlaid with medallions containing the dragon beast Jauzahr, or the hypothetical eighth planet responsible for the eclipse of the sun and the moon, alongside a seated figure surrounded by snakes with dragon heads (**8**). This theanthropic (both human and divine) figure and the connections to the cosmos

suggest it is a shamanic vessel. In the Spanish speaking regions of the Americas, ancient rituals required special ceremonial mortars like this one from the Pacopampa, Chavin de Huantar culture, Peru (**9**). It is in the shape of a feline and the pestle in the shape of a serpent, denoting two of the three shamanic realms, no doubt for preparing ceremonial plant teachers that allowed shamans to enter the third. A metate made of volcanic stone from the

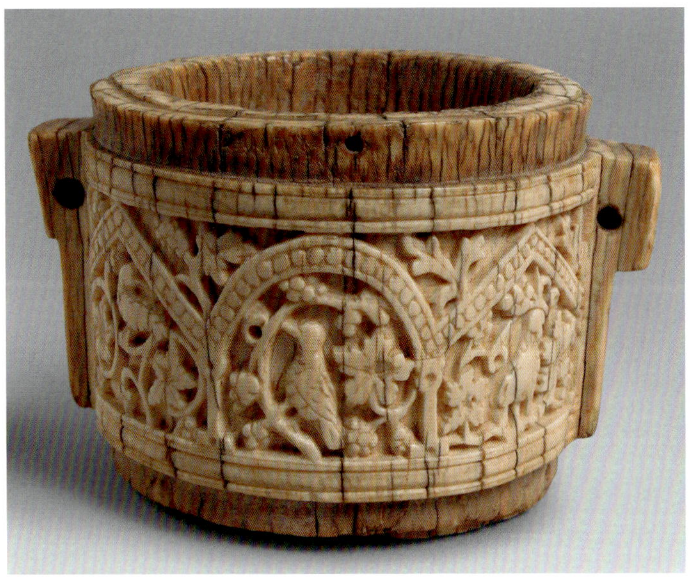

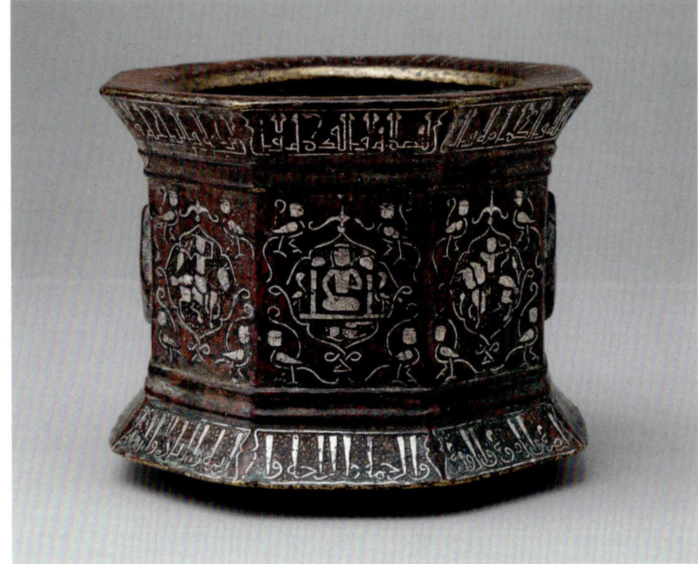

Guanacaste-Nicoya Culture, Nicoya Peninsula Region, Costa Rica, Central America, in the fourth to eighth century features an ornate tripod base and the head of a bird head—probably a parrot (**10**).

All of these artifacts provide evidence that throughout humanity, navigating and treating sickness and facilitating healing has remained a complex interplay of the physical and energetic or spiritual realms. In fact, though humanity has enriched our collective understanding of sickness and healing through the scientific method, the fundamental nature of sickness and healing continues to remain in this complex interplay. Whereas more modern practices in Western medical traditions focus mostly on the physical aspect of sickness, a practice that began in ancient Greece, this is in stark contrast with our ancestral practices, from which we have much to learn.

Two Healing Modalities

Traditionally living cultures have two main types of healing modalities that for the most part are deployed simultaneously to prevent or treat sickness and enable healing. The physical modality utilizes the natural world, medicinal plants and fungi, and even microbial and

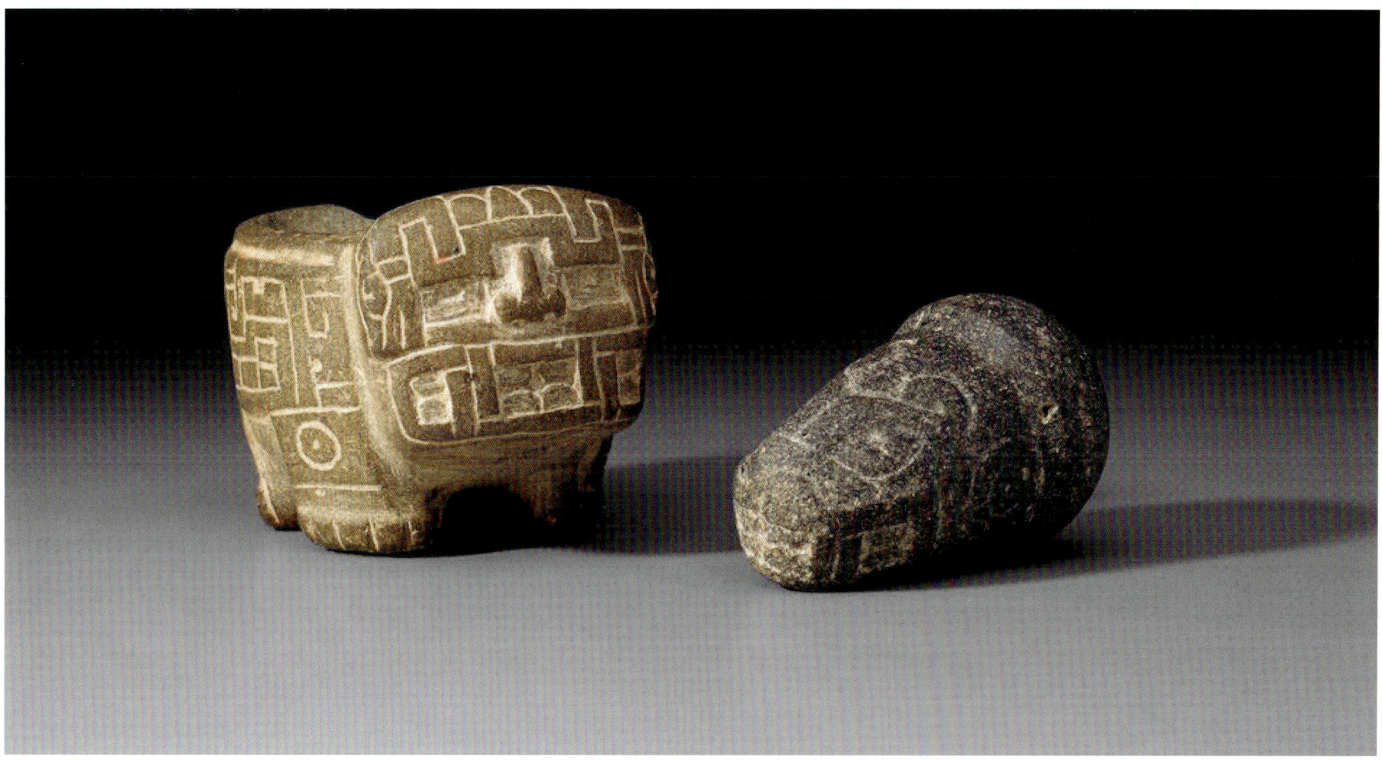

animal products, whereas the energetic or spiritual modality utilizes ceremony, ritual, divination and entheogenic practices of various sorts. These realms were viewed as inseparable, and navigating sickness and healing often required the collaboration of two or more healers. In dealing with the physical realm, there was a reliance on plant medicines and preparations administered by a traditional healer with herbal expertise discovered through millennia of shared learning with the natural world and passed on through oral lineages. The types of maladies they treated include wounds, infections, broken bones and the like.

The need to integrate the physical and spiritual worlds or realms gave rise to the shaman, who was oftentimes born into the practice through lineage or identified by predecessors based on talent, capabilities, or physical attributes (marked by gods, goddesses, or prevailing deities) (11). The shaman is trained to heal by entering the spirit world to communicate with and sometimes influence spirits or manipulate energy for the betterment of a patient and the community. Through ceremony and ritual, including the rhythmic oscillation of sound, meditation and breathing techniques, solitude and even isolation, vision questing and

10 Ceremonial Metate

Guanacaste-Nicoya culture, Costa Rica
300 – 700 CE
Stone
12 × 10 × 18 in., 30.5 × 25.4 × 45.7 cm
Metropolitan Museum of Art, New York
The Michael C. Rockefeller Memorial Collection
Bequest of Nelson A. Rockefeller, 1979

11 Dwarf Figure

Colima culture, West Mexico
100 BCE – 250 CE
Terracotta
9 ¾ in., 24.77 cm
Private Collection

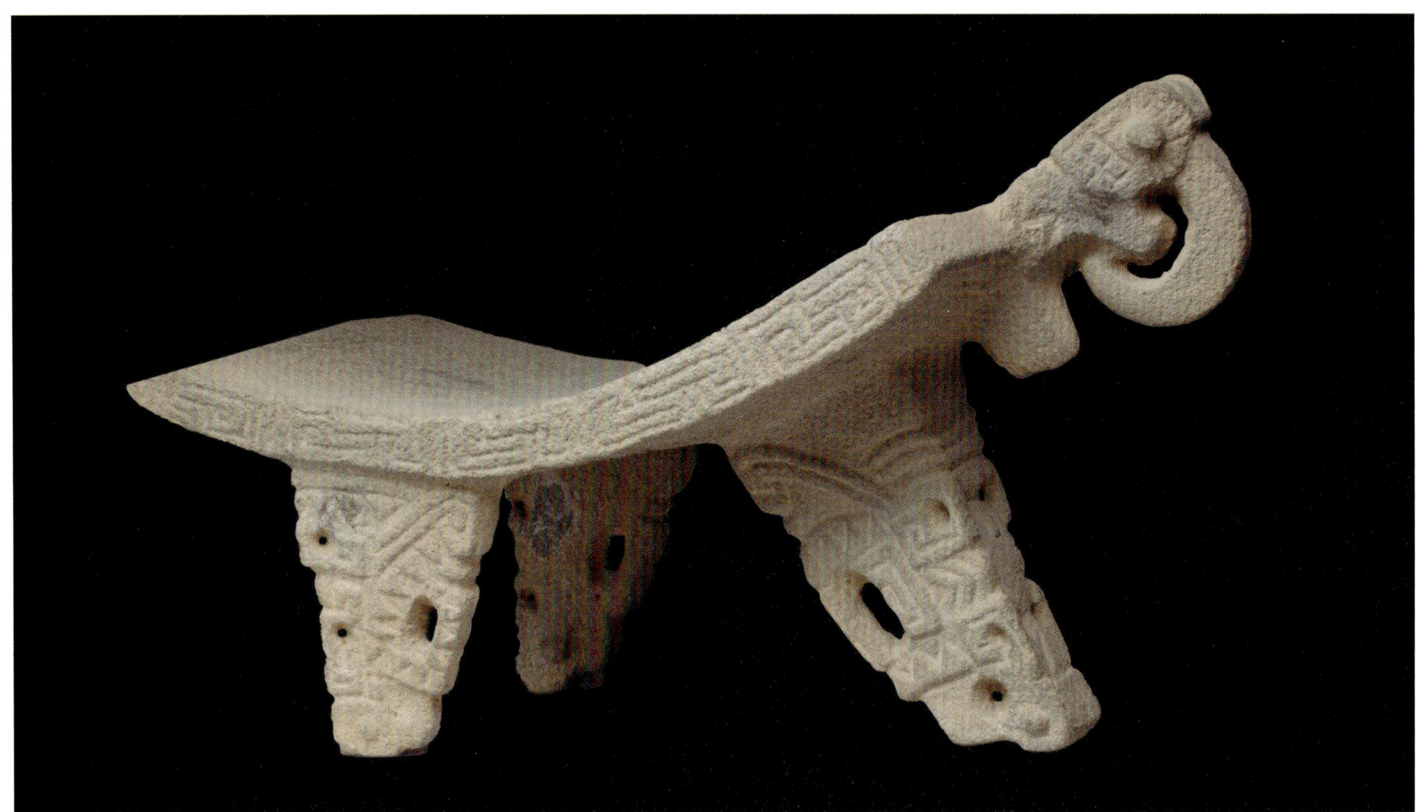

emergence, imbibing of entheogens and plant teachers, including a variety of psychedelic practices aimed at conscious expansion, these healers would "travel to the spirit realm" to heal from the other side and bring back visions and divinations for a vast array of reasons. Because they "walk in two worlds," shamans are held in high esteem and even revered by their communities.

The types of maladies they treat are physical but also include fear, soul loss, evil eye, possession, curses, and madness. These main healing modalities were most often practiced concurrently and though sometimes by the same person, it was more common that there was collaboration among specialists.

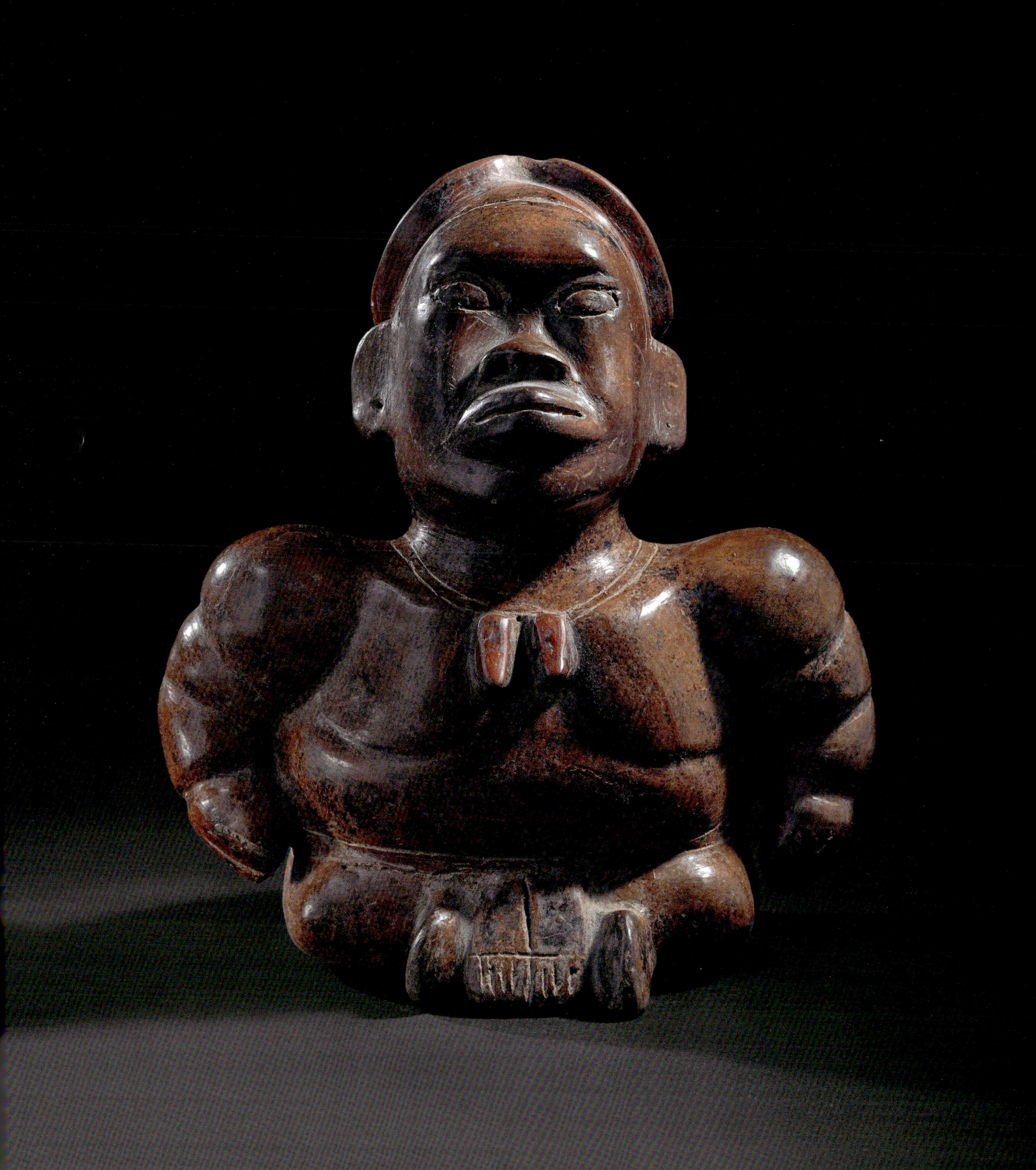

Herbalism and Medicinal Plants

Our earliest *Homo sapiens* ancestors probably practiced herbalism earlier than 70,000–60,000 BCE. These ancestors were eating plants that contained physiologically active and psychoactive compounds, and from the sciences of pharmacognosy and zoopharmacognosy we know that every animal on earth does so as well. In the so-called Flower Burial from roughly 70,000 BCE discovered in the Shanidar Cave, a Neanderthal adult of undetermined sex appears to have been buried with flowers from medicinal plants including yarrow, grape hyacinth, ephedra, a medicinal thistle, marshmallow, and others, still used in healing practices today. The study of a number of Paleolithic sites with significant material remains of plants suggests that the variety of species present cannot be explained as foodstuff alone since the proportion of medicinal plants represented is much greater than would have occurred naturally in those environments. In other words, the plants were gathered by our early ancestors for their medicinal properties. A prominent example is milk thistle, still lauded for its effective treatment of liver problems. These sites range from Gesher Benot Ya'aqov (780,000 BCE) to Atlit Yam (10,000 BCE). Importantly, the evidence ramps up at the beginning of the Neolithic period, when there was an explosion of medicinal plant usage likely driven by enhanced social transmission and more sophisticated social systems inclusive of resource exploitation and exchange. This stands to reason given that the Ice Age ended around then as well.

The frozen body of Ötzi the Iceman, discovered protruding from the Schnalstal/Val Senales Valley glacier in 1991, brings the ensuing Bronze Age to life before our eyes. Around 5300 BCE, Ötzi seems to have been traversing the Ötztal Valley Alps when he met his demise and was frozen in time carrying a flint dagger, a copper axe, and a deer hide quiver for arrows made from cornelian cherry, viburnum, and wayfaring trees. Interestingly, he also carried with him, or perhaps he wore, pieces of a birch polypore medicinal fungus threaded onto pieces of animal hide. As this has immunomodulatory, antibiotic, and hemostatic properties, he may have been using it to treat his wounds, though it was also widely used as tinder for starting fires. Ötzi's stomach contained remnants of bracken ferns, which he may have been using to treat intestinal parasites, and he was covered with around sixty marks that suggest tattooing, acupuncture sites, or perhaps both. The marks indicated focused work around the wrist and ankle joints, and scans revealed that Ötzi's joints were degenerating and likely causing him some pain—impetus for these healing tattoos. Traces of bog moss found along with the body indicate Ötzi was perhaps making himself some natural moss bandages. Considering all this, he seems to have been part of a culture with established traditional healing practices inclusive of tool, tattoo, and medicinal plant use.

Codification

The earliest codification of herbalism and medicinal plants currently dates to 3000 BCE. It takes the form of a Sumerian clay tablet from Nippur, Iraq, and lists fifteen prescriptions for common ailments such as headache. Some other seminal works followed that are currently dated to around 2000–1000 BCE. They include the Ebers Papyrus, an ancient Egyptian compilation of medical knowledge; the Vedic scriptures of India, which codify early Ayurveda; and the *Shennong Bencaojing* (*Divine Farmers Materia Medica*), attributed to Shen Nung, known as the Divine Farmer and renowned for birthing traditional Chinese herbalism and acupuncture, compiled in the third century BCE but likely older. Then came the works of the Greek physician Hippocrates and the Hippocratic Corpus, compiled around 400 BCE, followed by those of Galen around 200 BCE, and Avicenna around 600 CE. The modern-day herbal pharmacopoeia includes many of the very same herbal remedies found in these works. Indeed, many modern-day blockbuster medications—at least forty, but more likely closer to sixty percent—are derived from traditional medicinal plants. One of the first medications for high blood pressure, for example, came from *Rauwolfia serpentina* or Indian snakeroot, native to India and Asia and in use there for millennia. Similarly, the frontline diabetes medication Metformin is derived from *Galega officinalis* or French lilac, and cardiac glycosides like Digitalis and Digoxin that treat heart failure come from *Digitalis purpurea* or foxglove, and the list goes on and on.

Frequency of consensus speaks to the modern-day retention of ancient knowledge of healing plants and traditions, and it is quite apparent among some cultural groups. Importantly, indigenous cultural groups the world over continue to practice types of a more grass-roots herbalism; these were and remain prolific throughout the Americas, where the treatment of physical conditions continues to be tethered to energetic or spiritual realms. Many of these practices were rooted in simple diagnostics based on symptoms and rudimentary signs, such as easily observed wounds, fever, and cough, and techniques like eye, tongue, pulse, and reflex analysis and corresponding treatments based on bringing opposites, such as hot and cold, into balance. For example, if an individual had a hot condition such as fever, the treatment would be a plant in the cold category of that healer's repertoire.

One healing tradition with a significant frequency of consensus in the modern-day is that of the Maya of Central America, among whom many of the plants used in ancient times survive and are still in use. Depictions of modern-day Maya medicinal plants in ancient art include *Theobroma cacao* (cacao or chocolate), which the Maya referred to as the "food of the gods" (**12**); *Tynanthus guatemalensis,* a potent modern day medicinal plant that has important longevity activity; and *Protium copal*, a

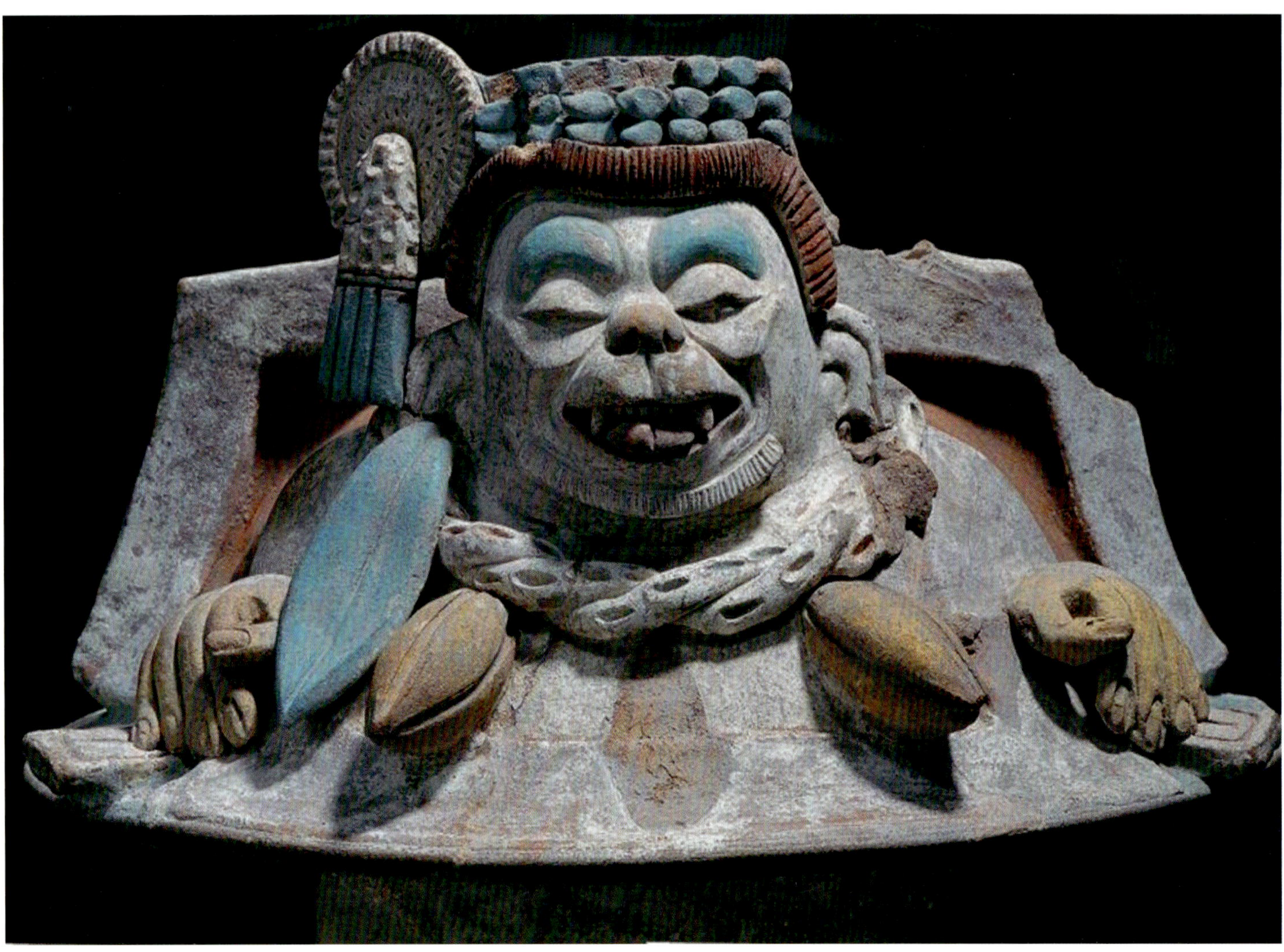

sacred incense for energetic clearing, a practice seen cross culturally in the use of sage, frankincense, myrrh, palo santo, cedar, and the like. The Maya used the K'AN glyph, meaning "precious, yellow," in murals and polychrome vessels. On ceremonial cacao drinking vessels, the glyph was a descriptor for an allspice-like flavoring ingredient, *T. guatemalensis* or Chibayel, which was a top selection for the treatment of diabetes and an exceptionally active extract in an antidiabetic assay for inhibition of protein glycation, which drives diabetes symptoms; the cross-section of this Chibayel vine is yellow in color and displays a cross as represented by the K'AN glyph (13). This is a revered longevity beverage used by both ancient and modern-day Maya.[2]

Shamanism

Just as there is evidence of herbalism among our earliest ancestors, so, too, is there evidence of shamanism in some of the earliest art. During the later Paleolithic period our earliest ancestors began leaving records

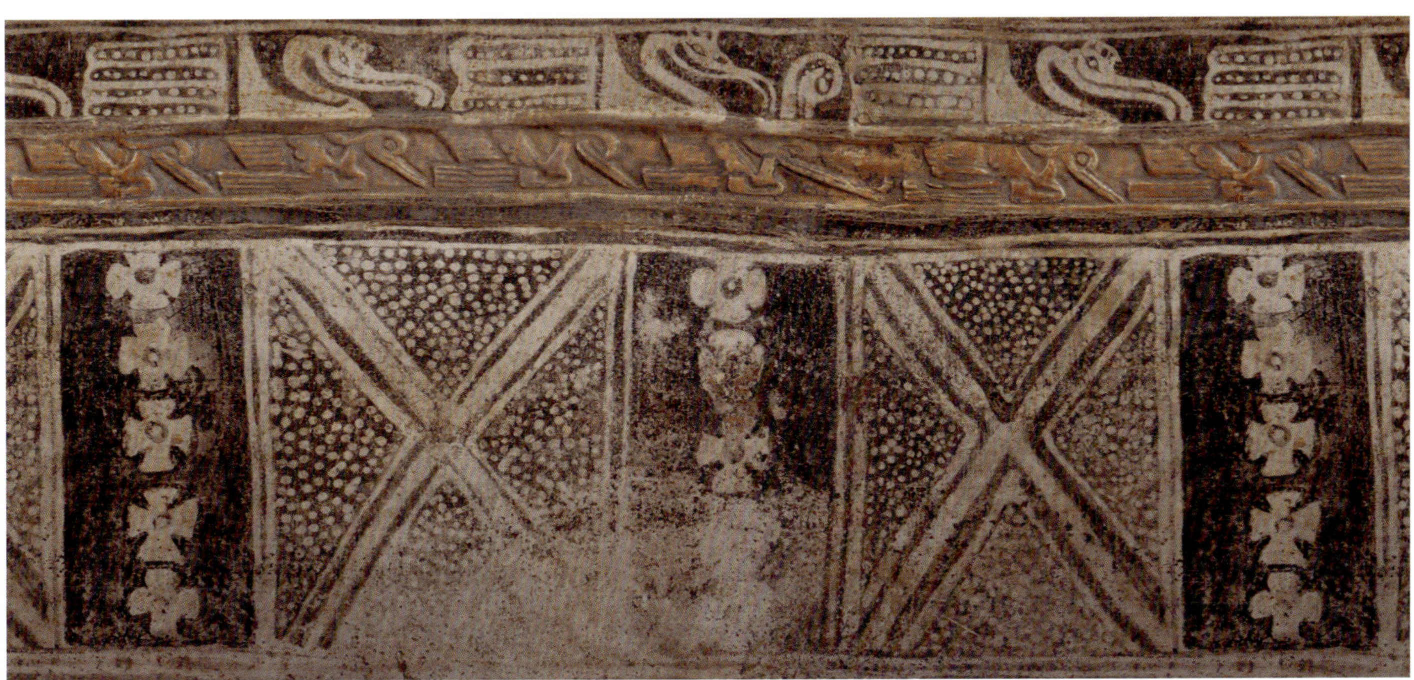

of their world and worldview (beginning evidently around 50,000 BCE) in the form of images, predominantly carved into or painted onto the walls of caves and in carvings. These were mostly depictions of hunts, animals as totems, and perhaps rituals to teach subsequent generations and to ensure the survival of herds. There were also female forms denoting fertility and childbearing, which ensured the survival of the species. These images of animals and, more rarely, composite human-animals, are records of shamanic journeying or visions seen by shamans in ritual trance states.

Trance states may be achieved in a multitude of ways including the rhythmic oscillation of sound or through the use of entheogens derived from plants, cacti, or fungi, but also from the secretions of animals such as certain toads. Entheogens, also known as plant teachers, have been revered through the ages by healers for their psychedelic and perceived healing effects. They are ingested by a shaman or other ritual specialist in order to produce visions and gain insight and healing through bringing balance and understanding. This Inca face beaker made around 1300–1500 is in the form of *Bufo*

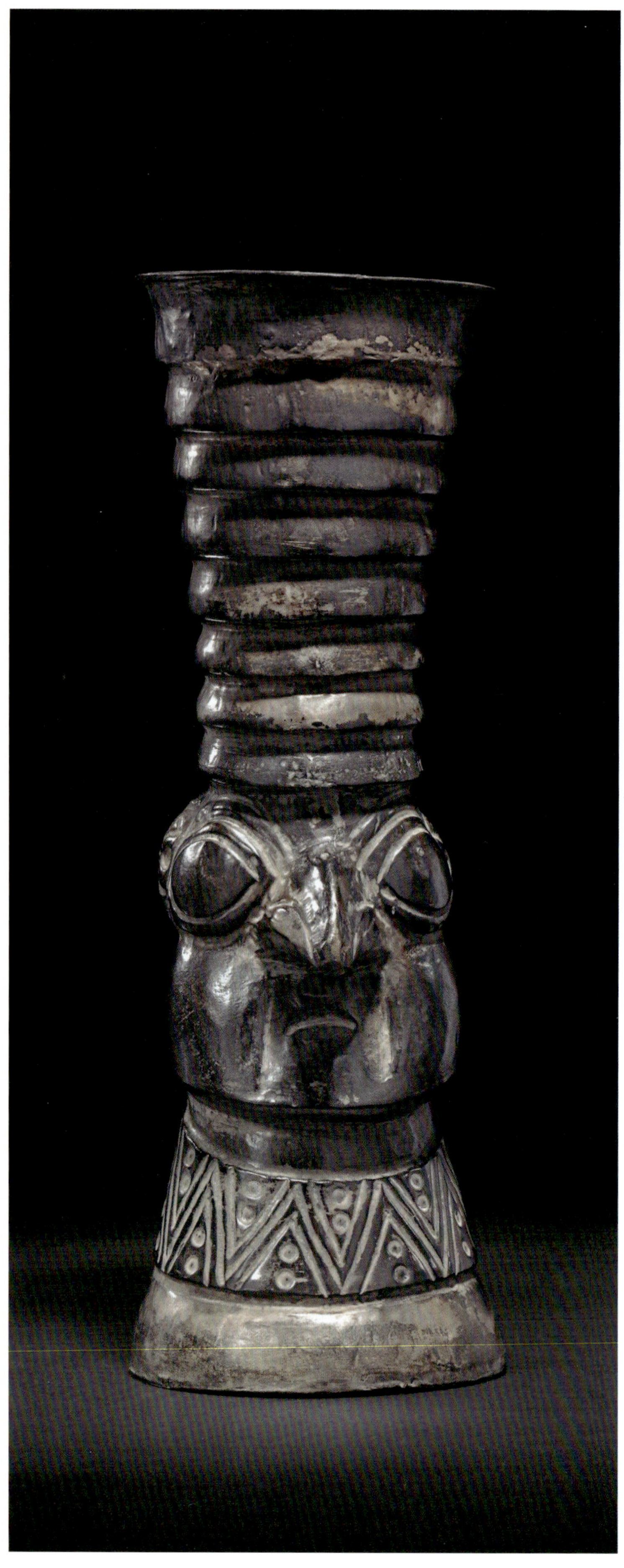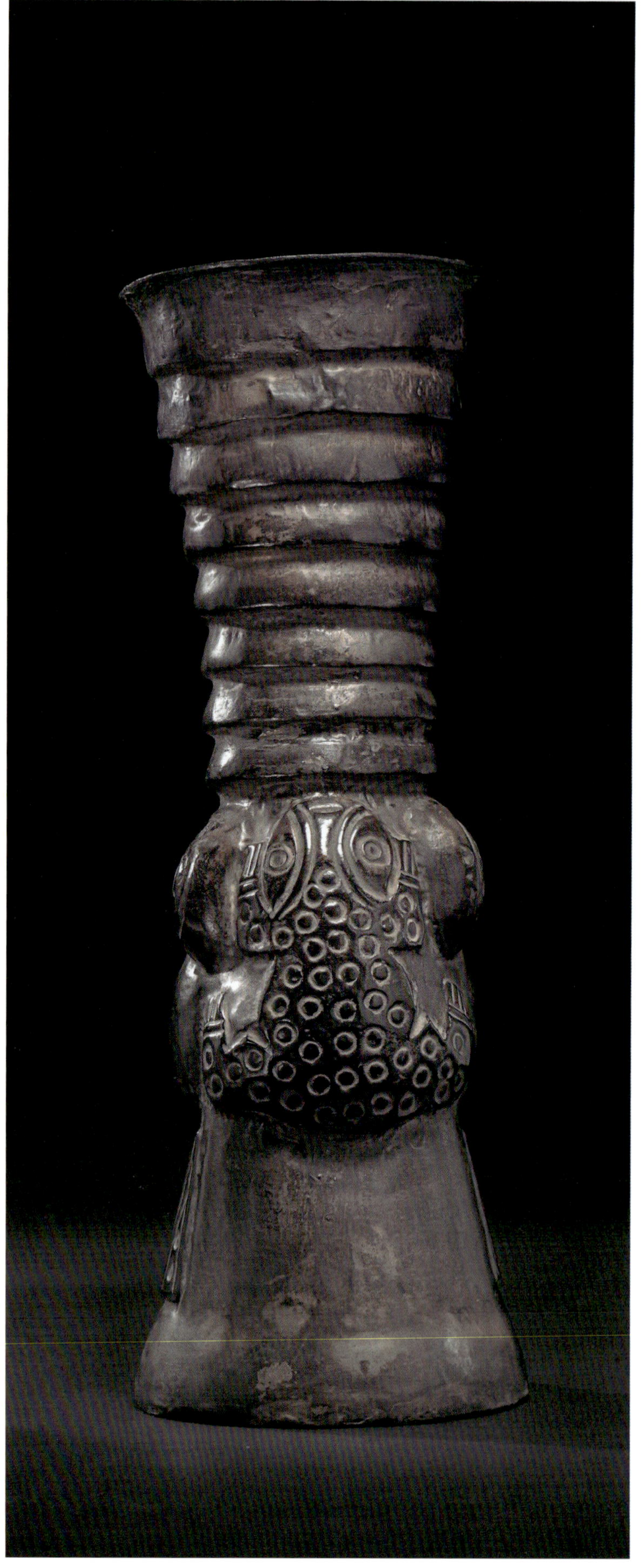

14 **Beaker with Frog**

Chimu/Inca culture, Peru
1300 – 1500
Silver
13 in., 33.02 cm
The Stuart Handler Collection

15 **The Lion-Human of
Hohlenstein-Stadel**

40,0000 – 35,000 BCE
Mammoth ivory
11.06 in., 28.1 cm
Museum Ulm, Germany

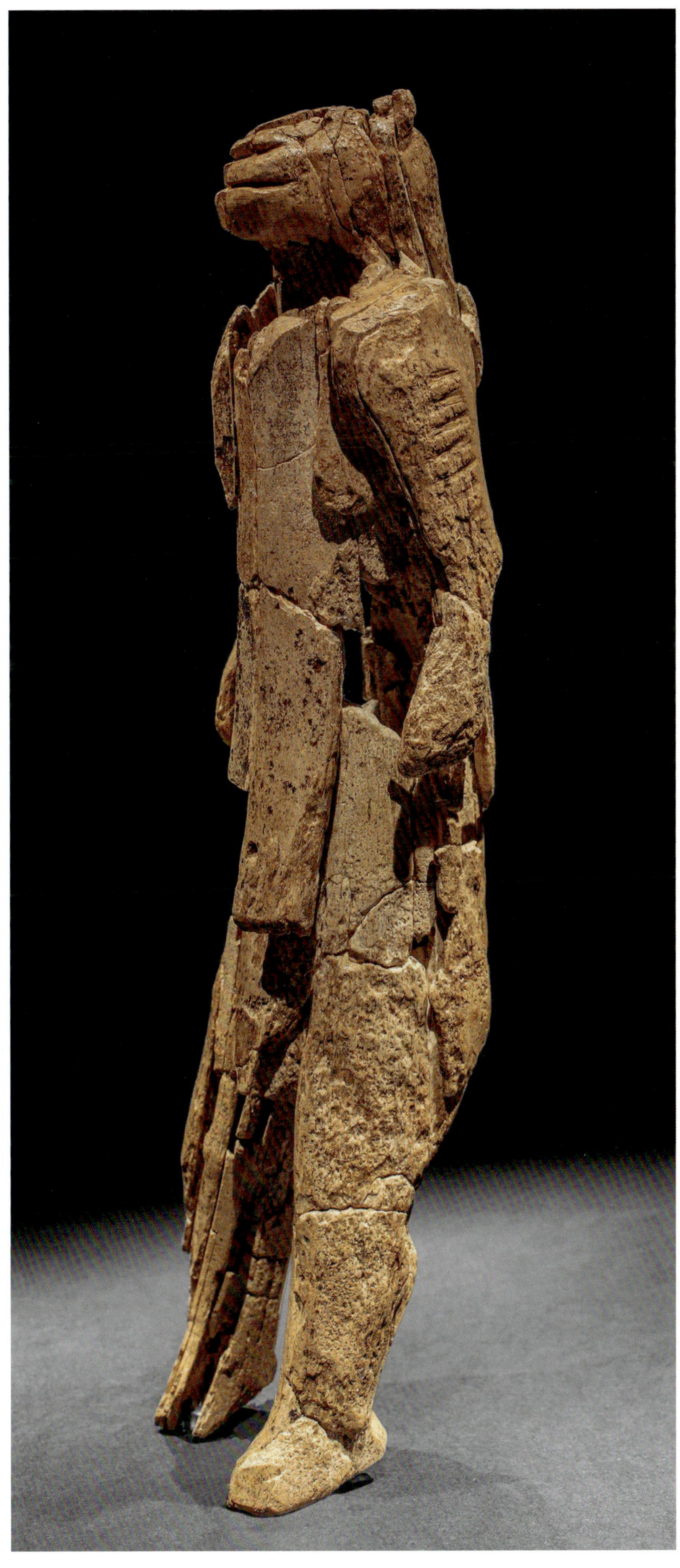

marinus or cane toad, which produces bufotoxins with psychoactive properties (**14**). The bufotoxins were blended with *chicha*, a traditional fermented beverage made from a variety of local wild plants including quinoa or maize, for shamanic purposes and drunk from such a beaker.

Another ancient common practice in shamanism is therianthropy, or the belief in the ability of humans to metamorphose into other animals by means of shapeshifting. One of the world's oldest carvings is a half-human, half-lion of mammoth ivory from about 40,000 BCE discovered in the Hohlenstein-Stadel cave in Germany in 1939 (**15**). Another example of this phenomenon is found in a depiction from Chauvet Cave, Vallon-Pont-d'Arc, France, from about 40,000–35,000 BCE. Here a bison man straddles a woman whose right arm seems to be transforming into the head of a lion. And one of the major deities of the ancient Central American cultures is Quetzalcóatl, whose name is derived from the Nahuatl word *quetzalli*, meaning "tail feather of the quetzal bird," and *coatl*, meaning "snake." Initially he was a god of vegetation related closely to water and earth and later to celestial bodies, in particular the evening and morning stars. We also have many surviving depictions of chimeras (**16** and **17**), which are composite creatures with, for example, a lion's head, a goat's body, and a serpent's tail, as well as depictions of anthropomorphized animals (animals exhibiting human form).

The fact that many of the early cave paintings and sculptures related to shamanism seem to have been inspired by the surface configurations of their media—for example, the three-dimensionality or shape of a rock or other media, and outcropping or relief patterns—lends support to the idea that some, and likely most, of these shamanic visions were prompted by the unique features of the media and that the ensuing art was a pictographic record of their visions. Some good examples include the spotted horse and negative handprints from Pech-Merle, France, made around 23,000 BCE, and the Reclining Woman from La Magdeleine Cave, Tarn, France, from around 12,000 BCE. These images seem to have emerged for the most part in what is now Spain and France, and they continued to be made into the Neolithic period. Similar depictions include early works from Anatolia and Mesopotamia, Persia (which is roughly now Turkey, Syria, and Iraq), Egypt, and then Greece and Rome. Some good examples are the bird man of Göbekli Tepe (in modern-day Turkey) from 10,000 BCE, and Oannes and the Apkallu, fish man/God (**18**) and bird man figures of ancient Mesopotamia. A clay Apkallu figurine from the ninth century BCE depicts a bird-headed human with four large wings (**19**). It was found under a floor in a palace in the ancient Assyrian city of Nimrud in Mesopotamia, where it was probably placed by a shaman to ritually protect the interior space of the building. It resembles the winged eagle-headed figures carved in relief on the walls of palaces, such as this Apkallu relief panel from the Northwest Palace at Nimrud, also from the ninth

16   Chimera of Arezzo

Estruscan culture, Italy
400 BCE
Bronze
30.9 in., 78.5 cm
National Archaeological Museum,
Florence, Italy

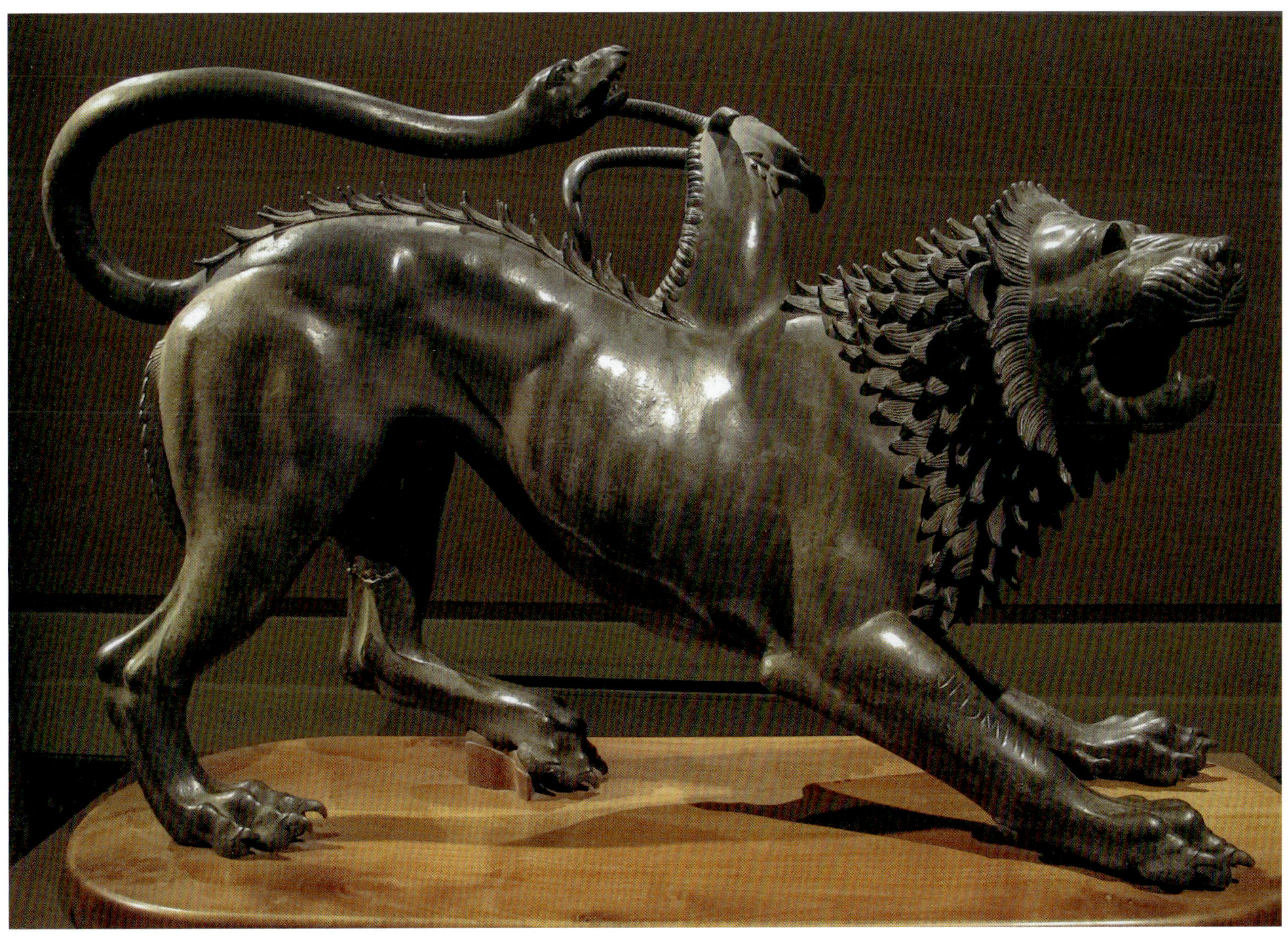

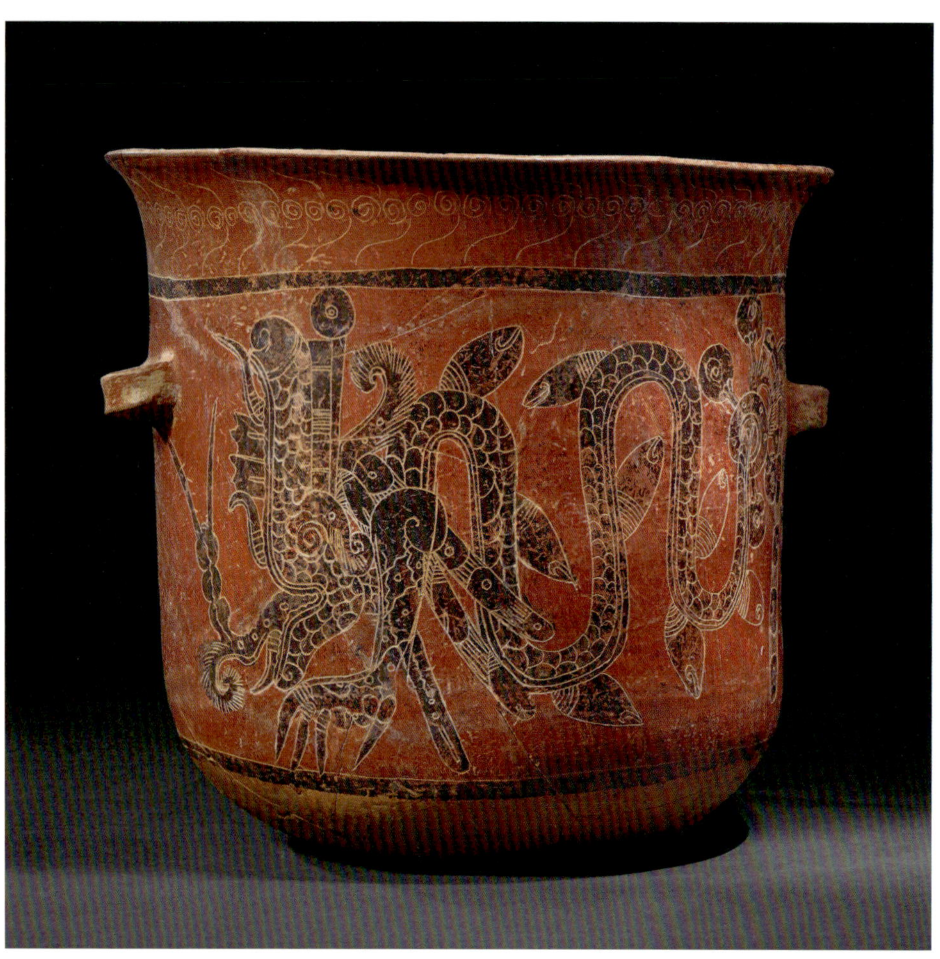

17 **Serpent Vessel**

Mixtec culture, South Central Mexico
1200 – 1500
Terracotta
12 ¾ × 13 ¼ in., 32.39 × 33.66 cm
Private Collection

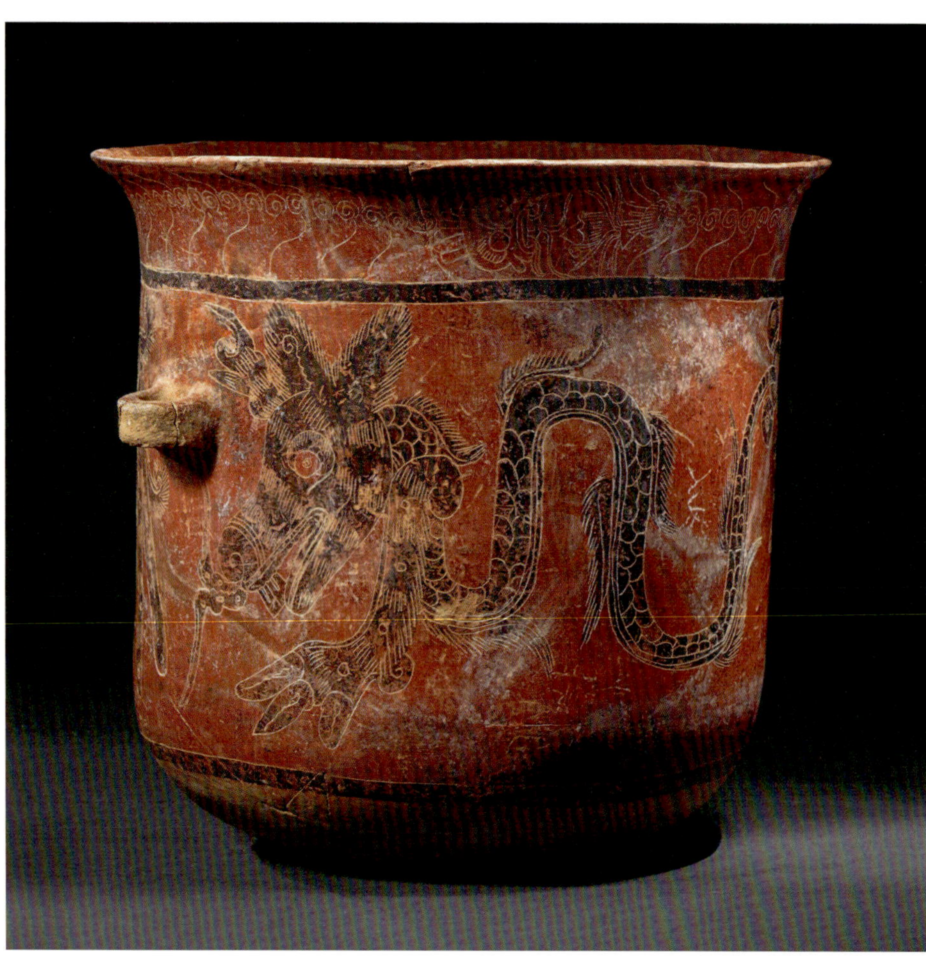

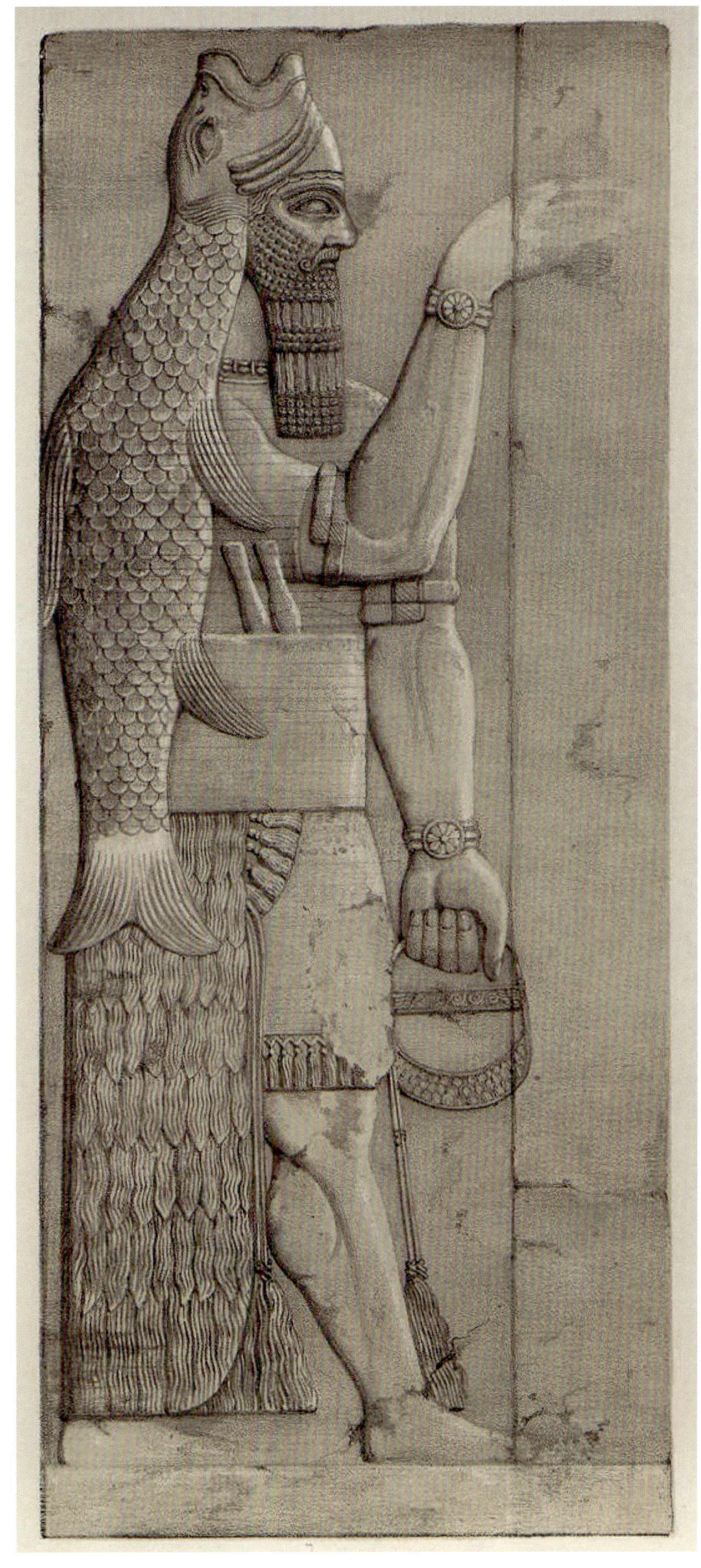

18 Fish God

Plate 6 from Austin Henry Layard, ed., *A Second Series of the Monuments of Nineveh: Including Bas-Reliefs from the Palace of Sennacherib and Bronzes from the Ruins of Nimroud from Drawings Made during a Second Expedition to Assyria, Northern Iraq* (London, 1853)

19 Apkallu

Assyrian culture, Nimrud (ancient Kalhu),
Northern Iraq
900 – 800 BCE
Terracotta
5 ⁹⁄₁₆ × 3 ¼ × ¹⁵⁄₁₆ in., 14.2 × 8.3 × 3.3 cm
Metropolitan Museum of Art, New York
Rogers Fund, 1954

20 Relief Panel

Assyrian culture, Nimrud (ancient Kalhu),
Northern Iraq
883 – 859 BCE
Gypsum alabaster
93 × 70 × 4 ¼ in., 236.2 × 177.8 × 10.8 cm
Metropolitan Museum of Art, New York
Gift of John D. Rockefeller Jr., 1932

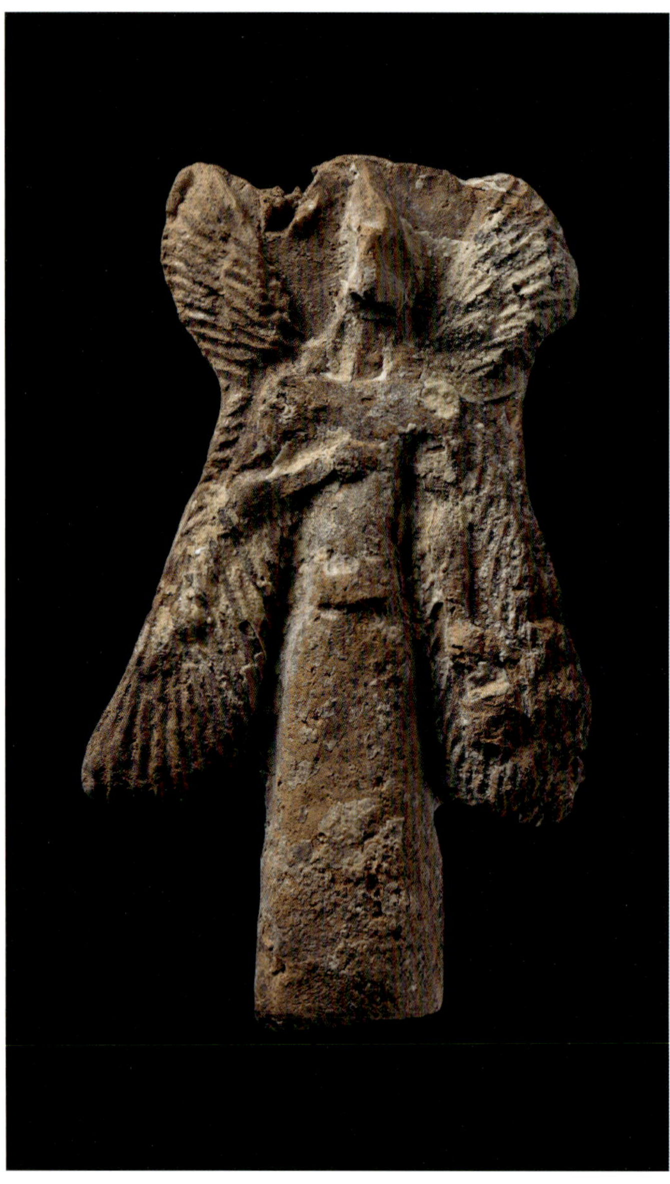

century BCE (**20**). Carvings such as this often flanked either the Assyrian king or a stylized "sacred tree."

Therianthropy was carried into the Americas as well, as exemplified by the Lanzon, a carved stone monument at Chavin de Huantar, a ceremonial center in the northern highlands of Peru. The Lanzon is a tall, wedge-shaped stone with a therianthropic, supernatural anthropomorph with a human body and feline head and powerful taloned hands uniting cosmos and earth. Accompanying it are complex chimeric, therianthropic shapeshifting jaguar, caiman, raptor, serpent, and human elements, along with sacred geometry. Similar depictions are found on a multitude of ceremonial vessels from the Chavin culture; this one held shamanic brew for the ceremonial altar (**21**). The powerful depictions of anaconda jaguar and raptor condor represent the push and the pull of divine feminine and masculine energies of forest and rivers and mountains. This is in the context of the three shamanic realms: the lower represented by the serpent, the middle by the feline, and the upper by the avian.

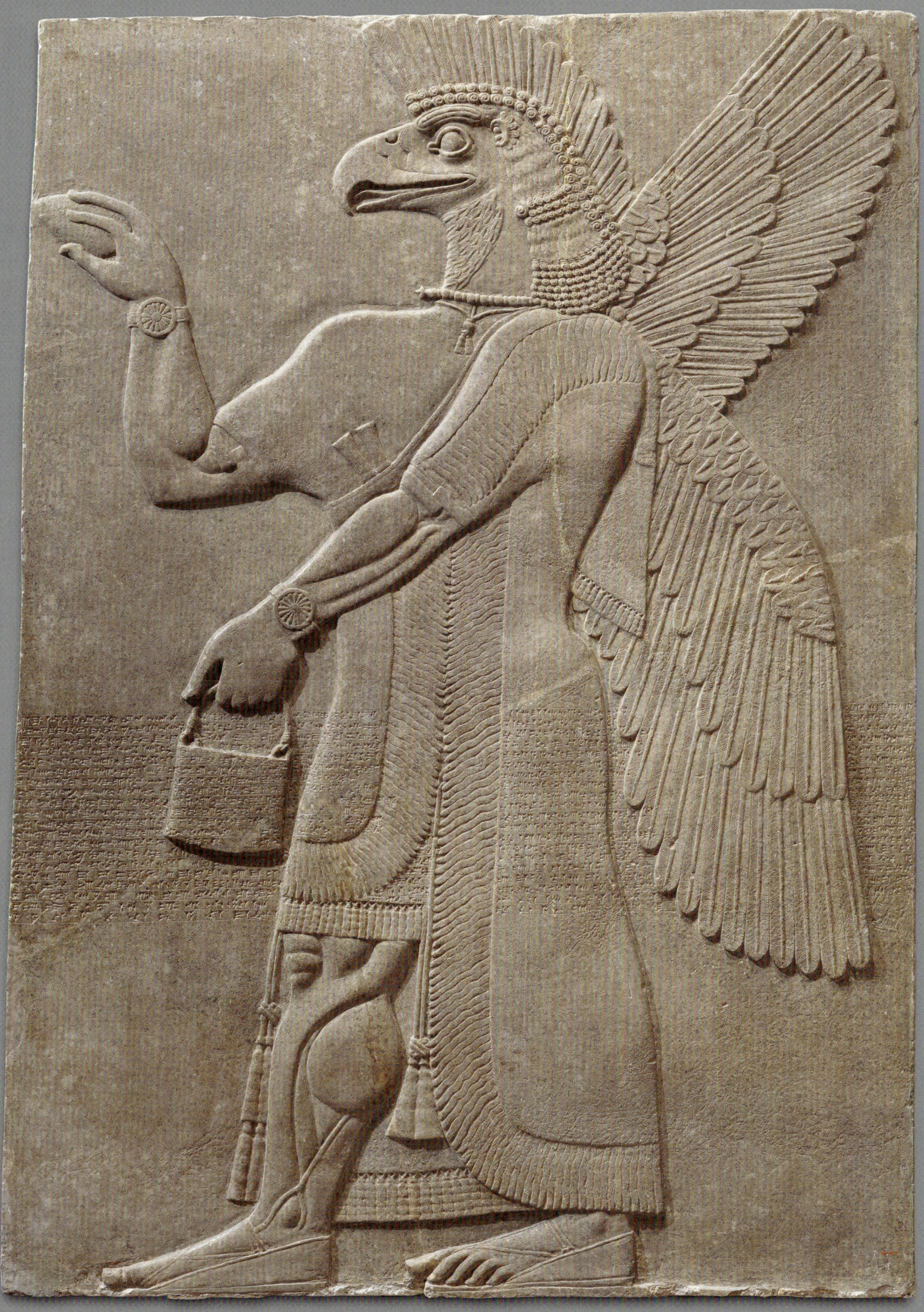

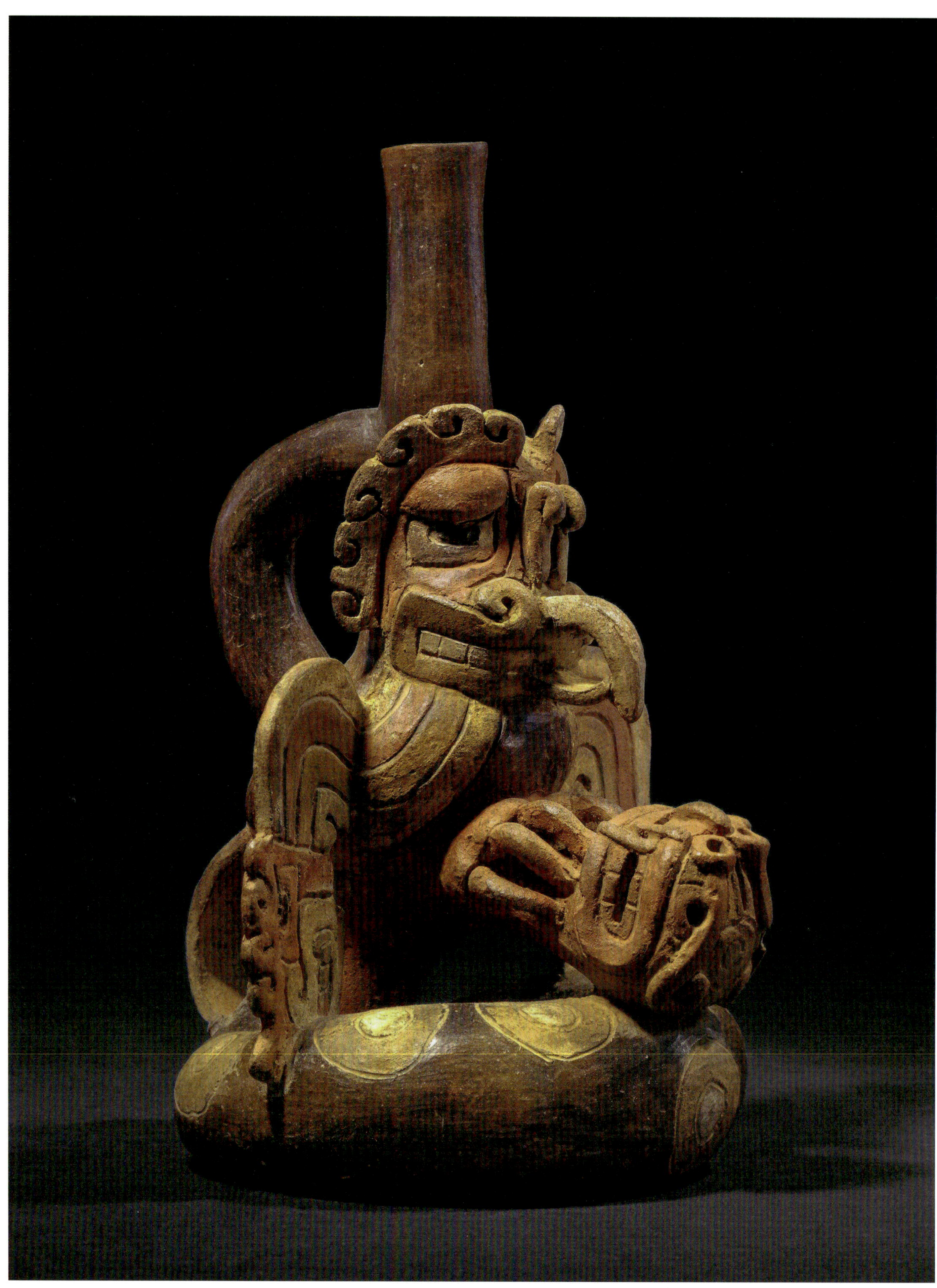

21 Spouted Vessel with Raptor and Serpent

Chavin culture, Northern Peru
900 – 200 BCE
Terracotta
10 ⅛ × 6 ¾ in., 25.72 × 17.15 cm
Private Collection

Healing Systems

Through the vast majority of history, our ancestors existed with and participated in shared learning with our natural world. Through this process, which is akin to the scientific method—i.e., observe, hypothesize, experiment, conclude—they built a repository of healing knowledge. For example, certain botanicals were observed to produce a kind of brightly colored visual or olfactory indicator that allures or distracts insects, birds, and animals, informing them about what to eat and what not to eat. In addition to observing the behavior of animals, they also learned from careful study and observation of the plants themselves, e.g., their morphologic and physical features, energetics, and habitat associations. So, if a tree had red sap, perhaps it was good for blood flow or wound healing. If a leaf was shaped like a uterus, it might be good for woman's health, hormonal balance, or birthing. They would then cautiously try it in those applications and if it worked, they would add it to their repertoire. Over time, they amassed vast pharmacopoeias, knowledge grew and coalesced, and as hunter-gatherers became agricultural societies and civilizations rose, healing systems were formed. Oral traditions of healing oftentimes have thousands of years of history and over the years have brought to the forefront some of the prominent healing techniques of today.

Some Far Eastern traditions have noble lineages in different forms of healing reaching back millennia. A Zen type of mindfulness philosophy and practice emerged in southern India thousands of years ago, perhaps around 4000–3000 BCE, with some scholars asserting it was earlier than 8000 BCE. It manifests the concept of *prana*, meaning "life force." Prana is one of the most comprehensive concepts linking different abstract thought systems in ancient India. It connects energetic concepts in sickness and healing and tethers life force with concepts of the three worlds, the humors, the elements, and the chakras, which serve as congruent overlays on a common underlying set of life processes and practices aimed at strengthening and balancing. Dozens of modes of healing throughout the Indic areas, including dietary, yogic, tantric, tribal, and folk, imbue this concept in one form or another. This grew into Yoga, Siddha, and Ayurveda and seeded diverse concepts in life energies and energetic healing the world over.

Yoga is a physical, mental, and spiritual practice that aims to still the mind and promote health through the induction of physical and mental well-being. It typically emphasizes *dyana* or "meditation," *pranayama* or "breathing techniques," and *asanas* or "physical movements and postures." Practice of these enables energies to ascend the seven chakras and into consciousness.

Siddha is one of the oldest traditional medicine systems of humanity and remarkably it remains one of three indigenous medical sciences recognized in India by the Central Government (along with Ayurveda and Unani). Siddha is less widely known than Ayurveda and Unani and is relatively localized to the southern states

Buddha of Medicine Bhaishajyaguru (Yaoshi fo)

China
Yuan dynasty, 1319
Water-based pigment over foundation of clay
mixed with straw
24 ft. 8 in. × 49 ft. 7 in., 751.8 × 1511.3 cm
Metropolitan Museum of Art, New York
Gift of Arthur M. Sackler, in honor of his parents,
Isaac and Sophie Sackler, 1965

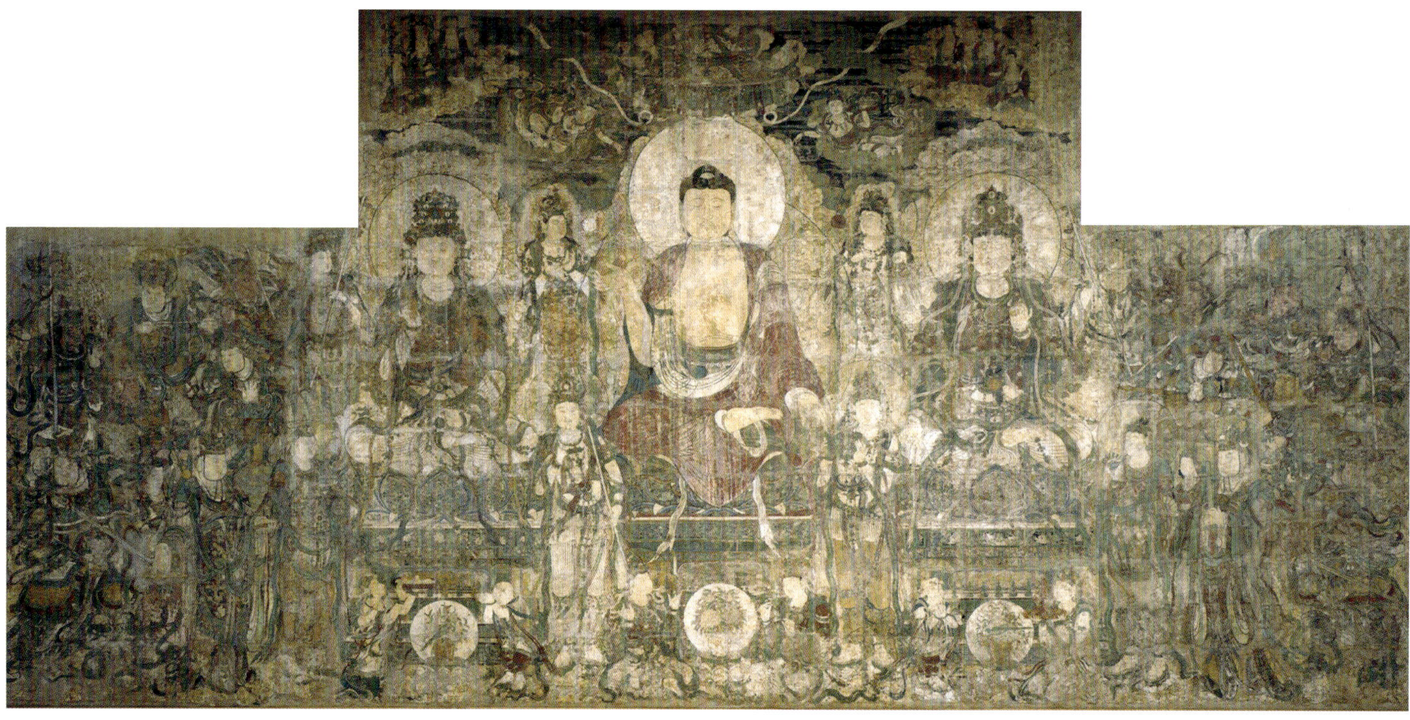

of India. Though its point of origin remains obscure, it is thought to have originated in the Indian subcontinent around 3000 BCE. Referred to as *Siddha Vaidyam* or "mother medical science" by practitioners, it is believed by them that most of the popular medical sciences and health care of the past and even present era derive from Siddha. The system maintains that the microcosm and macrocosm are one and the same. Like Ayurveda, it views sicknesses as imbalances in three bio-energies: *vata*, *pitta*, and *kapha*,

referred to collectively as *doshas*. These imbalances are treated by administering a wide range of elixirs prepared from medicinal plants, herbs, metals, minerals, and other ingredients. A sort of alchemy practice and biological transmutation is inherent to this system as well.

Ayurveda, meaning "science/wisdom of life," addresses the uniqueness of each person in an effort to promote protection from sickness and the act of healing from within. It takes a comprehensive approach inclusive of spirituality and lifestyle and advocates careful consideration of and harmony with nature. Similar to Siddha, the three *doshas* are observed and the basis of treatment is the balancing of *doshas* through lifestyle modifications like dietary change, herbal treatments, hygiene, spiritual practices, and detoxification practices—all aimed at the facilitation of *oja*—our life's energy.

Traditional Chinese Medicine

Healing practices including aspects of physical, mental, spiritual, and environmental interconnectedness played an important role in the transmission of Buddhism throughout Asia. This mural, made in China around 1319, depicts Bhaishajyaguru (Yaoshi fo), the Buddha of Medicine, wearing a red robe and attended by an assembly of related deities, including two seated bodhisattvas who hold symbols for the divine masculine and feminine, the sun and the moon (**22**). Elements of these systems moved out of India via the Silk Road, an ancient trade route linking China with the West, and helped inform elements of Traditional Chinese Medicine, including the underlying philosophy of balancing and strengthening *qi* or "vital life force," similar to *prana* and *oja*, via practices such as Qi Gong, Tai Chi and other martial arts, meditation, herbal medicine, acupuncture, and cupping and moxibustion, which work on similar principles as acupuncture

but with burning "moxa," usually dried mugwort, and applying negative pressure through combustion in a cup over an acupuncture or pressure point or meridian energy channel.

Millennia of human interactions with the Asiatic ecology produced a suite of beliefs and technologies surrounding health maintenance and remediation. The healing systems of the great river valley civilizations are the culmination of generations of intuitive and inquisitive interactions with the non-human world. These epistemes, or ways of interpreting reality, developed as the mythical Chinese dynasties arose from the mists of antiquity. By 6000 BCE, grasses were being domesticated and cultivated at Neolithic village sites along both the Yellow and Yangtze Rivers. Cliff carvings dating to 6,000 BCE found at the village site of Damaidi, in the Weining Mountains, portray herding of domesticated animals along with hunting and celestial imagery, trees, and mountains. Healing was necessarily both physical and energetic or spiritual, and as specialists developed, they consulted oracles written in the cracks of shells and bones. The origins of writing evolved along with the healing arts, birthing codification of systems of healing. As disease was thought to arise from causes such as upsetting the ancestors, disrupting natural balances, being cursed, the evil eye, demons, or having an entity enter the body, the remedy necessitated placating ancestors with suitable rituals or asking for their help in expelling demons.

The shaman became a mediator skilled at moving between worlds, communicating with the ancestors and

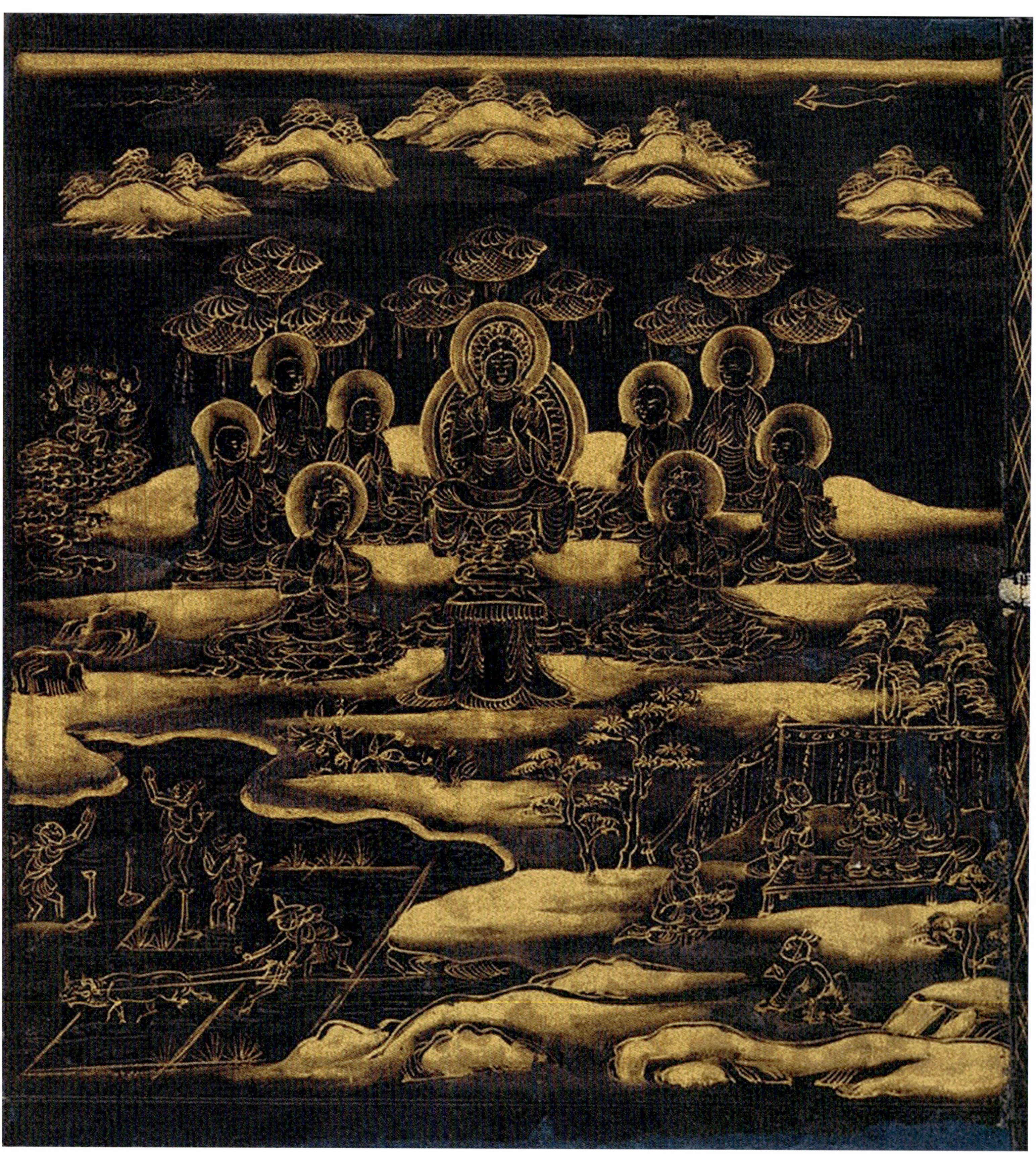

23 Parable of the Medicinal Herbs

Chapter 5 of the Lotus Sutra
Japan
Heian period, 1100 – 1200
Handscroll; gold and silver ink on indigo-dyed paper
10 1/16 in. × 34 ft. 8 3/4 in., 25.6 × 1058.6 cm
Metropolitan Museum of Art, New York
Seymour Fund, 1965

24 Detail of an Ancient Acupuncture Model

Emperor College, Santa Monica, California

deities and returning with remedies and advice. The demarcations gleaned from fire-cracked oracle bones and tortoise shells morphed into written language, allowing a flourishing of culture that included the distilling of generations of philosophical ideations and medicinal practices into texts such as the *Huangdi Neijing* (The Yellow Emperor's Classic of Internal Medicine) or the herbal classic *Shennong Bencaojing*. Then came later works, for example, the Lotus Sutra (**23**) and even models for teaching acupuncture (**24**).

As villages grew in size, cultures moved from consuming diets of foraged plants—fruits, nuts, seeds, greens, roots and tubers, mushrooms—to diets based primarily on cultivated grains and vegetables. Legend tells us that Shen Nung was boiling up some spring water under a tree when a few leaves blew by on the wind, a couple of which settled into the pot and created a delightful and healing beverage. Placing herbs in boiled water was a common practice and decoctions and teas soon became the primary form of herbal medicine regionally. Traditional knowledge of anatomical arrangements and functions, examination, diagnosis, and over a hundred treatments appeared in writing for apprentices and royal physicians to learn. The therapies described included acupuncture, massage, moxibustion, and therapeutic applications for dozens of medicinal herbs, minerals, and even certain animal parts.

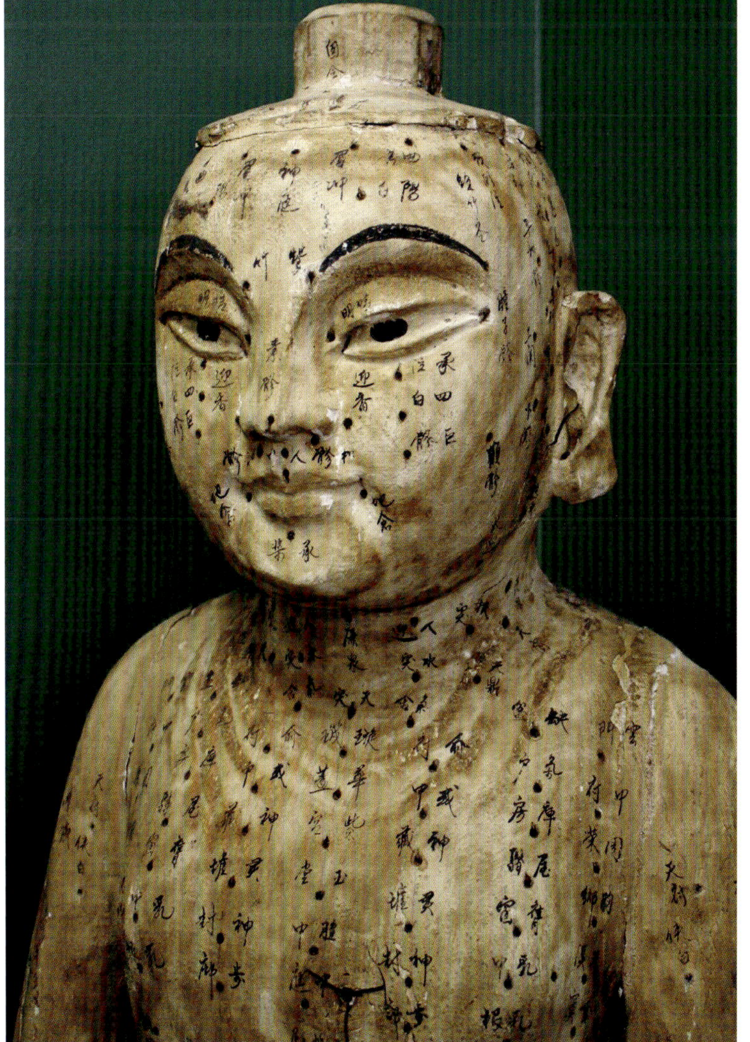

Thousands of years of experience and innumerable texts have contributed to the development of one of the oldest and most complex systems of traditional medicine. The Traditional Chinese Medicine corpus continues to be an invaluable source of healing herbals even in the development of blockbuster pharmaceuticals such as Viagra (inspired by vasodilation action by *Gingko biloba*) and the powerful antimalarial developed from *Artemisia annua*, or sweet wormwood. The title of Sun Simiao's seventh-century work, *Qianjin Yaofang*, says it well: Prescriptions Worth a Thousand Pieces of Gold.

Hippocrates and the Hippocratic Method

The burgeoning of modern Western medicine, which began with Hippocrates of Kos around 400 BCE (**25**), is distinguished by a more-or-less physical focus and essentially a rejection of the supernatural, energetic, or spiritual realms. Hippocrates is perhaps the best-known ancient physician in the modern-day West, where every physician must take the Hippocratic oath to "do no harm." This is, in part, why he is known there as the father of modern medicine. Another is that he wrote, or inspired, the Hippocratic Corpus (**26**), which gathered the main, extant medical texts of the day and compiled them into his theory of the four humors to explain the main causes of illness in people. This was his attempt at focusing on symptoms of illness and root causes as opposed to aspects he discounted as mere superstition, and it included clinical descriptions of fevers, phthisis,

puerperal convulsions, epilepsy, and other disorders. His theory proposed that the body consists of four humors (black bile, blood, phlegm, and yellow bile, each representing different aspects of human beings) and connected them to the four elements (earth, air, water, and fire) as well as the four seasons to describe sickness. For example, too much earth caused melancholy, while too much air made one sanguine, too much water made one phlegmatic, and too much fire made one choleric. Treatment attempted to balance the opposites.

Hippocrates and those he guided would first prescribe food as a remedy (one of his most touted quotes is "Let food be thy medicine and medicine be thy food") along with physical and mental activity, time in nature, and the application of heat and cold, as well as exercise in a regimen designed to bring balance to the imbalanced humor. In the case of a hot, dry sickness like fever, for example, it was believed that yellow bile was to blame. The physician would then work to increase the opposite, phlegm, through cold baths. If there was too much phlegm, such as with an upper respiratory sickness with phlegm production, the prescription would include heating the body up through hot baths, blankets, rest, and also wine. This system relied heavily on herbal medicine and other practices, such as inducing vomiting and diarrhea, and even bloodletting.

It is important to note that during Hippocrates' era, the conception of sickness and healing moved away from the supernatural and toward what is now understood as medicine, science, logic, and philosophy. Rather than viewing the prevailing deities of the time as responsible

25 **Portrait of Hippocrates**

Flanders
1574
Etching, with engraving, on cream laid paper
7 ¹³⁄₁₆ × 7 ⅞ in., 19.8 × 20 cm
Art Institute of Chicago
Gift of Mrs, Robert Sonnenschein

26 **Hippocratic Corpus**

Translated from Greek into Latin by
Marcus Fabius Calvus (1440 – 1527)
Rome
1525
Photo courtesy of Christie's

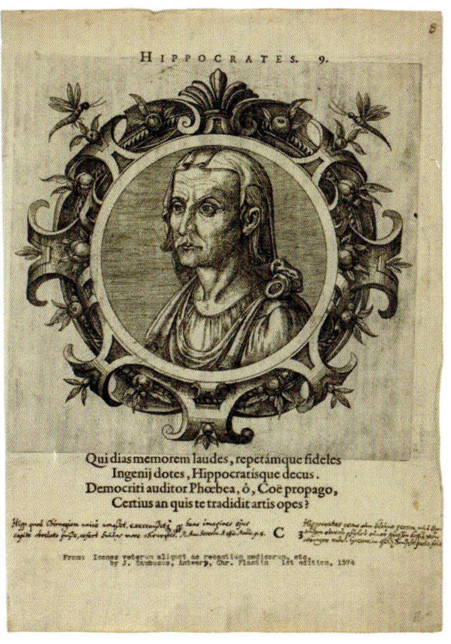

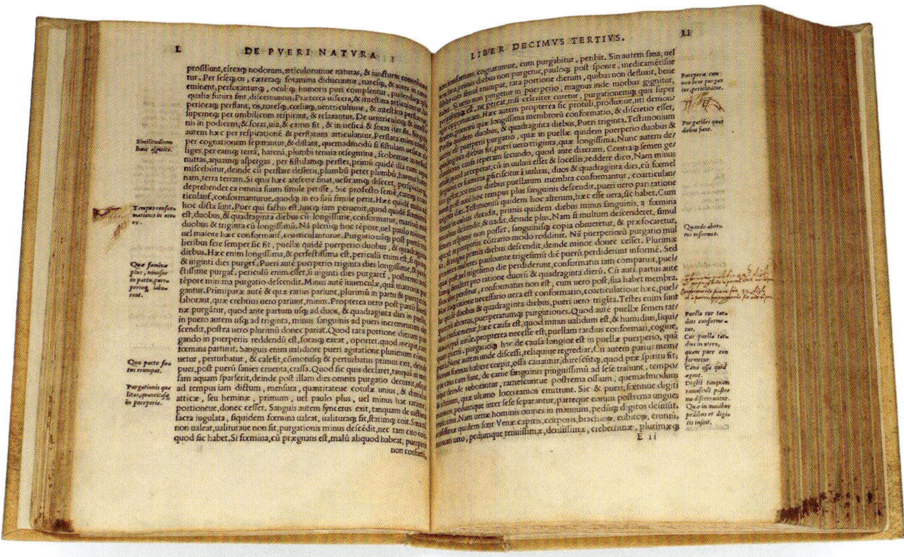

for sickness and seeking their assistance in healing through ritual, offerings, and prayer, sickness became viewed less as a transgression and more as an imbalance in the body caused by a variety of factors. For perhaps the first time in history, sickness and healing were regarded from a perspective of philosophy about the human body and its inextricable links to the natural world and cosmos, with Hippocrates driving much of this shift. The belief in immortals, gods, goddesses, and other deities as the causative agents in sickness and the instruments by which healing occurred segued to more of a scientific and medical paradigm. The humors became the dominant practice regionally for some 2500 years thereafter, as they were widely disseminated by the Greek physician and surgeon Galen, who practiced in the Roman Empire around 200 BCE, and whose efforts established the paradigm of the humors in the Middle Ages.

Perso-Arabic Unani in the Middle East was also shaped by way of Hippocrates. An influential medical treatise handed down to Unani was *De Materia Medica* (**27**), written by Greek physician Dioscorides around 100 BCE. Unani is healing based on the principles of nature.

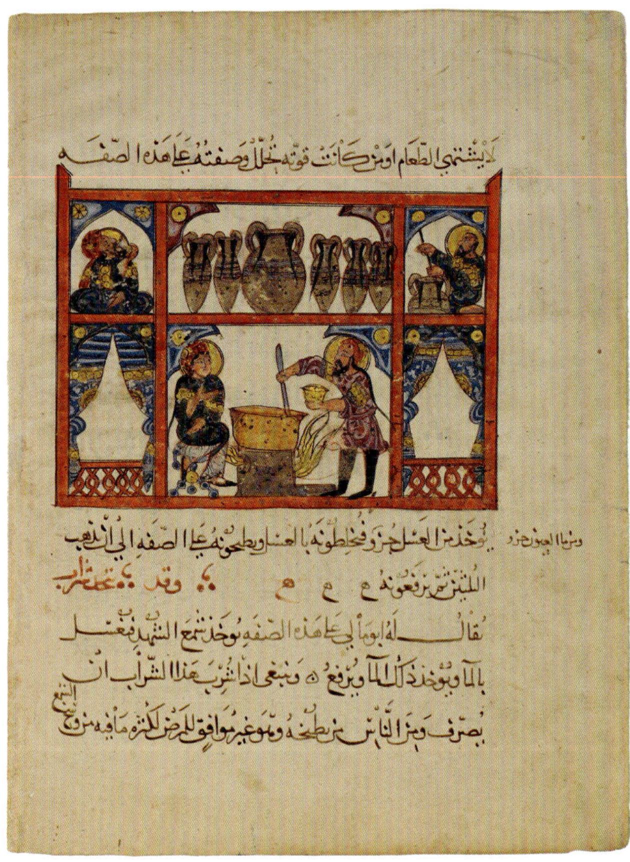

27 **Preparing Medicine from Honey**

From a dispersed manuscript of an
Arabic translation of *De Materia of Dioscorides*
Baghdad, Iraq
1224
Ink, opaque watercolor, and gold on paper
12 ⅜ × 9 in., 31.4 × 22.9 cm
Metropolitan Museum of Art, New York
Bequest of Cora Timken Burnett, 1956

The Americas: Herbalism and Shamanism

As ancient Greece and Rome became the epicenter for a movement toward medicine, natural sciences, logic, and philosophy as opposed to the supernatural, herbalism and shamanism were still widely practiced throughout the Americas by bands and tribal communities too numerous to mention, all the way up to chiefdoms and states like the Iroquois Confederacy of North America, the proto-Aztec, Olmec, Aztec, Maya of Central America, and the Moche, Nazca, Chavin, and Inca Empires of South America. The intricate systems of healing that developed in the Americas over millennia reflect commonalties rooted in the cultural and ecological nuances of the landscape and ecosystems. Many of its impressive civilizations had risen and fallen long before Europeans ever colonized the land and documented their invasion. The great city centers and princely palaces offered high levels of medical training and apprenticeships, extensive materia medicas, and well stocked medicinal plant gardens driven my millennia-old apothecaries and pharmacopoeias.

Mesoamerica

Many sources testify to the wealth of ethnopharmacological knowledge held by indigenous practitioners of the healing arts. The first book of medicinal plants actually written on the American Continent was the *Libellus Medicinalibus Indorum Herbis*, translated into Latin by Juan Badiano from the Nahuatl original written in 1552 by Indigenous physician

Its practitioners, or *hakims*, relied on natural healing based on principles of harmony and balance. Their goal was to bring balance to imbalance through the unification of physical, mental, and spiritual realms. While its main doctrine can be traced back to Hippocrates, it was later refined and developed by the Arabs and in particular by the Muslim physician and scholar Avicenna around 600. Like prior systems, there was a presence of the four elements—earth, water, fire and air—but also a more sophisticated consideration of balance among hot, cold, moist, and dry. There was even a compounded aspect to that; hot and dry, hot and moist, cold and dry, and cold and moist. Mesopotamian, Persian, and Egyptian systems of healing intersected with and informed Unani as well as other prevailing systems regionally.

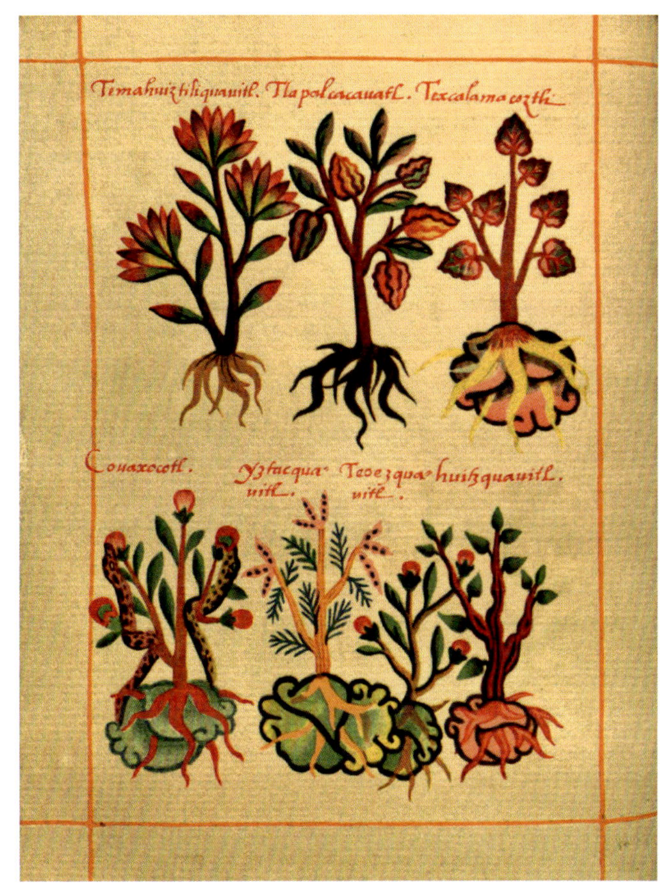

Martin de la Cruz of the Colegio de Indios de la Santa Cruz de Tlatelolco. It is the only surviving account of the detailed ethnobotany of the Aztecs written by Aztecs. The herbal covers regions of the body in thirteen chapters, as well as offering more general remedies and formulas, and includes colorful depictions in native pigments and detailed information on over 180 different medicinal herbs (**28**). It mentions the Nahuatl names of some forty additional herbs and includes both unfamiliar species such as the cardiotonic Mexican magnolia, or *Magnolia mexicana*, who's heart shaped flower is called *Yolloxochitl*, as well as more familiar plants such as cacao or *Theobroma cacao*, which is chocolate and referred to as *Tlapalcacauatl*. Similarly, the vanilla orchid, *Vanilla planifolia*, is referred to as *Tlilxochitl*, and yarrow, *Achillea millefolium,* referred to as *Tlalquequetzal*—this is the very same plant found in the Neanderthal Flower Burial in Shanidar Cave half a world away and some 65,000 years prior.

The most comprehensive work we have on Aztec lifeways and views on field and forest is a series of twelve books called the Florentine Codex, written by the Franciscan Friar Bernardino de Sahagún in the sixteenth century, which includes over 2,000 illustrations by Nahua peoples. Book eleven, dubbed "Earthly Things," is an eloquent documentation of the natural world as viewed by sixteenth-century Aztecs. Both the Florentine Codex and the *Historia de las Plantas de la Nueva España* by Spanish Physician Francisco Hernández document the wide use of medicinal plants in Mesoamerica at the time of conquest. Written accounts from the contact era describe Tenochtitlan, the great Aztec capital, as a city of gardens. The Nahuatl word *xóchitl* or "flower" and thus *xochitla*, meaning "flower place," the pleasure gardens of royal palaces were denoted as *xochitecpancalli*. In his well-studied memoirs from the late sixteenth century, the Spanish conquistador Bernal Díaz del Castillo, who participated in the Spanish conquest of the Aztec Empire, remarks that Moctezuma's Huaxtepec gardens were "the best that I have ever seen in all my life." The extensive hillside gardens at Netzahualcóyotl's palace in Texcoco included canals bringing in fresh spring water to reservoirs, bathing areas, and fountains spilling past orchards, and by sumptuously scented, ornamental flowers of entheogens grown only by the elites. These were often depicted in art via anthropomorphic or even phytomorphic means (**29**).

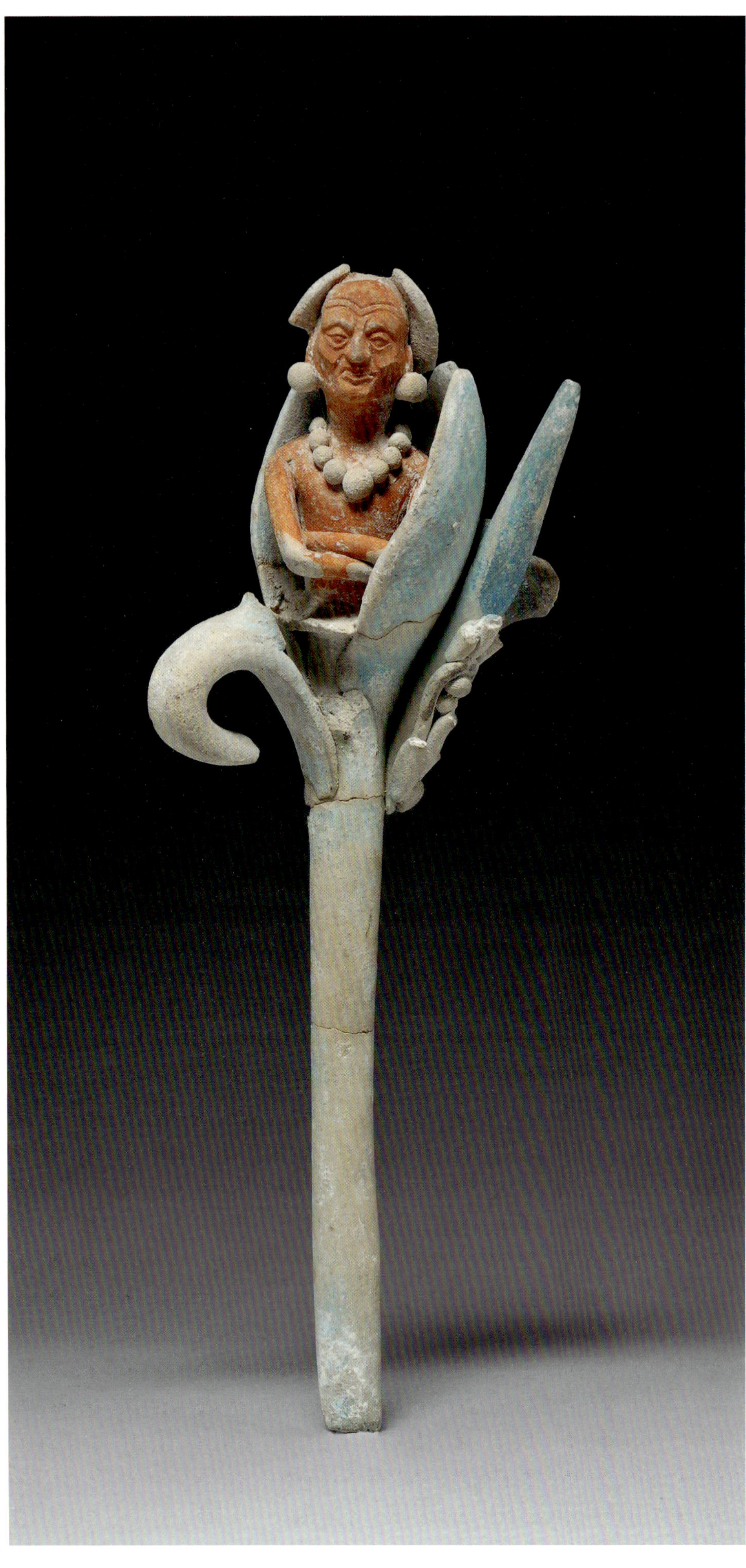

29 Anthropomorphic and Phytomorphic Whistle

Maya culture, Mexico
650 – 800 CE
Ceramic
6 ¾ × 2 ⅜ × 1 ¼ in., 17.15 × 6.03 × 3.18 cm
Dumbarton Oaks Museum,
Washington, DC
Photo by Joseph Mills

30 Man Holding Heart

Olmec culture, Las Bocas, Puebla, Mexico
1600 – 350 BCE
Terracotta
4.49 in., 11.4 cm
Private Collection

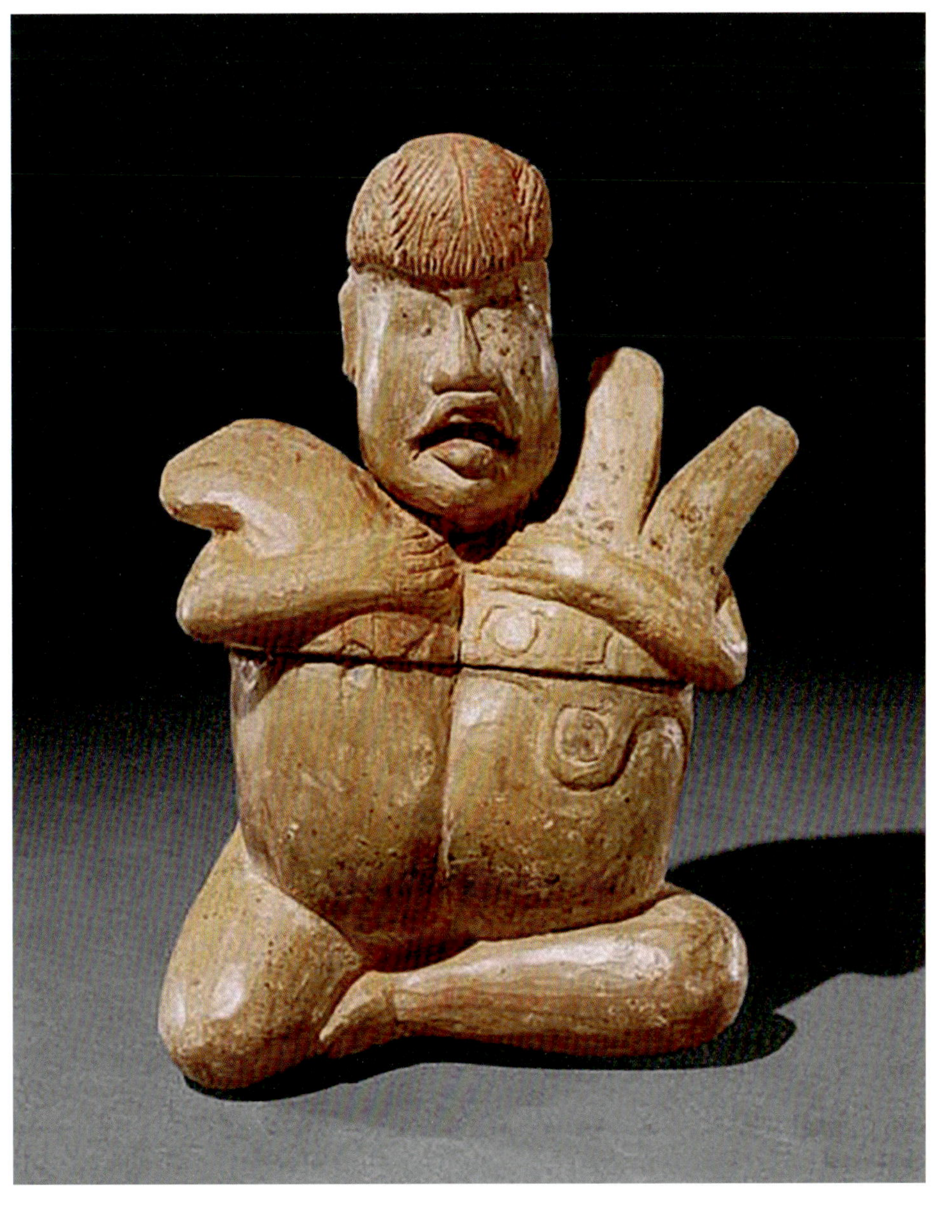

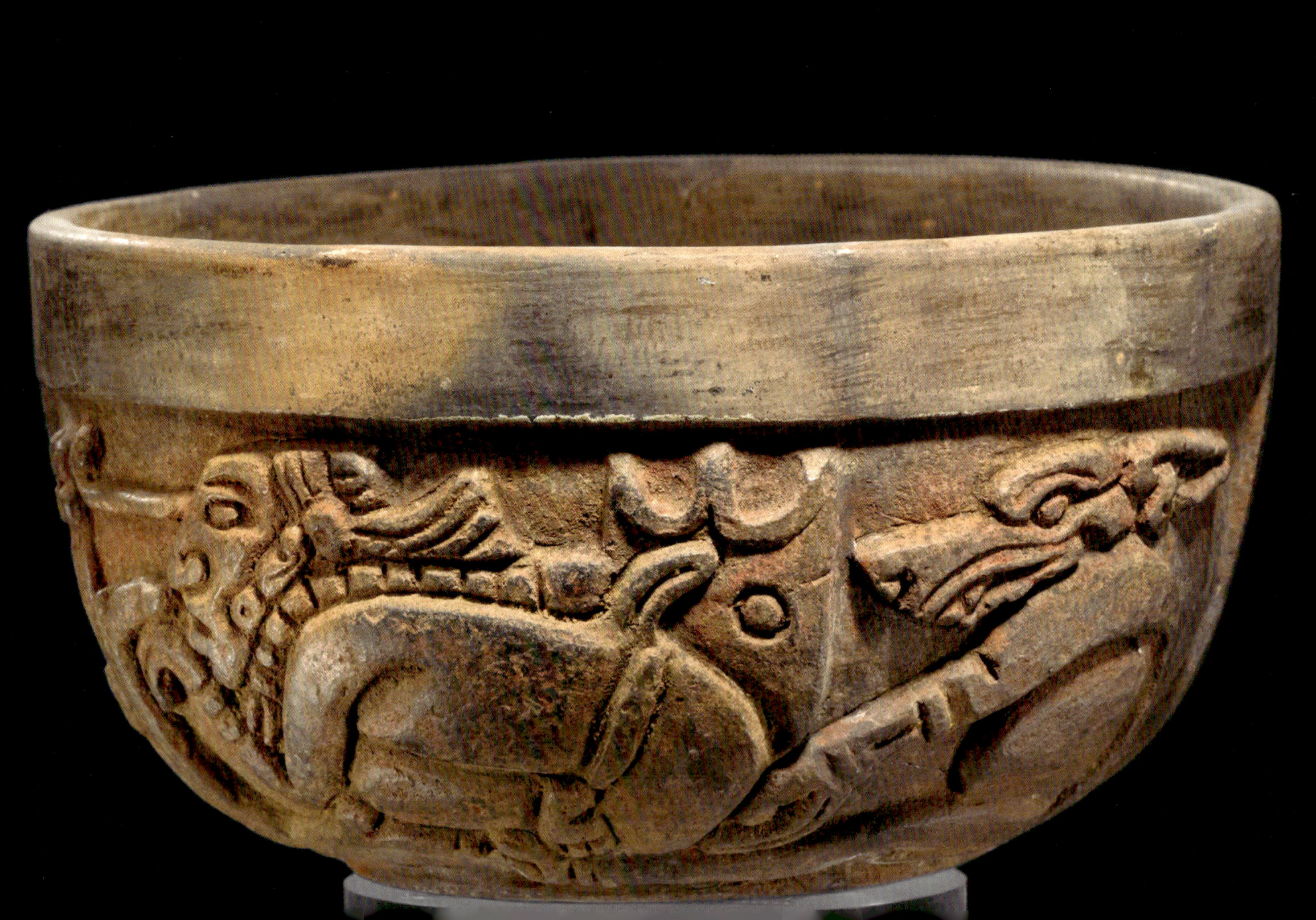

31 Carved Bowl

Maya culture, Mexico
600 – 800 CE
Terracotta
3 ½ in., 8.89 cm
Private Collection

32 Rollout photograph of Enema Beaker

Maya culture, Mexico
600 – 900 CE
Blackware ceramic
6.85 in. high, 17.4 cm
Princeton University Art Museum, New Jersey
Bequest of John B. Elliott, Class of 1951
Photo by Justin Kerr

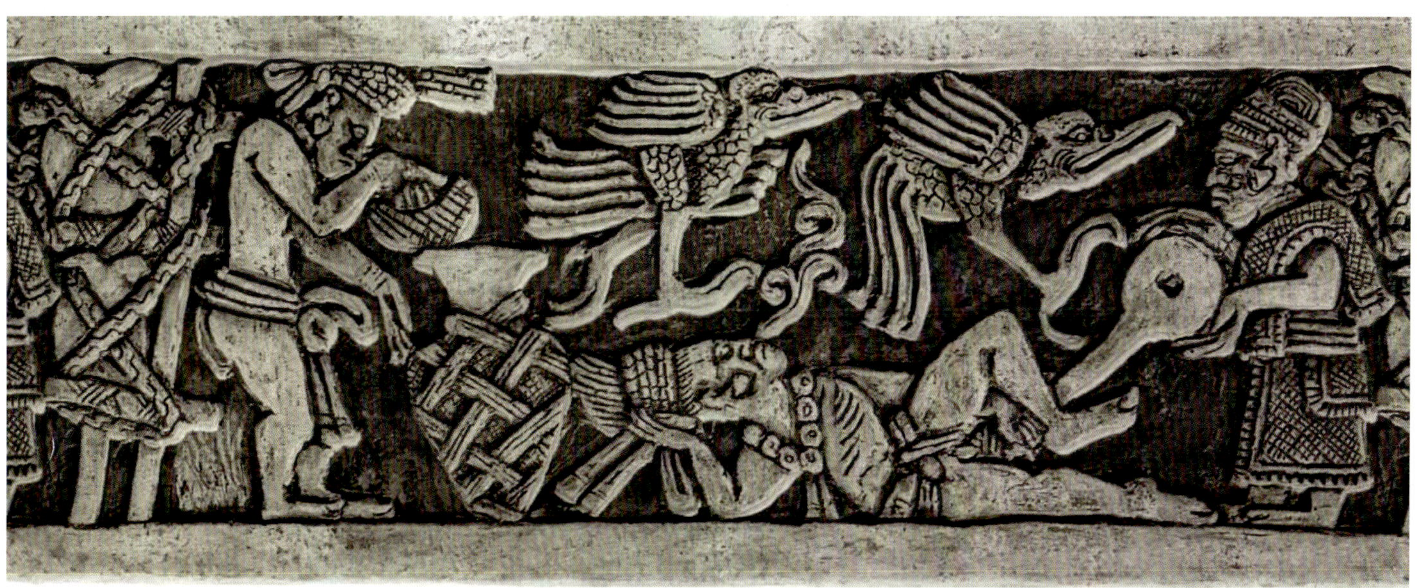

Many of the cultural attributes, motifs, signets of office, and conventions in language, mathematics, and calendrics that are seen in Classic Maya or contact era Aztec culture took form among the ancient cities of the Olmec people. The heart was perhaps the most sacred organ in Mesoamerican traditions—as it was in ancient Egyptian and many other cultures. By Olmec times we have a sculptural portrayal of an anatomical heart (30). The legendary dedication of the Templo Mayor in 1487 was consecrated by the sacrifice of thousands of human hearts still beating as they were extracted from the chest cavities of the sacrificial offerings—a practice not uncommon in ancient Mesoamerica.

One of the best-known motifs in Olmec art is the man-jaguar transforming between realms. This "were-jaguar" figure appears widely in the archaeological record in forms ranging from small greenstone figurines to larger carved basalt monuments. This anthropomorphic deity once again reflects the human propensity for therianthropy. This motif is carried into Maya and Aztec artworks and story by the notion of *nagual*—that is the belief in the ability to transform into one's animal spirit or shapeshift, which allows part of the consciousness to run wild through field, forest, and jungles, scaling high peaks and soaring through the clouds into the infinite blue; this represents the ascension through the three levels of the shamanic realms.

In Mesoamerican cultures, enemas were incorporated in ritual purifications that also included fasting, cleansing, sweat lodges or *temazcals*, and even, on occasion,

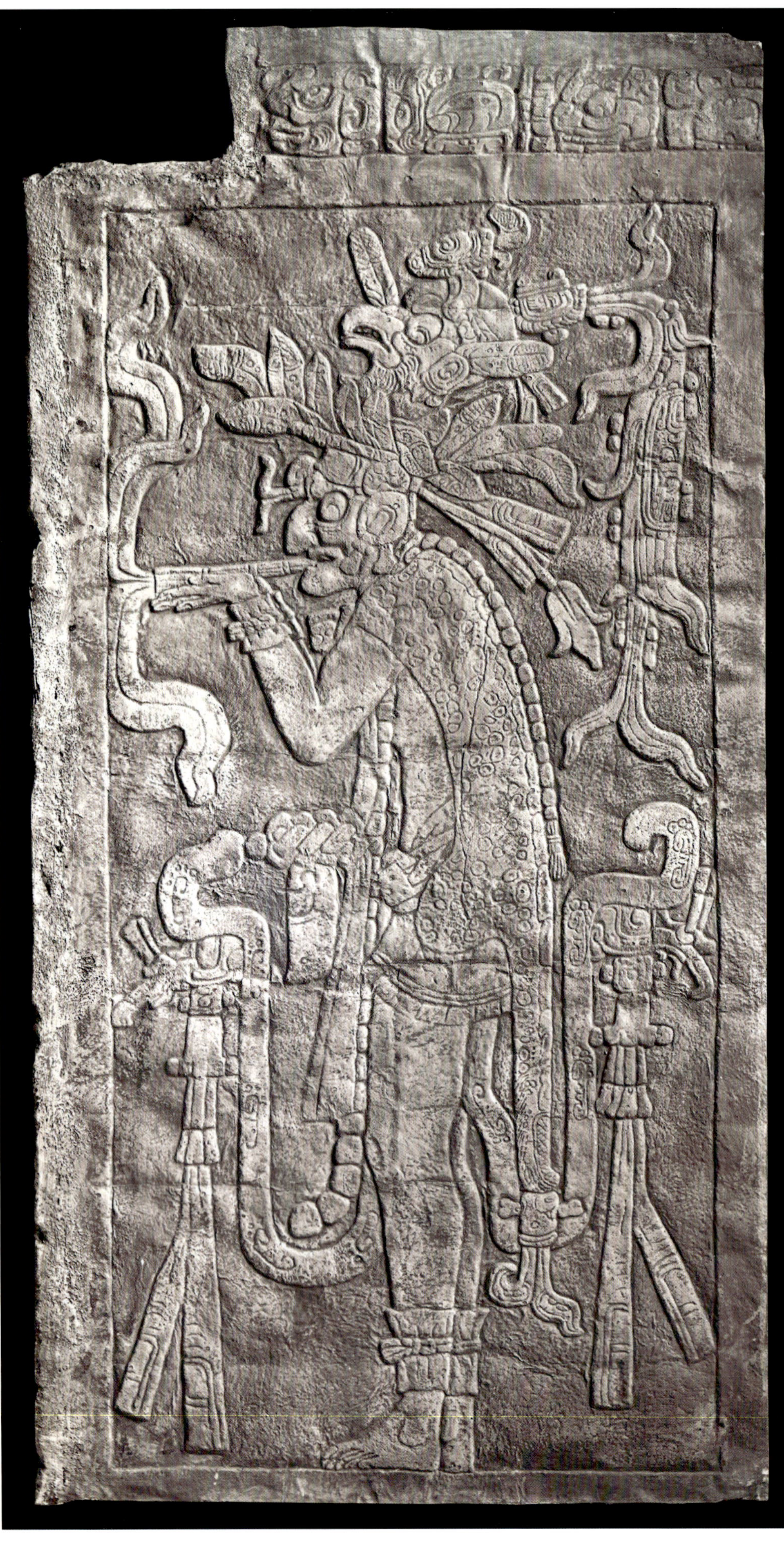

33 God L' or the Smoking God

Maya culture, Temple of the Cross,
Palenque, Chiapas, Mexico
600 – 700 CE
Bas-relief

Maya culture, Mexico
600 – 800 CE
Terracotta
8 ⁷⁄₁₆ × 7 ¹⁵⁄₁₆ × 1 ¹⁵⁄₁₆ in., 21.5 × 20.2 × 4.9 cm
Princeton University Art Museum, New Jersey
Gift of Shelby White in honor of Gillett G. Griffin

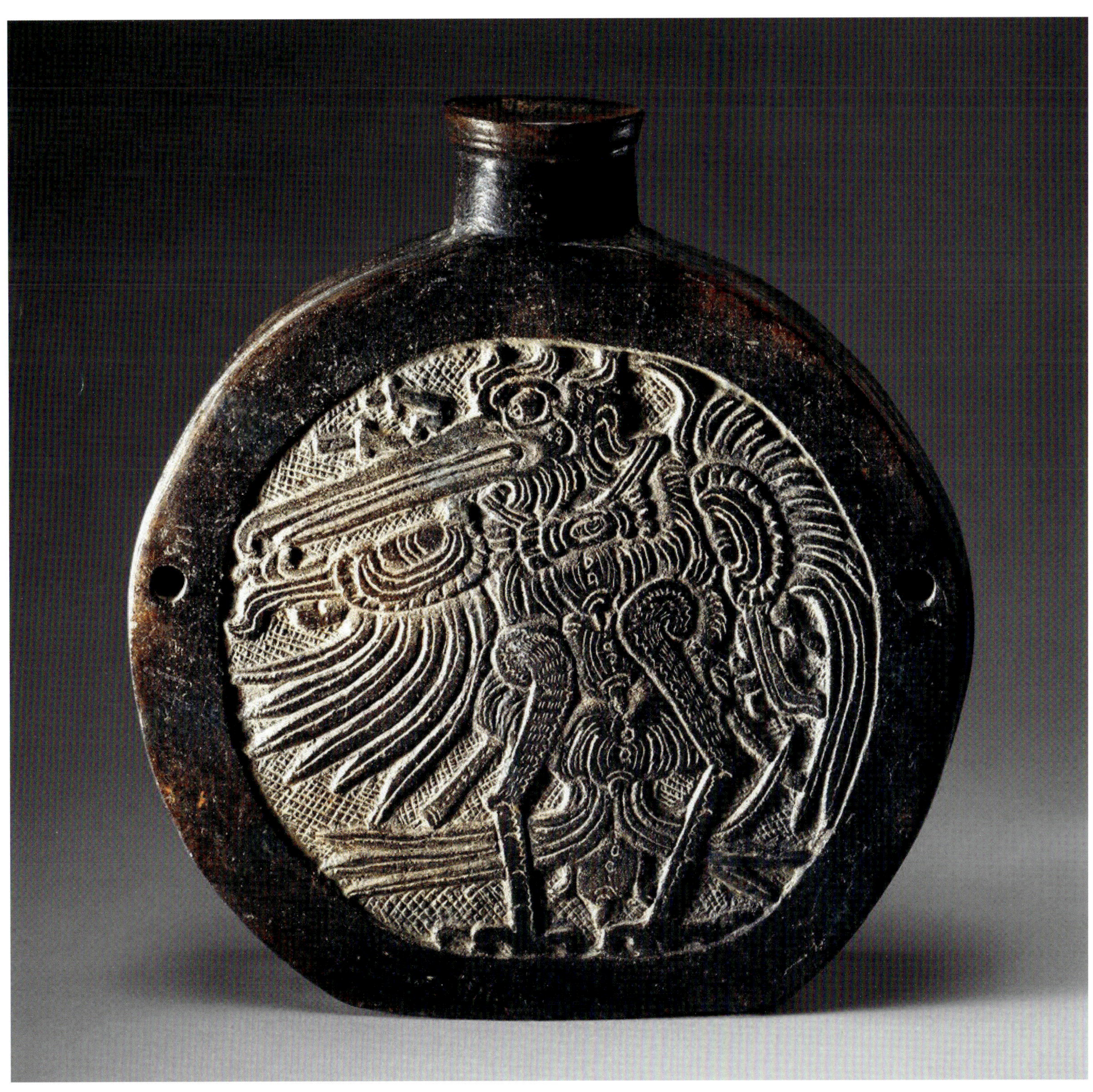

bloodletting. Rituals like these were undertaken to fortify the individual physically, emotionally, and mentally, and to induce visions and connect with ancestors. In Yucatec Maya, the word for enema is *halab*, and other regional dictionaries similarly denote *hal-ab* or *halab tz'ak* as "a medicinal purge or enema." Maya ceramic vessels vividly depict this ritual act. While the Maya were not shy about their medicinal enemas, scholars are surprisingly quiet around the matter. A Maya bowl from the lowlands region made around 600–800 depicts a ceremonial shamanic journeying enema being administered by an anthropomorphic wolf-man (**31**). Another Maya vessel depicts enemas being administered ritually (**32**). Images portraying the administration of medicinal or ritual enemas appear in carved stone, on polychrome vessels, and painted into codices. The brews included such intoxicants as cacao; tobacco; fermented brews of honey, pineapple and agave; various infusions of medicinal plants and trees; and entheogens like morning glory, water lily, Datura, Amanita, Psilocybe, and other mushrooms, as well as other things. The administration of these brews via enema enhances their effects and bypasses unpleasant side effects of oral administration, like vomiting. Enemas are still used for cleanses and to treat dysentery and constipation in highland Maya (and lowland Amazonian) healing systems today. Cultural depictions of these activities are accompanied by flowering plants suggesting tobacco, water lily, or a similar flowering species that may have been administered via the enema.

Tobacco was and remains an important shamanic entheogen through the ages, cross culturally and globally (**33** and **34**). Mexican buckeye, *Ungnadia speciosa*, and mescal bean, *Sophora secundiflora*, are found in archaeological sites dating back to the Paleolithic at Bonfire Shelter and several other rock shelter sites in what is now Texas and Northern Mexico. The Bonfire site yielded *Sophora* seeds from its lowest occupational stratum, known as Bone Bed II, dated to over 8000 BCE. At Cueva Candelaria near the borderlands, necklaces made of bone and what appear to be mescal bean seeds were found and at Murrah Cave in Texas, buckskin loincloth decorated with mescal beans was documented. The first European mention of *Sophora secundiflora* occurs about 1539, when Cabeza de Vaca's party reported seeing the red seeds. The seeds known as *ololiuhqui* utilized by the Aztec were likely *Ipomoea corymbosa*.

South America

South America similarly had a richness of ancient civilizations with healing traditions. The concentration of rich shamanic traditions in Peru dates back to at least the time of the Moche peoples from 100–800, but more likely to ancient Caracol and beyond. The use of coca has been demonstrated thousands of years back among highland Andean cultures; it is chewed ceremoniously, as shown in this Narino figure, for its stimulating effects at social gatherings, in rituals to commune with one's ancestors, and also medicinally to treat *soroche* (mountain or altitude sickness) (**35**). The utilization of *Huachuma* or San Pedro cactus, *Echinopsis pachanoi*, which figures prominently

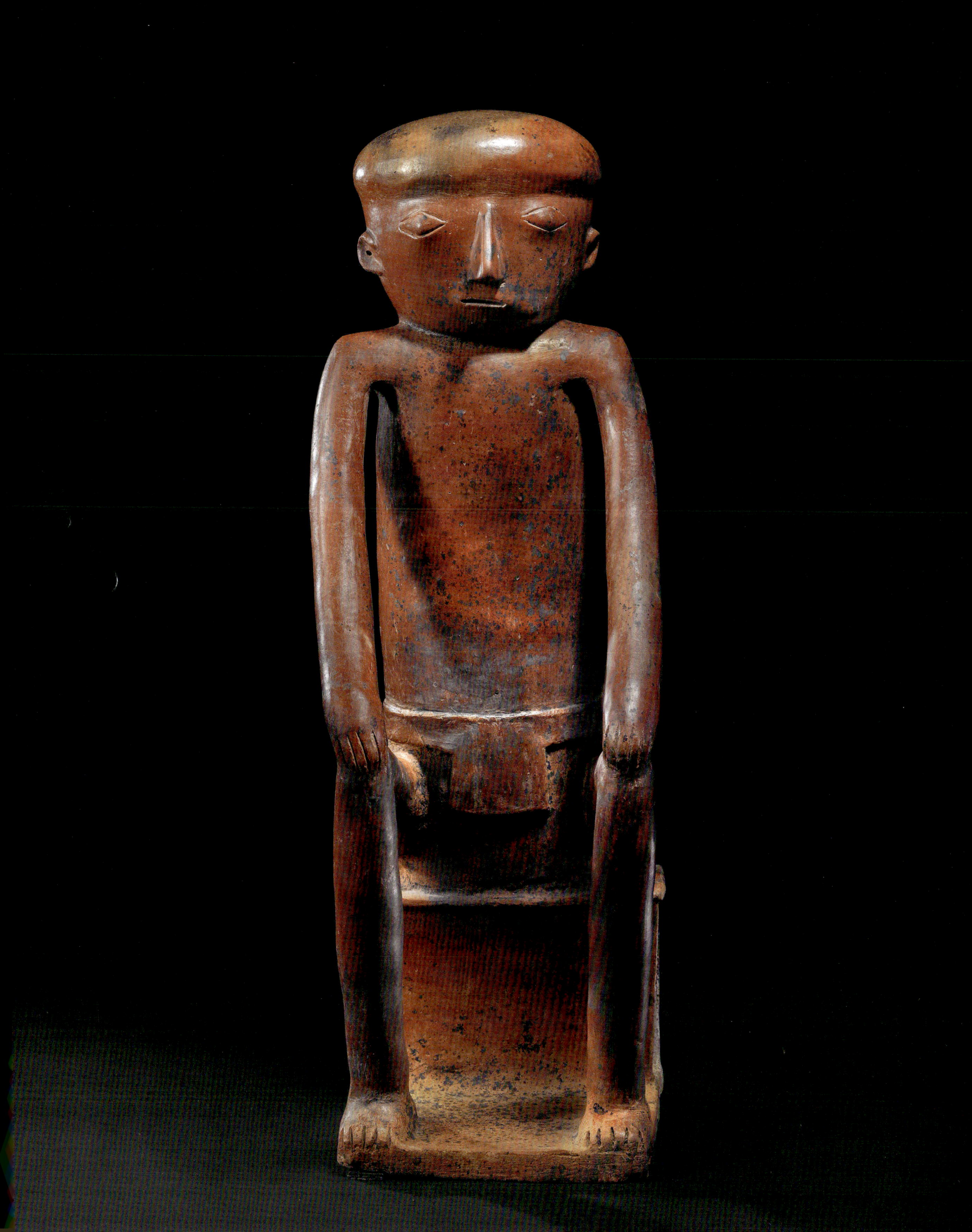

Shipibo culture,
San Francisco de Yarinacocha, Peru
1965
Terracotta
9.01 × 11.02 in., 23 × 28 cm
National Museum of the American Indian,
Washington, DC

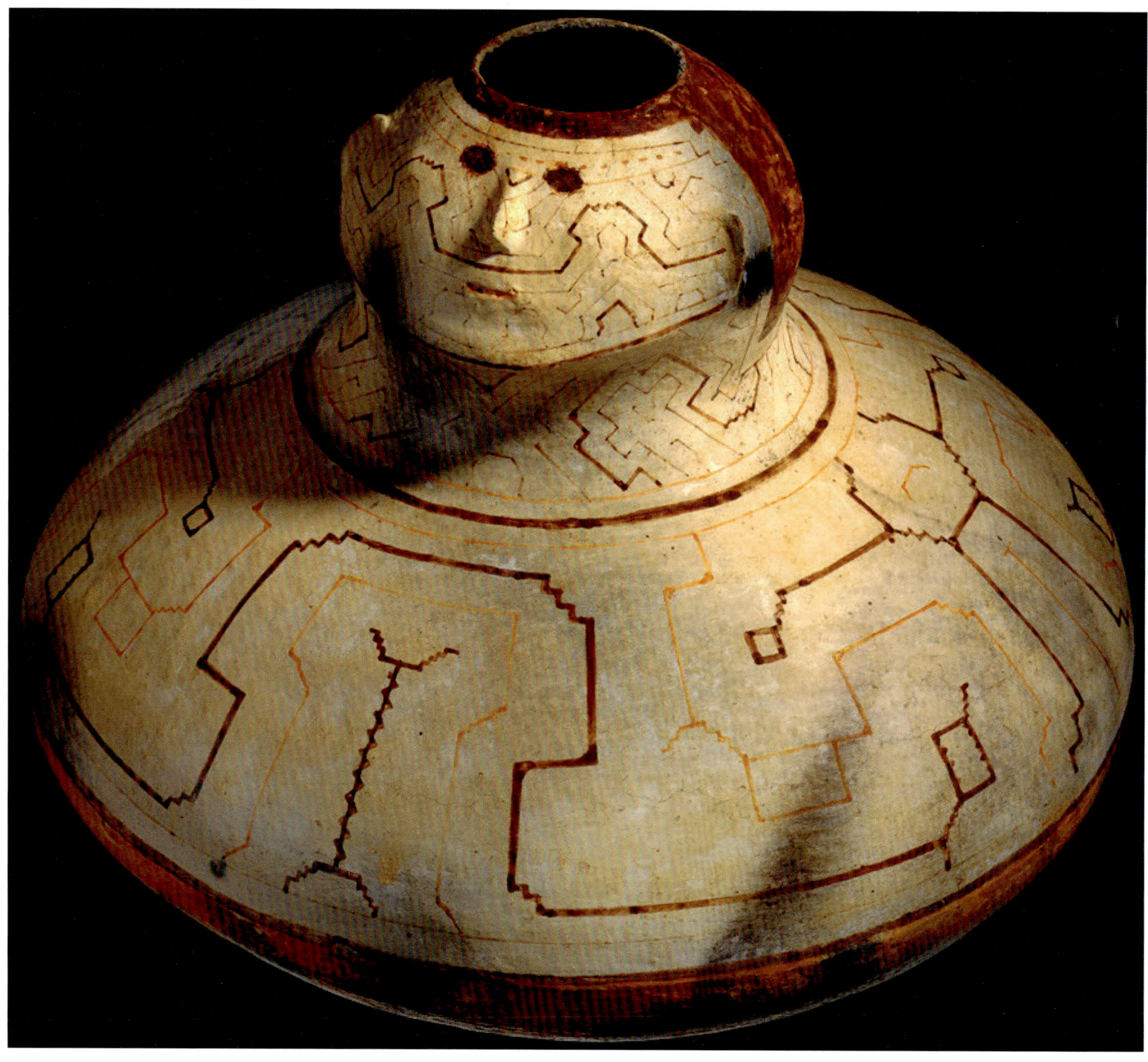

today in Andean healing practices, was well depicted in Moche art and that of the earlier Chavin or Cupisnique (1200–200 BCE) cultures. In the Andes, healings often took place at a *mesa* (ceremonial alter) on *huacas* (sacred sites) where shrines or other monuments were erected. These *huacas* were connected by "ceremonial energetic lines" aligned astronomically and called *ceque* in Quechua, an Andean dialect. Other cultures had their own versions of *huaca* and *ceque*. The Maya, for example, called them *sacbe* or "white road," paved white limestone roads connecting temples as sacred sites and modeled after *ochbe* (meaning "great white road" or the Milky Way)—viewed as the spirit realm or cosmic womb by many ancient peoples.

Our human ancestors all migrated out of Africa around 100,000 BCE. Throughout the millennia, we relied on celestial bodies and in particular Pole Stars in navigation—sometimes a single star, sometimes a star cluster, and sometimes no star. These stars are the ones most closely aligned with our northern and southern poles. They were relied on so heavily because they appear at the center of the night sky, where the rest of the stars rotate around them in an annual dance as earth spins. There is also a slight wobble of earth's axis, which is why the Pole Stars change throughout the ages. For example, Polaris is our northern pole star now, whereas in 5000 BCE our ancestors relied on Thuban for navigation. One can envisage them navigating out of Africa northward across Beringia and then throughout the Americas southward. In doing so, the night sky would shift in a multitude of ways, not the least because the farther one is from the equator, the

less prominent is the Milky Way. The entire Milky Way is visible (if one watches the whole year) at the equator. This is important in terms of cosmic connections, entheogens, and shamanic journeying. Farther north there is a reliance on "points" of light or caps of mushrooms, cacti, and seeds, whereas at the equator there is a reliance on more elongated entheogens like tall cacti and, importantly, the umbilicus to our cosmic womb. This cosmic umbilicus is none other than *Banisteriopsis caapi* or "vine of the soul"— one of two principal ingredients in the powerful shamanic brew Ayahuasca, the other being *Psychotria viridis*. The vine of the soul spirals up the canopy in the rainforest into the great white road or Milky Way. These aspects are prominently reflected in shamanic journeying regionally in practice and art.

The word *icaro* stems from the Andean Quechua word *icarai*, meaning "to blow." *Icaro* are magical chants that are sung or whistled by shamans during Ayahuasca ceremonies. They are said to come directly from the plants through shamanic journeying. Their purpose is to bring on "knowing" through the visionary trance state in which it is possible to reach greater understanding and hear and even see the sounds of the universe. *Icaro* also denotes the traditional artisanal, oscillatory pattern of the Shipibo people in the present day. They visually depict the rhythmic oscillations of sound, light, and the energy of the universe (**36**). Meanwhile five thousand years ago and half a world away in predynastic Egypt, we find similar depictions of rhythmic oscillations of sound, light and the energy of the universe (**37**).

Egypt
Predynastic, Naqada II period,
3400 – 3300 BCE
Terracotta
8 in., 23 cm
Private Collection
Photo courtesy of Christie's

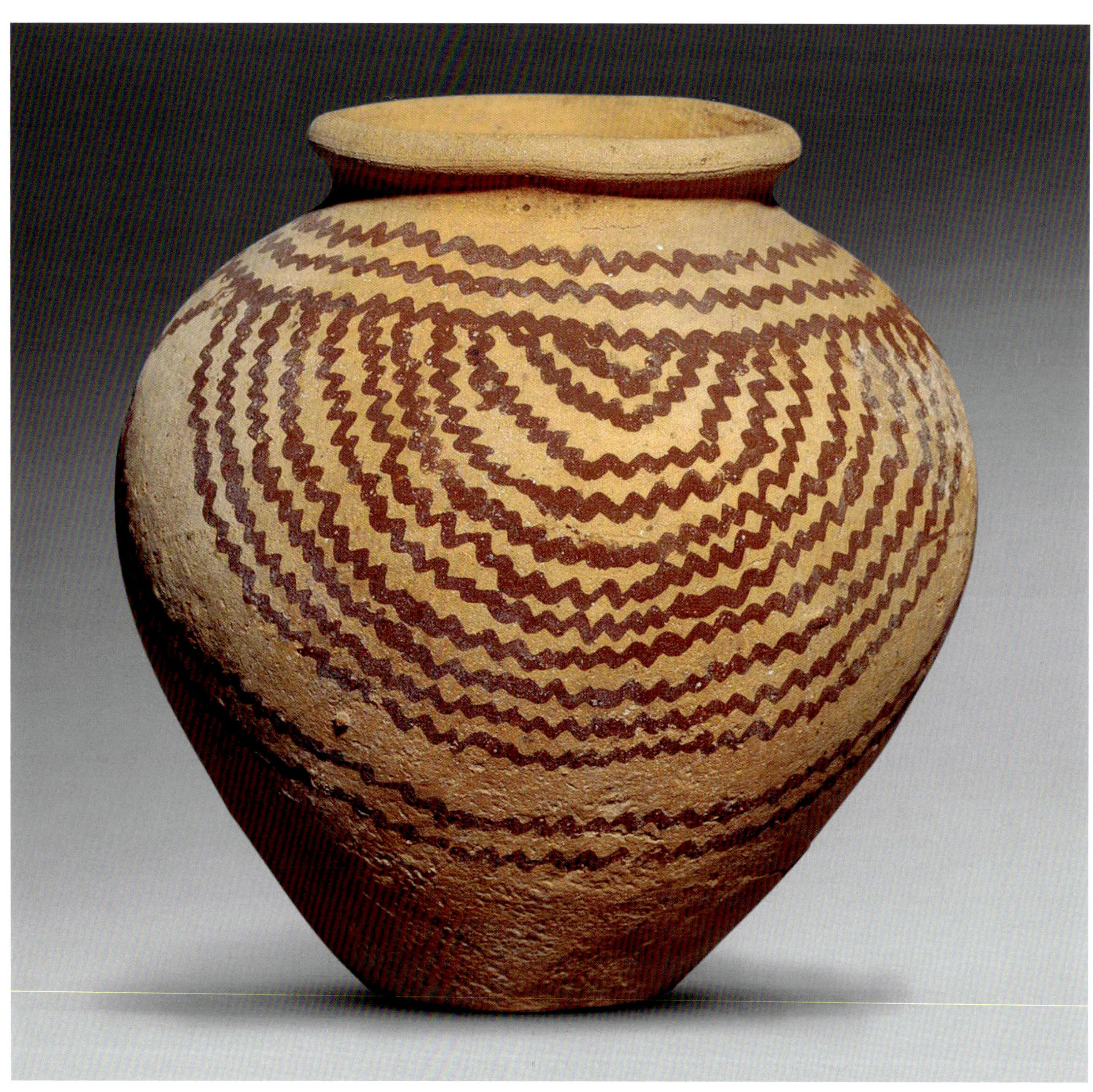

Conclusion

Throughout humanity, navigating and treating sickness and facilitating healing has largely remained a complex interplay among what we view as physical aspects of the body, inextricably intertwined with energetic or spiritual realms. In fact, though we have enriched our understanding of sickness and healing through the practice of the art and science of medicine and the scientific method and all that it brings, the fundamental nature of sickness and healing continues to remain in this complex interplay, where much discovery awaits.

Whereas more modern practices in Western medical traditions focus mostly on the physical aspect of sickness, a practice that began in ancient Greece, this is in stark contrast to our ancestral practices and the vast majority of traditional practices the world over since time immemorial. Our collective record in art displays these common threads in humanity visually for all to see. Our global healing practices, fueled by our ancestral roots, survive today in full force. In fact, according to the World Health Organization's Traditional Medicine Strategy, eighty percent of our planetary population relies on traditional healers for primary healthcare.[3]

The vast majority of our ancestors believed themselves to be caretaker inhabitants of the land and inextricably intertwined with all that is around, above, and below us. Accordingly, methods of treating sickness and promoting healing and health maintenance include elements of the mind-body, spirit, and environment—both social and natural worlds.[4] We ought not forget this. Indeed, we can leverage our ancestral wisdom and knowledge in sustaining health and healing into our future.

The bountiful visual record, which includes art that depicts various aspects of sickness and healing through the ages, illustrates this fact. We would do well to learn from our ancestors and our elders who survive them. Traditions and our longest-lived elders the world over continue to demonstrate simple strategies for navigating sickness and healing and facilitating health, wellness, and longevity through a simple set of practices observed since time immemorial that include traditional philosophy and outlook, lifestyle, and diet and nutritional practices.[5]

Our elders and traditions demonstrate that through a relatively comprehensive but simple set of practices we can enhance our vitality and promote longevity in a sustainable fashion—just as we have always done, using sustainable traditional healing systems that effectively prevent, mitigate, and treat sickness, facilitate healing, heighten consciousness, and contribute to healthy, happy, vibrant communities, thus ensuring the survival of our species and our traditions—for people and planet.

1   T. Pesek, L. Helton, and M. Nair, "Healing Across Cultures: Learning from Traditions," *EcoHealth* 3, no. 2 (2006): 114–18.

2   J. Ferrier, T. Pesek, F. Caal, V. Cal, M. Balick, J. Arnason, "A Classic Maya Mystery of a Medicinal Plant and Maya Hieroglyphs," *Heritage* 3, no. 16 (2020): 275–82.

3   World Health Organization, Programme on Traditional Medicine, *WHO Traditional Medicine Strategy 2002–2005* (Geneva: World Health Organization, 2002) and *WHO Traditional Medicine Strategy 2014–2023* (Geneva: World Health Organization, 2013).

4   Pesek, Helton, and Nair, "Healing Across Cultures."

5   T. Pesek, R. Reminick, and M. Nair, "Secrets of Long Life: Cross-Cultural Explorations in Sustainably Enhancing Vitality and Promoting Longevity via Elders' Practice Wisdom," *Explore: The Journal of Science and Healing* 6, no. 6 (2010): 352–58.

IX

RELIGION AND RITUALS

ALEX W. BARKER

Strong son of God, immortal love,
Whom we, that have not seen thy face,
By faith, and faith alone, embrace,
Believing where we cannot prove;

Thine are these orbs of light and shade;
Thou madest life in man and brute;
Thou madest death; and lo, thy foot
Is on the skull which thou hast made . . .

Alfred Lord Tennyson,
"In Memoriam,"
1850

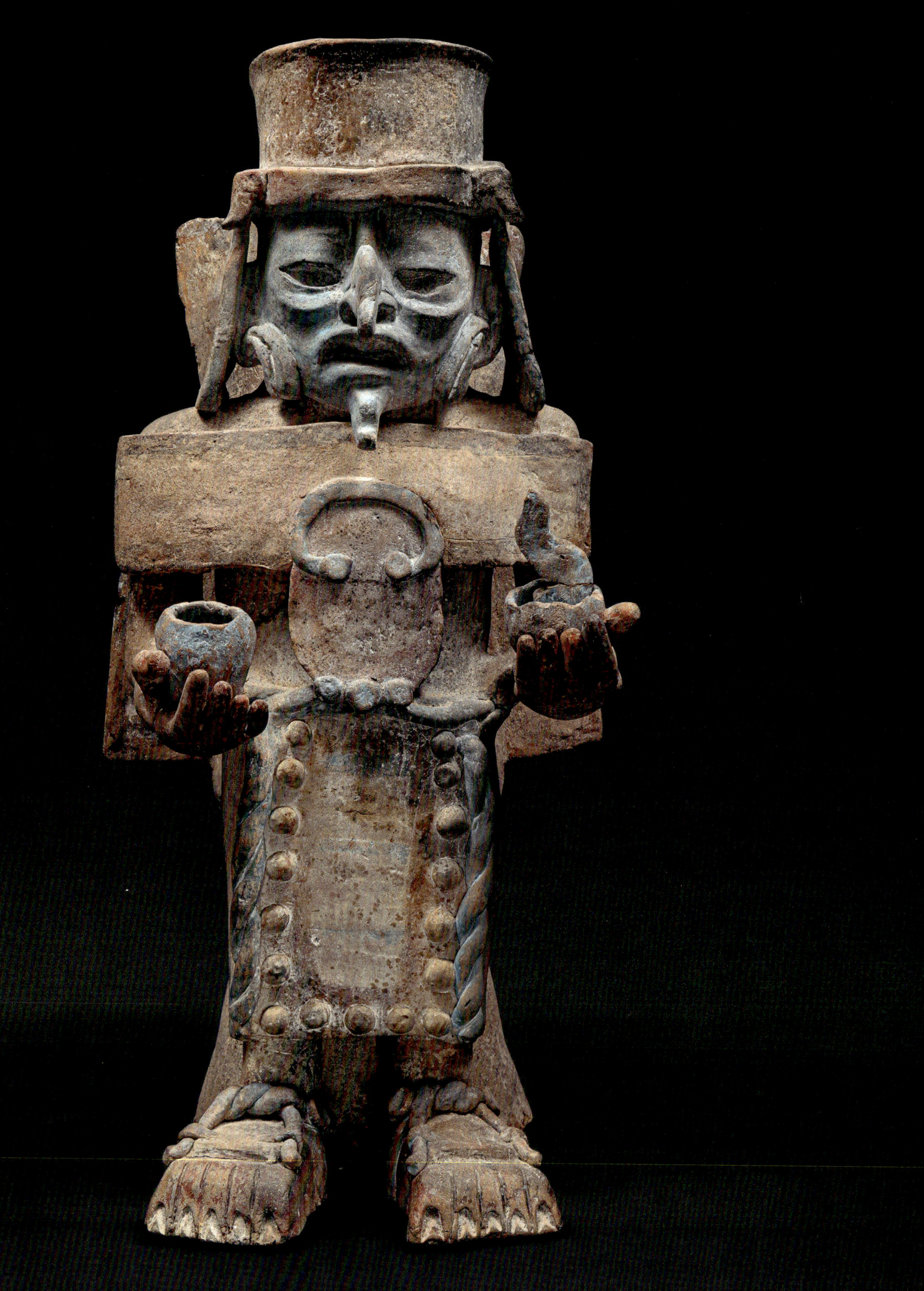

Mayapan Figural Censer

Maya culture, Yucatan, Mexico
1200 – 1450
Terracotta
26 × 12 × 16 in., 66.04 × 30.48 × 40.64 cm
Private Collection

The natural world is a dangerous and unpredictable place—fire and flood, dearth and death constantly loom around the next corner or the turn of the next season. Taken at face value, the notion that life is without purpose and subject entirely to chance is daunting at best and could easily lead to despair, or to social dissolution and lives that are, in the words of philosopher Thomas Hobbes in *Leviathan* (1651), "nasty, brutish, and short." Indeed, in a cross-cultural study, anthropologist Elizabeth Colson found that societies undergoing increasing privation begin by pulling together in mutual aid, but as conditions worsen and hope for improvement through common action wanes, they pull apart and fragment until even families dissolve into individual competition and conflict pitting one against another.[1]

Religions provide a way of finding supernatural order, meaning, and agency in this otherwise chaotic natural cosmos, and all societies have some form of religious belief and ritual practice. Even latter-day societies that claim to reject religion simply replace one kind of symbolic and sacred doctrine with another, equally based in and reliant on mythic belief and rituals, even if the content is ostensibly secular. Religions play a necessary role in society, regardless (or at least largely regardless) of their specific content.

None of this, I might add, questions the truth of any particular creed or faith; religion and ritual serve these functions in all human societies, and whether some religions reveal truth is well beyond the modest scope of this chapter. I wish to explore the commonality of religion and ritual across societies, not their specific contents.

Two caveats are necessary, however. First, scholars who seek cross-cultural regularities almost always find them, and as often as not this reflects *apophenia* (the tendency for the human mind to see patterns in any mass of data if one looks hard enough) rather than insight. Much ink has been spilled seeking universalities of religion, and such studies almost always find patterns in the content of belief that confirm a scholar's own inclinations. This is even more true when patterns in artistic depictions of such beliefs are sought, as the tendency to see patterns is even more pronounced in assessing visual forms (where it is termed *pareidolia*). Perhaps the most immediately familiar examples are the appearance of something looking like a human face in the pattern of shadows cast by Martian landforms, or of an image of Jesus in the burned areas of a piece of toast.

Second, representations reflect the symbolic systems of the community producing a visual work, but those symbolic representations may not accurately reflect their lived experiences. Elaborate Egyptian funerary boats both express metaphorical ideas of the passage from life to death to afterlife and also reference the familiar everyday experiences of a civilization focused on the Nile and its cycles (1). But communities choose what aspects of their experience to highlight rather than reflecting the fullness of daily life. The Inca Empire encountered by the Spanish conquistadors in highland Peru was an

Egypt
Middle Kingdom, Dynasty 12,
1981 – 1975 BCE
Wood, paint, plaster, linen twine, linen fabric
54 ½ × 20 ⅞ × 14 ¹⁵⁄₁₆ in., 138.5 × 53 × 38 cm
Metropolitan Museum of Art, New York
Rogers Fund and Edward S. Harkness Gift, 1920

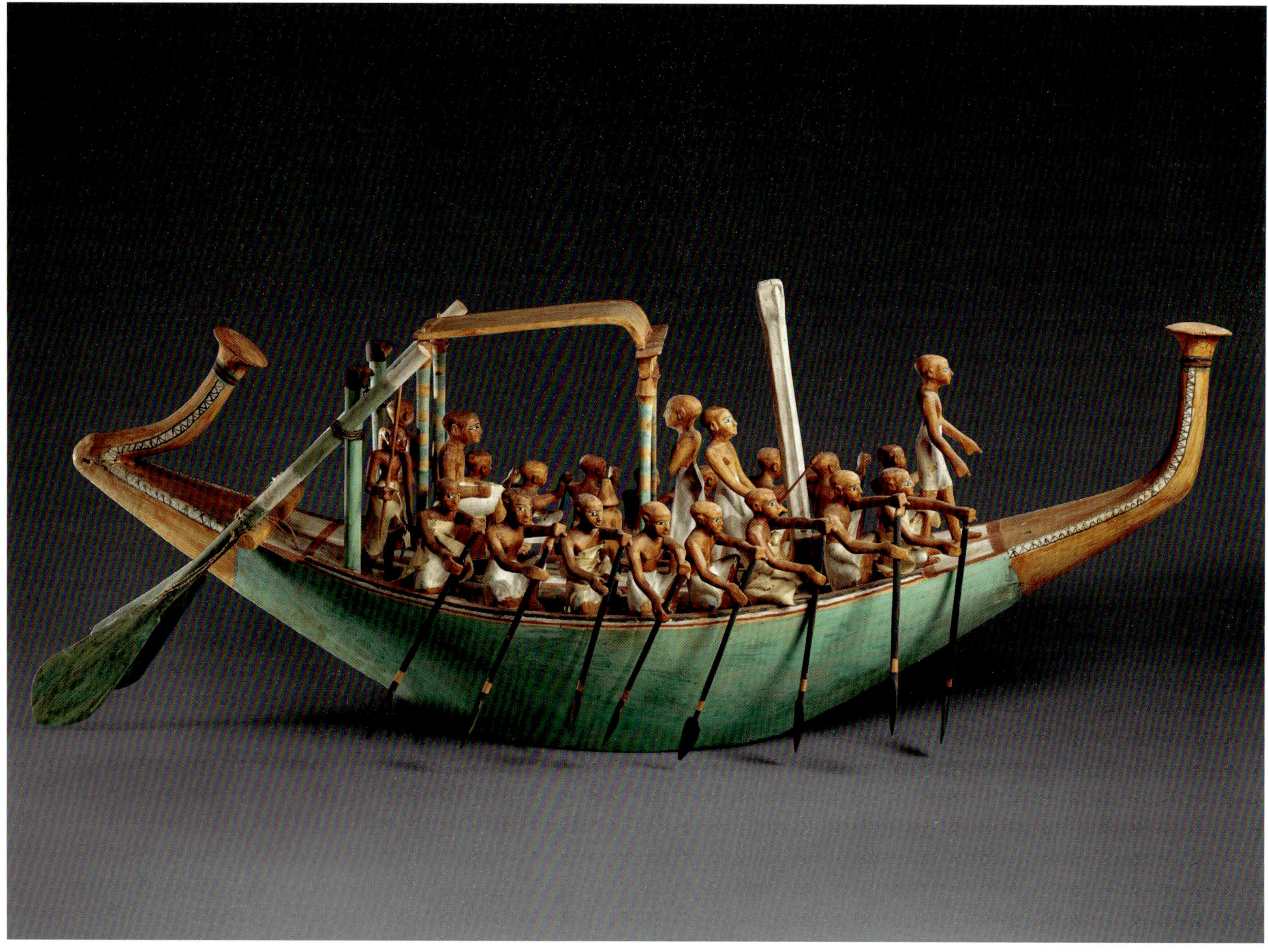

2 Repoussé Plate Depicting Birdman
Cahokian and Etowah cultures, United States
1200 – 1300
Copper
National Museum of Natural History,
Washington, DC

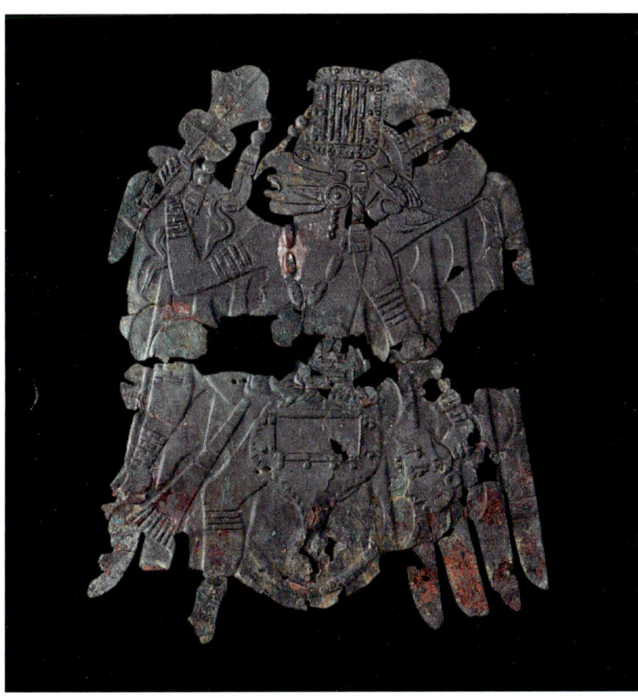

aggressively expansionary and militarist state, yet relatively little of its art emphasizes this. Conversely much art produced by the earlier Peruvian Moche culture includes warriors and scenes of conflict, but it is unclear whether this accurately reflects the daily lives of Moche communities rather than the way their religious symbol systems influenced how they understood or imagined their role in the world. Ancient Mississippian (ca. 1000–1500) art of the American midcontinent depicts striding winged figures brandishing maces and severed heads, but a careful analysis of such depictions shows two different beings, each holding the others head (**2**). Whether this represents endemic warfare or ritual cycles of redemption and rebirth is a matter of interpretation and assumption rather than fact. And while warfare and violence are nominally eschewed in Christian doctrine, untold multitudes died in wars between Christian states and their neighbors—Christian or not. The relationships between behaviors and beliefs are complex, and it is rarely easy to distinguish between them except by assessing multiple lines of artistic and archaeological evidence simultaneously.

Religion can be defined in two quite different ways. Functional definitions of religion, such as those with which I opened this chapter, discuss what religion does, how it works. In general, it is easier to draw cross-cultural comparisons of religions in functional terms, by showing how they achieve similar goals or use similar rhetorical or expository strategies, than to use substantive definitions of religion such as Max Weber's—which posits that religion is "a belief in a supernatural power that is unable to be scientifically explained"—because Weber's terms already position the discussion ethnocentrically, making religion a residual that cannot (yet) be explained by a more reliable "science," rather than a culturally meaningful mode of explanation in its own right.[2]

Anthropologist Clifford Geertz, for example, offered one of the most widely employed definitions of religion: "a system of symbols which act to establish powerful,

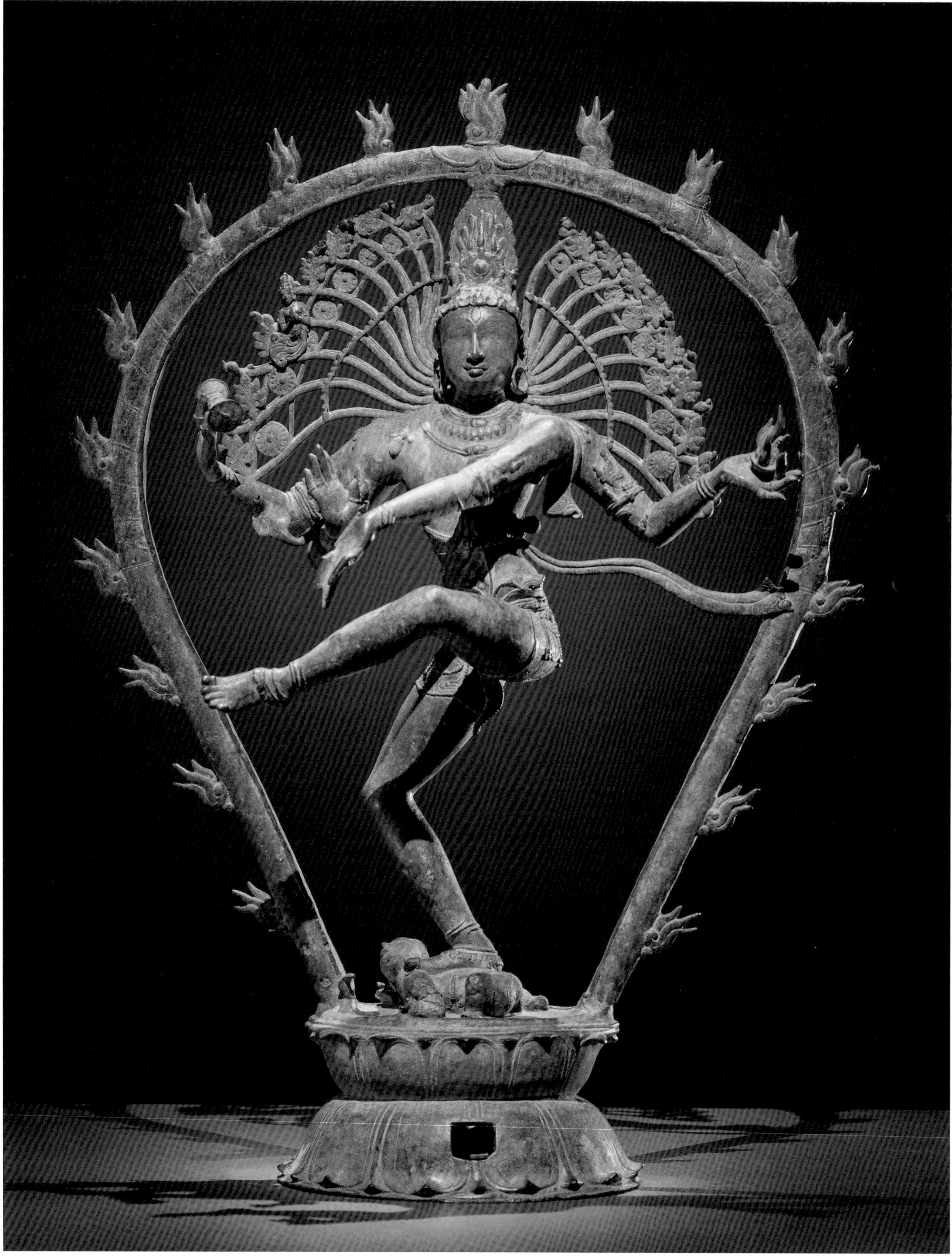

pervasive, and long-lasting moods and motivations in men by formulating conceptions of a general order of existence and clothing these conceptions with such an aura of factuality that the moods and motivations seem uniquely realistic."[3] There is perhaps no clearer illustration of the ubiquity of religion and ritual than the fact that one might casually replace "religion" with "culture" as the term Geertz is defining without losing the meaning or encountering any significant cognitive dissonance. For my purposes, however, the definition lacks one necessary substantive element making religion more than another word for culture—religion and rituals also concern the transcendent, the uncanny, or an "otherness" distinct from the observed everyday world, although communities differ widely in what this constitutes. Hindu iconography, for instance, often depicts divinities with multiple arms to indicate the multiplicity of their dimensions and aspects, not as a depiction of the grotesque (**3**).

I use the term transcendent instead of supernatural for two related reasons. First, for most societies the distinction between natural and supernatural is arbitrary, and religions intrinsically blur and destroy such separations. One might even restate Geertz's definition by saying that religions create an aura of factuality making their particular system of symbols seem entirely necessary and natural. Religion and ritual domesticate the sacred and make the supernatural seem a uniquely necessary part of the natural order. Second, religion and ritual bring individuals or communities into contact with a profound otherness, transcendent in both senses of

the term, as both beyond the usual limits of experience or comprehension and being universally applicable or significant. Supernatural connotes something other than everyday occurrence; transcendent connotes something beyond experience.

Joseph Campbell, a professor of literature who popularized the comparative study of myth in the 1970s, proposed a series of distinct functions for myth and religious belief. While many scholars debate the relative importance of the various roles he proposed, and his larger generalities regarding the unity of myth have been broadly challenged, the clarity of his explanation of myth's roles could hardly be improved. He argued that myth and religion have four quite distinct and sometimes contradictory functions: 1) metaphysical functions, which offer a sense of the transcendent and of mystery; 2) cosmological functions, which provide an explanation for why the world exists and why it operates in the ways it does; 3) sociological functions, encompassing a set of norms for how people are expected to act and thereby creating a sense of community and shared group identity; and 4) psychological functions, which guide an individual through life's passages and also provide a sense of individual identity and a charter for nonconformity and independence as a counterbalance to the norms established by myth's sociological functions. Nor are these wholly independent roles; knowing what makes events happen (the cosmological function) may allow an individual to influence these causes to one's advantage, gaining wealth, love, stature, power, or averting mischance, and thereby gain confidence and surety (the psychological function). Ijo shrines (*ifiri* or *iphiri*) of the Niger Delta, for example, celebrate and embody the aggressiveness and warlike spirit of individuals, families, or clans and thereby serve to ward off violence or threats (**4**).

Early social evolutionists like Edward B. Tylor and James Frazer argued that religion and beliefs in the supernatural arose from naturalistic observation of powerful physical forces like storms, while Herbert Spencer suggested animistic (the belief that all things— plants, animals, object—have spirits or souls) origins from psychological phenomena like dreams. Emil Durkheim disagreed, suggesting instead that religion reflects the social energy and euphoria of collective action, of groups of people coming together for common purpose and experiencing what Durkheim called "collective effervescence."[4] Whatever thing or idea that collective energy is projected onto becomes the sacred, and it serves to further focus and sharpen the sense of collectivity and "effervescence," a oneness with a larger group—a fact that leads some to view sports fandom as a kind of civic, totemic religion. Durkheim himself was generally careful to avoid using the term "god," but instead referred to "the sacred object," thus allowing him to include both supernatural beings (e.g., the Hindu deity Shiva) as well as sacred ideas (e.g., the Four Noble Truths of Buddhism). Importantly, however, these projections often involve tangible objects, allowing things to become sacred, to

become the focus (albeit not necessarily the object) of devotion.

In some respects, the distinction between the familiar and the uncanny, or the normal and the transcendent, mirrors Mircea Eliade's argument for a profound and irreducible separation of the sacred and the profane.[5] For Eliade, the sacred speaks to origins and meanings, to the way things came to be, and hence offers a structure and coherence to life that the profane secular world cannot provide. Only in origins, in the cosmic beginning of things, can certainty be found. Primordial time is marked by the appearance of the sacred, which in coming into being creates order. Eliade believed that for many societies, only hierophanies (manifestations of the sacred) give order to experience and provide a yardstick for the behavior and expectation of everyone in a society. Thus, both individuals and societies seek to return to these first principles and origins to find purpose, and he argues that the sacred always represents a return to the primordial and that ritual steps from the secular to the sacred beginning of time. Eliade's larger argument is premised on his understanding of Australian Aboriginal totemic belief and "dreamtime"; later scholars have rejected parts of his arguments based on either his somewhat suspect and poorly nuanced treatment of Aboriginal conceptions of time, cultural landscapes, and belief, or his attempt to generalize these temporal constructs into universal principles.

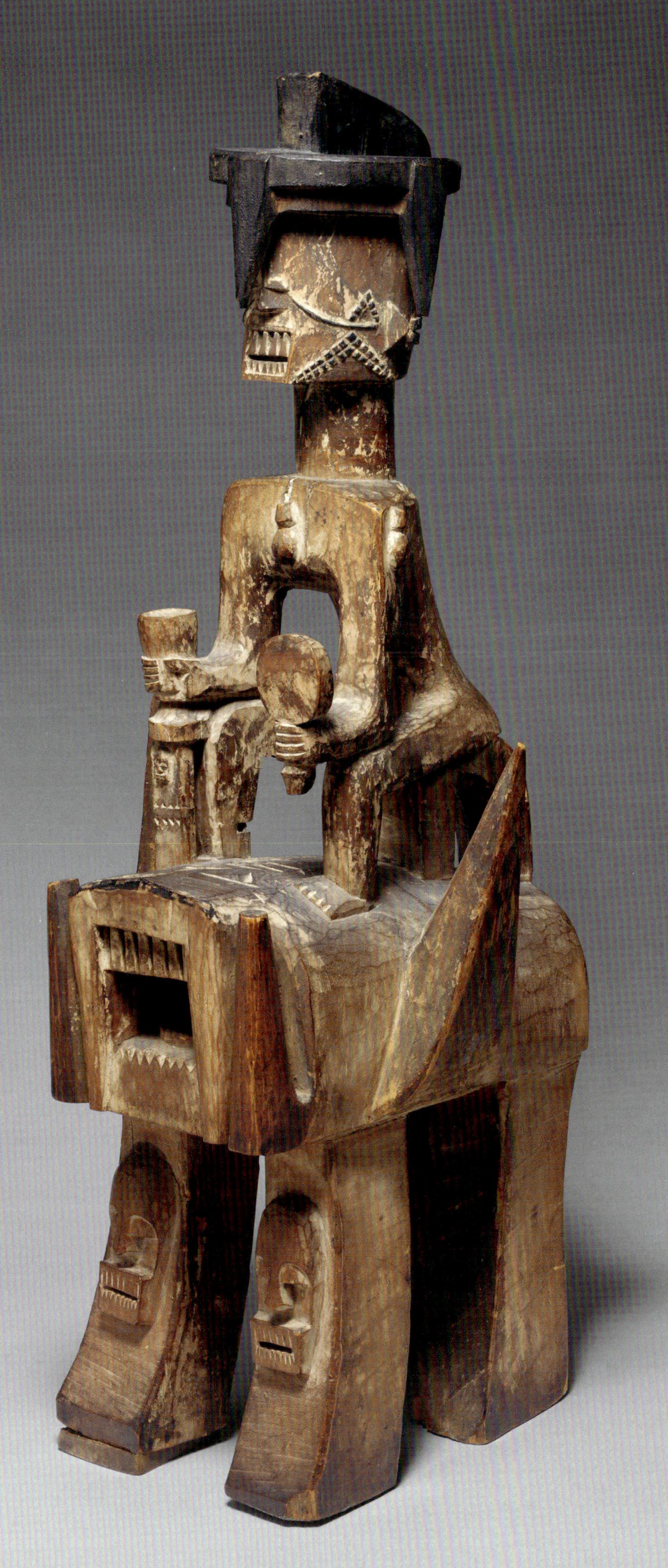

Part of the difficulty lies in the symbolic systems being employed; there are elements of the eternal in the "dreamings" (an "everywhen" in Aboriginal belief, both past and present) and "songlines" (dreamtracks that link paths across the landscape to origins) of Aboriginal belief that do not lend themselves to Eliade's distinctions between past and present, just as the term "totemic ancestors" implies a linear temporality at odds with a consubstantial identity, both in and out of time, directly linking people and place less *through* than *regardless of* time. The early Christian Church wrestled with these same issues; theologians like Boethius (480–524) grappled with the eternality of the divine and ended up distinguishing a deity for whom all times are the same, manifested in changing but everlasting ways in a temporal, physical, and imperfect world. Death often serves as the transition from temporal to eternal; Chinese Jin dynasty (265–316) funerary urns are thought to have served as eternal dwellings for the souls of the deceased (**5**).

Both time and space have religious dimensions and take on sacral qualities. In most Native American societies, the four directions have supernatural qualities and are acknowledged in religious practice. Aztec ritual honors the four directions, and a range of cultures including both Daoist Chinese and certain Muslim groups bless the four corners of a house before moving in. The four directions, and tetrads in general, play a central role in much symbolism across the Americas, and George Dumezil has argued that the number three and triads play

an equally central role in Indo-European symbolism.[6] But while space has sacred dimensions and most religions and many rituals are mapped onto specific parts of the landscape, ranging from Uluru/Ayers Rock, which is sacred to Indigenous Australians; to Mecca, sacred to Muslims or, more generally, Abrahamic Jerusalem; to specific spirits associated with the cardinal directions, the temporal dimension seems to loom larger in most ritual contexts. The Komuku-ten Guardian of the West, for example, is one of the four Shintennō who defend the four cardinal directions of the Buddha's realm (**6**).

While one might question whether all religion seeks a return to a primordial, sacred time, religion and time are always closely linked, and time's origin is usually described in sacral terms. Sometimes it is as simple as explaining why time is divided into night and day. In traditional Japanese Shinto belief, for example, Amaterasu, the ruler of heaven and the sun, orders her brother Tsukiyomi, ruler of the moon, to visit the food *kami* (divine being) Uke-mochi on earth. Tsukiyomi slays Uke-mochi when he learns she produces the earth's food by defecating and vomiting; Amaterasu banishes Tsukiyomi from her sight and thus day and night are separated, with Amaterasu ruling the day's sun and Tsukiyomi the night's moon. Calendar years are established through the sacred Amaterasu as well, with the *showa* date (the regnal year of the emperor, widely used for official documents) set by the accession ceremony of the new emperor, ending with the *daijosai*,

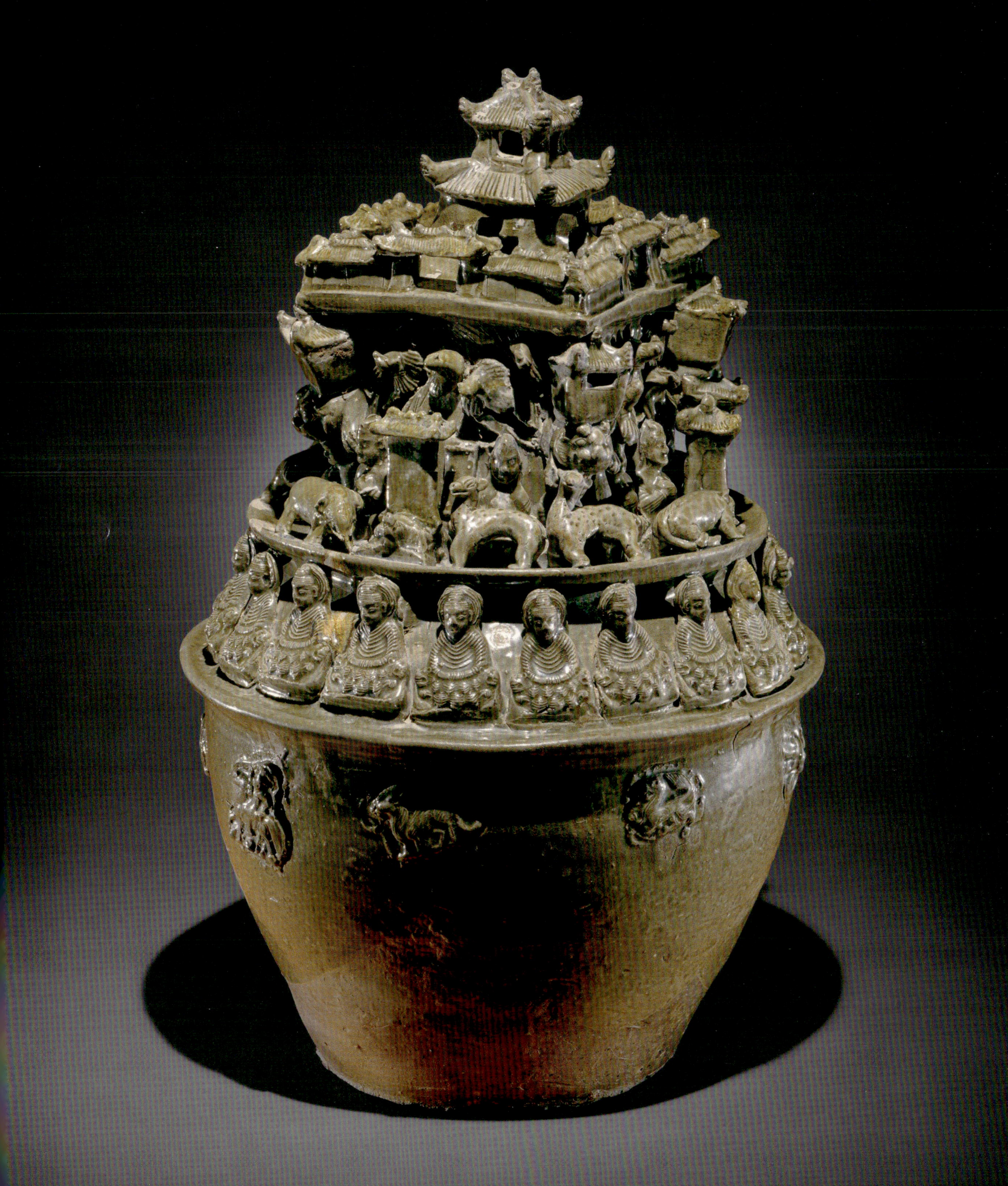

when the new emperor spends the night with Amaterasu. Other deities reflect this concern with sacral time; Amaterasu's brother Raijin, god of thunder, is often depicted with three fingers on each hand, representing past, present and future, although the depiction of Raijin and Fujin by Tawaraya Sotatsu (ca. 1600–1700) focuses instead on the tension between space (Fujin's four fingers represent the cardinal directions) and time (**7**).

Likewise, seasonality is often explained as having a sacred origin. In the familiar Greek myth of Hades and Persephone, Hades, lord of the underworld, abducts Persephone, daughter of Demeter, goddess of the harvest, and carries her to the underworld. Demeter's anger is such that she makes the world barren, until the gods intervene and force Hades to return Perspehone. Before she leaves the underworld, however, she is persuaded to eat four pomegranate seeds, and having eaten food in the underworld, she cannot return to the land of the living; a compromise is struck allowing her to stay with Hades for part of the year and return to her mother for the rest. When Persephone is with her mother, the earth is warm and abundant, but it cools and becomes barren when she is with Hades. The same basic pattern is present in a range of ancient Near Eastern societies. In Sumer (the earliest civilization of southern Mesopotamia, which flourished ca. 4500–1900 BCE), it is the return of the goddess Inanna/Ishtar, and in Egypt a three-season calendar is marked in part by the return of the goddess Isis.

My point in sharing these stories is not to suggest similarities in substance but rather in function. By explaining observed daily and annual patterns in sacred terms, these just-so stories reinforce the naturalness of religious belief, providing a kind of empirical evidence for the unobserved supernatural order in the real-world recurrence of the seasons. All of these ancient cultures, as it happens, had a sophisticated understanding of annual solar calendars, and they adopted religious explanations of the seasonal round not from lack of empirical knowledge but because it made such changes meaningful and allowed the potential to intercede in them or influence their effects.

In much of ancient Mexico, time was measured in calendar round cycles defined by two interlocking calendars, one a solar, secular cycle of 365 days (Mayan *haab'*, or Aztec *xiuhpōhualli*) and the other a ritual cycle of 260 days (Mayan *tzolk'in*, or Aztec *tōnalpōhualli*); those two epicycles only lined up once every fifty-two years, and they produce a remarkably accurate calendar with less imprecision than the Julian and Gregorian calendars used in Europe.[7] While the same calendar round system was used across a broad area and dates back to at least the fifth century BCE, the Maya believed it was communicated to humans by the god Itzamna (who was designated "God D" before archeologists learned to read Mayan

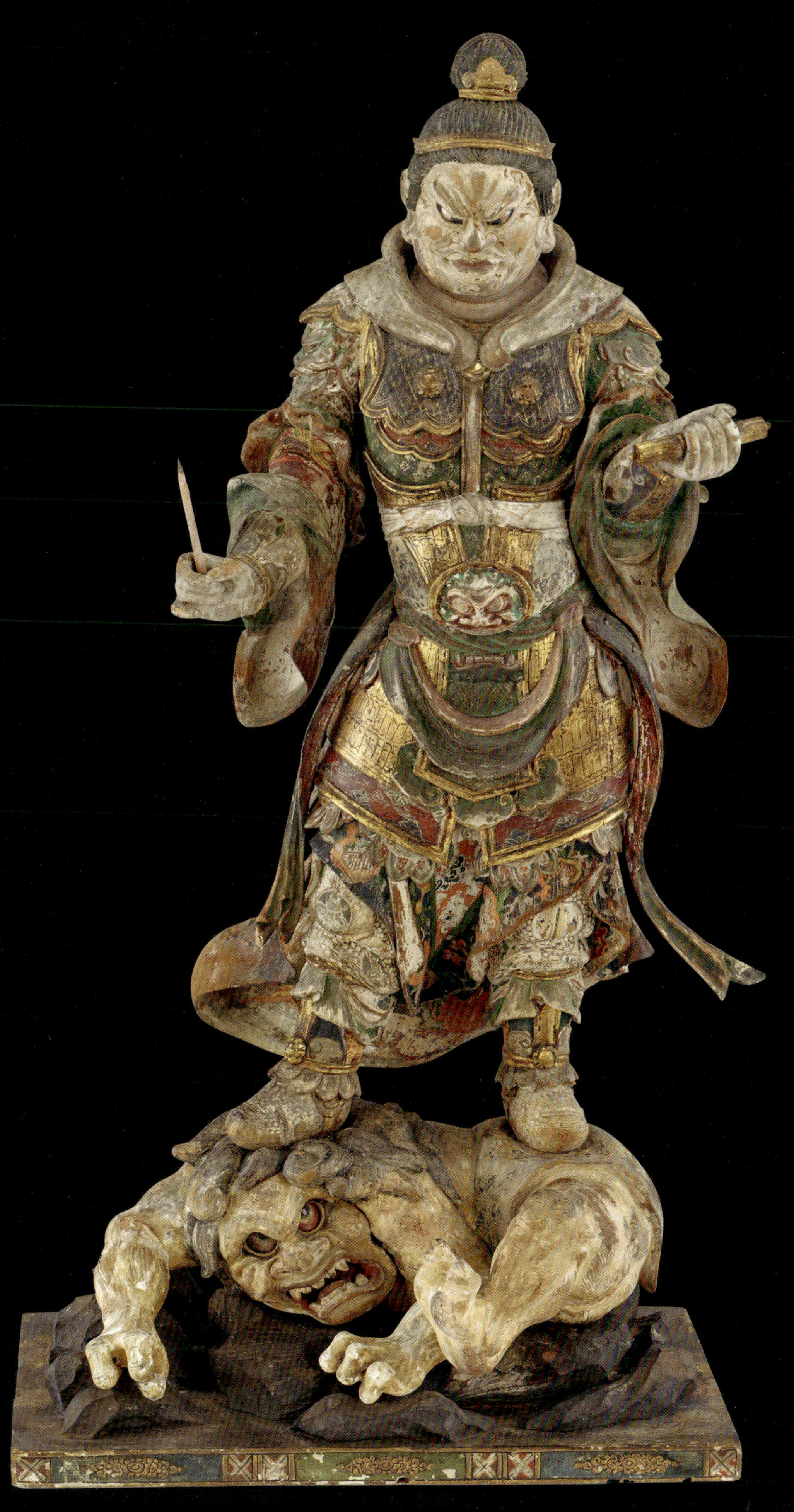

7 Wind God and Thunder God

Tawaraya Sotatsu (Japan, 1570 – 1643)
1600 – 1700
Pair of two folded screens; ink and color on paper
covered with gold leaves
66.85 × 60.83 in., 169.8 × 154.5 cm (each)
Ninna-ji Temple, Kyoto, Japan

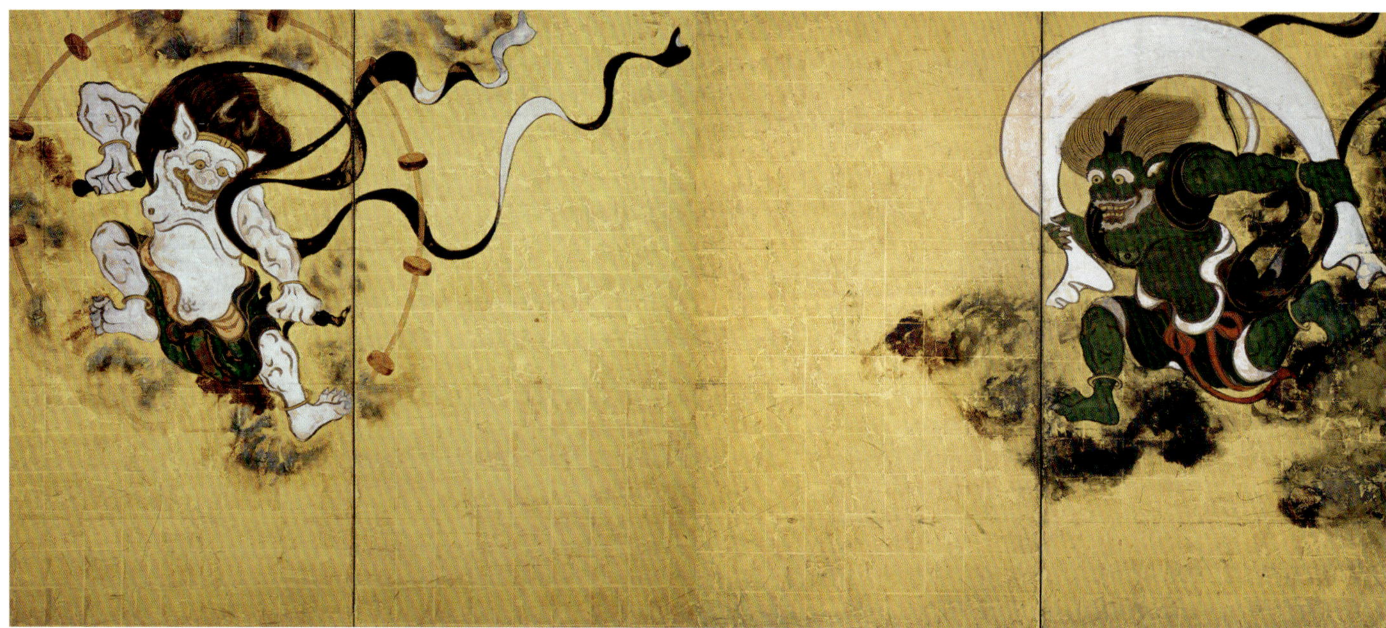

inscriptions), who is also credited with teaching writing
and medicine (**8**). Ancient Egyptian belief similarly
accepted a combination of linear calendrical (*djet*) and
cyclical seasonal/diurnal (*neheh*) time, although they
did not form an epicyclic round, and many societies
have a combination of secular solar calendars based
on earth's rotation around the sun and ritual calendars
using different cycles. Chinese, Babylonian, and Jewish
lunisolar calendars all create ritual events whose dates
appear to vary, as do movable feasts in the Christian
liturgical calendar.

Understandings of time usually involve a combination
of linear (e.g., calendrical dates) and cyclical (seasonal
or diurnal) elements, but some societies conceive of
time in cyclic rather than linear terms. Cosmologies of
ancient Mesoamerica (present-day Mexico and Central
American countries) emphasize the cyclicity of ages, with
the world being created, developing, declining, and being
destroyed as a series of specific iterations. A celebrated
mantle from Paracas, Peru, some two thousand years
old and recently repatriated by museums in Sweden,
depicts this progression of time as a series of unique

 Dresden Codex, Page 9

Maya culture, Mexico
1000 – 1100
Tree bark
8 × 20 in., 20.32 × 50.8 cm
(each page, accordion style)
Museum of the Saxon State Library,
Dresden, Germany

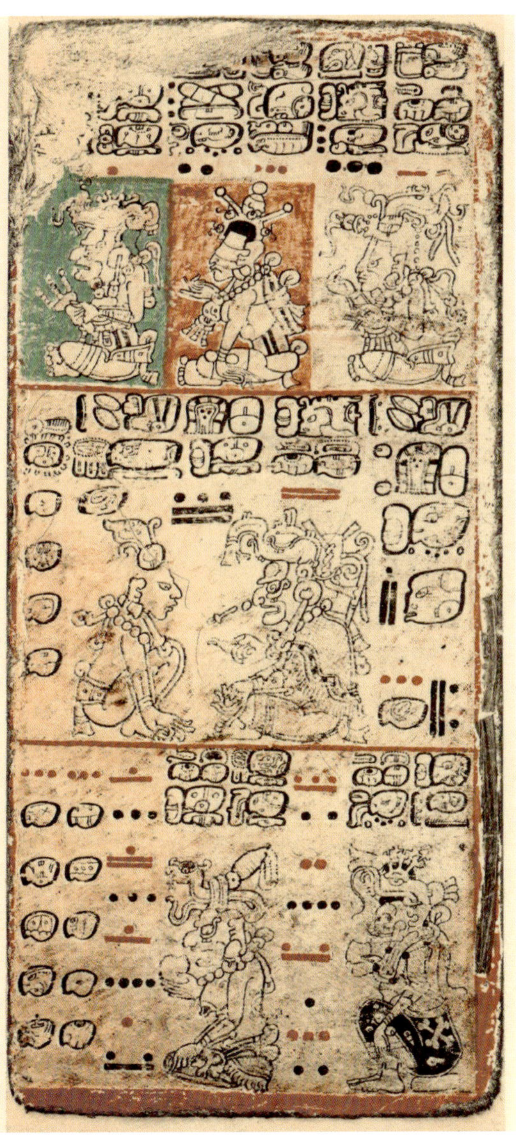

tiled panels (**9**). Hindu and Buddhist conceptions of time also assume long-term cycles (*yuga* cycles, which in turn aggregate into *kalpa* aeons). Other religions assume either cycles or a succession of stages; ancient Greek cosmogonies presuppose succeeding cycles or stages of creation, especially through the Greek poet Hesiod's (active ca. 700 BCE) notion of a succession of Gold, Silver, Bronze, Age of Heroes, and Iron ages. Other religions, by contrast, privilege the linearity of time, either as proceeding from a putative beginning (as does Newtonian science) or ticking down to an end (e.g., the Norse Ragnarok or the Judeo-Christian Armageddon); much Western thought since the Enlightenment in the late seventeenth and eighteenth centuries seems to include elements of both linear and terminal time, with the end coming for either eschatological or technological reasons. These are, necessarily, broad generalities, and temporal constructs are usually more complex when examined in detail, hence special cases ranging from the Christian premillennial dispensationist Rapture, the Vaishnavist Kalki and Kali Yuga, and the purely secular (and rather Bayesian) Carter catastrophist argument all assume an end of time on a more selective basis.[8]

Religion and ritual similarly give meaning to the cycles of human life—birth, puberty, marriage, death, and a range of other events that mark both the progression of a single lifetime and an initiation into a bewildering array of possible organizational forms that structure and regulate societies. Entry in (or passage through) these stages is marked by rites and reflected in works of art depicting such

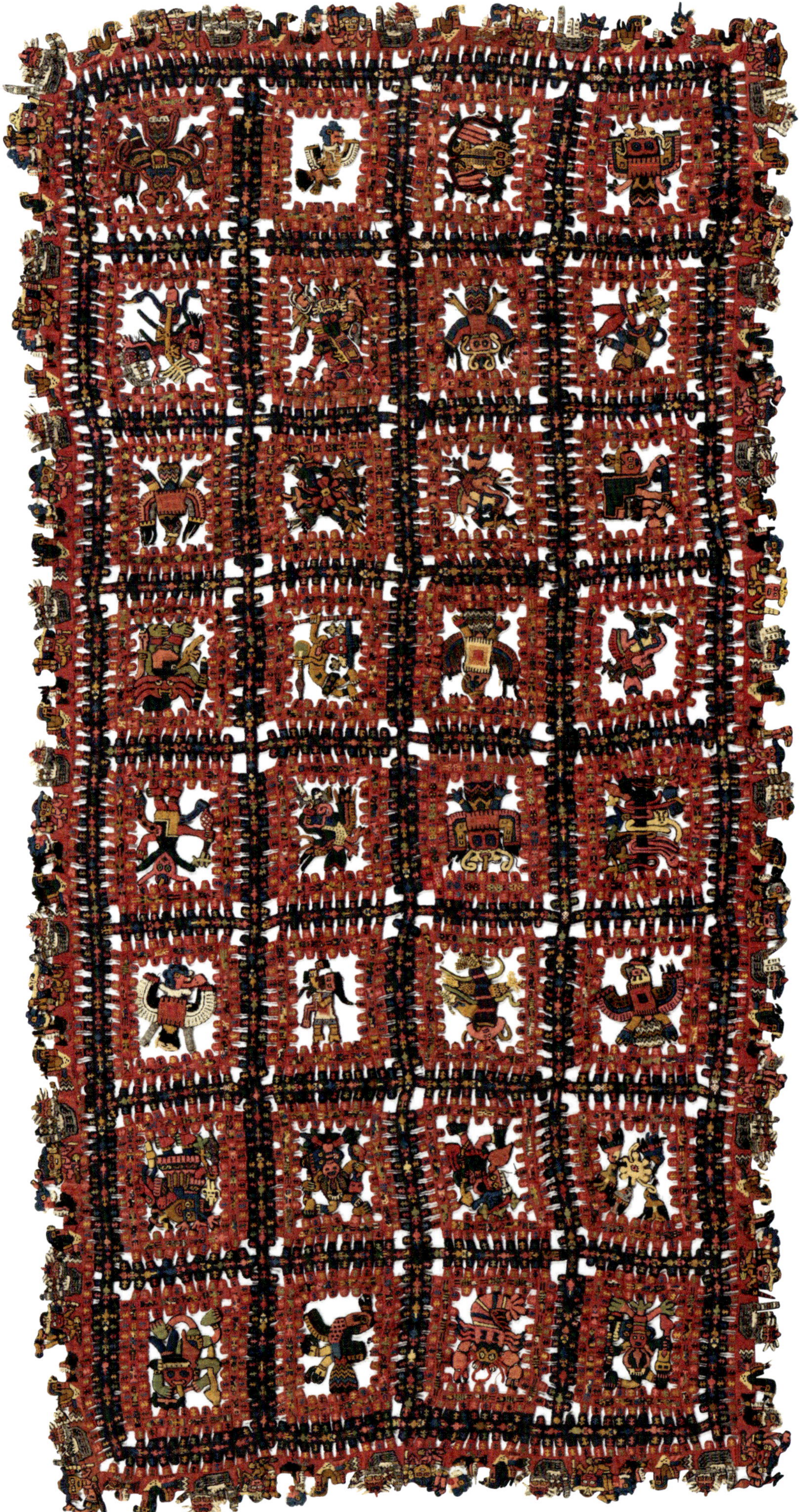

Paracas culture, Peru
160 BCE – 80 CE
Woven embroidery on cotton
40.95 × 20.87 in., 104 cm × 53 cm
National Museum of Archeology,
Anthropology, and History, Lima, Peru

rituals. Because of their social importance, such rituals of life's progressions and passage of power are often depicted, celebrated, and reified in art. In some cases, such as birth or death, the events and circumstances are self-evident, but many others are purely social constructs where the "who" and "when" depend on tradition and circumstance, as in this Recuay effigy vessel from Peru showing a fertility scene (**10**). But while the content of these rituals may be idiosyncratic, their role is not. Anthropologist Elman Service, for example, argues that as smaller and more simply organized societies aggregate into larger groupings, "sodalities" (age-grades, secret societies, confraternal or consororal associations) appear, both to break the larger social landscape into more manageable pieces and to create ready-made go-betweens to smooth the disputes that come with more people living more closely.[9] The logic can be visualized as a spreadsheet; everyone belongs to descent groups (columns) and sodalities (rows); for any two people currently at odds, there are others belonging to the same row but a different column, and a different column but the same row, able to step in and intercede and with a vested interest in doing so, and thus countering the centrifugal forces constantly pulling communities apart.

Anthropologist Arnold van Gennep suggests that rites of passage, regardless of the kind of passage they make or mark, generally include three stages.[10] First is a preliminary or separation phase (called "separation") serving to distance an individual from his or her former state (for example, "setting aside childish things"). Next is a liminal stage ("marge"), in which the individual is in an in-between state and groups of initiates in this state begin to bond with one another as sharing an experience foreign to others. Anthropologists Victor Turner and Mary Douglas have observed that such rites are perceived as dangerous, either symbolically or physically, and position the individual outside the usual social categories.[11] Finally, there is an incorporation or reaggregation phase ("aggregation") in which the individual re-enters society with their new status and in some respects a new identity. While the results of psychological research are mixed, there is at least some data to support the idea that the more intense the discomfort or suffering an individual endures during rites of passage, the more attractive the new status is likely to seem. Some rites carry with them their own perils (childbirth, for one), while for others the hazards are created for the purpose or framed as existential, psychological perils.

Latter-day Western societies have their own rites of passage, ranging from bar and bat mitzvahs to sweet sixteen and Latina *quinceañera* celebrations; even within academic settings, graduation ceremonies or traditions surrounding completion of competency examinations like the German *Abitur* and eastern European *Matura* tests are secular rituals serving the same function, and scholars like John Keegan have long observed that transitional experiences like military boot camp are not simply for drill and physical conditioning but are also rites of passage that distance recruits from society in ways allowing social strictures against killing to be relaxed and refocused.[12]

  Fertility Scene Vessel
Recuay culture, Peru
200 BCE – 600 CE
Terracotta
6 ⅝ × 7 ¾ in., 16.83 × 19.69 cm
Walters Art Museum, Baltimore

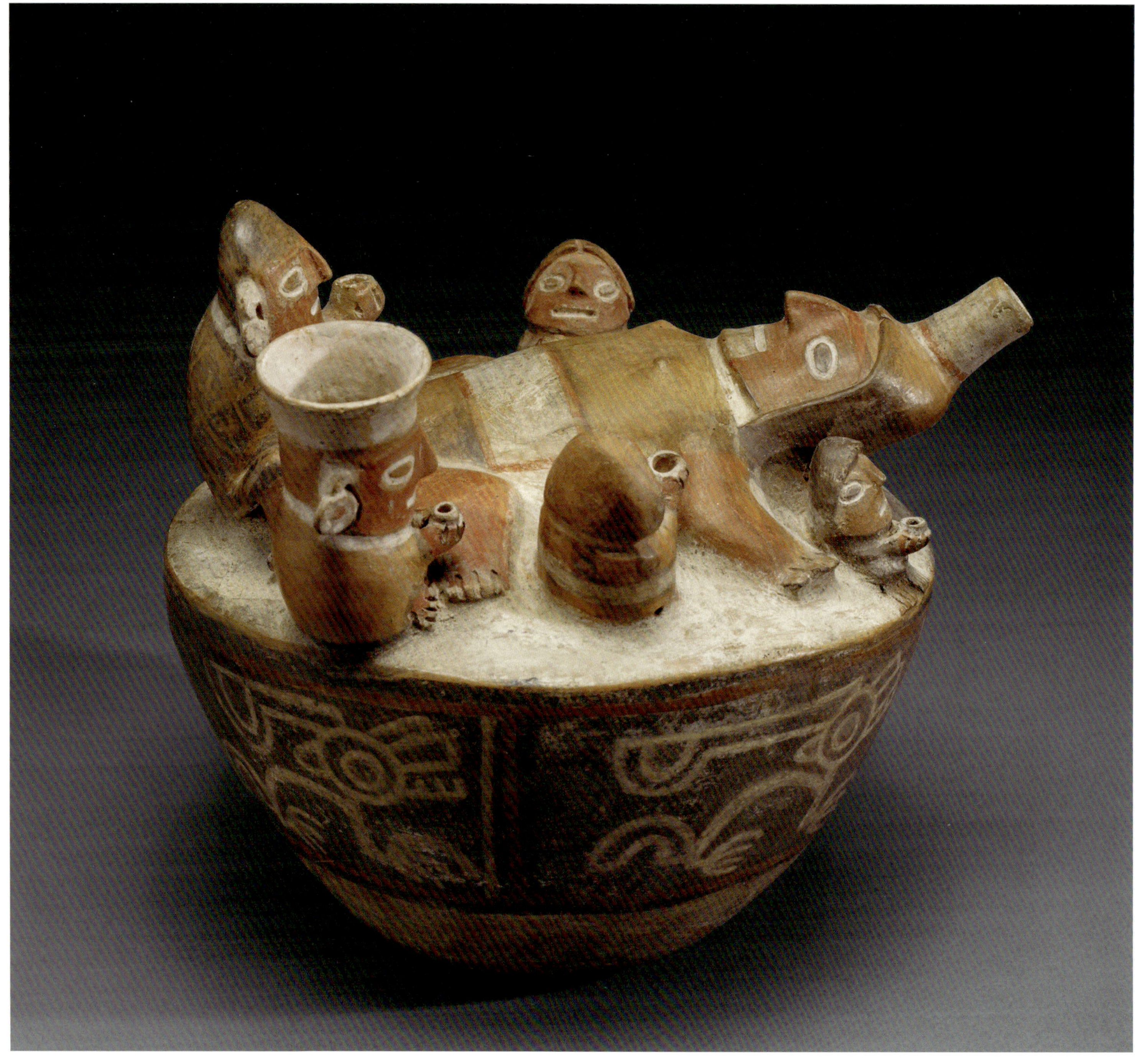

11 **Masks**

New Ireland, Papua New Guinea
1800 – 1900
Wood, pigment, bark cloth, shell, seeds,
vegetable fiber, cord
17.52 × 7.87 × 13.78 in., 44.50 × 20 × 35 cm
British Museum, London, England
Gift of Francis Russell, 9th Duke of Bedford

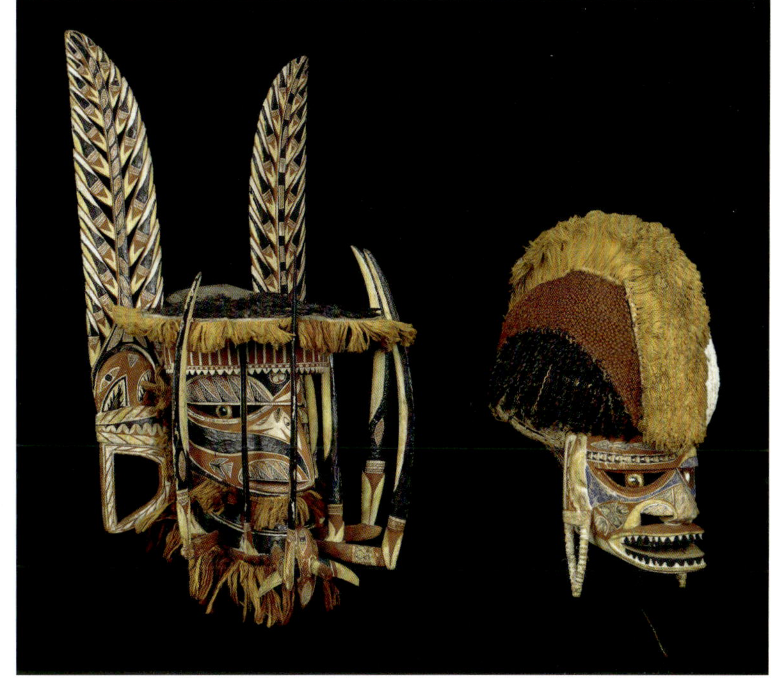

Other chapters in this volume explore many of these life passage events in greater detail, but most of them need to be understood as rituals and manifestations of religious symbol systems at work. Campbell's distinction between the four roles of ritual is useful conceptually but, as noted, different rites of passage or similar events may serve one, more, or all of the functions. A child's birthday party marks an anniversary of birth, cements and expands social networks among age-mates (often of both child and parents), reinforces social training and behavioral expectations, and serves as an affirmation and celebration of individuality. In many cases the representation of rites of passage in art also needs to be understood not in terms of the specific individual or event depicted but as statements made by others about that event's social significance. Funerals, for example, are really for and about the living. While archaeologists generally assume that an individual's status in death reflects their status in life, the only certainty is that the resulting burial tableau was created by the living to mark and denote that death in ways they deemed appropriate and necessary.

Malanggan rituals of the north coast of New Ireland, Papua New Guinea, honor a deceased individual and provide an opportunity for the role of the dead individual to be refilled by new initiates. Just as a unique individual dies and is replaced by a different individual, *malanggan* art has traditionally been used once then replaced with new objects, continuously renewing the creative cycle (11). But these rituals simultaneously and perhaps more importantly mend the rift in society caused by that death, affirming the primacy of clan and descent groups, resolving debts or disputes, and mediating the associated transfers of property and land rights. Preparation for the *malanggan* ritual cycle can take years, and while they are always held in the name of someone who has died, the deceased person is less the focus of the ceremony than its titular cause.

West African Senufo *poro* age-grade societies have a similar range of social responsibilities, including accompanying the deceased during funeral ceremonies. The fierce *kponyungo* helmet masks (sometimes called "firespitters") are worn by *poro* members in their roles simultaneously accompanying the deceased and

 Helmet Mask (*Kponyungo*)
Senufo culture, Ivory Coast
1900s
Wood
38 in., 96.5 cm
Private Collection
Photo courtesy of Sotheby's,
New York

 **Spouted Vessel with
Raptor and Serpent**
Chavin culture, Northern Peru
900 – 200 BCE
Terracotta
10 ⅛ × 6 ¾ in., 25.72 × 17.15 cm
Private Collection

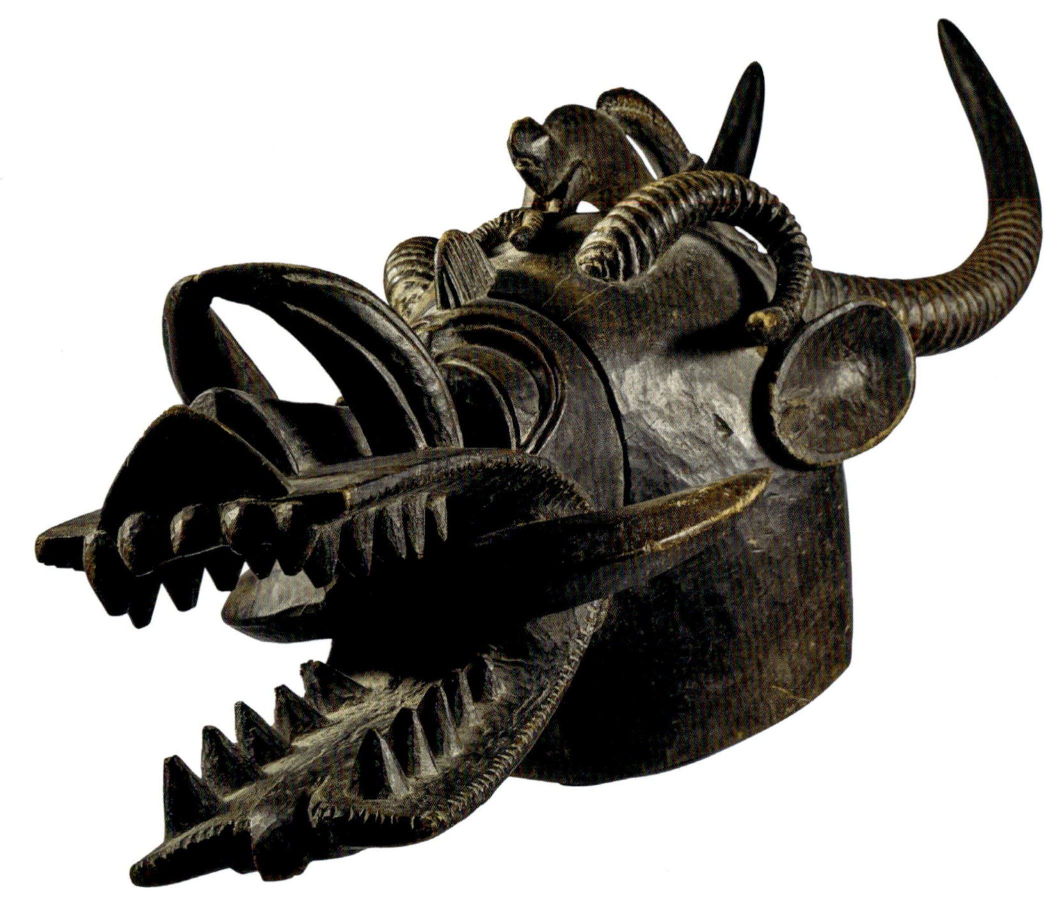

protecting the remainder of the community from malevolent spirits (**12**). Their wearers and the rituals they enact are about the dead but primarily serve integrative and apotropaic (warding off evil) functions for the living.

Such masks illustrate several commonalities in ritual art. Most obviously, the fantastic creatures depicted are at once otherworldly and composed of selected features of more everyday animals—hyena, crocodile, wild boar, and so on—assembled into a chimera of fearsome aspects of familiar beasts. Representations of supernatural spirits frequently denote the otherworldly as composites of known forms and obvious parallels can be drawn with the Egyptian pantheon; Greek monsters (the term "chimera," meaning composite animal, comes from a mythical lion-serpent-goat monster slain by the Greek hero Bellerophon, also known for taming the composite winged horse Pegasus); Harappan seals (carved steatite seals often featuring a unicorn-composite bull, associated with the early South Asian civilizations of Harappa and Mohenjo-Daro (ca. 2600–1900 BCE); Chinese *pixiu* (mythical composite beasts, including one-antlered male *tiānlù* associated with wealth, and two-antlered female *bìxié* warding off evil) from the Han dynasty (ca. 206 BCE–220 CE); Mesoamerican gods; Mississippian-period engraved shell carvings; and so on.

Second, and conversely, their creativity is bounded in prescribed ways, because their symbols need to be understood and meaningful to those seeing them in use. Ritual representations may be enormously imaginative, but they need to be recognizable to other participants in the same ritual performance or consumers of the same ritual messages. For this reason, carvers making *kponyungo* masks often make duplicates or identical sets, so that the familiar symbolic meanings and complex associations will

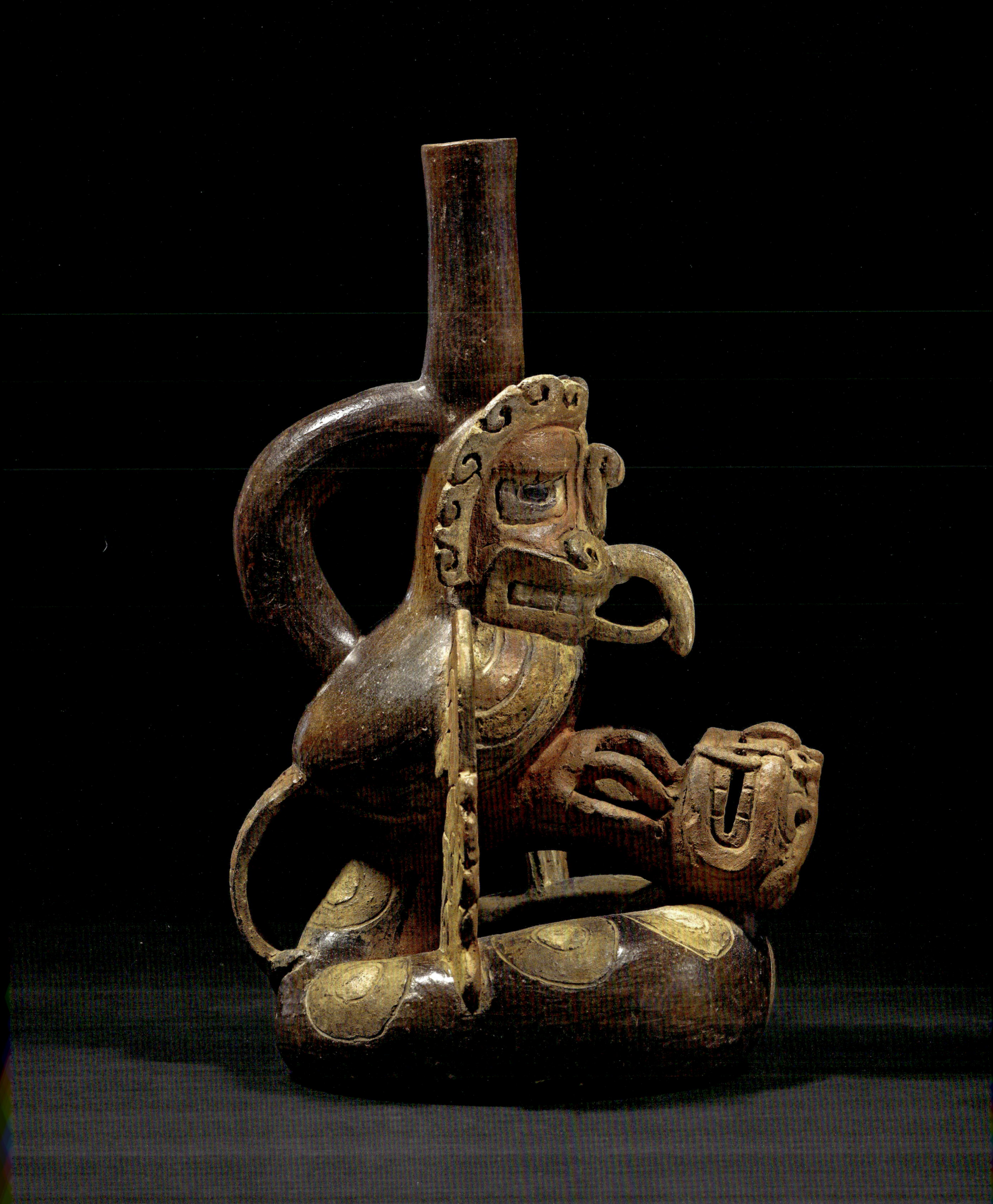

14 Madonna of the Goldfinch

Raphael (Italy, 1483 – 1520)
1505 – 06
Oil on panel
42.1 × 30.3 in., 107 × 77 cm
Uffizi Gallery, Florence, Italy

not be compromised if a specific mask is lost or destroyed. Just as a skilled musician can improvise endless riffs around a familiar tune, artists create fantastical and imaginative objects that nevertheless adhere to specific and recognizable canons that shape and underscore the social meanings and significance of the rituals in which they feature.[13]

Third, while such objects must be recognizable and decipherable to those empowered to know the ritual's meaning, they also embody esoteric knowledge through more subtle or arbitrary symbolic associations, making their meanings unclear or cryptic to outsiders. Throughout the Americas, feline, avian, and ophidian (serpent) symbolism recurs in different forms and combinations; regularly anthropomorphized to include human elements, they use selected symbols to reference complex and nuanced beliefs we can, at best, only partially reconstruct, as in this anthropomorphized bird and serpent stirrup pot from ancient Peru (**13**). While archeologists can often extend meanings from historical periods into later periods of prehistory, extending these understandings to earlier civilizations like the Chavin in Peru, the Olmec in Mexico, or Neolithic assemblages from Europe may not be valid; later civilizations may have appropriated symbols without assimilating their earlier meanings. The assemblage of elements and the ways they are combined are not arbitrary and their juxtaposition or specific elements of the design may communicate esoteric meanings to initiates that escape the notice of the casual or uninitiated observer. Even within a canon as well

known and studied as European Renaissance art of the fifteenth to sixteenth century, such symbols range from the familiar and well understood—such as the use of the European goldfinch as a symbol of the Crucifixion because its head bears a red flash supposedly gained when it pulled one of the thorns from Jesus's forehead (**14**)—to the unexplained, such as a common but cryptic hand gesture in which the third and fourth fingers are held tightly together, and the second and fifth fingers are spread (**15**).

Finally, the socially defined power of ritual objects often depends on their being consecrated in some way. The *kponyungo* mask being actively used has power but the backup mask does not; similarly Congo *nkisi* power figures (see below) are simply statues until certain ritually powerful materials are secreted within them; False Face Society masks among the Haudenosaunee (Iroquois) became powerful after they were initiated into the Society; and in Catholic and Anglican belief, common objects like water, chrism (oil), and the wine and wafer used in the Mass are inert but made supernaturally powerful after consecration by a priest.

Katsinam "dolls" of the Hopi of the American Southwest are a slightly different example of the same principle (**16**). *Katsinam* are spirits that visit the Hopi pueblos in the first half of each year and serve as intercessors or intermediaries between people and deities; propitiation of or friendship with the *katsinam* is crucial for Hopi health and harvest. They include spirits representing places, plants, animals, ancestors, or natural phenomena, and they are impersonated or represented by ceremonial

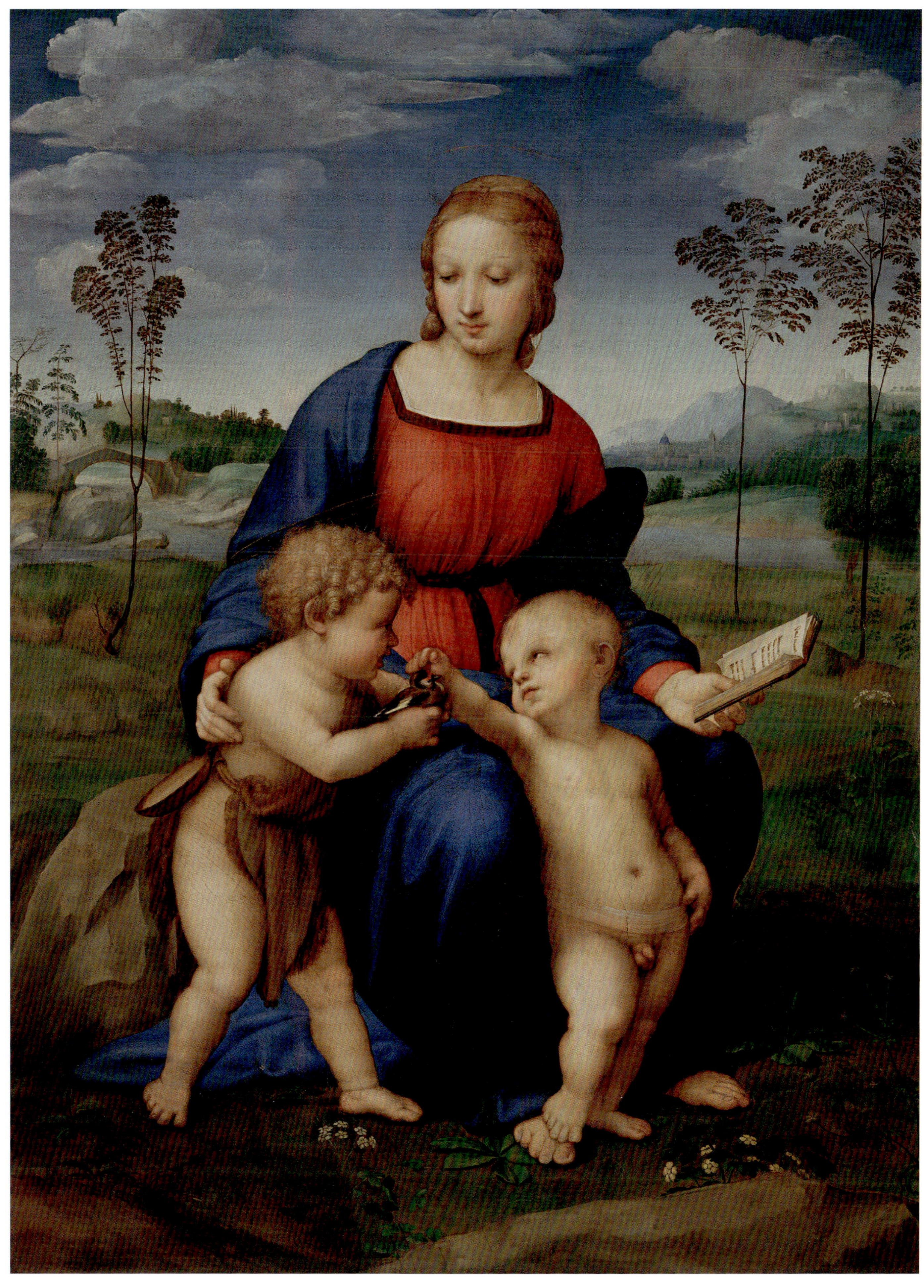

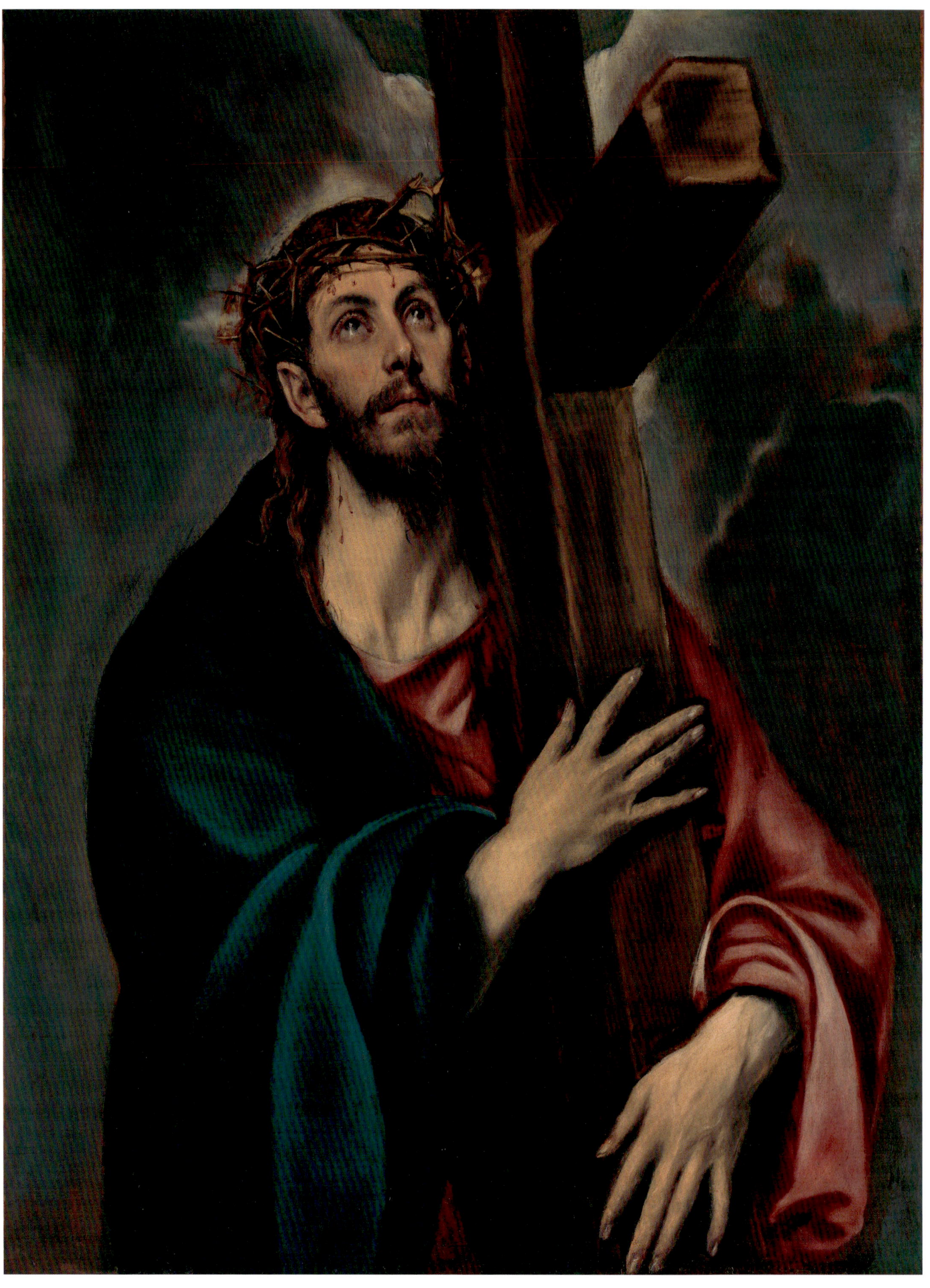

dancers from the community at specific events. Miniature models of these *katsinam* (called *katsintithu*) are carved from cottonwood root and given by a mother's brothers to uninitiated girls at specific ceremonies in the spring and summer, not as toys but as aids to learning the attributes of the some 200 *katsinam* inhabiting their cosmos.[14]

By providing explanations for what causes things to happen, religions also implicitly create opportunities for individuals and communities to interact with these supernatural forces or structures and, perhaps, intervene in and influence events. These interventions are expressed through rituals; some cause change (making it rain, for example, or curing illness), while others maintain the proper order of things (keeping the cosmos chugging along as it should or ensuring that individuals understand and fulfill their changing roles in the community over the course of their lives). Ritual practice thus provides some degree of agency for humans otherwise adrift in an indifferent world, letting them control or influence the forces shaping their experience. One indication of the importance of such agency is that all religions—no matter how omnipotent or beneficent the deity or deities involved—believe that worship and ritual impacts how supernatural beings or forces act on the natural world. Cosmogonies explain why the universe came to be and how it works, but in most religions, some degree of human intervention is needed for it to continue, if for no other reason than to keep the gods from punishing humans for their lack of interest. Most religions include a *memento mori* function, as in this ancient Peruvian stirrup

cup, which is a reminder of human mortality and a promise of either rebirth, afterlife, or redemption from death by divine means (**17**).

But how does one speak to the transcendent, intercede with the numinous? Whether simple or elaborate, rituals create a context in which gods or spirits listen. In some cases, such as certain Haudenosaunee mask rituals, the mask itself is imbued with power and gives the wearer the ability to act on behalf of certain supernatural forces. In others, such as the transubstantiation of the bread and wine used in the Catholic Mass, the ritual summons the deity and transforms these substances into his body and blood, which is consumed by the community of faithful as an act of communion (as noted below, more complexly organized societies with hierarchies of rights and specializations of function tend to have sacerdotal rites, in which a religious specialist, such as a priest, must officiate). Often specific words, ceremonies, or songs must be used, and knowledge of these actions and their proper use is frequently restricted to specific groups or individuals. And in some cases, certain objects or bundles are required for the actions to have effect—tangible, sacral objects that are understood to have power in their own right. In much Native American belief, sacred bundles are necessary to specific rituals; their contents are closely guarded and have symbolic associations that may limit usage to particular clans or group members. Current understandings of the Craig Mound at Spiro, Oklahoma, the source of a remarkable

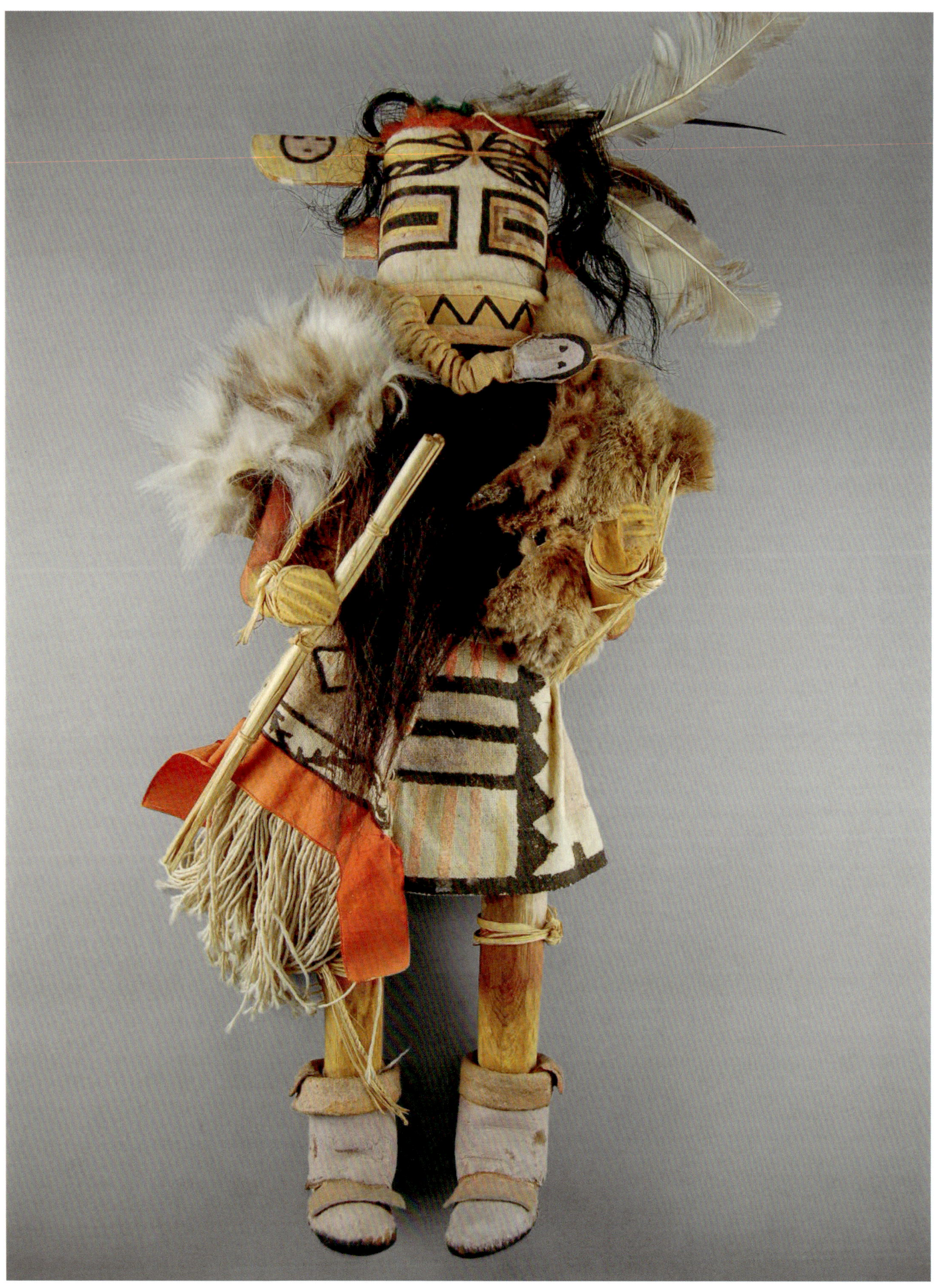

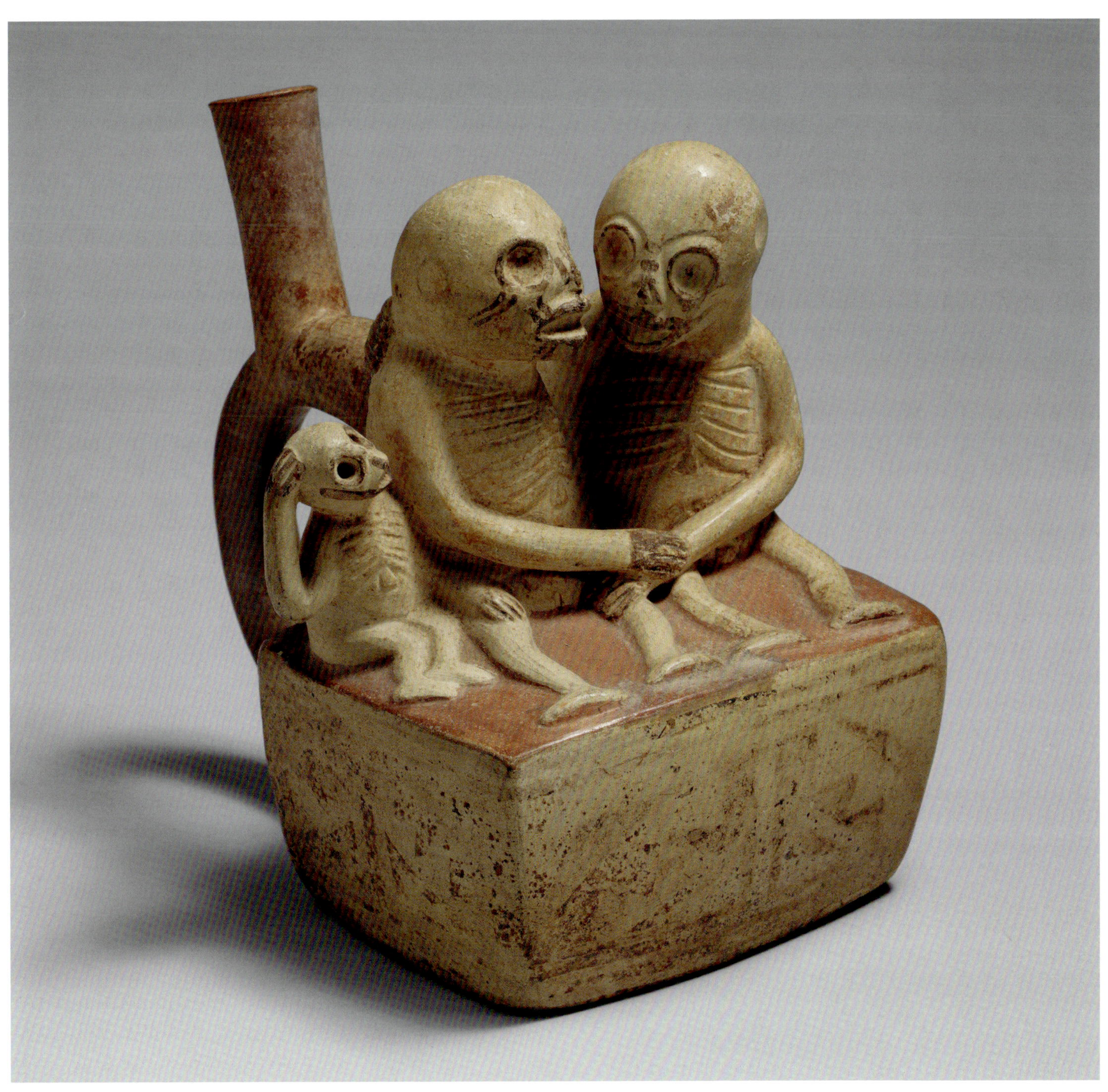

collection of late prehistoric ritual art, suggest the objects were talismans of considerable age, brought together from a broad region and arranged as a tableau or diorama recapitulating the cosmogonic origins of creation to revitalize a society facing severe stress. While the resulting tableau includes objects that may be sacred bundles, the entire assemblage may itself have served as a large-scale bundle.

Through ritual, believers can both interpret the will of supernatural spirits and learn—and perhaps alter—the course of events. One of the most widespread forms of such rituals is cleromancy or sortilege, in which decisions are made on the basis of casting lots. This can range from simple decision-making based on a binary outcome (e.g., heads or tails), to complex interpretations based on arrangements and patterns. In much of central Africa, basket divination was common. In this ritual a diviner would shake a basket containing a range of objects and interpret the meaning of the resulting pattern. In Cameroon, traditional diviners use a range of casting techniques, including leaf cards, which could be interpreted after being cast or placed in a vessel with an animal (often a ground spider, which was held to have magical properties), and the cards' displacement and rearrangement interpreted. Somatomancy interprets body parts (e.g., palm reading), theriomancy interprets the behavior of animals, haruspicy the entrails of sacrificed animals, horoscopy the positions of stars, and the list is nearly endless. Often the diviner employs knowledge of

context and tradition, replying with a series of cryptic or metaphorical phrases that allow meanings to be construed rather than clearly defined; anthropologist Victor Turner described such divination as a form of social analysis in which the diviner used his/her knowledge to bring hidden tensions or conflicts to light.[15] The Chinese *I Ching* book of divination (first written in the Western Zhou period, ca. 1000–750 BCE) is an obvious example, where the possible combinations of the thrown yarrow stalks relate to hexagrams with cosmological and moral implications connected to Daoist, Confucian, and Buddhist teachings. In the classical world, both the Delphic oracle of ancient Greece and the Sibylline Books of ancient Rome provided oracular guidance in notoriously cryptic forms, often with complex moral and didactic messages. Delphi has aspects of both prophecy and cleromancy, however; when Pythia, the oracle, was not available, inquirers could ask "yes/no" questions of the priests, who would cast colored beans to determine the answer.

Even the most elementary forms of divination may offer social benefits. Omar Khayyam Moore suggested that cleromancy regarding the location of game among the Labrador Naskapi hunters was crucial because while the results were essentially random, they were beneficial in a context where fixed hunting patterns could be dangerous.[16]

Whether such rituals represent magic or religion is largely a matter of definition. While some scholars see a sharp division between the two (James Frazer for

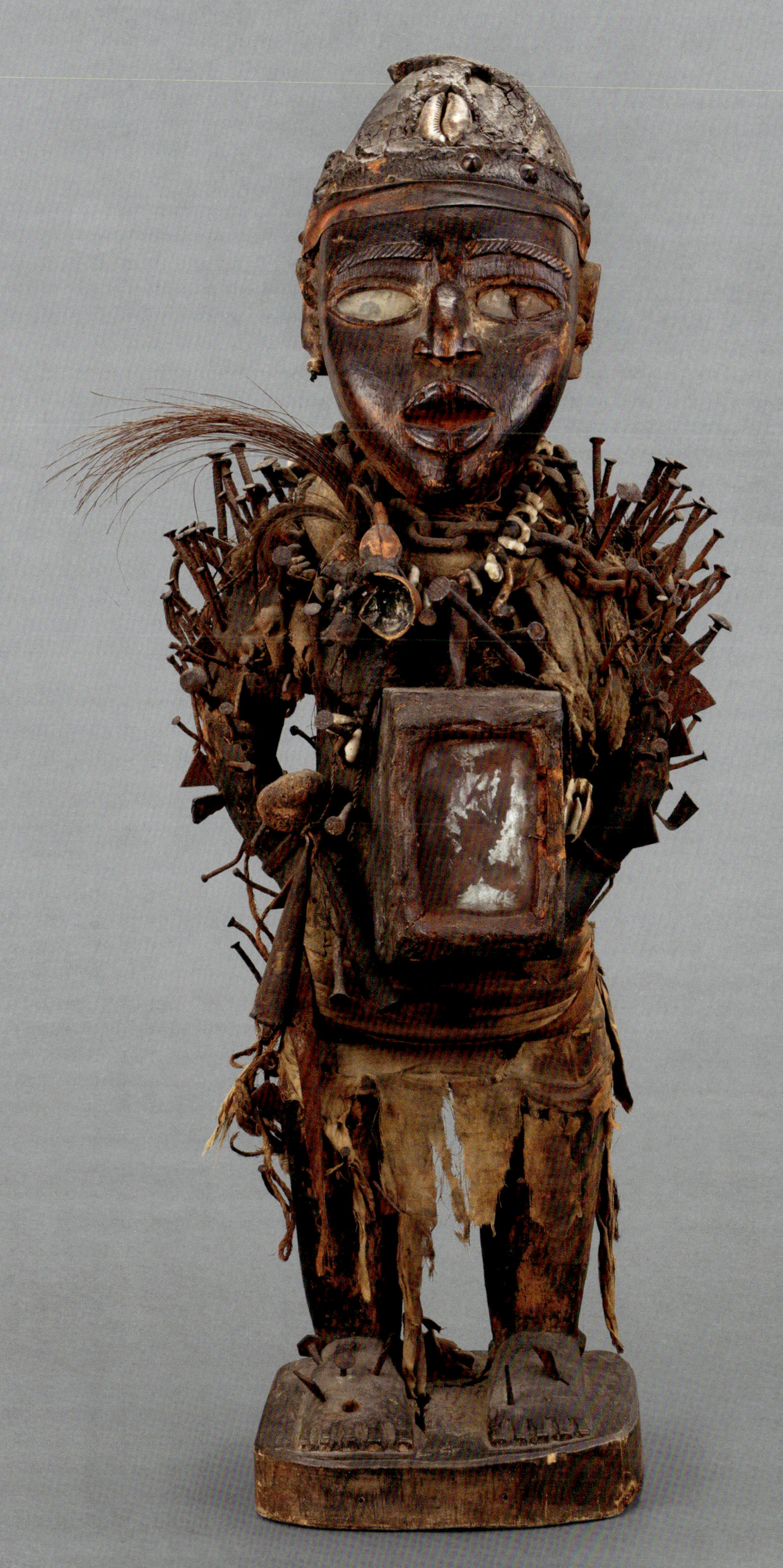

one), it may be more useful to see the distinction as one of socially specific categorization. Religion may be understood as the socially accepted and normative communal relationship with transcendental or uncanny powers, while magic marshals such forces for personal ends. Gods perform miracles and mortals perform magic, but both are part of the symbolic system religion encodes and encompasses.

Just as religions create and sustain social order by making conventions seem both natural and supernaturally sanctioned, ritual and supernatural powers punish the wayward. Consider, for example, the *minkisi* of the Yombe of the Congo (**18**). Each *nkisi nkondi* figure (*minkisi* figures are in the form of a human—others, like *nkisi kozo* taking the form of dogs, are also common) was produced by an artist, then transferred to a *nganga* (ritual specialist), who gave the lifeless artwork power by investing it with supernatural elements, including ritually important substances placed in the figure's head and belly. Objects—often nails or pieces of metal—are driven into the figure to solemnize oaths and settle disputes; the *nkisi nkondi* (literally "hunter spirit") ensures that these oaths are kept and malefactors punished, and the spirit represented by the figure is responsible for taking vengeance on the guilty. In ancient Greek belief, the *erinyes*, or furies, whose wrath could be called down upon those who violated covenants or the natural order of things, occupied the same role; and the Han dynasty Chinese *xiezhi* (a mythical creature with the inherent

ability to distinguish right and wrong, also known from Japan as *kaichi* or *shin'yo*) serves an equivalent function, and hence was traditionally depicted on public buildings as a symbol of justice.

Many societies also observe the converse: when misfortune befalls an individual or community, it is presumed to be punishment for an undisclosed sin or moral failure; moral failure in this context specifically means a failure to observe the normative rules of behavior specified within a given religious system of belief. There is no real difference between the Batswana belief that a thunderbolt killing an individual is proof of some prior misbehavior and an American televangelist blaming hurricane damage on a community's failure to follow Biblical precepts. Instead of assuming that supernatural forces will punish wrongdoers, both affirm the consequent and explain mischance as evidence of unseen misdeeds. For believers, this provides empirical proof of the efficacy of supernatural sanctions.

Sometimes misfortune is held to result not from mischance or punishment of hidden sins but from malevolence, and beliefs in witchcraft are widespread. In a highly influential study, E. E. Evans Pritchard argued that witchcraft among the Azande of South Sudan served to explain the relationship between humans and unfortunate events.[17] Nor was this mere credulity; if a structure fell down while people were inside, the Azande fully understood that its supports had been eaten by termites, but the moment of collapse and the

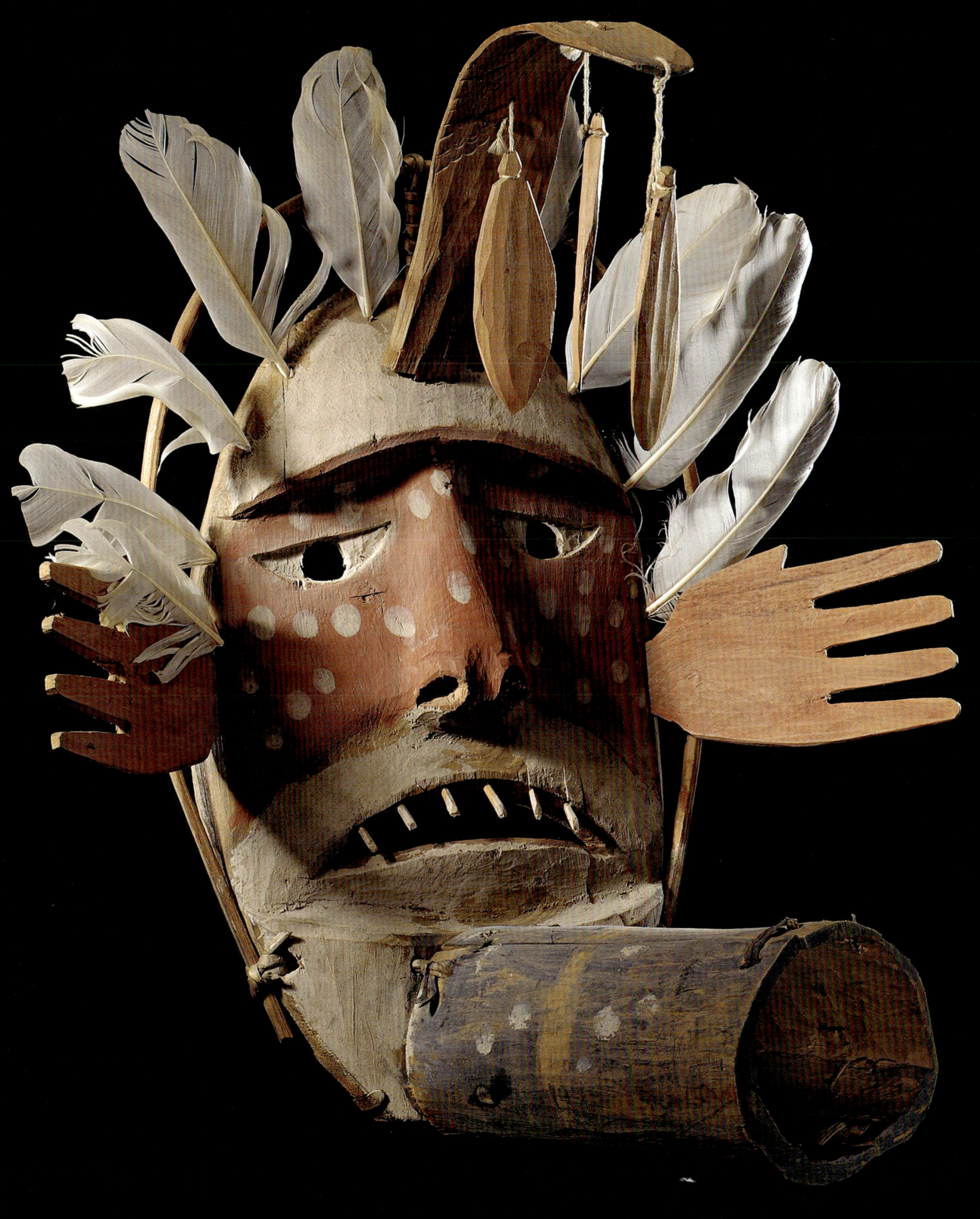

fact that people were inside at the time were explained as witchcraft. "Why" questions admit to multiple answers. Both the act of witchcraft and its punishment are ritual acts, allowing societies to address the "why me?" questions widely felt in times of misfortune in terms of their larger religious symbolic systems. Witchcraft also serves as a means of indirectly regulating conduct and maintaining social norms, since antisocial acts or disruptive attitudes may engender accusations of witchcraft and their accompanying sanctions. Witchcraft need not actually take place for its indirect effects to be felt.

While most religions are deeply concerned with morality, at least in the sense of codes of proper behavior, this does not always equate to supernatural notions of good and evil. Certainly, some religions are strongly dualistic. Zoroastrian cosmology of the Sassanid Empire (the last Iranian empire before the Muslim conquests of the seventh to eighth centuries) places the evil Ahriman as the opponent of the beneficent and omniscient—but not omnipotent—Ahura Mazda, with the natural world being contested between the two (although other forms of Zoroastrianism are more overtly monotheistic, with Ahriman occupying a lesser role).[18] Much Christian thought finds evil a deeply problematic concept, one that is at odds with an omnipotent deity, and evil is often treated less as a thing in itself than the absence of good. Many Native American societies have hero twin stories, by contrast, and while one of the twins may

be associated with chaos and wildness, and the other with order and humanity, they are rarely treated as inherently good or bad and often cosmic order depends on their juxtaposition. Many communities see spirits or supernatural beings as neither good nor bad but powerful and giving shape to events. Yup'ik masked dancing serves to make the numinous realm of spirits visible and facilitates the movement of beings between worlds (**19**). Frequently deities exhibit both positive and negative aspects; in Hindu thought deities (but especially Vishnu) may have a whole series of avatars that are expressed at different times or in different contexts (**20**). Hindu iconography often depicts deities with superhuman traits, showing both their superiority over humans and different simultaneous aspects of their divinity, such as maker and breaker, creator and destroyer.

An expectation of reciprocity applies in most societies; when one asks, one must also give, and seeking to placate, propitiate, or gain benefits from otherworldly powers may require a sacrifice. Indeed, the English term derives from the Latin *sacra* (sacred object) and *facere* (to perform). While sacrifice is common around the world and appears in most religious practice, both its logic and its form vary considerably. Gifts of value, either made of precious materials or requiring a large investment of time or skill, are one form of sacrifice. Sometimes the gift creates a reciprocal obligation (such as the celebrated *kula* exchange rings of the Trobriand Islands and nearby

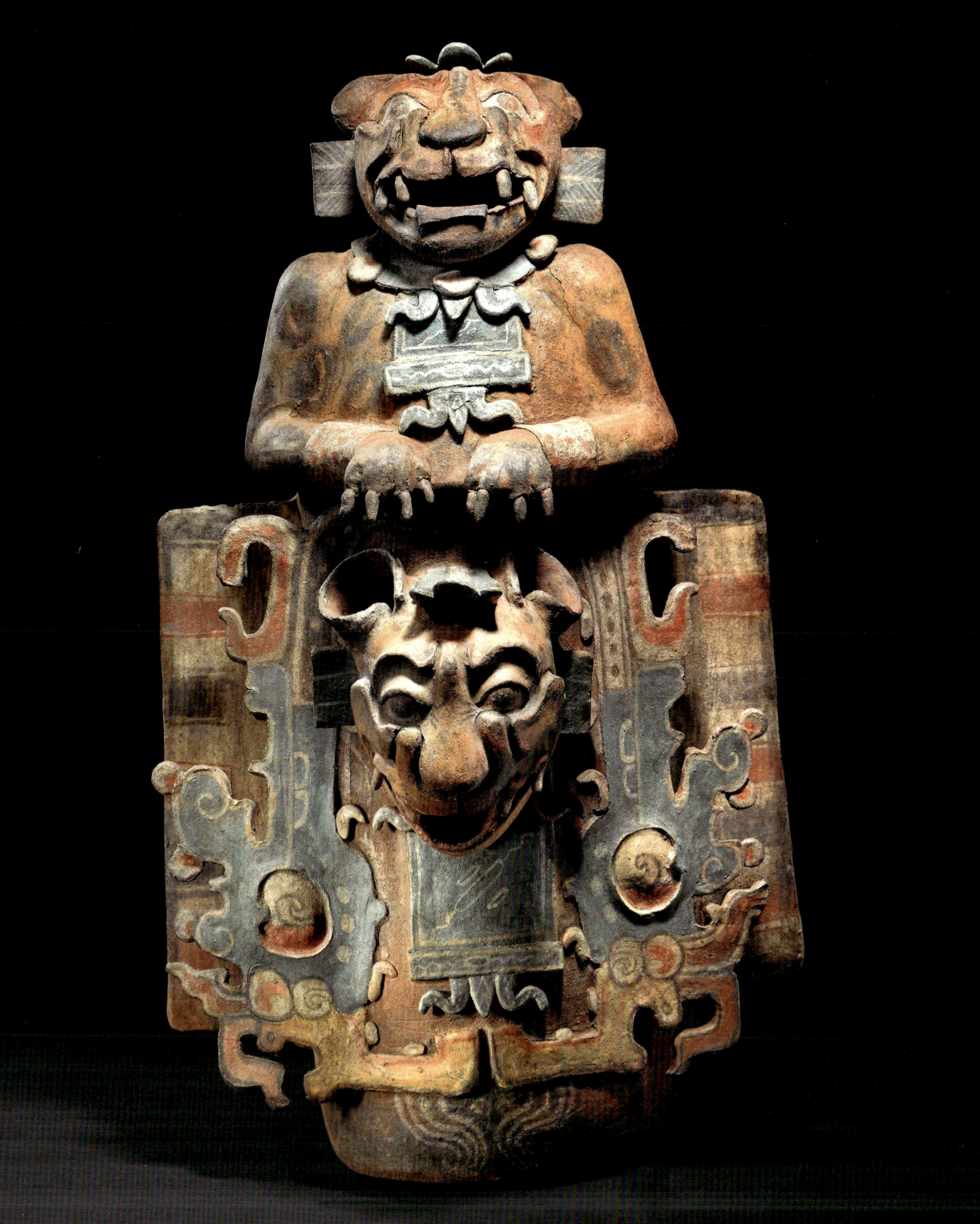

and incense use in religious ritual is common throughout East and South Asia. Islam and Christianity include incense in liturgies and worship, and Judaism uses it as part of the *havdalah* ceremony ending Shabbat (the Jewish sabbath), as well as retaining the formula for the *ketoret* incense used only in the Temple, held against the day of its rebuilding. Many—perhaps most—Native American societies use incense or smoke as a central element in ritual, often in the form of cedar, sweetgrass, or sage, to bless and purify. Mesoamerican societies used incense in similar ways, and Mesoamerican art often depicts the clouds of smoke that were believed to carry messages to divinities or ancestors and to bring answers back, and that served as visual metaphors for clouds and rain. In Aztec belief incense was such an important offering that the *tlamacazqui* priests burned it nine times daily; the midnight ceremony was so important that every priest was to wake at midnight to offer incense and blood through autosacrifice. For the Maya, incense fed the gods and ancestors, and as the world's *axis mundi* was believed to be a great ceiba tree, *incensarios* (censers) in the shape of the great ceiba trees allowed the smoke to follow the world tree to the heavens, while those in the shape of jaguars recalled the Jaguar God of Terrestrial Fire, also associated with the underworld and said to represent the night sun and the passage of the sun through the hours of darkness (**26**).

Capturing the ineffable in physical form challenges artists in all cultures. For some, the act itself becomes problematical, and some societies develop prohibitions on depicting the sacred or, like much of Islam, on most forms of representational art. This was not always the case, however, as Islamic art includes triumphs of both representation and technical achievement, and it boasts a particularly rich tradition of figural manuscript and miniature illustration, as in this depiction of courtly life from mid-sixteenth century Iran (**27**). One method for depicting sanctity is the halo, which is used for largely analogous iconographic purposes by Hindu, Buddhist, Christian, Egyptian, ancient Roman, and ancient Greek artists, although the full semantic meaning and significance varies. In Eastern Orthodox Christianity this debate over meaning contributed to the fourteenth-century schismatic Hesychast controversy concerning the "uncreated light" emanating from Christ at the transfiguration at Mount Tabor, and haloes were held to be depictions or manifestations of this sacred "Tabor light."[20]

Art does not merely represent the divine but can also summon it. The Hindu concept of *darshan* (from the Sanskrit for "viewing") treats the seeing of a representation of the divine as a reciprocal act—the viewer beholds the divinity and the divinity beholds and blesses the viewer. One looks at Ganesha and Ganesha looks back; art becomes a means of mediation between the human and the divine (**28**). While *darshan* is an unusually clear expression of this idea, it is widespread in religious art. The Byzantine Empire was divided from 726–843 by contention over the sanctity of icons. Veneration of icons was a key part of eastern Christian belief, but opponents (iconoclasts) argued it fetishized objects and verged on idolatry; the eventual restoration of icons by Empress

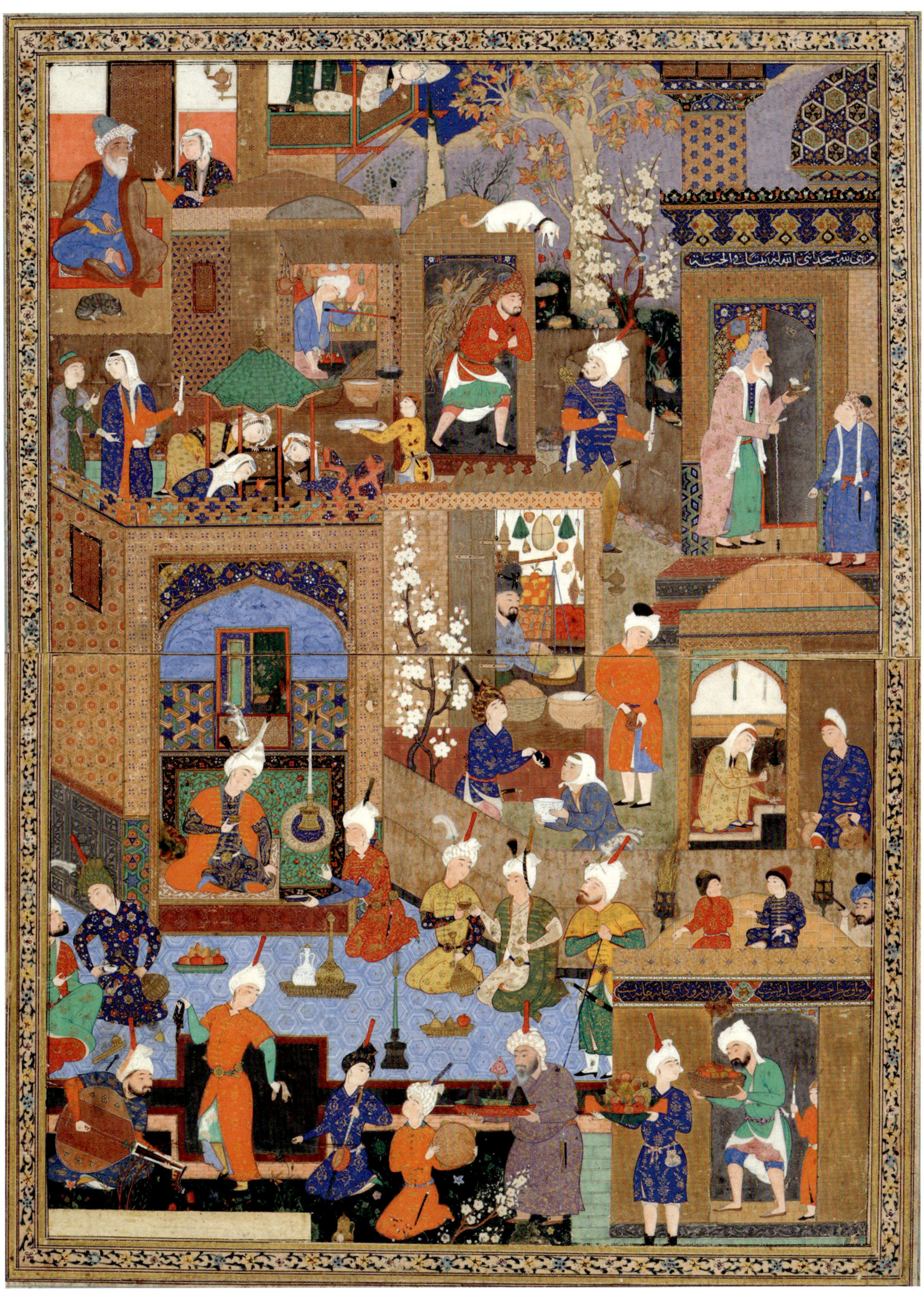

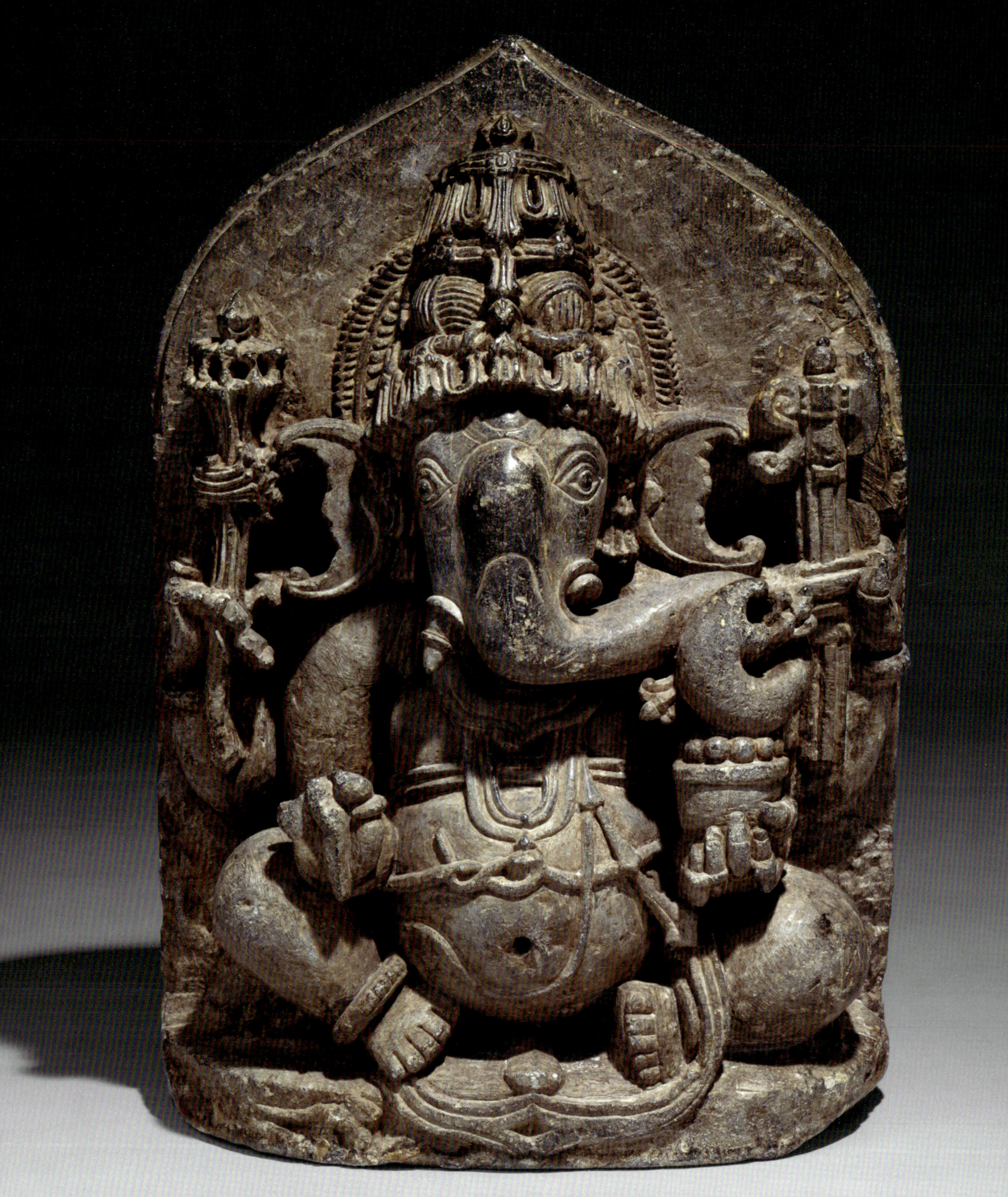

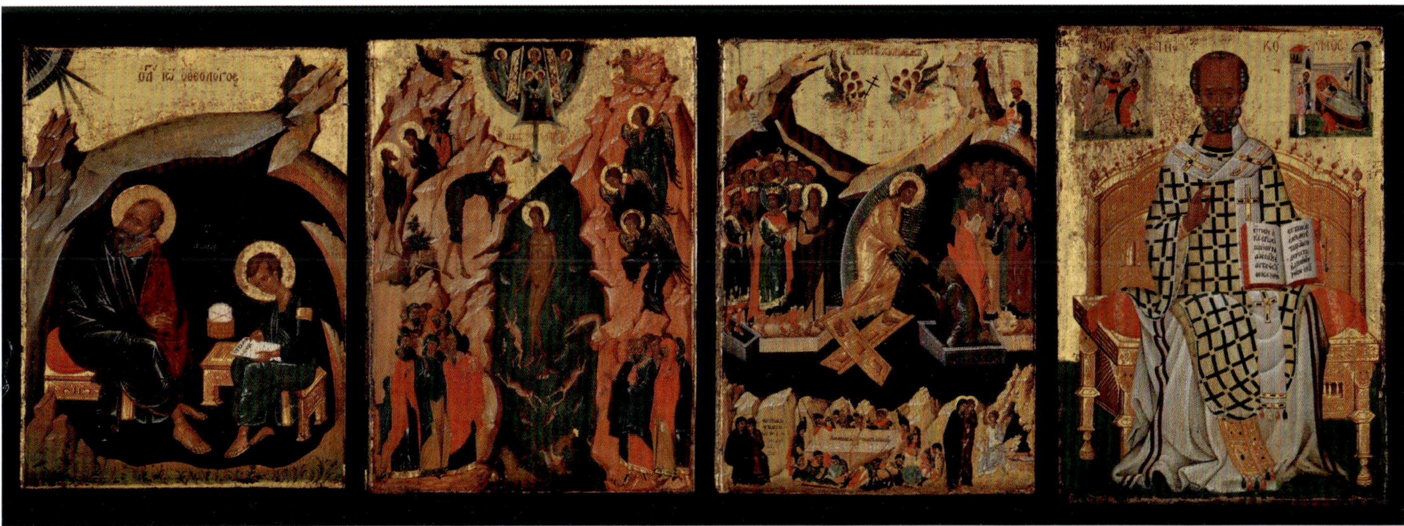

Theodora in 843 is still celebrated in the Eastern Church as the Feast of Orthodoxy (**29**). Within medieval European Christianity, Abbot Suger (1081–1151) of St.-Denis in France argued that beautiful art and the light-filled architecture of the Gothic style elevated the mind so it could properly approach and accept the numinous.

The possession of tangible sacred objects also provides legitimacy for both the social order and, at least in more complex societies, for the persons occupying positions of power. In Japan, the imperial regalia—the Three Sacred Treasures—are said to be the sword presented by Susoo to Amaterasu to placate her anger, and the gem and mirror that lured her from the cave where she had withdrawn in her anger, plunging the world into darkness; these were later given to her grandson Ninigi-no-Mikoto, grandfather of Japan's first emperor, and are still presented to the new emperor as part of his accession. In Britain, perhaps the most sacred piece of the coronation regalia is the twelfth-century spoon used to anoint the monarch with holy oil; its sacrality is partly due to the fact that it is the only piece of the older monarchic regalia that escaped destruction during the Commonwealth. This anointing is part of the complex myth of European divine kingship that Ernst Kantorowicz called the king's two bodies: 1) a body natural, subject to age, infirmity and death; and 2) a body politic, mystical, unseen, and transcendent.[21]

Divine kingship is nearly ubiquitous in monarchical societies, as it works at several levels. First, it provides a religious foundation for secular power, buttressing the exercise of physical force with moral authority. Second, it makes disloyalty to the monarch not simply treason but blasphemy, a point newly Anglicanized preachers were instructed to emphasize by their Tudor masters in sixteenth-century England. Treachery against one's husband in Tudor England was petty treason, but treachery against one's monarch was high treason and thereby an offense against god; familial, political and ritual hierarchies all became mutually reinforcing.

Objects can also have power in their own right. Many cultures have accounts of objects of power, and anthropologist Alfred Gell suggested that in many societies, art objects, once created, have their own agency and foster instrumental action.[22] By their technical virtuosity and command of the symbolic systems shared by artist and viewer, they create interactions, obligations, and shared intentionality. Trobriand canoe prows, for example, are treated as cognitive traps that captivate the viewer's mind through manipulation of their shared aesthetic and symbolic grammar—a form of object-based magic, if you will. Ritual art objects, once created, go about and do things.

While each religion represents a symbolic system as unique and dynamic as its community of practice, and most have multiple layers of nuance and esoteric detail, commonality of belief is profound and constantly leads to the recombination of different religious elements or to the adoption of beliefs and symbols from one religion or community into another. Sometimes this practice is intentional; different tribes of the North American Plains in the nineteenth century grafted new rituals from neighboring groups onto existing practices as a way of creating linkages between communities. Similarly, the early spread of Christianity in the Levant and Europe was aided by co-opting existing sacred places and holidays—All Saints Day/All Souls Day, for example, borrows traditions from Celtic Samhain (the harvest festival that also marks the autumnal equinox and the turn from days of light to days of darkness), including its conflation with Halloween, since Celtic day-reckoning begins the night before.

Sometimes the process results from one group viewing the sacred representations of another group and reinterpreting them through their own lenses—not absorbing or sharing beliefs, but simply appropriating the iconography of another religion and reinterpreting it in their own symbolic terms. The so-called Ram in the Thicket—a famous work recovered from archaeological excavations of the Sumerian Ubaid-period royal cemeteries at Ur (modern Tell el-Muqayyar in Iraq; the burial context dates to ca. 2600 BCE)—bears that name because the excavator interpreted a depiction of a goat feeding in a tree in terms of his own Biblical tradition of Abraham's sacrifice of a ram caught by his horns in a thicket, rather than its original Sumerian iconography invoking Inanna/Ishtar, whose symbol is the eight-pointed flower decorating the tree, and her consort Dumuzi/Tammuz, whose symbol is the goat. The cult of Inanna/Tammuz survived in some areas until the eighteenth century; like the myth of Persephone, the myth of Innana and Tammuz explains seasonality as Innana's annual consignment to and return from the underworld (in some versions Tammuz annually returns). But because religion makes a given view of the world seem natural and certain, the excavator (Sir Leonard Woolley) saw the work in terms of his own Christian religious beliefs rather than the beliefs of the artisans who crafted it or the elite individuals with whom it was buried.

Frazer and others argued that this myth of the dying-and-returning-god was universal, but more recent scholarship sees it as a core feature of Near Eastern religions and mystery cults that is not shared worldwide.[23] Even in the case of Inanna and Tammuz, its role is controversial, and some versions of the myth have one or the other god being continually reborn while in others the death is final. This points to a core problem in examining commonalities in religion (and many other cultural traits): since religion represents a symbolic system, communities living in close proximity or having close historical or ancestral connections are likely to share elements because of contact and contingency rather than universalist commonality. And the links can be indirect: French and Russian military units of the nineteenth century carried or wore eagles to ritually recall the legions of Rome, while British units wore them to ritually commemorate capturing French eagles at the Battle of Waterloo against Napoleon in 1815.

This familiar process of syncretism—of religious borrowing or convergence—was extensive in some societies; the Roman Republic and later Roman Empire constantly absorbed new deities into its pantheon, sometimes by simple addition, and often by recombining elements from different religious traditions and linking them to existing deities. Roman deities mirror the main Greek pantheon (Zeus/Jupiter, Ares/Mars, and so on), but with countless lesser divinities linked to places and peoples conquered and assimilated. In Roman-era Egypt, for example, "polytheophoric" personal names combining two or more gods became commonplace from the second to fourth centuries, with separate deities such as Hermanubis emerging as composites of the Greek god Hermes and the Egyptian god Anubis, distinct deities that shared certain roles and functions in the cosmopolitan belief systems of Ptolemaic Egypt (**30**). While many empires allow territories to retain local deities, they need not be as intensely syncretic as Rome; one of the first schools of ethnography was established in ancient China so officials could understand the territories they governed without fully syncretizing their various symbolic systems.

Few topics have been the focus of more diverse, contradictory, and, for the most part, purely ethnocentric scholarly attention than the classification of religions. What seems to unite such efforts is an assumption that the author's religious beliefs, whatever they may be, are the most advanced and sophisticated. Linguist Max Müller and theologian Cornelius Tiele offered influential classificatory systems in the late nineteenth and early twentieth century, the former organizing historical relationships along racialist lines, the latter creating a graduated scale based on increasing concern with ethical and universally redemptive doctrines.[24] During roughly the same period, E. B. Tylor developed evolutionary theories positing animism, or the belief in

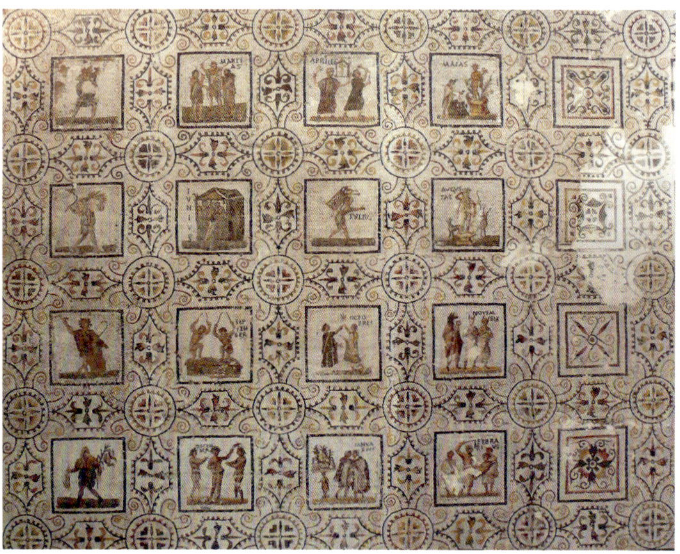

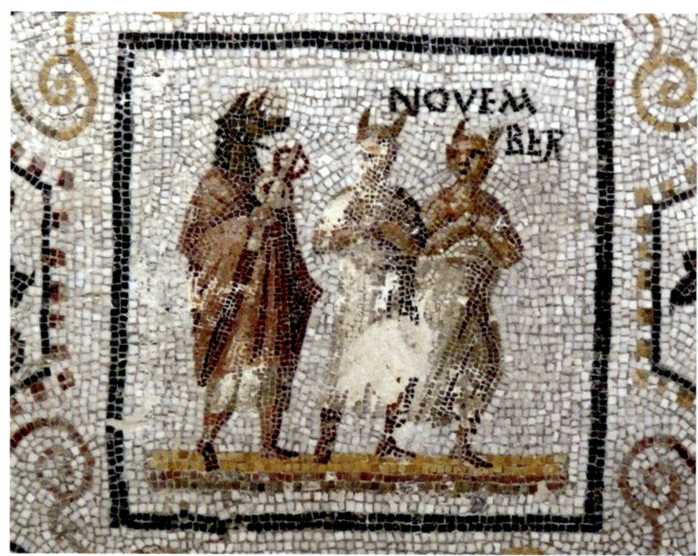

spirits or spiritual beings, as the most primitive form of religion,[25] while James Frazer developed a more elaborated evolutionary schema of religion moving from magic to religion to science.[26] More recently, Joseph Campbell proposed an evolutionary classification that largely paralleled cultural evolutionary formulations current during the same period in American cultural anthropology with his "Way of the Animal Powers" (shamanism and animal totems) corresponding to bands and tribes such as the "Hopewellian" occupants of Ohio some two thousand years ago, who created this mica cutout (**31**);[27] "Way of the Seeded Earth" (agrarian cultures focusing on mother goddess and fertility rituals) corresponding to more complexly organized tribes and chiefdoms; "Way of the Celestial Lights" (city states with pantheons of ruling gods, and a shift to masculine gods) corresponding to early states; and "Way of Man" (more individual-centric

religions and philosophies focusing on psycho-spiritual rather than literal-historical beliefs) associated with empires and modern states.[28] Unsurprisingly given Campbell's own scholarly interests and training, his classification is biased toward Old World societies and the development of both Western intellectual traditions and the six most widespread latter-day world religions.

Do religions evolve? Geertz's definition as reformulated here offers a partial answer. Because religions are symbol systems that make a particular social order seem given, they are closely and necessarily linked to how societies are organized. Societies characterized by gathering and hunting tend to have religion and rituals focusing on animal spirits and the immanence of place; these are the meaningful contexts of their lived experience. This does not, however, equate to simplistic. Aboriginal Australian kinship systems, for example, are among the

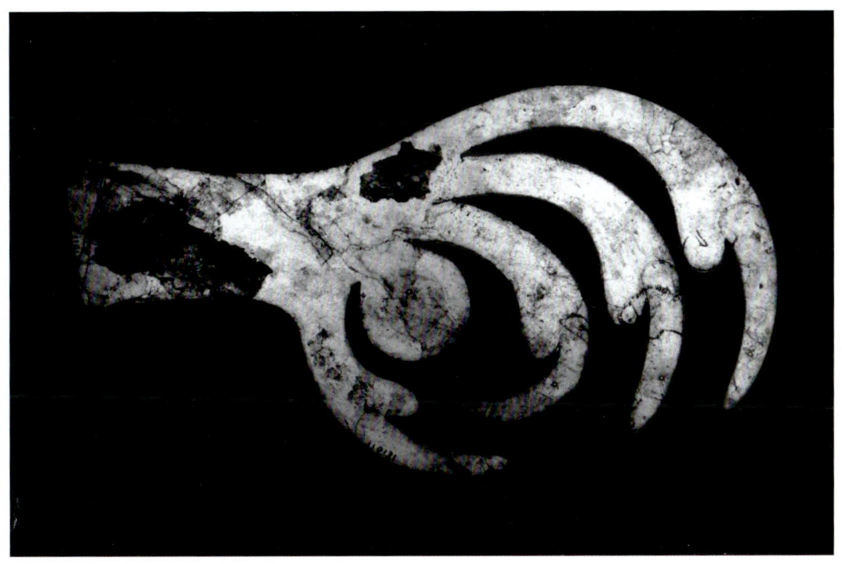

31 Eagle Foot Effigy

Woodland, Hopewell cultures,
United States
200 BCE – 500 CE
Mica (mineral dust)
Field Museum of Natural
History, Chicago

most complex in the world and corresponding religious conceptions encompassing places, obligations, and relationships linked to these elaborate classificatory systems are equally nuanced. Dreamtime and songlines enact and reflect a rich tapestry of landscapes, descent groups, rights, and obligations every bit as nuanced and complex as those of more hierarchical societies. Such societies generally do not have economic specialization, thus while there may be considerable esoteric knowledge associated with religious beliefs, its forms are generally related to the experiences and economies of the community and adepts are part-time religious specialists.

Much of religious practice and ritual involves mediating between humans and spirits, with individuals particularly skilled at such mediation in non-agricultural societies generally categorized by scholars as "shamans." The term itself comes from Evenki Tungus herders/hunters of Siberia, but it has been applied more broadly to religious practitioners who mediate between human and spirits, providing healing, divination, identification and punishment of wrongdoers, and correction of social wrongs or shortages, often through rituals characterized by trance states and spirit guides. While generally associated with herders and hunters, more complex societies often include shamanic practice; ancient Marajo chiefdoms in lowland Brazil, for example, seem to have had a long tradition of female shamans. Scholars who study religions of this kind are divided regarding why it arises and seems widespread. One school argues that it provides valuable benefits to the community because through altered states of consciousness and cognition, ritual practitioners are better able to synthesize subtle cues to resolve group conflicts, cure individual maladies, or predict the location of game.[29] The other school grants

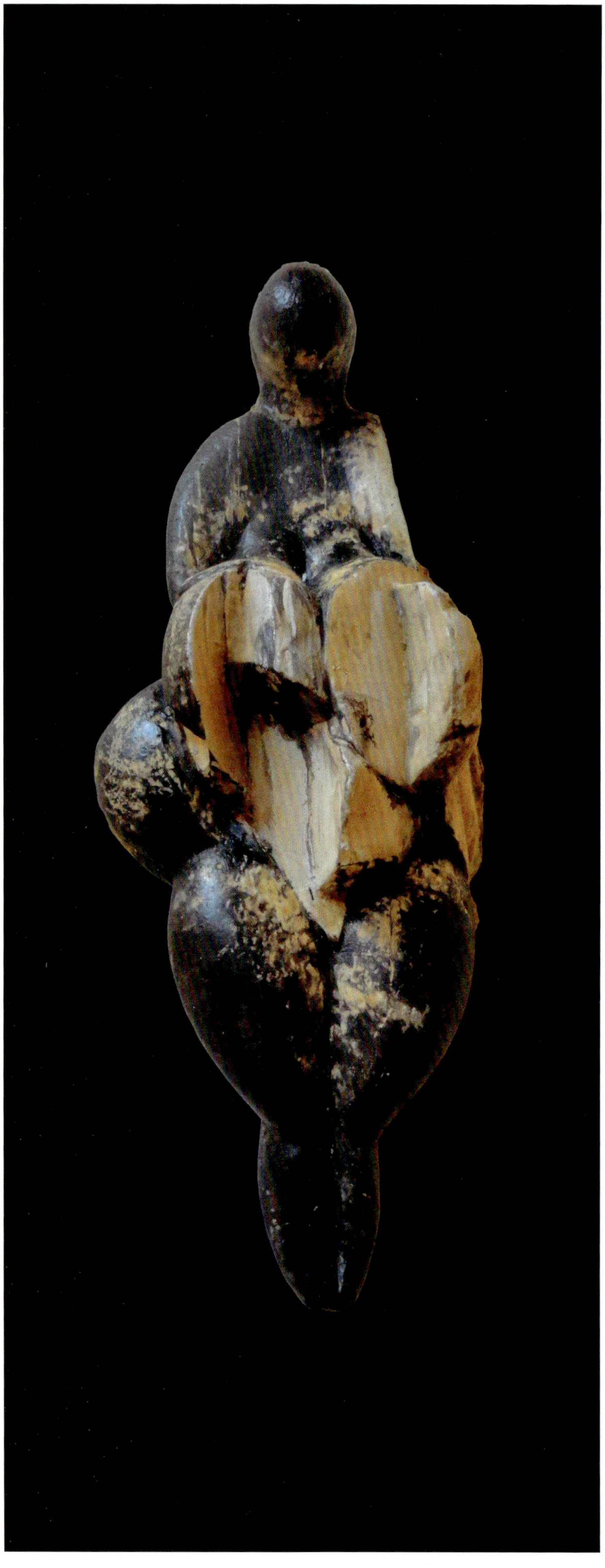

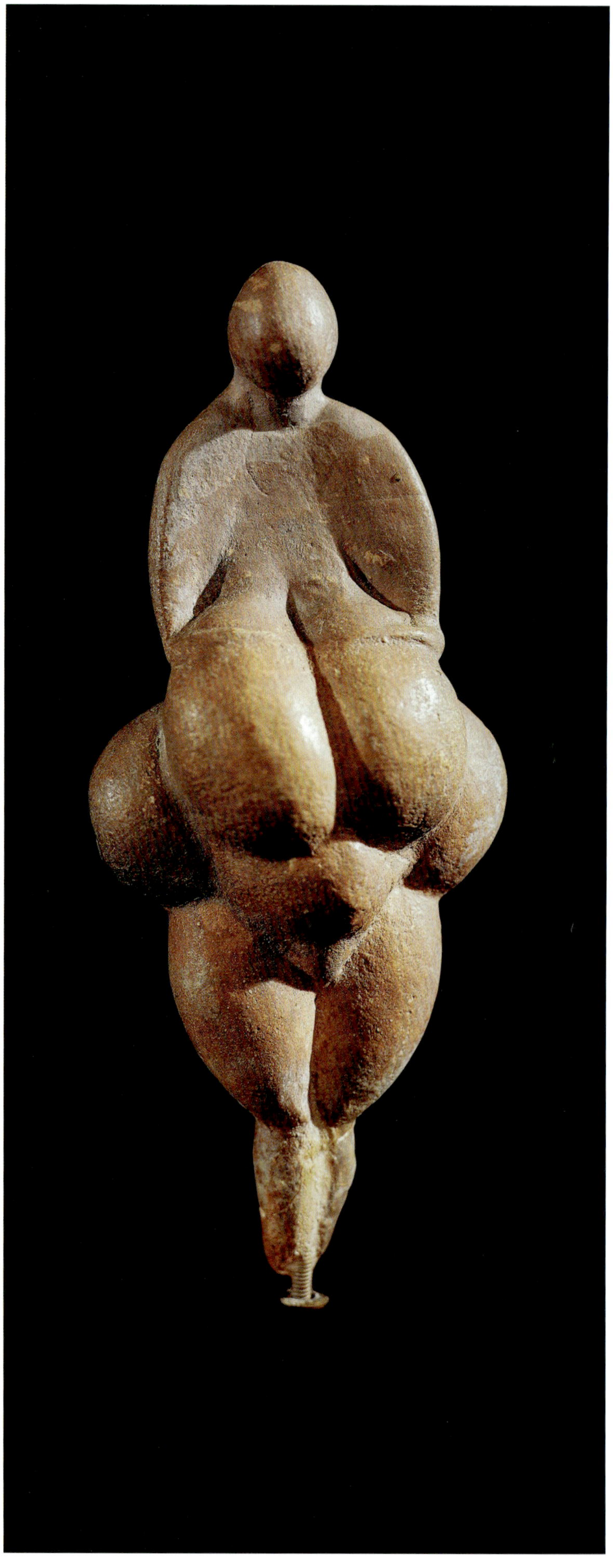

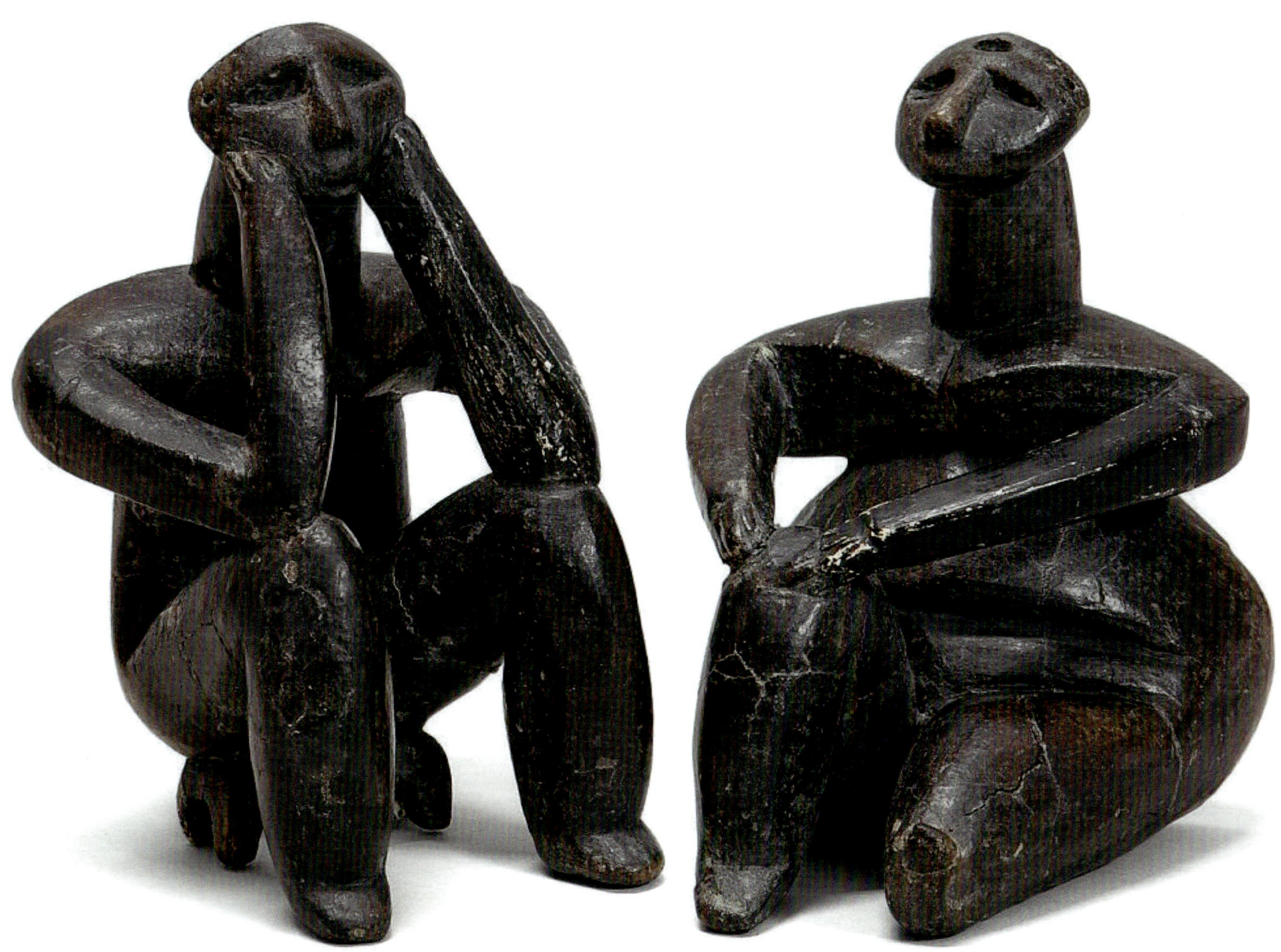

these benefits to the community but argues that they arise because of the community's belief rather than through the efficacy of the ritual practitioner.[30]

More sedentary societies, and those practicing agriculture, tend toward religions and rituals focusing on fertility and fecundity of the soil; just as all aspects of the environment may be personified and imbued with spiritual importance in communities based on gathering and hunting, communities based on agriculture focus belief and rituals on seasons, weather, and the apotheosis of agricultural production in all its applicable forms. Campbell and other scholars—most notably Marija Gimbutas—suggested such societies focus on a mother goddess as a widely shared trait (**32**), eventually displaced by male-dominated deities or pantheons.[31] Gimbutas went so far as to argue for a matriarchal and female-focused Neolithic culture shared across Europe that was displaced by patriarchal Bronze Age Indo-Europeans from the Pontic steppes (the plains north of the Black and Caspian seas), who introduced societies dominated by male warriors. In some respects, Gimbutas's theories echo those of Johann Jakob Bachofen, who argues for a similar sequence of promiscuity to matriarchy to patriarchy in *Das Mutterrecht* (1861), but focused archaeological work has not supported these ideas. Part of the problem may lie in assuming societies must be dominated by one or the other gender instead of including roles for each. Figurines from a Romanian Neolithic site (Hamangia culture, ca. 5000 BCE) are some of the earliest depictions of introspection and are commonly interpreted as matching

male and female figures, although the gender of the "male" figure is actually ambiguous (**33**). Campbell seems to have adopted Gimbutas's theory because it allowed a more compelling evolutionary schema (animism to matriarchies to patriarchies to individualism), but it does not fit available evidence. As roles become more specialized, religious practitioners become full-time, and as the specialization process continues, sacerdotal religions—in which a separate priesthood is required for ceremonies and to mediate between humans and spirits—emerge. And since religious symbolic systems are enmeshed in the ways society as a whole is organized, with this emergence comes sacerdotal states in which the leader is not only divinely appointed but the focal point of the belief system.

Campbell's next posited stage focuses on city states and celestial knowledge. Like many scholarly categorizations, his distinctions work better for Mediterranean and European histories than those of other regions. Ancient Mesoamerican beliefs among groups including the Maya and Aztec were profoundly focused on agriculture, sacrifice, and regeneration, but these beliefs were inseparably bound to celestial observations and cycles using sophisticated and precise astronomical calculations; they do not comfortably fit the Apollonian, classical civilization mode assumed by Campbell's schema. His final stage optimistically sees religion and ritual in personal terms of spiritual or psychological growth. In some ways Campbell's evolutionary schema simply recapitulates his separation of the four roles of religion and ritual, with different stages embodying or amplifying each.

Such efforts to find commonality across cultures for the substance of belief have proven controversial, in part because of the ease of picking out details that suggest similarities that would not be apparent in a more complete context (cherry-picking one's data), and because of uncertainty as to whether beliefs are shared through universal underlying structures or simply because of contact, diffusion, and imitation between groups (questioning the independence of samples being compared—also known as Galton's Problem and first posed in the late nineteenth century in response to anthropologist E. B. Tylor's cross-cultural comparisons). While it is possible to place religions along an evolutionary schema, they are better understood as adaptations or accommodations to the ways in which societies are organized, and societies with more economic specialization and social hierarchies have correspondingly more specialized and hierarchical religious systems and associated rituals. Over time communities may become more or less specialized or hierarchical; while religious and ritual systems are likely to change in response, they do so more slowly because of the contingency of social changes and the lag effect of social tradition.

Roy Rappaport suggests that language and ritual are necessarily linked, not as envelope and message, but because ritual blunts the two deadly fangs with which language threatens social order.[32] Language allows enormous creativity, but for all its adaptive benefits it also allows two vices: 1) the ability to lie; and 2) the ability to imagine other versions of doctrine. Ritual creates public performances of statements that simultaneously say (communicate) and perform (enact) their truth. In his conception ritual creates the armature of actionable, reliable semantic reality on which the social order is hung. If religion is a symbol system making the world meaningful and intelligible, ritual utterance serves as the guarantor that the symbols are shared and not endlessly encoded and recoded by each participant.

Religion and ritual thus play a number of simultaneous roles. First, they make the unknown meaningful. Individual knowledge is limited and the natural world can seem bleak and cruel. Religion offers metaphysical explanations that invoke something greater, something transcendent, irrespective of how that concept is mediated within a given society. By explaining why the world exists and how it operates, religion's cosmological function also offers a blueprint for how to make changes or influence events. If one knows what—or perhaps more precisely who—brings back the summer's warmth, one knows whose intercession or goodwill is required to chase the chill. Religions take the unknowable and random and give it purpose, and in doing so they offer the promise of influencing outcomes—or, in mundane and secular terms, of converting unpredictability into risks that can be addressed, whether those risks involve warfare or famine, childbirth or sickness.

Beliefs create and sustain social bonds, forging communities of practice and performance that leave societies more resilient and with an increased sense of group identity. This element is particularly important since it may explain, in part, the universality of religious belief. Regardless of the precise content of belief, participation in belief makes communities stronger and the ties binding people together more robust, so that rituals—at some level—always "work" and prove beneficial. The psychological function includes both charters for life's major transitions, simultaneously marked and mediated through rites of passage and through tropological metaphor between the epic quests of gods or heroes (which Campbell argues assume consistent cross-cultural forms) and one's own trials and tasks in achieving self-mastery.

Campbell's belief that the modern world shifts responsibility for these functions from religion to individual creators like artists and philosophers was warranted by *Star Wars* creator George Lucas, who credited the form of his Skywalker film cycle to the influence of Campbell's thought. *Star Wars* speaks to modern audiences because it serves the functions of ritual, largely by parroting and pirating its forms. Since religions as symbolic systems may serve ritual functions even when their content is ostensibly secular, this should come as no surprise, but it suggests that the common forms of ritual and belief meet a shared need and will persist. Whether these forms are universal and unchanging or constantly evolving as societies grow and transform is a far more complicated question—one perhaps only the gods can answer.

1   Elizabeth Colson, "In Good Years and in Bad: Food Strategies of Self-Reliant Societies," *Journal of Anthropological Research* 35, no. 1 (1979): 18–29.

2   Max Weber, *The Protestant Ethic and the Spirit of Capitalism*, trans. Talcott Parsons (New York: Charles Scribner and Sons, 1958).

3   Clifford Geertz, *The Interpretation of Cultures* (New York: Basic Books, 1973).

4   Edward Burnett Tylor, *Primitive Culture* (London: John Murray, 1871); James Frazer, *The Golden Bough: A Study in Comparative Religion* (London: Macmillan, 1890); Herbert Spencer, *Principles of Sociology* (London: Williams and Norgate, 1876); Emil Durkheim, *The Elementary Forms of the Religious Life*, trans. Joseph Swain (London: George Allen and Unwin, 1915).

5   Mircea Eliade, *The Myth of the Eternal Return: Cosmos and History* (Princeton: Princeton University Press, 1971).

6   Georges Dumézil, *Flamen-Brahman* (Paris: P. Geuthner, 1935).

7   The Julian calendar was introduced ca. 45 BCE and was used in Europe until at least the sixteenth century. It was succeeded by the Gregorian calendar, which more accurately tracked leap days and years; the new calendar was introduced in 1582 but not immediately accepted in some areas, and it was more than three hundred years before the Julian calendar was fully superseded.

8   The dispensationist rapture is a conservative Christian belief that Christ's return will be in two phases, beginning with a return for "his" saints (the Rapture, when the faithful will seem to vanish from the

temporal world), and a later return to reign. The Vaishnavist Kalki and Kali Yuga refer to the prophesied tenth and final incarnation of the Hindu god Vishnu, ending this cycle of existence. Brandon Carter introduced the Carter catastrophist model in the 1980s; it is a purely secular statistical model that shows, mathematically, that the human race is likely to go extinct soon. In part it reflects the built-in assumptions of Bayesian statistics, but while there are some compelling philosophical rebuttals to the argument, the math actually (and depressingly) works. It offers an interesting thought experiment in response to Max Weber's definition of religion as belief in a supernatural that cannot be scientifically explained, since it makes our continued existence as a species increasingly unexplainable by science—albeit not, I am happy to say, by philosophy.

9   Elman Service, *Primitive Social Organization: An Evolutionary Perspective* (New York: Random House, 1971).

10 Arnold van Gennep, *The Rites of Passage*, trans. Monika Vizedom and Gabrielle Caffee (Chicago: University of Chicago Press, 1960).

11 Mary Douglas, *Purity and Danger* (Harmondsworth: Penguin, 1966); Victor Turner, *The Forest of Symbols* (Ithaca: Cornell University Press).

12 John Keegan, *A History of Warfare* (New York: Random House, 1993).

13 Art historians, archaeologists, anthropologists, and other scholars focusing on tangible ritual forms have developed a copious literature on these canons and can sometimes identify fakes or forgeries because the replicator got the elements right without understanding the specific ways they needed to be combined. Alas, it is equally true that forgers can create works that pass inspection because they so closely exhibit the forms and features experts expect to see—sometimes from a close reading by the forger of the scholar's own works. Part of the archaeologist's concern over objects with unknown provenance is uncertainty over whether a work belongs to the canon or just successfully meets his or her expectations for it.

14 In response to growing market demand by non-Hopi for *katsintithu*, slightly altered versions that do not precisely represent the actual spirits are produced for sale.

15 Victor Turner, *Revelation and Divination in Ndembu Ritual: Symbol, Myth, and Ritual* (Ithaca: Cornell University Press, 1975).

16 Omar Khayyam Moore, "Divination: A New Perspective," *American Anthropologist* 59, no. 1 (1957): 69–74.

17 E. E. Evans Pritchard, *Witchcraft, Oracles and Magic Among the Azande* (Oxford: Clarendon Press, 1937).

18 Some sects of Christianity, such as Marcionism and Manichaeism, were ultimately denounced as heretical because they also accepted such dualism. They believed in a struggle between good and evil in ways that made the two forces seem balanced, leaving more canonical forms of Christianity to wrestle with the paradoxes of explaining evil in a world nominally ruled by a benevolent and omnipotent deity.

19 Joseph Watts, Oliver Sheehan, Quentin Atkinson, Joseph Bulbulia, and Russell Gray, "Ritual Human Sacrifice Promoted and Sustained Evolution of Stratified Societies," *Nature* 532 (2016): 228–31.

20 Nor is this an entirely historical footnote, as in 1996 Pope John Paul II expressed support for Hesychastic thought.

21 Ernst Kantorowicz, *The King's Two Bodies: A Study in Medieval Political Theology* (Princeton: Princeton University Press, 1957).

22 Alfred Gell, *Art and Agency: An Anthropological Theory* (Oxford: Clarendon Press, 1998).

23 For example, Mark S. Smith, "The Death of Dying and Rising Gods in the Biblical World," *Scandinavian Journal of the Old Testament* 12 (1998), 257–313, and Jonathan Z. Smith, "Dying and Rising Gods," *Encyclopedia of Religion* (New York: Macmillan, 2005), 2535–40.

24 Max Müller, *Lectures on the Origin and the Growth of Religion as Illustrated by the Religions of India* (London: Longmans, Green, 1878); Cornelis P. Tiele, *Outlines of the History of Religion to the Spread of the Universal Religions* (London: Trübner, 1877).

25 See note 3.

26 See note 3.

27 These terms belie the complexity of the societies themselves. Hopewell cultures from the Middle Woodland period (ca. 200 BCE to 500 CE) shared artistic styles across thousands of miles (from Florida to Ontario, and Louisiana to Wisconsin), traded valuable raw materials across eastern North America, and created mounds and earthworks in disparate and widely separated river valleys.

28 Joseph Campbell, *Historical Atlas of World Mythology* (New York: Harper and Row, 1983–89).

29 M. Winkelman, "Shamanism and Cognitive Evolution" *Cambridge Archaeological Journal* 12 (2002): 71–101.

30 Manvir Singh, "The Cultural Evolution of Shamanism" *Behavioral and Brain Sciences* 41 (2018): 1–62.

31 Marija Gimbutas, *The Civilization of the Goddess: The World of Old Europe* (San Francisco: Harper, 1991).

32 Roy A. Rappaport, *Ritual and Religion in the Making of Humanity* (Cambridge: Cambridge University Press, 1999).

X

DEATH

ROBERT B. PICKERING

Tomorrow, and tomorrow, and tomorrow,
Creeps in this petty pace from day to day
To the last syllable of recorded time,
And all our yesterdays have lighted fools
The way to dusty death. Out, out, brief candle!
Life's but a walking shadow, a poor player
That struts and frets his hour upon the stage
And then is heard not more, It is a tale
Told by an idiot, full of sound and fury,
Signifying nothing.

William Shakespeare,
Macbeth,
1606

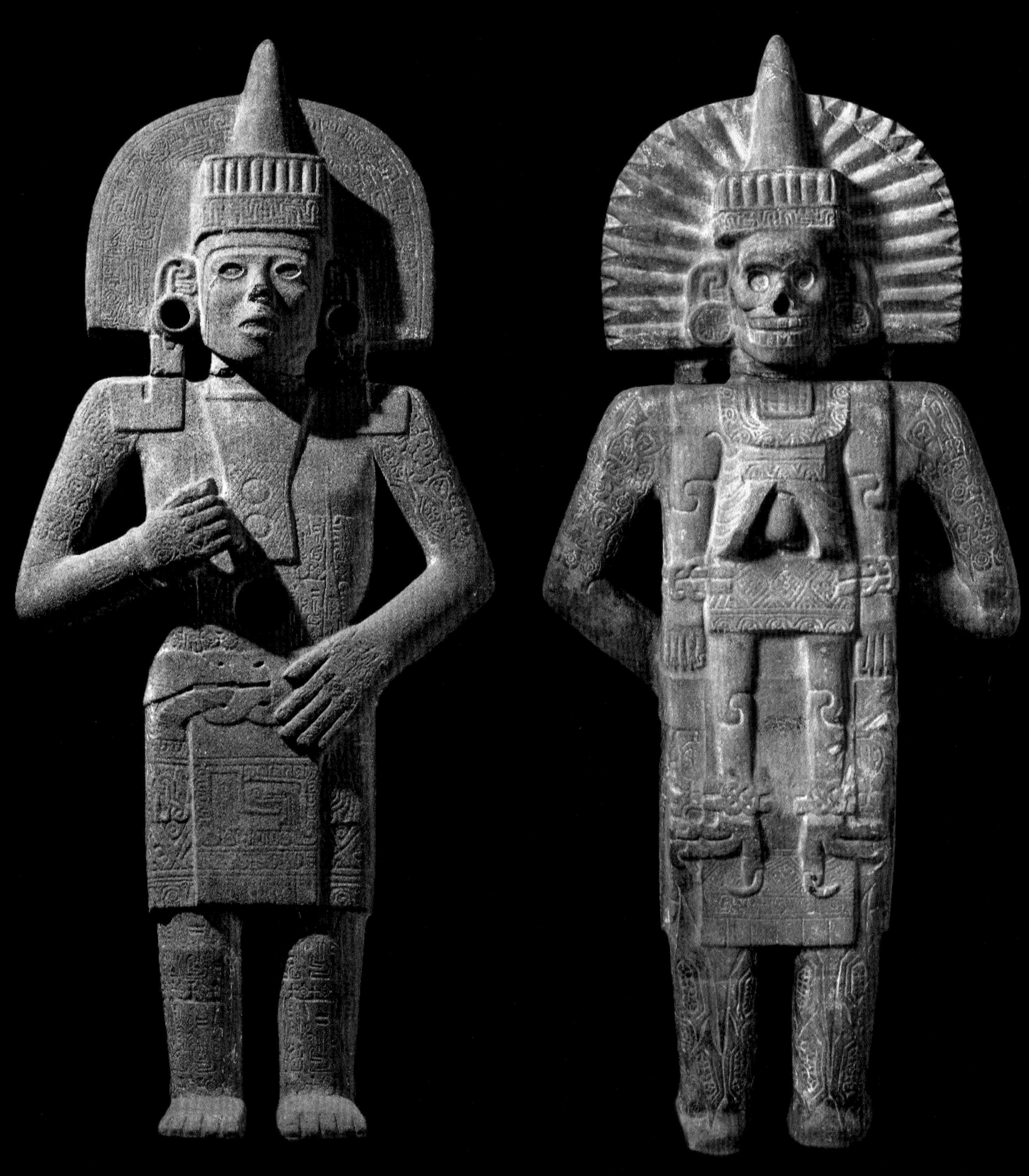

Life-Death Figure, Front and Back Views

Huastec culture, Mexico
900 – 1250
Sandstone
62 ⅜ × 26 × 11 ½ in., 158.4 × 66 × 29.2 cm
Brooklyn Museum, New York
Frank Sherman Benson Fund and the
Henry L. Batterman Fund

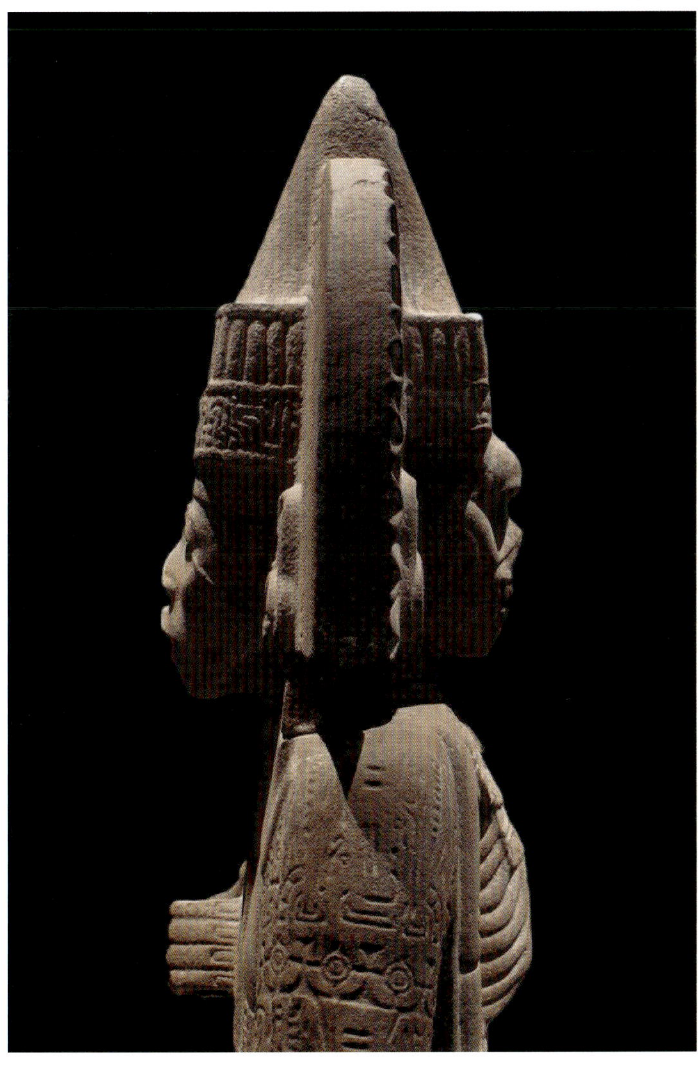

Life-Death Figure (front and back, detail)

Photo: Steven Zucker

Prologue
Thanatopsis:
Contemplations of Death

This volume and chapter address the idea that humans around the globe share many of the same life experiences and stresses related to death. Celebration, anxiety, and grief are part of life and part of the recognition of death. Art commemorates those events and feelings in culturally prescribed ways. While the details may differ, the themes are universal.

In recent decades, the study of human remains and mortuary behavior—how cultures cope with death—has become a sensitive and sometimes emotional subject. In response, museums are removing human remains and mortuary objects from their exhibits and websites. Ethics policies that result from consultation with descendant communities offer guidelines about appropriate procedures for researching or depicting the dead and mortuary objects. Museums hold objects from the past, but they exist in the present and serve contemporary audiences and are sensitive to evolving thinking and practice.

This author believes that exploring death and mortuary practices in a culturally sensitive context is not only achievable but important.

Introduction

Everyone dies. That is not a new idea. Indeed, a mark of sentient humanness is thinking about death and its meanings. As mental faculties developed in our early hominid ancestors, addressing the question of what happens when someone dies became an engrossing topic in human cultures worldwide. To maintain personal sanity and cultural survival, every society developed ways of explaining and coping with death. These ideas are core to diverse philosophies and religions. Ironically, thinking about death helps individuals appreciate life and accept their inescapable fates.

Before the development of writing, oral stories were vehicles for sharing and passing on knowledge about how to live and how to die. Storytellers used objects from the natural world and human-made artifacts as symbols or metaphors to help people understand their messages. As myth scholar Joseph Campbell opined in a series of television interviews, *The Power of Myth* with Bill Moyers, the problem is that most people see the metaphor but miss the idea behind it. For example, the Egyptian pharaoh Akhenaten (1372–1336 BCE) created a revolutionary monotheistic religion with the sun as the metaphor for the power of the one god, Aten. His religion was not sun-worship, but a recognition of a greater power behind it.

With the invention of writing, stories about the afterlife were codified as revered cultural stories. Campbell proposed that some stories from deep time survive as archetypes that continue in various forms to this day.[1] There are important reasons why death has occupied so much human attention. Death is the final act of this life and the first act of whatever comes next, even if that is non-existence. In confronting death, images and objects help people cope with the complicated feelings, realities, and transitions between the living and the dead.

Human Patterns Emerge

Although other species acknowledge the death of a group member, humans appear to be the only beings that commemorate the passing in material ways. Some of the earliest archaeological evidence of ancient hominids reveals efforts to prepare the physical body by creating a special place for it, such as a pit, and by placing objects with the dead. One of the earliest examples comes from Shanidar Cave in Iraq in the Paleolithic period. Shanidar is an important and controversial Neanderthal site because of burial practices described by Ralph Solecki and his team that excavated portions of the site through the 1950s.[2] Solecki's team uncovered ten Neanderthal skeletons representing adult women and men, and children. He claims that these Neanderthals repeatedly returned to the same site to inter their dead. In the lab, soil samples from near the bodies, outside the abdominal areas, revealed relatively high concentrations of plant pollen. The location of the pollen is significant. If it came from the abdominal area, it might have been ingested as food. Solecki proposed that finding pollen deposits outside the body indicated that people intentionally placed a quantity of flowers around the dead.

In 2014, another British team returned to Shanidar to excavate adjacent portions of Solecki's 1950s digs.[3] The team found remains of two more Neanderthals, each placed within separate curved-base depressions, dated to ca. 55,000–45,000 years ago. The 2014 excavations support Solecki's interpretations. Shanidar has profound implications for what it means to be human. Intentional burial in a special location (the cave), intentional placement of bodies in proximity to each other, in specific body positions, and contributing cultural items (chert flakes) and flowers near the body represent many of the elements of disposal of the dead practices elaborated upon during the last 50,000 years.

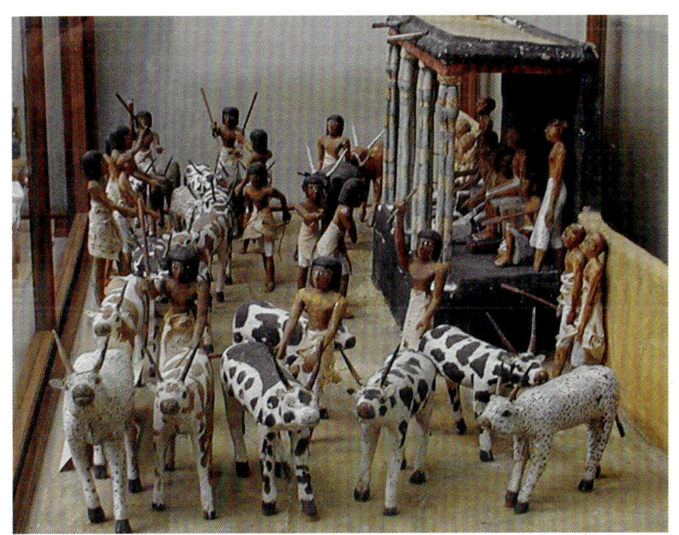

Concepts of Afterlife

Death sends people into the unknown. Is it heaven, Valhalla, or some other wonderful, everlasting place? In Homer's *Odyssey* (8th century BCE) the afterlife was rather dull; lively, heroic actions were the domain of the living. Will the spirit wander in a not-live/not-dead realm? Does death send one into the great void of non-existence? Each society answers these questions, but in all cases, it is a leap of faith to accept the conclusions.

Cultures create images of what they hope will be true. Frequently, perceptions of the afterlife look much like this life. In at least three parts of the world, ceramic tableaux or scenes were placed in tombs along with the dead, denoting continuity into the afterlife. Ancient Egyptians believed that objects placed in tombs reflected the eternal. Often using soft wood, Egyptian artists created scenes of the everyday life of farmers, women grinding grain, soldiers marching, and even gardens, painted to add individual details to the people and the animals depicted (1). As the act of carving hieroglyphic incantations in stone made them real, so, too, did these tableaux represent desires for the afterlife.

During China's long history, contributions for the afterlife of the deceased, especially for the elite, were numerous, exquisitely made, and often comprised of rare raw materials. Jade was not only beautiful, but it

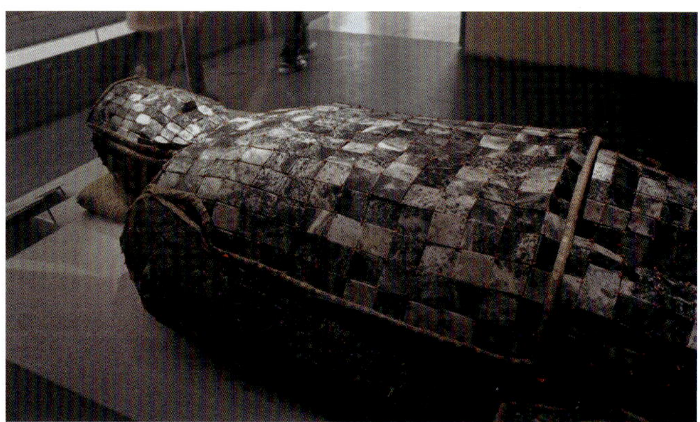

symbolized ritual power. As early as the Han dynasty (206 BCE–220 CE), the imperial dead were encased in jade burial suits made of hundreds of thin jade plaques held together with gold wire (**2**). Elaborate jade coverings provided magical protection to the body and soul throughout eternity. Jade disks (*bi*) were symbols of heaven and were interred with the dead for thousands of years beginning at least as early as 3400 BCE (**3**). According to Teng Shu-P'ing, *bi* represent early attempts to interpret cosmological concepts, with the disk representing a covering sky that revolves around a central axis.[4]

During China's Tang dynasty (618–906), fine polychrome slipped ceramics were placed in noble and royal tombs. Tang ceramicists also were known for their spectacular large animal figures, such as this standing horse, itself a symbol of power and prestige (**4**).

Scenes from life also were part of the mortuary offerings in west Mexico and Peru. Examples from west Mexico include representations of the Mesoamerican ballgame, rituals, and village scenes. These are not visions of the afterlife but what Hasso Von Winning and Olga Hammer called "anecdotal sculptures."[5]

Architectural structures including depictions of west Mexico's distinctive tiered, circular pyramids and houses were crafted from low-fired clay.

Humans and animals modeled on the tableaux are smaller and less refined than the large hollow figures for which this region is known, but they depict similar body adornment, clothing, and decoration (**5**). Identifying objects being held by large figures and the clothing they wear provides contextual insights for interpreting the smaller tableaux figures. This author has suggested these figures and the tableaux represent real people and their achievements in life. Putting them in the tomb signified their accomplishments, eternally.[6]

Ceramic scenes from Peru often take the form of hollow vessels. An enigmatic example shows skeletal humans overseeing the ritual (**6**). Additional skeletal figures carrying staffs surround the scene. Similar vessels depict living humans overseeing the interment of mummy bundles. A variant of this theme appears to show the placing of a mummy bundle in the mountains, a common practice in pre-Hispanic Peru.

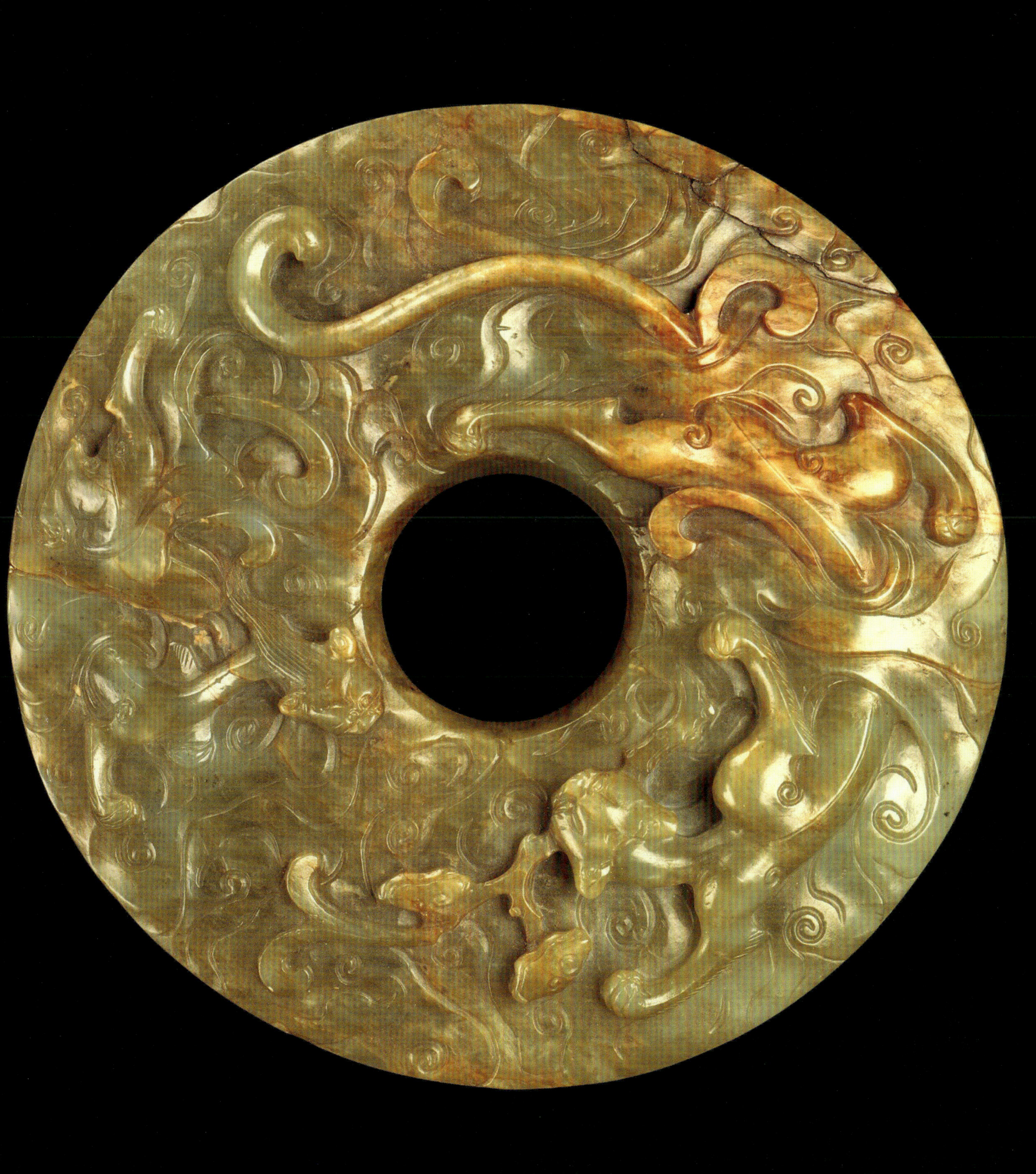

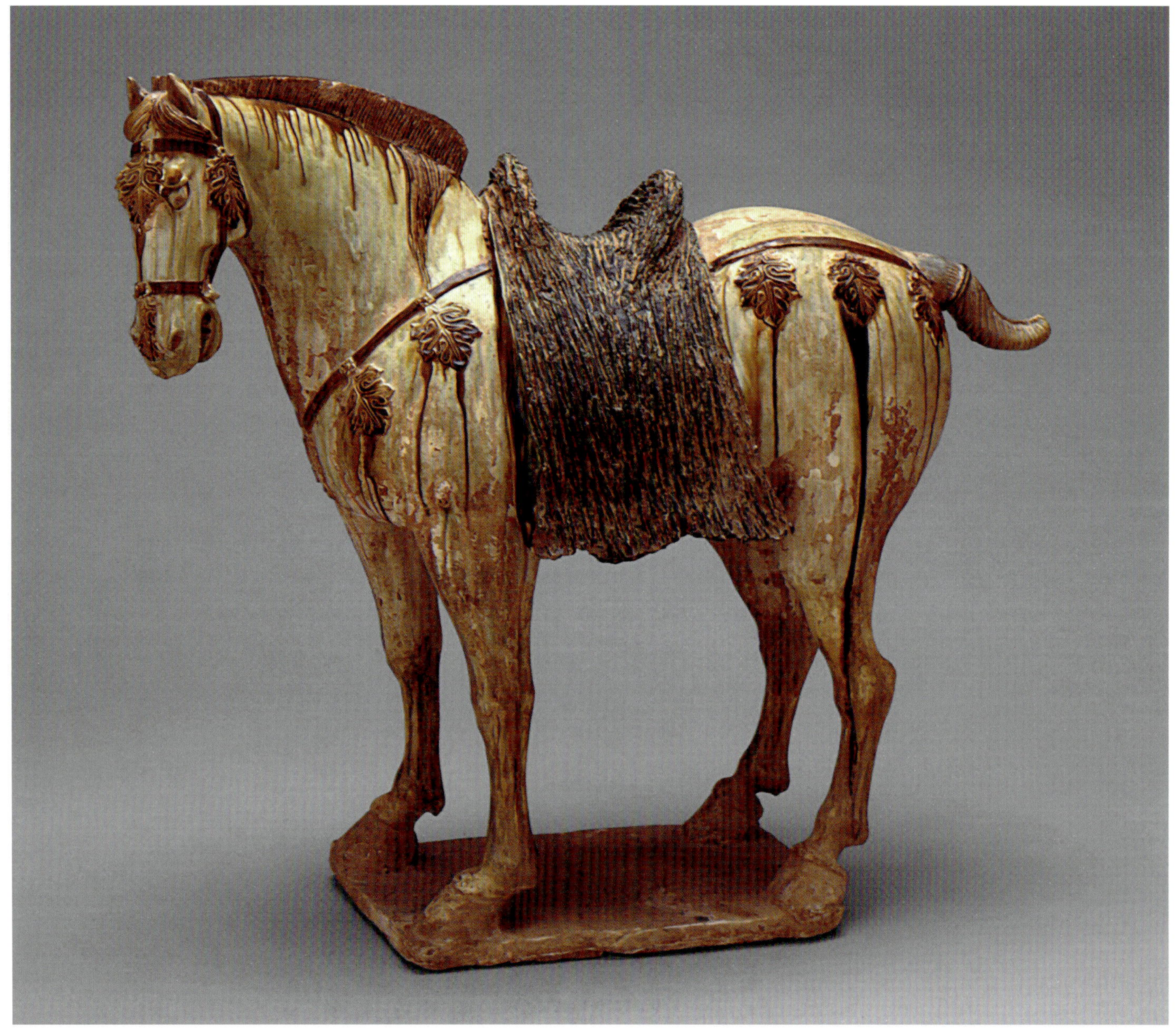

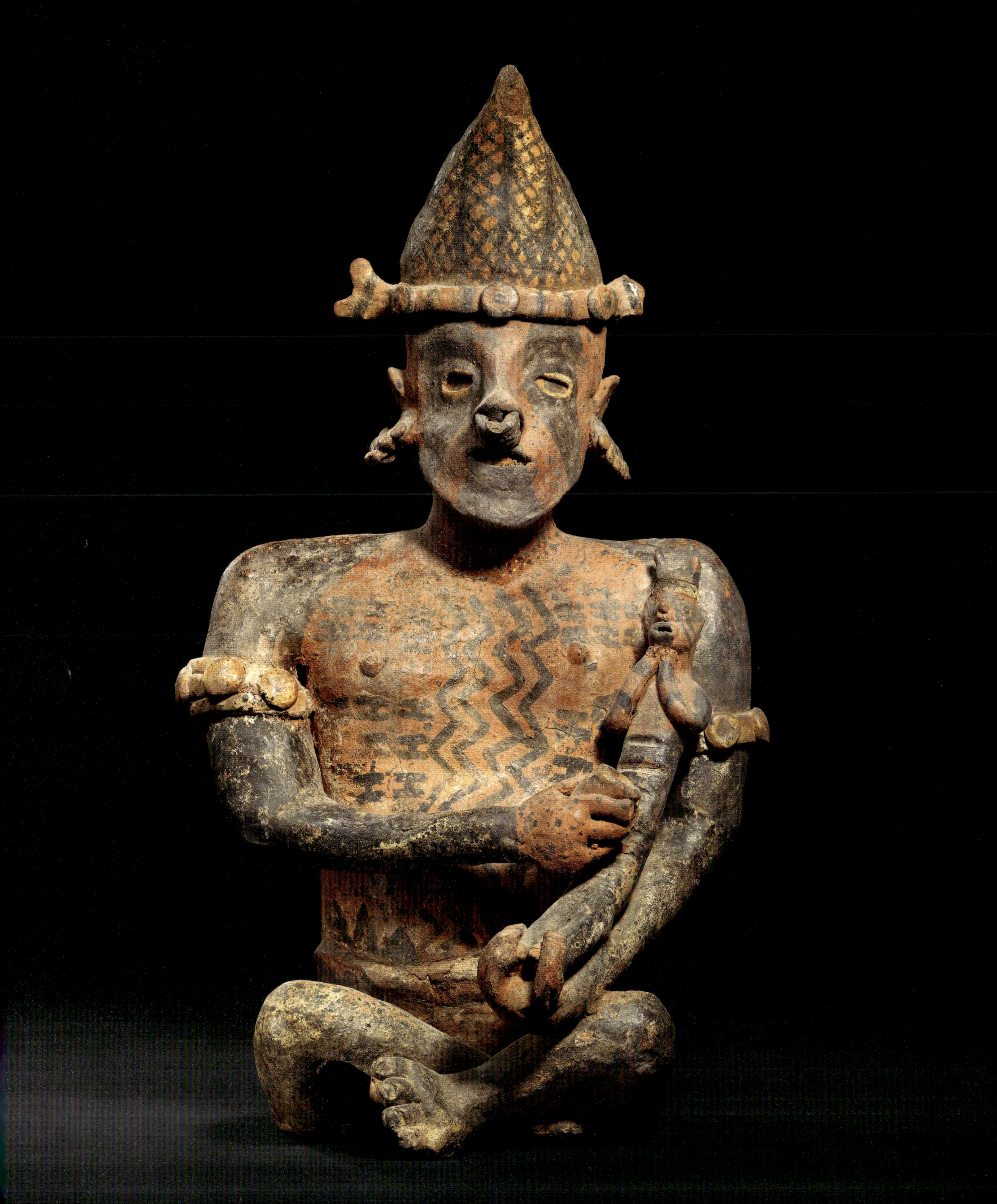

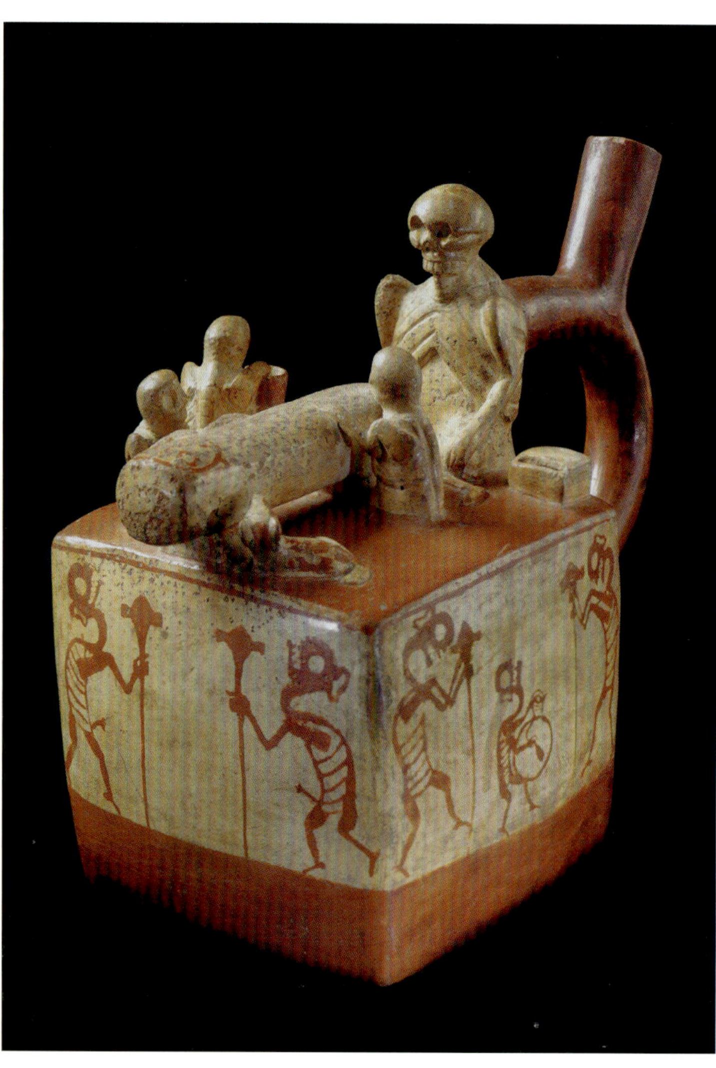

The Sacred Remains

Not every society, past and present, views human remains, their handling, and their display in the same manner, but every culture has its own prescribed behaviors and rituals. A Greek funerary plaque portrays the grief of the survivors (**7**), while a Greek amphora shows the special treatment befitting a warrior's death. Burial, mummification, public display, and dismemberment for consumption by scavengers represent diverse methods cultures employ to dispose of human remains (**8**). In Christian religious communities in Europe from about the thirteenth century forward, human remains were deposited in catacombs and were meant to be viewed. Religious beliefs encouraged displaying the dead as an exercise to contemplate life and death. Similarly, many paintings from the Italian Renaissance depict saints holding skulls evoking similar acts of contemplation without the macabre display of actual human remains (**9** and **10**).

Buddhist traditions frequently depict skulls and skeletons to evoke contemplations on life and death. In feudal Japan, the elite carried finely made *inro* (a case for small objects) and attached *netsuke* (a counterweight to the *inro*). These items represented the owner's high status and the subject matter conveyed a message that the owner wanted others to see. This small but intricately carved skeleton was a continuous reminder to the wearer of life's end (**11**). Fine *netsuke* can be thought of as monumental sculpture in miniature, a form that combines high artistic achievement and often an important message inherent in the depiction.

This emaciated fasting Buddha Shakyamuni (3rd–5th century) is a stone sculpture that represents enlightenment and the conquest of earthly needs and desires to emphasize the fleeting nature of this life in comparison to the eternal (**12**). In Tibetan Buddhist tradition, actual human bones are incorporated in ritual objects. This vessel from Eastern Tibet uses the upper cranial portion of a skull as a ritual cup (**13**).

In contrast, some cultures believe the material body is very important for a proper transition to the afterlife. They go to extraordinary lengths to preserve not only the body but also the deceased's identity. The mummification process developed over thousands of years in ancient Egypt is the iconic example. Book II of Herodotus's *History* (ca. 430 BCE) provides the most complete description of the mummification process and the varying contexts for mummification.[7] When Herodotus was writing, everyone, not just the pharaoh or other royals, was mummified in preparation for resurrection and a wonderful afterlife. Specially trained priest-embalmers prepared the body, physically and spiritually. Treating the physical body included placing the remains on a massive stone embalming slab after removal of the brain and internal organs, except for the heart. The body was then covered

with natron (sodium carbonate) to facilitate desiccation. Afterward, priests anointed, wrapped, and equipped the body with specific amulets for ritual protection.

In Colombia and adjacent parts of Central America, skeletonized remains were placed in ceramic funerary urns with anthropomorphic features (**14**). While aspects of the body and personal adornment are not as detailed as they are in figures from west Mexico, the images likely represent the deceased. Compare the stylized Colombian figure to a Roman marble sarcophagus lid depicting a couple casually reclining on a couch as they might wish to be in eternity (**15**). More than a millennium earlier, *larnax* (chest-shaped coffins) were repositories for the remains of the elite Minoan dead (**16**). While these examples come from different times and parts of the world, a common thread is that elaborate mortuary containers, sarcophagi, or urns were placed in tombs rather than graves. Creating the special space was a privilege of the social elite.

Funerary sculptures, separate from sarcophagi, depicted the deceased as they wanted to be remembered. A late classical Greek marble stele of a seated woman (mid-4th century BCE) is a sensitive portrayal while a similar female figure (2nd–1st century BCE) offers a more stoic or formal representation (**17** and **18**). The marble funerary altar of a Roman man with a dog (1st half of 1st century CE) may suggest a religious connection to Egypt from Yemen (**19**). Modern viewers may see the dog as a pet, an

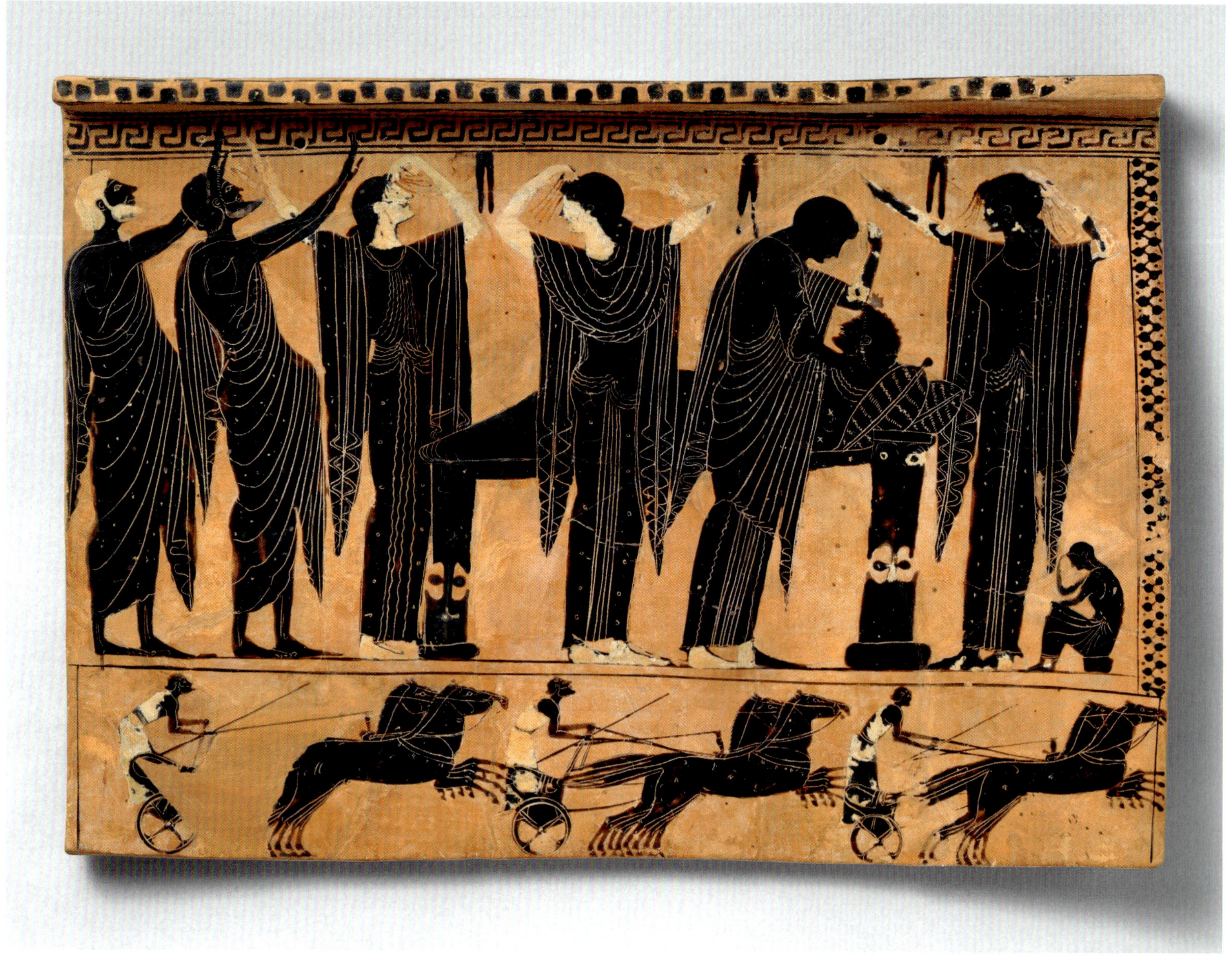

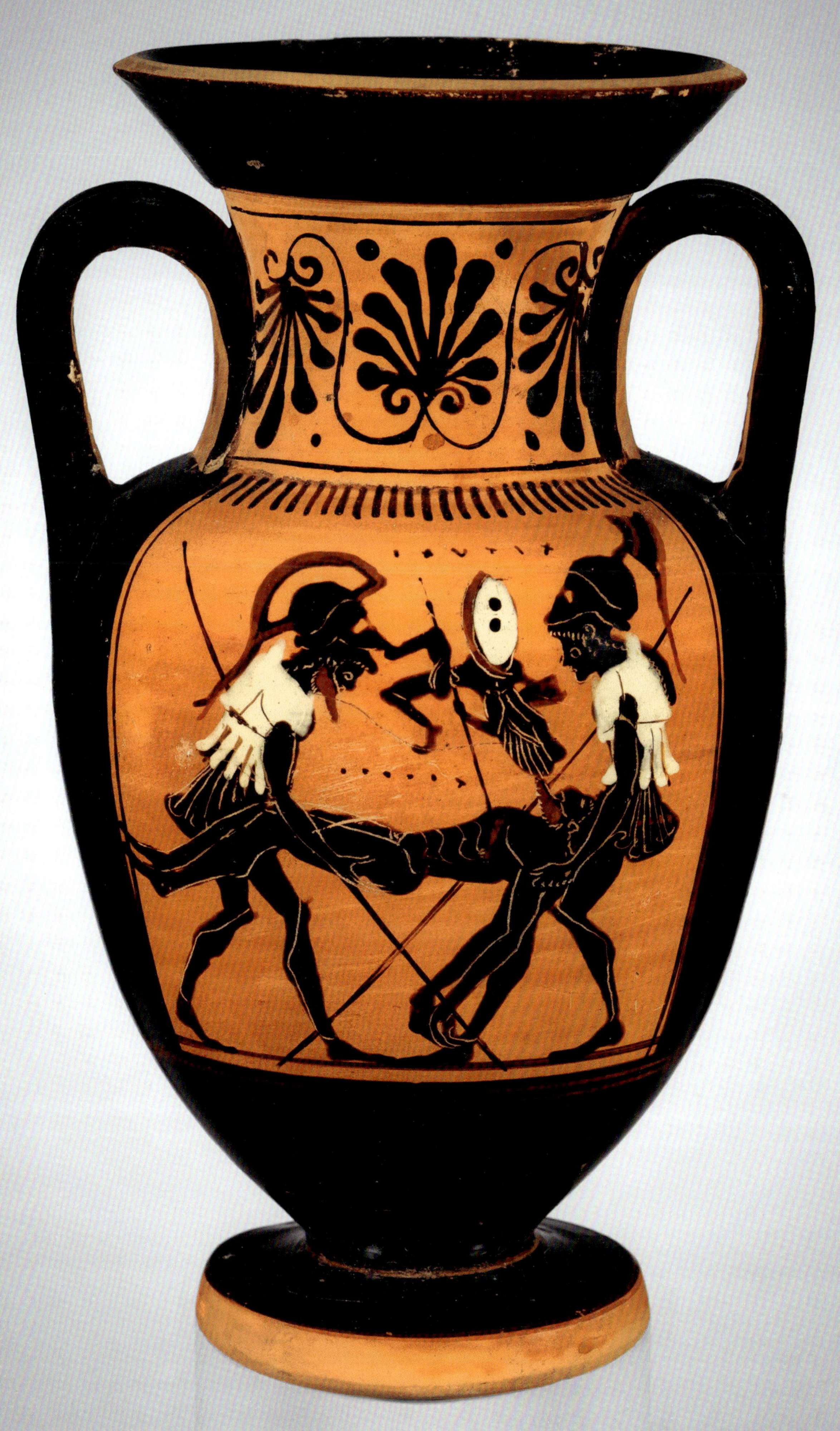

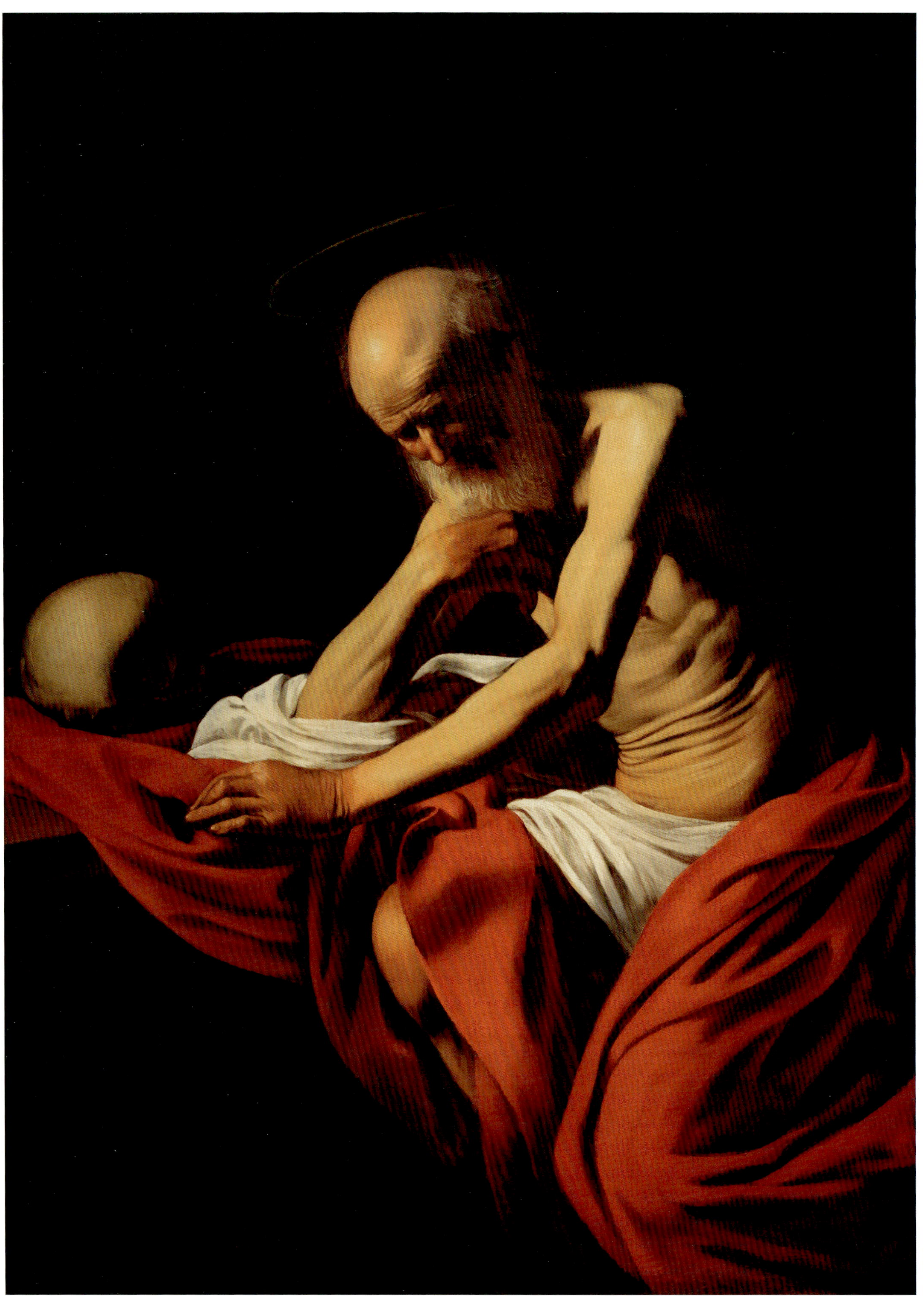

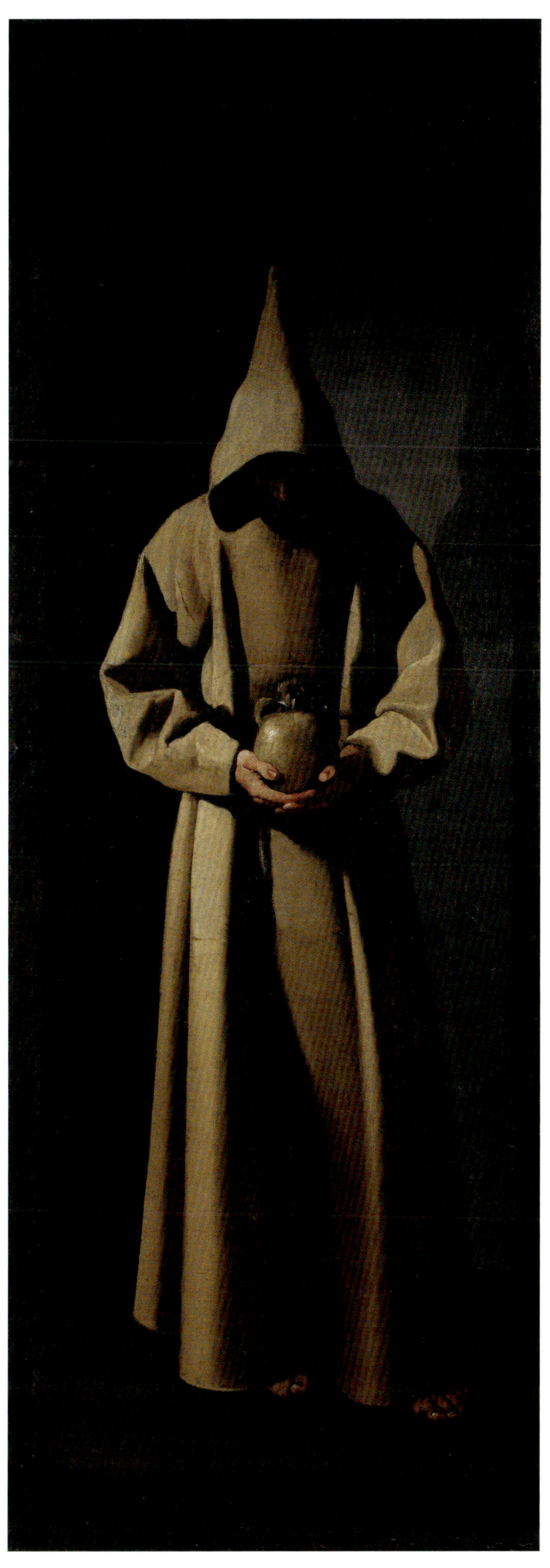

9 **Saint Jerome in Meditation**

Caravaggio (Italy, 1571 – 1610)
1605
Oil on canvas
55.3 × 40 in., 140.5 × 101.5 cm
Museum of Montserrat, Barcelona, Spain

10 **Saint Francis Contemplating a Skull**

Francisco de Zubaran (Spain, 1598 – 1664)
1635
Oil on canvas
36 × 12 in., 91.4 × 30.5 cm
Saint Louis Art Museum

11 **Skeleton**

Japan
1800 – 1900
Ivory with staining, *sumi*
1 3/16 × 1 15/16 in., 4.6 × 2.5 × 2.3 cm
Los Angeles County Museum of Art (LACMA)
Raymond and Frances Bushnell Collection

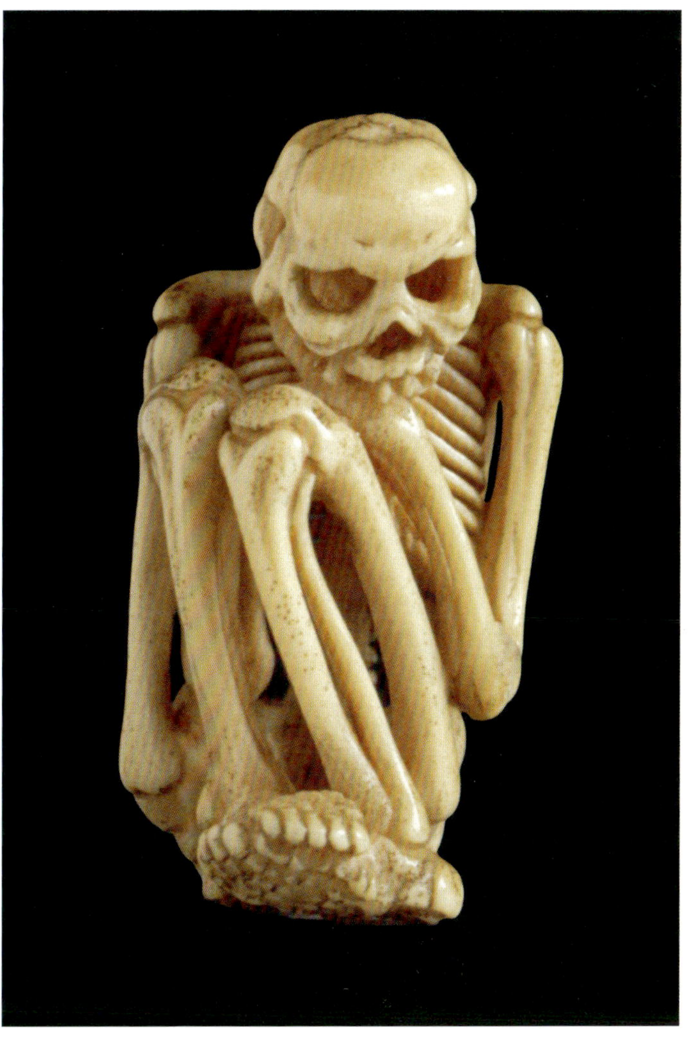

12 **Fasting Buddha Shakyamuni**

Ancient region of Gandhara, Pakistan
Kushan period, 200 – 400 CE
Schist
10 $^{15}/_{16}$ in., 27.8 cm
Metropolitan Museum of Art, New York
Samuel Eilenberg Collection, Ex Coll.: Columbia
University, Purchase, Rogers, Dodge, Harris
Brisbane Dick and Fletcher Funds, Joseph Pulitzer
Bequest, and Lila Acheson Wallace Gift, 1987

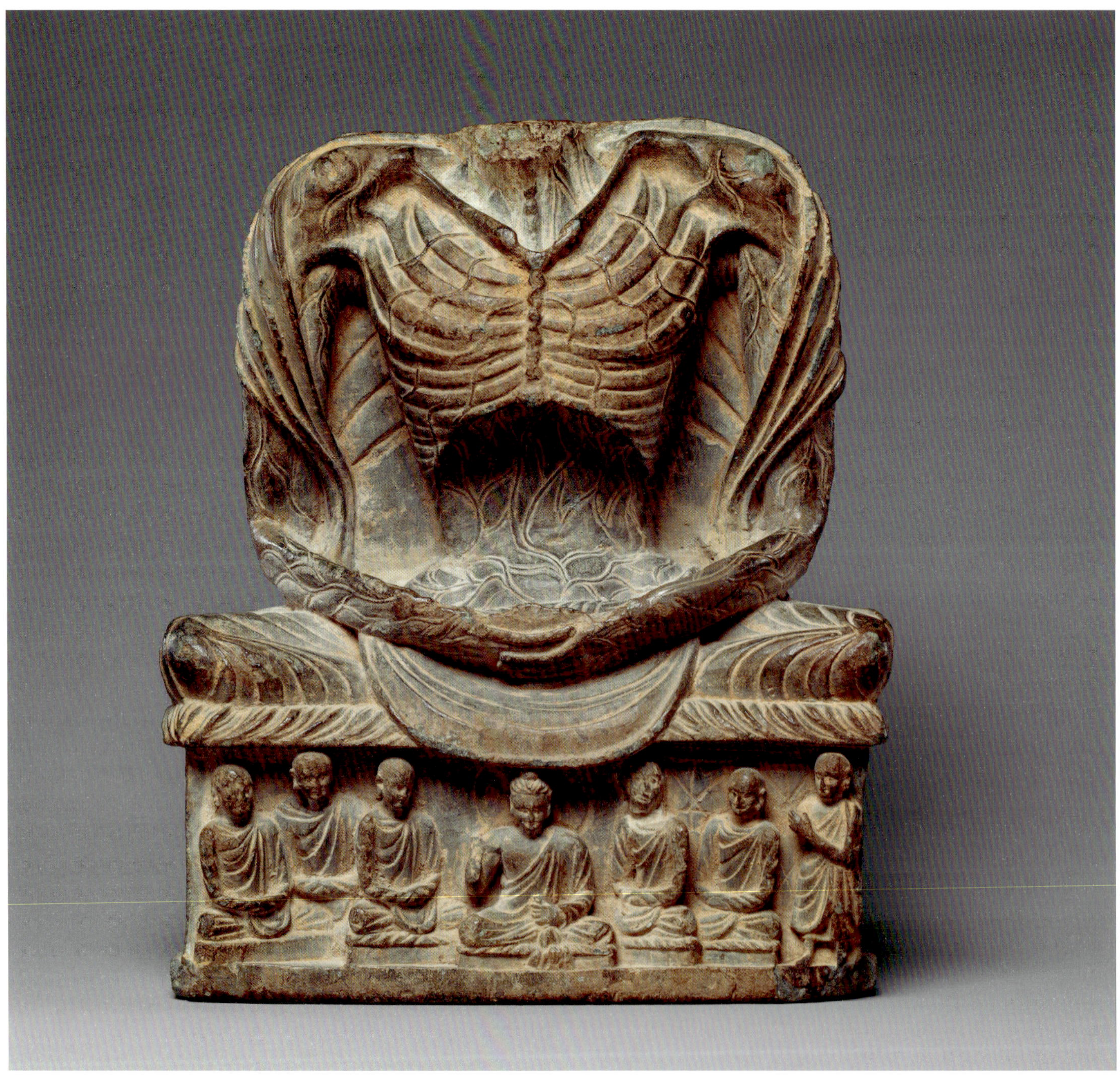

13 Skullcup with Lid

Kham region, Eastern Tibet, China
1700 – 1800
Gilt silver
6 ½ × 8 × 6 in., 16.51 × 20.32 × 15.24 cm
Los Angeles County Museum of Art (LACMA)
Purchased with funds provided by Anna Bing Arnold

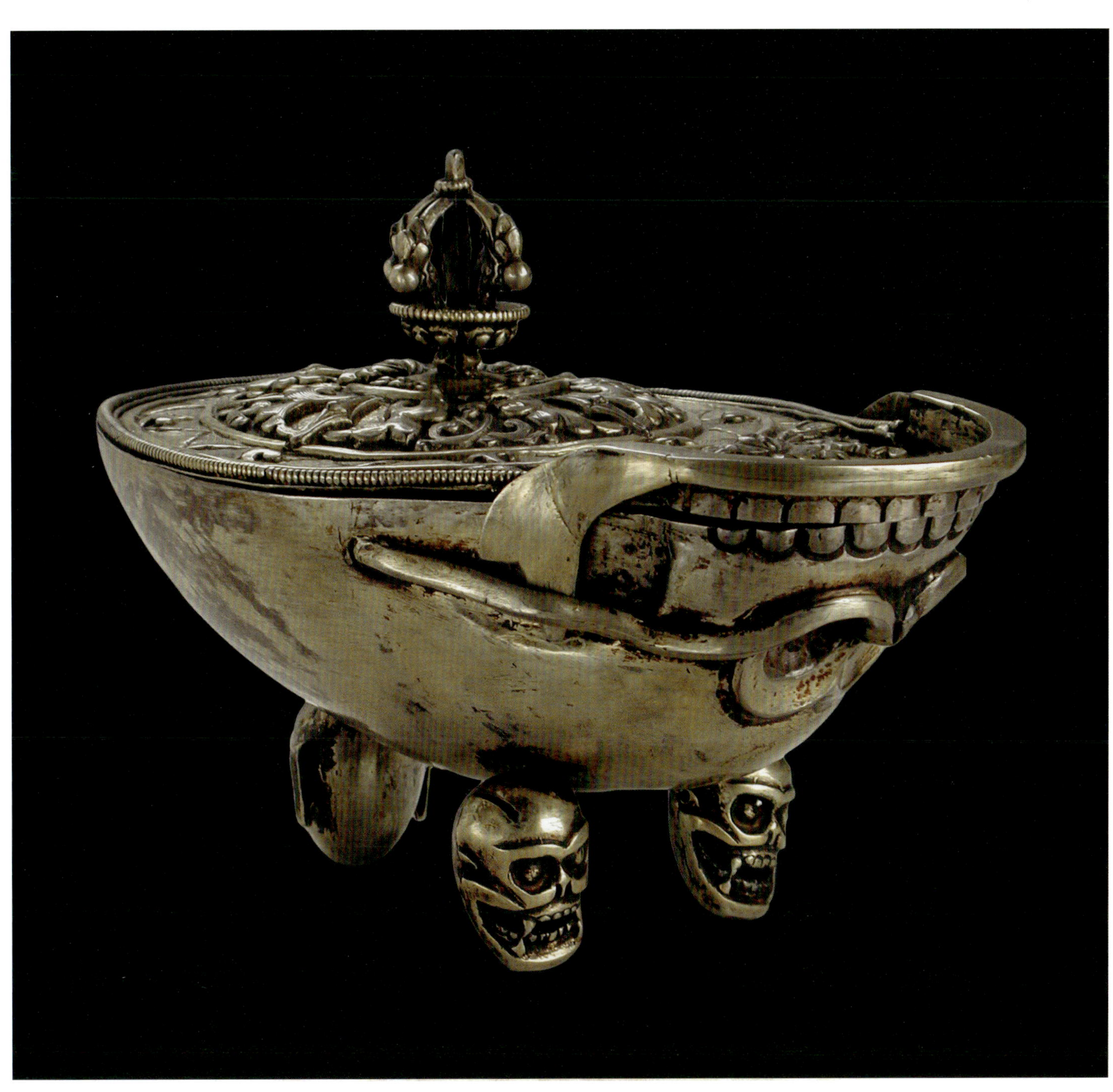

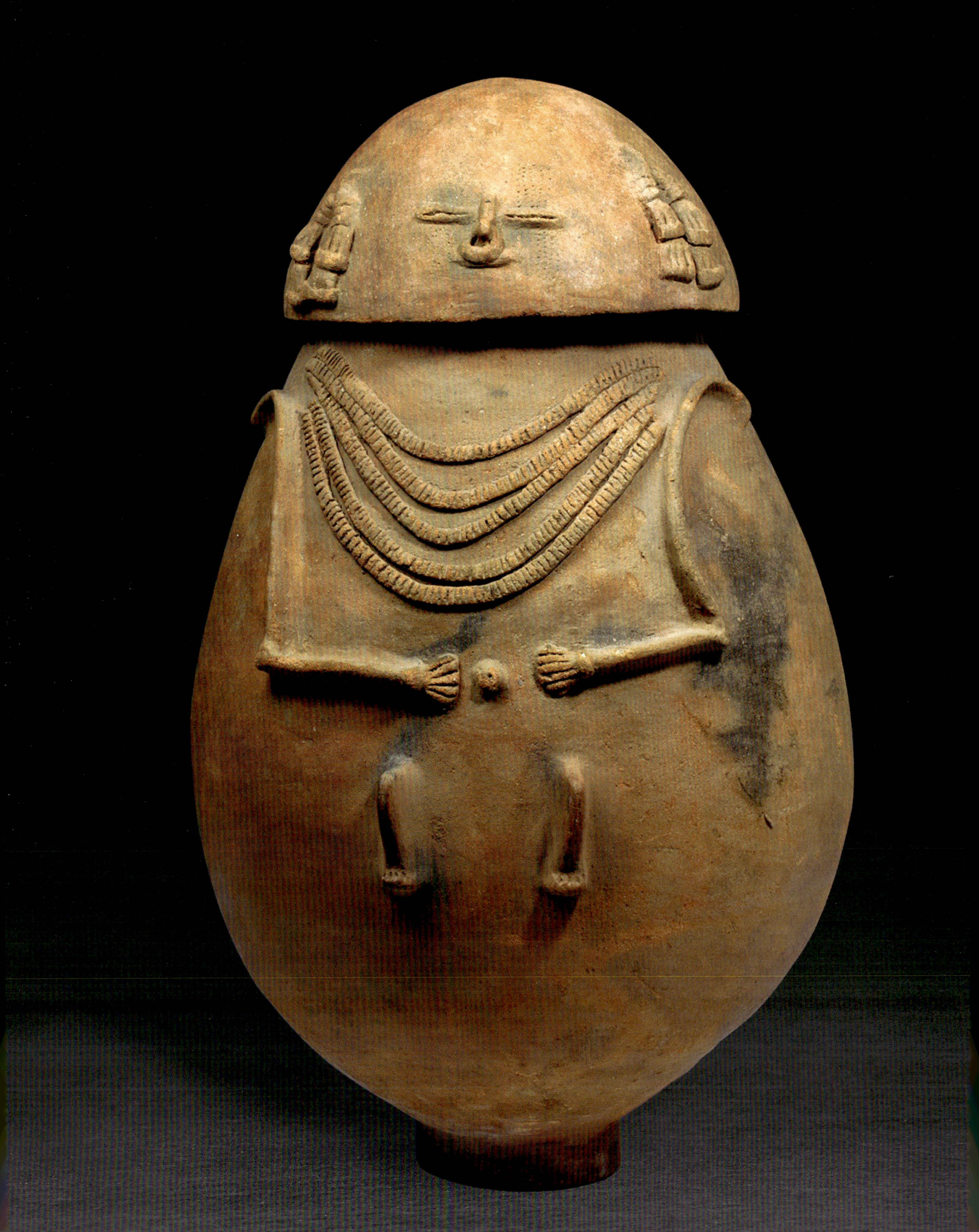

14 Chimila Burial Effigy Urn

Rio Magdalena, Colombia
1000 – 1500
Terracotta
25 ½ in., high, 64.77 cm
Private Collection

15 Sarcophagus Lid with Reclining Couple

Roman culture, Italy
Imperial period, Severan dynasty, 220 CE
Marble
91 in., 231.1 cm
Metropolitan Museum of Art, New York
Purchase, Lila Acheson Wallace Gift, 1993

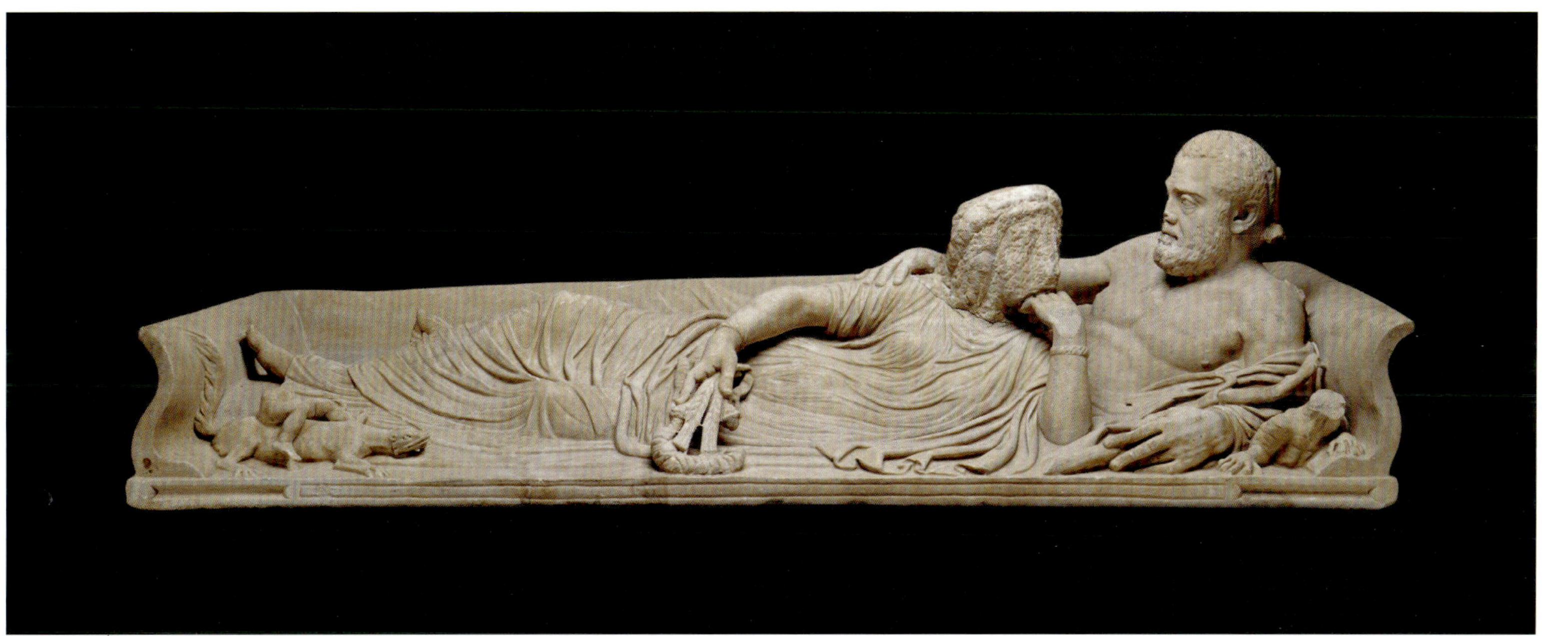

16 Chest-Shaped Coffin

Minoan culture, Crete
1250 BCE
Terracotta
40 × 18 × 42 ¼ in., 101.6 × 45.7 × 107.3 cm
Metropolitan Museum of Art, New York
Anonymous Gift, in memory of Nicolas
and Mireille Koutoulakis, 1996

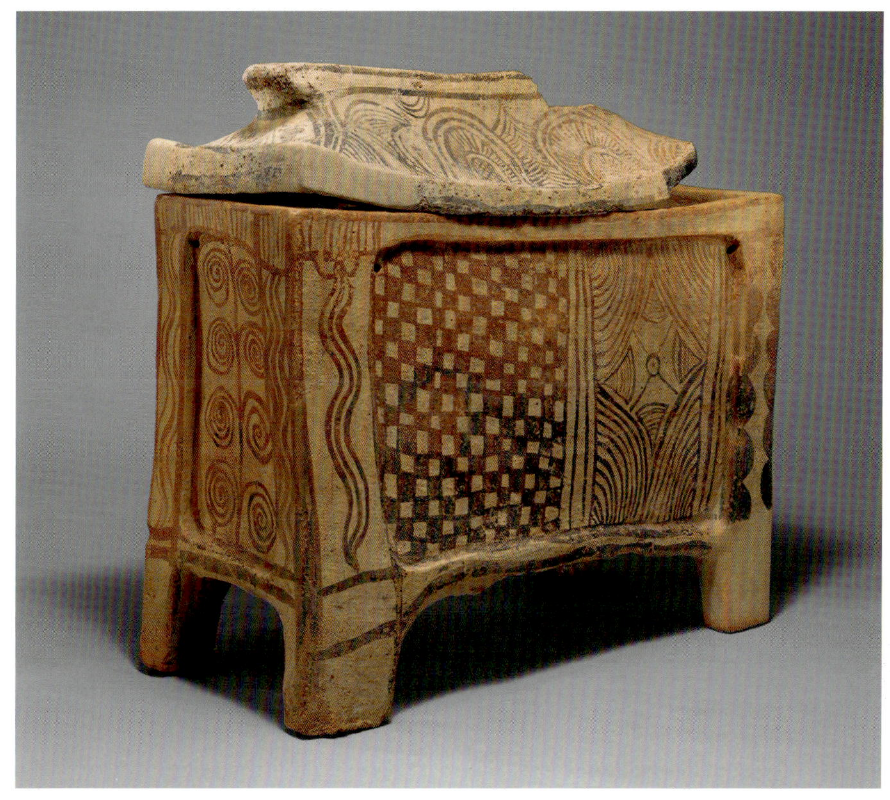

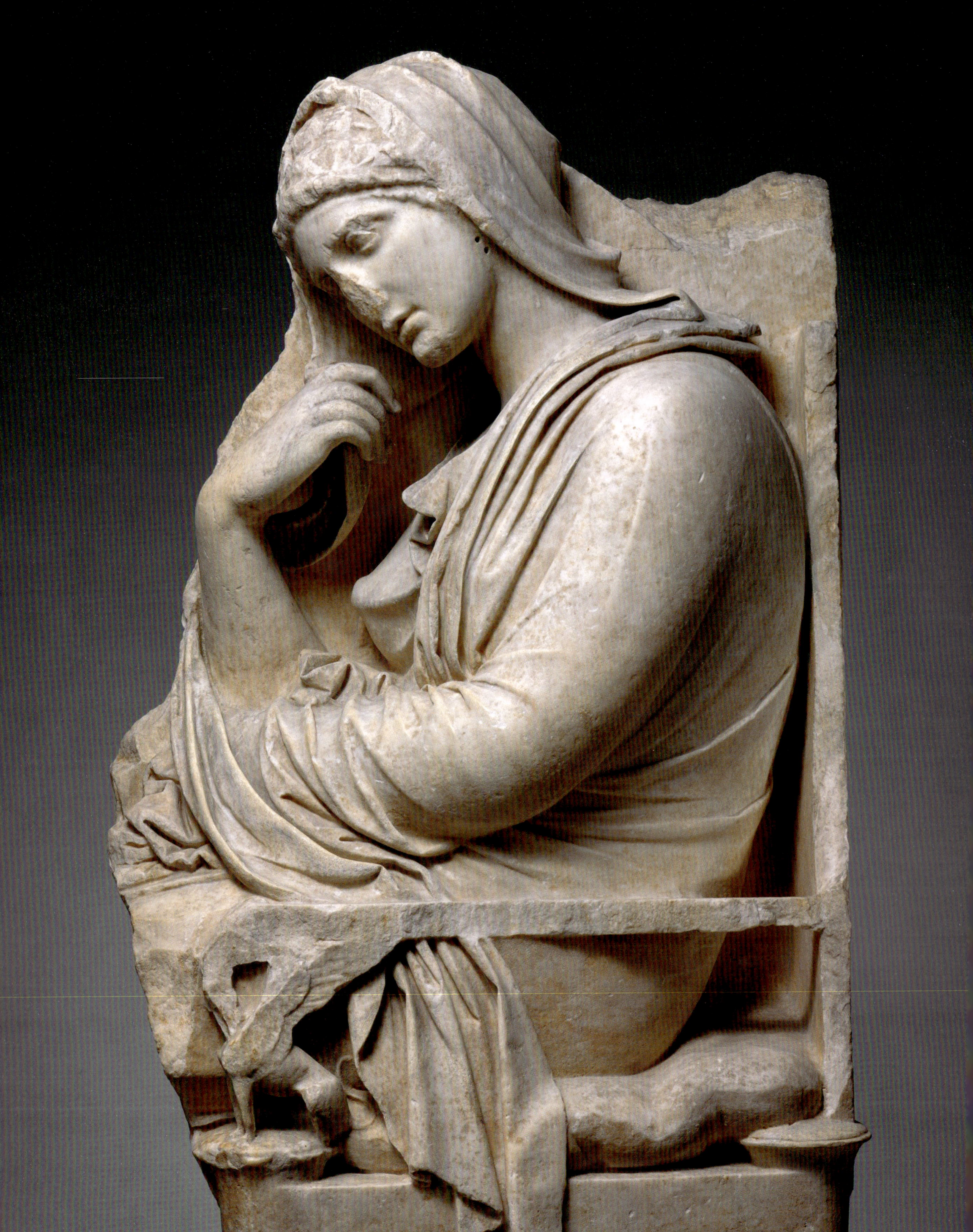

17 **Stele (Grave Marker) of a Woman**

Attic culture, Greece
350 BCE
Marble
48 ¹⁄₁₆ in., 122 cm
Metropolitan Museum of Art, New York
Harris Brisbane Dick Fund, 1948

18 **Funerary Monument with a Seated Woman**

Cyprus
Late Hellenistic period, 200 – 100 BCE
Limestone
42 × 17 ½ × 6 ¾ in., 106.7 × 44.5 × 17.1 cm
Metropolitan Museum of Art, New York
The Cesnola Collection, Purchased by
subscription, 1874 – 76

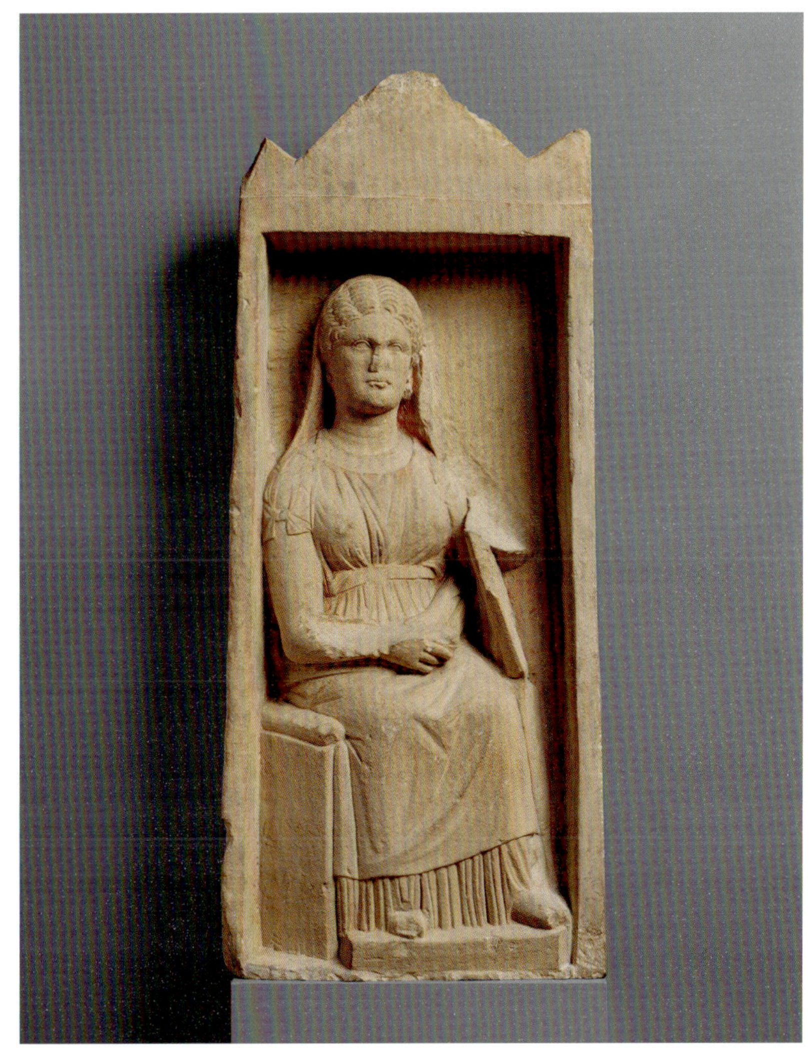

19 **Funerary Altar**

Roman culture, Italy
Early Imperial period,
Julio-Claudian dynasty, 1 – 50 CE
Marble
34 × 29 × 20 in., 86.3 × 73.7 × 51 cm
Metropolitan Museum of Art, New York
Gift of Lewis, Elaine, Jacob, Rachel, Ezra,
and Joseph Dubroff, in celebration of the
Museum's 150th Anniversary, 2018

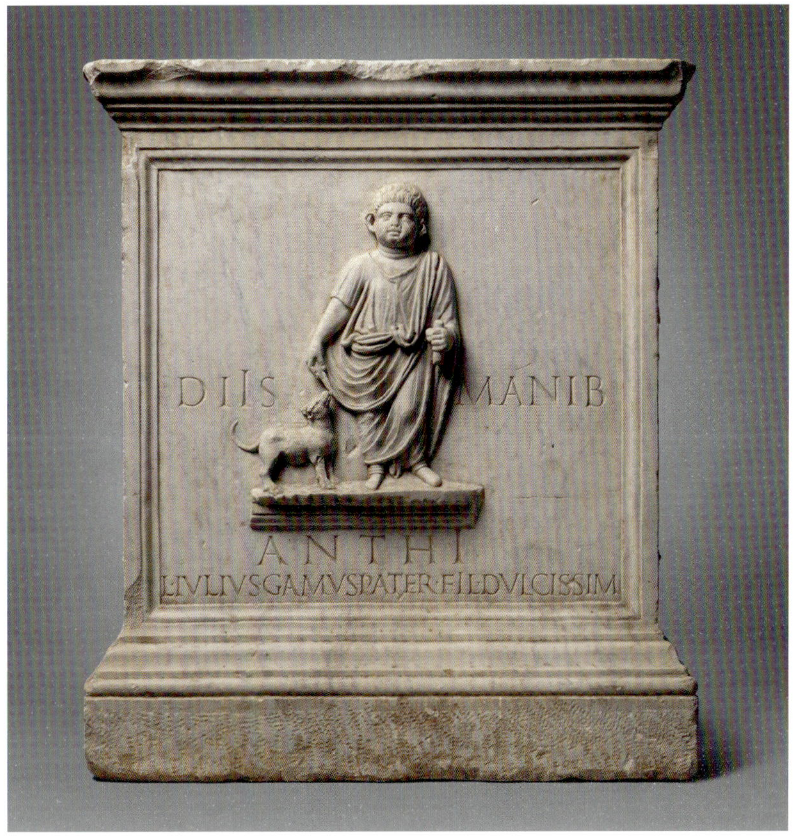

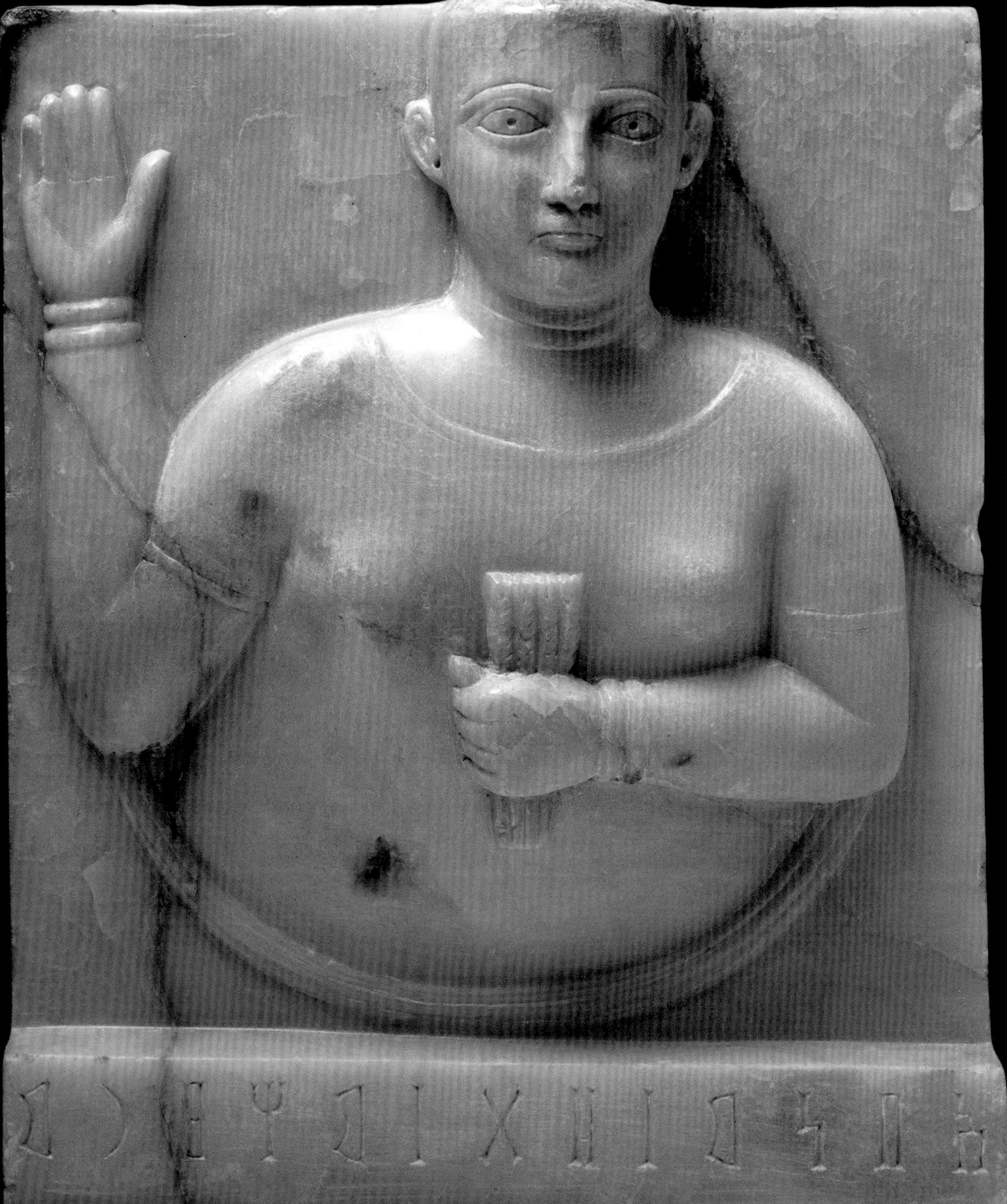

interpretation based on our own view of dogs. During the early Coptic period, however, the jackal-headed Anubis deity transformed into a dog that accompanied the dead into the next world. Long before the introduction of Islam to the Arabian Peninsula, Egyptians and Greeks left their artistic marks in Yemen. The style and form of this first-century BCE mortuary portrait is similar to Egyptian examples (**20**).

From roughly 900 to 1450, Mississippian culture encompassed most of the American southeastern states and extended as far west as Cahokia, America's monumental prehistoric city on the Illinois side of the Mississippi river across from St. Louis. From around the latter part of this period (ca. 1300–1450), the site now known as Spiro Mounds in eastern Oklahoma emerged as one of the most important in North America. Within this tradition, ceramic head pots depict solely male individuals. Moreover, each head pot depicts individuals with their own unique patterns of facial decorations (**21**).[8] On some examples, the mouth is closed and the lips appear to be sewn together. Very likely, the vessel represents a preserved human head. However, is this a so-called trophy head taken in combat, or did the head pot honor an important ancestor? That question is still open. Examples have been found in a relatively limited area that includes the central Mississippi Valley areas of northeastern Arkansas and adjacent southeastern Missouri, as well as a few from sites in the Carden Bottoms vicinity of the Arkansas River Valley.

More enigmatic are abstract masks made from sections of Busycon shells found in the Gulf of Mexico (**22**). They

appear to have been placed over the faces of the dead, but their significance is not known. Genuine examples are few in number compared to head pots. Perhaps they represent a special spiritual status. They do not have the individualistic characteristics of head pots that date to the same period.

In some cultures, the dead were adorned with masks and other regalia specifically for their journey to the next life (**23–25**). The gold, silver, and copper used in these similar examples from Peru ca. 300–1300 were highly valued as materials since they did not deteriorate and were eternal in the same sense that the deceased hoped to have eternal life. From a technical perspective, the use of these metals and their alloys provided impervious color that enhanced the form of the masks.

In Peru's ancient Moche culture (ca. 100 – 700), head pots rather than skulls commemorate exclusively male leaders. Christopher Donnan's extensive discussion of the manufacture, use, and interpretation of the head pots provides important cultural contexts and interpretations.[9] He notes that multiple head pots of the same individual were made and that pots representing the same person at different ages may have commemorated events at different life stages. For an elite individual, proper body preparation included attaching a facemask of precious metals to the mummy bundle.

West Mexico's so-called shaft tomb culture produced distinctive large, expressive human figures, as well as animal figures. As mentioned previously, these figures depict men and women in various posture/gesture combinations, wearing adornments, and carrying a

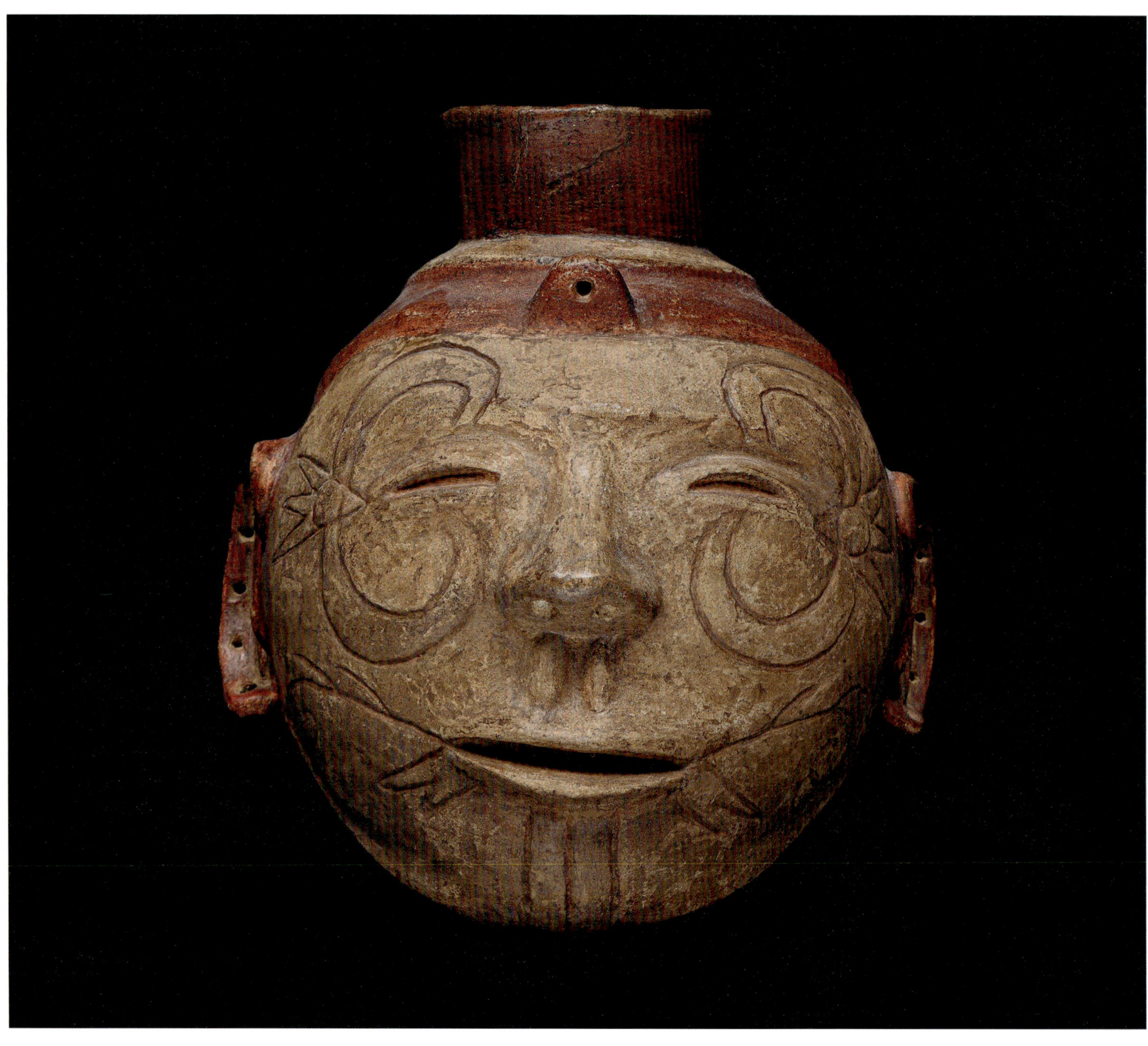

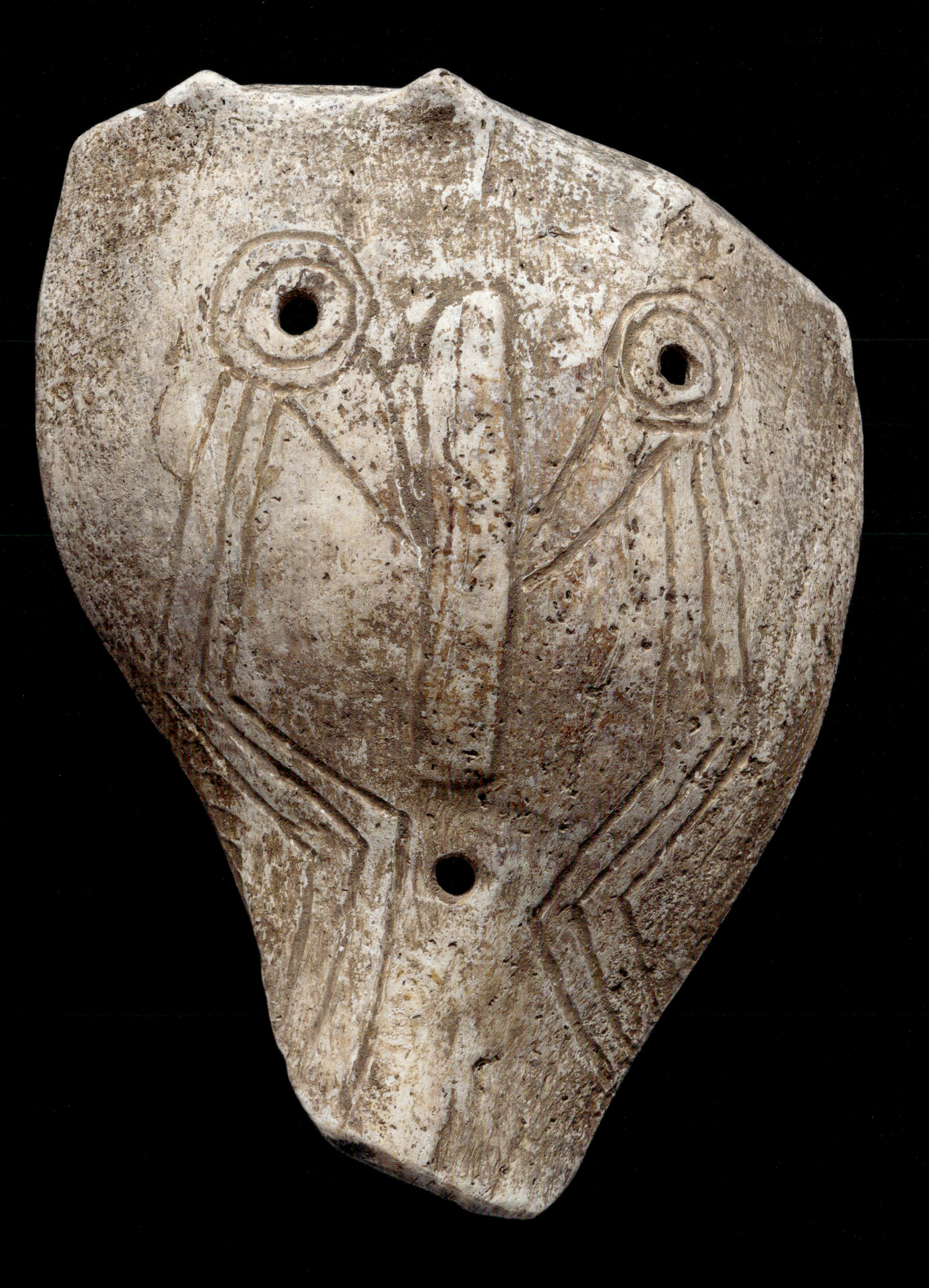

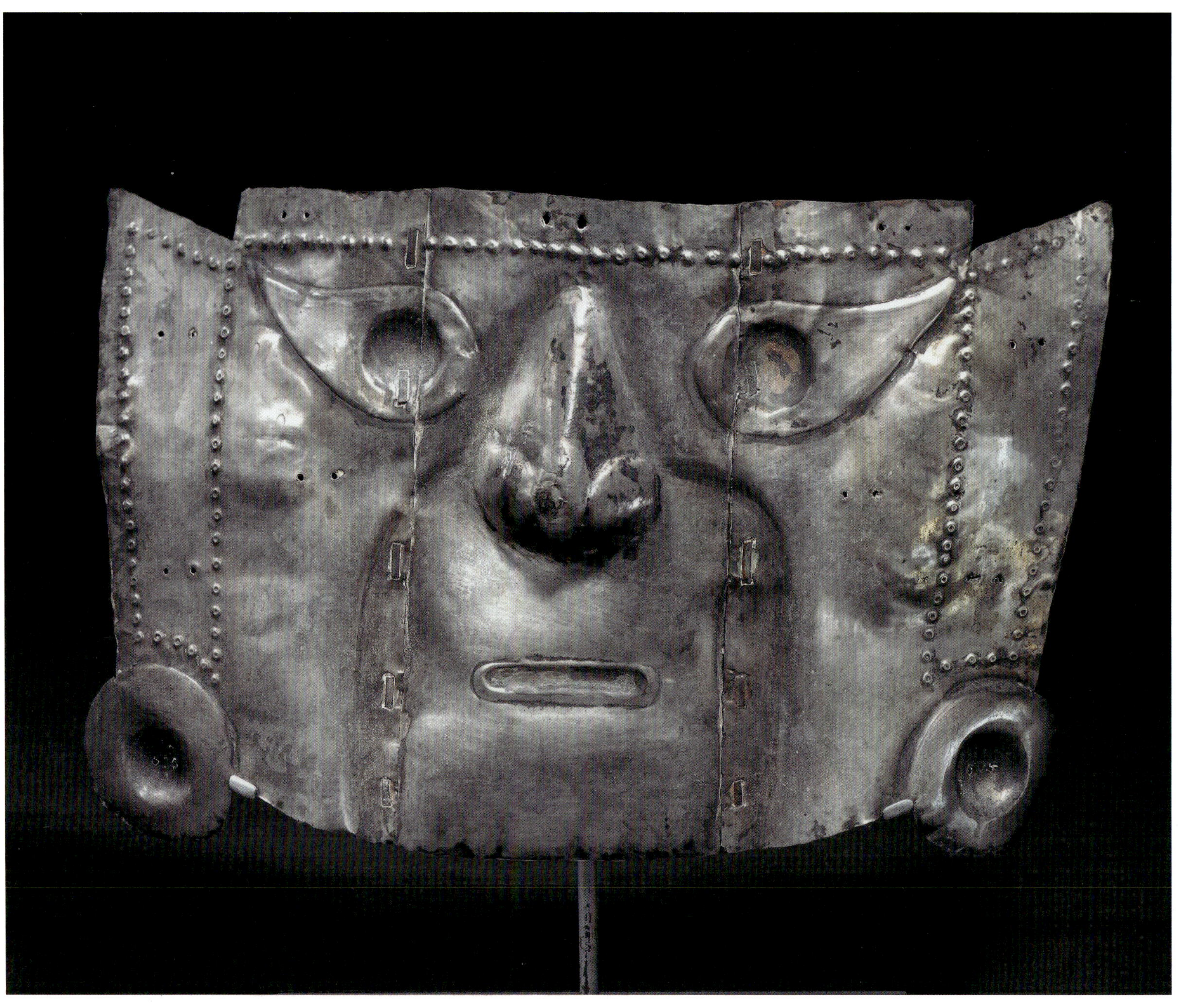

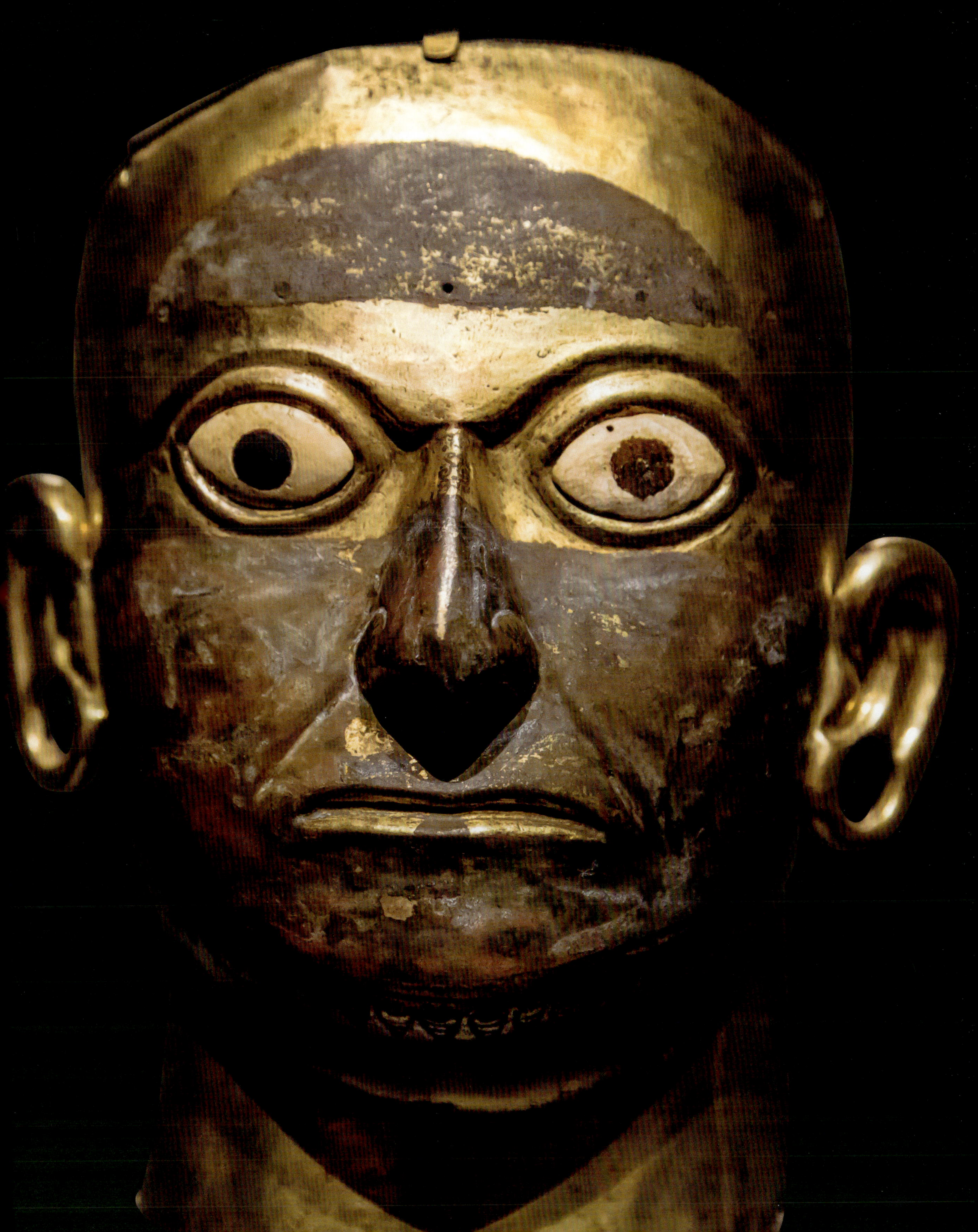

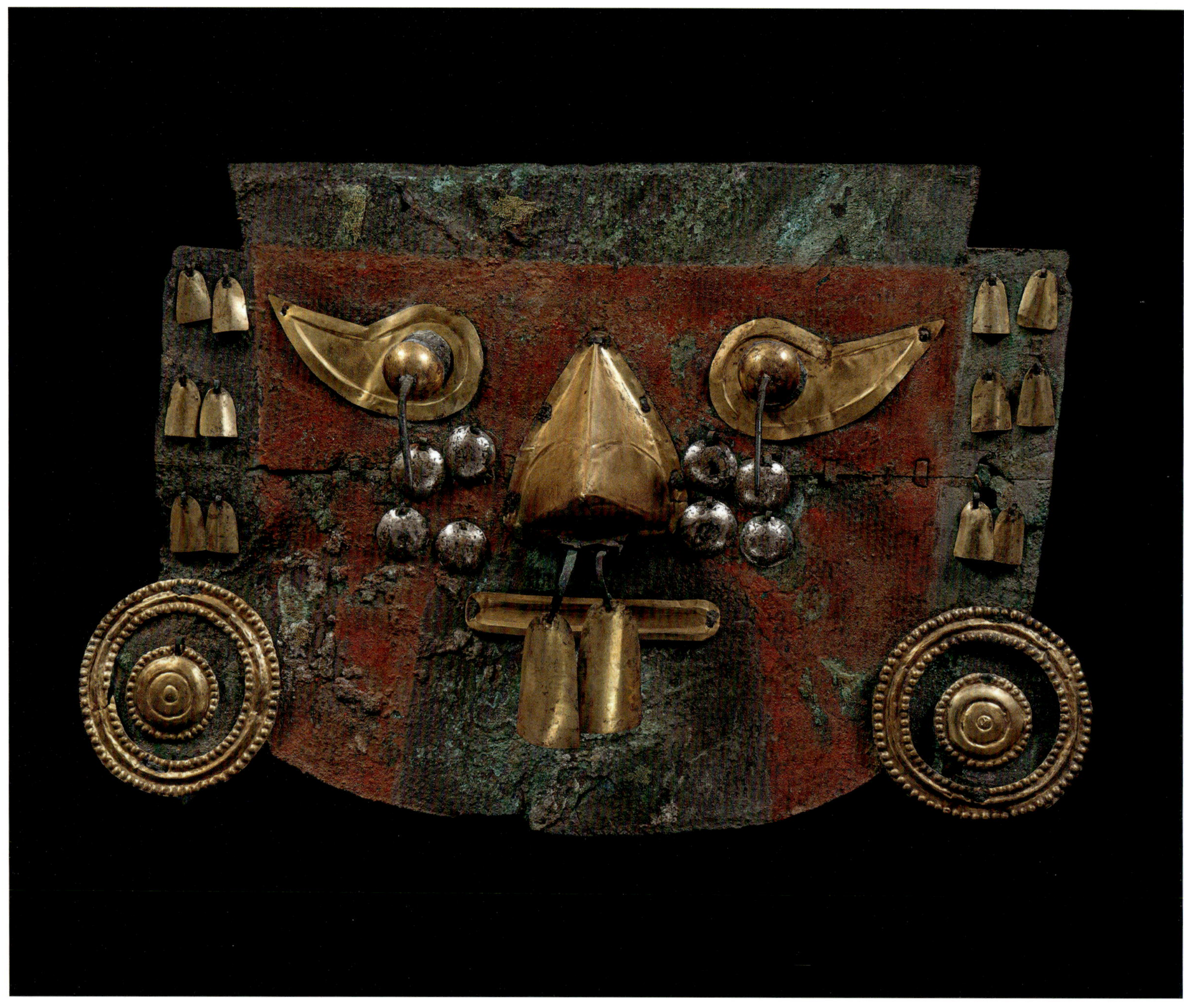

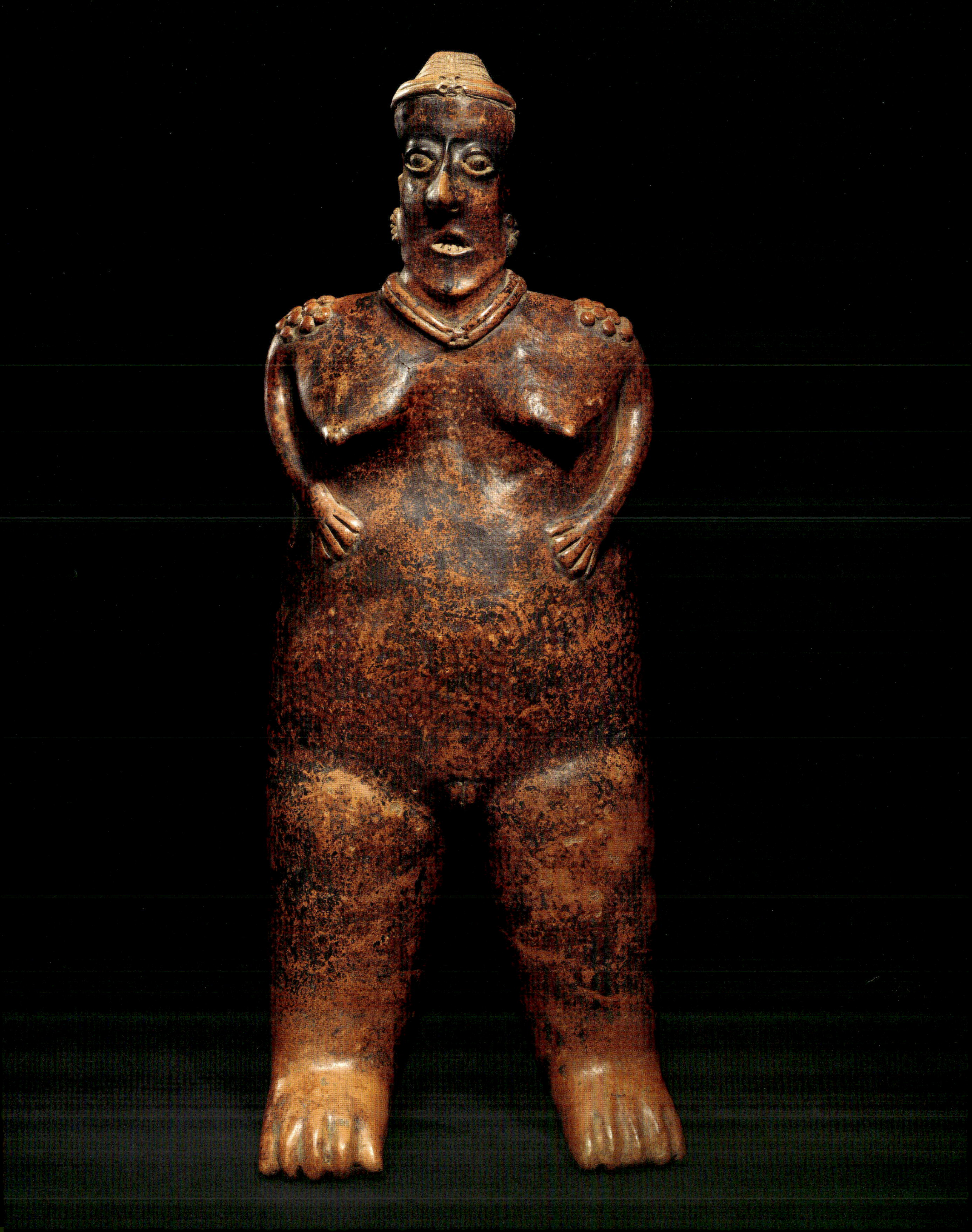

variety of objects. For males, warrior and ballgame player figures appear frequently. For women, many figures appear to refer to pregnancy. Hollow ceramic female figures are known in different west Mexican artistic styles, but they share common gender, posture/gesture combinations, facial expressions, and depiction of body decoration (**26**). Very likely, these figures represent pregnancy, but what aspect? Do they commemorate the pregnancy of a specific woman? Do they represent a desire to be pregnant or perhaps the birthing of an infant in an elite family? The figures might represent and commemorate the personal sacrifice of a woman who died in childbirth. Without contextual data, determining a precise meaning is elusive.

One of the most significant revelations from the Huitzilapa excavation was the verification that the juxtaposition of groups of hollow ceramic human figures was associated with specific individuals. Intuitively, it makes sense that female figures are associated with female remains and male figures with male remains, but so few tombs have been excavated by archaeologists that the data is limited. Based on the Huitzilapa example, this author proposed that these detailed and finely made figures represent the achieved status of the deceased.[10]

Social Impact of Death

The days of our years are threescore years and ten;
 and if by reason of strength they be fourscore years,
 yet is their strength labor and sorrow;
 for it is soon cut off, and we fly away.
(Psalm 90:1011)

My name is Ozymandias, King of Kings;
Look on my Works, ye Mighty, and despair!
Nothing beside remains. Round the decay
Of that colossal Wreck, boundless and bare
The lone and level sands stretch far away.
(Percy Bysshe Shelley, "Ozymandias," 1818)[12]

Prophets and poets have written about life's brevity, even for the rich and powerful. The Ramesseum, the massive mortuary temple of Ramesses II (reigned 1279–1213 BCE), is the monument that inspired Percy Bysshe Shelley's poem "Ozymandias." His message that even great kings and their mighty works do not last forever is a lesson for every generation.

Broadly speaking, a death requires two things—preparing the dead for the after-life and preparing the living for the after-death. Every culture establishes ways to satisfy both needs. Death, however, is much more than just the cessation of life. The death of a person, a member of the family and the larger society, is a loss that everyone confronts. To paraphrase a line from the film *Star Wars*, death is a rift in the Force.

Deaths have physical and psychological implications for the living that vary with the biological and familial characteristics of the deceased. As individuals grow, they develop knowledge and skills that benefit themselves, their families, and society. They integrate themselves into the social web. The death of a newborn baby is sad, indeed, but the impact is likely limited to the family. In contrast, the death of a person recognized for their knowledge, skills, and power has extensive effects. The recent passing of Queen Elizabeth II (1926–2022) was the largest, most extensive display of mortuary ritual for any death in a generation. She was the most recognized woman in the world, in addition to being the center point of more than 1,000 years of British tradition. The funerary events commemorated all of her social roles from grandmother to primary actor on the world stage.

Even in small-scale societies, deaths require adjustment. For example, the loss of an elder deprives a community of that person's accumulated wisdom, knowledge, and experience. If the community subsists by hunting and gathering, lost knowledge about food sources endangers it. Loss of wise elders leaves a hole in the spiritual life of communities that must be filled to sustain the living.

The living also must prepare for their own continuity. They need to protect themselves from any perceived evil caused by the dead, while they replace the dead in their spiritual, family, and work roles. Who leads the ceremonies? Who now finds food for the family? Societies have answered these questions by creating paths to succession or replacement. If a mother dies, perhaps her sister, or sisters, adopt the children, especially the young ones. If a spiritual leader dies, an appropriately

trained apprentice steps into the leader's role. In so-called egalitarian societies (after more than a century of ethnographic research, egalitarian societies have revealed more social distinctions than previously thought), in which each household expects to make all or most of their clothing and tools, junior members step up to do the work.

Regardless of who dies, the social fabric is torn; the relationships between the deceased and the living, and more important, among those who survive, are changed. Death is acknowledged, but life must go on. Death is like casting a stone into the quiet surface of water. Each one causes a ripple. Depending on the deceased's importance, the ripples will be small or tsunami-like in scale.

The Kota (Bakota) people of Gabon honor important clan ancestors with abstract figures of wood covered in thin copper. The head is recognizable, with hair and facial features that are clearly identifiable, while the rest of the body is more impressionistic. These figures surmounted the bone repositories of revered clan ancestors and served as spiritual guardians that protected the living (**27**). Paul Wingert describes this abstract form as representing a change from conveying personal emotional feelings toward the deceased to greater emphasis on the deceased's wealth and importance.[13] He suggests that this change of form parallels changes in fifteenth-century European tomb sculptures that also evolved from simple and naturalistic to more abstract forms.

An example from the Torres Straits of Australia combines stylized human features surmounted by a frigate bird that represents spiritual power in many cultures of the western Pacific (**28**). More subtle, the mask

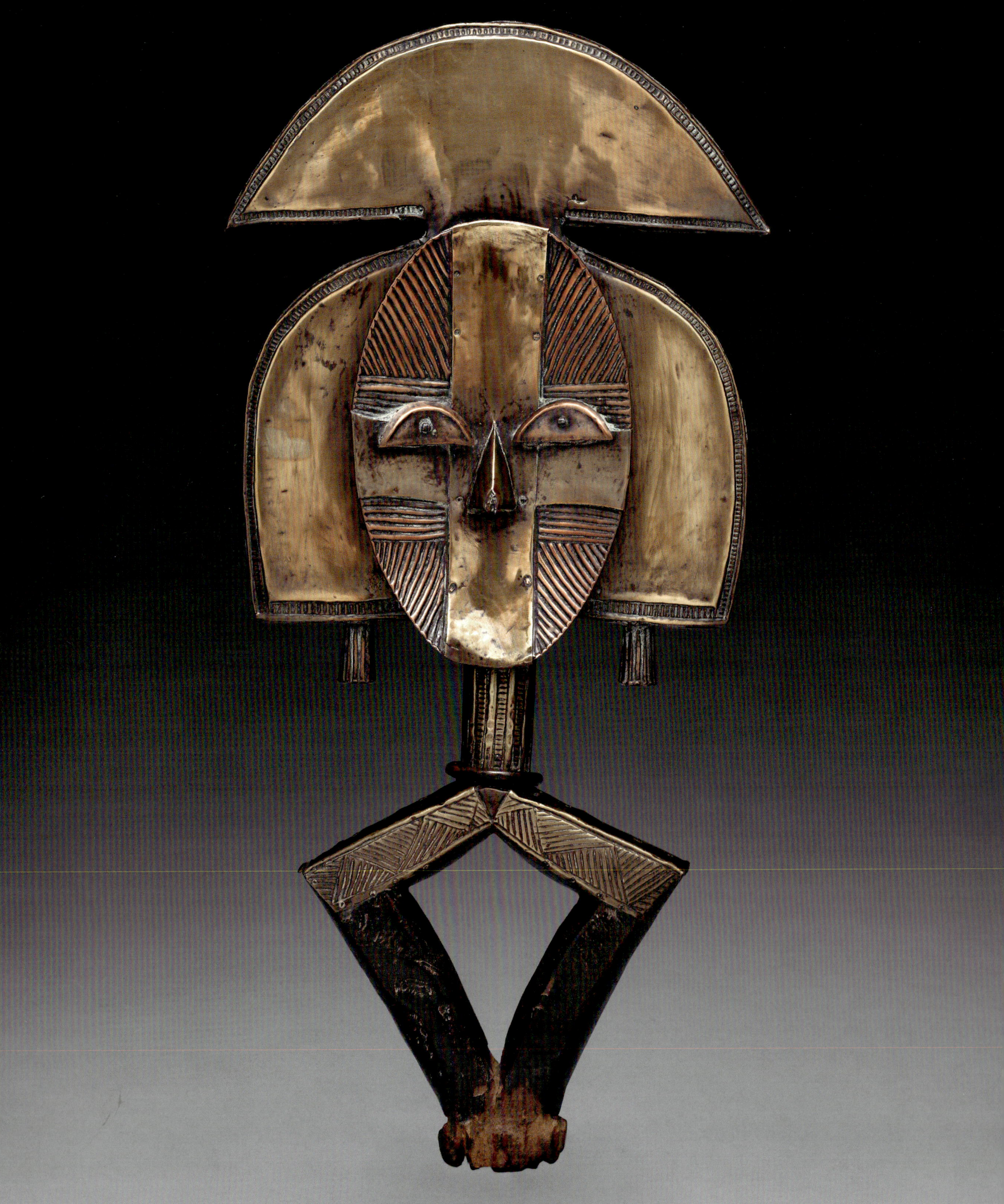

27 Sculptural Element from a Reliquary Ensemble (*Mbulu Ngulu*)

Kota-style maker, Gabon
1800 – 1900
Wood, copper alloy, and iron
24 x 19 ¹³⁄₁₆ x 1 ²⁄₁₆ in., 61 x 27.5 x 3 cm
Cleveland Museum of Art
Purchase from the J. H. Fund

28 Mask

Torres Strait Islander culture,
Mabuiag Island, Queensland, Australia
1850 – 1900
Turtle shell, wood, cassowary feathers, fiber,
resin, shell, paint
21 ½ x 25 x 22 ¾ in., 54.6 x 63.5 x 57.8 cm
Metropolitan Museum of Art, New York
The Michael C. Rockefeller Memorial Collection,
Purchase, Nelson A. Rockefeller Gift, 1967

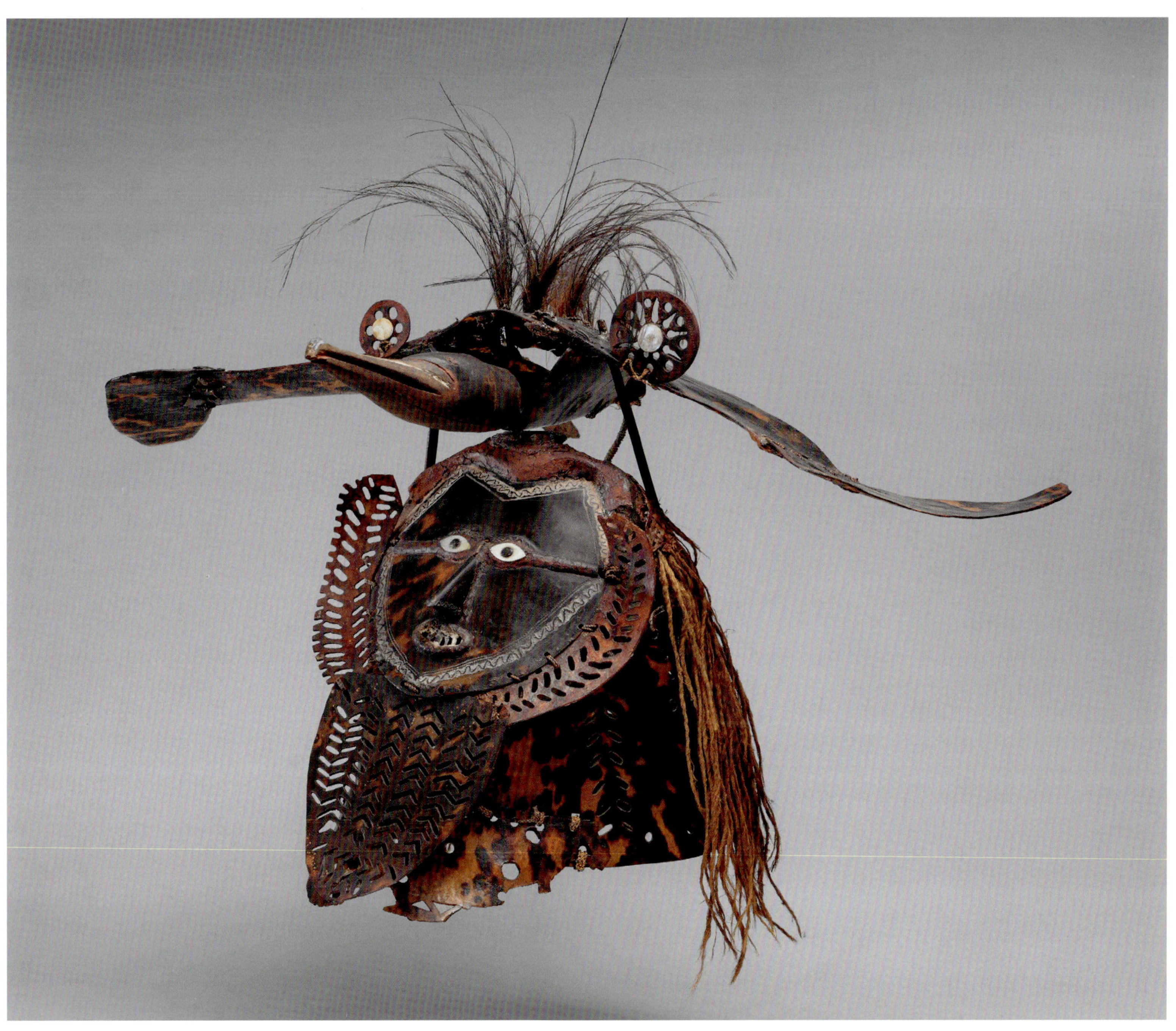

is made of sea turtle shell, a species that lives in the ocean but also needs to come to land to reproduce. The mask thus combines elements of the sky, sea, and land with the human who wears it.

Protecting the Living from the Dead

Dealing with the dead is dangerous business. Perhaps they do not want to leave this life, or even worse, they want to harm the living. Spiritualists create rationales and practices to protect people from the dangers of the dead. Rituals, incantations, offerings, and memorials exist to appease the dead's spirit and protective performances to thwart any negative impact on the living.

Sometimes, even mention of the dead invited evil. The Navajo people of the American Southwest have a tradition of dangerous witches. If someone died in a house or other building, it was abandoned to avoid any potential contact with evil. In some societies, when a person dies, their names are never spoken again and newborns are never named after an ancestor, regardless of how revered they were.

Sometimes, the dead need protection from themselves. Perhaps one of the best examples is the heart scarab that is an essential part of ancient Egyptian mummification practices. The shape of the heart scarab itself was powerfully protective because of its association with Khepri, the young sun god. The flat underside of the stone scarab was engraved with spell 30B from the Book of the Dead, a collection of mortuary texts that dates

back to ca. 1550 BCE. During the embalming process and after the internal organs were removed (the lungs, liver, intestines, stomach, and brain), a stone scarab was placed in the body cavity near the heart.

Ancient Egyptians believed that at the judgement of the dead, Anubis, the jackal-headed god, weighed the heart against the feather of the goddess Ma'at, known as the feather of truth. If the heart was lighter than the feather, the deceased passed into the next life; if not, Ammit, the hippopotamus monster, immediately devoured the person and they ceased to exist, forever. The protective text reads:

> *Oh my heart of [my] mother! Oh my heart of [my] mother!*
> *My heart of my different ages! Do not stand as a witness!*
> *Do not oppose me in the tribunal! Do not show your hostility*
>   *against me before the Keeper of the Balance! For you are*
>   *my ka which is in my body, the protector who causes my*
>   *limbs to be healthy!*
> *Go forth (for yourself) to the good place to which we hasten!*
> *Do not cause our name to stink to the entourage who make men*
>   *in heaps!*
> *What is good for us is good for the judge! May the heart stretch*
>   *(i.e. be happy) at the verdict! Do not speak lies in the presence*
>   *of god!*
> *Behold You are distinguished, existing (as a justified [meaning*
>   *worthy of rebirth] one)!*[14]

Elaborate, decorated, and hieroglyph-inscribed coffins also offered magical protection to the deceased. A sarcophagus at the Denver Museum of Nature and Science was a sacred

29 Takiyasha the Witch and the Skeleton Spectre

Utagawa Kuniyoshi (Japan, 1798 – 1861)
1843 – 1847
Ukiyo-e woodblock print triptych
Honolulu Museum of Art

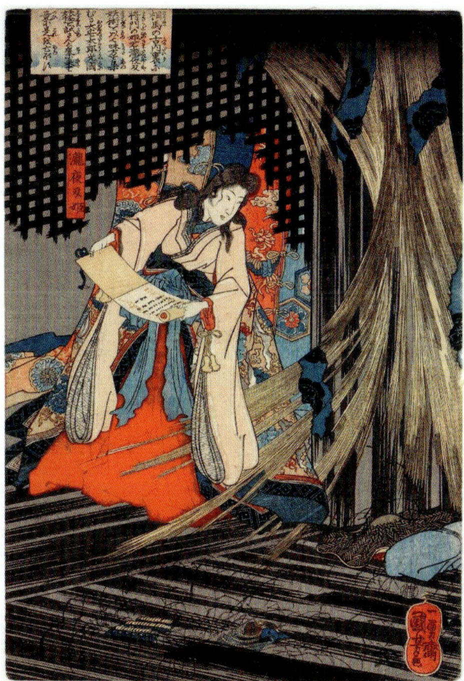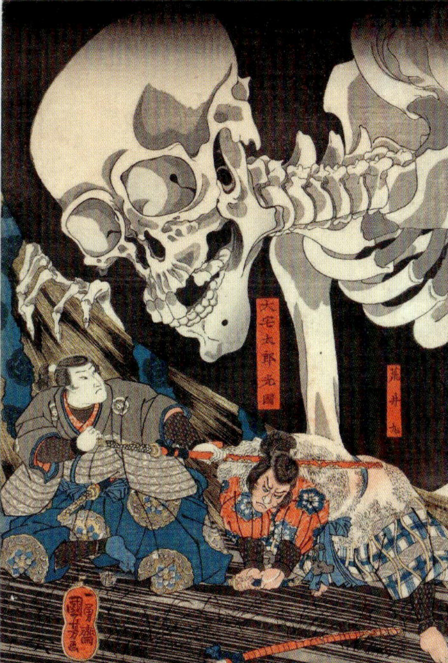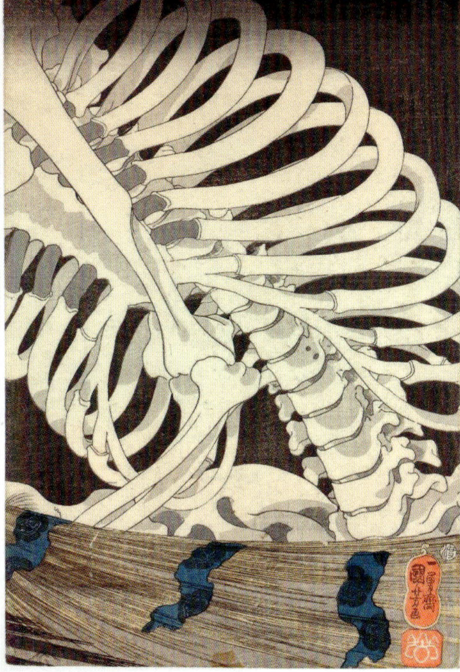

receptacle. The mummy lays directly on the image of the god Osiris, who is associated with resurrection and everlasting life. On the left side of the coffin, the goddess Isis, known as the Queen of Heaven and Great Lady of Magi and identified by her step crown, and on the right, the goddess of death and protector of souls Nephthys, wearing a crown representing a basket, encompass the mummy with all of their protective powers.

Horror movies take advantage of our fear of the dead and what they might do. Those movies are designed to scare people as well as to entertain, but for most of human history, the fear of the dead was real. Appeasing the dead, wearing protective amulets, or reciting protective incantations and prayers made people feel safe. Ancient Egyptian rituals, magic, and amulets influenced ancient Greek and Roman practices as well as those of early Christians, who also incorporated incantations and spells for protection from the dead into their rituals.[15]

Japan's tradition of terrifying ghosts provided inspiration for many *ukiyo-e* woodblock print masters.

Tokugawa Tsunayoshi Visiting Nikkō Shrine

Tsukioka Yoshitoshi (Japan, 1839 – 1892)
1875
Woodblock print
7 x 9 ½ in., 17.8 x 24.1 cm
Los Angeles County Museum of Art (LACMA)
Herbert R. Cole Collection

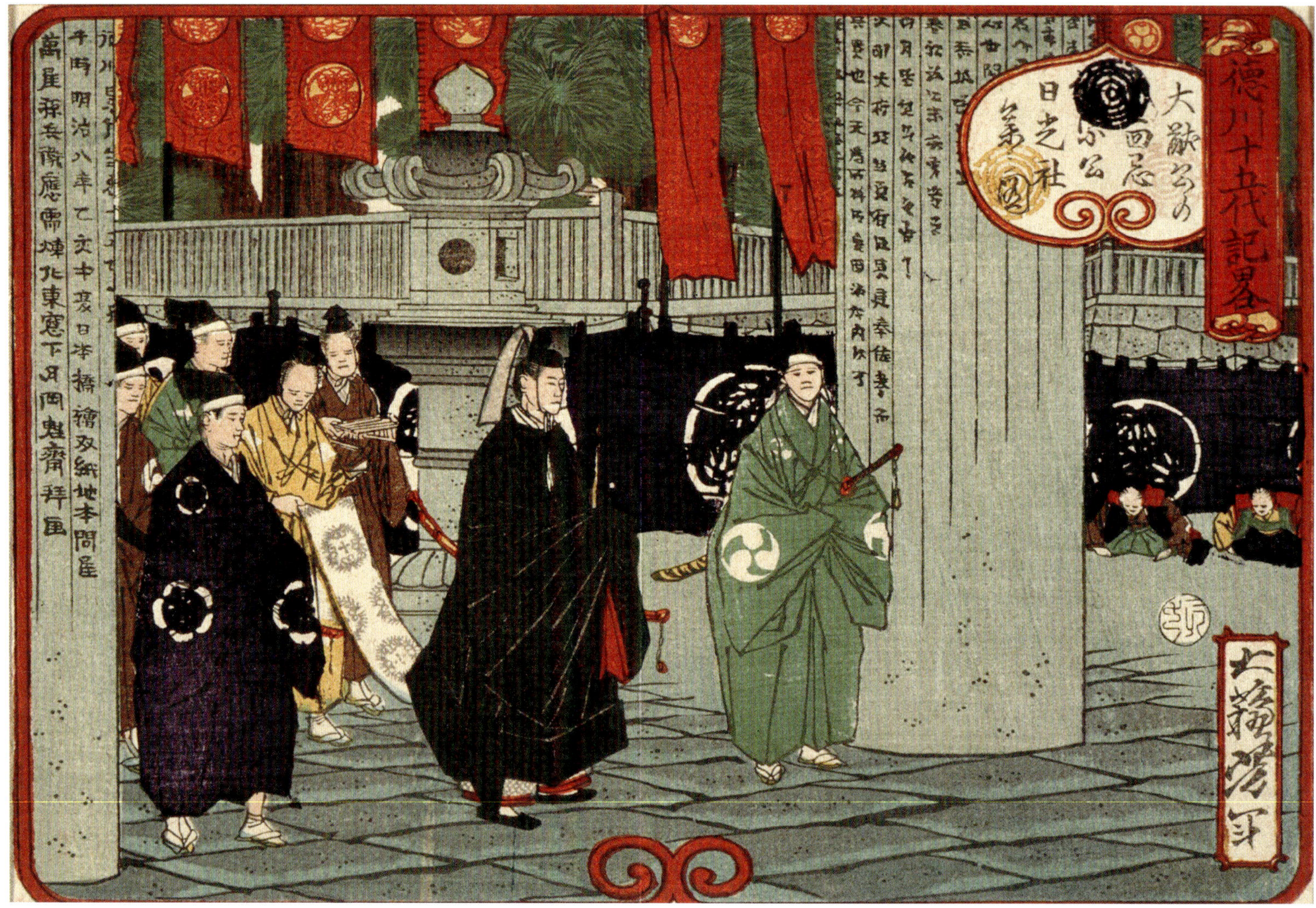

Utagawa Kuniyoshi created a powerful triptych that portrayed a giant skeleton summoned by a witch to haunt the palace of warlord Taira Masakado (903–940) (**29**). The threatening skeleton represented the ghosts of soldiers killed in a failed rebellion. Honoring the dead through appropriate rituals commemorates the dead and protects the living. The Tokugawa Tsunayoshi, the fifth shogun in that dynasty, leads a procession into the Nikkō mortuary shrine to honor his illustrious ancestors (**30**).

In modern times, a fear of ghosts and malevolent spirits is less common but the psychological impact of death remains. Elizabeth Kübler-Ross succinctly defined five stages of the grieving process after a death: denial, anger, bargaining, depression, and acceptance.[16] Anyone who has lost a loved one recognizes their own journey through this maze of emotions.

In some cultures, the dead provide guidance rather than danger. In nineteenth- and early twentieth-century men's houses of highland New Guinea, the preserved heads of revered ancestors were displayed in honored places and were consulted or petitioned when needed. At times, men retained just the skull of their ancestor, or the skull with the mandible attached by a woven cord. Other times, the skulls of the deceased were over-modeled with sunbaked mud that provided life-like contours, while paint and actual hair were used to provide a more realistic appearance. This practice emphasizes that while a physical line separates the living and the dead, the family includes both. Male ancestors in highland New Guinea were also portrayed in other forms and displayed in village men's houses. Spirit or *gope* boards are hand-carved figures of ancestral spirits that protect the living from evil and death.

A Proper Send-Off

Thousands of years before the first pharaoh, Egyptians buried their dead in desert sands, often covered with nothing more than a woven reed mat. No doubt, these ancient folks observed that the arid climate and sands preserved the body. Reliance on the desert's natural dryness and heat evolved into intentional mummification. For at least 3,000 years—through the Old, Middle, and Late Kingdoms, as well as the Ptolemaic and Roman periods in Egypt—bodies were mummified to preserve as much of their life likenesses as possible. However, determining who deserved mummification also evolved over the millennia. In the Old Kingdom (ca. 2700–2200 BCE), only the pharaoh was mummified, and through that practice, he achieved eternal life. A lifelike corpse was essential so that the *ba*, the *ka*, and the *akh*, all spiritual entities, could recognize their human host. The *akh* was particularly important as it determined if the person was worthy of an afterlife. Eventually, mummification and its implications for eternal life extended from the pharaoh to his family, then to nobles, and eventually to everyone who could afford it. Under the Egyptian pharaohs, beautiful images constructed of cartonnage, consisting of layers of linen and plaster, and decorated with paint, gold leaf, and hair, presented powerful portraits of the deceased (**31**). During

Egypt
New Kingdom, Dynasty 18, 1427 – 1390 BCE
Cartonnage, gesso, paint, gold, copper alloy, faience
14 ¹⁵⁄₁₆ x 15 ¹⁵⁄₁₆ x 7 ½ in., 38 x 40.5 x 19 cm
Metropolitan Museum of Art, New York
Theodore M. Davis Collection,
Bequest of Theodore M. Davis, 1915

the reign of the Greek Ptolemies, painted images of the dead were inserted in the mummy's wrappings (**32**). The mummification process was expensive and required up to ninety days, according to Herodotus. People wanted the best mummification they could afford even if that meant sacrificing some pleasures of this world in order to prepare for eternal life.

Ancient Egyptians believed that just as pharaoh called people to service in this life, so, too, could the gods call the deceased to service in the afterlife. For that reason, they created *ushabti* (also known as *shabti* or *shawabti*), small mummiform figures that stood in for the deceased in the land of the dead. Pharaohs were entombed with *ushabtis* of a quality of workmanship befitting their status. The *ushabti* of 19th-Dynasty pharaoh Siptah were made of carved and polished alabaster stone (**33**), while most individuals' *ushabtis* were made of faience, a blue-green glazed clay or wood. Royals and nobles had access to more expensive materials, including stone and gold. *Ushabti* were placed in elaborately decorated wooden casks with the deceased (**34** and **35**).

Cultures across the world commemorate the status and important achievements of the living when they die. The elites in highly stratified societies commission the most sumptuous architecture and the greatest assemblages of objects. The pyramids and elaborate mortuary temples of Egypt are some of the best-known examples. The royal pyramids testify to the knowledge, power, and importance of the pharaohs. Around the base of the great pyramids on the Giza Plateau, lesser

royals and nobles built their own mortuary temples to be near the god kings and to ensure that the living continued to perform proper rituals on their behalf. These magnificent mortuary monuments continue to be spectacular reminders of pharaonic power and prestige.

The first Qin emperor of China, Qin Shi Huang (259–210 BCE), sought eternal life and believed it could be achieved by drinking magical potions and preparing a mortuary monument on a scale not seen before or since. Thousands of workers toiled to create an entire terracotta army, each soldier with an individualized face and armed appropriately with real weapons, not replicas. The time and cost of materials and the scale of the effort involved is breathtaking, only the best being suitable for the person who unified China. Two elements of the emperor's extravagant tomb stand out. First, much of the military equipment deposited in it could have armed living soldiers, so in a sense, the emperor was demonstrating that his empire was wealthy enough to bury these riches without endangering his rule. Second, everything was buried out of the view of the living. The mortuary temples and pyramids of Egypt were on sacred ground but they were visible architectural monuments, even if their contents were not. The Qin emperor's ostentatious display was not for mortal eyes—it was created for the afterlife.

The royal bronzes and ivories of Benin provide an example of sumptuous and finely crafted objects made for deceased royals for veneration by the living. The images, busts, and accoutrement of royalty and kingship were cared for and displayed in shrines to deceased royals. Some of the busts are lifelike portraits while other objects

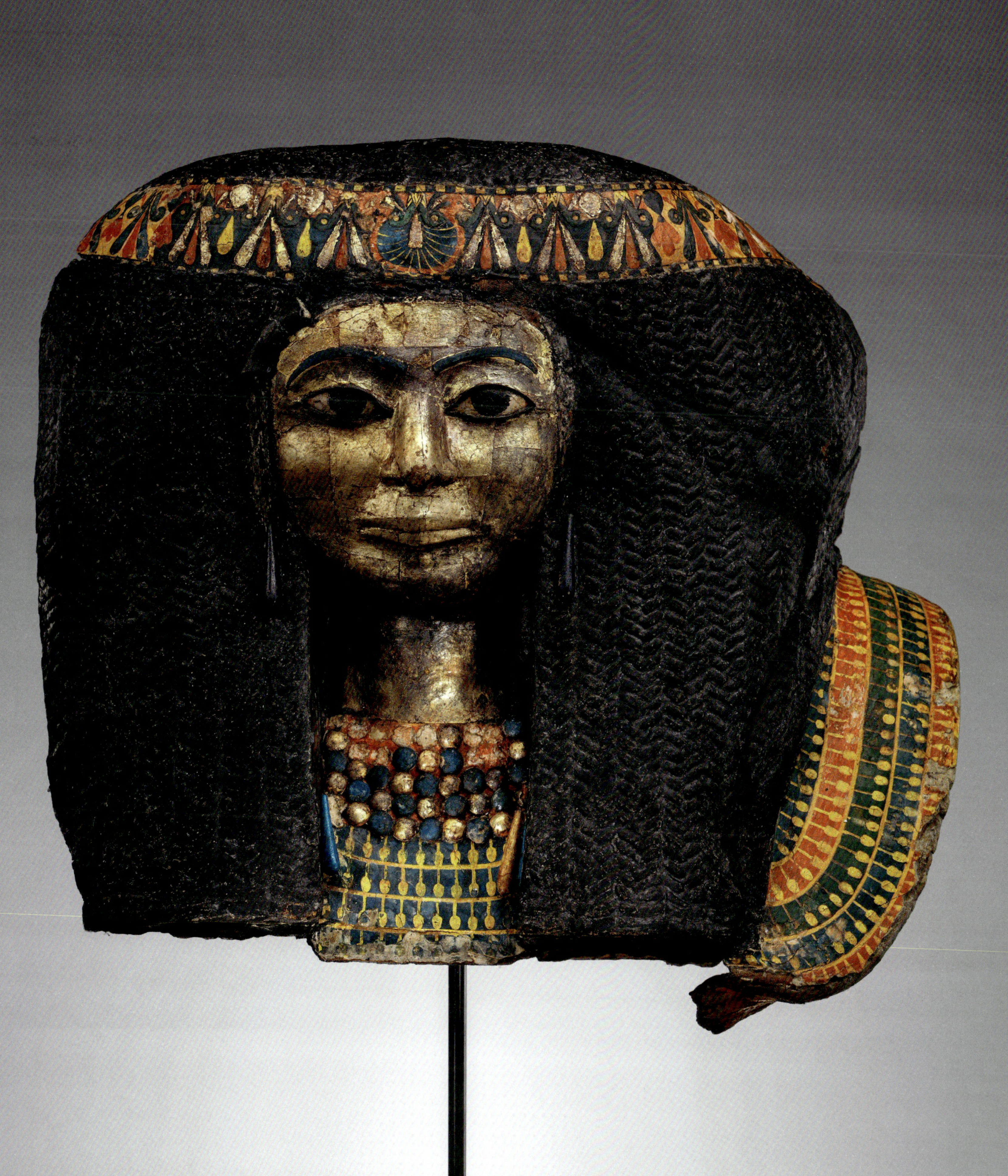

32 **Mummy Portrait of a Youth**

Egypt
150 – 200 CE
8 x 5 ⅒ in., 20.3 x 13 cm
Encaustic on wood
Getty Center, Los Angeles

33 *Shabti* of Siptah

Egypt
New Kingdom, Ramesside, Dynasty 19,
1194 – 1188 BCE
Travertine (Egyptian alabaster), paint
8 ¼ in., 20.9 cm
Metropolitan Museum of Art, New York
Gift of Theodore M. Davis, 1914

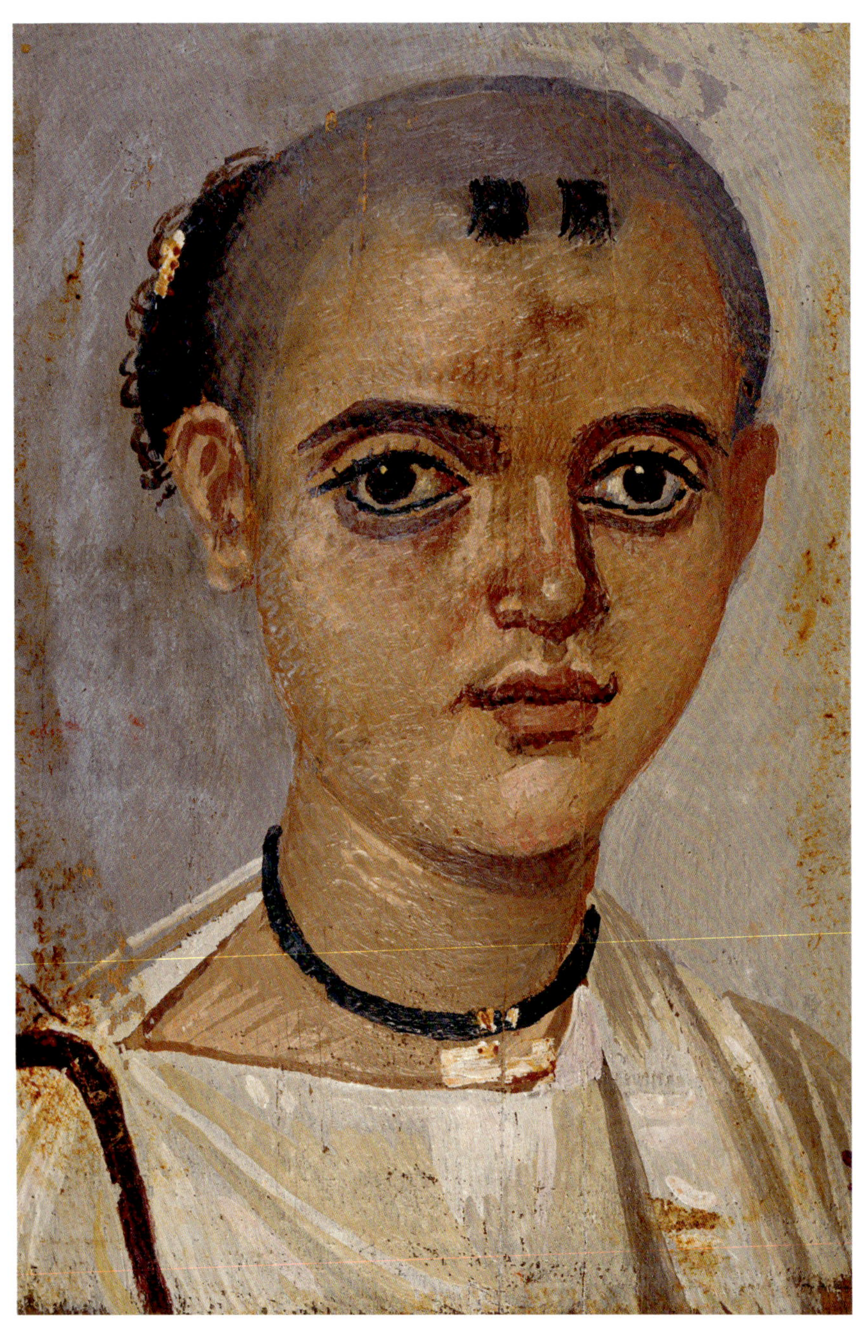

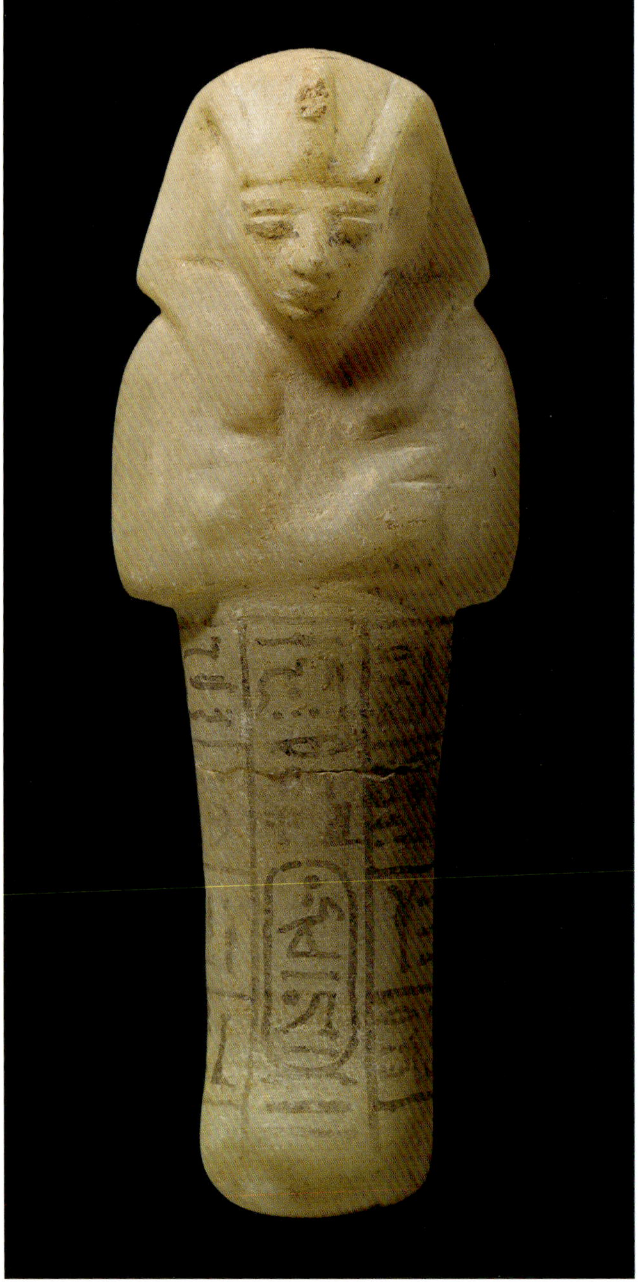

34 *Shabti* **Coffin of Wahneferhotep**

Egypt
Middle Kingdom, Dynasty 12 – 13,
1981 – 1640 BCE
Wood, paint, gold leaf
9 ⅞ x 4 ⅛ x 6 ⅛ in., 25.1 x 10.4 x 15.5 cm
Metropolitan Museum of Art, New York
Rogers Fund and Edward S. Harkness
Gift, 1914

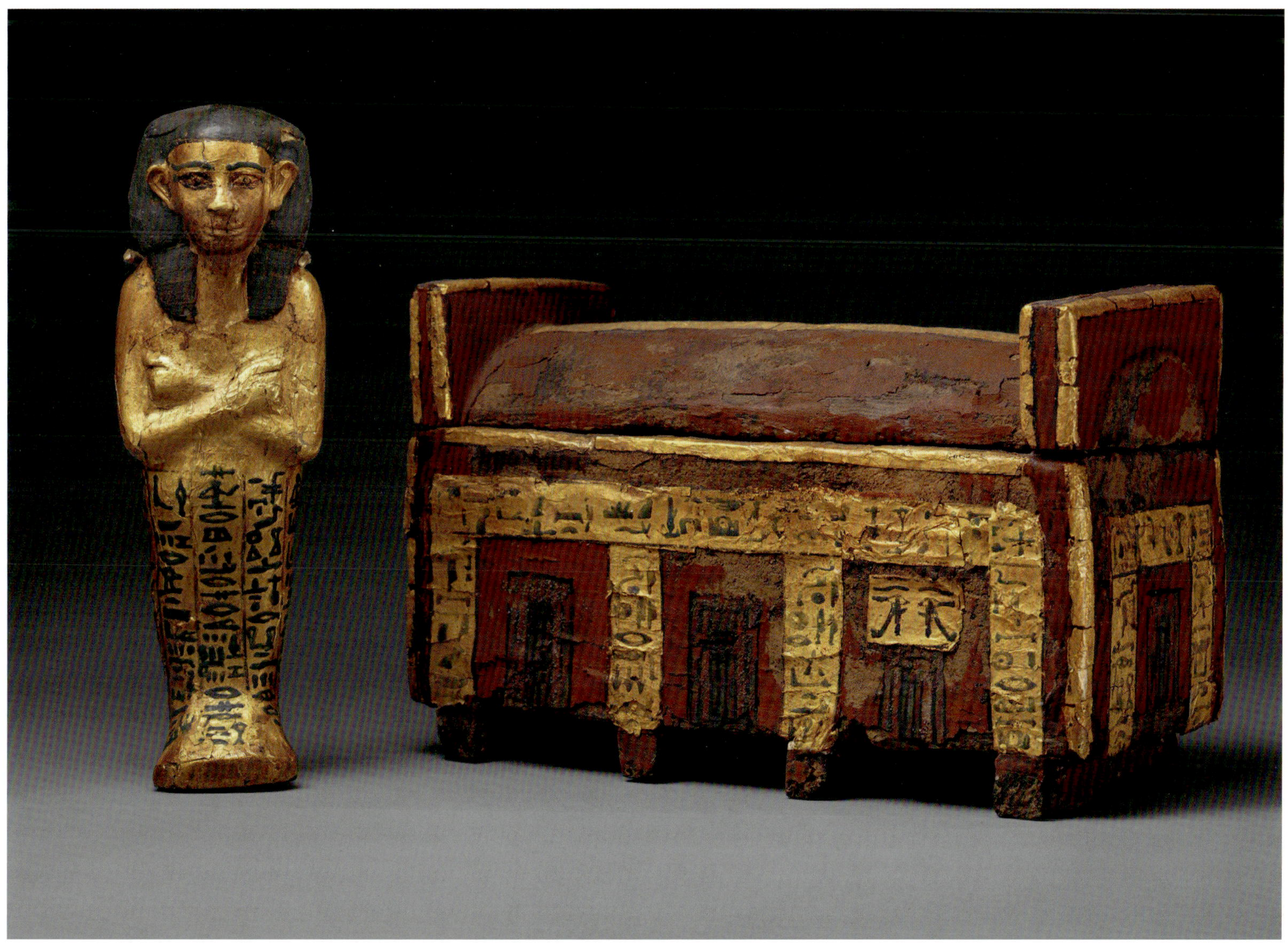

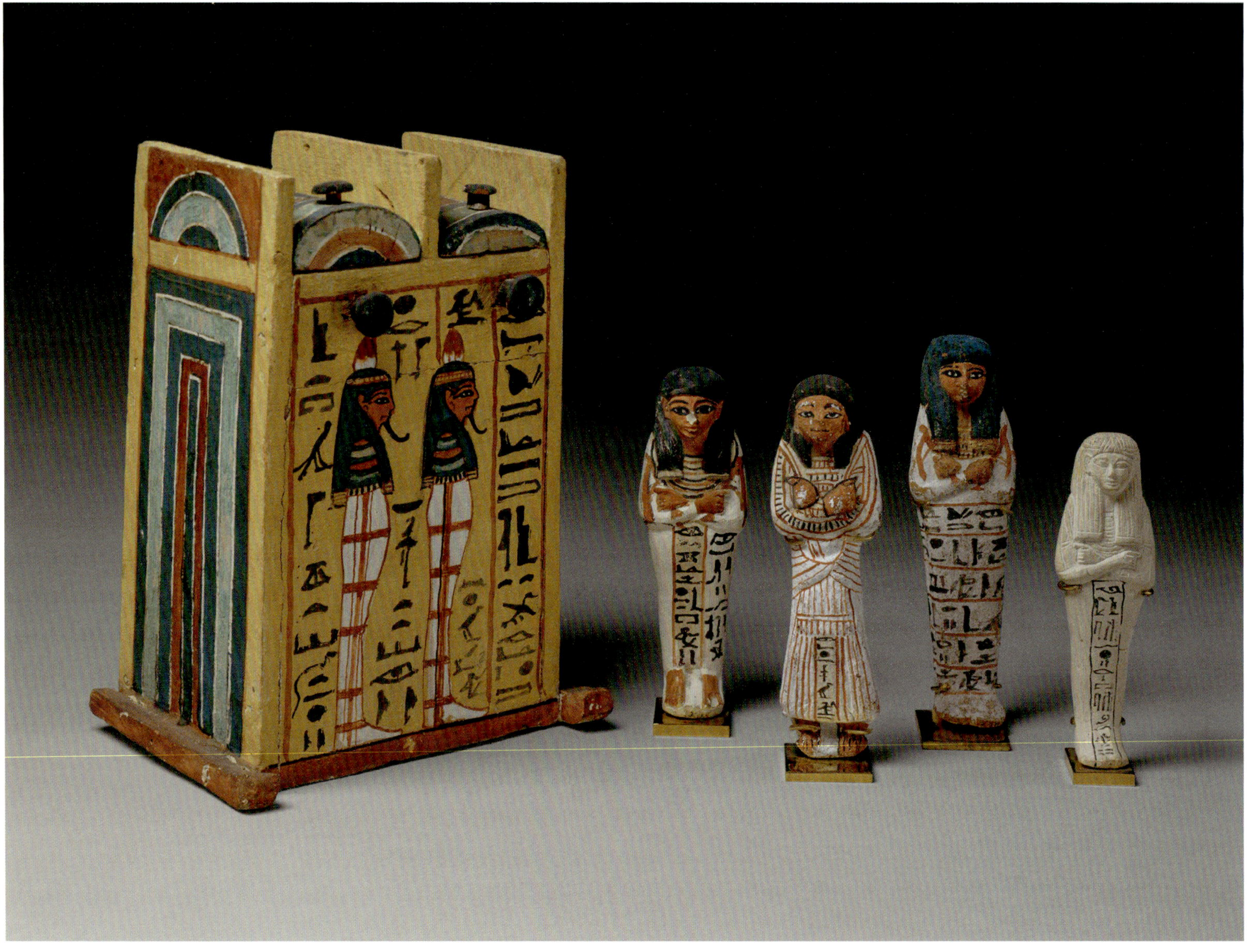

symbolize the dynasty's power and prestige. Ironically, the looting of the Benin royal shrines during the British Punitive Expedition of 1897 revealed these finely crafted cultural treasures to Europe and the rest of the world, where some questioned whether African artists could create such refined and exquisitely made bronzes and ivories. Today's art historians recognize the mastery of Benin artists and see the Benin figures as some of the finest bronzes and ivories made anywhere in the world (**36**). Their nobility and serenity denote high artistic conceptualization and achievement. It is important to note the individualized busts reflect the royals who they represent. The British attack on the royal shrines of Benin were controversial from the beginning, especially as some of the looted objects were sold to pay for the raid itself. In recent years, mounting social pressure is forcing the return of these treasures. They are not merely art objects, but continue to be important cultural properties and icons.

In the seventeenth to mid-eighteenth century, the Akan people of Ghana also created elegant memorial heads (*nsodie*) of royals but also of couriers and servants to sustain the royals in the afterlife (**37**). The figures are made of terracotta and have stylized features.

Not all societies were ruled by kings or emperors. Although virtually every society evidences some social, economic, religious, and/or political stratification, there may be few layers or many depending on the size and scale of the society. However, every society needs and values the knowledge and work of its members. Adults produce food and create tools, clothing, and shelter. They protect the community and its children, and they train them to be future adults. A death in this group brings not just grief but actual loss. People who live on the land—those who hunt, fish, gather, and grow crops—are especially important to their communities. The harsher the environment, the more important their knowledge of foods, seasons, and weather are for survival. Their passing may cause immediate danger of starvation.

These cultures, too, have mortuary rituals and behaviors that acknowledge life and commemorate death. At its most basic level, a death affects the immediate family. For most of human history, the loss of newborns and babies under two years of age was common (**38**). Mortality rates in this age group top fifty percent in some cultures. In contemporary times, some societies are plagued by famine and insufficient medical systems. They, too, suffer high infant mortality. How does a society deal with such sad but common losses? Can it bear to invest itself and its emotional stability in these brief fleeting lives? In some cultures, an infant must survive for at least a year or two to be considered fully human and part of the society. Often, crossing these age thresholds is a time for celebration, naming, and accepting the baby into the social fabric. Some ancestral Puebloan societies of the American southwest believed that if a baby died under four days old, it had a chance of being reborn into the same family. For that reason, they were buried under the floor, nearby.[17] The belief that the spirit survives and returns provides some comfort after an infant death.

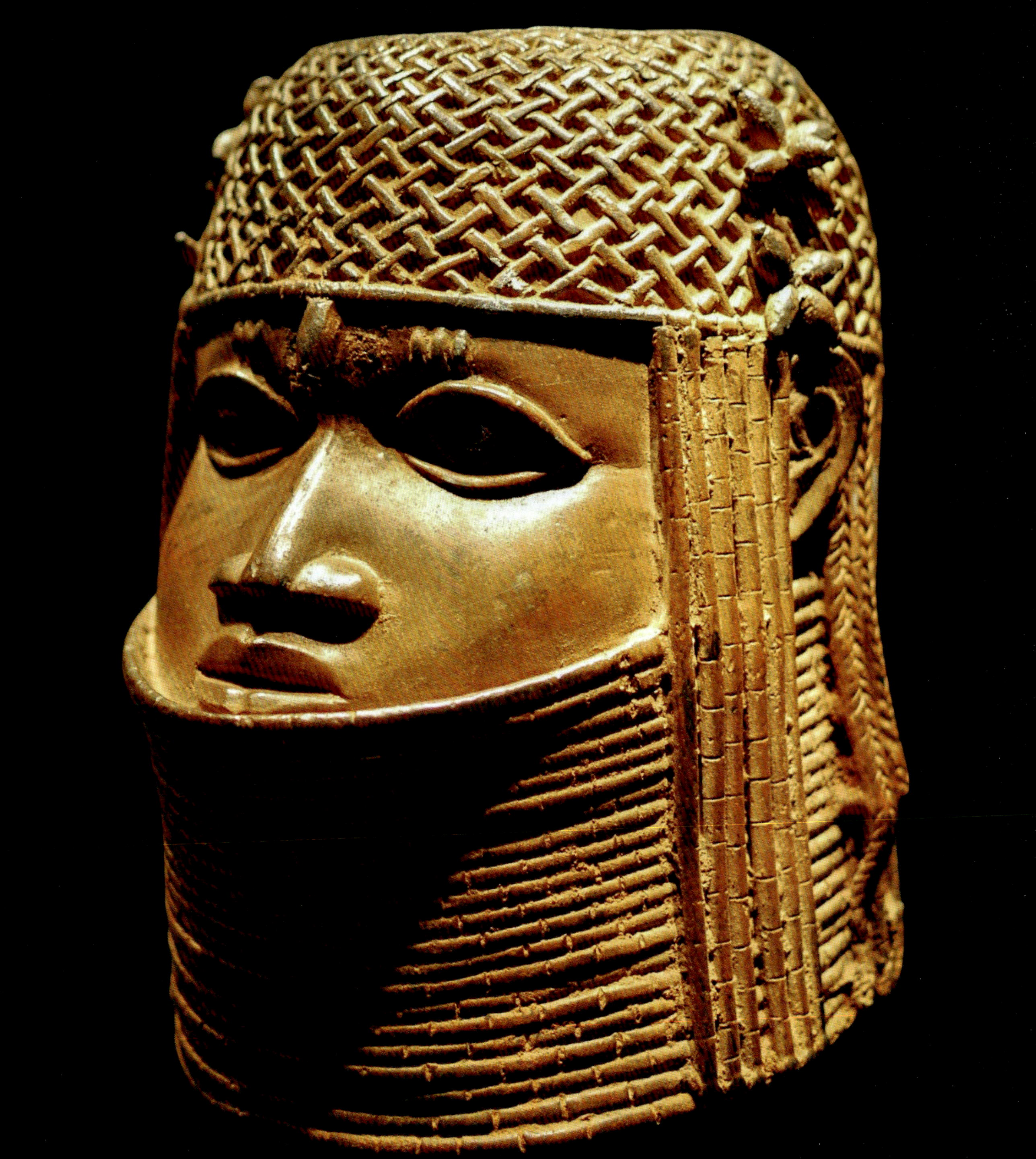

36 Cast Ceremonial Head of an *Oba*

Edo culture, Benin City, Nigeria
1600 – 1800
Bronze
Bristol Museum & Art Gallery, England

37 Memorial Head (*Nsodie*)

Akan culture, Ghana
1600 – 1750
Terracotta, roots, quartz fragments
8 x 5 ½ x 4 ¾ in., 20.3 x 14 x 12.1 cm
Metropolitan Museum of Art, New York
The Michael C. Rockefeller Memorial Collection,
Purchase, Nelson A. Rockefeller Gift, 1967

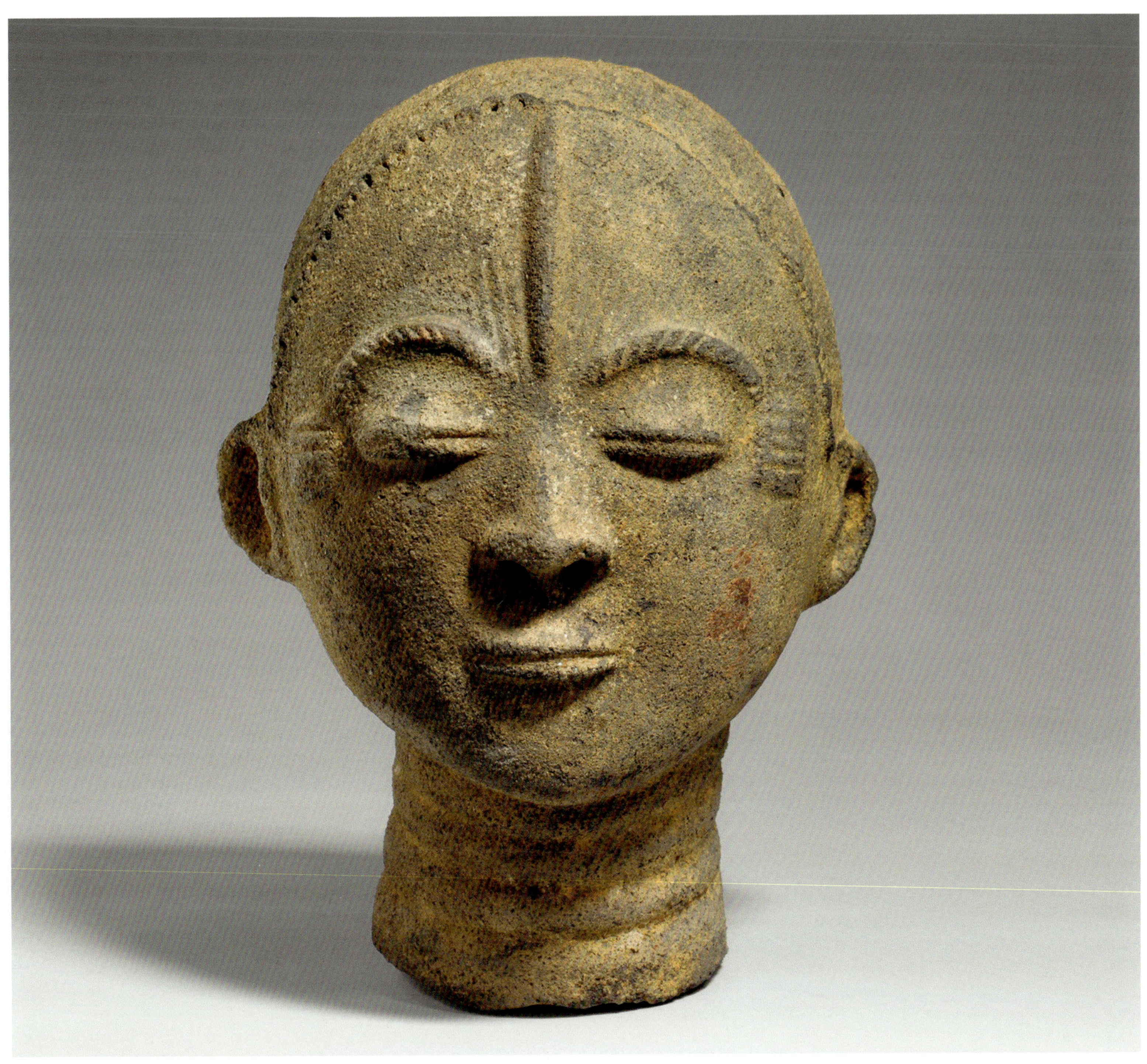

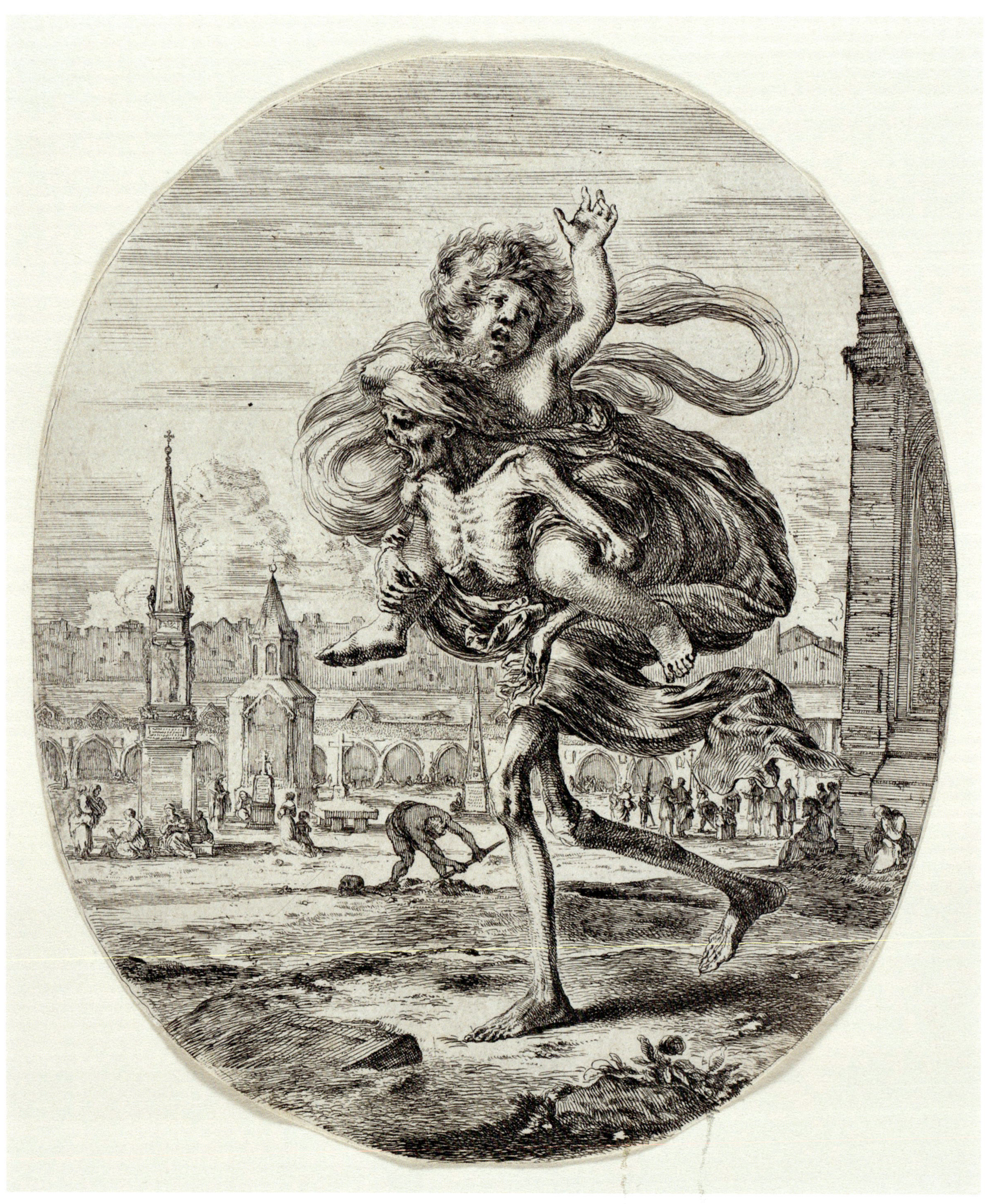

Objects for the Dead

[T]he sick man having been appointed by the Autmoin to die . . . all the relations and neighbors assembled, with the greatest possible solemnity, he delivers his funeral oration; he recites his heroic deeds, gives some directions to his family, recommends his friends; finally says adieu…as to gifts, they make none at all; but, quite different from us, the survivors give some to the dying man. (Pére Pierre Biard, SJ)[18]

Regardless of status or personal achievement, the dead must be properly equipped for their journey, often with personal adornment and tools, and sometimes with extensive offerings of food and clothing as well as animal and human sacrifices. These contributions are intentional, culturally important, and reflect cultural beliefs and values.

In hunting societies, spears and other weapons often are part of the contributed grave goods. Spears, bows and arrows, or other weapons equipped the deceased for hunts on the celestial plain, just as they did in this life. Of course, royals always had elaborate versions of these objects. An intriguing example comes from the tomb of the pharaoh Tutankhamun (ca. 1333–1323 BCE). Two nearly identical knives represent the duality of functional versus symbolic tools. The hilts and sheaths are similar in design and made primarily of gold. The difference between the daggers is the metal in the blades: one is made of gold, which signifies a ritual purpose, and the other is made of iron, signifying a functional purpose. According to recent analysis by Matsui Takafumi et al., the steel blade has its own amazing story and may have been the more important of the two.[19] Their analysis strongly indicates that the steel came from a meteor—truly a heavenly gift for a divine king. It is probable that the steel was not refined in Egypt but in Mitanni, an extensive kingdom that included northern Iraq, Syria, and part of Turkey. This unique knife may have been a gift from King Tasratta (14th century BCE) to Amenhotep III (ca. 1391–ca. 1354 BCE), Tutankhamun's grandfather.

Vessels for food and drink frequently are contributed goods for the afterlife. While some may have been used in everyday life before being interred, others may be specially created mortuary gifts or they may commemorate important events or achievements of the deceased. A lidded, polychrome Mayan cup carries a glyphic inscription below the rim that identifies the sixth-century Maya lord who owned it (**39**). The inscription also identifies the ritual drink's primary ingredients; a probable translation is "chilled and fruity cacao corn drink."[20]

In many parts of the world, the burning of incense is part of the mortuary ritual and the later celebrations. This example from Southwestern Arabia depicts an ibex (**40**). Incense might have multiple functions, including covering the smell of the dead, creating an appropriate ritual atmosphere, or even transporting prayers to the gods.

Cultures as far apart as Asia and the Americas sometimes included models of houses used by the living that also were desired abodes in the afterlife. During

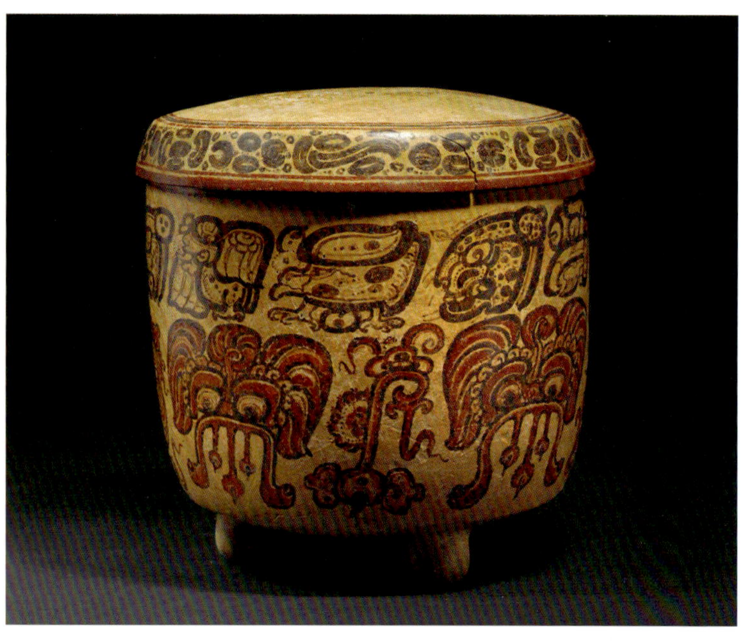

39 Tripod Lidded Vessel with Glyphs and Butterflies

Maya culture, Mexico
500 – 600 CE
Terracotta
9 ¾ x 8 ¾ in., 24.77 x 22.23 cm
The Stuart Handler Collection

40 Incense Burner

Southwestern Arabia
500 BCE
Bronze
10 ⅞ x 9 ⁵⁄₁₆ x 9 ⅛ in., 27.7 x 23.7 x 23.2 cm
Metropolitan Museum of Art, New York
Gift of Dr. Sidney A. Chariat, in memory of
his parents Newman and Adele Chariat, 1949

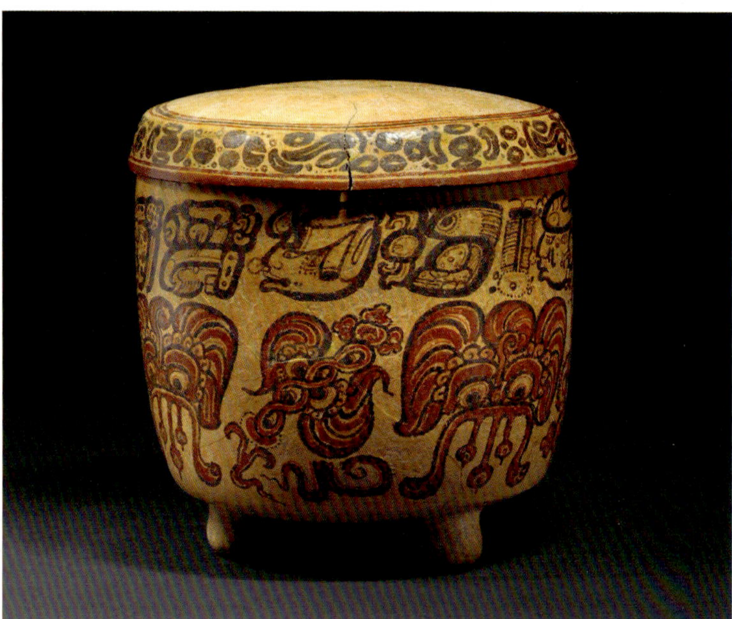

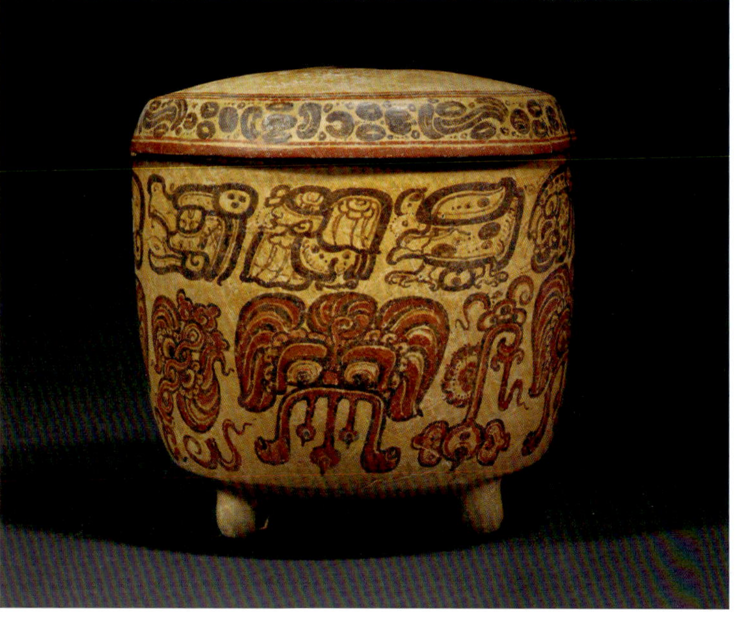

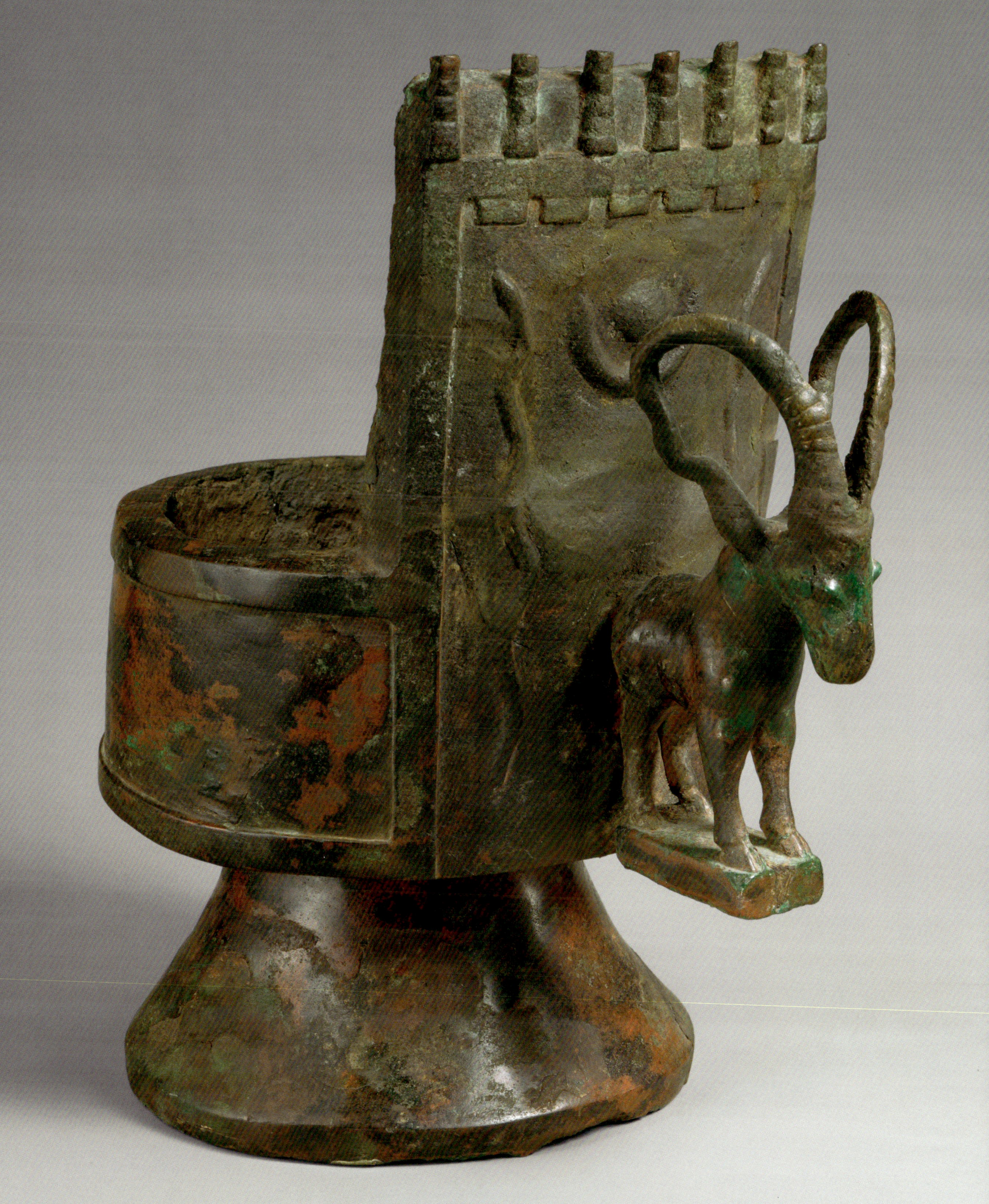

41 **Funerary Sculpture of a Double-Courtyard Residential Compound**

Shanxi Province, China
Middle Ming dynasty, 1450 – 1550
Earthenware with white slip, pigments, and green glaze
21 x 36 x 72 in., 53.3 x 91.4 x 182.9 cm
Los Angeles County Museum of Art (LACMA)
Gift of Mrs. Blanche Wilbur Mill

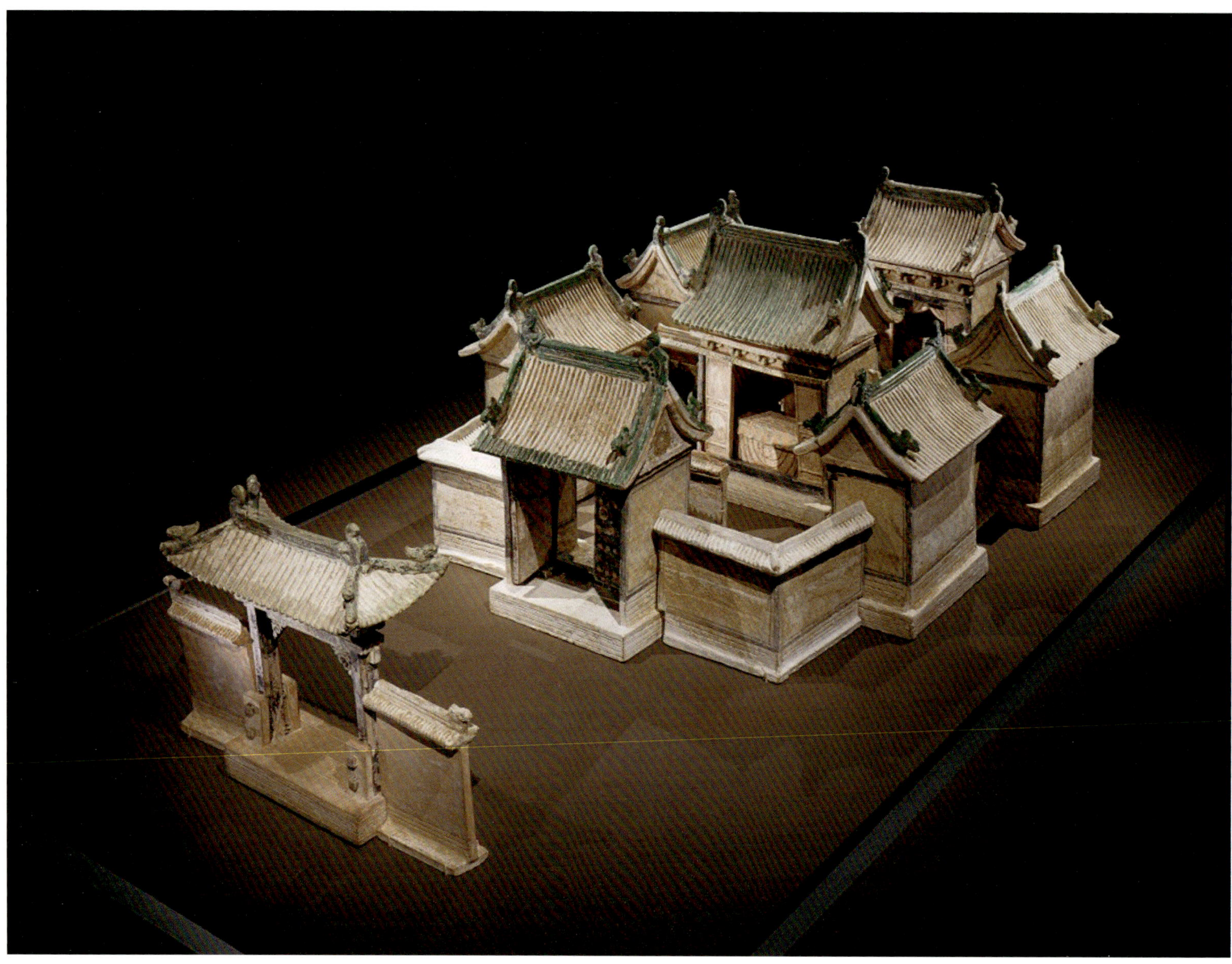

the Han dynasty in China (206 BCE–220 CE), elaborate models of houses, temples, and everyday activities were created from fired clay. Chinese families were the core of social structure, and one model depicts a magnificent compound in which the multigenerational family could live together (41).

In the shaft tombs of west Mexico, ca. 300 BCE–500 CE, ceramic houses complete with people engaged in various activities and, sometimes, dogs, were placed in the tomb. Complex examples have a lower component with seated people below the main floor of the house, which also depicts people. One interpretation is that the two levels represent the living family above and the family ancestors below. Shaft tomb excavation by Lorenza Lopez and Jorge Ramos at Huitzilapa may have revealed an actual analog in that the opening of the shaft tomb is in the floor of a house on a raised banquet.[21]

In the Americas, dogs frequently are associated with death and mortuary ritual. In some indigenous American cultures, they were sacrificed for feasts as late as the nineteenth century. Sometimes pure black or pure white dogs were considered to be imbued with spiritual power and were thus especially prized as sacrifices. In North America and on both sides of the Mississippi, dogs were sacrificed as part of the mortuary feast. According to ethnographer David Bushnell, "Dogs were among the gifts presented to the dying man by his friends and 'they kill these dogs in order to send them on before him into the other world' and they were eaten at the feast prepared at the time of death."[22]

The Aztecs had a special role for dogs, believing that Xolotl, a dog-monster, was the brother and evil twin of Quetzalcoatl, the feathered serpent deity of the Aztecs who lived in the underworld. Xolotl accompanied and protected the sun during its nightly journey through the underworld to emerge in the east each day. More than a thousand years earlier in western Mexico, polished red Colima-style ceramic dogs may have had a parallel task. Perhaps this earlier tradition represents dogs accompanying the dead through the underworld as Xolotl did the sun.

The challenge for archaeologists is to organize and analyze these objects and the information they convey and, more importantly, to interpret the meaning of these ancient remnants to help today's people understand their shared yet diverse human past. Jewelry and amulets, for example, often adorn the dead, perhaps as they may have in life. Today's observer often sees ancient jewelry as decorative, but at the same time, the form and material of the jewelry often had significance known to the wearer and the community in which they lived.

Sacrifice for Honor and Deities

Although everyone dies, causes of death vary and each type of death may require special recognition and treatment. For example, many cultures glorify and celebrate those who die in battle. These heroes inspire others by their ultimate sacrifice. Their names and deeds become myths and legends.

The European story of Sir Gawain and the Green Knight exemplifies an individual's willing self-sacrifice to maintain his own noble character.[23] Mythologist Joseph

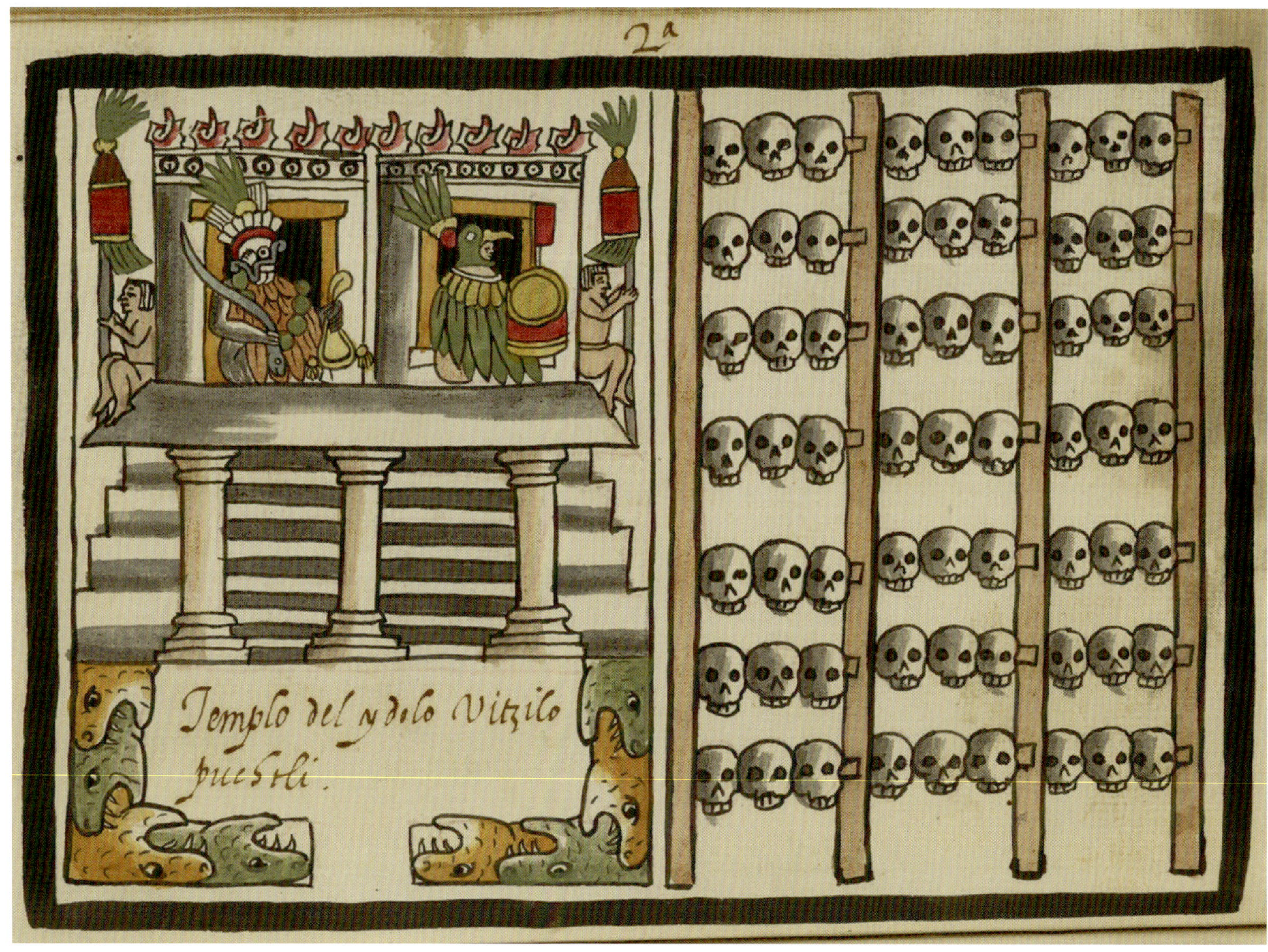
2ª
Templo del ydolo Vitzilo
puestli.

43 Relief Frieze

Coptic Christian
400 CE
Marble
Staaliches Museum,
Schwerin, Germany

Campbell classifies this as an archetypal story.[24] The Hopi have a story that parallels the risk and reward of taking a mystical journeying that could end in death: "A prominent young man might be invited to undertake the perilous trip so that he could return and tell his people what the opposite world was like. All such things served to alleviate the mystery of death and to mitigate the fear."[25]

Some cultures performed intentional human sacrifice for religious reasons. Hernán Cortés (1485–1547) and his Spanish conquerors were amazed at the size and grandeur of Tenochtitlán, the Aztec capital in present-day Mexico. They marveled at its massive architecture and compared the city favorably to Venice. At the same time, they were horrified to see the Tzompantli, an architectural structure near the Templo Mayor where the skulls of sacrificed human victims were displayed for all to see (**42**). By the end of the conquest, some of the Spaniards and at least one horse shared this dubious honor. In the Aztec world, one of the main functions of war was to capture victims, preferably high-ranking warriors, for religious sacrifice to honor the deity Huitzilopochtli and demonstrate his power over foreign gods. Human sacrifice to honor the gods, maintain balance between cosmic powers, or simply to demonstrate a ruler's control has occurred in cultures around the globe.

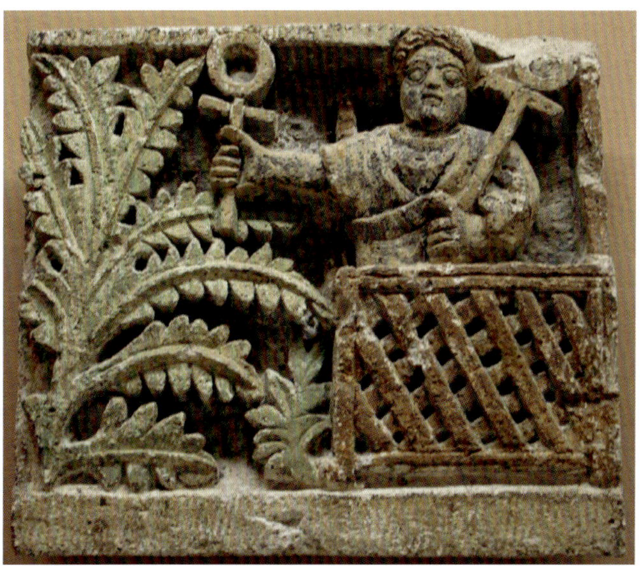

Conclusion

Art and death are intertwined. More than the human remains themselves, art related to death and mortuary behavior is a lasting commemoration that reminds the living of their own mortality while acknowledging those who have gone before. The works may be as ephemeral as the burning of paper offerings or as permanent as carved stone.

Those who observe these death-related works from ancient or distant cultures appreciate their beauty and

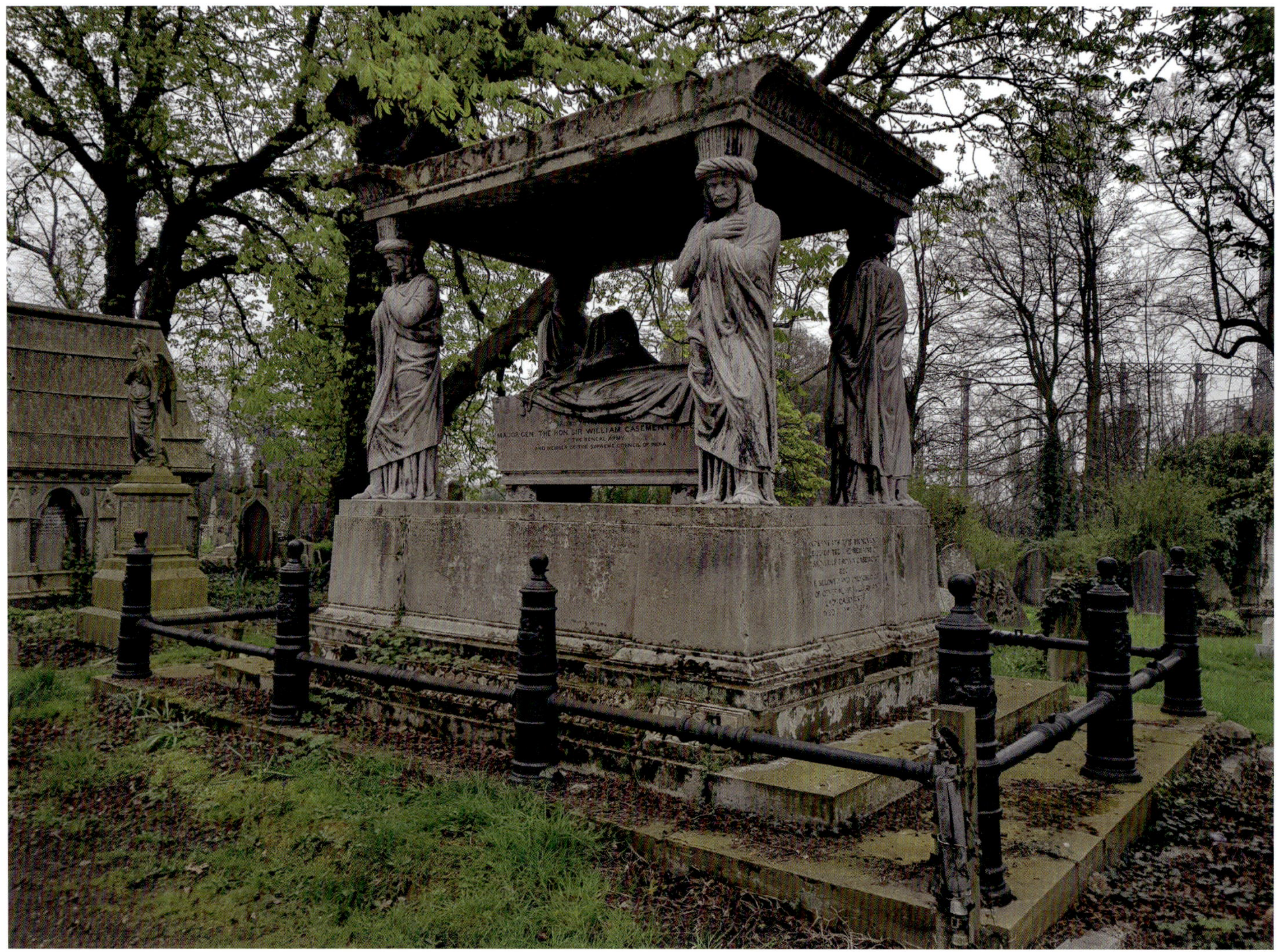

marvel at the artistry and skills of the makers. On a
deeper level, these objects are true *memento mori* that
should remind the living of the path that every person
follows. Memorializing the dead is as old as humanity
itself. Every new generation must address the issues
for themselves. This carved limestone architectural
element includes a portrayal of an ankh, a symbol
of eternal life in ancient Egyptian religion, into early

Coptic imagery (**43**). Today, we still borrow iconic
imagery from the distant past to help cope with the
eternal journey (**44**). Between these two poles of
appreciation are fascinating stories from each culture.
Taken together, these objects and stories are reminders
of our common humanity. In that sense, the objects are
memento vivere, reminding us that we must live.

1   Joseph Campbell, *The Hero with a Thousand Faces* (Princeton: Princeton University Press, 1968).

2   Ralph S. Solecki, *Shanidar, the First Flower People* (New York: Knopf, 1971).

3   Emma Pomeroy, Paul Bennet, Chris O. Hunt, Tim Reynolds, Lucy Farr, Marine Frouin, James Holman, Ross Lane, Charles, French, and Graeme Barker, "New Neanderthal Remains associated with the 'Flower Burial' at Shanidar Cave," *Antiquity* 94, no. 373 (2020): 11–26.

4   Teng Shu-P'ing, "The Original Significance of *Bi* Disks: Insights Based on Liangzhu Jade *Bi* with Incised Symbolic Motifs," *Journal of East Asian Archaeology* 2, no. 1–2 (2000): 165–94.

5   Hasso von Winning and Olga Hammer, *Anecdotal Sculpture of Ancient West Mexico* (Los Angeles: Ethnic Arts Council of Los Angeles, 1972).

6   Robert B. Pickering, "The Huitzilapa Tomb: Significance for Mortuary Behavior Studies," Paper presented at the Annual Meeting of the Society for American Archaeology, New Orleans, LA, April 10–14, 1996.

7   *History*, book 2:85–90, in *Herodutus*, trans. A. D. Godley, 4 vols. (London: Loeb Classical Library, 1920–25), 1: 369–75, http://onlinebooks.library.upenn.edu/webbin/book/lookupid?key=olbp71364.

8   J. F. Cherry, *The Headpots of Northeast Arkansas and Southern Pemiscot County, Missouri* (Fayetteville: University of Arkansas Press, 2009).

9   Christopher B. Donnan, *Moche Portraits from Ancient Peru* (Austin: University of Texas Press, 2004).

10   Pickering, "The Huitzilapa Tomb."

11   King James Version.

12   *The Best of Shelley*, ed. Newman I. White (New York: Ronald Press, 1932), 96.

13   Paul S. Wingert, *Primitive Art: Its Traditions and Styles* (New York: Oxford University Press, 1962), 57.

14   E. A. Wallis Budge, ed. and trans., *Book of the Dead* (New York: Gramercy Books 1960) 576–85.

15   Marvin Meyer and Richard Smith, *Ancient Christian Magic: Coptic Texts of Ritual Power* (San Francisco: Harper Press, 1994).

16   Elizabeth Kübler-Ross, *On Death and Dying* (New York: Scribner, 1997).

17   Tyler A. Hamilton, *Pueblo Gods and Myths* (Norman: University of Oklahoma Press, 1972), 50.

18   David I. Bushnell, *Native Cemeteries and Forms of Burial East of the Mississippi*, Smithsonian Institution, Bureau of American Ethnology, Bulletin 71 (Washington DC: Government print office, 1920), 12.

19   Takafumi Matsui, Ryota Moriwaki, Eissa Zidan, Tomoko Arai, "The Manufacture and Origin of the Tutankhamen Meteoritic Iron Dagger," *Meteoritics and Planetary Science* 57 (2022): 747–58, https://doi.org/10.1111/maps.13787.

20   Alexandre Tokovinine, personal communication, September 21, 2022.

21   Lorenza Lopez Mestas Camberos and Jorge Ramos de la Vega, "Excavating the tomb at Huitzilapa," in *Ancient West Mexico: Art and Archaeology of the Unknown Past*, ed. Richard F. Townsend (New York: Thames and Hudson, 1998), 53–70.

22   Bushnell, *Native Cemeteries and Forms of Burial East of the* Mississippi, 13.

23   Y.R. Porsor, *Gawain and the Green Knight: Adventures at Camelot* (New York: MacMillan Publishing, 1979).

24   Campbell, *The Hero with a Thousand Faces*.

25   Tyler, *Pueblo Gods and Myths*.

Further reading

Bourget', Steve. *Sex, Death, and Sacrifice in Moche Religion and Visual Culture*. Austin, University of Texas Press, 2006.

Cuevas, E. and R. B. Pickering. "The Ancient Ceramics of West Mexico." *American Scientist* 91, no. 3 (2003): 242–49.

Handler, Stuart, Hugh Thomson, and Joanne Stuhr. *Traveling with Cortés and Pizarro: Discovering Fine Pre-Columbian Art*. Milan: 5Continents, 2018.

Pickering, Robert B. and Cheryl Smallwood-Roberts. *West Mexico: Ritual and Identity*. Tulsa: Thomas Gilcrease Institute of American History and Art, 2016.

Pickering, Robert B. and Christopher S. Beekman. "A Historical Overview of Shaft Tomb Archaeology in West Mexico." In *Shaft Tombs and Figures in West Mexican Society: A Reassessment*, edited by Christopher S. Beekman and Robert B. Pickering, 1–22. Tulsa: Thomas Gilcrease Institute of American History and Art, 2016.

Pickering, Robert B. and Christopher S. Beekman. "Future Directions for Research." In *Shaft Tombs and Figures in West Mexican Society: A Reassessment*, edited by Christopher S. Beekman and Robert B. Pickering, 207–11. Tulsa: Thomas Gilcrease Institute of American History and Art, 2016.

Wiersma, Juliet B. *Architectural Vessels of the Moche*. Austin: University of Texas Press, 2015.

No man is an Iland, intire of itself; every man
is a peece of the Continent, a part of the maine;
if a Clod bee washed way by the Sea, Europe
is the lesse, as well as if a Promontorie were, as
well as if a Manor of thy friends or of thine
owne were; any man's death diminishes me,
because I am involved in Mankinde;
And therefore never send to know for whom
the bell tolls; it tolls for thee.

John Donne, Meditation XVII,
Devotions upon Emergent Occasions,
1624

AFTERWORD

Stuart Handler

After reading these chapters and seeing the artwork illustrating them, I hope you are as amazed and changed by the experience as I was. As editor, I have read the book many times, and each time I came away with a deeper understanding of my own life and human experience in general. What I took for granted and obvious was that my problems in life were singular ones. I thought no one has experienced my problems and challenges of growing up, raising a family, making a living, and suffering illnesses like I have. This book brought me closer to my own humanity.

I learned in stark reality that all human beings have experienced the same things I have; that I am essentially the same as the first human that stepped foot on this earth. I realized that I am in a bigger family, the family of humankind, than my own. I thought that this modern, global world I live in confronted me with different and more complex challenges and problems than other humans have ever had, and then I realized how challenging it would be to have to go out and hunt for your food every day and to shelter yourself against attacks from animals and other humans.

I have had the privilege of seeing thousands of photos of art humans have made throughout their existence and selecting 400 to represent the human experience. It was a sobering and astounding experience to see what the human brain has created to help make sense out of life. I look at things differently now and, I trust, you will too.

The book ends, appropriately, with a chapter on death. Humans know that this end must come to all living things, but humans were given the gift of art as their legacy to tell others that followed: "We were there, do not forget us."

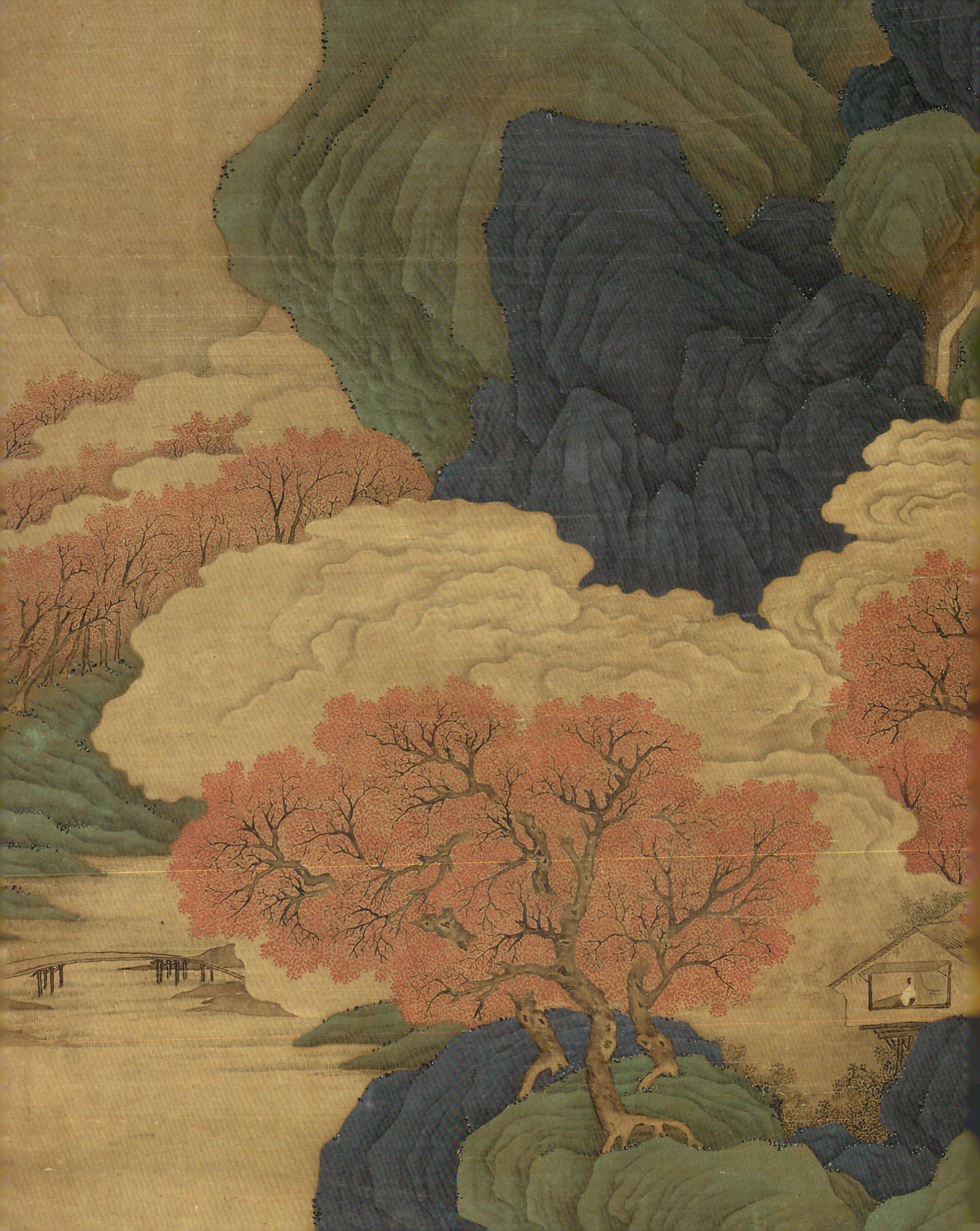

Map of the World around 1794

Plate 1 of *School Atlas to Cummings' Ancient and Modern Geography* (Boston, 1813)

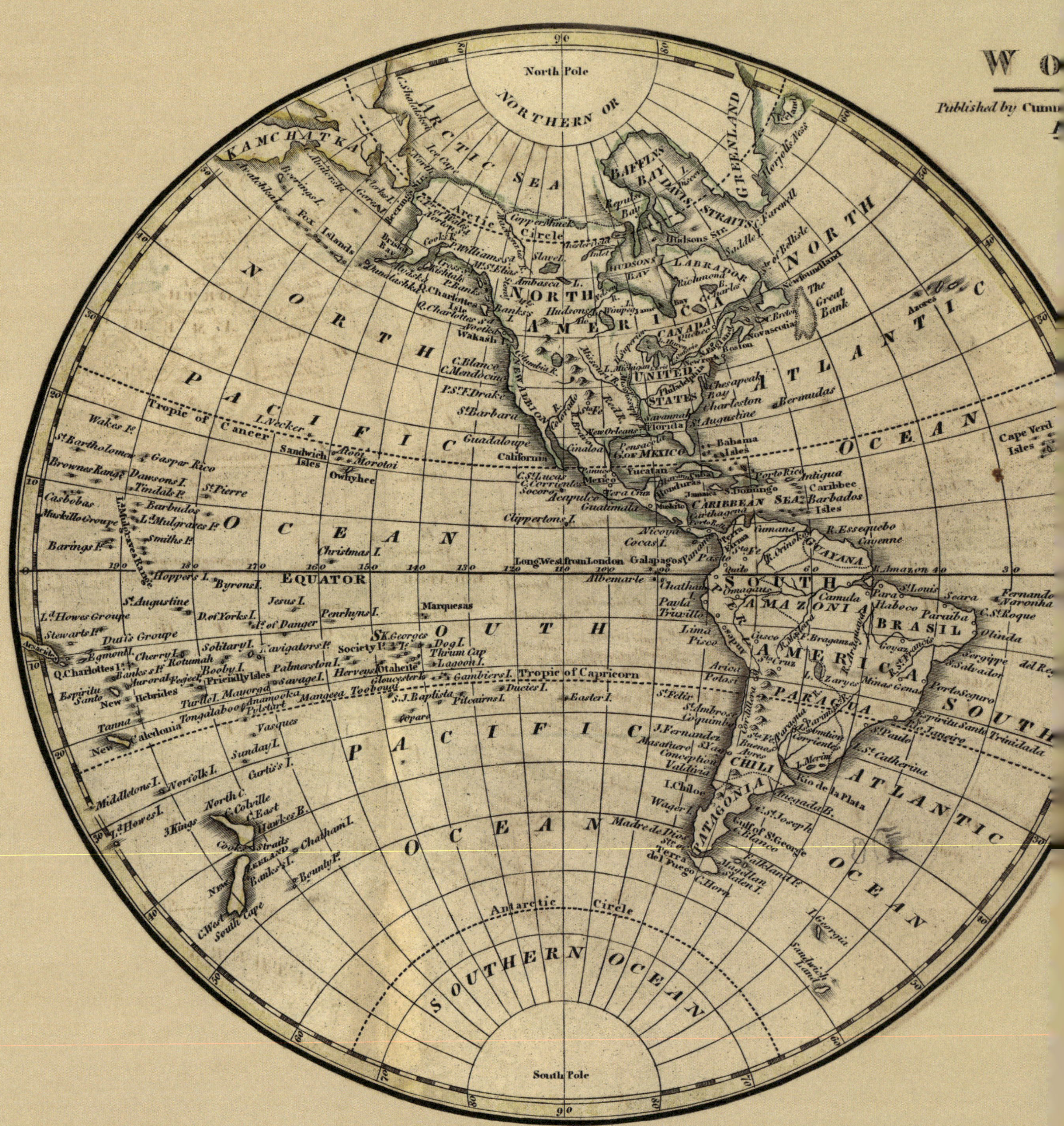
WO
Published by Cumm
North Pole
NORTHERN OR
KAMCHATKA
ARCTIC SEA
BAFFINS BAY
GREENLAND
DAVIS STRAITS
Fox Islands
Arctic Circle
Cook I.
P. Williams S.
NORTH
LABRADOR
HUDSONS BAY
CANADA
Newfoundland
The Great Bank
NORTH
Q. Charlottes
Wakash
C. Blanco
C. Mendocino
NORTH AMERICA
Hudsons
Quebec
Nova Scotia
Boston
ATLANTIC
Azores
NEW ALBION
P. St. F. Drake
St. Barbara
UNITED STATES
Chesapeak Bay
Charleston
Bermudas
OCEAN
PACIFIC
Tropic of Cancer
L. Necker
Wakes I.
St. Bartholomew
Gaspar Rico
Sandwich Isles
Morotoi
Guadaloupe
California
Sinaloa
Florida
St. Augustine
Cape Verd Isles
Brownes Range
Dawsons I.
Tindals R.
St. Pierre
Owyhee
G. MEXICO
Bahama Isles
Casbobas
Muskillo Groupe
Barbudos
L. Mulgraves Is.
Morotoi
Socorro
Acapulco
Vera Cruz
Honduras
Porto Rico
Antigua
Caribbee Isles
Barbados
Barings I.
Smiths I.
Christmas I.
Guatimala
Mosquito
CARIBBEAN SEA
OCEAN
Long West from London
Galapagos
R. Orinoco
GUAYANA
R. Essequebo
Cayenne
Hoppers I.
Byrons I.
EQUATOR
Albemarle
Nicoya
Cocas I.
Quito
Panama
Amazon
St. Louis
Scara
Fernando Noronha
L.d Howes Groupe
St. Augustine
D. ei Yorks I.
Jesus I.
Penrhyns I.
Marquesas
SOUTH
Paula
Truxillo
Lima
SOUTH
AMAZONIA
BRASIL
C. St. Roque
Olinda
Stewarts I.
Dui's Groupe
Solitary I.
Navigators I.
Society I.
St. Georges
Dog I.
Thrum Cap
Pisco
BRASIL
Sergippe
Salvador
del Re
Q. Charlottes I.
Cherry I.
Rotumah
Booby I.
Friendly Isles
Palmerston I.
Herveys I.
Otaheite
Savage I.
Gambiers I.
Tropic of Capricorn
Ducies I.
Easter I.
Porto Seguro
Espiritu Santo
New Hebrides
Turtle I.
Mayoroa
Tongataboo
Anamooka
Mangeea
Teeboo
S. J. Baptista
Pitcairns I.
Minas Genaes
PARAGUA
St. Paulo
R. Janeiro
Trinidada
Tanna
New Caledonia
Vasques
PARAGUA
Conception
St. Catherina
Middleton I.
Norfolk I.
Sunday I.
PACIFIC
CHILI
Rio de la Plata
SOUTH
3 Howes I.
3 Kings
North C.
C. Colville
East
Hawkes B.
Curtis's I.
Valdivia
I. Chiloe
ATLANTIC
Cooks Straits
Chatham I.
PATAGONIA
Wager I.
Gulf of St. George
C. St. Joseph
ZEELAND
Banks's I.
Madre de Dios
Tierra del Fuego
C. Horn
Falkland Is.
OCEAN
N.a West
South Cape
Antarctic Circle
Georgia
Sandwich Land
SOUTHERN OCEAN
South Pole